PRINCIPLES AND APPLICATIONS OF OPTICAL COMMUNICATIONS

MAX MING-KANG LIU
Quickturn Design Systems, Inc.

IRWIN

Chicago • Bogotá • Boston • Buenos Aires • Caracas
London • Madrid • Mexico City • Sydney • Toronto

©Richard D. Irwin, a Times Mirror Higher Education Group, Inc. company, 1996

Irwin Book Team

Publisher: *Tom Casson*
Senior sponsoring editor: *Scott Isenberg*
Senior marketing manager: *Brian Kibby*
Project Editor: *Rebecca Dodson*
Production supervisor: *Lara Feinberg*
Assistant manager, graphics: *Charlene R. Perez*
Designer: *Keith McPherson*
Compositor: *Interactive Composition Corporation*
Typeface: *10/12 Times Roman*
Printer: *R. R. Donnelley & Sons Company*

 Times Mirror
Higher Education Group

Library of Congress Cataloging-in-Publication Data

Ming-Kang Liu, Max
    Principles and applications of optical communications / Max Ming
-Kang Liu
      p. cm.
    Includes bibliographical references and index.
    ISBN 0-256-16415-0
    1. Optical communcations.   I. Title.
TK5103.59.M57   1996
621.382'7—dc20

95–25240

Printed in the United States of America
1 2 3 4 5 6 7 8 9 0 D O C 2 1 0 9 8 7 6 5

To the Allwisdom: "Let there be light," Genesis 1:3.
&
To my parents Yee-Tang, Pei-Yu, and my wife Ai-Ching
–MKL

PREFACE

Optical communication is a fascinating study subject for its practical importance and its extreme broad disciplines. Lightwave technology developed over the last two decades has greatly changed our lives. Today, undersea and underground optical fibers of large capacity carry more than 80 percent of the total traffic we generate. Because of this rapid development, many high bandwidth services such as high definition television (HDTV), video teleconferencing, and the Broadband Integrated Services Digital Network (B-ISDN) are being actively planned for deployment in the near future.

At the same time, lightwave technology is based on broad disciplines. For example:

- Electromagnetic (EM) wave background is needed to analyze propagation modes in an optical fiber. When we need to design polarization maintaining fibers, even more advanced EM knowledge such as birefringence is required.

- Semiconductor device background is needed to design semiconductor light sources and detectors. When we need to design and tune single frequency light sources such as distributed feedback lasers (DFB), advanced EM analysis is also needed.

- Advanced mathematics is needed to understand the use of the inverse scattering technique in analyzing fiber soliton transmissions, which is being actively studied for very long distance transmission without using repeaters.

- Broad communication background is needed to design proper modulation and detection schemes. This includes how to design a line code for ac-coupling detection, how to design a high speed timing recovery circuit, and how to design an equalizer to minimize the bit error rate (BER) under noise and fiber dispersion. When a higher receiver sensitivity is required, coherent detection and/or optical amplification is needed. Various advanced noise analyses are then required.

- High speed networking background is needed to properly integrate optical elements with other networking elements. Sufficient knowledge is needed to design a good network architecture such as wavelength division multiple access (WDMA) networks that can maximize the strength of lightwave technology.

PURPOSE OF THIS BOOK

Over the last few years, there have been many good books on this subject. However, due to the broad disciplines of the subject, there are three strong needs that have not been well fulfilled.

First, due to the broad disciplines, many important topics have not been sufficiently explained. Frequently, important results are simply cited without explanations or derivations. Many times, a large list of references is given for readers to dig into by themselves. I feel this is not satisfactory because of the following two reasons:

1. Many results depend on some assumptions, operating conditions, and the current technology development. As underlying conditions and/or technology change, results would be invalid. If a reader does not understand the full background, he or she would be limited in applying them properly. For example, a single frequency distributed feedback (DFB) laser diode can generate a single longitudinal mode output. However, under different conditions, there can be two main modes. Then what are the important factors that determine the emission output, and how to control them? It is thus important to understand its theory.

2. If readers cannot understand a property or equation at least in principle, they can only memorize results. As a result, what they learn will quickly fade away.

Second, although lightwave technology has been driven by the needs of high-speed communications, it is based on many device technologies such as optical fibers, laser diodes, optical amplifiers, optical tunable filters, and photonic switches. Therefore, when focusing discussion on devices, many books lack detailed system discussion. This will have curious readers asking the following questions:

What are the driving forces behind the technology development?

What are their limitations from the communication perspective?

As the fiber transmission capacity becomes higher and higher, how can other parts of a communication network be designed to increase the overall capacity?

To help answer these questions, this book provides design rationale and limitations for the various devices discussed. The book also discusses important system design concepts in detail. The discussion will help readers to propose new device designs for their communication needs and to use optical devices in their maximum strengths for practical systems.

Third, again due to the many disciplines involved, it is difficult to find a book that can help readers understand many different lightwave topics. For example, a device person can have difficulty understanding noise analysis and equalizer design, and a system person will likely be confused by the many types of light sources designed. To improve this understanding, this book provides a comprehensive discussion on many important topics, illustrates them with many examples, and has many appendices. To help readers understand difficult material, the book explains important equations or concepts with minimal mathematics and with as much physical meaning as possible. For example, in Chapter 4 on optical fibers, the concept and quantification of fiber dispersion in fiber transmission is explained with minimal treatment of the Maxwell wave equations. In Chapter 18 on fiber solitons, the physical meaning of each term in the nonlinear Schröndinger equation is explained and derived. To further help readers apply what is discussed, many examples are given to illustrate important concepts and to show practical applications numerically. Finally, for serious readers who wish to see the derivations and learn difficult theories inside out, appendices are given to meet their different needs and backgrounds. For example, various noise analyses, DFB laser diode rate equation derivations, and solutions of the nonlinear Schröndinger equation using the inverse scattering method are given.

CONTENTS OF THIS BOOK

This book consists of four parts: Overview, Basic Communication Blocks, Networking, and Signal Processing. Part I has two chapters which overview a communication system and a communication network. Important elements in the communication process are introduced, and various related optical components are described. These two chapters will help readers to understand (1) the driving forces in lightwave technology development for optical communications, (2) state-of-the-art lightwave technology, and (3) optical system and networking design and integration.

Part II has five chapters, which explain (1) light generation, (2) propagation, and (3) detection. These chapters explore important technologies and their principles in point-to-point communications. They also serve as a foundation for subsequent disussion in Parts III and IV. To help readers to design a communication system and evaluate the transmission performance, important noise analyses and receiver design issues are discussed in great detail.

Part III has four chapters which cover important optical networking aspects and supporting optics devices. Specifically, various multiplexing and switching techniques in optical communication networks are explained, and various innovative device designs are described. Design issues and trade-offs are discussed in detail to help readers apply what was learned previously.

Part IV has seven chapters which cover important and advanced topics in optical communications. On the transmitter side, both direct and indirect modulations are discussed in detail. The DFB laser diode, which is one of the most important single-frequency light sources used today, is also discussed. On the receiver side, coherent detection and timing recovery are explained. This helps readers to understand advanced detection schemes and timing recovery techniques in high-speed digital communications. Finally, on the subject of light signal transmission, recent technology developments on optical amplifiers and fiber solitons are discussed. These recent breakthroughs were developed to overcome the transmission loss and dispersion problems over a very long distance.

USE OF THIS BOOK

This book is self-sufficient as much as possible. However, due to the vast subjects it covers, some minimal background is required. This includes an understanding of calculus, differential equations, time-invariant linear systems, Fourier transforms, p-n junction physics, and traveling waves. These prerequisites should not be a problem for most senior students in electrical engineering. For readers who have deficiencies in some of these areas, they can make up by reading basic textbooks on related subjects. This book provides appendices for readers who do not have sufficient background on some important topics of EM theory, quantum physics, optics, probability theories, and communication theory.

This book can be used as an introductory course at the senior level or as an advanced optical communications course at the first-year graduate level. It can also be used for courses emphasizing either devices and/or systems. For a one semester course, teachers can use the following suggested table to select materials according to the course level and focus.

Course	Introductory	Advanced
Systems	Chaps. 1–2; Part of Chaps. 3–11	Chaps. 6, 7, 12, 15, 16, and Part of Chaps. 8–11, 17, 18
Devices	Chaps. 1–5; Part of Chaps. 9 and 11	Chaps. 9, 11–15, 17, and 18

For an introductory course on systems, instructors should cover Chapters 1–2 in detail. This gives students a solid background on the bigger picture of optical communication. Instructors can then selectively choose materials in Chapters 3–11. For example, instructors can choose materials in Chapters 3–7 to explain the design criteria of light sources for communications, derive the attenuation and dispersion limits in fiber transmissions, and describe the shot noise in the photodetection process. Also, instructors can choose materials in Chapters 8–11 to explain important multiplexing and switching techniques in optical network communications.

For an introductory course on devices, instructors should still cover Chapters 1–2 in detail. This allows students to learn about the use of each optical device discussed subsequently. After this, instructors can discuss Chapters 3–5 on light sources, fibers, and detectors in detail. Chapters 9 and 11 can be used to explain important wavelength multiplexing and photonic switching devices, basic transmission performance such as quantum limits, and the basic receiver block diagram.

For an advanced course on systems, a background in basic communication and semiconductor devices is assumed. Instructors can then describe noise analysis, receiver design, and direct modulation covered in Chapters 6, 7, and 12. Instructors are also encouraged to discuss coherent communications, line coding, and timing recovery techniques covered in Chapters 15 and 16. Materials in Chapters 8–11, 17, and 18 on communication systems and networks can be selectively discussed.

For an advanced course on devices, basic device knowledge discussed in Chapters 3–5 is assumed. Instructors can then describe various modulators, advanced light sources, wavelength multiplexing devices, photonic switches, hybrids, polarization controllers, fiber amplifiers, and optical fiber solitons covered in Chapters 9, 11–15, 17, and 18.

ACKNOWLEDGEMENTS

The start of this book was initially invited and encouraged by Mr. Howard Aksen, who is the Presisdent of Aksen Associates and was associated with Richard D. Irwin. During my writing, I was a faculty member at the Department of Electrical and Computer Engineering of the University of Arizona, where I developed and taught an optical communications course from 1989 to 1995. Many students in the class from 1993 to 1995 provided very valuable feedback and corrections which were incorporated into this text.

While writing the book, I found many new technology developments reported by creative and hard-working scientists and engineers. This makes me very humble. I thus would like to thank all of these people, without whom I would have nothing to write. Due to my limited ability, only a small portion of the work is referred and/or discussed in the book.

Since lightwave technology research and development consist of many facets, I have no way to comprehend all of them by myself. I would like to thank the following people who have helped my understanding of the technical contents in one way or another: Professor Fow-Sen Choa of the University of Maryland on lightwave devices, Dr. Tai-Yen Zhang on optical fiber solitons, Mr. Bob Burroughs and Dr. Qun Shi of Panasonic Technology, Inc., on subcarrier multiplexing, and many of my former graduate students including Panayiotis Modestou, Antonios C. Vrahas, Marc-Jules B. Moretti, Jaeyon Kim, and John Staab.

To put many topics in precise and clear words and in the right place is also challenging to me. I thus greatly appreciate many constructive comments on organization and content from the reviewers, including (in alphabetical order) David R. Anderson of the University of Iowa, Daniel J. Blumenthal and John A. Buck of Georgia Institute of Technology, Yung Jui Chen and Fow-Sen Choa of the University of Maryland, Baltimore County, Costas N. Georghiades of Texas A&M University, Gary A. Hallock of the University of Texas at Austin, Richard P. Kenan of Georgia Institute of Technology, Paul K. Pruncal of Princeton University, and Richard Ziokowski of the University of Arizona.

Finally, I would like to thank the editorial team of Richard D. Irwin for the professional publishing work and my strong management support at Quickturn Design Systems. I also would like to express my deep gratitude to my wife for her support, patience, encouragement, and most importantly, love during this lengthy writing period.

COMMENTS AND CORRECTIONS

To make this book a better contribution to the society, it takes the collective wisdom from all of you. Please send your valuable comments, suggestions, criticisms, questions, etc., to max.liu@quickturn.com. I will not, however, answer problems at the end of each chapter. Ask your instructor instead. If you like, I will put your IP address in my e-mail list so that I can inform you of any corrections and useful points made by other readers.

BRIEF CONTENTS

PART 1
OVERVIEW 1

Chapter 1
INTRODUCTION 3

Chapter 2
FROM POINT-TO-POINT TO NETWORKING 31

PART 2
BASIC COMMUNICATION BLOCKS 71

Chapter 3
LIGHT SOURCES 73

Chapter 4
OPTICAL FIBERS 121

Chapter 5
LIGHT DETECTION 181

Chapter 6
NOISE IN OPTICAL COMMUNICATIONS 225

Chapter 7
INCOHERENT DETECTION 287

PART 3
NETWORKING 359

Chapter 8
TIME-DOMAIN MEDIUM ACCESS 361

Chapter 9
WAVELENGTH-DOMAIN MEDIUM ACCESS 415

Chapter 10
SUBCARRIER MULTIPLEXING 489

Chapter 11
PHOTONIC SWITCHING 523

PART 4
SIGNAL PROCESSING 589

Chapter 12
DIRECT MODULATION 591

Chapter 13
DISTRIBUTED-FEEDBACK LASER DIODES AND MODULATION 639

Chapter 14
EXTERNAL MODULATION 685

Chapter 15
COHERENT DETECTION   753

Chapter 16
TIMING RECOVERY AND LINE CODING   815

Chapter 17
OPTICAL AMPLIFICATION   853

Chapter 18
OPTICAL FIBER SOLITON TRANSMISSION   897

Appendix A
IMPORTANT PHYSICAL AND MATHEMATICAL CONSTANTS   943

Appendix B
INTERNATIONAL SYSTEM OF UNITS (SI)   945

Appendix C
IMPORTANT PHYSICAL CONSTANTS OF III–V COMPOUNDS   947

Appendix D
IMPORTANT VARIABLE DEFINITIONS   949

Appendix E
USEFUL MATHEMATICAL FORMULAS   981

Acronyms   985

Index   990

CONTENTS

PART 1

OVERVIEW   1

Chapter 1

INTRODUCTION   3

1.1   Communication Systems   4
1.2   Baseband versus Passband   6
1.3   Analog versus Digital   9
1.4   Coherent versus Incoherent   12
1.5   Modulation and Line Coding   14
1.6   Advantages of Optical Communications   16
1.7   Components in Optical Communications   16
1.8   Advances in Optical Communications and System Applications   18
1.9   Summary   22
        Appendix 1–A: The Concept of dB   22
        Problems   24
        References   27

Chapter 2

FROM POINT-TO-POINT TO NETWORKING   31

2.1   Basic Needs from a Communication Network   32
2.2   Basic Network Communication Process   34
        2.2.1   Signaling   34
        2.2.2   Information Exchange   34
2.3   Medium Access Control   38
        2.3.1   Shared Resources in Medium Access   39
        2.3.2   Deterministic versus Statistic Medium Access   44
        2.3.3   Multiple Access in Optical Communications   44
2.4   Switching   45
        2.4.1   Criteria of a Switch   45
        2.4.2   Switch Architectures   47
        2.4.3   Circuit Switching versus Packet Switching   50
        2.4.4   Switching in Optical Communications   51
2.5   Topology   52
        2.5.1   Physical Topology   52
        2.5.2   Logical Topology   54
        2.5.3   Topology Considerations in Optical Communications   54
2.6   Speed Bottlenecks in Optical Network Communications   58
2.7   Design Solutions to Speed Bottlenecks   60
        2.7.1   Solution 1: Optical Domain Implementation   60
        2.7.2   Solution 2: Simple Processing in Exchange for Transmission Inefficiency   62
        2.7.3   Solution 3: Parallel Implementation   64
2.8   High-Speed Applications   64
2.9   Summary   65
        Problems   67
        References   68

PART 2

BASIC COMMUNICATION BLOCKS   71

Chapter 3

LIGHT SOURCES   73

3.1   Criteria for Light Sources in Optical Communications   74
3.2   Semiconductor Light Sources   79
        3.2.1   P-N Junction   80
        3.2.2   Heterostructures   82
3.3   Light-Emitting Diodes   85
3.4   Laser Principles   88
        3.4.1   External Pumping   88
        3.4.2   Light Amplification   89
        3.4.3   Positive Optical Gain: Population Inversion   90

3.5   Cavity Confinement 92
    3.5.1   Gain-Guided Lasers 92
    3.5.2   Weakly Index-Guided Lasers 94
    3.5.3   Strongly Index-Guided Lasers 95
3.6   Fabry-Perot Laser Diodes 96
    3.6.1   Power Loss and Gain 96
    3.6.2   Longitudinal Modes 98
3.7   Single (Longitudinal) Mode Laser
    Diodes 99
    3.7.1   DFB Lasers 99
    3.7.2   DBR Lasers 100
    3.7.3   Coupled-Cavity Lasers 100
3.8   Other Important Types of Laser Diodes 103
    3.8.1   Quantum-Well Lasers 104
    3.8.2   Tunable Lasers 108
3.9   Summary 111
    Appendix 3–A: Fabry-Perot Resonator 112
    Problems 115
    References 117

Chapter 4

OPTICAL FIBERS   121

4.1   Optical Fiber Structures and Types 122
    4.1.1   Single-Mode and Multimode Fibers 122
    4.1.2   Refractive Index Profile 124
    4.1.3   Noncircular Symmetric Fibers 126
4.2   Fiber Attenuation and Attenuation
    Limits 126
    4.2.1   Attenuation Sources 126
    4.2.2   Receiver Sensitivity and Power
        Budget 131
    4.2.3   Attenuation Limits 133
4.3   Light Propagation in Optical Fibers 135
    4.3.1   Signal Propagation by Geometrical
        Optics 135
    4.3.2   Propagation Modes 138
4.4   Fiber Dispersion 140
    4.4.1   Intramodal Dispersion 141
    4.4.2   Intermodal Dispersion 143
    4.4.3   Total Fiber Dispersion 145
    4.4.4   Modal Dispersion at Longer
        Distance 145
    4.4.5   Dispersion Limits 146
4.5   Advanced Optical Fibers 151

4.5.1   Dispersion-Shifted and Multiply-Clad
        Fibers 151
4.5.2   Polarization Maintaining Fibers 153
4.6   Summary 158
    Appendix 4–A: Basics of Wave
    Propagation 159
    4–A.1   Wave Equations 159
    4–A.2   Waves in a Dielectric Medium 161
    4–A.3   Waves in Waveguides 162
    Appendix 4–B: Group Velocity 165
    Appendix 4–C: Waveguide Dispersion
    Analysis 167
    Appendix 4–D: Dispersion of Graded-Index
    Fibers 171
    Appendix 4–E: Total Fiber Dispersion
    Derivation 173
    Problems 175
    References 178

Chapter 5

LIGHT DETECTION   181

5.1   Quantum Efficiency and Reponsivity 183
5.2   Photoconductors 186
5.3   Photodiodes 189
5.4   PIN Diodes 191
    5.4.1   Reverse Bias and Electric Field
        Distribution 193
    5.4.2   Frequency Response 196
5.5   Avalanche Photodiodes 197
    5.5.1   Electric Field Distribution 198
    5.5.2   Current Multiplication 200
    5.5.3   Frequency Response 205
5.6   Advanced Light-Detection Devices 211
    5.6.1   Metal-Semiconductor-Metal
        Photodetectors 211
    5.6.2   Separate Absorption and Multiplication
        APDs 214
    5.6.3   Integrated PIN/FET Receivers 214
    5.6.4   Phototransistors 215
    5.6.5   Dual Wavelength Photodetectors 216
5.7   Summary 217
    Appendix 5–A: Avalanche Photodiode
    Frequency Response Derivation 218
    Problems 219
    References 222

Chapter 6

NOISE IN OPTICAL COMMUNI–CATIONS 225

6.1 Effects of Noise and Distortion 227
6.2 Noise Characterization 229
    6.2.1 Probability Density Function 230
    6.2.2 Power Spectral Density 232
6.3 Noise and Distortion Reduction Techniques 232
    6.3.1 Wiener Filtering in Analog Communications 234
    6.3.2 Matched Filtering in Digital Communications 235
6.4 Shot Noise from PIN Diodes 237
    6.4.1 Power Spectral Density of Shot Noise 237
    6.4.2 Quantum Limit 238
6.5 Thermal Noise 240
6.6 Avalanche Noise in APDs 243
6.7 Relative Intensity Noise in Laser Diodes 246
    6.7.1 Intrinsic RIN 247
    6.7.2 RIN Due to Reflection 248
6.8 Phase Noise from Laser Diodes 248
    6.8.1 Linewidth Broadening Because of Phase Noise 249
    6.8.2 Phase Noise in Coherent Communications 250
6.9 Mode Partition Noise 251
6.10 Total Noise 254
6.11 Intersymbol Interference and Jitter 256
6.12 Summary 257
    Appendix 6–A: Probability and Random Variables 258
    6–A.1 Intuitive Definition of Probability 258
    6–A.2 Axiomatic Approach 258
    6–A.3 Basic Properties of Probability 259
    6–A.4 Random Variables 262
    6–A.5 Mean, Variance, Expectation, and Moments 263
    6–A.6 Moment and Characteristic Functions 264
    6–A.7 Important Density Functions 265
    6–A.8 Central Limit Theorem 266
    Appendix 6–B: Random Process and Power Spectral Density 267
    Appendix 6–C: Shot Noise Power Spectral Density 270

Appendix 6–D: Avalanche Photodiode Excess Noise Factor Derivation 272
Appendix 6–E: Phase Noise 274
Problems 279
References 285

Chapter 7

INCOHERENT DETECTION 287

7.1 Analog Signal Detection 288
7.2 Binary Digital Signal Detection 290
7.3 Signal, Intersymbol Interference, and Noise Formulation 292
7.4 Bit Error Rate Neglecting Intersymbol Interference 295
7.5 Bit Error Rate Including Intersymbol Interference 297
7.6 Receiver Sensitivity 302
    7.6.1 Zero ISI and Extinction Ratio 303
    7.6.2 Nonzero ISI and Extinction Ratio 308
7.7 Received Pluse Determination 309
7.8 Receiver Equalizer Design 312
7.9 AC Coupling and DC Wander 318
7.10 Other Design Issues in Digital Transmissions 322
    7.10.1 APD Multiplication Gain Optimization 322
    7.10.2 APD Gain and Power Penalty in Multiple Access 325
    7.10.3 Extinction Ratio 329
    7.10.4 Use of Repeaters 330
7.11 Front-End Amplifiers 333
    7.11.1 High-Impedance Amplifier 333
    7.11.2 Transimpedance Amplifier 336
    7.11.3 Allowable Dynamic Range 339
7.12 Summary 341
    Appendix 7–A: Spectrum and Power of Signal-Dependent Noise 344
    Appendix 7–B: Zero Intersymbol Interference 344
    Appendix 7–C: Received Pulse Determination Considering the Chirping Effect 346
    Appendix 7–D: Pulse-Broadening Analysis 351
    Problems 353
    References 358

PART 3

NETWORKING   359

Chapter 8

TIME-DOMAIN MEDIUM ACCESS   361

8.1   Time-Division Multiple Access   362
    8.1.1   Medium Access and Time Compression   364
    8.1.2   Slot Size, Compression Delay, and Access Efficiency   366
8.2   Optical Domain Time-Division Multiple Access   368
8.3   Time-Division Multiplexing   371
    8.3.1   Frame Structure   372
    8.3.2   Frequency Justification   376
8.4   SONET   382
    8.4.1   SONET Frame and Layered Structure   383
    8.4.2   Pointer Processing   386
    8.4.3   Optical Interface   390
8.5   Fiber Distributed Data Interface   393
    8.5.1   Dual-Ring Topology and Clock Distribution   394
    8.5.2   Optical Component Specifications   394
    8.5.3   Data Frame and Token Format   397
    8.5.4   Synchronous and Asynchronous Access   398
    8.5.5   FDDI-II and FDDI Follow-on LAN   399
8.6   Broadband ISDN   403
    8.6.1   Broadband Network   403
    8.6.2   Local Loop   406
8.7   Summary   408
    Problems   410
    References   413

Chapter 9

WAVELENGTH-DOMAIN MEDIUM ACCESS   415

9.1   System and Component Overview   416
    9.1.1   System Characteristics   416
    9.1.2   Components   422
9.2   Wavelength-Division Multiple Access Network Access and Routing   425
    9.2.1   Logical Configurations and Routing in Fixed Tuning WDMA   425
    9.2.2   Dynamic Tuning WDMA   432
    9.2.3   Frequency Reuse   433
9.3   Transmission Performance in Wavelength-Division Multiplexing   438
    9.3.1   Incoherent Detection   439
    9.3.2   Coherent Detection   441
9.4   Tunable Sources   443
    9.4.1   Tunable Laser Arrays   444
    9.4.2   Waveguide Grating Router and Optical Amplifiers   446
    9.4.3   Frequency Tuning and Stabilization   446
9.5   Frequency-Independent Coupling   449
9.6   Frequency-Dependent Multiplexing   454
    9.6.1   Grating   454
    9.6.2   Mach-Zehnder Interferometry   457
    9.6.3   Waveguide Grating Router   461
9.7   Demultiplexing, Optical Filtering, and Add-Drop Multiplexing   464
    9.7.1   Spatial-Domain Demultiplexing–Grating   464
    9.7.2   Frequency-Domain Discrimination   470
    9.7.3   Polarization-Domain Demultiplexing   475
9.8   Summary   477
    Problems   480
    References   484

Chapter 10

SUBCARRIER MULTIPLEXING   489

10.1   Basic Subcarrier Multiplexing System   490
    10.1.1   Modulation Schemes   490
    10.1.2   RF Mixing and Laser Modulation   496
    10.1.3   Photocurrent Detection and Carrier-to-Noise Ratio   497
10.2   Analog TV Transmission   499
10.3   Nonlinear Distortion   499
10.4   Nonlinear Distortion Analysis   503
10.5   Digital Subcarrier Multiplexing Transmission   508
10.6   Combination of Subcarrier Multiplexing and Wavelength-Domain Medium Access   510
10.7   Summary   513
    Appendix 10–A: Carrier-to-Noise Ratio Analysis for FM Transmission   514
    Appendix 10–B: Nonlinear Distortion Analysis   515

Problems   518
References   520

Chapter 11

PHOTONIC SWITCHING   523

11.1   Switching Architectures   524
    11.1.1   System Considerations   524
    11.1.2   Crossbar and Double Crossbar   525
    11.1.3 N-Stage Planar   527
    11.1.4   Clos   528
    11.1.5   Benes   528
    11.1.6   Dilated Benes   529
    11.1.7   Self-Routing   531
    11.1.8   Batcher Sorting Network   533
    11.1.9   Batcher-Banyan Network   534
    11.1.10   Crossover and Extended Perfect Shuffle   534
11.2   Spatial-Domain Photonic Switching   538
    11.2.1   Design Criteria   538
    11.2.2   Mechanical Switches   539
    11.2.3   Waveguide Switches   540
    11.2.4   Bistable Devices   546
    11.2.5   Self-Electro-Optic Effect Devices   554
    11.2.6   Free-Space Interconnections   564
11.3   Multidimensional Photonic Switching   568
    11.3.1   Wavelength-Domain Switching   568
    11.3.2   Time-Domain Switching   569
    11.3.3   Self-Routing and ATM Switching   572
11.4   Summary   572
    Appendix 11–A: N-Stage Planar Waveguide Switch   574
    Appendix 11–B: Rearrangeable Network   576
    Appendix 11–C: Switching Control for a Dilated Benes Network   577
    Appendix 11–D: Batcher Sorting Network   579
    Problems   582
    References   585

PART 4

SIGNAL PROCESSING   589

Chapter 12

DIRECT MODULATION   591

12.1   Direct Modulation for Light-Emitting Diodes   592
    12.1.1   Rate Equation and Steady State Solution   592
    12.1.2   Pulse Input Response: Digital Signal Modulation   595
    12.1.3   Small Signal Response: Analog Signal Modulation   600
12.2   Rate Equations of Laser Diodes   603
    12.2.1   Dynamics in a Laser Diode   603
    12.2.2   Laser Rate Equation for Carrier Density   605
    12.2.3   Rate Equation for Photon Density   606
12.3   Steady State Solution of Laser Diodes   608
12.4   Pulse Input Response of Laser Diodes: Digital Signal Modulation   612
    12.4.1   Stage 1: $t < t_d$ and $N_{ph} \approx 0$ 613
    12.4.2   Stage 2: $t_d < t < T_0$, Where T_0 Is the Bit Period   615
    12.4.3   Stage 3: $t > T_0$ 619
    12.4.4   Pulse Response Modeling   619
12.5   Small Signal Response of Laser Diodes: Analog Signal Modulation   620
12.6   Limitations of Direct Modulation   624
    12.6.1   Frequency Chirping   625
    12.6.2   Mode Partition   627
    12.6.3   Linewidth Broadening   630
12.7   Summary   630
    Appendix 12–A: Fabry-Perot Laser Diode Rate Equations   631
    Problems   636
    References   638

Chapter 13

DISTRIBUTED-FEEDBACK LASER DIODES AND MODULATION   639

13.1   Coupled-Mode Rate Equations   640
    13.1.1   Boundary Conditions   644
    13.1.2   Steady State Equations   645
13.2   Threshold Solutions   645
    13.2.1   Zero-Reflection DFB Lasers   648
    13.2.2   Single-Window DFB Lasers   649
    13.2.3 $\lambda/4$-Shift DFB Lasers   652
    13.2.4   Double-Cleaved DFB Lasers   655
13.3   Direct Current Characteristics   658
13.4   Modulation Characteristics   669
    13.4.1   Pulse Modulation   669
    13.4.2   Single-Tone Modulation   670
13.5   Summary   672

Appendix 13–A: Distributed-Feedback
Coupled-Mode Equations 674
Appendix 13–B: Threshold Equations of
DFB Lasers 679
Problems 682
References 683

Chapter 14

EXTERNAL MODULATION 685

14.1 Desirable Properties from an External
Modulator 686
14.2 Principles of External Modulation 688
14.3 Wave Propagation in Anisotropic
Media 689
    14.3.1 Anisotropic Materials 689
    14.3.2 Plane Wave Propagation 690
    14.3.3 Birefringence 693
    14.3.4 Normal Surfaces 695
    14.3.5 Index Ellipsoid 695
14.4 Electro-Optic Modulation 699
    14.4.1 Modulation of Refractive Indices 699
    14.4.2 Longitudinal and Transverse
        Modulators 709
14.5 Electro-Optic Phase Modulators 713
14.6 Electro-Optic Amplitude
Modulators 714
    14.6.1 Polarization Filtering 714
    14.6.2 Field Interference 715
    14.6.3 Waveguide Coupling 717
14.7 Modulation Bandwidth and Switching Power
of Electro-Optic Modulators 720
14.8 Acousto-Optic Modulation 725
    14.8.1 Elasto-Optic Coefficients 725
    14.8.2 Bragg Diffraction 732
    14.8.3 Raman-Nath or Debye-Sears
        Diffraction 734
14.9 Acousto-Optic Bragg Amplitude
Modulators 735
14.10 Deflection Efficiency, Driving Power, and
Bandwidth of Acousto-Optic
Modulators 737
14.11 Summary 740
Appendix 14–A: Waveguide Coupling 742
Appendix 14–B: Acousto-Optic
Coupling 746
Problems 748
References 751

Chapter 15

COHERENT DETECTION 753

15.1 Basic Principles of Coherent Detection 754
    15.1.1 Optical Mixing 754
    15.1.2 Homodyne and Heterodyne
        Detections 755
15.2 Signal and Noise Formulations in Coherent
Detection 756
15.3 On-Off Keying 764
    15.3.1 Signal Representation and
        Demodulation 764
    15.3.2 OOK Fundamental Detection
        Performance 765
15.4 Phase-Shift Keying 770
    15.4.1 Signal Representation and
        Demodulation 770
    15.4.2 Binary PSK Fundamental
        Performance 770
15.5 Differential Phase-Shift Keying 771
    15.5.1 DPSK Demodulation 771
    15.5.2 DPSK Fundamental Performance 773
15.6 Frequency-Shift Keying 775
    15.6.1 Signal Representation and
        Demodulation 775
    15.6.2 FSK Fundamental Performance 776
15.7 Performance Summary 777
15.8 Polarization-Shift Keying 780
    15.8.1 State of Polarization and Stokes
        Parameters 780
    15.8.2 Stokes Receiver 782
15.9 Carrier Recovery in Coherent Detection 784
15.10 Effects of Phase Noise 789
    15.10.1 Effect of Phase Noise in DPSK 790
    15.10.2 Effect of Phase Noise in Envelope
        Detection 792
    15.10.3 Effect of Phase Noise in FSK 794
    15.10.4 Effects of Phase Noise in Other
        Coherent Detection Techniques 795
15.11 Summary 795
Appendix 15–A: Polarization Controllers
and Isolators 798
Appendix 15–B: Four-Port Hybrids 801
Appendix 15–C: Six-Port 90° Hybrid
Analysis for Carrier Recovery 806
Appendix 15–D: Rician and Rayleigh
Distributions 807
Problems 808
References 811

Chapter 16

TIMING RECOVERY AND LINE CODING   815

16.1 Bandpass Filtering for Timing Recovery   817
16.2 The Q-Factor in Bandpass Filtering   819
16.3 Surface Acoustic Wave Filters   822
16.4 Phase-Locked Loops   824
16.5 Preprocessing for Bandpass Filtering   827
16.6 Line Codes for Timing Recovery   829
16.7 Fixed Transition Codes   835
16.8 Scrambling   837
    16.8.1   Maximum-Length Pseudo-Random Sequence Generation   840
    16.8.2   Frame-Synchronized Scrambler   841
    16.8.3   Self-Synchronized Scrambler   842
16.9 Summary   843
    Appendix 16: Properties of the Maximum-Length Sequences   845
    Problems   848
    References   851

Chapter 17

OPTICAL AMPLIFICATION   853

17.1 System Applications   854
17.2 System Criteria   855
17.3 Semiconductor Amplifiers   857
    17.3.1   External Pumping and Rate Equation   857
    17.3.2   Amplifier Gain, Pumping Efficiency, and Bandwidth   859
    17.3.3   Fabry-Perot Amplifiers   863
    17.3.4   Interchannel Interference   868
17.4 Erbium-Doped Fiber Amplifiers   869
    17.4.1   Optical Pumping   869
    17.4.2   Rate Equations and Amplifier Gain   874
17.5 Noise from Optical Amplification   880
    17.5.1   Amplified Spontaneous Emission Noise   880
    17.5.2   Noise Figures   881
17.6 System Design   884
17.7 Summary   887
    Appendix 17–A: Amplified Spontaneous Emission Noise Derivation   889
    Appendix 17–B: Noise Power after Photodetection   890

Problems   892
References   895

Chapter 18

OPTICAL FIBER SOLITON TRANSMISSION   897

18.1 Fiber Nonlinearity and Wave Equations   898
18.2 Physical Meaning of the Nonlinear Schrödinger Equation   900
    18.2.1 V_g^{-1}: Pulse Propagation   900
    18.2.2 β_2 or $-(\lambda/\omega)D_{intra}$: Pulse Broadening   901
    18.2.3 $j\gamma|A_1|^2$: Self-Phase Modulation and Spectrum Broadening   903
    18.2.4   Balance between Fiber Dispersion and Nonlinearity   903
18.3 One-Dimensional Soliton Solutions   906
18.4 Field Experiments   910
18.5 Applying Solitons for Digital Transmission   912
    18.5.1   Soliton Generation   912
    18.5.2   Fiber Attenuation and Optical Amplification   914
    18.5.3   Amplifier Noise and Timing Jitter   918
    18.5.4   Transmission Bit Rate   919
18.6 Summary   921
    Appendix 18–A: Inverse Scattering Technique   923
    Appendix 18–B: Derivation of the Gordon-Haus Limit   933
    Problems   936
    References   939

Appendix A

IMPORTANT PHYSICAL AND MATHEMATICAL CONSTANTS   943

Appendix B

INTERNATIONAL SYSTEM OF UNITS (SI)   945

Appendix C

IMPORTANT PHYSICAL CONSTANTS OF III–V COMPOUNDS   947

Appendix D
IMPORTANT VARIABLE DEFINITIONS
949

Appendix E
USEFUL MATHEMATICAL
FORMULAS   981

ACRONYMS   985

INDEX   990

1

OVERVIEW

To help readers gain an overview of the lightwave technology developed over the last two decades, Part 1 discusses fundamentals of optical communication systems and networks. A communication system is a point-to-point transmission link consisting of a transmitter on one end and a receiver on the other end. When the transmission distance is long, repeaters and/or in-line amplifiers are added.

Chapter 1 describes basic communication blocks in point-to-point communication systems. This introduction describes the trend of lightwave technology development and covers some important design issues in optical communications. The end of the chapter summarizes state-of-the-art development in lightwave technology.

Chapter 2 explains important networking concepts and speed bottlenecks in optical communications. A communication network consists of switching nodes that are interconnected through transmission lines. The switching function connects any two parties on the network. Chapter 2 also describes various network designs to improve the overall network throughput as lightwave technology is incorporated.

1

INTRODUCTION

Communication is an important part of our daily lives. It helps us to get closer to one another and exchange important information. The communication process involves information generation, transmission, reception, and interpretation. The primary task of communication engineers is to provide accurate and fast information exchange services for users who want to communicate with one another. As needs for various types of communication, such as images, voice, video, and data communications, increase, demands for large transmission capacity also increase. This need for large capacity has driven the rapid development of lightwave technology to support worldwide digital telephony and analog cable television distribution. As a background for the subsequent chapters on the principles and applications of optical communications, this chapter summarizes the important blocks in a communication system and reviews the development of lightwave transmission technology.

1.1 COMMUNICATION SYSTEMS

An optical or lightwave communication system is a **communication system** that uses lightwaves as the carrier for transmission. A communication system in this book is referred to as a point-to-point transmission link. When many transmission links are interconnected with multiplexing or switching functions as depicted in Figure 1.1, they are called a **communication network**. A communication network allows us to communicate with one another via shared transmission facilities. Important elements of a communication network and how lightwave technology can be used in high-speed networks will be discussed in detail in the next chapter.

Each communication link shown in Figure 1.1 consists of three basic components: a transmitter, a channel, and a receiver [1]. As illustrated in Figure 1.2, the transmitter converts the input message to a form suitable for transmission through the communication channel, which is a medium guiding the transmitted signal to the receiver. In most cases, the final received signal is corrupted by noise. In Figure 1.2, the noise comes from the channel, but this is only illustrative. In optical fiber communication systems, noise from the fiber channel is negligible. On the other hand, there are multiple noise sources from both the transmitter (light source) and the optical receiver. In addition to noise, the received signal can also be corrupted by distortion from a nonideal channel. Therefore, the challenge of the receiver design is to recover the transmitted signal from the corrupted form.

Example 1.1	**BASIC OPTICAL FIBER COMMUNICATION SYSTEM** In optical fiber communications, the key component in the transmitter is a light source, the channel is an optical fiber, and the receiver consists of a photodiode and a detection circuit. The light source can be a light emitting diode (LED) or a laser diode (LD). The light source is used to convert an electrical signal to an optical signal, which can propagate inside the fiber. An optical fiber is an optical waveguide that primarily consists of a core and a cladding layer. The light signal is confined within the core layer and propagates. The photodetector at the receiver converts the light signal back to an electrical signal, which is used for final signal detection or demodulation. These components will be discussed in detail in subsequent chapters. ∎

In a practical communication system, the transmitter and receiver can be further broken down into many smaller blocks. For example, a transmitter may consist of blocks performing source coding, channel coding, line coding, modulation, and signal amplification. And a receiver may include blocks performing equalization, retiming, detection, demodulation, and decoding. These blocks are illustrated in Figure 1.3. In optical communications, because transmission speeds are usually very high, simple coding, retiming, and equalization are important in the system design [2]. Example 1.2 explains the use of these blocks. Further illustration is given in Problem 1–2.

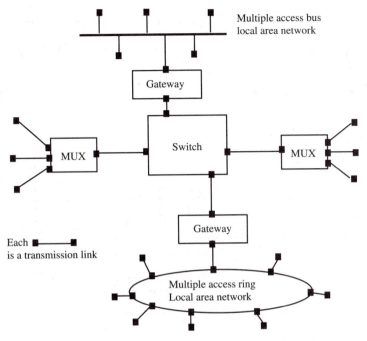

Figure 1.1 A communication network of interconnected links and subnetworks.

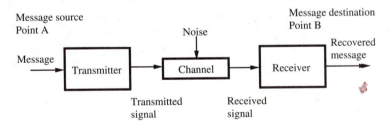

Figure 1.2 A point-to-point transmission link.

DIGITIZED IMAGE TRANSMISSION A digitized image is an image sampled in pixels (picture elements) and quantized into binary bits (0's and 1's). Because a digitized image consists of many bits (e.g., a 24 bits per pixel color image of 1000×1000 pixels has 24 megabits or 3 megabytes), source coding is frequently used to reduce the number of bits in transmission. When bits are transmitted in the channel, they can be corrupted by noise or adjacent bits called intersymbol interference (ISI). This corruption results in possible detection errors for the transmitted bits. Because source coding is liable to transmission errors, channel coding is often used to detect and correct error bits by adding extra parity

Example 1.2

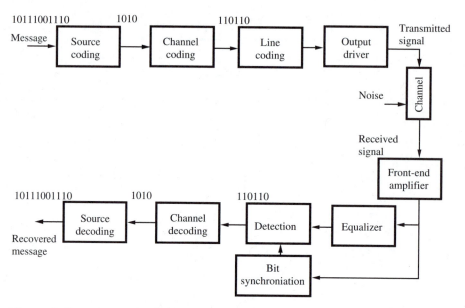

Figure 1.3   A more detailed look at a communication system.

check bits or redundant bits. In addition, line coding is used to achieve certain properties in the transmitted waveform, such as dc balance and sufficient transitions. This use of line coding will be further explained in Chapter 16. At the receiver side, due to added noise and distortion from transmission, an equalizer is used to maximize the detection performance. Bit timing synchronization is used to recover the original transmitter bit clock for sampling and detecting the transmitted bits. ∎

There are many different communication systems in which signals are transmitted and detected in different ways. Differences in communication systems can be characterized in three aspects: (1) baseband versus passband, (2) analog versus digital, and (3) coherent versus incoherent detection. These important aspects are discussed below for better understanding of various optical communication systems.

1.2 BASEBAND VERSUS PASSBAND

A signal can be transmitted in different frequency bands. If the signal is transmitted over its original frequency band, the transmission is called **baseband transmission**. On the other hand, if the signal is shifted to a frequency band higher than its original baseband, it is called **passband transmission**. Some baseband and passband signals are illustrated in Figure 1.4.

Signals as a function of time   Corresponding spectrum

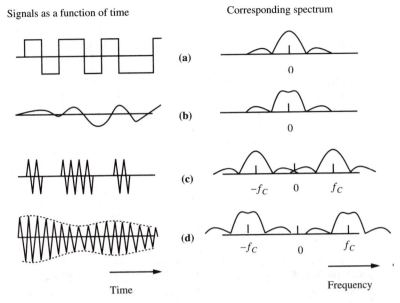

Time   Frequency

Figure 1.4   Illustration of baseband and passband signals: (a) a baseband binary signal, (b) a baseband continuous signal, (c) an amplitude modulated passband signal from the binary baseband signal, and (d) an amplitude modulated passband signal from the continuous baseband signal.

Shifting a baseband signal to a passband can be achieved by multiplying the baseband signal by a high frequency carrier:

$$s_{AM}(t) = m(t)\cos(\omega_c t) \qquad [1.1]$$

where $m(t)$ is the baseband signal, $\cos(\omega_c t)$ is the carrier, and s_{AM} is called an **amplitude modulated** passband signal because its amplitude is proportional to the baseband signal (see Figure 1.5) [3][4]. According to the Fourier transform, the spectra of $s_{AM}(t)$ and $m(t)$ are related by

$$S_{AM}(\omega) = \mathcal{F}\{s_{AM}(t)\} = \frac{1}{2}M(\omega - \omega_c) + \frac{1}{2}M(\omega + \omega_c) \qquad [1.2]$$

where $M(\omega)$ is the Fourier transform of $m(t)$. This equation shows that the output spectrum consists of two frequency shifts of the baseband signal by an amount $\pm\omega_c$.

The high frequency carrier can be generally expressed as

$$c(t) = A\cos[\omega_c t + \phi(t)].$$

Because it is a function of not only its amplitude A but also its phase $\phi(t)$ and frequency $\omega_c/2\pi$, another way to shift a baseband signal to a passband signal is to modulate the phase or frequency according to the baseband signal. This is illustrated in Example 1.3.

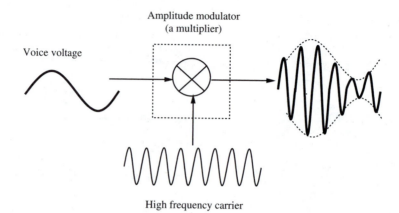

Amplitude modulator
(a multiplier)

Voice voltage

High frequency carrier

Figure 1.5   Illustration of amplitude modulation.

Example 1.3

FREQUENCY MODULATION   In FM the instantaneous frequency of the carrier $f(t)$ is the sum of a fixed high frequency term f_c plus a small term proportional to the baseband signal. That is, an FM signal of the form

$$s_{FM}(t) = A\cos[\theta(t)] \tag{1.3}$$

has instantaneous frequency

$$f(t) = \frac{1}{2\pi}\frac{d\theta(t)}{dt} = f_c + \frac{k_{FM}}{2\pi}m(t) \tag{1.4}$$

where the instantaneous frequency is by definition the time derivative of the phase divided by 2π, and k_{FM} is called the modulation index.

Therefore, in contrast with AM signals, the amplitude or the envelope A of an FM signal is constant, but its instantaneous frequency moves up and down around f_c. The amount of frequency deviation is determined by both the modulation index and the input message signal. Detailed discussion on FM can be seen in [3][4]. ∎

Why Passband?   There are several reasons to shift a baseband signal to passband. First, some transmission media have either a large loss or high noise at low frequencies. For example, optical fibers have a cutoff frequency below which electromagnetic waves have a high loss. Therefore, we need to convert a baseband signal to a lightwave for transmission over optical fibers. Similarly, in seawater communications, either extremely low frequency (ELF) of a few hundred Hz or blue light in the visible frequency range is chosen because of the low attenuation (this is why seawater is blue) [5].

Another reason for passband transmission is to multiplex multiple signals in the same transmission medium. For example, AM/FM radio and TV channels are multiplexed in the frequency domain by a process called frequency division multiplexing (FDM) [3], where each channel is centered around a preassigned carrier frequency. AM, FM, and TV are in the frequency ranges of 530–1700 kHz, 88–108 MHz, and 54–88 MHz plus 120–600 MHz, respectively. In optical communications, the carrier is in the visible or infrared frequency range. If the amplitude of a light signal is proportional to a baseband signal (except for a possible dc shift), the amplitude modulation is similar to that in AM/FM radio. As in radio, one can multiplex several optical signals of different carrier frequencies in the same fiber. This multiplexing in the frequency domain allows multiple transmissions at the same time. This same FDM technique in optical communications is called wavelength division multiplexing (WDM) [6]–[8].

FDM is sometimes done in several hierarchical layers. This is called subcarrier multiplexing (SCM). In the case of optical communications, the first step of frequency multiplexing is in the radio frequency (RF) domain. The combined radio signal is then used to modulate a light carrier [9]–[12]. Example 1.4 illustrates an important application based on SCM.

VIDEO TRANSMISSION OVER OPTICAL FIBERS   Cable television signals are traditionally amplitude modulated and frequency multiplexed over the 54–600 MHz band (excluding the 88–108 MHz FM band). As optical fiber transmission has become more cost-effective, many cable operators have used video transmission over fibers in video signal distribution [13][14]. To transmit these analog video signals that have already been multiplexed in the RF domain, SCM is a natural choice. In this approach, the multiplexed signal directly modulates the output light intensity of a laser diode. This subcarrier modulation is illustrated in Figure 1.6. In this system, there are two steps of carrier shifts. The first carrier shift is from the baseband to the RF band, and the second shift is from the RF band to the optical band. ■

Example 1.4

Careful observation of Example 1.4 reveals that the higher the carrier frequency, the more information it can carry. For example, in optical SCM transmission, the optical carrier is used to carry RF carriers. A higher carrier frequency can carry more information because it is the carrier frequency that determines the radio or lightwave propagation characteristic. When the frequency change caused by modulation is small compared to the carrier frequency, there is no significant change in wave propagation. As a result, for a given percentage of frequency deviation, we can transmit more information by increasing the carrier frequency. Figure 1.7 shows that lightwaves are five to six decades higher than microwaves in frequency, where each decade is 10 times higher in frequency, which is the fundamental reason for a large transmission capacity (several THz or thousands of GHz) in optical communications.

1.3 ANALOG VERSUS DIGITAL

Another important characteristic in communications is the **discreteness** of a message that is transmitted. In Example 1.2, a digitized image is transmitted in discrete binary bits (two levels). This is called digital communication. On the other hand, in the previous AM and

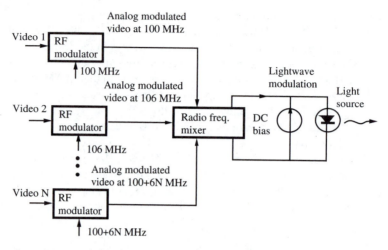

Figure 1.6   Illustration of subcarrier multiplexing for cable TV signals. Carrier frequencies shown are not the same as those used in real systems.

FM examples, input signals have a continuous waveform. This is called analog communication. Two digital communication examples are illustrated below.

Example 1.5	**AMPLITUDE-SHIFT KEYING** When the input signal to the AM modulator in Equation (1.1) is not continuous but instead has a finite number of discrete values, we have the digital counterpart of amplitude modulation called amplitude-shift keying (ASK). A four-level ASK signal is illustrated in Figure 1.8. As we can see, it is a passband digital signal, although only one carrier cycle per bit interval is drawn for illustration simplicity. ∎

Example 1.6	**U-INTERFACE OF ISDN** A baseband version of the four-level amplitude modulated signal is used in the U-interface of the integrated services digital networks (ISDN) [15]. The U-interface is the user interface between the ISDN network and its subscribers. In this defined interface, the bit rate is 160 kb/s, including 144 kb/s for user data and 16 kb/s for framing and control. Because of the four levels, each symbol carries two information bits. Therefore, the baud rate is 80 kilobauds per second. ∎

Because a digital signal has only a finite number of discrete levels, digital communication is in general more immune to noise than analog communication. For example, if noise in the channel is relatively small compared to the distance between two adjacent levels, original messages can still be recovered correctly in the presence of noise. However, in analog communication, once noise is added to the transmitted signal, it cannot be easily re-

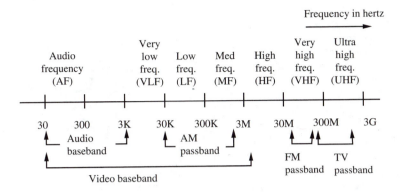

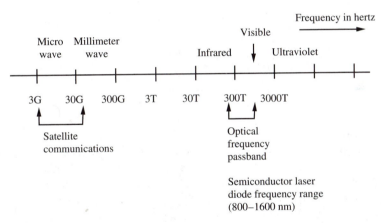

Figure 1.7   Electromagnetic spectrum from dc to lightwaves.

moved. This noise effect can accumulate when several analog transmission links are cascaded. Because of this noise effect, many analog communication systems have been converted to digital. For example, most voice transmissions in current telephone networks are digital, where voice signals are sampled, quantized in bits, and transmitted digitally [3]. This allows us to hear crystal clear sound over a long distance.

ADVANTAGE OF DIGITAL COMMUNICATION   In analog communication, if the transmitted signal power is 0.1 mW and the noise power in the channel is 1 μW, the signal-to-noise ratio is **Example 1.7**

$$\text{SNR} = \frac{0.1 \text{ mW}}{1 \text{ } \mu\text{W}} = 100.$$

On the other hand, in binary digital transmission, a SNR of 100 can have a bit error detection probability lower than 10^{-22} (see Chap. 6). This implies that on average there is fewer than one bit in error

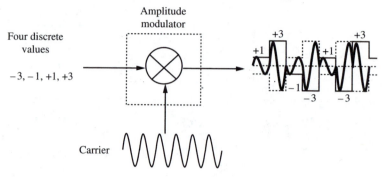

Figure 1.8   Illustration of four-level ASK signal.

if we transmit 10^{22} bits. Therefore, the ratio of the number of correct transmitted bits to that of error bits is 10^{22}, much higher than the SNR of 100. ∎

The trade-off for better transmission quality in digital communication is a larger transmission bandwidth. That is, when analog signals are sampled and transmitted digitally, they require a larger bandwidth than if transmitted as an analog signal. For example, a 3 kHz voice signal sampled at an 8 kHz rate and quantized at 8 bits per sample requires a 64 kHz bandwidth in digital transmission,[1] and 6 MHz video can require 45 MHz with moderate compression.

1.4 COHERENT VERSUS INCOHERENT

When a transmitted signal is received, we need to detect what was originally transmitted. If the signal is passband, it must be shifted back to the baseband. There are two different ways to do this: coherent and incoherent detections. In coherent detection, a different carrier source at the receiver side is used to demodulate the received signal or to shift the passband signal back to the baseband. This carrier is generally called the **local carrier** and is synchronized to the received signal in frequency and phase. On the other hand, in incoherent detection, there is no use of the local carrier [3][4]. Instead, some nonlinear processing is used to extract the amplitude or envelope of the passband signal.

---

[1] A spectral efficiency of 1 bit/Hz is assumed. This means a 100 percent excess bandwidth with respect to the minimum Nyquist bandwidth. See Chapter 7 for detail.

COHERENT DETECTION   In AM transmission, let the transmitted signal be of the form given in Equation (1.1). If we can recover the same carrier, ω_c, at the receiver, we can simply recover the original message signal by multiplying the received signal by the same carrier and passing the product through a low-pass filter. That is, $m(t)$ can be recovered from the low frequency part of

$$s_{AM}(t)\cos(\omega_c t) = \frac{1}{2}[m(t) + m(t)\cos(2\omega_c t)]. \ \blacksquare$$

Example 1.8

INCOHERENT DETECTION   For an AM signal

$$s_{AM}(t) = [1 + k_{AM}m(t)]\cos(\omega_c t)$$

where k_{AM} is the modulation index (small enough so that $|k_{AM}m(t)|$ is always smaller than 1). By taking the square of this AM signal, we have

$$s_{AM}(t)^2 = k_{AM}m(t) + \frac{1}{2} + \frac{1}{2}[k_{AM}m(t)]^2 + \frac{1}{2}[1 + k_{AM}m(t)]^2\cos(2\omega_c t).$$

The first term is the desirable signal term with a proportional constant k_{AM}. The second term is the dc term and is not important. The third term can be neglected if k_{AM} is small enough. The last term is a high frequency term and can be eliminated by low-pass filtering. Therefore, we can approximately recover the original signal $m(t)$ simply by taking the square of the received signal and using a low-pass filter. This detection process is commonly referred to as **envelope detection** and is incoherent because no local carrier is used. $\blacksquare$

Example 1.9

From the above two examples, we see that a primary trade-off between coherent and incoherent detection is implementation complexity versus detection performance. Coherent detection requires a local carrier and associated carrier recovery. Furthermore, the carrier source must be single frequency (see Chap. 3). In incoherent detection, on the other hand, we suffer distortion and limited signal power (small k_{AM}) in exchange for detection simplicity. In optical communications, most systems use incoherent detection for implementation simplicity at high speeds.

PHOTON COUNTING   In the so-called on-off-keying (OOK) optical communications, the light source in a transmitter is turned on if the input binary bit is "1" and turned off if it is "0." At the receiver, we can simply use a photodiode that converts received photons into photocurrent. By integrating the current or counting the received photons, we can detect whether "1" or "0" is transmitted by comparing the integrated value with a threshold. That is, "1" will be detected if the integrated value is greater than the threshold, and "0" will be detected if otherwise. In this detection scheme, the use of a local optical carrier is unnecessary. $\blacksquare$

Example 1.10

Example 1.11

QUANTUM LIMIT   The quantum limit is the theoretical lower limit on the average signal energy needed to achieve a specified bit error rate in digital communication. For example, the quantum limit is 10 photons per bit to get a bit error rate (BER) of 10^{-9} (see Chap. 6). In practice, when OOK signaling and photon-counting detection as described in Example 1.10 are used, we need a few hundred photons to get the same BER performance [16]. On the other hand, if coherent detection is used, the required number of photons can be much smaller and closer to the quantum limit. ∎

1.5 MODULATION AND LINE CODING

The concept of modulation has been discussed in the previous AM and FM examples. Similar to modulation that converts a baseband signal to a passband signal, line coding converts a binary input sequence into a suitable waveform for transmission. Because of similar functions, line codes are also called **modulation codes**.

Modulation and line coding are used for different communication systems. In general, modulation can be used in both digital and analog communications. On the other hand, line coding maps a finite set of signals to another set of signals with certain properties such as dc balance or frequent level transitions (see Chap. 16 for detail). Therefore, line coding is always used in digital communication, whether baseband or passband. Use of modulation and line coding is illustrated in Examples 1.12 and 1.13.

Example 1.12

MODULATION SCHEMES   AM and FM have been described in the previous examples. They are used for analog passband communications. In addition to modulating the amplitude or frequency of a carrier, we can modulate the phase of the carrier. This is called phase modulation (PM). Specifically, a PM signal has the following general form:

$$s_{PM}(t) = A\cos[\omega_c t + k_{PM} m(t)] \qquad \textbf{[1.5]}$$

where ω_c is the central carrier frequency, k_{PM} is the PM modulation index, and $m(t)$ is the modulating signal or information.

If the baseband signal, $m(t)$, in Equations (1.1), (1.4), and (1.5) is discrete and has M different levels, $\pm 1, \pm 3, \ldots, \pm(M-1)$, we have the corresponding digital counterparts called M-level ASK (amplitude-shift keying), FSK (frequency-shift keying), and PSK (phase-shift keying). ∎

Example 1.13

RZ AND NRZ CODES   Two of the simplest and most common line codes are the return-to-zero (RZ) and non–return-to-zero (NRZ) codes. These two codes are illustrated in Figure 1.9. These codes transform binary bits, 1's and 0's, into pulses of different durations. RZ is better than NRZ from the timing recovery consideration. For example, if there is a long sequence of 1's, the transmit-

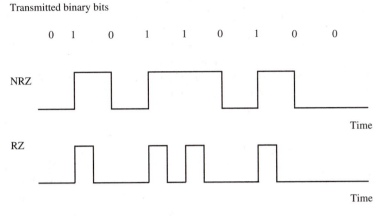

Figure 1.9 RZ and NRZ line codes.

ted NRZ signal is a constant. This constant signal makes it impossible for the receiver to detect how many bits are transmitted. On the other hand, if RZ is used, the transmitted signal is a periodical pulse train. The period equals the bit interval. Therefore, it is easy for the receiver to detect the transmitted bits. To avoid a long sequence of 0's using the RZ code, additional schemes such as **zero substitution**, discussed in Chapter 16, can be used.

RZ signaling can be considered a special case of amplitude modulation where the carrier frequency is set equal to the bit rate. This observation tells that the spectrum of an RZ signal is a frequency shift of its NRZ counterpart in both positive and negative directions by the amount of the bit rate. Therefore, the spectrum of an RZ signal is wider than that of the NRZ counterpart. ∎

Detailed discussion on modulation and line coding in optical communications can be seen in Chapters 12, 13, and 16. Different combinations of modulation schemes, analog/digital, and coherent/incoherent detections for some important optical communications are summarized in Table 1.1.

Table 1.1 Important types of optical communication systems.

Types	Analog	Digital
Incoherent	CATV via SCM	OOK
Coherent	—	OOK, DPSK, FSK

1.6   ADVANTAGES OF OPTICAL COMMUNICATIONS

Because the objective of a communication system is to transmit messages, a communication system is evaluated by its transmission capacity, distance, and fidelity. Recent active research and development in optical fiber communications has been driven by its many advantages, such as large capacity and long-distance transmission. Important advantages of optical fiber communications are discussed below.

- **Large transmission capacity.**   As mentioned earlier, when signals are carried by higher frequency carriers, more information can be transmitted. For example, the capacity in microwave communication is around several hundred MHz, and it is several thousand GHz in optical communication. As a result, transmission capacity in optical communication is not limited by the optical channel but by the electronic speeds. This motivates the use of parallel transmissions such as WDM.

- **Low loss.**   Another important advantage is the low transmission loss in optical fibers. Because of recent advancements, fiber attenuation can be as low as 0.2 dB/km at a wavelength of 1.55 μm.[2] In contrast, depending on the specific carrier frequency and the gauge of the cable, microwave waveguide loss is on the order of 1 dB/km and twisted-pair wires is around 10 dB/km [17]. In other words, if only loss is considered, optical fibers can transmit signals 5 times farther than waveguides and 50 times farther than twisted-pair wires.

- **Immunity to interference.**   Because of the waveguide nature and easy isolation, optical signals can be easily confined in a fiber without any external interference. In contrast, twisted-pair and radio transmissions have significant crosstalk and multipath interference.

- **High-speed interconnections.**   Optical communication is also well suited for high-speed interconnections. Unlike electrical signals, which require a careful control of impedance matching, optical signals can be easily transmitted and received through free space or fiber connections [18].

- **Parallel transmission.**   Because optical signals can be transmitted in free space, parallel transmission in three dimensions is possible. This provides powerful ways to interconnect large numbers of processors for parallel processing, photonic switching, and optical computing [19][20].

1.7   COMPONENTS IN OPTICAL COMMUNICATIONS

As mentioned in Example 1.1, there are three basic components in every optical fiber communication system: light source, optical fibers, and light detector. In addition to these three key components, an optical network can have other components, including (1) optical couplers and splitters to combine and separate optical signals, (2) optical filters such as Fabry-

---

[2] The concept of dB will be explained in Appendix 1–A.

Perot resonators to select optical signals at a particular frequency, (3) photonic switches for switching optical signals, (4) isolators to avoid undesirable reflections, (5) polarizers to maintain the light polarization, and (6) external modulators to modulate the phase or amplitude of a light carrier [21]. Example 1.14 illustrates the use of these components.

A WDM SWITCHING NETWORK   A photonic WDM switching network is illustrated in Figure 1.10 [22]. In this example, each laser diode in the transmitter is operated at a different carrier frequency. They are combined via an optical coupler. The combined signal is sent to a splitter by an optical fiber. The splitter directs the received signal to each of the optical filters. Each filter is a passband filter at a selected optical frequency. Therefore, each signal on the transmitted side can be routed to any detector on the receiving side. Therefore, this system performs photonic switching. The received signal is coherently detected at the receiver where a polarizer aligns the polarization between the received signal and the local oscillator signal. ∎

Example 1.14

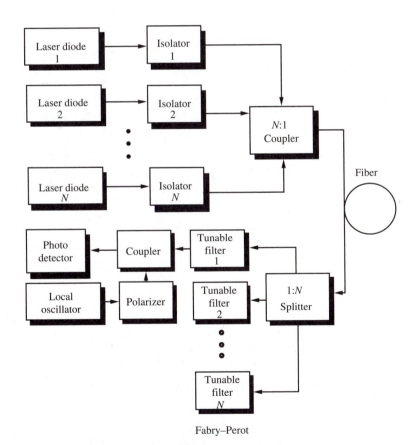

Fabry–Perot

Figure 1.10   Illustration of optical communication components.

1.8 ADVANCES IN OPTICAL COMMUNICATIONS AND SYSTEM APPLICATIONS

The development of optical communication technology has passed through several generations [17],[23]–[25]. The two primary objectives of these efforts have been larger transmission capacity and longer transmission distance. Advances of lightwave technology to improve the capacity–distance product are summarized in Figure 1.11.

To improve the capacity–distance product, higher output power and smaller fiber attenuation are essential to longer transmission distance, and good spectral coherence is key to higher transmission speeds. Therefore, most efforts have been made (1) to improve the output power and spectral coherence of light sources and (2) to reduce fiber attenuation and dispersion.

The spectral coherence of a light source output can be described by the histogram of its output photons according to their frequency and phase. As illustrated in Figure 1.12, the higher the coherence, the narrower the histogram or power spectral density (PSD) of the output photons.[3] Because photons of different frequencies propagate at different velocities in a fiber, an optical pulse will become broader as it travels along the fiber. This phenome-

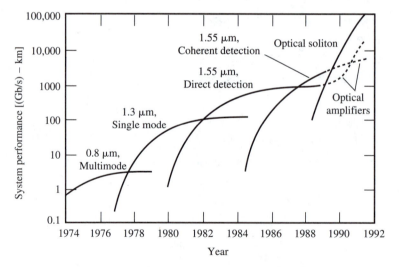

Figure 1.11   Advances of lightwave technology over the last two decades. As illustrated, the technology has developed through five generations, with each newer generation reaching a higher capacity–distance plateau.

SOURCE: Reprinted, by permission, from Agrawal, *Fiber-Optic Communication Systems* [26]. © 1992 by John Wiley and Sons.

[3] A more rigorous definition of spectral coherence requires the use of the PSD. Because its physical meaning is the power distribution of a signal in the frequency domain, we can consider it as a histogram of photons in frequency. For a detailed discussion of PSD, see Chapter 6.

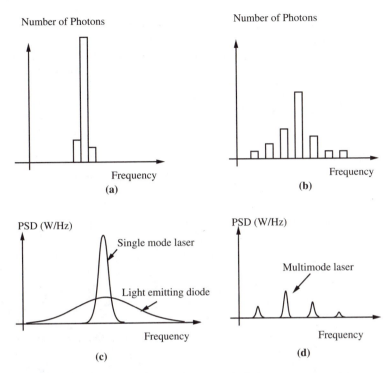

Figure 1.12 Illustration of coherence of a light source output: (a) a photon histogram of high coherence, (b) a photon histogram of low coherence, (c) PSDs of a typical single-frequency laser diode and a light emitting diode, and (d) PSD of a multimode laser diode.

non is called **fiber dispersion**. Because pulse broadening limits the minimum allowable pulse separation in transmission, spectral coherence and fiber dispersion are important factors for large capacity transmission.

The five generations of lightwave technology can now be described from the viewpoint of the improvements made in the capacity–distance product. A summary of key breakthroughs in these generations is given in Table 1.2.

First Generation   In the first generation, multimode fibers (MMF) and direct bandgap GaAs semiconductors were used. Multimode fibers allow multiple propagation modes that result in large modal dispersion. GaAs devices operate at the 800–900 nm wavelength range in which fibers do not have the lowest attenuation (> 5 dB/km) or dispersion. Therefore, both transmission distance and speed were limited in the first generation.

Second Generation   As fiber and material technology advanced, single-mode fibers (SMF) and other III–V compound semiconductors were used in the second generation. Single-mode fibers have much smaller dispersion because there is no modal dispersion due

Table 1.2   Summary of the five generations of lightwave technology development.

Generation	Light Sources	Wavelength (nm)	Fiber Attenuation (dB/km)	Fiber Dispersion	Detection
First	GaAs LED and FP LD	800–900	>5	Large	Incoherent
Second	III–V FP LD	1300	1 at 1330 nm	Minimal at 1300 nm	Incoherent
Third	III–V DFB LD	1300 and 1550	0.2 at 1550 nm	Minimal at 1300 nm	Incoherent
Fourth	III–V DFB and DBR LD	1300 and 1550	0.2 at 1550 nm 0.5 at 1300 nm	Dispersion shifted fiber for zero dispersion at 1550 nm	Coherent
Fifth	III–V DFB and DBR LD	1300 and 1550	Optical amplifiers	Optical solitons	Incoherent and coherent

NOTE: FP stands for Fabry–Perot type lasers, DFB stands for distributed feedback lasers, and DBR stands for distributed Bragg reflector lasers. DFB and DBR are single-frequency lasers.

to multiple propagation modes. III–V compounds such as InGaAsP operated at a wavelength of 1300 nm [27]. At this wavelength, fiber attenuation is approximately 0.4–0.6 dB/km, and fiber dispersion is essentially zero if higher-order contributions are ignored (see Chap. 4 for details). Therefore, transmission distance and speed are essentially limited by attenuation.

Third Generation   In the third generation, further improvement in semiconductor lasers made it possible to generate single longitudinal mode light signals at wavelengths of 1300 and 1550 nm. The coherence of the output light is much improved because of the single-mode output. At 1550 nm, the minimum attenuation of 0.2 dB/km can also be achieved. However, the dispersion is larger than that at 1300 nm. To get the minimum dispersion and attenuation, dispersion-shifted fibers have been used (see Chap. 4) for transmission at 1550 nm.

Example 1.15   Consider a typical optical transmission link with good receiver design that can tolerate a power loss of 20 dB at 1 Gb/s. When the bit rate is either increased or decreased, the allowable power loss is assumed to be proportionally decreased or increased.

In the first generation, if an MMF used for transmission at 850 nm has an attenuation of 5 dB/km, the transmission distance can be up to 4 km, which gives a capacity–distance product of 4 Gb/s-km. Since a typical graded-index MMF has a dispersion on the order 0.1 nsec/km, a transmission distance of 4 km means a dispersion of $4 \times 0.1 = 0.4$ nsec, which is a significant portion of the 1 nsec bit interval at 1 Gb/s. Therefore, the bit rate cannot go any higher, and, as shown in Figure 1.11, the capacity–distance product is around 4 Gb/s-km.

In the second generation, a typical SMF has an attenuation of 0.5 dB/km at 1300 nm. As a result, the transmission distance can go up to 40 km, which gives a capacity–distance product of 40 Gb/s-km. Because there is little dispersion at 1300 nm, this product can be improved by operating the system at a higher bit rate, for example, 10 Gb/s. In this case, the allowed power loss reduces to 10 dB at 10 Gb/s, and the transmission distance reduces to 20 km. The capacity–distance product, however, increases to 200 Gb/s-km. As Figure 1.11 shows, the product is actually smaller because of other high-speed limitations in practice.

In the third generation, assume an SMF has an attenuation of 0.2 dB/km at 1550 nm. The transmission distance can thus go up to 100 km at 10 Gb/s. Therefore, the capacity–distance product increases to 1000 Gb/s. Because single frequency laser diodes are also used in this generation, the dispersion problem at 1550 nm is not a concern. ∎

Fourth Generation   In the first three generations, signals were detected incoherently. In the fourth generation, coherent detection was used to enhance the receiver's sensitivity. With coherent detection, received signals are amplified by the local carrier, which makes the system performance limited by shot noise.

SHOT NOISE LIMIT IN COHERENT DETECTION   When coherent detection is used in the fourth generation, as discussed in Chapter 15, systems can achieve a detection performance of 50 photons per bit. At 1550 nm, this means an energy of

Example 1.16

$$E_b = 50 \times hf = 50 \times 6.63 \times 10^{-34} \times \frac{c}{1550 \times 10^{-9}} = 6.4 \times 10^{-18} \text{joule}$$

per bit. Therefore, at 10 Gb/s, the required received optical power is

$$P_{rx} = E_b \times 10^{10} = 64 \text{ nW} = -42 \text{ dBm}.$$

When we have a transmission power of 0 dBm, the tolerable power loss is 42 dB. At a 0.2 dB/km fiber attenuation and neglecting the dispersion effect from using a single frequency source, the distance limit is 210 km, and the capacity–distance product is 2100 Gb/s-km. ∎

Fifth Generation   At the time of this writing, we are in the fifth generation. To eliminate the attenuation and dispersion limits, optical amplifiers and optical fiber solitons have been developed. Optical amplifiers amplify optical signals directly in the optical domain. Research in optical fiber amplifiers has become sufficiently mature, and repeaterless systems have been demonstrated over hundreds of kilometers [28]. At the same time, research in nonlinear fiber soliton transmission has been successfully demonstrated with negligible dispersion over thousands of kilometers [29].

SOLITON EXPERIMENTS   In the recent optical fiber soliton experiments discussed in Chapter 18, transmission at a distance of more than 10,000 km and at a bit rate higher than 10 Gb/s has been demonstrated. Along the transmission line, power loss due to fiber attenuation is compensated by the use of erbium-doped fiber amplifiers (EDFA), and the pulse shape is maintained unchanged by the balance between fiber dispersion that broadens the pulse and fiber nonlinearity that compresses the pulse. From these breakthroughs, a capacity–distance product of more than 10^5 Gb/s-km was achieved. ∎

Example 1.17

The efforts made in the five generations mentioned have been focused on point-to-point transmission. This is in part because optical fiber communication has been essentially used in point-to-point long-distance transmission such as telephone networks. As the technology advances, it also becomes attractive to use optical fiber transmission for networking applications. For example, optical communication has been used for local area networks such as fiber distributed data interface (FDDI) [30] and various wavelength division multiple access (WDMA) networks [31][32]. In the near future, we will see optical fibers wired near or even in our homes. These are the so-called fiber-in-the-loop [33] and fiber-to-the-home [34]. A review of optical networking is given in Chapter 2, and a more detailed discussion can be found in Part 3.

1.9 SUMMARY

1. A communication network consists of interconnected links, each of which has three basic elements: transmitter, channel, and receiver.

2. A communication system is a point-to-point transmission link that can be done by (1) baseband or passband transmission, (2) digital or analog modulation, and (3) coherent or incoherent detection.

3. All optical communication systems are passband at visible or infrared frequencies. They can be digital or analog, coherent or incoherent.

4. Line coding and modulation are used to convert input signals into forms suitable for transmission. Line coding is used for digital transmission, and modulation is used for passband communications.

5. Advantages of optical fiber communication include (1) large transmission capacity, (2) low attenuation, (3) interference immunity, (4) high-speed interconnection capability, and (5) parallel transmission.

6. The focus of lightwave technology development in the past has been to increase transmission distance and capacity. Low-loss fibers and single-mode light sources are the keys to accomplishing these objectives.

APPENDIX 1-A: THE CONCEPT OF DB

The decibel, or "dB," is a unit that is 10 times the logarithm base 10 of a power ratio. It is frequently used to describe the SNR, fiber attenuation, amplifier gain, and so on. Therefore, this appendix explains the concept of the dB and its use. For two power quantities x and y of the same dimension, the power ratio in dB is defined as

$$(x/y) \text{ dB} \stackrel{\text{def}}{=} 10 \times \log_{10}(x/y).$$ **[1.6]**

For example, if an incident lightwave of 1 mW suffers a 3 dB loss through an optical wave-guide, the output y is related to input by

$$3 \text{ dB} = 10 \times \log_{10}(1/y).$$

Therefore, the output power is

$$y = 1 \text{ mW} \times 10^{-3/10} = 0.5 \text{ mW}.$$

The attenuation of a fiber is characterized by α dB/km. It means that over a distance of L km, we have

$$10 \times \log_{10} \left(\frac{P_{in}}{P_{out}} \right) = \alpha L$$

or

$$\frac{P_{out}}{P_{in}} = 10^{-\alpha L/10}.$$

For example, if the attenuation is 3 dB/km and because $10^{-3/10} = 0.5$, the output power reduces by a factor of 2 every kilometer. If $L = 10$ km, the total attenuation is 0.001 or 30 dB.

Although dB is defined for a ratio of two power quantities, it can also be extended for only one quantity with a reference quantity specified. For example, to express the output power of a light source in dB, a common reference power is 1 mW. For an output power of 4 mW, the ratio in dB is

$$10 \times \log_{10} \left(\frac{P_{out}}{P_{ref}} \right) = 10 \times \log_{10}(4) = 6 \text{ dB}.$$

To indicate the reference power of 1 mW, 4 mW in dB is written as 6 dBm instead of 6 dB, where "m" is added to denote the 1 mW reference power.

One important reason for using dB is to simplify the arithmetic involved. This is illustrated in Example 1.18.

Assume the output power of a laser diode is 5 dBm and the light is transmitted over a fiber of 4 km of attenuation 2 dB/km. If there are 2 couplers with 1 dB loss each, the final power can be easily calculated as

$$P_{out} = 5 \text{ dBm} - 2 \text{ dB/km} \times 4 \text{ km} - 2 \times 1 \text{ dB} = -5 \text{ dBm}$$

or 0.3 mW.[4] The total system attenuation is $2 \times 4 + 2 = 10$ dB. The calculation is simple and straightforward.

Example 1.18

---

[4] Because addition/subtraction of logarithms of the power ratios is equivalent to multiplication/division of the power ratios themselves, only the power expressed in dBm has units, and it is *not* incorrect to add/subtract a quantity in dBm by another quantity in dB.

On the other hand, we can calculate the power using real values. For 5 dBm power, it is 3.1 mW; 2 dB/km loss is equivalent to an attenuation of 0.63 every km traveled in the fiber. For 1 dB coupling loss, it is an attenuation of 0.79. Therefore, the final output power is

$$P_{out} = 3.1 \times 0.63^4 \times 0.79^2 = 0.3 \text{ mW}.$$

Clearly, this approach is less elegant. ∎

One care should be noted in computing dB for signals in electronic circuits. Since dB is defined for the ratio of two power quantities and the power is proportional to the square of a voltage or current signal, the ratio in dB of voltage or current signals (x, y) is defined as

$$(x/y) \text{ dB} = 10 \log_{10}(x^2/y^2) = 20 \times \log_{10}(x/y).$$

Example 1.19   If an operational amplifier has a voltage gain of 10, its corresponding dB value is $20 \log_{10}(10) = 20$ dB. In other words, the power ratio of the output to input is 100 or 20 dB. ∎

PROBLEMS

Problem 1–1 Communication Networks: If there are 50 users who want to talk to each other, find the number of point-to-point links for the following two cases.

a. Only point-to-point links are used.

b. A crossbar switch of size 50×50 is provided.

Problem 1–2 Components in a Communication System: Consider a binary digital transmission. The message consists of the following binary bits: 01 10 01 01 00 01 01 01 01 10 01 10 01 11 01 10. As shown, these bits have been grouped in two-bit blocks.

a. *Source coding:* A source coder is given as follows. The message is first partitioned into two bits per block. For each two-bit block, we have the coding rule given in Table 1.3. Find the encoded output according to the rule given. What is the compression ratio?

Table 1.3   The source encoding table of Problem 1–2.

Input Block	Encoded Output
00	110
01	0
10	10
11	111

b. *Missing bits and error multiplication:* If the encoded bits from *a* are transmitted to the receiver with the first bit incorrectly detected, use the same mapping above to decode the original message. Compare the final decoded output with the original message. How many error bits did the one error bit in transmission cause? This observation illustrates the need for error correction codes.

c. *Channel coding:* The (7,4) Hamming code is a one-bit error correction code that encodes four-bit blocks into seven bit blocks. If the input block is denoted by $\hat{X}$ and the output block is denoted by $\hat{Y}$ (both are in row vectors), the Hamming code has the following rule:

$$\hat{Y} = \hat{X} \begin{bmatrix} 1 & 1 & 0 & 1 & 0 & 0 & 0 \\ 0 & 1 & 1 & 0 & 1 & 0 & 0 \\ 1 & 1 & 1 & 0 & 0 & 1 & 0 \\ 1 & 0 & 1 & 0 & 0 & 0 & 1 \end{bmatrix}$$

Find the Hamming encoded output from the source encoded output in *a*. Note that the matrix product given above uses modulo 2 summation.

d. *Line Coding:* Draw the waveform of the transmitted signal using NRZ and RZ respectively for the first seven bits of *c*.

e. *Channel:* If the channel has an impulse response $h(t)$ given by

$$h(t) = \begin{cases} \frac{1}{T_0} e^{-t/T_0} & \text{if } t \geq 0 \\ 0 & \text{if } t < 0 \end{cases}$$

find the received waveforms from the RZ and NRZ signals in *d*, where T_0 is the bit interval.

f. *ISI and Equalization:* If the received signal is directly sampled at every bit interval, find the linear combination relationship that gives the sampled values in terms of the transmitted bits. That is, if the received signal has a sampled value r_k at kT_0 (for NRZ) or $kT_0 - T_0/2$ (for RZ), find the coefficients x_l that give

$$r_k = \sum_l x_l b_{k-l}$$

where b_k's are the transmitted bits (0's and 1's). ISI is the contribution of adjacent bits to the current sampled value. That is,

$$ISI_k = \sum_{l \neq 0} x_l b_{k-l}.$$

Problem 1–3 Fiber Capacity:

a. In digital telephone networks today, each voice is a 64 Kb/s channel. Calculate how many voice channels a single optical fiber link of 500 Mb/s can carry.

b.   In analog cable TV today, each video channel occupies a 6 MHz bandwidth. If an optical fiber has a 1 GHz bandwidth, calculate how many video channels a fiber can carry.

Problem 1–4 Analog versus Digital: In an analog communication system, assume the total noise power at the receiver is 1 μW. Find the required received signal power to have a signal-to-noise ratio of 1000 or 30 dB. If we use analog to digital conversion, transmit the signal digitally, and assume each bit error is equivalent to 1 mW noise power with respect to 10 mW signal power, find the required received power for the same SNR. Assume the bit error detection probability is of the form:

$$P_E(\gamma) = \frac{1}{\sqrt{2\pi\gamma}} e^{-\gamma/2} \text{ if } \gamma \gg 1$$

where

$$\gamma = \frac{\text{received signal power}}{\text{total noise power at the receiver}}.$$

If γ is smaller than 1, $P_E(\gamma)$ is around 1/2. Note that the equivalent SNR in the case of digital transmission is

$$\text{SNR} = \frac{10 \text{ mW}}{1 \text{ mW}} \frac{1}{P_E(\gamma)}.$$

Problem 1–5 Cable versus Fibers: Consider two digital transmission systems. One uses coaxial cable and the other uses optical fibers. If both systems have transmission power of 10 mW and a total receiver noise power of 5 μW, find the bit error probabilities of the two systems over 10 km. Use the P_E given in Problem 1–4. Assume cable attenuation is 5 dB/km and fiber attenuation is 0.5 dB/km.

Problem 1–6 Coherent Detection: Consider an AM coherent detection system. The received signal can be expressed as

$$s_{AM}(t) = m(t)\cos(\omega_c t).$$

If the local carrier is

$$c(t) = \cos(\omega_c t + \Delta\omega t + \theta)$$

find the detected output according to the detection method discussed in the example of AM coherent detection. This problem illustrates the importance of phase and frequency synchronization.

Problem 1–7 Fiber Attenuation: Low attenuation has been one important objective in the research and development of optical fiber communication. Consider the following scenarios.

a.   If 90 percent of the transmitted power is retained every kilometer, find the maximum transmission distance such that the total percentage of the power retained is greater than 0.1 percent.

b. If the power retention percentage is improved from 90 percent to 95 percent, find the new maximum transmission distance under the same consideration. This problem illustrates the significance of fiber attenuation to the maximum possible transmission distance.

Problem 1–8 Use of dB: If the output of a light source is 0 dBm and the minimum required input power to an optical receiver is −20 dBm, find the upper limit for the fiber attenuation if the transmission distance is 40 km. Assume there is an additional 5 dB loss due to fiber coupling and splicing.

REFERENCES

1. C. E. Shannon, "A Mathematical Theory of Communication," *Bell System Technical Journal,* vol. 27 (July 1948), pp. 379–423.

2. M.-K. Liu and D. G. Messerschmitt, "A Fixed Transition Coding for High Speed Timing Recovery in Fiber Optics Networks," *Proceedings of the International Conference on Communications* (*ICC*), vol. 1 (1987), pp. 188–92.

3. B. P. Lathi, *Modern Digital and Analog Communication Systems*, 2nd ed. Holt, Rinehart and Winston, 1989.

4. S. Haykin, *Communication Systems*, 2nd ed. John Wiley and Sons, 1983.

5. J. D. Jackson, *Classical Electrodynamics*, 2nd ed. John Wiley and Sons, 1975.

6. C. A. Brackett, "Dense Wavelength Division Multiplexing Networks: Principles and Applications," *IEEE Journal of Selected Areas in Communications*, vol. 8, (August 1990), pp. 948–64.

7. I. P. Kaminow, "Non-Coherent Photonic Frequency-Multiplexed Access Networks," *IEEE Network*, March 1989, pp. 4–12.

8. L. G. Kazovsky, "Multichannel Coherent Optical Communications Systems," *Journal of Lightwave Technology*, vol. 5 (August 1987), pp. 1095–1102.

9. R. Olshansky, V. A. Lanzisera, and P. M. Hill, "Subcarrier Multiplexed Lightwave Systems for Broadband Distribution," *Journal of Lightwave Technology*, vol. 7 (September 1989), pp. 1329–42.

10. W. I. Way, "Subcarrier Multiplexed Lightwave System Design Considerations for Subcarrier Loop Applications," *Journal of Lightwave Technology*, vol. 7 (November 1989), pp. 1806–18.

11. J. E. Bowers, "Optical Transmission Using PSK-Modulated Subcarriers at Frequencies to 16 GHz," *Electronics Letters*, vol. 22 (1986), pp. 1119–21.

12. T. E. Darcie, "Subcarrier Multiplexing for Multi-access Lightwave Networks," *Journal of Lightwave Technology*, vol. 5 (August 1987), pp. 1103–10.

13. Stephen D. Dukes, "Photonics for Cable Television System Design," *Communications Engineering and Design*, May 1992, pp. 34–48.

14. David E. Robinson, "Video-on-Demand: The Cable Advantage," *Communications Engineering and Design*, March 1992, p.78.

15. David G. Messerschmitt, "Design Issues for the ISDN U-Interface Transceiver," *IEEE Journal of Selected Areas in Communications,* vol.4 (November 1986), pp. 1281–93.

16. John R. Barry and Edward A. Lee, "Performance of Coherent Optical Receivers," *Proceedings of the IEEE*, August 1990, pp. 1369–94.

17. Paul S. Henry, "Introduction to Lightwave Transmission," *IEEE Communications Magazine*, May 1985, pp. 12–16.

18. D. H. Hartman et al., "Board-level High-Speed Photonic Interconnection: Recent Technology Developments," *Proceedings of the SPIE*, vol. 994 (1988), pp. 57–64.

19. G. Pauliat and G. Rossen, "Large Scale Interconnections Using Dynamic Gratings," *International Optical Computing Conference, SPIE,* vol. 700 (1986), pp. 202–08.

20. J. A. Neff, "Optoelectronic Arrays for Hybrid Optical/Electronic Computing," *Digital Optical Computing II, SPIE*, vol. 1215 (1990), pp. 44–54.

21. *IEEE Communications Magazine: Special Issue on Lightwave Systems and Components*, October 1989.

22. Tadahiko Yasui and Hirokazu Goto, "Overview of Optical Switching Technologies in Japan," *IEEE Communications Magazine*, vol. 25 (May 1987), pp. 10–15.

23. Paul S. Henry, "Lightwave Primer," *IEEE Journal of Quantum Electronics*, vol. 21, no. 12 (December 1985), pp. 1862–79.

24. E. E. Basch and T. G. Brown, "Introduction to Coherent Optical Fiber Transmission," *IEEE Communications Magazine*, vol. 23, no. 5 (May 1985), pp. 23–30.

25. T. Li, "Advances in Optical Fiber Communications: An Historical Perspective," *IEEE Journal on Selected Areas in Communications*, vol. 1 (April 1983), pp. 356–72.

26. G. P. Agrawal, *Fiber-Optic Communication Systems*, John Wiley and Sons, 1992.

27. P. D. Wright et al., "InGaAsP Double Heterostructure Lasers ($\lambda=1.3\mu$m) with Etched Reflectors," *Applied Physics Letters*, vol. 36, no. 7 (April 1980), pp. 518–20.

28. Y. Park et al., "Over 285 km Repeaterless, Dispersion-Free Transmission at 2.488 Gbit/s Using Er-Doped Fiber Amplifiers in Coherent Detection and Direct Detection," *Proceedings of International Conference on Communications (ICC) '91*, vol. 38, no. 2 (1991), pp. 1205–09.

29. L. F. Mollenauer et al., "Demonstration of Error-Free Solition Transmission over more than 15,000 Km at 5 Gb/s Single-Channel, and over more than 11,000 Km at 10 Gb/s in Two-Channel WDM," *Electronics Letters,* vol. 28, no. 8 (April 1992), pp.792–94.

30. F. E. Ross, "An Overview of FDDI: The Fiber Distributed Data Interface," *IEEE Journal on Selected Areas in Communications,* vol. 7 no. 7 (September 1989), pp. 1043–51.

31. H. Kobrinski et al., "Demonstration of High Capacity in the Lambdanet Architecture: A Multiwavelength Optical Network," *Electronics Letters*, vol. 23 (1987), pp. 824–26.

32. M.-S. Chen et al., "A Media-Access Protocol for Packet-Switched Wavelength Division Multiaccess Metropolitan Area Networks," *IEEE Journal on Selected Areas in Communications*, August 1990, pp. 1048–57.

33. TR-909, "Generic Requirements and Objectives Fiber in the Loop Systems," Bellcore, 1992.

34. M.-K. Liu, "From Fiber to the Home to Full Broadband ISDN," *Proceedings of Supercomm/ICC*, 1990, pp. 547–51.

2

FROM POINT-TO-POINT TO NETWORKING

Chapter 1 discussed important aspects of point-to-point communications and presented an overview of the lightwave technology developed over the last two decades. In practice, point-to-point links are seldom used by themselves. Instead, they are used together with other networking equipment, such as multiplexers and switches, for network communications. Chapter 2 explains the basic network communication process and introduces important aspects of a communication network, including medium-access control, switching, and network topology. To explain how lightwave technology can help to improve the overall speed of a communication network, the chapter points out some speed bottlenecks that occur when high-speed point-to-point optical fiber links are used. The chapter then provides solutions to remove the bottlenecks and improve the overall throughput.

2.1   BASIC NEEDS FROM A COMMUNICATION NETWORK

Chapter 1 explained that the function of a point-to-point transmission link is to send information from one point (source) to another (destination). When we want to send information to a different place or to talk to a different person, it becomes inconvenient and expensive to set up a new point-to-point link. To solve this problem, a communication network can be used, which includes functions such as multiplexing, switching, and signaling to provide (1) **connectivity** among people and (2) **cost sharing** for affordability

The need for connectivity can be easily seen from our daily communications for business and for building friendships. Today, through the worldwide telephone network, we can call or fax almost anyone in the world. This convenience allows us to quickly exchange information and improves our living quality.

Example 2.1	**THE TELEPHONE NETWORK** The telephone network allows us to talk to practically anyone by simply dialing that person's phone number. If the person moves to a different place, we can still talk to him or her by dialing the new number. If we are out of town and still want to be reached, we can ask the telephone company to forward any incoming calls to wherever we are. Furthermore, the telephone network allows us to set up a conference call so that a group of people can talk to each other. ■

Example 2.1 shows that the significance of connectivity is threefold.

1. It allows us to communicate with **one another**.
2. It allows us to communicate **wherever** we are.
3. It allows us to communicate **in groups**.

To achieve this threefold connectivity, the network must be able to set up all desirable connections. Without it, one has to use dedicated point-to-point transmission lines. This is not only expensive but practically impossible. This same threefold connectivity is also true and important in data communications, as illustrated in Example 2.2.

Example 2.2	**INTERNET AND E-MAIL** In addition to the telephone network, another important network that has begun to affect our lives in the last few decades is the Internet. The Internet is a successful evolution from the ARPANET in the 1960s for computer communications [1]. Today, government agencies, companies, and most universities in the world can all communicate via the Internet. One of the most important and successful Internet services is **electronic mail** or **e-mail**. With this mail utility, we now can send data messages to anyone else on the Internet.

E-mail service can provide the same threefold connectivity mentioned in Example 2.1. That is, it allows us to send messages to one another, allows us to forward e-mail messages from one com- |

puter to another, and allows us to set up an alias group so that any e-mail sent to the group name will be broadcast to all people in the group. ■

Although connectivity is important, it must also be affordable. Consequently, another need from a communication network is low-cost connectivity. The key to achieving this is to have a large number of users sharing the same transmission and switching equipment in the network. The concept of cost sharing is illustrated in Examples 2.3 and 2.4.

PHONE LINE CONCENTRATION   In the telephone network, each telephone line is connected to a central office. In the office, phone lines are first connected to a **concentrator** [2]. When we pick up our telephone handset, the concentrator in the central office detects this and connects our phone line to a **register**. After the register receives the dialing number, it informs the switch in the central office to set up the right connection. In general, the number of input lines to the concentrator is much larger than the number of output lines. Therefore, the concentrator can significantly reduce the cost for call control and switching. That is, phone concentration allows us to share the cost of registers and switches. ■

Example 2.3

ETHERNET™   Ethernet™ is a local area network (LAN) for computer communications within a small area (around 1 km in diameter) [3]. As illustrated in Figure 2.1, the physical implementation of an Ethernet™ can be as simple as a coaxial cable with taps connected to computers. Therefore, the coaxial cable is the shared medium for computers to send and receive data. If a computer finds the cable is idle or no one is sending data, it can transmit its data to the network. This "sense and transmit" strategy is referred to as **carrier-sense multiple access** (CSMA) and is part of the access protocol of Ethernet™. Because of the simplicity of the protocol, Ethernet™ has become one of the most important LANs. ■

Example 2.4

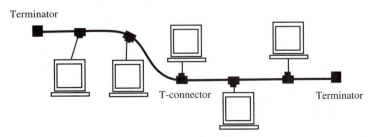

Figure 2.1   Cable is the shared medium of Ethernet™.

2.2 BASIC NETWORK COMMUNICATION PROCESS

To understand how a communication network provides connectivity and to learn how to design an optical communication network, this section explains the basic communication process in a communication network.

2.2.1 SIGNALING

Different from point-to-point communications, network communications in general require a call setup so that data can be properly switched through the network. For example, a call setup is required in the telephone network so that the multiplexers and switches can be configured for the requested call. To set up an incoming call, the network needs to know the call destination and needs to check the availability of the switching and transmission resources. If the call cannot be set up, it will be blocked. During the call, the network also monitors the transmission quality and status of the call. For example, the telephone network constantly checks if either of the two parties has ended the call. If so, the network will release all switching and transmission resources used for the call. The communication process for call setup and call monitoring in a network is generally referred to as **signaling**.

In computer communications, there can be a similar call setup process as in the telephone network. That is, a call request is first sent to the network for proper switching and multiplexing configurations. Once it is done, a call ID is assigned, and data is sent to and switched in the network according to its ID. In contrast to a physical circuit connection in the telephone network, the call ID in data communications is called a **virtual circuit identifier** (VCI), and the call is a logical connection called a **virtual circuit**.

The call setup process in computer communications can sometimes be skipped for simplicity. In this case, there is no VCI, and data is switched according to its destination address. When the size of the data is large, it will be sent in several separate blocks called **packets**. Each packet carries its destination address for switching. In contrast to a virtual circuit, packets from the same data source can be switched through different physical paths in the network. This can result in out-of-sequence packets due to variation in transmission delay. This type of data communications is commonly referred to as **datagram**.

2.2.2 INFORMATION EXCHANGE

After proper call setup, information can be exchanged between the source and destination. During the information exchange period, the "connection," or the switching and transmission facilities used for the call, remains unchanged. This connection is called a **call** in telephony, and is called a **session** in data communications.

The information exchange process in a network can be further broken down into the following four steps.

1. Application data processing: processing source data before transmission.
2. Transmitted data processing: processing transmitted data before it is sent to the network.
3. Network access: accessing and sending data to the network.
4. Traffic switching: routing and switching data in the network.

These four steps of information exchange in telephone and data communications are illustrated below.

DIGITAL TELEPHONY FOR PLAIN OLD TELEPHONE SERVICE (POTS) In digital telephony, voice is first digitized into bits. The basic transmission bit rate of each voice channel is 64 kb/s. This is frequently referred to as DS0 (DS stands for digital signal). The voice transmission process in this case is described below.

1. Application data processing. Voice is first sampled and quantized into a bit stream of 64 kb/s. The quantization is done according to the $\mu-255$ law in North America or A-LAW in Europe [4]. At the receiver side, the received digital data are decoded and converted back to the original analog voice signal.

2. Transmitted data processing. The digitized bit stream is encoded according to the DS0 signal format for transmission. At the receiver side, the original bit timing is recovered, and transmitted bits are detected from the received electrical signal.

3. Network access. The DS0 signal is multiplexed in the time domain with other DS0 signals. In North America, 24 DS0 signals are multiplexed into a higher bit rate signal called DS1 or T1 [5]. This is called time-division multiplexing (TDM) and will be explained in detail in Chapter 8.

4. Traffic switching. Each DS0 channel is individually switched by circuit switches in the telephone network to the final destination. This traffic switching is thus called **circuit switching**.

The four-step voice communication process described is illustrated in Figure 2.2.

OSI PROTOCOL LAYERS IN DATA COMMUNICATIONS As mentioned earlier, information bits such as e-mail messages are transmitted between computers in packets, which are switched or routed according to their destination addresses or VCIs. In contrast to circuit switching in the telephone network, this type of network communications is called **packet switching**. According to the open-system interconnect (OSI) reference model [1], packet switching in data communications is divided into seven hierarchical protocol layers.

1. Application layer. Accept and process user commands.
2. Presentation layer. Prepare transmitted data in a standardized format.

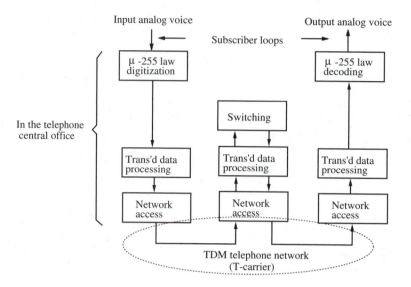

Figure 2.2   The voice transmission process in a telephone network.

3. **Session layer.**   Set up a communication session or call for a given application.

4. **Transport layer.**   Partition large-size data into small packets for transmission and restore them at the destination.

5. **Network layer.**   Switch and route individual packets.

6. **Data-link layer.**   Ensure accurate transmission of individual packets.

7. **Physical layer.**   Perform physical transmission.

To illustrate the seven protocol layers, consider a multitasking computer running two simultaneous communication applications, one is called **ftp** (file transfer protocol), and the other is **telnet** (remote login to another computer). Application ftp allows us to transfer files over the network, and application telnet allows us to use the local computer as a terminal to communicate with a remote computer. The communication processes for the two applications are described below.

1. **Application data processing.**   In this step, user commands are interpreted and processed. For example, in ftp, when a user enters the command: "get hello," ftp interprets the command and sends a file called "hello" from the remote site to the local computer. In the OSI model, this command processing belongs to the **application layer**.

Once a file transfer command is received, the **presentation layer** of the application program ftp converts the file content to a mutually understandable format between the source and destination computers. This is necessary when communication is between two different types of computers.

2. **Transmitted data processing.** Once the source data is prepared in a standardized format, it is sent to the **session layer** in the OSI model. In general, there is one session per ap-

plication. In the scenario considered, there are two sessions, one for ftp and one for telnet. The same session can be used for multiple transmissions as long as the application is active. For example, multiple file transfers can occur over the same ftp session.

One session per application allows the destination to sort arrival packets. When a packet is received, it is sent to the right session for further processing. This allows multiple communication applications through the same physical access.

For file transfer in ftp, a complete file is separated into packets for transmission. At the final destination, the original file is restored from all packets received. In the OSI model the **transport layer** does this packetization and depacketization.

To switch packets in the network, the transmitter also gives each packet a packet header that contains either its VCI or destination address. According to the OSI model, the **network layer** does this packet header processing. The network layer also checks whether there are any transmission errors and, if it detects errors, sends a packet retransmission request to the sender.

3. Network access. Once a complete packet is formed from the above processing, it is sent to the network according to the access protocol of the given network. The access protocol is generally called **medium access control** (MAC) and is specified in the **data-link layer** of the OSI model. Once the network is accessed, packets are transmitted according to the specified transmission technology. The **physical layer** of the OSI model describes the physical transmission.

4. Traffic Switching. When there are intermediate switching nodes in the network, packets are processed and forwarded until they reach the final destination node. In each intermediate node, only the last three layers of the OSI model are performed. Specifically, the physical layer is performed to send and receive data; the data-link layer is performed to access the network and control transmission errors; and the network layer is performed for proper packet switching.

The network communication process discussed for data communications is illustrated in Figure 2.3.

The discussion of the seven OSI layers shows two primary advantages of this hierarchical structure. First, it provides a much easier way to organize and implement the complex communication protocols. By specifying the interface between adjacent protocol layers, implementation of one layer can be made transparent to other layers. For example, if we want to replace the cable transmission by fiber optics, we only need to modify the physical and data-link layers. All other upper layers can remain unchanged.

Another reason for having different protocol layers is to permit heterogeneous communications. Heterogeneous communications are communications between either two types of data terminal equipment (DTE) or two types of networks. For example, consider communications between an IBM PC and an Apple Macintosh. We note that the two computers have different physical implementations, architectures, and network adaptors from various vendors. By standardizing data representations and protocol interfaces, we can communicate smoothly between the two computers in spite of different actual implementations of machine codes, system calls, and interrupt handling.

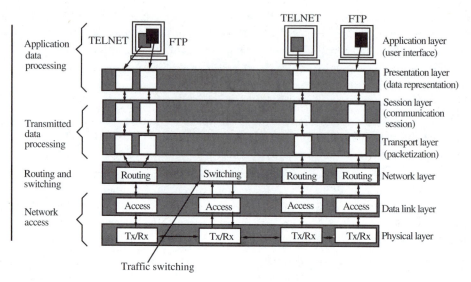

Figure 2.3   The data communication process and the seven OSI protocol layers.

2.3   MEDIUM ACCESS CONTROL

The previous section explained the basic network communication process. In the past, many types of networks were built in different transmission technologies and for different types of traffic. For example, telephone networks and computer networks use two different switching technologies (circuit switching versus packet switching) to carry two different types of traffic (voice versus data). To understand how lightwave technology can be best used for high-speed network communications, the next three sections explain in detail the three aspects of network design: medium-access control, switching, and network topology.

Medium-access control determines how a transmission node sends data to the shared medium. Because the shared medium in general has a much higher speed than the user data rate, medium-access control can also be considered as an interface between low-speed user data and the high-speed network backbone.

According to the relationship between the shared medium and the transmission nodes, there are two types of medium-access control: **multiplexing** and **multiple access**. As illustrated in Figure 2.4, when a centralized device is used between the transmission nodes and the shared medium, it is called multiplexing and the device is called a **multiplexer**. On the other hand, when all nodes are directly connected to the shared medium, the type of medium-access control is called **multiple access**.

In multiplexing, the multiplexer serves as the interface between the transmission nodes and the medium, and the transmission nodes do not need to be concerned with how

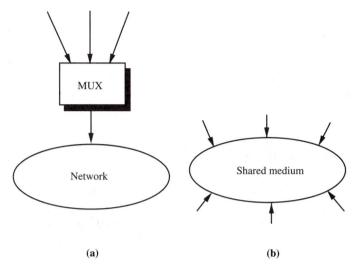

Figure 2.4   (a) Multiplexing and (b) multiple access.

to get access to the network. One important multiplexing example is TDM used in telephone networks. Because users cannot directly access the shared medium, the network is better protected. On the other hand, one disadvantage of this approach is its inflexibility to add new nodes and channels.

In multiple access, communication nodes that talk to each other are distributed over a large geographical area. One important example of multiple access is Ethernet, illustrated in Example 2.4. Because it is generally difficult to synchronize communication nodes in accessing the shared medium, multiple access has a lower medium-access efficiency than multiplexing. For example, traffic in Ethernet can have collisions due to finite propagation delays (see Problem 2–5). Furthermore, because nodes are directly connected to the shared medium, malfunctions from a node can easily damage the shared medium and affect transmissions of other nodes.

2.3.1 SHARED RESOURCES IN MEDIUM ACCESS

Medium-access schemes can be classified according to the form of the shared resource. Three important forms in medium access are: **time**, **frequency**, and **code**.

Time Domain One intuitive medium access is to share the medium in the time domain. That is, each information source gets a portion of time to send its data. This is called time-division multiplexing (TDM) in multiplexing and time-division multiple access (TDMA) in multiple access [6].

In TDM, as shown in Figure 2.5*a*, lower bit-rate signals are bit- or byte-interleaved into a higher bit-rate signal. Accordingly, the multiplexed output consists of **time slots,** each of which carries one bit or byte for one input signal. To demultiplex time slots or to recognize which slots belong to which original inputs at the receiver end, time slots are grouped into **frames,** which have additional overhead bits for frame and slot synchronization. As shown in Figure 2.5*a*, the number of time slots in a frame is equal to the total number of input signals, and when one input gets access to one slot, it continues to use the same slot in each frame for transmission.

To perform multiplexing in TDM, input signals should have the same bit clock. If not, a premultiplexing process that adjusts the input clocks to a common clock is needed. As will be illustrated later in the chapter and explained in detail in Chapter 8, this is called **frequency justification** and is not a trivial process at high speeds.

In TDMA, similar to TDM, communication nodes send their data to the shared medium during the assigned time slots. Different from TDM, however, lower bit-rate signals are first stored in a buffer before transmission. As shown in Figure 2.5*b*, when a node gets its time slot, it transmits all bits stored in the buffer at a high speed. To relax the synchronization requirement, data bursts or time slots in TDMA are separated by **guard time**. With this guard time, transmissions over different time slots can have different bit clocks. As will be illustrated in Example 2.26, this can simplify the timing recovery process and avoid the need of frequency justification.

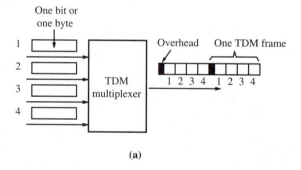

(a)

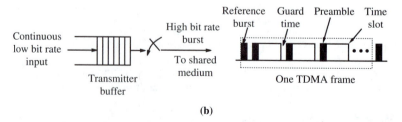

(b)

Figure 2.5   Illustration of time-domain medium access:
(*a*) TDM, and (*b*) TDMA.

To overcome the inefficiency due to guard time, time slots in TDMA are much larger in size than those in TDM. To facilitate timing recovery at the receiver end, each TDMA time slot also includes a preamble at the beginning.

TDMA IN SATELLITE COMMUNICATIONS   TDMA is used in the INTELSAT system. For BG-42 to BG-65 systems, the time frame is 2 msec in length [7]. The instantaneous transmission bit rate of the system is 120.832 Mb/s. If one time slot in the system is used to carry one T1 channel, or 1.544 Mb/s, the time slot size should be at least

Example 2.5

$$T_s > 2 \text{ msec} \times \frac{1.544}{120.832} = 25.6 \, \mu\text{sec}.$$

If we allocate 30 μsec for each slot including guard time and preamble, we can have up to $2000/30 = 66$ time slots in one TDMA frame. ∎

Example 2.5 demonstrates that TDMA provides an easy solution to medium access. One of its main disadvantages, however, is the guard time required. When the time slot size T_s is large compared to the guard time, this is not a problem. However, T_s can be small in optical communications. This will reduce the actual total network throughput even though we have a high transmission bit rate from the fiber optics.

TDMA ACCESS EFFICIENCY   Assume we have a TDMA optical network and the instantaneous transmission bit rate is increased to 1 Gb/s. If each time slot is used to carry the same T1 service, or a rate of 1.544 Mb/s, the time slot size is now

Example 2.6

$$T_s = \frac{1.544 \times 2 \text{ msec}}{1000} = 3 \, \mu\text{sec}.$$

If the guard time is still 4 μsec, the network can have up to $2000/(3 + 4) = 285$ slots, and the network throughput is

$$\text{throughput} = 285 \times 1.544 = 440 \text{ Mb/s}.$$

This is only 44 percent of the maximum possible throughput. ∎

Time slots in the TDMA considered above are used on a preassigned basis. That is, each user is required to reserve a time slot every frame before it can start transmitting data. Below we consider an example that does not require reservation.

Example 2.7	**ALOHA** Another well-known multiple-access scheme based on a time-domain medium access is called ALOHA [8], which can be considered as the ancestor of Ethernet. In this scheme, several nodes share the same RF band for transmission. When one transmission node has data to send, it sends all of its data regardless of the current channel condition. Therefore, there is a high probability of a collision with another transmission. To reduce the collision probability and improve the network utilization, Ethernet uses a modified version called carrier-sense multiple access with collision detection (CSMA/CD). According to the scheme, a node detects the channel before transmission and will transmit its data only when the channel is detected as being idle. During the transmission, the node also detects whether there is any collision. It will stop transmission immediately if a collision is detected. ∎

Frequency Domain Another alternative method of accessing the shared medium is to transmit signals in different frequency bands. In radio communications, this is called frequency division multiplexing (FDM) in the case of multiplexing and frequency division multiple access FDMA in the case of multiple access. In optical communications, this is called wavelength-division multiplexing (WDM) and wavelength-division multiple access (WDMA), respectively.

In general, frequency-domain medium access is similar to TDMA. For example, there is no need to synchronize the bit clocks of input signals. Furthermore, similar to the guard time used to separate time-slot channels, a guard band between frequency channels is needed to avoid interchannel interference.

In optical communications, frequency domain medium access is an important method to increase the total transmission capacity over optical fibers. For example, output signals from a large number of light sources operating at different wavelengths can be coupled and transmitted over one single optical fiber.

Example 2.8	**WDM** Consider a dense WDM system of 100 channels with channel separation of 10 GHz. If the first channel is operated at a wavelength of 1500 nm, its corresponding frequency is

$$f_1 = \frac{c}{\lambda} = 2 \times 10^{14} \text{ Hz.}$$

Because the channel separation is $\Delta f = 10$ GHz, the carrier frequency of the next channel is

$$f_2 = f_1 + 10^{10} = 2.0001 \times 10^{14} \text{ Hz}$$

and the corresponding wavelength is $\lambda_2 = 1499.93$ nm. For 100 channels, this means a total spectrum width of 7 nm. When transmission is over optical fibers, this is not a problem, and WDM can achieve a very high throughput.

However, because the output wavelength can vary as temperature or bias current changes, the channel separation $\Delta\lambda$ may be too small. A typical wavelength shift due to temperature is 0.1 nm/K for single-mode lasers. Compared to the 0.07 nm channel separation, we see it is difficult to have a close channel separation in WDM without a good frequency stablization scheme. Some innovative frequency stablization techniques are given in Chapter 9. ∎

Code-Domain Medium Access Code-division medium access (CDMA) is an abstraction from time- and frequency-domain medium access. In this case, the form of the shared resource is not a physical quantity but a logical "code" or "key." Consider Example 2.9.

DIRECT SEQUENCE SPREAD SPECTRUM   Assume transmitter i has a single symbol s_i to transmit (either 1 or -1). To send the symbol over the shared medium, the transmitter uses a key or a function of time $\phi_i(t)$, which is generally periodic over a symbol interval. With this key, instead of sending s_i directly, transmitter i sends out.

$$e_i(t) = s_i \phi_i(t).$$

If several such $e_i(t)$ signals are sent from other transmitters, the total signal is

$$e(t) = \sum_j e_j(t) = \sum_j s_j \phi_j(t).$$

To receive only signal $e_i(t)$ and reject other signals, the receiver uses the same key, $\phi_i(t)$, and correlates it with the received signal $e(t)$. That is, the receiver performs the following decoding:

$$\hat{s}_i = \int_0^T e(t)\phi_i(t)dt = \sum_j s_j \int_0^T \phi_j(t)\phi_i(t)dt$$

where T is the symbol interval. If the keys chosen are orthogonal or

$$\int_0^T \phi_i(t)\phi_j(t)dt = \begin{cases} 0 & \text{if } i \neq j \\ 1 & \text{if } i = j \end{cases}$$

then $\hat{s}_i = s_i$. This shows the use of keys or codes for medium access. An example of orthogonal keys is a set of passband carriers. In this case, CDMA reduces to FDMA. ∎

Example 2.9

Codes, $\phi_i(t)$'s, in practice are not exactly orthogonal. That is, there is a small, nonzero correlation between two different codes. As a result, unwanted signals cannot be completely eliminated. When the unwanted signals are stronger in power than the wanted signal, the interference can be significant. This is referred to as the **near–far** problem.

2.3.2 DETERMINISTIC VERSUS STATISTIC MEDIUM ACCESS

Medium access schemes can also be classified according to *how* the shared resource is obtained, whether it is in the form of time, frequency, or code. There are two main types in this classification: **deterministic** and **statistic**.

In deterministic multiple access, acquisition of the resource is made on a preassigned basis. For example, in TDM, a time slot is preassigned to a call during the call-setup process. After the assignment, the call can use the same time slot in each frame for its voice transmission.

In statistic multiple access, acquisition of the resource is made on a dynamic basis according to the current traffic demands. In other words, the resource is shared according to the "needs" at the time. In general, there is a fair possibility that more than one node is contending for the same resource. A medium-access control protocol in the OSI data-link layer thus needs to resolve this conflict.

Example 2.10

SLOTTED ALOHA VERSUS TDMA   An improved version of the ALOHA system is called **slotted ALOHA.** In this modified scheme, the time domain is divided into time slots within which data can be transmitted. To overcome different propagation delays in the network, guard time separates adjacent time slots. Therefore, this is the same time-slot structure as used in TDMA.

The difference between slotted ALOHA and TDMA is the way to get access to time slots. In slotted ALOHA, the time slot is randomly acquired according to the current traffic. In TDMA, slots are preassigned during the call request and reserved for the same call during the entire call period. Therefore, slotted ALOHA is statistic multiple access, and TDMA is deterministic multiple access. ∎

2.3.3 MULTIPLE ACCESS IN OPTICAL COMMUNICATIONS

In optical communications, there are practical systems operating on both the time-domain and frequency-domain medium accesses. As the earlier discussion and illustrations show, time-domain medium access is attractive if simple implementation is a primary consideration. For example, there is no need to stabilize the laser output frequency as in WDM, and there is no need to use a tunable filter or a tunable laser diode to tune to the selected channel. Instead, only a basic optical transceiver is needed for each communication node. As will be shown later, the main disadvantage of time-domain medium access is the speed bottleneck from modulation and multiplexing.

On the other hand, the main advantage of frequency-domain medium access is a higher throughput. By having multiple transmissions at the same time, we can multiply the total transmission bit rate by the number of parallel transmissions. The main disadvantage is the need of the more advanced wavelength devices. Detailed discussion on time-domain and frequency-domain medium access is given in Chapters 8 and 9.

2.4 SWITCHING

Switching is the network function that routes traffic to different destinations. As illustrated in Figure 2.6, a basic switch consists of three components: (1) the input/output (I/O) interface, (2) the switching fabric, and (3) the switching control. The I/O interface performs necessary signal format conversion and synchronization. It then sends input traffic to the switching fabric for routing. The switching control determines the switching fabric configuration to form desirable connections between input and output ports.

CROSSBAR SWITCH   One of the earliest circuit switches and simplest in structure is the crossbar switch as illustrated in Figure 2.7. An $N \times N$ crossbar switch has N^2 crosspoints. By closing the crosspoints, the switch can connect any input port to any output port. To avoid signal collision, two input lines cannot be connected to the same output. ∎

Example 2.11

2.4.1 CRITERIA OF A SWITCH

Switches for routing input signals to their output ports are designed based on the following objectives.

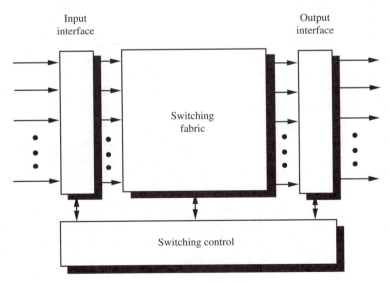

Figure 2.6   A block diagram of a switch.

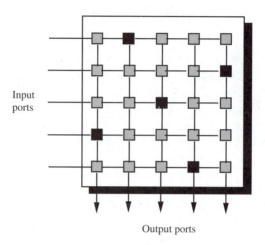

Input ports

Output ports

Figure 2.7   A crossbar switch.

1. Maximum throughput. The throughput of a switch is the total number of bits per second that can be switched through. To achieve a larger throughout, we can increase either the total number of I/O ports or the bit rate of each line. In other words, to maximize the switch throughput, we need a large switch and a high transmission bandwidth in the switching fabric.

2. Maximum switching speed. The switching speed is how fast the switching configuration of the switching fabric can change. This criterion is important when input traffic is time-division multiplexed or packet switched. In this case, the switching configuration needs to be changed rapidly.

3. Minimum number of crosspoints. For an $N \times N$ crossbar switch, the number of crosspoints is N^2. Therefore, as the size of the switch increases, the number of crosspoints can be extremely large and the implementation cost is high. Thus various multistage switching architectures have been designed to reduce the number of crosspoints.

4. Minimum blocking probability. This is an important criterion in circuit switching, in which a switching path needs to be set up when a new call comes in. If there is a path that can accommodate the call request, the new call can be accepted. Otherwise, it is rejected or blocked. The probability of having a call blocked is called the **blocking probability**.

There are two types of blocking probabilities. When the incoming call requests an output port that is occupied, it is called **external blocking**. If the requested output port is not occupied but no internal cross point is available to route the input to the output, it is called **internal blocking**. In general, the external blocking probability is subject to external traffic conditions, while the internal blocking probability is subject to the switch design.

5. Minimum delay and loss probability. This is an important criterion in packet switching, where input packets are switched to the output according to their VCIs or destination addresses. Similar to blocking in circuit switching, two packets may contend for the same output. To solve this problem, one packet is passed while the other is stored in a buffer, but buffering introduces additional delay. If the buffer is full, further incoming packets will be discarded. Therefore, a good packet switch design should minimize buffering delay and the loss probability.

6. Scalability. As traffic intensity grows, the switch size must increase to accommodate more traffic and maintain the same switching performance. Although it is always possible to replace the old switch with a new, larger switch, it is undesirable, because replacing a switch is generally very expensive. Therefore, it is desirable to incrementally increase the size of the existing switch as the traffic intensity grows.

7. Broadcasting and multicasting. To provide conferencing and multimedia applications in which a group of people communicate with each other in data, voice, and video, it is desirable for the switch to broadcast or multicast input traffic to multiple output ports.

2.4.2 SWITCH ARCHITECTURES

The above switching criteria have led to various types of switching architectures. This subsection introduces some important types. Detailed discussion on photonic switch designs is given in Chapter 11.

Multiple-Stage Switches The crossbar switch illustrated in Example 2.11 is one of the most basic types of circuit switches. Its main disadvantage is the large number of crosspoints required. One way to reduce the number of crosspoints is to use multiple stages. A three-stage spatial circuit switch is illustrated in Figure 2.8, where there are r switches of size $n \times m$ at the first stage, m switches of size $r \times r$ at the second stage, and r switches of size $m \times n$ at the third stage.

In this three-stage switch, an $N(=nr) \times N$ switch has only $2mN + mr^2$ crosspoints, as compared to N^2 for a one-stage crossbar switch. For example, if $n = r$, the total number is $3mN$. This is a much smaller number than N^2 if $3m < N$.

A potential problem of a multistage switch is its possible internal blockings. That is, even if two inputs are not contending for the same output port, there can be a conflict in configuring the switch to satisfy all the requested connections.

Clos [9] has given a condition to ensure no internal blocking for the three-stage switch. It is

$$m \geq 2n - 1. \qquad \textbf{[2.1]}$$

To understand this condition, consider a connection request from input port 1 to output port 1. There are m paths that can be used through the middle stage. However, the other $n - 1$ output ports of the same $n \times m$ switch at the first stage may have used $n - 1$ of the m paths in the input direction to the second stage. Similarly, in the output direction from the second stage, $n - 1$ paths of the total m path may have been used to route traffic to the $n \times m$ switch of output port 1 in the third stage. In the worst case, the two sets of $n - 1$ paths do not overlap. Therefore, we need one additional middle switch to provide the con-

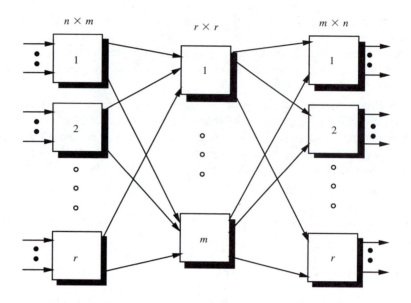

Figure 2.8   A three-stage spatial switch.

nection, which makes $m = 2n - 1$ the minimum number of paths needed to avoid the possibility of internal blocking.

Two-Dimensional Switches Another variation from basic spatial circuit switches is to combine switching in both the space and time domains. One important example of such two-dimensional switches used in TDM digital telephony is called the **time-space-time** (TST) switch shown in Figure 2.9.

In the first stage of the switch, time slots of each T1 frame arriving at a digital circuit switch will be switched in the time domain into different time slots of the same frame. This time-domain switching is referred to as **time-slot interchange** (TSI) and is implemented by memory buffers.

In the second stage, time slots from different input lines are switched spatially. The spatial switching configuration changes every time slot. After this spatial switching, switched time slots in the same frame will be switched again in the time domain.

The importance of this TST switching is threefold. First, it provides individual switching for each time slot. Because each slot corresponds to a DS0 voice channel, this switching provides individual voice-channel switching.

Second, by performing switching partially in the time domain, we can significantly reduce the number of spatial crosspoints. For example, if there are l T1 input lines to the switch, the number of crosspoints is l^2. On the other hand, if we perform purely spatial switching for each DS0 channel, the number of spatial crosspoints in a crossbar structure will be $(24l)^2$. Therefore, the size of the spatial switch is reduced by a factor of $24^2 = 576$.

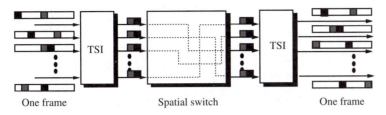

One frame   Spatial switch   One frame

Figure 2.9   A TST switch in TDM digital telephony.

Finally, we can note that the TST switch is logically equivalent to the three-stage pure spatial circuit switch discussed earlier. Therefore, by expanding the number of time slots m according to the Clos condition, we can build a nonblocking TST switch.

NON-BLOCKING TST SWITCH   Consider a TST switch where each input is a T1 line consisting of 24 DS0 slots. According to the Clos nonblocking condition, the minimum number of slots that need to be expanded at the first TSI stage is $24 \times 2 - 1 = 47$. In other words, each TSI at the first stage maps 24 input slots to 47 output slots, and the middle spatial switch changes its switching configuration 47 times over one T1 frame period. At the final TSI stage, 47 slots are mapped back into 24 slots. ∎

Example 2.12

Scalable Switches As mentioned earlier, scalability is an important property so that a switch can maintain the same blocking probability as traffic demand increases. In general, switches can cascade to make a larger switch. However, its internal blocking probability can substantially increase. In optical communications, as illustrated in Example 2.13, scalability can be achieved from the frequency domain.

WDM SWITCH   A WDM photonic switch using a star coupler is shown in Figure 2.10. A star coupler is a multiport optical device that couples a certain number of input signals, mixes them uniformly if ideal, and distributes them to all output ports. In this arrangement, an optical filter is used at each output port to select one of the input signals at wavelength λ_i.

    In this approach, signals are switched according to their wavelengths. When we want to increase the switch size, we can just increase the number of wavelength channels. Because the output filter can select any of the inputs, this WDM switch has no internal blocking and is logically equivalent to a crossbar switch.

    The two main disadvantages of this switch are power loss as the switch size increases and the need of tunable light sources and filters. Detailed discussion is given in Section 2.5 and Chapter 11. In practice, the size of the switch is limited by how many wavelength channels can be multiplexed and tuned to. ∎

Example 2.13

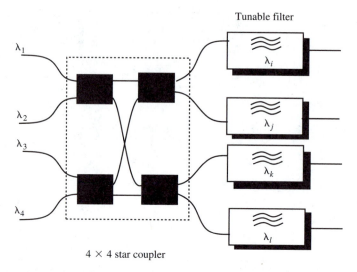

Figure 2.10   Illustration of a 4 × 4 WDM photonic switch.

2.4.3   CIRCUIT SWITCHING VERSUS PACKET SWITCHING

The switching configuration that governs how an input is connected to an output can be either predefined during the call setup or dynamically set up according to the destination information of the input data. These two different types of switching are called **circuit switching** and **packet switching**, respectively.

The switches discussed earlier are usually used as circuit switches. That is, their cross-points, time-slot interchanges, and wavelength tunings are predefined. One type of packet switch is illustrated in Example 2.14.

Example 2.14	**BATCHER-BANYAN SWITCH** A Batcher-Banyan switch is a combination of a sorting (Batcher) network [10] and a routing (Banyan) network [11]. A 4 × 4 B-B switch is illustrated in Figure 2.11.

As shown, the number on each input line represents the final output port number the packet should be sent to. At the end of the Batcher network, input packets are sorted in an ascending order according to their destination output ports. Once they are sorted, the Banyan network routes individual packets to their final output ports.

Specifically, in the Batcher network, each 2 × 2 block compares the destination port numbers of the two input packets. It sends the packet of a higher number to one of its two outputs according to the arrow shown. In the Banyan network, if we represent the destination output port number as a two-bit binary number, the first stage of the network routes input packets according to the most significant bit, and the second stage routes packets according to the least significant bit. As shown in Chapter 11, this sorting–routing combination guarantees no internal blocking.

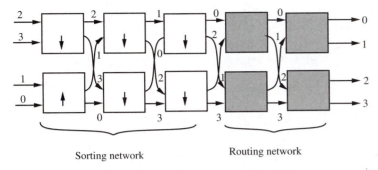

Sorting network   Routing network

Figure 2.11   A Batcher-Banyan packet switch.

This example shows that traffic switching is dynamic according to the destinations of the input packets. In other words, there is no predefined switching configuration. Therefore, there is a fair chance that two input packets may contend for the same output port. To solve this, many modified designs that include buffering have been proposed to reduce the blocking probability. ∎

Historically, circuit switching was introduced for voice traffic [12]. Because voice is a continuous signal in the time domain, packet switching is not preferable for its random delay and possible packet loss. Furthermore, because of the "predefined" nature in circuit switching, it is in general used together with deterministic multiplexing. This can be seen from the TST switch discussed earlier (and shown in Fig. 2.9).

On the other hand, packet switching was introduced for data communications. Because a computer may not continuously send packets into the network during the communication session, packet switching is preferred and is in general used together with statistical multiplexing. This use of packet switching and statistical multiplexing can greatly improve the transmission efficiency of data that come in bursts.

2.4.4   SWITCHING IN OPTICAL COMMUNICATIONS

Both circuit switching and packet switching have been used in optical communication networks. By predefining the switching configuration in circuit switching, the switching control can be simplified and does not need to be processed in real time. Therefore, circuit switching is generally a preferable choice in optical communications where transmission speeds are high.

On the other hand, in packet switching, as transmission speeds become higher and higher, packet duration becomes shorter and shorter. As a result, the speed requirement of changing the switching configuration also becomes tougher. For example, when the switch is large, the switching speed will be limited by the internal bus capacitance.

When photonic switching is considered, packet buffering in packet switching poses another problem. Because photons cannot be "stored" as electrons (i.e., photons have no stationary mass), it is difficult to buffer photons other than by introducing delay lines. As a result, many packet switching designs that employ buffering to reduce blocking probability cannot be easily employed in photonic switching.

2.5   TOPOLOGY

The topology of a communication network describes how communication entities are connected to each other. There are three basic types of topology: ring, star, and bus. There can be various combinations of these three basic topologies to form a more complex topology. The advantages and trade-offs of these topologies are discussed below.

2.5.1   PHYSICAL TOPOLOGY

Bus is a common and important topology in LANs where coaxial cables are used. In optical communications, as illustrated in Figure 2.12a, it can be made of a single optical fiber with hybrids attached for coupling between the bus and nodes. A hybrid is a four-port device with two inputs and two outputs. As will be explained in detail in Chapter 15, a hybrid can be designed so that the power coupling coefficient from the bus to a node is x ($0 < x < 1$), and the in-line coupling coefficient from the upstream bus to the downstream bus is $1 - x$, assuming no other power loss. The single-bus topology allows only unidirectional transmission in optical communications. To provide transmission from downstream to upstream, we can use either a double bus or a re-entrant single bus as shown in Figures 2.12b and 2.12c, respectively. A re-entrant single bus, instead of using hybrids, uses two-to-one couplers and one-to-two splitters.

When the two ends of a single bus are looped around and connected, this creates a ring topology as illustrated in Figure 2.13. In this case, only one ring is needed to provide communications among all nodes. However, a double or dual-ring is usually used for better reliability and network connectivity in case of possible fiber cuts. This can be seen from Figure 2.13c and is illustrated by Example 2.15.

Example 2.15	**SELF-HEALING RING** Ring topology has been used in optical communication networks for reliability. As illustrated in Figure 2.13, a double ring of opposite transmission directions is used to protect against fiber cuts. If one section in the ring is cut, two adjacent nodes can loop around the two fibers. This reconfiguration maintains the connectivity of the rest of the network. ■

In the ring topology, as illustrated in Figure 2.13, the coupling between the ring and a node can be either active or passive. Passive coupling provides better reliability and simpler implementation because there are no active components in the ring. The disadvantage

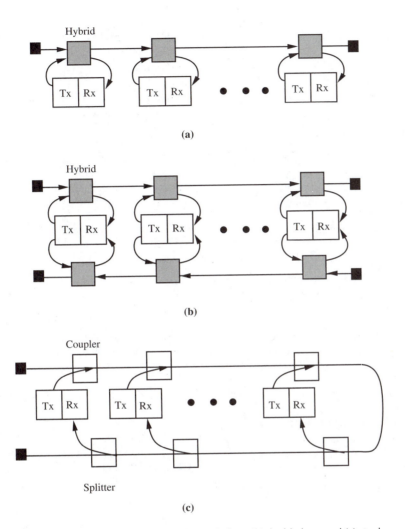

Figure 2.12   Bus topology: (a) single bus, (b) double bus, and (c) single re-entrant bus.

is coupling loss similar to the bus. On the other hand, if active coupling is used, each local transceiver regenerates the bus signal. Therefore, the network is subject to active component failure.

Another important type of topology is the star. In this case, all signals come to the star, which can either combine all the inputs and broadcast them to all the output ports or switch inputs to different output ports. In the first case, the star can be as simple as a passive star coupler or it can be an active one with power amplification. In the second case, the star contains a switch.

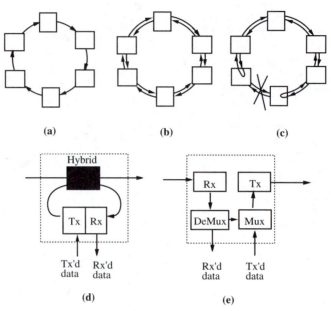

Figure 2.13   Ring topology: (*a*) single ring, (*b*) dual ring, (*c*) loop-around when there is a fiber cut, (*d*) passive coupling, and (*e*) active coupling.

2.5.2 LOGICAL TOPOLOGY

In contrast to the physical topology, which determines the physical connection of network entities, the logical topology is the logical connection of the network. This concept of logical topology can be understood from Example 2.16.

Example 2.16   **LOGICAL RING FROM PHYSICAL STAR**   As illustrated in Figure 2.14, a logical ring can be implemented from a physical star using WDMA. By properly defining the transmitter wavelength and receiver tuning frequency at each node, all the nodes can be connected as a ring. ∎

2.5.3 TOPOLOGY CONSIDERATIONS IN OPTICAL COMMUNICATIONS

To decide which topology to use in designing an optical communication network, there are two important considerations: power loss and the dynamic range of the received signal.

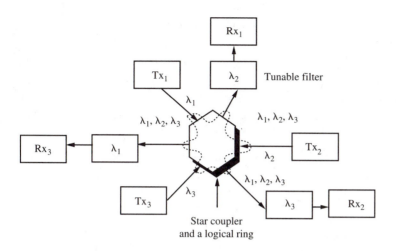

Figure 2.14   A logical ring from a physical WDM star.

Power Loss As illustrated in Example 2.4, it is easy in RF communications to use T-connectors to access the signal in the cable without causing significant signal attenuation. In optical communications, a typical T-connector can have a power loss of 1 dB. If we put several T-couplers in series, the total power loss can be significant. Therefore, a bus topology is not preferred in optical communications when the number of nodes is large. A more quantitative discussion on the power loss is given below.

Consider either a single or a double bus of N nodes. Assume the power coupling from the bus to a node (or vice versa) is $10^{-\alpha/10}x$, and the in-line coupling from the upstream to downstream is $10^{-\alpha/10}(1 - x)$, where $0 < x < 1$ and α is the coupling loss in dB. As a result, for the worst case of N couplings through the bus, the total power loss is

$$\eta_{bus} = (1 - x)^{N-2}x^2 10^{-\alpha N/10}$$
$$= 10(N - 2)\log_{10}(1 - x) + 20\log_{10} x - \alpha N \text{ dB.} \qquad \textbf{[2.2]}$$

Equation (2.2) shows that x cannot be too close to one or too close to zero. In space either of the two limits, η_{bus} will be close to zero. Therefore, there exists an optimum x value that can maximize η_{bus}. If we take the derivative of Equation (2.2) with respect to x, the condition for the optimum x is

$$-\frac{N - 2}{1 - x} + \frac{2}{x} = 0.$$

This gives

$$x_{bus,opt} = \frac{2}{N}. \qquad \textbf{[2.3]}$$

Substituting the above expression into Equation (2.2) and assuming $N \gg 1$, we get

$$\eta_{bus,opt} \approx \frac{1}{e^2}\left(\frac{2}{N}\right)^2 10^{-\alpha N/10} = -[2.6 + 6\log_2 N + \alpha N] \text{ dB.} \qquad \textbf{[2.4]}$$

Example 2.17

SINGLE BUS LOSS   Consider a numerical example with $\alpha = 1$ dB. At $N=10$

$$\eta_{bus,opt} = -(2.6 + 19.9 + 10) = -32.5 \text{ dB}$$

and at $N = 100$

$$\eta_{bus,opt} = -(2.6 + 39.9 + 100) = -142.5 \text{ dB.}$$

Clearly, power loss increases significantly when N is increased from 10 to 100. ∎

Consider the single re-entrant bus. The worst case power loss between the two left-most nodes can be similarly derived and is given by

$$\eta_{r.bus} = x(1-x)^{2N-3}x10^{-\alpha(2N-1)/10}$$
$$= 20\log_{10} x + 10(2N-3)\log_{10}(1-x) - \alpha(2N-1)\text{dB.} \qquad \textbf{[2.5]}$$

It can be easily verified that the optimum x in this case is

$$x_{r.bus,opt} = \frac{2}{2N-1} \qquad \textbf{[2.6]}$$

and

$$\eta_{r.bus,opt} \approx \frac{1}{e^2}\left(\frac{1}{N}\right)^2 10^{-\alpha(2N-1)/10} = -[8.68 + 6\log_2 N + \alpha(2N-1)] \text{ dB.} \quad \textbf{[2.7]}$$

Example 2.18

RE-ENTRANT BUS LOSS   If we follow the same assumptions as the previous example, we have

$$\eta_{r.bus,opt} = -(8.68 + 19.93 + 19) = -47.6 \text{ dB}$$

for $N = 10$, and

$$\eta_{r.bus,opt} = -(8.68 + 39.86 + 199) = -247.5 \text{ dB}$$

for $N = 100$. The power loss is even worse in this case. ∎

For an $N \times N$ star coupler, because the total signal is equally distributed over the N output ports, there is at least a power loss factor of $1/N$ for each input due to distribution.

In practice, there is additional loss from the coupler. To take this into consideration, one must know how many internal couplings a signal goes through. As illustrated in Figure 2.10, there are two stages of hybrids for the 4×4 star coupler. In general, for an $N \times N$ star coupler, there are $\log_2 N$ stages. Therefore, if each stage has a power loss of α in dB, the total additional power loss is $\alpha \log_2 N$ in dB. From the discussion, the output to input power ratio of an $N \times N$ star coupler is

$$\eta_{star} = \frac{1}{N} 10^{-\alpha \log_2 N} = -(10 \log_{10} N + \alpha \log_2 N) \text{ dB}$$

or

$$\eta_{star} = -(3 + \alpha) \log_2 N \text{ dB}. \qquad \textbf{[2.8]}$$

POWER LOSS OF A STAR COUPLER   Follow the same assumptions of the previous example. For $N = 10$, | **Example 2.19**

$$\eta_{star} = -4 \times 3.32 = -13.3 \text{ dB}$$

and for $N = 100$

$$\eta_{star} = -4 \times 6.64 = -26.6 \text{ dB}.$$

Thus, the power loss problem is not as significant as that in the bus topology. ∎

Dynamic Range   Because a receiver can receive signals from different transmitters on the same network, the received signal power can vary over a certain range. The power ratio of the maximum received power to the minimum power is called the **dynamic range**. As will be discussed in Chapter 7, an optical receiver can only properly receive signals within a finite dynamic range, beyond which the signal can be either too weak to be detectable or too strong to be useful. Therefore, the dynamic range is also an important consideration in selecting the topology.

In the star topology, the received signal power from each transmitter has equal power if the star coupler is made symmetrical and the transmission paths have equal attenuation. Therefore, the dynamic range is simply 1 or 0 dB.

On the other hand, in the single-bus or ring topology, the received power varies. If the received signal comes from the immediate upstream node, the received power is

$$P_{max} = P_0 x^2 10^{-2\alpha/10}$$

where P_0 is the transmission power. On the other hand, if the transmission is between the two farthest separated nodes (two end nodes in the bus or two adjacent nodes in the ring where the downstream node transmits data to the upstream), the received power is

$$P_{min} = P_0 x^2 (1-x)^{N-2} 10^{-N\alpha/10}.$$

Therefore, the dynamic range is

$$\text{DR}_{bus} = \frac{10^{(N-2)\alpha/10}}{(1-x)^{N-2}} = (N-2)[-10\log_{10}(1-x) + \alpha] \text{ dB.} \qquad \textbf{[2.9]}$$

Thus, the dynamic range in dB is approximately linearly proportional to the number of nodes. When N is large and the optimum, $x_{bus,opt} = 2/N$, is used,

$$\text{DR}_{bus} \approx e^2 10^{(N-2)\alpha/10} = [8.7 + (N-2)\alpha] \text{ dB.} \qquad \textbf{[2.10]}$$

Similarly, for the re-entrant bus topology, the dynamic range is

$$\text{DR}_{r.bus} = \frac{10^{(2N-4)\alpha/10}}{(1-x)^{2N-4}}$$

or

$$\text{DR}_{r.bus} \approx e^2 10^{(2N-4)\alpha/10} = [8.7 + 2(N-2)\alpha] \text{ dB} \qquad \textbf{[2.11]}$$

when $x = x_{r.bus,opt} = 2/(2N-1)$ is used.

Example 2.20	**DYNAMIC RANGE IN BUS TOPOLOGY** If the optical receiver used in the bus topology can allow only a dynamic range of 30 dB, at $\alpha = 1$ dB, the single bus topology can support only

$$N = \frac{30 - 8.7}{\alpha} + 2 = 23.$$

nodes, and the re-entrant bus topology can support only

$$N = \frac{30 - 8.7}{\alpha} + 2 = 12. \quad \blacksquare$$

2.6   SPEED BOTTLENECKS IN OPTICAL NETWORK COMMUNICATIONS

As more users are connected to the network, more data per second is transmitted over the network. As a result, one challenging question that constantly faces network operators is how to increase the network throughput to meet the growing demands for connectivity. The rapid development of lightwave technology is driven by this motivation.

From the previous discussion, one can recognize that increasing the transmission speed alone is not sufficient. In addition to networking overhead, due to various signaling and switching processes required in network communications, both high transmission speeds and processing power are required to increase the overall network throughput. Over the last few decades, most parts of a communication network have been implemented using integrated circuit (IC) technology. That is, various point-to-point transmission blocks such as driver and encoder circuits discussed in Chapter 1 and various networking blocks such as multiplexers and switches are based on IC technology.

As lightwave technology is introduced, we have ample bandwidths from fiber optics (thousands of GHz). However, the state-of-the-art switching speed from the silicon IC technology remains on the order of 1 GHz. When many practical factors are considered, the speed can be even lower. Therefore, as lightwave technology is introduced, the electronics part of the network becomes the speed bottleneck. This electronic bottleneck can be reflected in various ways in network communications as illustrated in Examples 2.21–2.23.

OPTICAL SIGNAL MODULATION   One speed bottleneck due to electronics in optical communications is direct modulation. As mentioned in Chapter 1, to modulate the light carrier for information transmission, we can turn on and off a laser diode according to the transmitted bit, 1 or 0. The faster we can switch on and off the laser diode, the faster we can transmit.

Example 2.21

A typical laser diode can respond to a switching speed of around 10 GHz. If Emitter Coupled Logic devices are used to drive the laser diode, however, the highest transmission speed is limited to 1 GHz, the switching speed limit of ECL devices. To solve this problem, GaAs technology has been used to increase the modulation speed. However, this technology is relatively immature and can only be integrated on a small scale as compared to the silicon technology.

Even when the GaAs technology is used, due to its speed limit and the modulation bandwidth of laser diodes, the transmission rate still cannot go beyond the order of 10 GHz, which is still much smaller than the several thousand GHz bandwidth of optical fibers. ■

MULTIPLEXING   In digital telephony, slower bit-rate signals are multiplexed into a higher bit-rate signal for transmission. When the slower bit-rate input signals are of the same frequency, multiplexing is basically a parallel–to–serial conversion process. Unfortunately, in many cases, the input signals have different frequencies. For example, although the frequency of DS1 or T1 signals in digital telephony is specified to be 1.544 Mb/s [5], it is only a nominal clock rate. In reality, there is a small plus-minus deviation. When several T1 signals of slight difference in frequency come to the multiplexer, they cannot immediately be interleaved. Instead, their frequencies must first be **justified,** or aligned to a common frequency. This frequency justification in general involves buffering and timing synchronization. Therefore it is not a straightforward process. When multiplexing is performed at higher and higher speeds, the electronic processing of frequency justification can become the speed bottleneck. ■

Example 2.22

TRAFFIC SWITCHING   Because most switches are made electronically, traffic switching in a network can also become the speed bottleneck as the transmission speed increases. To solve the switching bottleneck in optical communications, photonic switching technology provides one possible solution. ■

Example 2.23

The three examples illustrated are in fact the three important speed bottlenecks in optical communications: modulation, multiplexing, and switching. The next section presents important design solutions to these speed bottlenecks.

2.7 DESIGN SOLUTIONS TO SPEED BOTTLENECKS

There are three design solutions to the speed bottlenecks discussed above. In general, these solutions can be used at the same time, and the best combination depends on the specific applications that the network is designed for. For better understanding of these solutions, examples are provided in the following discussion. More detailed discussion can be found in Part 3 of the book.

2.7.1 SOLUTION 1: OPTICAL DOMAIN IMPLEMENTATION

As pointed out earlier, it is the electronics that limits the network throughput in optical communications. To solve the problem, one intuitive approach is to implement the network optically wherever possible. That is, we want to take advantage of the large optical bandwidth and avoid unnecessary optical-to-electronic and electronic-to-optical conversions. Motivated by this viewpoint, the concept of **all optical** communication networks has been proposed. In this notion, all key components of a network such as multiplexing, transmission, and switching are implemented optically. The journey to all optical communications is illustrated in Figure 2.15.

As shown, there are four evolutionary steps. The first step, as discussed in Chapter 1, implements optical-domain point-to-point transmissions. This step is quite mature and has been widely deployed in real systems. In the second step, optical-domain multiple access such as WDMA can be used to provide multiple transmissions at the same time. This optical-domain multiplexing step has been successfully demonstrated in some test networks such as Lambdanet [13] and Rainbow [14]. These test networks are all based on WDMA and require tunable light sources and receivers. The third step adds optical-domain switching to switch traffic. A photonic switch implementation will be illustrated shortly. Due to coupling and power-splitting loss, optical amplification in general is necessary at the same time. Compared to optical-domain transmissions and multiplexing, photonic switching is relatively immature and needs additional development for practical use. Because the communication process requires other complicated processing such as signaling, optical-domain computations that perform network operations would be the final step to achieve all-optical networking.

| **Example 2.24** | **PHOTONIC SWITCHING**   A photonic switch directly switches the light signals from inputs to outputs. A 4×4 photonic switch made of optical waveguides with coupling control is illustrated in Figure 2.16. By changing the refractive index of the waveguides, a lightwave can be coupled from one waveguide to another. This allows one input to be switched to one of the two outputs. The switching theory of these waveguide couplers is explained in Chapters 11 and 14. ∎ |

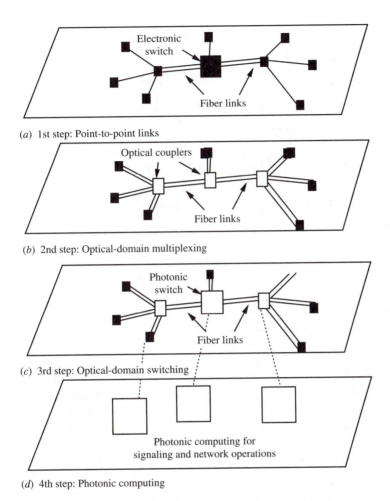

(a) 1st step: Point-to-point links

(b) 2nd step: Optical-domain multiplexing

(c) 3rd step: Optical-domain switching

(d) 4th step: Photonic computing

Figure 2.15   Four evolutionary steps to achieve an all-optical communication network: (a) optical-domain point-to-point transmissions, (b) optical-domain multiplexing and demultiplexing added, (c) photonic switching added, and (d) optical computing added.

Photonic switching can eliminate the speed bottleneck in two ways. First, it eliminates the need for electronic-to-optic and optic-to-electronic conversions. In other words, there is no need of electronic processing. Second, because optical waveguides by definition can support lightwave propagation, the channel bandwidth is broad enough for modulated light signals. Therefore, other than attenuation being introduced, photonic switching can essentially eliminate the speed bottleneck in switching.

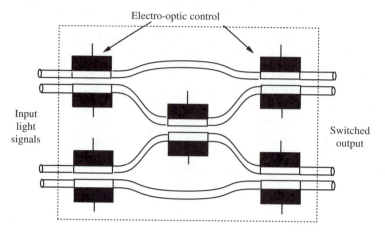

Figure 2.16   Illustration of a 4 × 4 electro-optic photonic switch.

2.7.2 SOLUTION 2: SIMPLE PROCESSING IN EXCHANGE FOR TRANS-MISSION INEFFICIENCY

Because IC technology is much more powerful in its signal processing capability than its optics counterpart, optics cannot practically replace electronics in every part of a communication network. When electronics technology is necessary, one way to overcome the speed bottleneck is to simplify the processing itself. In general, simplifying processing may cause a certain transmission inefficiency. As long as the loss in efficiency is smaller than the gain from the speed increase, this is still worthwhile. This exchange for simple processing can be understood from Examples 2.25 and 2.26.

Example 2.25

SONET   Synchronous optic network (SONET) is a recently standardized worldwide lightwave transmission system [15]. It is a TDM system similar to the T-carrier in digital telephony. As mentioned in Example 2.22, the multiplexing and demultiplexing are complex and speed-limited processes. When the T-carrier system was designed by AT&T, transmission efficiency was one of the highest considerations. As a result, the bit rates in the T-carrier hierarchy have no simple relationship. For example, the T1 rate at 1.544 Mb/s is not a simple multiple of 64 kb/s Pulse Code Modulation voice. One primary reason for this irregular bit timing relationship is to minimize the overhead bits in doing frequency justification (see Chap. 8). However, this complicates the timing recovery, which is another difficult process at high speeds (see Chap. 16).

To overcome the high-speed multiplexing problem in TDM, SONET uses an innovative frequency justification technique called **pointer processing.** Instead of performing frequency justification at a higher TDM level as in T-carriers, SONET performs at the *same* level. Once all low-speed signals are frequency justified with respect to the same local clock, they can be multiplexed to a high-speed signal by straightforward byte interleaving. This minimizes the high-speed processing requirement. In exchange for the simpler multiplexing and demultiplexing, SONET uses more overhead bits than the T-carrier. Detailed discussion on SONET is given in Chapter 8. ∎

TIME-SLOT SWITCHING   Other than photonic switching, one way to improve the switching speed is to simplify the switch design. In a typical TST circuit switch discussed earlier, input signals need to be synchronized in time slots before switching. This is illustrated in Figure 2.17a. Slot synchronization is necessary to allow the spatial switch to change its crosspoints at the same time.

  To synchronize the input signals, input signals must be regenerated and the recovered bits need to be stored in a buffer. To regenerate the signals, bit timing recovery is needed. However, as will be discussed in Chapter 16, bit timing recovery is in general expensive and difficult at high speeds. Therefore, to avoid timing recovery, the system needs to avoid synchronization among input signals. To achieve this, time slots can be separated by guard time. As illustrated in

Example 2.26

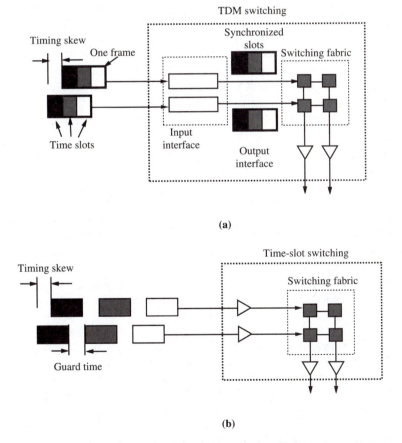

(a)

(b)

Figure 2.17   Illustration of (a) TDM switching and (b) time-slot switching.

Figure 2.17b, as long as the timing skew of the arrival slots is within the guard time, timing recovery of each individual input signal is unnecssary and slot timing can be derived from any one of the inputs. This trade-off between the simple switch design and guard-time inefficiency is called **time-slot switching** [16]. Switches based on this design have been demonstrated at a speed of 250 Mb/s [17][18]. ∎

2.7.3   SOLUTION 3: PARALLEL IMPLEMENTATION

Another alternative to solving the speed bottleneck is to have multiple identical processing in parallel. Ideally, the throughput can be multiplied by the total number of parallel processings.

Example 2.27	**WDM** As noted in Example 2.21, the transmission bit rate is limited by how fast the laser diode can be modulated. One way to overcome this is to have parallel transmissions in the frequency or wavelength domain. If N transmitters are operating at wavelength $\lambda_1, \ldots, \lambda_N$, there are N parallel transmissions. As explained earlier, this is called WDM. Modulating $N = 100$ laser diodes at a speed of 1 Gb/s allows a total throughput of 100 Gb/s. To avoid interchannel interference, the channel separation can be set at 10 GHz. As a result, for 100 channels, the total bandwidth is 1000 GHz. This is well within the fiber transmission bandwidth. ∎

2.8   HIGH-SPEED APPLICATIONS

Although lightwave technology is being rapidly developed to replace many parts of a communication network for higher throughput, it is still expensive if the ample bandwidth is not well utilized. For example, there is no apparent reason to replace Ethernet by fiber optics in a small office environment. Therefore, the widespread use of lightwave technology will also strongly depend on potential high-speed applications. Without applications or the need, the economic factor of lightwave technology is more challenging than its technological counterpart. This section describes some important high-speed applications that have benefited or will benefit from lightwave technology.

Medical Imaging An X-ray image of 1000×1000 pixels and 24 bits per pixel has a total size of 24 Mbits. Typically, the total retrieving and transmission delay should be within 3 seconds. Therefore, if the transmission delay is required to be within 1 second, the transmission rate should be at least 24 Mb/s. To support multiple simultaneous medical imaging transmissions, we thus need a high-speed fiber-optics network.

CATV and HDTV Distributions TV signal distribution is another important application. Current community antenna TV (CATV) systems can support 40–75 analog TV channels. With SCM transmission (discussed in Chapter 1), 150 channel transmissions have been reported. When analog TV is converted to digital, such as high-definition TV (HDTV), the total transmission bandwidth will be much larger. Furthermore, most current CATV services are broadcast. To provide pay-per-view and interactive video services, the required transmission bandwidth will be even much higher.

Video Conferencing and Multimedia Video communication has been a dream of many people since telephony; however, it requires a very large transmission bandwidth. Depending on the quality and compression algorithms, digital video signals can have a bit rate from 1 Mb/s to 100 Mb/s. This rate is 16–1600 times higher than the voice rate of 64 kb/s. Thus video requires a much higher speed not only in transmission but also in switching.

High Performance Computing To integrate several remotely separated computers into a supercomputer for various computation intensive applications, a high-speed backbone network is crucial. As a result, several gigabit networks are being designed and implemented to provide a national-level gigabit network in the United States. Important gigabit testbeds include Aurora, Blanca, Casa, Nectar, and Vistanet [19].

2.9 SUMMARY

1. A communication network is an interconnection of network entities such as multiplexers and switches through point-to-point links. With multiplexing and switching functions, any two users on the network can be connected.

2. The significance of connectivity that a network can provide is threefold. It allows users to communicate (1) with one another, (2) wherever they are, and (3) in groups.

3. To achieve connectivity, a communication network performs two primary functions: signaling and information exchange. To set up an incoming call request, to monitor the transmission quality of the call, and to detect the termination of the call, the switching nodes in the network need to constantly exchange call information. This process is called signaling. Once a call is set up, user information can be exchanged between two end nodes.

4. The information exchange process can be divided into four steps: application data processing, transmitted data processing, network access, and traffic switching.

5. In computer communications, the four information exchange steps are organized in seven protocol layers according to the OSI model. From top to bottom, they are the application layer, presentation layer, session layer, transport layer, network layer, data-link layer, and physical layer. The first two layers belong to application data processing, the next two layers and the bottom physical layer belong to transmitted data processing, the network layer performs the switching function, and the data-link layer performs the network access function.

6. In addition to transmission, various types of network design can be grouped into three areas: medium access control, switching, and topology. Medium access allows low-speed user data to be transmitted over high-speed networks, switching allows user data to be switched to the final destination, and topology describes how network nodes are interconnected.

7. There are two primary types of medium access: multiplexing and multiple access. When a single device serves as an interface between low-speed users and the high-speed network, it is called multiplexing, and the device is called a multiplexer. On the other hand, when geographically distributed nodes share the same medium, the medium access is called multiple access. In this case, there is no multiplexer and nodes access the network directly.

8. Medium access methods can be grouped according to what communication resource is shared and how it is shared. There are three different domains in which the communication resource can be shared: time, frequency, and code. A given type of shared communication resource can be acquired either deterministically or statistically. In the first case, the resource is preallocated before a call request is granted. Once granted, the resource is reserved for the call until it terminates. In the latter case, the resource is shared according to the current needs.

9. According to how the communication resource is acquired, there are two corresponding switching methods: circuit switching and packet switching. Circuit switching is used for deterministic resource sharing, and packet switching is used for statistical resource sharing. To minimize the need of high-speed processing in optical communications, circuit switching is in general preferable to packet switching.

10. Various types of switching architectures have been designed to achieve (1) maximum switching throughput, (2) maximum switching speed, (3) minimum number of crosspoints, (4) minimum blocking probability, (5) minimum delay and loss probability, (6) scalability, and (7) broadcasting and multicasting capability.

11. There are three basic types of topology that can be used to connect network nodes: bus, ring, and star. In general, the bus is not preferred in optical communications because of a large power loss and a large dynamic range. The ring is used in optical communications because it is reliable. The star topology is another important choice in optical communications because it has a small power loss compared to the bus.

12. As the transmission bandwidth from fiber optics rapidly increases, other parts of a communication network can become the speed bottleneck. Important bottlenecks include signal modulation and detection, switching, and medium access.

13. There are three basic solutions to the speed bottleneck problem. First, optics can replace electronics implementation. Because IC technology can provide much more sophisticated processing, this first solution is not always applicable. The second solution is to exchange transmission efficiency for simpler high-speed processing. Simpler high-speed processing maximizes the speed of available electronics. The third solution is to use parallel implementation. WDM in optical communications is an example.

14. High-speed optical communication networks need high-speed applications to justify the cost. Important high-speed applications include: medical imaging, TV signal distribution, video communications, and high-performance computing.

PROBLEMS

Problem 2–1 Connectivity: List all possible services that can currently be obtained from the telephone network in terms of the threefold significance of connectivity.

Problem 2–2 Signaling: When you send registered mail, the post office must trace the mail and ensure its correct delivery. Explain how the post office in this case plays a role similar to signaling in network communications.

Problem 2–3 Information Exchange: Describe our regular mail communications in terms of the four information exchange steps described in the text.

Problem 2–4 TDMA: Guard time in TDMA is necessary to overcome finite timing skew of user nodes. If the guard time required is T_g and the time slot size is T_s, find the dependence of the access efficiency η upon the guard time and frame size, where the access efficiency is the ratio of the active transmission duration in one TDMA frame to the frame size, which is given by

$$T_f = N(T_g + T_s) = N(5 + T_s)$$

where N is the number of time slots per frame and is assumed to be a fixed number.

Problem 2–5 CSMA/CD: Assume an Ethernet consists of a single bus of 1 km.

a. If the propagation velocity over the cable is 1×10^8 m/sec, what is the longest propagation delay between two nodes on the bus?

b. Explain possible scenarios to have a collision.

c. From *a* and *b*, how would the propagation delay affect the packet collision probability?

Problem 2–6 Circuit Switching versus Packet Switching: To travel from San Francisco to New York, one can either drive a car or take an airplane. Which of these two ways is similar to packet switching in network communications, and which is similar to circuit switching? Explain why.

Problem 2–7 Clos Switch:

a. To implement an $N \times N$ switch in three stages, what will be the optimum number of middle switches to ensure nonblocking and to minimize the total number of crosspoints?

b. From *a* what will be the asymptotic expression of the total number of crosspoints as N becomes large? How does this compare to N^2, the total number of crosspoints for the same size crossbar switch?

Problem 2–8 Transmission Bandwidth Increase of TST Switch: Assume you want to implement a nonblocking three-stage TST switch of size $N \times N$. Group n input channels into one TDM frame for TSI in the first stage. Assume $N = nr$. How much should the transmission bandwidth of the switching fabric of the middle spatial switch be increased compared to the pure spatial crossbar switch?

Problem 2–9 Nonblocking TST Switch: If a 20×20 spatial switch has a transmission bandwidth of 1.280 Mb/s, what is the maximum possible throughput in Mb/s of the switch when it is used in combination with TSIs to form a *nonblocking* three-stage TST switch? Assume inputs to the TSIs in the first stage consist of DS0 64 kb/s slots.

Problem 2–10 Bus Topology: Consider a single bus with $N = 50$ nodes attached. Assume power coupling from the bus to a user node is 20 percent and there is an additional 1 dB loss at each coupler.

    a. Calculate the total power loss from the first node to the last node.

    b. Calculate the dynamic range of the received power.

Problem 2–11 Star Topology: Assume an ideal (lossless) $N \times N$ star coupler is used in a star network. If the power budget or the total loss allowed is 30 dB, find the upper limit of the star size N. If a power loss of 1 dB is assumed in each coupling stage of the star coupler, what is the new upper limit? How significant is the change?

REFERENCES

1. A. S. Tanenbaum, *Computer Networks,* 2nd ed., Prentice-Hall, 1988.

2. R. F. Rey, technical ed., *Engineering and Operations in the Bell System,* 2nd ed., AT&T Bell Labs, 1983.

3. R. M. Metcalfe and D. R. Boggs, "Distributed Packet Switching for Local Computer Networks," *Communications of ACM*, July 1976, pp. 395–404.

4. S. Haykin, *Communication Systems,* 2nd ed., John Wiley and Sons, 1983.

5. J. Bellamy, *Digital Telephony*, 2nd ed., John Wiley and Sons, 1991.

6. S. J. Campanella and D. Schaefer, "Time-Division Multiple-Access Systems," chap. 8 of *Digital Communications: Satellite/Earth Station Engineering*, by K. Feher, Prentice-Hall, 1983.

7. "INTELSAT TDMA/DS1 System Specification (TDMA/DS1 Traffic Terminals)," BG-42-65E B/6/80, Intelsat, Washington, DC, June 26, 1980.

8. N. Abramson, "The ALOHA System—Another Alternative for Computer Communications," *AFIPS Conference Proceedings*, vol. 44 (1975), pp. 201–15.

9. C. Clos, "A Study of Non-Blocking Switching Networks," *Bell System Technical Journal*, March 1953, pp. 406–27.

10. K. E. Batcher, "Sorting Networks and Their Applications," *AFIPS, Proceedings of Spring Joint Computer Conference*, vol. 32 (1968), pp. 307–14.

11. A. Huang and S. Knauer, "Starlite: A Wideband Digital Switch," *Proceedings of Globecom*, 1984, pp. 121–25.

12. V. E. Benes, *Mathematical Theory of Connecting Networks and Telephone Traffic,* Academic Press, 1965.

13. M. S. Goodman et al., "The LAMBDANET Multiwavelength Network: Architecture, Applications, and Demonstrations," *IEEE Journal on Selected Areas in Communication,* vol. 8, no. 6 (1990), pp. 995–1003.

14. F. J. Janniello et al., "A Prototype Circuit-Switched Multi-Wavelength Optical Metropolitan Area Network," Journal of Lighwave Technology, vol. 11, No. 5-6 (1993), pp. 777-82.

15. R. Ballart and Y. C. Ching, "SONET: Now It's the Standard Optical Network," *IEEE Communications Magazine*, vol. 27, no. 3 (March 1989), pp. 8–15.

16. M. K. Liu, D. G. Messerschmitt, and D. A. Hodges, "Time Slot Switching for Integrated Services in Fiber Optic PBX/LAN," *IEEE Transactions on Communications,* vol. 37, no. 7 (July 1989), pp. 685–93.

17. H. J. Shin and D. A. Hodges, "A 250 Mb/s CMOS Crosspoint Switch," *Digest of Technical Papers*, IEEE International Solid-State Circuits Conference, February 1988, pp. 114–15, 320–321.

18. G. A. Hayward et al., "High Speed 16×16 CMOS Crosspoint Switch," *Electronics Letter*, vol. 21, no. 20 (1985), pp. 923–25.

19. Darleen L. Fisher, "Getting up to Speed on Stage-Three NREN: Gigabit Testbed Lessons on Architectures and Applications," *Proceedings of IEEE Globecom,* 1991, pp. 954–58.

2

BASIC COMMUNICATION BLOCKS

Part 2 comprises five chapters covering the basic optical communication blocks. A basic point-to-point optical communication system consists of an optical transmitter, an optical channel, and an optical receiver.

The main component of an optical transmitter is its light source, which converts an electrical signal into a light signal. Chapter 3 gives important design criteria of a light source for communications, then explains various light source designs, including light emitting diodes (LEDs) and laser diodes (LDs), driven by these criteria. This chapter also presents principles of advanced laser diode designs, such as distributed feedback (DFB) lasers, quantum well lasers, and tunable lasers.

Chapter 4 discusses optical fibers. Wave propagation in various types of optical fibers is explained with minimal mathematics. The primary objectives of this chapter are to help readers (1) know the driving forces behind optical fiber development and (2) understand the two important fiber transmission limits: attenuation limits and dispersion limits.

Chapter 5 describes photodiodes used in light signal detection. There are two primary types of photodiodes: p-intrinsic-n (PIN) and avalanche photodiodes (APD). The chapter presents in detail their operational principles, design issues, trade-offs, and response speeds.

Chapters 3, 4, and 5 cover the basic blocks in point-to-point optical communications. Chapters 6 and 7 are devoted to the comprehensive noise analysis, performance evaluations, and receiver design needed to improve and evaluate the end-to-end transmission performance. Readers will have a solid system analysis background after thoroughly reading these two chapters.

3

LIGHT SOURCES

In optical communications, a transmitter consists of a light source and a modulation circuit. The light source generates an optical frequency carrier, and the modulation circuit modulates the carrier according to the transmitted signal. This chapter discusses important light sources used in optical communications. Light carrier modulation will be discussed in detail in Chapters 12 and 13.

3.1 CRITERIA FOR LIGHT SOURCES IN OPTICAL COMMUNICATIONS

Chapter 1 explained that a carrier is characterized by its amplitude, frequency, and phase. An ideal carrier can be expressed as

$$c(t) = A \cos(\omega_c t + \phi) \tag{3.1}$$

where its amplitude A, circular frequency ω_c, and phase ϕ are time-invariant. In practice, however, a light source output driven by a constant current source has the following form:

$$c(t) = \sum_i A_i \cos[\omega_{c,i} t + \phi_i(t)] \tag{3.2}$$

where each carrier at frequency $\omega_{c,i}$ represents a **longitudinal mode** (explained in section 3.6), and $\phi_i(t)$ is a random phase noise. The carrier with the largest amplitude A_i is called the **main mode** and the others are called **side modes.** A multimode source is not good for communications. The following example illustrates two problems of multimodes.

Example 3.1	**PROBLEMS OF MULTIMODE SOURCES** Consider a light source generating three longitudinal modes:

$$c(t) = A_{-1} \cos[(\omega_c - \Delta\omega)t] + A_0 \cos(\omega_c t) + A_1 \cos[(\omega_c + \Delta\omega)t]$$

where the random phase noise $\phi_i(t)$ for each carrier is ignored here. If the carrier is amplitude modulated by a square pulse with duration T_0, the transmitted signal has the form

$$p(t) = rect(t, T_0)c(t) = rect(t/T_0) \{A_{-1} \cos[(\omega_c - \Delta\omega)t]$$

$$+ A_0 \cos(\omega_c t) + A_1 \cos[(\omega_c + \Delta\omega)t]\} \stackrel{\text{def}}{=} p_{-1}(t) + p_0(t) + p_1(t)$$

where $rect(t, T_0)$ is a unit rectangle pulse of duration T_0. If the three modes propagate in a fiber at speeds $v_g - \Delta v_g$, v_g, and $v_g + \Delta v_g$, respectively, the received pulse over distance L is

$$r(t) = p_{-1}(t - \tau_{-1}) + p_0(t - \tau_0) + p_1(t - \tau_1)$$

where

$$\tau_0 = \frac{L}{v_g}$$

and

$$\tau_{\pm 1} = \frac{L}{v_g \pm \Delta v_g} \approx \tau_0 (1 \mp \frac{\Delta v_g}{v_g})$$

if $\Delta v_g \ll v_g$. The detected photocurrent is proportional to the square of the received signal:

$$i_{out}(t) = \mathcal{R}|r(t)^2| \approx \mathcal{R} \{A_{-1}^2 rect[(t - \tau_{-1}), T_0]$$

$$+ A_0^2 rect[(t - \tau_0), T_0] + A_1^2 rect[(t - \tau_1), T_0] \}$$

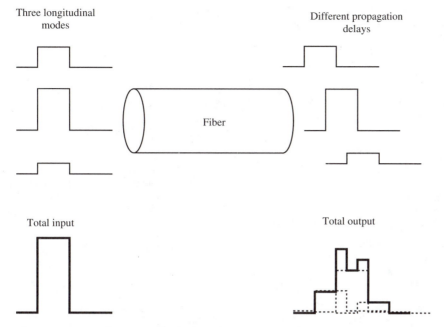

Figure 3.1   Illustration of pulse broadening because of multiple carriers and fiber dispersion.

where $\mathcal{R}$ is the responsivity in photodetection and the high-frequency cross terms have been dropped. Therefore, the final detected pulse has a broader width of $T_0 + 2(\Delta v_g/v_g)\tau_0$. This pulse broadening is illustrated in Figure 3.1 and results from a phenomenon called **fiber dispersion.** See Chapter 4 for a detailed discussion.

Another problem of multimode sources occurs when coherent detection is used. Consider the same carrier and modulating pulse. Assume no dispersion and that the pulse is coherently demodulated at the receiver. If the local carrier is also multimode of the form

$$c_{loc}(t) = B_{-1}\cos[(\omega_c - \Delta\omega)t] + B_0\cos(\omega_c t) + B_1\cos[(\omega_c + \Delta\omega)t]$$

we have

$$p(t)c_{loc}(t) = \frac{1}{2}rect(t, T_0)\times$$

$$\left[\sum_{i=-1}^{1} A_i B_i + \sum_{i\neq j} A_i B_j \cos[(i - j)\Delta\omega t] + \text{ terms at optical frequencies}\right].$$

Thus the demodulated output has many undesirable harmonics at multiples of $\Delta\omega$. ∎

In addition to multiple carriers, a light source output expressed in Equation (3.2) has other problems. For example, the amplitudes A_i in Equation (3.2) can fluctuate and result in a random power distribution among the longitudinal modes. This random intensity fluctuation causes two kinds of laser noise: **relative intensity noise** (RIN) and **mode partition noise** (MPN).

| **Example 3.2** | **PROBLEM OF PHASE NOISE**   Consider a light source generating a single longitudinal mode carrier |

$$c(t) = A_0 \cos[\omega_c t + \phi_n(t)]$$

where $\phi_n(t)$ is the phase noise. Although Chapter 6 will explain and quantify the noise, one problem is obvious here. Assume the carrier is phase modulated and coherently detected at the receiver. According to Equation (1.5), the transmitted signal has the following form:

$$s_{PM}(t) = A_0 \cos[\omega_c t + k_{PM} m(t) + \phi_n(t)].$$

An ideal phase demodulator that extracts the phase term of the signal with respect to $\omega_c t$ would give the following demodulated output:

$$\hat{m}(t) = k_{PM} m(t) + \phi_n(t).$$

Therefore, the output is distorted by the phase noise $\phi_n(t)$. To reduce its effect, we need to use a large k_{PM}. The trade-off is a larger transmission bandwidth. ■

Because of the problems of multiple longitudinal modes and phase noise, as illustrated in Examples 3.1 and 3.2, significant efforts have been made to generate only a single mode and to reduce noise. When various system applications are considered, there are additional requirements. For example, a large output power and a high linearity are needed for analog transmission, and tunability is needed for wavelength-domain multiplexing and switching. To understand the motivations behind various light-source designs, criteria of light sources for use in telecommunications are given below.

- **Single longitudinal mode.**   For the reason illustrated earlier, many single longitudinal mode (often simply called single-mode) lasers have been introduced such as distributed feedback (DFB) lasers [1] and distributed Bragg reflection (DBR) lasers [2]–[4]. They are based on the same principle of Bragg reflection to generate only a single mode.

- **Low noise.**   There are several kinds of laser noise including phase noise, relative intensity noise (RIN), and mode partition noise (MPN). A low noise is important to achieve a low bit error rate (BER) in digital communication and a sufficiently large SNR in analog communications. These types of noise will be explained in detail in Chapter 6.

- **Small linewidth.**   If there is no phase noise, the power spectral density (PSD) of the carrier in Equation (3.1) is a sum of two delta functions at $\pm \omega_c$. Because of the phase noise in Equation (3.1), the PSD is not a sum of delta functions but has a finite nonzero width around each $\pm\omega_c$. In the wavelength domain, the width of the spectrum is called the linewidth. In general, the more coherent the output light (or smaller phase noise), the smaller the linewidth. As illustrated in Example 3.2, phase noise or nonzero linewidth is undesirable in coherent communications. For incoherent communications, a nonzero linewidth results in pulse dispersion, similar to the case of multimodes illustrated in Example 3.1.

- **High output power.**   A high output power can either provide a large received SNR or allow a longer distance transmission. To achieve a high output power, light sources should be designed with a high external coupling efficiency and a high optical confinement.

- **Low threshold current.**   For laser diodes, lasing cannot start until the bias current is higher than a minimum value called the **threshold current,** I_{th}. As will be explained in Chapter 12, the output power is proportional to $(I - I_{th})$ where I is the bias current. Therefore, a lower threshold current allows a smaller bias current for the same output power. This alleviates the power dissipation problem in driving the laser diode.

- **Wavelength.**   Lightwaves at different wavelengths have different propagation characteristics. First-generation laser diodes operated at a wavelength around $0.87\ \mu$m using GaAs laser diodes. To have a lower fiber attenuation and dispersion, the quaternary alloy technology of III–V compounds has been successfully developed. The wavelength is now increased to $1.3\ \mu$m and $1.55\ \mu$m.

- **Large modulation bandwidths.**   As explained in Chapter 1, information in passband communication is transmitted via carrier modulation. In optical communications, there are two major modulation techniques: **direct modulation** and **external modulation.** Because it is simple, direct modulation is most frequently used. This technique uses the transmitted signal to drive the light source directly. In this case, the light source should respond fast enough to the time-varying input signal. Therefore, the modulation bandwidth should be as large as possible. In external modulation, an external device modulates the continuous wave (CW) output from the light source. A large modulation bandwidth from the light source is unnecessary in this case.

- **Small linewidth broadening.**   When a light source is directly modulated, its output linewidth is broadened. This linewidth broadening comes from the refractive index modulation of the light source. Because linewidth broadening results in pulse dispersion, it should be minimized. Quantum-well lasers have been reported for small linewidth broadening [5] and will be discussed later.

- **Linearity.**   For analog communications, signal distortion due to light source nonlinearity should be minimized. Nonlinearity will introduce higher harmonic terms and crosstalk. Analysis of nonlinearity is discussed in detail in Chapter 10 on subcarrier multiplexing (SCM).

- **Tunability.**   For applications such as wavelength division multiplexing (WDM), the capability to tune the wavelength of a laser diode is essential. A tunable laser diode has two or more external contacts that allow users to tune the output wavelength. A good tunable laser diode should have a tunable range of several thousand GHz.

From data given in [6]–[8], a sample list of state-of-the-art laser diodes for fiber communications at wavelengths of 1.30 μm and 1.55 μm are shown in Tables 3.1 and 3.2. These commercial laser diodes are designed in various ways to achieve a larger output power, lower threshold current, smaller linewidth, higher modulation bandwidth, lower noise, and higher tunability. To provide a better stability of output power and wavelength, an advanced laser diode is packaged with a photodetection circuit to monitor output power, an isolator to reject reflection from output coupling, and an electronic cooler circuit to stabilize the operating temperature.

Table 3.1 Characteristics of some state-of-the-art continuous wave InGaAsP laser diodes.

Manufacturer	Model No.	Wavelength (nm)	Linewidth (nm)	Output Power (mW) at mA	I_{th} (mA)	Remarks
BT&D	LSC2110	1300	3.00	1@45	20	
	XMT1300-1.2	1300	3.00	1@45	20	1.2 GB/s bandwidth
AT&T	237	1310	3.00	0.02@25	12	Very low I_{th}
	215	1300	—	2.5	18	
Epitaxx	ELA13-23B-FJS	1300	5	0.2@20	10	Very low I_{th}
NEC	NDL5730P	1300	2.00	2@40	20	
	NDL5650	1300	0.1	8@50	20	DFB
	NDL5730	1300	2.00	8@50	20	Internal monitor
	NDL5800P	1310	0.10	8@50	20	DFB, 2.5 GB/s on subcarrier
Toshiba	TOLD332S	1310	0.10	0.7@50	20	low RIN
	300S	1300	0.1	4.0@50	20	DFB
Fujitsu Microelectronics	FLD 130F2RH	1310	50 MHz	5.0	—	DFB, 33 dB side mode suppression
Mistsubishi Electronics America	FU-31LD	1300	3.0	2.5@40	20	Backfacet monitor
	ML-7901	1300	5.0	6.0@40	20	
	FU-42SLD-D	1300	3.0	10@100	20	
	ML-7901A	1300	3.0	26@100	20	High power
Lasertron	QLM1300MW	1300	3.0	1.0	—	12 GHz on subcarrier
Stantel	LYC7M1	1300	3.0	5.0@55	25	
Ortel	1515A	1310	5.0	2.0@70	20	10 GHz analog
	1540A	1300	< 1	4@65	15	5 GHz DFB
BT&D	TSL1000-1550	1550	< 100 kHz	0.5@100	20	Tunable over 40 nm, TE cooler

Table 3.1 (concluded)

Manufacturer	Model No.	Wavelength (nm)	Linewidth (nm)	Output Power (mW) at mA	I_{th} (mA)	Remarks
NEC	NDL 5850C	1550	0.1	5.0@55	25	DFB, 2.5 GB/s
	NDL 5650	1550	0.1	5.0@50	25	DFB
Toshiba	TOLD350S	1550	0.1	4.0@50	20	DFB
	TOLD350	1550	4.0	4.0@55	25	FP laser
Fujitsu	FLD150F3CH-AL	1550	0.2	100		DFB
Mistsubishi	ML-9701	1550	3.0	6.0@40	20	
Stantel	LYC 11M1	1550	0.1	5.0@80	50	DFB
Micracor	ML-02A/02B	1480–1560	10^{-6}	<5	—	Tunable external cavity

NOTE: (1) The list is by no means an exact representation of all advanced laser diodes. (2) Data given may have been changed by the original manufacturers. Please refer to the original data sheets for exact values. (3) Those laser diodes of a linewidth of 0.1 nm can actually have much smaller linewidths. The linewidth of 0.1 nm comes from the optical spectrum analyzer resolution.

Table 3.2 Detailed characteristics of DFB laser diodes in the TOLD33x series and TOLD38x series from Toshiba.

Item	Condition	Typical Value	Remarks
Threshold current	CW	20 mA	From linear extrapolation
Optical power	$I = 50$ mA	0.7 mW	
Wavelength	at 0.7 mW output	1310/1550 nm	TOLD332S/TOLD382S
Spectral linewidth	at 0.7 mW CW	20 MHz	
Side-mode suppression	at 0.7 mW output	35 dB	
Rise/fall time	$I_{bias} = I_{th}$	0.3 nsec	Modulation current is 30 mA
RIN	at 0.7 mW output	-145 dB	
Monitor current	at 0.7 mW output	0.1 mA	
Isolation ratio	at 0.7 mW output	30 dB	
Cooler capacity ΔT_c		maximum 35 °C	

NOTE: These laser diodes are usually packaged with an internal cooler circuit for temperature stability, a photodetector for output power stability, and an isolator for output wavelength stability.

3.2 SEMICONDUCTOR LIGHT SOURCES

Semiconductor light sources are the most important kind of light sources used in optical communications. Their small size, low cost, and low power consumption are among the reasons for the popularity. More significantly, they can generate light signals at wavelengths 1.3 μm and 1.55 μm, where the minimum fiber attenuation and/or dispersion can be achieved.

There are two types of semiconductor light sources: light emitting diodes (LEDs) and laser diodes (LDs). This section explains their common p-n junction structure where light is generated.

3.2.1 P-N Junction

The core of a semiconductor light source is its p-n junction, often referred to as the **active layer**. As depicted in Figure 3.2, the p-n junction is an interface between an N-type doped layer and a P-type doped layer.[1] Therefore, a semiconductor light source has essentially the same p-n junction as any semiconductor diode. However, there are two key differences between semiconductor light sources and ordinary p-n junction diodes.

The first difference is that the material used must have a direct energy bandgap. As shown in Figure 3.3, a semiconductor has (1) a conduction band above which electrons stay and (2) a valence band below which holes stay. In a direct bandgap material such as

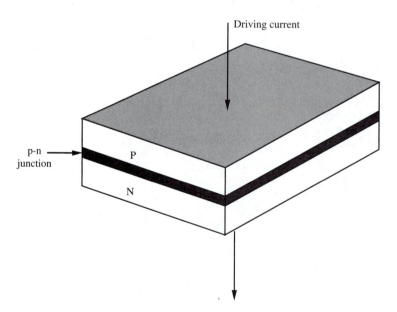

Figure 3.2   Illustration of a p-n junction.

---

[1] An N-type doped layer has free electrons from its N-type dopants, and a P-type doped layer has free holes from its P-type dopants. For background on p-n junction physics, read any standard textbook such as [9].

GaAs, electrons and holes have their minimum energies at the same momentum. In an indirect bandgap material such as silicon, on the other hand, the energy bands have different momenta at their minimum energies. Due to conservation of momentum, an electron and a hole at the same momentum can directly recombine and generate a photon. When they have different momenta, a third agent such as the semiconductor lattice has to be involved in the recombination process.

From the above observation, the significance of direct bandgap is twofold. First, a high direct electron and hole recombination (EHR) rate can be achieved because electrons and holes have the highest population at their minimum energy states. Second, because the energy release from each direct EHR is around the energy bandgap E_g, according to the Planck-Einstein relationship [11], photons generated by direct EHRs are around the same frequency

$$f = \frac{E_g}{h} \qquad \qquad [3.3]$$

where h is the Planck constant. If EHRs are not direct but take place through an intermediate interaction with the material lattice, each recombination can generate two particles (not necessarily photons) of smaller energies ΔE_1 and ΔE_2 with $E_g = \Delta E_1 + \Delta E_2$. Because ΔE_1 and ΔE_2 are undefined and random, indirect EHRs result in an undesirable wide spectrum.

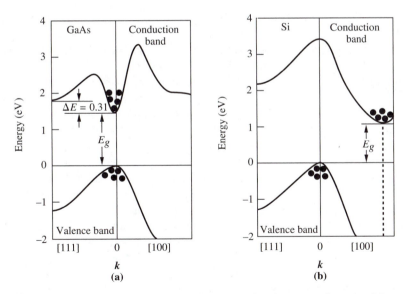

Figure 3.3   Illustration of direct and indirect bandgaps as a function of the momentum (k): (a) GaAs and (b) Si.

SOURCE: Reprinted, by permission, from Neaman, *Semiconductor Physics & Devices* [10]. ©1992 by Richard D. Irwin, p.85.

Example 3.3	**EMMISSION WAVELENGTH OF GAAS** Silicon is an excellent semiconductor material for electronics. However, as shown in Figure 3.3, it is not a direct bandgap material and is thus poor for use in a light source. If silicon were to be direct bandgap, the optoelectronic integrated circuit (OEIC) technology would have been much easier to realize.

The material used for first-generation light sources is GaAs. Its energy bandgap is 1.43 eV at 300K. From Equation (3.3), we have

$$\lambda = \frac{c}{f} = \frac{ch}{E_{\hat{g}}} = \frac{3 \times 10^8 \times 6.625 \times 10^{-34}}{1.43 \times 1.6 \times 10^{-19}} = 0.87 \ \mu\text{m}. \ \blacksquare$$

The second key difference between semiconductor light sources and other semiconductor diodes is their light confinement and coupling structures. When photons are generated in the active layer, they must be confined within the layer and efficiently coupled to an external device such as a lens or an optical fiber. In the next subsection, a very important light confinement structure called the **heterostructure** is discussed.

3.2.2   HETEROSTRUCTURES

Because of the large cavity loss, it is not possible to operate a laser diode at room temperatures using the simple p-n junction structure. The concept of heterostructures was first introduced in 1963 independently by two research groups [12][13]. In 1969, room temperature semiconductor laser diodes became a reality with the use of heterostructures [14]–[16]. A heterostructure is a junction of two materials of different energy bandgaps crystally joined. The junction is thus called a **heterojunction**.

An n-P heterojunction (capitalized P denotes the larger bandgap material) is depicted in Figure 3.4. Because of the energy gap difference, we can see a jump of the valence band at the junction. To confine both carriers and photons within the active layer, as illustrated in Figure 3.5, a **double heterostructure** (DH) is used. In the N-n-P DH illustrated, the center N-type material has a smaller energy gap.

A heterostructure provides both carrier (electrons and holes) and optical confinement. First, because of the energy jump or block at the heterojunctions, as illustrated in Figure 3.5, electrons and holes are confined in the active layer. Second, because the refractive indices of the wider bandgap materials are smaller than that of the smaller bandgap active layer, the DH forms an optical cavity, and photons are confined within the active layer. The principle of this photon confinement due to refractive index difference is the same principle of light propagation used in optical fibers. See Chapter 4 for a detailed discussion.

When photons and carriers are effectively confined in the same active layer, carriers can strongly interact with photons and generate large optical outputs. Therefore, heterostructures are used in all LEDs and LDs today. One critical constraint in building heterostructure LEDs and LDs is that the lattice constants of materials used should be closely matched. If there is a large difference in the lattice constant, it is difficult to grow one material on top of the other, causing many material defects at the junction. Figure 3.6 gives

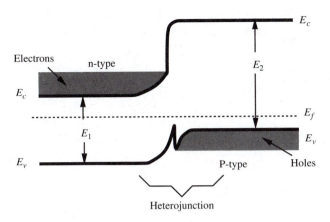

Figure 3.4 Illustration of an n-P heterostructure.

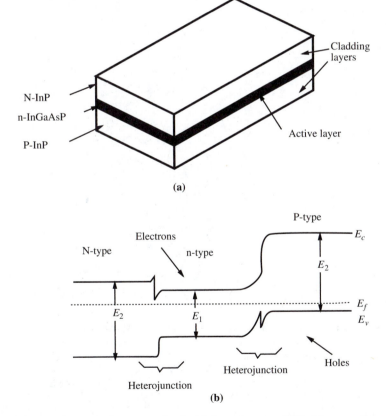

Figure 3.5 Illustration of a double heterostructure (DH): (*a*) geometrical illustration and (*b*) energy-band diagram.

the lattice constants of the III–V compound family and their energy bandgaps [17]. One popular combination is InGaAsP for its small bandgap and InP for its larger bandgap.

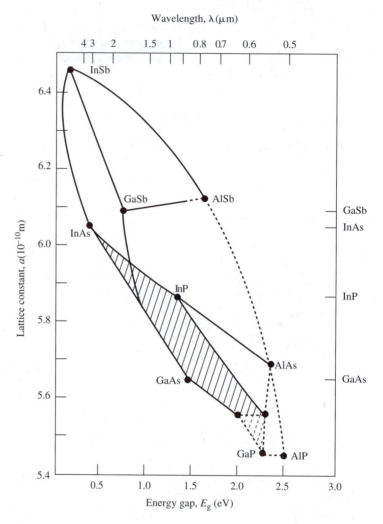

Figure 3.6   Lattice constant versus bandgap of the III–V compound family. The solid lines correspond to direct bandgap materials and the dashed lines correspond to indirect bandgap materials. The shaded area shows the quaternary compound $In_{1-x}Ga_xAs_yP_{1-y}$. The lattice match to InP occurs at $x = 0.8$ and $y = 0.65$.

Example 3.4

IN GAASP / INP HETEROSTRUCTURE   Consider an InGaAsP laser with InP cladding. Figure 3.6 shows that InP has a lattice constant of 5.9×10^{-10} m. To operate the active InGaAsP layer at 1.5 μm and have the same lattice constant, we need a compound $In_{1-x}Ga_xAs_yP_{1-y}$ in the shadow region. Note that the line that connects InAs and InP represents $InAs_yP_{1-y}$, and the line that connects InAs and GaAs represents $In_{1-y}Ga_yAs$. Therefore, if $In_{1-y}Ga_yAs$ is used instead as the active layer, the emission wavelength is at around 2.0 μm with $y \approx 0.4$. ∎

3.3   LIGHT-EMITTING DIODES

Light-emitting diodes are semiconductor diodes that emit **incoherent light** when they are biased by a forward voltage or current source. Incoherent light is an optical carrier with a rapidly varying random phase. In other words, the phase term in Equation (3.1) is a rapidly varying function of time. This random phase results from independent EHRs. That is, the phase and frequency of a photon generated from an EHR are different from those of photons from other EHRs. Therefore, incoherent light has a broad spectrum. Figure 3.7 illustrates a typical light spectrum of a GaAlAs LED. The linewidth is of the order of 0.1 μm with the central wavelength around 0.87 μm.

The linewidth of a light source can be defined in different ways. One common definition is called **full-width half-maximum** (FWHM), which is the width between two 50 percent points of the peak intensity. As a numerical example, the FWHM of the linewidth in Figure 3.7 is approximately 0.03 μm.

There exists a simple relationship between the linewidth and the spectrum width. Because

$$\lambda f = c$$

where c is the speed of light, by taking the total derivative, we have

$$f\partial\lambda + \lambda\partial f = 0.$$

For a given linewidth $\Delta\lambda$, we thus have

$$\boxed{\frac{|\Delta\lambda|}{\lambda} = \frac{|\Delta f|}{f}, \quad |\Delta\lambda| = c\frac{|\Delta f|}{f^2}, \quad |\Delta f| = c\frac{|\Delta\lambda|}{\lambda^2}}$$ **[3.4]**

where Δf is the corresponding spectral width.

Example 3.5

SPECTRAL WIDTH & LINE WIDTH CONVERSION   For the FWHM linewidth of 0.03 μm of the AlGaAs LED given above, the FWHM spectrum width is

$$\Delta f = f\frac{\Delta\lambda}{\lambda} = \frac{c}{\lambda^2}\Delta\lambda = 12 \text{ THz}.$$

Note that 12 THz is a very large spectrum compared to most baseband signal bandwidths. Example 3.2 demonstrates that it is impractical to perform phase or frequency modulation using LEDs. As a result, only amplitude modulation is used for LEDs in practice. ∎

The spectrum width of LEDs depends on the material, temperature, doping level, and light coupling structure [19]. For AlGaAs devices, the FWHM spectrum width of LEDs is about $2kT/h$, where k is the Boltzmann constant and T is temperature in Kelvin. For InGaAsP devices, it is about $3kT/h$ [20]. As the doping level increases, the linewidth also increases [21].

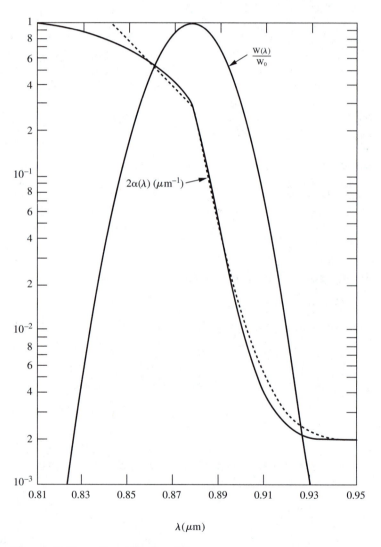

Figure 3.7   Linewidth of an LED.

SOURCE: Reprinted, by permission, from Marcuse, "LED Fundamentals," p. 819 [18]. © 1977 by IEEE.

TEMPERATURE DEPENDENCE OF LINEWIDTH   For an AlGaAs LED operated at 300K,

| Example
| 3.6

$$\Delta f = 2\frac{1.38 \times 10^{-23} \times 300}{6.62 \times 10^{-34}} = 12.4 \text{ THz}.$$

This is about the same value obtained from the previous example. ∎

The spectrum width also depends on the light coupling structure of the LED. The light coupling structure couples photons out of the active layer. As illustrated in Figures 3.8 and 3.9, there are two different light coupling structures: **surface emitting** [22] and **edge emitting**. The first type couples light vertically away from the layers and is called a surface-emitting or Burrus LED. The second type couples light out in parallel to the layers and is called an edge-emitting LED.

Because of self-absorption along the length of the active layer, edge emitting LEDs have smaller linewidths than those of surface-emitting diodes [19]. In addition, because of the transverse waveguiding, the output light has an angle around 30° vertical to the active layer [23]. On the other hand, because surface-emitting LEDs have a large coupling area, it is easier to interface them with fibers (self-aligned). Also, they can be better cooled because the heat sink is close to the active layer.

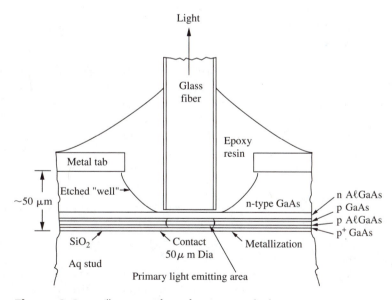

Figure 3.8   Illustration of a surface-emitting diode.

SOURCE: Reprinted, by permission, from Saul, Lee, and Barrus, Chapter 5 "Light Emitting Diode Devices Design," p.197, of Semiconductor & Semimetals, vol. 22, Part C, edited by Tsang[19]. © by Academic Press, 1985.

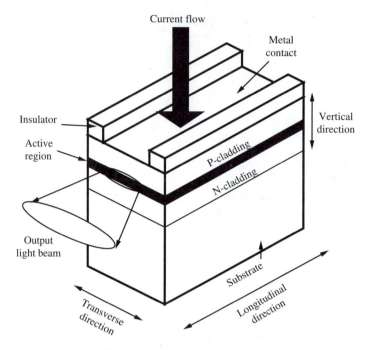

Figure 3.9   Illustration of an edge-emitting diode.

3.4 LASER PRINCIPLES

Another important type of light source used in optical fiber communications is the laser diode (LD). A basic laser diode structure is similar to that of the edge-emitting LED illustrated in Figure 3.9. By adding an additional structure for transverse photon confinement, a coherent carrier close to what is expressed in Equation (3.1) can be generated. Like any other lasers, the principles of semiconductor lasers are based on **(a) external pumping** and **(b) internal light amplification**.

3.4.1 EXTERNAL PUMPING

When a laser has several energy states, external pumping excites carriers to a higher energy state. When they return to the ground state, they release energy and generate photons. As an illustration, Figure 3.10 shows a simple two-level system in which carriers (e.g., electrons) can stay at one of the two energy states E_1 and E_2. When there is no external pumping, most carriers stay at the ground state E_1 because of thermal stability. When there is external pumping, on the other hand, carriers at E_1 can be excited to E_2.

The energy system of semiconductor lasers is shown in Figure 3.11, where E_c is the conduction band energy and E_v is the valence band energy. External pumping in this case

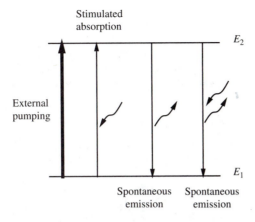

Figure 3.10   A two energy-level system.

is achieved by current injection, which supplies electrons and holes to their conduction band and valence band, respectively. When electrons and holes recombine, as in LEDs, they generate photons.

3.4.2 LIGHT AMPLIFICATION

Photon generation from external pumping is not sufficient for coherent light generation. An additional amplification mechanism is needed to multiply photons of the same frequency and phase. In a laser, this is made possible by a quantum phenomenon called **stimulated emission**. When the optical loss in a laser cavity is small from a good optical confinement, a net positive amplification gain from stimulated emission can be achieved. As a result, coherent photons can be built up.

As shown in Figure 3.10, several photon emission and absorption processes exist in a two-level atomic system. When a carrier is pumped to the upper state, it can come back to the ground state either spontaneously or by stimulation. The corresponding photon generation processes are called **spontaneous emission** and **stimulated emission**, respectively. In spontaneous emission, photons generated have random phases and frequencies. As a result, the light is incoherent. On the other hand, photons generated from stimulated emission have the same phase and frequency as the stimulating photons. Therefore, for coherent light generation, stimulated emission needs to dominate over spontaneous emission. In addition to photon emission, Figure 3.10 shows that photons can also be absorbed to excite carriers from the ground state to the upper state. This is called **stimulated absorption**.

Electrons and holes in a semiconductor have emission and absorption processes similar to those discussed above. As shown in Figure 3.11, electron hole pairs (EHPs) are generated by external current injection and stimulated photon absorption. They can later

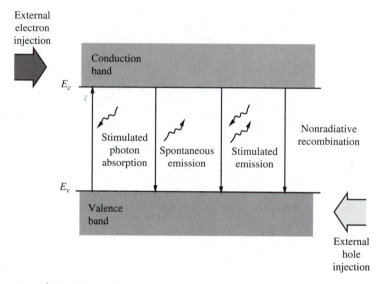

Figure 3.11   Carrier recombination and photon emission in a semi-conductor laser diode.

recombine either spontaneously or by stimulated emission. Because of leaky current at the p-n junction, there is also nonradiative carrier recombination in semiconductors.

3.4.3   POSITIVE OPTICAL GAIN: POPULATION INVERSION

In the equilibrium state, carriers have the same rate between the two states. Thanks to Einstein, we have

$$A_{21}N_2 + B_{21}N_2 S = B_{12}N_1 S + R_p \qquad \textbf{[3.5]}$$

where S is the photon energy density (joule/$m^3\cdot$Hz), N_1 and N_2 are carrier densities (1/m^3) at E_1 and E_2 respectively, B_{12} is the stimulated absorption rate coefficient, B_{21} is the stimulated emission rate coefficient, A_{21} is the spontaneous emission rate coefficient (1/sec), and R_p is the external pumping rate in a unit volume (1/m^{3}sec). Therefore, the left-hand side of Equation (3.5) is the total rate from E_2 to E_1, and the right-hand side is the total rate from E_1 to E_2.

From Equation (3.5), when there is no external pumping ($R_p = 0$), the photon energy density S in equilibrium is

$$S = \frac{A_{21}/B_{21}}{(B_{12}N_1/B_{21}N_2) - 1} = \frac{8\pi h f^3 n^3}{c^3}\left(\frac{1}{e^{hf/kT} - 1}\right) \text{ [joule/m}^3\cdot\text{Hz]} \qquad \textbf{[3.6]}$$

where the last equality comes from the Planck-Boltzmann's black-body radiation distribution. Equation (3.6) implies $B_{12} = B_{21}$ and $A_{21}/B_{21} = 8\pi h f^3 n^3/c^3$, where n is the refractive index of the medium.

EMMISION AT THERMAL EQUILIBRIUM At 300K thermal equilibrium and without external pumping, the ratio of stimulated emission rate to spontaneous emission rate is calculated as follows. If the photon wavelength is 1.5 μm or 2×10^{14} Hz in frequency, from Equation (3.6),

Example 3.7

$$\frac{B_{21}S}{A_{21}} = \frac{1}{e^{hf/kT} - 1} = [e^{(6.62 \cdot 10^{-34} \cdot 2 \cdot 10^{14})/(0.026 \cdot 1.6 \cdot 10^{-19})} - 1]^{-1} = 1.5 \times 10^{-14}.$$

Thus stimulated emission in this case is extremely insignificant. ∎

To increase the stimulated emission rate, the light intensity S must be increased. In general, the light intensity increases at a rate proportional to $(B_{21}N_2 - B_{12}N_1)S$, which is the photon stimulated emission rate minus the photon stimulated absorption rate. Building up the light intensity thus requires that

$$B_{21}N_2 > B_{12}N_1.$$ **[3.7]**

This condition is commonly referred to as **population inversion** and requires that $N_2 > N_1$ when $B_{21} = B_{12}$.

To achieve population inversion, the external pumping rate (R_p) needs to be greater than the spontaneous emission rate. This can be seen by rearranging Equation (3.5) as

$$S = \frac{R_p - A_{21}N_2}{B_{21}N_2 - B_{12}N_1}.$$ **[3.8]**

Because $S > 0$, R_p needs to be higher than the spontaneous emission rate ($A_{21}N_2$) when $B_{21}N_2 > B_{12}N_1$.

CURRENT INJECTION FOR POSITIVE GAIN Consider an InGaAsP laser diode. Its spontaneous emission rate is given by $A_{21}N_0$, with N_0 being a constant around the doping concentration. If we assume $A_{21} = 10^9$ sec^{-1} and $N_0 = 10^{24}$ 1/m^3, the pumping rate required for population inversion is

Example 3.8

$$R_p > A_{21}N_0 = 10^{33} \text{ 1/m}^3\text{sec.}$$

If the active layer of the diode has dimensions of 100 μm long, 5 μm wide, and 0.1 μm thick, the corresponding injection current required is

$$I = qR_p \times 10^{-4} \times (5 \times 10^{-6}) \times 10^{-7} > 80 \text{ mA.}$$

Population inversion thus requires an injection current of at least 80 mA. ∎

Because of a high cavity loss, photons generated in LEDs are not well confined but leak out quickly. As a result, the population inversion condition given by Equation (3.7) is not sufficient to build up the light intensity S, and most of the emissions in LEDs come from spontaneous emission. To have a low threshold current above which stimulated emission can dominate, various optical confinement structures discussed next become critical.

3.5   CAVITY CONFINEMENT

As illustrated in Figure 3.12, a laser cavity is a rectangular cavity of six walls, all of which should provide good photon and carrier confinement to reduce the cavity loss. Among these six walls, two are at the longitudinal ends of the cavity which need to couple light out, and two are the heterojunctions which achieve both carrier and photon confinement from the energy bandgap and refractive index differences, respectively. Therefore, the only additional confinement needed is at the transverse sides of the junction plane.

To provide the confinement at the two transverse sides, three structures have been used: (1) **gain-guided**, (2) **weakly index-guided**, and (3) **strongly index-guided lasers**. These confinement structures are discussed in detail below.

3.5.1   GAIN-GUIDED LASERS

A gain-guided laser has a structure that confines transverse current flow. Three basic types of gain-guided laser diodes are depicted in Figure 3.13. The oxide-stripe laser [24] is the same basic heterostructure laser shown in Figure 3.9 and uses the P-contact on the top to define the current flow region. Therefore, little current flows under the SiO_2 dielectric layer. The second type uses either a proton stripe [25] or a deuteron stripe [26] to create a

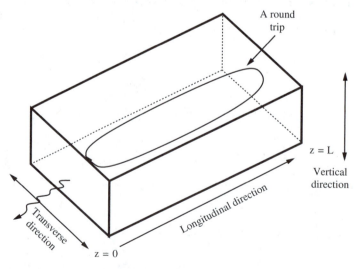

Figure 3.12   Illustration of a laser cavity.

high-resistivity region by which the transverse current flow is restricted. The third type has a junction stripe [27] where most current flows through the P-type area converted by zinc diffusion, and little current flows under the reversed-bias n-p junction.

In these gain-guided lasers, there is no physical confinement for photons on the two transverse sides. In fact, the high-current region has a lower refractive index and poor optical confinement. In addition, there is no physical confinement for carriers except for the proton- or deuteron-type lasers. Therefore, gain-guided lasers do not have a strong transverse confinement and thus have a large threshold current. As illustrated in Figure 3.14, the threshold current is around 100 mA. In addition, because of the weak transverse confinement, there can be several transverse modes.[2] As the driving current increases, the current density distribution changes in the active layer, which results in shifts of transverse modes. These shifts can be seen from the "kinks" in the nonlinear light versus current (L–I) characteristics.

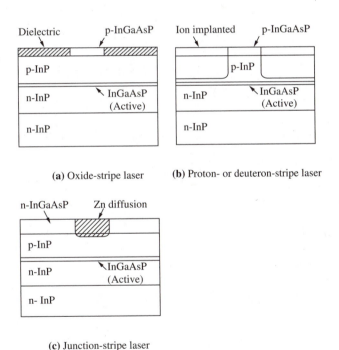

(a) Oxide-stripe laser   (b) Proton- or deuteron-stripe laser

(c) Junction-stripe laser

Figure 3.13   Three different gain-guided index structures.

SOURCE: Reprinted, by permission, from Dutta Chapter 9 of *Optical Fiber Transmission* edited by E.E. Basch "Optical Sources," p. 275, Figure 10 [28]. © 1987 by McGraw-Hill.

[2]Transverse modes are different sets of wavefunctions that satisfy the wave equations in the cavity. Similar to longitudinal modes that are determined by the longitudinal direction of the cavity (see Section 3.6), transverse modes are determined by the transverse current distribution or gain in the cavity. Chapter 4 discusses the concept of the waveguide and resonator modes in more detail.

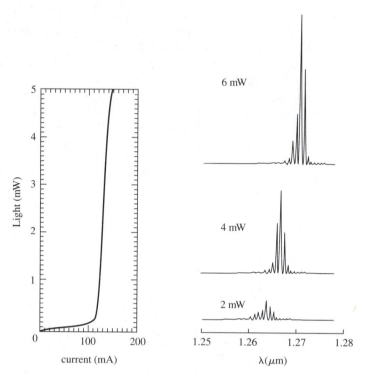

Figure 3.14   (a) Light power versus input current; (b) output optical spectrum.

SOURCE: Reprinted, by permission, from Schwartz et al., "Stripe Geometry," p. 841 [26]. © 1984 by IEEE.

3.5.2 WEAKLY INDEX-GUIDED LASERS

To provide a better confinement, especially for photons, index difference must be introduced on the two transverse sides. Laser diodes with structures that add the index difference are called index-guided lasers. In weakly index-guided diodes, a waveguide structure of a different material is grown below or above the active layer. This provides an index change up to 1 percent at the two transverse sides.

As shown in Figure 3.15, when a waveguide (P-type InP) is grown above the active layer (InGaAsP), it is called a **ridge waveguide** index-guided diode [29], and when a waveguide is grown below the active layer (N-type InP), it is called a **rib waveguide** diode [30]. With index-guiding, carriers and photons are better confined. Therefore, the threshold current is smaller, typically from 40 to 60 mA.

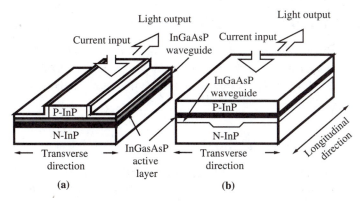

Figure 3.15   Illustrations of (a) ridge waveguide and (b) rib waveguide weak index-guiding.

3.5.3 STRONGLY INDEX-GUIDED LASERS

Instead of adding a waveguide structure below or above the active layer in weakly index-guided diodes, strongly index-guided lasers have a physical structure on the two transverse sides of the active layer to introduce an index change of around 0.2. Two important strongly index-guided lasers are illustrated in Figure 3.16. They are called **buried-heterostructure** (BH) lasers [31]–[33]. Intuitively speaking, strongly index-guided lasers introduce another two heterojunctions on the two transverse sides (total four heterojunctions) to provide both carrier and photon confinement. Because of the excellent confinement, the threshold current at room temperatures can be as low as 10 mA.

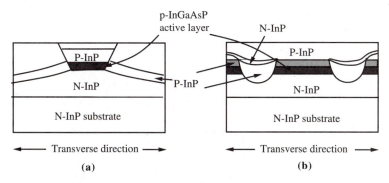

Figure 3.16   Illustrations of buried heterostructures: (a) etched-mesa (EM-BH) and (b) double-channel-plannar (DCP-BH).

3.6 FABRY-PEROT LASER DIODES

With cavity confinement discussed above, a basic LD that has a rectangular cavity is equivalent to a Fabry-Perot (FP) resonator (see Appendix 3–A). An LD that has a simple rectangular cavity is thus called an FP LD. In this section, we describe basic gain/loss and longitudinal mode properties of an FP LD.

3.6.1 POWER LOSS AND GAIN

When photons are reflected back and forth between the two FP cavity ends, they experience both gain and loss. The gain comes from stimulated emission, and the loss comes from medium absorption and partial reflections at the two cavity ends. In the steady state, the gain and loss are equal. From this condition, the required gain from stimulated emission can be derived. Chapter 12 shows how to use the required gain to find the laser threshold current.

For simple discussion, assume the wavefunction of a lightwave is a scalar and has a value A (a complex variable) at point $z = 0$.[3] From Figure 3.12, the wave traveling to the right can be expressed as

$$E^+(z) = Ae^{(j\beta_z - \alpha/2 + g/2)z}$$

where β_z is the propagation constant along the z-axis, and α and g are the distributed medium loss and gain, respectively. The time dependence factor $e^{-j\omega t}$ of the field is dropped for its irrelevance, and the power of the traveling wave is proportional to $e^{(g-\alpha)z}$. At $z = L$, the wavefunction has value $Ae^{(j\beta_z - \alpha + g)L}$. Assuming the cavity end on the right has a reflection coefficient of r_2, the reflected wave traveling to the left can be written as:

$$E^-(z) = r_2 A e^{(j\beta_z - \alpha/2 + g/2)(2L-z)}.$$

The round trip is complete after the left-traveling wave is reflected back by the left mirror with reflection coefficient r_1. Therefore, the conditions of a unit round trip gain in the steady state are

$$r_1 r_2 e^{(g-\alpha)(L)} = 1 \qquad\qquad \textbf{[3.9]}$$

and

$$2L\beta_z = 2m\pi \qquad\qquad \textbf{[3.10]}$$

where m is an integer. Equation (3.9) can be expressed as

---

[3] The text uses "waves" and "photons" interchangeably to describe optical signals. Quantum physics teaches that every particle has both the wave and particle nature. Therefore, every photon has its wavelength or frequency, as already shown in Equation (3.3). Because the number of photons in the cavity is proportional to the total optical power, the corresponding wave's amplitude is proportional to the square root of the photon density in the cavity. This concept will be used in Chapter 6 on phase noise and again pointed out in Chapter 12 when the power-current characteristic is derived.

$$g = \alpha - \frac{1}{L} \times \ln(r_1 r_2) = \alpha + \alpha_m = \alpha_{tot} \qquad \textbf{[3.11]}$$

where α_m accounts for the reflection loss at the cavity ends.

Equation (3.11) is the gain-loss condition at the steady state, and Equation (3.10) is the phase condition for the laser wavelength. This second condition is the basis for the longitudinal modes that will be discussed shortly.

THRESHOLD GAIN FOR LASER EMISSION Assume the active layer of a laser diode is GaAs with dielectric constant $\epsilon_r = 13.2$, the distributed loss is 1000 dB/m, and the cavity length $L = 1000 \mu$m. The required gain in the steady state can be computed as follows. | **Example 3.9**

First, from electromagnetic wave theory, the reflection coefficient at normal incidence from a dielectric medium of refractive index n_1 and reflected by an external medium of refractive index n_2 is

$$r = \frac{n_2 - n_1}{n_2 + n_1}. \qquad \textbf{[3.12]}$$

In the case of GaAs laser, $\epsilon_1 = \epsilon_r = 13.2$ and $\epsilon_2 = 1$ (air). Therefore, $n_1 = \sqrt{\epsilon_r} = 3.63$, and $n_2 = 1$. Consequently,

$$r_1 = r_2 = \frac{1 - n_1}{1 + n_1} = -0.568$$

Because the cavity loss given above is in terms of dB/m, it must be converted to what is shown in Equation (3.9). If α_{dB} is the loss in dB/m, over a distance L m, then

$$10^{-(\alpha_{dB}/10)L} = (e^{-\alpha L/2})^2.$$

Taking the logarithm of both sides gives

$$\alpha_{dB} = 4.34\alpha. \qquad \textbf{[3.13]}$$

Therefore, 1000 dB/m loss is equivalent to $\alpha = 230$ m^{-1}.

From Equation (3.11), the required gain at the steady state is,

$$g = 230 - \frac{1}{10^{-3}} \ln(0.568^2) = 1360 \text{ 1/m} = 5910 \text{ dB/m.} \blacksquare$$

The gain-loss condition in Equation (3.11) is only applicable to the steady state. Before the laser reaches its steady state, the gain is greater than the total loss. This builds up the radiation field in the laser by stimulating more photons from carrier recombinations. As the laser field is being built up, there are more stimulated emissions or EHRs. This brings down the carrier density and also the gain. Finally, a steady state is reached where the stimulated emission rate is in equilibrium with the carrier supply or generation rate. Therefore, the output power is determined by the injected current supply. The carrier recombination and photon emission dynamics will be discussed in detail in Chapter 12.

3.6.2 LONGITUDINAL MODES

Substituting $\beta_z = 2\pi n/\lambda$ into the round-trip phase condition given by Equation (3.10), we have

$$\lambda_m = \frac{2Ln}{m} \qquad [3.14]$$

where n is the refractive index of the gain medium and λ_m is the mth longitudinal mode. When m is a large integer, the longitudinal mode separation between λ_m and λ_{m+1} is

$$\Delta\lambda_{long} = \lambda_m - \lambda_{m+1} = 2Ln\left\{\frac{1}{m} - \frac{1}{(m+1)}\right\} \approx 2Ln\frac{1}{m^2} = \frac{\lambda^2}{2Ln}. \qquad [3.15]$$

Thus, at a given λ, the longitudinal mode separation is proportional to the square of the wavelength and inversely proportional to the length of the cavity.

When carriers are generated by an externally injected current, depending on their energy distributions in the conduction and valence bands, they contribute to stimulated emissions at different longitudinal modes. The distribution of this emission contribution determines the gain distribution, which is centered around a frequency slightly higher than that of the energy bandgap. Figure 3.17 illustrates a typical gain profile of a laser diode. A Gaussian or para-

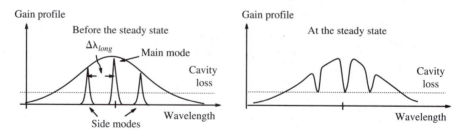

Figure 3.17 Illustration of gain profile and possible longitudinal modes.

bolic gain profile is generally assumed in modeling. As illustrated, only those longitudinal modes with initial gains (before reaching the steady state) higher than the cavity loss can exist. Note that the main mode is not necessarily at the peak of the gain profile.

Example 3.10 | **LONGITUDINAL MODE SEPARATION** If the cavity of a given InGaAsP laser has length $L = 500$ μm and the wavelength interval is [1.54, 1.56] μm within which the gain profile is greater than the minimum required gains, find the longitudinal mode separation and the number of possible modes. Also, what is the corresponding mode separation in GHz? Assume the refractive index is 3.63.

From Equation (3.15),

$$\Delta\lambda_{long} = \frac{\lambda^2}{2Ln} = \frac{1.55^2}{2 \times 500 \times 3.63} = 0.6618 \text{ nm}$$

The number of longitudinal modes is simply

$$\frac{1560 - 1540}{0.6618} = 30$$

Also, the mode separation in frequency is

$$\Delta f_{long} = \frac{c}{\lambda^2} \times \Delta\lambda_{long} = \frac{3 \times 10^{14}}{1.55^2} \times 0.6618 \times 10^{-3} = 82.6 \text{ GHz.} \blacksquare$$

3.7 SINGLE (LONGITUDINAL) MODE LASER DIODES

FP laser diodes generate undesirable multiple longitudinal modes. A different kind of laser diode called the single (longitudinal) mode laser can suppress side modes and generate only one main longitudinal mode. Important single-mode lasers include: DFB (distributed feedback) lasers, DBR (distributed Bragg reflector) lasers, and cleaved-coupled-cavity (C^3) lasers.

3.7.1 DFB LASERS

DFB lasers [1] use Bragg reflection to suppress undesirable modes. As illustrated in Figure 3.18, there is a periodic structure inside the cavity with the period equal to Λ. Because of the periodic structure, a forward traveling wave has interference with a backward traveling wave. To have constructive interference, the round trip phase change over one period

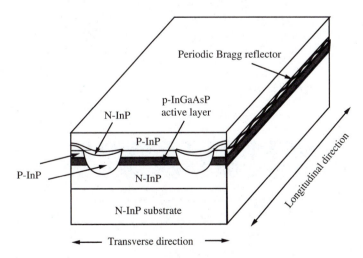

Figure 3.18   Illustration of a buried-heterostructure DFB LD.

should be $2\pi m$, where m is an integer and is called the order of the Bragg diffraction. With $m = 1$, the first order Bragg wavelength is:

$$2\pi = 2\Lambda \frac{2\pi n}{\lambda_B}$$

or

$$\boxed{\lambda_B = 2\Lambda n.}$$ **[3.16]**

Therefore, the period of the periodic structure determines the wavelength of the single-mode light output.

In reality, a periodic DFB structure generates two main modes with symmetric offsets from the Bragg wavelength [1]. To generate only one mode at the Bragg wavelength, a phase-shift of $\lambda/4$ can be used to remove the symmetry [34][35]. As illustrated in Figure 3.19, the periodic structure has a phase discontinuity of $\pi/2$ at the middle, which gives an equivalent $\lambda/4$ phase shift. Detailed discussion on the principle of $\lambda/4$ phase-shift DFB lasers is given in Chapter 13.

3.7.2 DBR LASERS

DBR lasers [4] use the same Bragg reflection principle to generate only one longitudinal mode. The difference between DBR and DFB lasers is that DBR lasers have the diffraction structure outside the laser cavity, as shown in Figure 3.20. With this arrangement, the laser control (laser cavity) and the frequency control (Bragg reflection cavity) can be done separately.

3.7.3 COUPLED-CAVITY LASERS

A **coupled-cavity** laser has two FP resonant cavities, which can be both active (called **cleaved-coupled-cavity** or C^3 lasers) [36] or one active and one passive [37]. These lasers are illustrated in Figure 3.21. In either case, the basic principle to generate only a single longitudinal mode is illustrated in Figure 3.22. The wavelength of the longitudinal mode

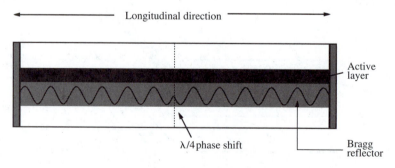

Figure 3.19   Illustration of a $\lambda/4$ phase-shift DFB LD.

that can pass through both cavities should satisfy the constructive interference condition, Equation (3.14). Thus

$$\lambda = \frac{2L_1 n}{m_1} = \frac{2L_2 n}{m_2} \qquad \textbf{[3.17]}$$

where m_1 and m_2 are two integers. With λ satisfying Equation (3.17) and using Equation (3.15), the modal separation is

$$\Delta\lambda_{long} = M_1 \frac{\lambda^2}{2L_1 n} = M_2 \frac{\lambda^2}{2L_2 n} \qquad \textbf{[3.18]}$$

where M_1 and M_2 are two mutually prime integers such that

$$\frac{L_1}{M_1} = \frac{L_2}{M_2} \overset{\text{def}}{=} L_0 \qquad \textbf{[3.19]}$$

From the above condition,

$$\Delta\lambda_{long} = \frac{\lambda^2}{2n L_0} \qquad \textbf{[3.20]}$$

MODE SEPARATION OF C³ LASERS Suppose $\lambda = 1.55\,\mu m$, $L_1 = 20\,\mu m$, $L_2 = 75\,\mu m$, and the refractive index n is 3.5. Considering L_0 as the largest common factor of L_1 and L_2 gives $L_0 = 5\,\mu m$ with $M_1 = 4$ and $M_2 = 15$. As a result,

$$\Delta\lambda_{long} = \frac{1.55^2}{7.0 \times 5} = 68.6 \text{ nm.} \quad \blacksquare$$

Example 3.11

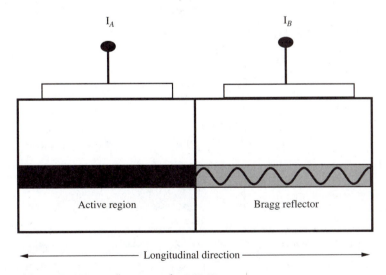

Figure 3.20   Illustration of a DBR LD.

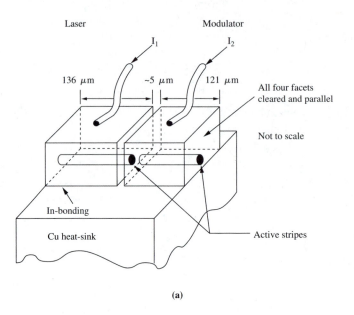

Laser

Modulator

I_1

I_2

136 μm

~5 μm

121 μm

All four facets
cleared and parallel

Not to scale

In-bonding

Cu heat-sink

Active stripes

(a)

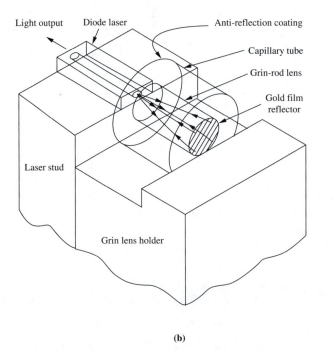

Light output

Diode laser

Anti-reflection coating

Capillary tube

Grin-rod lens

Gold film
reflector

Laser stud

Grin lens holder

(b)

Figure 3.21   Illustration of coupled-cavity LDs: (*a*) active-active, and (*b*) active-passive.

SOURCE: (*a*) Reprinted, by permission, from Tsang et al., "High-Speed," p. 650 [36]. © 1983 by American Institute of Physics. (*b*) Reprinted, by permission, from Liou et al., "Single Longitudinal-Mode," p. 729 [37]. © 1984 by American Institute of Physics.

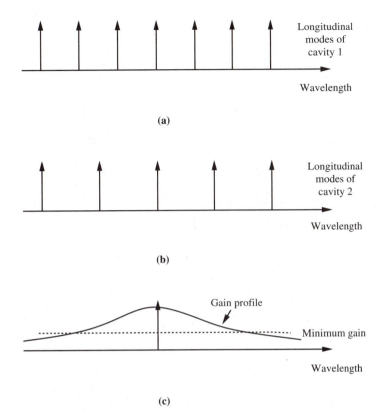

(a)

(b)

(c)

Figure 3.22   Principle of coupled-cavity laser diodes: (a) longitudinal modes of cavity 1, (b) longitudinal modes of cavity 2, and (c) only one common mode whose gain is greater than the loss in the gain profile.

When the modal separation is large enough, there is only one possible longitudinal mode that has enough gain in the gain profile to lase. For C^3 lasers, one of the current signals can be used for modulation, and the other can be used to control the output light wavelength. This is illustrated in Figure 3.23. When the current increases, the refractive index of the cavity decreases. From Equation (3.17), the output light wavelength decreases.

3.8   OTHER IMPORTANT TYPES OF LASER DIODES

There are other important types of laser diodes designed with specific objectives. This section considers two important types. The first type is called a **quantum-well** laser, which is designed for higher temperature stability, higher modulation frequency, lower linewidth enhancement, and lower threshold current. The second type is called a **tunable** laser, which is designed to provide tunability for applications such as WDMA.

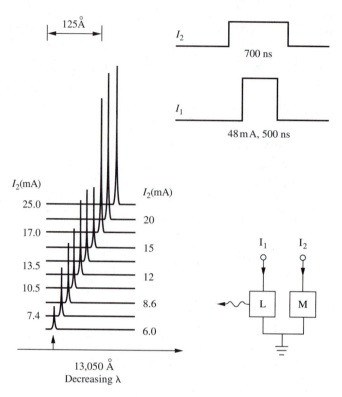

Figure 3.23   Frequency modulation of the C³ Laser.

SOURCE: Reprinted, by permission, from Tsang et al., "High-Speed," p. 650
[36]. © 1983 by American Institute of Physics.

3.8.1   QUANTUM-WELL LASERS

Because of a very thin active layer (e.g., 50Å), quantum-well lasers [38]–[40] have discrete energy levels, as illustrated in Figure 3.24. The thickness of the active layer of a typical quantum-well laser diode is around 1000 Å (0.1 μm).

The reason that the energy bands become discrete as the active layer becomes thinner comes from quantum mechanics, according to which the energy bands for electrons in the conduction band can be expressed as

$$E_{ic} = E_c + \frac{h^2}{8d^2} \frac{i^2}{m_e} \quad i = 1, 2, 3, \ldots \qquad \textbf{[3.21]}$$

and the energy bands for holes in the valence can be expressed as

$$E_{jh} = E_v - \frac{h^2}{8d^2} \frac{j^2}{m_h} \quad j = 1, 2, 3, \ldots \qquad \textbf{[3.22]}$$

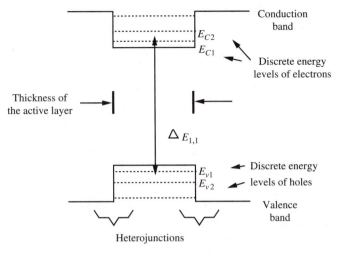

Figure 3.24 Illustration of the discrete energy levels of a quantum-well laser.

where d is the thickness of the active layer, m_e and m_h are the effective mass of electrons and holes, respectively, and i and j are integers. From the discrete energy levels, the possible energy gaps are

$$\Delta E_{i,j} = E_g + \frac{h^2}{8d^2}(\frac{i^2}{m_e} + \frac{j^2}{m_h})$$ [3.23]

with $E_g \overset{\text{def}}{=} E_c - E_v$. Note that the smaller the thickness of the active layer d, the larger the $\Delta E_{i,j}$ and the larger the difference among the $\Delta E_{i,j}$'s. Because d is small, the second term in the above equation can be a significant fraction of E_g. Therefore, we can adjust d to change the wavelength of the output light as illustrated in Figure 3.25.

EMISSION WAVELENGTHS OF QUANTUM-WELL LASERS For a GaAs quantum-well laser, $E_g = 1.43$ eV. If $d = 5$ nm, using $i = j = 1$ in Equation (3.23) gives

Example 3.12

$$\frac{h^2}{8d^2}(\frac{1}{m_e} + \frac{1}{m_h}) = 0.25 \text{ eV}$$

where $m_e = 0.068m_0$, $m_h = 0.5m_0$, and $m_0 = 9.11 \times 10^{-31}$ kg are assumed. This 0.25 eV is a significant increase from E_g of 1.43 eV. Therefore, the output light wavelength is reduced to

$$\lambda_{1,1} = \frac{hc}{(1.43 + 0.25)q} = 0.74 \ \mu\text{m}.$$

See Example 3.3 for comparison.

One can also calculate the energy difference between $\Delta E_{1,1}$ and $\Delta E_{2,1}$. If $\lambda_{1,1} = 1.5\ \mu$m, then

$$\Delta E = \Delta E_{2,1} - \Delta E_{1,1} = \frac{h^2}{8d^2}\frac{3}{m_e} = 0.66\ \text{eV}$$

and

$$|\lambda_{21} - \lambda_{11}| = 0.74 - \frac{hc}{(1.43 + 0.25 + 0.66)q} = 0.21\ \mu\text{m}.$$

This illustrates a large mode separation. Therefore, photons have a high energy concentration around $\Delta E_{1,1}$. ∎

Because the wavelength is strongly determined by Equation (3.23), quantum-well lasers have less temperature dependence and lower linewidth broadening under modulation. It has been shown that the threshold current I_{th} of both FP and quantum-well lasers has a temperature dependence given by

$$I_{th} = I_0 e^{T/T_c}$$

[3.24]

where T_c is called the **characteristic temperature** of the laser diode. For FP laser diodes, T_c is around 60 °C; and for quantum-well lasers, T_c is around 100 °C [41].

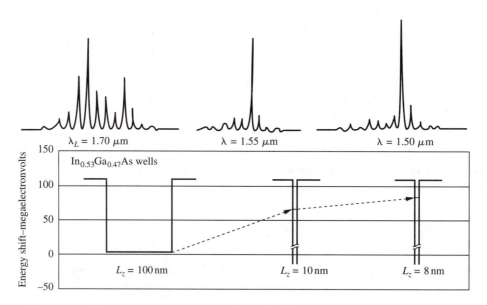

Figure 3.25   Output wavelength as a function of the active layer thickness.

SOURCE: Reprinted, by permission, from Temkin et al., "1.5–1.6 μm," p. 845 [39]. © 1987 by *American Institute of Physics.*

Linewidth broadening is a phenomenon whereby the output linewidth becomes broader as the light source is under direct modulation. For example, the DFB and C^3 lasers will no longer be single mode under high-speed modulation. This linewidth broadening is caused by refractive index modulation of the laser cavity. For the same reason, the chirping effect can also be observed, where the emission wavelength changes approximately as a linear function of time during modulation. As shown in Figure 3.26, the amount of wavelength shift due to chirping in quantum well lasers is about half that of conventional FP lasers [42]. The linewidth broadening and chirping effects will be discussed in more detail in Chapter 12.

Although quantum-well lasers have a smaller temperature dependence and linewidth broadening under modulation, the carrier and optical confinement is usually poor because of the very thin active layer. To overcome this problem, **multiple quantum well** (MQW) structures have been used [43]. As illustrated in Figure 3.27, active layers of smaller energy bandgaps are interleaved with cladding layers that have larger energy bandgaps. Just like heterostructures, this interleaved quantum-well structure provides better carrier and photon confinement.

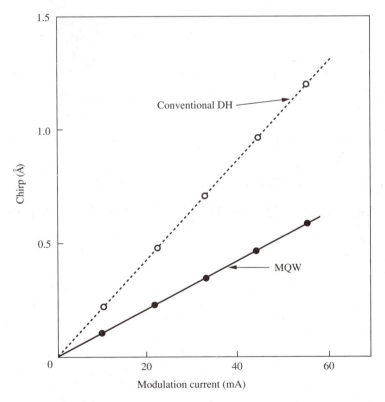

Figure 3.26   Chirping effect comparison between MQW and FP lasers in terms of peak-to-peak wavelength shift.

SOURCE: Reprinted, by permission, from Dutta et al., p. 19 [42]. © 1985 by *American Institute of Physics*.

3.8.2 TUNABLE LASERS

As mentioned earlier, C^3 lasers can be tuned in frequency by controlling one of their current inputs. In general, tunability is important for applications such as wavelength division multiplexing (WDM) and frequency division multiplexing (FDM).

Three basic types of tunable laser diodes based on DBR structures are shown in Figure 3.28 [4]. They all have an active region (denoted by A) and a Bragg reflection region (denoted by B). For better tuning, some DBRs also include a phase control region (denoted by P). In general, the output wavelength can be electrically tuned by adjusting the bias current of either B (Bragg reflection), P (phase), or both.

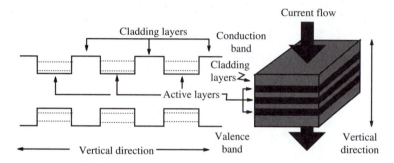

Figure 3.27   Illustration of multiple quantum well lasers.

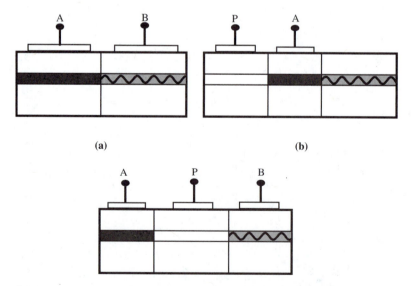

Figure 3.28   Tunable DBR lasers: (*a*) Bragg reflector tuning, (*b*) phase-section tuning, and (*c*) both Bragg and phase tuning.

Tunability of DBR lasers can be understood as follows. First, the combination of the active and phase regions can be considered as a special kind of FP laser (with one facet of zero reflection), and the Bragg reflection region can be considered as an optical filter. Therefore, the final emission output is the filtered output by the Bragg reflector from the emission input of the FP section. Because of the narrow spectrum width of the Bragg filter, only one longitudinal mode can pass through the filter and other longitudinal modes are suppressed.

When the bias current of the Bragg reflector is changed, from Equation (3.16), the Bragg wavelength decreases as the current increases (see Chap. 12 for the refractive index dependence on the bias current). This means the central wavelength of the bandpass Bragg filter shifts to a lower wavelength as the bias current increases. If the central wavelength

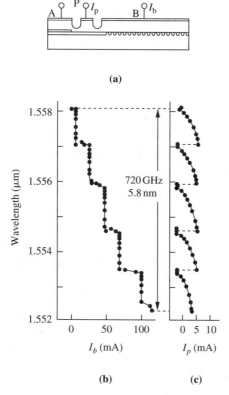

Figure 3.29   DBR-tuning frequency response: (a) Configuration (b) Bragg tuning only and (c) phase tuning only.

shift is not large enough, the same longitudinal mode from the FP section will pass through. Therefore, the wavelength of the emission output remains essentially unchanged. This can be seen from Figure 3.29*b*. When the current or central wavelength shift is large enough, the current longitudinal mode will be suppressed and an adjacent longitudinal mode will take over. This is reflected by a sudden drop in wavelength, as shown in Figure 3.29*b*.

When the bias current of the phase section changes, its refractive index decreases. Because the phase section is part of the FP section, from Equation (3.14), the decrease of refractive index results in a decrease of wavelengths of all longitudinal modes. This can be seen from Figure 3.29*c*. When both Bragg and phase controls are properly controlled at the same time, as shown in Figure 3.30, a continuous wavelength tuning over 3.1 nm is achieved [4]. At $\lambda = 1.55$ μm, this is equivalent to a 380 GHz tunable frequency range.

Figure 3.31 illustrates two kinds of tunable lasers based on DFB. The first kind has a second-phase control section, and the second kind has two active control sections. Because the Bragg reflection is inside the DFB laser section, tuning the active region changes the wavelengths of the longitudinal modes and the central wavelength of the Bragg filter at the same time. Therefore, compared to DBR lasers, it is much more difficult to tune a DFB laser. The characteristics of output wavelengths of DFB lasers will be discussed in Chapter 13.

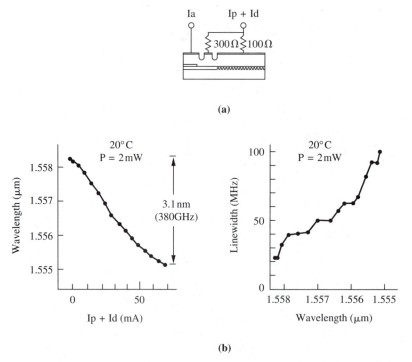

Figure 3.30   Both Bragg and phase-tuning frequency response of DBR lasers: *(a)* bias circuit and *(b)* frequency response.

SOURCE: Reprinted, by permission, from Kobayashi and Mito, "Single Frequency and Tunable Laser Diodes," Fig. 18a, p. 1630 [4]. © 1988 by IEEE.

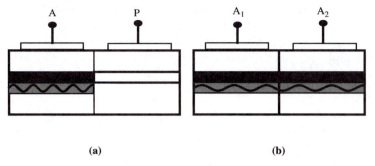

Figure 3.31 Tunable DFB lasers: (a) phase-section tuning and (b) two-active-section tuning.

3.9 SUMMARY

1. Important properties of a light source for optical fiber communications include: single mode, low noise, small linewidth, high output power, low threshold current (for laser diodes), wavelength at 1.3 or 1.5 μm, large modulation bandwidth, small linewidth broadening under direct modulation, high linearity, and tunability.

2. Two key requirements of making a good semiconductor light source are (1) direct bandgap and (2) heterostructures. A direct bandgap is necessary to have efficient photon generation from electron-hole recombinations (EHRs). Heterostructures are necessary to confine photons and carriers in the active layer.

3. Light emitting diodes generate incoherent light, where each EHR is independent of the others. Therefore, photons generated have independent phase and frequencies. Depending on the specific device, the output spectrum width (Δf) is several (2–3) kT/h, and the corresponding linewidth ($\Delta\lambda$) is several $(\lambda^2/c)(kT/h)$.

4. The principle of laser generation is based on (1) external pumping and (2) light amplification or stimulated emission. In semiconductor lasers, external pumping is through current injection, and stimulated emission is through EHRs. To have a positive light amplification gain at a low bias current, a good cavity confinement that reduces the cavity loss is critical. Because LEDs do not have good cavity confinement, they cannot generate laser light before overheating.

5. To reduce cavity loss and threshold current, in addition to the confinement by the heterostructure (vertical direction) and reflecting mirrors (longitudinal direction), gain-guiding and index-guiding structures have been used for confinement in the transverse direction.

6. Laser light is coherent; photons generated from stimulated emission have the same phase and frequency photons.

7. In an FP laser diode, because the coherent light is reflected back and forth between two cavity ends, their round-trip phase change should equal a multiple of 2π. Therefore, only certain frequencies can exist. They are called longitudinal modes. In general, FP lasers have multiple longitudinal modes at the output and are called multimode lasers.

8. To generate only a single mode, various structures have been developed. These include DFB, DBR, and C^3 laser diodes.

9. Quantum well lasers have very thin active layers. As a result, they have discrete energy levels, and when they are directly modulated, they have small linewidth broadening compared to other laser diodes.

10. Tunable laser diodes are important to WDM, WDMA, and coherent communications. Three- and two-section DBR and DFB tunable lasers can provide a tuning range of several hundred GHz.

APPENDIX 3-A: FABRY-PEROT RESONATOR

This appendix explains the theory of FP interference. (For more detailed discussion, [44] is a good reference.) Consider the FP resonator shown in Figure 3.32 as an optical filter, where an incident lightwave comes from the left-hand side of the cavity and leaves the cavity from the right-hand side. Assume the cavity has a refractive index n. If the incident wave has an amplitude A_{in}, the output wave can be expressed as:

$$A_{out} = tt'A_{in}D + tt'rr'A_{in}D^3 + tt'(rr')^2 A_{in}D^5 + \ldots$$

$$= tt'A_{in}D \sum_{i=0}^{\infty} (rr')^i D^{2i} = tt'A_{in}D \frac{1}{1 - rr'D^2}$$

where

$$D = e^{j2\pi nL/\lambda} \qquad \text{[3.25]}$$

Incident wave

Output wave

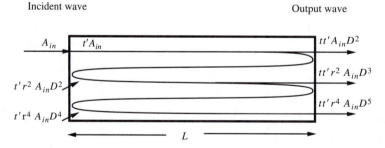

A_{in} $t'A_{in}$

$tt'A_{in}D^2$

$tt'r^2 A_{in}D^3$

$t'r^2 A_{in}D^2$

$tt'r^4 A_{in}D^5$

$t'r^4 A_{in}D^4$

L

Figure 3.32   Illustration of the Fabry-Perot interference.

is the one-way phase shift factor, t' and r' are the transmission and reflection coefficients at the left end, and t and r are the transmission and reflection coefficients at the right end. For convenience, we define $D = e^{j\delta/2}$, where

$$\delta = \frac{4\pi n L}{\lambda} \qquad\qquad [3.26]$$

is the round-trip phase shift. Therefore,

$$A_{out} = D \frac{tt'}{1 - rr'e^{i\delta}} A_{in}.$$

If we define $T = t^2$, $T' = t'^2$ as being the power transmissivities and $R = r^2$, $R' = r'^2$ as being the power reflectivities, the relationship between the input and output power is

$$P_{out} = |A_{out}|^2 = \left| \frac{tt'}{1 - rr'e^{i\delta}} \right|^2 |A_{in}|^2 = \frac{TT'}{1 + RR' - 2(RR')^{1/2}\cos(\delta)} P_{in}$$

$$= \frac{TT'}{(1 - \bar{R})^2 + 4\bar{R}\sin^2(\delta/2)} P_{in}$$

where $\bar{R} \overset{\text{def}}{=} (RR')^{1/2}$. If we define

$$F \overset{\text{def}}{=} \frac{4\bar{R}}{(1 - \bar{R})^2} \qquad\qquad [3.27]$$

we have

$$P_{out} = \frac{TT'}{(1 - \bar{R})^2} \frac{1}{1 + F\sin^2(\delta/2)} P_{in}. \qquad\qquad [3.28]$$

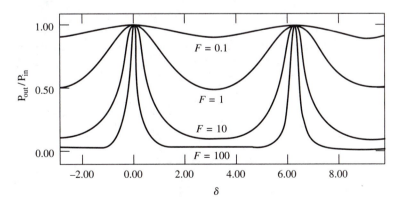

Figure 3.33   Fabry-Perot transmission as a function of δ.

The parameter F is called the **coefficient of finesse,** and the power ratio P_{out}/P_{in} given by Equation (3.28) is known as the **Airy** function. When the cavity ends are lossless, or $T = 1 - R$ and $T' = 1 - R'$, P_{out}/P_{in} can have peaks at unity if $R = R'$. The power ratio at several F's is plotted in Figure 3.33. The illustration shows that the larger the coefficient of finesse, the narrower the fringes. From Equation (3.28), P_{out} is a periodic function of δ with period 2π.

The width of each fringe can be calculated as follows. First, if $\delta = 2\pi m \pm \epsilon/2$, then

$$\frac{P_{out}}{P_{in}} = \frac{1}{1 + F \sin^2(\epsilon/4)} \qquad \textbf{[3.29]}$$

The full-width half-maximum (FWHM) width of each fringe is defined as the width between two half-maximum points of a fringe. When F is large, the value ϵ corresponding to the half-maximum point is

$$\epsilon \approx \pm \frac{4}{\sqrt{F}}.$$

The **finesse** $\mathcal{F}$ of the FP resonator is defined as

$$\mathcal{F} \stackrel{\text{def}}{=} \frac{2\pi}{|\epsilon|} = \frac{\pi}{2}\sqrt{F} = \pi \frac{R^{1/2}}{(1-R)}. \qquad \textbf{[3.30]}$$

This result shows that a very high reflectivity is needed to have a large finesse, $\mathcal{F}$.

The importance of $\mathcal{F}$ can be seen from the dependence of δ on the wavelength given by Equation (3.26). From the equation, note that the product $\delta\lambda$ is a constant. Therefore,

$$\left|\frac{\Delta\delta}{\delta}\right| = \left|\frac{\Delta\lambda}{\lambda}\right|$$

where $\Delta\delta$ is the width of each fringe and $\Delta\lambda$ is the corresponding linewidth. Therefore, the smaller the δ, the smaller the linewidth when the FP resonator is used as a bandpass filter.

From the definition of $\mathcal{F}$ given by Equation (3.30) and the 2π period of δ, note that $\mathcal{F}$ can be interpreted as the spectrum resolution of the resonator. When the resonator is used as a spectrum analyzer, a sawtooth voltage signal is used to modulate the refractive index of the resonator. This sweeps the peak of the resonator response over a 2π period. The frequency content of the power of an incident light signal can thus be scanned over the period.

Example 3.13 | **FINESSE OF FP RESONATORS**   For $\bar{R} = 0.9$,

$$F = \frac{4 \times 0.9}{0.01} = 360$$

and

$$\mathcal{F} = \pi \frac{0.9^{1/2}}{0.1} = 30.$$

For $\bar{R} = 0.99$,

$$F = \frac{4 \times 0.99}{0.0001} = 39600$$

and

$$\mathcal{F} = \pi \frac{0.99^{1/2}}{0.01} = 312.$$

Therefore, a very high reflectivity is necessary to have a finesse of a few hundreds. For a typical In-GaAsP laser diode with simple cleaving at its two ends, $R = 0.30$ and

$$F = \frac{4 \times 0.3}{(1 - 0.3)^2} = 2.45.$$

The corresponding finesse is

$$\mathcal{F} = \frac{\pi}{2}\sqrt{F} = 2.46.$$

This small finesse requires an additional filtering structure to make a semiconductor laser a good and clean light source. ∎

PROBLEMS

Problem 3–1 Multimode Light Source: Assume the output of a light source has two longitudinal modes with equal power and separated by a frequency of 10 GHz.
   a. If the corresponding difference in propagation speed is 10 km/sec along a given fiber, draw the pulse output over a distance of (*i*) 10 km, and (*ii*) 100 km. Assume the average propagation speed is 2×10^8 m/sec and the input pulse is a rectangular pulse 10 nsec wide. Neglect attenuation in transmission.
   b. In on-off keying, let each 10-nsec pulse be used to represent a bit "1." What will be the output waveform over 40 km if four input bits 1010 are transmitted at the bit rate of 100 Mb/s. Using the same assumptions given in *a*, can you tell what is transmitted?

Problem 3–2 Phase Noise: Phase noise in laser diodes comes from random spontaneous emissions (Chap. 6). Let the coherent component in the light output be $I \gg 1$ and the spontaneous emission component be $\exp(jx)$, where x is a random value from 0 to 2π. If we define $I + \exp(jx) = \hat{I}\exp(j\theta)$, what is the phase θ in terms of x and I? Note that θ is the phase shift due to the random spontaneous emission.

Problem 3–3 Low Threshold Current: The output power of a laser diode family is given by

$$P_{out} = A(I - I_{th})$$

for $I > I_{th}$ and zero otherwise. Let $A = 1$ mW/mA. If the bias current I is 70 mA, find the output power for $I_{th} = $ (a) 30 mA, (b) 50 mA, and (c) 100 mA. What is the ratio of the output power at 50 mA to that at 30 mA?

Problem 3–4 Heterostructures and Output Wavelength: From Figure 3.6, what is the lattice constant of InP? At the same lattice constant, find the energy bandgap for InGaAs. Calculate the corresponding output wavelength.

Problem 3–5 Output Linewidth of LEDs: If the linewidth of an LED at 300K is 0.01 μm, find the operating temperature to reduce the FWHM spectrum width to 10 GHz. For simplicity, assume the central wavelength is 0.9 μm and stays the same when temperature changes.

Problem 3–6 Light Coupling:

a. If the dielectric constant of the active layer of a Burrus LED is 12, find the transmissivity T at the LED–air interface.

b. If an intermediate fluid layer with dielectric constant 6 is added, find the combined transmissivity at the LED–fluid–air interface. Note that the transmissivity is one minus the reflectivity R, which is the amplitude squared of the reflection coefficient r.

c. If the LED is connected to a fiber with its core refractive index equal to 1.5, find the combined transmissivity through the LED–fluid–air–fiber coupling.

Problem 3–7 Cavity Confinement: Assume the cavity confinement is improved so that the cavity distribution loss is reduced from 1000 m^{-1} to 500 m^{-1}. If the cavity has a refractive index of 3.6 and a length of 1000 μm, find the improvement ratio of the total distribution loss.

Problem 3–8 Longitudinal Modes: If the gain profile of a laser diode of cavity length $L = 1000$ μm has $\lambda_{min} = 1.399$ μm and $\lambda_{max} = 1.400$ μm, find the mode separation and the total number of propagation modes. Assume the refractive index of the device is 3.0. If you want to have only one longitudinal mode, what is the maximum possible cavity length?

Problem 3–9 Cavity Loss: If a laser diode has length $L = 800\,\mu$m and dielectric constant 15, find the minimum distributive gain in dB/m. Assume the distributed loss is 1200 dB/m.

If the distributive gain is 4000 dB/m, at the same cavity length, what will be the minimum reflectivity at the cavity ends to generate laser light? Similarly, at the distributive gain of 4000 dB/m and the same dielectric constant of 15, what is the minimum cavity length L?

Problem 3–10 FP Laser Diode: Consider a FP laser made of InGaAsP with refractive index 3.5.

a. If the device has a gain profile

$$g(\lambda) = g_0 e^{-(\lambda - \lambda_0)^2 / \sigma^2}$$

with $g_0 = 1500$ m^{-1}, $\sigma = 10$ nm, and distributed cavity loss $\alpha_m = 1000$ m^{-1}, find the lower limit of the cavity length for lasing.

b. If the device has a longitudinal length $L = 2000$ μm and the same gain profile given in a, find the number of longitudinal modes. Let $\alpha_m = 500$ m^{-1} and $\lambda_0 = 1.5$ μm.

Problem 3–11 C³ Laser: A C³ laser has two cavities of lengths 800 μm and 1000 μm. Find the mode separation. Assume the central wavelength is 1.5 μm and the refractive index of the two cavities is 3.0.

Problem 3–12 DFB Laser: If a DFB laser diode has a cavity length of 1000 μm, find the period of the Bragg reflector structure so that the output wavelength is 1.5 μm. Let the refractive index of the cavity be 3.0.

Problem 3–13 Tunable DBR Laser: If the tunable wavelength range of a DBR laser is from 1.552 μm to 1.558 μm, find the corresponding frequency range. If the channel separation is 10 GHz, how many WDM channels can this laser be tuned to?

Problem 3–14 Quantum Well Laser: For a given quantum well laser, assume $m_e = 0.1 m_0$ and $m_h = 0.5 m_0$. Find the maximum thickness of the active layer so that the frequency separation of the two lowest frequency modes is 100 GHz.

Problem 3–15 Fabry-Perot Resonators: To achieve a finesse of 400, find the required reflectivity R at the two facets. If mode separation is 50 GHz, what is the FWHM bandwidth of each passband?

Problem 3–16 Reflection from Fabry-Perot Resonator:

a. Perform an analysis similar to that given in Appendix 3–A to show that the ratio of the reflected power to the incident power is given by

$$\frac{P_{ref}}{P_{in}} = \frac{(r - r')^2 + 4\bar{R}\sin^2(\delta/2)}{(1 - \bar{R})^2 + 4\bar{R}\sin^2(\delta/2)}.$$

In the analysis, you need to add all reflected rays. From [44] or Equation (3.12), note that the reflection coefficient at the left end is $-r'$ when the ray comes from outside of the cavity.

b. From a and Equation (3.28), show the conservation of energy if $T = 1 - R$ and $T' = 1 - R'$.

REFERENCES

1. H. Kogelnik and C. V. Shank, "Coupled-Wave Theory of Distributed Feedback Lasers," *Journal of Applied Physics*, vol. 43, no. 5 (May 1972), pp. 2327–35.

2. L. D. Westbrook et al., "Monolithic 1.5 μm Hybrid DFB/DBR Lasers with 5 nm Tuning Range," *Electronics Letters*, vol. 20 (November 1984), pp. 957–59.

3. S. Murata, I. Mito, and K. Kobayashi, "Spectral Characteristics for a 1.5 μm DBR Laser with Frequency-Tuning Region," *IEEE Journal of Quantum Electronics*, vol. 23 (June 1987), pp. 835–38.

4. K. Kobayashi and I. Mito, "Single Frequency and Tunable Laser Diodes," *Journal of Lightwave Technology*, vol. 6, no. 2 (November 1988), pp. 1623–33.

5. Y. Arakawa and A. Yariv, "Theory of Gain, Modulation Response, and Spectral Linewidth in AlGaAs Quantum Well Lasers," *IEEE Journal of Quantum Electronics*, vol. 21, no. 10 (October 1985), pp. 1666–74.

6. *Lasers & Optronics Buying Guide*: *Industry and Product Directory*, 1991.

7. *Laser Focus World*: *The Buyer's Guide*, vol. 29, 1994.

8. Toshiba Data Sheets of Fiber-Optic Semiconductor Devices for Optical Communications.

9. R. S. Muller and T. I. Kamins, *Device Electronics for Integrated Circuits*, John Wiley and Sons, 1977.

10. D. A. Neaman, *Semiconductor Physics & Devices,* Richard D. Irwin, 1992.

11. C. Cohen-Tannoudji, B. Diu, and F. Laloë, *Quantum Mechanics*, vol. 1, Chapter 1, "Waves and Particles," John Wiley and Sons, 1977.

12. H. Kroemer, "A Proposed Class of Heterojunction Injection Lasers," *Proceedings of the IEEE*, vol. 51, no. 12 (1963), pp. 1782–83.

13. Z. I. Alferov, R. F. Kazarinov, Authors certificate 181737 (USSR), 1963.

14. H. Kressel and H. Nelson, *RCA Reviews*, vol. 30 (1969), p. 106.

15. I. Hayashi et al., "A Technique for the Preparation of Low-Threshold Room Temperature Laser Diode Structures," *IEEE Journal of Quantum Electronics*, vol. 5 (April 1969), pp. 211–12.

16. Z. I. Alferov et al., *Soviet Physics: Semiconductors*, vol. 3 (1970), p. 1107; translated from *Fizika i tekhnika poluprovodnikov*, vol. 3 (1969), p. 1328.

17. J. Wilson and J. F. B. Hawkes, *Optoelectronics: An Introduction*, 2nd ed., Prentice Hall, 1989.

18. D. Marcuse, "LED Fundamentals: Comparison of Front- and Edge-Emitting Diodes," *IEEE Journal of Quantum Electronics*, vol. 13, no. 10 (October 1977), p. 819.

19. R. H. Saul, T. P. Lee, and C. A. Burrus, "Light-Emitting-Diode Device Design," Chapter 5, *Lightwave Communications Technology*, Part C, edited by W. T. Tsang, *Semiconductors and Semimetals*, vol. 22, Academic Press, 1985.

20. H. Temkin et al., "Temperature Dependence of Photoluminescence of n-InGaAsP," *Journal of Applied Physics*, vol. 52, no. 3 (1981), pp. 1574–78.

21. P. D. Wright et al., "InGaPAs-InP Double-Heterojunction High Radiance LED's," *IEEE Transactions on Electron Devices*, vol. 26 (1979), pp. 1220–27.

22. C. A. Burrus and B. J. Miller, "Small-Area, Double Heterostructure AlGaAs Electroluminescent Diode Sources for Optical-Fiber Transmission Lines," *Optical Communications*, vol. 4, (1971) Elsevier Science Publishers, pp. 307–9.

23. D. Botez and M. Ettenberg, "Comparison of Surface- and Edge-Emitting LED's for Use in Fiber Optical Communications," *IEEE Transactions on Electron Devices*, vol. 26, no. 8 (August 1979), pp. 1230–38.

24. J. J. Hsieh et al., "Room-Temperature CW Operation of GaInAsP/InP DH Diode Lasers Emitting at 1.1 μm," *Applied Physics Letters*, vol. 28 (1976), pp. 709–11.

25. G. D. Henshall et al., *Solid State and Electron Devices*, vol. 3, no. 1 (1979).

26. B. Schwartz et al., "Stripe Geometry InP/InGaAsP Lasers Fabricated with Deuteron Bombardment," *IEEE Transactions on Electron Devices*, vol. 31 (1984), pp. 841–43.

27. K. Oe and K. Sugiyama, "GaInAsP/InP Planar Stripe Lasers Prepared by Using Sputtered SiO_2 Film as a Zn Diffusion Mask," *Journal of Applied Physics*, vol. 51, no. 1 (1980), pp. 43–49.

28. N. K. Dutta, "Optical Sources for Lightwave System Applications," Chap. 9 of *Optical-Fiber Transmission*, edited by E. E. Basch, McGraw-Hill, 1987.

29. W. T. Tsang et al., "A New High-Power Transverse-Mode Stabilized Semiconductor Laser at 1.5 μm: The Heteroepitaxial Ridge-Overgrown Laser," *Applied Physics Letters*, vol. 45 (1984), pp. 1025–27.

30. S. E. H. Turley et al., "Properties of Inverted Rib-Waveguide Lasers Operating at 1.3 μm Wavelength," *Electronics Letters*, vol. 17, no. 23 (1981), pp. 868–70.

31. T. Tasukada, "GaAs-GaAlAs Buried-Heterostructure Injection Lasers," *Journal of Applied Physics*, vol. 45, no. 11 (1974), pp. 4899–4906.

32. M. Hirao et al., "Long-Wavelength InGaAsP/InP Lasers for Optical-Fiber Communication Systems," *Journal of Optical Communications*, vol. 1 (1980), pp. 10–14.

33. I. Mito et al., "InGaAsP Double-Channel Planar Buried-Heterostructure Laser Diode (DCPBH LD) with Effective Current Confinement," *IEEE Journal of Lightwave Technology*, vol. 1 (1983), pp. 195–202.

34. H. A. Haus and C. V. Shank, "Antisymmetric Taper of Distributed Feedback Lasers," *IEEE Journal of Quantum Electronics*, vol. 12, no. 9 (1976), pp. 532–39.

35. S. L. McCall and P. M. Platzman, "An Optimized $\pi/2$ Distributed Feedback Laser," *IEEE Journal of Quantum Electronics*, vol. 21, no. 12 (December 1985), pp. 1899–1902.

36. W. T. Tsang et al., "High-Speed Direct Single-Frequency Modulation with Large Tuning Rate in Cleaved-Coupled-Cavity Lasers," *Applied Physics Letters*, vol. 42 (1983), pp. 650–52.

37. K.-Y. Liou et al., "Single Longitudinal-Mode Stabilized Graded-Index-Rod External Coupled-Cavity Laser," *Applied Physics Letters*, vol. 45 (1984), pp. 729–31.

38. R. Dingle et al., "Quantum States of Confined Carriers in Very Thin $Al_xGa_{1-x}As$–$Al_xGa_{1-x}As$ Heterostructures," *Physics Review Letters*, vol. 33 (1974), pp. 827–30.

39. H. Temkin et al., "1.5–1.6 μm $Ga_{0.47}In_{0.53}As/Al_{0.48}In_{0.52}As$ Multiquantum Well Lasers Grown by Molecular Beam Epitaxy," *Applied Physics Letters*, vol. 42 (1983), p. 845.

40. N. Holonyak, Jr. et al., "Phonon Assisted Recombination and Stimulated Emission in Quantum Well $Al_xGa_{1-x}As$–GaAs Heterostructures," *Journal of Applied Physics*, vol. 51 (1980), pp. 1328–37.

41. G. P. Agrawal and N. K. Dutta, *Long-Wavelength Semiconductor Lasers,* Van Nostrand Reinhold, 1986.

42. N. K. Dutta et al., "Fabrication and Performance Characteristics of InGaAsP Multi-quantum Well Double Channel Planar Buried Heterostructure Lasers," *Applied Physics Letters*, vol. 46 (1985), pp. 19–21.

43. W. T. Tsang, "GaInAs/InP Multiquantum-Well Heterostructure Lasers Grown by MBE," *Applied Physics Letters*, vol. 44 (1984), pp. 288–90.

44. M. Born and E. Wolf, *Principles of Optics,* 6th ed., Pergamon Press, 1980.

4

OPTICAL FIBERS

This chapter presents basic optical fiber structures and explains how light propagates inside them. Optical fibers are a common transmission medium used in optical communications. Compared with other transmission media such as space and wires, optical fibers provide low attenuation and strong immunity to electromagnetic interference (EMI). Because of these advantages, optical fibers have been used in long-haul undersea and interoffice communications [1]–[3]. Recently, because of their cost effectiveness and better quality, fibers have also been used to replace cable for "cable" TV trunk distribution [4].

From the communication system point of view (Figure 1.2), optical fibers are the communication channel in which light propagates. Like any other transmission medium, signal attenuation and distortion in optical fibers are important degradation factors. This chapter discusses fiber attenuation and dispersion and explains how they limit transmission speed and distance. It also explains how to improve the speed and distance limits by reducing fiber attenuation and dispersion.

To quantify fiber attenuation and dispersion, one must understand various attenuation sources and know how light propagates inside a fiber. To explain light propagation, both geometrical optics and wave analysis are used. Detailed analysis of wave equations is purposely avoided, however, because the objective of this chapter is to illustrate important propagation properties with simple mathematics.

After explaining and quantifying fiber attenuation and dispersion, Chapter 4 derives attenuation and dispersion limits. These limits give upper bounds of transmission distance at a given transmission rate. If a system's transmission distance is limited by fiber attenuation, the system is called **attenuation limited**; otherwise, it is called **dispersion limited**. In general, most systems are attenuation limited at lower speeds (smaller than a few hundred Mb/s) and become dispersion limited at higher speeds.

This chapter considers optical fibers as a linear channel, where signals can be superimposed and fiber properties such as refractive indices are not modulated by the signals. Important nonlinear effects such as soliton propagations will be discussed in Chapter 18.

4.1 OPTICAL FIBER STRUCTURES AND TYPES

To guide light propagation, a basic optical fiber has a circular cross section as depicted in Figure 4.1. Although a practical fiber has many layers, only the core and cladding are important to light propagations. Both the core and cladding are typically made of silica glass. However, the core has a higher refractive index to confine light inside.

As light propagates inside a fiber, most of its power is confined in the core region, which is surrounded by the cladding. The cladding has a slightly lower optical density (or refraction index), typically between a fraction of 1 percent and a few percent. Most fibers have the cladding diameter around 125 μm. Its size is generally not important to light propagations. Outside the cladding are several layers of protection jackets. The jackets prevent the fiber surface from being scratched or cut by mechanical forces.

4.1.1 SINGLE-MODE AND MULTIMODE FIBERS

When a lightwave propagates inside the core of a fiber, it can have different EM field distributions over the fiber cross section. Each field distribution that meets the Maxwell equations and the boundary condition at the core–cladding interface is called a **transverse mode**.

Several transverse modes are illustrated in Figure 4.2. As shown, they have different electric field distribution over the fiber cross section. In general, different transverse modes propagate along the fiber at different speeds. As pointed out in Chapter 3, this results in dispersion and is undesirable. Fibers that allow propagation of only one transverse mode are called **single-mode fibers** (SMF). Fibers that allow propagation of multiple transverse modes are called **multimode fibers** (MMF).

The key in fiber design to having single-mode propagation is to have a small core diameter. This can be understood from the dependence of the **cutoff wavelength** λ_c of the fiber on the core diameter. The cutoff wavelength is the wavelength above which there can be only one single transverse mode. This is explained in Appendix 4–C, and λ_c is expressed as

$$\lambda_c = \frac{2\pi a}{V}(n_1^2 - n_2^2)^{1/2}$$

[4.1]

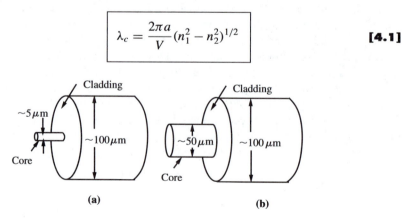

Figure 4.1   Basic structures of (a) single-mode and (b) multimode optical fibers.

where $V = 2.405$ for step-index fibers, a is the core radius, and n_1 and n_2 are the refractive indices of the core and cladding, respectively. This expression shows that fibers of a smaller core radius have a smaller cutoff wavelength.

CORE DIAMETER FOR SINGLE MODE   Because the two important wavelengths used in fiber transmissions are 1.30 μm and 1.55 μm, a cutoff wavelength smaller than 1.30 μm is needed to ensure single-mode propagation. To provide an additional safe margin, consider a cutoff wavelength of 1.2 μm. For $n_1 = 1.45$ and $n_2 = 1.449$, the corresponding core diameter is

Example 4.1

$$a = \frac{\lambda_c V}{2\pi} \frac{1}{(n_1^2 - n_2^2)^{1/2}} = 8.5 \ \mu\text{m}.$$

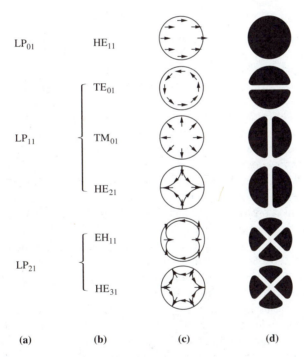

LP_{01}	HE_{11}		
LP_{11}	TE_{01}		
	TM_{01}		
	HE_{21}		
LP_{21}	EH_{11}		
	HE_{31}		
(a)	**(b)**	**(c)**	**(d)**

Figure 4.2   Some examples of low-order transverse modes of a step-index fiber. (*a*) Linear polarized (LP) mode designations, (*b*) exact mode designations, (*c*) electric field distribution, and (*d*) intensity distribution of the electric field component E_x.

Source: Reprinted, by permission, from Senior, *Optical Fiber Communications: Principles and Practice*, 2nd ed. [8]. ©1992 by Prentice-Hall International (UK) Ltd.

Typically, the core diameter is around 10 μm for single-mode fibers and around 50 μm for multimode fibers. ■

When the core diameter of a single-mode fiber is not much larger than the wavelength, there is a significant power portion or field penetration in the cladding. Therefore, it is necessary to define another parameter called **mode field diameter** (MFD). Intuitively, it is the "width" of the transverse field. Specifically, it is the **root mean square** (RMS) width of the field if the field distribution is Gaussian. When the field distribution is not Gaussian, the way to define the MFD is not unique. A good definition has been proposed in [5]. This MFD concept is useful when we want to determine the coupling or splicing loss of two fibers. In this case, it is the match of the MFD instead of the core diameter that is important to a smaller coupling or splicing loss.

4.1.2 REFRACTIVE INDEX PROFILE

Optical fibers can also vary in their refractive index distribution over the core and cladding of a fiber. Two basic types of refractive index profiles of multimode fibers are shown in Figures 4.3a and 4.3b, where one has a uniform profile in the core region, and the other has a smoother increase from the cladding–core boundary to the core center. These two types of fibers are called **step-index** and **graded-index** fibers, respectively. As will be discussed later, the motivation to use graded-index fibers is to equalize the group velocities of different propagation modes for minimal dispersion.

For single-mode fibers, there are also many different types of refractive index profiles. Some important examples are depicted in Figure 4.3C–J. The first one (Figure 4.3C) has the regular step-index profile. Both the core and cladding have constant refractive indices. The mode field diameter is between 9 and 10 μm, and the refractive index change is around 0.3 percent. Fibers of types d and e have different refractive indices in the cladding region. In general, the cladding portion immediately next to the core has the lowest refractive index. This type of fiber is called **depressed-cladding** (DC) fibers. In contrast, type c fibers are called **matched-cladding** (MC) *fibers*. These three types of fibers are used for single-mode transmissions in the wavelength region around 1300 nm. Development of these fibers later was adopted in the CCITT standards G.652 as shown in Table 4.1 [6].

In Figure 4.3f, a smaller core diameter (around 5 μm) or a smaller mode field diameter (7–9μm) is used. In Figures 4.3g and 4.3h, a triangle-shaped core refractive index profile is used, and the core diameter is around 6 μm. As will be discussed later in the chapter, these three fiber types have a higher waveguide dispersion so that the total fiber dispersion is zero at 1550 nm. They are called the **dispersion-shifted fibers.**

Fibers shown in Figures 4.3i and 4.3j have up-and-down refractive index profiles. They are called **multicladding** or **dispersion-flattened** fibers. Their core diameters are generally small, around 6 μm. These fibers have flat fiber dispersion characteristics over

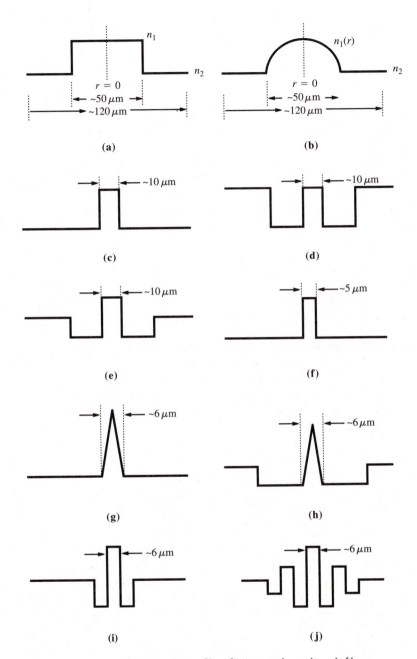

Figure 4.3 Refractive index profiles of (*a*) step-index multimode fibers, (*b*) graded-index multimode fibers, (*c*) match-cladding single-mode fibers, (*d*)–(*e*) depressed-cladding single-mode fibers, (*f*)–(*h*) dispersion-shifted fibers, and (*i*)–(*j*) dispersion-flattened fibers.

the 1300–1550 nm wavelength range. Detailed discussion will be given at the end of the chapter.

Table 4.1 CCITT Recommendation G.652.

Parameters	Specifications
Cladding diameter	125 μm
Mode field diameter	9–10 μm
Cutoff wavelength λ_c	1100–1280 nm
1550 nm bend loss	$\leq$ 1 dB for 100 turns of 7.5 cm diameter
Dispersion	$\leq$ 3.5 ps/nm·km between 1285 and 1330 nm
	$\leq$ 6 ps/nm·km between 1270 and 1340 nm
	$\leq$ 20 ps/nm·km at 1550 nm
Dispersion slope	$\leq$ 0.095 ps/nm^2·km

4.1.3 NONCIRCULAR SYMMETRIC FIBERS

In addition to fibers that have different core diameters and refractive index profiles, there are fibers that have a noncircular core or cladding. These noncircular structures are designed to introduce propagation mode asymmetry in the transverse plane. As will be discussed at the end of the chapter, this asymmetry reduces coupling of a lightwave from one polarization to another. As a result, these fibers are usually called **polarization-maintaining fibers** (PMF).

4.2 FIBER ATTENUATION AND ATTENUATION LIMITS

Optical fibers are not a lossless or distortionless medium. In fact, when optical fibers were first announced for communications 20 years ago, the loss was 20 dB/km. Now the loss can be as small as 0.2 dB/km, a significant improvement. This section discusses various attenuation sources in optical fibers. To minimize fiber attenuation, the light wavelength in fiber transmission has moved from 0.85 μm to 1.3 μm and 1.55 μm. To understand how fiber attenuation limits the transmission distance, the concepts of receiver sensitivity and power budget will be introduced.

4.2.1 ATTENUATION SOURCES

There are four primary attenuation sources.

Material Absorption Loss   There are two major types of material absorption loss: **intrinsic** and **extrinsic.** Intrinsic loss is caused by atomic resonances of fiber material. As shown in Figure 4.4, the absorption occurs in both the infrared and ultraviolet ranges. Extrinsic absorption is caused by the atomic resonances of external particles in the fiber. One important extrinsic absorption loss is due to water or the O-H bond, whose fundamental resonance frequency is 1.1×10^{14} Hz, or 2.8 μm in wavelength. Because the bond can absorb incident light at its resonant frequency and harmonics, there are absorption peaks at wavelengths $2.8/(n + 1)\mu$m. Several of them, at 1.40, 0.93, and 0.70 μm ($n = 1$, 2, and 3), are shown in Figure 4.5. Other absorption peaks, such as the one at 1.24 μm, are due to the interaction between the O-H bond and SiO_2 fiberglass.

Scattering Loss   There are four kinds of scattering loss in optical fibers: Rayleigh, Mie, Brillouin, and Raman scattering [8]. Rayleigh is the most important scattering loss and is shown in Figure 4.5. It is proportional to $1/\lambda^4$ and can be expressed as

$$\alpha_R = c_R \frac{1}{\lambda^4} \text{ [dB/km]} \qquad \text{[4.2]}$$

where c_R is called the Rayleigh scattering coefficient in $(dB/km) \cdot (\mu m)^4$. Practical measured values are shown in Figure 4.6 [7]. It ranges from 0.8 to 1.0 $(dB/km) \cdot (\mu m)^4$ and is a function of the refractive index difference between the core and cladding, the core diameter,

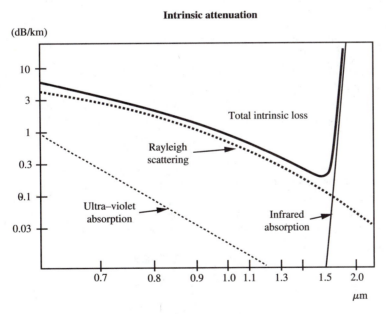

Figure 4.4   Intrinsic attenuation in optical fibers.

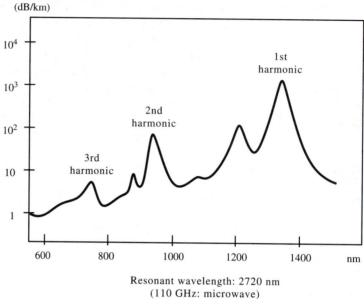

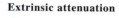

Figure 4.5   Extrinsic attenuation in optical fibers.

and the type of doped materials. In general, the larger the refractive index difference, the larger the Rayleigh scattering loss.

The total loss including the material loss and Rayleigh scattering loss is shown in Figure 4.7. As Figure 4.7 shows, infrared absorption is negligible compared to the Rayleigh scattering, and there are low attenuation "windows" at 1.3 μm and 1.55 μm. Therefore, most light sources are operated at these wavelengths for minimal attenuation.

Example 4.2

LOWER BOUND OF FIBER ATTENUATION   At the two low attenuation windows around 1.3 μm and 1.55 μm, both infrared and ultraviolet absorption can be neglected. Thus the theoretical lower limit of fiber attenuation can be calculated by considering only the Rayleigh scattering. For example, if the Rayleigh scattering coefficient is 0.9 dB/km(μm^4),

$$\alpha_R = 0.9 \frac{1}{1.3^4} = 0.32 \text{ dB/km}$$

and

$$\alpha_R = 0.9 \frac{1}{1.55^4} = 0.16 \text{ dB/km.}$$

at $\lambda = 1.3$ and 1.55μm, respectively. Practical fibers can have attenuation of 0.4 dB/km and 0.2 dB/km, respectively. ∎

Rayleigh and Mie scattering are linear scattering, where a partial power of a propagation mode is transferred to a radiation mode due to the inhomogeneity of either the refractive index (Rayleigh) or the waveguide surface (Mie). Brillouin and Raman scattering are nonlinear scattering, where a partial power of a propagation mode is transferred to a mode of a different frequency. Brillouin scattering can be considered as a light carrier modulation by thermal molecular vibrations. As a result, similar to what is given by Equation (1.2), the frequency of the modulated light is shifted up and down from the incident light carrier frequency. Raman scattering is similar to Brillouin except that the amount of the frequency shift is in the optical frequency range. Practically, both Brillouin and Raman scattering require large incident power, typically 100 mW for Brillouin and 1 W for Raman. Therefore, they are not important when the transmitted power is only a few mW.

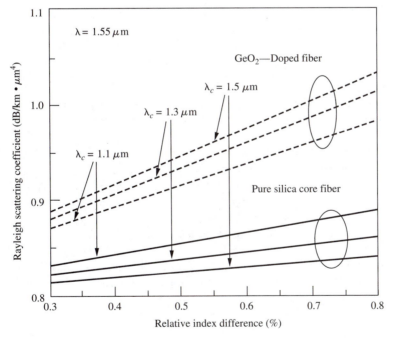

Figure 4.6   Rayleigh scattering loss coefficient.

SOURCE: Reprinted, by permission, from Ohashi et al., "Optical Loss Property" [7]. © 1992 by IEEE.

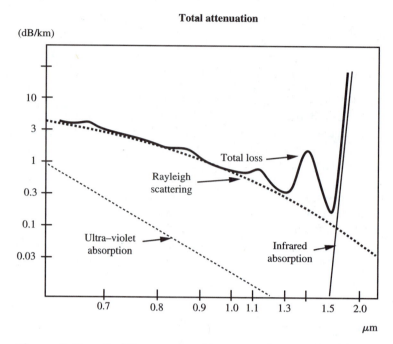

Figure 4.7   Total fiber attenuation. The extrinsic absorption due to the O-H bond of water varies with the fiber manufacturing process.

However, the nonlinear Raman scattering effect has been used for optical amplification called **stimulated Raman scattering** (SRS).

Bending Loss   Signals in optical fibers also suffer radiation loss at bends and curves because of evanescent modes generated. Practically, bending loss is not significant unless the bending curvature is in the order of 1 mm^{-1} or larger [8]. Because this is a large number for practical applications, bending loss can be neglected in general. However, when a transmission line is long and there are many turns, the accumulated bending loss can be significant. A smaller MFD can be used to reduce bending loss [9].

Coupling and Splicing Loss   A light signal will also be attenuated at a junction of two fibers connected either by a coupler or by splicing. The loss is caused by various reasons listed below.

- Extrinsic loss
    - misalignment in the core center.
    - tilt.
    - end gap.
    - end face quality.

- Intrinsic loss
  - core ellipticity.
  - mismatch in refractive index.
  - mismatch in mode field diameter.

Typically, coupling loss is around 0.2 dB and splicing loss is around 0.05 dB [10][11].

4.2.2 RECEIVER SENSITIVITY AND POWER BUDGET

Because of fiber attenuation, light power gets smaller as it propagates. As a result, fiber attenuation places an upper limit on the transmission distance and bit rate. This attenuation limit can be derived from the concepts of **receiver sensitivity** and **power budget**.

Receiver Sensitivity   In any communication system, a certain minimum received power is required to achieve a specified performance. This minimum power is called the receiver sensitivity. If the received power is lower than the minimum required power, the system will perform unsatisfactorily or may even be inoperational.

DIGITAL TRANSMISSION BER   In digital transmission, performance is based on the bit error rate (BER), which is the percentage of error bits received. One basic reason for having error bits is noise. If there is no noise, there is no error detection. Intuitively, the larger the signal power is than the noise power, the smaller the BER. From Chapter 6, the BER under white Gaussian noise (such as thermal noise) can be expressed as:

$$\text{BER} = \frac{1}{\sqrt{2\pi}} \int_{\sqrt{\gamma}}^{\infty} e^{-x^2/2} dx \overset{\text{def}}{=} Q(\sqrt{\gamma}) \approx \frac{1}{\sqrt{2\pi\gamma}} e^{-\gamma/2} \text{ when } \gamma \gg 1 \qquad \textbf{[4.3]}$$

where γ is the signal-to-noise ratio (SNR). If the BER is required to be smaller than 10^{-9}, γ or the SNR should be at least 36, or 16 dB.[1] Therefore, for a given total noise power in the system, the receiver sensitivity is 36 times the noise power. ∎

Example 4.3

FM THRESHOLD   In frequency modulation, the quality of the demodulated signal varies significantly around an SNR called the threshold. If the received SNR is above the threshold, there is not much difference in reception quality. If the received SNR is just a little bit below the threshold, however, the quality becomes significantly worse. We experience this when there is a strong fading in FM radio transmission. When the received SNR goes below the threshold, we sense a strong transition from good quality to clipping noise. Therefore, the threshold in FM is the minimum acceptable SNR, which determines the receiver sensitivity at a given noise level. ∎

Example 4.4

---

[1] At a given BER, the γ value can be calculated as follows. First, neglect the factor $1/\sqrt{2\pi\gamma}$ because it is much less γ dependent than the exponential term. Compute an approximated γ using only the exponential term, then substitute it in the factor $1/\sqrt{2\pi\gamma}$ to find a new γ. An accurate γ can be quickly obtained after a few such iterations.

Example 4.5	**PHOTON COUNTING** Photon counting is a basic method for optical signal detection. When digital on-off keying is used (i.e., bit "1" is transmitted by an optical pulse and bit "0" is transmitted by nothing), the idea of photon counting is to count the number of received photons over every bit interval. If the number is greater than a given threshold, the transmitted bit is detected as "1"; otherwise, it is detected as "0." In reality, the number of photons counted is random because of random electron–hole pair (EHP) generations in the photodetection process (see Chapter 6).[2] As a result, there is a nonzero probability that the number of counts due to "1" is smaller than the threshold. This nonzero probability is the BER. It can be reduced by increasing the transmission power for "1"s. In other words, for a given BER required, there is a minimum transmission power that can be derived in a manner similar to that used in Example 4.3. ∎

In addition to the minimum received power required, there is a power constraint at the transmitter side. For various reasons, such as technology limitations, power dissipation considerations, and government regulations, the output power from the transmitter has an upper bound. See Example 4.6.

Example 4.6	**LIMITS OF TRANSMITTER OUTPUT POWER** In optical communications, transmission power is determined by the light source used. To prevent overheating and avoid undesirable nonlinearities, the output power of a typical laser diode operated at CW (continuous wave) is in the range from 0.1 mW to several mW. In electronic communications, the output power of IC chips is limited by their power consumption and heat dissipation capability. If power consumption is too large, heat dissipation becomes a difficult job and may cause thermal oscillation. This explains why the powerful Pentium chip requires a separate cooling fan. In radio communications, radio transmission power in the United States is regulated by the Federal Communications Commission (FCC). According to Part 15, for example, radio power in the frequency band from 902 MHz to 928 MHz is required to be lower than 1 W. ∎

Power Budget   Given the required received power and available transmission power, the upper limit of the allowable power loss from transmission is called the **power budget.** Specifically, if the transmission power is P_{tx} and the minimum required receiving power is P_{min}, the power budget is the ratio:

$$\text{Power budget} = \frac{P_{tx}}{P_{min}}$$

or

$$\text{Power budget [dB]} \stackrel{\text{def}}{=} P_{tx} \text{ [dB]} - P_{min} \text{ [dB]}. \qquad \textbf{[4.4]}$$

---

[2] EHP generation is the inverse process of EHP recombination discussed in Chapter 3, where an incident photon excites an EHP to their conduction and valence bands, respectively.

If the transmission power is $P_{tx} = 1$ mW and the minimum required received power is $P_{min} = 0.1$ μW, the power budget is

$$\text{Power budget [dB]} = 10 \log_{10} 10^4 = 40 \text{ dB. } \blacksquare$$

Thus the total power loss in a transmission line must be below the power budget. In optical fibers, attenuation is expressed in terms of dB/km. Specifically, if a fiber is L km long and the attenuation is α_{fiber} dB/km, the total attenuation is $(\alpha_{fiber} L)$ dB. Thus, we need

$$\alpha_{fiber} L + \alpha_{coupling} N + \text{other loss} \leq \text{Power budget [dB]} \qquad \textbf{[4.5]}$$

where $\alpha_{coupling}$ is the coupling loss per connection and N is the total number of connections in the transmission line.

The power budget can be improved in several ways. For example, P_{tx} can be increased by increasing the laser diode output at the transmitter, and P_{min} can be reduced by using an avalanche photodetector as discussed in Chapter 5. The power budget can be further increased by using optical amplifiers, which are important to systems such as undersea transmission where attenuation is the limiting factor. Recent research efforts in optical amplifiers are discussed in Chapter 17.

4.2.3 ATTENUATION LIMITS

From the power budget equation (Equation 4.5), the transmission distance is limited by

$$L_{max} = \frac{1}{\alpha_{fiber}} \left\{ 10 \log_{10} P_{tx} - 10 \log_{10} P_{min} - \text{other loss [dB]} \right\} \qquad \textbf{[4.6]}$$

where α_{fiber} is in units of dB/km and P_{min} is the receiver sensitivity or the minimum power required for a given transmission performance such as SNR (analog communication) or BER (digital communication). If the transmitter output power P_{tx} and fiber attenuation α_{fiber} are given, achievable transmission distance based on attenuation is essentially limited by P_{min}.

If P_{min} is 1 mW or 0 dBm, P_{min} is -45 dBm, α_{fiber} is 0.2 dB/km, $\alpha_{coupling} = 1$ dB, $N = 2$ and other loss in the system is 5 dB, the power budget is 45 dB. Then,

$$L_{max} = \frac{45 - 5 - 2}{0.2} = 190 \text{ km. } \blacksquare$$

Dependence of Receiver Sensitivity on Bit Rate In digital communication, the minimum required received power increases as the transmission bit rate increases. In most cases, they are linearly proportional. This can be seen from two perspectives. First, as the bit rate increases, the bandwidth of the signal increases. Therefore, the receiver needs to have a larger bandwidth to receive the signal. As the receiver bandwidth increases, more noise power passes through. To maintain the same received SNR, the signal power thus should also be proportionally increased.

Another way to see the dependence of receiver sensitivity on bit rate is from the photon counting example given earlier. To count the number of incident photons, photodiodes are used to convert photons to photocurrent. The more photons coming to the photodiode, the more photocurrent will be generated. To maintain the same detection performance, one must maintain the same average number of photons detected. Consequently, when the counting (bit) interval decreases, the photon incoming rate or input optical power should be proportionally increased.

As will be explained in Chapter 7, the receiver sensitivity P_{min} is linearly proportional to the transmission bit rate when the total receiver noise is dominated by shot noise. In this case,

$$P_{min} = B \times \frac{P_0}{B_0} \quad \text{or} \quad P_{min}[\text{dB}] = P_0[\text{dB}] + 10\log_{10}(B/B_0) \qquad \textbf{[4.7]}$$

where B is the bit rate, and P_0 is the receiver sensitivity at bit rate B_0. Substituting Equation (4.7) into Equation (4.6) we have

$$
\begin{aligned}
L_{max} &= \frac{1}{\alpha_{fiber}}[(P_{tx} - P_0)\text{dB} - 10\log_{10}(B/B_0) - \text{other loss}] \\
&= L_{max,0} - \frac{10}{\alpha_{fiber}}\log_{10}(B/B_0).
\end{aligned}
\qquad \textbf{[4.8]}
$$

This equation is the attenuation limit, or how large L_{max} can be at a given B. Figure 4.8 illustrates a typical attenuation limit according to the equation.

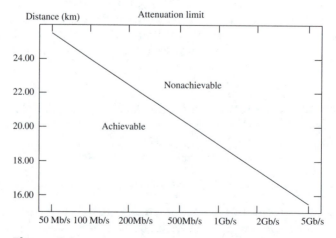

Figure 4.8   An attenuation limit at $\alpha_{fiber} = 2$ dB/km.

ATTENUATION LIMIT   Suppose P_{tx} −other loss = 1 dBm and the minimum required received power at $B_0 = 100$ Mb/s is $P_0 = 20$ nW. If the system operates at $B = 500$ Mb/s, the minimum required received power increases to $P_{min} = 20 \times (500/100) = 100$ nW or -40 dBm. At a fiber attenuation of $\alpha_{fiber} = 2$ dB/km, the upper limit of the transmission distance is

Example 4.9

$$L_{max} = \frac{1 - (-40)}{2} = 20.5 \text{ km}. \blacksquare$$

4.3 LIGHT PROPAGATION IN OPTICAL FIBERS

In addition to attenuation, fiber dispersion is another limiting factor in lightwave transmission. Dispersion is a phenomenon that photons of different frequencies or modes propagate at different speeds. As a result, a light pulse gets broader as it propagates along the fiber. This section first explains the basic physics of light propagation in optical fibers. The next section discusses various dispersion contributions in optical fibers and the dispersion limits.

Signal propagation in optical fibers can be described by either geometrical optics or Maxwell's equations. Geometrical optics is a good approximation when the wavelength of light is relatively small compared to the system's dimensions. On the other hand, solving Maxwell's equations can tell the exact story but is much more mathematically complex. This section uses both methods to study light propagation, but avoids complex mathematics such as solving wave equations in optical fibers. Instead, it stresses the relationship between geometrical optics and wave functions. This approach shows the insight of the physics of lightwave propagation with minimal mathematics.

4.3.1 SIGNAL PROPAGATION BY GEOMETRICAL OPTICS

The geometrical optics model for fiber propagation is illustrated in Figure 4.9, where incident light from a light source emits "rays" to a fiber in different directions. From Snell's refraction law, each ray will go partially into the cladding region or be totally reflected

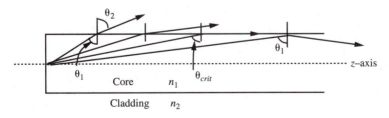

Figure 4.9   Light propagation using geometrical optics.

back depending on its incident angle θ_1 at the core–cladding boundary. More specifically, a ray will go partially into the cladding if a θ_2 exists such that

$$n_1 \sin(\theta_1) = n_2 \sin(\theta_2) \qquad \textbf{[4.9]}$$

where n_1 and n_2 are the refractive indices of the core and cladding respectively. Because $n_1 > n_2$, a complete internal reflection is possible if

$$\theta_1 > \sin^{-1}\left(\frac{n_2}{n_1}\right) \overset{\text{def}}{=} \theta_{crit}. \qquad \textbf{[4.10]}$$

That is, the corresponding ray will be totally reflected back to the core. As a result, a ray will propagate along the fiber without loss (other than various attenuation sources discussed earlier) if the incident angle θ_1 satisfies Equation (4.10).

Figure 4.9 provides two further, important observations First, rays with different $\theta_1 > \theta_{\text{crit}}$, have different z-component velocities. Specifically, for a ray of θ_1 its z component velocity is

$$v_z = \frac{c}{n_1} \sin(\theta_1). \qquad \textbf{[4.11]}$$

This velocity dependence on θ_1 results in different propagation delays or dispersion. To reduce dispersion, graded-index fibers mentioned earlier can be used. Ray propagation in a graded-index fiber is illustrated in Figure 4.10. As shown, although rays of larger θ_1 propagate in a shorter distance, they travel through a higher refractive index region. On the other hand, rays of smaller θ_1 travel a longer distance but through a lower refractive index region. As a result, graded-index fibers can equalize the propagation delay of different propagation rays, and greatly reduce the fiber dispersion.

Another important observation is that rays at larger θ_1's have larger z-component velocities, and consequently smaller radial velocities. Intuitively, we see that the larger the radial velocity, the higher the penetration of the light power into the cladding region. As the wave analysis will demonstrate shortly, rays of larger radial velocities correspond to higher propagation modes. When the radial velocity becomes too large or $\theta_1 > \theta_{\text{crit}}$, the ray will propagate into the cladding and never come back.

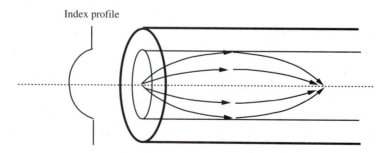

Index profile

Figure 4.10   Ray propagation in a graded-index fiber.

The critical angle condition of Equation (4.10) from geometrical optics gives the condition of propagatable rays. When θ_{cirt} is large or n_2 is very close to n_1, the incident ray has to be closely parallel to the fiber axis. Therefore, it is more difficult to inject light into the fiber for propagation. To quantify the ease of coupling light into a fiber for propagation, a parameter called the **numerical aperture (NA)** defined by

$$NA \stackrel{\text{def}}{=} \sqrt{n_1^2 - n_2^2} \qquad \textbf{[4.12]}$$

has been used. Because n_1 is close to n_2 in optical fibers, $n_1^2 - n_2^2 = (n_1 + n_2)(n_1 - n_2) \approx 2n_2^2 [(n_1 - n_2)/n_2]$. NA in Equation (4.12) can thus be approximated by

$$NA \approx \left[(2n_2^2) \left(\frac{n_1 - n_2}{n_2} \right) \right]^{1/2} = n_2(2\Delta)^{1/2} \qquad \textbf{[4.13]}$$

where

$$\Delta \stackrel{\text{def}}{=} \frac{n_1 - n_2}{n_2} \approx \frac{n_1 - n_2}{n_1} \qquad \textbf{[4.14]}$$

is the ratio of the refractive index difference.

The physical meaning of NA can be seen as follows. From Figure 4.11, an incident ray that can propagate in the fiber should be within the solid angle given by

$$\Omega = \frac{\text{cone area}}{d^2} = 2\pi [1 - \cos(\theta_{in})] = 4\pi \sin^2 (\frac{\theta_{in}}{2}) \approx \pi \sin^2(\theta_{in})$$

when $\theta_{in} \ll 1$. From Figure 4.11 and Equation (4.10),

$$\sin(\theta_{in}) = n_1 \cos(\theta_{crit}) = n_1[1 - \sin^2(\theta_{crit})]^{1/2} = (n_1^2 - n_2^2)^{1/2} = NA. \qquad \textbf{[4.15]}$$

Therefore,

$$\Omega \approx \pi(n_1^2 - n_2^2) = \pi NA^2. \qquad \textbf{[4.16]}$$

This shows that the larger the NA, the larger the solid angle within which incident light can propagate.

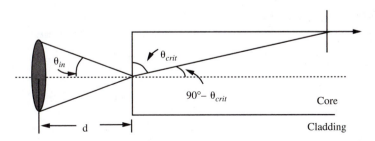

Figure 4.11   The physical meaning of numerical aperture.

Example 4.10	**GEOMETRICAL OPTICS** Suppose $n_1 = 1.50$ and $n_2 = 1.47$. From the discussion, we have

$$\theta_{crit} = \sin^{-1}(1.47/1.50) = 78.5°$$

$$v_{z,max} = c/1.5 = 0.667c$$

and

$$v_{z,min} = c\sin(\theta_{crit})/1.5 = 1.47c/1.5^2 = 0.653c.$$

The unit distance propagation delay difference is thus $0.035c^{-1}$, and

$$NA = (1.5^2 - 1.47^2)^{1/2} = 0.3. ■$$

4.3.2 PROPAGATION MODES

Geometrical optics discussed above is only an approximation of actual wave propagation. A more exact picture requires using Maxwell's equations. Fortunately, to understand only the propagation characteristics and fiber dispersion, we can avoid the most complicated mathematics. For detailed wave analyses, readers may find [8] and [12]–[15] useful.

Because of the boundary condition at the core–cladding interface (the counterpart of Snell's law, Equation [4.9], in geometrical optics), only a finite set of wave functions satisfying the Maxwell equations can propagate in a fiber, each of which is called a **propagation mode.** In Appendix 4–A, the concept of propagation modes is illustrated using rectangular waveguides. The same concept can be applied to circular waveguides. In this case, the wave function (either an electric field or a magnetic field) of a propagation mode can be expressed as:

$$\Psi_i(r, \phi, z) = A_i(r, \phi)e^{j(\omega t - \beta_{zi} z)} \qquad \qquad \textbf{[4.17]}$$

where i is the index to propagation mode ψ_i, $A_i(r,\phi)$ is the transverse field distribution, and β_{zi} is the z-axis propagation constant. As the equation shows, the wave function is a function of time t and spatial parameters r, ϕ, and z. The cylindrical coordinate is used here because an optical fiber is a circular waveguide. In the equation, the factor $e^{j(\omega t - \beta_{zi} z)}$ describes a traveling wave propagating along the fiber (z) axis.

z-Direction Propagation Constant   From the concept of propagation modes, discussed in Appendix 4–A, β_{zi} satisfies the following **dispersion equation:**

$$\boxed{\beta_1^2 = \left(\frac{n_1\omega}{c}\right)^2 = \beta_{zi}^2 + \kappa_i^2} \qquad \qquad \textbf{[4.18]}$$

where $\beta_1 = n_1 w/c$ is the propagation constant of a wave at frequency ω and in a homogeneous dielectric medium of refractive index n_1, and κ_i is the **eigenvalue** or propagation constant in the transverse direction of propagation mode i. Since each propagation mode has a real κ_i, β_{zi} satisfies the following inequality:

$$\beta_i^2 - \beta_{zi}^2 = \kappa_i^2 > 0. \qquad \text{[4.19]}$$

As discussed in Appendix 4–A, a rectangular waveguide of dimension a by b has an eigenvalue $\kappa_{m,n} = \pi(m^2/a^2 + n^2/b^2)^{1/2}$ for the $\text{TE}_{m,n}$ mode. Therefore, the larger the index values m and n or the higher the order of the transverse mode, the larger the eigenvalue. This means a smaller z-direction propagation constant β_{zi}. This property is also true of circular waveguides and optical fibers. Therefore, the higher the propagation mode or the larger the index i, the larger the κ_i and the smaller the β_{zi}. When κ_i exceeds β_1, β_{zi} becomes imaginary, and the mode has an exponential decay as it propagates.

Equation (4.19) is the propagation condition for the waves inside the core. There is a similar but different condition for them in the cladding:

$$\beta_{zi}^2 - \beta_2^2 > 0 \qquad \text{[4.20]}$$

where $\beta_2 = n_2\omega/c$. This condition requires no radial propagation in the cladding; in other words, the wave in the cladding is evanescent. Equations (4.19) and (4.20) together require β_{zi} in the following range:

$$\boxed{\frac{n_2}{n_1} < \frac{\beta_{zi}}{\beta_1} < 1.} \qquad \text{[4.21]}$$

This condition is the wave analysis counterpart of Equation (4.10) from geometrical optics. Equation (4.12) shows that the closer n_2 is to n_1, the smaller the NA and the more difficult it is to inject a propagatable ray. Similarly, Equation (4.21) shows that the smaller the NA, the smaller the allowable range of β_{zi}. As a result, there are fewer propagation modes.

z-Direction Propagation Velocity   Similar to the observation made in geometrical optics that the velocity of ray propagation depends on the incident angle θ_1, the z-direction velocity v_{gi} of a propagation mode i is a function of its propagation constant β_{zi}. From Appendix 4–B, v_{gi} is given by

$$v_{gi} = \frac{\partial \omega}{\partial \beta_{zi}} \qquad \text{[4.22]}$$

which is commonly known as the **group velocity** and tells how fast the *power* of a light signal propagates. This is different from the **phase velocity,** given by $v_{pi} = \omega/\beta_{zi}$ which tells how fast the *phase* of the light signal changes.

Although the exact computation of the group velocity v_{gi} requires the knowledge of β_{zi} as a function of ω Equation (4.19) can be used to find an approximation when the frequency dependence of κ_i is small. In this case,

$$\frac{\partial \beta_{zi}}{\partial \beta_1} \approx \frac{\beta_1}{\beta_{zi}}.$$

Because $\beta_1 = n_1\omega/c$

$$\frac{\partial \beta_1}{\partial \omega} = \frac{1}{c}\frac{\partial(n_1\omega)}{\partial \omega} = \frac{1}{c}(n_1 + \omega\frac{\partial n_1}{\partial \omega}) \overset{\text{def}}{=} \frac{n_{1g}}{c} \overset{\text{def}}{=} \frac{1}{v_g} \qquad \text{[4.23]}$$

where

$$n_{1g} = n_1 + \omega \frac{\partial n_1}{\partial \omega} \qquad \text{[4.24]}$$

is called the **group refractive index.** From the above results, using the chain rule, we have

$$v_{gi} = \frac{\partial \omega}{\partial \beta_{zi}} = \left(\frac{\partial \beta_{zi}}{\partial \omega}\right)^{-1} = \left(\frac{\partial \beta_{zi}}{\partial \beta_1}\frac{\partial \beta_1}{\partial \omega}\right)^{-1} \approx \left(\frac{\beta_1}{\beta_{zi}}\frac{n_{1g}}{c}\right)^{-1} = \frac{c}{n_{1g}}\frac{\beta_{zi}}{\beta_1} = v_g \frac{\beta_{zi}}{\beta_1}. \qquad \text{[4.25]}$$

Comparing this result with Equation (4.11) shows that the ratio of β_{zi} to β_1 is equivalent to $\sin(\theta_1)$ or the ratio of v_z to c/n_1 in Figure 4.9. Because each propagation mode has its β_{zi} each mode has a different propagation delay. This is consistent with the earlier propagation observation from geometrical optics that incident rays of different angles have different z-direction velocities.

Example 4.11	**GROUP VELOCITY** If $n_2/n_1 = 0.99$, Equation (4.21) gives the condition for the ratio β_{zi} to β_1 as $$0.99 < \frac{\beta_{zi}}{\beta_1} < 1.00.$$ If $\beta_{zi}/\beta_1 = 0.999$ and n Equation (4.25), gives the group velocity as $$v_{gi} \approx \frac{c}{1.5}\frac{\beta_{zi}}{\beta_1} = 0.666c. \qquad \blacksquare$$

This section has used both geometrical optics and wave analysis to describe light propagation. To calculate dispersion or delay variation due to different frequencies or propagation modes, however, only the wave analysis approach can be used. The next section derives fiber dispersion with minimal wave theory.

4.4 FIBER DISPERSION

As mentioned earlier, the group velocity v_{gi} in Equation (4.25) is a function of frequency and propagation modes. If an optical pulse consists of components at different frequencies and different propagation modes, different propagation delays from these components will result in a broader pulse at the other end of the fiber. This dispersion phenomenon was illustrated in Figure 3.1.

In general, there are three kinds of fiber dispersion: (1) **material dispersion** or **chromatic dispersion,** (2) **waveguide dispersion,** and (3) **modal dispersion.** The first two types of dispersion are attributable to the frequency dependence of the propagation velocities, and their summation is commonly referred to as **intramodal dispersion** or **group ve-**

locity dispersion (GVD). The third type of dispersion, also called **intermodal dispersion,** is due to the dependence of the propagation velocities on different propagation modes. From this classification, single mode fibers have only intramodal dispersion. The rest of this section presents a derivation of these three types of dispersion and discusses their effects on lightwave transmission.

4.4.1 INTRAMODAL DISPERSION

Intramodal dispersion can be understood as follows. Because the group velocity of a given propagation mode is frequency dependent, the unit propagation delay (i.e., the inverse of the group velocity) is also frequency dependent. The Taylor series expansion can be used to express the unit delay at a given wavelength λ as

$$\tau_g = \tau_g(\lambda_0) + (\lambda - \lambda_0)\frac{\partial \tau_g}{\partial \lambda} + 0.5(\lambda - \lambda_0)^2 \frac{\partial^2 \tau_g}{\partial \lambda^2} + \dots \qquad \textbf{[4.26]}$$

where $\tau_g(\lambda_0)$ is the unit distance propagation delay at the central wavelength λ_0. From the expansion, the intramodal dispersion is defined by

$$D_{intra} \overset{\text{def}}{=} \frac{\partial \tau_g}{\partial \lambda} = \frac{\partial}{\partial \lambda}\left(\frac{1}{v_g}\right) = \frac{\partial}{\partial \lambda}\left(\frac{\partial \beta_z}{\partial \omega}\right) \qquad \textbf{[4.27]}$$

where the index i to β_{zi} is dropped for simplicity. Equation (4.26) thus reduces to

$$\tau_g \approx \tau_g(\lambda_0) + (\lambda - \lambda_0)D_{intra} + 0.5(\lambda - \lambda_0)^2 \frac{\partial D_{intra}}{\partial \lambda}. \qquad \textbf{[4.28]}$$

If we keep only the first two terms, the pulse width increase due to intramodal dispersion D_{intra} is given by

$$\Delta \tau_g = D_{intra}\Delta \lambda \qquad \textbf{[4.29]}$$

where $\Delta \lambda$ is the linewidth of the light signal.

To find $D_{intra,}$ using the definition given in Equation (4.27) and the chain rule gives

$$D_{intra} = \frac{\partial}{\partial \lambda}\left(\frac{\partial \beta_z}{\partial \beta_1}\frac{\partial \beta_1}{\partial \omega}\right).$$

From Equation (4.23), D_{intra} reduces to

$$D_{intra} = \frac{1}{c}\frac{\partial n_{1g}}{\partial \lambda}\frac{\partial \beta_z}{\partial \beta_1} + \frac{n_{1g}}{c}\frac{\partial}{\partial \lambda}\left\{\frac{\partial \beta_z}{\partial \beta_1}\right\} \overset{\text{def}}{=} D_{material} + D_{waveguide} \qquad \textbf{[4.30]}$$

where

$$D_{material} \overset{\text{def}}{=} \frac{1}{c} \frac{\partial n_{1g}}{\partial \lambda} \frac{\partial \beta_z}{\partial \beta_1} \approx \frac{1}{c} \left(-\lambda \frac{\partial^2 n_1}{\partial \lambda^2} \right) \frac{\beta_1}{\beta_z} \approx \frac{1}{c} \left(-\lambda \frac{\partial^2 n_1}{\partial \lambda^2} \right)$$ **[4.31]**

is the material dispersion, and

$$D_{waveguide} \overset{\text{def}}{=} \frac{n_{1g}}{c} \frac{\partial}{\partial \lambda} \left(\frac{\partial \beta_z}{\partial \beta_1} \right)$$ **[4.32]**

is the waveguide dispersion. From the above definitions, note that $D_{material}$ is a parameter independent of the propagation mode and solely depends on the frequency dependence of the refractive index n_1. $D_{material}$ of typical silica optical fibers as a function of the wavelength is shown in Figure 4.12. The waveguide dispersion, $D_{waveguide}$ on the other hand, depends on the propagation mode i, which is in turn determined by the optical waveguide structure. In general, the computation of waveguide dispersion is quite involved. Approximation techniques exist for when $\Delta = (n_1 - n_2)/n_2$ is small. Detailed discussion on the waveguide dispersion computation is given in Appendix 4–C.

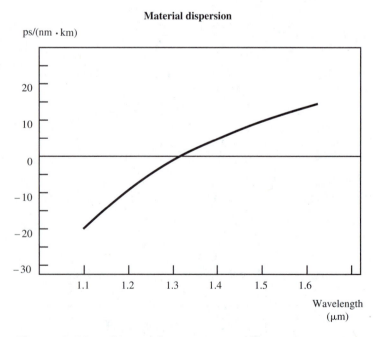

Material dispersion

ps/(nm · km)

Figure 4.12   Material dispersion in optical fibers.

4.4.2 INTERMODAL DISPERSION

Another kind of dispersion is called **intermodal** (or simply modal) dispersion. As mentioned earlier, it is caused by different propagation delays of different propagation modes. This can be seen from Equation (4.19), where β_{zi} is different for different propagation modes. Therefore, the corresponding group velocity v_{gi} in Equation (4.22) is also different. Specifically, modal dispersion can be defined as

$$D_{modal} = \frac{1}{v_{g,min}} - \frac{1}{v_{g,max}} = \tau_{g,max} - \tau_{g,min} \qquad \textbf{[4.33]}$$

where $\tau_{g,max}$ and $\tau_{g,min}$ are the maximum and minimum unit group propagation delays, respectively. This section examines modal dispersion in both step-index and graded-index fibers. Detailed discussion on the modal dispersion of graded-index fibers is given in Appendix 4–D.

Step-Index Fibers   One can estimate the modal dispersion of step-index fibers from geometrical optics. Substituting the two limiting cases $\theta_1 = \theta_{crit}$ and $90°$ into Equation (4.11) gives

$$\tau_{g,max} \approx \frac{n_{1g}}{c} \frac{1}{\sin(\theta_{crit})} = \frac{n_{1g}}{c} \frac{n_1}{n_2} \qquad \textbf{[4.34]}$$

and

$$\tau_{g,min} \approx \frac{n_{1g}}{c}. \qquad \textbf{[4.35]}$$

The modal dispersion is thus

$$D_{modal} = \tau_{g,max} - \tau_{g,min} \approx \frac{n_{1g}}{c}\left(\frac{n_1}{n_2} - 1\right) = \frac{n_{1g}}{c}\Delta. \qquad \textbf{[4.36]}$$

This simple result shows that the intermodal dispersion in step-index fibers is proportional to the refractive index difference. Because *NA* is proportional to $\Delta^{1/2}$, there is a trade-off between the coupling efficiency and dispersion.

MODAL DISPERSION OF STEP-INDEX FIBERS   Consider a step-index fiber at $\lambda = 0.85$ μm with radius $a = 50$ μm. The group refractive index $n_{1g} = 1.457$ and $\Delta = 0.005$. From Equation (4.36), the modal dispersion is

$$D_{modal} = \frac{1.457}{3 \times 10^5} \times 0.005 = 24 \text{ nsec/km.} \qquad \blacksquare$$

Example 4.12

Graded-Index Fibers   The refractive index profile of graded-index fibers can generally be expressed as

$$n(r) = \begin{cases} n_1(1 - 2\Delta[(r/a)]^\alpha)^{1/2} & \text{for } r < a \\ n_1(1 - 2\Delta)^{1/2} = n_2 & \text{for } r \geq a \end{cases} \qquad \textbf{[4.37]}$$

where α is a parameter that can be optimized for minimal modal dispersion.

Intermodal dispersion in graded-index fibers cannot be easily found using geometrical optics. However, the delay equalization illustrated in Figure 4.10 suggests that the modal dispersion is much smaller than that in step-index fibers. As shown in Appendix 4–D, when

$$\alpha = 2(1 - \Delta) \qquad \textbf{[4.38]}$$

the modal dispersion is minimized and given by

$$\boxed{D_{modal} = \frac{n_{1g}}{c} \frac{\Delta^2}{8}.} \qquad \textbf{[4.39]}$$

Thus the modal dispersion for graded-index fibers is much smaller than that of step-index fibers, given by Equation (4.36), because of the Δ^2 factor. It has also been shown [16] that the longitudinal propagation constant $\beta_{z,m}$ of each propagation mode can be approximated by

$$\beta_{z,m} \approx \beta_1 \left[1 - 2\Delta\left(\frac{m}{M}\right)^g\right]^{1/2} \qquad \textbf{[4.40]}$$

where $g = \alpha/(\alpha + 2)$ and

$$M \approx a^2\beta_1^2\left(\frac{\alpha\Delta}{\alpha + 2}\right) \qquad \textbf{[4.41]}$$

is the total number of propagation modes.

Example 4.13

MODAL DISPERSION OF GRADED-INDEX FIBERS   Consider a graded-index fiber of radius $a = 50$ μm. At $\lambda = 1.3$ μm, assume $n_1 = 1.65$, $n_{1g} = 1.66$, $n_2 = 1.64$,   and $n_2 = 1.65$. Therefore,

$$\Delta = \frac{0.01}{1.64} = 0.0061$$

and

$$\alpha = 2(1 - \Delta) = 1.99.$$

The total number of propagation modes is

$$M = 50^2 \times (2\pi \times 1.65/1.3)^2 \times \frac{1.99 \times 0.01}{1.64 \times (1.99 + 2)} = 481$$

and the modal dispersion is

$$D_{modal} = \frac{1.65}{c} \times \frac{0.0061^2}{8} = 25.6 \text{ ps/km.} \qquad \blacksquare$$

4.4.3   TOTAL FIBER DISPERSION

From both the intramodal and intermodal dispersions, one can obtain the total dispersion. Instead of adding them directly, it is given by the following square sum expression:

$$D_{total}^2 = D_{intra}^2 \Delta\lambda^2 + D_{modal}^2 \qquad \textbf{[4.42]}$$

where $\Delta\lambda$ is the linewidth (in nm) of the light spectrum. A proof of this square sum expression is given in Appendix 4–E.

TOTAL DISPERSION   Consider a fiber of $n_{1g} = 1.75$ and $\Delta = 50$ nm Also assume the intramodal dispersion of the fiber is 10 ps/km·nm and the linewidth of the light source is $\Delta\lambda = 50$ nm. The modal dispersion and the total dispersion of the fiber can be calculated as follows. First, if the fiber is a step-index fiber, the modal dispersion is given by

$$D_{modal} = n_{1g}\Delta/c = 58.3 \text{ nsec/km}.$$

Because $D_{intra}\,\Delta\lambda = 0.5$ nsec/km, the total dispersion is

$$D_{total} = (58.3^2 + 0.5^2)^{1/2} = 58.3 \text{ nsec/km}.$$

Similarly, if the fiber is a graded-index fiber,

$$D_{modal} = (n_{1g}/c)(\Delta^2/8) = 58.3 \times 0.01/8 = 73 \text{ ps/km},$$

and the total dispersion is

$$D_{total} = (0.5^2 + 0.073^2)^{1/2} = 0.51 \text{ nsec/km}.$$

Clearly, graded-index fibers have a much smaller modal and total dispersion. ∎

Example 4.14

Because an optical fiber is considered a communication channel, the total fiber dispersion is often used to characterize the fiber's transmission bandwidth. Because the total propagation delay difference is proportional to $D_{total}L$, the fiber bandwidth is defined as

$$B_{fiber} \stackrel{\text{def}}{=} \frac{1}{D_{total}L}. \qquad \textbf{[4.43]}$$

This means the larger the total dispersion and the longer the distance, the lower the transmittable bit rate.

4.4.4   MODAL DISPERSION AT LONGER DISTANCE

In general, dispersion is linearly proportional to L, the total transmission distance. When modal dispersion dominates and the fiber is longer than a critical length, however, the total

Dispersion (ns)

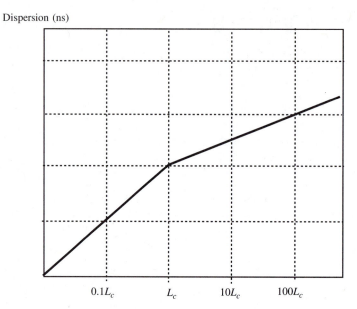

Figure 4.13   The reduction in modal dispersion due to mode coupling.

dispersion is not proportional to the length linearly but to its square root. This dependence on L is depicted in Figure 4.13. The smaller distance dependence on L when $L > L_c$ is due to mode coupling, which is power transfer among propagation modes and becomes significant when L is greater than a critical distance L_c. As a result, depending on the current propagation mode, photons travel sometimes faster (large group velocity) and sometimes slower (small group velocity). This speed variation makes the dispersion only proportional to the square root of the total length.

The above dispersion dependence on distance can be understood from probability theory, according to which, the variance of the sum of N independent random variables of equal variance σ^2 is $N\sigma^2$. In the case of fiber dispersion, one can partition the total distance L into N sections so that $L = NL_c$. Over each of these sections, photons or the lightwave stays at one propagation mode. Because modal dispersion depends on the propagation mode, and mode coupling from one section to another is random, total dispersion squared is simply the sum of dispersion squared in each section. That is, $D_{total}^2 = ND_{section}^2$, where $D_{section}^2$ is the dispersion squared of each section. Therefore, D_{total} is proportional to $\sqrt{N}$ or $\sqrt{L}$.

4.4.5   DISPERSION LIMITS

Similar to fiber attenuation, fiber dispersion places another upper bound for the maximum transmission distance at a given bit rate. This is called the **dispersion limit** and can be understood as follows. When binary bits of 1's and 0's are transmitted, as illustrated in Figure 4.14, they are transmitted in a sequence of optical pulses. Assume each pulse has width T_0

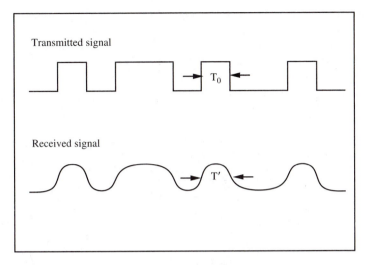

Figure 4.14   Transmitted and received optical pulses.

equal to the bit period. When pulses arrive at the other end of the fiber, they become broader because of fiber dispersion. Assume the received pulse has width T' with $T' > T_0$ Because of the pulse broadening, pulses overlap and 0's are interfered by adjacent pulses. This interference is called intersymbol interference, and the result is an increase of the BER.

In general, the BER will not be significantly increased until $\Delta T' = T' - T_0$ becomes too large. A rule of thumb is that if

$$\Delta T = T' - T_0 = D_{total}L \leq \frac{T_0}{4} = \frac{1}{4B}$$ **[4.44]**

the BER will not be degraded significantly [17]. More detailed discussion on this is given in Chapter 7.

In practical optical fiber communication systems, pulse broadening is not caused by fiber dispersion alone. Other factors such as the rise time of the light source and receiver can also contribute to pulse broadening. Similar to the square sum of the total fiber dispersion, the total pulse broadening is a square sum of all these factors (see Appendix 7–C for proof). Therefore,

$$\Delta T^2 = \tau_t^2 + \tau_r^2 + (D_{total}L)^2$$ **[4.45]**

where τ_t, and τ_r, are the rise times of the transmitter and receiver, respectively. Combining Equations (4.44) and (4.45) gives

$$\tau_t^2 + \tau_r^2 + (D_{total}L)^2 < \left(\frac{1}{4B}\right)^2 .$$ **[4.46]**

This is the general expression for the dispersion limit.

Example 4.15

DISPERSION LIMIT   If both the optical transmitter and receiver have a rise time of 2 nsec and the total fiber dispersion is 1 nsec/km, then the dispersion limit is

$$8 + L^2 < \frac{1}{16B^2}$$

where L is in km and B is in Gb/s. Thus, the highest speed achievable is $B = 88$ Mb/s ($L = 0$). At $L = 10$ km, the highest achievable speed reduces to 24 Mb/s. ∎

According to the dependence of D_{total} on the bit rate, three special cases of dispersion limits are considered below.

Type 1: Fiber Dispersion Independent of Bit Rate   From the total dispersion expression in Equation (4.42), dispersion ΔT can be independent of B when either intermodal dispersion dominates or when $\Delta\lambda$ does not depend on B. For example, in step-index multimode fibers, the modal dispersion is much larger than the intramodal dispersion. In single mode or graded-index multimode fibers, if the light source used is an LED or a multimode FP laser diode where the linewidth of the source is much greater than B, $\Delta\lambda$ will be independent of B.

In either case, Equation (4.46) gives

$$\boxed{D_{total}L < \left[\left(\frac{1}{4B}\right)^2 - \tau_t^2 - \tau_r^2\right]^{1/2}.}$$ **[4.47]**

For convenience, let

$$B_{max} \overset{\text{def}}{=} \frac{1}{4(\tau_t^2 + \tau_r^2)^{1/2}}$$ **[4.48]**

be the maximum achievable bit rate. Then,

$$\boxed{L < L_{max} = \frac{1}{4D_{total}}\left(\frac{1}{B^2} - \frac{1}{B_{max}^2}\right)^{1/2}.}$$ **[4.49]**

Note that D_{total} has the dimension sec/km.

Example 4.16

TYPE 1: DISPERSION LIMIT   If $B_{max} = 10$ Gb/s and $D_{total} = 0.25 B_{max} = 10$ Gb/s and $D_{total} = 0.25$ nsec/km, Equation (4.49) gives

$$L_{max} = (1 \text{ km})\left(\frac{1}{B^2} - 0.01\right)^{1/2}$$

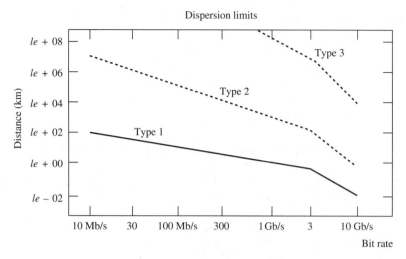

Figure 4.15   The three types of dispersion limits. Type 1 is independent of bit rate, type 2 is proportional to bit rate, and type 3 is proportional to bit rate squared.

where B is in Gb/s. Thus, when $B \ll 10$ Gb/s, L is linearly inversely proportional to B. This dispersion limit is shown as Type 1 in Figure 4.15. ∎

Type 2: Fiber Dispersion Proportional to Bit Rate   When single-mode fibers are used, there is no intermodal dispersion. In addition, if a single mode light source and external modulation (see Chap. 14) are used, the output linewidth $\Delta\lambda$ will be on the order of B. Specifically, from the AM modulation discussed in Chapter 1, the spectrum width under external modulation can be as low as $2B$ (lower band plus upper band). Depending on the modulation scheme, the spectrum width of the modulated light signal takes the form

$$\Delta f = k_b B$$

where $k_b = 2$ for AM modulation. Since the linewidth $\Delta\lambda$ is related to the spectrum width by $\Delta\lambda = (\lambda^2/c)\Delta f$ (see Equation [3.4]), we have

$$D_{total} = D_{intra} \times \Delta\lambda = D_{intra} \times (k_b B)\frac{\lambda^2}{c}. \qquad \textbf{[4.50]}$$

Combining Equations (4.46) and (4.50) gives

$$L \leq \frac{c}{4k_b\lambda^2}\frac{1}{D_{intra}}\frac{1}{B}\left(\frac{1}{B^2} - \frac{1}{B_{max}^2}\right)^{1/2}. \qquad \textbf{[4.51]}$$

When $B \ll B_{max}$, L is inversely proportional to B^2.

Example 4.17

TYPE 2: DISPERSION LIMIT   Suppose $B_{max} = 10$ Gb/s, $D_{intra} = 20$ psec/nm $\cdot$ km at $\lambda = 1.3\mu$m, and $k_b = 2$. The dispersion limit is

$$L_{max} = 1100\frac{1}{B}\left(\frac{1}{B^2} - \frac{1}{B_{max}^2}\right)^{1/2}$$

where B is in Gb/s and L is in km. This dispersion limit is plotted as Type 2 in Figure 4.15. ∎

Type 3: Fiber Dispersion Proportional to Bit Rate Squared   In addition to using single mode fibers, single mode light sources, and external modulation, one can further improve the dispersion limit, if the lightwave is at either 1.3 μm, or 1.55 μm, using dispersion-shifted fibers (see next section). In this case, $D_{intra} = 0$, and the second-order term in Equation (4.26) must be included. Thus

$$\Delta\tau_g \approx \frac{1}{2}\frac{\partial D_{intra}}{\partial\lambda}(\lambda - \lambda_0)^2 \qquad \textbf{[4.52]}$$

where λ_0 is the wavelength at which $\frac{\partial D_{intra}}{\partial\lambda} = 0$. If λ_0 is also at the center of the linewidth $\Delta\lambda$, the maximum deviation of $|\lambda = \lambda_0|$ is

$$\max|\lambda - \lambda_0| = \frac{\Delta\lambda}{2} = \frac{\lambda^2 k_b}{2c}B.$$

Therefore, the fiber dispersion is

$$\Delta\tau_g \approx \frac{1}{2}\frac{\partial D_{intra}}{\partial\lambda}\left(\frac{\lambda^2 k_b}{2c}B\right)^2 \qquad \textbf{[4.53]}$$

and the dispersion limit is

$$L < \frac{1}{2d\,D_{intra}/d\lambda}\left(\frac{2c}{\lambda^2 k_b}\right)^2\frac{1}{B^2}\left(\frac{1}{B^2} - \frac{1}{B_{max}^2}\right)^{1/2}. \qquad \textbf{[4.54]}$$

Example 4.18

TYPE 3: DISPERSION LIMIT   Using the same assumed parameters as the previous example and assuming $\partial D_{intra}/\partial\lambda = 80$ (psec/km$\cdot$nm$\cdot\mu$m), Equation (4.54) gives

$$L < 2.0 \times 10^8 \frac{1}{B^2}\left(\frac{1}{B^2} - \frac{1}{B_{max}^2}\right)^{1/2}$$

where B is in Gb/s and L is in km. This dispersion limit is plotted as Type 3 in Figure 4.15. ∎

Example 4.19

COMPONENT SELECTION GUIDELINES   Figure 4.16 superimposes two attenuation limits (using results from Example 4.8 and assuming fiber attenuation 2 dB/km at 1.30 μm and 0.2 dB/km at 1.55 μm) with the three dispersion limits described earlier. This figure provides important information for selecting suitable transmission components for a given optical communication system.

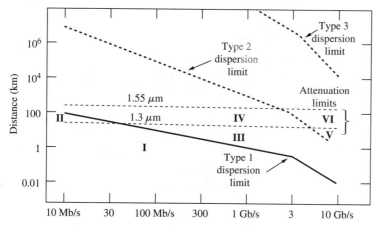

Figure 4.16   Superposition of both dispersion and attenuation limits. Curves are obtained from the data used in the examples.

The figure shows six possible operation zones. For systems operating at low speeds (zones I and II), multimode fibers and non-single-frequency light sources can be used. For longer distance transmission (zone II), the 1.55 μm wavelength is preferred over the 1.3 μm for lower fiber attenuation.

For systems operating at higher speeds, single-mode fibers and single-frequency light sources are needed. Operating at zero dispersion ($D_{intra} = 0$), however, does not significantly improve the dispersion limit because of another limit: B_{max}. Therefore, to take advantage of zero dispersion, one must improve the speed of transceivers at the same time. ∎

4.5 ADVANCED OPTICAL FIBERS

In addition to multimode and single-mode fibers discussed earlier, there are other fiber types used in optical fiber communications. Among them, two important types are **dispersion shifted fibers** and **polarization maintaining fibers.** Dispersion shifted fibers provide zero dispersion at 1.55 μm so that both dispersion and attenuation can be minimized. Polarization-maintaining fibers maintain the polarization of light signals as they propagate. This is critical in coherent communications where the performance is sensitive to the polarization state of the received signal.

4.5.1 DISPERSION-SHIFTED AND MULTIPLY CLAD FIBERS

Both **dispersion-shifted** and **multiply clad** fibers are designed to minimize fiber dispersion. Dispersion-shifted fibers minimize dispersion at one point: 1.55 μm, where the fiber

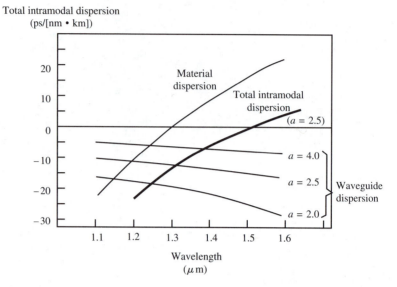

Figure 4.17   Total intramodal dispersion as a function of wavelength.

attenuation is at its minimum. On the other hand, multiply clad fibers are designed to minimize fiber dispersion over a wide wavelength range.

Because D_{intra} is the sum of $D_{material}$ and $D_{waveguide}$, as illustrated in Figure 4.17, D_{intra} can be made zero by adjusting $D_{waveguide}$ in dispersion-shifted fibers. There are two methods to adjust $D_{waveguide}$. First, the refractive index profile of the core can be changed. As shown in Figure 4.3*g* and *h*, a triangular refractive index profile can be used for this purpose.

Another way to adjust $D_{waveguide}$ is to change the core diameter. As Appendix 4–C explains, $D_{waveguide}$ is a function of a parameter V defined by

$$V \overset{\text{def}}{=} ka(n_1^2 - n_2^2)^{1/2} \approx \beta_1 a(2\Delta)^{1/2}. \qquad [4.55]$$

Because V is proportional to k or f, V is commonly referred to as the **normalized frequency.** Comparing it with the definition of the numerical aperture (*NA*) shows that V and *NA* are similar quantities. From Equation (4.89) and Figure 4.27 in Appendix 4–C, $D_{waveguide}$ can be reduced to zero by reducing V when $V = 1.4$ Therefore, as illustrated in Figure 4.17, one can achieve $D_{intra} = 0$ at 1.55 μm by reducing V through reducing the core radius a.

Example 4.20   **DISPERSION SHIFTED FIBERS**   Consider a fiber that has $n_1 = 1.45$, $n_2 = 1.44$, and $a = 4.0$ μm. At $\lambda = 1.55$ μm,

$$V = \frac{2\pi \times 4.0}{1.55}(1.45^2 - 1.44^2)^{1/2} = 2.76.$$

When a is reduced to 2.5 μm,

$$V = \frac{2\pi \times 2.5}{1.55}(1.45^2 - 1.44^2)^{1/2} = 1.7$$

From Equation (4.89), the waveguide dispersion is

$$D_{waveguide} = -\frac{n_{1g} - n_{2g}}{c\lambda}\left[\frac{V\partial^2(Vb)}{\partial V^2}\right] \approx -\frac{n_1 - n_2}{c\lambda}\left[\frac{V\partial^2(Vb)}{\partial V^2}\right] \qquad \textbf{[4.56]}$$

where b is a parameter defined in Equation (4.90). From Figure 4.27, $[V\partial^2 (Vb)/\partial V^2] \approx 0.02$ and 0.4 at $a = 4.0$ and 2.5 μm, respectively. Therefore, the waveguide dispersion is

$$D_{waveguide} = -\frac{1.45 - 1.44}{(3 \times 10^5[\text{km/sec}]) \times (1550[\text{nm}])} \times 0.02 = -0.43 \text{ psec/km·nm}$$

at $a = 4.0$ μm, and

$$D_{waveguide} = -\frac{1.45 - 1.44}{(3 \times 10^5[\text{km/sec}]) \times (1550[\text{nm}])} \times 0.4 = -8.6 \text{ psec/km·nm}$$

at $a = 2.5$ μm. This negative waveguide dispersion can be used to cancel the positive material dispersion at 1.55 μm. ∎

For a small dispersion over a wide wavelength range, multiply clad fibers can be used. A **doubly** clad [18] and a **quadruply** clad [19] fiber are illustrated in Figure 4.3*i* and *j*. Their low dispersion over a wide wavelength range is illustrated in Figure 4.18. These multiply clad fibers have two zero-dispersion points. Detailed analysis and numerical computations for these fibers can be found in [20].

4.5.2   POLARIZATION-MAINTAINING FIBERS

Polarization is an important property of an electromagnetic wave. It is the direction of the electric field (or magnetic field) perpendicular to the propagation direction. As illustrated in Figure 4.19, if the polarization stays the same during propagation, it is called **linearly polarized;** if it rotates circularly in the plane perpendicular to the propagation direction, it is called **circularly polarized.** In general, a wave of any polarization can be decomposed into two waves with polarizations perpendicular to each other (e.g., $\hat{x}$ and $\hat{y}$). If the two components have the same phase, the combined wave is linearly polarized. If the two have a phase difference of 90°, on the other hand, the combined wave is circularly polarized. When the two perpendicular polarizations are defined, the **polarization state** of a wave is characterized by the relative phase and the amplitudes of the two perpendicular polarizations. See Chapter 15 for a detailed discussion.

In a circular fiber, because of circular symmetry, two perpendicularly polarized waves have the same propagation constant. Therefore, the polarization state of the

Total intramodal dispersion
(ps/[nm · km])

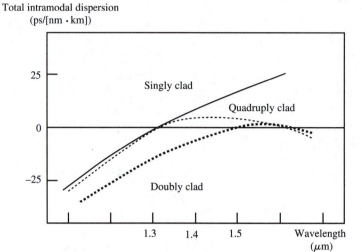

Figure 4.18   Dispersion characteristics of multiply clad fibers.

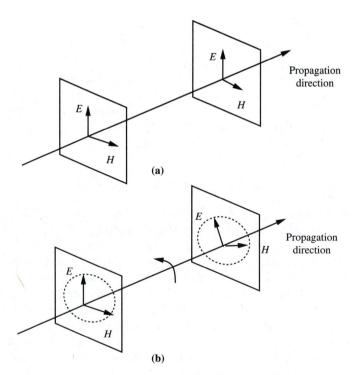

Figure 4.19   (*a*) Linear polarization and (*b*) circular polarization.

wave stays the same throughout the propagation. However, a practical fiber has a slight and random ellipticity along its axis. As a result, as the waves propagate, their propagation constants fluctuate, and the polarization state at the end of propagation is different from the initial one. For example, if the incident wave is linearly polarized and the two perpendicular modes experience a relative $90°$ phase change during propagation, the wave will become circularly polarized. To maintain the polarization state for systems whose performance is polarization sensitive thus requires polarization-maintaining fibers.

Circular Fibers   One intuitive way to maintain polarization is to make the fiber as circular as possible. One parameter used to characterize the circular symmetry of a fiber is called **birefringence,** which is defined by

$$\mathcal{B} \stackrel{\text{def}}{=} \frac{\beta_x - \beta_y}{k} = n_x - n_y \qquad \textbf{[4.57]}$$

where $k = \omega/c = 2\pi/\lambda$, β_x and β_y are the propagation constants of the two perpendicular polarizations, and n_x and n_y are the corresponding effective refractive indices.

BIREFRINGENCE   A low propagation constant difference, $\Delta\beta = \beta_x - \beta_y = 0.4$ deg/m, in a "spun-fiber" has been reported [21]. From Equation (4.57), the corresponding birefringence is

$$\mathcal{B} = \frac{0.4 \times \lambda}{360} = 1.7 \times 10^{-9}.$$

In a typical fiber, on the other hand, the birefringence is around 10^{-6}. ∎

Example 4.21

Single-Polarization or Differential Polarization Fibers   Another way to maintain polarization is to introduce a differential mechanism that cuts off one of the polarizations. To achieve this, one must introduce a large enough $\mathcal{B}$. As a result, the effective refractive indices n_x and n_y in the core are different. From Equation (4.1), the two polarizations have different cutoff wavelengths (substituting n_1 by n_x or n_y).

However, as pointed out earlier, Equation (4.1) is the single-mode condition. That is, from Figure 4.23, there is one and only one propagation mode (HE_{11}) if the wavelength is above λ_c or when $V < 2.4$. Therefore, even when a large $\mathcal{B}$ is introduced, both polarizations can still propagate. To suppress one polarization, use of a different index profile shown in Figure 4.20a has been suggested [22]. As illustrated in Figure 4.20b, this index profile modifies the β_z/k-V characteristic and cuts off the x-polarization completely when V is between $V_{c,y}$ and $V_{c,x}$.

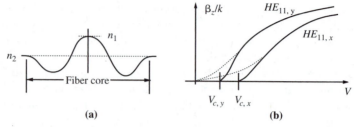

Figure 4.20   Polarization maintaining by differential attenuation: (a) the index profile and (b) the β_z/k-V characteristic, where the solid lines correspond to the index profile of (a) and the dotted lines correspond to the step-index profile.

Two-Polarization or Linearly Birefringent Fibers   When the birefringence $\mathcal{B}$ is large enough (on the order of 10^{-4}), coupling from one polarization to another is difficult [23]. Therefore, two polarizations will not be mixed, and the polarization state can be maintained if only one polarization is transmitted initially. To characterize mode coupling in polarization-maintaining fibers, a parameter h was introduced and defined by [24]:

$$10 \log_{10} \frac{P_x}{P_y} \overset{\text{def}}{=} 10 \log_{10}[\tanh(hL)] \qquad \textbf{[4.58]}$$

where P_y is the power of the initial polarization after a transmission distance L, and P_x is coupled power of the other polarization. The use of the tanh function can be understood as follows. When $hL \ll 1$, $\tanh(hL \approx hL)$. Therefore, hL is the coupling ratio from P_x to P_y. When hL becomes large, there can be mutual coupling from either direction. Therefore, $P_x/P_y = \tanh(hL) \rightarrow 1$ as $hL \rightarrow \infty$. Some two-polarization-maintaining fibers and their h values are summarized in Table 4.2 [24].

Example 4.22

ORTHOGONAL POLARIZED MODE COUPLING   If L_p is denoted as the distance over which $P_x/P_y = 1/p$ ($p > 1$), Equation (4.58) yields

$$L_p = \frac{\ln(p+1) - \ln(p-1)}{2h} \qquad \textbf{[4.59]}$$

Therefore, for a long distance at a given p, h should be as small as possible. As a numerical example, for $p = 9$ and $h = 10^{-6}\text{m}^{-1}$,

$$L_9 = 0.22 \times 10^6 = 220 \text{ km.}$$

This result says there is a 10% power coupling over a distance of 220 km by using a birefringence fiber of $h = 10^{-6}\text{m}^{-1}$. ∎

Table 4.2

Characteristics of representative polarization-maintaining fibers.

Types	Names	$\mathcal{B}$	h (1/m)	Loss (dB/km)	Wavelength (μm)
HB with GE	Elliptical core	4.2×10^{-4}	30×10^{-6}	85	0.85
	Side pit	0.5×10^{-4}	1×10^{-6}	5	1.15
	Side tunnel	4.2×10^{-4}	—	—	1.06
HB with SE	Elliptical cladding	7.2×10^{-4}	1.2×10^{-6}	5	0.63
	Elliptical jacket	3.0×10^{-4}	1.0×10^{-6}	0.8	1.55
	Panda	3.0×10^{-4}	0.5×10^{-6}	0.25	1.55
	Panda, SP	5.9×10^{-4}	(44 dB)	0.3	1.30
	Bow-tie	4.8×10^{-4}	—	3.6	0.85
	Bow-tie, SP	6.7×10^{-4}	(42 dB)	1.0	0.82
	Flat-clad	2.5×10^{-4}	5.9×10^{-6}	2.6	0.85
	Flat-clad, SP	4.7×10^{-4}	(34 dB)	1.0	0.63

NOTE: GE=geometrical effect, SE=stress effect; HB=high birefringence; SP=single polarization.

Many different ways of introducing birefringence are summarized in Table 4.2. One effective way to introduce a large birefringence is through mechanical stress. Fibers of this kind are called **stress-induced** polarization-maintaining fibers. A few examples are illustrated in Figure 4.21 [25]–[27]. In these fibers, borosilicate used as cladding for lower refractive index provides the desirable mechanical stress.

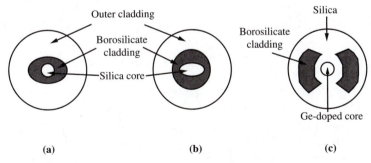

(a) **(b)** **(c)**

Figure 4.21 Stress-induced polarization-maintaining fibers: (a) elliptically deformed cladding, (b) elliptically deformed core, and (c) panda or bow-tie.

4.6 SUMMARY

1. An optical fiber consists of a core and a cladding layer. The core has a slightly higher refractive index than the cladding. This higher refractive index provides the guiding mechanism for light propagation inside the core.

2. According to the core diameter, there are single-mode and multimode fibers. When the core diameter is small enough, the cutoff wavelength of the fiber can be made lower than the operating wavelength. When this is the case, there is only one transverse mode. A typical single-mode fiber has a core diameter around 10 μm, and a typical multimode fiber has a core diameter around 50 μm.

3. According to the refractive index profile in the core, there are two common types of multimode fibers: step-index and graded-index. Step-index fibers have a constant index in the core, and graded-index fibers have a continuous index decrease from the center to the core–cladding boundary.

4. Fiber attenuation and dispersion limit the transmission capacity and distance. Fiber attenuation is caused by photon absorption, scattering, fiber bending, and coupling. Most optical fiber communication systems operate at wavelengths 1.3 μm and 1.55 μm for low fiber attenuation. Fiber attenuation can be as low as 0.2 dB/km at 1.55 μm.

5. Fiber dispersion is caused by different propagation velocities of components in the lightwave. There are three types of dispersion: material or chromatic dispersion, waveguide dispersion, and modal dispersion. Material dispersion and waveguide dispersion together are called the intramodal dispersion.

6. If the light output of a light source has a finite nonzero bandwidth, different frequency components propagate in different speeds. Dispersion caused by different frequency components is called intramodal or group velocity dispersion. Therefore, unless the light output is a continuous wave (CW), single-frequency carrier, there is intramodal dispersion.

7. Modal dispersion is caused by different velocities of different propagation modes. In single-mode fibers, there is only one propagation mode. Therefore, there is no modal dispersion. In step-index multimode fibers, modal dispersion is in general much larger than intramodal dispersion. Graded-index fibers have been used to reduce the large modal dispersion.

8. To reduce intramodal dispersion, dispersion-shifted fibers have been used for zero dispersion at 1.55 μm. At this wavelength, both minimum dispersion and minimum attenuation can be achieved. To provide a low intramodal dispersion over a wide wavelength range, multiclad fibers have been proposed.

9. In addition to attenuation and dispersion, polarization is another important factor to systems whose transmission performance is polarization dependent. As a result, polarization-maintaining fibers have been introduced, where birefringence or anisotropy is introduced by mechanical stress to minimize coupling from one polarization mode to another.

APPENDIX 4-A: BASICS OF WAVE PROPAGATION

Because light waves are electromagnetic waves, they can be described by the Maxwell wave equations. This appendix provides some background for readers who want to know more about wave propagation discussed in the various parts of the book.

A.1   WAVE EQUATIONS

The Maxwell equations consist of four equations describing the time dependence of the electric field $\mathcal{E}$ and magnetic field $\mathcal{H}$. A simplified set is given below by assuming no free space charges.[3] This is sufficient to understand wave propagations in a dielectric medium. The four equations are

$$\nabla \times \mathcal{E} = -\mu_0 \frac{\partial \mathcal{H}}{\partial t} \qquad \textbf{[4.60]}$$

$$\nabla \times \mathcal{H} = J + \frac{\partial \mathcal{D}}{\partial t} \qquad \textbf{[4.61]}$$

$$\nabla \cdot \mathcal{D} = 0 \qquad \textbf{[4.62]}$$

$$\nabla \cdot \mathcal{H} = 0 \qquad \textbf{[4.63]}$$

where J is the current density,

$$\mathcal{D} = \epsilon_0 \mathcal{E} + \mathcal{P} \qquad \textbf{[4.64]}$$

is called the **electric flux density** or **displacement,** and $\mathcal{P}$ is called the **induced polarization** by the electric field $\mathcal{E}$ in the medium. Constants ϵ_0 and μ_0 are the vacuum **permittivity** and **permeability** with the product equal to

$$\epsilon_0 \mu_0 = \frac{1}{c^2}$$

where c is the speed of light in a vacuum. The concept of P will be explained shortly. Examples 4.23 and 4.24 below illustrate the above Maxwell equations.

WAVE EQUATIONS IN VACUUM SPACE   In a vacuum, there is not any medium. As a result, there is no induced polarization or current. In other words, both $\mathcal{P}$ and J are zero. Therefore, the Maxwell equations reduce to   **Example 4.23**

$$\nabla \times \mathcal{E} = -\mu_0 \frac{\partial \mathcal{H}}{\partial t} \qquad \textbf{[4.65]}$$

| [3] See Chapter 3 of [28] for a general set of the Maxwell equations.

$$\nabla \times \mathcal{H} = \epsilon_0 \frac{\partial \mathcal{E}}{\partial t}$$

$$\nabla \cdot \mathcal{E} = 0$$

$$\nabla \cdot \mathcal{H} = 0.$$

These four equations describe the dependence between $\mathcal{E}$ and $\mathcal{H}$. One can eliminate $\mathcal{H}$ and get an equation for only $\mathcal{E}$. Taking the curl of $\nabla \times \mathcal{E}$ gives

$$\nabla \times \nabla \times \mathcal{E} = -\mu_0 \frac{\partial}{\partial t}(\nabla \times \mathcal{H}) = -\epsilon_0 \mu_0 \frac{\partial^2}{\partial t^2} \mathcal{E}.$$

Vector calculus gives the identity

$$\nabla \times \nabla \times \mathcal{E} = \nabla(\nabla \cdot \mathcal{E}) - \nabla^2 \mathcal{E} = -\nabla^2 \mathcal{E}.$$

Therefore, the wave equation for the electric field in vacuum is

$$\nabla^2 \mathcal{E} - \frac{1}{c^2} \frac{\partial^2}{\partial t^2} \mathcal{E} = 0. \qquad \textbf{[4.66]}$$

The solution to Equation (4.66) has the following general form:

$$\mathcal{E}(x, y, z, t) = a_+ \mathcal{E}^+(\bar{k} \cdot \bar{r} - \omega t) + a_- \mathcal{E}^-(\bar{k} \cdot \bar{r} + \omega t) \qquad \textbf{[4.67]}$$

where $\bar{r} = (x, y, z)$ is the position vector, $\bar{k} = (k_x, k_y, k_z)$ is the wave propagation vector, and ω is the angular frequency with

$$\frac{\omega^2}{c^2} = k_x^2 + k_y^2 + k_z^2.$$

The physical meaning of the wave solution given by Equation (4.67) can be understood as follows. First, consider the special case that $k_y = k_z = 0$. In this case, the argument $\bar{k} \cdot \bar{r} - \omega t$ reduces to $k_x r_x - \omega t = k_x[r_x - (\omega/k_x)t]$. This means the wave $\mathcal{E}^+$ propagates in the $\hat{x}$ direction at a velocity of ω/k_x. In general, when k_y or k_z is not zero, $\mathcal{E}^+$ is a wave propagating in the positive $\bar{k}$ direction at velocity c. Similarly, $\mathcal{E}^-$ represents a wave propagating in the negative $\bar{k}$ direction. ■

**Example
4.24**

PLANE WAVE   A special case of Equation (4.67) is the plane wave with

$$\mathcal{E}(x, y, z, t) = E e^{j(\omega t - kz)} \hat{x}. \qquad \textbf{[4.68]}$$

Here, the electric field has only one component in the x direction and propagates in the z direction. Substituting this electric field into Equation (4.65) and taking time integration give

$$\mathcal{H} = \frac{k}{j\mu_0 \omega} E_x e^{j(\omega t - kz)} \hat{y} = -j\sqrt{\frac{\epsilon_0}{\mu_0}} E e^{j(\omega t - kz)} \hat{y}.$$

Thus both the electric field and magnetic field are perpendicular to the wave propagation. ■

A.2   WAVES IN A DIELECTRIC MEDIUM

A dielectric medium is a medium in which a nonzero polarization $\mathcal{P}$ is induced by an external electric field $\mathcal{E}$. To understand the physical meaning of $\mathcal{P}$, consider a medium made of positive and negative charges (e.g., protons and electrons). When an electric field is present, it separates the positive and negative charges. This charge separation results in an additional electric field. This additional electric field is called the induced polarization.

Different media respond differently to a given external electric field. When the medium is linear and isotropic, $\mathcal{P}$ is linearly proportional to $\mathcal{E}$ and can be expressed as

$$\mathcal{P} = \epsilon_0 \chi \mathcal{E} \qquad\qquad \textbf{[4.69]}$$

where χ is called the **electric susceptibility.** With this definition, the electric flux density is

$$D = \epsilon_0 \mathcal{E} + \mathcal{P} \stackrel{\text{def}}{=} \epsilon_0 \epsilon_r \mathcal{E}$$

where

$$\epsilon_r = 1 + \chi \qquad\qquad \textbf{[4.70]}$$

is called the **dielectric constant.**

REFRACTIVE INDEX OF A DIELECTRIC MEDIUM   For an electromagnetic field in a dielectric medium without current, Equation (4.61) reduces to | **Example 4.25**

$$\nabla \times \mathcal{H} = \epsilon_r \epsilon_0 \frac{\partial \mathcal{E}}{\partial t}.$$

Using the same procedure described earlier, the wave equation for the electric field is

$$\nabla^2 \mathcal{E} - \frac{\epsilon_r}{c^2} \frac{\partial^2}{\partial t^2} \mathcal{E} = 0.$$

Therefore, the only difference of this equation from Equation (4.66) is that the wave propagation velocity changes from c to c/n, where

$$n = \sqrt{\epsilon_r}$$

is the refractive index of the medium. ∎

LOSSY DIELECTRIC MEDIUM   The current term in the wave equation can be included to represent the power loss of wave propagation. In this case, the induced current is related to the electric field by | **Example 4.26**

$$J = \sigma \mathcal{E}$$

where σ is called the **conductivity.** If the electric field has a time dependence $e^{j\omega t}$, the induced current density also has the same time dependence. Therefore, this current effect is included in the electric susceptibility as follows. From Equation (4.61),

$$J + \frac{\partial \mathcal{D}}{\partial t} = \frac{\partial}{\partial t}(\frac{J}{j\omega} + \mathcal{D}) = \frac{\partial}{\partial t}(\epsilon \mathcal{E})$$

with

$$\epsilon = \epsilon_r \epsilon_0 - j\frac{\sigma}{\omega} = \epsilon_0(1 + \chi - j\frac{\sigma}{\epsilon_0 \omega}).$$

The dielectric constant thus has a complex form with its imaginary part representing either loss (if negative) or gain (if positive). ∎

If $\mathcal{D}$ is substituted in Equation (4.61) from Equation (4.64), the wave equation for the electric field reduces to

$$\nabla^2 \mathcal{E} - \frac{1}{c^2}\frac{\partial^2}{\partial t^2}\mathcal{E} = \mu\frac{\partial^2}{\partial t^2}\mathcal{P}. \qquad \textbf{[4.71]}$$

This is the form used to derive the laser diode rate equations in Chapter 12.

A.3 WAVES IN WAVEGUIDES

Waveguides are structures within which electromagnetic waves are guided for propagation. As illustrated in Figure 4.22, there are two important kinds of waveguides: rectangular and circular. Important examples of these two kinds of waveguides are laser diode cavities and optical fibers, respectively.

Although it is quite different in mathematics to solve wave equations in rectangular and circular waveguides, many physical concepts, such as boundary conditions and propagation modes, are the same. Because it is much easier to solve wave equations for a rectangular waveguide, those will be considerd here to illustrate important concepts of waveguide propagation.

Let $\hat{z}$ be the longitudinal direction of the waveguide along which a wave propagates. By decomposing the wave into transverse and longitudinal fields, the electric and magnetic fields can be expressed as

$$\mathcal{E}(x, y, z, t) = \overline{E}(x, y)e^{j(\omega t - \beta_z z)}$$

$$\mathcal{H}(x, y, z, t) = \overline{H}(x, y)e^{j(\omega t - \beta_z z)}$$

where $\overline{E}$ and $\overline{H}$ are the transverse factors of the corresponding fields, and $e^{j(\omega t - \beta_z z)}$ is the common longitudinal factor. Substituting the above expressions into Equations (4.60) and (4.61) and assuming $J = 0$, we have

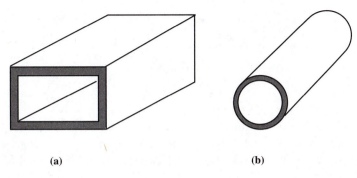

(a) **(b)**

Figure 4.22   Illustration of (a) a rectangular waveguide and (b) a circular waveguide.

$$\frac{\partial E_z}{\partial y} + j\beta_z E_y = -j\omega\mu_0 H_x \qquad\qquad \textbf{[4.72]}$$

$$-j\beta_z E_x - \frac{\partial E_z}{\partial x} = -j\omega\mu_0 H_y \qquad\qquad \textbf{[4.73]}$$

$$\frac{\partial E_y}{\partial x} - \frac{\partial E_x}{\partial y} = -j\omega\mu_0 H_z \qquad\qquad \textbf{[4.74]}$$

and

$$\frac{\partial H_z}{\partial y} + j\beta_z H_y = j\omega\epsilon E_x \qquad\qquad \textbf{[4.75]}$$

$$-j\beta_z H_x - \frac{\partial H_z}{\partial x} = j\omega\epsilon E_y \qquad\qquad \textbf{[4.76]}$$

$$\frac{\partial H_y}{\partial x} - \frac{\partial H_x}{\partial y} = j\omega\epsilon E_z \qquad\qquad \textbf{[4.77]}$$

where $\epsilon = \epsilon_r$. These six equations can be used to solve E_x, E_y, H_x, and H_Y in terms of E_z and H_z. For example, E_y (or H_x) can be obtained from Equations (4.72) and (4.76) by eliminating H_x (or E_y). Specifically,

$$E_x = -\frac{1}{\beta^2 - \beta_z^2}\left(j\beta_z \frac{\partial E_z}{\partial x} + j\omega\mu_0 \frac{\partial H_z}{\partial y}\right) \qquad\qquad \textbf{[4.78]}$$

$$E_y = \frac{1}{\beta^2 - \beta_z^2}\left(-j\beta_z \frac{\partial E_z}{\partial y} + j\omega\mu_0 \frac{\partial H_z}{\partial x}\right) \qquad\qquad \textbf{[4.79]}$$

$$H_x = \frac{1}{\beta^2 - \beta_z^2}\left(j\omega\epsilon \frac{\partial E_z}{\partial y} - j\beta_z \frac{\partial H_z}{\partial x}\right) \qquad\qquad \textbf{[4.80]}$$

and

$$H_y = -\frac{1}{\beta^2 - \beta_z^2}\left(j\omega\epsilon\frac{\partial E_z}{\partial x} + j\beta_z\frac{\partial H_z}{\partial y}\right) \qquad \textbf{[4.81]}$$

where

$$\beta = \omega\sqrt{\epsilon\mu_0} = \frac{n\omega}{c}$$

is the propagation constant of the waveguide medium.

    The above results show that the transverse fields (in the x and y directions) can be independently represented by the longitudinal fields E_z and H_z. If E_z is zero, the solution is called **transverse electric** (TE) waves, and if H_z is zero, the solution is called **transverse magnetic** (TM) waves.

    In addition to Equations (4.78)–(4.81), electromagnetic waves that are **propagatable** in a rectangular waveguide also need to satisfy certain boundary conditions. Waves that satisfy both Equations (4.78)–(4.81) and the boundary conditions are called **propagation modes.** The concept of boundary conditions is illustrated in Example 4.27.

Example 4.27

Consider TE waves in a metallic rectangular waveguide with transverse sizes a and b. In this case, E_z is completely zero and the electric field parallel to the waveguide boundary should also be zero to meet the boundary condition. Therefore, $H_z(x, y)\,H_z(x, y)$ should have the following form:

$$H_z(x, y) = H_{m,n}\cos(\pi m x/a)\cos(\pi n y/b) \qquad \textbf{[4.82]}$$

where m and n are two integers. With this form,

$$E_x(x, y) = -\frac{j\omega\mu_0}{\beta^2 - \beta_z^2}\frac{\pi n}{b}H_{m,n}\cos(\pi m x/a)\sin(\pi n y/b)$$

and

$$E_y(x, y) = \frac{j\omega\mu_0}{\beta^2 - \beta_z^2}\frac{\pi m}{a}H_{m,n}\sin(\pi m x/a)\cos(\pi n y/b).$$

It is easy to verify that

$$E_x(x, 0) = E_x(x, b) = E_y(0, y) = E_y(a, y) = 0.$$

In other words, $H_z(x, y)$ in Eq. (4.82) meets the boundary conditions and is a propagation mode. Specifically, it is called the TE$_{m,n}$ mode.

    From equation (4.66), β_z satisfies the below equality.

$$\left(\frac{\pi m}{a}\right)^2 + \left(\frac{\pi n}{b}\right)^2 + \beta_z^2 = \beta^2. \qquad \textbf{[4.83]}$$

This is usually called the **dispersion relationship** for the TE$_{m,n}$ mode because it describes the relationship between wave propagation constant β_z and frequency $\omega = c\beta/n$. For convenience, let us define

$$\kappa_{m,n}^2 = \left(\frac{\pi m}{a}\right)^2 + \left(\frac{\pi n}{b}\right)^2$$

where $\kappa_{m,n}$ is called the **eigenvalue** of the propagation mode $TE_{m,n}$. If $a > b$, the smallest eigenvalue is that of the $TE_{1,0}$ mode. ∎

The above discussion on rectangular waveguides can be generalized to circular waveguides. From Equation (4.83), the general dispersion relationship can be written as

$$\beta^2 = \beta_z^2 + \kappa_i^2 \qquad \textbf{[4.84]}$$

where k_i is the eigenvalue of the ith mode of the given waveguide. To find k_i for circular waveguides, one can apply the same concept of boundary conditions. However, the form for E_z or H_z satisfying the boundary condition is much more involved. Appendix 4–C provides further discussion on this.

APPENDIX 4–B: GROUP VELOCITY

The concept of group velocity is important to understanding lightwave propagation and quantifying fiber dispersion. In general, there are two different velocities: group velocity and phase velocity. To see the meanings of these velocities, let us first consider a traveling wave with the following form:

$$e(t, z) = E_0 \cos(\omega_0 t - \beta z).$$

Therefore, its Fourier transform with respect to time is

$$E(\omega, z) = E_0 \pi \left[\delta(\omega - \omega_0)e^{-j\beta z} + \delta(\omega + \omega_0)e^{j\beta z}\right].$$

This means that a plane wave has a constant frequency. This constant frequency wave is called a **monochromatic** wave and is also called a continuous wave (CW). In this case, the phase velocity is defined as

$$v_p \overset{\text{def}}{=} \frac{\omega_0}{\beta}. \qquad \textbf{[4.85]}$$

Thus, phase velocity is the velocity of a constant phase plane that moves in the propagation direction.

For the plane wave considered, its amplitude or power is constant over the entire space, independent of time and position. In other words, one cannot tell "where" the wave is. Actually, it is everywhere. On the other hand, for two plane waves with a slight difference in frequency and wave number,

$$e(t, z) = E_0 \cos(\omega_1 t - \beta_1 z) + E_0 \cos(\omega_2 t - \beta_2 z)$$

using trignometric identities gives

$$e(t, z) = 2E_0 \cos(\Delta\omega t/2 - \Delta\beta z/2) \cos(\overline{\omega} t - \overline{\beta} z)$$

where $\Delta\omega \overset{\text{def}}{=} \omega_2 - \omega_1$ and $\Delta\beta \overset{\text{def}}{=} \beta_2 - \beta_1$ are assumed small, compared to $\overline{\omega} \overset{\text{def}}{=} (\omega_2 + \omega_1)/2$ and $\overline{\beta} \overset{\text{def}}{=} (\beta_1 + \beta_2)/2$ respectively. Thus the envelope of the combined wave has a veleocity

$$v_g = \frac{\Delta\omega}{\Delta\beta}.$$

This is called the group velocity. As the derivation shows, it means the propagation velocity of *energy*.

The concept of group velocity can be generalized from the two monochromatic waves to a "wave packet" of the following form:

$$e(t, z) = \int a(\omega) e^{j[\omega t - \beta(\omega)z]} d\omega.$$

In this form, $a(\omega)$ is the amplitude spectrum density and $a(\omega)d(\omega)$ can be considered the amplitude of a monochromatic wave at frequency ω. Let $\overline{\omega}$ be the mean frequency of the wave packet and $\overline{\beta} = n(\overline{\omega})\overline{\omega}/c$ be the corresponding wave number. With these definitions, the wave packet $e(z, t)$ takes the following form:

$$e(t, z) = A(z, t) e^{j(\overline{\omega} t - \overline{\beta} z)}$$

where $A(z, t)$ is the amplitude of the wave packet. This expression says that the wave packet has an amplitude $A(z, t)$ that modulates a CW carrier at frequency $\overline{\omega}$. From the above two equations,

$$A(z, t) = \int a(\omega) e^{j[(\omega - \overline{\omega})t - (\beta - \overline{\beta})z]} d\omega.$$

If the amplitude density $a(\omega)$ is only large in a small frequency spread, the following approximation holds:

$$\beta(\omega) - \overline{\beta} \approx \frac{\partial\beta}{\partial\omega}(\omega - \overline{\omega}).$$

Thus,

$$A(z, t) = \int a(\omega) e^{j(\omega - \overline{\omega})(t - z/v_g)} d\omega$$

where

$$\boxed{v_g \overset{\text{def}}{=} \frac{\partial\omega}{\partial\beta}} \qquad \textbf{[4.86]}$$

is the group velocity. The above expression of $A(z, t)$ shows that each wave component at a different frequency travels at the same speed of v_g. In other words, the wave packet or its amplitude travels at the group velocity v_g.

APPENDIX 4–C: WAVEGUIDE DISPERSION ANALYSIS

This appendix derives the waveguide dispersion of weakly guided step-index optical fibers. It avoids solving wave equations by taking a different and simpler approach.

From Equation (4.32) and using the chain rule we have

$$D_{waveguide} = \frac{n_{1g}}{c} \frac{\partial}{\partial \lambda} \left(\frac{\partial \beta_z}{\partial \beta_1} \right) = \frac{n_{1g}}{c} \frac{\partial \beta_1}{\partial \lambda} \frac{\partial}{\partial \beta_1} \left(\frac{\partial \beta_z}{\partial \beta_1} \right)$$

$$= \frac{n_{1g}}{c} \left(\frac{-2\pi n_{1g}}{\lambda^2} \right) \frac{\partial}{\partial \beta_1} \left(\frac{\partial \beta_z}{\partial \beta_1} \right) = -\tau_g \frac{2\pi n_{1g}}{\lambda^2} \frac{\partial}{\partial \beta_1} \left(\frac{\partial \beta_z}{\partial \beta_1} \right)$$

[4.87]

where $\tau_g = n_{1g}/c$. To find the factor $\dfrac{\partial}{\partial \beta_1} \left(\dfrac{\partial \beta_z}{\partial \beta_1} \right)$, one uses the V factor deined in Equation (4.55). As explained earlier, V is the wave analysis version of NA that characterizes how easily an optical signal can be coupled into the fiber. Figure 4.23 shows β_z/β_1 versus V. When $V < 2.4$, there is only one propagation mode, HE_{11}.

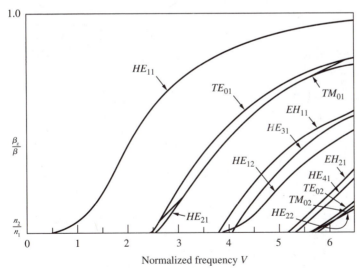

Figure 4.23 β_z to β_1 ratio at different V.

Source: Reprinted by permission, from Gloge, "Weakly Guiding Fibers"[29]. ©1971 by *Optical Society of America*.

From the definition of V given by Equation (4.55), V is proportional to β_1 if Δ is relatively independent of β_1 and V. In this case,

$$\frac{\partial}{\partial \beta_1}\left(\frac{\partial \beta_z}{\partial \beta_1}\right) = \frac{\partial}{\partial \beta_1}\left[\frac{\partial}{\partial \beta_1}\left(\frac{\beta_z}{\beta_1}\beta_1\right)\right] = \frac{\partial}{\partial \beta_1}\left[\frac{\partial}{\partial \beta_1}\left(\frac{\beta_z}{\beta_1}\right)\beta_1 + \frac{\beta_z}{\beta_1}\right]$$

$$= \beta_1 \frac{\partial^2}{\partial \beta_1^2}\left(\frac{\beta_z}{\beta_1}\right) + 2\frac{\partial}{\partial \beta_1}\left(\frac{\beta_z}{\beta_1}\right) = \frac{1}{\beta_1}\left[V^2\frac{\partial^2}{\partial V^2}\left(\frac{\beta_z}{\beta_1}\right) + 2V\frac{\partial}{dV}\left(\frac{\beta_z}{\beta_1}\right)\right].$$

The last equality is from the fact that V is linearly proportional to β_1. Therefore, the final expression for $D_{waveguide}$ is

$$D_{waveguide} = -\tau_g \frac{n_{1g}}{n_1\lambda}\left[V^2\frac{\partial^2}{\partial V^2}\left(\frac{\beta_z}{\beta_1}\right) + 2V\frac{\partial}{\partial V}\left(\frac{\beta_z}{\beta_1}\right)\right]. \qquad \textbf{[4.88]}$$

The terms within the brackets can be estimated from curves of β_z/β_1 versus V as shown in Figure 4.23. For small V and mode HE_{11}, the bracketed term in Equation (4.88) can be positive (or negative $D_{waveguide}$), so it is possible to use small V or a to cancel $D_{material}$ or to have zero D_{intra}. This is the basic principle of dispersion-shifted fibers.

Example 4.28

EIGENVALUE APPROXIMATION   To get a numerical estimate of the bracketed term in Equation (4.88), one can use the following approximation for $\kappa_{HE_{11}}$:

$$\kappa_{HE_{11}} \approx \frac{2.4}{a}\frac{2}{\pi}\arctan\left[\frac{\pi/2}{2.4/a}\beta_1(2\Delta)^{1/2}\right] = \frac{2.4}{a}\frac{2}{\pi}\arctan\left[\frac{\pi}{2}\frac{V}{2.4}\right]$$

where $\kappa_{HE_{11}}$ is the eigenvalue of mode HE_{11} and $V = (2\Delta)^{1/2}\alpha\beta_1$ from Equation (4.55). In this approximation, the use of an arctan function comes from Figure 4.24. As it shows, the first crosspoint of curves A and B from the left side is strongly determined by curve B, which is close to an arctan function. The parameters used in the arctan function are determined from the following considerations. When $V \ll 1, \beta_z/\beta_1 \approx 1 - \Delta$, and the eigenvalue to β_1 ratio is $\kappa_{HE_{11}}/\beta_1 = [1 - (1 - \Delta)^2]^{1/2} \approx (2\Delta)^{1/2}$. When $V \gg 1$, from Figure 4.24, the eigenvalue approaches a constant $2.40/a$. These two limits and the arctanlike curve of the eigenvalue give the above approximation. Therefore

$$\frac{\beta_z}{\beta_1} = \left[1 - \frac{\kappa_{HE_{11}}^2}{\beta_1^2}\right]^{1/2} \approx \left[1 - \frac{(2\Delta)\frac{4.8^2}{\pi^2}\arctan^2(\pi V/4.8)}{V^2}\right]^{1/2}.$$

This approximation at $\Delta = 0.0067$ is shown in Figure 4.25. The corresponding bracket term in Equation (4.88) normalized by Δ is plotted in Figure 4.26. ∎

Example 4.29

APPROXIMATED WAVEGUIDE DISPERSION   If $|\lambda^2 \times \delta^2 n_1/\delta\lambda^2| = 0.025$, $\lambda = 1.3$ μm, $n_1 = 1.45, n_{1g} = 1.46, V = 2$, and $\Delta = 0.0067$, then

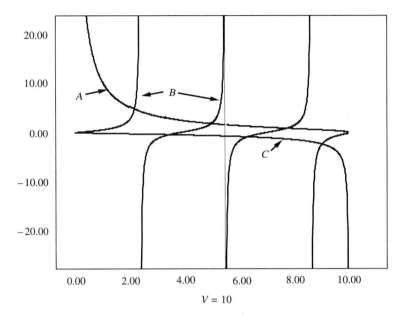

Figure 4.24 Eigenvalues can be obtained from the intersections of the curves shown, where curve A is $\gamma K_1(\gamma a)/\kappa K_0(\gamma a)$, curve B is $J_1(\kappa a)/J_0(\kappa a)$, and curve C is $-\kappa K_1(\gamma a)/\gamma K_0(\gamma a)$. The horizontal variable is κa and $\gamma a = \sqrt{V^2 - (\kappa a)^2}$. These curves come from the boundary condition $J_\nu(\kappa a)/J_{\nu-1}(\kappa a) = -\kappa K_\nu(\gamma a)/\gamma K_{\nu-1}(\gamma a)$.

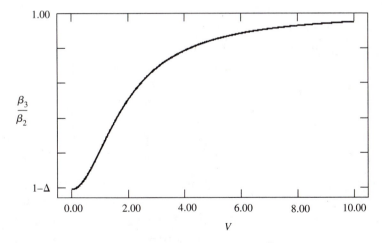

Figure 4.25 Approximated β_z to β_1 ratio at different V.

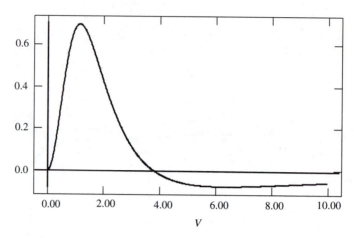

Figure 4.26   Approximated numerical value for the factor

$$\left[V^2 \frac{\partial^2}{\partial V^2}\left(\frac{\beta_z}{\beta_1}\right) + 2V\frac{\partial}{\partial V}\left(\frac{\beta_z}{\beta_1}\right) \right] \Big/ \Delta.$$

$$D_{material} = \left| \lambda^2 \times \frac{\partial^2 n_1}{\partial \lambda^2}\right| \frac{1}{c\lambda} = \frac{0.025}{1.3\ \mu\mathrm{m} \times 3 \times 10^5\ \mathrm{km}} = 64\ \mathrm{nsec}/\mu\mathrm{m}{\cdot}\mathrm{km}.$$

According to Figure 4.26 and Equation (4.88)

$$D_{waveguide} = -\frac{n_{1g}^2}{n_1 c\lambda} \times 0.0067 \times 0.4 = -10\ \mathrm{nsec}/\mu\mathrm{m}{\cdot}\mathrm{km}. \quad \blacksquare$$

According to Gloge [30], there is another and more common expression for D_{intra} in weakly guiding fibers ($\Delta \ll 1$):

$$D_{intra} = \frac{1}{c}\frac{\partial n_{2g}}{\partial \lambda} - \frac{n_{1g} - n_{2g}}{c\lambda}\left[\frac{V\partial^2(Vb)}{\partial V^2}\right] \tag{4.89}$$

where b is defined as

$$b \overset{\text{def}}{=} \frac{\beta_z^2/k^2 - n_2^2}{n_1^2 - n_2^2} \tag{4.90}$$

and $\kappa = 2\pi/\lambda = \beta_1/n_1$. Comparing this with Equation (4.32), shows that the first term is the material dispersion. To verify that the second term is the waveguide dispersion, first note that

$$b \approx \frac{\beta_z/k - n_2}{n_1 - n_2} \tag{4.91}$$

or

$$\beta_z \approx k[n_2 + (n_1 - n_2)b] = n_2 k(1 + b\Delta) \qquad \textbf{[4.92]}$$

in weakly guiding fibers. Therefore,

$$\frac{\beta_z}{\beta_1} \approx 1 - \Delta + b\Delta$$

is a linear function of b. Thus,

$$\frac{n_{1g} - n_{2g}}{c\lambda} V \frac{\partial^2 (Vb)}{\partial V^2} = \frac{n_{1g} - n_{2g}}{c\lambda} \left(V^2 \frac{\partial^2 b}{\partial V^2} + 2V \frac{\partial b}{\partial V} \right)$$

$$\approx \tau_g \lambda \left[V^2 \frac{\partial^2}{\partial V^2} \left(\frac{\beta_z}{\beta_1} \right) + 2V \frac{\partial}{\partial V} \left(\frac{\beta_z}{\beta_1} \right) \right].$$

This demonstrates the equivalence between the waveguide dispersion given by Equation (4.88) and the second term of Equation (4.89).

WAVEGUIDE DISPERSION FROM GLOGE Assume the same conditions as in the previous example, and use Figure 4.27 to calculate the waveguide dispersion [29]. Because $Vd^2(Vb)/dV^2$ is 0.2 at $V = 2$ from the figure, the waveguide dispersion is **Example 4.30**

$$D_{waveguide} = -\frac{1.46 \times 0.0067 \times 0.2}{\lambda c} = -5.0 \text{ nsec.} \quad \blacksquare$$

APPENDIX 4-D: **DISPERSION OF GRADED-INDEX FIBERS**

According to Gloge and Marcatili [16], the propagation constant of propagation mode m in a graded-index fiber with an index profile given by Equation (4.37) is

$$\beta_{z,m} = \beta_1 \left[1 - 2\Delta \left(\frac{m}{M} \right)^g \right]^{1/2} \qquad \textbf{[4.93]}$$

where $g \overset{\text{def}}{=} \alpha/(\alpha + 2)$ and M is the total number of propagation modes given by

$$M = a^2 \beta_1^2 \left(\frac{\alpha \Delta}{\alpha + 2} \right). \qquad \textbf{[4.94]}$$

From Equation (4.93), the unit propagation delay for mode m is:

$$\tau_{g,m} = \frac{\partial \beta_{z,m}}{\partial \omega} = \frac{\partial}{\partial \omega} \left\{ \beta_1 \left[1 - 2\Delta \left(\frac{m}{M} \right)^g \right]^{1/2} \right\} \qquad \textbf{[4.95]}$$

$$= \frac{\partial}{\partial \omega} \left\{ \frac{n_1}{c} \omega \left[1 - 2\Delta \left(\frac{m}{M} \right)^g \right]^{1/2} \right\}.$$

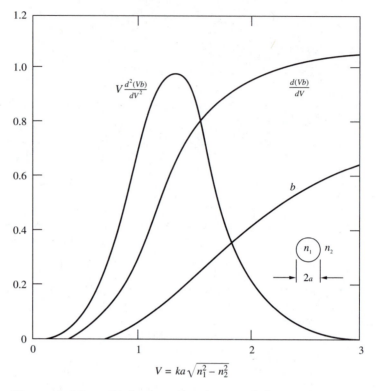

Figure 4.27   The factor used by Gloge to calculate waveguide dispersion.

SOURCE: Reprinted by permission, from Gloge, ``Dispersion in Weakly Guiding Fibers,'' p. 2442 [30].© 1971 by *Optical Society of America.*

To perform differentiation, note that M is a function of ω. Equation (4.94) enables the definition

$$f_m = \left(\frac{m}{M}\right)^g = K_m \omega^{-2g} \qquad \textbf{[4.96]}$$

where K_m is a parameter independent of ω. Therefore,

$$\frac{df_m}{d\omega} = -\frac{2g}{\omega} f_m.$$

Ignoring the effect of $\partial n_1 / \partial \omega$ (because it is much smaller than the modal dispersion effect in practice) gives

$$\tau_{g,m} = \frac{n_1}{c}(1 - 2\Delta f_m)^{1/2} + \frac{n_1}{c} \times 2\Delta f_m g \times (1 - 2\Delta f_m)^{-1/2}$$

$$= \frac{n_1}{c}[1 - 2\Delta f_m(1 - g)](1 - 2\Delta f_m)^{-1/2}.$$

Because Δ is a small number, $\tau_{g,m}$ can be expanded in a Taylor series of Δ:

$$\tau_{g,m} = \frac{n_1}{c}[1 - 2\Delta f_m(1 - g)]\left(1 + \Delta f_m + \frac{3}{2}\Delta^2 f_m^2 + \cdots\right)$$

$$\approx \frac{n_1}{c}\left[1 + \Delta f_m(2g - 1) + \Delta^2 f_m^2(2g - 0.5)\right]. \qquad \textbf{[4.97]}$$

To calculate modal dispersion, one finds propagation modes that give the minimum and maximum τ_g. The minimum dispersion occurs when the delays at the two endpoints are $f_0 = 0$ and $f_M = 1$. That is,

$$\tau_{g,1} = \frac{n_1}{c}$$

and

$$\tau_{g,M} = \frac{n_1}{c}\left[1 + (2g - 1)\Delta + (2g - 0.5)\Delta^2\right]$$

are the same. In this case, the corresponding or the optimum g satisfies the equation

$$(2g_{opt} - 1) = -\Delta(2g_{opt} - 0.5). \qquad \textbf{[4.98]}$$

This reduces to

$$g_{opt} = \frac{1 + 0.5\Delta}{2(1 + \Delta)} \approx 0.5(1 - 0.5\Delta). \qquad \textbf{[4.99]}$$

Because $g = \alpha/(\alpha + 2)$,

$$\alpha_{opt} = \frac{2g_{opt}}{1 - g_{opt}} \approx 2(1 - \Delta). \qquad \textbf{[4.100]}$$

Under the above condition, modal dispersion can be computed as the difference between $\tau_{g,0}$ and $\tau_{g,m}$ with $f_m = 0.5$. That is,

$$D_{modal} = \tau_{g,0} - \tau_{g,m} = \frac{n_1}{c}\left\{0.25\Delta^2 - 0.125\Delta^2\right\} = \frac{n_1}{c}\frac{\Delta^2}{8}. \qquad \textbf{[4.101]}$$

Thus, D_{modal} for graded-index fibers is proportional to Δ^2, much smaller than D_{modal} of step-index fibers.

APPENDIX 4–E: TOTAL FIBER DISPERSION DERIVATION

The square sum expression of the total fiber dispersion given by Equation (4.42) can be understood as follows [31]. Assume that a pulse consists of components of different frequencies and propagation modes:

$$p(t) = \sum_{i,m} p(t, \lambda_i, m) \qquad \textbf{[4.102]}$$

where i is the index to different frequency components, and m is the index to different propagation modes. The root mean square (RMS) pulse width is defined as

$$\Delta w \overset{\text{def}}{=} \left[\sum_{i,m} (\tau_{i,m} - \overline{\tau})^2 p(\lambda_i, m) \right]^{1/2} \qquad \textbf{[4.103]}$$

where $p(\lambda_i, m)$ is the percentage power of pulse $p(t, \lambda_i, m)$ with respect to the total power, and $\overline{\tau}$ is the average delay over both i and m. That is,

$$\overline{\tau} = \sum_{i,m} \tau_{i,m} p(i, m).$$

Using

$$\tau_{i,m} - \overline{\tau} = \tau_{i,m} - \overline{\tau_m} + \overline{\tau_m} - \overline{\tau} \qquad \textbf{[4.104]}$$

where

$$\overline{\tau_m} = \sum_i \tau_{i,m} \frac{p(i, m)}{p(m)} \qquad \textbf{[4.105]}$$

and $p(m) = \Sigma_i\ p(\lambda_i, m)$, then

$$(\tau_{i,m} - \overline{\tau})^2 = (\tau_{i,m} - \overline{\tau_m})^2 + (\overline{\tau_m} - \overline{\tau})^2 + 2(\tau_{i,m} - \overline{\tau_m})(\overline{\tau_m} - \overline{\tau}). \qquad \textbf{[4.106]}$$

The sum of the last term on the right-hand side of Equation (4.106) over i is zero because of Equation (4.105). Thus, from Equation (4.103),

$$(\Delta w)^2 = \sum_m \left[D_{intra,m}^2 p(m) + (\overline{\tau_m} - \overline{\tau})^2 p(m) \right] = \sum_m \left[D_{intra,m}^2 p(m) + D_{modal}^2 \right] \qquad \textbf{[4.107]}$$

where

$$D_{intra,m}^2 = \sum_i (\tau_{i,m} - \tau_m)^2 \frac{p(i, m)}{p(m)} \qquad \textbf{[4.108]}$$

and

$$D_{modal}^2 = \sum_m (\overline{\tau_m} - \overline{\tau})^2 p(m). \qquad \textbf{[4.109]}$$

Denoting

$$D_{intra}^2 = \sum_m D_{intra,m}^2 p(m) \qquad \textbf{[4.110]}$$

as the average intramodal dispersion results in the square sum expression given by Equation (4.42).

PROBLEMS

Problem 4–1 Fiber Attenuation: If a fiber has an attenuation of 4.5 dB/km, find the ratio of the output power to the input power over 10 km distance. If the input power is -3 dBm, what is the output power in mW?

Problem 4–2 Fiber Attenuation: Assume two fibers have attenuations x and y dB/km, respectively ($x > y$). Find the distance over which the ratio of the power loss is 2.

Problem 4–3 Photon Detection: If a fiber has an attenuation of 5 dB/km and the power coupled from the light source to the fiber is 10 mW, find
  a. The received power if the fiber has a length of 10 km.
  b. The number of photons (if all detected) in 1 nsec. Assume the wavelength is 1.5 μm.

Problem 4–4 Receiver Sensitivity: If at least 500 photons must be received on average for a given detection performance and the fiber has an attenuation of 0.6 dB/km, find the attenuation limit (distance versus bit rate) if the transmission power coupled to the fiber is 5 mW. Assume all photons received can be detected and the wavelength is 1.5 μm. What is the upper limit for the bit rate if $L = 10$ km? How about the case if $L = 50$ km?

Problem 4–5 Power Budget: If the transmission power is 2 mW and the minimum required received power is 0.1 μW, calculate the power budget in dB. To decrease the power budget by 3 dB, what will the new transmission power (received power unchanged) be in dBm?

Problem 4–6 Power Budget: If a given fiber has an attenuation of 1 dB/km and the total coupling and splicing loss is 6 dB, find the minimum power budget needed to transmit 50 km. On the other hand, if the power budget is only 35 dB, how can a signal be transmitted using the same fiber? To transmit 50 km, what is the maximum tolerable fiber attenuation? Assume the same coupling and splicing loss in each case.

Problem 4–7 Attenuation and Power Budget: Assume the fiber attenuation of a given fiber is $\alpha_{fiber} = 0.4$ dB/km, and the minimum required input power is 0.5 μW at 50 Mb/s for a given receiver.
  a. Find the minimum power budget for a transmission of 100 km. Assume there is a coupler every 15 km at a coupling loss of 0.5 dB each, and neglect coupling loss at the source and photodetector.
  b. Find and plot the attenuation limit for the conditions given in *a*. Assume the available power budget at 50 Mb/s is 50 dB. When you plot the attenuation limit, find L_{max} at $B = 5$, 50, and 500 Mb/s.
  c. With the same conditions in *a*, if the light source at the transmitter side has output power of 10 mW, find the actual power budget at 50 Mb/s. Is this good enough?
  d. With the same conditions in *a* except that the transmission distance is 200 km, how many repeaters are needed to transmit data at 200 Mb/s? Do not take dispersion into consideration, but assume the same coupling loss condition of *a*.

Problem 4–8 Geometric Optics: For a step-index fiber with $n_1 = 1.47$ and $n_2 = 1.465$, find (*a*) the critical angle, (*b*) the numerical aperture, and (*c*) the range of the propagation velocity along the fiber.

Problem 4–9 Light Propagation: For a step-index fiber, assume its core index is $n_1 = 1.45$ and the cladding index is $n_2 = 1.44$. Also assume the free space wavelength of the light is 1.5 μm.

    a. What is the numerical aperture (NA)?

    b. What is the critical angle θ_{crit}?

    c. What is the range of the propagation velocity along the fiber axis according to geometrical optics?

    d. What is the fiber dispersion according to geometrical optics?

    e. For propagation modes, what is the range of propagation constant β_z along the fiber axis if the free space wavelength is 1.2 μm?

Problem 4–10 Light Propagation: Suppose a step-index fiber has a refractive index $n_1 = 1.50$ in the core and $n_2 = 1.49$ in the cladding.

    a. At $\lambda = 1.5$ μm, find the propagation condition for β_z.

    b. Find the corresponding condition of the eigenvalue of propagation modes.

Problem 4–11 Group Velocity: Under the same assumptions of Problem 4–10, find the possible range of the group velocity of propagation modes. What is the dispersion in this case? Also, if the group velocity is in the middle of the group velocity range, what is the corresponding eigenvalue?

Problem 4–12 Dispersion Equation: Assume a propagation mode of an optical fiber has the following dispersion relationship:

$$\left(\frac{2\pi n_1}{\lambda}\right)^2 = \beta_1^2 = \beta_z^2 + \beta_z/a$$

where $a = 30$ μm is the diameter of the core. Let the refractive indices of the core and cladding be 1.50 and 1.49, respectively.

    a. Find the cutoff wavelength above which the mode cannot propagate. Express this cutoff wavelength in terms of n_1, n_2, and a.

    b. Find the group velocity as a function of the wavelength at 1.30 μm. Let $n_{1g} = 1.55$.

    c. At 1.30 μm, assume the material dispersion is zero. Find the intramodal dispersion of this propagation mode.

Problem 4–13 Intramodal Dispersion: The waveguide dispersion, according to Gloge [30], is given by

$$D_{waveguide} = -\frac{n_{1g} - n_{2g}}{c\lambda}\left[\frac{Vd^2(Vb)}{dV^2}\right]$$

where b is a parameter given by $(\beta_z/k - n_2)/(n_1 - n_2)$. For a given fiber, assume $n_{1g} - n_{2g} = 0.004$, $NA = 0.04$, and $a = 10$ μm. Use Figure 4.27 to find the waveguide dispersion at $\lambda = 1.6$ μm. If the material dispersion of a given fiber is 15 ps/nm·km, find the total intramodal dispersion.

Problem 4–14 Intermodal Dispersion of Graded-Index Multimode Fibers: For a graded-index fiber with $n_1 = 1.50$ and $NA = 0.2$, find the modal dispersion.

Problem 4–15 Intermodal Dispersion of Step-Index Multimode Fibers: For a step-index fiber with $n_1 = 1.5$, find the refractive index n_2 such that the dispersion is 10 nsec/km.

Problem 4–16 Total Dispersion: Consider the following three kinds of fiber with $\Delta = 0.005$, $n_{1g} = 1.6$, linewidth $\Delta\lambda = 0.5$ nm, and $D_{material} = 15$ ps/km·nm. Calculate the total dispersion for each case.

a. Single-mode fiber with $D_{waveguide} = -5$ ps/km·nm.
b. Multimode step-index fiber with $D_{waveguide} = 5$ ps/km·nm.
c. Multimode graded-index fiber with $D_{waveguide} = 5$ ps/km·nm.

Problem 4–17 Dispersion: Calculate various kinds of dispersion for the following fibers and light sources. Use Figure 4.27.

a. Find the modal dispersion of a step-index multimode fiber with $n_1 = 1.48$, $n_2 = 1.45$. Assume $n_{1g} = n_1$ and $n_{2g} = n_2$.
b. Find the modal dispersion of a graded-index multimode fiber with the same indices as in a.
c. For the same graded-index fiber as in b, if the intramodal dispersion is 30 ps/km · nm and the light source has a linewidth 2 nm, find the total dispersion.
d. Find the intramodal dispersion of a step-index single-mode fiber with the same indices as in a. In addition, assume the wavelength is 1.4 μm and the core diameter is 4 μm. Assume $D_{material} = 0$ at 1.4 μm.
e. For the same single-mode fiber as in d, but operated at a wavelength of zero intramodal dispersion, what is the the total dispersion if $\partial D_{intra}/\partial\lambda = 100$ps/km·nm^2 and linewidth $\Delta\lambda = 1$ nm.

Problem 4–18 Dispersion Limit: Assume the fiber dispersion is 1 nsec/km. Find the dispersion limit (distance versus bit rate) if the total dispersion at the receiving end should be less than 25 percent of the bit interval. Let $B_{max} = 1$ Gb/s.

Problem 4–19 Dispersion Limit: For a laser diode operating at wavelength 1.55 μm and a dispersion-shifted, single-mode fiber with $D_{intra} = 0$ at 1.55 μm, plot the dispersion limit as a function of the bit rate at $\partial D_{intra}/\partial\lambda = 100$ psec/km·nm·μm. Assume the linewidth of the light output is 0.01 nm and $B_{max} = 10$ Gb/s.

Problem 4–20 System Design: Suppose your supervisor asks you to design an optical fiber link with the following requirements:

1. Transmission rate $= 500$ Mb/s.
2. Transmission distance $= 50$ km.
3. Maximum allowable BER $= 10^{-9}$.

In the market, you find the following components:

Fibers: Two types of fibers are available: one single-mode and one step-index multimode. For both types of fibers, $n_1 = 1.47$, $n_2 = 1.46$, $n_{1g} = 1.50$, $n_{2g} = 1.49$, $D_{intra} = 20$ psec/km·nm at $\lambda = 1.55$ μm, $D_{intra} = 0$ at $\lambda = 1.30$ μm, $\partial D_{intra}/\partial\lambda = 0.1$ psec/km·nm^2 at $\lambda = 1.30$ μm, $\partial D_{intra}/\partial\lambda = 0.081$ psec/km·nm^2 at

$\lambda = 1.55$ μm, and $\alpha_{fiber} = 1$ dB/km at $\lambda = 1.30 \mu$m and 0.2 dB/km for $\lambda = 1.55$ μm. Assume $B_{max} = \infty$ and $k_b = 2$.

Light Sources: Two types of light sources are available: one single frequency laser diode and one multimode of a linewidth of $\Delta\lambda = 0.1 \mu$m. Both light sources can be operated at $\lambda = 1.30$ μm or 1.55 μm and have an output power of 1 mW.

Receivers: Only one kind is available. The photodetector can detect signals at both $\lambda = 1.3$ μm and 1.55 μm. At BER $= 10^{-9}$ and transmission rate $B = 100$ Mb/s, the minimum input power required is -30 dBm for both wavelengths. The receiver follows the rule that P_{min} is linearly proportional to the bit rate.

Couplers: Two kinds of couplers are available. The first kind connects single-mode fibers to light sources or photodetectors, and its loss is 0.5 dB per connection. The second kind connects multimode fibers to light sources or photodetectors, and its loss is 0.1 dB per connection.

For each possible combination of the above components, please find:

- *a.* The attenuation limit and plot it.
- *b.* The dispersion limit and plot it.
- *c.* Which combinations satisfy the specifications. For each of the other combinations, indicate whether it is the attenuation, the dispersion, or both that do not satisfy the specifications.

Problem 4–21 Dispersion-Shifted Fibers: Assume the material dispersion of a fiber at $\lambda = 1.4$ μm is 10 ps/nm·km.

- *a.* Find V so that the total intramodal dispersion is zero. Assume $n_{1g} - n_{2g} = 0.01$. Use Equation (4.56) and Figure 4.27.
- *b.* Find the corresponding core radius a if $n_1 = 1.5$ and $n_2 = 1.49$.

Problem 4–22 Polarization-Maintaining Fibers:

- *a.* If $\Delta\beta = \beta_x - \beta_y$ of a fiber is 10 deg/m, find the corresponding birefringence at $\lambda = 1.5$ μm.
- *b.* If the power coupling over a transmission distance of 100 km is required to be within 1 percent, find the required h value.

REFERENCES

1. S. Cheng et al., "Single Mode Lightwave Transmission Experiments at 432 and 144 Mb/s," *Proceedings of the Integrated Optics and Optical Fiber Communication Conference*, 28C2-3, 1983.

2. A. Mitchell et al., "Progress on Repeaterless Submarine Systems," *Proceedings of the International Conference on Communications*, 1991, pp. 1210-16.

3. Y. Iwamoto, "Optical Fiber Submarine Communications and Its Evolution," *Anritsu News,* vol. 6, no. 27 (1986).

4. S. D. Dukes, "Photonics for Cable Television System Design," *Communications Engineering and Design*, May 1992, pp. 34–48.

5. K. Petermann, "Mode-Field Characteristics of Single-Mode Fiber Designs," *Conference Records of OFC/IOOC*, 1987, p. 39.

6. P. Kaiser and D. B. Keck, "Fiber Types and Their Status," chapter 2 of *Optical Fiber Telecommunications II*, edited by S. E. Miller and I. P. Kaminow, Academic Press, 1988.

7. M. Ohashi et al., "Optical Loss Property of Silica-Based Single-Mode Fibers," *Journal of Lightwave Technology*, vol. 10, no. 5 (May 1992), pp. 539–543.

8. J. M. Senior, *Optical Fiber Communications: Principles and Practice*, 2nd ed., Prentice-Hall International (UK), 1992.

9. H. G. Haag et al., "Optical Fiber Cables for Subscriber Loops," *Journal of Lightwave Technology*, vol. 7, no. 11 (November 1989), pp. 1667–74.

10. W. C. Young and D. R. Frey, "Fiber Connectors," chapter 7 of *Optical Fiber Telecommunications II*, edited by S. E. Miller and I. P. Kaminow, Academic Press, 1988.

11. S. C. Mettler and C. M. Millter, "Optical Fiber Splicing," chapter 6 of *Optical Fiber Telecommunications II*, edited by S. E. Miller and I. P. Kaminow, Academic Press, 1988.

12. W. B. Jones, *Optical Fiber Communication Systems*, Holt, Rinehart, and Winston, 1988.

13. D. Marcuse, "Selected Topics in the Theory of Telecommunications Fibers," Chapter 3 of *Optical Fiber Telecommunications II*, edited by S. E. Miller and I. P. Kaminow, Academic Press, 1988.

14. J. E. Midwinter, *Optical Fibers for Transmission*, John Wiley and Sons, 1979.

15. G. Keiser, *Optical Fiber Communications*, 2nd ed., McGraw-Hill, 1991.

16. D. Gloge and E.A.J. Marcatili, "Multimode Theory of Graded-Core Fibers," *Bell System Technical Journal*, (November 1973), pp. 1563–78.

17. P. S. Henry, "Lightwave Primer," *IEEE Journal of Quantum Electronics*, vol. 21, no. 12, (December 1985), pp. 1862–79.

18. S. Kawakami and S. Nishida, "Characteristics of a Doubly Clad Optical Fiber with a Low-Index Cladding," *IEEE Journal of Quantum Electronics*, vol. 10, (1974), pp. 879–87.

19. L. G. Cohen et al., "Low-Loss Quadruple-Clad Single-Mode Lightguides with Dispersion below 2 ps/km·nm over the 1.28 μm–1.65 μm Wavelength Range," *Electronics Letters*, vol. 18, no. 24, (1982), pp. 1023–24.

20. W. L. Mammel and L. G. Cohen, "Numerical Prediction of Fiber Transmission Characteristics from Arbitrary Refractive-Index Profiles," *Applied Optics*, vol. 21, (1982), pp. 699–703.

21. A. J. Barlow et al., "Production of Single-Mode Fibers with Negligible Intrinsic Birefringence and Polarization Mode Dispersion," European Conference on Optical Communication '81, September 1981, Copenhagen.

22. T. Okoshi, "Polarization-Maintaining Optical Fibers," Chapter 4 of *Optoelectronic Technology and Lightwave Communications Systems*, edited by Chinlon Lin, New York: Van Nostrand Reinhold, 1989.

23. I. P. Kaminow, "Polarization Maintaining Fibers," *Applied Scientific Research*, vol. 41 (1984), pp. 257–70.

24. J. Noda et al., "Polarization-Maintaining Fibers and Their Applications," *Journal of Lightwave Technology*, vol. 4, no. 8 (August 1986), p. 1071.

25. V. Ramaswamy et al., "Birefringence in Elliptically Clad Borosilicate Single-Mode Fibers," *Applied Optics*, vol. 18 (1979), pp. 4080–84.

26. N. Shibata et al., "Fabrication of Polarization Maintaining and Absorption-Reducing Fibers," *Journal of Lightwave Technology*, vol. 1 (1983), pp. 38–43.

27. R. D. Birch, et al., "Fabrications of Polarization Maintaining Fibers Using Gas-Phase Etching," *Electronics Letters*, vol. 18 (1982), p. 1030.

28. S. Ramo, J. R. Whinnery, and T. Van Duzer, *Fields and Waves in Communications Electronics*, 2nd ed., John Wiley and Sons, 1984.

29. D. Gloge, "Weakly Guiding Fibers," *Applied Optics*, vol. 10 (October 1971), pp. 2252–58.

30. D. Gloge, "Dispersion in Weakly Guiding Fibers," *Applied Optics*, vol. 10, no. 11 (November 1971), pp. 2442–45.

31. R. Olshansky, "Pulse Broadening in Graded-Index Optical Fibers," *Applied Optics*, vol. 15, no. 2, (February 1976), pp. 483–491.

LIGHT DETECTION

This chapter describes light detection principles and practical light detection devices. Light detection is a process that converts incident light into an electrical photocurrent. A light detection device is used at the front end of every optical receiver to generate a photocurrent proportional to the incident light intensity.

There are two main types of light detection devices: **photoconductors** and **photodiodes**. They are both semiconductor devices. Photoconductors' conductivity increases when the intensity of incident light increases. This results in a higher current at a fixed voltage bias. On the other hand, photodiodes absorb photons and generate photocurrent and are the primary type used in communication systems for their high response speeds.

There are two types of photodiodes commonly used: PIN (P-type, intrinsic, N-type) diodes and avalanche photodiodes (APDs). PIN diodes have a sandwich p-i-n semiconductor structure. APDs have an additional layer that has a strong electric field to excite more electron–hole pairs (EHPs) for a larger photocurrent. APDs thus have a current gain greater than unity.

From the communication point of view, a good light detection device should have a high current gain to generate a large photocurrent at a given incident light power. At the same time, it should respond fast to the incident light (a large bandwidth) and add minimal noise. Because the received light signal is generally weak, the added noise is critical to the receiver sensitivity and performance. Noise and speed characteristics of some commercially available PINs and APDs are shown in Table 5.1 [1]. Detailed noise and detection performance discussion will be given in Chapters 6 and 7.

To improve the receiver sensitivity and response speeds, various advanced photodetectors based on InGaAs and InP/GaAs have been studied and developed. These include **metal-semiconductor-metal** (MSM) photodetectors, **separate absorption and multiplication** (SAM) APDs, and **heterophototransistors** (HPTs). Because of good photon absorption of InGaAs in the wavelength range 1.3–1.5 μm and good electrical properties of InP and GaAs, they can achieve a better detection performance. Furthermore, because InGaAs and InP/GaAs have close lattice constants, they can be integrated into **optoelectronic integrated circuits** (OEICs) for integrated light signal detection, amplification, and waveguiding.

Table 5.1 Light detection characteristics of some commercially available photodiodes.

Manufacturer	Model No.	Type	Gain	Responsivity (A/W) @ λ (nm)	Area Diameter (mm)	NEP (W/Hz$^{1/2}$)	Rise Time (nsec)
UDT Sensors	PIN-HS008	Si/PIN	—	0.4 @ 830	0.2 × 0.2	6.3×10^{-15}	0.35
NEC	NDL1202	Si/APD	600	0.7 @ 850	—	—	1.0
Germanium Power Devices	GM4	Ge/PN	—	—	0.3	8×10^{-13}	1.0
NEC	NDL5102	Ge/APD	350	—	0.03	—	0.3
Antel Optronics	AR-D25	InGaAs/PIN	—	—	0.08	1×10^{-10}	0.04
Antel Optronics	AR-D30	InGaAs/APD	30	—	0.08	1×10^{-10}	0.05
AT&T	117	InGaAs/APD	40	—	0.08	—	2.5 Gb/s
BT&D	PDC4310	InGaAs/PIN	—	0.8	0.025	—	0.009 @ 25 GHz
BT&D	PDT0412	InGaAs/PIN	—	—	0.09	—	5.0
GE Canada	C30616E	InGaAs/PIN	—	—	0.05	6.0×10^{-14}	0.1
GE Canada	C30644E	InGaAs/APD	30	—	0.05	6.0×10^{-12}	0.1
Mas Tech-Oki	OD150-90	InGaAs/PIN	—	0.8	90	$I_d = 1$ nA	1.0
Mas Tech-Oki	OD150-1000	InGaAs/PIN	—	0.8	1000	$I_d = 30$ nA	20.0
UDT Sensors	PIN 35–075	InGaAs/PIN	—	0.8 @ 1300 0.9 @ 1550	0.08	1×10^{-15}	1.0
Laser Diode	LPDF0120	InGaAs PIN/FET	—	—	0.075	2×10^{-12}	−40 dBm @ 120 MHz
Laser Diode	LPDF0250	InGaAs PIN/FET	—	—	0.075	4×10^{-12}	−35 dBm @ 250 MHz

NOTE: I_d is the dark current, and responsivity is the output photocurrent to incident light power ratio at unity gain. NEP stands for noise equivalent power with units W/Hz$^{1/2}$, which is defined as the required incident power to have a zero dB SNR over a bandwidth $B = 1$ Hz. (See Chapter 6 for detailed discussion.) Silicon photodiodes in general have the smallest NEP and operate in the wavelength range 300–1100 nm with peak responsivity at around $\lambda = 1000$ nm; Ge detectors operate at the wavelength range 600–1500 nm with peak responsivity at around $\lambda = 1400$ nm; and AlGaAs detectors operate at 1000–1700 nm with peak responsivity at around $\lambda = 1600$ nm.

5.1 QUANTUM EFFICIENCY AND RESPONSIVITY

One common characteristic of every light detection device is its light absorption ability. Light absorption is mainly determined by the absorption coefficient α of the detection device and the wavelength of the incident light. As illustrated in Figure 5.1, for an absorption layer of thickness d and absorption coefficient α, the fraction of light power absorbed is $(1 - e^{-\alpha d})$.

Figure 5.2 gives the absorption coefficient of various materials as a function of wavelength. The figure shows that the absorption coefficient of each material drops sharply when the wavelength exceeds a certain value. This sharp drop occurs when the energy of incident photons is smaller than the energy bandgap of the material. That is, when $hf < E_g$ or

$$\lambda > \frac{hc}{E_g} = \frac{1.24}{E_g[\text{eV}]}[\mu\text{m}] \qquad \textbf{[5.1]}$$

photons cannot be absorbed to excite EHPs.

To quantify the photon absorption ability, a parameter called the **quantum efficiency** (η) is used. It is the ratio of the number of excited EHPs to the total number of incident photons. Including the reflection at the device interface, the quantum efficiency for the device illustrated in Figure 5.1 is

$$\eta = (1 - R)(1 - e^{-\alpha d}) \qquad \textbf{[5.2]}$$

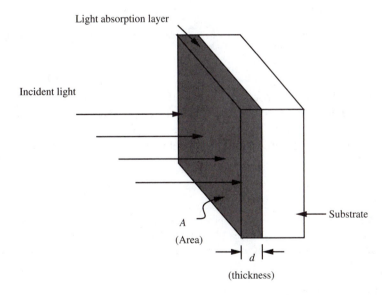

Figure 5.1 Photon absorption of a light detection device.

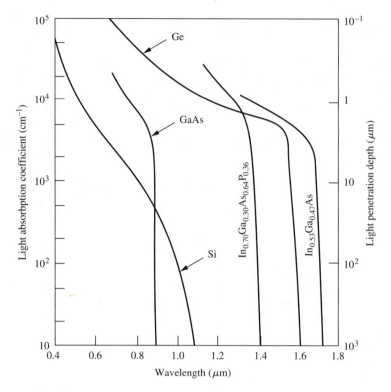

Figure 5.2   Photon absorption coefficient of various materials.

SOURCE: Reprinted, by permission, from Campbell Chapter 14, "Photodetectors for Long-Wavelength Lightwave Systems," edited by C. Lin. p. 367 [2]. ©1989 by Van Nostrand Reinhold.

where $R = r^2$ is the reflectivity at the front interface.[1] This equation assumes that a large fraction of the incident power is absorbed. Therefore, reflection at the substrate interface is neglected. Equation (5.2) shows that the quantum efficiency can be increased by having (1) a smaller reflectivity R, (2) a larger absorption coefficient α, or (3) a larger thickness d.

Example 5.1

QUANTUM EFFICIENCY   Consider a photodetection device whose photon absorption layer has a thickness of 10 μm with refractive index $n = 3.5$ and absorption coefficient $\alpha = 10^5$ m^{-1}. Under these assumptions, the reflection coefficient at the front interface is $r = (3.5 - 1)/(3.5 + 1) = 0.56$.

---

[1] The definition of the quantum efficiency by Equation (5.2) assumes every photon absorbed generates an EHP. Therefore, it is more formally referred to as the **external** quantum efficiency. When a photodiode is at reverse bias, most photons absorbed can contribute to the final photocurrent. This results in a high internal quantum efficiency, and Equation (5.2) can be considered as an approximation of the total quantum efficiency.

The corresponding reflectivity is $R = r^2 = 0.31$. The fraction of absorption in the absorption layer is $1 - e^{-\alpha d} = 0.63$. Therefore, the quantum efficiency is

$$\eta = (1 - 0.31) \times 0.63 = 0.43.$$

If an index-matching fluid of refractive index 2.0 is inserted between the device and the air, then $r_1 = 1/3 = 0.33$ at the air–fluid interface, and $r_2 = 1.5/5.5 = 0.27$ at the fluid–device interface. The net transmissivity is then $T = 1 - R = (1 - r_1^2)(1 - r_2^2) = 0.83$ and the quantum efficiency is

$$\eta = 0.83 \times 0.63 = 0.52. \blacksquare$$

Once the quantum efficiency of a light detection device is known, the corresponding **responsivity** $\mathcal{R}$ of the device is defined as

$$\boxed{\mathcal{R} = \frac{\eta q}{hf} = \frac{\eta \lambda}{1.24} \text{ A/W}} \qquad \textbf{[5.3]}$$

where the wavelength (λ) is in the unit of μm, h is the Planck constant, and f is the frequency in Hz. From the definition, the responsivity of a detection device is the ratio of the output photocurrent to the the incident light power when the current gain is unity. Responsivities of important light detection materials are shown in Figure 5.3. The shaded region indicates the range of variation of practical devices due to different quantum efficiencies.

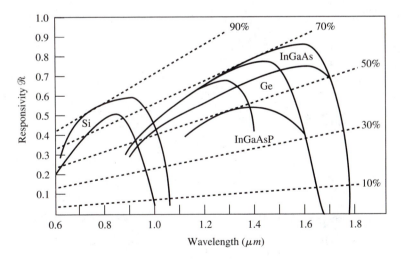

Figure 5.3 Responsivities of typical light detection devices.

SOURCE: Reprinted, by permission, from Hoss, *Fiber Optic Communications, Design Handbook*, p. 77 [3]. ©1990 by Prentice-Hall.

Also note that the responsivity in general increases as the wavelength increases. This can be simply understood from Equation (5.3), where $\mathcal{R}$ is linearly proportional to λ. However, because of the wavelength cutoff condition of Equation (5.1), the responsivity has a sudden drop.

5.2 PHOTOCONDUCTORS

There are two main types of photoconductors: **intrinsic** and **extrinsic**. An intrinsic photoconductor is an intrinsic semiconductor. Its conductivity increases when electrons are excited from the valence band to the conduction band. When there is incident light onto the photoconductor, electrons and holes are excited. As a result, the conductivity increases. On the other hand, an extrinsic photoconductor is a semiconductor with either N-type or P-type doping. Its conductivity increases when electrons (or holes) are excited from their N-type (or P-type) impurity levels. This is illustrated in Figure 5.4. Because intrinsic photoconductors require photons of much higher energies, they exhibit a strong long-wavelength cutoff effect. This can be understood from Equation (5.1).

Because extrinsic photoconductors have free carriers, they have low resistance. This is undesirable from the thermal noise consideration. As will be explained in the next chapter, the mean square current noise is proportional to the conductance. Therefore, the conductance of a photoconductor should be made as small as possible. From this consideration, intrinsic photoconductors are better than extrinsic ones.

The current gain and frequency response of an intrinsic photoconductor are derived as follows. At an incident light power of P_{in}, the amount of the carrier density increase (electrons and holes) is

$$\Delta n = \Delta p = \eta \frac{P_{in}}{hf} \tau_e \frac{1}{V} \qquad \textbf{[5.4]}$$

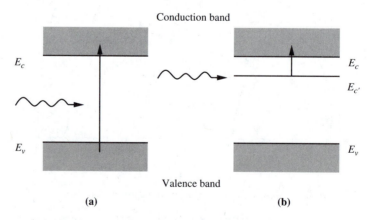

Conduction band

E_c

E_c

$E_{c'}$

E_v

E_v

Valence band

(a)   (b)

Figure 5.4   Energy band diagrams of (a) intrinsic and (b) extrinsic photoconductors.

where τ_e is the relaxation time of the photoconductor material and V is the volume of the absorption layer. Because the conductivity σ_c of a semiconductor is

$$\sigma_c = q(\mu_n n + \mu_p p)$$

where μ_n and μ_p are the mobilities of the electrons and holes, respectively [4], the increase of conductivity due to the incident light is

$$\Delta\sigma_c = \frac{q\eta}{hf} P_{in}(\mu_n + \mu_p)\tau_e \frac{1}{V}. \qquad [5.5]$$

The conductivity is related to the conductance G_c by

$$G_c = \frac{A}{d}\sigma_c$$

where A and d are the area and thickness of the photoconductor. Therefore,

$$\Delta G_c = \frac{q\eta}{hf} P_{in}(\mu_n + \mu_p)\tau_e \frac{1}{d^2}.$$

If the photoconductor is in series with a bias resistance R_F as shown in Figure 5.5, the amount of increased current is

$$\Delta i = \frac{V_{DD}}{R_F + R_c - \Delta R_c} - \frac{V_{DD}}{R_F + R_c} \approx \frac{|\Delta R_c|}{(R_c + R_F)^2} V_{DD} = \frac{R_c^2 V_{DD}}{(R_c + R_F)^2} \Delta G_c$$

$$= \frac{R_c^2 V_{DD}}{(R_c + R_F)^2} \left[\frac{q\eta}{hf} P_{in}(\mu_n + \mu_p)\tau_e \frac{1}{d^2} \right]. \qquad [5.6]$$

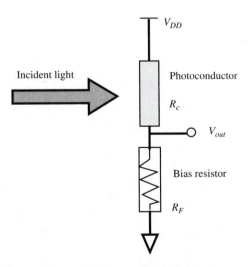

Figure 5.5   Circuit connection of a photoconductor for light detection.

If

$$\tau_t \stackrel{\text{def}}{=} \frac{d}{v_n} = \frac{d}{\mu_n E} = \frac{d^2}{\mu_n V_{DD}} \frac{R_c + R_F}{R_c} \qquad \textbf{[5.7]}$$

is defined as the **electron transit delay** across the conductor, Δi can be expressed as

$$\Delta i = \left[\frac{\eta q}{hf} P_{in} \right] \frac{\tau_e}{\tau_t} \left(1 + \frac{\mu_p}{\mu_n} \right) \frac{R_c}{R_c + R_F} \qquad \textbf{[5.8]}$$

and the photocurrent gain is defined as

$$G \stackrel{\text{def}}{=} \frac{\Delta i / q}{P_{in}/hf} = \eta \frac{\tau_e}{\tau_t} \left(1 + \frac{\mu_p}{\mu_n} \right) \frac{R_c}{R_c + R_F}. \qquad \textbf{[5.9]}$$

In general, $\tau_e \gg \tau_t$; therefore, photoconductors can have a large current gain.

Example 5.2	**CURRENT GAIN OF PHOTOCONDUCTORS** It can be shown (see Problem 5–4) that the optimum bias resistance R_F is $R_c/4.0$. Given this and assuming $\mu_p/\mu_n = 0.2$ and $\eta = 0.4$,

$$G = 0.4 \times 1.2 \times 0.8 \times \frac{\tau_e}{\tau_t} = 0.38 \frac{\tau_e}{\tau_t}.$$

If the photoconductor has a thickness $d = 10$ μm and is made of InGaAs with electron mobility $\mu_n = 10,000$ cm²/V-s, τ_t at a bias voltage $V_{DD} R_c/(R_c + R_F) = 15$ V is

$$\tau_t = \frac{d^2}{15\mu_n} = 6.7 \text{ psec.}$$

If the relaxation time constant $\tau_e = 1$ nsec, the current gain is

$$G = 0.38 \times \frac{1000}{6.7} = 57.$$

If the photoconductor were made of Si instead, it would have a much higher τ_e, typically between 1 μsec and 1 msec [5]. At $\tau_e = 1$ μsec,

$$G = 0.38 \times \frac{10^6}{6.7} = 5.7 \times 10^4.$$

This is 1000 times that of InGaAs. ∎

The frequency response of the current gain has a low pass characteristic [5] and can be given by

$$H(f) = \frac{1}{1 + j2\pi f \tau_e}. \qquad \textbf{[5.10]}$$

Therefore, the 3 dB bandwidth is

$$B_{3dB} = \frac{1}{2\pi \tau_e}. \qquad\qquad \textbf{[5.11]}$$

Comparing Equations (5.9) and (5.11) shows that there is a trade-off between the current gain and 3 dB bandwidth.

BANDWIDTH OF PHOTOCONDUCTORS At the assumed τ_e values in the previous example for In-GaAs and Si, the 3 dB bandwidths according to Equation(5.11) are 160 MHz and 160 kHz, respectively. ∎ | **Example 5.3**

Because of a large τ_e compared to the transit delay τ_t, photoconductors are not useful for high-speed communications. The photodiodes discussed next are a better choice.

5.3 PHOTODIODES

As mentioned earlier, there are two main types of photodiodes: PINs and APDs. The structure of a typical PIN diode is shown in Figure 5.6, where photons are coupled to the left-hand side of the diode and pass through an intrinsic region. A photon with sufficient energy (hf) can excite an electron–hole pair. If the pair is in the presence of a large electric field, the electron and hole will be separated and move quickly in opposite directions, resulting in a photocurrent. If the pair is in the presence of a small or zero electric field, they move slowly and may even recombine and generate heat. Therefore, a strong electric field in the depletion region is essential.

Because one absorbed photon generates one EHP in PINs, the photocurrent is a linear function of the input optical power P_{in}:

$$\boxed{I_{ph} = \eta \frac{q}{hf} P_{in} = \left(\eta \frac{\lambda}{1.24} \right) P_{in} = \mathcal{R} P_{in}} \qquad\qquad \textbf{[5.12]}$$

where η is the quantum efficiency discussed earlier and λ is the wavelength in μm.

Figure 5.7 shows the I-V characteristics at different input power levels. At zero input power, the reverse bias current is called the **dark current**. The total current is thus

$$I_{tot} = I_d + I_{ph} = I_d + \mathcal{R} P_{in}. \qquad\qquad \textbf{[5.13]}$$

For APDs, because of the current gain from EHP multiplications, the generated photocurrent is

$$I_{ph} = M_{apd} \mathcal{R} P_{in} \qquad\qquad \textbf{[5.14]}$$

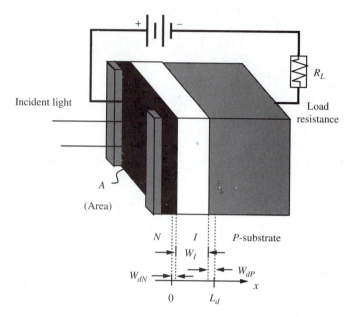

Figure 5.6   A PIN diode.

where M_{apd} is the multiplication gain of the APD. For PINs, the same equation holds, with $M_{apd} = 1$.

Unlike LEDs and LDs, photodiodes are generally operated at reverse bias for detection in optical communications. There are several reasons for this reverse bias operation:

1. Photodiodes have a large resistance at reverse bias. This allows a large bias or load resistance for high impedance detection. As Chapter 7 will explain, a large input resistance can minimize the input current noise.

2. The electric field in the absorption region is large with reverse bias. As a result, carriers generated from photon absorption move quickly to the external circuit. This implies fast response.

3. The width of the depletion region is large at reverse bias. This results in a small junction capacitance and, consequently, a small RC time constant. This also means a fast response.

The reverse-bias detection is also called **photoconductive** (PC) **detection**. This is in contrast to another operation mode called **photovoltaic** (PV) **detection**, where the bias voltage is zero. The advantage of PV detection is its zero dark current at zero bias voltage. However, because it has a small depletion width and electric field, the response speed is low. Therefore, PV detection is mainly used in instrumentation and not appropriate for high-speed detection. In high-speed optical communications, PIN and APD diodes are all operated in the PC mode.

The dark current I_d from the reverse bias is undesirable because it adds not only to the total current output but also to the total noise. It contributes to the so-called **shot noise** at the photodetection output (see Chapter 6). In general, the shot noise power is proportional

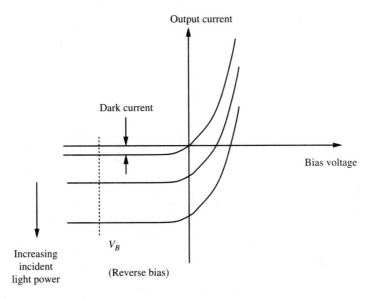

Figure 5.7 I-V characteristic of a reverse-bias PIN.

to the total current output. Therefore, it is important for a photodiode to have as small a dark current as possible. Figure 5.8 shows the dark current density of some photodetection materials. The figure shows that Si photodiodes give the smallest dark current density. On the other hand, Ge photodiodes have the largest dark current density. This dark current characteristic can be observed from the NEP of practical devices shown in Table 5.1. Because there is current leakage under reverse bias, it should be noted that the actual dark current can depend strongly on the device packaging.

5.4 PIN DIODES

As depicted in Figure 5.6, a PIN diode has an intrinsic layer (I) between an N-type and P-type layers. The N- and P-type layers usually have relatively higher doping levels compared to the lightly doped intrinsic layer. In practice, the intrinsic layer is not exactly intrinsic. It can be lightly N- or P-type doped.

Quantum Efficiency Because of the sandwich structure of photodiodes, the quantum efficiency expression given earlier in Equation (5.2) needs to be modified. As illustrated in Figure 5.6, incident photons first come to the N-type layer from the left-hand side. Because (1) the N-type layer can absorb incident photons and (2) photocurrent is generated in the intrinsic I-type layer, the modified expression for the quantum efficiency is

$$\eta = (1 - R)e^{-\alpha_N W_N}(1 - e^{-\alpha_I W_I})$$

[5.15]

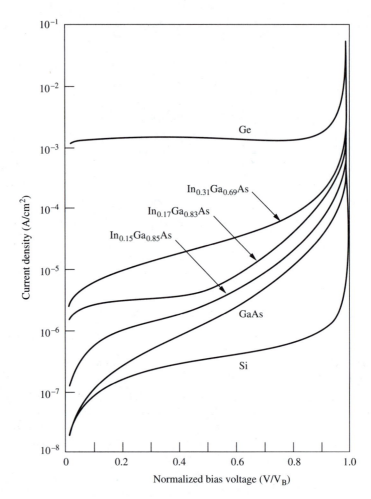

Figure 5.8   Dark-current density as a function of the normalized voltage for Ge, InGaAs, GaAs, and Si photodiodes. The normalized voltage is V/V_B, where V_B is the breakdown voltage.

| SOURCE: Reprinted, by permission, from Susa et al. [6]. ©1980 by IEEE.

where W_N and W_I are the thickness of N-type and I-type layers, respectively, and α_N and α_I are the photon absorption coefficients of the N-type and I-type layers, respectively. In this expression, the small reflection at the I–P interface is neglected.

Example 5.4   **QUANTUM EFFICIENCY OF PIN DIODES**   Using the same assumptions given in Example 5.1 and assuming $W_N = 1.0 \ \mu$m, there is an additional attenuation factor

$$e^{-\alpha W_N} = 0.9.$$

Therefore, when there is no matching fluid, the quantum efficiency reduces to

$$\eta = 0.43 \times 0.9 = 0.39.$$

When the matching fluid is used,

$$\eta = 0.52 \times 0.9 = 0.47. \blacksquare$$

5.4.1   REVERSE BIAS AND ELECTRIC FIELD DISTRIBUTION

As mentioned earlier, PIN diodes are reverse biased in normal operation. The reverse bias sweeps away all free charges between the N–I interface and the I–P interface. Consequently, there are only space charges left, which result in a high electric field. This high electric field region is called the depletion region and is the place where useful photocurrent is generated.

The relationship between the charge density $\rho(x)$ and the electric field $E(x)$ is described by the Poisson equation [7]:

$$\frac{\partial E}{\partial x} = \frac{1}{\epsilon_r \epsilon_0} \rho(x)$$

or

$$E(x) = \frac{1}{\epsilon_r \epsilon_0} \int_{-\infty}^{x} \rho(x') dx'. \qquad [5.16]$$

The voltage $V(x)$ by definition is related to the electric field by

$$\frac{\partial V}{\partial x} = -E(x)$$

or

$$V(x) = -\int_{-\infty}^{x} E(x') dx'. \qquad [5.17]$$

From the charge distribution shown in Figure 5.9b and Equation (5.16), the slope of the electric field is $qN_D/\epsilon_r \epsilon_0$, $-qN_I/\epsilon_r \epsilon_0$, and $-qN_A/\epsilon_r \epsilon_0$ in the N-, I-, and P-type layers, respectively. Here the intrinsic layer is assumed to be slightly P-type doped. Therefore, if the maximum electric field is E_{max} at the N–I interface, the depletion width on the N-type side is

$$W_{dN} = \epsilon_r \epsilon_0 \frac{E_{max}}{qN_D}. \qquad [5.18]$$

The electric field at the I–P interface is

$$E_{IP} = E_{max} - W_I \frac{qN_I}{\epsilon_r \epsilon_0} \stackrel{\text{def}}{=} E_{max}(1 - \Delta) \qquad [5.19]$$

where

$$\Delta \stackrel{\text{def}}{=} \frac{qN_I W_I}{\epsilon_r \epsilon_0 E_{max}}$$

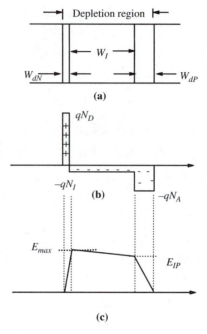

Figure 5.9   Charge and electric field distribution in a PIN diode: (a) depletion region, (b) charge density, and (c) electric field distribution.

is the electric field drop. The depletion width on the P-type side is thus

$$W_{dP} = \epsilon_r \epsilon_0 \frac{E_{max}}{q N_A} - W_I \frac{N_I}{N_A}.$$ [5.20]

By integrating the electric field shown above according to Equation (5.17), the total voltage across the depletion region is found to be

$$V_{PIN} + V_{bi} = \frac{1}{2}[E_{max} W_{dN} + (E_{max} + E_{IP})W_I + E_{IP} W_{dP}]$$

or

$$V_{PIN} + V_{bi} = \frac{\epsilon_r \epsilon_0}{2q} E_{max}^2 \left[\frac{1}{N_D} + \frac{(2 - \Delta)\Delta}{N_I} + \frac{(1 - \Delta)^2}{N_A} \right]$$ [5.21]

where

$$V_{bi} = V_T \ln \left(\frac{N_D N_A}{n_i^2} \right)$$

is the built-in junction voltage [4], and n_i is the intrinsic carrier density. Note that Δ is positive when the intrinsic region is P-type. It is negative otherwise.

If V_{PIN} just depletes the intrinsic layer (or $E_{IP} = 0$), it is called the **reach-through voltage**. In other words, it is the minimum voltage to deplete the intrinsic region. If a smaller voltage is applied across the PIN diode, carriers have a smaller drift velocity, which results in a slower response. On the other hand, the applied bias voltage should be low enough to avoid junction breakdown.

REVERSE BIASED PIN Consider an N$^+$-P-P$^+$ PIN diode with doping levels 10^{21}, 10^{19}, and 10^{20} m^{-3}, respectively. Assume its dielectric constant is $\epsilon_r = 11.8$ and the intrinsic region width is 20 μm. From the relation $dE/dx = qN/\epsilon_r \epsilon_0$, | **Example 5.5**

$$\frac{dE(x)}{dx} = \begin{cases} 1.53 \times 10^{12} \text{ V/m}^2 & \text{N-type layer} \\ -1.53 \times 10^{10} \text{ V/m}^2 & \text{Intrinsic layer} \\ -1.53 \times 10^{11} \text{ V/m}^2 & \text{P-type layer} \end{cases}$$

where $q/\epsilon_r \epsilon_0 = 1.53 \times 10^{-9}$ V$\cdot$m. At reach-through, $\Delta = 1$ and $E_{max} = qN_I W_I/\epsilon_r \epsilon_0$. Therefore,

$$V_{PIN} + V_{bi} = \frac{q}{2\epsilon_r \epsilon_0} W_I^2 \left(\frac{N_I^2}{N_D} + N_I \right)$$

$$= 0.5 \times 1.53 \times 10^{-9} \times (20 \times 10^{-6})^2 \times 10^{19} = 3.06 \text{ V}.$$

Assuming $n_i = 10^{12}$ m^{-3},

$$V_{bi} = 0.026 \times \ln(10^{17}) = 1.02 \text{ V}.$$

This gives $V_{PIN} = 2.04$ V. If $E_{max} = 10^6$ V/m,

$$\Delta = 1.53 \times 10^{-9} \times \frac{10^{19} \times 2 \times 10^{-5}}{10^6} = 0.31.$$

Then,

$$V_{PIN} + 1.02 = 0.5 \times \frac{10^{12}}{1.53 \times 10^{-9}} \left(\frac{1}{10^{21}} + \frac{1.69 \times 0.31}{10^{19}} + \frac{0.69^2}{10^{20}} \right) = 19 \text{ V}.$$

Consequently,

$$E_{IP} = E_{max}(1 - 0.31) = 6.9 \times 10^5 \text{ V/m}$$

$$W_{dN} = \frac{10^6}{1.53 \times 10^{12}} = 0.65 \ \mu\text{m}$$

and

$$W_{dP} = \frac{6.9 \times 10^5}{1.53 \times 10^{11}} = 4.5 \ \mu\text{m}. \ \blacksquare$$

5.4.2 FREQUENCY RESPONSE

The response time of a PIN diode is fundamentally limited by the transit delay of electrons and holes through the depletion region. The frequency response can be obtained from the following simplified model.

If one assumes light is completely absorbed in the N-type region of the diode in Figure 5.6, in other words, neglecting the interaction between carriers and photons in the intrinsic region, one can derive the frequency response using simplified carrier density transport equations [8]–[11]. Under this simplified model, the total output current density is given by

$$J_{out}(t) = \frac{1}{L_d} \int_0^{L_d} \left[J_n(x, t) + J_p(x, t) \right] dx \qquad \textbf{[5.22]}$$

where $L_d = W_{dN} + W_I + W_{dP}$ is the total depletion region width, and $J_n(x, t)$ and $J_p(x, t)$ are the electron and hole current densities in the depletion region satisfying the following transport equations:

$$\frac{\partial J_n(x, t)}{\partial t} - v_n \frac{\partial J_n(x, t)}{\partial x} = 0 \qquad \textbf{[5.23]}$$

and

$$\frac{\partial J_p(x, t)}{\partial t} + v_p \frac{\partial J_p(x, t)}{\partial x} = 0 \qquad \textbf{[5.24]}$$

Here v_n and v_p are the drift velocities of electrons and holes, respectively. Solving these two equations requires using the following two boundary conditions:

$$J_n(0, t) = \frac{q\eta}{hf} \frac{P_{in}(t)}{A}$$

and

$$J_p(0, t) = 0.$$

These boundary conditions are based on the approximation that all photon absorption at $x = 0$.

If the incident light is AM modulated and has the following form:

$$P_{in}(t) = P_0(1 + k_m e^{j\omega_m t}) \qquad \textbf{[5.25]}$$

one can solve Equations (5.23) and (5.24) and have

$$J_n(x, t) = J_0 + k_m J_0 e^{j\omega_m (t + x/v_n)}$$

and

$$J_p(x, t) = 0.$$

Therefore, the average photocurrent density from Equation (5.22) is

$$J_{out}(t) = J_0 \left[1 + k_m \frac{v_n}{j\omega_m L_d} (e^{j\omega_m L_d/v_n} - 1) e^{j\omega_m t} \right].$$

From this, the signal component has a transfer function

$$H(\omega) = \frac{1}{j\omega\tau_t}(e^{j\omega\tau_t}-1) = e^{j\omega\tau_t/2}\frac{2\sin(\omega\tau_t/2)}{\omega\tau_t} = e^{j\omega\tau_t/2}\text{sinc}(\omega\tau_t/2\pi)$$

where $\tau_t = L_d/v_n$ is the transit delay of electrons. The 3 dB bandwidth is when $|H(\omega_{3dB})|^2 = 0.5$. In other words,

$$|H(\omega_{3dB})|^2 = \text{sinc}(\omega_{3dB}\tau_t/2\pi)^2 = 0.5.$$

This gives $\omega_{3dB}\tau_t = 2.8$ or

$$\omega_{3dB} = \frac{2.8}{\tau_t} \text{ or } f_{3dB} = \frac{0.45}{\tau_t}. \qquad\qquad \textbf{[5.26]}$$

PIN DIODE FREQUENCY RESPONSE   Suppose $L_d = 30 \ \mu$m and $v_n = 3 \times 10^5$ m/sec. The transit delay is: **Example 5.6**

$$\tau_t = \frac{L_d}{v_n} = 100 \text{ psec.}$$

Therefore, the 3 dB bandwidth ($f_{3dB} = \omega_{3dB}/2\pi$) of this PIN device is 4.5 GHz. ∎

How to Improve Response Speed   As discussed above the response bandwidth of a PIN diode is inversely proportional to the transit delay. At a given drift velocity, therefore, the key to a high-speed response is a small width of the intrinsic region. Equation (5.15) shows, however, that this smaller width will result in a smaller quantum efficiency. Therefore, there is a trade-off between speed and quantum efficiency. See Problem 5–10 for illustration.

Even when the quantum efficiency is not a concern, the detection speed cannot be increased by reducing the intrinsic width. When the intrinsic width is small, the junction capacitance of the photodiode at reverse bias can become significant. When an external resistor is used for current–voltage conversion, the equivalent RC circuit can have a large time constant and become the new speed limit. Careful examination of the practical photodiodes listed in Table 5.1 shows this to be the case. This can be seen from the strong correlation between the speed (rise time) and the active area of the diode. When the area is large, the junction capacitance also becomes large, which results in a large time constant or rise time. The relative importance of transit delay and the RC time constant is illustrated in Problem 5–11.

5.5 AVALANCHE PHOTODIODES

A typical APD diode is illustrated in Figure 5.10. In addition to the N, I, and P layers in PIN diodes, it has a high doping P$^+$ layer between the N and I layers. As a result, it has a high electric field that accelerates electrons and holes with high momenta, which in turn excite more electron–hole pairs.

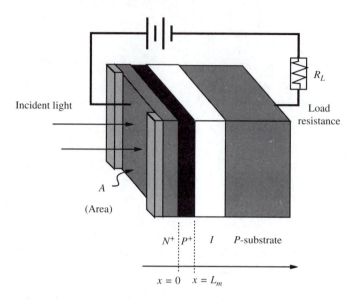

Figure 5.10   An APD diode.

5.5.1 ELECTRIC FIELD DISTRIBUTION

The electric field distribution in an APD diode is illustrated in Figure 5.11. The region between the N^+ and P^+ layers has a high electric field where carrier multiplication takes place. The I-type layer has a smaller electric field, so there is no multiplication. EHPs generated in the I-type layer are called the **primary** EHPs. EHPs generated by the primary EHPs in the multiplication region are called the **secondary** EHPs.

The geometry and doping levels of an APD must be chosen carefully to produce a fast device that operates at a reasonable reverse-bias voltage. As illustrated in Figure 5.11a, when the doping level of the multiplication region P^+ is too heavy, a high E_{max} is required to deplete the intrinsic region. Because a high E_{max} can cause device breakdown, this should be avoided. However, when E_{max} is not large enough to deplete the intrinsic region, the drift velocity is small. This implies a slow device.

On the other hand, as illustrated in Figure 5.11b, if the doping is too light in the multiplication region P^+, the intrinsic region has a high electric field. This implies a large reverse bias, which is undesirable from practical power supply considerations.

Example 5.7

REVERSED BIASED APD Consider an APD detector like that shown in Figure 5.10 with $\epsilon_r = 11.8$. If the multiplication region has a width of 1 μm, the intrinsic region has a width of 10 μm, and the doping levels of N^+ and P^+ are at the same level, 10^{21} m^{-3}, the minimum voltage required to start depleting the intrinsic region is

$$V_{min} = \frac{1}{2} E_{max} L_m = \frac{1}{2} \frac{q N_A}{\epsilon_r \epsilon_0} L_m^2 = 0.77 \text{ V}.$$

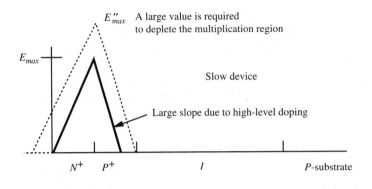

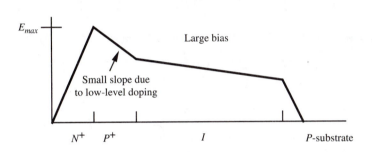

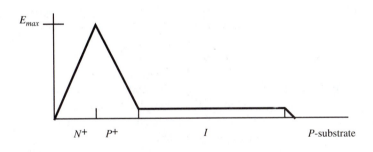

Figure 5.11 The electric field distribution at different doping levels of the multiplication region P^+: (a) doping level is too high and requires a large E_{max}, (b) doping level is too low and requires a large reverse bias, and (c) doping level is proper.

This voltage is small, and the corresponding peak electric field is

$$E_{max} = \frac{2V_{min}}{L_m} = 1.53 \times 10^6 \text{ V/m.}$$

At the same doping level of the N^+ layer, if the device has a heavily doped P^+ layer of $N_A = 10^{22}$ m^{-3}, the peak electric field to deplete the multiplication region is

$$E_{max} = \frac{qN_A}{\epsilon_r \epsilon_0} L_m = 1.53 \times 10^7 \text{ V/m.}$$

This value is too high and can easily cause device breakdown.

Now assume the device has a lightly doped P^+ layer of $N_A = 10^{20}$ m^{-3}. For $E_{max} = 10^7$ V/m to achieve enough multiplication gain, the electric field at the multiplication and intrinsic interface is

$$E_{P+I} = 10^7 - \frac{qN_A}{\epsilon_r \epsilon_0} L_m = 9.8 \times 10^6 \text{ V/m.}$$

At the same intrinsic width of 10 μm, the total voltage across it is approximately

$$V \approx 98 \text{ V.}$$

This voltage is too large for practical reasons. ∎

5.5.2 CURRENT MULTIPLICATION

The avalanche multiplication process is illustrated in Figure 5.12. As shown, primary electrons come to the multiplication region and initiate the multiplication process. As illustrated, a primary electron can excite several secondary EHPs on its way to the anode. At a high electric field or bias, secondary EHPs generated can pick up large momenta and generate more secondary EHPs. If the reverse bias is larger than a certain threshold, this multiplication process can last forever. This is called the **avalanche breakdown** and the corresponding threshold voltage is called the **breakdown voltage**.

The capability for electrons and holes to excite EHPs is characterized by the ionization coefficients α and β, respectively, which represent the multiplication ratio per unit length (in the unit of 1/m). Typical ionization coefficients as a function of the electric field are shown in Figure 5.13. From the figure, note that

1. Electron ionization coefficients of Si and GaAsSb are higher than hole ionization coefficients. For Ge, GaAs, and InGaAs, the opposite is true.

2. Ge has the largest electron and hole ionization coefficients. On the other hand, Si has the smallest hole ionization coefficient. Otherwise, the ionization coefficients are approximately the same.

From the definitions of the ionization coefficients of electrons and holes, the transport equations of electrons and holes in the steady state in the multiplication region can be written as

$$-\frac{dJ_n(x)}{dx} = \alpha(x)J_n(x) + \beta(x)J_p(x) \qquad \textbf{[5.27]}$$

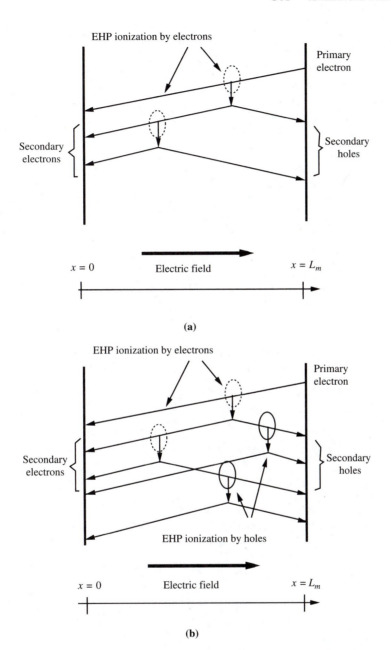

Figure 5.12   The multiplication process: (a) $k = 0$; (b) $k = 1$.

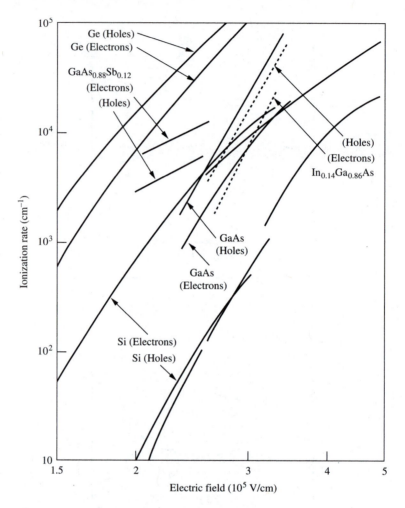

Figure 5.13   Ionization coefficients as a function of the electric field of important photodiode materials.

SOURCE: Reprinted, by permission, from Melchior, "Detectors for Lightwave Communications" [10]. ©1977 by *American Institute of Physics*.

and

$$\frac{dJ_p(x)}{dx} = \alpha(x)J_n(x) + \beta(x)J_p(x) \qquad \textbf{[5.28]}$$

where J_n and J_p are the current densities of electrons and holes in the multiplication region.

EHP MULTIPLICATION BY ONLY ELECTRONS If only electrons can excite EHPs in the multiplication region, then $\beta = 0$. Because the multiplication process is initiated by the electrons at $x = L_m$, one can have the following boundary conditions:

$$J_p(0) = 0 \qquad\qquad \textbf{[5.29]}$$

Example 5.8

and

$$J_n(L_m) = J_{PIN} \qquad\qquad \textbf{[5.30]}$$

where J_{PIN} is the current density generated from the intrinsic layer. Given these boundary conditions, the solution to the transport equations is

$$J_n(x) = J_{PIN}e^{\alpha(L_m-x)} \ \text{ for } 0 < x < L_m$$

and

$$J_p(x) = J_{PIN}e^{\alpha L_m} - J_{PIN}e^{\alpha(L_m-x)}.$$

Therefore, the current multiplication gain is

$$M_{apd,0} \stackrel{\text{def}}{=} \frac{J_n(0)}{J_n(L_m)} = e^{\alpha L_m}. \ \blacksquare \qquad\qquad \textbf{[5.31]}$$

From Equations (5.27) and (5.28), note that the total current density ($J = J_n + J_p$) is a constant. Therefore,

$$-\frac{dJ_n}{dx} = (\alpha - \beta)J_n + \beta J \qquad\qquad \textbf{[5.32]}$$

and

$$-\frac{dJ_p}{dx} = (\alpha - \beta)J_p - \alpha J \qquad\qquad \textbf{[5.33]}$$

Because J is a constant, the above equations are first-order linear differential equations, and the solution of $J_n(x)$ to Equation (5.32) can be given by:

$$J_n(x) = J_1 e^{-(\alpha-\beta)x} + J_2 \qquad\qquad \textbf{[5.34]}$$

where J_1 and J_2 are constants to be solved. The corresponding J_p from Equation (5.32) is

$$J_p(x) = -J_1 e^{-(\alpha-\beta)x} + (J - J_2).$$

Substituting $J_n(x)$ given by Equation (5.34) in Equation (5.32) gives

$$(\alpha - \beta)J_2 + \beta J = 0.$$

The boundary conditions given by Equations (5.29) and (5.30) then give

$$J_1 = -\frac{\alpha}{\beta}J_2$$

and

$$J_2 = \frac{J_{PIN}}{1 - (\alpha/\beta)e^{-(\alpha-\beta)L_m}}.$$

As a result,

$$J_n(x) = \frac{k - e^{-\alpha(1-k)x}}{k - e^{-\alpha(1-k)L_m}} J_{PIN} \qquad \textbf{[5.35]}$$

and

$$J_p(x) = -\frac{1 - e^{-\alpha(1-k)x}}{k - e^{-\alpha(1-k)L_m}} J_{PIN} \qquad \textbf{[5.36]}$$

where

$$\boxed{k \stackrel{\text{def}}{=} \frac{\beta}{\alpha}.} \qquad \textbf{[5.37]}$$

The total current density J is thus

$$J = J_n(x) + J_p(x) = \frac{k - 1}{k - e^{-\alpha(1-k)L_m}} J_{PIN} \qquad \textbf{[5.38]}$$

and the multiplication gain is

$$\boxed{M_{apd,0} = \frac{J_n(0)}{J_n(L_m)} = \frac{J}{J_{PIN}} = \frac{(1-k)e^{\alpha L_m(1-k)}}{1 - ke^{\alpha L_m(1-k)}}.} \qquad \textbf{[5.39]}$$

In the above derivation, electrons are assumed to be the primary carriers that initiate the secondary EHP generations. For a different type of APD for which holes are the carriers that initiate the multiplication process, symmetry gives the following gain expression:

$$\boxed{M_{apd,h} \equiv \frac{J_p(0)}{J_p(L_m)} = \frac{(1-1/k)e^{\beta L_m(1-1/k)}}{1 - (1/k)e^{\beta L_m(1-1/k)}}.} \qquad \textbf{[5.40]}$$

| **Example 5.9** | **APD MULTIPLICATION GAIN**   Consider two special cases of Equations (5.39) and (5.40). First, when $k = 0$, it is easy to verify that Equation (5.39) reduces to Equation (5.31). Second, when $k = 1$ or $\alpha = \beta$, $M_{apd} = 1/(1 - \alpha L_m)$. (Why?) In this case, if $\alpha L_m = 1$, the gain is infinite; that is, if there is a strong enough field that has $\alpha = 1/L_m$, the multiplication can continue forever without providing any photocurrent. ∎ |

The multiplication gain as a function of α at different values of k is shown in Figure 5.14. When α becomes large enough, the gain becomes infinite. The voltage to achieve this infinite gain is called the **breakdown voltage**. Some typical values of the breakdown voltage are shown in Table 5.2. In general, Si has the largest breakdown voltage, and Ge the smallest. As a result, Si can sustain a high electric field, which allows it to have a high current gain. Although Ge has the lowest breakdown voltage, as Figure 5.13 shows, it has high ionization coefficients. Therefore, a good current gain still can be achieved.

An empirical equation to express the multiplication gain as a function of reverse bias voltage is

$$M_{apd,0} = \frac{1}{1 - (\frac{V}{V_B})^{n_B}} \qquad \text{[5.41]}$$

where n_B depends on the material and doping profile. Typically, it can vary from 2 to 10.

Table 5.2

Typical APD characteristics.

Devices	Ionization Ratio	Gain	Breakdown Voltage
Si	0.1	100–1000	200 V
Ge	2.0	50–500	5–50 V
InGaAs	1.5	20–50	50–100 V

5.5.3 Frequency Response

Because of the multiplication process, APDs have a slower frequency response compared to PIN diodes. As illustrated in Figure 5.12, carriers in the multiplication region can continue to generate secondary carriers at a large multiplication gain. As a result, the photocurrent impulse response has a long duration, and the frequency response is slow.

Similar to the simplified model used in the PIN diode frequency analysis, the frequency response of an APD can be analyzed by adding time dependent terms to Equations (5.27) and (5.28). As a result, the transport equations can be written as [11]:

$$\frac{1}{v_n} \frac{\partial J_n(x,t)}{\partial t} - \frac{\partial J_n(x,t)}{\partial x} = \alpha(x) J_n(x,t) + \beta(x) J_p(x,t) \qquad \text{[5.42]}$$

and

$$\frac{1}{v_p} \frac{\partial J_p(x,t)}{\partial t} + \frac{\partial J_p(x,t)}{\partial x} = \alpha(x) J_n(x,t) + \beta(x) J_p(x,t). \qquad \text{[5.43]}$$

If the incident light is assumed to have the same form given by Equation (5.25), $J_n(x, t)$ and $J_p(x, t)$ can be expressed as

$$J_n(x, t) = J_{n0}(x) + J_{n1}(x)e^{j\omega_m t} \tag{5.44}$$

$$J_p(x, t) = J_{p0}(x) + J_{p1}(x)e^{j\omega_m t} \tag{5.45}$$

where $J_{n0}(x)$ and $J_{p0}(x)$ are the dc components corresponding to P_0, and $J_{n1}(x)$ and $J_{p1}(x)$ are the ac components corresponding to $P_0 k_m e^{j\omega_m t}$. To derive the frequency response, only the ac components of the above transport equations will be used.

With these assumptions, in the multiplication region where $0 < x < L_m$, Equation (5.42) and (5.43) reduce to

$$\frac{\partial J_{n1}(x)}{\partial x} + a J_{n1}(x) + \beta J_{p1}(x) = 0 \tag{5.46}$$

and

$$\frac{\partial J_{p1}(x)}{\partial x} - b J_{p1}(x) - \alpha J_{n1}(x) = 0 \tag{5.47}$$

where

$$a \stackrel{\text{def}}{=} \alpha - \frac{j\omega_m}{v_n} \tag{5.48}$$

and

$$b \stackrel{\text{def}}{=} \beta - \frac{j\omega_m}{v_p} \tag{5.49}$$

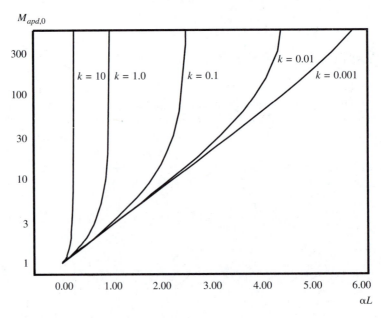

Figure 5.14 DC gain $M_{apd,0}$ versus α at various k values.

In the intrinsic region, the same equations ([5.23] and [5.24]) for PIN diodes can be used. From the time dependence factor $e^{j\omega_m t}$,

$$\frac{\partial J_{n1}(x)}{\partial x} - \frac{j\omega_m}{v_n} J_{n1}(x) = 0 \qquad \textbf{[5.50]}$$

and

$$\frac{\partial J_{p1}(x)}{\partial x} + \frac{j\omega_m}{v_p} J_{p1}(x) = 0 \qquad \textbf{[5.51]}$$

for $L_m < x < L_m + L_d$, where L_d is the depletion width of the intrinsic region.

The boundary conditions are

$$J_{n1}(x = L_m) = k_m J_0 \qquad \textbf{[5.52]}$$

and

$$J_{p1}(x = 0) = 0. \qquad \textbf{[5.53]}$$

Detailed derivation of $J_{n1}(x)$ and $J_{p1}(x)$ is given in Appendix 5–A. The results are

$$J_{n1}(x) = J_0 k_m \frac{(r_2 + a)e^{r_1 x} - (r_1 + a)e^{r_2 x}}{(r_2 + a)e^{r_1 L_m} - (r_1 + a)e^{r_2 L_m}} \qquad \textbf{[5.54]}$$

and

$$J_{p1}(x) = -J_0 k_m \alpha \frac{e^{r_1 x} - e^{r_2 x}}{(r_2 + a)e^{r_1 L_m} - (r_1 + a)e^{r_2 L_m}} \qquad \textbf{[5.55]}$$

for $0 < x < L_m$, where r_1 and r_2 are the two solutions to the eigenvalue equation (5.65). In other words, r_1 and r_2 are from the following expression:

$$r_{1,2} = -\frac{1}{2}(a - b) \pm [\frac{1}{4}(a - b)^2 + (ab - \alpha\beta)]^{1/2}. \qquad \textbf{[5.56]}$$

The average current output is defined as

$$J_{ac} = \frac{1}{L_m + L_d} \int_0^{L_m + L_d} [J_{p1}(x) + J_{n2}(x)] dx. \qquad \textbf{[5.57]}$$

The multiplication gain M_{apd} is defined to be the ratio of the average current density over $0 < x < L_m$ to $k_m J_0$. That is,

$$M_{apd} \stackrel{\text{def}}{=} \frac{\int_0^{L_m} [J_{n1}(x) + J_{p1}(x)] dx / L_m}{k_m J_0}$$

$$= \frac{(r_2 + a - \alpha)r_2(e^{r_1 L_m} - 1) - (r_1 + a - \alpha)r_1(e^{r_2 L_m} - 1)}{L_m r_1 r_2 [(r_2 + a)e^{r_1 L_m} - (r_1 + a)e^{r_2 L_m}]}. \qquad \textbf{[5.58]}$$

At dc or $\omega_m = 0$, this gives the same result given by Equation (5.39) (see Problem 5–14).

Figures 5.15 and 5.16 show the ac gain M_{apd} as a function of the normalized frequency $\omega_m \tau_t$ at different dc gains. In these results, it is assumed that $v_n = v_p$. Using Equation (5.57), one can find the 3 dB frequency at which

$$\left| \frac{J_{ac}}{k_m J_0} \right|^2 = 0.5.$$

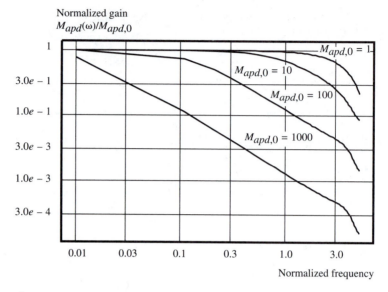

Figure 5.15   Frequency response at different values of $M_{apd,0}$; $k = 0.1$.

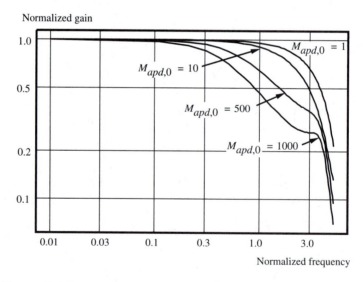

Figure 5.16   Frequency response at different values of $M_{apd,0}$; $k = 0.001$.

From Equations (5.54), (5.55),(5.66), and (5.67) in Appendix 5–A,

$$J_{ac} = \frac{L_m}{L_m + L_d} J_{ac}^{(1)} + \frac{L_d}{L_m + L_d} J_{ac}^{(2)}$$

where

$$J_{ac}^{(1)} = k_m J_0 \frac{(r_2 + a - \alpha)r_2(e^{r_1 L_m}-1) - (r_1 + a - \alpha)r_1(e^{r_2 L_m}-1)}{L_m r_1 r_2[(r_2 + a)e^{r_1 L_m} - (r_1 + a)e^{r_2 L_m}]} \qquad \textbf{[5.59]}$$

is the average current density over the multiplication region, and

$$J_{ac}^{(2)} = k_m J_0 \left[\left(\frac{e^{j\omega_m L_d/v_n}-1}{j\omega_m L_d/v_n} \right) - \alpha \frac{e^{r_1 L_m} - e^{r_2 L_m}}{(r_2 + a)e^{r_1 L_m} - (r_1 + a)e^{r_2 L_m}} \left(\frac{e^{j\omega_m L_d/v_p}-1}{j\omega_m L_d/v_p} \right) \right] \qquad \textbf{[5.60]}$$

is the average current density over the intrinsic region.

Figure 5.17 shows the normalized 3 dB bandwidth ($\omega_B \tau_t$) as a function of the dc multiplication gain $M_{apd,0}$ at different k's and at $L_d = 0$, where $\tau_t = L_m/v_n$. In other words, there is no intrinsic region. In this case, the response bandwidth is entirely determined by the multiplication region. A line $kM_{apd,0} = 1$ is superimposed in the figure. When $kM_{apd,0} < 1$ (above the line), the normalized 3 dB bandwidth stays in a small range around 1.0. When $kM_{apd,0} > 1$ (below the line), on the other hand, the 3 dB bandwidth is inversely proportional to $M_{apd,0}$. In other words, the following empirical formula holds when $kM_{apd,0} > 1$:

$$(\omega_{3dB} \tau_t)(kM_{apd,0}) = N$$

where N is between 3 (when $k = 1.0$) and 0.5 (when $k = 0.001$). In other words,

$$\omega_{3dB} \approx \begin{cases} \dfrac{N}{\tau_t} & \text{when } kM_{apd,0} < 1 \\[2ex] \dfrac{N}{\tau_t kM_{apd,0}} & \text{when } kM_{apd,0} > 1 \end{cases} \qquad \textbf{[5.61]}$$

at $L_d = 0$. This shows that the larger the multiplication gain at dc, the smaller the 3 dB bandwidth when $kM_{apd,0} > 1$.

When $L_d = 0$, the time delay due to the intrinsic region should be included, which results in a smaller 3 dB bandwidth. The 3 dB bandwidth as a function of the dc multiplication gain at various k's and L_d/L_m's is given in Figure 5.18. Using equations (5.26) and (5.61), one can get the following approximation:

$$\frac{1}{\omega_{3dB}} = \begin{cases} \dfrac{\tau_t}{N} + \dfrac{L_d}{L_m} \dfrac{\tau_t}{2.8} & \text{when } kM_{apd,0} < 1 \\[2ex] \dfrac{\tau_t}{N}(kM_{apd,0}) + \dfrac{L_d}{L_m} \dfrac{\tau_t}{2.8} & \text{when } kM_{apd,0} > 1. \end{cases} \qquad \textbf{[5.62]}$$

Since $\tau_t = L_m/v_n$ is the transit delay over the multiplication region, note that $(L_d/L_m)\tau_t = L_d/v_n$ is the transit delay over the intrinsic region.

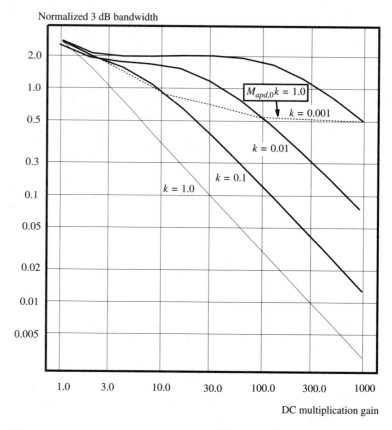

Figure 5.17   Normalized 3 dB bandwidth as a function of dc gain $M_{apd,0}$ at various values of k; $L_d/L_m = 0$.

| Example 5.10 | **APP FREQUENCY RESPONSE**   When $kM_{apd,0} = 1.0$, |

$$(\omega_B \tau_t)^{-1} = \frac{1}{N} + \frac{L_d}{L_m} \frac{1}{2.8}.$$

At $L_d/L_m = 1.0$ and $N = 30$, the normalized frequency is around 1.45 for different k values. At $L_d/L_m = 10.0$, the normalized frequency is limited by the intrinsic region and around 0.28. These results are consistent with Figure 5.18.

When $kM_{apd,0} > 1$,

$$(\omega_B \tau_t)^{-1} = \frac{kM_{apd,0}}{N} + \frac{L_d}{L_m} \frac{1}{2.8}.$$

Figure 5.18 shows that the normalized 3 dB bandwidths all approach the value $2.8/(L_d/L_m)$ when $(L_d/L_m)/2.8 > kM_{apd,0}/N$. ∎

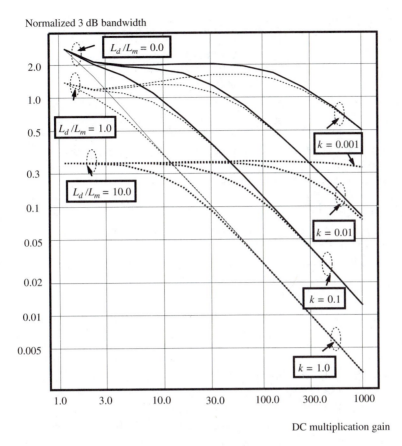

Figure 5.18   Normalized 3 dB bandwidth as a function of dc gain $M_{apd,0}$ at various values of k and L_d/L_m.

5.6   ADVANCED LIGHT-DETECTION DEVICES

In addition to the PIN diodes and APDs commonly used in optical communications, there are other innovative structures for better detection response time, receiver sensitivity, current gain, or quantum efficiency. Central to these devices, the primary material used is In-GaAs, which has good photon absorption in the wavelength range 1.3–1.5 μm. Because it also has a close lattice match with GaAs or InP, which have good electrical properties, In-GaAs photodetectors can be integrated with GaAs or InP FETs and waveguides into OEICs.

5.6.1   METAL-SEMICONDUCTOR-METAL PHOTODETECTORS

Metal-semiconductor-metal (MSM) photodetectors (PDs) based on InGaAs/InP or In-GaAs/GaAs have attracted a lot of research interest for their higher photodetection sensitivities, higher response speeds, and easy integration with field effect transistors (FETs) and optical waveguides [12]–[16]. Compared to PIN diodes, MSM PDs have a lower junction capacitance per unit area [12], which is the basis for high sensitivity and speeds, as will be explained shortly.

As shown in Figure 5.19a, an MSM PD has a structure similar to a p-i-n photodiode, but with the P-type and N-type semiconductors replaced by metal contacts. To provide a high electric field in the middle semiconductor for high speed photodetection, an MSM PD needs a high-barrier metal–semiconductor Schottky junction [4].[2] A low Schottky barrier in general has a large dark current and consequently a high noise power. Because the Schottky barrier of the metal–InGaAs junction is low, as shown in Figure 5.19b, an intermediate InAlAs layer and a graded layer are generally used.

The top view of an MSM PD is shown in Figure 5.19b. It shows that two metal contacts are interleaved in an **interdigitated** structure. This interleaving structure reduces the fringing effect in a simple two-plate capacitor as illustrated in Figure 5.19c. A lower capacitance can thus be achieved [12].

Because the incident light can be partially blocked by the interdigitated metal structure, an MSM PD has a lower quantum efficiency. According to [12], the quantum efficiency of an MSM PD is given by

$$\eta_{msm} = \frac{q}{hf} \frac{d}{d+w} (1 - e^{-\alpha D})$$ [5.63]

where w is the width of interdigitated metal contacts, d is the interdigit finger spacing, α is the photon absorption coefficient, and D is the depth of the MSM photodetector. Thus, the quantum efficiency is reduced by a factor $d/(d + w)$ compared to photodiodes.

Although MSM PDs have a lower quantum efficiency, they can still have a higher receiver sensitivity because of a lower capacitance. As explained in Chapter 7, the photodetector is followed by a front-end amplifier for photocurrent amplification. If a high-impedance FET amplifier is used, according to Equation (7.123), the output noise power due to the front-end amplifier (not including the shot noise) is given by

$$\sigma_{a,FET}^2 = 2kT\Gamma \frac{(2\pi C_{in})^2}{g_m} B^3 J_2$$ [5.64]

where Γ is a device-dependent parameter typically between 0.5 and 3.0, g_m is the transconductance of the FET, B is the bandwidth of the photodetector, and J_2 is a dimensionless parameter and a function of the receiver transfer function (see Chapter 7 for a detailed explanation). Because the noise power is proportional to the square of the total capacitance C_{in} at the FET input, a small capacitance results in a lower noise power or a higher receiver sensitivity.

Thus, receiver sensitivity can be maximized by increasing the finger spacing until the frequency response is limited by the transit delay given by Equation (5.26). At this maximum spacing, the capacitance and noise power given by Equation (5.64) are minimized.

---

[2] A Schottky junction is a metal–semiconductor junction.

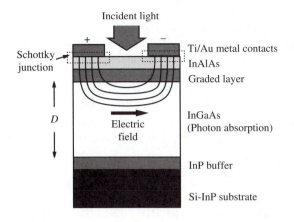

(a)

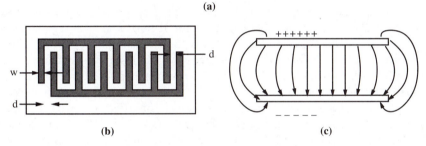

(b)   (c)

Figure 5.19   (*a*) Cross-sectional view of an MSM PD. (*b*) Top view of an MSM PD with an interdigitated structure. (*c*) Illustration of the fringing effect of a simple two-plate capacitor.

SENSITIVITY GAIN FROM MSM PD   Consider an InGaAs MSM PD design that requires a bandwidth of $B = 100$ GHz. If the drift velocity is $v = 10^6$ m/sec, the maximum possible finger spacing is

	Example 5.11

$$d = v\tau_t = v\frac{2.8}{2\pi B} = 4.6 \ \mu\text{m}.$$

At this spacing, the capacitance of a PIN is

$$C_{pin} = \frac{\epsilon_r}{d} = \frac{13.2 \times \epsilon_0}{4.6 \times 10^{-6}} = 25 \ \text{F/mm}^2$$

where the dielectric constant of InGaAs is assumed to be 13.2. Depending on the fringing effect, the actual capacitance can increase 20% or more. On the other hand, the capacitance per unit area of an MSM photodetector at 4.6 μm spacing is only 10 F/mm^2[12]. When C_{pin} is increased 20% by the fringing effect, the capacitance ratio is

$$\frac{C_{pin} \times 1.2}{C_{msm}} = \frac{1.2 \times 25}{10} = 3.0.$$

In other words, when both the shot noise and input capacitance of the FET can be ignored, the noise power from Equation (5.64) is reduced by a factor of 9.

On the other hand, if the metal contacts of the MSM PD have a width $w = 5\mu m$, the quantum efficiency from Equation (5.63) is reduced by a factor of

$$\frac{\eta_{msm}}{\eta_{pin}} = \frac{d}{w + d} = \frac{4.6}{4.6 + 5} = 0.48$$

which means the signal power (photocurrent squared) is reduced by a factor of $0.48^2 = 0.23$. Considering both the noise power and signal power reductions, the SNR is increased by a factor $9 \times 0.23 = 2.07$ or 3.2 dB. ∎

5.6.2 SEPARATE ABSORPTION AND MULTIPLICATION APDS

Separate absorption and multiplication (SAM) photodetectors are APDs that use different materials at the absorption region and multiplication region, with each region optimized for its respective function. As depicted in Figure 5.20, the absorption region is made of InGaAs that has a smaller bandgap to absorb longer wavelength photons, and the multiplication region is made of InP that has a larger energy bandgap to pass long wavelength photons and to sustain a higher reverse bias. As shown in Figure 5.20, incident photons can pass through InP and generate EHPs inside InGaAs. Compared to narrow bandgap InGaAs, where a breakdown occurs at an electric field of around 2×10^5 V/cm, InP can sustain a much higher electric field ($> 5 \times 10^5$ V/cm). Therefore, a higher multiplication gain can be achieved.

5.6.3 INTEGRATED PIN/FET RECEIVERS

An integrated PIN/FET receiver is depicted in Figure 5.21. With this structure, the photocurrent detected can be immediately amplified. Because of the integrated design, it has a smaller parasitic capacitance at the transistor input. Therefore, a higher speed can be achieved.

From the circuit point of view, it is a simple combination of a PIN diode and a FET. However, from the device point of view, the integrated PIN/FET is an example of OEIC technology that requires separate materials optimized for photodetection and electrical current amplification, respectively. In the past, there have been different material combinations including GaAs/GaAs [17], AlGaAs/GaAs [18], InGaAs/InGaAs [19], and InGaAs/InP [20]–[22], where the first material is used for the PIN diode, and the second is used for the FET.

In general, GaAs and InP are good materials for FETs, and InGaAs and AlGaAs are good for PIN diodes. A receiver sensitivity of −34.5 dBm at 100 Mb/s has been reported [21]. However, because of the limited transconductance gain from the FET, this is still not as good as the best hybrid circuits.

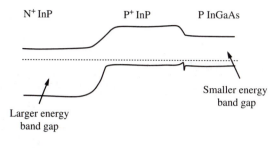

N⁺ InP   P⁺ InP   P InGaAs

Smaller energy band gap

Larger energy band gap

(a) Zero bias

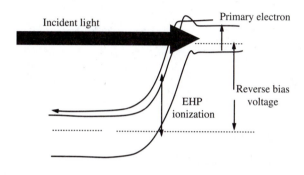

Incident light   Primary electron

Reverse bias voltage

EHP ionization

(b) Reverse bias

Figure 5.20   Energy-band diagrams of a SAM device under (a) zero bias and (b) reverse bias.

5.6.4   PHOTOTRANSISTORS

Different from the PIN/FET, a phototransistor is a single device that detects light and amplifies the current. A typical heterophototransistor (HPT) is shown in Figure 5.22, where the base (P-InGaAs) and collector (N-InGaAs) together function as a photodiode at reverse bias. Adding the emitter (N-InP) creates an n-p-n transistor. The material InP is used for the emitter because of its large bandgap. Therefore, little incident light is absorbed through it.

Phototransistors of high incident light sensitivity (around 1 nW) and high current gain (> 100) have been reported [23]. Because the switching speed of the transistor depends on how fast the base-emitter capacitor charges or discharges, the speed of a phototransistor strongly depends on the incident light power, which generates the current to charge the base-emitter capacitor. Therefore, their use for high-speed and high-sensitivity communications is limited.

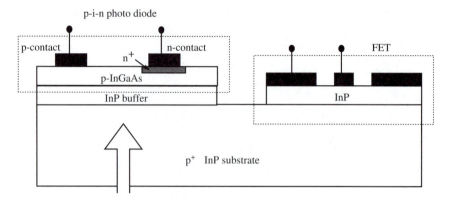

Figure 5.21   An InGaAs/InP PIN/FET photodetector. In general, there are multiple FETs in one chip for higher gains.

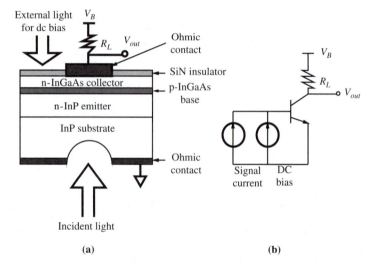

Figure 5.22   A heterophototransistor (HPT): (*a*) structure and (*b*) equivalent circuit. Note that both InP layers and the N-type InGaAs layer have large energy bandgaps so that incident photons will not be absorbed. Only the P-type InGaAs base can absorb the light because of its smaller bandgap.

5.6.5 DUAL WAVELENGTH PHOTODETECTORS

Another interesting and clever photodetection device for dual-wavelength detection is shown in Figure 5.23. It was first proposed by Campbell et al. [24] to detect two optical signals at two different wavelengths simultaneously. It is thus attractive to applications such as wavelength-division multiplexing (WDM).

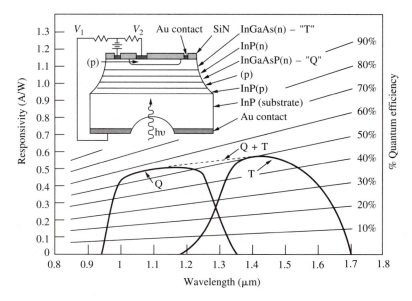

Figure 5.23   Structure of a dual wavelength photodetector and its responsivity as a function of wavelength.

SOURCE: Reprinted, by permission, from Campbell et al., "Wavelength-Discriminating Photodetector" [26]. © 1983 by *IEE*.

As shown in Figure 5.23, the device has two p-n photodiodes in parallel. One is made
of P-InGaAs (T) and N-InGaAs, and the other is made of P-InP and N-InGaAsP (Q). The
two materials (T and Q) have different compositions so that the T material absorbs light of
longer wavelengths (around 1.5 μm), and the Q material absorbs light of shorter wavelengths (around 1.1 μm). As shown in Figure 5.23, these Q and T photodiodes have their
own load resistors, whose voltage outputs are denoted by V_1 and V_2, respectively.

As shown in Figure 5.23, it is important to place the Q-type material before the T-type
material from the incident light direction. If the incident light has a short wavelength, the
Q-type material will absorb the light. On the other hand, if the incident has a long wavelength, it will pass through the Q-type material and be absorbed by the T-type material. At a
33 Mb/s experiment, the receiver sensitivities measured were −38.5 and −39.7 dBm at a
BER of 10^{-9}. The measured crosstalk was −19 and −30 dB for the short and long wavelength
ranges, respectively. The much higher crosstalk for the short wavelength range is because
light of long wavelengths must first pass through the short-wavelength absorbing material.

5.7 SUMMARY

1. A photodetector converts incident light into photocurrent from photon absorption and
electron–hole pair generation. The efficiency that quantifies the photon absorption is called

the quantum efficiency. A large quantum efficiency is desirable for a larger photocurrent. However, to have a higher efficiency, a thicker absorption layer is required. This results in a longer transit delay, or slower response.

2. From the communication point of view, a light detection device should not only generate a large photocurrent, but also needs to respond to the incident light as fast as possible and add minimal noise. In general, these cannot all be satisfied at the same time.

3. The ratio of the number of EHPs generated to the number of absorbed photons is called the photocurrent gain. To have a large photocurrent, a large gain is desirable. However, a higher current gain generally comes together with a slower response and more noise.

4. Photoconductors generate photocurrent at a constant voltage bias from an increase of their conductivity due to incident light. In general, they can have a large photocurrent gain. However, their response speeds are limited by their relaxation time constants, which are generally large for Si (in the order of 1 μsec) and small for InGaP (in the order of 1 nsec) devices.

5. PIN and APD diodes are semiconductor diodes with an intrinsic region that generates EHPs from photon absorption and converts them into photocurrent by a large internal electric field. APD diodes have an additional multiplication layer that allows primary EHPs to excite secondary EHPs through ionization. Therefore, APDs have a larger current gain. However, they generally have a slower response speed when the gain is large.

6. Because of the low capacitance, MSM devices are attractive for high-speed detection and receiver sensitivity. They have a similar p-i-n structure with the P- and N-type semiconductor layers replaced by metal contacts. When InGaAs is used for MSM photodetection, it can be easily integrated into OEICs with FETs made of GaAs or InP.

7. SAM devices optimize photon absorption and EHP multiplication by using different bandgap materials. Specifically, InGaAs is used for photon absorption because of its smaller energy bandgap, and InP is used for multiplication because of its larger bandgap and higher breakdown voltage.

APPENDIX 5-A: AVALANCHE PHOTODIODE FREQUENCY RESPONSE DERIVATION

This appendix provides more detailed mathematics for the APD frequency response analysis.

Multiplication Region   In the multiplication region where $0 < x < L_m$, assume $J_{n1}(x)$ and $J_{p1}(x)$ have an exponential form Ce^{rx}; substituting this into Equations (5.46) and (5.47) gives

$$(r + a)J_{n1} = -\beta J_{p1}$$

and

$$(r - b)J_{p1} = \alpha J_{n1}.$$

These two equations require r to satisfy the following eigenvalue equation:

$$r^2 + (a - b)r + (\alpha\beta - ab) = 0. \qquad \textbf{[5.65]}$$

Therefore, two solutions, r_1 and r_2, to Equation (5.65) have the form given by Equation (5.56). From this,

$$J_{n1}(x) = c_1 e^{r_1 x} + c_2 e^{r_2 x}.$$

From Equation (5.46),

$$J_{p1}(x) = -\frac{1}{\beta}[c_1(r_1 + a)e^{r_1 x} + c_2(r_2 + a)e^{r_2 x}].$$

Using the boundary conditions given by Equations (5.52) and (5.53),

$$c_1 = \frac{r_2 + a}{(r_2 + a)e^{r_1 L_m} - (r_1 + a)e^{r_2 L_m}} k_m J_0$$

and

$$c_2 = -\frac{r_1 + a}{(r_2 + a)e^{r_1 L_m} - (r_1 + a)e^{r_2 L_m}} k_m J_0.$$

These give us the solutions of J_{n1} and J_{p1} given by Equations (5.54) and (5.55).

Intrinsic Region   For the current densities $J_{n1}(x)$ and $J_{p1}(x)$ in the intrinsic region, according to Equations (5.50) and (5.51) and the boundary conditions at $x = L_m$,

$$J_{n1}(x) = J_0 e^{j\omega_m (x - L_m)} \qquad \textbf{[5.66]}$$

and

$$J_{p1}(x) = J_{p1}(L_m)e^{j\omega_m (x - L_m)} \qquad \textbf{[5.67]}$$

for $L_m < x < L_m + L_d$.

PROBLEMS

Problem 5–1 Quantum Efficiency: From Figure 5.2, which materials are appropriate for light detection at wavelength 1.55 μm? If the material has an absorption coefficient of 1×10^4 1/cm, find the corresponding quantum efficiency by Equation (5.2). Assume the refractive index of the material is 3.5 and the thickness of the absorption layer is 1 μm. How can you increase the quantum efficiency by 20% using the same material?

Problem 5–2 Photoconductor Gain: If a given photoconductor has a quantum efficiency of 0.5, thickness of 20 μm, relaxation time constant of 1 nsec, and electron and hole mobilities of 8000 cm^2/V-sec and 2000 cm^2/V-sec, respectively, calculate the photocurrent gain. Assume $R_c \gg R_F$ and the bias voltage is 10 volts.

Problem 5–3 Photoconductor Bandwidth: Use the same assumptions given in Problem 5–2. What is the 3 dB bandwidth of the device? What is the gain–bandwidth product? How can you adjust the thickness to improve the product? Is there any limit to doing so?

Problem 5–4 Photoconductor Output Resistance: Assume a photoconductor has a resistance R_C in series with a load resistance R_L. Find the optimum resistance R_L that yields the maximum signal to noise ratio. Note that for a conductor of conductance G, the equivalent thermal current noise power is $4kT\,BG$, and the signal current power is the square of the photocurrent given by Equation (5.6).

Problem 5–5 Quantum Efficiency of PIN: If $W_N = 0.1\ \mu$m and $W_I = 1\,\mu$m for a PIN diode, find the optimum absorption coefficient α_{opt} to give the maximum quantum efficiency. What is the general expression of α_{opt} in terms of W_N and W_I? If the reflection coefficient r at the fiber–PIN interface is 0.3, find the corresponding optimum quantum efficiency.

Problem 5–6 Bias of PIN: Consider a silicon PIN diode that has an N^+-P-P^+ structure with $N_D = 10^{20}$ m^{-3}, $N_I = 10^{18}$ m^{-3}, and $N_A = 10^{19}$ m^{-3}. Assume the intrinsic width W_I is 10 μm, $n_i = 10^{12}$ m^{-3}, and $\epsilon_r = 11.8$.

   a. Find the reach-through voltage.

   b. If the applied reverse-bias voltage is 15 V, what are W_{dn}, W_{dp}, and the maximum electric field?

Problem 5–7 Field Distribution and Drift Velocity: For the same doping distribution as given in Problem 5–6:

   a. Find the electric field at the I-P interface if the peak electric field is 4×10^6 V/m. Assume the intrinsic region has a width of 20 μm.

   b. If the electron mobility is 8000 cm^2/V-sec, find the drift velocity and the corresponding drift delay. For simplicity, use the average field in the intrinsic region in calculating the velocity.

   c. To reduce the delay by half, what will be the penalty in terms of the quantum efficiency? Assume the same mobility and E_{max}.

Problem 5–8 PIN Photodiode Design: For a given PIN diode, if the coupling interface between the diode and the fiber has a reflectivity $r^2 = 0.4$, find W_N of the N^+ layer and W_I of the intrinsic layer so that the total quantum efficiency is 0.4. Assume the material has an absorption coefficient of $\alpha = 10^5$ m^{-1}. Consider the following two conditions in finding W_N and W_I:

   a. The N^+ layer absorbs only 10% of the incident light.

   b. The N^+ layer passes the same percentage of the incident light that was absorbed in the intrinsic layer.

Problem 5–9 Frequency Response of PIN: Consider an ideal PIN diode for which the intrinsic region of the diode is truly intrinsic ($N_I = 0$) and has a width of 10 μm.

   a. If the drift velocity is 1×10^6 m/sec at $E_{max} = 10^6$ V/m, find the 3 dB bandwidth.

   b. How could you increase the 3 dB bandwidth by a factor of 10 while keeping the intrinsic region the same width? What is the trade-off?

Problem 5–10 Trade-off between Quantum Efficiency and Bandwidth: For a given PIN diode shown in Figure 5.6, $W_N = 2\,\mu\text{m}$, and the material has the following properties: $\alpha = 10^5\,\text{m}^{-1}$ (photon absorption coefficient), dielectric constant $\epsilon_r = 9.0$ and electron mobility $\mu_n = 5000\,\text{cm}^2/(\text{Volt}\cdot\text{sec})$. The electric field E_{max} is maintained at a constant 10^5 V/m in the intrinsic region. If the PIN diode is used to receive a digital signal at 100 Mb/s and the transit delay is required to be smaller than 20% of the bit period, find the valid range of W_I to meet the speed requirement and at the same time have a quantum efficiency greater than 0.5.

Problem 5–11 Frequency Response and Junction Capacitance: Assume the drift velocity of a PIN diode is 1×10^6 V/m at a given bias condition.

a. Give the 3 dB bandwidth as a function of the intrinsic region width. Neglect the depletion widths in the N^+ and P^+ regions.

b. If the diode has an opening area of $2.5 \times 10^{-9}\,\text{m}^2$ and a dielectric constant of 14, give the reverse bias junction capacitance as a function of the intrinsic region width. Neglect the depletion width in the N^+ and P^+ regions.

c. For the detection circuit shown in Figure 5.6, can you keep decreasing the intrinsic region width to increase the 3 dB bandwidth? If the load resistance R_L is $100\,\text{k}\Omega$, what will be the width of the intrinsic region at which the bandwidth cannot be further increased effectively? Note that the cutoff frequency of a low-pass RC filter is at $1/(2\pi RC)$.

Problem 5–12 APD Field Distribution: For a given APD detector illustrated in Figure 5.10, at a peak electric field of 10^6 V/m, draw the field distribution if the doping distribution is $N_D = 10^{21}\,\text{m}^{-3}$ at the N^+ region, $N_A = 2 \times 10^{20}\,\text{m}^{-3}$ at the substrate, $N_I = 0$ at the intrinsic region, and $N_A = 10^{21}\,\text{m}^{-3}$ at the P^+ multiplication region. Assume the multiplication region and intrinsic region have widths of $0.5\,\mu\text{m}$ and $20\,\mu\text{m}$, respectively. Use $\epsilon_r = 11.8$. What is the total voltage from the electric field integration?

Problem 5–13 APD Gain Computation: Under the same assumptions given in Problem 5–12, find the multiplication gain if the electron ionization constant $\alpha = 2 \times 10^6$ 1/m and the ionization ratio $k = 0.4$.

Problem 5–14 APD dc Gain: Show that at $\omega = 0$, Equation (5.58) reduces to Equation (5.39).

Problem 5–15 Choice of k for APDs: From Figure 5.17, it is clear that one should use a small k to achieve a larger multiplication gain and bandwidth product. On the other hand, Equation (5.39) and Figure 5.14 show that a higher αL_m is needed to achieve the same multiplication gain. Find the values of αL_m at $M_{apd,0} = 100$ for $k = 0.1$ and $k = 0.001$ using Equation (5.39). What is the corresponding normalized 3 dB bandwidth using Figure 5.14? What is the disadvantage of having a larger αL_m value?

Problem 5–16 APD Bandwidth Computation: Assume the transit delay of an APD device over the multiplication region is 0.1 nsec.

a. Find the 3 dB bandwidth from Equation (5.62) if $k = 0.1$, $M_{apd,0} = 200$, $N = 0.5$, and $L_d/L_m = 10$.

b. For a different device with the same assumptions as in *a* except $k = 0$ and $N = 3.0$, what is the new multiplication gain? What is the new 3 dB bandwidth?

REFERENCES

1. *Fiberoptic Product News: 1990–1991 Buying Guide,* Elsevier, 1990.

2. J. C. Campbell, "Photodetectors for Long-Wavelength Lightwave Systems," Chapter 14 of *Optoelectronic Technology and Lightwave Communications Systems,* edited by Chinlon Lin, New York: Van Nostrand Reinhold, 1989.

3. R. J. Hoss, *Fiber Optic Communications, Design Handbook,* Prentice-Hall, 1990.

4. S. M. Sze, *Physics of Semiconductor Devices,* 2nd ed., John Wiley and Sons, 1981.

5. S. R. Forrest, "Optical Detectors for Lightwave Communication," Chapter 14 of *Optical Fiber Telecommunications II,* edited by S. E. Miller and I. P. Kaminow, Academic Press, 1988.

6. N. Susa et al., "Vapor Phase Epitaxially Grown InGaAs Photodiodes," *IEEE Transactions on Electron Devices,* vol. 27 (January 1980), pp. 92–98.

7. S. Ramo, J. R. Whinnery, T. Van Duzer, *Fields and Waves in Communication Electronics,* 2nd ed., John Wiley and Sons, 1984.

8. A. Yariv, *Optical Electronics,* 4th ed., Holt, Rinehart and Winston, 1991.

9. W. T. Read, "A Proposed High-Frequency Negative-Resistance Diode," *Bell System Technical Journal,* vol. 37 (1958), p. 401–46.

10. H. Melchior, "Detectors for Lightwave Communications," *Physics Today,* vol. 30 (November 1977), pp. 32–39.

11. R. B. Emmons, "Avalanche-Photodiode Frequency Response," *Journal of Applied Physics,* vol. 38, no. 9 (August 1967), pp. 3705–14.

12. D. L. Rogers, "Integrated Optical Receivers Using MSM Detectors," *Journal of Lightwave Technology,* vol. 9, no. 12 (December 1991), pp. 1635–38.

13. J. S. Parker and G. Bosman, "Noise Characteristics of an InGaAs Interdigitated Metal-Semiconductor-Metal Photodetector (MSM-PD)," *IEEE Transactions on Electron Devices,* vol. 39, no. 6 (June 1992), pp. 1282–87.

14. J. S. Wang et al., "11 GHz Bandwidth Optical Integrated Receivers Using GaAs MESFET and MSM Technology," *IEEE Photonics Technology Letters,* vol. 5, no. 3 (March 1993), pp. 316–21.

15. W. Ng et al., "High-Efficiency Waveguide-Coupled $\lambda = 1.3$ μm InGaAs/GaAs MSM Detector Exhibiting Large Extinction Ratios at *L* and *X* Band," *IEEE Photonics Technology Letters,* vol. 5, no. 5 (May 1993), pp. 514–17.

16. M. Fallahi et al., "Grating Demultiplexer Integrated with MSM Detector Array in InGaAs/AlGaAs/GaAs for WDM," *IEEE Photonics Technology Letters,* vol. 5, no. 7 (July 1993), pp. 794–97.

17. R. M. Kolbas et al., "Planar Monolithic Integration of a Photodiode and a GaAs Pre-amplifier," *Applied Physics Letters*, vol. 43 (1983), pp. 821–23.

18. O. Wada et al., "AlGaAs/GaAs P-I-N Photodiode/Preamplifier Monolithic Photoreceiver Integrated on Semi-insulating GaAs Substrate," *Applied Physics Letters*, vol. 46 (1985), pp. 981–83.

19. R. F. Leheny et al., "An Integrated PIN/JFET Photoreceiver for Long Wavelength Optical Systems," *Technical Digest: International Electronics Device Meeting*, 1981, pp. 276–79.

20. S. Hata et al., "Planar InGaAs/InP PINFET Fabricated by Be Ion Implantation," *Electronics Letters*, vol. 20 (1984), pp. 947–48.

21. K. Kasahara et al., "Monolithically Integrated $In_{0.53}Ga_{0.47}As$-PIN/InP-MISFET Photoreceiver," *Electronics Letters*, vol. 20 (1984), pp. 314–15.

22. B. Tell et al., "Monolithic Integration of a Planar Embedded InGaAs PIN Detector with InP Depletion Mode FET's," *IEEE Transactions on Electron Devices*, vol. 32 (1985), pp. 2319–21.

23. J. C. Campbell et al., "Small-Area High-Speed InP/InGaAs Phototransistor," *Applied Physics Letters*, vol. 39 (1981), pp. 820–21.

24. J. C. Campbell et al., "Dual-Wavelength Demultiplexing InGaAsP Photodiode," *Applied Physics Letters*, vol. 34 (1979), pp. 401–2.

25. K. Ogawa et al., "Wavelength Division Multiplexing Experiment Employing Dual-Wavelength LED's and Photodiodes," *Electronics Letters*, vol. 17 (1981), pp. 857–59.

26. J. C. Campbell et al., "Wavelength-Discriminating Photodetector for Lightwave Systems," *Electronics Letters*, vol. 19 (1983), pp. 672–74.

6

NOISE IN OPTICAL COMMUNICATIONS

Previous chapters focused on light signal generation, transmission, and detection. In parallel with this, various kinds of noise are also generated, transmitted, and added to the final detected photocurrent. When the transmission channel is not ideal, the waveform of the transmitted signal is also distorted. As a result, the transmitted signal cannot be perfectly recovered, and it is an important task to minimize the effects of noise and distortion at the receiver end. In analog communications, this means maximizing the *signal-to-noise ratio* (SNR); in digital communications, this means minimizing the *bit error rate* (BER). This chapter discusses various noise sources in optical communications. More detailed analysis and equalization techniques for both noise and distortion will be given in Chapter 7.

In optical communications, noise can come from both the transmitter and receiver. In addition to **thermal noise**, which occurs in essentially every electronic circuit, there are **phase noise**, **relative intensity noise** (RIN), and **mode partition noise** (MPN) from the light source at the transmitter side, and **shot noise** and **excess (avalanche gain) noise** from the photodetector at the receiver side.

There are additional noise sources in advanced systems. For example, when optical amplifiers are used to overcome power loss, they add so-called **amplified spontaneous emission** (ASE) noise to the amplified signal. In wavelength-division multiplexing (WDM) and subcarrier multiplexing (SCM) systems in which multiple channels are transmitted through the same optical fiber, there can also be **adjacent channel interference** (ACI) or **crosstalk**, which is the interference from adjacent channels because of the power spectrum overlap. Because adjacent channels are statistically independent of the channel tuned to, they can be considered as another noise source.

In addition to noise and crosstalk, there can be signal distortion because of a nonideal channel. In optical communications, distortion can come from fiber dispersion and device nonlinearity. Depending on the format of signal transmission, channel distortion results in different effects. In analog communications, signal distortion means a loss in fidelity. In digital communications, signal distortion results in **intersymbol interference** (ISI), which in turn causes an excessively high bit error rate.

Various noise and crosstalk sources discussed can be considered as *waveform domain* noise. That is, they cause random distortion of the signal's waveform. In digital communications, there can also be *time domain* noise called **jitter**. Jitter is the timing error of the recovered bit clock with respect to the received data sequence. In digital communications, the recovered clock is used to sample the received signal for detection. As a result, a timing error will sample the received signal at a wrong timing and result in a large error detection probability. In general, jitter comes from imperfect bit timing recovery. In optical fiber soliton transmission, as discussed in Chapter 18, individual pulses (solitons) can also have random propagation velocities because their speed depends on their spectral contents. When optical amplifiers are used in transmission, the spectral contents of solitons are distorted by ASE noise. Over a long distance (thousands of kilometers), a small and random velocity change can result in a significant timing error.

Unlike thermal noise, most noise sources in optical communications are signal dependent. That is, when the signal level increases, the noise level also increases. For example, shot noise power is linearly proportional to the photocurrent generated. Relative intensity noise and mode partition noise power are even worse, being proportional to the photocurrent squared.

Table 6.1 summarizes important noise and distortion sources mentioned above. This chapter will discuss some important ones. Among all noise sources, shot noise is the most fundamental and important. This is because all other noise sources can *theoretically* be reduced to zero (e.g., use a single-mode laser and external modulation to reduce MPN, use a long cavity to reduce phase noise and RIN, and avoid the use of optical amplifiers to reduce ASE), but shot noise is intrinsic in photocurrent generation and can never be reduced to zero. The performance limit caused by shot noise is called the **quantum limit**, which is used as a benchmark for evaluating the performance of many real systems.

Table 6.1 Summary of various noise, crosstalk, and distortion sources.

Noise Source	From	Importance	Where Discussed
Thermal Noise	Resistors	Universal	Chapters 6, 7
Phase noise	Laser diodes	Important in coherent communications	Chapters 6, 15
RIN	Laser diodes	Important in SCM	Chapters 6, 7, 10
MPN	Multimode lasers under high modulation	Important in high-speed transmissions	Chapter 6
Shot noise	Photodetection	Very important and places the fundamental quantum limit	Chapters 6, 7, 15
Avalanche noise	APDs	Important when the APD gain is high	Chapters 6, 7
ASE	Optical amplifiers	Important when optical amplifiers are used	Chapter 17
Crosstalk	Adjacent channels	Important in WDM and SCM systems	Chapters 9, 10
ISI	Channel distortion	Important in digital systems	Chapters 6, 7
Jitter	Timing recovery and soliton transmission	Important in digital systems	Chapters 6, 16, 18

6.1 EFFECTS OF NOISE AND DISTORTION

To know the noise effects quantitatively, consider a basic point-to-point communication system shown in Figure 1.2. Let the transmitted signal be $s(t)$, the channel impulse response be $h(t)$, and the channel noise be $n(t)$. The received signal $r(t)$ is thus given by

$$r(t) = s(t) \otimes h(t) + n(t) \stackrel{\text{def}}{=} q(t) + n(t) \qquad \text{[6.1]}$$

where $\otimes$ denotes the convolution and $q(t) \stackrel{\text{def}}{=} s(t) \otimes h(t)$.

If the channel is ideal, it introduces only a certain delay and loss. Therefore, the impulse response of an ideal channel is given by

$$h(t) = a\delta(t - \tau) \qquad \text{[6.2]}$$

where a is a constant factor representing transmission loss (if $a < 1$) and τ is the propagation delay. When $h(t)$ is not ideal, Equation (6.1) shows that the received signal is corrupted by both noise and channel distortion.

Effect in Analog Communications In analog communications, the received signal quality can be characterized by the following ratio:

$$\gamma_Q \stackrel{\text{def}}{=} \frac{E[s(t)^2]}{E[|s(t) - r(t)|^2]} \qquad \text{[6.3]}$$

where $E[x]$ denotes the expectation or average of signal x.[1] Therefore, $E[s(t)^2]$ is the average signal power and $E[|s(t) - r(t)|^2]$ is the mean square error (MSE) with respect to the original signal $s(t)$.

When the channel is ideal, γ_Q reduces to the signal-to-noise ratio (SNR) given by

$$\gamma_Q = \text{SNR} = \frac{E[s(t)^2]}{E[n(t)^2]} \qquad \text{[6.4]}$$

where $E[n(t)^2]$ is the average noise power.

TWO TONE TRANSMISSION Consider a transmission of two sinusoidal signals:

$$s(t) = \cos(\omega_1 t) + \cos(\omega_2 t).$$

Because the transmission loss is different at different frequencies, assume the received signal is given by

$$r(t) = \cos(\omega_1 t) + a \cos(\omega_2 t)$$

Example 6.1

---

[1] In general, both s(t) and r(t) are random processes, and their expectations can be calculated if their probability density functions are known. For most real signals, their expectations can be calculated by simple time average. See Appendix 6–B for a detailed discussion.

where the propagation delay is ignored. The ratio of the signal power to the MSE is thus

$$\gamma_Q = \frac{E[|\cos(\omega_1 t) + \cos(\omega_2 t)|^2]}{E[|(1-a)\cos(\omega_2 t)|^2]} = \frac{2}{(1-a)^2}.$$

As a numerical example, if $a = 0.9$, $\gamma_Q = 200$, or 23 dB. ∎

Example 6.2

THERMAL NOISE   If the noise from transmission is only due to thermal noise, the noise power is given by (see Section 6.5)

$$E[n(t)^2] = 2kTB$$

where k is the Boltzmann constant, T is the temperature in Kelvin, and B is the receiver bandwidth in Hz. If the channel is ideal or adds no distortion,

$$\gamma_Q = \text{SNR} = \frac{E[s(t)^2]}{2kTB}.$$

As a numerical example, if the signal power is –30 dBm and $B = 100$ MHz,

$$\text{SNR} = \frac{10^{-6}}{4 \times (1.38 \times 10^{-23}) \times 300 \times 10^8} = 1.2 \times 10^6 = 60.8 \text{ dB.} \blacksquare$$

Effect in Digital Communications   In digital communications, the consideration is a little bit different. Instead of minimizing the MSE, the objective is to recover the original bits transmitted with a minimal error detection probability. Consider a pulse amplitude modulated (PAM) signal transmitted over a channel. The received signal is given by

$$r(t) = \sum_k A_k p(t - kT_0) + n(t) \qquad \text{[6.5]}$$

where A_k is the amplitude of the kth pulse, $p(t)$ is the received pulse, and T_0 is the interval between two consecutive pulses. To detect the transmitted amplitude A_k, the received signal is first sampled at $kT + \tau$ for a certain τ within $(0, T_0)$. From Equation (6.5), the sampled output is

$$r_k \overset{\text{def}}{=} r(kT + \tau) = \sum_i A_i p[(k-i)T + \tau] + n_k \qquad \text{[6.6]}$$

$$\overset{\text{def}}{=} \sum_i A_i p_{k-i} + n_k = A_k + \sum_{i \neq k} A_i p_{k-i} + n_k$$

$$= A_k + \text{ISI}_k + n_k$$

where $p_i \overset{\text{def}}{=} p(iT + \tau)$ and $n_k \overset{\text{def}}{=} n(kT + \tau)$. Equation (6.6) shows that the sampled output consists of three terms: signal (A_k), noise (n_k), and distortion ($\sum_{i \neq k} A_i p_{k-i}$). In digital communications, the last distortion term is called the intersymbol interference (ISI) because it is caused by adjacent symbols and pulses.

Because of noise and ISI, r_k and A_k are not necessarily the same. A digital receiver thus needs to "guess" what amplitude is transmitted from the received r_k. The process of finding a likely $\hat{A}_k$ from the sampled value r_k is called **detection**. If $\hat{A}_k = A_k$, detection is correct; if $\hat{A}_k \neq A_k$, detection is incorrect. Because both noise and ISI are unpredictable, the detection performance is characterized by the error detection probability:

$$P_E = P(\hat{A}_k \neq A_k | r_k). \qquad \textbf{[6.7]}$$

Therefore, the smaller the error detection probability, the better the transmission performance.

PROBABILITY OF ERROR DETECTION   Assume A_k is either -A or A in Equation (6.5) and let $p(t)$ be a unit rectangular pulse of duration from 0 to T_0. If the signal is sampled at $kT_0 + 0.5T_0$, the sampled output is **Example 6.3**

$$r_k = r(kT_0 + 0.5T_0) = A_k p(0.5T_0) + n_k = A_k + n_k.$$

In this case, there is no ISI.

To detect the original transmitted amplitude A_k, one can perform **threshold detection** according to the received sample r_k. Specifically, setting the threshold at 0,

$$\hat{A}_k = \begin{cases} A & \text{if } r_k > 0 \\ -A & \text{if } r_k \leq 0. \end{cases}$$

From this detection, the error detection probability is given by

$$\begin{aligned} P_E &= P(r_k < 0 | A_k = A) P(A_k = A) \\ &\quad + P(r_k > 0 | A_k = -A) P(A_k = -A) \\ &= P(n_k < -A) P(A_k = A) \\ &\quad + P(n_k > A) P(A_k = -A). \end{aligned}$$

This probability can be evaluated when the probability distribution function of n_k is known. ∎

In Example 6.3, the transmitted amplitude can assume two different values, $\pm A$. Therefore, each pulse carries one bit, and the error detection probability P_E is called the bit error rate (BER). When A_k can take 2^b different values, each pulse carries b bits and P_E is called the **symbol error rate**. With proper coding between the amplitude A_k and b input bits, most detection errors result in only one error bit, and the BER is approximately related to P_E by

$$\text{BER} \approx \frac{P_E}{b}. \qquad \textbf{[6.8]}$$

6.2   NOISE CHARACTERIZATION

As the above discussion makes clear, it is important to know the noise characteristics to evaluate the distortion and error detection probability. This section describes two primary noise characteristics: the **probability density function** (PDF) and the **power spectral density** (PSD).

6.2.1   PROBABILITY DENSITY FUNCTION

The noise sample n_k considered earlier is a random variable. As explained in Appendix 6–A, every random variable has a PDF. For continuous random variables, their PDFs are continuous functions; for discrete random variables, their PDFs are a summation of delta functions. When the PDF of a random variable is known, various statistics of the random variable can be computed.

Let $f_X(x)$ be the PDF of a continuous random variable X. By definition, the probability for $a < X < b$ is

$$Prob(a < X < b) = \int_a^b f_X(z)dz.$$

When the above integration is over $(-\infty, x]$, the probability as a function of x is called the **probability distribution function** or **probability accumulation function**. That is,

$$F_X(x) \overset{\text{def}}{=} \int_{-\infty}^{x} f_X(z)dz. \qquad [6.9]$$

From this, $f_X(x)$ is the derivative of the probability accumulation function $F_X(x)$. Various important PDFs are given in Appendix 6–A.

Example 6.4

GAUSSIAN NOISE   Consider a Gaussian noise $n(t)$ of zero mean and variance σ^2. Its PDF is given by

$$f_n(x) = \frac{1}{\sqrt{2\pi\sigma^2}} e^{-x^2/2\sigma^2}. \qquad [6.10]$$

From this, the noise power is $E[n^2] = \sigma^2$. If the signal is an AM signal of the form $m(t)\cos(\omega_c t)$, then

$$E[s(t)^2] = \frac{1}{2}E[m(t)^2]$$

and

$$\text{SNR} = \frac{E[m(t)^2]}{2\sigma^2}.$$

As a numerical example, if $\sigma^2 = 1$ nW and $E[m(t)^2] = 1$ μW, SNR $= 500 = 27$ dB. ∎

Example 6.5

BER UNDER GAUSSIAN NOISE   (Continued from Example 6.3) If noise n_k is Gaussian with the PDF given by Equation (6.10), then

$$P(n_k < -A) = \int_{-\infty}^{-A} f_n(x)dx.$$

Similarly,

$$P(n_k > A) = \int_{A}^{\infty} f_n(x)dx.$$

Because of the importance of Gaussian noise, these two probabilities are commonly expressed in terms of the Q-function or the complementary error function $erfc()$. The definition of the Q-function is

$$Q(x) \stackrel{\text{def}}{=} \frac{1}{\sqrt{2\pi}} \int_{x}^{\infty} e^{-y^2/2}dy. \qquad \text{[6.11]}$$

Therefore, $Q(0) = 0.5$ and $Q(\infty) = 0$. The definition of the error function is

$$erf(x) \stackrel{\text{def}}{=} \frac{2}{\sqrt{\pi}} \int_{0}^{x} e^{-y^2}dy = \frac{2}{\sqrt{2\pi\sigma^2}} \int_{0}^{x\sqrt{2\sigma^2}} e^{-y^2/2\sigma^2}dy \qquad \text{[6.12]}$$

and the definition of the complementary error function is

$$erfc(x) \stackrel{\text{def}}{=} 1 - erf(x). \qquad \text{[6.13]}$$

Therefore, $erf(\infty) = erf\,c(0) = 1$. From the definitions,

$$Q(x) = \frac{1}{2}erfc(x/\sqrt{2}). \qquad \text{[6.14]}$$

As a result,

$$P(r_k > 0|A_k = -A) = P(r_k < 0|A_k = A)$$
$$= Q(A/\sigma) = \frac{1}{2}erfc(A/\sqrt{2\sigma^2}).$$

Because

$$SNR = \frac{E[s(t)^2]}{\sigma^2} = \frac{A^2}{\sigma^2},$$

$$P_E = P(r_k > 0|A_k = -A) = P(r_k < 0|A_k = A) \qquad \text{[6.15]}$$
$$= Q(\sqrt{SNR}) = \frac{1}{2}erfc(\sqrt{SNR/2}).$$

This P_E dependence on SNR is shown in Figure 6.1. The following approximation for $Q(x)$ makes calculation easier:

$$Q(x) \approx \frac{1}{\sqrt{2\pi x^2}}e^{-x^2/2} \text{ if } x \gg 1. \qquad \text{[6.16]}$$

This equation shows that, the larger the SNR, the smaller the P_E. As a result, it is important to maximize the SNR to reduce the error probability. ∎

In practice, a noise sample n_k can also be a discrete random variable. For example, in optical communications, one can count the number of incident photons over a certain interval. In this case, n_k is the difference between the average number of photons and the actual number counted. This discrete noise in photon counting will be discussed in detail in Section 6.4.

6.2.2   POWER SPECTRAL DENSITY

Another important characteristic of noise is the power spectral density (PSD). Mathematically, it is defined as the Fourier transform of the autocorrelation function of the noise. Physically, it describes the frequency content of the noise power. In other words, for a given PSD $S_n(\omega)$ of noise $n(t)$, the integration

$$\int_{\omega_1}^{\omega_2} S_n(\omega) \frac{d\omega}{2\pi}$$

gives the portion of the noise power within the frequency range from ω_1 to ω_2. If the integration is over the entire frequency range, it gives the average noise power. That is,

$$E[n(t)^2] = R_n(0) = \int_{-\infty}^{\infty} S_n(\omega) \frac{d\omega}{2\pi} \qquad \textbf{[6.17]}$$

where $R_n(0)$ is the autocorrelation of $n(t)$ at $\tau = 0$. See Appendix 6–B for detailed discussion on the autocorrelation function and PSD of a random process.

Example 6.6

WHITE NOISE   White noise has a constant power spectral density. That is,

$$S_n(\omega) = \frac{N_0}{2}.$$

Therefore, over a frequency band of B, the power is

$$P_n = \int_{-2\pi B}^{2\pi B} \frac{N_0}{2} \frac{d\omega}{2\pi} = N_0 B.$$

Because the total power of white noise is infinite, a true white noise does not physically exist. However, if the PSD of a noise is flat over the frequency range of interest, it still can be considered as white noise. ∎

6.3   NOISE AND DISTORTION REDUCTION TECHNIQUES

When the PSDs of a signal and noise are known, we can use filtering and equalization techniques to reduce the effects of noise and distortion [1]. It is thus instructive to see some key design concepts. Since detailed discussion of this subject is beyond the scope of the

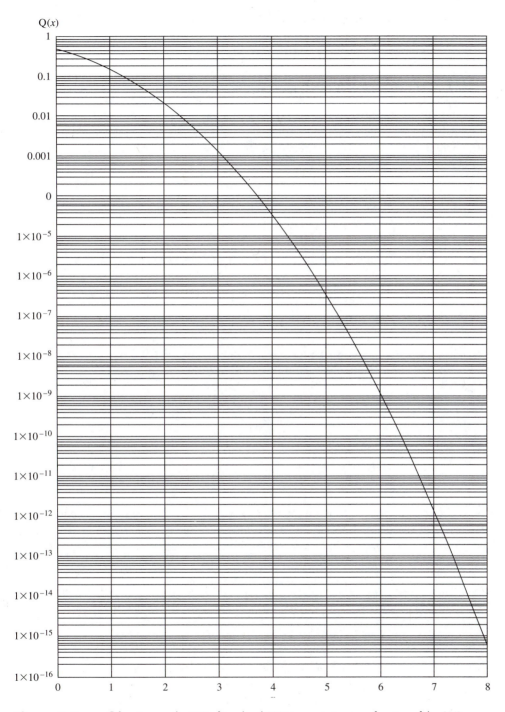

Figure 6.1 Q-function, or the BER of two-level PAM transmission as a function of the SNR.

book, readers who want to study various noise sources in optical communications directly can skip this section.

6.3.1   WIENER FILTERING IN ANALOG COMMUNICATIONS

In analog communications, the objective is to maximize the performance measure given by Equation (6.3). To achieve this, a filter called an *equalizer* following the receiver front-end is commonly used. From the received signal given by Equation (6.1), the equalized output is

$$r_{out}(t) = r(t) \otimes h_{eq}(t) = q(t) \otimes h_{eq}(t) + n(t) \otimes h_{eq}(t)$$
$$\stackrel{\text{def}}{=} s_{out}(t) + n_{out}(t)$$

where $h_{eq}(t)$ is the impulse response of the equalizer. Therefore, the MSE is

$$\text{MSE} = E[|r_{out}(t) - s(t)|^2] = E[|s_{out}(t) - s(t)|^2] + E[n_{out}^2]$$
$$\stackrel{\text{def}}{=} \text{MSE}_s + E[n_{out}^2]$$

where the noise and signal are assumed to be statistically independent. As Appendix 6–B shows, the two terms on the right-hand side can be written as

$$E[n_{out}^2] = \int S_n(\omega)|H_{eq}(\omega)|^2 \frac{d\omega}{2\pi}$$

and

$$\text{MSE}_s \stackrel{\text{def}}{=} E[|s_{out} - s(t)|^2] = \int S_s(\omega)|H(\omega)H_{eq}(\omega) - 1|^2 \frac{d\omega}{2\pi}$$

where $S_s(\omega)$ is the PSD of the original signal and $H(\omega)$ is the transfer function of the channel. Let H_{opt} be the optimum transfer function of the equalizer that gives the minimum $\text{MSE}_{s,min}$. If $H_{eq} = H_{opt} + \delta H$, by expanding the factor $|H(\omega)H_{eq}(\omega) - 1|^2$, the MSE reduces to

$$\text{MSE} = \text{MSE}_{min} + 2\Re \left\{ \int [S_n H_{opt}^* + S_s|H|^2(H_{opt}^* - 1)]\delta H \frac{d\omega}{2\pi} \right\}$$
$$+ \int (S_n + S_s|H|^2)|\delta H|^2 \frac{d\omega}{2\pi}$$

where $\Re\{z\}$ denotes the real part of z. Because the last term on the right-hand side of the above equation is always positive, the middle term should always be zero to ensure $\text{MSE} \geq \text{MSE}_{min}$ for any δH. As a result, the optimum $H_{opt}(\omega)$ satisfies the following condition:

$$S_n H_{opt} + S_s|H|^2(H_{opt} - 1) = 0$$

or

$$H_{opt}(\omega) = \frac{S_s(\omega)|H(\omega)|^2}{S_s(\omega)|H(\omega)|^2 + S_n(\omega)}. \qquad \textbf{[6.18]}$$

The optimum filter given by Equation (6.18) may not necessarily be implementable (i.e., its inverse Fourier transform may not necessarily have a finite duration). Therefore, it is called the **noncausal Wiener filter**.

WIENER FILTER FOR WHITE NOISE   Consider a band-limited signal with $S_s(\omega) = A\,rect(\omega - 2\pi B, 4\pi B)$, an ideal channel with $H(\omega) = 1$, and a white noise with $S_n(\omega) = N_0/2$, where $rect(x, a)$ is defined as a unit rectangular function over an interval $(0, a)$. Therefore, the PSD of the signal is unity if $|\omega| < 2\pi B$ and is zero otherwise. From Equation (6.18), the optimum filter is

Example 6.7

$$H_{opt}(\omega) = K\,rect(\omega - 2\pi B, 4\pi B)$$

where $K = A/(A + N_0/2)$. This result says the optimum filter is simply an ideal low-pass filter (LPF) at the same cutoff frequency as the signal's band. Because this low-pass filtering does not distort the signal and at the same time rejects noise outside the signal's frequency band, this LPF result is quite understandable. However, this ideal LPF is not implementable because it is not causal. ∎

WIENER FILTER FOR LOW PASS NOISE   Consider the same $S_s(\omega)$ in the previous example, but assume

Example 6.8

$$S_n(\omega) = \frac{N_0/2}{1 + (\omega/\omega_c)^2}.$$

The optimum filter is

$$\begin{aligned}
H_{opt}(\omega) &= \frac{rect(\omega - 2\pi B, 4\pi B)}{1 + (N_0/2A)/[1 + (\omega/\omega_c)^2]} \\
&= \frac{rect(\omega - 2\pi B, 4\pi B)}{1 + N_0/2A}\,\frac{1 + (\omega/\omega_c)^2}{1 + (\omega/\omega_c)^2/(1 + N_0/2A)}.
\end{aligned}$$

This result shows that the filter consists of two factors: the same ideal LPF as in the previous example and a filter whose gain increases as the frequency increases. Because the input noise is strong in the low frequency range, this additional filter is included to attenuate the noise at the low frequency range and enhance the SNR at the high frequency range. When the input SNR is small (proportional to A/N_0), including the additional filter becomes important. ∎

6.3.2   MATCHED FILTERING IN DIGITAL COMMUNICATIONS

In digital communications, instead of minimizing the MSE as in analog communications, one must minimize the error detection probability P_E. If a similar equalizer $h_{eq}(t)$ is used after the receiver front end, the filtered output from Equation (6.5) is

$$r_{out}(t) = \sum_k A_k p_{out}(t - kT_0) + n_{out}(t)$$

where $p_{out}(t) = p(t) \otimes h_{eq}(t)$. If we sample the signal at every T_0, the sampled output at $(k + 1)T_0$ is

$$r_{out,k} = A_k p_{out}(T_0) + n_{out,k}$$

where we define $r_{out,k} = r_{out}[(k + 1)T_0]$ and $n_{out,k} = n_{out}[(k + 1)T_0]$. In the above expression, $p_{out}(jT_0)$ terms for $j \neq 1$ are ignored.[2] Because the filtered noise $n_{out,k}$ is still Gaussian, from Equation (6.15),

$$P_E = Q\left[\frac{Ap_{out}(T_0)}{\sigma_{n_{out}}}\right].$$

To minimize P_E, $p_{out}(T_0)/\sigma_{n_{out}}$ must be maximinized, or

$$\left[\frac{p_{out}(T_0)}{\sigma_{n_{out}}}\right]^2 = \frac{|\int P(\omega)H_{eq}(\omega)e^{j\omega T_0}d\omega/(2\pi)|^2}{\int S_n(\omega)|H_{eq}(\omega)|^2 d\omega/(2\pi)} \qquad \textbf{[6.19]}$$

where $P(\omega)$ is the Fourier transform of $p(t)$. If $H_{eq}(\omega) = H_{pre}(\omega)H_{post}(\omega)$ such that

$$|H_{pre}(\omega)|^2 = \frac{1}{S_n(\omega)} \qquad \textbf{[6.20]}$$

then

$$\left[\frac{p_{out}(T_0)}{\sigma_{n_{out}}}\right]^2 = \frac{1}{2\pi}\frac{|\int P(\omega)H_{pre}H_{post}(\omega)e^{j\omega T_0}d\omega|^2}{\int |H_{post}(\omega)|^2 d\omega}.$$

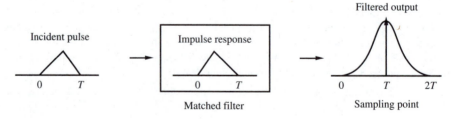

Figure 6.2   A matched filter.

| [2] Chapter 7 considers the ISI effect caused by nonzero $p_{out}(jT_0)$, for $j = 1$.

According to the Schwartz inequality [2],

$$\left(\frac{p_{out}(T_0)}{\sigma_{n_{out}}}\right)^2 \le \frac{1}{2\pi}\frac{\int |P(\omega)H_{pre}e^{j\omega T_0}|^2 d\omega \int |H_{post}(\omega)|^2 d\omega}{\int |H_{post}(\omega)|^2 d\omega} = \int \frac{|P(\omega)|^2}{S_n(\omega)}\frac{d\omega}{2\pi}.$$

The equality holds when $H_{post}(\omega) = K P^*(\omega)H_{pre}^*(\omega)e^{-j\omega T_0}$ for some constant K. Therefore, the optimum $H_{opt}(\omega)$ is

$$\boxed{H_{opt}(\omega) = K P^*(\omega)H_{pre}^*(\omega)e^{-j\omega T_0}H_{pre}(\omega) = K\frac{P^*(\omega)e^{-j\omega T_0}}{S_n(\omega)}.}$$ **[6.21]**

This optimum filter is called the **matched filter**.

MATCHED FILTER UNDER WHITE NOISE   For white noise $S_n(\omega)$ is a constant. If $K = S_n(\omega)$, the optimum filter is   **Example 6.9**

$$H_{opt}(\omega) = P^*(\omega)e^{-j\omega T_0}.$$

The inverse transform of this gives

$$h_{opt}(t) = p(T_0 - t).$$

This matched filter is illustrated in Figure 6.2. ∎

6.4   SHOT NOISE FROM PIN DIODES

The photocurrent from a PIN diode given by Equation (5.12) is a constant when the incident light power is a constant. In practice, because of random EHP generation, the photocurrent has a random fluctuation from its average value. This random fluctuation is called shot noise and is the most fundamental noise in optical communications. This section gives a derivation of the PSD of a shot noise and explains its quantum limit as an ultimate detection performance limit in direct detection.

6.4.1   POWER SPECTRAL DENSITY OF SHOT NOISE

Shot noise $n_{shot}(t)$ as a function of time at the photodiode output is defined to be

$$n_{shot}(t) \stackrel{\text{def}}{=} i_{ph}(t) - I_{ph}$$ **[6.22]**

where $i_{ph}(t)$ is the photocurrent and I_{ph} is its average. From the derivation given in Appendix 6–C, the two-sided PSD of a shot noise is given by

$$S_{shot}(\omega) = q(I_{ph} + I_d)|H_{pin}(\omega)|^2 \approx q(I_{ph} + I_d) \qquad \textbf{[6.23]}$$

where I_d is the dark current and $H_{pin}(\omega)$ is the Fourier transform of the impulse response of the PIN diode due to an EHR. Because $H_{pin}(\omega)$ is generally flat over a large frequency range, it can be dropped from Equation (6.23). In other words, shot noise can be considered as a white noise over most relevant frequency ranges. If this is the case, the shot noise power over a bandwidth B is

$$\overline{n_{shot}^2} = \int S_{shot}(\omega) \times \frac{d\omega}{2\pi} \approx 2q(I_{ph} + I_d)B = 2q(\mathcal{R}P_{in} + I_d)B. \qquad \textbf{[6.24]}$$

Example 6.10

SHOT NOISE POWER   Consider an incident optical signal of $P_{in} = -40$ dBm at wavelength $\lambda = 1.55\mu$m. If the quantum efficiency of photodetection is $\eta = 0.5$, the average photocurrent is

$$I_{ph} = 0.5 \times 10^{-7} \frac{1.55}{1.24} = 63 \text{ nA}.$$

When the dark current is ignored, the root mean square of the shot noise over a bandwidth of B = 1 GHz is

$$(\overline{n_{shot}^2})^{1/2} = (2qI_{ph}B)^{1/2} = (2 \times 1.6 \times 10^{-19} \times 63 \times 10^{-9} \times 1 \times 10^9)^{1/2} = 4.5 \text{ nA}.$$

The SNR due to shot noise is thus

$$\text{SNR} = \frac{I_{ph}^2}{\overline{n_{shot}^2}} = \left(\frac{63}{4.5}\right)^2 = 20\log_{10}(63/4.5) = 23 \text{ dB}. \blacksquare$$

6.4.2 QUANTUM LIMIT

As pointed out earlier, all noise sources except shot noise can theoretically be reduced to zero. Because the shot noise power from photodetection is proportional to the incident light power or average photocurrent, however, as long as there is a light signal, there is shot noise. This section presents a derivation of the fundamental detection performance due to shot noise. At a specified BER, one must know what is the minimum number of photons per bit required. This minimum number is called the quantum limit.

The quantum limit due to shot noise can be derived from the following consideration. If on-off keying (OOK, discussed in Chapter 1) is used to transmit binary bits, an optical pulse is transmitted for bit "1" and nothing (no pulse) for bit "0". At the receiver side, to detect whether a pulse is transmitted or not, one can count the number of incident photons over the bit interval T_0. When the number of photons counted is greater than a certain threshold, a pulse or "1" is detected; otherwise, "0" is detected. This photon counting process can be easily implemented by integrating the photocurrent generated for a duration T_0 and is called **integration-and-dump** in communications.

From Chapter 5, for an incident light signal of power P_{in}, the average number of EHPs generated over T_0 is

$$\overline{N} = \Lambda = \eta \frac{P_{in}}{hf} T_0 \tag{6.25}$$

where η is the quantum efficiency of the photodiode. Because photocurrent generation is a Poisson process [3], the actual number of EHPs generated over T_0 is a Poisson random variable, and the probability of having N EHPs counted over T_0 is given by

$$P[N] = \frac{\Lambda^N}{N!} e^{-\Lambda}. \tag{6.26}$$

Note that when $\Lambda = 0$ or $P_{in} = 0$, $P[0] = 1$. This means there is no possibility of having any EHPs generated. Therefore, to detect whether an optical pulse or bit "1" is transmitted, one can set the threshold at 0.5. That is, if N is greater than 0.5, one can be sure that an optical pulse is transmitted. On the other hand, if N counted is zero, it is determined that no pulse is transmitted. Because $P[N]$ can be zero even when P_{in} or Λ is nonzero, from Equation (6.26), the error detection probability is given by

$$P_E = e^{-\Lambda} p_1 \tag{6.27}$$

where p_1 is the prior probability of sending bit "1." At a given P_E value, the quantum limit N_q is the average number of EHPs per bit required to achieve the specified P_E. From Equation (6.27), the quantum limit is given by

$$\boxed{N_q = p_1 \Lambda = p_1 \ln \left(\frac{p_1}{P_E} \right).} \tag{6.28}$$

QUANTUM LIMIT   As a numerical example, consider $p_1 = 0.5$ and $p_E = 10^{-9}$. Then,

$$N_q = 0.5 \times \ln(5 \times 10^8) = 10.$$

This means an average of 10 EHPs generated per bit is required to achieve a BER of 10^{-9}. ∎

Example 6.11

In Example 6.11, the detection threshold is 0.5. When Λ is large and other noise in the system is considered, the threshold needs to be much larger. In this case, computation of the error detection probability becomes a series summation of the Poisson probability functions given by Equation (6.26). This is illustrated below.

Assume $\Lambda = 100$ and the threshold is set at 39.5. When OOK is used for transmitting binary bits, the BER can be expressed as

$$P_E = p_1 P(0|1) = 0.5 \sum_{i=0}^{39} P(i, \Lambda = 100) = 3.76 \times 10^{-12}.$$

Example 6.12

If we use the central limit theorem (see Appendix 6–A) and approximate the number of EHPs as a Gaussian distribution, then

$$P_E \approx 0.5 \times \frac{1}{\sqrt{200\pi}} \int_{-\infty}^{39.5} e^{-(N-100)^2/200} dN = 5 \times 10^{-10}.$$

Therefore, Gaussian approximation in this case is a conservative estimation of the actual BER. ■

6.5 THERMAL NOISE

Thermal noise, a **white Gaussian noise,** is one of the most common kinds of noise encountered in communication systems. Thermal noise is caused by radiation from random motion of electrons. Because it is a Gaussian noise, the PDF of thermal noise is Gaussian as given by Equation (6.10). This Gaussian distribution comes from the fundamental central limit theorem, which states that if the number of noise contributors (such as the number of electrons in a crystal) is large and they are statistically independent, the combined noise distribution is Gaussian. Because of this theorem, shot noise was approximated as Gaussian noise in Example 6.12.

From thermodynamics, the PSD of thermal noise is given by

$$S_T(\omega) = \frac{h\omega}{2\pi} \left(\frac{1}{2} + \frac{1}{e^{h\omega/2\pi kT} - 1} \right) \qquad \textbf{[6.29]}$$

where k is the Boltzmann constant (1.38×10^{-23} J/K) and T is the temperature in Kelvin [2]. The first term in Equation (6.29) is from quantum mechanics. When $kT \gg h\omega/2\pi$, the power spectrum is almost a constant and equal to kT. From this approximation, thermal noise is a white noise with the following PSD:

$$S_T(\omega) = kT. \qquad \textbf{[6.30]}$$

The inverse Fourier transform gives the following autocorrelation for thermal noise:

$$R_T(\tau) = E[n_T(t)n_T(t + \tau)] = kT\delta(\tau). \qquad \textbf{[6.31]}$$

If the noise is filtered over a finite frequency band B, the filtered power spectrum will be zero outside the frequency band, and the average power is

$$\sigma^2 = R_T(0) = \int_{frequency\ bands} kT\,df = 2kTB. \qquad \textbf{[6.32]}$$

This calculation is illustrated in Figure 6.3.

Example 6.13

THERMAL NOISE POWER AT ROOM TEMPERATURE   At room temperature, $T = 300$ K, the white noise approximation is true if

$$f \ll \frac{2kT}{h} = 12.5 \text{ THz}.$$

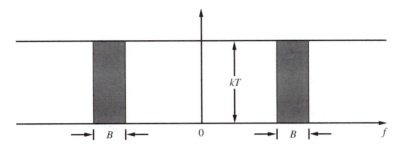

Figure 6.3   Power spectral density of thermal noise.

Because most applications operate at a frequency much lower than 12 THz, the assumption is good. If the system operates from dc to 1 GHz, the average thermal noise power in the system is

$$\sigma^2 = R_T(0) = 2kTB = 8.3 \text{ pW.} \blacksquare$$

Thermal noise can be modeled as a voltage source of bandwidth B by:

$$\frac{\overline{v^2_{thermal}}}{2R} = 2kTB. \qquad\qquad \textbf{[6.33]}$$

Therefore, we have

$$\overline{v^2_{thermal}} = 4kTRB. \qquad\qquad \textbf{[6.34]}$$

In Equation (6.33), the factor of 2 in the denominator on the left-hand side is to account for the optimum power transfer efficiency. That is, 50 percent of the noise power from the equivalent voltage source contributes to the measurable noise power $2kTB$. The thermal current source can be similarly expressed as

$$\overline{i^2_{thermal}} = 4kTGB \qquad\qquad \textbf{[6.35]}$$

where $G = 1/R$ is the conductance.

EQUIVALENT THERMAL VOLTAGE AND CURRENT NOISE SOURCES   At $T = 300$ K, $R = 1$ kΩ, and $B = 1$ GHz, the equivalent voltage and current thermal noise sources have the root mean square values given by:

$$(\overline{v^2_{thermal}})^{1/2} = 0.13 \text{mV}$$

and

$$(\overline{i^2_{thermal}})^{1/2} = 0.13 \ \mu\text{A} \blacksquare$$

Example 6.14

If the thermal noise is included with the shot noise discussed earlier, the SNR at the photodiode output can be expressed as

$$
\begin{aligned}
\text{SNR} &= \frac{(\mathcal{R}P_{in})^2}{2qB(\mathcal{R}P_{in} + I_d + 2V_T G)} \\
&= \frac{I_{ph}^2}{2qB(I_{ph} + I_d + 2V_T G)}
\end{aligned}
\qquad \textbf{[6.36]}
$$

where $V_T = kT/q$ is the **thermal voltage** and G is the conductance of the load resistor. Note that when the photocurrent I_{ph} is large enough, thermal noise can be neglected. This motivates the use of APDs. However, there is an additional noise generated from the multiplication process. This will be discussed in the next section.

Example 6.15

THERMAL NOISE IN PHOTODETECTION   At $T = 300$ K, the thermal voltage V_T is 26 mV. Consider a photodiode that has a responsivity $\mathcal{R} = 0.8$ A/W and a dark current $I_d = 10$ nA. If $G = 1 \times 10^{-5}$ S and $P_{in} = -30$ dBm, the total noise power over a bandwidth $B = 1$ GHz is

$$
\begin{aligned}
\sigma_n^2 &= 2qB(\mathcal{R}P_{in} + I_d + 2V_T G) = 3.2 \times 10^{-10} \times (8.0 \times 10^{-7} + 10^{-8} + 2 \times 2.6 \times 10^{-7}) \\
&= 3.4 \times 10^{-16} \text{ A}^2.
\end{aligned}
$$

Because the signal power is $I_{ph}^2 = 6.4 \times 10^{-13} \text{A}^2$ the signal-to-noise ratio is

$$
\text{SNR} = \frac{6.4 \times 10^{-13}}{3.4 \times 10^{-16}} = 1.9 \times 10^3 = 32.7 \text{ dB}.
$$

In the above computation the shot noise dominates the thermal noise power. However, when the incident light power decreases by a factor of 10, the thermal noise will dominate. In this case,

$$
\text{SNR} = \frac{6.4 \times 10^{-15}}{1.12 \times 10^{-16}} = 57 = 17.6 \text{ dB}.
$$

The SNR drops by 15 dB when the light power drops by only 10 dB. This illustrates the need of a small thermal noise power at a low incident light power. ∎

Noise Equivalent Power   An important parameter that is used to quantify the output noise power of a photodiode is called the **noise equivalent power** (NEP). It is defined as the required incident light power to have a zero dB SNR over a bandwidth of 1 Hz. Solving Equation (6.36) for P_{in} gives

$$
\text{NEP}_{pin} = \frac{1}{\mathcal{R}}\hat{q}\left(1 + \sqrt{1 + 2(I_d + V_T G)/\hat{q}}\right)
\qquad \textbf{[6.37]}
$$

where $\hat{q} = q \times (1 \text{ Hz})$ and the subscript *pin* indicates the use of a PIN diode in photodetection. When the shot noise power due to $\mathcal{R}P_{in}$ is negligible compared to $I_d + V_T G$ or when $2(I_d + V_T G) \gg \hat{q}$,

$$\text{NEP}_{pin} \approx \frac{1}{\mathcal{R}}[2q(I_d + 2V_T G)]^{1/2} \text{ W/Hz}^{1/2}. \qquad \textbf{[6.38]}$$

Thus NEP is the noise power due to dark current and thermal noise.

TYPICAL NEP USING PIN   As a numerical example, consider a PIN diode of $I_d = 1$ nA and $G = 1 \times 10^{-5}$ S. Thus

Example 6.16

$$2(I_d + V_T G) = 2 \times (1 \times 10^{-9} + 0.026 \times 10^{-5}) = 5.22 \times 10^{-7} \gg 1.6 \times 10^{-9} \text{ A}.$$

Therefore, at $\mathcal{R} = 0.8$,

$$\text{NEP}_{pin} = 3.6 \times 10^{-13} \text{ W/Hz}^{1/2}. \quad \blacksquare$$

6.6   AVALANCHE NOISE IN APDS

Because of the multiplication or avalanche process, the photocurrent generated by an APD has an even larger fluctuation. This larger current fluctuation comes from the random secondary EHP generation by each primary EHP. In other words, the total photocurrent fluctuation is contributed by both primary and secondary EHP generation. The total noise is called the APD noise, and the contribution from the random secondary generation is called the **excess noise**, which is quantified by a factor called the **excess noise factor**.

Probability Density Function and Moment Generating Function   The PDF of the total number of EHPs from an APD is a function of the APD gain and its ionization ratio. The probability function and the moment generating function have been derived by McIntyre [4] and Personick [5], respectively. The probability function of having n primary electrons and r secondary EHPs is

$$P(n, r) = n \left[\frac{(1-k)(M_{apd}-1)}{M_{apd}} \right]^{(n+r)/(1-k)} \left[\frac{\Gamma(\frac{n+r}{1-k})}{(n + kr)r!\,\Gamma(\frac{n+kr}{1-k})} \right] \qquad \textbf{[6.39]}$$

where M_{apd} is the gain of the N-type APD,[3] k is the hole to electron ionization ratio as defined by Equation (5.37), and $\Gamma(x)$ is the Gamma function [4].

Personick [5] took a different approach and derived the moment generating function for $P(n, r)$. By definition, the moment generating function of n is

$$M_n(s) = \sum_r P(n, r)e^{sr}.$$

| [3] For P-type APDs, the same equation can be used by replacing k with $1/k$.

Because each primary electron independently generates its secondary EHPs,

$$P(n, r) = \underbrace{P(1, r) \otimes P(1, r) \otimes \ldots \otimes P(1, r)}_{n \text{ convolutions}}.$$

Therefore,

$$M_n(s) = M_1^n(s).$$

From [5], the moment generating function of $M_1(s)$ is

$$M_1(s) = e^s[(1 - a)M_1(s) + a]^b \qquad \textbf{[6.40]}$$

where

$$b \overset{\text{def}}{=} \frac{1}{(1 - k)} \qquad \textbf{[6.41]}$$

and

$$a \overset{\text{def}}{=} \frac{1 + k(M_{apd}-1)}{M_{apd}}. \qquad \textbf{[6.42]}$$

It has been shown that the two results (Equations [6.39] and [6.40]) are equivalent [6] [7] if s in Equation (6.40) is smaller than a critical value [8]. Detailed discussion is given in Appendix 6–D.

Excess Noise Factor Given the moment generating function by Equation (6.40), the APD noise can be computed as follows. As discussed in section 6.4.2 on the quantum limit due to shot noise, the number of primary electrons generated over a time duration T_0 at incident power P_{in} is given by Equations (6.25) and (6.26). Therefore, the total moment generating function of the APD output v is

$$M_v(s) = \sum_{k=0}^{\infty} e^{-\Lambda} \frac{\Lambda^k}{k!} (M_1(s)^k = e^{-\Lambda} e^{\Lambda M_1(s)}. \qquad \textbf{[6.43]}$$

The mean square APD noise is defined as

$$\overline{n_{apd}^2} \overset{\text{def}}{=} E[(v - \bar{v})^2]$$

From Appendix 6–D,

$$\overline{n_{apd}^2} = \Lambda M_1''(0) = \Lambda M_{apd}^3[1 - (1 - a)^2 b]. \qquad \textbf{[6.44]}$$

Comparing this with shot noise and including the APD gain M_{apd}, the excess noise factor can be defined as

$$F_{apd} = \frac{\overline{n_{apd}^2}}{\Lambda M_{apd}^2} = M_{apd}[1 - (1 - a)^2 b]. \qquad \textbf{[6.45]}$$

From Appendix 6–D, this can be expressed in terms of k and M_{apd}:

$$
\begin{aligned}
F_{apd,e} &= M_{apd}\left[1 - (1-k)\frac{(M_{apd}-1)^2}{M_{apd}^2}\right] \\
&= kM_{apd} + (1-k)(2 - \tfrac{1}{M_{apd}})
\end{aligned}
$$

[6.46]

where the secondary EHP generation is assumed to be initiated by electrons. For APDs whose secondary EHP generation is initiated by holes,

$$
\begin{aligned}
F_{apd,e} &= M_{apd}\left[1 - (1-\tfrac{1}{k})\frac{(M_{apd}-1)^2}{M_{apd}^2}\right] \\
&= \tfrac{1}{k}M_{apd} + (1-\tfrac{1}{k})(2 - \tfrac{1}{M_{apd}}).
\end{aligned}
$$

[6.47]

For convenience, the excess noise factor sometimes is also expressed as

$$
F_{apd} = M_{apd}^x
$$

[6.48]

where x is around 0.4 for silicon, 0.6 for InGaAs, and 1.0 for germanium.

APD Noise Power and Spectral Density   As with shot noise, the PSD of an APD noise can be computed. When the frequency response of a given APD is white over the interested frequency range, the APD noise power over a frequency range B is

$$
\begin{aligned}
\overline{n_{apd}^2} &= 2q(\mathcal{R}P_{in} + I_d)M_{apd}^2 B F_{apd} \\
&= 2q(I_{ph}M_{apd} + I_d M_{apd}^2)B F_{apd}
\end{aligned}
$$

[6.49]

where the dark current I_d is included and is defined when $M_{apd} = 1$, and the corresponding two-sided PSD is

$$
\begin{aligned}
S_{apd}(\omega) &= q(\mathcal{R}P_{in} + I_d)M_{apd}^2 F_{apd} \\
&= q(I_{ph}M_{apd} + I_d M_{apd}^2)F_{apd}.
\end{aligned}
$$

[6.50]

Including the thermal noise, the SNR at the APD output can now be expressed as

$$
\begin{aligned}
\text{SNR} &= \frac{(\mathcal{R}P_{in})^2}{2q B[(\mathcal{R}P_{in} + I_d)F_{apd} + 2V_T G/M_{apd}^2]} \\
&= \frac{I_{ph}^2}{2q B[(I_{ph} + I_d M_{apd})F_{apd} + 2V_T G/M_{apd}]}.
\end{aligned}
$$

[6.51]

Note that the thermal noise will become relatively unimportant as M_{apd} increases. If the excess noise factor F_{apd} can be kept small, a higher SNR can be achieved.

Example 6.17	**APD EXCESS NOISE** As a numerical example, if $M_{apd} = 100$ and $k = 0$,

$$F_{apd} = 100(1 - \frac{99^2}{100^2}) = 2.$$

This means a 3 dB degradation in SNR with respect to the case considering only shot noise. ∎

Noise Equivalent Power Using APD   From Equation (6.51) and the NEP expression of a PIN diode given by Equation (6.38), the NEP of an APD can be expressed as

$$\text{NEP}_{apd} = \frac{1}{\mathcal{R}} \sqrt{2q(I_d F_{apd} + 2V_T G / M_{apd}^2)}.$$ **[6.52]**

Comparing this expression with Equation (6.38) shows that the NEP of an APD can be greatly reduced by a large multiplication gain when thermal noise is strong and the excess noise factor is not too large.

Example 6.18	**NEP OF APD** Assume that the APD in the previous example is used. That is, $M_{apd} = 100$ and $F_{apd} = 2$. Under the same conditions as in Example 6.16,

$$\text{NEP}_{apd} = \frac{1}{0.8} \sqrt{2q(2 \times 10^{-9} + 0.026 \times 10^{-9})} = 2.5 \times 10^{-14} \text{ W/Hz}^{1/2}.$$

This is about 9 dB lower than that in Example 6.16, which means an increase of the receiver sensitivity. ∎

6.7 RELATIVE INTENSITY NOISE IN LASER DIODES

Relative intensity noise (RIN) is the intensity fluctuation at a laser diode output. Similar to phase noise, discussed in the next section, it is primarily caused by random spontaneous emission. Different from phase noise, which is critical to coherent communication (Chapter 15) and soliton transmission (Chapter 18), RIN is important in analog communications, such as in SCM (see Chapter 10).

If incident light to a light detector has power $P_{in} + \Delta P_{in}$, where ΔP_{in} is the zero mean intensity noise, RIN is defined as

$$\text{RIN} \stackrel{\text{def}}{=} \frac{E[\Delta P_{in}^2]}{B P_{in}^2} = \frac{2S_{rin}}{P_{in}^2}$$ **[6.53]**

where B is the bandwidth of the signal and S_{rin} is the two-sided PSD of $\Delta P_{in}(t)$.

Because the photocurrent at the photodetector output is proportional to the incident light power, the mean square of the photocurrent fluctuation can be written as

$$E[\Delta i_{rin}^2] = \text{RIN}(I_{ph}^2 B) = \text{RIN}(M_{apd}\mathcal{R}P_{in})^2 B. \qquad [6.54]$$

If the PSD of the RIN in the photocurrent output is $S_{rin} = 50$ (pA)^2/Hz, and the signal photocurrent is

$$I_{ph}(t) = 100\,[1 + k_m s_m(t)]\,\mu\text{A}$$

where k_m is the modulation index for the message signal $s_m(t)$, then

$$\text{RIN} = \frac{2 \times 50 \times 10^{-24}}{100^2 \times 10^{-12}} = 1 \times 10^{-14}\ \text{Hz}^{-1} = -140\ \text{dB/Hz}.$$

If k_m is 0.1 and $s_m(t) = \cos(\omega_m t)$, at a bandwidth of 6 MHz the CNR (carrier-to-noise ratio) is

$$\text{CNR} = \frac{1}{2}\frac{k_m^2}{\text{RIN} \times B} = \frac{5 \times 10^{-3}}{6 \times 10^{-8}} = 8.3 \times 10^4 = 49\ \text{dB.} \ \blacksquare$$

Example 6.19

In addition to spontaneous emission, laser RIN can also be caused by modal instabilities and reflection at the diode–fiber interface. Therefore, RIN can be factored into two components: intrinsic RIN, which is caused by spontaneous emission and internal modal instabilities, and extrinsic RIN, which is caused by reflection.

6.7.1 INTRINSIC RIN

Experimental results [9] show that intrinsic RIN is proportional to

$$\text{RIN} \propto \left(\frac{I_B}{I_{th}} - 1\right)^{-3} \propto \left(\frac{I_{th}}{P_{tx}}\right)^3 \qquad [6.55]$$

where I_B is the bias current and I_{th} is the threshold current of the diode. From this equation, we see that a smaller threshold current device has a smaller RIN at a given power output.

Intrinsic RIN also depends on the modulation frequency [10]. RIN as a function of the modulation frequency is shown in Figure 6.4. At the low modulation frequency range, the RIN follows Equation (6.55). As the modulation frequency increases, the dependence of RIN on the factor $I_B/I_{th} - 1$ becomes insignificant.

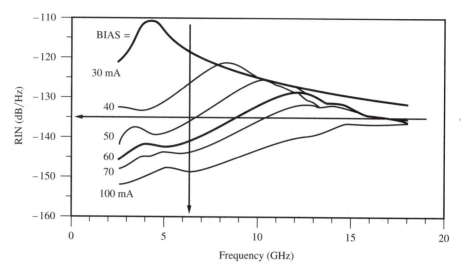

Figure 6.4   RIN as a function of modulation frequency. RIN of an InGaAsP DH diode.

Source: Reprinted, by permission, from Olshansky et al., "Subcarrier Multiplexed Lightwave System,"
[10]. © 1989 by IEEE.

6.7.2   RIN DUE TO REFLECTION

On the path from the light source to the light detector, there can be several light reflection points. The closest reflection point is at the laser diode and fiber interface. This reflection has a low frequency behavior and can be reduced by using antireflection (AR) coating.

The reflection by the far end of the fiber or by other optical components can result in peaking in the noise power spectrum. For a fiber of length L, the peaking frequency is

$$f_p = \frac{c}{2n_f L} \qquad \qquad \textbf{[6.56]}$$

where n_f is the refractive index of the fiber. For example, for a fiber 10 meters long and $n_f = 1.5$, the peaking frequency is $f_p = 10$ MHz. For an even longer length, this peaking will not be significant, because it is in the LF bands. Sato has performed various tests to measure the increase of RIN because of the far-end reflection [9]. Depending on the reflection power percentage, RIN can increase up to 20 dB due to reflection. Therefore, this can be significant in analog video communications.

6.8   PHASE NOISE FROM LASER DIODES

As mentioned earlier, phase noise is caused by random spontaneous emissions in a laser diode. If there is no spontaneous emission, the output light spectrum consists of delta functions (each delta function $\delta[\omega - \omega_i]$ corresponding to one longitudinal mode at frequency ω_i). When there are random spontaneous emissions, the spectrum is no longer a sum of delta functions. Instead, the spectrum is broadened and has a finite nonzero linewidth around each ω_i.

6.8.1 LINEWIDTH BROADENING BECAUSE OF PHASE NOISE

To see the effect of linewidth broadening, consider a continuous wave light output of a single-mode laser given by

$$x(t) = e^{j[\omega_c t + \phi(t)]} \tag{6.57}$$

where ω_c is the center frequency and $\phi(t)$ is the phase noise. If $\phi(t) = 0$, $x(t)$ is at a single frequency and its PSD is a delta function. When there is phase noise, according to Appendix 6–E the PSD due to phase noise is given by

$$S_x(\omega) = \frac{2t_{coh}}{1 + t_{coh}^2(\omega - \omega_c + \alpha_{lw}R_{sp}/2I)^2} \tag{6.58}$$

where R_{sp} is the spontaneous emission rate (1/sec), α_{lw} is the linewidth broadening factor (1/sec) defined in Equation (6.120), I is the total number of photons in the laser cavity (dimensionless), and t_{coh} is the **coherence time** given by

$$t_{coh} \overset{\text{def}}{=} \frac{4I}{R_{sp}(1 + \alpha_{lw}^2)}. \tag{6.59}$$

Equation (6.59) shows that t_{coh} is proportional to I, or the output optical power. Therefore, the larger the optical power, the larger the coherence time. The spectrum given by Equation (6.58) is commonly referred to as a **Lorentzian spectrum**. Its FWHM bandwidth (spectral width between two half-magnitude points) is

$$\Delta\omega_{3dB} = \frac{2}{t_{coh}} = \frac{2R_{sp}}{4I}(1 + \alpha_{lw}^2). \tag{6.60}$$

Therefore, the larger the output optical power, the smaller the 3 dB linewidth (or the more coherent the output signal). Good single-frequency laser diodes today can have a 3 dB bandwidth around 100 kHz (see Table 3.1).

SPECTRUM WIDTH OF A SINGLE FREQUENCY LASER Consider a numerical example. If $I^{1/2} = 160$, $\alpha_{lw} = 5.5$, and $R_{sp} = 720$ GHz, then | **Example 6.20**

$$t_{coh} = \frac{4I}{R_{sp}(1 + \alpha_{lw}^2)} = 4.4 \text{ nsec}$$

and

$$\Delta f_{3dB} = \frac{2}{2\pi t_{coh}} = 72 \text{ MHz.}$$ ∎

The above discussion points out that phase noise broadens the linewidth of a light source output. Chapter 4 explained that a large linewidth results in a large fiber dispersion. Therefore, a small phase noise or a high coherence time is desirable. In coherent communications where the phase of a light carrier is modulated according to the transmitted information, phase noise is even more critical. As will be discussed in Chapter 15, phase noise poses a lower bound of the modulation bit rate. If the bit rate is too low or the bit interval is too long, phase noise can result in a significant phase change over the bit interval, which will cause an excessively high bit error rate.

6.8.2   PHASE NOISE IN COHERENT COMMUNICATIONS

In addition to the linewidth broadening effect discussed above, phase noise can directly corrupt the phase or frequency of a modulated carrier in coherent communications. As explained in Appendix 6–E, the phase noise $\phi(t)$ given by Equation (6.57) consists of two components: one deterministic that results in a frequency shift from ω_c and one random that broadens the linewidth. Because a constant frequency shift has no effect on phase or frequency modulated carriers, only the random phase component must be considered. Denote it by $\phi_r(t)$. From Appendix 6–E, the autocorrelation of the time derivative of $\phi_r(t)$ is given by

$$R_{\dot{\phi}_r}(\tau) = \Delta\omega_{3dB}\delta(\tau).$$ **[6.61]**

By taking the Fourier transform, the corresponding PSD is

$$S_{\dot{\phi}_r}(\omega) = \Delta\omega_{3dB}.$$ **[6.62]**

Because $\dot{\phi}_r$ is the time derivative of $\phi_r(t)$, the PSD of the phase noise is

$$S_{\phi_r}(\omega) = \frac{S_{\dot{\phi}_r}(\omega)}{\omega^2} = \frac{\Delta\omega_{3dB}}{\omega^2}.$$ **[6.63]**

Since the time derivative of a phase is frequency, $\dot{\phi}_r$ represents a *frequency noise*. Equation (6.62) shows that the frequency noise caused by shot noise is a white noise, and when FSK is used the frequency separation must be large enough compared to $\Delta\omega_{3dB}$. On the other hand, Equation (6.63) shows that the phase noise is proportional to $1/f^2$, which means a strong noise in the low-frequency range. When phase modulation is used, the bit rate must be high enough that the effect of phase noise can be minimized.

6.9 MODE PARTITION NOISE

Mode partition noise (MPN) is caused by mode competition inside a multimode FP laser cavity. As a result, even though the total power is constant, the power distribution over different modes is random. Because different modes have different propagation delays in fiber transmission, random power distribution results in random power variation at the receiving end. This power fluctuation due to mode competition is called MPN.

Because the power competition among all longitudinal modes is not fully understood, an exact description of the PDF is not available. However, similar to RIN, it is well known that the noise power of MPN is proportional to the signal power [11]. As a result, an error floor can be reached when MPN becomes dominant. This section presents basic properties of MPN and explains the error floor phenomenon [11].

Suppose a given laser diode has N longitudinal modes and each has a relative power a_i, $i = 1, \ldots, N$. By definition, the sum of these a_i's satisfies

$$\sum_{i=1}^{N} a_i = 1. \tag{6.64}$$

Because each a_i at a certain time is a random variable, the average relative power for mode i is given by

$$\overline{a_i} = E[a_i] = \int a_i \times \text{PDF}(a_1, \ldots, a_N) da_1 \ldots da_N.$$

If the waveform of mode i received is $f_i(t)$, the combined received signal is

$$r(t) = \sum_i a_i f_i(t). \tag{6.65}$$

If the signal is sampled at time t_0, the variance of the sampled signal is

$$\sigma^2 = E[r(t_0)^2] - E[r(t_0)]^2. \tag{6.66}$$

From Equations (6.65) and (6.66),

$$\sigma^2 = \sum_{i,j} f_i(t_0) f_j(t_0) (\overline{a_i a_j} - \overline{a_i}\,\overline{a_j}). \tag{6.67}$$

To simplify the expression, Ogawa introduces a constant k_{mpn}, which is defined as

$$k_{mpn}^2 \overset{\text{def}}{=} \frac{\sum_{i,j} [f_i(t_0) - f_j(t_0)]^2 (\overline{a_i a_j} - \overline{a_i}\,\overline{a_j})}{\sum_{i,j} [f_i(t_0) - f_j(t_0)]^2 \overline{a_i a_j}} \overset{\text{def}}{=} \frac{N}{D} \tag{6.68}$$

where

$$D \stackrel{\text{def}}{=} \sum_{i,j} [f_i(t_0) - f_j(t_0)]^2 \overline{a_i a_j}$$

$$= \sum_i f_i(t_0)^2 \overline{a_i} - 2 \sum_i \sum_j f_i(t_0) f_j(t_0) \overline{a_i a_j} + \sum_j f_j(t_0)^2 \overline{a_j}$$

$$= 2 \sum_i f_i(t_0)^2 \overline{a_i} - 2 \left[\sum_i f_i(t_0) \overline{a_i} \right]^2 \qquad \text{[6.69]}$$

and

$$N \stackrel{\text{def}}{=} \sum_{i,j} [f_i(t_0) - f_j(t_0)]^2 (\overline{a_i a_j} - \overline{a_i}\,\overline{a_j})$$

$$= \sum_{i,j} [f_i(t_0)^2 - 2 f_i(t_0) f_j(t_0) + f_j(t_0)^2](\overline{a_i a_j} - \overline{a_i}\,\overline{a_j})$$

$$= 0 - 2 \sum_{i,j} f_i(t_0) f_j(t_0)(\overline{a_i a_j} - \overline{a_i}\,\overline{a_j})$$

$$= 2 \sum_{i,j} f_i(t_0) f_j(t_0)(\overline{a_i a_j} - \overline{a_i}\,\overline{a_j}) = 2\sigma^2. \qquad \text{[6.70]}$$

Therefore, from Equations (6.67)–(6.70),

$$\sigma^2 = k_{mpn}^2 \times \frac{1}{k_{mpn}^2} \times \sigma^2 = k_{mpn}^2 \frac{D}{N}\sigma^2 = k_{mpn}^2 \frac{D}{2}$$

$$= k_{mpn}^2 \left\{ \sum_i f_i(t_0)^2 \overline{a_i} - \left[\sum_i f_i(t_0)\overline{a_i} \right]^2 \right\}. \qquad \text{[6.71]}$$

Because $\overline{a_i}$ is the average power distribution, which can be measured experimentally, the last expression for σ^2 is a convenient form to compute σ^2 at a given k_{mpn}. See Example 6.21 for illustration.

Example 6.21

CONSTANT CROSS-CORRELATION   Assume the cross-correlation coefficient between any two modes is a constant. That is, assume

$$R_{i,j} = \frac{E[a_i a_j]}{E[a_i]E[a_j]} = \alpha.$$

From this assumption and Equation (6.68), k_{mpn}^2 becomes independent of the waveforms $f_i(t)$ and is

$$k_{mpn}^2 = 1 \frac{\overline{a_i a_j} - \overline{a_i}\,\overline{a_j}}{\overline{a_i a_j}} = 1 - \alpha$$

for any different i and j. Summing over j ($j \neq i$) on both the numerator and denominator[4], gives

---

| [4] This can be done because their ratio is independent of j and equal to k_{mpn}^2.

$$k_{mpn}^2 = \frac{\overline{a_i(1-\overline{a_i})} - \overline{a_i}(1-\overline{a_i})}{\overline{a_i}(1-\overline{a_i})} = \frac{\overline{a_i^2} - \overline{a_i}^2}{\overline{a_i} - \overline{a_i}^2}. \tag{6.72}$$

In practice, $\overline{a_i}$ and $\overline{a_i^2}$ can be measured. Therefore, the above expression allows one to find the value k_{mpn}. As a numerical illustration, assume there are three longitudinal modes of $\overline{a_{-1}} = 0.2$, $\overline{a_0} = 0.7$ and $\overline{a_1} = 0.1$. If the power variation of the main mode is $\overline{a_0^2} - \overline{a_0}^2 = 0.01$, then

$$k_{mpn}^2 = \frac{0.01}{0.7 - 0.49} = 0.05. \quad \blacksquare$$

MPN Caused by Attenuation   Although MPN is caused by random mode partition, it can be manifested by different mechanisms. For example, it can be manifested by fiber attenuation caused by frequency discrimination. For illustration, assume

$$f_i(t_0) = \begin{cases} 0 & \text{if } 1 \leq i < n \text{ or } m < i \leq N \\ A & \text{if } n \leq i \leq m. \end{cases}$$

From Equation (6.71),

$$\sigma^2 = k_{mpn}^2 A^2 \left(\sum_{i=n}^m \overline{a_i} \right) \left(1 - \sum_{i=n}^m \overline{a_i} \right). \tag{6.73}$$

This expression shows that the noise power is proportional to the average power of the modes that pass through multiplied by the average power of the modes that do not pass through. More important, note that σ^2 is proportional to A^2, the square of the optical power. Therefore, when MPN dominates, the SNR cannot be improved by simply increasing the transmitting power.

Because longitudinal modes from an FP laser diode are close in frequency, they have essentially the same fiber dispersion. Therefore, MPN due to fiber attenuation is not important in practice. A more important manifestation is fiber dispersion.

MPN Caused by Fiber Dispersion at High Speeds   When fiber dispersion is significant, one can assume the received waveform of each mode as

$$f_i(t_0) = Ap(i\,\Delta\tau)$$

where for simplicity i is assumed from $-N$ to N. In this case, the received waveforms are different only by a certain time delay due to dispersion. To evaluate MPN, assume a raised-cosine pulse for $p(t)$. That is,

$$p(t) = \begin{cases} 1 + \cos(2\pi t/T) & \text{if } |t| \leq T/2 \\ 0 & \text{otherwise} \end{cases}$$

and

$$\Delta\tau = D_{intra} L \Delta\lambda_{long}$$

is the delay difference between adjacent longitudinal modes due to dispersion ($\Delta\lambda_{long}$ is the longitudinal mode separation in wavelength). From these assumptions,

$$f_i(t_0) \approx 2A - \frac{A}{2}\left(2\pi\frac{i\Delta\tau}{T}\right)^2.$$

From Equations (6.69) and (6.71),

$$\sigma^2 = k_{mpn}^2\frac{D}{2} = k_{mpn}^2 A^2\frac{1}{8}\left(2\pi\frac{\Delta\tau}{T}\right)^4\left[\sum_{i,j}(i-j)^2\bar{a}_i\bar{a}_j\right]. \qquad \textbf{[6.74]}$$

This result leads to the following observations: (1) because noise power is proportional to the square of the received optical power, the SNR cannot be improved by just increasing the transmission power, (2) noise power is proportional to the fourth power of the fiber dispersion, and (3) noise power is proportional to the fourth power of $1/T$ or the bit rate. Therefore, mode partition noise becomes more important when fiber dispersion is significant or when data rates are high.

6.10   TOTAL NOISE

The above discussion presented various kinds of noise in optical communications. This section summarizes their total effect on the final signal detection. As illustrated in Figure 6.5, the total noise at the photodetector output and front-end amplifier input is

$$n_{tot}(t) = n_{mpn}(t) + n_{rin}(t) + n_{apd}(t) + n_{th}(t) \qquad \textbf{[6.75]}$$

where n_{mpn}, n_{rin}, n_{apd}, and n_{th} are the mode partition noise, relative intensity noise, APD noise, and thermal noise, respectively. If a PIN diode is used instead of an APD, $n_{apd}(t)$ should be replaced by $n_{shot}(t)$. Because phase information is not detected in direct detection, phase noise is not included in Equation (6.75).

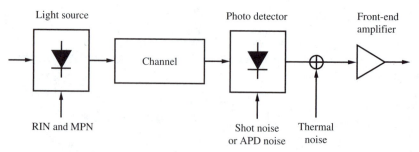

Figure 6.5   Total current noise at the photodetector output.

Because each noise has a different PDF, the total PDF of $n_{tot}(t)$ can be analytically intractable. Using Gaussian approximation for each noise source can simplify calculations. According to the central limit theorem, discussed in Appendix 6–A, this is a reasonable approximation. As a result, the total noise has a zero mean noise and variance equal to the sum of the variance of each noise source. That is,

$$E[n_{tot}^2] = E[n_{mpn}^2] + E[n_{rin}^2] + E[n_{apd}^2] + E[n_{th}^2]. \qquad \textbf{[6.76]}$$

From Equations (6.35), (6.49), (6.54), (6.73), and (6.74),

$$E[n_{tot}^2] = K_{mpn}I_{ph}^2 + \text{RIN}I_{ph}^2 B + 2q(I_{ph}M_{apd} + I_d M_{apd}^2)F_{apd}B + 4kTBG \qquad \textbf{[6.77]}$$

where $I_{ph} = M_{apd}\mathcal{R}P_{in}$ and K_{mpn} is a proportionality constant for the MPN. The corresponding PSD under white noise approximation is

$$S_{tot}(\omega) = \mathcal{K}_{mpn}I_{ph}^2 + \frac{1}{2}\text{RIN}I_{ph}^2 + q(I_{ph}M_{apd} + I_d M_{apd}^2)F_{apd} + 2kTG \qquad \textbf{[6.78]}$$

where $\mathcal{K}_{mpn}$ is a spectral proportionality constant for the MPN.

TOTAL CURRENT NOISE POWER FROM PHOTODETECTION   For a given optical communication system, at room temperature, assume $\mathcal{R} = 0.5$ A/W, $P_{in} = $ dBm, $K_{mpn} = 10^{-4}$, RIN $= -140$ dB/Hz, $I_d = 0$, $F_{apd} = 2$, $M_{apd} = 100$, G $=1$ $(k\Omega)^{-1}$ and B $=500$ MHz. From these data, the average total photocurrent is

Example 6.22

$$I_{ph} = \mathcal{R}P_{in}M_{apd} = 5 \ \mu\text{A}.$$

The total current noise power is thus

$$E[n_{tot}^2] = 10^{-4} \times (2.5 \times 10^{-11}) + (5 \times 10^{-6}) \times (2.5 \times 10^{-11}) + (3.2 \times 10^{-19}) \times$$

$$(5 \times 10^{-6}) \times 10^2 \times 10^9 + 4 \times (1.38 \times 10^{-23}) \times 300 \times 10^{-3} \times (5 \times 10^8)$$

$$= 2.5 \times 10^{-15} + 1.25 \times 10^{-16} + 1.6 \times 10^{-13} + 8.3 \times 10^{-15}$$

$$= 1.7 \times 10^{-13} \ \text{A}^2.$$

Therefore, the ratio I_{ph} to $(E[n_{tot}^2])^{1/2}$ is

$$\frac{I_{ph}}{E[n_{tot}^2]^{1/2}} = 12 = 22 \ \text{dB}.$$

In this case, the strongest contribution to the total noise is from APD noise. If the received power increases from –40 dBm to –20 dBm, then $I_{ph} = 500 \ \mu$A, and

$$E[n_{tot}^2] = 10^{-4} \times (2.5 \times 10^{-7}) + (5 \times 10^{-6}) \times (2.5 \times 10^{-7}) + (3.2 \times 10^{-19}) \times$$

$$(5 \times 10^{-4}) \times 10^2 \times 10^9 + 4 \times (1.38 \times 10^{-23}) \times 300 \times 10^{-3} \times (5 \times 10^8)$$

$$= 2.5 \times 10^{-11} + 1.25 \times 10^{-12} + 1.6 \times 10^{-11} + 8.3 \times 10^{-15}$$

$$= 4.2 \times 10^{-12} \ \text{A}^2.$$

Therefore, the total noise is dominated by MPN. Also, the ratio I_{ph} to $(E[n_{tot}^2])^{1/2}$ is now increased to

$$\frac{I_{ph}}{E[n_{tot}^2]^{1/2}} = 240 = 48 \text{ dB.} \quad \blacksquare$$

6.11 INTERSYMBOL INTERFERENCE AND JITTER

As pointed out in Chapter 1, intersymbol interference (ISI) in digital optical communications is due to pulse broadening, which can be caused by fiber dispersion, slow photodiode response, and other sources such as low-pass filtering in the receiver. Because the binary bits in a digital signal are random and determined by the source data, ISI is also random. An equalizer is generally used to minimize ISI. However, an equalizer optimized to reduce ISI may enhance noise at the same time. Thus there is a trade-off between noise and ISI. As explained in Chapter 7, ISI can be an important factor and a raised-cosine equalization is commonly used to reduce ISI.

As mentioned earlier, jitter is the time domain noise of the recovered bit clock. This is illustrated in Figure 6.6. In practice, jitter can be caused by either noise (called **random jitter**) or ISI (called **systematic jitter**). Because jitter is not an amplitude noise, it is not important unless it becomes large ($>$ 25 percent; see Chapter 7). When jitter is large, the received signal may not be sampled at the optimum timing, and this results in a higher BER. In a transmission link that has many repeaters, jitter can accumulate and cause problems [1].

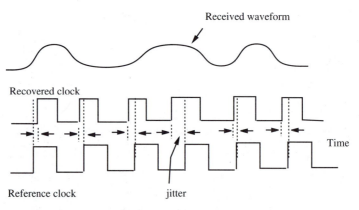

Figure 6.6   Timing jitter at signal transitions.

6.12 SUMMARY

1. Noise and distortion are important performance limiting factors in signal detection. They result in a smaller SNR or higher BER. In analog communications, the SNR should be maximized, and in digital communications, the BER should be minimized.

2. Two important characteristics of a noise are the PDF and PSD. They allow one to calculate the SNR and BER. In addition, an optimum filter can be designed to minimize the BER or maximize the SNR.

3. Thermal noise is a white Gaussian noise due to random thermal radiation. Because of the central limit theorem and the flat spectrum of white noise, white Gaussian noise is often used to approximate other kinds of noise.

4. Shot noise in optical communications is caused by random EHP generations in a photodiode. The number of EHPs generated over a given time interval is a Poisson distribution. Shot noise defined as the photocurrent fluctuation is a filtered Poisson process. Its spectrum is often considered white for simplicity.

5. Because shot noise is intrinsic to photocurrent generation, it places a fundamental performance limit called the quantum limit. When all other noise sources are ignored, the quantum limit is the minimum number of photons per bit required for a specified BER. At a BER of 10^{-9} and a 100 percent quantum efficiency, the quantum limit from incoherent detection is 10 photons per bit.

6. APD noise in optical communications is due to both random primary and secondary EHP generations. Because of the additional secondary EHP generations, APDs have a higher noise power (after normalization by the APD gain). This is quantified by the excess noise factor.

7. RIN in optical communications is caused by the intensity fluctuation due to both random spontaneous emissions in a laser diode and reflections from external couplings. RIN can be important to intensity modulated signals, especially in analog communications. In general, a smaller RIN can be achieved by a higher bias current, smaller threshold current, smaller reflectivity, or lower speed modulation.

8. Phase noise in optical communications is the phase fluctuation caused by random spontaneous emissions in a laser diode. As a result, it broadens the carrier's linewidth. This can be a limiting factor in coherent communications.

9. Mode partition noise in optical communications is caused by random power distribution among longitudinal modes. Because of fiber dispersion, this can cause random signal fluctuation at the receiver end. Like RIN, the noise power is proportional to the signal power. Therefore, RIN and MPN are fundamental factors that cause the error floor.

10. ISI is caused by a limited transmission bandwidth or channel distortion. In optical communications, for example, it can be caused by a small modulation bandwidth of the light source or by fiber dispersion. To reduce ISI, equalization is a common technique used at the receiver end.

11. Jitter is the time domain noise primarily caused by imperfect timing recovery due to random noise and ISI. In optical fiber soliton transmission, jitter can also be caused by ASE noise from optical amplification. In general, jitter is only important in digital communications, and is not critical until it becomes large compared to the bit interval (> 25 percent).

APPENDIX 6–A: PROBABILITY AND RANDOM VARIABLES

This appendix provides the necessary background of probability theory for readers to understand the discussion in this chapter. Most of the examples are also important in communication theory.

6A.1 INTUITIVE DEFINITION OF PROBABILITY

If a given experiment is performed n times (with $n \gg 1$) and an event $\mathcal{A}$ occurs n_A times, the **relative frequency** (n_A/n) of event $\mathcal{A}$ gives an indication of how likely it is that the event will occur. When $n \to \infty$, the limiting relative frequency is called the **probability** of event $\mathcal{A}$. That is,

$$P(\mathcal{A}) = \lim_{n \to \infty} \frac{n_A}{n}.$$

Therefore, the probability of an event means the relative frequency of its occurrence among many other possible events. In general, for a given experiment (e.g., throwing a die), every possible outcome can be called an **event**, and the total collection of all possible events is called the **sample space** of the experiment.

6A.2 AXIOMATIC APPROACH

A more rigorous approach to defining the probability of an event is called the axiomatic approach. In this approach, three things must be defined: (i) a sample space Ω, (ii) a collection of the subsets $\mathcal{F}$ of the sample space, and (iii) a **probability function** P defined over the collection.

To understand the meaning of the above three terms, consider the simple example of throwing a die. The sample space Ω in this case is $\{1, 2, 3, 4, 5, 6\}$. The collection $\mathcal{F}$ is then the set made of all subsets of $\{1, 2, 3, 4, 5, 6\}$. For example, $\{2, 4, 6\}$ is an element of $\mathcal{F}$, which means an event of even numbers. With the collection $\mathcal{F}$ defined, the probability function P is a mapping between an element or event of $\mathcal{F}$ and a real number between 0 and 1.

To have a well-defined probability function over a collection of events, the collection $\mathcal{F}$ should form a σ-**field**. A σ-field is a nonempty collection of subsets of Ω satisfying the following two conditions:

1. If A is in $\mathcal{F}$, $A^c \overset{\text{def}}{=} \Omega - A$ is also in $\mathcal{F}$. A^c is called the complement of A.

2. For a countable number of A_n's in $\mathcal{F}$, $n = 1, 2, \ldots$, the union and the intersection of A_n's are also in $\mathcal{F}$.

The physical meaning of these conditions can be understood as follows. The first condition tells that if $\mathcal{A}$ is a possible event, "$\mathcal{A}$ will not occur" is also a possible event. The second condition tells that if $\mathcal{A}$ and $\mathcal{B}$ are two possible events, (1) "either $\mathcal{A}$ or $\mathcal{B}$ will occur" and (2) "both $\mathcal{A}$ and $\mathcal{B}$ will occur" are also possible events. Note that the definition implies that Ω and ϕ (the empty set) are in the σ-field $\mathcal{F}$.

For a given σ-field $\mathcal{F}$ of the sample space Ω, the probability function P defined over $\mathcal{F}$ should satisfy the following conditions:

1. $P(\Omega) = 1$.

2. $P(A) \geq 0$,   for any A in $\mathcal{F}$.

3. If $A_n, n = 1, 2, 3, \ldots$, are mutually disjoint sets in $\mathcal{F}$, then

$$P(A_1 + A_2 + \ldots) = P(A_1) + P(A_2) + \ldots.$$

The set $(\Omega, \mathcal{F}, P)$ is called a **probability space** defined on $\mathcal{F}$.

6A.3 BASIC PROPERTIES OF PROBABILITY

Conditional Probability   For two events A and M in $\mathcal{F}$, the **conditional probability** $P(A|M)$ is defined by

$$P(A|M) \overset{\text{def}}{=} \frac{P(AM)}{P(M)}$$

where AM is the intersection of A and M that means both events A and M occur. Consider Example 6.23.

BINARY TRANSMISSION   In binary transmission, a transmission error causes a transmitted "1" to be received as "0" or a transmitted "0" to be received as "1." If A is the event that there is a transmission error and M is the event that a "1" is transmitted, the event AM is that a "1" is transmitted and a "0" is erroneously received. The probability $P(A|M)$ is the error probability given "1" is transmitted. For convenience, this $P(A|M)$ is usually written as $P(0|1)$. ∎

Example 6.23

THE BINARY SYMMETRIC CHANNEL MODEL   The **binary symmetric channel** (BSC) model is a common model used in communications. It can be described as follows. When a binary bit "0" is sent over a channel, the probability for the received bit to be "0" is $1 - q$, and the probability for the received bit to be "1" is q. Similarly, if a binary bit "1" is transmitted, the probability for the received bit to be "0" is q, and the probability for the received bit to be "1" is $1 - q$. This BSC model is illustrated in Figure 6.7.

Example 6.24

If the probability for a source bit to be "1" is p, the average error detection probability is the probability of detecting an error when "1" is transmitted plus the probability of detecting an error when 0 is transmitted, or

$$P_E = P(0|1)p + P(1|0)(1 - p) = qp + q(1 - p) = q. \blacksquare$$

There are several special cases for the conditional probability. If $A \subseteq M$, then $P(A|M) = P(A)/P(M)$. If $M \subseteq A$, then $P(A|M) = 1$. And if M and A are disjoint, then $P(A|M) = 0$.

Independent Events   Two events $\mathcal{A}$ and $\mathcal{B}$ (their corresponding subsets are A and B) are called **independent** if

$$P(AB) = P(A)P(B).$$

If A and B are independent, $P(A|B) = P(A)$ and $P(B|A) = P(B)$. Inversely, if one of these two conditions is satisfied, A and B are independent.

Example 6.25	**TWO BIT TRANSMISSION** As mentioned earlier, the bit error rate (P_E) in binary digital transmission is the probability that a bit is incorrectly detected. Assume two bits are transmitted. Let event $\mathcal{A}$ be the transmission error of the first bit and event $\mathcal{B}$ be the transmission error of the second bit. If these two events are assumed to be independent, then

- The probability that both bits are incorrectly detected is P_E^2.
- The probability that only one bit is incorrectly detected is $2P_E(1 - P_E)$.
- The probability of no transmission error is $(1 - P_E)^2$. $\blacksquare$

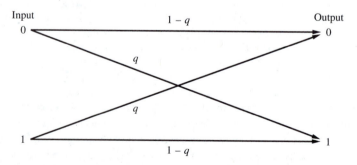

Figure 6.7   The binary symmetric channel model.

Bayes' Theorem   To describe Bayes' theorem, it is useful to first define the concept of **partition**. A partition $\mathcal{P}$ is a collection of subsets of the sample space Ω that are mutually disjoint and whose union equals Ω. Thus, for a subset B and a partition $\mathcal{P} = \{A_1, A_2, \ldots, A_n\}$ of Ω,

$$P(B) = P(B|A_1)P(A_1) + P(B|A_2)P(A_2) + \ldots + P(B|A_n)P(A_n)$$

where

$$P(B|A_i) = \frac{P(BA_i)}{P(A_i)} = \frac{P(A_i|B)P(B)}{P(A_i)}$$

From the above two equations,

$$P(A_i|B) = \frac{P(B|A_i)P(A_i)}{P(B)} \qquad\qquad \textbf{[6.79]}$$

$$= \frac{P(B|A_i)P(A_i)}{P(B|A_1)P(A_1) + P(B|A_2)P(A_2) + \ldots + P(B|A_n)P(A_n)}.$$

$P(A_i)$s are usually called the **a priori** probabilities and $P(A_i|B)$s are called the **a posteriori** probabilities (the probabilities for A_i's when an event B is observed). Therefore, Baye's theorem tells how to find a posteriori probabilities from a priori probabilities and conditional probabilities $P(B|A_i)$.

A POSTERIORI PROBABILITY OF ERROR DETECTION   In digital transmission, assume the probability to transmit a "1" is p, the probability to transmit a "0" is $q = 1 - p$, and the error detection probability is P_E. Let event Y_i be the output at the detector, where $i = 0, 1$. From the assumptions, $P(X_1) = p$, $P(X_0) = 1 - p$, and $P(Y_0|X_1) = P(Y_1|X_0) = P_E$. According to Bayes' theorem,

$$P(X_1|Y_0) = \frac{pP_E}{pP_E + q(1 - P_E)}. \quad\blacksquare$$

Example 6.26

Bayesian Detection   Detecting a digital signal requires *guessing* whether "1" or "0" is transmitted from the received signal y. To obtain the best performance, one must maximize the probability of a correct guess. There are two important detection methods.

1. **Maximum likelihood (ML) detection.**   One claims that the bit just transmitted is "0" if $P(y|0) \geq P(y|1)$, and "1" if $P(y|1) \geq P(y|0)$.

2. **Maximum a posteriori probability (MAP) Detection.**   Here one claims bit "i" is transmitted ($i = 0, 1$) if $P(i|y)$ is the largest. Therefore, this detection maximizes the a posteriori probability $P(i|y)$. To find out which a posteriori probability is the largest, one must use Bayes' theorem for computation. From Equation (6.79), the MAP detection reduces to choosing the largest $P(y|i)P(i)$.

When the a priori probabilities $P(i)$'s are the same, the two detection methods become equivalent. In general, MAP detection gives better detection performance but requires more computation. On the other hand, ML detection is easy to implement and is used in most practical applications.

Example 6.27	**ML DETECTION** Assume the transmitted output i can be either 0 or 1 and the received output y can be 0, 1, or 2. Also assume $P(y|0) \geq 0.5, 0.5, 0$, respectively, for $y = 0, 1, 2$; and $P(y|1) = 0, 0.5,$ 0.5, respectively, for $y = 0, 1, 2$. Then, the ML detection yields 0, 0/1, 1 if $y = 0, 1, 2$, respectively. In this case, when y is 1, one can randomly pick 1 or 0. ■

Example 6.28	**MAP DETECTION** From Example 6.27, further assume the a priori probabilities $P(i) = 0.75,$ 0.25 for $i = 1$, respectively. In this case, $P(y|0)P(0) = 3/16, 3/16, 0$, and $P(y|1)P(1) = 0, 1/16, 1/16$ for $y = 0, 1$, and 2, respectively. Therefore, the MAP detection yields 0, 0, 1 when $y = 0, 1, 2$, respectively. ■

Example 6.29	**ERROR PROBABILITY** According to the detection rules in Examples 6.27 and 6.28, detection is correct when y is either 0 or 2. When $y = 1$, however, the detection may be erroneous. The probability to make such an error is called the error probability. In ML detection, because "0" or "1" is randomly picked when $y = 1$, the error probability for ML is

$$P(\text{"1" is claimed and } y = 1 \,|\, \text{"0" is transmitted})P(0)$$
$$+ \; P(\text{"0" is claimed and } y = 1 \,|\, \text{"1" is transmitted})P(1)$$
$$= 0.25 \times 0.75 + 0.25 \times 0.25 = 0.25$$

On the other hand, the error probability for MAP is

$$P(y = 1 \text{ and "1" is transmitted}) = P(y = 1 \,|\, 1)P(1) = 0.5 \times 0.25 = 0.125$$

Therefore, MAP performs better detection than ML. ■

6A.4 Random Variables

A **random variable** (RV) is a mapping between events in a probability space $(\Omega, \mathcal{F}, P)$ and numerical values. In practical applications, each RV has its own physical meaning.

Example 6.30	**DISCRETE RANDOM VARIABLE** A random variable X for the human population at a given time is a discrete random variable. That is, the human population cannot be any number but positive integers. For example, $P(X = 50 \text{ million at year } 2000) = 10^{-10}$ means the probability of having 50

million people at year 2000 is 10^{-10}. To find the probability that the population will be between 45 million and 50 million, simply do the following summation:

$$P(\text{population between 45 and 50 million}) = \sum_{x\,=\,45,000,000}^{50,000,000} P(X = x). \blacksquare$$

RANDOM VARIABLE FOR ERROR TRANSMISSION   In digital transmission, one can assign "0" in the event of a correct transmission of a bit and "1" for an incorrect transmission. Therefore, the RV is used to indicate the occurrence of a transmission error. ∎ | **Example 6.31**

For a given RV X, the function

$$F_X(x) = Prob(X \le x) \quad \text{for } -\infty < x < \infty$$

is called the **probability distribution** or **accumulation function** of RV X. Note that X is capitalized to indicate it as a RV, and the lowercase x is a certain number. Because the probability of any event is non-negative, the function F_X should be always monotonically increasing. The distribution function can be either a continuous or a step function. If it is continuous, the RV is called a *continuous* RV; otherwise, it is called a *discrete* RV.

CONTINUOUS RANDOM VARIABLE   If RV X is defined as the time between two customers coming to a bank, the distribution function is a continuous function over a certain range, say $F_X(x) = 1 - exp(-x/T)$ for $x \ge 0$. This is called an **exponential distribution**. ∎ | **Example 6.32**

The **probability density function** (PDF) $f_X(x)$ is defined as the derivative of the distribution function. If the RV X is discrete, taking values x_i with probability $P(X = x_i)$,

$$f_X(x) = \sum_i P(X = x_i)\delta(x - x_i).$$

Because $F_X(x)$ is monotonically increasing, the PDF $f_X(x)$ should always be non-negative.

6A.5 MEAN, VARIANCE, EXPECTATION, AND MOMENTS

Given a PDF, the following definitions are important.

1. Mean. The mean, η, of a continuous RV X is defined as

$$\eta_X = \int x f_X(x)dx$$

and is

$$\eta_X = \sum_i x_i P_X(x_i)$$

for a discrete RV.

2. **Variance.** The variance, σ^2, of a continuous RV is defined as

$$\sigma_X^2 = \int (x - \eta_X)^2 f_X(x) dx = \int x^2 f_X(x) dx - \eta_X^2.$$

One can similarly define it for discrete RVs.

3. **Expectation.** The expectation of a function $g(x)$ for a given PDF $f_X(x)$ is defined as

$$E_X[g(x)] = \int g(x) f_X(x) dx.$$

Therefore, mean and variance are the special cases of expectations of a given PDF. Specifically,

$$\eta_X = E_X[x]$$

and

$$\sigma_X^2 = E_X[(x - \eta)^2] = E_X[x^2] - E_X^2[x].$$

4. **Moments.** Moments are expectations of powers of the random variable. Specifically,

$$m_n = E[x^n]$$

is called the **nth order moment**. Here the index X is dropped for simplicity.

6A.6 MOMENT AND CHARACTERISTIC FUNCTIONS

Just like the Laplace and Fourier transforms for a time-domain signal, similar transforms can be performed for a given PDF. Here are two definitions:

1. **Characteristic function $\Phi(\omega)$.**

$$\Phi_X(\omega) \stackrel{\text{def}}{=} \int f_X(x) e^{j\omega x} dx = E[e^{j\omega x}] = \mathcal{F}\{f_X(x)\}^*$$

where $\mathcal{F}\{\cdot\}$ is the Fourier transform and $\mathcal{F}\{f_X(x)\}^*$ is the complex conjugate of $\mathcal{F}\{f_X(x)\}$. The above equation says that the characteristic function is the complex conjugate of the Fourier transform of the PDF. From the inverse Fourier theorem, the characteristic function also uniquely defines the PDF of an RV. In addition, because $f(x) \geq 0$,

$$|\Phi_X(\omega)| \leq \int |f_X(x) e^{j\omega x}| dx = \Phi_X(0).$$

2. **Moment generating function $M_X(s)$.**

$$M_X(s) \stackrel{\text{def}}{=} \int_{-\infty}^{\infty} f_X(x) e^{sx} dx = E_X[e^{sx}].$$

Therefore, the moment generating function is similar to the Laplace transform with integration over $(-\infty, \infty)$ instead of $(0, \infty)$. In general, for some $f_X(x)$'s that do not decrease fast enough as $|x| \to \infty$, the moment generating function may diverge as $|s|$ increases.

6A.7 IMPORTANT DENSITY FUNCTIONS

The mean, variance, characteristic function, and moment generating function of some important PDFs are discussed below. For simplicity, the index X is dropped.

Normal or Gaussian Distribution   The PDF of a normal distribution is

$$f(x) = \frac{1}{\sigma\sqrt{2\pi}} e^{-(x-\eta)^2/2\sigma^2}$$

and is commonly denoted by $N(\eta, \sigma)$. Because $f(x)$ is symmetric with respect to η, $E[(x - \eta)] = 0$. Therefore, η is the mean of the distribution. Also, from integration by parts, note that σ^2 is the variance of the distribution:

$$\frac{1}{\sigma\sqrt{2\pi}} \int x^2 e^{-x^2/2\sigma^2} dx = x \left(\frac{\sigma^2}{\sigma\sqrt{2\pi}} e^{-x^2/2\sigma^2} \right) \Big|_{-\infty}^{\infty} + \sigma^2 E[1] = \sigma^2.$$

The characteristic function can be computed as follows:

$$\Phi(\omega) = \frac{1}{\sqrt{2\pi\sigma^2}} \int e^{-(x-\eta)^2/2\sigma^2} e^{j\omega x} dx$$

$$= \frac{1}{\sqrt{2\pi\sigma^2}} \int e^{-(x-\eta-j\omega\sigma^2)^2/2\sigma^2} e^{j\omega\eta - \omega^2\sigma^2/2} dx = e^{j\omega\eta - \omega^2\sigma^2/2}.$$

Substituting $j\omega$ for s in the above computation, one has the moment generating function given by

$$M(s) = \exp(\eta s + \sigma^2 s^2/2).$$

Uniform Distribution   For a uniform distribution between x_1 and x_2, the PDF is

$$f(x) = \begin{cases} \dfrac{1}{(x_2 - x_1)} & x_1 \le x \le x_2 \\ 0 & \text{otherwise.} \end{cases}$$

It is easily shown that the mean is $\eta = (x_1 + x_2)/2$ and the variance is $\sigma^2 = (x_1 - x_2)^2/12$. Also, from the Fourier transform of a rectangle function, the characteristic function is given by

$$\Phi(\omega) = \frac{1}{(x_2 - x_1)} \int_{x_1}^{x_2} e^{j\omega x} dx = e^{j\omega\eta} \text{sinc}[\omega(x_2 - x_1)/2\pi].$$

Poisson Distribution   The Poisson distribution is a discrete distribution of non-negative integers:

$$P(X = k) = e^{-\lambda}\frac{\lambda^k}{k!}, \quad k \geq 0.$$

In this case,

$$\eta = \sum_{k=1} kP(X = k) = a\sum_{k=1} P(X = k-1) = \lambda.$$

and

$$\sigma^2 = \sum_{k=1} k^2 P(X = k) - \lambda^2 = \sum_{k=1}[k(k-1) + k]P(X = k) - \lambda^2 = \lambda.$$

The characteristic function is,

$$\Phi(j\omega) = \sum_k e^{j\omega k} P(X = k) = \exp[\lambda(e^{2'\omega} - 1)]$$

and the moment generating function is thus

$$M(s) = \exp[\lambda(e^s - 1)]$$

6A.8 CENTRAL LIMIT THEOREM

The central limit theorem states that for most RVs satisfying certain basic properties, the average of the RV over a large number of repeated experiments is approximately a normal distribution. Specifically, the theorem states that for n *independent* and *identically* distributed (i.i.d.) random variables X_i, $i = 1, \ldots, n$, the normalized sum

$$\overline{X} = \frac{X_1 + \ldots + X_n}{\sigma\sqrt{n}}$$

will approach $N(\eta, 1)$ as n approaches infinity, where η and σ^2 are the mean and variance of the distribution of each X_i.

An intuitive proof is as follows. Because

$$\exp(j\omega x) = 1 + j\omega x - \omega^2 x^2 + o(\omega^3 x^3)$$

when ωx is small enough, the following approximation holds:

$$\Phi(\omega) = E[\exp(j\omega x)] = 1 - \sigma^2\omega^2/2 + o(\omega^3) \approx e^{-\sigma^2\omega^2/2}$$

if the mean of X is zero (assumed for simplicity) and the higher-order moments exist (more relaxed conditions are possible). As a result, if n is large so that $\omega/\sigma\sqrt{n}$ is small enough,

$$\Phi_{\bar{x}}(\omega) = \Phi^n\left(\frac{\omega}{\sigma\sqrt{n}}\right) \approx e^{-\omega^2/2}.$$

Therefore, $\overline{X}$ will approach N(0,1) as n approaches infinity. This is called the central limit theorem.

APPENDIX 6–B: RANDOM PROCESS AND POWER SPECTRAL DENSITY

This appendix provides the background of random or stochastic processes. In communications, a signal generated by a transmitter or received by a receiver is generally a random process. A random process is defined as a sequence of random variables. That is, at any given time, a random process is a random variable, and the collection of these random variables over a certain period of time is a random process. To describe how the values of a random process at different times are related, a function called the **autocorrelation** function is used. Its Fourier transform is called the power spectral density (PSD). The PSD is an important characteristic of a random process.

Specifically, for a random process $n(t)$, its autocorrelation function is defined as

$$R_n(t_1, t_2) \overset{\text{def}}{=} E[n^*(t_1)n(t_2)] \qquad \textbf{[6.80]}$$

is the complex conjugate of n and $E[\cdot]$ is the expectation function. Because there are two random variables $n(t_1)$ and $n(t_2)$ in the expectation, it is called a **joint expectation**.

BINARY PULSE AMPLITUDE MODULATED (PAM) SIGNALS   A PAM signal has the form: | **Example 6.33**

$$X(t) = \sum_{n=-\infty}^{\infty} A_n h(t - nT) \qquad [6.81]$$

where $h(t)$ is a pulse of duration from 0 to T and each A_n is a random variable. For binary PAM signals, it is assumed that A_n is either 1 or –1 with equal probability and that A_n is independent of A_m if $n = m$. That is,

$$R_A[n, m] \overset{\text{def}}{=} E[A_n A_m] = \begin{cases} E[A_n]E[A_m] = 0 & \text{if } n \neq m \\ E[1] = 1 & \text{if } n = m \end{cases}.$$

Therefore,

$$R_X(t_1, t_2) = \begin{cases} E[X(t_1)]E[X(t_2)] = 0 & \text{if } t_1 \text{ and } t_2 \text{ are not} \\ & \text{in the same bit interval} \\ h(t_1 - kT)h(t_2 - kT) & \text{if both } t_1 \text{ and } t_2 \text{ are} \\ & \text{in the interval } [kT, (k+1)T]. \end{cases}$$ ∎

In many cases, $R_X(t_1, t_2) = R_X(t_2 - t_1) = R_X(\tau)$. That is, the autocorrelation is a function of only the difference of the two time points. A random process with this property in addition to a constant mean (i.e., a time independent $E[X(t)]$) is called a **wide-sense stationary process**. It should be noted that the autocorrelation function in the above PAM example is not a function of only the time difference. To make it a function of only the time difference, communication theorists use the following time-average definition for the autocorrelation function:

$$R_X(\tau) = \lim_{T' \to \infty} \frac{1}{2T'} \int_{-T'}^{T'} X(t)X(t+\tau)dt. \qquad \textbf{[6.82]}$$

This definition is equivalent to the formal definition given by Equation (6.80) if the signal is **autocorrelation-ergodic**.[5] Example 6.34 illustrates the use of this definition to compute the correlation function.

Example 6.34

AUTOCORRELATION OF PAM SIGNALS   Consider the PAM signal from Example 6.33. is $R_X(\tau)$ now calculated as

$$R_X(\tau) = \lim_{T' \to \infty} \frac{1}{2T'} \int_{-T'}^{T'} \sum_n A_n h(t - nT) \sum_m A_m h(t + \tau - mT)dt.$$

Consider $T' = NT$. By substituting $m = n + r$

$$R_X(\tau) = \lim_{N \to \infty} \frac{1}{2NT} \sum_r \int_{-NT}^{NT} \sum_n A_n A_{n+r} h(t - nT)h[t + \tau - (n+r)T]dt$$

$$= \sum_r \lim_{N \to \infty} \frac{1}{2NT} \int_{-NT}^{NT} \sum_n A_n A_{n+r} h(t - nT)h[t + \tau - (n+r)T]dt$$

$$= \sum_r \left(\lim_{N \to \infty} \frac{1}{2NT} \sum_n A_n A_{n+r} \right) \int_{-\infty}^{\infty} h(t)h(t + \tau - rT)dt.$$

Because the autocorrelation $R_A[A_n A_m] = 0$ if $n \neq m$ the only nonzero term in the above summation is due to $r = 0$. This gives

$$R_X(\tau) = \frac{1}{T} \int_{-\infty}^{\infty} h(t)h(t + \tau)dt. \qquad \textbf{[6.83]}$$

In general, if the input sequence of A_n's has a given autocorrelation function

$$R_A[r] = E[A_n A_{n+r}] = \lim_{N \to \infty} \frac{1}{2N+1} \sum_{n=-N}^{N} A_n A_{n+r}$$

then

$$R_X(\tau) = \frac{1}{T} \sum_r R_A[r] \int_{-\infty}^{\infty} h(t)h(t + \tau - rT)dt. \qquad \textbf{[6.84]}$$

---

[5] A random process $x(t)$ is called **mean-ergodic** if its mean is constant and can be obtained by the time average. A random process $x(t)$ is called **correlation-ergodic** if its correlation can be obtained by the time average of $x(t)x(t + \tau)$ In general, for an expected quantity y of $x(t)$, the process is called **y-ergodic** if it can be obtained from the time average.

Consider a special case to evaluate the integration. Assuming $h(t)$ is a rectangular pulse over $(0, T)$ of constant amplitude 1, the value of the integration is then proportional to how much $h(t)$ and $h(t + \tau)$ overlap in time. The result is

$$R_X(\tau) = \begin{cases} 1 - |\tau|/T & \text{if } |\tau| < T. \\ 0 & \text{otherwise.} \end{cases} \blacksquare$$

The Fourier transform of the autocorrelation is called the power spectral density (PSD). That is,

$$S_X(\omega) \overset{\text{def}}{=} \int_{-\infty}^{\infty} R_X(\tau)e^{-j\omega\tau}d\tau. \qquad [6.85]$$

For a PAM signal, from Equation (6.84),

$$S_X(\omega) = \frac{1}{T} \sum_r R_A[r] \int_{-\infty}^{\infty} \int_{-\infty}^{\infty} h(t)h(t + \tau - rT)e^{-j\omega\tau}d\tau dt$$

or

$$S_X(\omega) = \frac{1}{T} \sum_r R_A[r]e^{-j\omega rT}|H(\omega)|^2 \overset{\text{def}}{=} \frac{1}{T} S_A(\omega)|H(\omega)|^2 \qquad [6.86]$$

where $S_A(\omega) \overset{\text{def}}{=} \sum_r R_A[r]e^{-j\omega rT}$. From the properties of linear systems, if $X(t)$ is the input to a linear time invariant filter, the power spectral density of the output signal $Y(t)$ is

$$S_Y(\omega) = S_X(\omega)|H(\omega)|^2 \qquad [6.87]$$

where $H(\omega)$ is the transfer function of the filter. This can also be verified as follows. From

$$R_Y(\Delta t) = E[Y(t)Y(t + \Delta t)] = E\left[\int X(\tau)h(t - \tau)d\tau \int X(\tau')h(t + \Delta t - \tau')d\tau'\right]$$

$$= \int R_X(\tau' - \tau)h(t - \tau)h(t + \Delta t - \tau')d\tau d\tau'$$

by taking the Fourier transform and noting that

$$e^{-j\omega\Delta t} = e^{-j\omega(t+\Delta t-\tau')}e^{j\omega(t-\tau)}e^{-j\omega(\tau'-\tau)}$$

one obtains Equation (6.87).

PSD OF FILTERED OUTPUT Consider the same PAM signal example (Examples 6.33 and 6.34). From Equation (6.83), the power spectral density is

Example 6.35

$$S_X(\omega) = \frac{1}{T} \int_{-\infty}^{\infty} h(t)h(t+\tau)e^{-j\omega\tau} dt d\tau$$

$$= \frac{1}{T} \int_{-\infty}^{\infty} h(t) \left[\int_{-\infty}^{\infty} h(t+\tau)e^{-j\omega(\tau+t)} d\tau \right] e^{j\omega t} dt = \frac{1}{T}|H(\omega)|^2.$$

Therefore, if the signal $X(t)$ passes through a filter with impulse response $g(t)$, the output is

$$Y(t) = X(t) \otimes g(t) = \sum_n A_n h_1(t - nT)$$

where

$$h_1(t) = h(t) \otimes g(t).$$

Thus

$$S_Y(\omega) = \frac{1}{T}|H_1(\omega)|^2 = \frac{1}{T}|H(\omega)|^2|G(\omega)|^2$$

where $G(\omega)$ is the Fourier transform of $g(t)$. ∎

From Equation (6.87), the physical meaning of the PSD definition can be understood as follows. First, from the inverse Fourier transform note that

$$\frac{1}{2\pi} \int_{-\infty}^{\infty} S_X(\omega)d\omega = R_X(0) = E[X(t)^2] = \text{average power.} \qquad \textbf{[6.88]}$$

Therefore, the total integration of the power spectral density is the average signal power. With this understanding, if we use a narrow bandpass filter $H(\omega)$, Equation (6.87) says that the power of the signal at the filter output is the power of the original signal within the narrow frequency band. Therefore, $S_X(\omega)$ is the power per Hz or power density at frequency ω.

APPENDIX 6-C: SHOT NOISE POWER SPECTRAL DENSITY

This appendix presents a derivation of the PSD of a shot noise. From the EHP generation process discussed in Chapter 5, the photocurrent $i_{ph}(t)$ can be expressed as

$$i_{ph}(t) = q \sum_i h(t - t_i) = q \sum_i \delta(t - t_i) \otimes h_{pin}(t) \overset{\text{def}}{=} i_\delta(t) \otimes h_{pin}(t) \qquad \textbf{[6.89]}$$

where t_i is the generation time of the ith EHP, $h_{pin}(t)$ is the normalized impulse response of the PIN diode, and

$$i_\delta(t) \stackrel{\text{def}}{=} q \sum_i \delta(t - t_i) \qquad\qquad \text{[6.90]}$$

is the impulse photocurrent train caused by EHRs at t_i's. By definition, $h_{pin}(t)$ satisfies the following normalization condition:

$$\int_{-\infty}^{\infty} h_{pin}(t)dt = 1.$$

In practice, photodiodes have a fast response time and $h_{pin}(t)$ can be approximated as the $\delta(t)$ function. From Equation (6.90), the expected integrated current over a period Δt and divided by q is

$$E\left[\frac{1}{q}\int_t^{t+\Delta t} i_\delta(t)dt\right] = E\left[\int_t^{t+\Delta t} \sum_i \delta(t - t_i)dt\right] = \frac{\mathcal{R}P_{in}}{q}\Delta t \stackrel{\text{def}}{=} \Lambda \qquad \text{[6.91]}$$

where $\mathcal{R}$ is the responsivity of the photodetector. Therefore,

$$E\left[i_\delta(t)\right] = q\frac{\Lambda}{\Delta t} = \mathcal{R}P_{in} = \frac{\eta q}{hf}P_{in}. \qquad\qquad \text{[6.92]}$$

This result is consistent with Equation (5.12). The shot noise n_δ corresponding to $i_\delta(t)$ is defined as

$$n_\delta(t) \stackrel{\text{def}}{=} i_\delta(t) - \overline{i_\delta(t)}. \qquad\qquad \text{[6.93]}$$

To find the PSD of this shot noise, consider a new signal $x(t)$ defined as

$$x(t) \stackrel{\text{def}}{=} \text{number of EHPs within } (t, t + \Delta t) - \Lambda.$$

From this definition,

$$n_\delta(t) = \lim_{\Delta t \to 0} q\frac{x(t)}{\Delta t}$$

$$E[x(t)] = 0$$

and

$$R_x(\tau) = E[x(t)x(t + \tau)] = \left(1 - \frac{|\tau|}{\Delta t}\right)\Lambda \quad \text{for } |\tau| < \Delta t \qquad \text{[6.94]}$$

$$\text{otherwise.}$$

Equation (6.94) can be derived as follows. If $|\tau| > \Delta t$, $x(t)$ and $x(t + \tau)$ do not overlap; therefore, $E[x(t)x(t + \tau)] = 0$. If $\tau = 0$, $R_x(0)$ is the variance of $x(t)$, which is Λ from the Poisson distribution property. In general, for $|\tau| < \Delta t$, the fraction of overlap over Δt is $(1 - |\tau|/\Delta t)$. This gives Equation (6.94).

By taking the Fourier transform of Equation (6.94), the PSD of $x(t)$ is given by

$$S_x(\omega) = \Delta t \times \text{sinc}^2\left(\omega\frac{\Delta t}{2\pi}\right)\Lambda. \qquad \textbf{[6.95]}$$

Since $n_\delta(t) \approx x(t)(q/\Delta t)$, when Δt is very small,

$$S_\delta(\omega) = \lim_{\Delta t \to 0}\left\{\left(\frac{q}{\Delta t}\right)^2 S_x(\omega)\right\} = q I_{ph}. \qquad \textbf{[6.96]}$$

Including the impulse response $h_{pin}(t)$ in Equation (6.89) and using Equation (6.87) from Appendix 6–B, one has the PSD of the shot noise given by

$$S_{shot}(\omega) = q(I_{ph} + I_d)|H_{pin}(\omega)|^2 \approx q(I_{ph} + I_d) \qquad \textbf{[6.97]}$$

where the dark current I_d is included.

APPENDIX 6–D: AVALANCHE PHOTODIODE EXCESS NOISE FACTOR DERIVATION

From Equation (6.40),

$$M_1'(s) = M_1(s) + e^s b[(1-a)M_1(s) + a]^{b-1}(1-a)M_1'(s)$$

$$= M_1(s) + b(1-a)\frac{M_1(s)}{(1-a)M_1(s) + a}M_1'(s).$$

Rearranging this equation,

$$M_1'(s) = \frac{(1-a)M_1(s) + a}{(1-a)(1-b)M_1(s) + a}M_1(s). \qquad \textbf{[6.98]}$$

From the basic definition of the moment generation function,

$$M_1(s) = \sum_r P(1, r)e^{sr}. \qquad \textbf{[6.99]}$$

The reason we have summation instead of integration here is because the random variable r (number of secondary EHPs) is discrete. From this definition, it is clear that $M_1(0) = 1$. Furthermore, because

$$M_1'(s) = \sum_r r P(1, r)e^{sr}$$

one has $E[r] = M_1'(0) = M_{apd}$, the multiplication gain. From Equation (6.98),

$$M_1'(0) = M_{apd} = \frac{1}{(1-a)(1-b)+a} = \frac{1}{1-b+ab}.$$

This gives

$$a = \frac{1 + k(M_{apd} - 1)}{M_{apd}}.$$

For convenience, one can define

$$M_1'(s) \overset{\text{def}}{=} \frac{f_1(s)}{f_2(s)} M_1(s) \qquad\qquad \textbf{[6.100]}$$

where

$$f_1(s) \overset{\text{def}}{=} (1-a)M_1(s) + a \qquad\qquad \textbf{[6.101]}$$

and

$$f_2(s) \overset{\text{def}}{=} f_1(s) - (1-a)bM_1(s). \qquad\qquad \textbf{[6.102]}$$

At $s = 0$,

$$f_1(0) = 1 \;\text{ and }\; f_2(0) = 1 - (1-a)b = \frac{1}{M_{apd}}.$$

Going back to Equation (6.100) and taking another derivative, one obtains

$$M_1''(s) = \frac{f_1(s)}{f_2(s)} M_1'(s) + \frac{f_1'(s)f_2(s) - f_1(s)f_2'(s)}{f_2^2(s)} M_1(s). \qquad\qquad \textbf{[6.103]}$$

From Equation (6.43),

$$\bar{v} = \frac{d}{ds}e^{\Lambda(M_1(s)-1)}|_{s=0} = \Lambda M_1'(0) = \Lambda \frac{f_1(0)}{f_2(0)} = \Lambda \frac{1}{1-(1-a)b}$$

and

$$\overline{v^2} = \frac{d^2}{ds^2}e^{\Lambda(M_1(s)-1)}|_{s=0} = \Lambda M_1''(0) + [\Lambda^2 M_1'(0)]^2.$$

From the two equations above,

$$E\left[(v - \bar{v})^2\right] = \overline{v^2} - \bar{v}^2 = \Lambda M_1''(0).$$

From Equation (6.103),

$$M_1''(0) = \frac{f_1(0)}{f_2(0)} M_1'(0) + \frac{f_1'(0)f_2(0) - f_1(0)f_2'(0)}{f_2^2(0)}.$$

Since

$$f_1'(0) = (1-a)M_1'(0) = \frac{(1-a)}{f_2(0)}$$

and

$$f_2'(0) = f_1'(0) - (1-a)bM_1'(0) = (1-a)(1-b)M_1'(0) = \frac{(1-a)(1-b)}{f_2(0)}$$

one obtains

$$M_1''(0) = \frac{1}{f_2(0)^2} + \frac{(1-a) - (1-a)(1-b)/f_2(0)}{f_2(0)^2} \qquad \textbf{[6.104]}$$

$$= \frac{f_2(0) + (1-a)ab}{f_2(0)^3} = M_{apd}^3[1 - (1-a)^2b].$$

Therefore,

$$\overline{n^2_{apd}} = E[(v - \overline{v})^2] = \Lambda M_1''(0) = \Lambda M_{apd}^3[1 - (1-a)^2b].$$

Comparing this with the variance of the shot noise Λ and including the gain factor M_{apd}^2, the APD noise can be expressed in terms of the excess noise factor F_{apd} as

$$\overline{n^2_{apd}} \stackrel{\text{def}}{=} \Lambda M_{apd}^2 F_{apd}$$

where

$$F_{apd} \stackrel{\text{def}}{=} M_{apd}[1 - (1-a)^2b].$$

From the equation next to Equation (6.102),

$$\frac{M_{apd} - 1}{M_{apd}} = \frac{1-a}{1-k}$$

where $b = 1/(1-k)$ from Equation (6.41) is substituted. Thus

$$F_{apd} = M_{apd}\left[1 - (1-k)\left(\frac{M_{apd} - 1}{M_{apd}}\right)^2\right].$$

APPENDIX 6-E: PHASE NOISE

This appendix gives a derivation for the PSD of a light carrier under phase noise and the PSD of phase noise itself. To begin, consider the light output of a single-mode laser diode given by

$$x(t) = e^{j\omega_c t + j\phi(t)} \stackrel{\text{def}}{=} e^{j\omega_c t} \times y(t) \qquad \textbf{[6.105]}$$

where $\phi(t)$ is the random phase due to spontaneous emissions.

Linewidth Broadening   To see the effect of linewidth broadening, first find the autocorrelation function of $x(t)$, which is defined by

$$R_x(\tau) = E[x^*(t)x(t+\tau)] = e^{j\omega_c\tau}E[e^{-j\phi(t)}e^{j\phi(t+\tau)}] = e^{j\omega_c\tau}E[e^{j\Delta\phi}] \quad \textbf{[6.106]}$$

where

$$\Delta\phi \overset{\text{def}}{=} \phi(t+\tau) - \phi(t) = \sum_{i=1}^{N}\Delta\phi_i \quad \textbf{[6.107]}$$

and N is the random number of spontaneous emissions over period $\tau > 0$.

Because the probability of having $N = k$ spontaneous emissions over τ is Poisson,

$$P(N = k) = \frac{(R_{sp}\tau)^k}{k!}e^{-(R_{sp}\tau)}$$

where R_{sp} is the spontaneous emission rate. Therefore,

$$R_x(\tau) = e^{j\omega_c\tau}\sum_{k=0}^{\infty}E[e^{j\Delta\phi_i}]^k\frac{(R_{sp}\tau)^k}{k!}e^{-(R_{sp}\tau)} = e^{j\omega_c\tau}e^{R_{sp}\tau(e_\phi - 1)} \quad \textbf{[6.108]}$$

where

$$e_\phi \overset{\text{def}}{=} E[e^{j\Delta\phi_i}].$$

To find $e_\phi = E[e^{j\Delta\phi_i}]$, one must know the physics. This is illustrated in Figure 6.8, where the coherent carrier has a magnitude of $\sqrt{I}$ and I is normalized as the total number of photons in the cavity.[6] When there is a spontaneous emission, there is an immediate phase change $\Delta\phi_i'$, as illustrated in Figure 6.8a. From the figure,

$$I^{1/2} + e^{j\phi_i} = (I + \Delta I)^{1/2}e^{j\Delta\phi_i} \quad \textbf{[6.109]}$$

where ϕ_i is the random phase of the spontaneously emitted photon and $\Delta\phi_i$ is the simultaneous phase change with respect to the coherent carrier phase. Comparing the amplitude squares of the two sides of Equation (6.109), one obtains

$$\Delta I = 2\sqrt{I}\cos(\phi_i) \quad \textbf{[6.110]}$$

and

$$\Delta\phi_i' = \frac{\sin(\phi_i)}{\sqrt{I}} \quad \textbf{[6.111]}$$

when I is large. Equation (6.110) shows that there is a significant intensity change for only one spontaneous emission. This change results in a relaxation oscillation as pointed out by [12]. After some time, the relaxation oscillation brings the intensity back to the steady state

---

[6]Because I denotes the total number of photons in a laser cavity, I is a dimensionless representation of the laser power in the cavity. Therefore, $\sqrt{I}$ is a dimensionless representation of the lightwave magnitude.

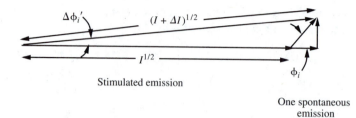

Stimulated emission

One spontaneous emission

(a)

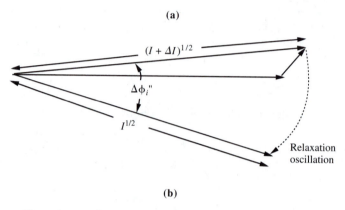

Relaxation oscillation

(b)

Figure 6.8   Phase changes due to one spontaneous emission: (a) instantaneous phase change and (b) delay phase change due to relaxation oscillation.

value I. However, at the same time, there is an additional phase change $\Delta\phi_i''$ due to this relaxation process, as illustrated in Figure 6.8. From Equation (6.122), to be derived shortly, this second phase change is

$$\Delta\phi_i'' = -\frac{\alpha_{lw}}{2I} - \frac{\alpha_{lw}}{\sqrt{I}}\cos(\phi_i) \qquad \text{[6.112]}$$

where α_{lw} is called the **linewidth broadening factor**, defined by Equation (6.120). The total phase change is thus

$$\Delta\phi_i = \Delta\phi_i' + \Delta\phi_i'' = -\frac{\alpha_{lw}}{2I} + \frac{1}{\sqrt{I}}[\sin(\phi_i) - \alpha_{lw}\cos(\phi_i)]. \qquad \text{[6.113]}$$

Because ϕ_i is uniformly distributed over $[0, 2\pi)$,

$$E[e^{j\Delta\phi_i}] = e^{-j\alpha_{lw}/2I} E[e^{j(\sin\phi_i - \alpha_{lw}\cos\phi_i)/\sqrt{I}}]$$

$$\approx e^{-j\alpha_{lw}/2I} E\left[1 - \frac{(\sin\phi_i - \alpha_{lw}\cos\phi_i)^2}{2I}\right]$$

$$= e^{-j\alpha_{lw}/2I}\left[1 - \frac{1 + \alpha_{lw}^2}{4I}\right] \approx 1 - j\frac{\alpha_{lw}}{2I} - \frac{1 + \alpha_{lw}^2}{4I}$$

when I is large. Thus, from Equation (6.108),

$$R_x(\tau) = e^{j\omega_c\tau}e^{-j(\alpha_{lw}R_{sp}/2I)\tau}e^{-[R_{sp}(1+\alpha_{lw}^2)/4I]\tau}$$

for $\tau > 0$. Because $R_x(\tau) = R_x^*(-\tau)$,

$$R_x(\tau) = e^{j\omega_c\tau}e^{-j(\alpha_{lw}R_{sp}/2I)\tau}e^{-[R_{sp}(1+\alpha_{lw}^2)/4I]|\tau|}$$

$$\overset{\text{def}}{=} e^{j(\omega_c - \alpha_{lw}R_{sp}/2I)\tau}e^{-|\tau|/t_{coh}}$$

[6.114]

where

$$t_{coh} \overset{\text{def}}{=} \frac{4I}{R_{sp}(1 + \alpha_{lw}^2)}$$

[6.115]

is called the **coherence time** for the output signal. Because t_{coh} is proportional to I, or the output optical power, the larger the optical power, the larger the coherence time. By taking the Fourier transform of Equation (6.114), the power spectrum is found to be

$$S_x(\omega) = \frac{2t_{coh}}{1 + t_{coh}^2(\omega - \omega_c + \alpha_{lw}R_{sp}/2I)^2}.$$

[6.116]

This is called the **Lorentzian spectrum**, and the FWHM bandwidth is

$$\Delta\omega_{3dB} = \frac{2}{t_{coh}} = \frac{R_{sp}}{2I}(1 + \alpha_{lw}^2).$$

[6.117]

Relaxation Phase Shift   The phase noise term $\Delta\phi_i''$ due to relaxation phase shift from spontaneous emission is derived below. The derivation is based on the rate equations (12.109) and (12.110) given in Appendix 12–A. Readers are encouraged to fully understand the rate equations before reading the following derivation.

From the discussion in Appendix 12–A and Equations (12.97)–(12.102),

$$\Gamma a(N - N_0) - \alpha_{int} = \frac{\omega}{n_0 c}\left(\chi_0'' + \chi_p'' - \frac{\sigma}{\epsilon_0\omega}\right).$$

The definitions of the variables above are given in Chapter 12. If

$$1 + \chi_0 + \chi_p' + j\left(\chi_0'' + \chi_p'' - \frac{\sigma}{\epsilon_0\omega}\right) \overset{\text{def}}{=} (n_0 + \Delta n' + j\Delta n'')^2$$

$$\approx n_0^2 + 2n_0(\Delta n' + j\Delta n'')$$

one has

$$\Gamma a(N - N_0) - \alpha_{int} = 2\frac{\omega}{c}\Delta n''.$$

Therefore, the rate equations (12.109) and (12.110) reduce to

$$\frac{dI}{dt} = v_g \frac{\omega}{c} \Delta n'' \tag{6.118}$$

and

$$\frac{d\phi}{dt} = -\frac{1}{2} v_g \frac{\omega}{c} \Delta n'. \tag{6.119}$$

Here $I = A^2$ is used for intensity (dimensionless). If

$$\boxed{\alpha_{lw} \stackrel{\text{def}}{=} -\frac{\Delta n'}{\Delta n''}} \tag{6.120}$$

is defined as the **linewidth broadening factor**, then

$$\frac{d\phi}{dt} = \alpha_{lw} \frac{dI/dt}{I}. \tag{6.121}$$

In the case of one spontaneous emission, both sides of Equation (6.121) can be integrated from $t = t_i$ to $t = \infty$. Because I is essentially a constant and $I(\infty) - I(t_i) = -\Delta I = 1 + I^{1/2}\cos(\phi_i)$, the relaxation phase shift $\Delta\phi_i''$ is given by

$$\Delta\phi_i'' = \phi(\infty) - \phi(t_i) = -\alpha_{lw}\left(\frac{1}{I} + \frac{\cos(\phi_i)}{I^{1/2}}\right). \tag{6.122}$$

PSD of Phase Noise   The statistics of phase change $\Delta\phi_i$ itself are derived below. Equation (6.121) shows that the phase change due to one spontaneous emission has a constant term $-\alpha_{lw}/2I$ and a random zero-mean term $[\sin(\phi_i) - \alpha_{lw}\cos(\phi_i)]/\sqrt{I}$. The constant term results in a frequency shift of the carrier, and the random term causes random phase fluctuation of the carrier. Because the frequency shift is constant, it has no effect on information transmission. On the other hand, the random phase term can corrupt the transmitted information when either phase or frequency modulation is used. To quantify its effect, define

$$\Delta\phi_{i,r} \stackrel{\text{def}}{=} \frac{1}{\sqrt{I}}[\sin(\phi_i) - \alpha_{lw}\cos(\phi_i)] \tag{6.123}$$

as the random phase change due to the ith spontaneous emission, and

$$\phi_r(t) \stackrel{\text{def}}{=} \sum_i \Delta\phi_{i,r} u(t - t_i) \tag{6.124}$$

as the random phase function of the output carrier

$$x(t) = e^{j(\omega_c - \alpha_{lw}R_{sp}/2I)t} e^{j\phi_r(t)}.$$

In Equation (6.124), $u(t)$ is a unit step function and t_i is the occurrence time of the ith spontaneous emission.

Because ϕ_i is uniformly distributed between 0 and 2π, the variance of the random phase change at each spontaneous emission is

$$E[\Delta\phi_{i,r}^2] = \frac{1 + \alpha_{lw}^2}{2I} = \frac{2}{R_{sp}t_{coh}} = \frac{\Delta\omega_{3dB}}{R_{sp}}. \qquad \textbf{[6.125]}$$

Also, the autocorrelation of the time derivative $\dot{\phi}_r(t)$ is

$$R_{\dot{\phi}_r}(\tau) = E\{\dot{\phi}_r(t+\tau)\dot{\phi}_r(t)\}$$
$$= E\left[\lim_{\epsilon_1 \to 0} \frac{\phi_r(t+\tau+\epsilon_1) - \phi_r(t+\tau)}{\epsilon_1} \lim_{\epsilon_2 \to 0} \frac{\phi_r(t+\tau+\epsilon_2) - \phi_r(t+\tau)}{\epsilon_2}\right].$$

When $\tau \neq 0$, the phase changes within the two time intervals ϵ_1 and ϵ_2 are independent. Therefore, the correlation function is zero. When $\tau = 0$,

$$R_{\dot{\phi}_r}(0) = \lim_{\epsilon \to 0} E\left\{\frac{\Delta\phi^2}{\epsilon^2}\right\} = \lim_{\epsilon \to 0} \frac{(R_{sp})E[\Delta\phi_{i,r}^2]}{\epsilon^2}$$

noting the fact that there is an average number (R_{sp}) of spontaneous emissions during the time interval ϵ. Therefore,

$$R_{\dot{\phi}_r}(\tau) = \Delta\omega_{3dB}\delta(\tau) \qquad \textbf{[6.126]}$$

and

$$S_{\dot{\phi}_r}(\omega) = \Delta\omega_{3dB}. \qquad \textbf{[6.127]}$$

Because $\dot{\phi}_r$ is the time derivative of $\phi_r(t)$,

$$S_{\phi_r}(\omega) = \frac{S_{\dot{\phi}_r}(\omega)}{\omega^2} = \frac{\Delta\omega_{3dB}}{\omega^2} \qquad \textbf{[6.128]}$$

PROBLEMS

Problem 6–1 Noise Power: Consider a noise with the following PDF:

$$f_N(n) = \frac{1}{2\sigma}e^{-|n|/\sigma}.$$

Find the variance or the noise power.

Problem 6–2 Bit Error Rate: The BER illustrated in Example 6.3 is usually called the *raw* BER. Using an error correction code can reduce the BER significantly. Equivalently, it allows a smaller input SNR to produce the same final BER. The factor of this SNR reduction is called the **coding gain**. Consider the following. First, use Equations (6.15) and (6.16) to calculate the SNR required to have a BER of 10^{-8}. If an error correction code is used that reduces a raw BER of 10^{-4} down to 10^{-8}, find the corresponding SNR required. What is the ratio of the two SNRs in dB? This ratio is called the coding gain.

Problem 6–3 PSD and Noise Power: For a noise with the following PSD:

$$S_n(\omega) = N_0 \frac{1}{1 + (\omega/\omega_c)^2}$$

calculate the total noise power. If this noise is passed through an ideal low-pass filter with bandwidth $B = \omega_c/(2\pi)$, what is the output noise power?

Problem 6–4 Signal's Bandwidth: There are several ways to define a signal's transmission bandwidth.

a. The first definition is called the 3 dB bandwidth. The 3 dB bandwidth is the frequency at which the power spectrum density is half of the peak value. Based on this definition, find the 3 dB frequency of the following signal.

$$S_x(\omega) = S_0 \frac{1}{\sqrt{2\pi\sigma^2}} e^{-\omega^2/(2\sigma^2)}$$

If the signal is a passband signal, the frequency range between two half-maximum points is called the full-width half-maximum (FWHM).

b. Another definition is called the root mean square (RMS) bandwidth. The RMS bandwidth B_{RMS} of a signal $x(t)$ with its PSD of $S_x(\omega)$ is defined as

$$(2\pi B_{RMS})^2 \stackrel{\text{def}}{=} \frac{\int \omega^2 S_x(\omega) d\omega}{\int S_x(\omega) d\omega}. \qquad \textbf{[6.129]}$$

For the Gaussian PSD given in a, find its RMS bandwidth.

c. If the PSD of a given signal has null points (i.e., there are frequencies at which the PSD is zero), another definition of the bandwidth commonly used is its first null point. For an NRZ digital signal of bit rate $1/T_0$ with the following PSD:

$$S_x(\omega) = T_0 \text{sinc}^2(\omega T_0/2\pi)$$

find the null-point bandwidth.

Problem 6–5 Wiener Filtering: Consider a signal with the following PSD:

$$S_x(\omega) = \begin{cases} S_0[1 - (\frac{\omega}{\omega_B})^2] & \text{if } |\omega| < \omega_B \\ 0 & \text{otherwise.} \end{cases}$$

Assume a white noise $S_n(\omega) \neq N_0/2$ is added to the signal.

a. Find the output SNR if an ideal low-pass filter is used at the receiver with the cutoff frequency at $\omega_B/(2\pi)$.

b. Find the noncausal Wiener filter and the corresponding output SNR. How much does the SNR improve at $N_0/2S_0 = 1$?

Problem 6–6 Matched Filtering: A PAM signal $x(t) = \sum_k A_k p(t - kT_0)$ has $A_k = \pm A$ and the following triangle pulse:

$$p(t) = \begin{cases} 1 - |t|/T_0 & \text{if } |t| < T_0 \\ 0 & \text{otherwise.} \end{cases}$$

a. What is the corresponding matched filter under white Gaussian noise? What is the sampled value of the filtered signal at $t = 0$?

b. If the PSD of the white Gaussian noise is $N_0/2$, what is the noise power at the sampled time using the matched filter in a? If a single pulse is transmitted with $x(t) = Ap(t)$, what is the corresponding BER in terms of the Q-function?

c. For an ideal low-pass filter with its cutoff frequency at $1/T_0$, find the corresponding BER. What is the improvement in terms of the input signal power from using the matched filter? Use the result

$$\int_0^1 \frac{\sin(\pi x)}{\pi x} dx = 0.59.$$

Problem 6–7 Shot Noise: In a digital optical receiver, assume there is no other noise but dark current and shot noise due to the signal photocurrent. If the dark current is 16 pA and the bit rate is 10 Mb/s, find the minimum signal photocurrent and the threshold to have the average bit error rate less than 0.011. Assume the input signal is an NRZ signal and the photon counting technique is used for detection. In threshold detection, if the number of electrons received is greater than the threshold, "1" will be claimed, and if the number of electrons received is less than or equal to the threshold, "0" will be claimed. Note that the signal's photocurrent is zero for bit "0" and a high value for bit "1." Also, "0" and "1" are equally possible. Use Table 6.2 for computing the Poisson probabilities. Hint: for minimal signal photocurrent, the error probabilities $P(e|1)$ and $P(e|0)$ should be close to each other.

Table 6.2 $P(k \leq x) = \sum_{k=0}^{x}(\Lambda^k/k!)e^{-\Lambda}$.

Λ	x = 6	7	8	9	10	11	12	13
2.0	0.9955	0.9989	0.9998	1.0000	1.0000	1.0000	1.0000	1.0000
3.0	0.9665	0.9881	0.9962	0.9989	0.9997	0.9999	1.0000	1.0000
4.0	0.8893	0.9489	0.9786	0.9919	0.9972	0.9991	0.9997	0.9999
5.0	0.7622	0.8666	0.9319	0.9682	0.9863	0.9945	0.9980	0.9993
6.0	0.6063	0.7440	0.8472	0.9161	0.9574	0.9799	0.9912	0.9964
7.0	0.4497	0.5987	0.7291	0.8305	0.9015	0.9467	0.9730	0.9872
8.0	0.3134	0.4530	0.5925	0.7166	0.8159	0.8881	0.9362	0.9658
9.0	0.2068	0.3239	0.4557	0.5874	0.7060	0.8030	0.8758	0.9261
10.0	0.1301	0.2202	0.3328	0.4579	0.5830	0.6968	0.7916	0.8645
11.0	0.0786	0.1432	0.2320	0.3405	0.4599	0.5793	0.6887	0.7813
12.0	0.0458	0.0895	0.1550	0.2424	0.3472	0.4616	0.5760	0.6815
13.0	0.0259	0.0540	0.0998	0.1658	0.2517	0.3532	0.4631	0.5730
14.0	0.0142	0.0316	0.0621	0.1094	0.1757	0.2600	0.3585	0.4644
15.0	0.0076	0.0180	0.0374	0.0699	0.1185	0.1848	0.2676	0.3632
16.0	0.0040	0.0100	0.0220	0.0433	0.0774	0.1270	0.1931	0.2745
17.0	0.0021	0.0054	0.0126	0.0261	0.0491	0.0847	0.1350	0.2009

Table 6.2   Continued.

Λ	x = 6	7	8	9	10	11	12	13
18.0	0.0010	0.0029	0.0071	0.0154	0.0304	0.0549	0.0917	0.1426
19.0	0.0005	0.0015	0.0039	0.0089	0.0183	0.0347	0.0606	0.0984
20.0	0.0003	0.0008	0.0021	0.0050	0.0108	0.0214	0.0390	0.0661
21.0	0.0001	0.0004	0.0011	0.0028	0.0063	0.0129	0.0245	0.0434
22.0	0.0001	0.0002	0.0006	0.0015	0.0035	0.0076	0.0151	0.0278
23.0	0.0000	0.0001	0.0003	0.0008	0.0020	0.0044	0.0091	0.0174
24.0	0.0000	0.0000	0.0002	0.0004	0.0011	0.0025	0.0054	0.0107
25.0	0.0000	0.0000	0.0001	0.0002	0.0006	0.0014	0.0031	0.0065
26.0	0.0000	0.0000	0.0000	0.0001	0.0003	0.0008	0.0018	0.0038
27.0	0.0000	0.0000	0.0000	0.0001	0.0002	0.0004	0.0010	0.0022
28.0	0.0000	0.0000	0.0000	0.0000	0.0001	0.0002	0.0006	0.0013
29.0	0.0000	0.0000	0.0000	0.0000	0.0000	0.0001	0.0003	0.0007
30.0	0.0000	0.0000	0.0000	0.0000	0.0000	0.0001	0.0002	0.0004
31.0	0.0000	0.0000	0.0000	0.0000	0.0000	0.0000	0.0001	0.0002
32.0	0.0000	0.0000	0.0000	0.0000	0.0000	0.0000	0.0000	0.0001

Λ	x = 14	15	16	17	18	19	20	21
2.0	1.0000	1.0000	1.0000	1.0000	1.0000	1.0000	1.0000	1.0000
3.0	1.0000	1.0000	1.0000	1.0000	1.0000	1.0000	1.0000	1.0000
4.0	1.0000	1.0000	1.0000	1.0000	1.0000	1.0000	1.0000	1.0000
5.0	0.9998	0.9999	1.0000	1.0000	1.0000	1.0000	1.0000	1.0000
6.0	0.9986	0.9995	0.9998	0.9999	1.0000	1.0000	1.0000	1.0000
7.0	0.9943	0.9976	0.9990	0.9996	0.9999	1.0000	1.0000	1.0000
8.0	0.9827	0.9918	0.9963	0.9984	0.9993	0.9997	0.9999	1.0000
9.0	0.9585	0.9780	0.9889	0.9947	0.9976	0.9989	0.9996	0.9998
10.0	0.9165	0.9513	0.9730	0.9857	0.9928	0.9965	0.9984	0.9993
11.0	0.8540	0.9074	0.9441	0.9678	0.9823	0.9907	0.9953	0.9977
12.0	0.7720	0.8444	0.8987	0.9370	0.9626	0.9787	0.9884	0.9939
13.0	0.6751	0.7636	0.8355	0.8905	0.9302	0.9573	0.9750	0.9859
14.0	0.5704	0.6694	0.7559	0.8272	0.8826	0.9235	0.9521	0.9712
15.0	0.4657	0.5681	0.6641	0.7489	0.8195	0.8752	0.9170	0.9469
16.0	0.3675	0.4667	0.5660	0.6593	0.7423	0.8122	0.8682	0.9108
17.0	0.2808	0.3715	0.4677	0.5640	0.6550	0.7363	0.8055	0.8615
18.0	0.2081	0.2867	0.3751	0.4686	0.5622	0.6509	0.7307	0.7991
19.0	0.1497	0.2148	0.2920	0.3784	0.4695	0.5606	0.6472	0.7255
20.0	0.1049	0.1565	0.2211	0.2970	0.3814	0.4703	0.5591	0.6437
21.0	0.0716	0.1111	0.1629	0.2270	0.3017	0.3843	0.4710	0.5577
22.0	0.0477	0.0769	0.1170	0.1690	0.2325	0.3060	0.3869	0.4716

Table 6.2 Continued.

Λ	x = 14	15	16	17	18	19	20	21
23.0	0.0311	0.0520	0.0821	0.1228	0.1748	0.2377	0.3101	0.3894
24.0	0.0198	0.0344	0.0563	0.0871	0.1283	0.1803	0.2426	0.3139
25.0	0.0124	0.0223	0.0377	0.0605	0.0920	0.1336	0.1855	0.2473
26.0	0.0076	0.0142	0.0248	0.0411	0.0646	0.0968	0.1387	0.1905
27.0	0.0046	0.0088	0.0160	0.0274	0.0445	0.0687	0.1015	0.1436
28.0	0.0027	0.0054	0.0101	0.0179	0.0300	0.0478	0.0727	0.1060
29.0	0.0016	0.0033	0.0063	0.0115	0.0199	0.0326	0.0511	0.0767
30.0	0.0009	0.0019	0.0039	0.0073	0.0129	0.0219	0.0353	0.0544
31.0	0.0005	0.0011	0.0023	0.0045	0.0083	0.0144	0.0239	0.0379
32.0	0.0003	0.0007	0.0014	0.0028	0.0052	0.0093	0.0159	0.0260

Problem 6–8 Shot Noise: Assume the photocurrent output of a PIN diode has an average value of 32 nA. If the current is integrated over 1 nsec, what is the probability that the integrated value divided by q is lower than 10?

Problem 6–9 Quantum Limit:
a. Find the quantum limit at BER $= 10^{-6}$.
b. In on-off keying, assume the photodiode has a dark current I_d of 10 pA and the average photocurrent I_{ph} generated by signal "1" is 40 pA. Find the maximum transmission rate to give a bit error rate of 0.01. Assume 0's and 1's are equally likely. Also, what threshold should be used in your detection? Use Table 6.2 for computations.

Problem 6–10 Thermal Noise: When the input signal power is very weak, such as in satellite communications, a low operating temperature is a key to reducing thermal noise at the receiver front end. For illustration, consider a digital transmission system where the received signal power is 10 pW. Assume the receiver front-end amplifier has only thermal noise and the bandwidth is 200 MHz.
a. Find the input SNR at 300 K. Use Equations (6.15) and (6.16) to find the BER.
b. Find the operating temperature to reduce the BER to 10^{-6}.

Problem 6–11 Equivalent Thermal Noise Sources: Consider two parallel resistors of 10 and 30 kΩ. Find the equivalent thermal current source at 300 K. What is the equivalent voltage source? Assume a bandwidth of 1 GHz.

Problem 6–12 Multiplication Gain Noise:
a. For an APD at a given multiplication gain, if the electron ionization coefficient α is smaller than the hole ionization coefficient β, which type of APD ($n^+p^+pp^+$ or $p^+n^+nn^+$) should be used to minimize the excess noise factor? Explain why.
b. Explain how the multiplication gain affects the SNR in an optical receiver.

Problem 6–13 Multiplication Gain Noise: Assume an N-type APD is used with $k = 0.5$. Calculate the excess noise gain factor at gains of 10, 50, and 100. If the APD noise power is equal to the thermal noise at the receiver front end at a gain of 10, find the normalized total noise power at gains of 50 and 100 in terms of the total power at the gain of 10. The normalized total noise power is the total noise power divided by the squared gain.

Problem 6–14 Multiplication Gain Noise: For an N-type APD of a multiplication gain 50, find the excess noise factor at $k = 0.0, 0.5$, and 1.0. From the excess noise point of view, which k is the best at the same multiplication gain? From the discussion in Chapter 5, what is the trade-off of having such k?

Problem 6–15 Intrinsic RIN: Using Equation (6.55), find by what percentage the RIN decreases when the threshold current is reduced by 10, 20, and 30 percent at the same output power, respectively.

Problem 6–16 RIN: In an analog communication system, assume a RIN of -130 dB/Hz. Calculate the CNR at a modulation index of 0.2 and a bandwidth of 5 MHz. If the modulating signal $m(t)$ has mean square $\overline{m^2} = 0.1$, calculate the corresponding SNR.

Problem 6–17 Phase Noise: If the 3 dB bandwidth (in Hz) due to phase noise is required to be within 10 percent of the transmission bit rate, find the ratio of the coherent time to the bit period.

Problem 6–18 Phase Noise: If a given single-mode laser diode has a 3 dB bandwidth of 40 MHz, find the linewidth broadening factor α_{lw} if the normalized intensity is $I = 40,000$ and the spontaneous emission recombination rate is $R_{sp} = 500$ GHz. Also, explain how to reduce f_{3dB} to 4 MHz at the same α_{lw} and R_{sp}.

Problem 6–19 MPN: Assume a laser diode has three modes with a constant correlation of the intensities. If the intensity of a mode a_i has an average value of 0.4 and variance 0.004, find the value of the parameter k_{mpn}.

Problem 6–20 MPN: Assume a laser diode has three modes at its output. The relative intensities are 0.1, 0.8, and 0.1, respectively. Use Equation (6.74) to find the MPN power divided by signal power A^2. Assume $\Delta\tau/T = 0.1$ and $k_{mpn} = 0.1$.

Problem 6–21 Total Noise: For a given optical communication system operated at room temperature, assume $\mathcal{R} = 0.5$ A/W, $P_{in} = -30$ dBm, $K_{mpn} = 10^{-6}$, RIN $= -140$ dB/Hz, $F_{apd} = 5$, $M_{apd} = 100$, $G = 1$ $(k\Omega)^{-1}$, and $B = 500$ MHz.

    a. Find the total input current noise power using Equation (6.77). What is the total normalized power? The normalized power is the power divided by the APD gain squared.

    b. Which noise dominates the total noise? In what percentage?

    c. Calculate the ratio of the square of the average photocurrent to the total noise power.

Problem 6–22 Total Noise: Using the same assumptions as in Problem 6–21, find the signal-to-noise ratio defined in Problem 6–21c at an incident power P_{in} of -10, -20, and -40 dBm, respectively. In each case, which noise is the most important noise?

Problem 6–23 Conditional Probabilities: In a digital transmission system, the BER is P_{E1} when "1" is sent and P_{E0} when "0" is sent. If 6 1's and 4 0's are transmitted, what is the probability of having no error transmissions?

Problem 6–24 Expectation of Poisson Distribution: If n is a Poisson random variable with mean λ, find the expectation $E[1/(n + 1)(n + 2)]$.

Problem 6–25 Rayleigh Distribution: A Rayleigh distributed random variable X has the following PDF:

$$f_X(x) = \begin{cases} \dfrac{x}{\sigma^2} e^{-x^2/2\sigma^2} & \text{if } x \geq 0 \\ 0 & x < 0. \end{cases}$$

Find its mean and variance.

Problem 6–26 Bayes' Theorem: Assume that 1 out of every 1000 people is the victim of a cancer. A test has been developed that will show positive with 99 percent probability if a patient has the cancer. This test will also show positive with 10 percent probability if a patient does not have the cancer. What is the probability that a person has the cancer if his or her test is positive?

Problem 6–27 Characteristic Function: Assume X is a uniformly distributed random variable over the interval $[a, b]$. Find its characteristic function.

Problem 6–28 Maximum Likelihood Detection: Assume two possible transmitted symbols (X) are "0" and "1" and there are three possible received values (Y): 0, 0.5, and 1. Also assume the a priori probabilities $P(X = 0) = 0.2$ and $P(X = 1) = 0.8$ and the following transition probabilities: $P(Y = 0|X = 0) = 0.7$, $P(Y = 0.5|X = 0) = 0.2$, $P(Y = 1|X = 0) = 0.1$, $P(Y = 0|X = 1) = 0.1$, $P(Y = 0.5|X = 1) = 0.1$, and $P(Y = 1|X = 1) = 0.8$. Give the decision rules according to ML detection. What is the average BER?

Problem 6–29 Maximum A Posteriori Detection: Use the same assumptions as in the previous problem. Give the decision rules according to MAP detection. Also, calculate the average BER.

Problem 6–30 PSD Derivation: Find the PSD of an NRZ signal $x(t) = \sum_k A_k p(t - kT_0)$, where $p(t)$ is a unit rectangle pulse of duration T_0 and A_k is either 0 or A with equal probability.

Problem 6–31 Power from PSD: If the PSD of a signal is given by

$$S_x(\omega) = S_0 e^{-|\omega|/\omega_c}$$

find the signal power from dc to $\omega_c/2\pi$.

REFERENCES

1. E. A. Lee and D. G. Messerschmitt, *Digital Communication*, 2nd ed., Kluwer Academic Publishers Press, 1994.

2. M. Schwartz, "Performance of Point-to-Point Communication Systems: Limitations Due to noise," *Information, Transmission, Modulation, and Noise,* Chapter 6 of, 4th ed., McGraw-Hill, 1990.

3. A. Papoulis, *Probability, Random Variables, and Stochastic Processes,* 3rd ed., McGraw-Hill, 1991.

4. R. J. McIntyre, "The Distribution of Gains in Uniformly Multiplying Avalanche Photodiodes: Theory," *IEEE Transactions on Electron Devices,* vol. 19 (June 1972), pp. 703–13.

5. S. D Personick, "Statistics of a General Class of Avalanche Detectors with Applications to Optical Communication," *Bell System Technical Journal,* vol. 50 (December 1971), pp. 3075–95.

6. J. E. Mazo and J. Salz, "On Optical Communication via Direct Detection of Light Impulses," *Bell System Technical Journal,* vol. 55 (March 1976), pp. 347–69.

7. B. P. Balaban, P. E. Fleisher, and H. Zucker, "The Probability Distribution of Gains in Avalanche Photodiodes," *IEEE Transactions on Electron Devices,* vol. 23 (October 1976), pp. 1189–90.

8. M.-J. B. Moretti, "Bit Error Rate Computation in Optical Fiber Communications," masters thesis, Department of Electrical and Computer Engineering, University of Arizona, 1991.

9. K.-I. Sato, "Intensity Noise of Semiconductor Laser Diodes in Fiber Optic Analog Video Transmission," *IEEE Journal of Quantum Electronics,* vol. 19, no. 9 (September 1983), pp. 1380–91.

10. R. Olshansky et al., "Subcarrier Multiplexed Lightwave Systems for Broadband Distribution," *Journal of Lightwave Technology,* vol. 7 (September 1989), pp. 1329–42.

11. K. Ogawa, "Semiconductor Laser Noise: Mode Partition Noise," Chapter 8 of *Lightwave Communications Technology,* edited by W. T. Tsang, vol. 22 (1985), *Semiconductors and Semimetals,* Academic Press.

12. C. Henry, "Theory of the Linewidth of Semiconductor Lasers," *IEEE Journal of Quantum Electronics,* vol. 18 (Febuary 1982), pp. 259–64.

7

INCOHERENT DETECTION

Photodetection, described in Chapter 5, converts incident light into photocurrent, which is proportional to the power of the incident light and carries no information about the phase of the incident light. As a result, this detection is called **incoherent detection** or **direct detection.** This is in contrast to **coherent detection,** to be discussed in Chapter 15, which detects both the power and phase of the incident light.

Because incoherent detection only detects the power of the incident light, it is used primarily for intensity or amplitude modulated transmission. When phase or frequency modulation is used, coherent detection is necessary. As will be explained in Chapter 15, coherent detection can also amplify the power of the incident light, which can thus improve detection performance and help to approach the quantum limit.

This chapter focuses on incoherent detection for both analog and digital communications. In analog communications, both fiber dispersion and attenuation, discussed in Chapter 4, can be important. To minimize the effect of fiber dispersion, most existing analog transmission systems are based on 1.3 μm transmission. To minimize noise and to achieve a high signal-to-noise ratio (SNR) or carrier-to-noise ratio (CNR), laser RIN noise should be carefully controlled. In addition to dispersion and noise, nonlinear distortion can also be important. Nonlinear distortion in optical communications is primarily caused by the nonlinear characteristics of laser diodes near the threshold current. In a system that is not power limited or dispersion limited, nonlinear distortion can become the ultimate performance limit.

In digital communications, as discussed in Chapters 4 and 6, fiber dispersion and various noise sources are important degradation factors. Fiber dispersion can cause intersymbol interference (ISI), which can also be aggravated by inappropriate equalizer design and nonzero turn-on and turn-off delays of light sources and detectors. This chapter evaluates digital detection performance in terms of the bit error rate (BER) and discusses in detail various design considerations.

7.1 ANALOG SIGNAL DETECTION

A receiver block diagram for analog communications is shown in Figure 7.1. In addition to the photocurrent generated, noise from the front-end amplifier such as thermal noise and transistor junction noise is added. Because there is a dc bias in analog communications, ac-coupling is used to reject the dc component. Furthermore, to compensate for any channel distortion and to maximize the SNR, an equalizer, discussed in Chapter 6, is commonly used before the final signal output.

In analog communications, the amplitude-modulated signal at the output of the photodiode can be expressed as

$$i_{ph}(t) = I_0[1 + k_m m(t)] \qquad \textbf{[7.1]}$$

where I_0 is the dc current, $m(t)$ is the message signal, and k_m is the amplitude modulation index. From this expression, the SNR is given by

$$\text{SNR} = \frac{k_m^2 I_0^2 \overline{m(t)^2}}{\sigma_{n,out}^2} \qquad \textbf{[7.2]}$$

where $\sigma_{n,out}^2$ is the total noise power from Equation (6.77). Specifically, for a given receiver equalizer $H(\omega)$,

$$\sigma_{n,out}^2 = \int [q(I_0 M_{apd} + I_d M_{apd}^2) F_{apd} + \frac{\text{RIN}}{2} I_0^2 + S_a] |H(\omega)^2| \frac{d\omega}{2\pi} \qquad \textbf{[7.3]}$$

where I_d is the dark current, M_{apd} is the current gain of the photodiode (equal to unity if a PIN diode is used), F_{apd} is the excess noise factor of the photodiode, RIN is the relative intensity noise factor, and S_a is the PSD of the equivalent front-end amplifier input noise. In practice, MPN is not important in analog communications and is not included.

An equivalent photocurrent circuit is shown in Figure 7.2, where Z_{in} is the input impedance of the front-end amplifier, and v_a and i_a are the equivalent input voltage and current noise sources, respectively. Therefore, the PSD of the total equivalent input noise source of the front-end amplifier is

$$S_a(\omega) = S_i(\omega) + \frac{S_v(\omega)}{|Z_{in}(\omega)|^2}. \qquad \textbf{[7.4]}$$

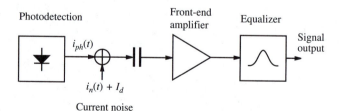

Figure 7.1 Block diagram of an analog receiver.

A common choice for $H(\omega)$ is a low-pass filter at a cut-off frequency B equal to or greater than the signal's bandwidth. In this case, the output SNR is

$$\text{SNR} = \frac{k_m^2 I_0^2 \overline{m(t)^2}}{[2q I_0 M_{apd} F_{apd} + \text{RIN} I_0^2 + (\mathcal{R} M_{apd} \text{NEP})^2] B} \qquad \textbf{[7.5]}$$

where

$$(\mathcal{R} M_{apd} \text{NEP})^2 B = 2q I_d M_{apd}^2 F_{apd} B + \int_{-2\pi B}^{2\pi B} S_a \frac{d\omega}{2\pi} \qquad \textbf{[7.6]}$$

is the signal independent noise power, and NEP is the noise equivalent power (defined in Chapter 6). When $m(t)$ is a cosine carrier, or $m(t) = \cos(\omega_m t)$, the above SNR reduces to the CNR given by

$$\text{CNR} = \frac{k_m^2 I_0^2}{2\sigma_{n,out}^2}. \qquad \textbf{[7.7]}$$

CNR OF ANALOG VIDEO TRANSMISSION   Consider an analog video transmission system where $I_0 = 1\ \mu\text{A}$, $I_d = 4\ \text{nA}$, $F_{apd} = 4$, $M_{apd} = 25$, RIN $= -140$ dB/Hz, and $S_a = 0$. If an ideal low-pass filter of bandwidth $B = 4.5$ MHz is used, the total noise power is

Example 7.1

$$\sigma_{n,out}^2 = 4.5 \times 10^6 \times (3.2 \times 10^{-19} \times 1.1 \times 10^{-6} \times 4 \times 25 + 10^{-14} \times 10^{-12})$$
$$= 1.58 \times 10^{-16}\ \text{A}^2$$

where $I_0 + M_{apd} I_d = 1.1 \times 10^{-6}$ A is used. If the modulation index is $m = 0.1$, the CNR is

$$\text{CNR} = \frac{m^2 I_0^2 / 2}{\sigma_{n,out}^2} = 32 = 15\ \text{dB}.$$

In this calculation, RIN is not important. However, a typical CNR is required to be around 50 dB. Therefore, the bias current level must be increased to, say, $I_0 = 1$ mA. In this case,

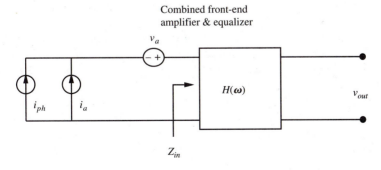

Combined front-end
amplifier & equalizer

v_a

$H(\omega)$

v_{out}

i_{ph} i_a

Z_{in}

Figure 7.2   A receiver model for optical signal detection.

$$\sigma_{n,out}^2 = 4.5 \times 10^6 \times (3.2 \times 10^{-19} \times 10^{-3} \times 10^2 + 10^{-14} \times 10^{-6})$$
$$= 4.5 \times 10^6 \times (3.2 + 1.0) \times 10^{-20} = 1.9 \times 10^{-13} \text{ A}^2.$$

RIN is now 25 percent of the total noise power, and the CNR reduces to CNR = 2.6×10^4 = 44 dB. ∎

The fiber transfer function given by Equation (4.43) shows that D_{total} must be minimized to maximize the transmission bandwidth. For this reason, most analog video transmission systems are operated at 1.3 μm, where fiber dispersion is minimized.

Example 7.2

FIBER BANDWIDTH   Consider a single-mode fiber of $D_{intra} = 20$ ps/nm·km at 1.55 μm and length $L = 50$ km. If the light source has a linewidth $\Delta\lambda = 1$ nm, the fiber bandwidth is

$$B_{fiber} = \frac{1}{D_{total}L} = 1 \text{ GHz}.$$

This can be critical for video transmission of a bandwidth around 1 GHz. ∎

In addition to noise and bandwidth considerations, nonlinearity is another problem in analog communications. In optical communications, for example, nonlinear distortion can come from laser clipping at the threshold and saturation at a high current bias. Two important parameters used in community antenna TV (CATV) to characterize nonlinear distortion are composite second order (CSO) distortion and composite third order beats (CTB) [1]. Detailed discussion on this subject is given in Chapter 10.

7.2   BINARY DIGITAL SIGNAL DETECTION

A basic block diagram for digital signal detection is shown in Figure 7.3. As illustrated, it consists of a photodetector, a front-end amplifier, an equalizer, a slicer (i.e. threshold detector), and a bit timing recovery circuit.

The photodetector converts incident light into photocurrent. The front-end amplifier amplifies the photocurrent with minimal added noise. The equalizer is used in combination with the front-end amplifier to achieve a certain receiver transfer function. For example, it can be used to compensate the low-pass response of the front-end amplifier, and, as explained in Chapter 6, it can also be designed to reduce ISI and maximize the SNR. The slicer performs threshold detection. In the case of binary transmission, it detects the equalized output as either high (greater than the threshold) or low (smaller than the threshold). To regenerate the original bit stream, the bit timing recovery circuit recovers the original transmitter clock from the received signal.

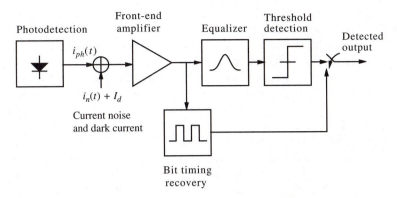

Figure 7.3   Block diagram of a typical digital receiver.

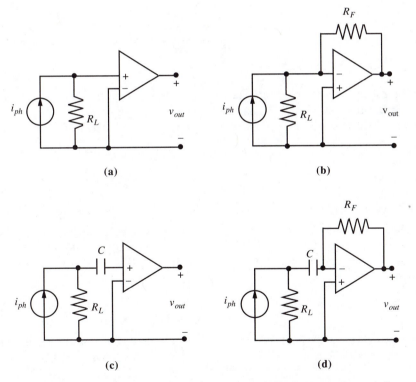

Figure 7.4   Illustration of different types of digital receivers: (a) dc-coupled
high-impedance, (b) dc-coupled transimpedance, (c) ac-coupled
high-impedance, and (d) ac-coupled transimpedance.

In optical communications, there are two main types of front-end amplifiers: **high-impedance** and **transimpedance** amplifiers. As illustrated in Figure 7.4, high-impedance amplifiers have a high input resistance (large R_L) to minimize the thermal noise, and transimpedance amplifiers have a feedback resistance (R_F) to accommodate a large dynamic range of input signals. The design and performance of these amplifiers will be discussed later in this chapter. Various literature on receiver design and performance evaluation can be found in [2]–[5].

Between the photodetector and the front-end amplifier, there are two types of signal coupling: **dc coupling** and **ac coupling**. The classification is determined by whether there is a capacitor or equivalent on the signal path between the photodetector and front-end amplifier. As mentioned earlier, the purpose of ac coupling is to reject the undesirable dc component of the photocurrent output. For example, in digital communications, the nonzero dark current is an undesirable term. For high-impedance amplifiers, the dark current results in a high voltage input to the front-end amplifier, which limits the dynamic range of the signal. When ac coupling is used, however, the dc component of the signal is filtered out. If the signal is not **dc balanced** or has some **dc wander** (i.e., the local time average of the signal is time varying), ac coupling can cause ISI. This ISI due to ac coupling will be explained later in the chapter.

7.3 SIGNAL, INTERSYMBOL INTERFERENCE, AND NOISE FORMULATION

To evaluate the transmission performance and to understand various design issues, it is useful to first formulate the signal, ISI, and noise at various stages of the digital receiver shown in Figure 7.3. To start, consider a binary digital signal at the photodetector output given by

$$i_{tot}(t) = \sum A_k p(t - kT_0) + I_d + i_n(t) = i_{ph}(t) + I_d + i_n(t) \qquad \textbf{[7.8]}$$

where

$$i_{ph}(t) = \sum A_k p(t - kT_0) \qquad \textbf{[7.9]}$$

is the photocurrent due to a pulse-amplitude modulated (PAM) signal, I_d is the dark current of the photodiode, and $i_n(t)$ is the noise current. In binary transmission using on-off-keying (OOK), A_k equals either a high value A_H for bit "1" or a low value A_L for bit "0." The ratio

$$\epsilon \overset{\text{def}}{=} \frac{A_L}{A_H} \qquad \textbf{[7.10]}$$

is called the **extinction ratio.** It is desirable to have $\epsilon = 0$ to allow for a larger noise margin. However, because of imperfect bias conditions in practice, it can be slightly greater than 0.

Signal   If the front-end amplifier and equalizer have a combined transfer function $H(\omega)$ as illustrated in Figure 7.2, the output of the equalizer is

$$y_{out}(t) = i_{tot}(t) \otimes h(t)$$

where $\otimes$ denotes convolution and $h(t)$ is the impulse response corresponding to the transfer function $H(\omega)$. The signal component of the output signal is thus

$$y_s(t) = i_{ph}(t) \otimes h(t) = \sum_k A_k p(t - kT_0) \otimes h(t) \overset{\text{def}}{=} \sum_k A_k p_{out}(t - kT_0). \qquad \textbf{[7.11]}$$

MATCHED FILTER OUTPUT   Consider a binary transmission system using NRZ line coding. Without fiber dispersion and other distortion, the signal current $i_{ph}(t)$ can be expressed as

Example 7.3

$$i_{ph}(t) = \sum_k A_k rect(t - kT_0, T_0)$$

where $rect(t, T_0)$ is the unit rectangle function of duration from 0 to T_0, the bit interval, and A_k is either $A_H = 1 \ \mu A$ for bit "1" or $A_L = 0$ for bit "0."

If the total impulse response $h(t)$ of the receiver is also a rectangle function of $R_L rect(t, T_0)$, the output pulse is a triangle function given by

$$p_{out}(t) = \begin{cases} R_L t & 0 \le t \le T_0 \\ R_L(2T_0 - t) & T_0 \le t \le 2T_0 \\ 0 & \text{otherwise.} \end{cases}$$

When the output is sampled at kT_0, the signal component at the equalizer output is $y_s(kT_0 + T_0) = R_L A_k T_0$ because $p_{out}(T_0) = T_0$ ∎

Intersymbol Interference   To detect the transmitted amplitude A_k, y_{out} at the equalizer output is sampled at the bit rate and compared with a threshold. As mentioned earlier, this is called **threshold detection.** From Equation (7.11), the sampled output at $kT_0 + \tau (0 < \tau \le T_0)$ is

$$y_{out,k} \overset{\text{def}}{=} y_{out}(kT_0 + \tau) = \sum_{k'} A_{k'} p_{out}([k - k']T_0 + \tau) + y_{n,k}$$

$$\overset{\text{def}}{=} A_k p_{out}[0] + ISI_k + y_{n,k} \qquad \textbf{[7.12]}$$

where the constant dark current term has been dropped for its irrelevance. In Equation (7.12),

$$ISI_k \overset{\text{def}}{=} \sum_{k' \ne k} A_{k'} p_{out}[k - k'] \qquad \textbf{[7.13]}$$

is the ISI term with $p_{out}[k] \overset{\text{def}}{=} p_{out}(kT_0 + \tau)$, and $y_{n,k}$ is the noise term given by

$$y_{n,k} \overset{\text{def}}{=} y_{n,out}(kT_0 + \tau).$$

The characteristics of output noise $y_{n,out}(t)$ will be discussed shortly.

Equation (7.12) shows that ISI and noise are two primary sources that cause $y_{out,k}$ to deviate from $A_k p_{out}[0]$ and result in error detection. Specifically, when $A_k = A_H$ and

$y_{out,k} < y_{th}$ or when $A_k = A_L$ and $y_{out,k} > y_{th}$, there is error detection, where y_{th} is the threshold used in the threshold detection. From this observation, the error detection probability is

$$P_E = p_0 P(y_{out,k} > y_{th} \mid A_k = A_L) + p_1 P(y_{out,k} < y_{th} \mid A_k = A_H) \quad \textbf{[7.14]}$$

where p_0 and p_1 are a priori probabilities for bits "0" and "1."

Example 7.4	**ISI DUE TO WRONG SAMPLING TIMES** (Continued from Example 7.3.) Note that there is no ISI when $\tau = T_0$. However, if the current signal is sampled at $kT_0 + T_0/2$ (i.e., $\tau = T_0/2$), then $p_{out}(\tau) = p_{out}(T_0 + \tau) = R_L/2$. Thus,

$$y_{out,k} = A_k \frac{R_L}{2} + A_{k-1} \frac{R_L}{2} + y_{n,k}.$$

In this case, $\text{ISI}_k = A_{k-1} R_L/2$, a significant quantity compared to the signal term $A_k R_L/2$. ∎

The threshold y_{th} considered above can be optimized to minimize the BER or P_E. This will be explained in the next section. In practical implementation, the threshold can be directly derived from the dc average of $y_{out}(t)$ through low-pass filtering. For equally possible 1's and 0's, y_{th} is halfway between the high and low values of $y_{out}(t)$.

Noise   From Equation (6.78), the two-sided PSD at the photodiode output is

$$S_{n,ph}(\omega, t) = q[i_{ph}(t)M_{apd} + I_d M_{apd}^2]F_{apd} + \frac{1}{2}\text{RIN}i_{ph}^2 + S_{MPN}(\omega) \quad \textbf{[7.15]}$$

where the last term is due to mode partion noise. Because $i_{ph}(t)$ is not a constant but depends on A_k's, the noise power spectrum is signal dependent and time varying. Because both the MPN and RIN are proportional to i_{ph}^2, the subsequent discussion uses RIN to represent both noise sources for simplicity. According to Appendix 7–A, the time-dependent noise PSD at the equalizer output can be expressed as:

$$S_{n,out}(\omega, t) = \int S_{n,ph}(\omega, t - t')H(\omega)h(t')e^{j\omega t'} dt' + S_a(\omega) |H(\omega)|^2. \quad \textbf{[7.16]}$$

If $S_{n,ph}$ is not a function of time, Equation (7.16) reduces to the standard form:

$$S_{n,out} = [S_{n,ph}(\omega) + S_a(\omega)] \mid H(\omega)|^2. \quad \textbf{[7.17]}$$

Also from Appendix 7–A, when $S_{n,ph}(\omega)$ is white or relatively independent of frequency (but time varying), the total noise power at the equalizer output is shown to be

$$\sigma_{n,out}^2(t) = S_{n,ph}(0, t) \otimes h(t)^2 + \int S_a(\omega) \mid H(\omega)|^2 \frac{d\omega}{2\pi}. \quad \textbf{[7.18]}$$

Consider Example 7.5 for illustration.

SIGNAL DEPENDENT CURRENT NOISE   (Continued from Example 7.3.) Assume a load resistance $R_L = 100 \, \text{k}\Omega$, excess noise factor $F_{apd} = 5$, $M_{apd} = 50$, $\text{RIN} = -140 \, \text{dB/Hz}$, $I_d = 2 \, \text{nA}$, and $S_a = 0$. From Equation (7.18),

| Example 7.5 |

$$\sigma_{n,out}^2(t) = \{1.6 \times 10^{-19} \times [i_{ph}(t) \times 50 + 5 \times 10^{-6}] \times 5$$
$$+ 0.5 \times 10^{-14} i_{ph}(t)^2\} \otimes [10^5 rect(t, T_0)]^2.$$

If t is evaluated at $(k+1)T_0$,

$$[i_{ph}(t) \otimes rect(t, T_0)^2]_{(k+1)T_0} = \int \sum_m A_m rect([k+1]T_0 - mT_0 - t', T_0) rect(t', T_0)^2 dt'$$
$$= \int_0^{T_0} \sum_m A_m rect[(k+1-m)T_0 - t', T_0] dt' = A_k T_0.$$

Similarly,

$$[i_{ph}(t)^2 \otimes rect(t, T_0)^2]_{(k+1)T_0} = A_k^2 T_0.$$

Therefore,

$$\sigma_{n,out}^2(kT_0) = [1.6 \times 10^{-19} \times (A_k + 1.0 \times 10^{-7}) \times 5 \times 50 + 0.5 \times 10^{-14} A_k^2] \times (10^5)^2 T_0.$$

When $i_{ph}(t)$ is at the low state or $A_k = 0$, the noise power in this example is solely due to the dark current. Specifically,

$$\sigma_{n,out}^2[(k+1)T_0] \, |_{A_k = A_L} \overset{\text{def}}{=} \sigma_{n,k,L}^2 = 4.0 \times 10^{-14} T_0 \, \text{V}^2 \text{sec}^2. \qquad \textbf{[7.19]}$$

When $i_{ph}(t)$ is at the high state,

$$\sigma_{n,out}^2[(k+1)T_0] \, |_{A_k = A_H} \overset{\text{def}}{=} \sigma_{n,k,H}^2 = 4.4 \times 10^{-13} T_0 \, \text{V}^2 \text{sec}^2. \qquad \textbf{[7.20]}$$

This example clearly shows that the the noise power is signal dependent. ∎

7.4   BIT ERROR RATE NEGLECTING INTERSYMBOL INTERFERENCE

To understand BER evaluation, let us first consider the simple case where ISI is neglected. A power penalty can be subsequently added when ISI is included. A more rigorous BER calculation including ISI is given in the next section.

Using Equation (7.12) and dropping the ISI term, we find the sampled output at the equalizer output is

$$y_{out,k} = A_k p_{out}[0] + y_{n,k}.$$

From the Gaussian approximation discussed in Chapter 6 and Equation (7.14), the BER is

$$P_E = p_1 Q \left(\frac{y_H - y_{th}}{\sigma_H} \right) + p_0 Q \left(\frac{y_{th} - y_L}{\sigma_L} \right) \qquad \textbf{[7.21]}$$

where $y_H = A_H p_{out}[0]$, $y_L = A_L p_{out}[0]$, y_{th} is the threshold, and σ_H^2 and σ_L^2 are the corresponding noise power at $A_k = A_H$ and A_L, respectively.

Optimum Threshold   The threshold y_{th} can be chosen to minimize the error detection probability. From the definition of the Q-function and taking the derivative of Equation (7.21) with respect to y_{th}, the optimum threshold is found to satisfy the following equation:

$$f(y_{th} \mid 1) = \frac{1}{\sigma_H \sqrt{2\pi}} e^{-(y_H - y_{th})^2/\sigma_H^2} = \frac{1}{\sigma_L \sqrt{2\pi}} e^{-(y_{th} - y_L)^2/\sigma_L^2} = f(y_{th} \mid 0) \quad \textbf{[7.22]}$$

where $p_0 = p_1$ is assumed and $f(y_{th} \mid i)$ is the PDF at $y = y_{th}$ when bit i is transmitted. This optimum threshold condition is illustrated in Figure 7.5.

In Equation (7.22), note that y_{th} is strongly determined by the exponential factors. Therefore, a suboptimum threshold satisfying

$$\frac{y_H - y_{th}}{\sigma_H} = \frac{y_{th} - y_L}{\sigma_L}$$

or

$$y_{th} = \frac{\sigma_L y_H + \sigma_H y_L}{\sigma_L + \sigma_H} \quad \textbf{[7.23]}$$

is used instead in practice. From this suboptimum value, the BER reduces to

$$P_E = Q\left(\frac{y_H - y_L}{\sigma_L + \sigma_H}\right). \quad \textbf{[7.24]}$$

Example 7.6   Consider an optical receiver in which a PIN diode is used for photodetection and the receiver filter is the same rectangle function as in the previous examples. At a load resistance R_L,

$$y_H - y_L = (A_H - A_L)T_0 R_L = \mathcal{R} P_{in} T_0 R_L$$

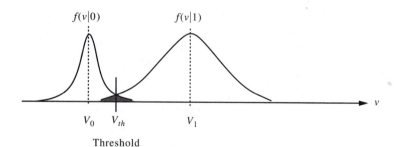

Figure 7.5   Illustration of optimum threshold detection.

where P_{in} is the peak received power due to bit "1," and the extinction ratio is assumed to be zero. Neglecting the receiver noise, we have

$$\sigma_H + \sigma_L = \left(\sqrt{2q(\mathcal{R}P_{in} + I_d)T_0} + \sqrt{2qI_dT_0} \right) R_L.$$

The bit error rate is thus

$$P_E = Q \left(\frac{\mathcal{R}P_{in}T_0^{1/2}}{\sqrt{2q(\mathcal{R}P_{in} + I_d)} + \sqrt{2qI_d}} \right).$$

At $P_{in} = 0.01\ \mu W$, $I_d = 1$ nA, $\mathcal{R} = 0.8$, and $T_0 = 1$ nsec,

$$P_E = Q \left(\frac{8 \times 10^{-9}}{\sqrt{3.2 \times 10^{-19}} \times (3 + 1)} \right) = Q(3.5) \approx 2.5 \times 10^{-4}$$

where Equation (6.16) is used to find $Q(3.5)$. ∎

7.5 Bit Error Rate Including Intersymbol Interference

In the previous section, the BER is calculated by neglecting the ISI. In this section, the effect of ISI is included and a more rigorous BER expression is derived.

Because both ISI and noise are signal dependent, the detection error probability depends on the input sequence $\{A_k\}$. For accurate error probability calculation, the detection error probability must be computed for each possible input sequence $\{A_k\}$ case and a statistical average is taken. When ISI is a function of many adjacent symbols, this can be a tedious process. For simplicity, one may consider only the worst case. That is, consider only the input sequence that gives the largest error probability. Because this error probability is generally much larger than others, it is the dominating term and is close to the actual BER.

DOMINANCE OF WORST CASE BER   Assume the sampled value at the equalizer output is

Example 7.7

$$y_{out,k} = A_k + 0.1A_{k-1} + 0.1A_{k+1} + y_{n,k} = A_k + ISI_k + y_{n,k}$$

where the noise term $y_{n,k}$ is assumed to be Gaussian and have a variance $\sigma_{n,out}^2$ independent of $\{A_k\}$. Because each A_k can assume two possible values, there are four possibilities for A_{k-1} and A_{k+1}. If they are equally likely,

$$P_E = \frac{1}{8} \times \sum_{u,v=A_H,A_L} P(A_H + 0.1u + 0.1v + y_{n,k} < y_{th}) +$$

$$\frac{1}{8} \times \sum_{u,v=A_H,A_L} P(A_L + 0.1u + 0.1v + y_{n,k} > y_{th}).$$

Choosing $y_{th} = 0.6(A_L + A_H)$ gives

$$P_E = \frac{1}{4} \left[Q \left(\frac{0.6(A_H - A_L)}{\sigma_{n,out}} \right) + 2Q \left(\frac{0.5(A_H - A_L)}{\sigma_{n,out}} \right) + Q \left(\frac{0.4(A_H - A_L)}{\sigma_{n,out}} \right) \right].$$

The first term is for the case $A_{k-1} = A_k = A_{k+1}$, the second term is for the case $A_{k+1} \neq A_{k-1}$, and the third term is due to a symbol sequence of either

$$S_H = \{\ldots, A_L, A_H, A_L, \ldots\} \tag{7.25}$$

where $A_k = A_H$, or

$$S_L = \{\ldots, A_H, A_L, A_H, \ldots\} \tag{7.26}$$

where $A_k = A_L$. As a numerical illustration, if $(A_H - A_L)/\sigma_{out} = 12$, using the Q-function approximation given by Equation (6.16), one has

$$P_E \approx \frac{1}{4\sqrt{2\pi}} \left(\frac{1}{7.2} \times e^{-7.2^2/2} + 2 \times \frac{1}{6} \times e^{-6.0^2/2} + \frac{1}{4.8} \times e^{-4.8^2/2} \right)$$

$$= 0.1 \times \left(7.7 \times 10^{-13} + 2.5 \times 10^{-9} + 2.1 \times 10^{-6} \right) = 2.1 \times 10^{-7}.$$

This illustration shows that the term $Q(\frac{0.4(A_H - A_L)}{\sigma_{out}})$ is much more significant than other terms. Therefore, the sequences given by Equations (7.25) and (7.26) contribute the most to the BER and are the worst case input sequences. The other sequences can be neglected in the BER computation. ∎

To evaluate the BER when ISI is considered, Equations (7.12) and (7.14) give

$$P_E = p_1 E \left[P(A_H p_{out}[0] + ISI_k + y_{n,k} < y_{th}) \right] \tag{7.27}$$
$$+ p_0 E \left[P(A_L p_{out}[0] + ISI_k + y_{n,k} > y_{th}) \right]$$

where $E[\cdot]$ is the expectation over possible sequences $\{A_k\}$. If $y_{n,k}$ is assumed to be Gaussian, the BER reduces to

$$P_E = E \left[p_1 Q \left(\frac{A_H p_{out}[0] - y_{th} - ISI_k}{\sigma_H} \right) + p_0 Q \left(\frac{y_{th} - A_L p_{out}[0] - ISI_k}{\sigma_L} \right) \right] \tag{7.28}$$

where σ_L^2 and σ_H^2 are the variances of $y_{n,k}$ when $A_k = A_L$ and A_H, respectively. Note that both σ_L^2 and σ_H^2 in general depend on the adjacent symbols. Considering only the worst case sequences given by Equations (7.25) and (7.26) gives

$$P_E \approx \left[p_1 p_0^2 Q \left(\frac{A_H p_{out}[0] - y_{th} - ISI_{k,H}}{\sigma_H} \right) \right.$$
$$\left. + p_0 p_1^2 Q \left(\frac{y_{th} - A_L p_{out}[0] - ISI_{k,L}}{\sigma_L} \right) \right]_{worst}. \tag{7.29}$$

From Equations (7.15) and (7.18), the output noise power can be decomposed as

$$\sigma_{n,out}^2 \overset{def}{=} \sigma_{sd}^2 + \sigma_{si}^2 \tag{7.30}$$

where

$$\sigma_{sd}^2 \overset{def}{=} \int \left[q F_{apd} M_{apd} i_{ph}(t - t') + \frac{RIN}{2} i_{ph}^2(t - t') \right] h^2(t') dt' \tag{7.31}$$

is the signal dependent noise component, and

$$\sigma_{si}^2 \overset{\text{def}}{=} \int \left[q I_d M_{apd}^2 F_{apd} + S_a(\omega) \right] \mid H(\omega) \mid^2 \frac{d\omega}{2\pi} \qquad \textbf{[7.32]}$$

is the signal independent noise component. Thus,

$$\sigma_H^2 = \sigma_{sd\,A_k=A_H}^2 \Big| + \sigma_{si}^2 \qquad \textbf{[7.33]}$$

and

$$\sigma_L^2 = \sigma_{sd\,A_k=A_L}^2 \Big| + \sigma_{si}^2. \qquad \textbf{[7.34]}$$

Example 7.8 illustrates the calculation of signal and various noise variances defined above.

ISI AND BER OF A FINITE SLOPE PULSE   Consider a received pulse $p(t)$ shown in Figure 7.6. It can be expressed as

$$p(t) = \begin{cases} \frac{t}{2\delta} + \frac{1}{2} & \text{if } |t| < \delta \\ 1 & \text{if } \delta < t < T_0 - \delta \\ -\frac{t - T_0}{2\delta} + \frac{1}{2} & \text{if } |t - T_0| < \delta \\ 0 & \text{otherwise.} \end{cases} \qquad \textbf{[7.35]}$$

Example 7.8

For the same receiver filter used in Example 7.3, or $h(t) = R_L rect(t, T_0)$ of duration T_0, the signal output sampled at $kT_0 + T_0$ is

$$y_{s,k} = R_L A_k \int_0^{T_0} p(t')dt' = R_L A_k (T_0 - \delta/2).$$

The ISI and noise power can be calculated as follows. For ISI, from Equation (7.13), the sampled ISI at $t = kT_0 + T_0$ is

$$\text{ISI}_k = R_L \int_0^{T_0} \Big\{ A_{k-1} p[kT_0 + T_0 - (k-1)T_0 - t'] \qquad \textbf{[7.36]}$$

$$+ A_{k+1} p[kT_0 + T_0 - (k+1)T_0 - t'] \Big\} dt'$$

$$= R_L A_{k-1} \int_{T_0}^{T_0+\delta} p(t')dt' + R_L A_{k+1} \int_{-\delta}^{0} p(t')dt'$$

$$= \frac{R_L \delta}{4} (A_{k-1} + A_{k+1}).$$

Using the worst case sequences given by Equations (7.25) and (7.26), one obtains

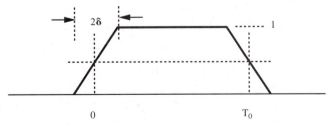

Figure 7.6   A finite slope pulse.

$$\text{ISI}_{k,H} = R_L A_L \frac{\delta}{2}$$

and

$$\text{ISI}_{k,L} = R_L A_H \frac{\delta}{2}.$$

Similarly, the signal dependent noise power at $t = kT_0 + T_0$ has variance

$$\sigma_{sd}^2 = R_L^2 \int_0^{T_0} \left\{ q F_{apd} M_{apd} i_{ph}[(k+1)T_0 - t'] + \frac{\text{RIN}}{2} i_{ph}[(k+1)T_0 - t']^2 \right\} dt'$$

$$= q R_L^2 M_{apd} F_{apd} \left[(A_{k-1} + A_{k+1})\delta/4 + A_k(T_0 - \delta/2) \right]$$

$$+ \frac{\text{RIN}}{2} R_L^2 \int_0^{T_0} \left[A_{k-1} p(2T_0 - t') + A_{k+1} p(-t') + A_k p(t') \right]^2 dt'$$

$$= q R_L^2 M_{apd} F_{apd} [(A_{k-1} + A_{k+1})\delta/4 + A_k(T_0 - \delta/2)]$$

$$+ \frac{\text{RIN}}{2} R_L^2 \left[(A_{k-1}^2 + A_{k+1}^2) \frac{\delta}{12} + A_k^2 \left(T_0 - \frac{5\delta}{6} \right) + (A_{k-1} + A_{k+1}) A_k \frac{\delta}{3} \right].$$

Under the same worst case sequences,

$$\sigma_{H,sd}^2 = q R_L^2 M_{apd} F_{apd} \left[A_L \delta/2 + A_H(T_0 - \delta/2) \right] \qquad \text{[7.37]}$$

$$+ \frac{\text{RIN}}{2} R_L^2 \left[A_L^2 \frac{\delta}{6} + A_H^2 \left(T_0 - \frac{5\delta}{6} \right) + A_L A_H \frac{2\delta}{3} \right]$$

and

$$\sigma_{L,sd}^2 = q R_L^2 M_{apd} F_{apd} \left[A_H \delta/2 + A_L(T_0 - \delta/2) \right] \qquad \text{[7.38]}$$

$$+ \frac{\text{RIN}}{2} R_L^2 \left[A_H^2 \frac{\delta}{6} + A_L^2 \left(T_0 - \frac{5\delta}{6} \right) + A_L A_H \frac{2\delta}{3} \right]$$

If the threshold is

$$y_{th} = R_L(A_H + A_L)T_0/2$$

the BER is approximately given by

$$P_E \approx \frac{1}{8} Q \left(\frac{R_L(A_H - A_L)(T_0 - \delta)}{2\sqrt{\sigma_{H,sd}^2 + \sigma_{si}^2}} \right) + \frac{1}{8} Q \left(\frac{R(A_H - A_L)(T_0 - \delta)}{2\sqrt{\sigma_{L,sd}^2 + \sigma_{si}^2}} \right).$$

This equation assumes equally possible 1's and 0's in transmission. ∎

Threshold Optimization   Given A_H, A_L, σ_H, σ_L, and the worst case ISI, the optimum threshold to minimize the P_E can be found as in the previous section. Taking the derivative of P_E with respect to y_{th} and equating it to zero gives

$$\frac{p_1 p_0^2}{\sigma_H} e^{-[A_H p_{out}(\tau) - y_{th} + ISI_{k,H}]^2 / 2\sigma_H^2} = \frac{p_0 p_1^2}{\sigma_L} e^{-[y_{th} - A_L p_{out}(\tau) - ISI_{k,L}]^2 / 2\sigma_L^2}.$$

Choosing the suboptimum threshold y_{th} that satisfies

$$\frac{A_H p_{out}(\tau) - y_{th} + ISI_{k,H}}{\sigma_H} = \frac{y_{th} - A_L p_{out}(\tau) - ISI_{k,L}}{\sigma_L}$$

gives

$$y_{th} = \left[\frac{A_H p_{out}(\tau) + ISI_{k,H}}{\sigma_H} + \frac{ISI_{k,L} + A_L p_{out}(\tau)}{\sigma_L} \right] \frac{\sigma_L \sigma_H}{\sigma_L + \sigma_H}. \qquad \textbf{[7.39]}$$

With this threshold, the BER reduces to

$$P_E = p_0 p_1 Q \left(\frac{(A_H - A_L) p_{out}(\tau) + ISI_H - ISI_L}{\sigma_L + \sigma_H} \right). \qquad \textbf{[7.40]}$$

This BER is worse than that without ISI. As a result, the power penalty due to ISI can be defined as

$$PP_{ISI} \overset{\text{def}}{=} 10 \log_{10} \left(\frac{A_{pp}(\delta = 0)}{A_{pp}(\delta) + ISI_H - ISI_L} \right). \qquad \textbf{[7.41]}$$

where $A_{pp}(\delta) \overset{\text{def}}{=} (A_H - A_L) p_{out}(\tau)$. Equation (7.41) gives the power penalty due to ISI for the incident light to achieve the same performance.

POWER PENALTY DUE TO ISI   Continue from the previous example, except use the suboptimum threshold given by Equation (7.39), which is

$$y_{th} = R_L \left(\frac{A_H (T_0 - \delta/2) + A_L \delta/2}{\sigma_H} + \frac{A_L (T_0 - \delta/2) + A_H \delta/2}{\sigma_L} \right) \frac{\sigma_L \sigma_H}{\sigma_L + \sigma_H}.$$

Example 7.9

The equation uses the fact that $p_{out}(\tau)|_{T_0} = T_0 - \delta/2$. Therefore,

$$A_{pp}(\delta) = R_L (A_H - A_L)(T_0 - \delta/2)$$

and

$$P_E \approx p_0 p_1 Q \left(\frac{R_L (A_H - A_L)(T_0 - \delta)}{\sigma_H + \sigma_L} \right).$$

Therefore, the power penalty is

$$PP_{ISI} = 10 \log_{10} \left(\frac{1}{1 - \delta/T_0} \right).$$

This power penalty as a function of δ/T_0 is illustrated in Figure 7.7. At $2\delta/T_0 = 1/4$, the power penalty is 0.6 dB, which is reasonably small. Therefore, pulse broadening 2δ less than $T_0/4$ is commonly used as the limit below which ISI can be neglected. ∎

Power penalty in dB

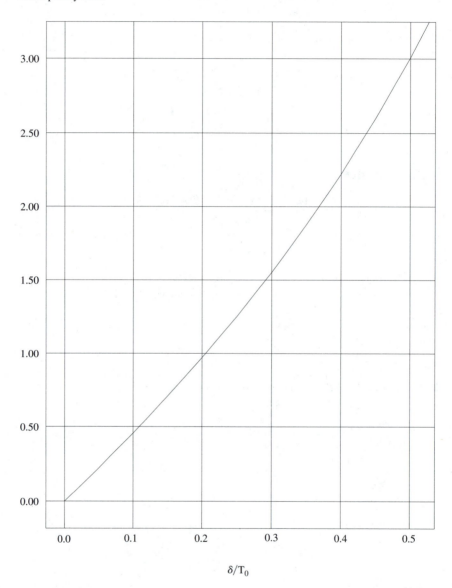

δ/T_0

Figure 7.7   Power penalty in dB due to ISI as a function of δ/T_0.

7.6 RECEIVER SENSITIVITY

Receiver sensitivity is defined as the minimum power of the incident light required to meet a specified detection performance. For binary transmission, as given by Equation (7.9), the average incident light power is

$$\overline{P_{in}} = \frac{1}{\mathcal{R}M_{apd}}(p_1 A_H + p_0 A_L)\frac{\int p(t)dt}{T_0} = \frac{1}{\mathcal{R}M_{apd}}(p_1 + p_0\epsilon)A_H\frac{p_T}{T_0} \qquad \textbf{[7.42]}$$

where

$$p_T \stackrel{\text{def}}{=} \int p(t')dt' \qquad \textbf{[7.43]}$$

is the pulse energy. At a given extinction ratio, the incident power is thus proportional to the current amplitude A_H of bit "1."

The receiver sensitivity can also be defined in terms of the minimum number of photons per bit required. At a quantum efficiency of η, it is given by

$$\overline{N} = \frac{\overline{P_{in}}T_0}{hf} = \frac{1}{\eta q M_{apd}}(p_1 + p_0\epsilon)A_H p_T. \qquad \textbf{[7.44]}$$

Because the Q-function is a monotonically decreasing function, at a specified P_E the argument in the Q-function of Equation (7.24) or (7.40) should be greater than a minimum value x_{min}, where

$$P_{E,min} \stackrel{\text{def}}{=} Q(x_{min}). \qquad \textbf{[7.45]}$$

For example, for a BER lower than 10^{-9}, the Q-function shown in Figure 6.1 gives $x_{min} = 6$. Combining the definition of x_{min} and Equation (7.40) gives

$$\frac{(A_H - A_L)p_{out}(\tau) + \text{ISI}_H - \text{ISI}_L}{\sigma_L + \sigma_H} \geq x_{min}. \qquad \textbf{[7.46]}$$

Using Equations (7.42), (7.44), and (7.46), one can compute the receiver sensitivity. This is explained in detail below.

7.6.1 ZERO ISI AND EXTINCTION RATIO

To easily understand the dependence of the receiver sensitivity on various receiver parameters and the transmission bit rate, first consider the simple case in which both ISI and the extinction ratio are zero. In this case, $A_L = \text{ISI}_H = \text{ISI}_L = 0$, and Equation (7.46) reduces to

$$\frac{A_H p_{out}(\tau)}{\sigma_L + \sigma_H} \geq x_{min} \qquad \textbf{[7.47]}$$

where σ_L^2 is given by Equation (7.32) and, from Equations (7.31) and (7.33), σ_H^2 is given by

$$\sigma_H^2 = \sigma_L^2 + q F_{apd} M_{apd} A_H \hat{p}_s \qquad \textbf{[7.48]}$$

where

$$\hat{p}_s \stackrel{\text{def}}{=} \int p(t')h^2(\tau - t')dt'. \tag{7.49}$$

RIN is ignored in Equation (7.48) because it is not important in digital communications. From Equation (7.47), $A_H = x_{min}(\sigma_L + \sigma_H)/p_{out}(\tau)$ at the receiver sensitivity. Substituting this into Equation (7.48) gives

$$\sigma_H^2 = \sigma_L^2 + q F_{apd} M_{apd} x_{min} \frac{\hat{p}_s}{p_{out}(\tau)}(\sigma_L + \sigma_H) \stackrel{\text{def}}{=} \sigma_L^2 + \xi \sigma_L(\sigma_L + \sigma_H) \tag{7.50}$$

where

$$\xi \stackrel{\text{def}}{=} \frac{q F_{apd} M_{apd} x_{min}}{\sigma_L} \frac{\hat{p}_s}{p_{out}(\tau)} \tag{7.51}$$

is a parameter that quantifies the relative importance between signal dependent noise and signal independent noise. According to its definition, ξ is dimensionless. Solving Equation (7.50) for σ_H/σ_L gives

$$\sigma_H = (1 + \xi)\sigma_L. \tag{7.52}$$

Therefore,

$$A_H = \frac{x_{min}(1 + \xi)\sigma_L}{p_{out}(\tau)} = \frac{\sigma_L^2}{q F_{apd} M_{apd} \hat{p}_s}\xi(1 + \xi)$$

where the last equality comes from the substitution of $x_{min}/p_{out}(\tau)$ using Equation (7.51). Substituting A_H, given above, into Equation (7.42) gives the receiver sensitivity:

$$\boxed{\overline{P_{in}} = \frac{p_1 hf}{\eta F_{apd} M_{apd}^2} \frac{\sigma_L^2}{q^2 T_0} \frac{p_T}{\hat{p}_s}\xi(1 + \xi).} \tag{7.53}$$

Cases When $\xi \ll 1$ and $\xi \gg 1$ Two extreme cases of the receiver sensitivity given by Equation (7.53) are of interest: $\xi \ll 1$ and $\xi \gg 1$. When $\xi \ll 1$, from Equation (7.52), $\sigma_H^2 \approx \sigma_L^2$. In this case, shot noise is insignificant compared to signal independent noise such as thermal noise and receiver noise, and the receiver sensitivity is linearly proportional to ξ. On the other hand, when $\xi \gg 1$, $\sigma_H^2 \gg \sigma_L^2$ and shot noise is the dominant noise source. As a result, the receiver sensitivity is linearly proportional to ξ^2. An approximated log-log plot of $\overline{P_{in}}$ versus ξ is illustrated in Figure 7.8a. The slope clearly doubles at the junction $\xi = 1$.

Example 7.10

RECEIVER SENSITIVITY AT LARGE THERMAL NOISE   If both $p(t)$ and the receiver filter $h(t)$ are the unit rectangle function from 0 to T_0, then $\hat{p}_s = p_T = T_0$. From Equation (7.32),

$$\frac{\sigma_L^2}{T_0} = q I_d + \int S_a \mid H \mid^2 df.$$

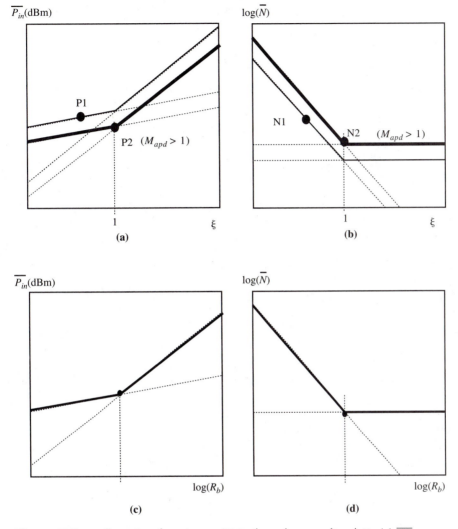

$\overline{P}_{in}$(dBm)

P1

P2 $(M_{apd} > 1)$

1   ξ

(a)

$\log(\overline{N})$

N1

N2 $\quad (M_{apd} > 1)$

1   ξ

(b)

$\overline{P}_{in}$(dBm)

$\log(R_b)$

(c)

$\log(\overline{N})$

$\log(R_b)$

(d)

Figure 7.8   Illustration of receiver sensitivity dependence on ξ and R_b: (a) $\overline{P}_{in}$ as a function of ξ, (b) $\overline{N}$ as a function of ξ, (c) $\overline{P}_{in}$ as a function of R_b, and (d) $\overline{N}$ as a function of R_b. In *a* and *b*, $\xi = 1$ is the crossover point where the receiver sensitivity is determined by the signal independent noise ($\xi < 1$) or by the signal dependent noise ($\xi > 1$). In *a* and *b*, the receiver sensitivity can be improved by increasing the current gain (M_{apd}) when the noise is dominated by the signal independent noise.

Assuming $I_d = 10$ nA and the receiver noise is 10 times the shot noise due to dark current,

$$\frac{\sigma_L^2}{T_0} = 11 \times 1.6 \times 10^{-19} \times 10^{-8} = 1.76 \times 10^{-26} \ \text{C}^2/\text{sec}.$$

At $p_1 = 0.5$, $\eta = 0.8$, $M_{apd} = F_{apd} = 1$ (a PIN diode is used), and $\lambda = 1.55$ μm, the receiver sensitivity is

$$\overline{P_{in}} = \frac{0.5 \times hc}{0.8 \times 1.55 \times 10^{-6}} \times \frac{1.76 \times 10^{-26}}{q^2} \xi(1 + \xi) = 5.5 \times 10^{-8} \xi(1 + \xi) \text{ W.}$$

If $x_{min} = 6$ and $T_0 = 1$ nsec or $R_b = 1$ Gb/s, from Equation (7.51),

$$\xi = \frac{q x_{min}}{\sigma_L} = \frac{1.6 \times 10^{-19} \times 6}{(1.76 \times 10^{-26} \times 10^{-9})^{1/2}} = 0.23.$$

Thus $\overline{P_{in}} = 1.55 \times 10^{-8}$ W or -48.1 dBm. ∎

Bit Rate Dependence   To attain the attenuation and dispersion limits discussed in Chapter 4, it is necessary to know the bit rate dependence of the receiver sensitivity. According to the definitions of σ_L^2, p_T, and $\hat{p}_s$ given by Equations (7.34), (7.43), and (7.49), respectively, if the impulse response of the receiver filter $h(t)$ is dimensionless, they all are proportional to T_0, the bit interval.[1] As a result, from the definition of ξ given by Equation (7.51), ξ is proportional to $R_b^{1/2} = T_0^{-1/2}$.

Therefore, the bit rate dependence of the receiver sensitivity given by Equation (7.53) is determined by the factor $\xi(1 + \xi)$. When $\xi \ll 1$ (i.e., when signal independent noise dominates) the receiver sensitivity is proportional to ξ or $R_b^{1/2}$. When $\xi \gg 1$ (i.e., when shot noise dominates) the receiver sensitivity is proportional to ξ^2 or R_b. This bit rate dependence is illustrated in the log-log plot of Figure 7.8c.

Receiver Sensitivity in Photons   The receiver sensitivity discussed above can also be expressed in terms of the average number of photons per bit. From Equations (7.44) and (7.53),

$$\overline{N} = \frac{\overline{P_{in}} T_0}{hf} = \frac{p_1}{\eta q^2 F_{apd} M_{apd}^2} \frac{\sigma_L^2 p_T}{\hat{p}_s} \xi(1 + \xi).$$

Substituting for σ_L^2 using Equation (7.51) gives

$$\overline{N} = \frac{p_1 F_{apd} x_{min}^2}{\eta} \left(\frac{\hat{p}_s p_T}{p_{out}(\tau)^2} \right) \frac{1 + \xi}{\xi}. \tag{7.54}$$

Figure 7.8b illustrates the dependence of this result on ξ for $\xi \ll 1$ and $\xi \gg 1$. Because ξ is proportional to R_b and $\hat{p}_s p_T / [p_{out}(\tau)^2]$ is independent of T_0, the dependence on R_b has a similar function, as illustrated in Figure 7.8d.

---

[1] Note that σ_L^2 is in units of Coulomb squared (C^2) and proportional to T_0 numerically. Similarly, ξ is dimensionless and proportional to $R_b^{1/2}$ numerically.

QUANTUM LIMIT If both $p(t)$ and $h(t)$ are the unit rectangle function from 0 to T_0, $p_{out}(\tau) = \hat{p}_s = p_T = T_0$ at $\tau = T$. Then,

$$\overline{N} = \frac{p_1 F_{apd} x_{min}^2}{\eta} \frac{1+\xi}{\xi} \approx \frac{p_1 F_{apd} x_{min}^2}{\eta} \text{ if } \xi \gg 1. \qquad \textbf{[7.55]}$$

Example 7.11

If $x_{min} = 6$, $\eta = 1$, $F_{apd} = 1$, and $p_1 = 0.5$, then $\overline{N} = 18$. This is the quantum limit under Gaussian approximation.[2] ∎

RECEIVER SENSITIVITY UNDER HIGH EXCESS APD NOISES (Continued from Example 7.10.) Consider the use of an InGaAs APD of $M_{apd} = 20$. If the excess noise factor F_{apd} at $M_{apd} = 20$ is 5,

Example 7.12

$$\xi = \frac{q F_{apd} M_{apd} x_{min}}{\sigma_L} = 100 \times 0.23 = 23.$$

Therefore, the signal independent noise dominates. At this value, the receiver sensitivity is

$$\overline{P}_{in} = \frac{5.5 \times 10^{-8}}{F_{apd} M_{apd}^2} \xi(1+\xi) = 15.2 \text{ nW} = -48.2 \text{ dBm}$$

and

$$\overline{N} = p_1 F_{apd} x_{min}^2 (1 + \xi^{-1}) = 18 \times 5 \times 1.04 = 94.$$

This higher $\overline{N}$ is primarily due to the excess noise factor. ∎

Improvement of Receiver Sensitivity Figures 7.8a and 7.8b also show that the receiver sensitivity can be improved by increasing the current gain M_{apd} when $\xi < 1$. From Equations (7.32) and (7.51), note that when M_{apd} increases, ξ can increase if F_{apd} does not increase as fast as σ_L^2 / M_{apd}^2 decreases. Under this condition, as illustrated in the solid dark curves of Figure 7.8a and 7.8b, the receiver sensitivity can increase. Specifically, from Equations (7.53) and (7.54), $\overline{P}_{in}$ is smaller if $\xi(1+\xi)\sigma_L^2 / F_{apd} M_{apd}^2$ is made smaller, or, equivalently, $\overline{N}$ is smaller if $F_{apd}(1+\xi)/\xi$ is made smaller. This is illustrated in Figure 7.8a and 7.8b where $\overline{P}_{in}$ is moved down from P1 to P2 and $\overline{N}$ is moved down from N1 to N2. When the above conditions are not true, a larger M_{apd} can actually decrease the sensitivity because of a higher F_{apd} value. Analysis to find the optimum APD gain is given later in the chapter.

A sample list of commercially available digital data links at BER of 10^{-9} is given in Table 7.1 [6]. One can note that the receiver sensitivity is around -30 to -35 dBm for speed around 200 Mb/s. When the speed increases beyond 500 Mb/s, however, the receiver sensitivity drops quickly compared to the speed increase. One important cause for this is a high power penalty due to a large ISI at high speeds. This is discussed next.

| [2] When the exact Poisson distribution is used, the quantum limit is 9. See Equation (6.28) of Chapter 6.

7.6.2   NONZERO ISI AND EXTINCTION RATIO

When the ISI and extinction ratio are nonzero, calculating the receiver sensitivity becomes tedious. However, a similar dependence on ξ and R_b should be observed. The difference is an additional power penalty due to the nonzero ISI and extinction ratio. To see this, consider the finite slope pulse shown in Figure 7.6 for simplicity.

Table 7.1   Receiver sensitivity of some commercial digital data links.

Manufacturer	Model No.	λ (nm)	R_b (Mb/s)	$\overline{P_{in}}$ (dBm)
Artel	T/R2010	850	25	-36
AT&T	1252P, 1352P	870	55	-32
	1402, 1403	1310	125	-34
	1227, 1310	1300	650	-26.7
BT&D	DLX2040	1300	170	-34.0
	DL1040	1300	200	-35.5
Force	2553	1300	400	-25
	2556-650	1300	650	-18
	2538	1300	1260	-19
Laser Diode	LDDL 1100	1300	125	-31
	LDDL 1710	1300/1550	270	-35
	LDDL 2100	1300	500	-30
	LDDL 2115	1500	500	-33
	LDDL 2550	1300/1500	1200	-25
Ortel	3510B/4510B	1300	5000	-14
PCO	DTL-1300C	1300	220	-34
	FDT-1300	1300	125	-31
Siemens AG	V23804-E2-54	1310	200	-35

From Example 7.9, Equation (7.46) reduces to

$$R_L A_H \frac{(1 - \epsilon)(T_0 - \delta)}{\sigma_L + \sigma_H} \geq x_{min}.$$

When the signal independent noise dominates, or $\sigma_L \approx \sigma_H$,

$$R_L A_H \frac{(1 - \epsilon)(T_0 - \delta)}{2\sigma_L} \geq x_{min}.$$

Therefore, compared to the case $\epsilon = \delta = 0$, the power penalty is

$$PP = \frac{(1 + \epsilon p_0/p_1)}{(1 - \epsilon)(1 - \delta/T_0)}. \qquad \textbf{[7.56]}$$

As a numerical illustration, for $p_1 = p_0 = 0.5$, $\epsilon = 0.1$, and $\delta/T_0 = 0.5$, the power penalty is 3.5 dB.

When the signal independent noise is insignificant compared to the shot noise,

$$R_L A_H \frac{(1 - \epsilon)(T_0 - \delta)}{\sigma_{H,sd} + \sigma_{L,sd}} \geq x_{min}.$$

From Equation (7.37)

$$\sigma_H^2 \approx q R_L^2 M_{apd} F_{apd} A_H (T_0 - \delta/2) + \frac{RIN}{2} R_L^2 A_H^2 (T_0 - \frac{5\delta}{6}) \qquad \textbf{[7.57]}$$

where the second and higher order terms are neglected. In practice, the RIN term can be dropped in digital communications. Given these approximations,

$$\frac{(1 - \epsilon)^2 (1 - \delta/T_0)^2}{(1 - \delta/2T_0)} \frac{A_H T_0}{q M_{apd} F_{apd}} \geq x_{min}^2. \qquad \textbf{[7.58]}$$

Compared to the case of $\delta = \epsilon = 0$, the power penalty is thus

$$PP = 10 \log_{10} \left(\frac{(1 - \delta/2T_0)(1 + \epsilon p_0/p_1)}{(1 - \epsilon)^2 (1 - \delta/T_0)^2} \right). \qquad \textbf{[7.59]}$$

POWER PENALTY UNDER ISI AND STRONG SHOT NOISE   If $\delta/T_0 = 0.2$ and $\epsilon = 0.1$, | **Example**
the power penalty is | **7.13**

$$PP = 10 \log_{10} \left(\frac{0.9 \times 1.1}{0.9^2 \times 0.8^2} \right) = 2.8 \text{ dB}.$$

If δ/T_0 increases to 0.5,

$$PP = 10 \log_{10} \left(\frac{0.75 \times 1.1}{0.9^2 \times 0.5^2} \right) = 6.1 \text{ dB}.$$

Therefore, the power penalty increases rapidly as the bit rate ($1/T_0$) increases. ■

7.7 RECEIVED PULSE DETERMINATION

Determining the received pulse $p(t)$ in Equation (7.9) is important to the subsequent receiver filter design and consequently to the detection performance. When it is known, a proper receiver filter to minimize the BER can be chosen.

In general, the waveform of the received pulse $p(t)$ depends on the light source, modulation, line coding, fiber dispersion, and photodetector. For example, an LED light source has a wide spectrum. As a result, fiber dispersion can significantly broaden the pulse. On the other hand, if a single-frequency laser diode and external modulation are used, there is no chirping effect and pulse broadening due to fiber dispersion is minimal.[3] In this case, the received pulse $p(t)$ is close to the original one that modulates the external modulator.

| [3] See Chapter 12 for discussion of the chirping effect and Chapter 14 for external modulation.

Light Pulse $p_s(t)$ at the Transmitter Output   To derive the input pulse $p(t)$, start from the light source. From the step input response, discussed in Chapter 12, the pulse output from directly modulating a laser diode can be expressed as

$$p_s(t) = \begin{cases} 0 & \text{if } t < t_d \\ 1 - \cos(\omega_r[t - t_d])e^{-\alpha(t-t_d)} & \text{if } t_d < t < T_0 \\ [1 - \cos(\omega_r[T_0 - t_d])e^{-\alpha(T_0-t_d)}]e^{-\alpha_{off}(t-T_0)} & \text{if } t > T_0 \end{cases}$$ [7.60]

where t_d is the initial turn-on delay, ω_r is the relaxation oscillation frequency, α is the damping constant of the relaxation oscillation, and $\alpha_{off} \gg \alpha$ is the decay constant when the laser is turned off. A pulse given by Equation (7.60) is illustrated in Figure 7.9.

In Equation (7.60), the chirping effect is ignored for simplicity. (For a more complete analysis that includes the chirping effect, see Appendix 7–C.) When the turn-on delay t_d and the relaxation oscillation of the laser diode are neglected, $p_s(t)$ can be further approximated as

$$p_s(t) \approx p_m(t) \otimes h_{LD}(t)$$ [7.61]

where $p_m(t)$ is the input pulse that drives the laser diode (a rectangle pulse for NRZ signaling), and $h_{LD}(t)$ is the impulse response of the laser diode. For simplicity, it can be modeled as a first-order low-pass filter with a cutoff frequency of $1/(2\pi\tau_{LD})$ (see Chapter 5). Therefore, the impulse response can be expressed as

$$h_{LD}(t) = \begin{cases} 0 & \text{if } t < 0 \\ \frac{1}{\tau_{LD}}e^{-t/\tau_{LD}} & \text{if } t > 0. \end{cases}$$ [7.62]

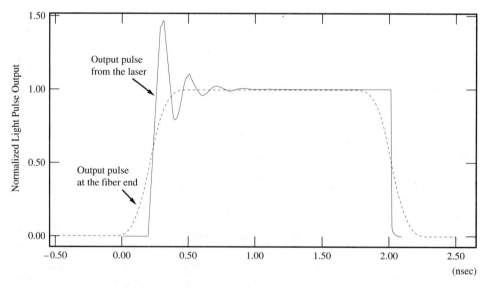

Figure 7.9   Pulse output from a laser diode and at the fiber end. The total fiber dispersion is $D_{intra}L\Delta\lambda = 0.2$ nsec. The original pulse width is 2 nsec, relaxation oscillation frequency is 5 GHz, damping constants are $\alpha = 8.0 \times 10^9$ sec^{-1} and $\alpha_{off} = 8.0 \times 10^{10}$ sec^{-1}, and initial time delay is $t_d = 0.2$ nsec.

If an LED is used, there is no time delay or relaxation oscillation. Instead, one must consider its rise time and fall time (see Chapter 12). For simplicity, it can be similarly modeled with the following impulse response:

$$h_{LED}(t) = \begin{cases} 0 & \text{if } t < 0 \\ \frac{1}{\tau_{LED}} e^{-t/\tau_{LED}} & \text{if } t > 0 \end{cases} \qquad \textbf{[7.63]}$$

where τ_{LED} is the time constant of the LED. Similar to Equation (7.61), the output pulse $p_s(t)$ is given by

$$p_s(t) = p_m(t) \otimes h_{LED}(t). \qquad \textbf{[7.64]}$$

Optical Channel The channel response of an optical fiber is determined by the fiber dispersion, fiber length, and source's spectrum. Consider a single-mode fiber of length L and intramodal dispersion D_{intra}, the propagation delay of a photon at wavelength λ is $\tau_g(\lambda) = \tau_{g0} + (\lambda - \lambda_0)D_{intra}L$, where τ_{g0} is the propagation delay at the reference wavelength λ_0. Therefore, if the light source has a normalized spectrum $g_s(\lambda - \lambda_0)$ so that

$$\int g_s(\lambda - \lambda_0)d\lambda = 1 \qquad \textbf{[7.65]}$$

the fiber channel can be modeled with the following impulse response:

$$h_{fiber}(t) = g_s\left(\frac{t - \tau_{g0}}{D_{intra}L}\right) \frac{1}{D_{intra}\Delta\lambda L}. \qquad \textbf{[7.66]}$$

The factor $1/(D_{intra}\Delta\lambda L)$ is introduced to have

$$\int h_{fiber}(t)dt = 1. \qquad \textbf{[7.67]}$$

From Appendix 7–D conditions given by Equations (7.65) and (7.67) are for energy conservation.

For LEDs or multimode laser diodes, the output light spectrum is commonly assumed to be Gaussian. If the linewidth is $\Delta\lambda$,

$$g_s(\lambda - \lambda_0) = \sqrt{\frac{2}{\pi \Delta\lambda^2}} e^{-2(\lambda - \lambda_0)^2/(\Delta\lambda)^2}. \qquad \textbf{[7.68]}$$

Note that this expression meets the condition given by Equation (7.65). From this, the channel impulse response is

$$h_{fiber}(t) = \sqrt{\frac{2}{\pi}} \frac{1}{D_{intra}L\Delta\lambda} e^{-2(t - \tau_{g0})^2/(D_{intra}L\Delta\lambda)^2}. \qquad \textbf{[7.69]}$$

For single-mode laser diodes, from the Lorentzian spectrum given in Chapter 6,

$$g_s(\lambda - \lambda_0) = \frac{2}{\pi \Delta\lambda} \frac{1}{1 + 4(\lambda - \lambda_0)^2/\Delta\lambda^2} \qquad \textbf{[7.70]}$$

and

$$h_{fiber}(t) = \frac{2}{\pi D_{intra} L \Delta\lambda} \frac{1}{1 + 4(t - \tau_{g0})^2/(D_{intra} L \Delta\lambda)^2}. \qquad \textbf{[7.71]}$$

Received Pulse   At the receiver end, the impulse response of the photodiode can be similarly modeled as a first-order low-pass filter. The impulse response is thus

$$h_{ph}(t) = \begin{cases} 0 & \text{if } t < 0 \\ \frac{1}{\tau_{ph}} e^{-t/\tau_{ph}} & \text{if } t > 0 \end{cases} \qquad \textbf{[7.72]}$$

where τ_{ph} is the time constant of the photodiode.

Given the output pulse $p_s(t)$, the channel impulse response $h_{fiber}(t)$, and the photodetector response $h_{ph}(t)$, the received pulse at the front-end amplifier input is given by

$$p(t) = p_s(t) \otimes h_{fiber}(t) \otimes h_{ph}(t). \qquad \textbf{[7.73]}$$

An output pulse according to Equations (7.60) and (7.68) at $D_{intra} L \Delta\lambda = 0.2$ nsec is illustrated in Figure 7.9, where $h_{ph}(t) = \delta(t)$ is assumed.

Simplified Model   For simplicity, $p(t)$ can be modeled as the one shown in Figure 7.6. From Appendix 7–D, the square of the pulse broadening parameter δ is the sum of mean square widths of the impulse functions of the source, fiber, and detector. That is, the total broadening effect can be approximated as

$$(2\delta)^2 = (\tau_{tx})^2 + (D_{total} L \Delta\lambda)^2 + (\tau_{ph})^2 \qquad \textbf{[7.74]}$$

where τ_{tx} is the turn-on or turn-off delay equal to either τ_{LD} for laser diodes or τ_{LED} for LEDs.

Example 7.14   **TOTAL PULSE BROADENING**   Assume $\tau_{LD} = 0.1$ nsec, $D_{intra} L \Delta\lambda = 0.2$ nsec, and $\tau_{ph} = 0.2$ nsec. Then

$$\delta^2 = \frac{1}{4}(0.01 + 0.04 + 0.04) = 0.0225 \text{ nsec}^2$$

and

$$\delta = 0.15 \text{ nsec. } \blacksquare$$

7.8   RECEIVER EQUALIZER DESIGN

As can be seen from Equation (7.18), the choice of the total receiver transfer function $H(\omega)$ determines the noise power and the signal. If an improper $H(\omega)$ is used, there will be either excessive noise power or significant signal distortion (i.e., ISI). This section discusses receiver design and the trade-off between noise and ISI.

When only noise is considered, Chapter 6 explains that the optimum filter is the matched filter. However, when ISI due to fiber dispersion is important, the matched filter is not necessarily the best choice to minimize the BER. Instead, optimum detection involves matched filtering, sampling, and sequence estimation [7][8]. In this optimum detection, the use of matched filtering and sampling at the bit rate generates a set of sufficient statistics (i.e., no information loss). All samples are then jointly detected to minimize the error detection probability.

In optical communications, this optimum detection is impractical for high-speed transmission. Furthermore, the detection technique is applicable only to Gaussian noise. When signal-dependent noise such as shot noise is important, the technique may not even be applicable. Therefore, depending on whether noise or ISI is stronger, two main types of filters are used in practice. When noise is a stronger factor, a low-pass filter or integration-and-dump is used. When ISI is a stronger factor, a raised-cosine filter is preferred. These two filters are discussed below.

Integration-and-Dump Filtering   Integration-and-dump has been considered in the previous examples. An implementation is illustrated in Figure 7.10, where the generated photocurrent is integrated every bit interval. At the end of integration, the integrated value is sampled and threshold detected. From Equation (7.9), the integrated output at time $kT_0 + T_0$ is

$$
\begin{aligned}
v_{out,k} &= \frac{1}{C} \int_{kT_0}^{(k+1)T_0} i_{tot}(t)dt \\
&= \frac{1}{C} \int_{-\infty}^{\infty} rect(kT_0 + T_0 - t, T_0)i_{tot}(t)dt \qquad \textbf{[7.75]} \\
&= \frac{1}{C} [rect(t, T_0) \otimes i_{tot}(t)]_{t=kT_0+T_0}
\end{aligned}
$$

where $rect(t, T_0)$ is the unit rectangle function from 0 to T_0. The last convolution expression shows that integration-and-dump is equivalent to matched filtering if $p(t)$ is an NRZ pulse. Furthermore, because the impulse response $rect(t, T_0)$ has a transfer function of a cutoff frequency $1/T_0$, integration-and-dump is low-pass filtering of bandwidth $1/T_0$.

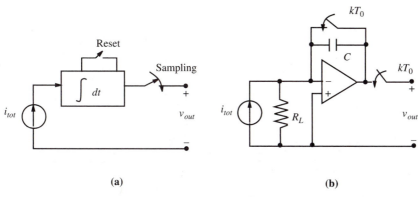

(a)   (b)

Figure 7.10   (a) Integration-and-dump detection and (b) implementation of integration-and-dump.

Example 7.15	**EQUIVALENCE TO PHOTON COUNTING** From Equation (7.75), photon counting detection used in the quantum limit calculation in Chapter 6 is the same as integration-and-dump. In that case, because only shot noise is considered and there is no ISI, integration-and-dump suffers no ISI. Its performance result gives the fundamental performance limit in optical signal detection. ∎

Raised-Cosine Filtering   When the received pulse $p(t)$ has a finite duration greater than one bit interval, the use of integration-and-dump results in ISI. As a result, the BER gets worse, as illustrated in Example 7.9. When ISI is a stronger factor than noise, an equalizer must be used to reduce ISI. Although in general this can enhance the noise power at the same time, it is still good if the final BER is reduced.

To reduce ISI, one approach is to force ISI to zero. This kind of equalizer is called the **zero-forcing** equalizer. When a given output pulse $p_{out}(t)$ with zero ISI is chosen, the zero-forcing equalizer has a transfer function (including that of the front-end amplifier) given by

$$H(\omega) = \frac{P_{out}(\omega)}{P(\omega)}$$

[7.76]

where $P(\omega)$ is the Fourier transform of $p(t)$.

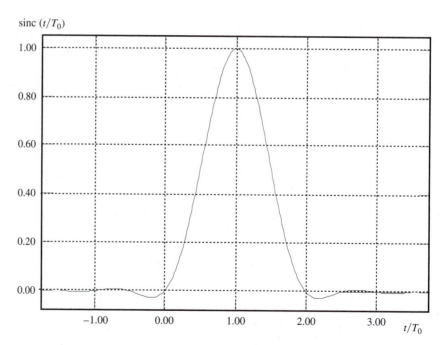

Figure 7.11   Raised cosine waveform of zero ISI at 100 percent excess bandwidth.

From Appendix 7–B, an important zero-forcing equalizer is called the **raised-cosine filter**. Its equalized output is given by

$$p_{out}(t) = \text{sinc}(2t/T_0 - 2) + \frac{1}{2}\text{sinc}(2t/T_0 - 3) + \frac{1}{2}\text{sinc}(2t/T_0 - 1) \qquad \textbf{[7.77]}$$

$$= \frac{1}{1 - 4[(t/T_0) - 1]^2}\text{sinc}(2t/T_0 - 2).$$

This pulse is illustrated in Figure 7.11. This definition says that

$$p_{out}(t)\,|_{kT_0} = \begin{cases} 1 & \text{if } k = 1 \\ 0 & \text{otherwise.} \end{cases} \qquad \textbf{[7.78]}$$

Therefore,

$$y_s(kT_0 + T_0) = \left[\sum_{k'} A_{k'}\,p_{out}(t - k'T_0)\right]_{kT_0 + T_0} = A_k.$$

Thus there is no ISI at the sample time A_k. The corresponding Fourier transform of $p_{out}(t)$ is

$$P_{out}(\omega) = \begin{cases} \frac{T_0}{2}[1 + \cos(\omega T_0/2)]e^{-j\omega T_0} & \text{if } |\omega T_0| < 2\pi \\ 0 & \text{otherwise.} \end{cases} \qquad \textbf{[7.79]}$$

Assuming the input pulse $p(t)$ is given by Equation (7.35), the corresponding Fourier transform is

$$P_{in}(\omega) = 2\frac{\sin(\omega T_0/2)}{\omega}\frac{\sin(\omega\delta)}{\omega\delta}e^{-j\omega T_0/2} = T_0\text{sinc}(fT_0)\text{sinc}(2\delta f)e^{-j\omega T_0/2}.$$

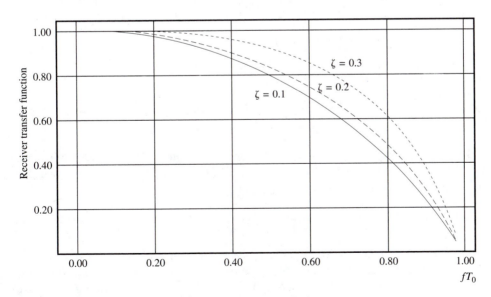

Figure 7.12 Frequency response of the raised-cosine filter; $\zeta = \delta/T_0$.

Therefore, the equalizer has the following transfer function

$$H(\omega) = \frac{P_{out}(\omega)}{P_{in}(\omega)} = \begin{cases} \frac{1+\cos(\omega T_0/2)}{2\mathrm{sinc}(\omega T_0/2\pi)\mathrm{sinc}(\omega\delta/\pi)}e^{-j\omega T_0/2} & \text{if } |\omega T_0| < 2\pi \\ 0 & \text{otherwise.} \end{cases} \qquad \textbf{[7.80]}$$

This transfer function at different values of $\zeta = \delta/T_0$ is shown in Figure 7.12.

Which Filter To Choose   Equation (7.40) shows that a good receiver design should compromise between noise and ISI. Specifically, a good receiver should have the argument in the Q-function as large as possible. From this observation one can decide when to use integration-and-dump and when to use raised-cosine filtering.

For the finite slope rectangle pulse $p(t)$ given by Equation (7.35), the performances of integration-and-dump and raised-cosine filtering are compared below. The BER performance of integration-and-dump has been discussed in Example 7.8. The BER of raised-cosine filtering is similarly computed below. Because raised-cosine filtering results in zero ISI,

$$\mathrm{ISI}_H = \mathrm{ISI}_L = 0.$$

Also from $p_{out}(T_0) = 1$,

$$(A_H - A_L)p_{out}(T_0) + \mathrm{ISI}_H - \mathrm{ISI}_L = (A_H - A_L). \qquad \textbf{[7.81]}$$

For noise power computation, from Equation (7.31),

$$\sigma_{H,sd}^2 = \int \left[q M_{apd} F_{apd} S_H(t - t') + \frac{\mathrm{RIN}}{2} S_H^2(t - t') \right] h^2(t')dt' \qquad \textbf{[7.82]}$$

where

$$S_H(t) = A_H[p(t + T_0) + p(t) + p(t - T_0)] \qquad \textbf{[7.83]}$$

is the worst case sequence for $A_k = A_H$, and

$$\sigma_{L,sd}^2 = \int \left[q M_{apd} F_{apd} S_L(t - t') + \frac{\mathrm{RIN}}{2} S_L^2(t - t') \right] h^2(t')dt' \qquad \textbf{[7.84]}$$

where

$$S_L(t) = A_H p(t + T_0) + A_L p(t) + A_H p(t - T_0) \qquad \textbf{[7.85]}$$

is the worst case sequence for $A_k = A_L$. The computation for the signal-independent noise term can be done according to Equation (7.32). To compare the performance for integration-and-dump and raised-cosine filtering, let us define

$$\eta_{eq} = \frac{\{(A_H - A_L)/(\sigma_H + \sigma_L)\}_{\text{raised-cosine}}}{\{(A_H - A_L)(1 - \delta/T_0)/(\sigma_H + \sigma_L)\}_{\text{integration-and-dump}}}. \qquad \textbf{[7.86]}$$

Thus, when $\eta_{eq} > 1$, raised-cosine filtering is better than integration-and-dump, and when $\eta_{eq} < 1$, integration-and-dump is better. Assuming $\epsilon = 0.1$, $F_{apd} = 2$, $M_{apd} = 20$, $I_d = 0$, $A_H = 1$ μA, $\delta/T_0 = 0.1$, and $S_a = 2 \times 10^{-23}$A^2/Hz, the performance comparison is illustrated in Figure 7.13. This illustration shows that integration-and-dump performs better than raised-cosine filtering only when δ/T_0 is small, less than 0.07. In other words, when $\delta/T_0 > 0.07$, it is advantageous to use raised-cosine filtering. In general, when $\delta/T_0 > 0.1$, raised-cosine filtering is a better choice.

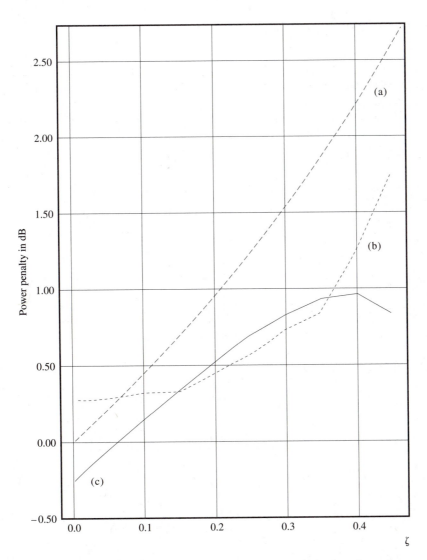

Figure 7.13 Performance comparison between integration-and-dump and raised-cosine filtering as a function of $\zeta = \delta/T_0$: (a) power penalty due to ISI using integration-and-dump, (b) power penalty due to noise enhancement using raised-cosine filtering, and (c) the difference of power penalty in dB of (a) and (b). $S_a = 2.0 \times 10^{-23}$ A^2/Hz.

7.9 AC COUPLING AND DC WANDER

As pointed out earlier, ac coupling is commonly used in optical signal detection to filter out undesirable dc components such as dark current and dc bias. However, when ac coupling is used, the dc component of the signal is also filtered out. If the signal is not dc balanced or has dc wander, ac coupling will result in signal distortion or ISI. To see this, consider Example 7.16 below.

Example 7.16

AC COUPLING BY RC FILTERING   Consider the ac-coupled circuit shown in Figure 7.14. Basic circuit analysis shows that

$$[i_{in}(t) - i_{out}(t)]R = v_c(t) + Ri_{out}(t).$$

$$i_{out}(t) = C\frac{dv_c(t)}{dt}.$$

Combining these two equations gives

$$RC\frac{di_{in}(t)}{dt} = i_{out}(t) + 2RC\frac{di_{out}(t)}{dt}.$$

For convenience, define

$$\tau_{rc} \stackrel{\text{def}}{=} 2RC.$$

Taking the Laplace transform of the differential equation then gives

$$\frac{\tau_{rc}}{2}[-i_{in}(0) + sI_{in}(s)] = \tau_{rc}[-i_{out}(0) + sI_{out}(s)] + I_{out}(s)$$

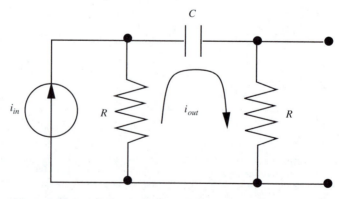

Figure 7.14   AC coupling by an RC filter.

or

$$I_{out}(s) = \frac{\tau_{rc}}{1 + s\tau_{rc}} [i_{out}(0) - i_{in}(0)/2] + \frac{s\tau_{rc}/2}{1 + s\tau_{rc}} I_{in}(s)$$

where $I_{out}(s)$ is the Laplace transform of $i_{out}(t)$. Transforming the equation back into the time domain gives

$$i(t) = [i_{out}(0) - i_{in}(0)/2]e^{-t/\tau_{rc}} + \frac{1}{2}i_{in}(t) - \frac{1}{2\tau_{rc}} \int_0^t i_{in}(u)e^{-(t-u)/\tau_{rc}} du.$$

Moving the time origin from 0 to $-\infty$ and assuming $i(-\infty) = x(-\infty) = 0$ one obtains

$$i_{out}(t) = \frac{1}{2}i_{in}(t) - \frac{1}{2\tau_{rc}} \int_{-\infty}^t i_{in}(u)e^{-(t-u)/\tau_{rc}} du.$$

The first term in the equation is the signal, and the second term is ISI due to $i_{in}(t')$, $t' < t$.

If the input current signal is a PAM signal as given by Equation (7.9),

$$i_{out}(t) = \frac{1}{2}i_{in}(t) - \frac{1}{2\tau_{rc}} \int_{-\infty}^t A_k p(u - kT_0)e^{-(t-u)/\tau_{rc}} du$$

$$= \frac{1}{2}i_{in}(t) - \frac{1}{2\tau_{rc}} \sum_k A_k \int_{-\infty}^t p(u - kT_0)e^{-(t-u)/\tau_{rc}} du.$$

Sampling $i_{out}(t)$ at $t = nT_0 + \tau$, $0 < \tau < T_0$, and assuming $p(t)$ has a finite duration from 0 to T_0 gives

$$i_{out}(nT_0 + \tau) = \frac{1}{2}A_n p(\tau) - \frac{1}{2}\sum_{k<n} A_k I_p \rho^{(n-k)} e^{-\tau/\tau_{rc}}$$

where

$$\rho \stackrel{\text{def}}{=} e^{-T_0/\tau_{rc}}$$

and

$$I_p \stackrel{\text{def}}{=} \frac{1}{\tau_{rc}} \int_0^{T_0} p(u)e^{u/\tau_{rc}} du.$$

The ISI term is thus

$$\text{ISI}_n = -\frac{1}{2}\sum_{k<n} A_k I_p \rho^{(n-k)} e^{-\tau/\tau_{rc}}. \qquad \text{[7.87]}$$

For a random input sequence $\{A_k\}$, the output current is illustrated in Figure 7.15 for NRZ and Figure 7.16 for biphase signals, respectively, where $p(t)$ is a rectangle pulse of duration T_0 for NRZ but for biphase signals is a positive rectangle pulse from 0 to $T_0/2$ and a negative rectangle pulse from $T_0/2$ to T_0. The illustrations in the figures are called the **eye diagram,** where the signal is retraced and superimposed on the same plot. ∎

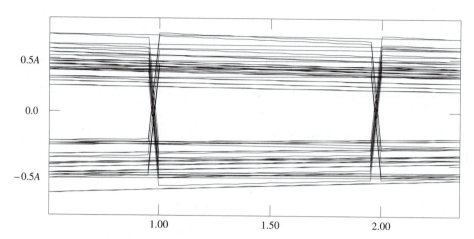

Figure 7.15   Eye diagram of a random NRZ signal after ac coupling, where $\tau_{rc} = 20T_0$ and A is the amplitude of the input NRZ pulse.

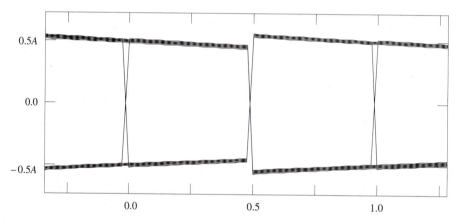

Figure 7.16   Eye diagram of a random biphase signal after ac coupling, where $\tau_{rc} = 20T_0$ and A is the peak-to-peak of the input biphase pulse.

Example 7.16 shows that the eye opening of the NRZ signal is much smaller than that of the biphase signal. This significant difference is because biphase has a much smaller ISI than NRZ. This is illustrated in Example 7.17.

Example 7.17   **ISI OF NRZ AND BIPHASE SIGNALS**   For NRZ signals,

$$I_p = e^{T_0/\tau_{rc}} - 1 = \rho^{-1} - 1.$$

Therefore,

$$ISI_n = -\frac{1}{2}(\rho^{-1} - 1)\sum_{k<n} A_k \rho^{n-k} e^{-\tau/\tau_{rc}}.$$

In the worst case, if all A_k's had the same value,

$$ISI_{worst} = -\frac{1}{2}e^{-\tau/\tau_{rc}}A_k.$$

For $A_n = 1$, the worst case is when A_k's are also 1. In this case, $ISI_{worst} = -e^{-\tau/\tau_{rc}}/2$, and

$$i_{out}(nT_0)\,|_{A_n=1} = 0.5 - 0.5e^{-\tau/\tau_{rc}} \approx 0.5\frac{\tau}{\tau_{rc}}.$$

Similarly, for $A_n = 0$, the worst case is when A_k's are also 0. In this case, $ISI_{worst} = 0$, and

$$i_{out}(nT_0)\,|_{A_n=0} = 0.0 - 0.0 = 0.$$

Therefore, the eye of NRZ at τ is $0.5\tau/\tau_{rc}$, which is very small when $\tau < T_0 \ll \tau_{rc}$.

For biphase signals,

$$I_p = -(e^{T_0/2\tau_{rc}} - 1) + (e^{T_0/\tau_{rc}} - e^{T_0/2\tau_{rc}}) = 1 - 2e^{T_0/2\tau_{rc}} + e^{T_0/\tau_{rc}} = (1 - \rho^{-1/2})^2.$$

In the worst case, when all A_k's are the same value,

$$ISI_{worst} = -\frac{1}{2}e^{-\tau/\tau_{rc}}\frac{1 - \rho^{1/2}}{1 + \rho^{1/2}}A_k.$$

If $\rho = e^{-T_0/\tau_{rc}}$ is close to 1 (i.e., $T_0 \ll \tau_{rc}$),

$$ISI_{worst} \approx -\frac{1}{2}e^{-\tau/\tau_{rc}}\frac{T_0}{4\tau_{rc}}A_k \approx 0.$$

Therefore, biphase codes have a much broader eye opening. ∎

As Example 7.17 demonstrates, a proper choice of pulse $p(t)$, such as the biphase pulse, can result in a small $I_p/(1 - \rho)$, which can have a small ISI. Another way to reduce ISI is to control the sequence $\{A_k\}$. This can be understood from Example 7.18.

LINE CODE FOR SMALL ISI Consider the use of NRZ signaling. For the kth input binary bit, the following coding rule is used to generate A_k's:

Example 7.18

$$\text{If } b_k = 1, \quad \text{then } A_{2k} = 1, \; A_{2k+1} = 0.$$
$$\text{If } b_k = 0, \quad \text{then } A_{2k} = 0, \; A_{2k+1} = 1.$$

This rule is essentially the same biphase coding. The only difference is that now only two symbols are transmitted for each input bit. In other words, the coding efficiency of biphase coding is only 50 percent to achieve dc balance. There are better codes, such as the **code mark inversion** (CMI) code discussed in Chapter 16 that can maintain dc balance and at the same time have a high coding efficiency. ∎

7.10 OTHER DESIGN ISSUES IN DIGITAL TRANSMISSIONS

This chapter has discussed various factors such as noise, ISI, and dc wander that are important in digital optical communications. This section presents some other design issues that are also important in practical systems.

7.10.1 APD MULTIPLICATION GAIN OPTIMIZATION

As mentioned earlier, using APDs can improve the receiver sensitivity when the excess noise factor is not large. In general, there exists an optimum gain value that maximizes the SNR.

In Equation (7.40), note that the numerator in the Q-function is a function of the signal and ISI. Therefore, it is proportional to the APD gain M_{apd}. From Equations (7.30)–(7.34), the denominator is

$$\sigma_H + \sigma_L = \sqrt{\sigma_{H,s}^2 + \sigma_a^2} + \sqrt{\sigma_{L,s}^2 + \sigma_a^2}$$

where σ_a^2 is the receiver noise independent of M_{apd}, and

$$\sigma_{x,s}^2 = q F_{apd}[M_{apd} S_x(\tau) + I_d M_{apd}^2] \otimes h^2(\tau) + \frac{\text{RIN}}{2} S_x^2(\tau) \otimes h^2(\tau)$$

is the signal-dependent noise. In the above equation, x denotes either H or L, and $S_x(\tau)$ is either $S_H(\tau)$ or $S_L(\tau)$ defined by Equations (7.83) and (7.85). Since $S_x(\tau)$ is proportional to M_{apd}, for convenience, let us define the following parameters that are M_{apd} independent:

$$\delta_x^2 \stackrel{\text{def}}{=} q \left(\frac{S_x(\tau)}{M_{apd}} + I_d \right) \otimes h^2(\tau)$$

and

$$\delta_{x,RIN}^2 \stackrel{\text{def}}{=} \frac{\text{RIN}}{2} \frac{S_x^2(\tau)}{M_{apd}^2} \otimes h^2(\tau).$$

Therefore,

$$\sigma_H + \sigma_L = M_{apd} \left[\sqrt{F_{apd}\delta_H^2 + \delta_{H,RIN}^2 + (\sigma_a^2/M_{apd}^2)} \right.$$
$$\left. + \sqrt{F_{apd}\delta_L^2 + \delta_{L,RIN}^2 + (\sigma_a^2/M_{apd}^2)} \right].$$

From the above formulations, the argument in the Q-function of Equation (7.40) is inversely proportional to

$$\gamma \stackrel{\text{def}}{=} \sqrt{F_{apd}\delta_H^2 + \delta_{H,RIN}^2 + (\sigma_a^2/M_{apd}^2)}$$
$$+ \sqrt{F_{apd}\delta_L^2 + \delta_{L,RIN}^2 + (\sigma_a^2/M_{apd}^2)}. \qquad \textbf{[7.88]}$$

Minimizing the BER thus requires minimizing γ. When M_{apd} is small, the term σ_a^2 can be significant; when M_{apd} is large, F_{apd} can be large and the term $F_{apd}\delta_x^2$ becomes significant. Therefore, there exists an optimal value for M_{apd}.

NORMALIZED NOISE POWER AS A FUNCTION OF M_{APD} As a numerical illustration, | **Example**
assume $\sigma_a^2 = 10\delta_H^2 = 100\delta_L^2$ and neglect the RIN noise. This gives | **7.19**

$$\gamma = \delta_L \left(\sqrt{10F_{apd} + \frac{100}{M_{apd}^2}} + \sqrt{F_{apd} + \frac{100}{M_{apd}^2}} \right).$$

From the excess noise factor derived in Chapter 6,

$$F_{apd} = kM_{apd} + \left(2 - \frac{1}{M_{apd}} \right)(1 - k) \approx kM_{apd} + 2(1 - k) \qquad \textbf{[7.89]}$$

when M_{apd} is large. Figure 7.17 shows γ/δ_L as a function of M_{apd}, where the minimal point is near $M_{apd} = 3.9$. ∎

Using Equation (7.88), the optimum M_{apd} can be derived by taking the derivative with respect to M_{apd} and equating it to zero. The result is

$$M_{apd}^3 \frac{\partial F_{apd}}{\partial M_{apd}} \left(\frac{\delta_H^2}{\sigma_H} + \frac{\delta_L^2}{\sigma_L} \right) = 2 \left(\frac{\sigma_a^2}{\sigma_H} + \frac{\sigma_a^2}{\sigma_L} \right). \qquad \textbf{[7.90]}$$

This expression can be simplified by neglecting the δ_L^2 term. Under this assumption,

$$M_{apd}^3 \frac{\partial F_{apd}}{\partial M_{apd}} = 2\frac{\sigma_a^2}{\delta_H^2}(1 + \frac{\sigma_H}{\sigma_L}). \qquad \textbf{[7.91]}$$

When $kM_{apd} \gg 1$, from Equation (7.89),

$$M_{apd}^3 \frac{\partial F_{apd}}{\partial M_{apd}} \approx kM_{apd}^3 \approx F_{apd}M_{apd}^2.$$

Therefore, if

$$h \stackrel{\text{def}}{=} \frac{F_{apd}\delta_H^2}{\sigma_a^2/M_{apd}^2} \approx \frac{kM_{apd}^3\delta_H^2}{\sigma_a^2} \qquad \textbf{[7.92]}$$

Equation (7.91) reduces to

$$h = 2(1 + \frac{\sigma_H}{\sigma_L}) = 2 \left(1 + \sqrt{\frac{F_{apd}\delta_H^2 + \sigma_a^2/M_{apd}^2}{\sigma_a^2/M_{apd}^2}} \right)$$

$$= 2(1 + \sqrt{1 + h}). \qquad \textbf{[7.93]}$$

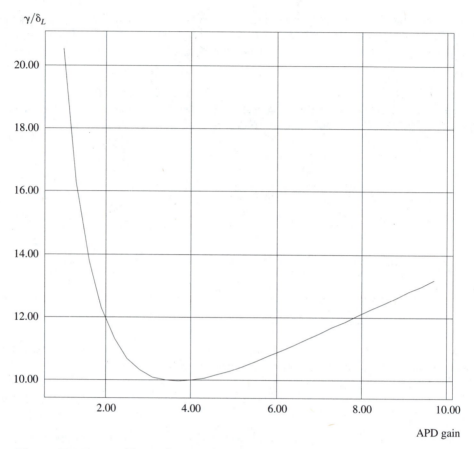

Figure 7.17 γ/δ_L as a function of M_{apd} at $k = 1.0$.

Solving this equation gives $h = 8$. Therefore, from Equation (7.92),

$$kM_{apd,opt}^3 \approx 8\frac{\sigma_a^2}{\delta_H^2}$$

or

$$M_{apd,opt} = \left(\frac{8\sigma_a^2}{k\delta_H^2}\right)^{1/3}.$$ **[7.94]**

At this optimum value, from Equation (7.88),

$$\gamma_{opt} \approx \frac{\sigma_a}{M_{apd}}(\sqrt{h+1}+1) = 2\left(k\delta_H^2\sigma_a\right)^{1/3}.$$ **[7.95]**

OPTIMUM APD GAIN   Under the same conditions as in the previous example, with $k = 1.0$,   **Example 7.20**

$$M_{apd,opt} \approx (8 \times 10)^{1/3} = 4.3.$$

This is close to the optimum value (3.9) given by the previous example. At this value,

$$\gamma_{opt} = \frac{4}{4.3}\sigma_a = 0.93\sigma_a. \quad \blacksquare$$

Equation (7.94) shows that M_{apd} increases as the signal-independent noise power increases. This increase suppresses the importance of the amplifier noise. On the other hand, when the incident power, or δ_H^2, increases, the optimum gain decreases. This decrease reduces the excess noise from the APD.

7.10.2   APD GAIN AND POWER PENALTY IN MULTIPLE ACCESS

For point-to-point communications, one can in principle know the incident power to the optical receiver and therefore find the optimum APD gain in the receiver design. In multiple access communications such as local area networking, however, the incident power is not a constant but a function of the distance between the source and receiver. If the source is close to the receiver, the incident power is large. If the source is far away from the receiver, the incident power is small. The range of possible incident power is called the **dynamic range** and has been discussed in Chapter 2. In this case, there is no single "optimum" M_{apd} for the incident power across the dynamic range. As a result, for a given M_{apd}, if it is not the optimum value for an incident power, the noise factor γ (defined earlier) is larger than the optimum one. The ratio gives us the power penalty.

The power penalty due to nonoptimum M_{apd} can be calculated as follows. Let the input power range from $\delta_{H,1}$ to $\delta_{H,2}$, and let an intermediate value $\delta_{H,m}$ be used to give the optimum gain $M_{apd,opt}$ according to Equation (7.94). For any value δ_H in the dynamic range, if its optimum gain value is used, according to Equation (7.95), its optimum γ is

$$\gamma_{opt} = 2\left(k\delta_H^2\sigma_a\right)^{1/3}$$

at a given k and σ_a. Its actual γ value at $M_{apd,opt}$, from Equation (7.88), is

$$\gamma = \frac{\sigma_a}{M_{apd,opt}}\left(\sqrt{\left[\frac{F_{apd}\delta_H^2}{\sigma_a^2/M_{apd,opt}^2} + 1\right]} + 1\right).$$

From Equation (7.92) and $h_{opt} = 8$,

$$\frac{8}{\delta_{H,m}^2} = \frac{F_{apd}}{\sigma_a^2/M_{apd,opt}^2}.$$

Therefore,

$$\gamma = \frac{\sigma_a}{M_{apd,opt}} \left[\sqrt{8(\delta_H/\delta_{H,m})^2 + 1} + 1 \right] = \left(\frac{k\delta_{H,m}^2 \sigma_a}{8} \right)^{1/3} \left[\sqrt{8(\delta_H/\delta_{H,m})^2 + 1} + 1 \right]$$

and the power penalty ratio is

$$\boxed{\frac{\gamma}{\gamma_{opt}} = \frac{\sqrt{8x + 1} + 1}{4} x^{-1/3}} \qquad \text{[7.96]}$$

where $x \overset{\text{def}}{=} (\delta_H/\delta_{H,m})^2$. The power penalty $10\log_{10}(\gamma/\gamma_{opt})$ as a function of $\delta_H^2/\delta_{H,m}^2$ is shown in Figure 7.18.

Given an input dynamic range from $\delta_{H,1}$ to $\delta_{H,2}$, an important question is *which* intermediate value $\delta_{H,m}$ should the optimum gain be based on? To see this, define

$$x_h \overset{\text{def}}{=} \frac{\delta_{H,2}^2}{\delta_{H,m}^2} \qquad \text{[7.97]}$$

and

$$x_l \overset{\text{def}}{=} \frac{\delta_{H,1}^2}{\delta_{H,m}^2}. \qquad \text{[7.98]}$$

Because $\delta_{H,sd}^2$ is proportional to the incident light power, the ratio x_h to x_l is the dynamic range. From Equation (7.96), when $x_h \gg 1$,

$$r_h \overset{\text{def}}{=} \frac{\gamma(x_h)}{\gamma_{opt}} \approx \frac{\sqrt{8x_h}}{4}(x_h)^{-1/3} = \left(\frac{x_h}{8} \right)^{1/6}.$$

Similarly, when $x_l \ll 1$,

$$r_l \overset{\text{def}}{=} \frac{\gamma(x_l)}{\gamma_{opt}} \approx \frac{1}{2}(x_l)^{-1/3} = \left(\frac{1}{8x_l} \right)^{1/3}.$$

To maximize the dynamic range at a given power penalty, $r = r_h = r_l$. Under this condition, $x_h = 8r^6$ and $x_l = \frac{1}{8r^3}$. Therefore,

$$DR = \frac{x_h}{x_l} = 64r^9 \qquad \text{[7.99]}$$

or

$$PP(dB) = 10\log_{10}(r) = \frac{10}{9}\log_{10}\left(\frac{DR}{64} \right). \qquad \text{[7.100]}$$

Equation (7.100) gives the power penalty in dB as a function of the input dynamic range. This power penalty dependence on the dynamic range is shown in Figure 7.19. From Equations (7.97) and (7.98),

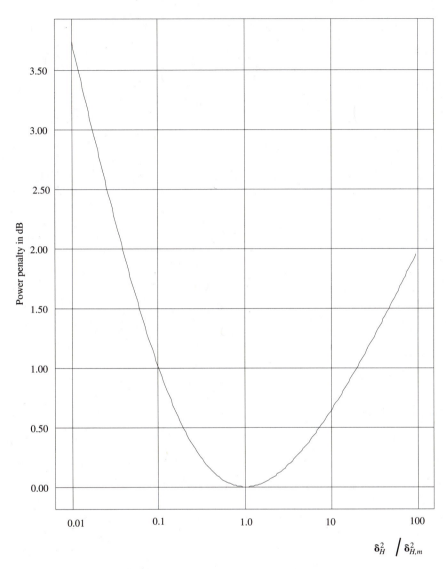

Figure 7.18 γ/γ_{opt} in dB as a function of $\delta_H/\delta_{H,m}$.

$$\delta_{H,m}^2 = \frac{\delta_{H,2}^2}{x_h} = \frac{2\delta_{H,2}^2}{\mathrm{DR}^{2/3}} \qquad \textbf{[7.101]}$$

or

$$\delta_{H,m}^2 = \delta_{H,1}^2 x_l = 2\delta_{H,1}^2 \mathrm{DR}^{1/3}. \qquad \textbf{[7.102]}$$

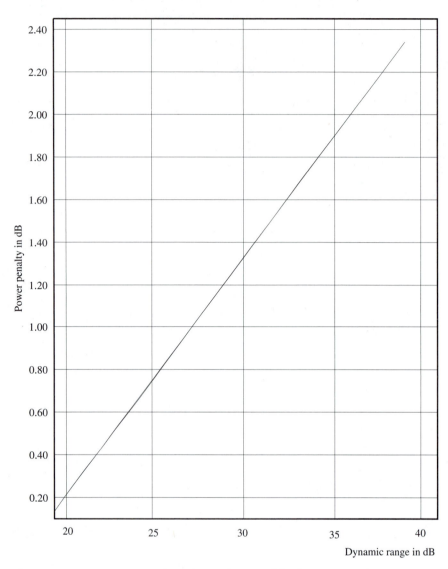

Figure 7.19   Power penalty in dB as a function of the dynamic range.

Example 7.21 | **POWER PENALTY**   If the dynamic range is 20 dB, or DR = 100, the power penalty due to nonoptimum gain is

$$10 \log_{10}(r) = \frac{10}{9} \log_{10}(100/64) = 0.22 \text{ dB}$$

where the optimum gain is set at

$$\delta_{H,m}^2 = 0.093\delta_{H,2}^2 = 9.3\delta_{H,1}^2. \quad \blacksquare$$

7.10.3   EXTINCTION RATIO

From the previous discussion, the argument of the Q-function in Equation (7.40) is proportional to $A_H - A_L = (1 - \epsilon)A_H$. Therefore, the extinction ratio can be important in the BER performance. To have the same BER, a nonzero extinction factor requires a higher incident power or a lower receiver sensitivity. Because $\sigma_H + \sigma_L$ is also a function of ϵ in general, the power penalty due to a nonzero extinction factor can be even worse.

To quantify the power penalty due to a nonzero extinction ratio, first assume

$$\delta_L^2 \approx \epsilon \delta_H^2$$

for simplicity. Therefore, from the definition of h given by Equation (7.92),

$$\sigma_H = \frac{\sigma_a}{M_{apd}} \sqrt{h + 1}$$

and

$$\sigma_L = \frac{\sigma_a}{M_{apd}} \sqrt{\epsilon h + 1}.$$

From the optimum condition of Equation (7.90),

$$h\left(1 + \epsilon\sqrt{\frac{1 + h}{1 + \epsilon h}}\right) = 2\left(1 + \sqrt{\frac{1 + h}{1 + \epsilon h}}\right). \quad \textbf{[7.103]}$$

This equation can be simplified as

$$\epsilon h^2 + (\epsilon + 1)h - 8 = 0. \quad \textbf{[7.104]}$$

From Equation (7.88), the corresponding optimum γ is

$$\gamma(\epsilon) = \frac{\sigma_a}{M_{apd,opt}(\epsilon)}(\sqrt{1 + h} + \sqrt{1 + \epsilon h}) \quad \textbf{[7.105]}$$

where

$$M_{apd,opt} = \left(\frac{h\sigma_a^2}{k\delta_H^2}\right)^{1/3} \quad \textbf{[7.106]}$$

with h satisfying Equation (7.104). From Equation (7.95),

$$\gamma(0) = \frac{4\sigma_a}{M_{apd,opt}(0)}.$$

Therefore,

$$\frac{\gamma(\epsilon)}{\gamma(0)} = \frac{M_{apd,opt}(0)}{M_{apd,opt}(\epsilon)} \frac{\sqrt{1+h} + \sqrt{1+\epsilon h}}{4}.$$

From Equation (7.106), we note that $M_{opt}(\epsilon)$ is proportional to $h^{1/3}$. Therefore,

$$\frac{\gamma(\epsilon)}{\gamma(0)} = \left(\frac{8}{h}\right)^{1/3} \left(\frac{\sqrt{1+h} + \sqrt{1+\epsilon h}}{4}\right). \qquad \textbf{[7.107]}$$

If the additional power factor $(1+\epsilon)$ for the incident power and another factor $(1-\epsilon)$ for a smaller numerator in the Q-function of Equation (7.40) are included, the total power penalty due to the extinction ratio is

$$PP(\epsilon) = \left[\frac{1+\epsilon}{1-\epsilon}\right] \frac{\gamma(\epsilon)}{\gamma(0)} = \left[\frac{1+\epsilon}{1-\epsilon}\right] \left(\frac{8}{h}\right)^{1/3} \frac{\sqrt{1+h} + \sqrt{1+\epsilon h}}{4} \qquad \textbf{[7.108]}$$

with h satisfying Equation (7.104). Using Equations (7.104) and (7.108) gives the power penalty in dB as shown in Figure 7.20.

7.10.4 USE OF REPEATERS

When a system is required to operate at a speed–distance product higher than either the dispersion limit or the attenuation limit, it needs to use repeaters, which are digital optical transceivers that detect, retime, and retransmit received signals. Therefore, each repeater can be considered a fully functional transceiver pair. When the bit error rate is low enough, digital signals can be regenerated without noise accumulation. This is one significant advantage of digital communications over analog communications.

For undersea transmissions and some other applications, because of cost, a higher reliability requirement, and the need of power supply, the use of repeaters is undesirable. Therefore, research and development for repeaterless systems using optical amplifiers have been active recently [9]. Using optical amplifiers at either the transmitter end or receiver end can improve the attenuation limit. Detailed discussion on optical amplifiers is given in Chapter 17.

In designing a system that requires repeaters, one basic question is *how* many repeaters are needed at a given specification? If the system is limited by attenuation, the number can be determined by the power budget and fiber attenuation. If the system is limited by dispersion, the number can be determined by the bit rate and fiber dispersion. These will be illustrated shortly. Once the number is determined, one must be cautious of the BER requirement for each repeater. Because the BER of each repeater is accumulated at each stage, the BER required at each stage should be lower than the original specification. More specifically, if P_E is the required end-to-end BER, with N repeaters plus the final receiver, the BER of each stage should be $P_{E,r}$ such that

$$1 - P_E = (1 - P_{E,r})^{N+1}.$$

When $P_{E,r}$ and P_E are much smaller than 1, the approximation

$$P_{E,r} = \frac{P_E}{N+1} \qquad \textbf{[7.109]}$$

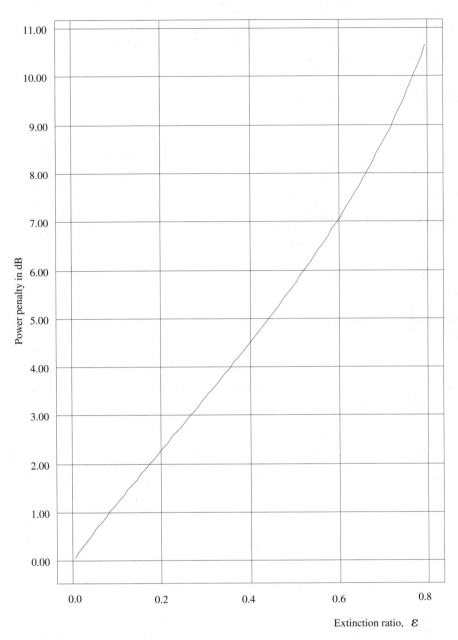

Figure 7.20   Power penalty due to nonzero extinction ratio.

holds. For example, if P_E required is 10^{-9}, the BER of each stage with nine repeaters should be 10^{-10}. Examples 7.22 and 7.23 illustrate the use of repeaters for attenuation- and dispersion-limited systems, respectively.

Example 7.22	**SYSTEM LIMITED BY ATTENUATION** Consider an optical communication system that needs to transmit data at a rate of 150 Mb/s and over a distance of 500 km. The BER is required to be $P_E = 10^{-9}$. The wavelength is chosen to be 1.3 μm, and single-mode fibers are used. Because intramodal dispersion is zero at 1.3 μm and there is no modal dispersion in single-mode fibers, fiber dispersion can be ignored. If fiber attenuation is 0.6 dB/km at 1.3 μm, the total attenuation is $0.6 \times 500 = 300$ dB. If the available power budget at BER $= 10^9$ is 30 dB, the system is significantly limited by attenuation. If there are 9 repeaters, or 30 dB power budget for each segment, the BER of each segment is 10^{-9} and the combined BER is 10^{-8}, which is not satisfactory. Therefore, there must be at least 10 repeaters. At this number, the fiber attenuation of each segment is 27.3 dB. In other words, there is additional power of 2.7 dB at BER $= 10^{-9}$. For $Q(x) \approx e^{-x^2/2}/\sqrt{2\pi x^2} = 10^{-9}$, $x = 6$, and for $Q(x) = 10^{-10}$, $x = 6.4$. The ratio 6.4:6 gives $10\log_{10}(6.4/6.0) = 0.3$ dB, so the additional power of 2.7 dB is sufficient to bring the BER of each segment below 10^{-10}. ∎

Example 7.23	**SYSTEM LIMITED BY DISPERSION** An optical communication system is required to transmit data at a rate of 630 Mb/s over a distance of 100 km. The BER is required to be $P_E = 10^{-9}$. The wavelength is chosen at 1.5 μm, and single-mode fibers are used. The light source is a Fabry-Perot laser diode of linewidth 5 nm. Assume the fiber dispersion at 1.5 μm is 10 psec/(nm·km), and assume the fiber attenuation at 1.5 μm is 0.2 dB/km. Under these assumptions, if there is no repeater, the total fiber attenuation is 20 dB, and the total fiber dispersion is

$$\Delta T = D_{intra} L \Delta \lambda = 5 \text{ nsec.}$$

For a bit interval $T_0 = 1.6$ nsec, this dispersion is too high. If the power budget is 25 dB, the system is not limited by attenuation but is significantly limited by the fiber dispersion. If the driver circuit for the light source and the light detector circuit have both a rise and fall time of 0.2 nsec, the allowable fiber dispersion is

$$0.2^2 + 0.2^2 + (\Delta T)^2 \leq \left(\frac{T_0}{4}\right)^2$$

or

$$\Delta T \leq 0.28 \text{ nsec.}$$

Therefore, the number of repeaters should be at least

$$N = \frac{5}{0.28} - 1 = 17.$$

This is a large number. To solve this problem, one must use a light source that has a much smaller linewidth, for example, a DFB laser diode. If the linewidth is reduced to 0.01 nm, the total fiber dispersion over 100 km is reduced to 0.01 nsec and no repeater is needed. ∎

7.11 FRONT-END AMPLIFIERS

As mentioned earlier, the objective of the front-end amplifier is to amplify the signal with minimal added noise. Since the photocurrent signal can be very weak at the front-end amplifier, the added amplifier noise is very critical to the subsequent detection.

As illustrated in Figure 7.4, two important types of front-end amplifiers are (1) high-impedance and (2) transimpedance amplifiers. High-impedance amplifiers are optimized from low noise consideration, which is important in long-distance point-to-point communications. Transimpedance amplifiers, on the other hand, are optimized from wide dynamic range consideration, which is important to multiple access.

7.11.1 HIGH-IMPEDANCE AMPLIFIER

An equivalent circuit for a high impedance amplifier is depicted in Figure 7.21, where the amplifier can be a bipolar junction transistor (BJT), a field effect transistor (FET), or an operational amplifier. From the equivalent circuit, the input impedance is

$$Z_{in}(\omega) = \frac{R_{in}}{1 + j\omega R_{in}C_{in}}$$ [7.110]

where R_{in} is the total input resistance with

$$G_{in} = 1/R_{in} = 1/R_L + 1/R_d + 1/R_a.$$

In the equation, R_d is the output resistance of the photodiode, R_L is the load resistance, and R_a is the front-end amplifier input resistance. Also, C_{in} is the total input capacitance, which can be expressed as

$$C_{in} = C_d + C_s + C_a$$

where C_d is the diode junction capacitance, C_s is the stray capacitance, and C_a is the front-end amplifier input capacitance.

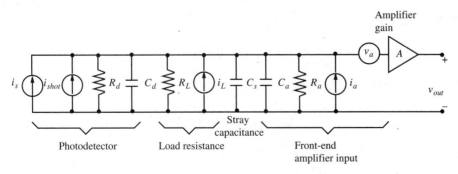

Figure 7.21 Equivalent circuit of high-impedance front-end amplifier.

From the input resistance R_{in}, there is a current thermal noise with the PSD given by

$$S_{th} = 2kTG_{in}. \tag{7.111}$$

From equations (7.4) and (7.18), the PSD of the receiver noise is

$$S_a(\omega) = S_i(\omega) + S_v(\omega)\frac{1 + (\omega R_{in} C_{in})^2}{R_{in}^2} = S_i(\omega) + \frac{S_v(\omega)}{R_{in}^2} + \omega^2 C_{in}^2 S_v(\omega). \tag{7.112}$$

Therefore, high-impedance amplifiers can have a minimal noise power by using a large R_{in}. When R_{in} is large enough, the middle term in Equation (7.112) can be dropped. Specific current and voltage sources at the input of different types of front-end amplifiers are shown below.

BJT Amplifier   For BJT devices, the PSD of the current noise source is qI_B, where I_B is the base current. Therefore, the total current noise source is

$$S_i = qI_B + 2kTG_{in} \approx qI_B \tag{7.113}$$

where the term $2kTG_{in}$ is dropped if G_{in} is small. Also, the voltage noise source for BJT is

$$S_v = \frac{2kT}{g_m} \tag{7.114}$$

where g_m is the equivalent transconductance of the transistor equal to

$$g_m = \frac{qI_C}{kT}. \tag{7.115}$$

The total PSD of receiver noise is thus

$$S_{a,BJT} \approx S_i + 2kT\frac{\omega^2 C_{in}^2}{g_m}. \tag{7.116}$$

From the PSD derived, if the total receiver transfer function is $H(\omega)$, the output noise power due to the front-end amplifier is

$$\sigma_{a,BJT}^2 = \int S_a(\omega) \mid H(\omega) \mid^2 \frac{d\omega}{2\pi} = \int [S_i(\omega) + \omega^2 C_{in}^2 S_v] \mid H(\omega) \mid^2 \frac{d\omega}{2\pi}$$

which can be conveniently expressed as

$$\sigma_{a,BJT}^2 = qI_B B J_0 + 2kT\frac{(2\pi C_{in})^2}{g_m} B^3 J_2 \tag{7.117}$$

where

$$J_i \stackrel{\text{def}}{=} \int \mid \hat{H}(x) \mid^2 x^i dx \quad \text{for } i = 0, 1, 2 \tag{7.118}$$

is a normalized parameter with

$$\hat{H}(x) \stackrel{\text{def}}{=} H(2\pi Bx).$$ **[7.119]**

BJT NOISE Consider an ideal low-pass filter $H(\omega)$ of a cutoff frequency B. In this case,

Example 7.24

$$\hat{H}(x) = \begin{cases} 1 & \text{if } |x| \leq 1 \\ 0 & \text{if } |x| > 1 \end{cases}$$

and

$$J_i = 2 \int_0^1 x^i \, dx = \frac{2}{i+1}.$$

The noise power given by Equation (7.117) thus reduces to

$$\sigma_{a,BJT}^2 = 2qI_B B + \frac{4}{3}kT \frac{(2\pi C_{in})^2}{g_m} B^3.$$

For the receiver filter $H(\omega)$ given by Equation (7.80) with $B = 1/T_0$,

$$\hat{H}(x) = \begin{cases} \frac{1+\cos(\pi x)}{2\text{sinc}(x)\text{sinc}(2x\delta/T_0)} & \text{if } |x| \leq 1 \\ 0 & \text{if } |x| > 1. \end{cases}$$

Numerical integration gives the following values:

δ/T_0	0.0	0.1	0.25
J_0	1.12	1.15	1.30
J_1	0.37	0.38	0.47
J_2	0.17	0.18	0.24

Because the signal output is normalized to unity (see Equation [7.78]), there is a stronger noise effect (larger J_i) as δ/T_0 increases.

Note that although raised-cosine filtering has smaller J_i's than ideal low-pass filtering, detection performance cannot be directly compared by their J_i's. For a fair comparison, one must take the ratio of the signal squared at the equalizer output to the noise power given by Equation (7.117). ∎

FET Amplifier For FET devices, the current noise source is

$$S_i = qI_G + 2kTG_{in} \approx 0$$ **[7.120]**

where I_G is the gate current and is close to zero. Similar to the voltage noise source in BJT, the voltage noise source is

$$S_v = \frac{2kT\Gamma}{g_m}$$ **[7.121]**

where Γ is a material dependent parameter. A typical value for Γ is from 0.5 to 3.0. Therefore,

$$S_{a,FET} \approx \omega^2 C_{in}^2 S_v = 2kT\Gamma \frac{\omega^2 C_{in}^2}{g_m} \qquad \textbf{[7.122]}$$

and the receiver noise output power is

$$\sigma_{a,FET}^2 = \int \omega^2 C_{in}^2 S_v \mid H(\omega) \mid^2 \frac{d\omega}{2\pi} = 2kT\Gamma \frac{(2\pi C_{in})^2}{g_m} B^3 J_2. \qquad \textbf{[7.123]}$$

Typical numerical values for BJT and FET devices are given in Table 7.2 [4] [11] [12].

Table 7.2   Typical numerical values for BJT and FET devices.

Parameters	Si JFET	Si MOSFET	GaAs MOSFET	Si BJT
Transconductance, g_m (mS)	5–10	30–50	15–50	qI_C/kT
Current gain, β	—	—	—	100–300
Gate-source capacitance, C_{gs} (pF)	3–6	0.5–0.8	0.2–0.5	—
Base-emitter capacitance (pF)	—	—	—	0.2–1.0
Γ	0.5–1.0	1.0–3.0	1.1–1.75	—
Gate or base current (nA)	0.01–0.1	< 0.01	1–1000	I_C/β
Cutoff frequency, f_T (GHz)	0.1–0.2	1–20	10–100	6–12

Example 7.25   **FREQUENCY DEPENDENCE OF BJT & FET NOISE POWER**   For raised-cosine filtering with NRZ input, the table in Example 7.24 shows $J_0 = 1.12$ and $J_2 = 0.17$. Let $C_{in} = 50$ pF, $\Gamma = 1.5$, and $g_m = 10$ mS for FET. At room temperature of $T = 300\,\text{K}$,

$$\sigma_{a,FET}^2 = 2.1 \times 10^{-38} B^3 \, \text{A}^2.$$

For BJT, if $I_B = 0.5$ mA and $I_C = 50$ mA, $g_m = 1.9$ S. Thus

$$\sigma_{a,BJT}^2 = 9.0 \times 10^{-23} B + 7.0 \times 10^{-41} B^3.$$

These noise powers as a function of bit rate B are illustrated in Figure 7.22. At low bit rates, FET has smaller noise than BJT. When the bit rate is high, BJT performs better because of a large transconductance g_m. ■

7.11.2   Transimpedance Amplifier

As illustrated in Figure 7.4, a transimpedance amplifier has a negative feedback resistance. The equivalent circuit is shown in Figure 7.23. In this circuit, in addition to the input photocurrent and noise, as in the case of high-impedance amplifiers, there is thermal nose (i_F) from the feedback resistor R_F.

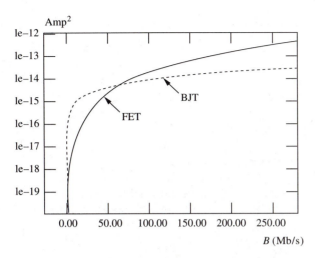

Figure 7.22 Noise power comparison between FET and BJT front-end amplifier.

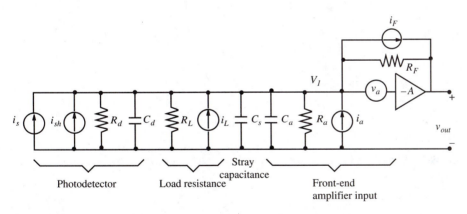

Figure 7.23 Equivalent circuit of transimpedance front-end amplifier.

The circuit analysis is more complicated than for high-impedance amplifiers. For simplicity, the amplifier gain A is assumed to be much greater than one and its input impedance is assumed to be infinity. Under these approximations, the signal output v_{out} satisfies the following equation:

$$i_{ph} = \frac{v_1}{Z_{in}} + \frac{v_1 - v_{out}}{R_F}$$

where

$$v_{out} = -Av_1. \qquad \textbf{[7.124]}$$

This gives

$$v_{out} = -\frac{i_{ph}R_F}{1 + 1/A + R_F/AZ_{in}} \approx -i_{ph}R_F.$$

[7.125]

Thus the output voltage is controlled by the feedback resistance and not by the amplifier gain. Furthermore, because the pole of Equation (7.125) is approximately $A/(R_F C_{in})$, at a large A, it is much higher than the signal's bandwidth. Therefore, the transimpedance amplifier can be considered as an all-pass filter with the transimpedance gain equal to $-R_F$.

PSD of Parallel Current Noise Sources   The output noise power spectrum is the superposition of the output due to each noise source. Because shot noise, RIN noise, thermal noise, and current noise of the front-end amplifier are all parallel to the signal photocurrent, their total output spectrum is R_F^2 times the sum of the individual spectra. That is,

$$S_{i,out} = R_F^2 \left(q F_{apd} M_{apd} i_{ph} + \frac{\mathrm{RIN}}{2} i_{ph}^2 + \frac{2kT}{R_{in}} + S_i \right).$$

PSD of Feedback Resistor   For noise output due to thermal current noise i_F,

$$\frac{v_1}{Z_{in}} + i_F + \frac{v_1 - v_{F,out}}{R_F} = 0.$$

Using Equation (7.124),

$$v_{F,out} \approx i_F R_F.$$

Therefore, the output noise power spectrum due to i_F is

$$S_{F,out} = 2kT R_F = R_F^2 \frac{2kT}{R_F}.$$

PSD of Voltage Noise Source   For noise output due to the voltage source v_a of the front-end amplifier,

$$-A(v_a + v_1) = v_{a,out}$$

and

$$\frac{v_1 - v_{a,out}}{R_F} + \frac{v_1}{Z_{in}} = 0.$$

These give

$$v_{a,out} \approx -R_F v_a \left(\frac{1}{R_F} + \frac{1}{Z_{in}} \right).$$

If

$$\frac{1}{R_p} = \frac{1}{R_F} + \frac{1}{R_{in}}$$

[7.126]

then

$$S_{v,out} = R_F^2 S_v \left(\frac{1}{R_p^2} + \omega^2 C_{in}^2 \right). \qquad \textbf{[7.127]}$$

Total PSD   Adding all the noise terms, the total noise output spectrum is

$$S_{n,out} = R_F^2 \left(q F_{apd} M_{apd}^2 i_{ph} + \frac{\text{RIN}}{2} i_{ph}^2 + \frac{2kT}{R_p} + S_i \right) + R_F^2 S_v \left(\frac{1}{R_p^2} + \omega^2 C_{in}^2 \right).$$
$$\textbf{[7.128]}$$

Dividing the output spectrum by the factor R_F^2 gives the equivalent input noise spectrum:

$$S_{n,in,trans} = q F_{apd} M_{apd}^2 i_{ph} + \frac{\text{RIN}}{2} i_{ph}^2 + \frac{2kT}{R_p} + S_i + S_v \left(\frac{1}{R_p^2} + \omega^2 C_{in}^2 \right). \quad \textbf{[7.129]}$$

Comparing this with that of the high-impedance amplifier gives

$$S_{n,in,trans} = S_{n,in,high} + \frac{2kT}{R_F} + \frac{S_v}{R_p^2} \qquad \textbf{[7.130]}$$

and

$$\sigma_{a,trans}^2 = \sigma_{a,high}^2 + \frac{2kT}{R_F} B J_0 + \frac{2kT}{g_m R_p^2} B J_0. \qquad \textbf{[7.131]}$$

Therefore, the transimpedance amplifier has two extra noise power terms due to (1) feedback resistance noise and (2) front-end amplifier voltage noise.

EXTRA NOISE OF TRANSIMPEDANCE AMPLIFIERS   Use the same BJT parameters in Example 7.25. Also assume $R_F \approx R_p = 100\text{k}\Omega$. In this case, the additional noise power is | **Example 7.26**

$$\frac{2kT}{R_F} B J_0 + \frac{2kT}{g_m R_p^2} B J_0 \approx \frac{2kT}{R_F} B J_0 = 9.3 \times 10^{-26} B.$$

This is not a significant increase for BJT. However, for FET, this can be significant because of a much smaller transconductance g_m. ∎

7.11.3 ALLOWABLE DYNAMIC RANGE

For a given front-end amplifier design, there is a window of the received signal power within which satisfactory performance can be achieved. The lower limit of this window is determined by the receiver sensitivity, which has been discussed in detail in Section 7.6. The higher limit of the window is determined by the receiver amplifier gain saturation discussed below.

Consider a high-impedance or transimpedance amplifier. Let

$$A_H G = v_{out}$$

where G is the transimpedance gain equal to either $R_{in}A$ (high-impedance amplifiers) or $R_F A_H$ (transimpedance amplifiers), and v_{out} is the voltage at the amplifier output. If the output v_{out} cannot be higher than V_D due to either bias or other circuit constraints, the photocurrent high level A_H needs to be lower than V_D/G for linear response. In other words, if $A_H > V_D/G$, the output v_{out} stays at the same value V_D. Although this distortion is fine in digital communications, the output noise power can continue to increase after signal saturation. At a high photocurrent level, the noise power can be dominated by the RIN noise. In this case,

$$\sigma_H + \sigma_L \approx \sigma_H = G\sqrt{\mathrm{RIN} \times A_H^2 B}.$$

Furthermore, in the ideal case that both ISI and the extinction ratio are zero, the argument of the Q-function in Equation (7.40) reduces to

$$x = \frac{V_D}{G A_H \sqrt{\mathrm{RIN}B}}.$$

This equation shows that A_H is upper bound before x becomes smaller than a minimum value. For example, if $x = 6$ for BER at 10^{-9},

$$A_H < \frac{V_D}{6G\sqrt{\mathrm{RIN}B}} = \frac{A_{H,sat}}{6\sqrt{\mathrm{RIN}B}} \qquad \textbf{[7.132]}$$

where

$$A_{H,sat} \stackrel{\text{def}}{=} \frac{V_D}{G}. \qquad \textbf{[7.133]}$$

From Equation (7.132), we see the larger the G, the smaller the upper limit for A_H, and a smaller dynamic range. Because the high-impedance amplifier has a much higher G than the transimpedance amplifier, the transimpedance amplifier has a larger dynamic range.

Example 2.27

ALLOWABLE DYNAMIC RANGE   If $G = 100\,\mathrm{k}\Omega$ for a transimpedance amplifier and $1\,\mathrm{M}\Omega$ for a high-impedance amplifier, the upper voltage limit for the transimpedance amplifier is 10 dB higher than that for the high-impedance amplifier. If the receiver sensitivity of the high-impedance amplifier is better than the transimpedance amplifier by 2 dB, the allowable dynamic range is 8 dB larger using the transimpedance amplifier.

For the transimpedance amplifier, assume the lower limit for A_H is 0.01 μA. At $V_D = 5$ V, RIN $= 10^{-14}$ dB/Hz, and B = 100MHz/s, the upper limit is

$$A_H < 8.3\ \mu\mathrm{A}.$$

This gives an allowable dynamic range of $10\log_{10}(8.3/0.01) = 29.2$ dB. ∎

In practice, the allowable dynamic range is degraded by a nonzero extinction ratio and ISI. For example, if there is a nonzero extinction ratio, the output low level due to A_L can still increase while A_H has reached its saturation point. This results in a smaller signal margin $v_{out,H} - v_{out,L}$. Similarly, for the worst case sequence given by Equation (7.26), when there is a nonzero ISI, the "tail" portion due to A_H from neighboring bits can still increase. Exact computation of the higher limit is even more involved when various circuit constraints such as nonlinearity and slew rate at large signal input are considered. Therefore, the higher limit is either practically determined from experiments or set by the saturation point given by Equation (7.132) [5].

A common technique to increase the allowable dynamic range is to use **automatic gain control** (AGC), which reduces (or increases) the APD gain when the received signal power is detected to be high (or low). In practice, the APD gain can be controlled by its reverse bias voltage. For actual circuit design on the AGC, see [10] for more details.

7.12 SUMMARY

This chapter has discussed and illustrated various design principles and performance evaluations for both analog and digital signal detection using incoherent detection. For digital signal detection, Figure 7.24 summarizes what has been discussed, which includes

- The optimum gain design for an APD (Section 7.10).
- Line code consideration for ac coupling and dc wander (Section 7.9).

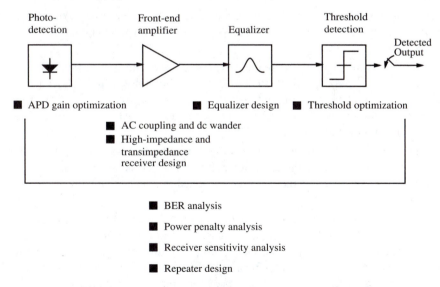

Figure 7.24   Summary of various design and performance evaluation subjects discussed for an incoherent digital receiver.

- Front-end amplifier design (Section 7.11).
- Equalizer design (Section 7.8).
- Optimum threshold design (Sections 7.4 and 7.5).
- Repeater design (Section 7.10.4).
- Various performance analyses, including
  - BER (Sections 7.4 and 7.5).
  - Power penalty due to nonzero ISI, extinction ratio, and a finite input dynamic range (in various sections).
  - Receiver sensitivity (Section 7.6).

Because many noise sources and ISI are signal dependent, simple and exact forms are usually unavailable. To show the design trade-offs and performance dependence on various parameters, this chapter instead used a finite slope pulse as the input pulse and assumed a unit rectangle pulse as the receiver filter (i.e., integration-and-dump) in most of the discussion. There were also many examples illustrating the analysis, design, and performance evaluations. For different received pulses and different receiver filters, readers can follow the same analysis procedure and obtain similar results. From the discussion and analysis, some general results and observations are summarized below.

1. In analog communication, one primary performance measure is the SNR or CNR. In general, when the SNR/CNR is required to be high (around 50 dB), RIN is a significant noise source and places an upper bound on the SNR/CNR. In addition to noise, nonlinearity from the laser diode characteristic can also be significant. To quantify the nonlinearity distortion, CSO (second-order distortion) and CTB (third-order distortion) are important parameters used in CATV applications (see Chapter 10 for detailed discussion.)

2. Transmission performance in digital communications is measured by the BER, which is in turn determined by the received signal power, noise power, intersymbol interference, crosstalk, and timing jitter.

3. In digital communications, there are two noise components at the input of the receiver front-end. One is signal dependent, such as RIN and shot noise, and the other is signal independent, such as thermal noise and amplifier input noise. The power of the signal dependent noise increases as the incident power increases. At a large incident power, signal-dependent noise dominates.

4. The ISI in optical communications can be caused by fiber dispersion, laser chirping, and a finite response time of the transmitter driver and photodetector circuits. The pulse broadening caused by each of these sources is added in a square sum according to Equation (7.74).

5. The BER can be calculated according to Equation (7.40) for a given input pulse waveform and receiver design. This expression is based on the assumption that the total noise is Gaussian. Therefore, it is called the Gaussian approximation. Other BER computation methods can be found in [3] and [4]. Because the expression depends on the pattern of the input sequence, the worst case sequence is used for simple computations.

6. The receiver sensitivity is the minimum incident power required to achieve a certain BER. When the thermal and amplifier noise are negligible compared to shot noise, the receiver sensitivity is linearly proportional to the bit rate.

7. The photocurrent pulse at the output of a photodiode in digital communications is mainly determined by the large signal response of the light source, fiber dispersion, and the photodiode response. When single-mode fibers are used, the equivalent fiber transfer function is determined by the output spectrum of the light source.

8. At high transmission bit rates, laser chirping causes linewidth broadening during the turn-on and turn-off transitions. As a result, it can further reduce the achievable distance–capacity product. To minimize the chirping effect, laser diodes with a small linewidth broadening factor α_{lw} should be used.

9. When ISI is not important, simple integration-and-dump receivers are attractive for minimal noise power. When ISI is important, raised-cosine filters should be used instead to minimize ISI.

10. When ac coupling is used to reject undesirable dc components, the dc level of the signal should also be maintained constant. This is called dc balance. If there is dc wander, it will pass through the ac coupling and cause a strong ISI. Using a proper line code, such as CMI, can reduce the dc wander and consequently ISI.

11. When an APD diode is used for photodetection, its gain can be optimized to minimize the BER. In general, when the noise from the receiver is large, the gain should be large to de-emphasize the receiver noise. When the incident light power is large, on the other hand, the gain should be small to minimize the excess noise.

12. In binary digital transmission, the extinction ratio is the ratio of the low signal value to the high signal value. In general, it should be as small as possible to maximize the noise margin at a given average signal power. A nonzero extinction ratio not only reduces the noise margin but also increases ISI. As a result, more transmission power is required to meet the same BER performance.

13. In digital communications, when systems are either limited by dispersion or attenuation, repeaters are needed to regenerate signals. The number of repeaters is determined by the available power budget, transmission rate, fiber attenuation, and fiber dispersion. Because the final BER is proportional to the total number of repeaters plus one, the required BER on each repeater link should be less than the end-to-end BER divided by the total number of repeaters plus one.

14. Two important types of front-end amplifiers are high-impedance and transimpedance amplifiers. High-impedance amplifiers can minimize the input noise but have a smaller dynamic range. Transimpedance amplifiers, on the other hand, have a little higher input noise power but can achieve a larger dynamic range, which is important in multiple access applications such as local area networking.

15. The allowable dynamic range of a given system is the input power range within which specified performance is met. In general, the lower limit is determined by the receiver sensitivity, and the upper limit is determined by the gain saturation of the receiver.

APPENDIX 7-A: SPECTRUM AND POWER OF SIGNAL-DEPENDENT NOISE

As noted earlier, the noise from the photodetector output is signal dependent. Therefore, the random process of the noise is nonstationary. Specifically, Equation (7.15) shows that the PSD of the current noise is a function of $i_{ph}(t)$, which is time dependent, as can be seen from Equation (7.9). When the current noise is passed through a filter with impulse response $h(t)$, the output noise is given by

$$y_{n,out}(t) = i_n(t) \otimes h(t).$$

This is also a nonstationary process. The PSD of this output noise is the Fourier transform of the autocorrelation

$$R_{n,out}(t, t + \tau) = E[y_{n,out}(t)y_{n,out}(t + \tau)].$$

Therefore,

$$
\begin{aligned}
S_{n,out}(\omega, t) &= \int R_{n,out}(t, t + \tau)e^{-j\omega\tau}d\tau \\
&= \int E[i_n(t - t')i_n(t + \tau - t'')]h(t')h(t'')e^{-j\omega\tau}d\tau dt'dt'' \\
&= \int R_{n,in}(t - t', t + \tau - t'')h(t')h(t'')e^{-j\omega\tau}d\tau dt'dt'' \\
&= \int S_{n,in}(\omega, t - t')H(\omega)h(t')e^{j\omega t'}dt'. \qquad \textbf{[7.134]}
\end{aligned}
$$

The variance of $y_{n,out}(t)$, which is needed to calculate the detection performance, can be obtained by integrating $S_{n,out}$ over the frequency domain. That is,

$$\sigma_{n,out}^2(t) = \int S_{n,out}(\omega, t)\frac{d\omega}{2\pi} = \int\int S_{n,in}(\omega, t - t')H(\omega)e^{j\omega t'}h(t')\frac{d\omega}{2\pi}dt'.$$

When $S_{n,in}(\omega, t - t')$ is a constant over the interested frequency range (white noise) or relatively broad compared to $H(\omega)$,

$$\sigma_{n,out}^2(t) \approx \int S_{n,in}(t - t')h(t')^2dt'. \qquad \textbf{[7.135]}$$

This means that the output variance is a weighted average of the input noise variance with the weight function $h(t)^2$.

APPENDIX 7-B: ZERO INTERSYMBOL INTERFERENCE

This appendix derives the condition for $p_{out}(t)$ in Equation (7.11) to have zero ISI. From the definition in Equation (7.13), the zero ISI condition is given by Equation (7.78). In other words,

$$p_{out}(t) \sum_i \delta(t - iT_0) = \sum_i p_{out}(iT_0)\delta(t - iT_0) = p_{out}(T_0)\delta(t - T_0).$$

Performing the Fourier transform on both sides gives

$$P_{out}(\omega) \otimes \sum_i e^{j\omega i T_0} = \frac{2\pi}{T_0} P_{out}(\omega) \otimes \sum_i \delta(\omega - i2\pi/T_0)$$

$$= \frac{2\pi}{T_0} \sum_i P_{out}(\omega - 2\pi i/T_0) = p_{out}(T_0)e^{-j\omega T_0}.$$

In other words, the condition for zero ISI is that

$$\boxed{\sum_i P_{out}(\omega - 2\pi i/T_0) = \text{constant.}} \qquad \textbf{[7.136]}$$

A special case that $P_{out}(\omega)$ has the minimal bandwidth is when

$$P_{out}(\omega) = \begin{cases} T_0 & |\omega| < \frac{\pi}{T_0} \\ 0 & \text{otherwise.} \end{cases} \qquad \textbf{[7.137]}$$

In other words, the minimal bandwidth of a zero ISI pulse is $1/2T_0$ or half of the bit rate. This is called the **Nyquist bandwidth** for zero ISI. It should be noted that this Nyquist bandwidth is different from the **Nyquist rate** used in the sampling theorem [8].

   An important class of zero ISI pulses commonly used in communication systems is called the **raised-cosine** family. They can be expressed as

$$P_{out}(\omega) = \begin{cases} T_0 & |\omega| < \dfrac{\pi}{T_0} - \Delta\omega \\ 0 & |\omega| > \dfrac{\pi}{T_0} + \Delta\omega \\ \dfrac{T_0}{2}\{1 \pm \sin(\pi[|\omega| \pm \pi/T_0]/[2\Delta\omega])\} & ||\omega| \pm \pi/T_0| < \Delta\omega. \end{cases} \qquad \textbf{[7.138]}$$

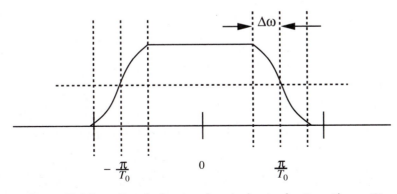

Figure 7.25   Transfer function of a raised-cosine function with zero ISI.

This transfer function is illustrated in Figure 7.25. It can be clearly seen from the illustration that $P_{out}(\omega)$ given by Equation (7.138) satisfies the condition of Equation (7.136). The ratio $\Delta\omega T_0/\pi$ is called the **excess bandwidth ratio.** At 100 percent excess bandwidth, $\Delta\omega = \pi/T_0$. The corresponding pulse is given in Equation (7.79).

APPENDIX 7–C: RECEIVED PULSE DETERMINATION CONSIDERING THE CHIRPING EFFECT

For laser diodes under direct modulation, the photocurrent pulse is more complex when the chirping effect is considered. As discussed in detail in Chapter 12, the chirping effect is caused by refractive index modulation of the laser cavity. As a result, the output spectrum $g_s(\lambda - \lambda_c)$ is time varying. For single-mode laser diodes, the range of wavelength shifts during turn-on and turn-off transitions can be much larger than that at the steady state linewidth.

For simple consideration, assume the *shape* of the spectrum is time invariant. Although this assumption may not be valid under large modulation, a time-varying spectrum shape is difficult to model and strongly depends on individual devices used. Therefore, only the case of time-invariant spectrum shape is considered here. With this assumption, the time-varying spectrum can be modeled as

$$g_s = g_s[\lambda - \lambda_0 - \Delta\lambda_c(t)]$$ **[7.139]**

where $\Delta\lambda_c(t)$ is the wavelength shift from the central wavelength λ_0 due to chirping. When a laser is turned on, the wavelength shift is negative and is called **blue shift.** When the laser is turned off, the wavelength shift is positive and is called **red shift.** Because the wavelength shift is proportional to the shift of the refractive index from its steady state value during modulation, we can have

$$\Delta\lambda_c(t) = \begin{cases} 0 & \text{if } t < t_d \\ -\beta_{chirp}\Delta\lambda\sin(\omega_r[t-t_d])e^{-\alpha(t-t_d)} & \text{if } t_d < t < T_0 \\ -\beta_{chirp}\Delta\lambda\sin(\omega_r[T_0-t_d])e^{-\alpha(T_0-t_d)}e^{-\alpha_{off}(t-T_0)} \\ +\beta_{chirp}\Delta\lambda(1-e^{-\alpha_{off}(t-T_0)}) & \text{if } T_0 < t \end{cases}$$ **[7.140]**

where β_{chirp} is the ratio of the peak wavelength shift due to chirping to the linewidth at the steady state. This wavelength shift due to chirping is illustrated in Figure 7.26. Given this wavelength shift, the pulse output at the other end of the fiber is

$$p(t) = \int \frac{1}{D_{intra}L} g_s\left(\frac{t - t_{g0} - t' - D_{intra}L\Delta\lambda_c(t')}{D_{intra}L}\right) p_s(t')dt'$$ **[7.141]**

where $p_s(t)$ is the pulse input to the fiber. Therefore, the fiber transfer function can be modified as

$$h_{fiber}(t) = \frac{1}{D_{intra}L} g_s\left(\frac{t + t_{g0} + D_{intra}L\Delta\lambda_c(t)}{D_{intra}L}\right).$$ **[7.142]**

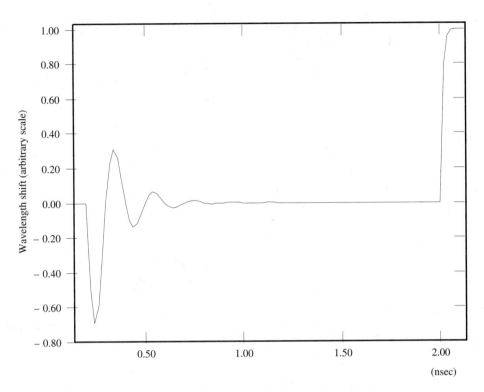

Figure 7.26   The wavelength shift due to chirping. Scale is arbitrary. The original pulse width is 2 nsec, relaxation oscillation frequency is 5 GHz, damping constants are $\alpha = 8.0 \times 10^9$ sec^{-1} and $\alpha_{off} = 8.0 \times 10^{10}$ sec^{-1}, and initial time delay is $t_d = 0.2$ nsec.

Various pulses with the chirping effect considered are illustrated in Figure 7.27.

A Simplified Model   Although the chirping effect can be computed numerically using Equation (7.141), it is instructive to use a simplified model to gain insight into the effect. The model first assumes an output pulse from a laser diode of a form similar to that given by Figure 7.6. That is, it assumes

$$p_s(t) = \begin{cases} \frac{t}{\delta_c} & \text{if } 0 < t < \delta_c \\ 1 & \text{if } \delta_c < t < T_0 \\ 1 - \frac{t-T_0}{\delta_c} & \text{if } T_0 < t < T_0 + \delta_c \\ 0 & \text{otherwise.} \end{cases} \qquad \textbf{[7.143]}$$

The first portion δ_c of the pulse is assumed to be the portion where the central wavelength linearly increases from $\lambda_0 - \beta_{chirp}\Delta\lambda$ to the steady state value λ_0. The tail portion δ_c of the pulse is assumed to be the portion where the central output wavelength linearly increases from the steady state value λ_0 to $\lambda_0 + \beta_{chirp}\Delta\lambda$. In the middle portion, the pulse is assumed to have a constant central wavelength λ_c.

Let $p_1(t)$ be the beginning portion of the pulse that has chirping with output wavelength linearly decreasing to the steady state. For $0 < t < \delta_c$, the propagation delay over distance L is

$$t_g(t) = t_{g0} + \frac{t - \delta_c}{\delta_c} D_{intra}\beta_{chirp}\Delta\lambda L$$

where t_{g0} is the propagation delay at the steady state wavelength. If $p_1(t)$ is partitioned into many small intervals,

$$p_1(t) = \lim_{\Delta t \to 0} \sum_i \frac{rect(t - t_i, \Delta t)}{\Delta t} p_1(t_i)\Delta t$$

where $t_i = i\Delta t$. The pulse after a distance L is

$$p_{1,out}(t, L) = \lim_{\Delta t \to 0} \sum_i \frac{rect(t - t_i - t_{g0} - \tau_c[t_i - \delta_c]/\delta_c, \Delta t)}{\Delta t} p_1(t_i)\Delta t$$

where

$$\tau_c \overset{def}{=} \beta_{chirp} D_{intra} L \Delta\lambda. \qquad\qquad \textbf{[7.144]}$$

By taking the limit $\Delta t \to 0$, one obtains

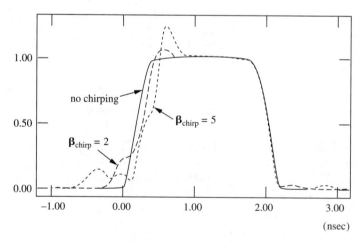

Figure 7.27   Pulse output at the fiber end with the chirping effect considered. Three β_{chirp} values are illustrated: 0 (no chirping), 2, and 5. The total fiber dispersion is $D_{intra}L\Delta\lambda = 0.2$ nsec. The original pulse width is 2 nsec, relaxation oscillation frequency is 5 GHz, damping constants are $\alpha = 8.0 \times 10^9$ sec^{-1} and $\alpha_{off} = 8.0 \times 10^{10}$ sec^{-1}, and initial time delay is $t_d = 0.2$ nsec.

$$p_{1,out}(t) = \int \delta[t - t'(1 + \tau_c/\delta_c) - t_{g0} + \tau_c]p_1(t')dt' \qquad [7.145]$$

$$= \frac{\delta_c}{\delta_c + \tau_c} p\left(\frac{t - t_{g0} + \tau_c}{1 + \tau_c/\delta_c}\right).$$

Similarly, for the tail portion of the pulse, which has chirping during the turn-off transition from T_0 to $T_0 + \delta_c$, the output over distance L is

$$p_{2,out}(t, L) = \lim_{\Delta t \to 0} \sum_i \frac{rect[t - t_i - \tau_c(t_i/\delta_c) - T_0 - t_{g0}, \Delta t]}{\Delta t} p_2(t_i + T_0)$$

$$= \int \delta[t - T_0 - t_{g0} - t_i(1 + \tau_c/\delta_c)]p_2(t' + T_0)dt' \qquad [7.146]$$

$$= \frac{\delta_c}{\delta_c + \tau_c} p_2\left(\frac{t - T_0}{1 + \tau_c/\delta_c}\right).$$

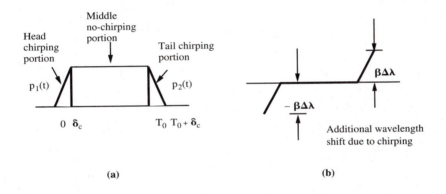

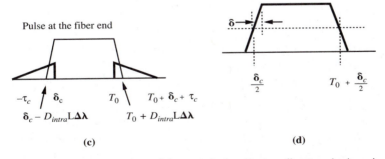

Figure 7.28   A simple model to include the chirping effect in pulse broadening: (a) original pulse with three partitions, (b) wavelength chirping of the pulse, (c) pulse broadening due to fiber dispersion, and (d) approximate broadened pulse.

The output pulse over distance L according to this simplified model is illustrated in Figure 7.28. Figure 7.28a shows the original pulse, which consists of three portions: the head, middle, and tail. The head and tail portions have chirping as shown in Figure 7.28b. With fiber dispersion, the pulse at the fiber end is illustrated in Figure 7.28c. Here the effect of fiber dispersion on the middle portion of the pulse is also considered. To quantify the chirping effect together with the fiber dispersion effect on pulse broadening, one can approximate the pulse shown in Figure 7.28c as the pulse in Figure 7.28d. To find the corresponding pulse

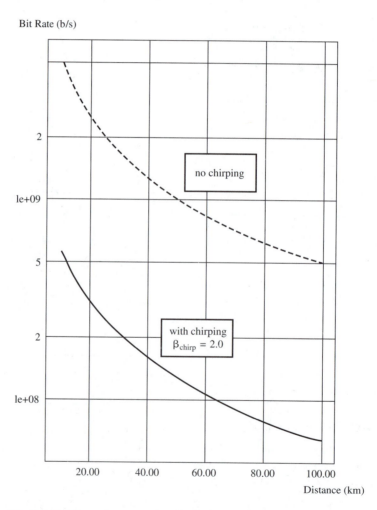

Figure 7.29   Dispersion limits with chirping and without chirping.
Parameters used are given in Example 7.28.

broadening factor δ in Figure 7.6, equate the power of the head portion of the pulse between $-\tau_c$ and $\delta_c/2$ to the power of beginning portion of the pulse from $-\delta$ to 0 in Figure 7.6.

If $D_{intra}L\Delta\lambda = \tau_c/\beta_{chirp} < \delta_c/2$, the middle portion caused by fiber dispersion is still within $\delta_c/2$ and $T_0 + \delta_c/2$. Therefore, its broadening is not important, and the pulse broadening is purely due to chirping. In this case, the equivalent pulse broadening parameter δ is

$$\frac{1}{4}\delta = \frac{1}{2}\delta_c \left(\frac{\tau_c + \delta_c/2}{\tau_c + \delta_c} \right)^2. \qquad \text{[7.147]}$$

If $D_{intra}L\Delta\lambda > \delta_c/2$, the fiber dispersion for the middle portion should be included. In this case, the equivalent pulse broadening parameter δ is

$$\frac{1}{4}\delta = \frac{1}{2}\delta_c \left(\frac{\tau_c + \delta_c/2}{\tau_c + \delta_c} \right)^2 + \frac{1}{2}\frac{(\tau_c/\beta_{chirp} - \delta_c/2)^2}{(\tau_c/\beta_{chirp})}. \qquad \text{[7.148]}$$

DISPERSION LIMIT DUE TO CHIRPING   Assume $\delta_c = 0.2$ nsec, fiber dispersion $D_{intra}\Delta\lambda = 10$ psec/km, and $\beta_{chirp} = 2$. At $L = 100$ km, $D_{total}L = 1$ nsec and $\tau_c = 2$ nsec. Equation (7.148) gives

Example 7.28

$$\delta = 2 \times 0.2 \times \left(\frac{2.1}{2.2} \right)^2 + 2 \times 0.9^2 = 0.36 + 1.62 = 1.98 \text{ nsec.}$$

If $B = 1/(8\delta)$ is the dispersion limit, the bit rate over 100 km is limited below 63.1 Mb/s. On the other hand, if there is no chirping and $\delta_c = 0$, the bit rate is limited by $1/(2D_{total}L)$ or 500 Mb/s. The dispersion limits as a function of distance with and without chirping considered are illustrated in Figure 7.29. The parameters used are the same as given in this example. ∎

APPENDIX 7–D: PULSE-BROADENING ANALYSIS

If an input pulse passes through a filter with impulse response $h(t)$, the output pulse will become broader. This is a general fact from the Fourier transform and also becomes clear from the subsequent discussion. Before analyzing the pulse-broadening effect, this appendix derives a condition for $h(t)$ so that the output pulse has the same energy or time integration as the input pulse. Let the input pulse be $p(t)$; the output is

$$p_{out}(t) = \int p(t')h(t - t')dt'.$$

Integrating the above equation to get the total energy of the pulse gives

$$\int p_{out}(t)dt = \int p(t')dt' \int h(t'')dt''.$$

Therefore, to have the same time integration or $\int p_{out}(t)dt = \int p(t')dt'$,

$$\int h(t'')dt'' = 1. \qquad\qquad \textbf{[7.149]}$$

The root-mean-square (RMS) width of an impulse response $h(t)$ is defined as

$$\delta^2 \stackrel{\text{def}}{=} \int (t - \bar{t})^2 h(t)dt \qquad\qquad \textbf{[7.150]}$$

where $\bar{t}$ is the center point of the pulse or

$$\bar{t} = \int t \times h(t)dt.$$

Example 7.29

EXPONENTIAL PULSE   Consider an exponential pulse caused by RC low-pass filtering. That is,

$$h(t) = \begin{cases} 0 & \text{if } t < 0 \\ \frac{1}{\tau}e^{-t/\tau} & \text{otherwise.} \end{cases}$$

Given that

$$\bar{t} = \int t \times h(t)dt = \tau$$

and

$$\overline{t^2} = \int t^2 h(t)dt = 2\tau \int t \times h(t)dt = 2\tau^2$$

the RMS width of this exponential pulse is

$$\delta^2 = \overline{t^2} - \bar{t}^2 = \tau^2 \quad\blacksquare \qquad\qquad \textbf{[7.151]}$$

The rise time or fall time of a pulse is typically defined as the time interval from 10 percent to 90 percent or from 90 percent to 10 percent. Exact calculation of the rise or fall time depends on the individual pulse.

Example 7.30

RISE TIME OF FIRST ORDER RC LOW PASS FILTER   The step input response because of RC filtering given in Example 7.29 is

$$p(t) = 1 - e^{-t/\tau}.$$

Therefore, the rise time is

$$t_{on} = \tau \ln(9) = 2.2\tau. \quad\blacksquare$$

Example 7.30 demonstrates that the rise time is a little higher than two times the RMS width of the impulse response (Example 7.29). For simplicity, the rise time is usually set to twice the RMS width of the impulse response.

If there are several filters cascaded in a system, the contribution to the total pulse broadening is the sum of the mean square of each impulse response. This can be verified as follows. Suppose there are two filters in cascade, with impulse responses $h_1(t)$ and $h_2(t)$, respectively. For simplicity and without loss of generality, assume $\bar{t}_1$ and $\bar{t}_2$ are zero. In this case,

$$\int t \times h_1(t - \tau)h_2(\tau)d\tau dt = 0.$$

In other words, the center point of $h_1(t) \otimes h_2(t)$ is also zero. The corresponding RMS is

$$\delta^2 = \int t^2 h_1(t - \tau)h_2(\tau)d\tau dt = \int (t - \tau + \tau)^2 h_1(t - \tau)h_2(\tau)d\tau dt$$

$$= \int [(t - \tau)^2 + \tau^2 + 2(t - \tau)\tau]h_1(t - \tau)h_2(\tau)d\tau dt = \delta_1^2 + \delta_2^2.$$

This result shows that the combined pulse has a wider RMS than each individual pulse. As a special case, if $h_1(t)$ is replaced by an input pulse $p(t)$, the result shows that the output pulse from $h_2(t)$ is broader than the input. If a communication link has many filters in series, the pulse along the link becomes broader as it propagates.

In an optical fiber transmission system, assume the turn-on times of the transmitter and receiver are t_{tx} and t_{rx}, respectively. If the total fiber dispersion is $\Delta T = D_{intra}L\Delta\lambda$, the RMS width of the equivalent impulse response of the fiber is $\Delta T/2$. Therefore, the total RMS width of the combined transmitter, fiber, and receiver response is

$$\delta^2 = \left(\frac{\Delta T}{2}\right)^2 + \left(\frac{t_{tx}}{2}\right)^2 + \left(\frac{t_{rx}}{2}\right)^2. \qquad \textbf{[7.152]}$$

PROBLEMS

Problem 7–1 CNR in Analog Signal Detection: For an analog video transmission system, a PIN diode is used in photodetection. The average detected photocurrent is $I_0 = 10 \ \mu A$, the dark current is $I_d = 0.1 \ \mu A$, and the RIN is -135 dB/Hz. Ignore the thermal noise and amplifier input noise and let $B = 1$ GHz.

    a. Calculate the CNR at a modulation index of 0.2.

    b. What is the upper limit of the CNR by increasing I_0?

Problem 7–2 Bandwidth in Analog Signal Detection: If the intramodal dispersion of a fiber is 25 psec/nm·km, what is the maximum allowable linewidth of the light source output for a transmission bandwidth of 1 GHz over 50 km? In analog SCM video transmission, the wavelength is generally chosen at 1.3 μm. Why?

Problem 7–3 Signal and ISI: Assume the photocurrent output from an incident light signal has the following form:

$$i_s(t) = \sum_k A_k p(t - kT_0)$$

where $A_k = 1 \, \mu A$ or 0, and

$$p(t) = \begin{cases} e^{-t/T_0} & \text{if } t > 0 \\ 0 & \text{otherwise.} \end{cases}$$

If the signal is sampled at every T_0, find the signal component of the sampled value at kT_0. What is the corresponding ISI component?

Problem 7–4 Filtered Output: If the photocurrent output of Problem 7–3 passes through an integration-and-dump filter, find the corresponding sampled signal component and ISI.

Problem 7–5 Signal-Dependent Noise: Under the same assumptions of Problems 7–3 and 7–4, find the noise power output at $t = kT_0$ and in terms of $\{A_k\}$. Consider only the shot noise and RIN terms.

Problem 7–6 Worst Case Sequence: With the same assumptions in Problems 7–3 to 7–5, find the worst case sequences and corresponding values at the filtered and sampled output for the following cases.

    a. ISI_k when A_k is high.
    b. ISI_k when A_k is low.
    c. Signal-dependent noise power when A_k is high.
    d. Signal-dependent noise power when A_k is low.

Problem 7–7 BER Computation: Assume the sampled value at an equalizer output is

$$y_k = A_k + 0.2A_{k-1} + 0.1A_{k-2} + y_{n,k}$$

where A_k is equally likely to be high (A_H) or low (A_L), and $y_{n,k}$ is assumed to be Gaussian of a constant variance $\sigma_{n,out}^2$. Assume the threshold is $0.65(A_H + A_L)$.

    a. Express the exact BER in terms of A_H, A_L, and $\sigma_{n,out}^2$.
    b. Give the worst case sequences for $A_k = A_H$ and A_L, respectively. Express the corresponding approximated BER.
    c. Calculate the BER for each possible input sequence at $A_H - A_L = 10\sigma_{n,out}$. Use Equation (6.16) for the Q-function approximation.
    d. Show that the approximated result from *b* and *c* is reasonably good compared to the exact expression given by *a*.

Problem 7–8 Threshold Optimization of Zero ISI: Assume the sampled value at the equalizer output is

$$y_k = A_k + y_{n,k}$$

with the noise power of $y_{n,k}$ given by

$$\sigma_{n,k}^2 = 0.1 A_k (A_H + A_L).$$

Find the suboptimum threshold given by Equation (7.23) and the corresponding BER.

Problem 7–9 Threshold Optimization Including ISI: Using the sampled output given by Problem 7–7, find the suboptimum threshold given by Equation (7.39) and the corresponding BER. For simplicity, assume σ_L and σ_H have a ratio 1:4. Consider only the worst case sequences in the computation.

Problem 7–10 Receiver Sensitivity: Assume the sampled value of a received signal is

$$y_k = A_k T_0 + y_{n,k}$$

where T_0 is the bit period and the noise term $y_{n,k}$ is Gaussian of variance

$$\sigma_{n,out}^2 = \begin{cases} \sigma_H^2 = 50q A_H T_0 + 10^{-14} A_H^2 T_0 + \sigma_a^2 & \text{if } A_k = A_H \\ \sigma_L^2 = \sigma_a^2 & \text{if } A_k = A_L \end{cases}$$

with $\sigma_H^2 \gg \sigma_a^2$.

a. Find the minimum current value of A_H to have a BER of 10^{-9} in terms of T_0. Compute the numerical values for $T_0 = 10$, 1, and 0.1 nsec.

b. If A_k is equally likely to be the high or low value, find the minimum required incident light power at $T_0 = 10$, 1, and 0.1 nsec, respectively. Assume the photodiode has a responsivity of 0.5.

c. From b, find the minimum average number of incident photons per bit. Assume the photodiode has a quantum efficiency of 0.8.

Problem 7–11 Receiver Sensitivity: Assume the same conditions as in Problem 7–10 except that $y_{n,k}$ now is a signal-independent noise of variance $10^{-21} T_0$ C^2.

a. Find the minimum A_H at $T_0 = 10$, 1, and 0.1 nsec, respectively.

b. Find the corresponding incident optical power and number of photons per bit.

Problem 7–12 Pulse Broadening: If the light source and photodetector have turn-on times of 0.2 and 0.4 nsec, respectively, find the total pulse broadening factor 2δ from Equation (7.74) as a function of L, the fiber distance. Assume the total fiber dispersion $D_{intra} \Delta \lambda$ is 10 psec/km. What is the dispersion limit if δ should be within $T_0/8$?

Problem 7–13 Receiver Filter Design: Based on Problem 7–12, which filtering will you use, integration-and-dump or raised-cosine? Assume $B = (1/T_0) = 100$ Mb/s and consider $L = 10$, 50, and 100 km, respectively. What is the corresponding penalty due to pulse broadening? Use Figure 7.13 in the computation.

Problem 7–14 Raised-Cosine Filtering: The raised-cosine filter given by Equation (7.79) is a special case of the raised-cosine filter family given by Equation (7.138).

a. Show that the transfer function given by Equation (7.138) satisfies the Nyquist zero ISI criterion.

b. Derive the inverse Fourier transform of Equation (7.138).

c. What is the trade-off for having different $\Delta \omega$ values?

Problem 7–15 Eye Opening for AC Coupling: For a given NRZ pulse amplitude modulated (PAM) signal

$$x(t) = \sum_k A_k rect(t - kT_0, T_0)$$

follow Example 7.17 to find the worst case eye opening after ac coupling. In the computation, assume $T_0/\tau_{rc} = 0.1$, $\tau = T_0$, and A_k can be either $+1$ or -1 with the constraint that there are no 5 consecutive $+1$'s or -1's. In other words, there is at least one $+1$ and one -1 in every five consecutive bits.

Problem 7–16 DC Balance Line Code: In an ac-coupled receiver, the eye opening must be at least 80 percent of the peak-to-peak distance (i.e., the eye opening when there is no ac coupling). For the NRZ signal given in Problem 7–15, what is the upper limit in length of the sequence A_k's that can have consecutive $+1$'s or -1's? Let $T_0/\tau_{rc} = 0.01$ in this case.

Problem 7–17 APD Gain Optimization: In on-off keying digital transmission, assume the incident power is 0.2 μW when $A_k = A_H$. The total signal-independent noise power at the front-end amplifier output is $\sigma_{si}^2 = 10^{-14}$ A^2, where the front-end amplifier is an ideal low-pass filter of bandwidth B. For an APD of $k = 0.1$ and responsivity $\mathcal{R} = 0.5$, find the optimum gain. Neglect the RIN and ISI in the calculation.

Problem 7–18 Dyanmic Range and Power Penalty: In a multiple access optical network, assume the input dynamic range is 30 dB from 0.01 μW to 10 μW.
  a. What is the minimum power penalty because of the 30 dB input dynamic range?
  b. Using the same conditions as Problem 7–17, find the input power value on which the optimum APD gain is based. What is the corresponding optimum gain?

Problem 7–19 Extinction Ratio:
  a. Find the h value in Equation (7.104) with an extinction ratio of 0.2.
  b. Based on the h value computed, find the optimum gain. Use the same conditions as Problem 7–17.
  c. Calculate the power penalty in dB due to the nonzero extinction ratio.

Problem 7–20 Use of Repeaters: Consider an optical communication system that transmits data at a rate of 200 Mb/s and over a distance of 100 km. The BER is required to be 10^{-9}.
  a. At a fiber attenuation of 0.2 dB/km at $\lambda = 1.55$ μm, check whether the system is within the attenuation limit. Assume the power budget is 20 dB at a bit rate of 200 Mb/s.
  b. At a fiber dispersion of 15 ps/km, check whether the system is within the dispersion limit. Assume the light source and photodiode have a turn-on delay of 0.2 nsec.
  c. From *a* and *b*, find the number of repeaters to meet the specifications. What is the minimum required BER for each link?

Problem 7–21 Repeaterless System: Without using any repeaters for the system as specified in Problem 7–20, how can either the fiber dispersion or fiber attenuation be improved? What possible technologies can help this?

Problem 7–22 High-Impedance Front-End Amplifier and Equalizer Design: Design a high-impedance front-end amplifier and equalizer combination to meet the following specifications for analog communications: (1) a minimum CNR of 30 dB and (2) a bandwidth of 100 MHz.

a. Ignore the dark current, RIN, and the front-end transistor noise. Find the minimum photocurrent for a CNR of 30 dB. Assume the modulation index is 0.4.

b. If the total input capacitance is 40 pF, design the high-impedance front-end amplifier and equalizer. In your design, specify the total input resistance, the required photocurrent input to the amplifier, the cutoff frequency of the front-end amplifier, and the equalizer transfer function. Also, choose the input resistance so that the thermal noise is only one-fourth of the shot noise power at the required photocurrent.

c. If the constraint of b whereby the thermal noise is one-fourth of the shot noise power is relaxed, what is the trade-off with the receiver sensitivity?

Problem 7–23 System Design: An optical communication system operates at a bit rate of 1 Gb/s and over a distance of 50 km. The end-to-end bit error rate is required to be less than 10^{-9}. Assume the fiber used is single-mode and has an intramodal dispersion of 10 ps/nm-km and a fiber attenuation of 0.5 dB/km. Neglect all other losses and light source and photodiode rise/fall times. Also, assume the light source used is a laser with linewidth 0.5 nm.

For a system using no repeaters, find:

a. The required bandwidth of the receiver, if the total RMS pulse broadening can be as large as 50 percent of the bit interval.

b. The required input SNR to the receiver, assuming the relationship between the SNR and the bit error rate is

$$\text{BER} = Q(\sqrt{\text{SNR}}).$$

c. The required minimum photocurrent due to signal "1" at the minimum SNR given in b. Consider only shot noise due to the signal current and no other noise.

d. The transmitter optical power if the photodiode (PIN) has a responsivity $\mathcal{R} = 0.5$ A/W.

Problem 7–24 High-Impedance Receiver: You are assigned to design a high-impedance front-end amplifier and equalizer. The equivalent circuit is shown in Figure 7.21. The SNR has the following form:

$$\text{SNR} = \frac{I_{ph}^2}{\{2qI_{ph} + 4kT/R_{in} + S_i + S_v[1/R^2 + (2\pi BC)^2/3]\}\,B}.$$

Assume $I_{ph} = 100$ nA, $B = 100$ MHz, $C = 10$ pF, $T = 300$ K, $S_i = 10^{-26}\text{A}^2/\text{Hz}$, and $S_v = 10^{-21}$ V^2/Hz.

a. Find the minimum R_{in}, total parallel resistance to the front-end amplifier, to have at least an SNR of 30 dB.

b. What is the 3dB frequency f_{3dB} of the front-end amplifier with the resistance R_{in} from a?

Problem 7–25 Transimpedance Amplifier: If the input capacitance C_{in} is 50 pF and the amplifier gain $A = 20$, find the feedback resistance R_F for a bandwidth of 100 MHz. At this R_F, if photocurrent from a PIN diode is 0.1 μA, find the corresponding output voltage.

Problem 7–26 Dynamic Range: Consider an optical receiver that uses a PIN photodiode of a responsivity of 0.8 and a transimpedance front-end amplifier. The receiver sensitivity at a specified performance is 0.1 mW.

a. If the output photocurrent cannot be higher than 10 μA before gain saturation, calculate the input dynamic range of the receiver.

b. If the input dynamic range is required to be at least 30 dB, how could you adjust the feedback resistance R_F to meet the requirement? Assume the front-end output voltage needs to be limited below 5 V. Assume the thermal noise is negligible compared to other input noise.

Problem 7–27 Chirping Effect on Pulse Broadening: Assume a laser diode has a chirping time constant $\delta_c = 0.1$ nsec and frequency shift factor $\beta_{chirp} = 2.0$. At the fiber dispersion $D_{intra}\Delta\lambda$ of 8 psec/km, compute the equivalent pulse-broadening factor δ according to Equations (7.147) and (7.148) at $L = 10$, 50, and 100 km. What are the corresponding transmission bit rate limits due to dispersion?

REFERENCES

1. T. E. Darcie, "Subcarrier Multiplexing for Lightwave Networks and Video Distribution Systems," *IEEE Journal on Selected Areas in Communications*, vol. 8, no. 7 (September 1990), pp. 1240–48.

2. S. D. Personick, "Receiver Design for Digital Fiber Optic Communication Systems," parts 1 and 2, *Bell System Technical Journal*, vol. 52 (July–August 1973), pp. 843–86.

3. J. J. O'Reilly et al., "Optical Fiber Direct Detection Receivers Optimally Tolerant to Jitter," *IEEE Transactions on Communications*, vol. 34 (November 1986), pp. 1141–47.

4. C. W. Helstrom, "Computing the Performance of Optical Receivers with Avalanche Diode Detectors," *IEEE Transactions on Communications*, vol. 36 (January 1988), pp. 61–66.

5. T. V. Muoi, "Receiver Design for High-Speed Optical Fiber Systems," *Journal of Lightwave Technology*, vol. 2, no. 3 (June 1984), pp. 243–67.

6. *Fiberoptic Product News, 1990–1991 Buying Guide*, Elsevier, 1990.

7. J. G. Proakis, *Digital Communications*, 2nd ed., McGraw-Hill, 1989.

8. E. A. Lee and D. G. Messerschmitt, *Digital Communication*, 2nd ed., Kluwer Academic Publishers Press, 1994.

9. A. Mitchell et al., "Progress on Repeaterless Submarine Systems," *Proceedings of the IEEE International Conference on Communications (ICC)*, 1991, pp 1210–16.

10. B. Owen, "PIN-GaAs FET Optical Receiver with a Wide Dynamic Range," *Electronics Letters*, vol. 18 (July 1982), pp. 626–27.

11. G. Kaiser, "Optical Receiver Operation," chapter 7 of *Optical Fiber Communications*, 2nd ed., McGraw-Hill, 1991.

12. K. Ogawa et al., "A Long Wavelength Optical Receiver Using Short Channel Si MOSFET," *Bell System Technical Journal,* vol. 62 (May–June 1983), pp. 1181–88.

Because of the fast growing needs of networking services and rapid development of supporting technologies, lightwave technology research and development have expanded from point-to-point transmission to high-speed networking over the last decade. This expansion is critical to many broadband services, such as interactive video, medical imaging, and distributed computing that need not only high-speed transmission but also networking support such as medium access and switching.

In optical networking, there are different system considerations and design trade-offs because of different high-speed and optical implementation characteristics. To teach various issues and technology development, Part 3 discusses important medium access and switching solutions from both system and device perspectives: Chapters 8–10 discuss medium access principles and introduce various practical systems, and Chapter 11 describes important architectures and devices for high-speed photonic switching.

In Chapter 8, various time-domain medium access (TDoMA) schemes are discussed. These include (1) deterministic access schemes such as time-division multiplexing (TDM) and time-division multiple access (TDMA) and (2) statistical access schemes such as token passing. Because the supporting technology is most mature in this time-domain approach, many of these schemes have been standardized and even developed into commercial products. Synchronous optic network (SONET), Fiber distributed data interface (FDDI), and Asynchronous transfer mode (ATM) are a few examples that will be discussed in detail.

Different from time-domain access, multiple optical signals can also share the same medium in the frequency or wavelength domain. Chapter 9 discusses various system configurations and devices to support wavelength-domain medium access (WDoMA). In particular, Chapter 9 explains the concept of dynamic versus fixed tuning; describes various logical configurations including hypercube, deBruijn, and perfect shuffle networks; shows how wavelength channels can be reused; and discusses various WDoMA devices including tunable laser arrays, wavelength multiplexers, and demultiplexers.

Among many trade-offs between time-domain and frequency-domain medium access, a basic one is capacity versus complexity. In the time domain, implementation can be relatively simple, but the total capacity is limited. In the frequency domain, on the other hand, parallel transmission can be used to achieve a better fiber bandwidth utilization. Chapter 10 describes a low-cost alternative and compromise between these two medium-access schemes: subcarrier multiplexing (SCM), which first multiplexes radio frequency (RF) channels in the frequency domain and then uses a single optical carrier for transmission. SCM thus achieves the advantages of parallel transmission and simple implementation (no need of WDoMA devices) at the same time. Because of laser nonlinearity, however, there is intermodulation among the RF channels that limits the total transmission capacity. Chapter 10 will explain in detail SCM's basic principle, nonlinear distortion, and community antenna television (CATV) applications.

In addition to medium access, photonic switching must be provided in all-optical networking. Chapter 11 introduces various photonic switching technologies from both system and device perspectives. Specifically, it describes many important switching fabric interconnection architectures including cross-bar, N-stage planar, three-stage Clos, Benes, Banyan, Batcher, and cross-over networks. These different interconnection architectures have different characteristics, such as the total number of crosspoints, implementation complexity, switch size, and blocking probability. Chapter 11 also describes various photonic switch designs, including spatial switches using directional couplers and bistable devices, frequency domain switches using star couplers and filters, and time-domain switches using delay loops.

8

TIME-DOMAIN MEDIUM ACCESS

Chapter 2 discussed various medium access methods according to the form of the shared resource. When the form of the shared resource is in time, frequency, or code, we have time-domain, frequency-domain, and code-domain access, respectively. This chapter explains the basic principles of time-domain medium access (TDoMA) and shows some important standard systems.

To access the shared medium in the time domain, a transmission node needs to know (1) *when* and (2) *how long* it can send its data. As illustrated in Figure 2.5, one simple approach is to divide time into **frames** and partition each frame into a certain number of **time slots**. In this way, communication nodes can share the same medium by sending data in different slots. Once a slot is allocated during the call setup, a node can repeat the transmission in the same slot of each frame throughout the call duration. As mentioned in Chapter 2, this is called *deterministic* access and there is no traffic contention after the call setup.

As shown in Figure 2.5, data transmission in two adjacent slots can be continuous in bit timing or separated by guard time. To transmit data in different slots continuously, bit timings from different sources first need to be synchronized. This medium access scheme is called **time division multiplexing** (TDM). When a network is used for multiple access, it is impossible to synchronize the timings of all nodes distributed over the network. As a result, guard time that separates consecutive slot transmissions is necessary, and the medium access scheme is called **time division multiple access** (TDMA).

Because TDM requires bit timing synchronization, its implementation is more involved. To synchronize input bit rates, electronic implementation has to be used and direct optical domain multiplexing is not practically feasible. A TDM standard called Synchronous Optic Network (SONET) [1] has been designed for optical transmission. To avoid the electronic bottleneck in high-speed multiplexing, SONET introduces an innovative floating payload concept that can synchronize input signals at low speeds.

Because of no need for bit timing synchronization, TDMA can be done directly in the optical domain. An optical transmitter in this case gets access to the medium by transmitting an optical burst consisting of binary bits over a time slot. When all-optical networking is concerned, TDMA is an attractive choice compared to TDM. However, TDMA has a worse access efficiency than TDM because of the guard time.

In addition to TDMA and TDM, time-domain medium access can be done by token passing and random access. As discussed in Chapter 2, token passing and random access belong to the category of *statistical multiplexing*. In token passing, a transmission node can send data only when it holds the token. When it finishes transmission, it passes the token to the next node. An important token-passing fiber-based local area network called the Fiber Distributed Data Interface (FDDI) will be described. To support TDM traffic that requires deterministic access, a hybrid version called FDDI-II has also been defined. In random access, an optical transmission version of carrier-sense multiple access with collision detection (CSMA/CD) has been proposed [2]. However, because of the poor access efficiency from collisions, use of this approach is limited.

FDDI is primarily designed for local area networking. To provide long-haul broadband networking for video, voice, and data, the concept of **Broadband Integrated Services Digital Network** (B-ISDN) has been proposed. It is based on high-speed SONET transmission and a fixed-size packet switching technique called **asynchronous transfer mode** (ATM). To extend the optical fiber–based B-ISDN to end subscribers, various loop plans such as **fiber-in-the-loop** (FITL) and **fiber-to-the-home** (FTTH) have also been proposed.

8.1 TIME DIVISION MULTIPLE ACCESS

As illustrated in Figure 8.1, a TDMA frame consists of a **reference burst** and a certain number of time slots. The reference burst is used for frame synchronization and signaling, and the time slots are used to carry data.

The reference burst consists of three parts: a preamble, a start code, and control data. The preamble is a periodic bit sequence for bit timing synchronization. Depending on how rapid a synchronization can be achieved (see Chapter 16 on the quality factor), the pream-

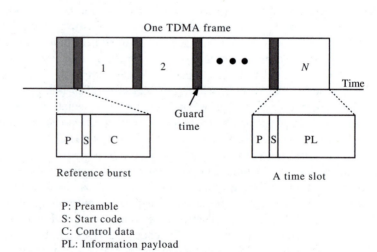

P: Preamble
S: Start code
C: Control data
PL: Information payload

Figure 8.1   A TDMA frame consisting of N slots.

ble length can range from 10 to several hundred symbols. Once the bit timing is established, the content in the rest of the reference burst can be read. Following the preamble is a unique start code indicating the end of the preamble and the start of the information portion of the reference burst. By recognizing the word, control data can be interpreted correctly. In general, control data carries information such as station timing, call setup status, and signaling information.

The reference burst in a TDMA frame is the overhead and occupies only a small portion of the frame. The rest of the frame is divided into time slots separated by guard time. Similar to the reference burst, each time slot consists of a preamble, a unique start code, and the information payload. Because of different propagation delays between stations, the guard time between time slots is necessary to avoid overlap between two consecutive time slots. This is illustrated in the following two examples.

SHARED MEDIUM   Consider a TDMA network made of a shared medium where a node can immediately receive what it just transmits. A single Ethernet coaxial cable and an ALOHA radio network (discussed in Chapter 2) are examples of such a shared medium.

Example 8.1

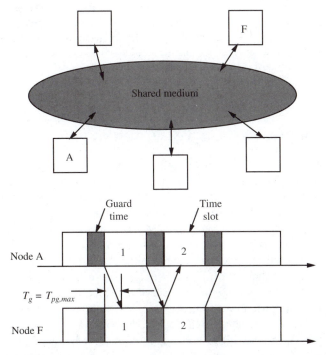

Figure 8.2   Required guard time of a shared TDMA network.

As illustrated in Figure 8.2, assume two nodes, A and F, attached to the network are the two farthest separated nodes with a propagation delay $T_{pg,max}$. In this case, if node A transmits its data at the beginning of a certain time slot and finishes the transmission at the end of the time slot, node F will receive the data $T_{pg,max}$ time later. When node F has data to send in the following slot, the size of the guard time, T_g, should be at least $T_{pg,max}$ to avoid transmission conflict.

In the above consideration, all the nodes are assumed to have the same frame timing. In practice, this is not easy to achieve. For example, if the frame timing is distributed from node A, a different node, say B, will get is frame timing by a backward shift of $T_{pg,AB}$ from the received timing from node A, where $T_{pg,AB}$ is the propagation delay between node A and node B. When the shift used is not equal to the actual propagation delay, the frame timings of nodes A and B are different. This timing difference is called the **timing skew**. To account for it, the guard time needs to be increased by the peak deviation of the timing skew. ■

Example 8.2	**CENTRALIZED STAR** Consider a different TDMA network where all the nodes are connected to a centralized star. A satellite network, for example, is a centralized star where the satellite is the star and many earth stations distributed over a large geographical area are connected through the satellite. To minimize the guard time size, the frame timings shown in Figure 8.3 can be used for each node. As shown, earth station i has different transmission and receiving timings, which are $T_{pg,i}$ earlier and later with respect to the timing at the satellite, and $T_{pg,i}$ is the propagation delay between the ith earth station and the satellite. Given this arrangement, all transmitted data from different earth stations have the same frame timing when they arrive at the satellite. As a result, there is no transmission overlap and the guard time can be reduced to zero. As mentioned earlier, this requires zero timing skew. When there is an error in estimating the delay from tracking the location of a satellite, the timing skew is nonzero, and a nonzero guard time equal to the peak timing skew needs to be included. ■

8.1.1   MEDIUM ACCESS AND TIME COMPRESSION

When nodes attached to a TDMA network have data to transmit, they need to wait for available time slots. In TDMA, a slot is obtained through a call setup process. Once a node is granted with an available slot, it can use the same slot in every frame throughout the call. As mentioned ealier, this medium access is called deterministic.

Because of the deterministic access, TDMA is primarily used for constant bit-rate transmission. To support such transmission, input bits of a constant bit-rate signal are first stored in a transmitter buffer. When the assigned time slot arrives, all the bits stored will be transmitted at a much higher speed. This process is illustrated in Figure 8.4. Clearly, data bits are compressed in time during the high-speed transmission. For this reason, TDMA is also called **time compression multiplexing**.

From the compression mechanism described, the payload size of a time slot can be determined for a constant bit-rate input. For an input signal of a bit rate B_s b/s, the total number of input bits during a time frame is $T_f B_s$, where T_f is the TDMA frame size. To transmit these bits over the payload of a time slot, the payload size $T_{s,pload}$ should be at least

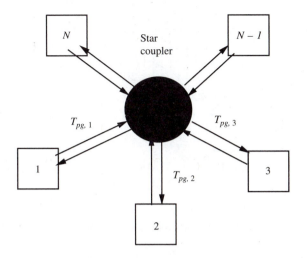

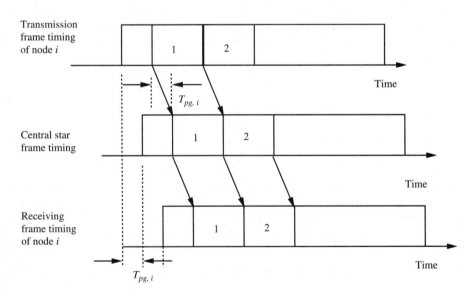

Figure 8.3   Required guard time of a centralized TDMA network.

$$T_{s,pload} = T_f \frac{B_s}{R} \qquad \text{[8.1]}$$

where R is the instantaneous transmission rate.

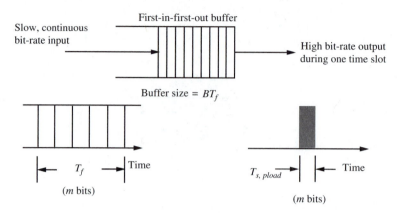

Figure 8.4   Concept of time compression multiplexing in TDMA.

| Example 8.3 | **DIGITAL TELEPHONY VIA TDMA**   Consider a TDMA system with frame size $T_f = 2$ msec and an instantaneous bit rate of 100 Mb/s. If a TDMA slot is used to carry one 64 kb/s digital PCM voice, the payload of the time slot size should be |

$$T_{s,pload} = 2 \times 10^{-3} \times \frac{64 \times 10^3}{10^8} = 1.28 \ \mu\text{sec}.$$

This is a small interval compared to the frame size. ∎

When input bits are stored in the time compression buffer, a compression delay is introduced. Because the bits transmitted in one slot are input bits received during the previous time frame, the compression delay is simply equal to the frame size. Therefore, to reduce compression delay (which can be critical to real time traffic), the frame size should be as small as possible. As will be shown shortly, however, a smaller frame size has a lower access efficiency. Therefore, there is a trade-off between compression delay and access efficiency.

8.1.2 SLOT SIZE, COMPRESSION DELAY, AND ACCESS EFFICIENCY

In addition to its payload, a time slot has an overhead for synchronization and signaling. Therefore, the time slot size, T_s, is

$$T_s = T_{s,oh} + T_{s,pload} \tag{8.2}$$

where $T_{s,oh}$ is the overhead size for preamble, signaling, and control.

From Equations (8.2) and (8.1), the time slot size is

$$T_s = T_{s,oh} + T_f \frac{B_s}{R}. \qquad \textbf{[8.3]}$$

At a given reference burst size T_{ref} and guard time T_g, the total number of time slots that can be accommodated within a frame is

$$N = \left\lfloor \frac{T_f - T_{ref}}{T_s + T_g} \right\rfloor = \left\lfloor \frac{R}{B_s} \frac{1 - T_{ref}/T_f}{1 + (R/B_s)(T_{s,oh} + T_g)/T_f} \right\rfloor. \qquad \textbf{[8.4]}$$

From Equation (8.4), note that N has an upper bound of $\lfloor (R/B_s) \rfloor$ and can be improved by increasing T_f. At a given T_g, T_{ref}, $T_{s,oh}$, and R/B_S, the upper bound can be approached when $T_f \gg T_{ref}$ and $T_f \gg (R/B_s)(T_{s,oh} + T_g)$.

At a given N, the access efficiency is defined as the ratio of the total data transmission time to the frame size. From Equation (8.4),

$$\eta_{TDMA} = \frac{N T_{s,pload}}{T_f} = \frac{N B_s}{R} = \frac{B_s}{R} \left\lfloor \frac{R}{B_s} \frac{1 - T_{ref}/T_f}{1 + (R/B_s)(T_{s,oh} + T_g)/T_f} \right\rfloor \qquad \textbf{[8.5]}$$

When T_f is large enough, the upper limit of the access efficiency is $(B_s/R)\lfloor R/B_s \rfloor$.

TDMA INTELSAT In INTELSAT [3], a time frame is 2 msec. The simultaneous transmission rate is 120.832 Mb/s. To carry one 2.048 Mb/sec CEPT1 channel (see the discussion of time division multiplexing in section 8.3), the payload size of each time slot is

| **Example** |
| **8.4** |

$$T_{s,pload} = \frac{2.048}{120.832} T_f = 33.9 \ \mu\text{sec}.$$

If the reference burst size is 10 μsec and the guard time plus slot overhead is 20 μsec, a TDMA frame can carry up to

$$N = \left\lfloor \frac{2000 - 10}{33.9 + 20} \right\rfloor = 36$$

slots, and the access efficiency is

$$\eta_{TDMA} = \frac{36 \times 33.9}{2000} = 61.02\%.$$

If the frame size is increased enough that $T_g + T_{s,oh}$ can be ignored, the upper limit of N is 58, and the upper limit of the access efficiency is

$$\eta_{TDMA} = \frac{58 \times 33.9}{2000} = 98.31\%.$$

This example shows that the larger the time frame size, the higher the access efficiency. ∎

Example 8.4 and the previous discussion on compression delay demonstrate that there is a trade-off between access efficiency and compression delay. Equation (8.4) shows that the efficiency is primarily determined by the factor $(R/B_s)(T_{s,oh} + T_g)/T_f$. Consequently, when $R \gg B_s$, the trade-off is more difficult to achieve. In this case, a larger T_f is needed to get the same factor $(R/B_s)(T_{s,oh} + T_g)/T_f$ at a given $T_{s,oh} + T_g$.

Example 8.5	**OPTICAL DOMAIN TDMA** Consider an optical TDMA system where optical signals are coupled into a shared optical fiber. If the instantaneous transmission rate is 5 Gb/s and each slot is used to carry a CEPT1 signal at the rate of 2.048 Mb/s, the ratio R/B_s is

$$\frac{R}{B_s} = 2441.4.$$

To achieve an access efficiency of 90 percent (neglecting the reference burst),

$$(R/B_s)(T_{s,oh} + T_g)/T_f = 0.11.$$

This implies $T_f = 2.2 \times 10^4 \times (T_{s,oh} + T_g)$. If $T_{s,oh} + T_g = 10\,\mu\text{sec}$, T_f must equal 220 msec, which can be too long for real-time traffic such as voice. On the other hand, if T_f is limited within 2 msec, the access efficiency is

$$\eta_{TDMA} = \frac{1}{1 + 12.205} = 7.6\%$$

which is very low. Thus it is important to reduce $T_g + T_{s,oh}$ and increase B_s in optical domain TDMA. ■

8.2 OPTICAL DOMAIN TDMA

In spite of the difficult trade-off mentioned above, optical domain TDMA is still attractive because of no need to synchronize bit timings among transmission nodes [4]. As a result, as long as the receiver knows the transmission bit rate (within the acquisition range), each transmission node can have its independent bit clock. Because the bit rate is usually high in optical domain TDMA, this clock independence that avoids the need of bit clock synchronization among transmission nodes is an important characteristic.

As illustrated in Examples 8.1 and 8.2, the star topology is preferred to minimize the effect of guard time. A block diagram of such an optical domain TDMA network is shown in Figure 8.5. To synchronize the access, a master frame timing needs to be distributed to all nodes. To achieve this, one of the nodes in the network is called the master node, which generates a reference burst every T_f. From detecting the reference burst, the frame timing can be established at every other node. If the given number of slots per frame is known, the slot timing can also be obtained.

To receive data over a certain time slot, a gating signal that is high during the slot interval is generated from the derived slot timing. As illustrated in Figure 8.5, data in this slot

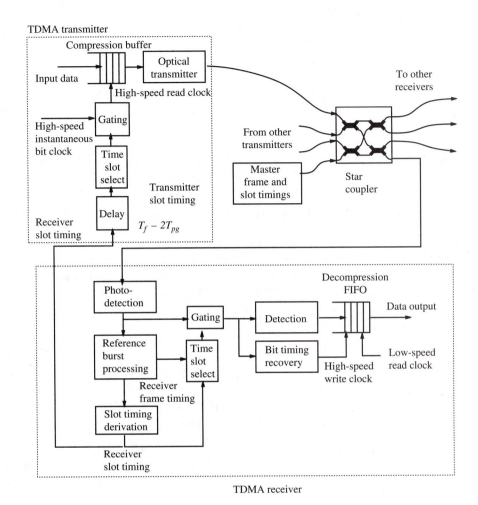

Figure 8.5   An optical domain TDMA implementation.

interval can pass through the gate, be detected, and then be stored in the decompression buffer. The received slot timing derived is also sent to the local transmitter to determine its slot timing for transmission. Because there is a finite propagation delay between the node and the star coupler, as shown in Figure 8.5, a certain delay is introduced at the local transmitter to get the transmitter slot timing.

The necessary delay between the transmission slot timing and receiver slot timing can be determined as follows. With respect to the framing timing at the master node, the receiver slot timing has a delay of $T_{M,pg} + T_{A,pg}$, where $T_{M,pg}$ is the propagation delay between the master node and the star coupler, and $T_{A,pg}$ is the propagation delay between the user node and the star coupler. Therefore, from Example 8.2, to have the same frame timing at the star coupler, the additional delay D_A is added so that

$$[T_{M,pg} + T_{A,pg} + D_A] + T_{A,pg} = T_{M,pg} \bmod T_f \qquad \textbf{[8.6]}$$

where $[T_{M,pg} + T_{A,pg} + D_A]$ is the relative delay of the transmitter frame timing at the user node with respect to the master frame timing. From Equation (8.6),

$$D_A = mT_f - 2T_{A,pg} \qquad \textbf{[8.7]}$$

where m is the smallest integer such that $mT_f - 2T_{A,pg} > 0$. Equation (8.7) shows that a large delay line is needed when T_f is large to have a high access efficiency.

Coupling Loss and Optical Amplification   When the number of nodes is large, the coupling loss and distribution loss from the star coupler can be significant. To compensate for the loss, erbium-doped fiber amplifiers (EDFA) can be used [5]. In this case, the star coupler must first be partitioned into an $N{:}1$ coupler and a $1{:}N$ splitter. From this arrangement, as shown in Figure 8.6, a single EDFA (see Chapter 17) can be inserted in between. For stable operations, isolators are used before and after the EDFA.

To determine the necessary power gain, the total power loss must be calculated for the arrangement shown in Figure 8.6. In general, there are three types of power loss. First, there can be a coupling loss at each coupling point (e.g., between the coupler and isolator). Second, when N signals are coupled by an $N{:}1$ coupler, there is a minimal $1/N$ power attenuation.[1] For the same reason, there is another power attenuation of $1/N$ through the $1{:}N$ splitter. When the coupler and splitter are not perfect, there is additional power loss inside them. This is the third type of power loss. In general, a $1{:}N$ splitter or $N{:}1$ coupler has $\log_2 N$ stages. If the additional power loss at each stage is α_{c2} dB, the total additional power loss is $\alpha_{c2} \log_2 N$ dB. Thus the total power loss is

$$\alpha_{tot,c} = M\alpha_{c1} + 2\log_2 N\alpha_{c2} + 10\log_{10} N^2 = M\alpha_{c1} + (2\alpha_{c2} + 6)\log_2 N \text{ dB} \qquad \textbf{[8.8]}$$

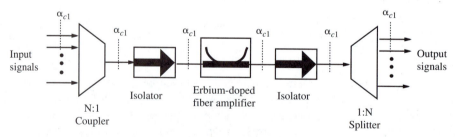

Figure 8.6   Use of an EDFA in optical domain TDMA.

---

[1] To understand this, assume each input has the same power, frequency, and phase. If the output wave is α times the summation of the incident waves, the output power is $\alpha^2 \times N^2 P_{in}$. Because of the conservation of energy, the output power cannot be greater than NP_{in}, the total input power. Therefore, α^2 cannot be greater than $1/N$.

where M is the number of couplings, α_{c1} is the coupling loss in dB, and α_{c2} is the internal coupling loss in dB of the splitter and coupler.

REQUIRED GAIN IN OPTICAL TDMA   For the arrangement shown in Figure 8.6, there are six couplings between an input fiber and output fiber. If $N = 16$, $\alpha_{c1} = 0.2$ dB, and $\alpha_{c2} = 0.1$ dB,

Example 8.6

$$\alpha_{tot,c} = (0.2 \times 6 + 6.1 \times 4) = 25.6 \text{ dB}.$$

If the overall power budget is PB in dB and the total fiber attenuation from transmission is α_f in dB, the EDFA gain should be at least

$$G + \text{PB} > \alpha_f + \alpha_{tot,c}.$$

For example, if α_f is 15 dB and PB is 20 dB, the required power gain from the EDFA should be at least 20.6 dB. ∎

Optical Domain Demultiplexing   In Figure 8.5, the optical TDMA signal is first photodetected and then detected during a given slot interval. Data in all other time slots are suppressed by the gating operation. To preserve the received signal waveform, the bandwidth of the gating device needs to be much larger than the instantaneous bit rate. As a result, the bandwidth of the gate can limit the total TDMA throughput.

To solve this problem, the gating function can be done in the optical domain. This is illustrated in Figure 8.7, where an electro-optical gate is used for a larger transmission bandwidth. In this approach, a programmable optical delay line is needed. As illustrated, the node shown uses the kth slot to transmit its data and receives data from the mth slot. As opposed to the electronic gating implementation shown in Figure 8.5, this approach requires a separate slot timing distribution from the master slot timing to every node.

8.3 TIME DIVISION MULTIPLEXING

TDM was first used in digital telephony, where multiple lower rate digital streams called **tributary signals** are interleaved in the time domain to form a higher rate digital signal. Similar to TDMA, TDM is a time-domain medium access scheme and each of its frames consists of a certain number of time slots. However, different from TDMA, data carried by different time slots are first synchronized in bit timing, and then interleaved by a higher bit clock. As will be discussed in detail shortly, the process of bit timing synchronization is called **frequency justification**, which is necessary when upstream signals have different bit clock frequencies.

Because all tributary signals are synchronized in bit timing, no guard time is required between adjacent time slots as in TDMA, and there is no need to include a preamble at the beginning of each time slot. When bit synchronization can be achieved, TDM is consequently a better choice than TDMA.

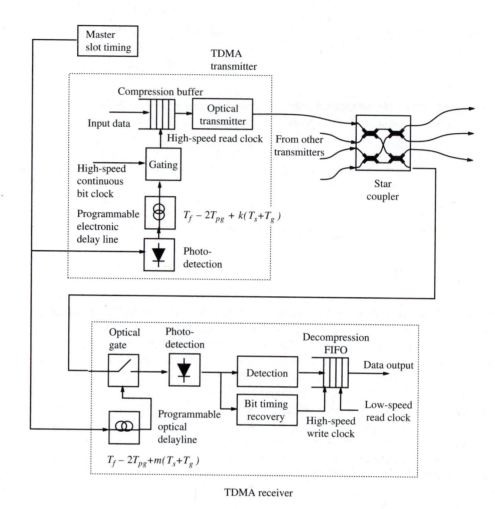

Figure 8.7 Optical domain gating in optical TDMA demultiplexing.

8.3.1 FRAME STRUCTURE

A TDM frame structure is illustrated in Figure 8.8. It consists of time slots to carry information bits of tributary signals. Because there is no need to include guard time and a preamble for each time slot, the time slot size in TDM is much smaller than that in TDMA for small compression delay. A typical slot size in TDM is only one byte.

In addition to time slots, a TDM frame consists of **overhead** bits for synchronization, signaling, and transmission maintenance. Synchronization bits are necessary to recognize frame boundaries and perform frequency justification; signaling is used to set up and maintain each circuit connection; and maintenance bits such as error check sequence are used to monitor the bit error rate of transmission.

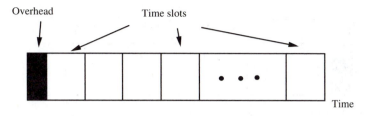

(a) One-dimensional frame structure

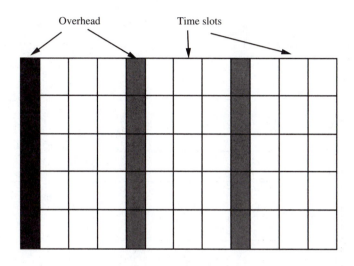

(b) Two-dimensional frame structure

Figure 8.8   TDM frame formats: (a) one-dimensional and (b) two-dimensional. In the second case, data are transmitted from left to right, and from top to bottom.

One of the most important TDM signals in North America is the T1 or DS1 signal (digital signal 1) shown in Figure 8.9. This is also referred to as CCITT recommendation G.733. Each frame of the T1 signal has a duration of 125 μsec and consists of 24 time slots (each slot is one byte). With this frame structure, each time slot can carry one standard pulse code modulation voice, which has one byte sampled voice every 125 μsec. In addition to the 24 slots, every T1 frame has a framing bit at the beginning. Therefore, the total number of bits per frame is 193 bits, and the total bit rate is 1.544 Mb/s.

As Figure 8.9 shows, T1 has no dedicated bits for signaling such things as call status. To carry signaling information, T1 frames are further grouped into **superframes**. As shown in Figure 8.10, one superframe consists of 12 frames. The 12 framing bits together form two framing patterns for the T1 demultiplexer to recognize the frame and superframe boundaries, respectively. With the superframe structure, certain (not all) least significant

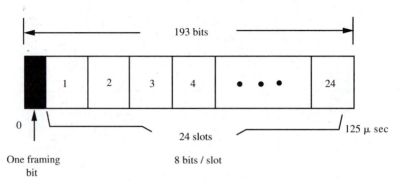

Figure 8.9   Frame format of T1.

A superframe

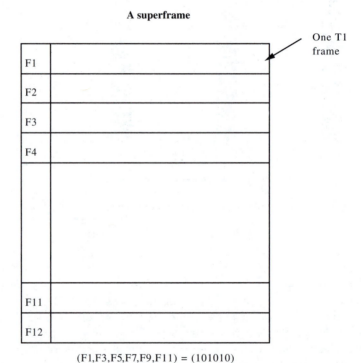

$(F1,F3,F5,F7,F9,F11) = (101010)$

$(F2,F4,F6,F8,F10,F12) = (001110)$

Figure 8.10   A superframe in T1, where (F1,F3,F5,F7,F9,F11) forms a pattern for T1 frame synchronization, and (F2,F4,F6,F8,F10,F12) forms another pattern for the superframe boundary recognition.

bits of regular time slots per superframe are used to carry signaling information. Such bits are called **robbered bits**.[2]

The counterpart of T1 in Europe is the CEPT1 or E1 (CCITT G.732) 30-channel system. As shown in Figure 8.11, the frame size is also 125 μsec, but each frame consists of 32 slots, with 2 slots (slot 0 and slot 16) used for framing and signaling and the remaining 30 slots used to carry 30 64-kb/s channels. From the design, the bit rate of CEPT1 is 2.048 Mb/s.

Compared to T1, CEPT1 is better engineered for several reasons. First, it uses one byte per frame for framing. Therefore, frame synchronization is faster and more accurate. Second, it uses a dedicated byte for signaling. In other words, there are no data bits robbed for signaling. Finally, the bit clock of CCITT G.732 is in a simple integer relationship (32 times) with 8 kHz. In T1, on the other hand, its clock is 193×8 kHz. This results in a more difficult DS0 timing recovery in T1 demultiplexing.

Why were the above factors not considered when T1 was designed? There were two simple reasons. First, it was designed earlier than CEPT1. Therefore, CEPT1 is an improved version of T1. Second, at the time T1 was designed, transmission cost was high. Therefore, the design philosophy was to minimize the overhead size. This led to the optimum design of only one overhead bit per frame. From the transmission cost point of view, this was indeed a smart design.

TDM Hierarchy TDM systems can form a hierarchy. That is, higher rate signals are multiplexed into an even higher bit-rate signal. As shown in Figure 8.12, four T1 (DS1) signals are multiplexed into a T2 (DS2) signal, and seven T2 (DS2) signals are multiplexed into a T3 (DS3) signal. Therefore, each T3 signal can carry $24 \times 4 \times 7 = 672$ PCM voices. On the other hand, the European CEPT standard has a uniform multiplexing of four tributary signals into a higher bit-rate signal.

The frame structure of the DS2 signal is shown in Figure 8.13. It is in a two-dimensional frame structure. More important, it has some new overhead bits, including control bits and stuffing bits. These additional bits are used for frequency justification, explained below.

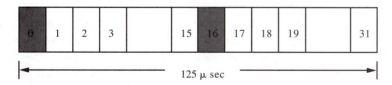

Figure 8.11   Frame format of CEPT1.

[2] Because it is the least significant bit in a PCM byte used for signaling, it will not distort the PCM voice signal significantly. On the other hand, if a T1 slot is used to carry data instead of PCM voice, only the first seven bits are guaranteed to be valid. As a result, the data channel rate per slot is only 56 kb/s instead of 64 kb/s.

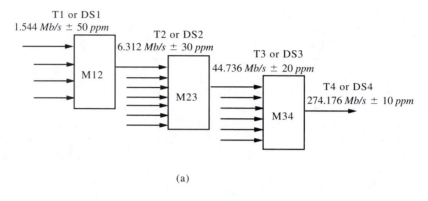

(a)

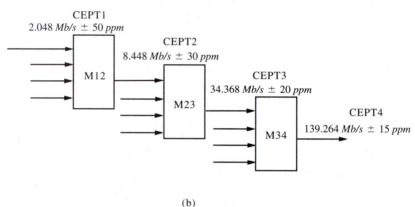

(b)

Figure 8.12   TDM hierarchy: (*a*) North American T-carriers and (*b*) European CEPT carriers.

8.3.2 FREQUENCY JUSTIFICATION

Lower bit-rate signals need to have the same bit clock when they are interleaved into a higher bit-rate signal. If the frequencies of the lower rate input signals are exactly the same, the TDM system is called **synchronous TDM**. Otherwise, it is called **asynchronous TDM**. For asynchronous TDM, lower rate signals of different frequencies cannot be multiplexed directly. They need an intermediate step called *frequency justification*, which aligns all input tributary signals to a common local clock. Below are described two primary techniques for this: **slip control** and **bit stuffing**.

Slip Control   Slip control is the easiest way of doing frequency justification. As illustrated in Figure 8.14, a random access memory (RAM) that allows simultaneous read and write is used. The RAM has a size of one frame of the tributary signal. When the tributary

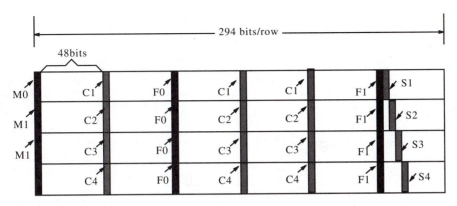

Figure 8.13 Frame format of DS1 or T2, where M0 and M1 are multiframing bits, F0 and F1 are framing bits, C1, C2, C3, and C4 are control bits indicating whether stuffing bits S1, S2, S3, and S4 carry data, respectively.

input bit rate is slower than the local (read) clock, the local frame timing will eventually catch up to the input frame timing. As a result, the previous frame will be retransmitted once. Similarly, if the input bit rate is faster than the local clock, the input frame timing can catch up to the local timing at a certain time point, and one frame of data that has just been written to the RAM will be replaced by the incoming data. As a result, the previous frame will be completely erased or dropped.

From the description, *one entire frame* is either dropped or retransmitted when a slip control is performed. This is necessary to maintain frame synchronization. Because one frame of data lost or added can be significant, slip control is only used in DS0 to DS1 multiplexing, where one DS0 frame is simply one voice byte and its loss or insertion is not critical.

ALLOWABLE SLIP RATE   In digital telephony, the end-to-end slip rate cannot be higher than one per five hours [6]. Because slips can occur at multiple points in the digital telephone network, the actual requirement for the slip rate is stronger. For a slip rate of one per 20 hours, for example, the clock frequency should be within

$$\Delta f \times 20 \times 3600 \leq 8 \text{ bits.}$$

This implies that $\Delta f < 1.1 \times 10^{-4}$ Hz. With respect to 64 kHz, this means a very high accuracy of 1.74×10^{-9}. ∎

Example 8.7

Bit Stuffing   To avoid a large frame drop or insertion, an alternative and more important method of frequency justification is called bit stuffing. In this approach, each frame of the multiplexed signal has certain overhead bits called stuffing bits to carry either tributary

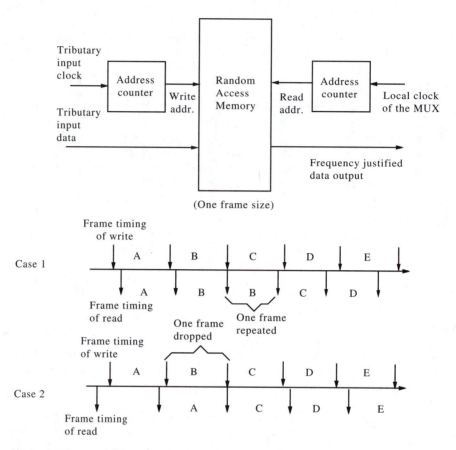

Figure 8.14   Slip control in frequency justification, where the address counters count cyclically from 0 to (frame size −1), and the memory allows simultaneous read and write. In case 1, the write clock is slower than the read clock, and in case 2, the write clock is faster than the read clock.

data or nothing (stuffing). A block diagram of bit stuffing in a multiplexer is illustrated in Figure 8.15. To understand the principle of bit stuffing, consider a practical example where four T1 signals are multiplexed into a T2 signal.

Because T1 signals from different sources can have different clock frequencies, the T1 rate of 1.544 Mb/s is only a nominal rate. According to the specification, it can have a ±50 ppm variation. As a result, it is necessary to perform frequency justification before T1 signals are multiplexed into a T2 signal. Because a T1 frame has 192 information bits, it will not be good to use the simple slip control for frequency justification.

As shown in Figure 8.13, a DS2 frame has four stuffing bits, each of which is used for one of the four T1 inputs. Each DS2 frame consists of four rows with 294 bits each, including 6 framing/control bits, 287 data bits, and 1 stuffing bit. If the local clock of the T2 multiplexer is f_2, the frequency range of input T1 signals that can be justified is

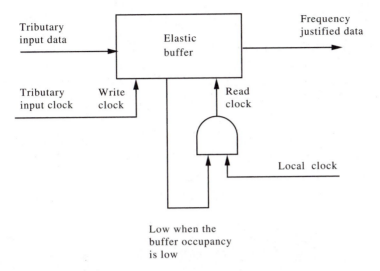

Tributary input data

Elastic buffer

Frequency justified data

Tributary input clock

Write clock

Read clock

Local clock

Low when the buffer occupancy is low

Figure 8.15 Bit stuffing in frequency justification. When the occupancy is too low, there will be no read for one bit cycle. The corresponding data output during the read clock bit interval is a stuff bit.

$$\frac{f_2}{4}\frac{287}{294} \le f_1 \le \frac{f_2}{4}\frac{288}{294} \qquad \textbf{[8.9]}$$

where the lower limit in Equation (8.9) is when the stuffing bit is never used to carry T1 data, and the upper limit is when the stuffing bit is always used to carry T1 data. When the stuffing bit is never used to carry data, there are 287 information bits out of 294 bits from each row. On the other hand, when the stuffing bit is always used to carry T1 data, there are 288 information bits out of 294 bits.

Because the nominal bit rate of T2 signals is set to $f_2 = 6.312$ Mb/s,

$$1.54043 \le f_1 \le 1.54580. \qquad \textbf{[8.10]}$$

In other words, bit stuffing used in T1 to T2 multiplexing can accommodate a T1 clock frequency range from 1.54043 to 1.54580 Mb/s. With respect to the nominal T1 clock of 1.5440 Mb/s, this means a tolerable variation range of [−3.57, 1.8] kHz, which is large enough for the specified ± 50 ppm variation or ± 77.2 Hz.

For a tributary signal within the justifiable frequency range, the proportion that the stuffing bits are used to carry data is called the **negative stuffing ratio**. The word "negative" means a stuffing bit is "not" used as stuffing. Therefore, the **positive stuffing ratio** means the proportion that the stuffing bits are not used to carry data. In the case of T1 to T2 multiplexing, the negative stuffing ratio at the nominal rates is

$$\frac{287 + r}{288} = \frac{1.54400}{1.54580} \qquad \textbf{[8.11]}$$

or $r = 0.665$. This means 66.5 percent of stuffing bits are used to carry data in a nominal T2 signal.

The stuffing ratio is important to the timing jitter of the recovered bit clock at the demultiplexer, where the stuffing bits are removed [7]. Therefore, the stuffing ratio in practical design can be first selected for minimal timing jitter. With this determined, the nominal rate of the multiplexed signal can be determined.

<table>
<tr><td>**Example 8.8**</td><td>**STUFFING RATIO** For a negative stuffing ratio $r = 0.5$, the nominal T2 clock f_2 should be</td></tr>
</table>

$$1.544 = \frac{f_2}{4}\frac{287 + 0.5}{294}$$

or $f_2 = 6.3156$ Mb/s.

Actually, $r = 0.665$ is found to be a good value for minimal time jitter at the M21 demultiplexer (demultiplexing T2 into T1) [7]. Therefore, the actual T2 rate is 6.312 Mb/s. ∎

Destuffing at the Demultiplexer When a TDM signal based on bit stuffing arrives at the demultiplexer, the stuffing bits need to be removed, and the original tributary bit clock needs to be reconstructed. For illustration, a block diagram of an M21 demultiplexer (T2 to T1 demultiplexing) is shown in Figure 8.16. It consists of an elastic buffer to store demultiplexed DS1 data and a bit timing recovery loop to recover the original DS1 clock.

To know whether a stuffing bit is used to carry data or not, control bits are used. As Figure 8.13 shows, three control bits are used for each stuffing bit.[3] Based on majority voting, when there are two or three control bits equal to one, the stuffing bit is interpreted as an information bit. Otherwise, if there are two or three control bits equal to zero, the stuffing bit is interpreted as a junk bit and will not be written into the demultiplexer elastic buffer.

The elastic buffer in the demultiplexer is a first-in–first-out (FIFO) buffer with input from one of the tributary signals. The write clock is derived from the clock of the multiplexed signal and equal to the maximal possible bit rate of the tributary signal. For example, in the case of T-carrier M21 demultiplexing, the write clock is

$$f_w = \frac{6.312}{4}\frac{288}{294} = 1.54580 \text{ Mb/s}.$$

When the stuffing bit does not carry data, the corresponding bit interval of the write clock is set to zero (or not transition). This avoids a junk bit written to the elastic buffer. Therefore, the write clock is called a **gapped clock**.

[3] Using multiple control bits protects against transmission errors. Because a wrong insertion or drop of an information bit can cause frame timing to be out of synchronization, a reliable interpretation of the stuffing bit is extremely important.

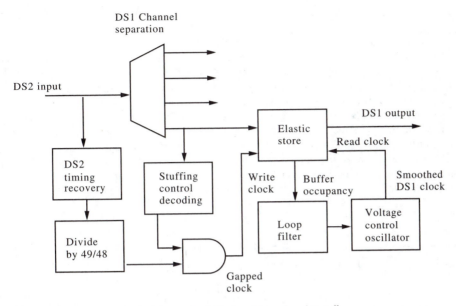

Figure 8.16 Demultiplexing of a DS2 signal based on bit stuffing.

The read clock of the elastic buffer is the recovered bit clock of the demultiplexed tributary signal. Unlike the gapped write clock, it is a smoothed clock at the same bit rate as the original transmitter clock. To recover this clock, the occupancy of the elastic buffer is used to drive the voltage control oscillator (VCO), whose output is the recovered, smooth clock. If the buffer occupancy is high, input to the VCO is high and the frequency of the VCO output is high. In the steady state, the average rate data written into the buffer is the same as the rate data read out of the buffer. As a result, if a "good" loop filter (low-pass) is used, the input to the VCO is a constant and the recovered clock is smooth. The loop formed by the elastic buffer, loop filter, and the VCO is a phase-locked loop (PLL) (see Chapter 16).

Because the write clock has a gap, it can have a sudden occupancy drop during the gap, as illustrated in Figure 8.17. Practical limitations of the loop filter design make it impossible to completely eliminate such a jump, and consequently there is a timing jitter in the recovered clock. This is well known as the **waiting time jitter** [7][8].

TIME JITTER FROM DESTUFFING   Equation (8.11) shows that approximately one third of stuffing bits are used to carry dummy data (i.e., junk). Therefore, in demultiplexing DS2 to DS1, there is a one-bit drop in the buffer occupancy every three stuffing opportunities, as illustrated in Figure 8.17. Because there is only one stuffing opportunity every DS2 frame, the buffer occupancy has a period of three DS2 frames. Since

$$T_{f,DS2} = \frac{4 \times 294}{6.312} = 186.3 \ \mu sec$$ **[8.12]**

Example 8.9

the buffer occupancy has a period around $3 \times 186.3 = 559$ μsec. This corresponds to a frequency of 1.8 kHz.

Figure 8.16 shows that the buffer occupancy signal is input to the loop filter. Because one of the primary functions of the loop filter is to minimize the input variation so that its output is close to a constant and the VCO output is near a certain frequency, the low-pass loop filter needs to have a low cutoff frequency. For example, if the loop filter is a first-order low-pass filter of a cutoff frequency of 100 Hz, the variation of the buffer occupancy signal can be attenuated by approximately 13 dB. However, because it is not completely zero, the small variation at the loop filter output or VCO input can still cause a small phase variation at the VCO output. This phase variation is the waiting time jitter.

To further reduce the jitter, one might think to use a low-pass filter at an even lower cutoff frequency. Since the bandwidth of the low-pass filter also determines the frequency acquisition range (see Chapter 16), it cannot be smaller than the DS1 clock variation range or 77.2 Hz (50 ppm). Therefore, a cutoff frequency of 100 Hz is already close to the lower limit. ∎

8.4 SONET

SONET, or synchronous optic network, is a TDM standard for transmission over optical fibers (the international version is called **synchronous digital hierarchy** or SDH). It is designed to simplify the process of frequency justification so that multiplexing and demultiplexing can be done at high speeds. To achieve this, SONET introduces an innovative **floating payload** concept for frequency justification, where the information payload is not fixed in location but floats with respect to the frame. To find the beginning of the floating payload, SONET uses **pointer processing**. As the following discussion makes clear, this

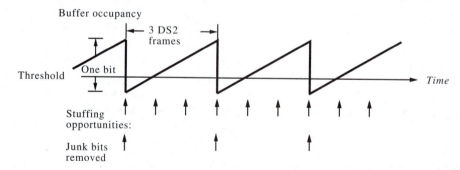

Figure 8.17   Illustration for the cause of waiting timing jitter in TDM demultiplexing. When a stuffing opportunity does not carry data, there is a gap in the gapped clock that writes DS1 data to the buffer. Therefore, there is a one-bit jump at the corresponding time. If a one-bit variation of the buffer occupancy is considered to be a phase of 2π, the buffer occupancy can also be considered to be the phase difference between the gapped write clock and the smoothed read clock.

new approach requires high-speed processing only at the transceiver end, and all clocks in SONET are multiples of its basic rate, 51.84 Mb/s.

8.4.1 SONET FRAME AND LAYERED STRUCTURE

As shown in Figure 8.18, a basic SONET frame has a two-dimensional structure and consists of 90 (columns) by 9 (rows) bytes. For the same reason as T1, the SONET frame has a duration of 125 μsec. Therefore, the transmission bit rate of the basic SONET signal is $90 \times 9 \times 8 \times 8 = 51.84$ Mb/s. This basic SONET signal is called STS-1, where STS stands

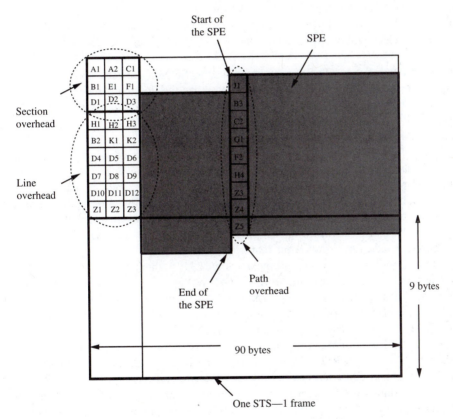

Figure 8.18 A SONET frame consists of 9 × 90 bytes, where the first three columns are the section and line overheads, and the remaining 87 columns are called the synchronous payload envelope (SPE). The SPE floats with respect to the frame. In other words, the first byte of the SPE can be anywhere in the 9 by 87 area. The first column of nine bytes in the SPE are path overhead, and the remaining 86 columns carry data.

for synchronous transmission signal. STS-1 is the lowest rate signal in SONET, and all other SONET signals have rates that are multiples of the basic rate. For example, an STS-N signal has a bit rate N times 51.84 Mb/s. Because STS-3 is the basic rate used in SDH, N is in practice a multiple of three. When an STS-N signal is used to modulate a laser diode for transmission, the corresponding signal is called OC-N, where OC stands for **optical carrier**.

Among the 90 columns, the first 4 are overhead, and the remaining 86 are payload. The first three overhead columns are called the section and line overheads, and the fourth is called the path overhead. As will be explained shortly, these section, line, and path overheads are used for operation and maintenance at different transmission levels.

The path overhead and the following 86 data columns form a structure called the **synchronous payload envelope** (SPE). Uniquely in SONET, as illustrated in Figure 8.18, this SPE floats with respect to the SONET frame. In other words, the first byte of the SPE can be anywhere in the 9×87 area. To recognize the beginning position of the SPE, two bytes in the line overhead are used as the SPE pointer. When the pointer is incremented by one, the position of the SPE is moved down by one byte. The change of the pointer value is called **pointer processing**, which will be explained in detail when frequency justification is considered.

Layered Structure   There are two reasons that SONET overheads are partitioned into section, line, and path. First, it is necessary to realize the floating payload concept for frequency justification, where section and line overheads are terminated at a SONET multiplexer and the path overhead, as a part of the SPE, will pass through. This will be elaborated in detail in the subsection on pointer processing.

The second reason for the layered structure is to facilitate simple transmission operation and maintenance. In general, an end-to-end transmission link consists of repeaters, multiplexers, and switches. Similar to the seven OSI layers in data communications discussed in Chapter 2, the transmission processing can be partitioned into different layers.

As illustrated in Figure 8.19, a section layer is between adjacent repeaters or between a repeater and a **line terminating equipment** (LTE). An LTE is a piece of equipment that multiplexes or adds/drops lower bit-rate tributary signals to/from a higher bit-rate signal. Therefore, a multiplexer or demultiplexer is an LTE. Other examples of LTE in digital transmission include add-drop multiplexers (ADMs) and digital cross-connects (DCSs).

A line layer in an end-to-end transmission link is between two LTEs or between one LTE and one **path terminating equipment** (PTE). A PTE examines the data in the payload for necessary processing. For example, a SONET STS-1 payload can carry a number of T1 signals. The equipment that maps T1 signals into the SONET STS-1 payload and reads data from it is a PTE. Other examples of PTEs include SONET switches, which switch individual PCM voices carried by the SPE.

Both section and line layer equipment do not examine the SPE. They only process their corresponding section and line overheads. For example, when a line consists of several sections, the line overhead is unchanged and the section overhead is modified from one section to another. On the other hand, at the end of an LTE, both section and line overheads are processed.

The top layer defined by SONET is the path layer, which is between two path terminators. Because the path overhead is associated with the data that will be processed in the PTE, they together form the SPE and float with respect to the SONET frame.

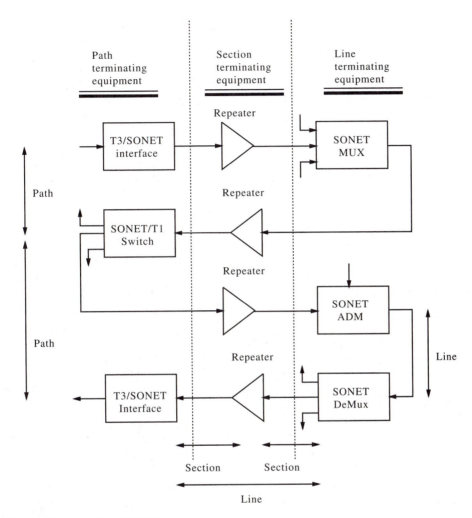

Figure 8.19 The SONET three-layer concept.

Detailed Overhead Description As shown in Figure 8.18, there are nine bytes in the section overhead: two bytes (A1, A2) for framing, one byte (BIP-8) for error detection, one byte (C1) to identify the current STS-1 signal, three bytes (D1–D3) for data communication, one byte (E1) for orderwire, and one byte (F1) for user use. The orderwire byte is to provide a 64 kb/s voice PCM channel for communication during maintenance or repair. The three D1–D3 bytes are used for data communications over the section layer.

There are 18 bytes for line overheads: three bytes (H1–H3) for pointer processing (to be explained shortly), one byte (B2) for line error detection, 9 bytes (D4–D12) for data communication, two bytes (Z1, Z2) for future use, one byte (E2) for orderwire, and two bytes (K1, K2) for automatic protection switching (APS). APS is used to protect against transmission failures between two line terminators. In practical transmission systems, a backup line is usually added to a certain number of working lines. When a working line is broken, two protection switches at the transmission ends will automatically switch on the backup line to replace the broken line.

The path overhead includes one byte (J1) called STS path trace to verify the continuous transmission of the path, one byte (B3) for error detection, one byte (C2) for labeling the STS path signal (unequipped, equipped, etc.), one byte (G1) for conveying the path-terminating status and performance back to the originating PTE, one byte (H4) for virtual tributary (VT)[4] multiframe synchronization, three bytes (Z3–Z5) for future use, and one byte (F2) for path user channel.

8.4.2 P OINTER P ROCESSING

As mentioned earlier, the floating SPE concept and the use of pointer processing come from the need for simpler implementation for frequency justification. Different from T-carrier where a tributary input at a multiplexer is frequency justified with respect to the frame of its *next higher* hierarchy, SONET performs frequency justification at the *same* STS-1 level. In other words, when N STS-1 signals are multiplexed, the section and line overheads of each STS-1 signal are terminated (note that a multiplexer is an LTE), and the SPE of an upstream STS-1 signal is mapped to the SPE of a local STS-1 signal. Because the local STS-1 signal is in synchronization with the local STS-1 clock of the multiplexer, all N STS-1 signals after payload mapping are frequency justified, and they can then be multiplexed by byte interleaving. Therefore, the nominal bit rate of STS-N is simply N times that of STS-1.

When L STS-N signals are multiplexed, each STS-N is first demultiplexed into N STS-1 signals, each of which is then frequency justified by the STS-1 clock of the multiplexer. After this, byte interleaving can be done for the $L \times N$ STS-1 signals. Thus SONET multiplexing always occurs at the STS-1 level. This is different from T-carriers. For example, to multiplex T1 signals into a T3 signal, four T1s are first multiplexed into one T2 and then multiplex seven T2s into one T3. This hierarchical multiplexing is not only tedious but complicates the bit clock relationships at different levels.

The same fixed-level multiplexing cannot be done for T or CEPT carriers. To perform frequency justification of a TDM frame within the same TDM frame, the following provisions are needed.

1. Consider a pseudo-signal PS-1 illustrated in Figure 8.20. Because the two PS-1 signals can have (slightly) different bit rates, the frame structure must have some space (stuffing bits) to accommodate the clock difference.

2. A PS-1 frame should consist of at least two parts: P1 (overhead) and P2 (payload). When the first PS-1 is frequency justified with respect to the second PS-1, only P2 is

---

| [4] A VT is designed to carry a T1 or CEPT1 signal. It has a similar floating payload structure for frequency justification.

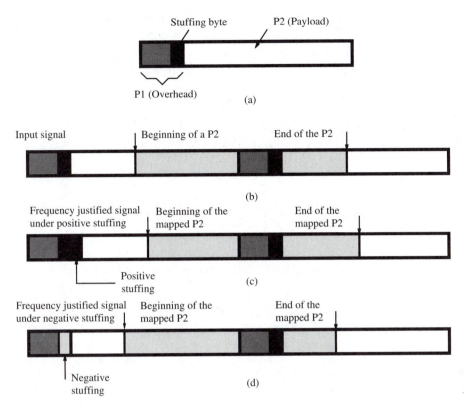

Figure 8.20 The floating payload concept for frequency justification: (a) a frame partitioned into two parts for the overhead and payload, respectively, (b) an input signal, (c) a mapped output when positive stuffing is performed, (d) a mapped output when negative stuffing is performed.

copied from the first PS-1 to the second PS-1. If there is no such partition, the entire frame must be copied. When the two signals have different bit clocks, this is impossible from bit conservation.

3. If the first PS-1 has a higher bit rate than the second PS-1, occasionally the stuffing space from P1 of the second PS-1 must be used to carry P2 data from the first PS-1. However, P2 has the same size in both PS-1 signals. Therefore, when a stuffing byte from P1 in the second PS-1 is used to carry a byte from P2 of the first PS-1, there is a one-byte shift in the subsequent mapping. In other words, the beginning of the next P2 is shifted up by one byte. This means P2 has to float with respect to P1.

4. If the first PS-1 has a lower bit rate than the second PS-1, sometimes a dummy byte must be filled into P2 of the second PS-1 (i.e., mapping must stop for one byte). Again, because P2 has the same size in both PS-1 signals, the subsequent bytes of P2 will be shifted down by one byte in mapping P2 from the first PS-1 to the second PS-1. In other words, the beginning of the next P2 is shifted down by one byte.

5. From the two above observations, P2 floats with respect to P1 in a PS-1 frame and can move in both directions. Thus a pointer is needed in P1 to locate the starting position of P2. When the starting position of P2 is shifted, the pointer value must be updated. This is called pointer processing.

The above discussion gives the primary rationale behind the SONET STS-1 frame structure design. The section and line overheads are the P1 discussed above, and the SPE is the P2. When a stuffing byte (H3) is used to carry an SPE byte, this is called negative stuffing. On the other hand, when a certain position in SPE (the byte right next to H3, not floating) is not used to carry SPE data, this is called positive stuffing.

When negative stuffing is performed, the pointer (H1, H2) will be decremented by one. To signal the demultiplexer of this change, there is an intermediate step for this decrement, where all the D bits of the previous pointer value are inverted (see Figure 8.21). Similarly, when positive stuffing is performed, the pointer will be incremented by one. Before this change, all I bits of the pointer will be inverted in the intermediate step.

Example 8.10	**ENCODING OF H1 AND H2 BYTES** The total range that H1 and H2 need to point to is from 0 to $(9 \times 87 - 1)$ or 782. Therefore, use of 10 bits out of the two H1 and H2 bytes is sufficient. As shown in Figure 8.21, only the 10 LSB bits of H1 and H2 are used for payload pointing, and the 4 MSB bits (N bits) are used for the new data flag. The four N bits are normally set to 0110. When there is a need to start a new SPE (a new pointer value), the four N bits can be set to 1001, and the 10 LSB bits of H1 and H2 can be of any value between 0 and 782. When stuffing is performed, either I bits or D bits are inverted (see Figure 8.21). For example, if the 16 bits of H1, H2 are [01100010, 00100010] (SPE starts at position 546), it will be encoded as [01100011, 01110111] during negative stuffing, and changed to [01100010, 00100001] in the next frame. If positive stuffing is performed instead, it will be [01100000, 10001000] with I bits inverted and changed to [00000010, 00100011] one frame later. ∎

Plesiochronous Network   According to the above description of pointer processing, the minimal interval for changing the pointer value for bit stuffing is three frames. This requires a certain minimum frequency accuracy. In fact, when the concept of the *synchronous* network was originally proposed [10], the clocks of all tributary signals were planned to be all the same. If this were the case, no frequency justification would be necessary, and high-speed multiplexing could be easily implemented. Because a real synchronous network requires a separate, reliable, and stable clock distribution, it is very expensive. As a compromise, SONET allows the use of independent but accurate clocks at line and path terminators. To ensure a high accuracy, their clocks should be traceable to at least Stratum 3 (a clock standard). This use of highly accurate but independent clocks is called **plesiochronous**.

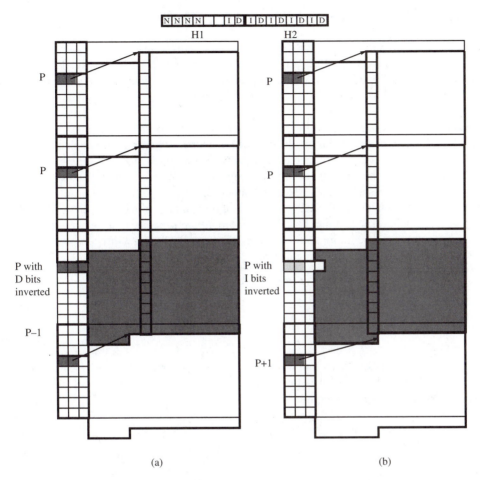

Figure 8.21 SONET pointer processing: (a) negative stuffing, where the H3 byte is used to carry data in the frame whose D bits of H1,H2 bytes are inverted; (b) positive stuffing, where the byte right next to the H3 byte is used as a dummy byte in the frame whose I bits of H1,H2 bytes are inverted.

MINIMUM CLOCK ACCURACY If the upstream STS-1 signal is higher in frequency than that of a SONET multiplexer by 1 ppm, the time it takes to perform one negative stuffing is

$$T = \frac{8}{1 \times 10^{-6} \times 51.84 \times 10^6} = 0.154 \text{ sec}$$

or $0.154/(125 \times 10^{-6}) = 1235$ STS-1 frames. To ensure a minimum three-frame period in performing stuffing, the clock accuracy should be within 412 ppm, which can be easily achieved. ∎

Example 8.11

8.4.3 OPTICAL INTERFACE

To allow transmission between SONET equipment made by different manufacturers, SONET also defines the optical interface between an optical transmitter and receiver [9]. Because SONET was primarily designed for long-distance transmission, only single-mode fibers and laser diodes can be used. Detailed specifications of the optical interface are given below.

Systems   In SONET, two different repeater spans are considered: (1) less than 25 km and (2) between 25 and 40 km. If the distance is above 40 km, a joint engineering by the transmitter manufacturer and receiver manufacturer is required. To maintain an end-to-end BER around 10^{-9}, the BER in each repeater span is specified to be less than 10^{-10}.

The line code used by SONET can be either return-to-zero (RZ) or not-return-to-zero (NRZ). In other words, a SONET receiver should be able to detect signals with either an RZ or NRZ pulse. To facilitate this detection, there are separate requirements of the rise time and relaxation oscillations for RZ and NRZ. Specifically, for a direct modulated pulse illustrated in Figure 8.22, NRZ signals need to satisfy

$$0.95T \leq \text{Rise time} + \text{On time} \leq 1.05T \qquad \textbf{[8.13]}$$

and

$$f_0 > \frac{2}{T} \qquad \textbf{[8.14]}$$

where f_0 is the relaxation oscillation frequency (see Chapter 12). The above conditions are valid for all SONET signals from OC-1 to OC-48.

RZ, on the other hand, requires that

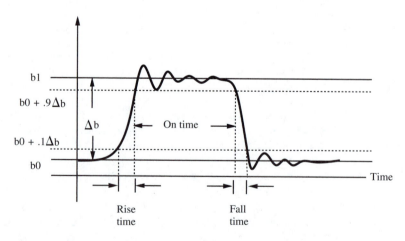

Figure 8.22   Optical pulse output specifications in SONET. The oscillations shown are called relaxation oscillations.

$$\text{Rise time} + \text{On time} + \text{Fall time} \leq \frac{2}{3}T \qquad \textbf{[8.15]}$$

and

$$\begin{aligned} f_0 &> \frac{2}{T} \quad \text{for OC-1 to OC-18} \\ f_0 &> \frac{3}{T} \quad \text{for OC-24 to OC-48.} \end{aligned} \qquad \textbf{[8.16]}$$

In addition to the above requirements, rise time and fall time for both RZ and NRZ need to be within the following values:

$$\text{Rise time} \leq \frac{T}{3} \quad \text{OC-1 to OC-48} \qquad \textbf{[8.17]}$$

and

$$\text{Fall time} \leq \begin{cases} \frac{T}{3} & \text{OC-1 to OC-18} \\ \frac{T}{2} & \text{OC-24 to OC-48.} \end{cases} \qquad \textbf{[8.18]}$$

Laser Diodes   Because the repeater span considered is within 40 km, multimode laser diodes may be used. In SONET, use of both multi- and single-mode laser diodes at wavelengths 1310 and 1550 nm is specified. However, to control fiber dispersion, SONET has different specifications for multimode and single-mode lasers.

For multiple mode laser diodes, a parameter $\Delta\lambda_{MSTM}$ is used. It is the linewidth in nm between two side modes whose power is one tenth of the main mode (−10 dB). As given in Table 8.1, $\Delta\lambda_{MSTM}$ cannot exceed a specified value for different SONET rates and output wavelength range.

Table 8.1   Spectral specifications of multimode laser diodes used in SONET.

Repeater Span (km)	$[\lambda_{min}, \lambda_{max}]$ (nm)	$\Delta\lambda_{MSTM}$ (nm)			
		OC-1	OC-3	OC-9	OC-12
≤ 25	1300–1320	30	15	10	8
	1285–1330	30	15	7	5.5
	1270–1340	30	15	5	3.5
	1540–1560	30	15	10	8
	1525–1575	30	15	7	5.5
$\geq 25, \leq 40$	1300–1320	25	10	7.5	6
	1285–1330	25	10	4.5	3.5
	1540–1560	25	10	7.5	6
	1525–1575	25	10	4.5	3.5

For single-mode laser diodes, a minimum sidemode suppression ratio of 25 dB is specified. In addition, $\Delta\lambda_{15}$ should be within 1.0 nm, where $\Delta\lambda_{15}$ is the full linewidth between two -15 dB points from the peak point. In addition, the center wavelength should be in the range [1280, 1340] at 1310 nm, and in the range [1525, 1575] at 1550 nm transmission.

Optical Fibers   SONET does not explicitly specify the physical dimensions of optical fibers that can be used. Instead, at 1310 nm transmission, it requires single-mode fibers with a maximum acceptable dispersion slope, $\partial D_{intra}/\partial\lambda$, equal to 0.1 ps/nm^{2}km, and the zero dispersion (D_{intra}) point should be within the range 1300–1320 nm. At 1550 nm, dispersion-shifted single-mode fibers should be used.

Example 8.12

WORST CASE PULSE BROADENING   From the above specifications, assume the zero dispersion point of a single-mode fiber used is at wavelength 1300 nm, and the central wavelength of a multimode laser diode is at 1330 nm. Therefore, at the maximum $\partial D_{intra}/\partial\lambda$ of 0.1 psec/nm^{2}km and the maximum $\Delta\lambda_{MSTM}$ given in Table 8.1 for OC-1, the pulse broadening is

$$\Delta\tau = \frac{1}{2}\frac{\partial D_{intra}}{\partial\lambda}\Delta\lambda_{MSTM}^2 L = \begin{cases} 1.13 \text{ nsec} & L = 25 \text{ km} \\ 1.25 \text{ nsec} & L = 40 \text{ km}. \end{cases}$$

Therefore, for OC-1 at 51.84 Mb/s, the pulse broadening is negligible compared to the bit interval of 19.3 nsec. ∎

Power Levels   Because the repeater span can vary and the interface point between the transmitter and receiver is not fixed, SONET does not explicitly specify the transmitter output power and receiver sensitivity. Instead, for a given repeater distance $L \leq 25$ km, SONET specifies the minimum power at the given interface point that the transmitter needs to provide.

Let L_{tx-i} be the distance between the transmitter and interface and L_{rx-i} be the distance between the receiver and interface (consequently $L = L_{tx-i} + L_{rx-i}$). From L_{tx-i} and L_{rx-i}, SONET uses the following rationale to specify the power P_I at the interface point. First, for a given bit rate, SONET assigns a certain power budget, PB (in dB), for the transmission section (see Table 8.2). If the coupling at the interface has a loss of 3 dB and the transmitter power is P_{tx}, the power measured at the interface should be at least

Table 8.2   Power budget specified in SONET.

OC-N	Power Budget in dB
OC-1	25
OC-3	23
OC-9	17.5
OC-12	17
OC-18	17

Table 8.2 Continued

OC-N	Power Budget in dB
OC-24	17
OC-36	17
OC-48	17

$$P_I \geq P_{tx} - (\text{PB} - 3)\frac{L_{tx-i}}{L_{tx-i} + L_{rx-i}} - 3.$$

If the transmitter power output can be in a range from -1 to -7 dBm,

$$-7 \text{ dBm} - \frac{L_{tx-i}}{L_{tx-i} + L_{rx-i}}(\text{PB} - 3) - 3 \leq P_I < -4 \text{ dBm}. \qquad \textbf{[8.19]}$$

Equation (8.19) is called the **dynamic interface power requirement** because the interface can be anywhere between the transmitter and receiver.

MINIMUM RECEIVED POWER REQUIRED   For OC-12–OC-48, the available power budget is the same 17 dB. If the interface point is set at the receiver end, the received power should be at least

$$P_{rx} = P_I = -7 - (17 - 3) - 3 = -24 \text{ dBm}.$$

This power requirement is an overkill for OC-12 but can be critical to OC-48. ∎

Example 8.13

8.5 FIBER DISTRIBUTED DATA INTERFACE

The SONET standard discussed above is designed for point-to-point transmissions. FDDI, developed by the ANSI X3T9.5 task group [11][12], on the other hand, is intended for high-speed local area networking. FDDI has a dual-ring topology and operates at a 100 Mb/s data rate.[5] It can connect up to 500 nodes and supports a maximum fiber length of 200 km. The maximum distance between adjacent nodes is 2 km.

Similar to TDMA and TDM, FDDI is based on time-domain medium access. However, the first version of FDDI does not have a fixed frame size as in TDMA or TDM. Instead, it uses a token-passing protocol with a variable packet size (each packet is called a

---

[5] FDDI uses a line code that maps every four input bits into a five-bit word. Therefore, the actual transmission bit rate is 125 Mb/s, with 80 percent, or 100 Mb/s, for data and 20 percent for redundancy. See Chapter 16 for details on its 4B5B line code.

[6] It is quite common in telecommunications that people use different terminologies for the same thing, and can use the same terminology for different things. Here, a "cycle" in FDDI-II is the same as a frame in TDM, and a frame in FDDI is similar to a slot in TDMA.

frame in FDDI). To support constant bit-rate traffic, FDDI was later modified. The second version is called FDDI-II and has the same 125 μsec cycle size as in T1 and SONET.[6]

8.5.1 DUAL-RING TOPOLOGY AND CLOCK DISTRIBUTION

An FDDI network based on the dual-ring topology is illustrated in Figure 8.23. As pointed out in Chapter 2, this dual-ring topology can maintain network connectivity even when there is a cable cut. To support up to 500 nodes on the ring, each node is an active node that detects bits from the upstream signal, stores them in a local buffer, and sends them downstream.

Because there can be up to 500 nodes, each node has its own clock to minimize jitter accumulation. In other words, a transmitter does not use its upstream clock derived from bit timing recovery to send data. To minimize timing difference among all local clocks, FDDI requires a clock accuracy of ± 50 ppm for each node. In this approach, the received signal and the local clock have different bit timings. To absorb this difference, the receiver buffer, shown in Figure 8.23, is an elastic buffer (i.e., with two separate read and write clocks), and the preamble used in each FDDI frame is not fixed but can be within a certain range.

Example 8.14	According to the specifications, an FDDI frame can have a maximum size of 4500 bytes. When a maximum length frame at 100 Mb/s is transmitted, its transmission time is

$$\Delta T = \frac{4500 \times 8}{10^8} = 3.6 \times 10^{-4} \text{ sec.}$$

Because the actual clock can vary, the above transmission time is only a nominal time. When the upstream node has a clock of $100\,\text{Mb/s} + 50$ ppm and the downstream node has a clock of $100\,\text{Mb/s} - 50$ ppm, over the same time interval, the number of bits that the downstream node can forward to the next node is less than what is received from the upstream node. Specifically, over the period of 4500 byte transmission, the downstream node has the following number of bits still stored in the elastic buffer:

$$4500 \times 8 - \frac{4500 \times 8}{10^8 \times (1 + 50 \times 10^{-6})} \times 10^8 \times (1 - 50 \times 10^{-6})$$

$$\approx 36{,}000 - 36{,}000(1 - 100 \times 10^{-6}) = 3.6.$$

To transmit these bits, as a result of the clock difference, a variable length of preamble is allowed. ∎

8.5.2 OPTICAL COMPONENT SPECIFICATIONS

To appeal to a wide range of users, optical components in FDDI have been chosen for minimal cost. As shown in Table 8.3, the transmitter according to the initial specification is required to have a minimum power of only −20 dBm and the receiver is required to have a minimum sensitivity of −31 dBm. This implies a power budget of 11 dB. Compared to the

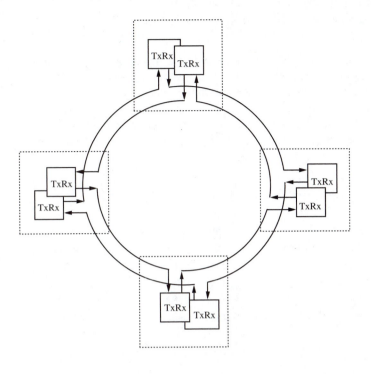

(a)

TxRx

From upstream   To downstream

Rx

TX

PLL

MAC

Recovered
bit clock

ES

Buf

Upstream
data

Local
100 MHz
clock

Local data to
transmit

PLL: Phase Lock Loop
ES: Elastic Store
MAC: Medium Access Control
Buf: Transmitter Buffer

(b)

Figure 8.23   (a) A dual ring FDDI; (b) detailed structure of each station.

power requirement in SONET, these specifications were motivated for the use of low-cost LED and PIN diodes at the transmitter and receiver, respectively.

For low attenuation and dispersion, low-cost multimode graded-index fibers are chosen. The core/cladding diameters are 62.5/125 μm, and the transmission wavelength is 1300 nm. The specifications also allow other sizes, including 50/125, 85/125, and 100/140. When these different fibers are used in the same link, care must be taken to control additional coupling loss caused by cross-section mismatch.

Table 8.3   Optical specifications in FDDI.

Components	Initial Specifications	Low-Cost Specifications
Transmitter output power	Min. –20 dBm	Min. –22 dBm
	Max. –14 dBm	Max. –14 dBm
Receiver sensitivity	Min. –31 dBm	Min. –29 dBm
	Max. –14 dBm	Max. –14 dBm
Fiber	Graded-index	Graded-index
	MMF, 62.5/125,	MMF, 62.5/125,
	50/125, 85/125,	50/125, 85/125,
	100/140	100/140, 200/230
Transmitter rise time	Max. 4 ns	0.6 – 5.0 ns
Receiver rise time	Max. 4.5 ns	0.6 – 5.0 ns

The fiber attenuation of 65/125 fibers is around 2 dB/km at 1300 nm. Therefore, for a link up to 2 km as specified, the total attenuation loss can be up to 4 dB. For a power budget of 11 dB, this means the total coupling power loss cannot exceed 7 dB.

After the initial FDDI specifications were completed in 1991, it was realized that transceiver cost could be a critical factor in the deployment. Therefore, a second version of specifications was introduced for even lower cost. In the new version, use of multimode graded-index fibers is unchanged, but lower cost 200/230 fibers are also permitted. To reduce the transceiver cost, the transmitter is allowed to have a minimum output power of –22 dBm (2 dB smaller than the previous version), and the receiver is allowed to have a minimum receiver sensitivity of –29 dBm. This new specification reduces the power budget from 11 dB to 7 dB. As a result, the allowable link length is reduced from 2 km to 500 m.

The bit error rate (BER) for each transmission link in FDDI is required to be less than 4×10^{-11}. For 500 nodes on the network and considering a cable cut, the worst case end-to-end BER is

$$\text{BER}_{worst} = 2 \times 500 \times 4 \times 10^{-11} = 4 \times 10^{-8}.$$

As pointed out earlier, specifications of the above optical components were driven by the low-cost consideration. However, when FDDI components became available in the market, people realized the real cost in practice was wiring and cable installation in an existing building. As a result, a twisted-pair version of FDDI has been proposed, where existing phone wires are used to provide 100 Mb/s transmission. With advanced coding and equalization techniques, this high bit-rate transmission is possible. Proprietary coaxial and shielded twisted-pair products at 100 Mb/s are available, but their transmission distance is currently limited to 50–100 m.

8.5.3   DATA FRAME AND TOKEN FORMAT

As mentioned earlier, FDDI is based on a token passing medium access protocol. When a node gets the token, it may transmit its data (having the token is not a sufficient condition for transmission). After it finishes transmission (up to 4500 bytes including the overhead), it will release the token and pass it to the next node. Therefore, as given in Figure 8.24, there are two packet formats in FDDI, one for the data frame and one for the token. The fields of the frame formats given in Figure 8.24 are explained below.

1. PA is the preamble field nominally consisting of 16 IDLE symbols (a maximum frequency signal that is used for establishing and maintaining clock synchronization), where a symbol has four information bits or five encoded bits (4B/5B code).

2. SD is the starting delimiter field. It consists of a two-symbol sequence (11000, 10001) that is uniquely recognizable. This unique pattern enables the receiver to recognize the symbol boundary and start processing the overhead that follows.

3. FC is the frame control field consisting of two symbols that define the frame type and its characteristics. It distinguishes between synchronous and asynchronous frames (see discussion below), the length of the address field (16 or 48 bits), and the kinds of frame (user data or network administration). The FC also distinguishes two kinds of tokens: *restricted* and *nonrestricted*. The restricted token is used in a special class of service that provides for extended dialogs among a limited set of cooperating stations.

4. DA is the destination address.

5. SA is the source address.

6. FCS is the frame checking sequence for transmission error detection.

Figure 8.24   Data frame and token formats in FDDI.

7. ED is the end delimiter field. It is a two-symbol sequence (01101, 01101) for tokens and one symbol (01101) for frames.

8. FS is the frame status field that includes at least three control indicator symbols: (1) an error has been detected by the destination station, (2) the destination station has recognized its address, and (3) the frame has been copied by the destination station. This FS field is modified by the destination station as a positive acknowledgment.

8.5.4 SYNCHRONOUS AND ASYNCHRONOUS ACCESS

In FDDI, two types of traffic are considered: synchronous and asynchronous. Synchronous traffic is time sensitive and requires an upper bound for its transmission delay. On the other hand, asynchronous traffic is time insensitive and consequently its transmission delay is not guaranteed.

To provide access for these two types of traffic, FDDI uses two separate mechanisms. For synchronous traffic, each node can transmit its data for a preassigned amount of time once it receives the token. The total time assigned to synchronous traffic for all nodes is equal to a value called **target token rotation time** (TTRT). TTRT is a variable and can be negotiated among all stations.

For asynchronous traffic, a station that receives the token still may not be able to send its data. It needs to compare a timer maintained by it and the specified TTRT. The timer is called the **token rotation time** (TRT), which is the time difference between the current time and the last time the token is received. When TRT is smaller than TTRT, it can transmit its asynchronous data for a duration up to THT = TTRT − TRT, where THT is called the **token holding time**. Therefore, the token-passing protocol in FDDI is called *timed* token passing.

There are two performance parameters important to evaluating the FDDI timed token-passing protocol: (1) the access efficiency (η_{FDDI}) and (2) the maximum access delay (D_{max}) [13]. The access efficiency is defined as the percentage of the time FDDI uses for data transmission, and the maximum access delay is the maximum delay that a node in FDDI can send its data.

Let D be the token passing delay around one loop when there is no traffic. From the medium access protocol described, the token rotation time is up to TTRT + D when there is only synchronous traffic, and the maximum medium access efficiency is

$$\eta_{FDDI,s} = \frac{\text{TTRT}}{\text{TTRT} + D} \approx 1 - \frac{D}{\text{TTRT}} \qquad [8.20]$$

if $D \ll$ TTRT. On the other hand, when there is only asynchronous traffic, the token rotation time is limited within TTRT, and the maximum amount of time used for transmission is TTRT − D. Therefore, the maximum medium access efficiency is

$$\eta_{FDDI,a} = \frac{\text{TTRT} - D}{\text{TTRT}} = 1 - \frac{D}{\text{TTRT}.} \qquad [8.21]$$

When there are both synchronous and asynchronous traffic, it can be assumed that an amount of time $T_s <$ TTRT is allocated for synchronous traffic and (TTRT − T_s − D) is allocated for asynchronous traffic in the steady state. Therefore, the overall performance is still $\eta_{FDDI,a}$.

At a given TTRT, there can be one TTRT for asynchronous traffic followed by another TTRT for synchronous traffic in one rotation. Therefore, the worst case access delay for synchronous traffic is $2 \times$ TTRT. For asynchronous traffic, on the other hand, the maximum access delay depends on the number of stations that are active. If there are N stations that have asynchronous traffic to send, the maximum access delay is on the order of $(N - 1) \times$ TTRT. In other words, when a node finishes its transmission, it needs to wait for $(N - 1)$ passes of the token (for the transmission of the other $N - 1$ nodes) before it gets the next transmission opportunity.

MAXIMUM ACCESS DELAY FOR ASYNCHRONOUS TRAFFIC   The token passing delay D in the absence of traffic is

$$D = \frac{L}{v_g} + NT_s = N\left(\frac{L_s}{v_g} + T_s\right) \qquad \textbf{[8.22]}$$

> **Example 8.15**

where v_g is the group velocity in the optical fiber, L is the total fiber length, L_s is the average fiber length between two adjacent nodes, N is the number of total stations in the ring, and T_s is the token processing time at each station. When $v_g = 2 \times 10^5$ km/sec, $L_s = 0.1$ km, $N = 100$, and $T_s = 1\ \mu\sec$,

$$D = 100 \times \left(\frac{0.1}{2 \times 10^5} + 1.0 \times 10^{-6}\right) = 0.15 \text{ msec.}$$

Therefore, to have an access efficiency of 90 percent, TTRT should be 1.5 msec.

When the average number of active stations is 20 percent of the total number of nodes, the maximum access delay for asynchronous traffic is

$$D_{max} = (20\% \times 100 - 1)\text{TTRT} = 19\text{TTRT} = 28.5 \text{ msec.} \quad \blacksquare$$

8.5.5 FDDI-II AND FDDI FOLLOW-ON LAN

In FDDI, both synchronous and asynchronous traffic cannot be guaranteed a fixed transmission delay. To support isochronous traffic such as T-carriers, a second version called FDDI-II has been developed [14][15]. In this modified version, time is partitioned into 125 μsec **cycles** as in T1 and SONET frames. To maintain accurate cycle timing, an 8 kHz clock from an **external timing reference** (ETR) is separately distributed to all nodes, as shown in Figure 8.25.

Over the 125 μsec cycle interval and at 100 Mb/s, there are 3125 symbols, or 1562.5 bytes. As shown in Figure 8.26 [15], among the 3125 symbols, there are 5 symbols used

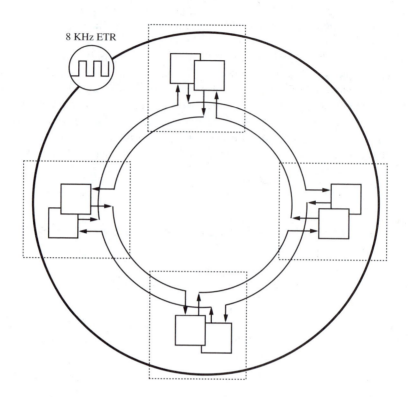

Figure 8.25   External 8 kHz timing distribution in FDDI-II.

for the preamble, 24 symbols for the cycle header, and 24 symbols known as the **packet data group** (PDG) used for packet data traffic. The remaining 3072 symbols, or 1536 bytes, in a cycle are divided into 16 **wide band channels** (WBCs) of 96 bytes each. At 125 μsec cycle time, each of the WBCs represents a constant bit channel at 6.144 Mb/s, which can be used to carry four T1 or three CEPT1 signals.

Each of the 16 WBCs can be individually assigned to carry isochronous traffic or asynchronous/synchronous traffic. To achieve this, as shown in Figure 8.27, the OSI model of FDDI-II has an additional layer between the physical layer and medium access layer called **hybrid ring control** (HRC). When HRC receives data from the physical layer, it demultiplexes traffic to either the regular MAC (packet) or I-MAC (isochronous) layer. If a WBC is used to carry isochronous traffic, HRC forwards its data to the I-MAC, and if the WBC is used to carry synchronous/asynchronous traffic, HRC forwards data to the regular MAC.

To tell the type of traffic a WBC carries, HRC reads the corresponding byte in the cycle header shown in Figure 8.28, where 16 symbols, P0–P15, are used to determine the traffic types of the corresponding WBCs (0–15). In addition to these 16 sym-

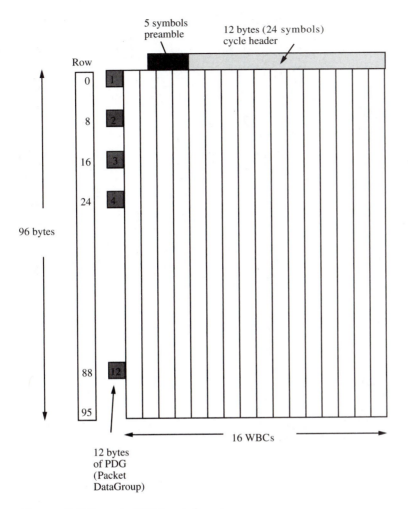

Figure 8.26 An FDDI-II cycle format.

bols, two symbols are used for the starting delimiter (SD), two symbols are used for the cycle sequence (CS) from 0 to 191, two control symbols, C1 and C2, are used when P0–P15 are changed, and two symbols are used for the **maintenance voice channel** (MVC) as a 64 kb/s PCM voice channel. In other words, it is similar to the orderwire bytes used in SONET.

In principle, when all the WBC channels are set to carry packet data, FDDI-II reduces to the basic FDDI operation. In this case, FDDI-II is said to be in the *basic mode*. When one or more WBC channels are used to carry isochronous traffic, FDDI-II is said

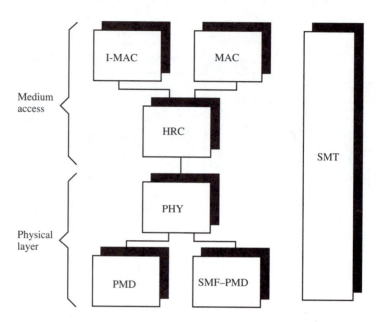

Figure 8.27   The protocol layers in FDDI-II.

SD	C1	C2	CS	P0	P1	• • • •	P14	P15	MVC

Figure 8.28   The cycle header format in FDDI-II.

to be in the *hybrid mode*. After FDDI-II is initialized, it is by default in the basic mode. To go to the hybrid mode, all stations have to negotiate. If all agree, they switch to the hybrid mode at the same time. When FDDI-II is in the basic mode, the SD field in the cycle header is (11000, 1001). When the mode is changed to hybrid, the SD field is changed to (11111, 00101).

FFOL: FDDI Follow-on LAN   As FDDI gains wide acceptance, it becomes important to have a backbone network to interconnect multiple FDDI networks. To achieve this, **FDDI follow-on LAN** (FFOL) was initiated in 1990 by Task Group X3T9.5 of ASC X3 to establish requirements and formal projects for a next generation local area network (LAN) [16][17]. Among many considerations, there is a general agreement that FFOL should allow interconnections between FDDI and SONET. Furthermore, it should provide an interface to exchange packet formats between FDDI and B-ISDN.

8.6 BROADBAND ISDN

In the early 1980s, the concept of providing various data and voice services for residential and business subscribers was realized through the standardization of the so-called **integrated services digital network** (ISDN) [18]. In ISDN, a subscriber can access a digital line of 144 kb/s using the existing two-wire subscriber loop. With advanced optical fiber technology, the concept of broadband ISDN (B-ISDN) quickly emerged to provide broadband services such as video.

To provide integrated voice, data, and video services, two areas need to be defined: the broadband network and the local loop. The broadband network switches and multiplexes various types of traffic within the network, and the local loop delivers traffic between the network and subscribers.

8.6.1 BROADBAND NETWORK

To provide high-speed switching and transmission, B-ISDN is based on SONET transmission and a fixed-size packet switching technique called **asynchronous transfer mode**

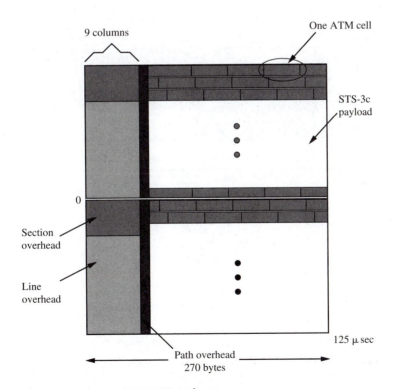

Figure 8.29   SONET STS-3c format.

(ATM). As mentioned earlier, the concept of pointer processing in SONET allows simple and high-speed multiplexing and demultiplexing. To facilitate high-speed switching, all packets, called cells, have the same size (53 bytes).

To carry fixed-size cells, cells are mapped to the SONET SPE. In B-ISDN, the basic rate is SONET STS-3c, which has the same rate of STS-3. However, instead of byte interleaving three STS-1 SPEs, the three SPEs are combined into a single SPE with only one column path overhead. Therefore, the "c" in STS-3c stands for concatenation. As illustrated in Figure 8.29, the rest of the SPE is used to carry ATM cells. Because an integer number of ATM cells cannot fit within one SPE, cells are continously mapped from one SPE to another.

To switch all voice, data, and video traffic, B-ISDN takes an integrated switching approach that all types of traffic are switched based on the same ATM packet switching. However, in the cell overhead, there are flags indicating the types of traffic so that an ATM switch can place different queuing priorities in switching cells.

According to the standards, an ATM cell has 53 bytes, consisting of five overhead bytes and 48 data bytes. To meet different traffic needs, the determination of the ATM size

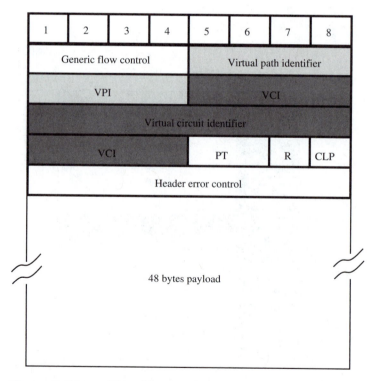

Figure 8.30   ATM cell format at the UNI, where VPI is virtual path identifier, VCI is virtual circuit identifier, PT is payload type, R is reserved, and CLP is cell loss priority.

was not an easy task. For voice, a large ATM size means a large compression delay (see discussion on TDMA) and a large buffer requirement. On the other hand, a small ATM size has a low efficiency because of the overhead. As a compromise, the ANSI T1S1 committee chose a payload size of 48 bytes, which corresponds to a delay of $48 \times 125 \ \mu\text{sec} = 6 \ \text{msec}$ for 64 kb/s PCM voice.

The formats of the five-byte overhead at the user–network interface (UNI) and network–network interface (NNI) are given in Figures 8.30 and 8.31, respectively [19]. The NNI is the interface for internal ATM switching equipment in the broadband network. On the other hand, the UNI is the interface between the network and subscriber communication terminals.

The 20-bit Virtual Circuit Identifier field in both interfaces is used for virtual circuit switching. The Virtual Path Identifier field is used for virtual path switching, which is similar to trunks in telephone networks. Each VPI carries a large number of virtual circuits that are switched identically according to the common VPI in the internal network. At the UNI, only 8 bits are allocated for VPI since there are not as many virtual paths as at the NNI. Also uniquely at the UNI, there is a 4-bit field for generic flow control. It is designed for protocol adaptation when the user has its own local area network.

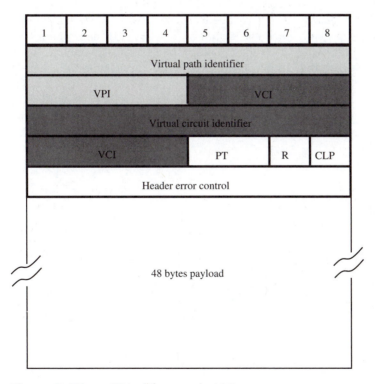

Figure 8.31   ATM cell format at the NNI.

Common to both the UNI and NNI, there is two-bit payload type field to indicate traffic types, such as **continuous bit rate** (CBR) traffic and **variable bit rate** (VBR) traffic. There is also a one-bit field for cell loss priority, which is used for internal ATM switches to determine the priority in dropping cells upon traffic congestion or buffer overflow. Finally, there is a one-byte field for error control of the overhead bits.

8.6.2 LOCAL LOOP

Because of many different considerations, such as cost, performance, compatibility, installations, and operation, there have been many different proposals for the local loop implementation. Although extension of B-ISDN/ATM/SONET in the broadband network is an obvious choice, it may not be the most cost-effective approach.

Multiplexing   To multiplex different types of traffic and send it to subscribers, time division multiplexing (TDM), wavelength division multiplexing (WDM), and subcarrier multiplexing (SCM) have all been proposed. In TDM, the B-ISDN/ATM/SONET combination used in the broadband network can simply be extended to end subscribers. The cost of this approach can be high when subscribers may only want to watch analog video.

To minimize the user cost, a WDM approach, illustrated in Figure 8.32, can be used [20]. As shown, there are two wavelength channels. At $\lambda_1 = 850$ nm, a low bit-rate channel is used to provide voice and data, and at $\lambda_2 = 1310$ nm, a high bit-rate channel (> 450 MB/s) is used to carry digital video. In this approach, only the low bit-rate channel can be initially offered to reduce the user's cost. The high bit-rate channel can be added as needed by simple WDM.

Another proposed low-cost approach is based on SCM [21]. As illustrated in Figure 8.33, all analog video, digital data, voice, and video such as HDTV can be first modulated by microwave carriers and then multiplexed. In this approach, several low bit-rate

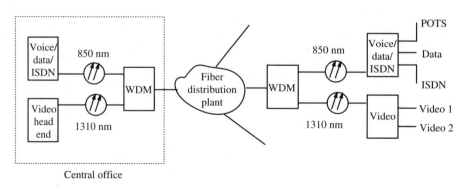

Figure 8.32   Two wavelength channels for the local loop.

signals (1.5 Mb/s for T1 carriers) can be modulated in a frequency band below 1 GHz, and several wideband channels (around 50 MHz) can be carried in the frequency range from 1 to 4 GHz. Each wideband channel can carry analog TV, digital HDTV, and DS3 signals. The combined signal is used to modulate the light carrier for transmission. As will be explained in detail in Chapter 10, one primary limitation of SCM is the nonlinear cross-product distortion.

Local Loop Alternatives   In the above discussion, optical local loops are extended to end subscribers. This is commonly referred to as fiber-to-the-home (FTTH) [22]. Because of the cost and difficulty in maintenance, an alternative approach called fiber-in-the-loop (FITL) has also been proposed [23].

In FITL, optical fibers are terminated at a point close to end subscribers. As illustrated in Figure 8.34, an optical fiber link in the loop is terminated at an optical network unit (ONU), or pedestal, which performs optical/electrical conversions and distributes multimedia data to a group of subscribers. This approach reduces the last mile cost from customers and at the same time provides the flexibility for future FTTH.

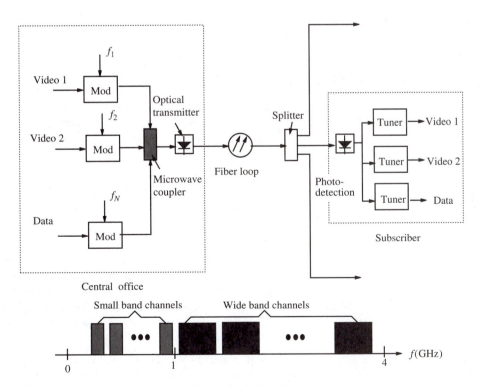

Figure 8.33   Subcarrier multiplexing for the local loop.

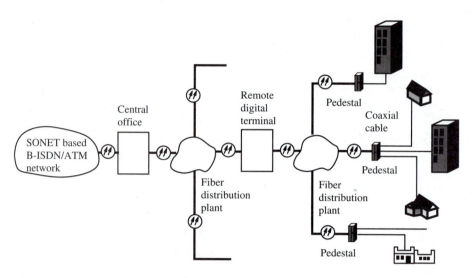

Figure 8.34   Fiber-in-the-loop.

8.7 SUMMARY

1. In time-domain medium access, stations send data over different time intervals. Different TDMA schemes differ primarily in how long a station can send its data and how long it has to wait before the next transmission. In TDM and TDMA, a station can send its data for a fixed time interval and can get access to the network over a fixed access delay. In token passing (e.g., FDDI) and random access (CSMA/CD), on the other hand, both the transmission interval and access delay are indeterministic.

2. In TDMA, time is divided into frames, which are fixed in size and are generally on the order of msec to overcome the guard time inefficiency. A TDMA frame consists of (1) a reference burst for frame synchronization and signaling and (2) a certain number of fixed-size time slots to carry data. There is also guard time between time slots to separate transmissions and to avoid possible transmission overlaps.

3. In TDMA, there is a trade-off between the access efficiency and compression delay. The access efficiency is the ratio of the total transmission time in a frame to the total frame time. The inefficiency is mainly due to guard time, which in turn is determined by the propagation delay and frame timing skew. To improve the access efficiency at a given guard time, the frame size must be increased, which increases the compression delay of storing lower-rate input data before slot transmission.

4. Because of no need to synchronize transmitters in bit clocks and the ability to tolerate frame timing skew, optical domain implementation of TDMA is practically attractive. In this case, an optical star coupler is needed to mix optical signals from all stations and then distribute the mixed signal in equal power to all receivers. To overcome the distribution power loss, erbium-doped fiber amplifiers can be used.

5. Similar to TDMA, TDM has a fixed frame size consisting of the overhead and a fixed number of slots. However, data in different TDM slots are synchronized in bit timing. Therefore, TDM does not need to include guard time, and its frame size (also slot size) is much smaller (typically 125 μsec for 64 kb/s PCM voice) than TDMA to reduce the compression delay.

6. In TDM, when tributary inputs have different bit clocks, their clocks must be synchronized before multiplexing. This process is called frequency justification and can be done by either slip control (drop or repeat a tributary frame) or bit stuffing (a stuffing bit that can carry tributary data or a dummy bit, depending on the buffer occupancy of the elastic store). In T-carriers, slip control is only done in DS0 to DS1 multiplexing. Higher TDM signal multiplexing is done by slip control.

7. In SONET, the lowest bit rate is 51.84 Mb/s and is denoted by STS-1. In SDH (an international version), the basic rate is STS-3. To facilitate high speed multiplexing and de-multiplexing in optical communication, SONET introduces a new bit stuffing technique called pointer processing.

8. In pointer processing, a two-byte word (called a pointer) in the overhead is used to point to the floating payload within each frame. When there is a need to perform stuffing (negative or positive), the payload will shift in position with respect to the frame. This technique maps the payload of an input STS-1 signal to that of a local STS-1 signal. Because of this STS-1 level mapping, complicated frequency justification is limited at the basic rate STS-1, and high-speed multiplexing is done by simple byte interleaving.

9. To permit communications between SONET transmitters and receivers made by different manufacturers, a dynamic optical interface is defined in SONET, which specifies the minimum power required for the transmitter to deliver at any point in a transmission section.

10. To provide high-speed networking in a local area, a 100 Mb/s token-ring standard called FDDI has been defined. Different from TDM or TDMA, the medium access is statistical. When a transmission node holds the token, it can transmit data for a variable duration. However, the time delay until it can hold the token again for the next transmission is not fixed. Therefore, FDDI was not designed for constant bit-rate traffic. Instead, it supports two types of traffic: synchronous and asynchronous.

11. Synchronous traffic in FDDI is time sensitive and requires an upper bound for the transmission delay. For a specified target token rotation time (TTRT), the maximum access delay is within two TTRT (one each for synchronous and asynchronous traffic). On the other hand, asynchronous traffic is time insensitive; its transmission delay depends on how many active nodes have asynchronous data to send. If there are N active nodes (if N is large), the delay is on the order of $N \times$ TTRT.

12. To achieve the delay upper bound for synchronous traffic, synchronous data can be sent for a preallocated fraction of one TTRT at every token pass. On the other hand, for asynchronous traffic, it can be sent only when (1) the node gets the token and (2) the token rotation time (TRT) is within the specified TTRT, where TRT is the time interval between two token passes. When TRT < TTRT, the time it can hold the token for asynchronous transmission is up to TTRT − TRT. The token-ring protocol of FDDI is thus called *timed* token-passing.

13. To support fixed bit-rate traffic in FDDI, an improved version called FDDI-II has been specified. In this case, a fixed cycle of 125 μsec rotates along the ring, and each cycle consists of 16 wideband channels (WBCs) at a rate of 6.144 Mb/s. In FDDI-II, all WBCs can be used for synchronous and asynchronous traffic (called basic mode) or can be individually assigned for asynchronous/synchronous traffic and isochronous traffic (called hybrid mode).

14. For wide acceptance, optical components in FDDI are chosen for minimal cost. For example, LEDs can be used as light sources, graded multimode fibers for transmission, and PIN diodes for photodetection. The original power budget specified was 11 dB. To further reduce the device cost, a low-cost version of FDDI allows a power budget of only 7 dB.

15. To provide broadband video, voice, and data services to both residential and business customers, the concept of the broadband integrated services digital network (B-ISDN) has been proposed. To achieve this requires both (1) a high-speed digital network that transmits and switches data and (2) a high-speed local loop that delivers multimedia data to end subscribers.

16. To transmit high-speed data, the basic rate used in B-ISDN is SONET STS-3c, which combines three STS-1 payloads for transmission at a rate over 150 Mb/s. To provide high-speed switching and multiplexing of data traffic, B-ISDN uses a fixed-size packet switching scheme called asynchronous transfer mode (ATM). This fixed-size packet switching simplifies timing and buffering implementation greatly in high-speed switching.

17. For various reasons, such as cost and smoother deployment, there are many approaches in the design of broadband local loops. First, a fiber-to-the-home (FTTH) approach has been proposed that extends the B-ISDN/SONET/ATM combination from the broadband network to subscribers. However, it is expensive and requires many changes from the subscribers. A compromise approach is called fiber-in-the-loop (FITL), where the fiber link from the local central office is terminated at a point near subscribers, from which traditional cables or twisted-pair wires are used to reach the end subscribers.

18. In addition to the time-domain based multiplexing approach in the local loop design, both wavelength-division multiplexing (WDM) and subcarrier multiplexing (SCM) approaches have been proposed. In WDM, two wavelength channels are used for low-speed traffic (voice and data) and high-speed video. The low-speed channel can initially be installed alone for minimal cost. To further reduce the cost of WDM devices, SCM that mixes both analog and digital signals in the microwave frequency range is a good alternative. However, its cross-product distortion should be controlled for good transmission performance.

PROBLEMS

Problem 8–1 Guard Time in TDMA: Consider a TDMA network using a star coupler in the center. As mentioned in the text, the guard time can be reduced to zero when the propagation delay is perfectly measured. In reality, this is not possible. If the propagation delay measured from a node to the central star has an error of $\pm 1 \, \mu$sec, find the required guard time as a result.

Problem 8–2 Access Efficiency in TDMA: If the guard time in a given TDMA network is 1 μsec and the preamble plus the start code in each slot has a total of 100 bits, find the access efficiency if the slot payload size is 6 μsec and the instantaneous bit rate is 100 Mb/s. Neglect the reference burst in the computation for simplicity.

Problem 8–3 Compression Delay in TDMA: Continue from Problem 8–2. If each slot is designed to carry a 2 Mb/sec signal, find the minimum frame size so that the access efficiency is at least 80 percent. Assume the same 100 Mb/s instantaneous bit rate but use a different slot size.

Problem 8–4 Access Efficiency in TDMA: Consider a TDMA system designed to carry a 2 Mb/s channel per slot. Suppose the guard time over the system is 10 μsec. Design such a system so that its access efficiency is greater than 90 percent and the compression delay is less than 1 msec. In the design, specify the number of slots per frame, frame size, and instantaneous bit rate, and give the actual access efficiency from the design. Assume the reference burst duration is 20 μsec and neglect the overhead time for each slot.

Problem 8–5 Effect of Access Efficiency at High-Speed TDMA: If the TDMA frame is fixed at 4 msec and each slot is designed to carry 1 Mb/s constant bit-rate traffic, find the upper bound of the instantaneous bit rate to ensure a minimum access efficiency of 90 percent. Assume the guard time plus the preamble of each slot is 10 μsec and neglect the reference burst size for simplicity.

Problem 8–6 Coupling Loss in Optical Domain TDMA: In an optical domain TDMA network using an EDFA as shown in Figure 8.6, find the number of input signals that can be coupled if (1) the total power budget is equal to the total fiber attenuation, and (2) the optical gain available from the EDFA is at most 30 dB. Assume no coupling loss at each interface and a coupling loss of 0.1 dB inside each stage of the splitter and coupler.

Problem 8–7 Framing Synchronization in TDM:
  a. As shown in Figure 8.10, frame boundaries can be identified by recognizing the 6-bit [101010] framing pattern. If frame synchronization is established once such a pattern is found, find the maximum time to establish the frame timing. For simplicity, assume there is no possibility for the payload to have the same framing pattern.
  b. In CEPT1, on the other hand, frame timing can be established by matching the eight-bit framing byte. Calculate the worst case time to establish the frame timing.

Problem 8–8 Slip Control: Consider the case of performing slip control for DS0 signals, and assume the local clock is 72 kHz and the input signal's clock is 64 kHz.
  a. Find the slip rate.
  b. Based on the slip control using a single RAM as described in the text, find the byte sequence read from the RAM if the input byte sequence is 1, 2, 3, 4, 5, 6, 7, 8, 9, 10, where each decimal value represents eight binary bits of the same value. Assume the read clock is initially one byte behind the write clock.

Problem 8–9 Bit Stuffing: If the negative stuffing ratio in M12 multiplexing is designed to be 1/3, find the nominal bit rate of T2.

Problem 8–10 SONET Pointer Processing: A SONET multiplexer is found to perform positive stuffing for an STS-1 input. In addition, the pointer value repeats a cycle over 30,000 frames. Find the relative clock difference between the input STS-1 and the local clock of the multiplexer. Assume the local clock is at the nominal clock rate of 51.84 Mb/s.

Problem 8–11 SONET Pointer Processing: Consider a SONET transmission path consisting of one SONET path terminator, one multiplexer, and another path terminator. Assume something is wrong with the transmission line and two technicians are checking the system at the two path terminators. For voice communications, they use the E2 byte of the line overhead. If the average slip rate is found to be once every hour, find the average rate that the pointer value is changed at the middle multiplexer for the SONET path considered.

Problem 8–12 SONET Optical Interface: In SONET, assume the zero-dispersion point of a single-mode fiber and the central wavelength of a multimode laser diode coincide at 1330 nm. Find the pulse broadening over a 40 km transmission. Assume $\partial D_{intra}/\partial\lambda$ is 0.1 psec/nm^{2}km and $\Delta\lambda_{MSTM}$ is at the maximum value given in Table 8.1 for OC-12.

Problem 8–13 SONET Optical Interface: Consider a SONET transmission over 25 km. Find the required power at the middle point of transmission for OC-3, OC-9, and OC-12.

Problem 8–14 FDDI Token Rotation Time and Access Efficiency: Assume an FDDI network has only asynchronous traffic. The token rotation time in the absence of traffic is $D = 10 \, \mu$sec, and the target token rotation time (TTRT) is set at 1 msec. If the asynchronous traffic has a total average bit rate of 50 Mb/s, find the actual average token rotation time and the access efficiency.

Problem 8–15 Worst Case FDDI Access Delay:
a. If an FDDI network has 50 nodes, find the total token passing delay D in the absence of traffic. Assume the total fiber length is 100 km, the propagation velocity is $v_g = 1 \times 10^5$ km/sec, and the token processing delay at each node is 10 μsec.
b. From (a), design the target token rotation time (TTRT) so that its maximum access efficiency for asynchronous traffic is 80 percent.

Problem 8–16 FDDI Optical Components:
a. In the original FFDI specifications, the power budget is 11 dB and the length between two adjacent nodes can be up to 2 km. If the total coupling loss is 5 dB, find the upper limit of the fiber attenuation for fibers to be used.
b. In the low-cost version, the power budget is 7 dB and the length between two adjacent nodes cannot be greater than 500 m. For the same amount of coupling loss, find the corresponding upper limit of fiber attenuation.
c. Comparing the results from (a) and (b), which one has a looser requirement on fibers? Why?

Problem 8–17 B-ISDN/ATM: Assume ATM cells are used to carry a constant bit-rate digital video at 45 Mb/s. If the whole 48-byte payload is used to carry the video, find the average number of ATM cells needed in every STS-3c frame.

REFERENCES

1. R. Ballart and C. Yau, "SONET—Now It's the Standard Optical Network," *IEEE Communications Magazine,* vol. 26, no. 3 (March 1989), pp. 8–15.

2. R. Schmidt et al., "Fibernet II: A Fiber Optic Ethernet," *IEEE Journal of Selected Areas in Communications,* vol. 1, no. 5 (November 1983), pp. 702–11.

3. K. Feher, "Time-Division Multiple Access Systems," Chapter 8 of *Digital Communications, Satellite/Earth Station Engineering,* Prentice-Hall, 1981.

4. F. Matera et al., "Proposal of a High-Capacity All-Optical TDMA Network," *Microwave and Optical Technology Letters,* vol. 5, no. 1 (January 1992), pp. 41–44.

5. S. Culverhouse, R. A. Lobbett, and P. J. Smith, "Optically Amplified TDMA Distributive Switch Network with 2.488 Gb/s Capacity Offering Interconnection to over 1000 Customers at 2 Mb/s," *Electronics Letters,* vol. 28, no. 17 (August 1992), pp. 1672–73.

6. J. E. Abate et al., "The Switched Digital Network Plan," *Bell System Technical Journal,* September 1977, pp. 1297–1320.

7. D. L. Duttweiler, "Waiting Timing Jitter," *Bell System Technical Journal,* vol. 51 (1972), p. 165.

8. P. E. K. Chow, "Jitter Due to Pulse Stuffing Synchronization," *IEEE Transactions on Communications,* vol. 21 (1973), p. 854.

9. ANSI T1.106, American National Standard for Telecommunications, "Digital Hierarchy—Optical Interface Specifications (Single Mode)," American National Standards Institute, Inc., 1988.

10. G. R. Ritchie, "SYNTRAN—A New Direction for Digital Transmission," *IEEE Communications Magazine,* vol. 23, no. 11 (November 1985), p. 20.

11. R. Jain, "FDDI: Current Issues and Future Plans," *IEEE Communications Magazine,* September 1993, pp. 98–105.

12. R. Jain, *FDDI Handbook: High Speed Networking Using Fiber and Other Media,* Addison Wesley, 1993.

13. R. Jain, "Performance Analysis of FDDI Token Ring Networks: Effect of Parameters and Guidelines Setting TTRT," *IEEE Communications Magazine,* vol. 2, no. 2 (May 1991), pp. 16–22.

14. T. Ichihashi et al., "Implementing Models of the FDDI-II Cycle Synchronization Technique," *Computer Communication,* vol. 15, no. 3 (April 1992), pp. 169–76.

15. F. E. Ross, "An Overview of FDDI: The Fiber Distributed Data Interface," *IEEE Journal on Selected Areas in Communications,* vol. 7, no. 7 (September 1989), pp. 1043–51.

16. F. E. Ross and R. L. Fink, "Overview of FFOL—FDDI Follow-On LAN," *Computer Communication,* vol. 15, no. 1 (January 1992), pp. 5–10.

17. J. R. Hamstra and R. L. Fink, "FFOL Transmission Services—Issues for an SMUX," *Computer Communication,* vol. 16, no. 3 (March 1993), pp. 177–83.

18. P. Bocker, *ISDN—The Integrated Services Digital Network: Concepts, Methods, Systems,* Springer-Verlag, 1988.

19. Bellcore, "Broadband ISDN Switching System Framework Generic Criteria," FA-NWT-001110, December 1990.

20. M. Balmes, J. Bourne, J. Mar, "Fiber to the Home: The Technology behind Heathrow," *IEEE Lightwave Communication Systems Magazine,* vol. 1, no. 3 (August 1990), pp. 25–29.

21. R. Olshansky, "Subcarrier Multiplexed Broadband: A Migration Path to BISDN," *IEEE Lightwave Communication Systems Magazine,* vol. 1, no. 3 (August 1990), pp. 30–34.

22. M. K. Liu, "From Fiber to the Home to Full Broadband ISDN," *Proceedings of IEEE ICC/SuperCom,* 1990, pp. 547–51.

23. G. R. Boyer, "A Perspective on Fiber in the Loop Systems," *IEEE Lightwave Communication Systems Magazine,* vol. 1, no. 3 (August 1990), pp. 6–11.

c h a p t e r
9

WAVELENGTH-DOMAIN MEDIUM ACCESS

Different from time-domain medium access (TDoMA), discussed in the previous chapter, wavelength-domain medium access (WDoMA) allows multiple transmissions and multiple access through sharing multiple wavelength carriers. This chapter presents various system and component aspects of WDoMA. Because the wavelength of an optical carrier is inversely proportional to its frequency, WDoMA is essentially the same as frequency-domain medium access that has long been used in radio communications, such as frequency division multiplexing (FDM).

Because of parallel transmissions in the wavelength domain, WDoMA avoids the speed bottleneck discussed in Chapter 2. Therefore, it has the potential to utilize a large transmission bandwidth of optical fibers. As shown in Figure 9.1, a typical fiber has a bandwidth of 100–150 nm [1]. Table 9.1 shows that this corresponds to a spectrum width of 18 THz at 1300 nm (at 100 nm fiber bandwidth) and 19 THz at 1550 nm (at 150 nm fiber bandwidth). Because current electronics technology and modulation bandwidths of laser diodes can operate only up to tens of GHz, parallel transmission from WDoMA is a key to high utilization of fiber bandwidths.

Table 9.1 Spectrum width (GHz) versus linewidths at 1300 nm and 1550 nm. This table gives a convenient conversion between linewidth in nm and spectrum width in Hz.

Central Wavelength (nm)	Linewidth (nm)	Spectrum Width (GHz)
1300	0.1	17.8
	1.0	177.5
	10.0	1775.2
1550	0.1	12.5
	1.0	124.9
	10.0	1248.7

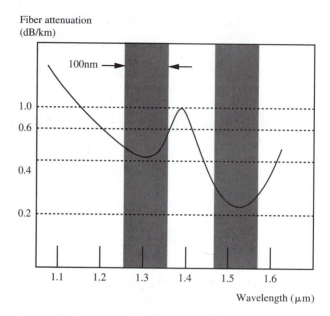

Figure 9.1 Available spectrum width from optical fibers.

Research work on WDoMA has been very active recently and can be grouped into two primary directions: systems and components. Work on systems is concerned with various networking architectures and medium access protocols to achieve a high throughput and short transmission delay, while work on components is concerned with various devices such as tunable lasers, arrays, filters and multi/demultiplexers for system needs. Because components can be limited in tuning speeds, size, and spectral resolution, a good system design should achieve a proper balance between system performance and component limitations.

This chapter provides detailed discussion on both systems and components. On systems, various tuning protocols and logical configurations in a WDoMA network are described. On components, various state-of-the-art components and their principles are discussed, including star couplers, grating devices, waveguide routers, tunable laser arrays, and optical filters.

9.1 **SYSTEM AND COMPONENT OVERVIEW**

Before detailed discussion, it is instructive to have an overview on various system and component aspects. This section introduces important system characteristics, describes key optic and electro-optic devices for WDoMA, and points out their criteria for system use.

9.1.1 **SYSTEM CHARACTERISTICS**

A WDoMA system in general can be characterized by its physical configuration, logical connectivity, channel separation, signal detection, and channel tuning protocol.

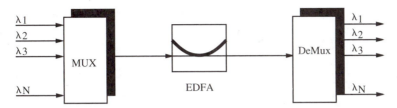

Figure 9.2 System configuration of a wavelength division multiplexing system. In general, the multiplexer and demultiplexer pair are designed specifically according to the wavelengths used. This can reduce the power loss in multiplexing and de-multiplexing. To further overcome power loss due to coupling and fiber attenuation, erbium-doped fiber amplifiers (EDFAs) can also be used.

WDM versus WDoMA   There are two basic system configurations in WDoMA: wavelength-division multiplexing (WDM) and wavelength-division multiple access (WDMA). In WDM, as shown in Figure 9.2, an $N:1$ multiplexer or coupler at the transmitter side is used to mix N input channels. The mixed signal at the output of the multiplexer is then transmitted through a single optical fiber. At the receiver end, a subset of the N signals can be demultiplexed by a grating device or tuned by coherent detection [2] (see Chapter 15 for details). Because multiplexing, fiber transmission, and demultiplexing introduce power loss, optical amplifiers can be inserted in the transmission line to boost the power [3].

In WDMA, as illustrated in Figure 9.3, multiple users can send and receive signals over a distributed network and use different wavelength channels. One example of the shared medium is an $N:N$ star coupler as shown in Figure 9.4a. In this arrangement, each node sends its data to one of the input ports of the star coupler, which mixes all input signals and then distributes them to all output ports. As a result, signals from all input ports can be received from any output port.

As shown in Figures 9.4b and 9.4c, a WDMA network can also be in a bus or ring topology. In this case, directional couplers or hybrids can be used to couple local signals to the shared medium. Compared to the star topology, however, when there are many nodes, the bus and ring topologies suffer a higher power loss and have a larger dynamic range, as discussed in Chapter 2.

Physical versus Logical Topology   By properly choosing the wavelengths at transmitters and receivers, a physical WDMA network can have different logical configurations. As illustrated in Figure 9.5a, with proper wavelength tuning, a logical ring can be formed when each node has a single pair of transceivers.

In principle, a node in a WDMA network can have multiple transmitters and/or receivers for better connectivity. For example, when each node has three pairs of transceivers, eight nodes in the network can form a hypercube network as shown in Figure 9.5b.

Dense versus Sparse WDoMA   According to how closely wavelength channels are separated, a WDoMA system can be classified as either dense or sparse. In general, channel

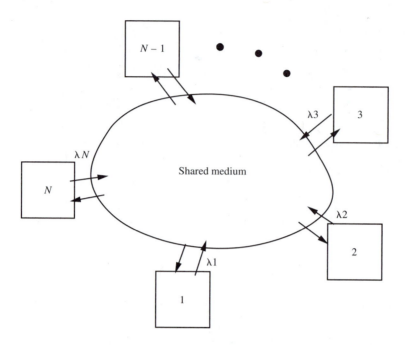

Figure 9.3   WDMA: All wavelength channels are coupled into the same shared medium and can be received by all nodes. Stations are geographically distributed over the shared medium, which can be in a physical star, bus, or ring topology interconnecting all the nodes. Because the operating wavelengths of transceivers of each node can vary, the interface between each station and the shared medium is generally based on wavelength independent coupling. As will be explained later, this has a higher power loss compared to wavelength dependent multiplexing in WDM.

separation of a dense WDoMA system is only a few times the channel bandwidth. For example, if the wavelength bandwidth is 1 GHz, a channel separation less than 10 GHz (or smaller than 0.1 nm in wavelength) is considered dense. On the other hand, if channel separation is greater than 100 GHz, it is considered sparse.

To maximize the total capacity, dense WDoMA is desirable. To achieve this, however, all tunable light sources, multiplexers, and demultiplexers need to be both high in tuning accuracy and frequency resolution. These usually imply a high implementation cost.

Coherent Detection versus Incoherent Detection   There are two techniques to tune to a wavelength channel: *coherent* and *incoherent*. As shown in Figure 9.6, coherent detection mixes the received optical signal with a local optical carrier. If the wavelength channel at λ_j is selected, the carrier frequency of the local oscillator is

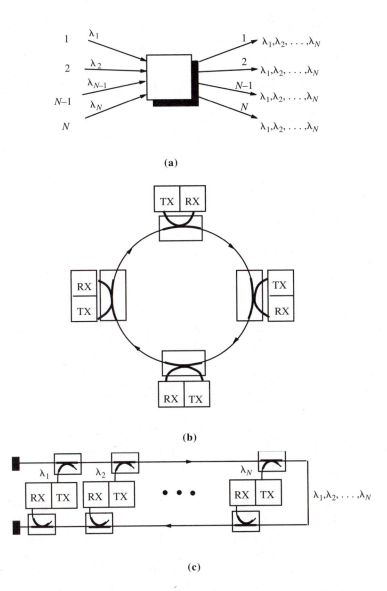

(a)

(b)

(c)

Figure 9.4   Different implementations of physical topologies for the shared medium in WDMA: (*a*) star, (*b*) ring, and (*c*) bus.

adjusted to be higher (or lower) than f_j by a radio frequency (RF) f_{IF}. After photodetection, a product term of the local oscillator and the channel being tuned to is generated. Because the product term is centered at frequency f_j, it can pass the IF (intermediate frequency) bandpass filter. All other product terms are outside the IF bandwidth and will be rejected.

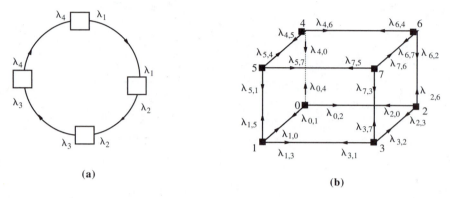

(a)

(b)

Figure 9.5   By properly setting the tuning wavelengths, different logical configurations can be formed: (a) logical ring with one transceiver pair at each node and (b) hypercube with three transceiver pairs at each node.

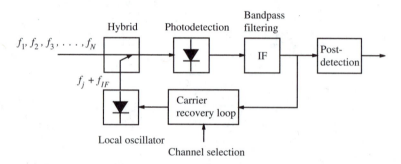

Figure 9.6   Wavelength channel tuning by coherent detection.

In principle, the coherent detection process described above has long been used in AM, FM, and TV broadcasting. Because a local oscillator made of a tunable laser diode can have a 50–100 nm tuning range and a narrow band IF filter can be easily implemented in the RF domain, coherent detection is attractive. However, as discussed in Chapter 15, coherent detection in optical communications requires a complex circuit to lock the local optical carrier to the incident light signal. As a result, it can be expensive.

To reduce the implementation cost, an alternative (shown in Figure 9.7) uses an optical filter to pass only the wavelength channel that is tuned to. In this case, incoherent detection, discussed in Chapter 7, can be used afterward. Compared to coherent detection, incoherent detection requires a narrow band optical filter.

Fixed Tuning versus Dynamic Tuning   A WDMA network can have its transceivers tuned at fixed frequencies or not. When the traffic intensity among stations is steady or does not fluctuate, fixed tuning provides a simple solution for interconnection. Some logical configurations shown previously in Figure 9.5 can be set up by fixed tuning.

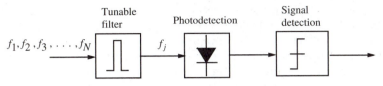

Figure 9.7 Wavelength channel tuning by incoherent detection with a tunable filter or demultiplexer before photodetection.

On the other hand, when there is a large variation in traffic intensity among stations, dynamic tuning provides a better throughput.

In dynamic tuning, transmitters and receivers can change their wavelength channels according to the traffic pattern. Based on the tuning protocol, dynamic tuning can also be done in three different ways: transmitter only, receiver only, and both. Common to these three methods, a good tuning protocol should be simple in implementation and high in performance (i.e., short delay and high throughput).

When dynamic tuning is done only at the transmitter side, the carrier frequency of the transmitter needs to be tuned to that of the destination receiver. Because there can be multiple transmitters that want to send data to the same receiver, an access control is necessary. In general, for a given wavelength channel, any proper TDoMA scheme discussed in Chapter 8 can be used.

When dynamic tuning is done only at the receiver side, destination receivers need to be informed of their source channels before transmission. This can be done by a separate signaling channel. In general, multiple receivers can be tuned to the same transmitter for multicasting. On the other hand, when the number of wavelength channels is limited and a group of transmitters share the same wavelength channel, they also need to resolve their access using an additional access protocol.

When dynamic tuning is performed at either the transmitter or receiver side, there can be blocking. For example, when tuning is performed at the transmitter side and a group of receivers share the same wavelength (when the number of wavelength channels is limited), a source transmitter cannot send its data if the wavelength of its destination is being used by another in the group. Similarly, when tuning is performed only at the receiver side and a group of transmitters share the same wavelength channel, a source transmitter cannot send its data and must wait if the wavelength is being used by another transmitter in the group.

From the above considerations, dynamic tuning at both the transmitter side and the receiver side is preferred to maximize the throughput. In this case, a good wavelength allocation algorithm and a separate signaling network for informing the transceiver pair are needed. When the total numbers of wavelength channels and stations are large, an efficient implementation for dynamic channel allocation becomes challenging.

Single-Hop versus Multihop As pointed out earlier, a physical WDMA network can have different logical configurations and can increase its connectivity by increasing the number of transceivers per node. A WDMA network is said to be **fully connected** or **single-hop** if a wavelength channel exists between any two nodes. For a network of N stations, this can be done by having one transmitter and $N - 1$ receivers at each station. As illustrated in Figure 9.8, each transmitter operates at a unique wavelength. Therefore, for a network of N nodes, there must be N wavelength channels. By having $N - 1$ receivers at each station tuned to the $N - 1$ wavelength channels of all other stations, the network has a logical connection shown in Figure 9.8. Clearly, it is a fully connected network. An example of this fully connected network is the LAMBDANET proposed by Bellcore [4].

When the size of the network is large, it is expensive to implement a fully connected network described above. Therefore, it may be necessary to accept a partially connected network to reduce the number of transceivers. In this case, two nodes may not be directly connected (i.e., there is no direct wavelength channel between the source transmitter and the destination receiver), and the network is called **partially connected** or **multihop.** Therefore, a number of intermediate nodes that receive data from one wavelength channel and forward it to another are needed. Logical configurations shown in Figure 9.5 are examples of multihop networks. A multihop network in general has a longer transmission delay and lower throughput because of intermediate buffering.

Packet Switching versus Circuit Switching   As discussed in Chapter 2, packet and circuit switching are two switching mechanisms to route data to their destinations. In WDMA, when transceivers periodically and deterministically tune their operating wavelengths, it is in the category of circuit switching. In this case, switching is performed in both the wavelength domain and time domain. This is similar to the space-and-time two-dimensional switching discussed in Chapter 2. On the other hand, when transceivers tune their wavelengths on a per packet basis, it is packet switching. In general, circuit switching is relatively simple in implementation and does not require a high tuning speed. On the other hand, packet switching is good for rapidly fluctuating traffic. When dynamic tuning is used according to packet destinations, a high throughput can be achieved.

9.1.2 COMPONENTS

To realize a WDoMA system, various optic and electro-optic devices are needed for carrier generations, multiplexing, and demultiplexing.

Tunable Light Sources   To fully utilize the large fiber bandwidth, light sources that can emit light over a large wavelength range (100 nm) are needed. Furthermore, for system operation such as dynamic tuning, it is highly desirable that they are tunable. To meet these requirements, various tunable laser diodes based on distributed-feedback (DFB), distributed Bragg-reflection (DBR), and multiple quantum-well (MQW) structures (discussed in Chapter 3) can be used. For satisfactory system operation, these devices have the following design criteria.

1. Large tunable range.   To transmit signals over a large fiber bandwidth, the tuning range of a laser diode should be as large as possible. This is of particular importance when dynamic transmitter tuning is used. On the other hand, for fixed tuning or dynamic receiver tuning, the tuning range needs only to overcome deviations of various operation conditions such as temperature, aging, and bias.

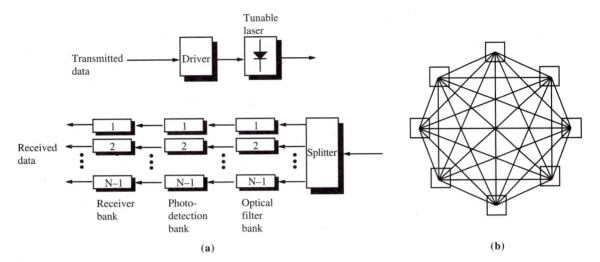

Figure 9.8   A fully connected, single-hop WDMA network: (a) implementation at each node and (b) logical configuration for $N = 8$.

2. Small linewidth.   To accommodate as many wavelength channels as possible in a given fiber bandwidth, the channel separation should be small. To achieve this, the laser linewidth should be small; otherwise, the interchannel interference (ICI) can be severe and cause a high bit error rate.

3. High frequency stability.   The output wavelength of a tunable laser can deviate because various factors change, such as temperature, bias current, and aging. To avoid channel interference and to simplify the task of receiver tuning, the output wavelength should be as stable as possible.

4. Rapid tuning.   When dynamic transmitter tuning is used, rapid tuning from one wavelength channel to another is important for efficient transmission and high-speed switching.

Multiplexers and Couplers In WDoMA, wavelength channels need to be coupled to the shared medium for transmission. To achieve this, a multiplexer or a coupler is used. A multiplexer is a device that mixes input signals of different wavelengths based on the principle of either grating (wave diffraction) or interference. As a result, multiplexer output is strongly input-wavelength dependent, and the wavelengths used in WDM or WDMA cannot be changed arbitrarily once the multiplexer is designed (unless it is also tunable).

A coupler, on the other hand, mixes input light based on the principle of power coupling. As a result, the mixed output is relatively wavelength independent. Couplers are inexpensive and flexible for different input wavelengths. The primary disadvantage of couplers is their relatively large power loss compared to multiplexers. The reason for this will be explained later in the chapter. Some important criteria for good multiplexers and couplers are given below.

1. **Large number of input ports.**   To accommodate a large number of wavelength channels, a multiplexer or coupler should be able to mix a large number of input signals. In general, a large number of input ports implies a larger device size, a more complex design, and larger power loss.

2. **Low power loss.**   When the incident light signals are mixed, there is a coupling loss. In general, the larger the multiplexer/coupler size, the larger the coupling loss.

3. **Equal mixing efficiency.**   When a number of wavelength channels are mixed, it is desirable that they experience approximately the same amount of power loss. This will simplify the receiver design (a small dynamic range is sufficient) and result in equal detection performance for different wavelength channels.

4. **Low polarization dependence.**   In general, the mixing efficiency of a frequency dependent multiplexer is polarization dependent. This can be due to the anisotropy of the multiplexer device. Polarization dependence can be reduced either by using isotropic material or improving the multiplexing design.

Demultiplexers and Splitters   When all wavelength channels are received at a receiver end, they need to be demultiplexed or filtered for selective detection. When incoherent detection is used, demultiplexing or filtering can be done in either the spatial domain (grating), frequency domain (wave interference or narrowband amplification), or polarization domain. They all have the following design objectives.

1. **Large free spectral range (FSR).**   One FSR is an interval between two wavelengths that have the same demultiplexing or filtering effect. In other words, two carriers with one FSR separation will be demultiplexed to the same output path or can both pass the filter. To avoid ambiguity in demultiplexing over a large frequency range, a large FSR is needed.

2. **High resolution.**   A demultiplexer or filter also needs to differentiate wavelength channels of close separation. This implies a large diffraction capability from grating devices or a narrow band from filtering devices. In general, the ratio of one FSR to the frequency resolution determines the number of WDoMA channels that can be accommodated in the system.

3. **Easy tuning control.**   For practical operation, it is desirable that the wavelength tuning can be done easily and is insensitive to offsets.

4. **Short tuning delay.**   For high-speed dynamic receiver tuning, the tuning device needs to go quickly from one channel to another. In general, demultiplexing or filtering devices based on either the electro-optic or acousto-optic effect are slower in tuning compared to semiconductor devices.

5. **Low power loss.**   Similar to wavelength channel mixing, there can be power loss because of various limitations. A low power loss can reduce the burden on the total power budget.

6. **Low polarization dependence.**   Similar to wavelength mixing, when tuning is not in the polarization domain, it is important to maintain the same channel tuning when input channels have different polarizations. On the other hand, if tuning is based on polarization,

channel tuning is sensitive to the input polarizations, and they should be aligned first before filtering or demultiplexing.

9.2   WAVELENGTH DIVISION MULTIPLE ACCESS NETWORK ACCESS AND ROUTING

In WDMA, wavelength channels are the shared resource. To access the network, each source node needs to first acquire a wavelength channel. To ensure proper transmission to the final destination, either the destination receiver must be tuned to the wavelength channel or there must exist an efficient routing algorithm that can forward the data to the destination. Over the last few years, many access protocols and routing algorithms have been proposed [5]–[7]. In general, a good WDMA access protocol should both perform satisfactorily and be easy to implement. That is, from the system perspective, the protocol should achieve a high access efficiency, high throughput, and low transmission delay. From the implementation perspective, the required tuning speeds of tunable devices should be feasible, the number of total wavelength channels needed should be attainable, and the channel allocation algorithm should be simple and fast.

   This section discusses routing algorithms for fixed tuning networks and switching performance for dynamic tuning networks. Frequency reuse, which reduces the number of wavelength channels required as the network size increases, and its possible implementations are also presented.

9.2.1   LOGICAL CONFIGURATIONS AND ROUTING IN FIXED TUNING WDMA

When the traffic pattern in a WDMA network is stationary, fixed tuning is a good choice to simplify the design and relax the fast tuning requirement. As mentioned earlier, by choosing the tuning wavelengths of individual transceivers properly, a WDMA network can have a logical configuration independent of its physical connection. Once the logical configuration is determined, simple and efficient routing algorithms can be derived. Below three important logical configurations and their routing algorithms are presented.

Hypercube   A hypercube configuration has been used in computer communications for multiprocessors [8]. For a given $N = 2^p$ nodes, each node has p pairs of transceivers connected to p different nodes in duplex. A hypercube network of $p = 4$ is illustrated in Figure 9.9.

   In a hypercube, each node has an address represented by a binary p-tuple $\overline{A} = (a_0, a_1, \ldots, a_{p-1})$. For two nodes whose addresses differ by only one bit, there exists a duplex link between them. When a node of address $\overline{A}_i$ has data to send to node $\overline{A}_j$, the data will be forwarded through k steps, where k is the number of different bits between $\overline{A}_i$ and $\overline{A}_j$. In the worst case, as a result, the number of hops is p, the same number as the transceiver pairs per node. When the traffic pattern is uniform, it can be easily verified that the average number of hops is $(p/2)N/(N-1)$ (see Problem 9–3).

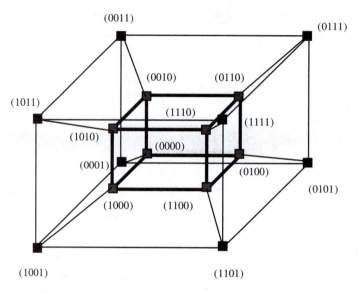

Figure 9.9   A 16-node hypercube at $p = 4$.

Example	**MULTI-HOP IN HYPERCUBE** Consider a hypercube network of $N = 128 = 2^7$ nodes. In this
9.1	case, each node has a 7-bit address $(b_0, b_1, b_2, b_3, b_4, b_5, b_6)$. To route data to the destination, the addresses of intermediate nodes on the route must be determined. To do this, first identify the address bits that are different between the source and destination. For those different bits, all the addresses of the intermediate nodes can be generated by changing those different bits one at a time and from left to right.

For example, if the source node has an address $(1,0,1,1,0,0,0)$ and the destination has an address $(0,0,0,1,1,0,1)$, the addresses have four different bits and it requires to route four hops. The intermediate nodes have the following addresses: $(0,0,1,1,0,0,0)$, $(0,0,0,1,0,0,0)$, $(0,0,0,1,1,0,0)$, and finally the destination $(0,0,0,1,1,0,1)$. ■

---

deBruijn Network   In a hypercube, the number of nodes is a power of 2. In addition, for a given N, it requires a large number of transceiver pairs. One way to relax these constraints is to use a deBruijn configuration [9] shown in Figure 9.10. Similar to hypercube, a node can have an address $\overline{A} = (a_0, a_1, \ldots, a_{H-1})$, where each a_i can be from 0 to $p - 1$. Therefore, the total number of nodes in a deBruijn configuration is $N = p^H$.

According to the above addressing scheme, a node of address $\overline{A}$ is connected in *simplex* (unidirection) to p nodes with addresses of the form $(a_1, a_2, \ldots, a_{H-1}, b)$, where b ranges from 0 to $p - 1$. From the given connectivity, when a node of address $\overline{A}_i$ sends data to another node of address $\overline{A}_j$, the source node needs to first find the longest *rightmost* subsequence in its address so that it matches the *leftmost* portion of the destination address.

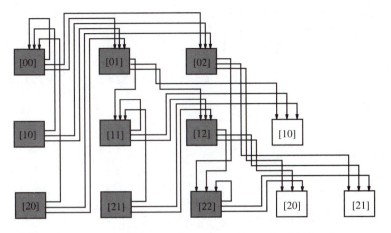

Figure 9.10   A deBruijn configuration with $p = 3$ and $H = 2$.

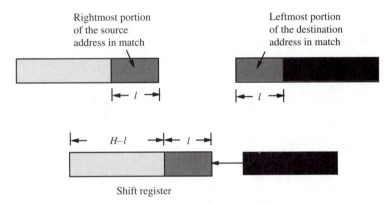

Figure 9.11   Longest match of the rightmost portion of the source address and the leftmost portion of the destination address determines the number of hops in a deBruijn configuration.

This is illustrated in Figure 9.11. If the length of the longest subsequence is l, the number of hops is $H - l$. Thus the maximum number of hops is H.

ROUTING IN DEBRUIJN   Consider a deBruijn configuration with $p = 3$ and $H = 6$. Assume the source and destination have addresses $(0, 2, 0, \underline{0, 0, 0})$ and $(\underline{0, 0, 0}, 1, 1, 2)$, respectively, where the bits underlined represent the longest portion of the rightmost portion of the source address and the leftmost portion of the destination address. According to the connection, the minimum distance route is thus from $(0,2,0,0,0,0)$, then $(2,0,0,0,0,1)$, $(0,0,0,0,1,1)$, and finally to $(0,0,0,1,1,2)$. ■

Example 9.2

When the traffic pattern is uniform, the probability of having the length of the longest sequence equal to l is approximately

$$P[l] \approx Ap^{-l}$$

where A is a constant that can be determined from normalizing the total probability. From

$$\sum_{l=0}^{H} P[l] = 1 = A\frac{1 - p^{-(H+1)}}{1 - p^{-1}}$$

$A = (1 - p^{-1})/(1 - p^{-(H+1)})$ and

$$P[l] \approx \frac{1 - p^{-1}}{1 - p^{-(H+1)}} p^{-l}. \qquad [9.1]$$

The average number of hops is thus

$$\overline{H} = \sum_{l=0}^{H} P[l](H - l) = H - \sum_{l=0}^{H} P[l]l$$

$$\approx H - \frac{p - (p-1)pH/N}{(p - 1)(p - N^{-1})}. \qquad [9.2]$$

When $N = p^H \gg 1$,

$$\boxed{\overline{H} \approx H - \frac{1}{p - 1} = H - \frac{1}{N^{1/H} - 1}.} \qquad [9.3]$$

Equation 9.3 shows that $\overline{H}$ is between H and $H - 1$. In other words, the routing usually takes the maximum number of hops to reach the destination.

Example 9.3

HYPERCUBE VERSUS DEBRUIJN   Compare the hypercube and deBruijn configurations of the same number of nodes $N = 2^9 = 8^3$. In this case, each node in the hypercube has 9 transceiver pairs and the average number of hops is approximately 4.5. On the other hand, the deBruijn only needs 3 transceiver pairs per node but averages 7.5 hops. ∎

Perfect Shuffle Network Another important logical configuration is called the perfect shuffle network (PSN) [5]–[7]. As shown in Figure 9.12, the network consists of k columns of p^k nodes. Each node is connected to p nodes in the next column. As a result, each node in a perfect shuffle network has p transceiver pairs, and the total number of nodes is

$$N = kp^k \qquad [9.4]$$

From the configuration, each node in a PSN is represented by a $(k + 1)$-tuple address $\overline{A} = (c, r_1, r_2, \ldots, r_k)$, where $0 \leq c \leq k - 1$ is the column address, and $0 \leq r_i \leq p - 1$ for

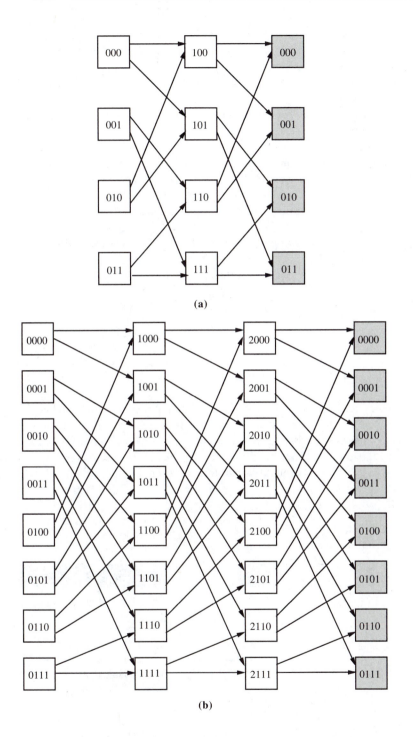

Figure 9.12 Perfect shuffle networks: (a) $k = p = 2$; (b) $k = 3$ and $p = 2$.

$i = 1, \ldots, k$ is the row address. As shown in Figure 9.12, node $(c, r_1, r_2, \ldots, r_k)$ is connected to nodes $(c', r_2, r_3, \ldots, r_k, R)$, where $c' = (c + 1) \bmod k$ and R ranges from 0 to $p - 1$.

From the given connectivity, to send data between two nodes on the same column or the same c address, it takes exactly k hops. This can be understood as follows. Because the column address is the same, there must be at least k hops. To reach the destination in k hops, the connection path consists of nodes with row addresses that are left-shifted versions of the source addresses, with the destination row address as the input in each shift. This is illustrated in Figure 9.13.

When the destination node and source node have different column addresses, the number of hops is at least $D = (k + c_d - c_s) \bmod k$, where c_d is the destination column address and c_s is the source column address. After these D hops, the column addresses can be made the same. Furthermore, the row addresses can also be made the same if the rightmost portion of the source row address of length $k - D$ is equal to the corresponding leftmost portion of the destination row address. If this is not the case, it will take another k steps as described earlier.

The maximum number of hops is thus

$$H_{max} = 2k - 1. \tag{9.5}$$

Furthermore, the average number of hops is

$$\overline{H} = \frac{1}{N-1} \left\{ (p^k - 1)k + \left[\sum_{D=1}^{k-1} \frac{1}{p^{k-D}} D + \sum_{D=1}^{k-1} \left(1 - \frac{1}{p^{k-D}} \right)(k+D) \right] p^k \right\} \tag{9.6}$$

where the first term is due to the case $D = k$, and the second term is due to $D < k$. In the first case, there are $p^k - 1$ possible destinations from a given source and it takes k hops in each case. In the second case, when there are $k - D$ bits matched (with probability $p^{-[k-D]}$), the number of hops is D; otherwise, the number of hops is $k + D$ with probability $1 - p^{-(k-D)}$. With straightforward manipulation, Equation (9.6) reduces to

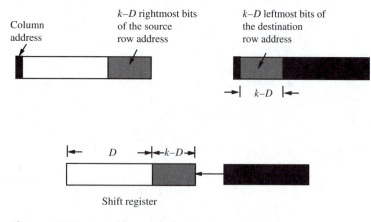

Figure 9.13   Address shifts from the source to the destination in a perfect shuffle network.

$$\overline{H} = \frac{1}{N-1}\left\{N\left[\frac{1}{2}(3k-1) - \frac{1}{p-1}\right] + \frac{k}{p-1}\right\}. \qquad \textbf{[9.7]}$$

When N is large,

$$\overline{H} \approx \frac{1}{2}(3k-1) - \frac{1}{p-1}. \qquad \textbf{[9.8]}$$

DESIGN TRADE-OFF   Equation (9.8) shows that the perfect shuffle network has a flexibility of trading the average number of hops with the number of transceiver pairs. For example, for a given N, because k decreases as p increases, $\overline{H}$ can be reduced by increasing p. Consider a network on the order of 450 nodes, which can be realized by either

Example 9.4

$$N_1 = 2 \times 16^2 = 512$$

or

$$N_2 = 6 \times 2^6 = 384.$$

For these two cases, increasing the number of transceiver pairs from 2 to 16 decreases the average number of hops from 7.5 to 2.4.

Equation (9.8) also indicates that an increase of $\overline{H}$ by 1.5 at a fixed p can increase the network size by approximately p times. ∎

A summary of the network size, the maximum number of hops, and the average number of hops of hypercube, deBruijn, and perfect shuffle networks is given in Table 9.2. For simple comparison, Figure 9.14 also shows the different average numbers of hops for different configurations and transceiver pairs (p).

Table 9.2   Summary of hypercube, deBrujin, and perfect shuffle configurations.

Configuration	N	H_{max}	$\overline{H}$
Hypercube	2^p	p	$p/2$
deBruijn	p^H	H	$H - \frac{1}{p-1}$
Perfect shuffle	kp^k	$2k-1$	$\frac{1}{2}(3k-1) - \frac{1}{p-1}$ when $N \gg 1$

Adaptive Routing   The routing algorithms for the three configurations discussed above are simple. However, they are good only when the traffic pattern is uniform. When the traffic pattern is nonuniform, it can suffer long transmission delay and/or high packet loss probability. For example, when several upstream nodes send data to the same downstream node, there will be heavy traffic congestion. To solve this problem, adaptive routing

Average number of hops

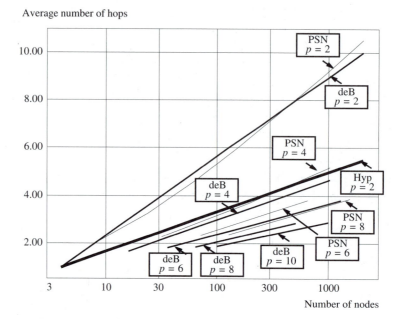

Figure 9.14   Average number of hops at different logical configurations and number of transceivers per node (p) for perfect shuffle network (PSN), deBruijn (deB), and hypercube (Hyp).

has been proposed [5]. In the proposed approach, data packets will be forwarded to a node that has minimal data in its receiver buffer. This can in principle balance the traffic and reduce the delay.

9.2.2 DYNAMIC TUNING WDMA

When the traffic pattern changes rapidly and high-speed tuning technology is available, a more efficient medium access control is to allow transceivers to tune dynamically. As a result, single-hop can be achieved by setting up a common wavelength channel between the source transmitter and destination receiver.

From the logical configurations discussed above, note that a wavelength channel can be mapped logically to a spatial channel. Therefore, dynamic tuning in WDMA is in principle logically equivalent to dynamic spatial switching. Consequently, dynamic tuning can be performed by borrowing switching techniques used in packet switching or circuit switching networks. Below dynamic tuning based on circuit switching is discussed and how to represent dynamic tuning with a spatial circuit switching network is explained. From the equivalence, the blocking probability can be evaluated according to Lee's approximation [59]. For packet switching, various algorithms can be found in [7].

To see the logical equivalence of a dynamic tuning WDMA network to a spatial switching network, first consider a WDMA network where dynamic tuning is done at both the transmitter and receiver side and each node has one transceiver pair. In this case, if the total number of nodes is N, the equivalent switching network is simply a single $N \times N$ crossbar switch as shown in Figure 9.15a. In other words, as long as the destination node is idle, the source node can find an available wavelength channel for transmission.

When each node has p transceiver pairs and all are tunable, the equivalent switching network consists of N deconcentrators, a $pN \times pN$ spatial switch (or p parallel $N \times N$ switches) and N concentrators. In this case, as long as the destination node has one idle receiver, a wavelength channel can be available for transmission.

When the number of nodes (N) is greater than the number of wavelength channels (N_λ), the equivalent switching network consists of concentrators, spatial switches, and deconcentrators. For example, if both transmitters and receivers are tunable, one can have the equivalent switching network shown in Figure 9.15b. As shown, there is an $N{:}N_\lambda$ switch, an $N_\lambda{:}N_\lambda$ switch, and an $N_\lambda{:}N$ switch. In this case, if the ratio N to N_λ is S, according to Lee's approximation, and the probability flow shown in Figure 9.16a, the blocking probability is

$$P_{bk} = [1 - (1 - Sp)^2]^{N_\lambda} \qquad \textbf{[9.9]}$$

where p is the active probability of each node.

When transceivers are not both tunable, the equivalent switching network shown in Figure 9.15b needs modifications. If only transmitters are tunable, as shown in Figure 9.15c, the switching network consists of an $N{:}N_\lambda$ switch, an $N_\lambda \times N_\lambda$ switch, and N_λ 1:S deconcentrators. On the other hand, if only receivers are tunable, as shown in Figure 9.15d, the switching network consists of N_λ concentrators, an $N_\lambda \times N_\lambda$ switch, and an $N_\lambda \times N$ spatial switch.

From Figure 9.16b or 9.16c and using the same Lee's approximation, the blocking probability is

$$P_{bk} = 1 - (1 - Sp)^2. \qquad \textbf{[9.10]}$$

BLOCKING PROBABILITY IN DYNAMIC TUNING   Assume $S = N_\lambda = 10$ and $N = 100$. When both transmitters and receivers are tunable, from Equation (9.9), the blocking probability at $p = 0.05$ is

Example 9.5

$$P_{bk} = [1 - (1 - 10p)^2]^{10} = 0.056.$$

On the other hand, when only either transmitters or receivers are tunable, from Equation (9.20), the blocking probability at the same p is

$$P_{bk} = 1 - (10p)^2 = 0.75$$

Therefore, it is important to have tunability at both the transmitters and receivers when Sp is close to 1. ∎

9.2.3 FREQUENCY REUSE

In a WDMA network where all wavelength channels are coupled in the same shared medium, the number of wavelengths required is

$$N_\lambda = pN \qquad \textbf{[9.11]}$$

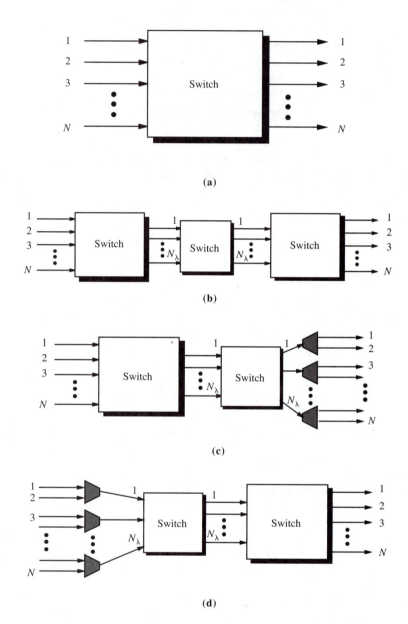

Figure 9.15 Equivalent spatial switching networks for dynamic wavelength tuning: (a) $N = N_\lambda$; (b) $N > N_\lambda$ and both transmitters and receivers are dynamically tunable—equivalence of tunability is represented by the two $N \times N_\lambda$ switches; (c) $N < N_\lambda$ and only transmitters are tunable—equivalence of the wavelength sharing is represented by the N_λ deconcentrators; (d) $N < N_\lambda$ and only receivers are tunable—equivalence of the wavelength sharing is represented by the N_λ concentrators.

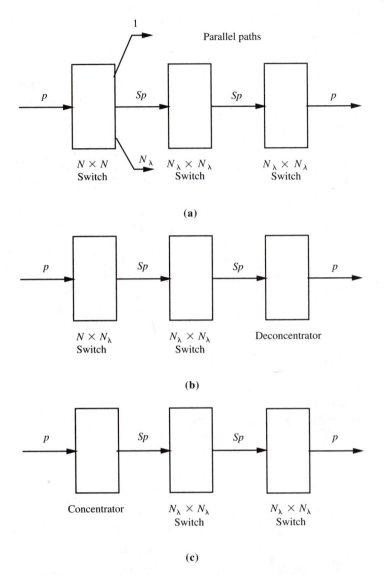

Figure 9.16 Probability flows of (a) dynamic tuning at both ends, (b) only at the transmitter side, and (c) only at the receiver side.

where N is the total number of nodes and p is the number of transceiver pairs per node. Therefore, when N and p are large, the number of channels can be too large to be implementable.

To reduce the number of wavelengths required, the concept of frequency reuse has been proposed. There are several approaches to achieving this. First, multiple shared media can be used for wavelength isolation. As illustrated in Figure 9.17, a logical hypercube configuration can be implemented by partitioning wavelength channels into three physical networks. As shown, for a network size of 8, the number of wavelength channels can be reduced from 24 to 8. As a result, frequency resolution is reduced by a factor of 3. However, three separate sets of fibers, couplers, and splitters are needed.

Another frequency reuse approach is to terminate the **wavelength channel** at its destination and reuse it for a different signal. As shown in Figure 9.18, with the use of optical add-drop multiplexers (ADMs), the number of wavelength channels reduces from 24 to only 5. An ADM implementation for this purpose will be discussed in Section 9.7.

The third approach to frequency reuse employs **wavelength converters** (WCs) [10]. As an example, consider the case that eight nodes are grouped into two WDMA networks shown in Figure 9.19. Assume each node has one transmitter and four receivers, where three of the four receivers receive signals from other nodes in the same group, and the fourth one receives signals from the other group through the WC. From this arrangement, full connectivity can be achieved by using five different wavelengths, where four wavelength channels are used for traffic within each group and one wavelength channel is used for intergroup traffic. Compared to the LAMBDANET, the number of wavelength channels is reduced from eight to five, and the number of receivers per node is reduced from seven to four. In general, when there is heavy intragroup traffic and light intergroup traffic, the above grouping and use of WCs make sense and can greatly reduce the hardware cost.

WCs can also be used in conjunction with photonic switches [11]. As illustrated in Figure 9.20, four nodes can be interconnected by two-stage 2×2 photonic switches, where each photonic switch routes two wavelength inputs, λ_1 and λ_2, to two different output ports. The routing can be determined by external tuning control (e.g., see the Mach-Zehnder interferometer implementation discussed in Section 9.6). Because the two wavelengths at the output of each 2×2 switch can be in different permutation, the following WCs are used to convert them to the desirable permutation.

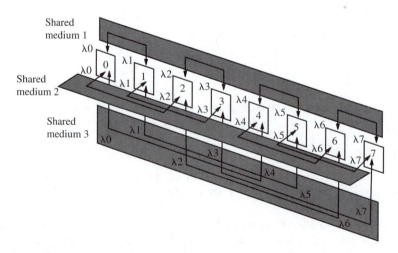

Figure 9.17   Frequency reuse by wavelength partitioning.

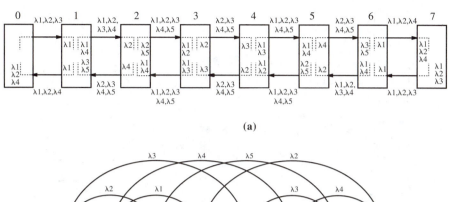

(a)

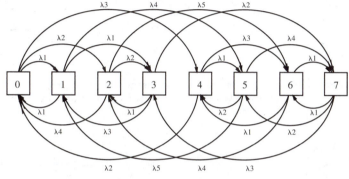

(b)

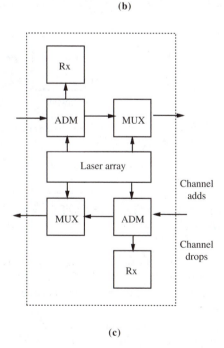

(c)

Figure 9.18 Frequency reuse by add-drop multiplexing: (*a*) physical connection, (*b*) logical connection, and (*c*) implementation of each node.

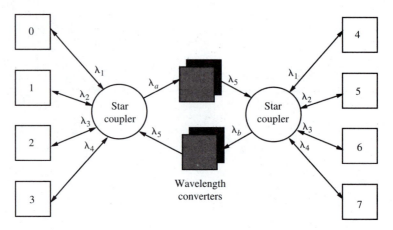

Figure 9.19   Frequency reuse by wavelength converters as optical gateways, where wavelengths λ_a and λ_b can be one of λ_1 to λ_4.

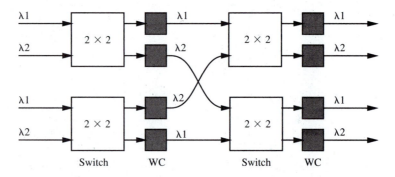

Figure 9.20   Frequency reuse by wavelength converters and wavelength photonic switches.

9.3 TRANSMISSION PERFORMANCE IN WAVELENGTH DIVISION MULTIPLEXING

When multiple wavelengths are multiplexed or coupled into a single optical fiber, they can interfere with each other. As illustrated in Figure 9.21, at a channel separation of $\Delta\omega$ (in circular frequency), there can be a strong interchannel interference (ICI) when $\Delta\omega$ is comparable to the bandwidth of each channel.

As mentioned earlier, channel tuning can be done by either coherent detection or optical filtering followed by incoherent detection. This section analyzes the ICI and the power penalty for both cases.

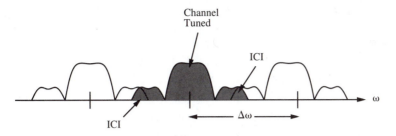

Figure 9.21   Interchannel interference.

9.3.1   Incoherent Detection

Analysis for ICI using incoherent detection has been studied in detail [12]. Below is a simple case where all WDM signals have the same polarization. This assumption leads to the worst case ICI, where all product terms from photodetection are included.

When the input channels have the same polarization, the total incident light can be considered as a scalar wave given by

$$x(t) = \sqrt{2P_{inc}} \sum_i a_i(t) \cos(\omega_i t + \phi_i)$$

where $a_i(t)$ is a pulse train of values 0 or 1 according to on-off keying (OOK). When $x(t)$ is filtered by an optical filter, such as a fiber Fabry-Perot filter, tuned at channel j,

$$y(t) = \sqrt{2P_{inc}} \sum_i h_j[i]^{1/2} a_i(t) \cos(\omega_i t + \phi_i)$$

where $h_j[i]$ is the frequency response of channel i. After photodetection, the photocurrent is

$$i_{ph}(t) = \mathcal{R}|y(t)|^2 \approx \mathcal{R}P_{inc} \sum_i h_j[i]a_i(t)$$

$$+ 2\mathcal{R}P_{inc} \sum_{i>k} h_j[i]^{1/2} h_j[k]^{1/2} a_i(t) a_j(t) \cos([i-k]\Delta\omega t) \qquad \textbf{[9.12]}$$

where $\mathcal{R}$ is the photodiode responsivity, $a_i(t)^2 = a_i(t)$ from OOK, $\Delta\omega$ is the channel separation, and all high-frequency terms ($\omega_i + \omega_k$) are dropped. From Equation (9.12), the total ICI power after low-pass filtering with a certain transfer function $H(\omega)$ is

$$P_{ICI} = \mathcal{R}^2 P_{inc}^2 \left[\sum_{i \neq j} h_j[i]^2 \int_{-\infty}^{\infty} S_a(\omega)|H(\omega)|^2 \frac{d\omega}{2\pi} + \sum_{i>k} h_j[i]h_j[k] \times \right.$$

$$\left. \int_{-\infty}^{\infty} [S_a^{(2)}(\omega - [i-k]\Delta\omega) + S_a^{(2)}(\omega + [i-k]\Delta\omega)]|H(\omega)|^2 \frac{d\omega}{2\pi} \right] \qquad \textbf{[9.13]}$$

where $S_a(\omega)$ is the power spectral density of the baseband OOK $a_i(t)$ signal, and $S_a^{(2)}(\omega) = S_a(\omega) \otimes S_a(\omega)$ is the convolution of $S_a(\omega)$ with itself. From the above expression, the **signal-to-interference ratio** (SIR) is

$$\text{SIR} = \frac{h_j[j]^2 \int_{-\infty}^{\infty} S_a(\omega)|H(\omega)|^2 \frac{d\omega}{2\pi}}{\int_{-\infty}^{\infty} \left\{ \sum_{i \neq j} h_j[i]^2 S_a(\omega) + \sum_{i > k} h_j[i] h_j[k] \left[S_a^{(2)}(\omega - [i-k]\Delta\omega) + S_a^{(2)}(\omega + [i-k]\Delta\omega) \right] \right\} \left| H(\omega) \right|^2 \frac{d\omega}{2\pi}} \qquad [9.14]$$

From Equations (9.13) and (9.14), ICI can be expressed as

$$P_{ICI} = \mathcal{R}^2 P_{inc}^2 \times \text{SIR}^{-1} \times h_j[j]^2 \int_{-\infty}^{\infty} S_a(\omega)|H(\omega)|^2 \frac{d\omega}{2\pi}. \qquad [9.15]$$

To find the SIR given by Equation (9.14), numerical computations from the given S_a and $H(\omega)$ can be used.

From Equation (9.15), the total equivalent noise power is

$$\sigma_{tot}^2 = \sigma_n^2 + P_{ICI} = q\mathcal{R}P_{inc} \sum_i h_j[i]^2 \int_{-\infty}^{\infty} |H(\omega)|^2 \frac{d\omega}{2\pi} + P_{ICI}$$

$$= \sigma_{n0}^2 \left[\sum_i h_j[i]^2 + h_j[j]^2 \text{SIR}^{-1} \text{SNR}_0 \right] \qquad [9.16]$$

where

$$\sigma_{n0}^2 = q\mathcal{R}P_{inc} \int_{-\infty}^{\infty} |H(\omega)|^2 \frac{d\omega}{2\pi} \qquad [9.17]$$

is the shot noise power in the case of a single channel and without the use of the optical filter, and SNR_0 is the corresponding signal-to-noise ratio given by

$$\text{SNR}_0 = \frac{\mathcal{R}^2 P_{inc}^2 \int_{-\infty}^{\infty} S_a(\omega)|H(\omega)|^2 \frac{d\omega}{2\pi}}{\sigma_{n0}^2} = \frac{\mathcal{R}^2 P_{inc}^2 \int_{-\infty}^{\infty} S_a(\omega)|H(\omega)|^2 \frac{d\omega}{2\pi}}{q\mathcal{R}P_{inc} \int_{-\infty}^{\infty} |H(\omega)|^2 \frac{d\omega}{2\pi}} \qquad [9.18]$$

Including the ICI in the total noise power, the actual SNR is

$$\text{SNR} = \frac{h_j[j]^2}{\sum_i h_j[i]^2 + h_j[j]^2 \text{SIR}^{-1} \text{SNR}_0} \text{SNR}_0. \qquad [9.19]$$

Power Penalty   From Equation (9.19), the power penalty or the additional power factor to compensate for the ICI is

$$P_p \overset{\text{def}}{=} \frac{\text{SNR}_0}{\text{SNR}} = \frac{\sum_i h_j[i]^2}{h_j[j]^2(1 - \text{SNR}/\text{SIR})}. \qquad [9.20]$$

FP FILTERING FOR INCOHERENT DETECTION   Consider a fiber FP filter with finesse, $\mathcal{F}$, equal to 100π used as the optical filter. If there are 50 WDM channels, $h_j[i]$ is

$$h_j[i] = \frac{1}{1 + (2\mathcal{F}/\pi)\sin^2([i-j]/100)} \qquad \text{[9.21]}$$

Example 9.6

where $i = 0, 1, \ldots, 49$. From numerical computation,

$$\sum_{i=0}^{49} h_j[i]^2 = 1.796.$$

From Equation (9.19), the power penalty is thus

$$P_p = 1.796 \frac{1}{1 - \text{SNR}/\text{SIR}}.$$

This shows that even when $\text{SIR} \gg \text{SNR}$, there is a power penalty of 1.796, or 2.54 dB, because of nonideal optical channel filtering. ∎

9.3.2 COHERENT DETECTION

ICI in the case of coherent detection has also been analyzed [13][14]. In this case, the received signal is mixed with a local oscillator. If the carrier frequency of the local oscillator is at $\omega_j - \omega_{IF}$, from Equation (15.9) given in Chapter 15, the photodetection output can be expressed as

$$i_{ph}(t) = 2\mathcal{R}\sqrt{P_{loc}P_{inc}} \sum_i a_i(t) \cos[(\omega_{IF}t + (i-j)\Delta\omega t + \phi_i(t)] \qquad \text{[9.22]}$$

where $\mathcal{R}$ is the responsivity of the photodiode, P_{loc} is the optical power of the local oscillator, P_{inc} is the peak power of the received optical signal, and $a_i(t)$ and $\phi_i(t)$ are the amplitude and phase of carrier i, respectively.[1]

From Equation (9.22), the interchannel interference from channel i is

$$ICI_i = 2\mathcal{R}\sqrt{P_{loc}P_{inc}}a_i(t) \cos[\omega_{IF}t + (i-j)\Delta\omega t + \phi_i(t)].$$

If the power spectral density (PSD) of $a_i(t)\cos(\phi_i[t])$ is $S_a(\omega)$ and the IF filter has a transfer function of $H(\omega)$, the total ICI power at the output of the IF filter is

$$P_{ICI} = 2\mathcal{R}^2 P_{loc}P_{inc} \sum_{i \neq j} \int_{-\infty}^{\infty} [S_a(\omega - \omega_{IF} - [i-j]\Delta\omega)$$

$$+ S_a(\omega + \omega_{IF} + [i-j]\Delta\omega)] \left| H(\omega) \right|^2 \frac{d\omega}{2\pi} \qquad \text{[9.23]}$$

---

1 When on-off keying (OOK) is used, $a_i(t)$ is a pulse train with peak values between 0 and 1 and $\phi_i(t)$ is a constant. On the other hand, when phase-shift keying (PSK) is used, $a_i(t) = 1$ and $\phi_i(t)$ is a pulse function with peak values 0 and π (binary PSK). For detailed discussion on various digital modulation schemes, see Chapter 15.

The signal-to-interference power ratio (SIR) is thus

$$\text{SIR} = \frac{\int_{-\infty}^{\infty} \left[S_a(\omega-\omega_{IF}) + S_a(\omega+\omega_{IF})\right] |H(\omega)|^2 \frac{d\omega}{2\pi}}{\sum_{i \neq j} \int_{-\infty}^{\infty} \left[S_a(\omega-\omega_{IF}-[i-j]\Delta\omega) + S_a(\omega+\omega_{IF}+[i-j]\Delta\omega)\right] |H(\omega)|^2 \frac{d\omega}{2\pi}}. \qquad \textbf{[9.24]}$$

From Equations (9.23) and (9.24),

$$P_{ICI} = 2\mathcal{R}^2 P_{loc} P_{inc} \times \text{SIR}^{-1} \int_{-\infty}^{\infty} \left[S_a(\omega - \omega_{IF}) + S_a(\omega + \omega_{IF})\right] |H(\omega)|^2 \frac{d\omega}{2\pi}. \qquad \textbf{[9.25]}$$

As with incoherent detection, the SIR given by Equation (9.24) can be obtained from numerical computations at the given $S_a(\omega)$ and $H(\omega)$. When ICI is added to the shot noise, the total noise power is

$$\sigma_{tot}^2 = \sigma_{n0}^2 + P_{ICI} = \sigma_{n0}^2[1 + \text{SNR}_0/\text{SIR}] \qquad \textbf{[9.26]}$$

where

$$\sigma_{n0}^2 = q\mathcal{R}P_{loc} \int_{-\infty}^{\infty} |H(\omega)| \frac{d\omega}{2\pi} \qquad \textbf{[9.27]}$$

and

$$\text{SNR}_0 = \frac{2\mathcal{R}^2 P_{loc} P_{inc} \int_{-\infty}^{\infty} [P(\omega - \omega_{IF}) + P(\omega + \omega_{IF})] |H(\omega)|^2 \frac{d\omega}{2\pi}}{\sigma_n^2}. \qquad \textbf{[9.28]}$$

Equation (9.26) tells that the total equivalent noise power increases as the signal power increases. Considering the total noise power, the actual SNR is

$$\text{SNR} = \frac{\text{SNR}_0}{1 + \text{SNR}_0/\text{SIR}}. \qquad \textbf{[9.29]}$$

When $\text{SNR}_0 \to \infty$,

$$\text{SNR} = \text{SNR}_0 \frac{1}{1 + \text{SNR}_0/\text{SIR}} \to \text{SIR}. \qquad \textbf{[9.30]}$$

This means the actual SNR is bounded on the high end by the SIR.

From Chapter 15, the error detection probability can be expressed as

$$P_E = Q(\sqrt{\gamma \text{SNR}}) \approx \frac{1}{\sqrt{2\pi \gamma \text{SNR}}} e^{-\gamma \text{SNR}/2} \qquad \textbf{[9.31]}$$

where Q is the Q-function and γ is a parameter depending on the modulation scheme. For heterodyne OOK, PSK, and FSK, γ is $\frac{1}{2}$, 2, and 1, respectively.

REDUCTION OF SNR DUE TO ICI   When the SNR_0 in the absence of ICI is 20 dB, or 100, at | **Example**
an SIR of 10 dB, 20 dB, and 30 dB, respectively, the actual SNR is 9.6 dB (9.1), 16.9 dB (50), and | **9.7**
19.6 dB (90.9), respectively. Clearly when $SNR_0 \gg SIR$, the actual SNR is strongly limited by SIR.
From Equation (9.31), the error detection probability is 3.7×10^{-6}, 7.8×10^{-13}, and 7.6×10^{-22},
respectively. ∎

Power Penalty   From Equations (9.28)–(9.31), the power penalty is

$$\frac{SNR_0}{SNR} = \frac{1}{1 - SNR/SIR}$$ **[9.32]**

where SNR can be determined from a specified P_E according to Equation (9.31).

POWER PENALTY IN OOK   For OOK and P_E at 10^{-9}, the required SNR is 72. At an SIR of | **Example**
30 dB, the power penalty is | **9.8**

$$P_p = \frac{1}{1 - 0.072} = 1.078 = 0.32 \text{ dB}.$$

When SIR decreases to 20 dB, the power penalty increases to

$$P_p = \frac{1}{1 - 0.72} = 3.57 = 5.53 \text{ dB}.$$

Therefore, the power penalty increases very fast when SIR is close to SNR. ∎

The power penalty for OOK at different normalized channel separations and IF frequencies is shown in Figure 9.22. Equation (9.24) shows that if $\Delta\omega = 2\omega_{IF}$, ω_{IF}, $1.5\omega_{IF}$, or $0.5\omega_{IF}$, there is a channel that coincides with the tuned channel. As a result, ICI or P_p is strong in these cases. Therefore, channel separation, $\Delta\omega$, in general should be at least several times greater than the IF frequency.

9.4 TUNABLE SOURCES

As mentioned earlier, WDoMA requires various advanced opto-electronic devices to implement carrier generation, coupling, and tuning. In the last few years, many interesting and innovative designs have been proposed. The remainder of this chapter presents various such designs and their principles.

In principle, discrete DFB, DBR, and MQW lasers, discussed in Chapter 3, can be used as tunable light sources in WDoMA. However, in either WDM or WDMA, it is desirable to build a large tunable laser array for cost-effective implementation. For example, Section 9.2

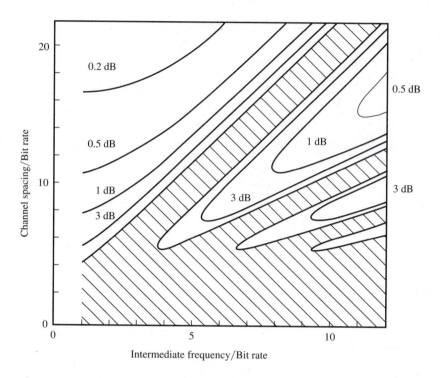

Figure 9.22   Constant power penalty curves at different channel separations and IF frequencies normalized with respect to bit rate.

SOURCE: Reproduced, by permission, from Suyama, Chikama, and Kuwahara, "Channel Allocation and Crosstalk Penalty," *Electronics Letters,* vol. 24, no. 20 [13]. © 1988 by *IEE.*

on WDMA indicates that it is desirable to use a large number of transceivers per node for high throughput and low transmission delay. In WDM, a large laser array can also be integrated with multiplexing devices, discussed in Section 9.6, for high-speed transmission.

When tunable light sources are used in a WDoMA system, it is important to maintain a precise and stable wavelength output. As discussed in Section 9.3, this is important in dense WDoMA to minimize ICI and to maintain a good transmission quality. This is also important when many frequency-dependent multiplexing devices, discussed in Section 9.6, are used.

9.4.1   TUNABLE LASER ARRAYS

For WDM applications, high-speed and tunable laser array designs of sizes up to 20 lasers have been reported recently [15]–[22]. Most laser arrays for WDM applications are based on the MQW and DBR combinations, where MQW is used as the active layer for low threshold current and DBR is used for frequency tuning. A typical MQW-DBR laser array is illustrated in Figure 9.23.

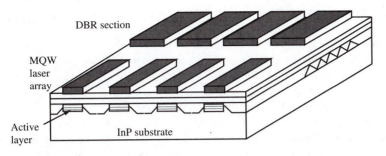

Figure 9.23 An MQW-DBR laser array.

To achieve tunability and generate different wavelength outputs, several design methods have been proposed. The first one uses a separate heating filament for each laser [15]. By passing different current to control the laser temperature, a 5 nm tunability can be achieved.

A second approach uses a built-in difference in the DBR sections. From the Bragg wavelength equation (see Chapter 3):

$$\lambda = 2n_B\Lambda \qquad \text{[9.33]}$$

where n_B is the refractive index of material in the DBR section and Λ is the period of the Bragg reflector, different wavelength outputs can be obtained by introducing different n_B or Λ in the design. For example, in [19], 20 wavelength channels ranging from 1459.2 nm to 1590.6 nm are generated by using fast electron lithography to form different grating periods from $\Lambda = 2262.5$–2500 Å and in 12.5 Å increments. In [20], another lithography technique called **synchrotron orbital radiation** is used to create different Λ. In [17] and [22], different n_B values are introduced by having different waveguide depth in processing.

TUNABILITY BY REFRACTIVE INDEX OR BRAGG REFLECTION Consider a GaAsInP MQW-DBR laser diode array that has n_B around 3.2. From Equation (9.33), Λ that generates 1550 nm emission is around 242.2 nm. A channel separation of 2 nm for WDM requires | **Example 9.9**

$$\Delta(n_B\Lambda) = 1.0 \text{ nm.}$$

When n_B is a variable and Λ is fixed at 221.4 nm,

$$\Delta n_B = 4.2 \times 10^{-3}.$$

On the other hand, if n_B is fixed at 3.2,

$$\Delta\Lambda = 0.3 \text{ nm.}$$

In general, because of practical processing limitations and variations, it is challenging to achieve a small and precise increment of either Δn_B or $\Delta\Lambda$ for dense WDM. ∎

9.4.2   WAVEGUIDE GRATING ROUTER AND OPTICAL AMPLIFIERS

Another innovative design of tunable light sources has been proposed by forming a positive feedback loop between optical amplifiers and the **waveguide grating router** (WGR) described in Section 9.6 [23]–[25]. In this approach, the WGR serves as an optical filter. When the net gain of the positive feedback loop is greater than unity or 0 dB, optical carriers with wavelengths determined by the WGR can be generated.

As shown in Figure 9.24, an array of four ring lasers and their wavelength multiplexing are implemented by forming four optical amplifiers and the WGR in rings. From Section 9.6, the wavelength that can pass from input port i to output j is $\lambda_{i+j} \overset{\text{def}}{=} \lambda_0 - (i + j)\Delta\lambda$. This wavelength relationship is summarized in Table 9.3. As a result, when the four ring lasers share the same half portion on the right-hand side of the WGR and through output ports 5 and 6, the four emission wavelengths are λ_{12}, λ_{10}, λ_8, and λ_6, respectively. Therefore, the four wavelengths are uniformly separated and multiplexed at the same time to the same right portion of the ring. By using a coupler from the ring, the multiplexed output can be sent into an external fiber.

Table 9.3   Wavelengths that can pass for a given pair of input and output ports of a waveguide grating router, where $\lambda_{i+j} \overset{\text{def}}{=} \lambda_0 - (i + j)\Delta\lambda$.

Out	Input							
	1	2	3	4	5	6	7	8
1	λ_2	λ_3	λ_4	λ_5	λ_6	λ_7	λ_8	λ_9
2	λ_3	λ_4	λ_5	λ_6	λ_7	λ_8	λ_9	λ_{10}
3	λ_4	λ_5	λ_6	λ_7	λ_8	λ_9	λ_{10}	λ_{11}
4	λ_5	λ_6	λ_7	λ_8	λ_9	λ_{10}	λ_{11}	λ_{12}
5	λ_6	λ_7	λ_8	λ_9	λ_{10}	λ_{11}	λ_{12}	λ_{13}
6	λ_7	λ_8	λ_9	λ_{10}	λ_{11}	λ_{12}	λ_{13}	λ_{14}
7	λ_8	λ_9	λ_{10}	λ_{11}	λ_{12}	λ_{13}	λ_{14}	λ_{15}
8	λ_9	λ_{10}	λ_{11}	λ_{12}	λ_{13}	λ_{14}	λ_{15}	λ_{16}

Another similar design based on the feedback loops of a WGR and optical amplifiers is shown in Figure 9.25. When amplifier i on the left and amplifier j on the right are turned on, the combination of two reflecting mirrors, the two lasers, and the WGR forms a laser with output wavelength at $\lambda_0 - (i + j)\Delta\lambda$. If all optical amplifiers on the left are turned on, wavelength channels $\lambda_0 - (i + j)\Delta\lambda$ for $i = 1$ to N can be generated and multiplexed.

9.4.3   FREQUENCY TUNING AND STABILIZATION

As pointed out earlier, accurate wavelength generation is important to proper wavelength multiplexing, interchannel interference, and tuning. The output wavelength of a

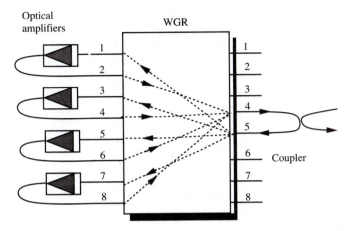

Figure 9.24   An array of ring lasers sharing the same waveguide grating router with fixed channel separation.

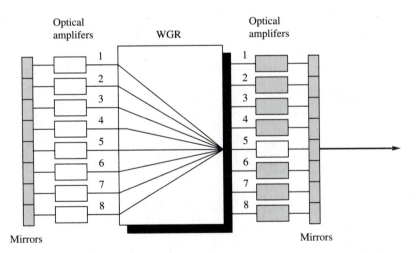

Figure 9.25   A laser array using optical amplifiers and a waveguide grating router. The shaded optical amplifiers are turned off.

tunable laser, however, can vary because of fabrication errors, temperature, bias current, and aging. A typical temperature coefficient of the output wavelength of a single-frequency laser is around 0.09 nm/C° [26]. From Table 9.1, this is around 10 GHz/C° at 1550 nm. To provide satisfactory system operation, mechanisms to stabilize output frequencies are needed.

Absolute Frequency Stabilization One way to maintain frequency stabilization is to use an absolute frequency source that is stable against various external conditions. In this approach, both channel separations and absolute frequencies can be maintained for proper channel multiplexing and tuning.

A design of absolute frequency stabilization is shown in Figure 9.26, where the atomic transition of argon at 1.2960 μm is used [27]. As shown, a hollow cathode lamp (HCL) that contains argon is used as the calibrator. When the output of the reference DFB laser is at the

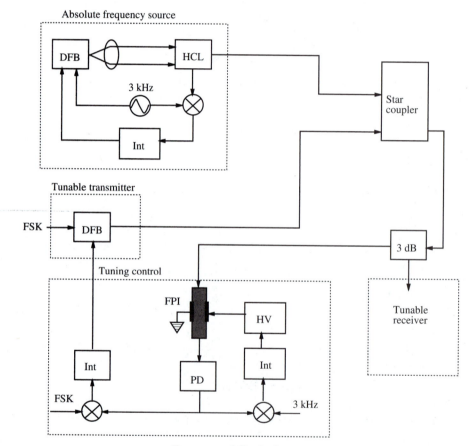

Figure 9.26 A design of absolute frequency stabilization. The DFB in the absolute frequency source is locked to the 1.2960 μm atomic transition of argon in the hollow cathode lamp (HCL). To lock all other DFB outputs, an FPI is used. It is biased in such a way that 1.2960 μm is one of its passing bands. All other DFB outputs are locked to the rest of the passing bands of the FPI by the frequency stabilization loop. From this arrangement, the channel separation is determined by the FSR of the FPI.

Ar $2p_{10}$–$3d_5$ 1.2960 μm transition, a voltage is induced at the cathode lamp. This induced voltage can then be used as a feedback to lock the DFB laser. The frequency-locked loop shown in Figure 9.26 is in principle equivalent to a phase-locked loop discussed in Chapter 16, with the DFB diode, the cathode lamp, and the integrator being equivalent to the voltage-controlled oscillator (VCO), phase detector (PD), and the loop filter, respectively. The additional oscillator at 3 kHz shown in Figure 9.26 is used to correlate the DFB output and reject all other undesired frequency contents in the cathode lamp voltage output.

To lock all other DFB sources with respect to the absolute frequency source, a **Fabry-Perot interferometer** (FPI) is used at each node. Based on the similar locking mechanism used in the reference frequency generation, the FPI is biased by a feedback voltage so that the reference wavelength 1.2960 μm can pass through. Once the FPI is properly biased, another loop for the local DFB is used to lock the DFB output wavelength to one of the passing bands of the FPI. When all FPIs used by different nodes have the same FSR, uniform channel separation of one FSR can be maintained.

Relative Frequency Stabilization   When absolute frequencies are not required, it is only necessary to ensure constant channel separation to avoid a large ICI. In this case, a single FPI can be used as the calibrator [28]. As shown in Figure 9.27, each star coupler output has all wavelength channels, which are individually controlled to pass the same FPI. The locking mechanisms of the wavelength output for each DFB are similar to the absolute frequency design in Figure 9.26.

The design shown in Figure 9.27 requires that all the laser diodes are local and share the same FPI. One modified design uses one FPI at each laser source, and uses a reference frequency source to align one passing band of all the FPIs [29]. From this alignment, each laser source is locked to another passing band of its local FPI. When FPIs do not have the same FSR, however, this approach can still cause a high ICI.

An improved design, shown in Figure 9.28, uses a single laser and a single FPI to generate N reference wavelengths, where N is the total number of wavelength channels [30]. These N references are generated one at a time by applying a stairlike input to the tuning control of the reference laser. From these references, all other laser diodes can be locked to their corresponding reference wavelengths by performing direct photodetection and correlation filtering using their own transmitted signal.

In this approach, all laser sources are indirectly locked to a single FPI. Therefore, precise frequency stabilization can be achieved. This scheme can also be used together with the absolute frequency stabilization design shown in Figure 9.26 by locking the FPI of the reference DFB to the argon transition. Furthermore, because each channel output is synchronized with its reference in both polarization and a constant IF frequency difference, a lock-in amplifier at the receiver side can be used to amplify the reference channel being tuned to. The amplified output can be used as the local oscillator for coherent detection.

9.5   FREQUENCY-INDEPENDENT COUPLING

As mentioned earlier, wavelength channels need to be coupled to the shared medium for transmission. To allow a node in WDMA to tune its wavelength channels for transmission,

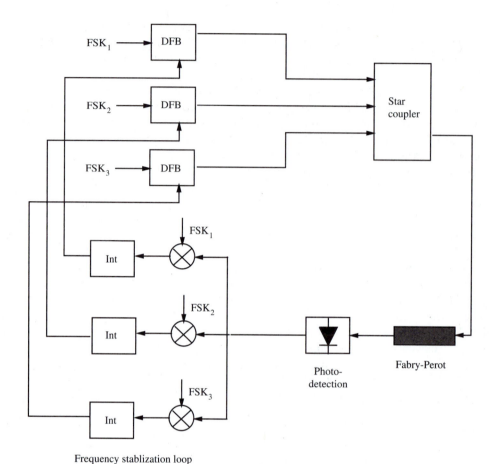

Frequency stablization loop

Figure 9.27   A design of relative frequency stabilization using one FPI resonator. All light sources are required to be local.

coupling should be made insensitive to the wavelength. For this purpose, a star coupler is commonly used. As illustrated in Figure 9.4a, a star coupler has N input ports and N output ports, with each output port consisting of all signals from the N input ports.

In the star coupler design, one important consideration is the total power loss. From conservation of energy, when the coupler is symmetric, the output power of each channel at each port is attenuated by at least a factor of N, the size of the star coupler. This $1/N$ coupling loss is called distribution loss because the incident light from one input port is distributed to N output ports. In addition to distribution loss, there is excess loss due to many couplings with loss such as internal power attenuation. As a result, the total coupling loss in a star coupler can be expressed as

$$\alpha_{tot} \text{ dB} = 10\log_{10}(N) + \alpha_{excess} \text{ dB.} \qquad \text{[9.34]}$$

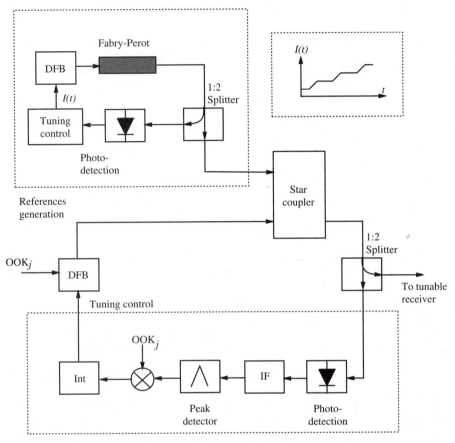

Figure 9.28   A relative frequency stabilization design using a single FPI. All light sources can be at different places.

In general, the excess loss depends on both the coupler design and size.

TOTAL STAR COUPLING LOSS   Consider a star coupler of size 100×100 and an excess loss of 3 dB; the total coupling loss of each channel is

Example 9.10

$$\alpha_{tot} = 20 + 3 = 23 \text{ dB}.$$

When N is large, from the logarithm function in Equation (9.34), note that star couplers have a smaller distribution loss compared to bus and ring networks. This has been pointed out in Chapter 2. ∎

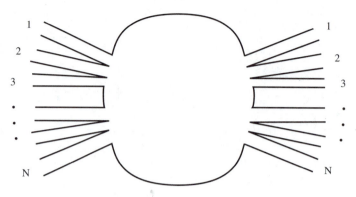

Figure 9.29   A planar waveguide as a star coupler.

A star coupler can be implemented in various ways. Important designs include single planar couplers, fused optical fibers, and combinations of 2×2 couplers. These are described below.

Single Planar Waveguide   A simple star coupler design employs a single planar waveguide structure shown in Figure 9.29 [31][2]. By properly designing the shape and dimension of the planar waveguide and directions of the input/output ports, the excess loss can be kept below 3 dB.

Fused Optical Fibers   Another star coupler design called **fused** optical fibers is shown in Figure 9.30. In this approach, fiber cores are fused together so lightwaves from different fibers can be coupled together. In general, when N is large, there can be a large excess power loss and it is difficult to achieve a uniform mixing.

Combination of 2×2 Couplers   To build a large $N \times N$ star coupler, another approach is to form an interconnected network of 2×2 couplers. As illustrated in Figure 9.31, an $N \times N$ star coupler with $N = 2^k$ can be implemented as a perfect shuffle network of $k \times (N/2)$ star couplers. This approach has the advantage that there is no size limit as long as $N = 2^k$. The disadvantage, is the need of many 2×2 couplers.

For a star coupler consisting of 2×2 couplers and of size $N = 2^k$, an optical path from input to output consists of k couplers. Therefore, if the excess loss at each coupler is α_{excess} dB, the total coupling loss is

$$\alpha_{tot} = 10 \log_{10} N + (\log_2 N)\alpha_{excess} = (3 + \alpha_{excess}) \log_2 N \text{ dB.} \qquad \textbf{[9.35]}$$

Example 9.11   **2 X 2 COUPLERS**   Consider a WDMA network that has a power budget of 30 dB. If the star coupler made of 2×2 couplers has an excess loss of 0.1 dB per coupler, the size of the star coupler cannot be greater than

$$N \leq 2^{\lfloor \frac{20}{3.1} \rfloor} = 64.$$

At $N = 64$, there are 6 stages, and the total excess loss is 0.6 dB, which is small compared to the distribution loss of $20 \log_{10} 64 = 18$ dB. ∎

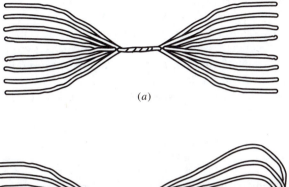

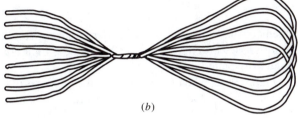

(a)

(b)

Figure 9.30   Fused fibers as a star coupler.

SOURCE: Reprinted, by permission, from Agrawal, *Fiber-Optic Communication Systems* [58]. © 1992 by John Wiley and Sons.

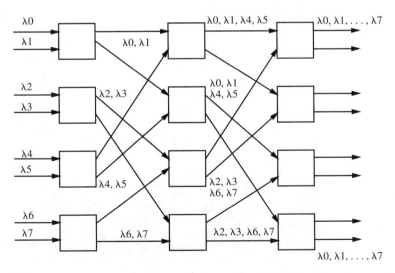

Figure 9.31   An 8 × 8 star coupler consisting of 2 × 2 couplers in a perfect shuffle configuration.

9.6   FREQUENCY-DEPENDENT MULTIPLEXING

In addition to star couplers, frequency-dependent multiplexers can be used to mix wavelength channels. In this case, there is no distribution loss. However, mixed outputs are strongly dependent on the wavelengths of input signals. Different from star couplers, multiplexers are thus primarily used in WDM. In WDMA, where nodes can tune their transmission wavelengths, use of frequency-dependent multiplexers is not suitable.

To implement a frequency-dependent multiplexer, there are two primary designs: grating and Mach-Zehnder interferometry. In the first case, light from different spatial directions is coupled together. In the latter case, light of different wavelengths is coupled together, with coupling coefficients dependent on the input wavelengths. These designs are described in detail below.

9.6.1   GRATING

Grating is an arrangement that imposes on an incident light a periodic phase variation [32]–[35]. When many phase-shifted versions of the incident light are superimposed, a spatially dependent intensity pattern is formed.

As illustrated in Figure 9.32, when the light is incident on a periodic structure of period Λ and at an incident angle α, the condition for constructive interference is

$$\Lambda[\sin(\alpha) - \sin(\beta)] = m\lambda \qquad \textbf{[9.36]}$$

where Λ is the period of the periodic structure, β is the reflection angle, and m is the order of interference. In general, only the case $m = 1$ as the first-order diffraction is considered.

A special and important kind of grating is called the **blazed grating** shown in Figure 9.33, which can be implemented by either a surface-relief metallized grating or a volume

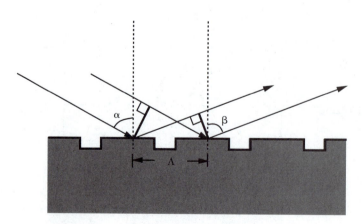

Figure 9.32   A reflection grating.

holographic grating [32]. In either case, the grating surface and the Bragg plane are at a fixed blazed angle α.

When additional focusing lenses are used in a grating setup (see Figure 9.34), it is desirable to have both the incident and reflected rays on the same horizontal path to provide autocollimation and to minimize the angular distortion. The setup for this condition is called **Littrow configuration** [35]. In this case, $\alpha = -\beta \stackrel{\text{def}}{=} \theta_B$, and Equation (9.36) ($m = 1$) reduces to

$$2\Lambda \sin(\theta_B) = \lambda. \qquad [9.37]$$

Note that Equation (9.37) is satisfied at only one wavelength. For other wavelengths, the incident angle needs to be different to have the same reflection angle $\beta = -\theta_B$. From this observation and Equation (9.36), an **angular dispersion factor** is defined as:

$$K_\lambda \stackrel{\text{def}}{=} \frac{d\alpha}{d\lambda} = \frac{m}{\Lambda \cos \alpha} = \frac{\sin \alpha - \sin \beta}{\lambda \cos \alpha}. \qquad [9.38]$$

When α is close to θ_B,

$$K_\lambda \approx \frac{2 \tan(\theta_B)}{\lambda}. \qquad [9.39]$$

From the angular dispersion factor defined, if the incident angle α that satisfies Equation (9.36) is θ_B at λ, the incident angle at wavelength $\lambda + \Delta\lambda$ that satisfies Equation (9.36) is

$$\alpha = \theta_B + K_\lambda \Delta\lambda \qquad [9.40]$$

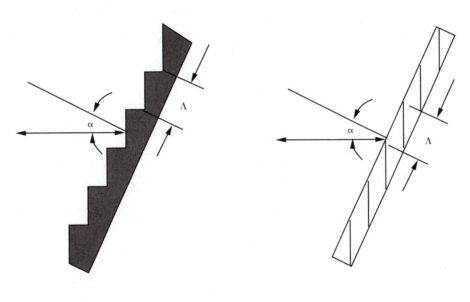

(a)   (b)

Figure 9.33   A blazed grating made of (a) surface-relief metal and (b) a hologram.

Equation (9.40) can be used to design a multiplexer as shown in Figure 9.34. In this arrangement, incident light from different fibers is first collimated by either a convex lens or a **graded-index** (GRIN) lens. From the collimation, light from the same fiber has the same incident angle at the grating. By properly placing input fibers in different vertical positions so that the incident angle (α) at the grating satisfies Equation (9.40), the diffracted light will be all in the same horizontal path ($\beta = -\theta_B$). With the use of the same lens, all diffracted light is focused back to the output fiber.

Specifically, the input fiber spacing, b, can be determined by the angular dispersion factor, K_λ, and channel separation, $\Delta\lambda$, as follows. Let f be the focal length of the collimating lens. From Figure 9.34, the incident angle separation is

$$\Delta\alpha = \frac{b}{f}$$

where $b \ll f$ is assumed. From Equation (9.40), the fiber spacing is

$$b = f K_\lambda \Delta\lambda. \qquad \textbf{[9.41]}$$

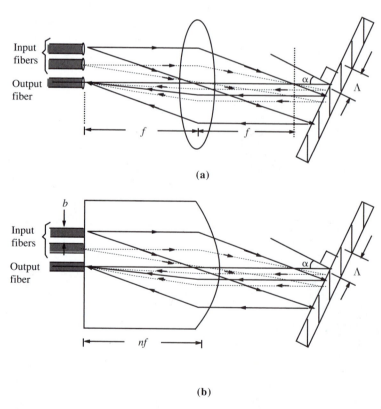

(a)

(b)

Figure 9.34   Wavelength multiplexing based on the Littrow configuration grating: (a) a convex lens is used for focusing; (b) a GRIN lens is used for focusing.

**Example
9.12**

WDM USING LITTROW CONFIGURATION If $\theta_B = 6.9°$ and $\lambda = 1550$ nm, the angular dispersion factor is

$$K_\lambda = \frac{2\tan\alpha}{\lambda} = 1.56 \times 10^{-4} \text{ nm}^{-1}.$$

When $\Delta\lambda = 1.0$ nm and $f = 10$ cm, fiber spacing is

$$b = 10 \times 1.56 \times 10^{-4} \times 1 = 1.56 \times 10^{-3} \text{ cm} = 15.6 \ \mu\text{m}.$$

From Equation (9.40), we note that the smaller the channel separation ($\Delta\lambda$), the larger the focal length, f, needed at a given b and K_λ. To reduce the multiplexer size, a modified design based on substrate-mode grating has been proposed [34]. ∎

9.6.2 MACH-ZEHNDER INTERFEROMETRY

Another emerging and important design of frequency-dependent multiplexers is based on Mach-Zehnder interferometry [36]–[38]. In this approach, an N:1 multiplexer is composed of $N - 1$ 2×2 Mach-Zehnder interferometers (MZIs) in m stages, where $N = 2^m$. To understand the principle, first consider the basic 2×2 MZI.

As shown in Figure 9.35, each 2×2 MZI consists of three stages: a 3-dB coupler, a two-branch phase shifter, and another 3-dB coupler. At each 3-dB coupling, the transfer matrix between the input and output waves can be expressed as

$$\begin{bmatrix} E_{out,1} \\ E_{out,2} \end{bmatrix} = \frac{1}{\sqrt{2}} \begin{bmatrix} 1 & j \\ j & 1 \end{bmatrix} \begin{bmatrix} E_{in,1} \\ E_{in,2} \end{bmatrix} \stackrel{\text{def}}{=} M_{3dB} \begin{bmatrix} E_{in,1} \\ E_{in,2} \end{bmatrix}. \qquad \textbf{[9.42]}$$

This 3-dB coupler is a special case of the four-port hybrid discussed in Chapter 15. For detailed discussion on the transfer function and its properties, see Appendix 15–B.

The phase shifter consists of two branches. When the two inputs come from the same light source, the light output from the two branches has a phase difference, $\Delta\phi$. Because

$$\Delta\phi = \frac{2\pi n_1}{\lambda} L_1 - \frac{2\pi n_2}{\lambda} L_2$$

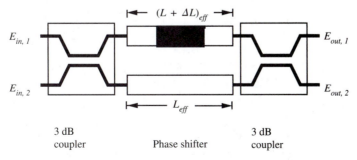

$E_{in,\,1}$ $(L + \Delta L)_{eff}$ $E_{out,\,1}$

$E_{in,\,2}$ L_{eff} $E_{out,\,2}$

3 dB coupler   Phase shifter   3 dB coupler

Figure 9.35   A MZI for wavelength multiplexing.

the phase difference can be introduced by either a different path length ($L_1 \neq L_2$) or a different refractive index ($n_1 \neq n_2$). For convenience,

$$L_{eff} \overset{\text{def}}{=} nL \qquad \qquad \textbf{[9.43]}$$

is defined as the effective waveguide length. As a result, $\Delta\phi = k\Delta L_{eff}$, with $k = 2\pi/\lambda$. At a given $\Delta\phi$, the output light from the two branches can be related to the input by

$$M_{shift} = \begin{bmatrix} e^{jk\Delta L_{eff}/2} & 0 \\ 0 & e^{-jk\Delta L_{eff}/2} \end{bmatrix} \qquad \textbf{[9.44]}$$

where the average phase shift is ignored for simplicity.

From Equations (9.42) and (9.44), the MZI can be characterized by the combined matrix

$$M_{MZI} = M_{3dB} M_{shift} M_{3dB} = j \begin{bmatrix} \sin(k\Delta L_{eff}/2) & \cos(k\Delta L_{eff}/2) \\ \cos(k\Delta L_{eff}/2) & -\sin(k\Delta L_{eff}/2) \end{bmatrix}. \, \textbf{[9.45]}$$

If the incident light inputs, $E_{in,1}$ and $E_{in,2}$, are at wavelengths λ_1 and λ_2, from Equation (9.45), the output power is

$$P_{out,1} = \sin^2(k_1\Delta L_{eff}/2)P_{in,1} + \cos^2(k_2\Delta L_{eff}/2)P_{in,2} \qquad \textbf{[9.46]}$$

and

$$P_{out,2} = \cos^2(k_1\Delta L_{eff}/2)P_{in,1} + \sin^2(k_2\Delta L_{eff}/2)P_{in,2} \qquad \textbf{[9.47]}$$

where $k_1 = 2\pi/\lambda_1$ and $k_2 = 2\pi/\lambda_2$.

From Equations (9.46) and (9.47), a proper ΔL_{eff} can be used to completely mix two inputs. Specifically, if

$$k_1\Delta L_{eff} = 2m_1\pi \qquad \qquad \textbf{[9.48]}$$

and

$$k_2\Delta L_{eff} = (2m_2 + 1)\pi \qquad \qquad \textbf{[9.49]}$$

with certain integers m_1 and m_2, then $P_{out,1} = 0$ and $P_{out,2} = P_{in,1} + P_{in,2}$. When $m_1 = m_2$, combining Equations (9.48) and (9.49) yields

$$(k_1 - k_2)\Delta L_{eff} = \pi. \qquad \qquad \textbf{[9.50]}$$

Because $k_1 - k_2 = 2\pi(f_1 - f_2)/c$,

$$\boxed{\Delta L_{eff} = \frac{c}{2\Delta f}.} \qquad \qquad \textbf{[9.51]}$$

Equation (9.51) gives the design of the MZI at a given frequency separation Δf.

Example	**REQUIRED DIFFERENCE OF WAVEGUIDE LENGTHS** If a 2×2 MZI is used as a multi-
9.13	plexer for two WDM channels at a frequency separation of 10 GHz, the effective waveguide difference should be

$$\Delta L_{eff} = \frac{3 \times 10^{14}}{2 \times 10^{10}} = 15 \text{ mm}.$$

When the refractive index is 1.5 in a silicon waveguide, the actual ΔL is 10 mm. ∎

Using the 2×2 MZI discussed above as the basic component, one can build a multiplexer of any size $N = 2^n$. For simple understanding, consider a multiplexer of size four illustrated in Figure 9.36. As shown, the four input signals are first multiplexed by two MZIs. The input frequencies from top to bottom are: f, $f + 2\Delta f$, $f + \Delta f$, and $f + 3\Delta f$. Therefore, from Equation (9.50), ΔL_{eff} of the two MZIs at the first stage satisfies

$$2\Delta f \Delta L_{eff,i}^{(1)} = \frac{c}{2} \qquad \textbf{[9.52]}$$

where $i = 0, 1$. As a result, $\Delta L_{eff,i}^{(1)}$ of each MZI in the first stage should be the same. However, a slight difference is needed (as will be explained shortly). Similarly, for the second stage,

$$\Delta f \Delta L_{eff}^{(2)} = \frac{c}{2}. \qquad \textbf{[9.53]}$$

From the above two equations,

$$\Delta L_{eff}^{(2)} = 2\Delta L_{eff}^{(1)}. \qquad \textbf{[9.54]}$$

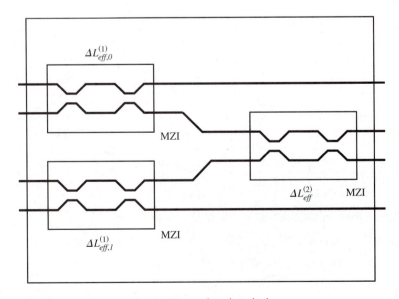

Figure 9.36   A 4×4 MZI wavelength multiplexer.

In addition to the above conditions, from Equations (9.48) and (9.49) and the arrangement shown in Figure 9.36, it is necessary that

$$k\Delta L_{eff,0}^{(1)} = 2m\pi \qquad \qquad \textbf{[9.55]}$$

and

$$(k + \Delta k)\Delta L_{eff,1}^{(1)} = (2m \pm 1)\pi. \qquad \qquad \textbf{[9.56]}$$

Because $2\Delta k \Delta L_{eff,i}^{(1)} = \pi$ from Equation (9.52), Equations (9.55) and (9.56) require that

$$k[\Delta L_{eff,1}^{(1)} - \Delta L_{eff,0}^{(1)}] = \pm\frac{\pi}{2}. \qquad \qquad \textbf{[9.57]}$$

This condition shows that $\Delta L_{eff,1}^{(1)}$ needs to be slightly different from $\Delta L_{eff,0}^{(1)}$. Example 9.14 illustrates this point.

Example 9.14

4:1 MZI MULTIPLEXER   Consider a 4:1 multiplexer based on the MZI discussed above. Assume the channel separation is 10 GHz and the longest wavelength channel is at 1550 nm. Thus from Equations (9.52) and (9.53),

$$\Delta L_{eff,0}^{(1)} \approx \Delta L_{eff,1}^{(1)} = \frac{c}{4\Delta f} = 7.5 \text{ mm}$$

and

$$\Delta L_{eff}^{(2)} = 2\Delta L_{eff,0}^{(1)} = 15 \text{ mm}.$$

The above ΔL_{eff} values are only approximations. From Equation (9.57),

$$\Delta L_{eff,1}^{(1)} - \Delta L_{eff,0}^{(1)} = \pm\frac{\lambda}{4} = \pm 387.5 \text{ nm}.$$

A precise $\Delta L_{eff,0}^{(0)}$ value can be determined if

$$k\Delta L_{eff,0}^{(0)} = 2m\pi$$

for a certain integer m. Over all possible choices, let $\Delta L_{eff,0}^{(1)} = 7.50045$ mm ($m = 4839$) as the one closest to 7.5 mm. From this, $\Delta L_{eff,1}^{(1)} = 7.50006$ mm. At these $\Delta L_{eff}^{(1)}$ values, from Equations (9.46) and (9.47), the lower branch output of the first MZI at the first stage is

$$P_{lower,0}^{(1)} = \cos^2(k\Delta L_{eff,0}^{(1)}/2)P_{in,0} + \sin^2(k\Delta L_{eff,0}^{(1)}/2 + 2\pi\Delta f \Delta L_{eff,0}^{(1)}/c)P_{in,1}$$

$$\approx P_{in,0} + (1 - 4.5 \times 10^{-10}\pi^2)P_{in,1}.$$

The upper branch output of the second MZI at the first stage is

$$P_{upper,1}^{(1)} = \sin^2[(k + \Delta k)L_{eff,1}^{(1)}/2]P_{in,2} + \cos^2[(k + 3\Delta k)L_{eff,1}^{(1)}/2]P_{in,3}$$

$$= \sin^2(\tfrac{\pi}{2} - \tfrac{\pi}{4} + 0.250002 \times \pi)P_{in,2} + \cos^2(\tfrac{\pi}{2} - \tfrac{\pi}{4} + 0.750006 \times \pi)P_{in,3}$$

$$= (1 - 2\pi^2 \times 10^{-12})P_{in,2} + (1 - 1.8\pi^2 \times 10^{-11})P_{in,3}.$$

This example shows that in principle there cannot be complete mixing. When the same design is used as a demultiplexer, there is crosstalk or interchannel interference. However, this incomplete mixing is negligible. ∎

9.6.3 WAVEGUIDE GRATING ROUTER

There is a recent innovative multiplexing design based on MZI called a **waveguide grating router** (WGR). As shown in Figure 9.37, a WGR consists of two star couplers and an MZI-based grating [39]–[42]. From the design, a large number of wavelength channels of uniform channel separation can be multiplexed through a single MZI.

The principle of the WGR for wavelength multiplexing can be understood as follows. In the first star coupler, a wavelength channel input is split uniformly in power and with a certain phase shift to all output ports. Specifically, if the incident wave at input port p of the first star coupler is E_{in}, the split lightwave that goes into output port s is

$$E_s = \frac{E_{in}}{\sqrt{N}} e^{j\phi_{p,s}} \qquad \textbf{[9.58]}$$

where $\phi_{p,s}$ is the phase shift in the star coupler from input port p to output port s. When the planar coupler has a focal length R, the phase shift is given by

$$\phi_{p,s} = \frac{2\pi n_{coupler}}{\lambda} d_{p,s} \qquad \textbf{[9.59]}$$

where $n_{coupler}$ is the refractive index of the planar coupler and

$$d_{p,s} = R\{[1 - \cos(p\alpha) - \cos(s\alpha')]^2 + [\sin(p\alpha) - \sin(s\alpha')]^2\}^{1/2} \approx R(1 - ps\alpha\alpha') \qquad \textbf{[9.60]}$$

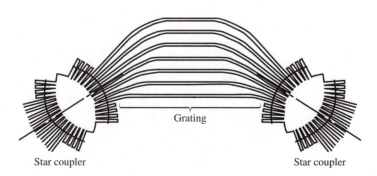

Figure 9.37 A waveguide grating router.

SOURCE: Reprinted, by permission, from Dragone, et al., "Integrated Optics $N \times N$ Multiplexer on Silicon," *IEEE Photonics Technology Letters*, vol. 3, no. 10 [39]. © 1991 by IEEE.

is the distance between the openings of the input and output ports. As shown in Figure 9.38, α and α' are the separation angles of input ports and output ports, respectively.

Once the light signal goes into the sth waveguide through the output port s of the first coupler, it experiences another phase shift proportional to the waveguide length. If the sth waveguide has a length

$$L_s = s\Delta L + L \qquad \textbf{[9.61]}$$

where ΔL is the length difference between adjacent waveguides, the phase shift from the waveguide is

$$\phi_s = \frac{2\pi n_{wgr}}{\lambda}(s\Delta L + L) \qquad \textbf{[9.62]}$$

where n_{wgr} is the refractive index of the waveguides. Once the signal arrives at the second star coupler, it is split again into all output ports. Similar to the phase shift in the first star coupler, the phase shift from input port s to output port q is

$$\phi_{s,q} = \frac{2\pi n_{coupler}}{\lambda}R(1 - sq\alpha\alpha'). \qquad \textbf{[9.63]}$$

From Equations (9.59)–(9.62), the total phase shift from input port p of the first star coupler, through the sth waveguide, and to output port q of the second star coupler is

$$\phi_{p,s,q} = \frac{4\pi n_{coupler}}{\lambda}R + \frac{2\pi n_{wgr}}{\lambda}(s\Delta L + L) - \frac{2\pi n_{coupler}}{\lambda}Rs(p+q)\alpha\alpha'. \qquad \textbf{[9.64]}$$

Therefore, the phase shift difference between two adjacent waveguides is

$$\Delta\phi_{p,q} \overset{\text{def}}{=} \phi_{p,s,q} - \phi_{p,s-1,q} = \frac{2\pi n_{wgr}}{\lambda}\Delta L - \frac{2\pi n_{coupler}}{\lambda}R(p+q)\alpha\alpha'. \qquad \textbf{[9.65]}$$

When all waves are superimposed through different waveguides, the total output power is

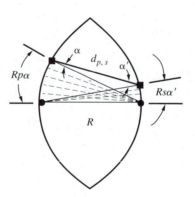

Figure 9.38 $d_{p,s}$ determination.

$$P_{p,q} = \frac{1}{M^2}\left|\sum_{s=0}^{M-1} e^{js\Delta\phi_{p,q}}\right|^2 P_{in} = \frac{1}{M^2}\frac{\sin^2(M\Delta\phi_{p,q}/2)}{\sin^2(\Delta\phi_{p,q}/2)}P_{in} \qquad \textbf{[9.66]}$$

where M is the total number of waveguides between the two planar star couplers. Therefore, when

$$\frac{\Delta\phi_{p,q}}{2} = \pi \qquad \textbf{[9.67]}$$

the output power will be close to the input power P_{in}. Let $\lambda_{p,q}$ be the wavelength that satisfies Equation (9.67). From Equation (9.65),

$$\boxed{\lambda_{p,q} = n_{wgr}\Delta L - n_{coupler}(p+q)R\alpha\alpha' \stackrel{\text{def}}{=} \lambda_0 - (p+q)\Delta\lambda} \qquad \textbf{[9.68]}$$

where

$$\Delta\lambda \stackrel{\text{def}}{=} n_{coupler}R\alpha\alpha' \qquad \textbf{[9.69]}$$

and

$$\lambda_0 = n_{wgr}\Delta L. \qquad \textbf{[9.70]}$$

Equation (9.68) gives the wavelength that can go from input port p to output port q, and Equation (9.69) gives the wavelength separation of WDM channels. From these equations, the wavelength difference between $\lambda_{p,q}$ and $\lambda_{m,n}$ is

$$\lambda_{p,q} - \lambda_{m,n} = (m+n-p-q)\Delta\lambda. \qquad \textbf{[9.71]}$$

A WGR DESIGN   Consider a WGR design of $R = 10$ mm, $R\alpha = R\alpha' = 5\ \mu$m, and $M = 16$. At $n_{coupler} = 1.5$, from Equation (9.69), the constant channel separation is

$$\Delta\lambda = 3.75 \text{ nm}.$$

At $\lambda = 1550$ nm, from Table 9.1, this corresponds to a channel separation of 470 GHz.

From Equation (9.70), if the refractive index of the grating waveguide is $n_{wgr} = 1.5$, the unit length difference ΔL between waveguides should be

$$\Delta L = \frac{1.55}{1.5} = 1.033\ \mu\text{m}. \quad\blacksquare$$

Example 9.14

From Equation (9.68), wavelength multiplexing can be done as follows. To multiplex wavelength channels at output port q of the second star coupler, the wavelength of incident light at input port p of the first star coupler should be $\lambda_{p,q} = \lambda_0 - (p+q)\Delta\lambda$. All these carriers will then pass through the WGR and arrive at the output port q of the second star coupler.

9.7 DEMULTIPLEXING, OPTICAL FILTERING, AND ADD-DROP MULTIPLEXING

When incoherent detection is used, a mechanism is needed to select one of the wavelength channels optically before photodetection. In general, this can be done in either the spatial domain, frequency domain, or polarization domain. In the spatial domain, wavelength channels are split into different spatial paths (grating) for detection. In the frequency domain, either an optical bandpass filter is used to suppress out-of-band channels or a narrow-band optical amplifier is used to amplify only the in-band channel. In the polarization domain, a wavelength channel is separated by a polarizing beam splitter if its polarization is orthogonal to that of other wavelength channels.

As mentioned earlier, there are two design criteria in demultiplexing wavelength channels: a large free spectral range (FSR) and a high spectral resolution. The fundamental reason that two wavelengths at one FSR separation have the same demultiplexed output is because wave interference has a periodic effect in phase. To avoid ambiguity, a large FSR is required. In general, the FSR of a demultiplexer is inversely proportional to the period of its grating or diffracting structure.

The spectral resolution of a demultiplexer, on the other hand, determines how closely two wavelength channels can be separated. In general, the resolution is inversely proportional to the device size that introduces wave interference. This can be understood from the Fourier transform, which says that the larger the size of an object in the spatial domain, the smaller the width of its Fourier transform in the spatial spectral domain. Detailed discussion on the FSR and spectral resolution of various demultiplexing devices is given below.

9.7.1 SPATIAL-DOMAIN DEMULTIPLEXING—GRATING

Grating is the primary method that splits wavelength channels in the spatial domain [43]–[49]. Although there are many designs, they all introduce interference among diffracted or reflected waves from a periodic structure. Presented below are three different designs: **diffraction grating** based on the Littrow configuration discussed earlier, **Bragg-reflection grating,** and **acousto-optic Bragg diffraction.**

Diffraction Grating   The same Littrow grating configuration shown in Figure 9.34 can be used as a wavelength demultiplexer if the light propagation directions are reversed [43][44]. In this case, different wavelength channels from the same input direction will be diffracted to different output directions according to Equation (9.36).

To see the FSR of the grating configuration, consider an incident wave at wavelength λ. From Figure 9.32, the phase difference between two adjacent diffracted rays is

$$\Delta\phi = \Lambda[\sin\alpha - \sin\beta]\frac{2\pi}{\lambda} \qquad \textbf{[9.72]}$$

where α is the incident angle and β is the diffraction angle. Therefore, the superimposed output power of N diffracted rays at angle β is proportional to

$$X = \left| \sum_{k=1}^{N} e^{jk\Delta\phi} \right|^2 = \left| \frac{\sin(N\Delta\phi/2)}{\sin(\Delta\phi/2)} \right|^2 \qquad \textbf{[9.73]}$$

where N is equal to the number of periods of the periodic structure. Equation (9.73) shows that the response, X, is a periodic function of $\Delta\phi$ and has a period 2π. Equation (9.72) indicates that $\Delta\phi$ is a function of λ. Therefore, there can be multiple wavelengths whose X's are maximized at the same diffraction angle β (i.e., their $\Delta\phi$'s are multiples of 2π). From this observation, one FSR is the wavelength range that corresponds to a 2π change of $\Delta\phi$. When two wavelengths are within one FSR, they are diffracted to different angles. On the other hand, as shown in Figure 9.39, lightwaves separated by one FSR are diffracted to the same angle β. Equation (9.72) allows the following definitions:

$$\lambda_m \overset{\text{def}}{=} \frac{2\pi \Lambda[\sin\alpha - \sin\beta]}{2m\pi} = \frac{\Lambda[\sin\alpha - \sin\beta]}{m} \qquad \textbf{[9.74]}$$

where λ_m is the wavelength at which $\Delta\phi = 2m\pi$. Therefore, the mth order FSR between λ_m and λ_{m+1} is

$$\text{FSR}_m \overset{\text{def}}{=} \lambda_{m+1} - \lambda_m = \frac{\Lambda[\sin\alpha - \sin\beta]}{m(m+1)} = \frac{\lambda_{m+1}}{m} = \frac{\lambda_m}{m+1}. \qquad \textbf{[9.75]}$$

Equation (9.75) shows that the larger the diffraction order (m), the smaller the FSR.

FSR OF LITTROW GRATING Consider a Littrow grating configuration of $\alpha = -\beta = 10°$ and $\Lambda = 5\ \mu\text{m}$. In this case,

Example 9.16

$$\lambda_m = \frac{2\Lambda \sin\alpha}{m} = \frac{1.73}{m}\ \mu\text{m}.$$

Therefore, the first FSR is from 0.87 ($m = 2$) to 1.73 μm ($m = 1$). ■

To find the spectral resolution, consider two wavelength channels at λ_m and $\lambda_m + \Delta\lambda$. From Equation (9.74), a difference $\Delta\lambda$ results in an angle separation of

$$\Delta\beta = \frac{m}{\Lambda \cos\beta}\Delta\lambda \qquad \textbf{[9.76]}$$

at the mth order diffraction. According to the **Rayleigh's resolution criterion** [35], the angle separation, $\Delta\beta$, between the two diffraction peaks should correspond to the peaks' minimum points, as shown in Figure 9.40. That is, for a given wavelength λ, $\Delta\beta$ should also be the difference between two diffraction angles whose corresponding $\Delta\phi$'s yield the maximum and the first minimum of X. From Equation (9.73), the difference between the two $\Delta\phi$'s that give the maximum and first minimum is $2\pi/N$. Thus from Equation (9.72),

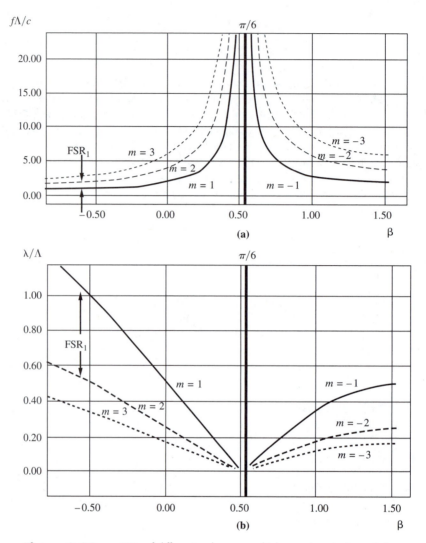

Figure 9.39   FSRs of different orders over which wavelength channels have the same diffraction direction. The incident angle, α, is assumed to be $\pi/6$. (a) Normalized diffracted frequency ($f\Lambda/c$) as a function of the diffraction angle at different diffraction orders. (b) Normalized diffracted wavelength (λ/Λ) as a function of the diffraction angle.

$$\frac{\Lambda \cos \beta}{\lambda_m} \Delta\beta = \frac{1}{N}. \qquad \textbf{[9.77]}$$

Combining Equations (9.76) and (9.77) gives

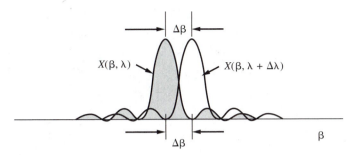

Figure 9.40 Minimum angle resolution criterion according to Rayleigh.

$$\Delta\lambda > \frac{\lambda_m}{mN} = \frac{\lambda_m}{\lambda_{m+1}} \frac{FSR_m}{N}. \tag{9.78}$$

Equation (9.78) says that a smaller channel separation can be achieved by having a large N and a smaller FSR. In addition, the total number of wavelength channels that can be accommodated in the system is

$$N_{ch} = \frac{FSR_m}{\Delta\lambda} = N\frac{\lambda_{m+1}}{\lambda_m}. \tag{9.79}$$

Note that N_{ch} is on the same order as N, the number of grating periods.

Continuing from Example 9.16, the number of wavelength channels within FSR_1 is

$$N_{ch} = \frac{N}{2}.$$

To provide 100 channels thus requires that $N = 200$. Because the period is 5 μm, the size of the periodic structure should be at least 1.0 mm. In addition, the channel separation should be at least

$$\Delta\lambda = \frac{2}{N}(1.73 - 0.87) = 8.6 \text{ nm.} \blacksquare$$

Example 9.17

Bragg-Reflection Grating Bragg reflection, used in DFB and DBR lasers, can also be used for wavelength demultiplexing. One interesting design is shown in Figure 9.41, where the fiber is placed on top of a fan-shaped grating. When the periodic interval is Λ and $\alpha = -\beta = \pi$, there is a strong reflection if the incident wavelength λ_m satisfies the Bragg-reflection equation (9.74) or

$$2n\Lambda = m\lambda_m \tag{9.80}$$

where n is the refractive index of the fiber. For a given λ_m, Λ of the grating in Figure 9.41 can be adjusted to meet Equation (9.80). To do this, the relative location between the grating

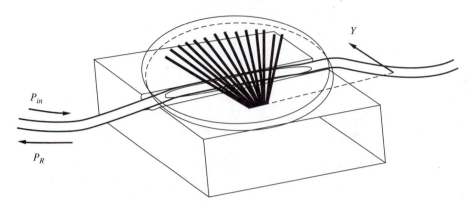

Figure 9.41   A fan-shaped grating is used to provide tunable Bragg reflection grating.

| SOURCE: Reprinted, by permission, from Sorin et al., "Tunable Single-Mode Fiber Reflective Grating Fil-
| ter," *Journal of Lightwave Technology*, vol. 5, no. 9 [45]. © 1987 by IEEE.

structure and the fiber can be moved. To find the FSR and spectral resolution, the same equations, (9.75) and (9.78), can be used by substituting $\alpha = -\beta = \pi$.

Another variation of Bragg-reflection grating is shown in Figure 9.42. In this case, the periodic grating is introduced in a loop section of a fiber. As shown, the loop junction is made to be a 3-dB coupler with the transfer matrix given by Equation (9.42). In Figure 9.42a, when the wavelength of incident light does not satisfy Equation (9.80), the output is a superposition of the incident light through two paths, one without any cross-coupling over the loop junction and one with two cross-couplings. Because each cross-coupling experiences a phase shift of 90°, the superimposed output is zero. On the other hand, if the incident wavelength satisfies the Bragg reflection condition, the incident light is reflected by the periodic structure. Thus this produces the two possible paths that go from input to output shown in Figure 9.42b. Each path has one cross-coupling. As a result, the two paths are in phase and the superposition of the two waves yields a strong output.

Bragg-Reflection Add-Drop Multiplexers   In many system applications, it is desirable to drop one wavelength channel and add another of the same wavelength. For example, as shown in Figure 9.18, ADMs are key elements to provide frequency reuse.

One ADM implementation based on Bragg-reflection grating is shown in Figure 9.43 [47][48]. Its operation principle is very similar to that of the fiber Bragg-reflection grating discussed above. As shown, the device consists of two 3-dB couplers and a Bragg reflector. The incident light at λ_1 is first split by the left-hand 3-dB coupler. When the wavelength λ_1 of the incident light satisfies Equation (9.80), it will be reflected by the grating. As shown in Figure 9.43b, there are two possible paths for the incident light reflected back to the output port 2. Because both paths experience the same 90° phase shift, the superposition at port 2 is in phase. At the same time, there are also two reflections from the grating to port 1. Because they are out of phase, the superposition is zero.

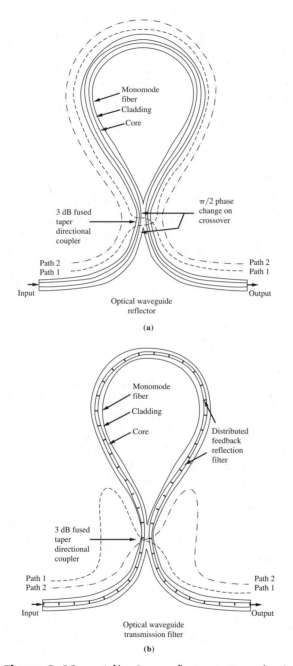

Figure 9.42 A fiber Bragg reflection grating with a 3-dB coupling over the loop junction.

SOURCE: Reprinted, by permission, from Hill, "Narrow Bandwidth Optical Waveguide Transmission Filters," *Electronics Letters*, vol. 23, no. 9 [46]. © 1987 by IEE.

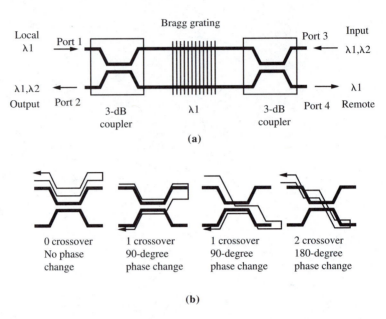

Figure 9.43   (a) An ADM with a Bragg reflection grating on top of an MZI. (b) Possible paths over the 3dB coupler for λ_1 from input port 1.

As shown in Figure 9.43, when there is a different light signal at the same wavelength λ_1 but from the right-hand side, it will be completely reflected to port 4 for the reason just explained. Therefore, the signal is dropped and can be detected. On the other hand, if the signal from the right-hand side is at a wavelength λ_2 different from λ_1, it is split by the right-hand 3-dB coupler, passes through the grating (because Equation [9.80] is not satisfied), and is combined again in phase at output port 2. (There is no output at port 1. Why?) Therefore, the incident signal at λ_2 is combined with the local signal at λ_1.

Acoustic Bragg Reflection   The same Bragg reflection can be used for demultiplexing when the grating is created by a periodic acoustic wave. As shown in Figure 9.44, the longitudinal acoustic wave can create an effective periodic grating at a period Λ. As a result, when the incident light is at the Bragg angle, θ_B, satisfying

$$2n \sin(\theta_B)\Lambda = \lambda \qquad \textbf{[9.81]}$$

where n is the refractive index of the acoustic medium, the light will be reflected as shown (see Chapter 14 for detail). When the wavelength of the incident light does not satisfy Equation (9.81), it will pass through without reflection. This achieves the demultiplexing needed.

9.7.2 FREQUENCY-DOMAIN DISCRIMINATION

Wavelength channels can also be filtered by selective suppression or enhancement in the frequency domain. As a result, the channel tuned to becomes much stronger in power than other channels.

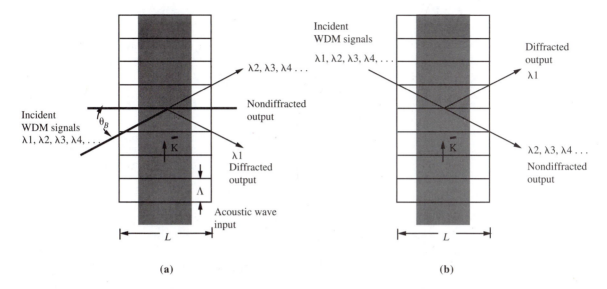

Figure 9.44   Bragg reflection grating from an acoustic chamber. There can be two kinds of interaction: (a) down-shift diffraction and (b) up-shift diffraction.

Fabry-Perot Interferometry   Fabry-Perot interferometry is a common technique used to pass a light signal whose wavelength is in resonance with that of a Fabry-Perot interferometer (FPI) [50]–[53]. As explained in Appendix 3A, the transmissivity of an FPI is given by

$$T(\delta) = \frac{P_t}{P_{in}} = \frac{1}{1 + (2\mathcal{F}/\pi)^2 \sin^2(\delta/2)} \qquad \textbf{[9.82]}$$

where $\mathcal{F}$ is the finesse and δ is given by

$$\delta = \frac{4\pi n L}{\lambda} \qquad \textbf{[9.83]}$$

with L being the cavity length and n the cavity refractive index.

Because the transmissivity is at its peaks when $\delta = 2m\pi$ (m is an integer), from Equation (9.83), wavelength channel tuning can be done by adjusting L or n. To adjust L, a piezoelectric crystal and an external voltage source can be used, as shown in Figure 9.26. In this arrangement, L is modulated by varying the bias voltage across the crystal. To adjust n, an electro-optic crystal can be used, as discussed in Chapter 14. From Equation (9.83), to tune from one channel to another with a separation of $\Delta\lambda$, the amount that nL needs to be changed is

$$\Delta(nL) = \Delta L_{eff} = \frac{nL}{\lambda} \Delta\lambda. \qquad \textbf{[9.84]}$$

FPI MADE OF PIEZOELECTRIC CRYSTAL   Consider an FPI made of a piezoelectric crystal with its length change determined by

Example 9.18

$$\Delta L = KL\Delta V \qquad\qquad \text{[9.85]}$$

where ΔV is the external voltage change and K is the material constant equal to $10^{-3}\ \text{V}^{-1}$. If channel separation, $\Delta\lambda$, is 1 nm and a tuning range for 100 channels is needed, at $\lambda = 1.5\ \mu\text{m}$, $n = 3.0$, and from Equation (9.84), the required voltage change is

$$\Delta V = 100\frac{\Delta L}{KL} = \frac{100}{K}\frac{\Delta\lambda}{\lambda} = 66.7\ \text{V}.$$

From the above equation, note that the required voltage is only a function of the material constant K and the ratio of the wavelength change. ∎

Equation (9.82) says that the transmissivity of an FPI is a periodic function of δ with period 2π. Therefore, from Equation (9.83), one FSR is given by

$$2\pi = \frac{4\pi nL}{\lambda^2}\text{FSR}$$

or

$$\text{FSR} = \frac{\lambda^2}{2nL}. \qquad\qquad \text{[9.86]}$$

At a given FSR, the number of channels that can be multiplexed is determined by the channel separation, $\Delta\lambda$. As shown in Figure 9.45, the number of channels is thus

$$N_{ch} = \frac{\text{FSR}}{\Delta\lambda}. \qquad\qquad \text{[9.87]}$$

To reduce ICI to an insignificant level, $\Delta\lambda$ should be large. From the narrow bandpass characteristic given by Equation (9.82), $\Delta\lambda$ can be set to the full-width half-maximum (FWHM) of the FPI, which corresponds to the width between two $T = 0.5$ points. From Equation (9.82),

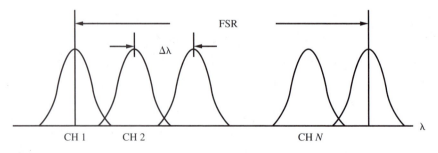

Figure 9.45   Wavelength channel allocations over one FSR.

$$\text{FWHM} = \frac{\text{FSR}}{\mathcal{F}} \qquad \textbf{[9.88]}$$

By setting channel separation, $\Delta\lambda$, equal to one FWHM of the FPI, from Equation (9.87), the number of channels is simply equal to the finesse $\mathcal{F}$.

FPI DESIGN   Equation (9.86) says that the FSR is inversely proportional to L. If $\lambda = 1550$ nm, $n = 1.5$, and $L = 100$ μm,

Example 9.19

$$\text{FSR} = 8 \text{ nm}.$$

To increase the FSR five times to 40 nm, L should be reduced to 20 μm. According to Equation (9.88), this FSR increase also causes an increase of the FWHM at a given finesse. At a finesse of 100, the FWHM increases from 0.08 nm to 0.4 nm when FSR increases from 8 nm to 40 nm. ∎

Mach-Zehnder Interferometry   If we reverse the light propagation directions, the MZI discussed in Section 9.6 for frequency-dependent multiplexing can also be used as a demultiplexer. Similar to an FPI, the performance of an MZI can be characterized by its transmissivity as a function of the incident wavelength. Without loss of generality, assume a demultiplexing path which has a transmissivity $\cos^2[(2\pi/\lambda) \times \Delta L_{eff,m}/2]$ at stage m. Therefore, the overall transmissivity of the path is

$$T(f) = \prod_{m=1}^{k} \cos^2 \left(\frac{2\pi f}{c} \frac{\Delta L_{eff,m}}{2} \right) \qquad \textbf{[9.89]}$$

where $k = \log_2 N$. From the multistage MZI design and Equation (9.51),

$$\Delta L_{eff,m} = \frac{c}{2^m \Delta f}$$

where Δf is the channel separation. From the trigonometric equality

$$\cos(x) = \frac{\sin(2x)}{2\sin(x)}$$

the overall transmissivity is

$$T(f) = \prod_{m=1}^{k} \cos^2 \left(\frac{\pi f}{2^m \Delta f} \right) = \left[\frac{\sin(\pi f/\Delta f)}{N \sin(\pi f/N \Delta f)} \right]^2. \qquad \textbf{[9.90]}$$

Equation (9.90) shows that the transfer function is periodic with period $N\Delta f$, which is one free spectral range. That is,

$$\text{FSR} = N\Delta f. \qquad \textbf{[9.91]}$$

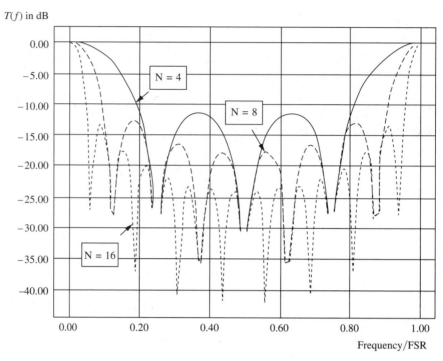

$T(f)$ in dB

Figure 9.46   Transmissivity as a function of the normalized frequency over one FSR at $N = 4$, 8, and 16.

The transmissivity as a function of f/FSR is shown in Figure 9.46 for $N = 4$, 8, and 16. Clearly the larger the N, the sharper the frequency response.

Example 9.20

SIDE LOBE SUPPRESSION OF MZI   According to Equation (9.90), the peak value of the first ripple is approximately at $f = 1.5\Delta f$. At this frequency, the transmissivity is

$$T(1.5\Delta f) = \left| \frac{1}{N \sin(1.5\pi/N)} \right|^2 \approx -13.4 \text{ dB}$$

when $N \gg 1$. This is consistent with Figure 9.46. ∎

Narrow-Band Optical Amplification   Instead of suppressing all wavelength channels that are not tuned to, another frequency-domain demultiplexing method is to amplify only the channel that is tuned to. This can be done by using a tunable single-fre-

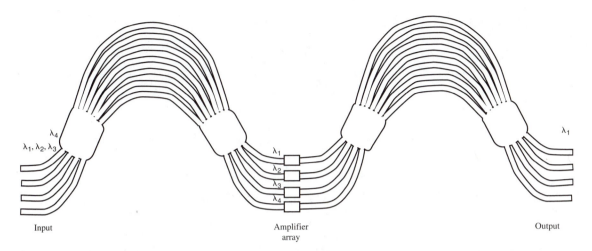

Figure 9.47   Use of optical amplifiers between two WGRs for filtering.

SOURCE: Reprinted, by permission, from Zirngibl et al., "Digitally Tunable Channel Dropping Filter/Equalizer," *IEEE Photonics Technology Letters,* vol. 6, no. 4 [55]. © 1994 by IEEE.

quency laser as a tunable narrow-band amplifier [54][55]. One system uses an MQW-DBR laser as the tunable narrow-band optical amplifier of a bandwidth as small as 6 MHz [54]. Another uses an array of semiconductor amplifiers together with two waveguide grating routers [55]. As shown in Figure 9.47, the first WGR separates the wavelength channels, and the second WGR combines them back. By turning on only one amplifier in the middle between the two WGRs, only one wavelength channel can appear at the output port.

9.7.3   POLARIZATION-DOMAIN DEMULTIPLEXING

When all WDM channels have the same polarization, as depicted in Figure 9.48, another way to demultiplex a wavelength channel is to rotate the polarization of the selected channel by 90° and then use either a polarizing beam splitter (PBS) for separation or a polarizer for filtering.

To rotate the polarization of the selected wavelength light signal, the basic principle is to provide a **polarization mode coupling** mechanism that is wavelength dependent. Polarization mode coupling is a phenomenon in which one polarization is coupled to its orthogonal polarization. When the wavelength of the incident light meets a certain wavelength-dependent coupling condition of the device, there will be a strong coupling between the two orthogonal polarization modes. When the wavelength does not meet the condition, there is no coupling and the incident light will pass through the device with its polarization unchanged.

To provide a wavelength-dependent mode coupling, a waveguide that is birefringent and has a periodic refractive index change can be used. A waveguide that is birefringent means different polarized lightwaves "see" different refractive indices. This happens when the

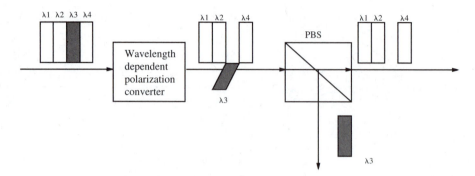

Figure 9.48   Wavelength tuning over the polarization domain.

waveguide is made of an anisotropic material and its dielectric constant is represented by a dielectric tensor (see Chapter 14 for details). When the period of the refractive index variation satisfies the condition

$$\Lambda(n_1 - n_2) = \lambda \tag{9.92}$$

a strong coupling can occur, where n_1 and n_2 are the effective indices of the two orthogonal polarizations.

The condition given by Equation (9.92) can be understood from the conservation of momentum. Because the momenta of the two orthogonal polarizations are $2\pi n_1/\lambda$ and $2\pi n_2/\lambda$, respectively, to couple from one to another requires a third momentum to meet the difference. Therefore, if the waveguide has a periodic refractive index change, the effective momentum is $2\pi/\Lambda$. From the conservation of momentum,

$$\frac{2\pi n_1}{\lambda} - \frac{2\pi n_2}{\lambda} = \pm \frac{2\pi}{\Lambda}$$

which leads to Equation (9.92). This same conservation of momentum is the principle behind the direct bandgap condition in semiconductor light sources discussed in Chapter 3, the diffraction grating discussed earlier, and acousto-optic modulation discussed in Chapter 14.

When the condition given by Equation (9.92) is met, the output power of the two modes over a coupling length L is

$$P_1(L) = P_1(0)\cos^2(\kappa L) \tag{9.93}$$

and

$$P_2(L) = P_1(0)\sin^2(\kappa L) \tag{9.94}$$

where κ is the coupling constant that depends on the waveguide, and $P_1(0)$ is the initial incident power of mode 0. Mode coupling, given by Equations (9.93) and (9.94), can be understood from a similar discussion given in Chapter 14.

From Equation (9.92), to tune to a lightwave at wavelength λ requires a certain refractive index $\Delta n = n_1 - n_2$ or a different period Λ. Once the condition given by Equation (9.92) is reached, the waveguide length for a complete switch-over is

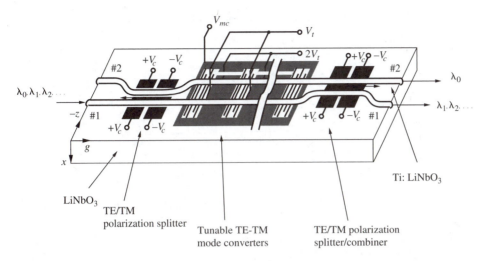

Figure 9.49 An electro-optic implementation for the wavelength dependent polarization converter.

Source: Reprinted, by permission, from Warzanskyj et al., "Polarization-Independent Electro-Optically Tunable Narrow-Band Wavelength Filter," *Applied Physics Letters*, vol. 53, no. 1 [56]. © 1988 by American Institute of Physics.

$$L_{\pi/2} = \frac{\pi}{2\kappa}. \qquad \textbf{[9.95]}$$

Electro-Optic Filters One way to implement a wavelength-dependent polarization coupler is shown in Figure 9.49 using two interleaved metal grids. This interleaved structure has a fixed period, Λ. Because the waveguide is made of an electro-optic crystal such as $LiNbO_3$, the difference in the refractive index can be modulated by the external voltage, which provides the wavelength tuning according to Equation (9.92).

Surface Acoustic Filters Another implementation is based on the **surface acoustic wave** (SAW) structure shown in Figure 9.50. As the figure shows, the periodic refractive index change is introduced by a longitudinal acoustic wave, which is generated by an **interdigital transducer** (IDT). When the waveguide material is acousto-optic, its refractive index can be modulated by the acoustic wave, whose intensity and period can be controlled by an external voltage applied to the IDT.

9.8 SUMMARY

1. WDoMA research has been active for parallel transmission over different wavelength channels. This parallel transmission overcomes the electronics bottleneck and allows systems to utilize tens of THz bandwidths from optical fibers.

2. Research work on WDoMA can be grouped into two primary areas: systems and components. Work on systems is concerned with network connectivity, interchannel interference,

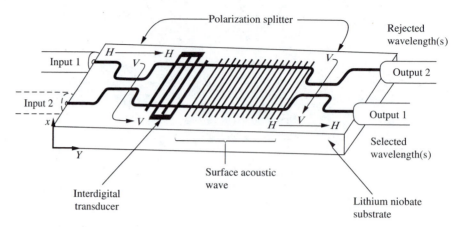

Figure 9.50 An acousto-optic implementation for the wavelength-dependent polarization converter.

SOURCE: Reprinted, by permission, from Smith et al., "Integrated Optic Acoustically Tunable Filters for WDM Networks," *IEEE Journal on Selected Areas in Communications*, vol. 8, no. 6 [57]. © 1990 by IEEE.

channel allocation, medium access, overall network throughput, and average transmission delay. Work on components is concerned with various device realizations for the system needs, such as tunable light sources, multiplexers/demultiplexers, and optical filters.

3. WDoMA systems can also differ in various aspects. According to the relative size between channel separation and channel bandwidth, WDoMA systems are either dense or sparse. Depending on the relative distance between transceivers, there is WDM where signals from a set of transmitters are multiplexed for transmission over a long distance and WDMA that provides multiple access for nodes distributed over a large geographic area. According to how the wavelength channels are selected and detected, there is also coherent detection which uses a local oscillator, and incoherent detection which uses an optical demultiplexer or filter before photodetection.

4. The connectivity of a WDMA network can be described by either its physical configuration which specifies how nodes are physically connected (such as bus, star, or ring), or its logical configuration which specifies how wavelengths of transceivers are set up for interconnection. The logical connectivity can be either fixed or dynamically changed through fixed tuning or dynamic tuning, respectively. Important examples of logical configurations include hypercube, deBruijn, and perfect shuffle. In general, a good logical configuration should provide a high throughput and short transmission delay.

5. For a given logical configuration, a transmission path between the source and final destination can be either direct (single-hop) or through several intermediate nodes (multihop). In general, single-hop is desirable but it can require a large number of transceiver pairs per node. Multihop is lower in implementation cost but can have a long transmission delay and lower throughput.

6. The logical configuration or wavelength channel allocation of a WDMA network can be either deterministic (circuit switching) or statistical (packet switching). In the latter case, wavelength channels are allocated on the basis of individual packets, which can achieve a high throughput and short delay but require fast tuning devices.

7. When the network size (number of nodes) is large, a large number of wavelength channels are required. Because the total number of wavelength channels can be limited by various device constraints, they need to be reused. There are several ways to achieve this. For example, a system can partition the wavelength channels physically over a number of disjoint media, reuse or add-drop a wavelength channel at its destination, or use wavelength converters to avoid wavelength conflicts.

8. In WDoMA, because the power spectral densities of adjacent channels can overlap, there is interchannel interference in detection. The signal-to-interference ratio (SIR) places an upper bound on the effective SNR that determines the detection performance. When the SIR is only slightly higher than the SNR in the absence of SIR for a certain BER performance, the actual required SNR is much larger than the effective SNR, which means a large power penalty. To reduce the power penalty and achieve a satisfactory transmission performance, a channel separation of 5–10 times the channel bandwidth is required.

9. To implement a WDoMA system, three basic components are needed: tunable sources, multiplexers/couplers, and demultiplexers/filters. Tunable sources are needed to operate at different wavelengths. For satisfactory system use, they need to have a large tuning range, single and stable frequency output, and short tuning delay. To meet these criteria, most tunable lasers are based on the MQW-DBR structure. Recently, use of multiplexers with optical amplifiers in a positive feedback loop has been proposed. The use of optical amplifiers provides the necessary gain for oscillation, and the use of multiplexers provides a frequency selection mechanism. When these are properly integrated, multiple wavelength carriers can be generated at fixed channel separation and multiplexed at the same time.

10. To mix multiple wavelength carriers in the same shared medium, either wavelength-independent star couplers or wavelength-dependent multiplexers can be used. Star couplers can provide uniform channel mixing and distribution independent of the input wavelengths. Therefore, they are useful in WDMA applications where input wavelengths can change, as in dynamic tuning. A large star coupler can be easily implemented by either a single planar cavity waveguide, fused optical fibers, or a combination of 2×2 couplers with proper interconnection. One primary limitation of frequency-independent couplers, however, is the large distribution loss that each wavelength channel experiences. In general, the loss is linearly proportional to the total number of output ports.

11. Wavelength-dependent multiplexers couple wavelength channels into a single output without distribution loss. However, proper mixing is strongly dependent on the input wavelengths, which implies a high accuracy of absolute wavelengths of incident carriers.

12. There are two primary methods to implement a frequency-dependent multiplexer: grating and Mach-Zehnder interferometry. In the first method, different wavelength inputs from different incident angles or paths are diffracted or reflected to the same output direction. In the second method, a multistage of 2×2 coupled waveguides is used. Because coupling from one waveguide to another is wavelength dependent, two input channels can be mixed by having one channel coupled from one waveguide to another and having the other channel stay in the same waveguide.

13. Demultiplexing is the inverse process of multiplexing. In general, demultiplexing can be done either in the spatial domain, where wavelength channels are split into different spatial paths; in the frequency domain, where a narrow bandpass filter or amplifier is used; or in the polarization domain, where the polarization of the selected channel is made orthogonal to that of others for polarization-dependent separation.

14. All demultiplexing implementations need a large free spectral range (FSR) and a high spectral resolution. When two wavelength channels are separated by one FSR, they are demultiplexed or filtered equally, which causes ambiguity. To increase the wavelength range without ambiguity, a large FSR is needed. The spectral resolution of a demultiplexer is its wavelength differentiability. The ratio of the FSR to the minimal channel separation that a demultiplexer can differentiate places an upper bound on the total number of channels in a shared medium.

PROBLEMS

Problem 9–1 Fiber Bandwidth: Assume a fiber has a bandwidth of 20 THz over a wavelength range around 1550 nm. If channel separation is 10 GHz and the bit rate for each channel is 2 Gb/s, find the maximum transmission capacity over the 20 THz bandwidth. At this maximum capacity, what is the multiplexer size when WDM is concerned?

Problem 9–2 WDMA Logical Configuration: If each node in a WDMA network has two transceiver pairs, describe how to tune the transceiver wavelengths to form a logical dual ring. Assume the network has 4 nodes.

Problem 9–3 Average Hops of Hypercube:
a. Show that there are C_k^p nodes that take k hops to reach, where C_k^p is the combinatorial equal to $\frac{p!}{k!(p-k)!}$.
b. From (*a*), show that the average number of hops is

$$\overline{H} = \frac{p}{2}\frac{N}{N-1}$$

when the traffic pattern is uniform.

Problem 9–4 Hypercube: Consider a hypercube of $N = 2^8 = 64$.
a. Describe a minimum routing path from the source [0,1,0,0,1,0,1,1] to the destination [0,0,0,1,1,1,1,1].
b. If the traffic pattern is symmetric and uniform, find the maximum network throughput. Assume the bit rate of each wavelength channel is 1 Gb/s.

Problem 9–5 deBruijn: Consider a deBruijn configuration of $N = 3^5$.
a. Describe a minimum routing path from the source [1,2,0,2,1] to [1,2,0,0,1]. How many hops are there?
b. If the traffic pattern is symmetric and uniform, find the maximum network throughput. Assume the bit rate of each wavelength channel is 1 Gb/s. Use Equation (9.3) to approximate the number of hops.

Problem 9–6 deBruijn: Consider the use of the deBruijn configuration for a WDMA network of at least 100 nodes.

    a. Design the network with the minimum number of hops. Specifically, give the average number of hops, maximum number of hops, and the number of transceiver pairs per node.

    b. Design the network with a minimum number of transceiver pairs.

    c. Which one of the above two cases gives the larger maximum network throughput? Use $N = p^H$ in your calculation.

Problem 9–7 Perfect Shuffle: Consider a perfect shuffle network of $k = 2$ and $p = 3$.

    a. Draw the logical connection of all nodes.

    b. Find the average number of hops.

    c. If the traffic pattern is uniform and symmetric, find the maximum throughput. Assume each wavelength channel has a bit rate of 1 Gb/s.

Problem 9–8 Perfect Shuffle:

    a. If perfect shuffle is used for a WDMA network of at least 100 nodes, design the network with a minimum number of transceivers. Calculate the average number of hops.

    b. From the design given in (*a*), find the maximum throughput if the traffic pattern is uniform and symmetric. Assume each channel has a bit rate of 1 Gb/s.

Problem 9–9 Dynamic Tuning: Consider a WDMA network of 100 nodes interconnected by a star coupler. Assume each node has only one transceiver pair and can be tuned to up to a total of 10 wavelength channels.

    a. If dynamic tuning is used only at the transmitter side, find the upper bound of the active probability of each node so that the blocking probability is less than 0.1 according to Lee's approximation.

    b. From (*a*), find the network utilization at the blocking probability of 0.1.

    c. Do (*a*) and (*b*) with dynamic tuning used at both the transmitter and receiver side.

Problem 9–10 Dynamic Tuning: Consider the same dynamic tuning WDMA network in Problem 9–9.

    a. If each wavelength channel has a bit rate of 10 Gb/s and each node has an average of 10 Mb/s data to transmit, find the active probability of each node using dynamic tuning only at the receiver side.

    b. Find the blocking probability of (*a*).

    c. If 50 percent of the data from each node is multicast to an average of 9 destinations, find the effective active probability of each node and the blocking probability if dynamic tuning is used only at the transmitter side. In this case, multiple transmissions are performed for the same data but to different nodes.

Problem 9–11 Frequency Reuse: If add-drop multiplexing is used for frequency reuse, find the number of wavelength channels needed for a hypercube of size $2^4 = 16$. Also show the wavelength interconnections similar to that given in Figure 9.18.

Problem 9–12 Frequency Reuse: If wavelength converters are used as optical gateways for frequency reuse:

a. Draw the physical interconnection of a WDMA network that has 24 nodes partitioned into three groups. Assume each node has one transceiver pair, nodes in the same group are connected by a star coupler, and one pair of wavelength converters is used between each two groups. What is the size of the star coupler in each group?

b. If each node has an active probability of 1 percent and the total outgoing traffic in each group is 50 percent of the intragroup traffic, find the blocking probability for intragroup and intergroup traffic, respectively. Assume one pair of wavelength converters is used at each gateway.

Problem 9–13 ICI in Incoherent Detection: Assume an optical filter has the following characteristic:

$$h_j[i] = e^{-4|i-j|}.$$

a. Find the SIR if the contribution from $S_a^{(2)}$ in Equation (9.14) is neglected.
b. Find the power penalty from (a) if the received SNR required is 20 dB.
c. Find the power penalty if the SIR is reduced by 10 dB because of $S_a^{(2)}$.

Problem 9–14 ICI in Coherent Detection: Assume the SIR of a given system can be expressed as

$$\text{SIR} = 4e^{\Delta f}$$

where Δf is the WDM channel separation in GHz. If the required SNR is 25 dB, find the necessary channel separation so that the power penalty is only 2 dB.

Problem 9–15 ICI in Coherent Detection: Assume the same SIR dependence on Δf given in Problem 9–14. If the BER is of the form

$$P_E = Q(\sqrt{\text{SNR}})$$

find the minimum channel separation so that the error floor is lower than $P_E = 10^{-10}$.

Problem 9–16 Tunable Light Source: For an MQW-DBR laser array that has output wavelengths around 1300 nm and channel separation of 0.2 nm, find the step change of Bragg period Λ. Assume the refractive index of the laser active layer is 3.5.

Problem 9–17 Frequency Stablization: Consider the absolute frequency stablization scheme shown in Figure 9.26.
a. If the FPI used to lock its local laser has a free spectral range of 1 nm, give the general expression for the output wavelength of a locked laser.
b. If the same scheme is used to lock 100 wavelength channels and the free spectral range of each FPI can have an error of ±0.01 nm, describe scenarios that can cause strong ICI. From this, explain the importance of the single FPI scheme shown in Figure 9.28.

Problem 9–18 Planar Waveguide Coupler: Consider a planar waveguide coupler of a size 10 × 10. Assume it has an excess power loss of 3 dB in addition to the distribution loss.
a. Find the total power loss of each channel through the coupler.
b. How can 90 input channels be coupled in terms of the 10 × 10 waveguide couplers? Also find the total power loss of each channel.

Problem 9–19 Star Coupler: If a star coupler is made of 2×2 couplers that have an excess loss of 0.1 dB, find the maximum size so that the total power loss is less than 30 dB.

Problem 9–20 Grating Multiplexing: Consider a WDM multiplexer based on the Littrow configuration shown in Figure 9.34. If channel separation is 0.2 nm and fiber separation is 10 μm, find the required angular dispersion factor. From this, find the Littrow angle, θ_B. In the calculation, assume the operating wavelength is around 1550 nm and the focusing lens has a focus of 10 cm.

Problem 9–21 MZI Multiplexing: Consider a 2×2 MZI used to multiplex two wavelength channels.

    a. If channel separation is 0.2 nm, find the required ΔL_{eff}. Assume the wavelength is centered at 1550 nm.

    b. If ΔL_{eff} is introduced by modulating the refractive index of the waveguide made of an electro-optic crystal, find the required refractive index change if the waveguide has a length of 100 mm.

Problem 9–22 MZI Multiplexing: Give a design of an 8:1 MZI multiplexer with a channel separation of 5 GHz. Assume the lowest wavelength is 1550 nm. In the design, specify ΔL_{eff} in each 2:2 MZI.

Problem 9–23 Waveguide Grating Router: Consider a WGR that can multiplex wavelength channels of unit separation $\Delta \lambda = 0.5$ nm.

    a. If the refractive index of the waveguide is $n_{wgr} = 1.6$, find the length difference between two waveguides so that the central wavelength, λ_0, is 1550 nm.

    b. If $\alpha = \alpha' = 0.01°$, find the radius, R, for the required channel separation from Equation (9.69). Assume $n_{coupler} = 1.5$.

Problem 9–24 Waveguide Grating Router: Consider the output power $P_{p,q}$ given by Equation (9.66). Find the minimal M value so that an incident wave at wavelength $\lambda = \lambda_{p,q} + \Delta \lambda$ will experience a power attenuation of at least 20 dB, where $\Delta \lambda$ is given by Equation (9.69). Assume $\Delta \lambda / \lambda_{p,q} = 0.01$.

Problem 9–25 Diffraction Grating Demultiplexing: Consider a diffraction grating used to demultiplex 100 wavelength channels of unit separation 0.5 nm.

    a. What is the required FSR? From this, give the corresponding wavelength range that covers $\lambda = 1530$ nm.

    b. If the incident angle is $\alpha = 60°$, find the angle range of β corresponding to the FSR given in (*a*) and at the same diffraction order m. Assume the grating period is $\Lambda = 1$ mm.

    c. Find the spectral dispersion factor $\partial \beta / \partial \lambda_m$ at the middle of the β range of (*b*).

Problem 9–26 Bragg-Reflection Grating Demultiplexing: Consider a Bragg-reflection grating with period $\Lambda = 3$ μm and refractive index 1.5. Find its first-order reflection wavelength and the corresponding FSR.

Problem 9–27 Fabry-Perot Filtering: Consider the use of an FPI for filtering WDM channels at 1 nm channel separation.

    a. If the FPI needs to accommodate 100 WDM channels, find the required FSR and its longitudinal length. Assume the center wavelength is 1550 nm and the refractive index is 1.5.

b. If the FPI is used for a 200-channel WDM system of channel separation 0.5 nm, what needs to be modified in the FPI design?

Problem 9–28 FPI versus MZI Demultiplexing: Consider the transmissivity of an FPI given by Equation (9.82) and that of an MZI given by Equation (9.90).

a. If N channels are uniformly separated over one FSR of an FPI, what is the largest transmissivity of out-of-tune channels? Assume $N = \mathcal{F} = 100$.

b. Do the similar computation for the case of MZI.

c. For the case where the wavelength of each channel can deviate from its correct position by 10 percent of the channel separation, repeat (*b*).

Problem 9–29 MZI Demultiplexing: If an MZI demultiplexer is used to demultiplex 256 channels of 5 GHz separation, give the maximum and minimum ΔL_{eff} values.

Problem 9–30 Polarization Demultiplexing: If a birefringent electro-optic waveguide that has a refractive index difference $\Delta n = 0.1$ is used for polarization demultiplexing, find the required period of the electrodes for a lightwave centered around 1550 nm.

REFERENCES

1. I. P. Kaminow, "Non-Coherent Photonic Frequency-Multiplexed Access Networks," *IEEE Network,* March 1989, pp. 4–12.

2. R. A. Linke, "Frequency Division Multiplexed Optical Networks Using Heterodyne Detection," *IEEE Network,* March 1989, pp. 13–20.

3. H. Toba et al., "16-Channel Optical FDM Distribution/Transmission Experiment Utilizing Er^{3+} Doped Fiber Amplifier," *Electronics Letters,* vol. 25, no. 14 (July 1989), pp. 885–87.

4. H. Kobrinski et al., "Demonstration of High Capacity in the Lambdanet Architecture: A Multiwavelength Optical Network," *Electronics Letters,* vol. 23, no. 16 (July 1987), pp. 824–26.

5. M. J. Koral and S. Z. Shaikh, "A Simple Adaptive Routing Scheme for Congestion Control in ShuffleNet Multihop Lightwave Networks," *IEEE Journal on Selected Areas in Communications,* vol. 9, no. 7 (September 1991), pp. 1040–51.

6. J.-F. P. Labourdette and A. S. Acampora, "Logically Rearrangeable Multihop Lightwave Networks," *IEEE Transactions on Communications,* vol. 39, no. 8 (August 1991), pp. 1223–30.

7. *Journal of Lightwave Technology*, Special issue on lightwave networks, no. 11, vol. 5/6 (May/June 1993).

8. P. W. Dowd, "Wavelength Division Multiple Access Channel Hypercube Processor Interconnection," *IEEE Transactions on Computers,* vol. 41, no. 10 (October 1992), pp. 1223–41.

9. P. Green, Jr., *Fiber Optic Networks*, Prentice Hall, 1993.

10. B. S. Glance et al., "New Advances on Optical Components Needed for FDM Optical Networks," *Journal of Lightwave Technology,* vol. 11, no. 5/6 (May/June 1993), pp. 882–89.

11. K. C. Lee and V. O. K. Li, "A Wavelength Convertible Optical Network,"*Journal of Lightwave Technology,* vol. 11, no. 5/6 (May/June 1993), pp. 962–70.

12. P. A. Humblet and W. M. Hamdy, "Crosstalk Analysis and Filter Optimization of Single- and Double-Cavity Fabry-Perot Filters," *Journal on Selected Areas in Communications,* vol. 8, no. 6 (August 1990), pp. 1095–1107.

13. M. Suyama, T. Chikama, and H. Kuwahara, "Channel Allocation and Crosstalk Penalty in Coherent Optical Frequency Division Multiplexing Systems," *Electronics Letters,* vol. 24, no. 20 (September 1988), pp. 1278–79.

14. L. G. Kazovsky, "Multichannel Coherent Optical Communications Systems," *Journal of Lightwave Technology,* vol. 5, no. 8 (August 1987), pp. 1095–1102.

15. Y. H. Lo, "4-Channel Integrated DFB Laser Array with Tunable Wavelength Spacing and 40-Gb/s Signal Transmission Capacity," *Journal of Lightwave Technology,* vol. 11, no. 4 (November 1993), pp. 619–23.

16. J. M. Verdiell, "8-Wavelength DBR Laser Array Fabricated with a Single-Step Bragg Grating Printing Technique," *IEEE Photonics Technology Letters,* vol. 5, no. 6 (1993), pp. 619–21.

17. Y. Katoh, "DBR Laser Array for WDM System," *Electronics Letters,* vol. 29, no. 25 (1993), pp. 2195–97.

18. P. N. Woolnough, "Fabrication of a 4-Channel DFB Laser Transmitter OEIC for 1550 nm Operation," *Electronics Letters,* vol. 29, no. 15 (1993), pp. 1388–90.

19. C. E. Zah et al., "1.5 μm Compressive-Strained Multiquantum Well 20-Wavelength Distributed Feedback Laser Arrays," *Electronics Letters,* vol. 28 (1992), pp. 824–26.

20. M. Nakao et al., "Distributed Feedback Laser Arrays Fabricated by Synchrotron Orbital Radiation Lithography," *IEEE Journal on Selected Areas in Communications,* vol. 8, no. 6 (August 1990), pp. 1178–82.

21. T. Sasaki et al., "Novel Tunable DBR-LDs Grown by Selective MOVPE Using a Waveguide Direction Bandgap Energy Control Technique," Digest of Conference on Optical Fiber Communications, 1992, Optical Society of America, p.282.

22. T. Sasaki et al., "10 Wavelength MQW-DBR Lasers Fabricated by Selective MOVPE Growth," *Electronics Letters,* vol. 30, no. 19 (1994), pp. 785–86.

23. H. Takahashi, H. Toba, and Y. Inoue, "Multiwavelength Ring Laser Composed of EDFAs and an Arrayed-Waveguide Wavelength Multiplexer," *Electronics Letters,* vol. 30, no. 1 (January 1994), pp. 44–45.

24. M. Zirngibl and C. H. Joyner, "High Performance, 12 Frequency Optical Multichannel Controller," *Electronics Letters,* vol. 30, no. 9 (April 1994), pp. 700–701.

25. M. Zirngibl and C. H. Joyner, "12 Frequency WDM Laser Based on a Transmissive Waveguide Grating Router," *Electronics Letters,* vol. 30, no. 9 (April 1994), pp. 701–2.

26. N. K. Dutta, "Optical Sources for Lightwave System Applications," Chapter 9 of *Optical-Fiber Transmission*, edited by E. E. B. Basch, SAMS, 1986.

27. Y. C. Chung et al., "WDM Coherent Star Network with Absolute Frequency Reference," *Electronics Letters,* vol. 24, no. 21 (October 1988), pp. 1313–14.

28. B. Glance et al., "Frequency Stablization of FDM Optical Signals," *Electronics Letters,* vol. 23 (1987), pp. 750–52.

29. B. Glance et al., "Frequency Stablization of FDM Optical Signals Originating from Different Locations," *Electronics Letters,* vol. 23 (1987), pp. 1243–45.

30. M. K. Liu, "Technique for Accurate Carrier Frequency Generation in OFDM System," USA Patent No. 5,239,400, August 24, 1993.

31. C. Dragone, "Efficient $N \times N$ Star Coupler Based on Fourier Optics," *Electronics Letters,* vol. 24, no. 15 (1988), pp. 942–44.

32. B. Moslehi et al., "Fiber-Optic Wavelength-Division Multiplexing and Demultiplexing Using Volume Holographic Gratings," *Optics Letters,* vol. 14, no. 19 (October 1989), pp. 1088–90.

33. J. B. D. Soole, "Wavelength Precision of Monolithic InP Grating Multiplexer/Demultiplexers," *Electronics Letters,* vol. 30, no. 8 (April 1994), pp. 664–65.

34. Y.-T. Huang et al., "Wavelength-Division-Multiplexing and -Demultiplexing by Using a Substrate-Mode Grating Pair," *Optics Letters,* vol. 17, no. 22 (November 1992), pp. 1629–31.

35. E. Hecht, *Optics*, 2nd ed., Addison-Wesley, 1987.

36. B. H. Verbeek et al., "Integrated Four-Channel Mach-Zehnder Multi/Demultiplexer Fabricated with Phosphorous Doped SiO_2 Waveguides on Si," *Journal of Lightwave Technology,* vol. 6, no. 6 (June 1988), pp. 1011–15.

37. N. Takato et al., "Silica-Based Integrated Optic Mach-Zehnder Multi/Demultiplexer Family with Channel Spacing of 0.01–250 nm, *IEEE Journal on Selected Areas in Communications,* vol. 8, no. 6 (August 1990), pp. 1120–27.

38. K. Oda et al., "A 16-Channel Frequency Selection Switch for Optical FDM Distribution Systems," *IEEE Journal on Selected Areas in Communications,* vol. 8, no. 6 (August 1990), pp. 1132–40.

39. C. Dragone et al., "Integrated Optics $N \times N$ Multiplexer on Silicon," *IEEE Photonics Technology Letters,* vol. 3, no. 10 (October 1991), pp. 896–99.

40. C. Dragone et al., "An $N \times N$ Multiplexer Using a Planar Arrangement of Two Star Couplers," *IEEE Photonics Technology Letters,* vol. 3, no. 9 (September 1991), pp. 812–15.

41. H. Obara et al., "Multiwavelength Routing Using Tunable Lasers and Arrayed-Waveguide Grating Multiplexers for Wavelength-Division and Space-Division Multiplexed Crossconnects," *Electronics Letters,* vol. 28, no. 23 (November 1992), pp. 2172–74.

42. S. Suzuki et al., "Polarization-Insensitive Arrayed Waveguide Grating Multiplexer with SiO_2-on-SiO_2 Structure," *Electronics Letters,* vol. 30, no. 8 (April 1994), pp. 642–43.

43. G. J. Cannell et al., "Practical Realization of a High Density Diode Coupled Wavelength Demultiplexer," *IEEE Journal on Selected Areas in Communications,* vol. 8, no. 6 (August 1990), pp. 1141–45.

44. P. A. Kirby, "Multichannel Wavelength Switched Transmitters and Receivers—New Component Concepts for Broadband Networks and Distributed Switching Systems," *Journal of Lightwave Technology,* vol. 8, no. 2 (February 1990), pp. 202–11.

45. W. V. Sorin et al., "Tunable Single-Mode Fiber Reflective Grating Filter," *Journal of Lightwave Technology,* vol. 5, no. 9 (September 1987), pp. 1199–1202.

46. K. O. Hill, "Narrow Bandwidth Optical Waveguide Transmission Filters," *Electronics Letters,* vol. 23, no. 9 (April 1987), pp. 465–66.

47. C. M. Ragdale et al., "Integrated Laser and Add-Drop Optical Multiplexer for Narrowband Wavelength Division Multiplexing," *Electronics Letters,* vol. 28, no. 8 (April 1992), pp. 712–14.

48. C. M. Ragdale et al., "Integrated Three Channel Laser and Optical Multiplexer for Narrowband Wavelength Division Multiplexing," *Electronics Letters,* vol. 30, no. 11 (May 1994), pp. 897–98.

49. A. Lord and J. M. Boggis, "Novel Single-Mode, Grating WDM Device Based Network," *Electronics Letters,* vol. 24, no. 11 (May 1988), pp. 672–74.

50. I. P. Kaminow et al., "FDM-FSK Star Network with a Tunable Optical Fiber Demultiplexer," *Electronics Letters,* vol. 23, no. 21 (October 1987), pp. 1102–3.

51. A. R. Chraplyvy et al., "Network Experiment Using an 8000 GHz Tuning-Range Optical Filter," *Electronics Letters,* vol. 24, no. 17 (1988), pp. 1071–72.

52. L. J. Cimini et al., "Optical-Fiber Fabry-Perot Frequency Discriminator for Communications Applications," *Electronics Letters,* vol. 23, no. 9 (April 1987), pp. 463–64.

53. K. Hirabayashi et al., "Tunable Liquid-Crystal Fabry-Perot Interferometer Filter for Wavelength-Division Multiplexing Communication Systems," *Journal of Lightwave Technology,* vol. 11, no. 12 (December 1993), pp. 2033–43.

54. F. S. Choa and T. L. Koch, "Static and Dynamical Characteristics of Narrowband Tunable Resonant Amplifiers as Active Filters and Receivers," *Journal of Lightwave Technology,* vol. 9, no. 1 (1991), pp. 73–78.

55. M. Zirngibl et al., "Digitally Tunable Channel Dropping Filter/Equalizer Based on Waveguide Grating Router and Optical Amplifier Integration," *IEEE Photonics Technology Letters,* vol. 6, no. 4 (April 1994), pp. 513–15.

56. W. Warzanskyj et al., "Polarization-Independent Electro-Optically Tunable Narrow-Band Wavelength Filter," *Applied Physics Letters,* vol. 53, no. 1 (July 1988), pp. 13–15.

57. D. A. Smith et al., "Integrated-Optic Acoustically-Tunable Filters for WDM Networks," *IEEE Journal on Selected Areas in Communications,* vol. 8, no. 6 (August 1990), pp. 1151–59.

58. G. P. Agrawal, *Fiber-Optic Communication Systems,* John Wiley and Sons, 1992.

59. C. Y. Lee, "Analysis of Switching Networks," *Bell System Technical Journal,* November 1955, pp. 1287–1315.

10

SUBCARRIER MULTIPLEXING

Optical subcarrier multiplexing transmission (SCM) is a multiplexing scheme where multiple signals are multiplexed in the radio frequency (RF) domain and transmitted over a single optical carrier. It is thus similar to wavelength-domain medium access (WDoMA) that provides simultaneous multiple transmissions in the frequency domain. Different from WDoMA, however, it does not require advanced wavelength division devices such as tunable light sources and de/multiplexers. Instead, only regular RF modulators, demodulators, and mixers are needed. SCM is consequently much simpler in implementation.

Optical SCM transmission has been recently deployed in community antenna television (CATV) systems for analog television video signal transmission [1]–[3]. In these systems, analog video signals modulated at the CATV carrier frequencies are mixed to drive a laser diode for transmission between a CATV headend and a subscriber loop distribution point. Because of the low fiber attenuation, optical SCM transmission does not require as many power amplifiers as in coaxial cable transmission.

In addition to analog TV transmission, SCM can be used for digital transmission and can be combined with WDoMA. As mentioned earlier in Chapter 8, SCM is a low-cost alternative to fiber-to-the-home (FTTH) [4]. In this case, subscribers can access both data and analog video services over a single optical fiber. Because of the intensity noise of laser diodes, nonlinear distortion from laser clipping and gain saturation of power amplifiers, and limited modulated bandwidths of RF devices, SCM has a limited transmission bandwidth (several GHz). To accommodate more channels, combining SCM and WDoMA has also been proposed [5][6]. When SCM is combined with WDM, groups of RF channels are carried by different wavelength channels. When SCM is combined with WDMA for multiple access, dynamic frequency tuning can be easily performed over the RF frequency domain.

This chapter discusses analog SCM transmission in detail. In particular, it analyzes the carrier-to-noise ratio (CNR) for both AM and FM transmission and discusses the nonlinear distortion caused by laser clipping. Applications of SCM for digital transmission and combination with WDoMA will be addressed, too.

10.1 BASIC SUBCARRIER MULTIPLEXING SYSTEM

The block diagram of a basic SCM transmission system is illustrated in Figure 10.1. An SCM system consists of (1) signal modulation, (2) RF domain mixing, (3) light carrier modulation, (4) photodetection, (5) RF power splitting, and (6) demodulation. Important aspects of these subsystems are given below.

10.1.1 MODULATION SCHEMES

Before RF domain mixing, each transmitted baseband signal is first modulated according to a certain modulation scheme. In analog communications, there are two common schemes: amplitude modulation (AM) and frequency modulation (FM) [7]. In digital transmission, quadrature amplitude modulation (QAM) [8][9], phase-shift keying (PSK) [10], and frequency-shift keying (FSK) [11] have all been studied.

Amplitude Modulation   In AM transmission, a baseband signal, $m(t)$, is used to modulate the amplitude of a carrier. Because there are two orthogonal carriers, $\cos(\omega_c t)$ and $\sin(\omega_c t)$, at the same frequency, an AM signal can be of the following general form:

$$x_{AM}(t) = m_c(t) \cos(\omega_c t) + m_s(t) \sin(\omega_c t) \qquad \textbf{[10.1]}$$

where $m_c(t)$ is called the **in-phase** baseband signal, and $m_s(t)$ is called the **quadrature-phase** baseband signal.

As shown in Figure 10.2, when the baseband signal, $m(t)$, has a bandwidth B, the required passband bandwidth is $2B$. This means twice the baseband bandwidth is required for passband transmission. However, when $m_c(t) = m_1(t)$ and $m_s(t) = m_2(t)$ are two independent baseband signals, as shown in Figure 10.2c, $x_{AM}(t)$ carries the two signals over the same $2B$ frequency band. The required passband bandwidth thus reduces to one B per signal, and the $x_{AM}(t)$ signal is called a **quadrature amplitude modulated** (QAM) signal.

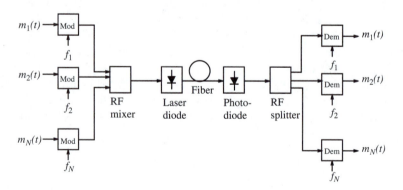

Figure 10.1   Block diagram of an SCM transmission system.

To achieve the same baseband transmission efficiency, the **single sideband** (SSB) technique can also be used [12]. As shown in Figure 10.3, if the quadrature-phase signal, $m_s(t)$, is the Hilbert transform of the in-phase signal, $m_c(t)$, then

$$\mathcal{F}\{m_c(t)\cos(\omega_c t)\} = \tfrac{1}{2}[M_c(\omega - \omega_c) + M_c(\omega + \omega_c)]$$

and

$$\mathcal{F}\{m_s(t)\sin(\omega_c t)\} = \frac{1}{2j}[H_h(\omega - \omega_c)M_c(\omega - \omega_c) - H_h(\omega + \omega_c)M_c(\omega + \omega_c)]$$

where

$$H_h(\omega) \stackrel{\text{def}}{=} \begin{cases} j & \text{if } \omega < 0 \\ -j & \text{if } \omega > 0 \end{cases}$$

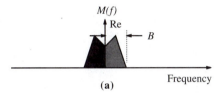

(a)

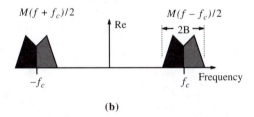

(b)

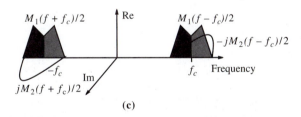

(c)

Figure 10.2 AM spectra of (a) baseband signal $m(t)$, (b) double sideband AM (DSB-AM) signal $m(t)\cos(\omega_c t)$, and (c) quadrature amplitude modulated (QAM) signal $m_1(t)\cos(\omega_c t) + m_2(t)\sin(\omega_c t)$. In these illustrations, it is assumed that the spectra of $m(t), m_1(t)$, and $m_2(t)$ are real.

is the transfer function of the Hilbert filter. As shown in Figure 10.3, the combined $x_{AM}(t)$ requires only the lower sideband of the double sideband signal for passband transmission.

Example 10.1

MONOTONE SSB   Consider a single tone signal $m(t) = \cos(\omega_m t)$. When it is transmitted according to VSB-AM, the modulated signal is

$$x_{AM}(t) = m(t)\cos(\omega_c t) = \tfrac{1}{2}\cos([\omega_c - \omega_m]t) + \tfrac{1}{2}\cos([\omega_c + \omega_m]t).$$

The Fourier transform of $x_{AM}(t)$ is

$$X_{AM}(\omega) = \tfrac{1}{4}[\delta(\omega - \omega_c + \omega_m) + \delta(\omega - \omega_c - \omega_m) + \delta(\omega + \omega_c - \omega_m) + \delta(\omega + \omega_c + \omega_m)].$$

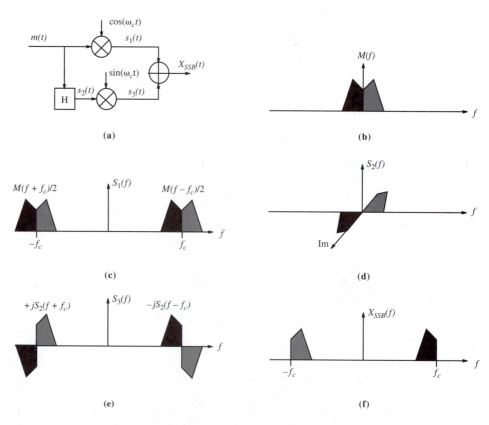

Figure 10.3   The SSB-AM scheme in the frequency domain: (a) block diagram, where H is the Hilbert transform, (b) the in-phase passband spectrum, (c) the baseband spectrum after Hilbert transform, (d) the quadrature-phase passband spectrum, and (e) the lower sideband SSB spectrum.

The spectrum has two delta functions on each side of $\pm \omega_c$. In other words, there is a double side band.

Alternatively, SSB-AM transmission can be used. Because the Fourier transform of $m(t)$ is $M(\omega) = [\delta(\omega - \omega_m) + \delta(\omega + \omega_m)]/2$, the Hilbert transform of $M(\omega)$ is $M_h(\omega) = [\delta(\omega - \omega_m) - \delta(\omega + \omega_m)]/2j$. Thus $m_h(t) = \sin(\omega_m t)$, and

$$m_h(t)\sin(\omega_c t) = \sin(\omega_m t)\sin(\omega_c t) = \tfrac{1}{2}\cos([\omega_c - \omega_m]t) - \cos([\omega_c + \omega_m]t).$$

From Equation (10.1), the SSB-AM signal is $x_{SSB}(t) = \cos([\omega_c - \omega_m]t)$, and the Fourier transform is

$$X_{SSB}(\omega) = \tfrac{1}{2}[\delta(\omega - \omega_c + \omega_m) + \delta(\omega + \omega_c - \omega_m)].$$

This corresponds to the lower sideband of $X_{AM}(\omega)$ but double in amplitude. ∎

In practice, because of the sharp transition of the Hilbert transfer function at $\omega = 0$, it is difficult to perform SSB modulation when the baseband signal has a strong dc power. In this case, a smoother slope filter shown in Figure 10.4a can be used. The resulting signal

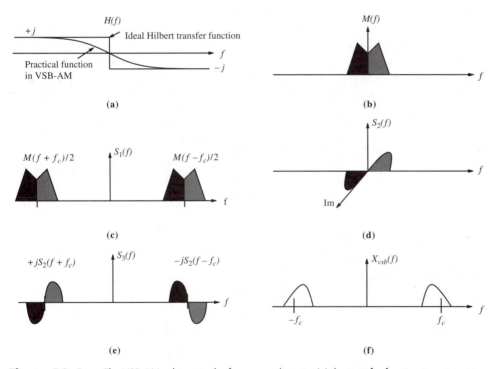

(a)

(b)

(c)

(d)

(e)

(f)

Figure 10.4   The VSB-AM scheme in the frequency domain: (a) the transfer function to get $m_s(t)$ from $m_c(t)$, (b) the in-phase passband spectrum, (c) the baseband spectrum after the transform, (d) the quadrature-phase passband spectrum, and (e) the lower sideband VSB spectrum.

has a spectrum shown in Figure 10.4*f*, which is called a **vestigial sideband amplitude modulated** (VSB-AM) signal. This modulation scheme is used in many TV transmission systems and will be discussed in detail later.

Frequency Modulation   In addition to AM, FM is another important modulation scheme used in analog communications, where the frequency of a given carrier is modulated according to the transmitted signal. Therefore, an FM signal can be expressed as

$$x_{FM}(t) = A \cos \left(\omega_c t + 2\pi k_f \int_{-\infty}^{t} m(t') dt' \right).$$ **[10.2]**

By taking the derivative of the phase term, the simultaneous frequency is

$$f(t) = f_c + k_f m(t)$$ **[10.3]**

which is a linear function of $m(t)$. If $m(t)$ is in the range $(-m_p, m_p)$, the instantaneous frequency is between $(f_c - k_f m_p)$ and $(f_c + k_f m_p)$. From this, it is possible to define

$$\Delta f \overset{\text{def}}{=} k_f m_p$$ **[10.4]**

as the **simultaneous peak frequency deviation**.

   In principle, the transmission bandwidth of an FM signal can be obtained from the Fourier transform of $x_{FM}(t)$ given by Equation (10.2). However, because the input signal is in the cosine function, the exact bandwidth in general cannot be found analytically. Instead, a simple estimation called **Carson's rule** [12] is commonly used. When $m(t)$ has a baseband spectral width B, the rule states that the passband bandwidth of FM transmission is approximately

$$B_{FM} \approx 2(\Delta f + B) = 2B(1 + \beta_{FM})$$ **[10.5]**

where

$$\beta_{FM} \overset{\text{def}}{=} \frac{\Delta f}{B}$$ **[10.6]**

is called the **frequency modulation index**.

Example 10.2

SINGLE PULSE FREQUENCY MODULATION   Consider a pulse signal that has an amplitude of -1 from $-T/2$ to 0 and an amplitude of $+1$ from 0 to $T/2$. In this case,

$$\int_{-\infty}^{t} m(t') dt' \overset{\text{def}}{=} z(t) = \begin{cases} -(t + T/2) & -T/2 < t < 0 \\ t - T/2 & 0 < t < T/2 \\ 0 & \text{otherwise.} \end{cases}$$

Therefore, the Fourier transform of Equation (10.2) is

$$X_{FM}(\omega) = \tfrac{1}{2} \mathcal{F} \left\{ e^{j\omega_c t + 2\pi k_f z(t)} + c.c \right\} = \tfrac{1}{2} [\delta(f - f_c) + \delta(f + f_c)] + J$$

where

$$J = \frac{1}{2}\int_{-T/2}^{T/2}[e^{-j2\pi[f-f_c-k_f z(t)]t} - e^{-j2\pi(f-f_c)t}]dt + \frac{1}{2}\int_{-T/2}^{T/2}[e^{-j2\pi[f+f_c+k_f z(t)]t} - e^{-j2\pi(f+f_c)t}]dt$$

$$= \frac{1}{2}\int_{-T/2}^{T/2}e^{-j2\pi[f-f_c-k_f z(t)]t}dt + \frac{1}{2}\int_{-T/2}^{T/2}e^{-j2\pi[f+f_c+k_f z(t)]t}dt - \frac{T}{2}\Big\{\text{sinc}[(f-f_c)T]$$

$$+ \text{sinc}[(f+f_c)T]\Big\}$$

$$= \frac{T}{4}e^{-j\pi k_f T}\Big\{\text{sinc}[(f-f_c+k_f)T/2]e^{j\pi(f-f_c+k_f)T/4}$$

$$+ \text{sinc}[(f-f_c-k_f)T/2]e^{-j\pi(f-f_c-k_f)T/4}\Big\}$$

$$+ \frac{T}{4}e^{j\pi k_f T}\Big\{\text{sinc}[(f+f_c-k_f)T/2]e^{j\pi(f+f_c-k_f)T/4}$$

$$+ \text{sinc}[(f+f_c+k_f)T/2]e^{-j\pi(f+f_c+k_f)T/4}\Big\}$$

$$- \frac{T}{2}\Big\{\text{sinc}[(f-f_c)T] + \text{sinc}[(f+f_c)T]\Big\}. \qquad \textbf{[10.7]}$$

A sketch of this spectrum is shown in Figure 10.5. The passband transmission bandwidth is approximately $B_{FM} = 2(k_f + 2/T)$, where $\Delta f = k_f$ in this case. Because the baseband bandwidth of the pulse $m(t)$ is $B = 2/T$ (same as the RZ pulse), $B_{FM} = 2(\Delta f + B)$, which is exactly equal to what Carson's rule predicted. ∎

Carson's rule (10.6) shows that when the modulation index, β_{FM}, is small ($\beta_{FM} < 0.5$), the bandwidth is not much larger than $2B$. This is called *narrow band FM*. When β_{FM} is large, the actual transmission bandwidth can be several times $2B$. This is called the *wide band FM*. As will be shown later, a large modulation index, β_{FM}, in *wideband FM* can improve the final SNR. In other words, a large transmission bandwidth can be used in exchange for a high SNR. In SCM, where a large SNR is difficult to achieve because of the laser noise and nonlinear distortion, wideband FM becomes an attractive modulation scheme [7].

Digital Modulation　In general, the same AM and FM modulations discussed above can be used to transmit digital signals. In this case, $m(t)$ has only a finite set of discrete levels. For example, in binary frequency-shift keying (FSK), $m(t)$ can be either 1 or 0 and in an NRZ pulse train. In M-level QAM, on the other hand, both the in-phase and quadrature-phase signals have $L = M^{1/2}$ discrete levels at $-(L-1)\Delta/2$, $-(L-3)\Delta/2, \ldots,$ $(L-3)\Delta/2$, and $(L-1)\Delta/2$, where Δ is the step size between two adjacent levels. A 64-level QAM signal, for example, has 8 discrete levels in both the in-phase and quadrature-phase terms. See Section 10.5 for detailed discussion.

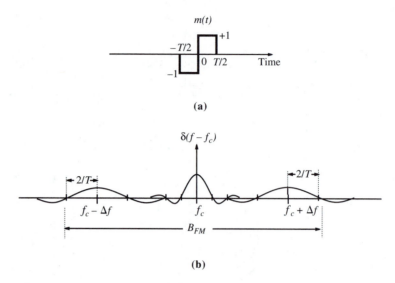

Figure 10.5   Carson's rule for a message signal $m(t)$ shown in (a) and the one-sided spectrum ($f > 0$) shown in (b). Only the relative magnitude (not phase) is shown for simplicity.

10.1.2 RF MIXING AND LASER MODULATION

In SCM, multiple modulated carriers, $x_j(t)$'s ($j = 1, \ldots, N$), given by Equations (10.2) or (10.3) are mixed in the RF domain before optical transmission. When the laser diode has a threshold current I_{th} and is biased at current I_b, the total driving current is given by

$$I_{tot}(t) = I_b + (I_b - I_{th}) \sum_j k_j x_j(t) \stackrel{\text{def}}{=} I_b + (I_b - I_{th}) x_{tot}(t) \qquad \textbf{[10.8]}$$

where k_j is the amplitude modulation index of the jth modulated carrier x_j, and $x_{tot}(t) \stackrel{\text{def}}{=} \sum_j k_j x_j(t)$.

If the total current, I_{tot}, is greater than the threshold current, the output light power is

$$P_{out}(t) = \mathcal{R}_{ld}[I_{tot}(t) - I_{th}] = \mathcal{R}_{ld}(I_b - I_{th})[1 + x_{tot}(t)]$$
$$= \mathcal{R}_{ld}(I_b - I_{th})[1 + \sum_j k_j x_j(t)] \stackrel{\text{def}}{=} P_b[1 + \sum_j k_j x_j(t)] \qquad \textbf{[10.9]}$$

where $\mathcal{R}_{ld}$ is the responsivity of the laser diode and P_b is the output power at bias. Because the total output power, $P_{out}(t)$, cannot be negative, there will be a clipping if $I_{tot}(t)$ is less than the threshold current. This results in **intermodulation distortion** and will be analyzed in detail later.

Example 10.3   **DISTORTION DUE TO CLIPPING**   If the modulation index of each channel is $k_j = 0.01$ and each x_j is over the range $[-1, 1]$, $x_{tot}(t)$ can be smaller than -1 if the total number of channels is greater than 100, even if the total ac power is only $0.5 \times k_j^2 \times 100 = 0.5\%$ of the dc power (assuming $N = 100$). Therefore, the number of SCM channels can be limited by the amount of nonlinear distortion due to clipping. ∎

10.1.3 PHOTOCURRENT DETECTION AND CARRIER-TO-NOISE RATIO

At the receiver side, the detected photocurrent from direct detection is

$$
\begin{aligned}
I_{ph}(t) &= \mathcal{R}_{pd} P_{out} 10^{-\alpha_f L/10} = \mathcal{R}_{pd}\mathcal{R}_{ld} 10^{-\alpha_f L/10}[I_{tot}(t) - I_{th}] \\
&= \mathcal{R}_{pd}\mathcal{R}_{ld}(I_b - I_{th})10^{-\alpha_f L/10}[1 + x_{tot}(t)] \stackrel{\text{def}}{=} I[1 + x_{tot}(t)]
\end{aligned}
\tag{10.10}
$$

where $\mathcal{R}_{pd}$ is the responsivity of the receiver photodiode, α_f is the fiber attenuation in dB/km, L is the fiber length in km, and

$$
I \stackrel{\text{def}}{=} \mathcal{R}_{ld}\mathcal{R}_{ph}(I_b - I_{th})10^{-\alpha_f L/10}
\tag{10.11}
$$

is the dc component of the photocurrent. From Equation (7.3) derived in Chapter 7, when the ac term is small compared to the dc current, the photocurrent noise power is

$$
\sigma_n^2 = [2q F I + \text{RIN} \times I^2 + (\mathcal{R}_{pd} \times \text{NEP})^2]B
\tag{10.12}
$$

where F is the excess noise factor and the receiver is assumed to have an ideal low-pass filter of bandwidth B.

SNR and CNR in AM Transmission For AM transmission, given by Equation (10.1), if each channel has the same modulation index, $k_j = k_m$, the received SNR is

$$
\text{SNR} = \frac{k_m^2 \overline{m^2} I^2}{\sigma_n^2} = \frac{k_m^2 \overline{m^2} I^2}{[2q F I + \text{RIN} \times I^2 + (\mathcal{R}_{pd} \times \text{NEP})^2]B}.
\tag{10.13}
$$

If $m(t)$ is a monotone carrier of unit amplitude, the corresponding carrier-to-noise ratio (CNR) is given by

$$
\text{CNR} = \frac{k_m^2 I^2}{2\sigma_n^2} = \frac{k_m^2 I^2}{2B[2q F I + \text{RIN} \times I^2 + (\mathcal{R}_{pd} \times \text{NEP})^2]}.
\tag{10.14}
$$

CATV TRANSMISSION Consider an SCM transmission system for CATV signals with $B = 6$ MHz, RIN $= -140$ dB/Hz, $I = 1$ mA, $F = 1$ (PIN photodiode is used), and NEP $= 0$. From Equation (10.12), the total noise power is

Example 10.4

$$
\sigma_n^2 = 6.0 \times 10^6 \times (3.2 \times 10^{-19} \times 10^{-3} + 10^{-14} \times 10^{-6}) = 6.0 \times 10^{-14} \text{ A}^2.
$$

If the modulation index, k_m, is 0.1, the CNR is

$$
\text{CNR} = \frac{k_m^2 I^2}{2\sigma_n^2} = 8.3 \times 10^4 = 49 \text{ dB}.
$$

The computation shows that the noise power is dominated by the laser RIN noise, which is the typical case in AM SCM transmission. If the modulation index is reduced to accommodate more CATV channels, the RIN noise also needs to be smaller to maintain the same CNR. Therefore, a low intensity noise from laser sources is critical to satisfactory AM SCM transmission. ∎

SNR and CNR in FM Transmission   In FM transmission, the actual CNR can be increased by increasing the modulation index, β_{FM}. As shown in Appendix 10–A, the effective SNR in CATV transmission is given by

$$\text{SNR}_{FM} = \left[6 \frac{\Delta f^2 B_{FM}}{B^3} \frac{\overline{m(t)^2}}{x_p^2} k_w \right] \text{CNR}_{FM} \stackrel{\text{def}}{=} G_{FM}\text{CNR}_{FM} \qquad \textbf{[10.15]}$$

where $\Delta f = k_f x_p$ is the peak frequency deviation, x_p is the peak value of the VSB-AM modulated signal of $m(t)$, B_{FM} is the passband FM transmission bandwidth, B is the baseband video bandwidth, and k_w is the gain factor from using transmission preemphasis and receiver deemphasis for noise reduction. The parameter

$$G_{FM} \stackrel{\text{def}}{=} 6 \frac{\Delta f^2 B_{FM}}{B^3} \frac{\overline{m(t)^2}}{x_p^2} k_w \qquad \textbf{[10.16]}$$

is called the FM gain factor with respect to the received CNR in FM transmission. Although it is the gain most literatures use [7][13][14], it is not the true improvement with respect to AM transmission. Because CNR_{FM} is smaller than CNR_{AM} by a factor B_{FM}/B_{AM}, where B_{AM} is the corresponding transmission bandwidth if AM is used, the actual gain from using FM with respect to VSB-AM is

$$G_{FM-AM} = 6 \frac{\Delta f^2 B_{AM}}{B^3} \frac{\overline{m(t)^2}}{x_p^2} k_w. \qquad \textbf{[10.17]}$$

Example 10.5

FM GAIN IN CATV   When FM is used for CATV transmission, a 6 MHz baseband VSB-AM signal is FM modulated. If the peak frequency deviation is set to $\Delta f = 10$ MHz, according to Carson's rule $B_{FM} = 2(\Delta f + B_{AM}) = 32$ MHz, where $B_{AM} = 6$ MHz. At the receiver end, the video signal is first FM demodulated and then VSB-AM demodulated. Because the video bandwidth after AM demodulation is $B = 4.2$ MHz,

$$6 \frac{\Delta f^2 B_{FM}}{B^3} = 6 \times \frac{100 \times 32}{4.2^3} = 259 = 24.1 \text{ dB}$$

where $\overline{m(t)^2}/x_p^2 = 1$ is assumed. Because a typical k_w is around 14 dB [14], the total gain is

$$G_{FM} = 24.1 + 14 = 38.1 \text{ dB}.$$

Also, because

$$\frac{B_{FM}}{B_{AM}} = 7.6 = 8.8 \text{ dB}$$

the actual gain with respect to VSB-AM is $38.1 - 8.8 = 29.3$ dB. From this large gain, a low RIN value required in AM, illustrated in Example 10.4, is not necessary here. ∎

10.2 ANALOG TV TRANSMISSION

Analog TV transmission is one primary application of SCM. In North America, an NTSC (National Television System Committee) TV signal has a bandwidth of 6 MHz. As shown in Figure 10.6, there is a video carrier and an audio carrier. The video signal is modulated according to VSB-AM, and the audio signal is modulated according to FM.

In TV broadcast or in cable transmission, the channel allocation over the VHF and UHF bands is shown in Figure 10.7. The first channel (called channel 2) is in the frequency range from 54 MHz to 60 MHz, where the video carrier is at 55.25 MHz and the audio carrier is at 59.75 MHz.

In TV transmission, the required CNR is in the range of 40–45 dB for VSB-AM and 15–20 dB for FM [7]. Examples 10.4 and 10.5 show that it is advantageous to use FM transmission if the RIN or received power is a problem. On the other hand, for low-cost implementation, VSB-AM is attractive because its format is directly compatible to TV broadcast and cable transmission.

10.3 NONLINEAR DISTORTION

In SCM, frequency channels are interleaved in the frequency domain. As a result, they are overlapped in the time domain. When the transmission channel (including the source driver and receiver amplifier) is nonlinear, there is intermodulation distortion from different RF carriers. In practice, there are several sources that cause nonlinear distortion. In coaxial cable transmission, for example, gain saturation of power amplifiers in the transmission line is a common cause. In optical fiber transmission, on the other hand, laser clipping is the primary source.

To explain the nature of intermodulation distortion, the ac component of the photocurrent output can be expanded as a polynomial series of $x_{tot}(t)$:

$$i_{ph} = a_1 x_{tot} + a_2 x_{tot}^2 + a_3 x_{tot}^3 + \ldots = a_1 x_{tot} + \sum_{i=2} a_i x_{tot}^i \overset{\text{def}}{=} a_1 x_{tot}(t) + x_{NLD}(t) \quad \textbf{[10.18]}$$

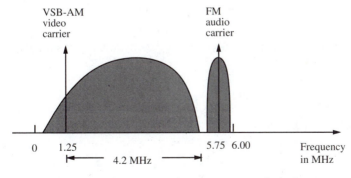

Figure 10.6 The spectrum of an NTSC TV signal. The frequencies shown are relative to the start of a TV channel band.

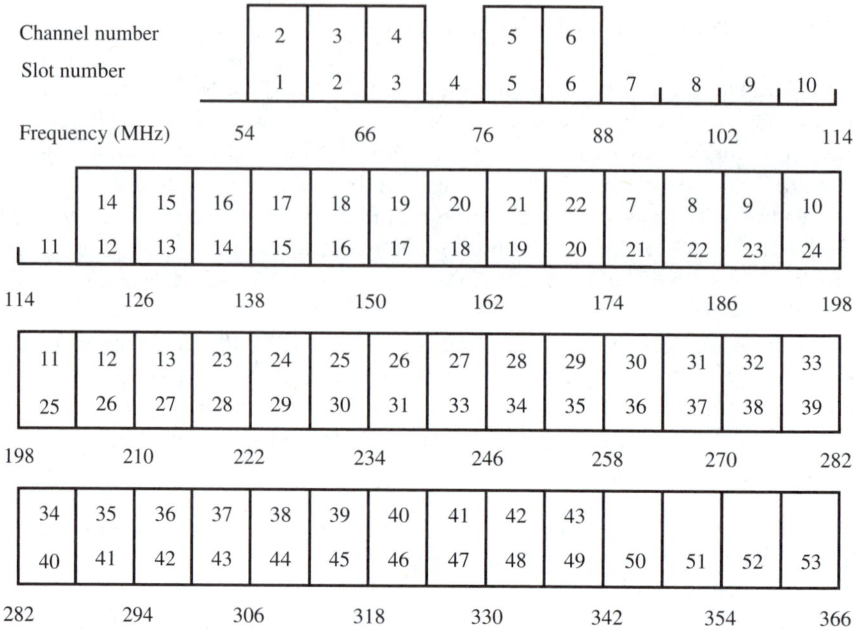

Channel number		2	3	4		5	6				
Slot number		1	2	3	4	5	6	7	8	9	10

Frequency (MHz)   54   66   76   88   102   114

11	14	15	16	17	18	19	20	21	22	7	8	9	10
	12	13	14	15	16	17	18	19	20	21	22	23	24

114   126   138   150   162   174   186   198

11	12	13	23	24	25	26	27	28	29	30	31	32	33
25	26	27	28	29	30	31	33	34	35	36	37	38	39

198   210   222   234   246   258   270   282

34	35	36	37	38	39	40	41	42	43			
40	41	42	43	44	45	46	47	48	49	50	51	52	53

282   294   306   318   330   342   354   366

Figure 10.7   The frequency channel allocation of a 42-channel CATV system. Note that there are several discontinuities in the channel allocation.

where a_i's are the coefficients that can be determined from the nonlinear function $i_{ph}(x_{tot})$, and $x_{NLD}(t)$ represents the total nonlinear distortion.

From Equation (10.1) or Equation (10.2), x_{NLD} consists of **intermodulation products** (IMPs) at frequency combinations $f_i \pm f_j$, $f_i \pm f_j \pm f_k$, etc. For example, the second-order distortion in AM transmission can be expanded as

$$x_{tot}(t)^2 = \sum_{i,j} x_i(t)x_j(t)$$

$$= \sum_{i,j} \left[m_{c,i}(t)m_{c,j}(t)\cos(\omega_i t)\cos(\omega_j t) + m_{s,i}(t)m_{c,j}(t)\sin(\omega_i t)\cos(\omega_j t) \right.$$

$$\left. + m_{c,i}(t)m_{s,j}(t)\cos(\omega_i t)\sin(\omega_j t) + m_{s,i}(t)m_{s,j}(t)\sin(\omega_i t)\sin(\omega_j t) \right].$$

Therefore, x_{tot}^2 has components at frequencies $|f_i \pm f_j|$. Similarly, for the third-order distortion, x_{tot}^3, there are components at $|f_i \pm f_j \pm f_k|$.

As Figure 10.7 shows, the video carrier frequency of a CATV channel (except channels 5 and 6) is 1.25 MHz higher from a multiple of 6 MHz. Therefore, for most channels, the video carrier frequency can be expressed as

$$f_i = (6c_i + 1.25) \text{ MHz} \qquad \textbf{[10.19]}$$

where $6c_i$ is the beginning frequency of channel i.

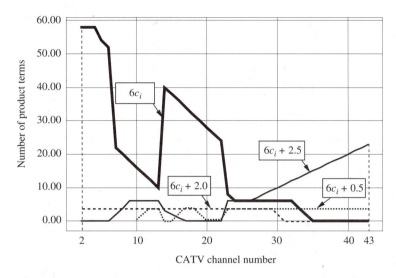

Figure 10.8   The number of product terms due to the second-order distortion.

For simple nonlinear distortion quantification, assume each RF signal $x_i(t)$ is a monotone signal and at frequency f_i. Therefore, the second-order distortion generates frequencies at

$$f_i \pm f_j = 6c_m, \quad \text{or} \quad 6c_m + 2.5 \text{ MHz}$$

where c_m is a certain integer. The above equation says that the second-order distortion carriers are at either 0 or 2.5 MHz from the start of a CATV frequency band. For the 42-channel system, the numbers of product terms at different carrier frequencies due to the second-order distortion are shown in Figure 10.8. We see lower band channels have a large number of product terms due to $|f_i - f_j|$, and upper-band channels have a large number of product terms due to $f_i + f_j$.

Similarly, for the fourth-order distortion, there are product terms at frequencies

$$f_i \pm f_j \pm f_k \pm f_l = 6c_m, \quad 6c_m \pm 2.5, \quad \text{or} \quad 6c_m + 5.0 \text{ MHz}.$$

The number of product terms of the 42-channel system due to the fourth-order distortion is shown in Figure 10.9. Most product terms are at the same two frequencies as the second-order distortion. However, the number of the product terms is much larger because the number of combinations is $O(N^3)$. In second-order distortion, the number of product terms is $O(N)$, where N is the number of SCM channels (see Problem 10–9).

From the above observation, an important parameter used to evaluate the nonlinear distortion in CATV is called the **composite second-order** (CSO) distortion. The CSO distortion ratio of a given CATV channel is a measurable quantity defined to be the ratio of the carrier power to the total nonlinear distortion power at the **CSO frequency**:

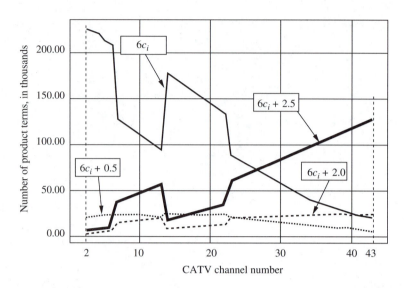

Figure 10.9 The number of product terms due to the fourth-order distortion.

$$\text{CSO} \overset{\text{def}}{=} \frac{\text{carrier power}}{\text{total distortion due to product terms at the CSO frequency}} \qquad \textbf{[10.20]}$$

where the CSO frequency of a given channel is defined to be either $6c_m$ or $6c_m + 2.5$ MHz, depending on which has more product terms, and $6c_m$ is the start frequency of channel m. As the definition indicates, the CSO is contributed to only by even-order distortions.

In contrast to the CSO, the third-order distortion generates product terms at frequencies

$$f_i \pm f_j \pm f_k = 6c_m \pm 1.25, \text{ or } 6c_m + 3.75 \text{ MHz.}$$

In general, as shown in Figure 10.10, most of the of third-order product terms are at the carrier frequencies (i.e., $6c_m + 1.25$). Similarly, for the fifth-order product terms,

$$f_i \pm f_j \pm f_k \pm f_l \pm f_m = 6c_m + 0.25, \quad 6c_m \pm 1.25, \quad \text{or} \quad 6c_m \pm 3.75.$$

Figure 10.11 shows some important fifth-order product terms from the 42-channel system. As shown, most product terms are still at the video carrier frequency. Therefore, the **composite triple beat** (CTB) ratio is a measurable quantity defined to be the ratio of the carrier power to the total nonlinear distortion at the video carrier frequency:

$$\text{CTB} \overset{\text{def}}{=} \frac{\text{carrier power}}{\text{total distortion power due to product terms at the carrier frequency}} \qquad \textbf{[10.21]}$$

As the definition and above discussion indicate, the CTB is contributed only from odd-order distortions.

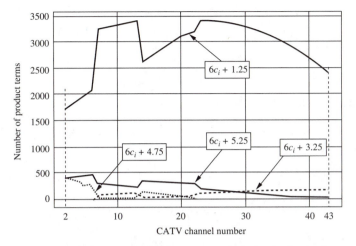

Figure 10.10   The number of product terms due to the third-order distortion.

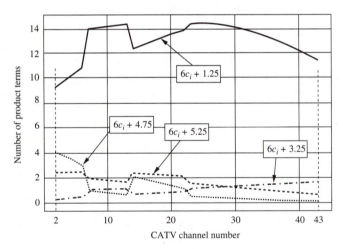

Figure 10.11   The number of product terms due to the fifth-order distortion.

10.4 NONLINEAR DISTORTION ANALYSIS

Several techniques have been proposed in the past to evaluate the nonlinear distortion [15]–[18]. One simple technique, given by Saleh [15], calculates the total nonlinear distortion that is below the threshold of the laser diode. This technique assumes the total ac signal,

$x_{tot}(t)$, has a Gaussian distribution. When N, or the total number of channels, is large and all carriers are asynchronous in phase, this is a valid assumption according to the central limit theorem (see Chapter 6). From Equation (10.9), the variance of $x_{tot}(t)$ is

$$E[x_{tot}^2] = \frac{N}{2}k_m^2 \stackrel{def}{=} \mu^2 \qquad \text{[10.22]}$$

where μ is the total modulation depth.

As illustrated in Figure 10.12, when $(I_b - I_{th})[1 + x_{tot}(t)] < 0$ or $x_{tot} < -1$, the laser output is zero. In other words, the total nonlinear power below clipping is

$$P_{NLD} = P_b \frac{1}{\sqrt{2\pi\mu^2}} \int_{-\infty}^{-1} (1 + x)^2 e^{-x^2/2\mu^2} dx = P_b \left[(1 + \mu^2)Q(\mu^{-1}) - \frac{\mu}{\sqrt{2\pi}} e^{-1/2\mu^2} \right]. \qquad \text{[10.23]}$$

The series expansion of the Q-function given by Equation (10.39) in Appendix 10–B gives

$$P_{NLD} \approx P_b \sqrt{\frac{2}{\pi}} \mu^5 e^{-1/2\mu^2}. \qquad \text{[10.24]}$$

If the nonlinear distortion power in each channel is uniformly distributed, from Equation (10.24), the **carrier-to-nonlinear-distortion ratio** (CNLD) in each channel is

$$\text{CNLD} = \frac{k_m^2 P_b/2}{P_{NLD}/N} = \sqrt{\frac{\pi}{2}} \mu^{-3} e^{1/2\mu^2}. \qquad \text{[10.25]}$$

Example 10.6

CNLD DUE TO SALEH   From Equation (10.25), if a CNLD of 70 dB is needed, the total modulation depth, μ, needs to satisfy

$$\sqrt{\frac{\pi}{2}} \mu^{-3} e^{1/2\mu^2} > 10^7$$

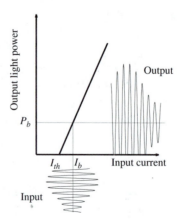

Figure 10.12   Nonlinear distortion due to laser clipping.

which results in the condition

$$\mu < 0.21.$$

From Equation (10.14), if the system is dominated by RIN $= -140$ dB/Hz and the required CNR is 45 dB, then

$$\frac{k_m^2/2}{2B \times 10^{-14}} > 10^{4.5}.$$

At $B = 6$ MHz, this implies

$$k_m^2 > 0.0076.$$

From Equation (10.22), the total number of channels is limited by

$$N = \frac{2\mu^2}{k_m^2} = 10.$$

This example illustrates the bandwidth limitation of SCM transmission due to nonlinear distortion. ∎

Saleh's method, discussed above, calculates only the total nonlinear distortion and cannot distinguish the CSO and CTB. Because a CATV system uses the CSO and CTB as part of the transmission specifications, Saleh's method is insufficient. Furthermore, from the number of product terms shown in Figures 10.8–10.11, the assumption of *uniform* nonlinear power distribution over all channels is invalid. As a result, several series expansion techniques have been proposed [16]–[18]. In [16], the laser I-P characteristic curve is approximated by a continuous curve, as illustrated in Figure 10.13. According to this, the ratio of the **carrier power to the nth-order intermodulation product power** (CIMP) at frequency ν can be shown to be

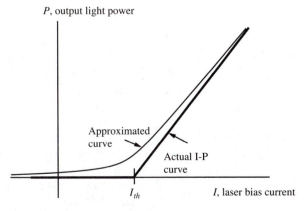

Figure 10.13   An I-P characteristic approximation for distortion analysis.

$$\text{CIMP}_{\nu}^{(n)} = \frac{\pi (4N)^{n-1} (n!)^2 a_1^2}{H_{n-2}^2 (1/\sqrt{2}\mu) K_{\nu}^{(n)}} e^{1/\mu^2} \qquad \textbf{[10.26]}$$

where $H_k(x)$ is the **Hermite function** of order k, $K_{\nu}^{(n)}$ is the number of products of order n at frequency ν, and $a_1 = 1 - Q(1/\mu)$ (see Appendix 10–B for derivation).

From Equation (10.16) and the definitions of the CSO and CTB,

$$\text{CSO} = \frac{P_c}{\displaystyle\sum_{n=2,4,\ldots} P_{cso}^{(n)}} = \frac{\pi e^{1/\mu^2} a_1^2}{\displaystyle\sum_{n=2,4,\ldots} [H_{n-2}^2 (1/\sqrt{2}\mu) K_{cso}^{(n)}]/[(4N)^{n-1}(n!)^2]} \qquad \textbf{[10.27]}$$

$$\text{CTB} = \frac{P_c}{\displaystyle\sum_{n=3,5,\ldots} P_{ctb}^{(n)}} = \frac{\pi e^{1/\mu^2} a_1^2}{\displaystyle\sum_{n=3,5,\ldots} [H_{n-2}^2 (1/\sqrt{2}\mu) K_{ctb}^{(n)}]/[(4N)^{n-1}(n!)^2]} \qquad \textbf{[10.28]}$$

where P_c is the carrier power.

Example 10.7

CIMP AT DIFFERENT ORDERS   From Equations (10.16) and (10.41),

$$\text{CIMP}_{\nu}^{(2)} = \frac{\pi a_1^2 (4N)}{K_{\nu}^{(2)}} 4 e^{1/\mu^2}$$

$$\text{CIMP}_{\nu}^{(3)} = \frac{\pi a_1^2 (4N)^2}{K_{\nu}^{(3)}} [18\mu^2] e^{1/\mu^2}$$

$$\text{CIMP}_{\nu}^{(4)} = \frac{\pi a_1^2 (4N)^3}{K_{\nu}^{(4)}} \frac{144\mu^4}{(1-\mu^2)^2} e^{1/\mu^2}$$

$$\text{CIMP}_{\nu}^{(5)} = \frac{\pi a_1^2 (4N)^4}{K_{\nu}^{(5)}} \frac{1800\mu^6}{(1-3\mu^2)^2} e^{1/\mu^2}.$$

At $\mu = 0.5$,

$$a_1 = 1 - Q(2) = 0.95.$$

For channel 2 in the 42-channel system, $K_{CSO}^{(2)} = 58$, $K_{CTB}^{(3)} = 1737$, $K_{CSO}^{(4)} = 225{,}972$, and $K_{CTB}^{(5)} = 9{,}326{,}580$. Therefore, $\text{CIMP}_{CSO}^{(2)} = 32.5$ dB, $\text{CIMP}_{CTB}^{(3)} = 40.5$ dB, $\text{CIMP}_{CSO}^{(4)} = 47.1$ dB, and $\text{CIMP}_{CTB}^{(5)} = 67.7$ dB. These results are consistent with what is shown in Figure 10.14. ∎

The Saleh's fundamental limit and CIMPs at different orders of channels 2 and 13 are shown in Figures 10.14 and 10.15. The second-order distortion is stronger than the third-order at channel 2. However, the second-order distortion is smaller at channel 13 for $\mu < 0.7$. This difference is mainly due to the large change of the product numbers of orders 2 and 3 between the two channels (see Figures 10.8 and 10.10). On the other hand,

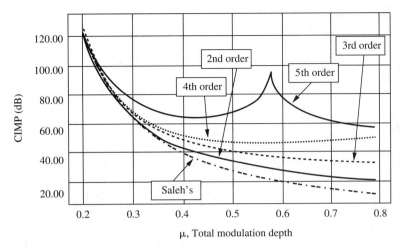

Figure 10.14 CIMP for orders 2–5 of CATV channel 2. For orders 2 and 4 the frequency is at 54 MHz, and for orders 3 and 5, the frequency is at the video carrier frequency, 55.25 MHz. The Saleh's fundamental limit is also superimposed for comparison.

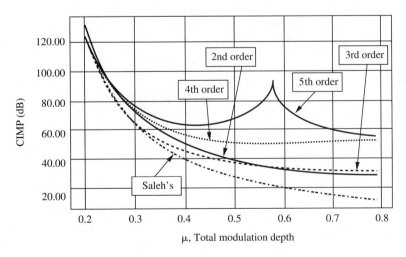

Figure 10.15 CIMP for orders 2–5 of CATV channel 13. For orders 2 and 4 the frequency is at 126 MHz, and for orders 3 and 5 the frequency is at the video carrier frequency, 127.25 MHz.

both the fourth- and fifth-order distortions are negligible, and the Saleh's result gives a conservative estimate of the nonlinear distortion.

10.5 DIGITAL SUBCARRIER MULTIPLEXING TRANSMISSION

Because of the simple and low-cost implementation, SCM has also been proposed for digital transmission [8]–[11]. By allocating additional channels for digital transmission, both analog and digital TV signals can be transmitted over the same fiber.

In digital transmission, either frequency or amplitude modulation can be used. A digital FM system proposed by [11] provides 20 100 Mb/s channels, where the channel separation is 200 MHz. In the design, the frequency separation of two FSK frequencies of each channel is set at 100 MHz.

From the intermodulation distortion discussed earlier, FSK can be sensitive to the product terms. That is, when the frequencies $f_i \pm f_j$ or $f_i \pm f_j \pm f_k$ fall in the interested frequency channel, there is an increased noise power. In other words, the effective CNR is reduced. As shown in Figure 10.16, the CNR can be reduced by 3–7 dB at a large 8 percent modulation depth.

To improve the spectrum efficiency, multilevel QAM can be used [8][9]. When the number of signal levels increases, however, the effects of noise and interchannel interference become more significant. To maintain the same transmission performance (i.e., bit error rate), the received SNR must be increased and the intermodulation distortion is controlled. According to Equation (10.13), the SNR can be increased either by increasing the modulation index, k_m, or by increasing the optical power before the RIN noise becomes too large. Because of clipping and power saturation of laser diodes, these increases cannot be arbitrary.

In M-level QAM transmission, the amount that the optical power needs to be increased can be seen as follows. Because there are $L = \sqrt{M}$ signal levels for both the in-phase and quadrature-phase carriers, the L levels are

$$-(L-1)\Delta/2, -(L-3)\Delta/2, \ldots, -\Delta/2, \Delta/2, \ldots, (L-1)\Delta/2$$

where Δ is the required peak-to-peak separation for M-level QAM transmission. When each of the L levels is equally likely, the average power is

$$\frac{2}{L} \sum_{k=1}^{L/2} (2k-1)^2 \frac{\Delta^2}{4} = \frac{L^2-1}{3} \frac{\Delta^2}{4}$$

Therefore, the required received SNR for M-level QAM transmission with respect to quatenary QAM is increased by a factor of

$$\frac{\text{SNR}_M}{\text{SNR}_4} = \frac{L^2-1}{3} = \frac{M-1}{3} \qquad\qquad \textbf{[10.29]}$$

where SNR_4 is the required SNR for 4-QAM transmission at a given bit error rate and receiver design. When $M = 2^m \gg 1$, the ratio can be simplified to

$$\frac{\text{SNR}_M}{\text{SNR}_4} \approx \frac{M}{3} = -4.77 + 3m \text{ dB.} \qquad\qquad \textbf{[10.30]}$$

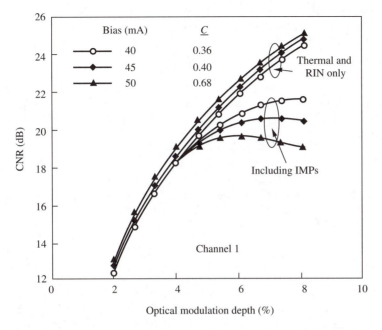

Figure 10.16   Received CNR at different laser bias and different laser modulation depth (%). There can be a significant drop because of IMP at a large modulation depth.

SOURCE: Reprinted, by permission, from Hill and Olshansky, "A 20-channel Optical Communication System," *Journal of Lightwave Technology*, vol. 8, no.4, p. 554 [11]. ©1990 by IEEE.

This result tells that the power penalty of QAM is approximately 3 dB/bit.

16-QAM   Consider a 160 Mb/s digital transmission using SCM. To reduce the transmission bandwidth, **16-QAM** is used. Because $\log_2(16) = 4$, there are 4 bits per symbol and the symbol rate is 40 Mbaud/s. If the NRZ pulse is used, the passband transmission bandwidth is 80 MHz.

Example 10.8

From Equation (10.29), the required SNR increases by a factor of

$$\frac{M-1}{3} = 5 = 7.0 \text{ dB}.$$

From Equation (10.13), if shot noise is the dominating term,

$$\text{SNR} \approx \frac{k_m^2 \overline{m^2} I}{2qBF}.$$

Because the transmission bandwidth is reduced by a factor of 4, the power penalty is $5/4 = 1.25$ or 1 dB.

For the above result to be true, shot noise must be much larger than RIN noise. From the above equation, if $k_m = 0.02$, $F = 1$, SNR = 15 dB, $\overline{m^2} = 0.5$, and $B = 160$ MHz, the required photocurrent, I, for 4-QAM transmission is

$$I = 8.1 \mu A.$$

When RIN = −140 dB/Hz, from Equation (10.13), the RIN power factor is $10^{-14}I/2q = 25.3$ percent of the shot noise power. Therefore, the laser noise in this case cannot be ignored. From Equation (10.13) or

$$\text{SNR} = \frac{k_m^2}{2B[2qFI^{-1} + \text{RIN}]}$$

the required I is 10.8 μA, or 1.34 times higher than the original 8.1 μA. When 16-QAM is used, the SNR is 5 times higher and B is 4 times smaller. The required photocurrent from similar computation is 15.8 μA, which is 1.46 times of 10.8 μA. In other words, the required received power increases by a factor of 1.46 instead of 1.25 because of RIN noise. ∎

When the received optical power increases, however, the interchannel interference also increases and can become a dominating term. To reduce it, the channel separation can be increased, which reduces the channel spectrum efficiency and defeats the original purpose of using multilevel signaling. To solve this, pulse shaping can be used. By choosing a QAM pulse such as a raised-cosine pulse with a much smaller spectral width, the interchannel interference can be significantly reduced [8].

10.6 COMBINATION OF SUBCARRIER MULTIPLEXING AND WAVELENGTH-DOMAIN MEDIUM ACCESS

Because of the nonlinear distortion discussed earlier, SCM can use only a small portion of the available fiber bandwidth. In analog AM-SCM CATV transmission, for example, a large transmission bandwidth ($\gg 1$ GHz) can cause a strong nonlinear distortion and is prohibited.

To explore a large available fiber bandwidth and reduce the expensive WDoMA implementation, SCM can be combined with WDoMA as a cost-effective alternative [5][6]. An SCM-WDM transmission system is illustrated in Figure 10.17. As shown, a number of RF channels are first multiplexed in the RF domain. Each of the multiplexed signals is used to drive a laser diode tuned at a distinct wavelength. These different optical signals can then be multiplexed in the optical wavelength domain. In principle, the same WDM devices discussed in Chapter 9 can be used to perform the optical domain multiplexing and demultiplexing.

The advantages of combining SCM with WDM over either SCM or WDM alone can be seen as follows. First, for a total number of $N = N_{RF}N_{Opt}$ frequency channels, the number of optical receivers can be reduced by a factor of N_{RF}. Because there are only N_{RF} channels added together to modulate one laser diode, the total modulation index, μ, is also reduced by a factor of $\sqrt{N_{Opt}}$, which can significantly reduce the nonlinear distortion.

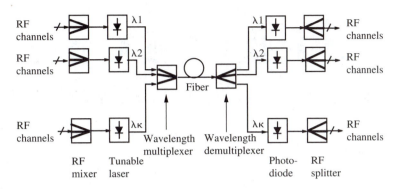

Figure 10.17   SCM and WDM combination.

The combination of SCM and WDM also has some minor disadvantages. First, as shown in Figure 10.18, the spectrum efficiency is reduced by at least a factor of 2 because both sidebands with respect to a wavelength carrier need to be transmitted. When a small channel wavelength separation is not critical, this smaller spectrum efficiency may not be important. Second, with respect to SCM, there is more interference from other wavelength channels. This can be an important factor when analog AM transmission is used.

When multiple access is concerned, it is also attractive to combine WDMA with RF FDMA. Because RF frequency tuning is much faster and more stable than optical domain tuning, fast dynamic frequency tuning can be done in the RF domain, and fixed frequency tuning and/or relatively low-speed switching can be done in the optical frequency domain. This two-level medium access is illustrated in Figure 10.19. As shown, each user node accesses the network in the RF domain, and every N_{RF} node forms an FDMA group, which consists of p parallel FDMA networks. If each FDMA group is considered an optical node in the WDMA network, there are p wavelength channels per optical node, and the WDMA network can be logically configured in various connections, such as perfect shuffle, discussed in Chapter 9.

For each user node to access one of the wavelength channels, it needs to tune its carrier frequency and uses the demultiplexer to direct the signal to the corresponding FDMA network. At a given WDMA logical configuration, the signal will be received by one of the FDMA networks. If the destination user node is reached, the signal will be demodulated and terminated. Otherwise, it will be demodulated and modulated for transmission over the WDMA network again (the dotted lines shown in Figure 10.19). The number of hops to reach the final destination will be determined by the given WDMA logical configuration, as discussed in Chapter 9.

From the discussion, the WDMA and FDMA combination can provide a total number of $N_{RF} N_\lambda / p$ RF end users for multiple access. Because there are only N_λ wavelengths instead of $N = N_\lambda N_{RF}$, the need for a large number of wavelength channels can be reduced and the number of intermediate hops reduced. On the other hand, this combination requires more complex FDMA implementation and needs proper RF tuning control. When N_{RF} and p are large, the implementation can be challenging.

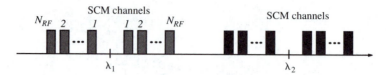

Figure 10.18   Spectrum of SCM and WDM combination.

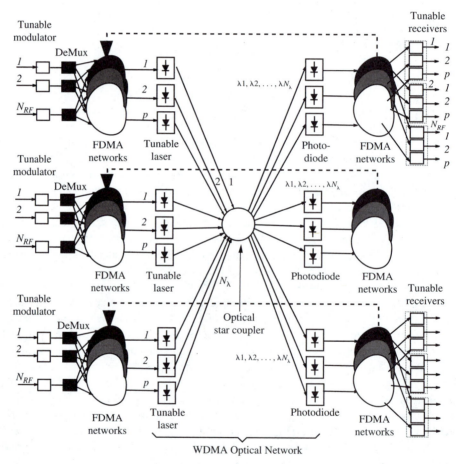

- - - - - -   RF channels that need to be forwarded over the WDMA optical network

Figure 10.19   FDMA and WDMA combination in multiple access. As shown, every N_{RF} node forms an FDMA group consisting of p FDMA networks and p laser drivers. At the given p wavelengths per FDMA group, the WDMA network can be configured in a certain logical connection. By properly tuning the RF modems and demultiplexers, the RF signals can reach the final destination over certain hops in the WDMA network.

10.7 SUMMARY

1. Similar to WDoMA, SCM is a frequency-domain multiplexing scheme. However, because multiplexing and demultiplexing are both performed in the RF domain, there is no need for advanced WDM devices. On the other hand, due to nonlinear distortion from laser clipping and limited modulation bandwidths of lasers and RF devices, SCM is limited in the total transmission bandwidth.

2. SCM is attractive to analog AM and FM CATV transmission. In this case, lower fiber attenuation can greatly reduce the number of power amplifiers needed between the CATV headend and distribution points. Furthermore, because there is no need to convert the RF signal format (e.g., no analog to digital and digital to analog conversions), implementation is simple.

3. One primary trade-off between AM and FM is the required CNR versus the transmission bandwidth. In general, AM requires a high CNR (40–45 dB for CATV) but needs a small transmission bandwidth (6 MHz for VSB-AM). On the other hand, FM requires a large transmission bandwidth (30–40 MHz) but can relax the required CNR level (15–20 dB). Because the laser RIN noise in SCM contributes a significant portion to the total noise power, the smaller CNR required by FM can avoid the need of extra low RIN laser sources.

4. In CATV transmission, each TV channel in VSB-AM modulation occupies a 6 MHz bandwidth. For most TV channels except channels 5 and 6, their frequency bands start at multiples of 6 MHz, and the video and audio carriers are at 1.25 and 5.75 MHz, respectively, from the start of frequency bands.

5. When the total SCM signals are mixed in the RF domain, there is a possibility that the total signal plus the bias current is lower than the threshold current of the laser diode. In this case, there is no optical output because of laser clipping. This results in nonlinear distortion and can be quantified by the carrier-to-nonlinear-distortion ratio (CNLD) and by the carrier-to-intermodulation-product ratio (CIMP). In general, the nonlinear distortion can be decomposed into intermodulation products (IMPs) at different orders and at different frequencies.

6. Among many different IMPs at different orders and frequencies in CATV, the two most important ones occur at the carrier frequency and at ± 1.25 MHz from the carrier frequency. The IMPs that occur at the carrier frequency are due to odd-order IMPs, and the carrier to the total IMPs at the carrier frequency is called the composite triple beat ratio (CTB). IMPs that occur at ± 1.25 MHz are due to even-order IMPs. For a given CATV channel, the frequency of either $+1.25$ or -1.25 MHz with respect to the carrier frequency is called the composite second-order (CSO) frequency, depending on which has the larger total IMPs. The carrier-to-total-IMPs ratio at the CSO frequency is called the composite second-order ratio (CSO).

7. Acceptable CSO and CTB in CATV is around 60–70 dB. To improve these values, the total modulation depth (μ) must be limited. Consequently, there is an upper bound for the allowable modulation index from the tolerable nonlinear distortion. When the modulation index, k_m, of each CATV channel is given from the required CNR, the number of CATV channels is limited by $2\mu^2/k_m^2$.

8. In addition to analog video transmission, SCM transmission can also be used for data transmission by allocating additional RF channels. In general, FSK, ASK, and PSK can all be used as the modulation schemes. For efficient spectrum use, multilevel signaling and pulse shaping can be used to reduce the transmission bandwidth and channel separation.

9. To increase the total transmission bandwidth of SCM and reduce the implementation cost of WDM, WDM and SCM can be combined. In this case, the total channel number is the product of the wavelength channel number and the SCM channel number.

10. When multiple access is concerned, WDMA and FDMA can also be combined. In this case, the network access of each node is over the RF domain, and a few RF channels are mixed and carried by one optical wavelength channel. Because RF transceivers can be tuned at a high speed, dynamic frequency tuning can be performed over the RF domain and use fixed-frequency tuning over the wavelength domain. This combination can reduce the number of intermediate hops and responds to fast traffic fluctuation.

APPENDIX 10-A: CARRIER-TO-NOISE RATIO ANALYSIS FOR FM CATV TRANSMISSION

This appendix analyzes the demodulated CNR using FM for video transmission. For the FM signal shown in Equation (10.2), one way to demodulate the transmitted signal is to differentiate the received signal and perform peak detection. Using this scheme, the FM demodulated output of a VSB-AM modulated signal $x_{vsb}(t)$ is

$$y(t) = 2\pi k_f k_m x_{vsb}(t) I$$

where k_m is the amplitude modulation index from VSB-AM. The signal power of the signal after VSB-AM demodulation is

$$S = (2\pi k_f k_m I)^2 \overline{m^2(t)} = (2\pi \Delta f)^2 (k_m I)^2 \frac{\overline{m^2(t)}}{x_p^2} \qquad \textbf{[10.31]}$$

where $\Delta f = k_f x_p$ is the peak frequency deviation and x_p is the peak value of $x_{vsb}(t)$.

If the baseband video signal's bandwidth is B (equal to 4.2 MHz for NTSC) and the noise power spectral density is N_0, the noise power is

$$\sigma_n^2 = 2N_0 \int_0^B (2\pi f)^2 |H(f)|^2 df = \frac{2N_0}{3}(2\pi)^2 B^3 k_w^{-1} \qquad \textbf{[10.32]}$$

where $H(f)$ is the low-pass filter used in FM demodulation when preemphasis at the transmitter side is used [12] and

$$k_w \overset{\text{def}}{=} \frac{\int_0^B (2\pi f)^2 df}{\int_0^B (2\pi f)^2 |H(f)|^2 df} \qquad \textbf{[10.33]}$$

is the gain factor from using the deemphasis filter $H(f)$. From the above results, the demodulated SNR is

$$\text{SNR}_{FM} = \frac{S}{\sigma_n^2} = \left[\frac{(k_m I)^2/2}{2N_0 B_{FM}} \right] \times \left[6\frac{\Delta f^2 B_{FM}}{B^3} \frac{\overline{m(t)^2}}{x_p^2} k_w \right]$$

or

$$\text{SNR}_{FM} = \text{CNR}_{FM} \left[6\frac{\Delta f^2 B_{FM}}{B^3} \frac{\overline{m(t)^2}}{x_p^2} k_w \right] \qquad \textbf{[10.34]}$$

where B_{FM} is the total passband FM transmission bandwidth and

$$\text{CNR}_{FM} = \frac{(k_m I)^2/2}{2N_0 B_{FM}} \qquad \textbf{[10.35]}$$

is the received CNR from FM transmission. From Equation (10.34), the SNR gain from using FM is

$$G_{FM} \stackrel{\text{def}}{=} 6\frac{\Delta f^2 B_{FM}}{B^3} \frac{\overline{m(t)^2}}{x_p^2} k_w. \qquad \textbf{[10.36]}$$

This gain factor is the gain used in most literatures comparing FM versus AM [7][13][14]; however, note that it is with respect to the received CNR $_{FM}$. Because CNR $_{FM}$ is smaller than CNR $_{AM}$ by a factor of B_{FM}/B_{AM} (B_{AM} is the corresponding transmission bandwidth if AM is used), the actual gain from using FM with respect to VSB-AM is

$$G_{FM-AM} = 6\frac{\Delta f^2 B_{AM}}{B^3} \frac{\overline{m(t)^2}}{x_p^2} k_w. \qquad \textbf{[10.37]}$$

APPENDIX 10–B: NONLINEAR DISTORTION ANALYSIS

This appendix gives detailed analysis of SCM nonlinear distortion, derives the Q-function series expansion for the Saleh's fundamental limit, and analyzes the CSO and CTB using a series expansion.

Q-Function Series Expansion To obtain the Saleh's fundamental limit on nonlinear distortion, the Q-function must be expanded in a Taylor series. Because

$$Q(x) \stackrel{\text{def}}{=} \int_x^\infty \frac{1}{\sqrt{2\pi}} e^{-y^2/2} dy$$

substituting $x + \epsilon$ for y gives

$$Q(x) = \int_0^\infty \frac{1}{\sqrt{2\pi}} e^{-(x+\epsilon)^2/2} d\epsilon = \frac{e^{-x^2/2}}{\sqrt{2\pi}} \int_0^\infty e^{-x\epsilon} \sum_{n=0}^\infty \frac{1}{n!} \left(\frac{\epsilon^2}{2} \right)^n d\epsilon$$

where

$$e^{-\epsilon^2/2} = \sum_{n=0}^{\infty} \frac{(-\epsilon^2/2)^n}{n!}$$

is substituted. Because

$$\int_0^{\infty} \epsilon^n e^{-x\epsilon} d\epsilon = n! x^{-n-1}$$

this gives

$$Q(x) = \frac{e^{-x^2/2}}{\sqrt{2\pi}\,x} \sum_{n=0}^{\infty} (-1)^n \frac{(2n)!}{2^n n!} x^{-2n} = \frac{e^{-x^2/2}}{\sqrt{2\pi}\,x}[1-x^{-2} + 3x^{-4} - \ldots] \qquad \textbf{[10.38]}$$

when $x \gg 1$.

CSO and CTB Analysis from I-P Characteristic Approximation   To find the CSO and CTB separately, the a_i coefficients in the Taylor series given by Equation (10.18) must be found. Because the laser I-P characteristic function is not differentiable at the threshold current, the laser I-P characteristic must first be approximated by a differentiable curve (see Figure 10.13). As suggested by [16], the curve considered is given by

$$f(x) = x + \frac{\mu}{\sqrt{2\pi}} e^{-x^2/2\mu^2} - x Q(x/\mu) = x + \frac{1}{\sqrt{2\pi\mu^2}} \int_x^{\infty} (x' - x) e^{-x'^2/2\mu^2} dx' \qquad \textbf{[10.39]}$$

where $x = 1 + x_{tot}$ and $P_{out} = \mathcal{R}_{pd}(I_b - I_{th}) f(x)$.

When μ is small, x is centered around 1, and $f(x)$ can be expanded in a Taylor series around $x = 1$. That is,

$$f(x) = \sum_{n=0}^{\infty} \frac{(x-1)^n}{n!} \frac{d^n f}{dx^n}\bigg|_{x=1} = \sum_{n=0}^{\infty} \frac{d^n f}{dx^n} x_{tot}^n.$$

From Equation (10.39),

$$f'(x) = 1 - \frac{1}{\sqrt{2\mu^2}} \int_x^{\infty} e^{-x'^2/2\mu^2} dx'$$

and

$$f''(x) = \frac{1}{\sqrt{2\mu^2}} e^{-x^2/2\mu^2}.$$

For higher orders,

$$f^{(n+2)} = \frac{1}{\sqrt{2\mu^2}} \frac{d^n}{dx^n} e^{-x^2/2\mu^2} = \frac{1}{\sqrt{2\mu^2}} (-\sqrt{2}\mu)^{-n} e^{-x^2/2\mu^2} H_n(x/\sqrt{2}\mu)$$

where $H_n(x)$ is the **Hermite function** of degree n [19]. As a summary,

$$f'(1) = 1 - Q(1/\mu)$$

$$f^{(n)}(1) = \sqrt{\frac{2}{\pi}} \mu e^{-1/2\mu^2} (-\sqrt{2}\mu)^{-n} H_{n-2}(1/\sqrt{2}\mu) \qquad \textbf{[10.40]}$$

for $n \geq 2$. Hermite functions of the first few orders and a recursive formula are given below [19].

n	$H_n(x)$
0	1
1	$2x$
2	$4x^2 - 2$
3	$8x^3 - 12x$
4	$16x^4 - 48x^2 + 12$
5	$32x^5 - 160x^3 + 120x$
n	$2xH_{n-1}(x) - 2(n-1)H_{n-2}(x)$

[10.41]

From the above results,

$$f(x) = \sum_{i=1}^{\infty} a_i(x-1)^i = \sum_{i=1}^{\infty} a_i x_{tot}^i = \frac{I(t) - I_b}{I_b - I_{th}}$$

where

$$a_1 = 1 - Q(1/\mu)$$

and

$$a_n = \sqrt{\frac{2}{\pi}} \mu e^{-1/2\mu^2} (-\frac{1}{\sqrt{2}\mu})^n \frac{H_{n-2}(1/\sqrt{2}\mu)}{n!} \quad n > 1.$$ [10.42]

Therefore, for $n > 1$, the nth order distortion power at frequency ν is

$$P_\nu^{(n)} = \frac{1}{2} \left[\frac{(I_b - I_{th})k_m^n a_n}{2^{n-1}} \right]^2 K_\nu^{(n)} = \frac{k_m^2}{2}(I_b - I_{th})^2 e^{-1/\mu^2} \frac{H_{n-2}^2(1/\sqrt{2}\mu)}{\pi(n!)^2(4N)^{(n-1)}} K_\nu^{(n)}$$ [10.43]

where $K_\nu^{(n)}$ is the number of product terms at frequency ν. In the above equation, all product terms are assumed to be incoherent with one another.

The total distortion at a certain frequency, ν, is a summation of $P_\nu^{(n)}$ over n. The frequency ν considered in practice is either the CSO frequency or the carrier frequency (for CTB) of a video channel. Because the carrier power of the channel is

$$P_c = (I_b - I_{th})^2 \frac{\mu^2}{N} a_1^2 = (I_b - I_{th})^2 \frac{k_m^2}{2} a_1^2$$

the carrier-to-the-nth-order-intermodulation-product ratio (CIMP) at frequency ν is

$$\text{CIMP}_\nu^{(n)} = \frac{P_c}{P_\nu^{(n)}} = \frac{\pi(4N)^{n-1}(n!)^2 a_1^2}{H_{n-2}^2(1/\sqrt{2}\mu)K_\nu^{(n)}} e^{1/\mu^2}.$$ [10.44]

Similarly, the CSO and CTB are given by

$$
\text{CSO} = \frac{P_c}{\displaystyle\sum_{n=2,4,\ldots} P_{cso}^{(n)}} = \frac{\pi e^{1/\mu^2} a_1^2}{\displaystyle\sum_{n=2,4,\ldots} [H_{n-2}^2(1/\sqrt{2}\mu) K_{cso}^{(n)}]/[(4N)^{n-1}(n!)^2]}
\qquad \textbf{[10.45]}
$$

$$
\text{CTB} = \frac{P_c}{\displaystyle\sum_{n=3,5,\ldots} P_{ctb}^{(n)}} = \frac{\pi e^{1/\mu^2} a_1^2}{\displaystyle\sum_{n=3,5,\ldots} [H_{n-2}^2(1/\sqrt{2}\mu) K_{ctb}^{(n)}]/[(4N)^{n-1}(n!)^2]}
\qquad \textbf{[10.46]}
$$

PROBLEMS

Problem 10–1 Hilbert Transform: Find the Hilbert transform of the following functions.

   a. $e^{j\omega_c t}$.

   b. $\text{sinc}(t/T)\cos(2\pi f_c t)$ with $f_c = 1/T$.

Problem 10–2 QAM Demodulation:

   a. For the QAM signal given by Equation (10.1), the message signals, $m_c(t)$ and $m_s(t)$, can be recovered by correlating the QAM signal with two carriers, $\cos(\omega_c t)$ and $\sin(\omega_c t)$, respectively. Specifically, the QAM signal can be multiplied by either of the carriers and the result sent to a low-pass filter. Describe the process in detail and derive the final output.

   b. If there is a phase shift of the two local carriers, find the outputs from the same demodulation process given in (*a*). Assume the two carriers are in the form $\cos(\omega_c t + \Delta\phi)$ and $\sin(\omega_c t + \Delta\phi)$, where $\Delta\phi$ is the relative phase shift.

Problem 10–3 SSB-AM Modulation: If $m(t) = \text{sinc}(t/T)$ is the baseband signal to be transmitted, find the passband SSB-AM signal at a carrier frequency $f_c \gg 1/T$.

Problem 10–4 FM Modulation: In FM broadcast, the peak frequency deviation is set at $\Delta f = 75$ kHz and the frequency band of a baseband stereo audio signal is 55 kHz. Find the modulation index, β_{FM}, and the FM transmission bandwidth using Carson's rule.

Problem 10–5 Digital QAM Modulation: Consider a 16-QAM digital transmission.

   a. Express the total modulated signal if the NRZ pulse is used. Assume the bit rate is T_b and the carrier frequency is f_c.

   b. Two signals, $x(t)$ and $y(t)$, are called **orthogonal** if

$$
\int_0^{T_B} x(t)y(t)dt = 0
$$

where $T_B = 4T_b$ is the symbol interval. They are further called **orthonormal** if

$$
\int_0^{T_B} x(t)^2 dt = \int_0^{T_B} y(t)^2 dt = 1.
$$

Show that $x(t) = \sqrt{\frac{2}{T_B}} \cos(2\pi f_c t)$ and $y(t) = \sqrt{\frac{2}{T_B}} \sin(2\pi f_c t)$ are two orthonormal signals if $8 f_c T_b$ is an integer.

c. For a single 16-QAM pulse from 0 to T_B, it can be considered as a linear combination of the two orthonormal functions given in (b). The pair of corresponding linear coefficients can be considered as a two-dimensional vector. Show all the 16 vectors in a two-dimensional space. This is called the vector space representation of the 16-QAM signal.

Problem 10–6 CNR in AM Modulation:

a. At a given modulation index (k_m), RIN, and bandwidth (B), express the upper limit of the CNR when $I \to \infty$, using Equation (10.14).

b. Similarly, at a given total modulation depth (μ), B, RIN, and specified CNR, express the maximum number of SCM channels that can be provided.

c. From (b), what is the allowable RIN value to accommodate 50 channels at $\mu = 0.5$, $B = 6$ MHz, and a maximum CNR of 45 dB?

Problem 10–7 CNR in FM Modulation: Consider a 4-MHz single-tone transmission using FM. Find the FM transmission gain, G_{FM}, if $B_{FM} = 40$ MHz and $k_w = 14$ dB.

Problem 10–8 AM versus FM in SCM Transmission: Consider an SCM system where the total available transmission bandwidth is 1 GHz, the total modulation depth, μ, is 0.6, and the laser RIN noise is –140 dB/Hz.

a. For VSB-AM transmission in CATV find the maximum number of 6-MHz CATV channels that can be provided. Assume the required CNR after demodulation is 45 dB.

b. For FM transmission, find the maximum number of CATV channels if $B_{FM} = 30$ MHz. Assume the same CNR after demodulation (not the received CNR) in (a) is required and the filtering gain is $k_\omega = 15$ dB.

Problem 10–9 Intermodulation Products: From Figures 10.8–10.11, find the ratios of peak values of $K_v^{(n)}$ to $(2N)^n$ for $n = 2, \ldots, 5$, where $N = 42$. For $n = 3$ and 5, v is at the carrier frequency, and for $n = 2$ and 4, v is at the CSO frequency.

Problem 10–10 Channel Number Limitation from Nonlinear Distortion: Consider the CIMP's of channel 2 shown in Figure 10.14.

a. Find the upper limit of the total modulation depth if the second-order CIMP is required to be 50 dB.

b. Find the lower limit of the individual channel modulation index, k_m, using VSB-AM. Assume the required CNR is 40 dB and the laser RIN noise is –140 dB/Hz.

c. From (a) and (b), find the maximum number of VSB-AM CATV channels.

d. If FM is used instead and the available transmission bandwidth is 12 GHz, find the maximum number of CATV channels using the same μ from (a). Assume $B_{FM} = 30$ MHz and the CNR gain with respect to AM is 10 dB.

Problem 10–11 CSO and CTB Distortion: Calculate the CSO and CTB of channel 13 at $\mu = 0.6$ using Equations (10.27) and (10.28), for the 42-channel system. The corresponding product numbers of channel 13 of 2, 3, 4, and 5 are 10; 3402; 96,540; and 14,447,160, respectively.

Problem 10–12 SNR in Digital QAM Transmission:

a. For a 4-QAM 200 Mb/s transmission system, if the required SNR is 20 dB and only shot noise is considered, find the required photocurrent. Assume $F = 1$, $\overline{m^2} = 1$, $B = 100$ MHz, and $k_m = 0.1$.

b. If 64-QAM is used instead, find the required photocurrent if shot noise is still the only noise source considered.

Problem 10–13 Combination of WDMA and SCM: To build a frequency-domain multiple access network using a WDMA and SCM combination for at least 1000 SCM channels, describe the network design if a perfect shuffle configuration is used in WDMA. The design should minimize the number of intermediate hops with two transceiver pairs at each optical node. Also assume each wavelength channel can carry up to 20 SCM channels.

REFERENCES

1. Stephen D. Dukes, "Photonics for Cable Television System Design," *Communications Engineering and Design,* May 1992, pp. 34–48.

2. T. E. Darcie, "Subcarrier Multiplexing for Lightwave Networks and Video Distribution Systems," *IEEE Journal on Selected Areas in Communications,* vol. 8, no. 7 (September 1990), pp. 1240–48.

3. J. A. Chiddix, H. Loar, D. M. Pangrac, L. D. Williamson, R. W. Wolfe, "AM Video on Fiber CATV Systems: Need and Implementation," *IEEE Journal on Selected Areas in Communications,* vol. 8, no. 7 (September 1990), pp. 1229–39.

4. R. Olshansky, "Subcarrier Multiplexed Broadband: A Migration Path to BISDN," *IEEE Lightwave Communication Systems Magazine,* vol. 1 no. 3 (August 1990), pp. 30–34.

5. S. C. Liew et al., "A Broadband Optical Network Based on Hierarchical Multiplexing of Wavelengths and RF Subcarriers," *Journal of Lightwave Technology,* vol. 7, no. 11 (1989) pp. 1825–35.

6. Y. H. Lee et al., "Performance Analysis of Wavelength Division and Subcarrier Multiplexing (WDM-SCM) Transmission Using Fibre Brillouin Amplification," IEE Proceedings-J, vol. 139, no. 4 (August 1992), pp. 272–79.

7. W. I. Way, "Subcarrier Multiplexed Lightwave System Design Considerations for Subcarrier Loop Applications," vol. 7, no. 11 (November 1989), pp. 1806–18.

8. M. K. Liu and P. C. Modestou, "Multilevel Signaling and Pulse Shaping for Spectrum Efficiency in Subcarrier Multiplexing Transmission," *Journal of Lightwave Technology,* vol. 12, no. 7 (July 1994), pp. 1239–46.

9. N. Kanno and K. Ito, "Fiber-Optic Subcarrier Multiplexing Video Transport Employing Multilevel QAM," *IEEE Journal on Selected Areas in Communications,* vol. 8, no. 7 (September 1990), pp. 1313–19.

10. J. E. Bowers, "Optical Transmission Using PSK-Modulated Subcarriers at Frequencies to 16 GHz," *Electronics Letters,* vol. 22 (1986), pp. 1119–21.

11. P. M. Hill and R. Olshansky, "A 20-Channel Optical Communication System Using Subcarrier Multiplexing for the Transmission of Digital Video Signals," *Journal of Lightwave Technology,* vol. 8, no. 4 (April 1990), pp. 554–60.

12. B. P. Lathi, *Modern Digital and Analog Communication Systems,* 2nd ed., Holt, Rinchart and Winston, 1989.

13. F. V. C. Mendis, "Interpretation of Signal/Noise Ratio Expressions in FM Video Transmission," *Electronics Letters,* vol. 25, no. 1 (January 1989), pp. 67–69.

14. F. V. C. Mendis, "CNR Requirements for Subcarrier-Multiplexed Multichannel Video FM Transmission in Optical Fiber," *Electronics Letters,* vol. 25, no. 1 (January 1989), pp. 72–74.

15. A. A. M. Saleh, "Fundamental Limit on Number of Channels in Subcarrier Multiplexed Lightwave CATV System," *Electronics Letters,* vol. 25, no. 12 (1989), pp. 776–77.

16. N. J. Frigo et al., "Clipping Distortion in Lightwave CATV Systems: Models, Simulations, and Measurement," *Journal of Lightwave Technology,* vol. 11, no. 1 (January 1993), pp. 138–46.

17. Q. Shi and R. Burroughs, private communications, Panasonic Technology, Inc., Princeton, New Jersey.

18. J. Staab, "Capacity Improvement of a Subcarrier Multiplexed System through the Use of Non-Uniform Modulation Indices," master's thesis, Department of Electrical and Computer Engineering, University of Arizona, June 1993.

19. I. S. Gradshteyn and I. M. Ryzhik, *Table of Integrals, Series, and Products,* Academic Press, 1965, p. 1033.

chapter

11

PHOTONIC SWITCHING

As introduced in Chapter 2, switching is a network function that routes traffic from one channel to another. To provide high switching throughputs and to avoid the electronics speed bottleneck, photonic switches that implement the I/O interface and switching fabric in optics, as shown in Figure 2.6, have been actively studied over the last decade [1][2].[1] For fast packet switching such as in B-ISDN/ATM that needs high-speed switching control, self-routing photonic switches that integrate switching control with switching fabrics in optics have also been demonstrated [3][4].

To simplify implementation of large photonic switches, 2-to-2 switches can be used as the building block. In general, with a multistage interconnection architecture, any switch size of 2^k can be built. In addition, with a good interconnection architecture, the number of 2-to-2 switching elements can be reduced while maintaining good switching performance, such as zero blocking probability.

Similar to multiple access, discussed in the previous chapters, photonic switching can be done in different domains such as space, time, wavelength, and polarization, where traffic is switched from one spatial line, time slot, wavelength channel, or polarization state to another. These different domain switchings have different system characteristics and require different physical implementation. For example, spatial-domain switching can configure different physical light paths but require complete spatial interconnections. Wavelength-domain switching, on the other hand, is attractive to WDoMA but requires precise wavelength control and tuning.

As mentioned in Chapter 2, switching complexity can be reduced by performing switching in multiple domains. For example, by performing time-space-time (TST) switching, the number of spatial crosspoints can be greatly reduced. In a WDoMA network, spatial switching can be similarly combined with wavelength-channel interchange (WCI) to form a large switch. In general, switchings in different domains and their combinations can be logically equivalent. For example, WCI is logically equivalent to time-slot interchange (TSI). As a result, the most convenient technology can be used to implement the same logical switching architecture and a similar switching control algorithm can be used to achieve the same switching performance.

---

[1] To simplify implementation, switching control can still be implemented in electronics and/or opto-electronics.

This chapter discusses various photonic switching devices and their interconnection architectures. Specifically, it presents some attractive nonblocking switches and self-routing networks that have small numbers of crosspoints. It also discusses various switching devices such as mechanical switches, waveguide couplers, and bistable devices. For high-speed WDoMA and TDoMA networking, this chapter explains wavelength- and time-domain switching and their combinations with spatial switching.

11.1   SWITCHING ARCHITECTURES

This section discusses some important switching architectures that use 2×2 switches as the basic building block. Although 2×2 switches can be realized in different technologies, they can be interconnected with the same architecture and similar system considerations.

11.1.1   SYSTEM CONSIDERATIONS

There are several criteria for a good switching architecture from system considerations. First, for a given switch size, N, the number of crosspoints or 2×2 switches should be as small as possible. When the number is large, implementation is expensive and the optical path is subject to large power loss and crosstalk. As a result, one primary design objective is to minimize the number of crosspoints.

To evaluate a switch design from its number of crosspoints, it can be compared with the lower bound, $\log_2(N!)$. This lower bound can be obtained from the following consideration. Because a switch works as a permutator that routes inputs to outputs according to a certain permutation, it needs to provide at least $N!$ different configurations. Because each crosspoint can provide two different configurations, a minimum number of $\log_2(N!)$ crosspoints are needed to configure $N!$ different routings or permutations.

Many switching architectures have been designed to minimize the number of crosspoints [5]. The three-stage Clos switch, discussed in Chapter 2, is one example. Another switching architecture, called the **Benes** network, can approach the lower bound asymptotically [6]. If internal blockings are acceptable, the number of crosspoints can be further reduced by using a self-routing network.

Optical paths should go through a minimal and equal number of crosspoints. Because each crosspoint introduces a certain power loss and crosstalk, a large number of crosspoints along a configured path require a large incident light power. Many multistage switches have thus been designed to have as few as $\log_2 N$ crosspoints along any configured path. Furthermore, to reduce power variation at the switch output and to avoid the near–far problem,[2] optical paths need to have the same number of crosspoints.

When a switch is designed to reduce the number of crosspoints in total and in each configured path, it can have a large internal blocking probability. In a multistage switch,

---

[2] When there is crosstalk through a crosspoint, even though the coupling coefficient is small, the weak input (the "far" signal) can be critically interfered by the other strong input (the "near" signal). This is called the near–far problem.

internal blocking occurs when there is no available route from the existing configuration. To reduce the blocking probability, the number of possible routes between inputs and outputs can be increased. The Clos switch, for example, can have a zero blocking probability when the number of middle-stage switches, which equals the number of possible routes, is large enough.

In some switching architectures, the internal blocking probability can be completely reduced to zero by using a good switching control or rearranging the current switching configuration. These cases are called wide-sense nonblocking and rearrangeably nonblocking, respectively. These different nonblocking conditions are defined below [6].

1. Strictly Nonblocking. A switch is strictly nonblocking if a connection path can always be found no matter what the current switching configuration is or what switching control algorithm is used.

2. Wide-Sense Nonblocking. A switch is wide-sense nonblocking if a connection path can always be found no matter what the current switching configuration is if a *good* switching control algorithm is used. In other words, the switch can have internal blockings if a poor switching control is used but will have no blocking if a good switching control is used.

3. Rearrangeably Nonblocking. A switch is rearrangeably nonblocking if a connection path can be found by rearranging the existing switching configuration.

WIDE-SENSE NONBLOCKING A 4×4 crossbar switch is shown in Figure 11.1. From its current connection of input 1 to output 2, shown in Figure 11.1*a*, there is internal blocking if input 2 is to be connected to 3. However, when the switching control algorithm illustrated in Figure 11.1*b* is used, there is no blocking. To connect input *i* to output *j*, the algorithm sets the switch in the *i*th row and *j*th column at the "BAR" state and sets all other switches on its left and below it at the "CROSS" state. Therefore, the crossbar switch is wide-sense nonblocking. ∎

Example 11.1

REARRANGEABLY NONBLOCKING A 4×4 3-stage switch is shown in Figure 11.2. To connect input 1 to output 4 from the current configuration shown in Figure 11.2*a*, there is no available path. Therefore, the connection is blocked. However, the blocking can be removed by rearranging the current configuration as shown in Figure 11.2*b*. This is a Benes switch of size 4, which is verified to be rearrangeably nonblocking in Appendix 11–B. ∎

Example 11.2

11.1.2 CROSSBAR AND DOUBLE CROSSBAR

Crossbar, shown in Figure 11.1, is a basic switching architecture that uses N^2 crosspoints to construct a switch of size N. In addition to its large number of crosspoints, there can be a large number of crosspoints in a configured path. According to the nonblocking

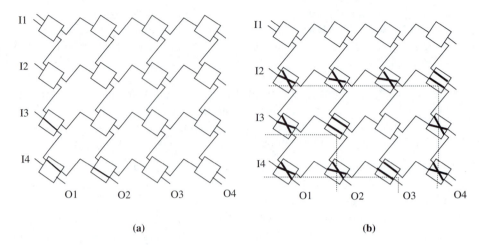

Figure 11.1   Blocking in a crossbar switch: (*a*) an internal blocking scenario when input 4 is to be connected to output 3, and (*b*) a nonblocking algorithm.

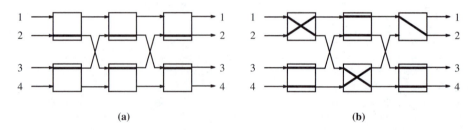

Figure 11.2   A rearrangeably nonblocking switch: (*a*) connection 1 to 4 is blocked from the current configuration 2 to 3 and 3 to 2, and (*b*) nonblocking after rearrangement.

switching control shown in Figure 11.1*b*, there can be a worst-case path that connects input 1 to output 4. In this case, the total number of crosspoints is 7. When the switch size is N, the worst-case number of crosspoints is $2N - 1$.

To reduce the number of crosspoints of an optical path for low power loss and crosstalk, a ***double crossbar*** architecture has been proposed [7]. As shown in Figure 11.3, outputs from each stage of the upper crossbar are connected to the corresponding stage of the lower crossbar. Furthermore, the connections are cyclically shifted between the rows of the two crossbars from one stage to another. That is, row i of the upper crossbar at stage j is connected to row $[(i - j) \bmod (N + 1)]$ of the lower crossbar.

According to the interconnection architecture of the double crossbar, one can have the following switching control. If input port i is connected to output port k, the connection will first go straight from input port i to stage j so that $[(i - j) \bmod (N + 1)] = k$. After

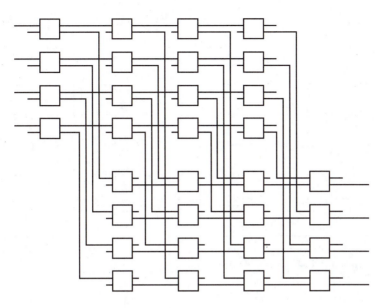

Figure 11.3   A double crossbar switch.

that, it will be switched to the lower crossbar and go straight to the output port k. Because different (i, k) pairs have different j's, the switch is wide-sense nonblocking. Furthermore, because there are j and $N - j + 1$ crosspoints in the upper and lower path respectively, the total number of crosspoints in every path is $N + 1$. Compared to the worst case $2N - 1$ in single crossbar, the loss and crosstalk is reduced approximately by half.

An apparent disadvantage of the double crossbar design is twice the number of the crosspoints needed for the single crossbar. When N is large, this can be a significant drawback. Figure 11.3 shows that there are also many crossovers of the connection paths between the two crossbars. When the paths are physically implemented by waveguides, a large number of crossovers will increase the fabrication cost and interconnection area. To avoid these problems, an N-stage planar switch discussed next becomes attractive.

11.1.3 *N*-STAGE PLANAR

An N-stage planar architecture of size 8 is illustrated in Figure 11.4 [8]. Because it has no crossovers, it is attractive to photonic switches made of directional couplers. Furthermore, it has only $N(N - 1)/2$ crosspoints (less than half of that in a single crossbar) and a maximum number of N crosspoints in a connection path (better than the double crossbar).

Because of the fewer number of crosspoints, one primary disadvantage of the N-stage planar switch is it is no longer wide-sense nonblocking. Instead, as verified in Appendix 11–A, it is rearrangeably nonblocking [8]. To have a smaller number of crosspoints and at the same time to provide zero blocking, the Clos switch can be used.

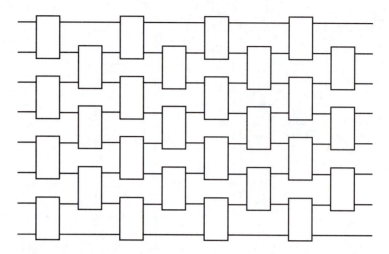

Figure 11.4   An N-stage planar switch of size 8.

11.1.4 CLOS

As explained in Chapter 2, a Clos 3-stage switch, shown in Figure 2.8, is strictly non-blocking if $m \geq 2n - 1$, where n is the input switch size of the first stage and m is the number of middle stage switches. As shown in Figure 2.8, however, a Clos switch has many crossovers when m is large. Therefore, it is not attractive to photonic switches made of directional couplers. When free-space interconnection is available, however, the problem can be solved using the 3D interconnection shown in Figure 11.5.

If rearrangeably nonblocking is acceptable, the number of middle switches can be further reduced. According to Slepian and Deguid [9] and verified in Appendix 11–B [10], the Clos switch is rearrangeably nonblocking if

$$m \geq n. \qquad \qquad \textbf{[11.1]}$$

One special example of rearrangeably nonblocking Clos switches is called the Benes switch [6]. It is of great importance because its number of crosspoints approaches the lower bound, $\log_2(N!)$.

11.1.5 BENES

As shown in Figure 11.6a, a Benes switch has a recursive three-stage architecture where the middle stage has another two three-stage Benes networks of half size. A specific example of an 8×8 switch is shown in Figure 11.6b.

From the recursive architecture, a Benes switch of size N has $2 \log_2 N - 1$ stages and $N/2$ crosspoints per stage. As a result, the total number of crosspoints of a Benes switch is

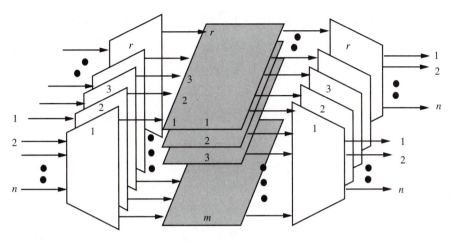

Figure 11.5 Three-dimensional interconnection of a three-stage Clos switch.

$N(2\log_2 N - 1)/2$. When N is large, it is approximately $N\log_2 N$, which is of the same order as the lower bound, $\log_2(N!)$.

Figure 11.6*a* shows that the Benes switch is a special case of the Clos switch that satisfies Equation (11.1). Therefore, it is rearrangeably nonblocking. To avoid its large number of crossovers, a 3D interconnection can be used, as shown in Figure 11.6*c*.

11.1.6 Dilated Benes

For a switch of many stages, crosstalk due to incomplete switching can accumulate over many stages and strongly interfere with the signal. To solve this problem, a variation of the Benes switch called the **dilated Benes** has been proposed [11]. The basic concept behind the approach is to make sure there is only one active input at each 2×2 switch. To understand the reason for this condition, consider a basic 2×2 switch. If S and X are its two inputs, the signal at the output port of S is

$$Y = (1 - \alpha)S + \alpha X$$

where α is the power fraction due to crosstalk. When there is only one active input, or $X = 0$, $Y = (1 - \alpha)S$ and there is no crosstalk.

In general, when there is a connection path in a multistage switch consisting of M 2×2 switches, the output at the signal's output port is

$$Y = (1 - \alpha)^M S + \alpha(1 - \alpha)^{M-1} X_1 + \alpha(1 - \alpha)^{M-2} X_2 + \ldots + \alpha X_M \qquad \textbf{[11.2]}$$

where X_i represents the other inputs of the 2×2 switch at stage i. When α is small,

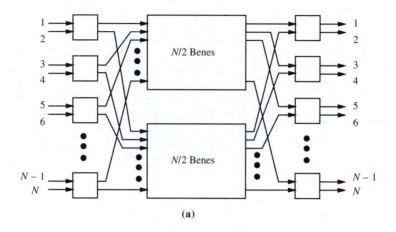

(a)

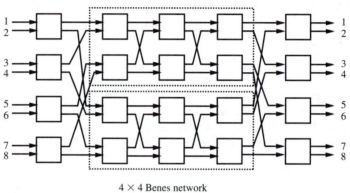

4 × 4 Benes network

(b)

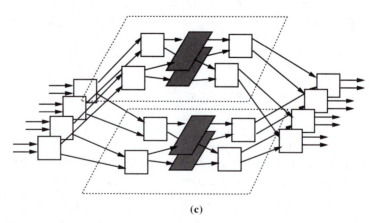

(c)

Figure 11.6   (a) Benes network in a recursive 3-stage Clos switch, (b) 8 × 8 Benes network, and (c) three-dimensional implementation of (b).

$$Y \approx (1 - \alpha M)S + \alpha \sum_{i=1}^{M} X_i.$$

This result indicates that the crosstalk is linearly proportional to αM.

When there is only one active input at each 2×2 switch, on the other hand, $X_1 = 0$ and $X_i = \alpha X'_{i-1}$. In other words, X_i is the crosstalk from its previous stage. Equation (11.2) thus reduces to

$$Y = (1 - \alpha)^M S + \alpha(1 - \alpha)^{M-2} X'_1 + \ldots + \alpha X'_{M-1}$$

$$= (1 - \alpha)^M S + \alpha^2 (1 - \alpha)^{M-2} X_2 + \ldots + \alpha^2 X_M \approx (1 - \alpha M)S + \alpha^2 \sum_{i=1}^{M-2} X_i.$$

[11.3]

Comparing Equation (11.3) with Equation (11.2) shows that crosstalk is smaller in the case of dilated Benes by a factor of α.

CROSSTALK REDUCTION   If $M = 10$ and $\alpha = 0.01$ (−20 dB crosstalk), Equation (11.2) says that the accumulated crosstalk can be up to $\alpha M = 0.1 = -10$ dB. On the other hand, Equation (11.3) indicates that the worst case crosstalk is around $\alpha^2(M-1) = 9 \times 10^{-4} \approx -30$ dB. In other words, there is a 20 dB improvement in crosstalk by requiring only one active input per 2×2 switch. ∎

Example 11.3

A recursively defined dilated Benes network of size N is shown in Figure 11.7a. It consists of three stages. In the first and third stages, there are N 2×2 switches with one active input and output per switch. In the middle stage, there are two $N \times N$ Benes networks. From this arrangement, traffic can be split into two subnetworks. Furthermore, from the switching control algorithm described in Appendix 11–C, each of the 2×2 switches at the input stage of the two $N \times N$ Benes switches has only one active input, and each of the 2×2 switches at the output stage of the two $N \times N$ switches has also only one active output. As a result, the two $N \times N$ Benes are two $N/2$ dilated Benes. Therefore, Figure 11.7a is a recursive definition of a dilated Benes of size N. The basic 2×2 dilated Benes is shown in Figure 11.7b. The recursive definition shows that all 2×2 switches in a dilated Benes network have only one active input.

11.1.7 SELF-ROUTING

Self-routing is attractive in packet switching where routing is performed at each switching stage according to the destination address of an input packet. In this case, there is an address decoding logic at each crosspoint. From this arrangement, a separate switching control to configure the switching fabric is unnecessary.

In practice, an input packet carries its routing information through either its virtual circuit identifier (VCI) (in virtual circuit) or its destination node address (in datagram). In either

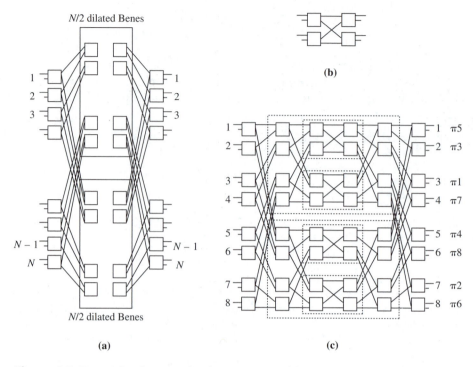

Figure 11.7 Dilated Benes networks: (a) recursive definition, (b) a 2 × 2 dilated Benes, and (c) an 8 × 8 dilated Benes.

case, it is mapped to a p-bit address corresponding to its output port, where $2^p = N$ is the switch size. When the packet is routed through the switch, one bit at a time of its p-bit address is used for switching at a stage. Therefore, a self-routing network in general has $p = \log_2 N$ switching stages. Some important self-routing networks, including the Banyan (routing), baseline (half of the Benes), omega or shuffle exchange, and flip (inverse shuffle), are illustrated in Figure 11.8 [10]. In principle, they are all logically equivalent.

Example 11.4

BANYAN ROUTING NETWORK   An 8 × 8 3-stage Banyan routing network is shown in Figure 11.8. If (b_1, b_2, b_3) is the triple binary output port address of an incoming packet, bit b_i will be used for routing at stage i. When b_i is 1, the packet will be routed to the lower output port at stage i. Otherwise, it will be routed to the upper port.

For example, if an incoming packet at input port 3 has an output address 6 (both in the range from 0 to 7) or (110), it will routed down in the first stage, stay down in the second stage, and then go up in the last stage.

If there is another incoming packet at input port 2 that has an output port address 5 (101), it needs to be routed down at the same first stage switch. Therefore, there is a switching conflict, or internal blocking, at the first stage. ∎

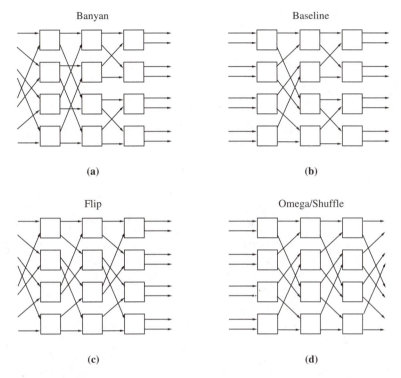

Figure 11.8   Self-routing networks: (a) Banyan, (b) baseline, (c) flip, and (d) omega or shuffle exchange

From Example 11.4, a self-routing network can have internal blocking. One simple technique to avoid this is to presort the input packets according to the output addresses. An important sorting network called the **Batcher** network will be discussed next. The combination of the Batcher and Banyan can provide a nonblocking self-routing network.

11.1.8 BATCHER SORTING NETWORK

The Batcher network can sort input packets according to their output port addresses in an ascending order. A recursive Batcher network architecture is shown in Figure 11.9. It consists of two main stages. In the first stage, it consists of two half-size Batcher networks that sort inputs into two monotonic subsequences: one increasing and one decreasing. The second stage then merges the two subsequences into one single ascending sequence. Figure 11.9 shows that the merging network is again in a recursive structure. According to the merging algorithm by Batcher [15], corresponding elements in the two subsequences are formed into pairs and compared. Those that are larger are grouped into one new subsequence, and those that are smaller are grouped into another. Each of the two subsequences is then split into half for similar comparisons. This process repeats until each of the final subsequences has only one element. Appendix 11–D verifies that the final outcome is a sorted sequence.

11.1.9 BATCHER-BANYAN NETWORK

As mentioned earlier, combining a sorting network and a self-routing network can provide zero internal blocking. One important example is the Batcher-Banyan network shown in Figure 11.10a.

To see the nonblocking property of the Batcher-Banyan network, assume the number of active inputs at the Batcher network is $L \leq N$. The network sorts the L active packets according to their output port numbers. As illustrated in Figure 11.10d, $L = 5$ active outputs will be placed on the top after Batcher sorting. As shown in Figure 11.10b, a Banyan routing network of size N can be considered as a two-stage network, where N inputs are routed in the first stage and directed to two Banyan networks of size $N/2$ in the second stage. Because the L inputs have been sorted, two inputs that come to the same switch at the first stage of the Banyan network have an output address difference of at least $N/2$. Therefore, there is no routing conflict in the first stage. Furthermore, the sorted order of two output substreams is maintained *cyclically*. That is, if we perform necessary cyclic shifts, the output addresses of the two subsequences are still in the ascending order. The above observations and the recursive Banyan routing indicate that there is no internal blocking. A routing example through the Banyan is illustrated in Figure 11.10d.

11.1.10 CROSSOVER AND EXTENDED PERFECT SHUFFLE

Self-routing networks and sorting networks discussed above require shuffle exchanges between adjacent stages. This can be complex using either waveguides or free-space interconnections. An interconnection network that is logically equivalent but simple in optics implementation is thus desirable. One such network, called the **crossover network** [12], is shown in Figure 11.11, where only simple prisms and beam-splitting mirrors are needed.

The logical equivalence of the crossover network to a self-routing network is given in [13]. To further reduce the blocking probability, fan-out and fan-in can be used before and after the crossover network, respectively. As depicted in Figure 11.12, a fan-out ratio of $F = 2$ is used. In general, a large F value can achieve a smaller blocking probability. Because the crossover and shuffle networks are equivalent, this three-stage network is referred to as the **extended generalized shuffle** (EGS) network [14].

To compare the various switching networks discussed, their important properties are summarized in Table 11.1.

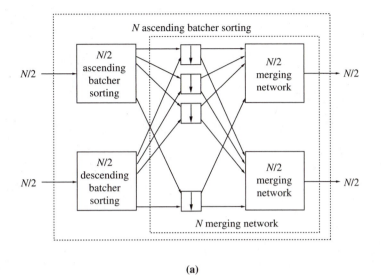

(a)

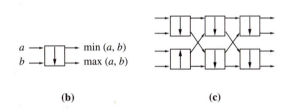

(b)   **(c)**

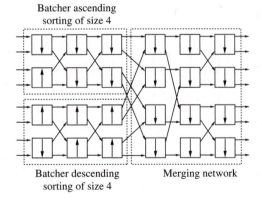

(d)

Figure 11.9   A Batcher network: (*a*) recursive definition, (*b*) basic
                   comparison block and definition, (*c*) a 4 × 4
                   Batcher, and (*d*) an 8 × 8 Batcher.

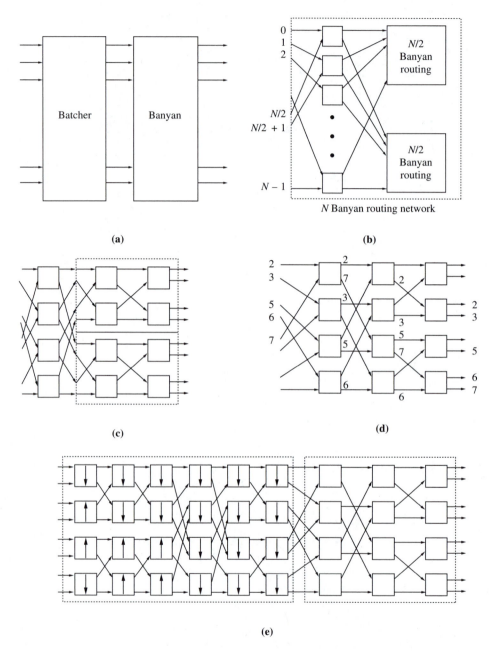

Figure 11.10   (a) A Batcher-Banyan network, (b) a recursive definition of the Banyan network, (c) an 8 × 8 Banyan based on the recursive definition, (d) a simplified 8 × 8 Banyan, and (e) an 8 × 8 Batcher-Banyan.

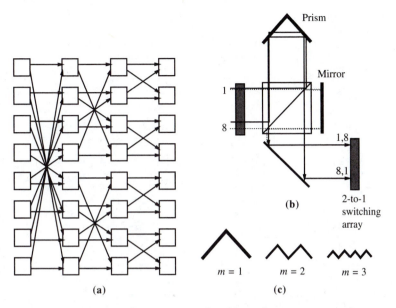

Figure 11.11 A crossover network: (*a*) logical interconnection of an 8 × 8 switch, (*b*) optics implementation between two stages, and (*c*) prisms used at different stages.

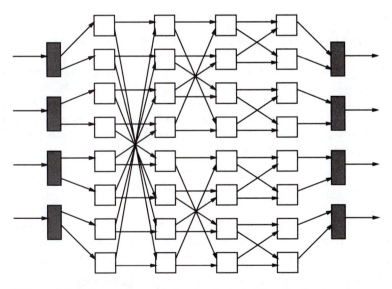

Figure 11.12 An extended generalized shuffle network, where $F = 2$ and the switch size is 4.

Table 11.1   Summary of various switching networks.

Architecture	Stages	Crosspoints	Maximum Number in a Configured Path	Minimum Number in a Configured Path	Non-Blocking	Crossovers
Crossbar	—	N^2	$2N-1$	1	Wide-sense	No
Double crossbar	$N+1$	$2N^2$	$N+1$	$N+1$	Wide-sense	Yes
N-stage planar	N	$N(N-1)/2$	N	$(N-1)/2$	Rearrangeably	No
Clos[1]	3	$2Nm + m(N/n)^2$	$2(n+r+m)-3$	3	Yes[1]	No in 3D
Benes[2]	$2p-1$	$N(p-1/2)$	$2p-1$	$2p-1$	Rearrangeably	No in 3D
Dilated Benes[3]	$2p$	$2Np$	$2p$	$2p$	Rearrangeably	No in 3D
Self-routing[2]	p	$Np/2$	p	p	No	No in 3D
Batcher[2]	$p(p+1)/2$	$Np(p+1)/4$	$p(p+1)/2$	$p(p+1)/2$	Yes[4]	No in 3D
Batcher-Banyan[2]	$p(p+3)/2$	$Np(p+3)/4$	$p(p+3)/2$	$p(p+3)/2$	Yes	No in 3D
Crossover	$p+1$	$N(p+1)$	$p+1$	$p+1$	No	No in 3D
EGS	p_F+1	$FN(p_F+1)$	p_F+1	p_F+1	No	No in 3D

Notes: [1] Assume crossbar switches are used in each stage. It is strictly blocking if $m > 2n-1$ or rearrangeably nonblocking if $m \geq n$. [2] $p = \log_2 N$. [3] $p_F = \log_2(FN)$, where F is the fan-out. [4] If idle input channels are assigned with unused output ports.

11.2   SPATIAL-DOMAIN PHOTONIC SWITCHING

In spatial switching, physical optical paths between input ports and output ports are configured according to the requested connections. This section will first introduce important design criteria to photonic spatial switches. Three types of spatial switching elements are then considered: mechanical switches, directional couplers, and bistable optical gates. These switches configure optical paths by moving optical fibers, changing the optical coupling characteristic of waveguides, and modulating the states of the bistable gates, respectively.

11.2.1   DESIGN CRITERIA

System considerations of switching architectures and general design criteria have been given in the previous section and in Chapter 2. Below are listed some specific criteria related to spatial-domain switching.

1. Low Power Loss.   In general, an optical path in a spatial photonic switch consists of couplers, splitters, and propagation paths made of waveguides or free-space links. Because each of these can lose power, it is important to have a minimal power loss design. When the total loss is large, optical amplifiers and/or active devices may be needed to regenerate the light signals.

2. Low Crosstalk. As mentioned earlier on dilated Benes networks, crosstalk occurs when input power is not completely switched to the desired output port. As a result, there is a small portion of input power occurring at other ports. When the switch has a large number of stages, the crosstalk can accumulate and eventually result in an unacceptable signal quality. Some possible causes of incomplete photonic switching include: fabrication errors, alignment and/or coupling errors, wavelength drifts, and polarization dependence on the incident light.

3. Polarization Independence. Photonic switches in general exhibit polarization dependence. For example, many waveguide switches use the electro-optic (EO) effect to change the switching state. By modulating the waveguide refractive index, incident light can be switched from one input to another. As explained in Chapter 14, the EO effect depends on the polarization of the input light. As a result, the voltage required to switch is polarization dependent. To minimize this dependence, various design techniques have been proposed and will be discussed later.

4. Simple Interconnection. Compared to the electronics counterpart, photonic switching requires quite different interconnection considerations. For example, when light propagation is directed by waveguides, the number of crossovers of one waveguide over another is a critical parameter. A large number of crossovers require a large number of deposition layers and can limit the switch size. When light propagation is directed by fibers, on the other hand, interconnection can become a mess when the size is large. When light propagation is over free space, grating and reflecting optic devices are needed to configure light propagation paths. In this case, precise optics and alignment are required.

5. Low Switching Energy. As mentioned earlier, a photonic switch in practice is made of 2-to-2 switching elements. When each switching element is changed from one state to another, a certain energy is required. At a given switch size, the switching power is proportional to the switching speed and the switching energy. Because the switching power is limited by the power dissipation capability, a low switching energy is important for large implementations and high-speed reconfigurations.

11.2.2 MECHANICAL SWITCHES

A mechanical switch configures light propagation paths through a mechanical mechanism. As shown in Figure 11.13, an array of 1-to-2 photonic switches has a movable portion so that input fibers can be coupled to one of the two output fiber arrays. In general, multiple 1-to-2 and 2-to-1 switching elements can be interconnected to form a larger switch. As shown in Figure 11.14, four 1-to-2 switches are used to form a 2-to-2 switch.

Because there is no need for advanced optics, a mechanical switch is attractive for its simple implementation. As a result, it is good for use in cross-connects and automatic protection switches (APSs) where the slow mechanical speed is not a concern. As illustrated in Figure 11.15, 1-to-2 switches can be used for 1:2 automatic protection switching (APS) and self-healing rings.

Mechanical switches have some limitations. When an input fiber is switched to a different fiber, for example, there can be a large coupling loss from misalignment. Wear can make precise alignment difficult after single-mode fibers are used for a long time. Another critical

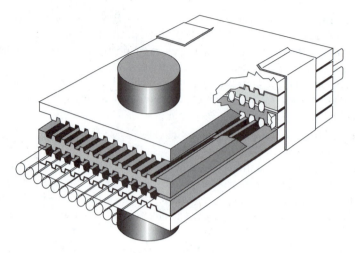

Figure 11.13   A mechanical photonic switch connecting a fiber array to one of the two output arrays. The input fibers are mechanically moved up and down during switching.

SOURCE: Reprinted, by permission, from Young and Curtis, "Single-Mode Fiber Switch with Simultaneous Loop-Back Feature," *Photonic Switching*, edited by Gustafson and Smith [16]. ©1988 by Springer-Verlag.

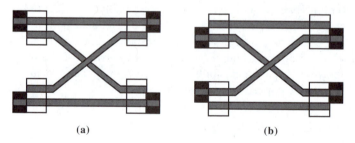

(a)   (b)

Figure 11.14   A 2-to-2 mechanical switch made of four 1-to-2 switching elements: (*a*) bar state and (*b*) cross state.

limitation of mechanical switches is the slow switching speed. It can take msecs and even seconds to move fibers from one position to another. Mechanical switches are thus not useful in applications such as TDM and ATM, where switching fabrics are reconfigured at high speeds.

11.2.3 WAVEGUIDE SWITCHES

A more popular switch design is based on the directional couplers depicted in Figure 11.16. As shown, the coupled waveguides provide the mechanism to switch incident light from one waveguide to another. An external voltage can be used to modulate the refractive

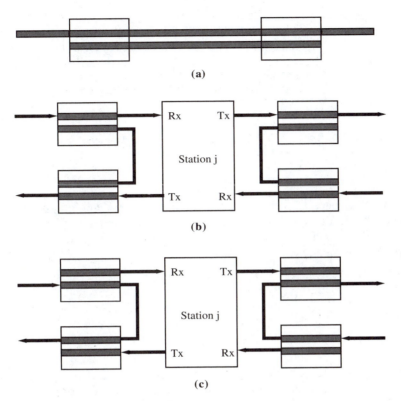

(a)

(b)

(c)

Figure 11.15 The use of 1-to-2 mechanical switches against fiber cuts and active node failure: (a) 1:2 APS against fiber cuts, (b) normal configuration of a node in a self-healing ring, and (c) optical loop-back against active node failure.

index of the waveguides through the EO effect, which can in turn modulate the light coupling between the waveguides.

In practice, most directional couplers used for photonic switching are made of Ti-LiNbO$_3$ [17]–[20]. They are attractive for low waveguide loss and high electro-optic coefficients. As shown in Figure 11.16, to achieve a higher refractive index, titanium is diffused into the LiNbO$_3$ substrate to form waveguides. A 16×16 Ti-LiNbO$_3$ waveguide switch has been reported [20]. For integration with III-V photodetectors, waveguide switches made of InP have also been considered [21]–[23].

Coupling Theory Below the switching principle of directional couplers is briefly explained. Detailed discussion and analysis on coupling theory can be found in Chapter 14 and Appendix 14–A.

When the two waveguides shown in Figure 11.16 are closely separated, the field distribution of an incident lightwave can extend from its input waveguide to the adjacent one.

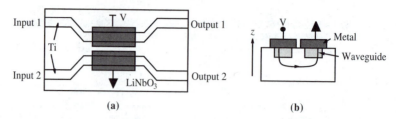

Figure 11.16   A 2-to-2 waveguide switch using directional couplers:
(a) top view and (b) cross-section.

As the wave propagates, the center of the field can move back and forth between the two waveguides. Depending on the coupling strength (κ) between the two waveguides, the coupling length (L) and the difference (δ) between the two waveguides, the power at the two output ports is given by

$$P_{out,1} = P_{in,1} - P_{out,2}$$
$$\text{[11.4]}$$

and

$$P_{out,2} = P_{in,1} \frac{\kappa^2}{\kappa^2 + \delta^2} \sin^2[(\kappa^2 + \delta^2)^{1/2} L]$$
$$\text{[11.5]}$$

where the incident light is at input port 1. From Appendix 14–A, the coupling constant, κ, is a function of the waveguide separation and the transversal mode of the incident light, and δ is defined by

$$\delta \overset{def}{=} \frac{1}{2} \times [(\beta_1 - \beta_2) + (\kappa_{11} - \kappa_{22})]$$
$$\text{[11.6]}$$

where $\beta_1 - \beta_2$ is the difference of the propagation constants of the two waveguides or

$$\beta_1 - \beta_2 = \frac{2\pi n_1}{\lambda} - \frac{2\pi n_2}{\lambda} \overset{def}{=} \frac{2\pi \Delta n}{\lambda}$$
$$\text{[11.7]}$$

and $\kappa_{11} - \kappa_{22}$ is the difference between the two self-coupling constants (i.e., coupling back to the same waveguide). When the two waveguides are geometrically identical, $\kappa_{11} = \kappa_{22}$; and when Δn is modulated by the EO effect,

$$\Delta n = rn^3 E = \frac{1}{2}rn^3 \frac{V}{d} \overset{def}{=} \gamma V$$
$$\text{[11.8]}$$

where r is the electro-optic coefficient of the waveguide, E is the electric field applied to the waveguide, V is the applied voltage, and d is approximately the waveguide separation (see Chapter 14). Combining Equations (11.7) and (11.8) gives

$$\beta_1 - \beta_2 = \frac{2\pi}{\lambda} \gamma V$$
$$\text{[11.9]}$$

where

$$\gamma \overset{\text{def}}{=} \frac{rn^3}{d}. \qquad [\textbf{11.10}]$$

To operate the coupling waveguides as a switch, L is usually set to

$$L = \frac{\pi}{2\kappa} \overset{\text{def}}{=} L_c. \qquad [\textbf{11.11}]$$

From Equations (11.4) and (11.5), there is thus a complete switchover when the two wave-guides are identical, or $\delta = 0$. In other words, if no voltage is applied to the waveguides shown in Figure 11.16, the switch is at the CROSS state.

To change the switch to the BAR state, a voltage can be applied, as shown in Figure 11.16. This results in a refractive index difference, or a nonzero δ. If δ is increased from 0 to $\sqrt{3}\kappa$, according to Equation (11.5), $P_{out,2} = 0$ because $\sin(2\kappa L_c) = 0$. The switch is thus at the BAR state. To have $\delta = \sqrt{3}\kappa$, from Equations (11.6) and (11.9), the required voltage is

$$V = \sqrt{3}\frac{\kappa}{\pi\gamma}\lambda = \frac{\sqrt{3}}{2\gamma}\frac{\lambda}{L_c}. \qquad [\textbf{11.12}]$$

LiNbO₃ SWITCH   Consider the LiNbO$_3$ waveguide switch shown in Figure 11.16, where the z-axis of the crystal is vertical to the waveguide plane and the y-axis is parallel to the propagation direction. Depending on the polarization of the incident wave,

$$r = r_{13} = 9.6 \times 10^{-12} \text{ m/V}$$

Example 11.5

for the TE mode and

$$r = r_{33} = 30.9 \times 10^{-12} \text{ m/V}$$

for the TM mode at $\lambda = 633$ nm. If $n_1 = 2.29, n_3 = 2.20$, and $d = 5\ \mu$m,

$$\gamma_{TE} = r_{13}n_1^3\frac{1}{d} = 2.3 \times 10^{-5} \text{ 1/V}$$

and

$$\gamma_{TM} = r_{33}n_3^3\frac{1}{d} = 6.6 \times 10^{-5} \text{ 1/V}$$

respectively. If $\kappa = 1.0 \times 10^3$ 1/m,

$$L_c = \frac{\pi}{2\kappa} = 1.57 \text{ mm}$$

From Equation (11.9), the required voltage is

$$V_{TE} = \frac{\sqrt{3}}{2}\frac{0.633}{1.57 \times 10^3}\frac{1}{2.3 \times 10^{-5}} = 15.2 \text{ V}$$

and

$$V_{TM} = \frac{\sqrt{3}}{2} \frac{0.633}{1.57 \times 10^3} \frac{1}{6.6 \times 10^{-5}} = 5.4 \text{ V}$$

respectively. The above numerical results show that the required voltage for the TE mode is approximately three times higher than for the TM mode. ∎

Reversal-β Directional Couplers   Because of fabrication errors, L in practice cannot be exactly equal to the required L_c. In this case, a complete switchover at zero bias cannot be achieved. As a result, there is undesirable crosstalk. To solve this problem, a modified design called **reversal-β** directional couplers, depicted in Figure 11.17, can be used [18].

As shown, the design uses two waveguide sections with opposite bias voltages. As a result, the two sections have opposite $\Delta\beta$ values. From the derivation given in Appendix 14–A, the output power of the two waveguides can be expressed by

$$P_{out,1}(L) = P_{in,1} \left\{ 1 - \frac{2\kappa^2}{\kappa^2 + \delta^2} \sin^2[(\kappa^2 + \delta^2)^{1/2}L/2] \right\}^2 \qquad \textbf{[11.13]}$$

and

$$P_{out,2}(L) = P_{in,1} - P_{out,1}(L). \qquad \textbf{[11.14]}$$

According to these equations, the switch at zero bias (or $\delta = 0$) is at the CROSS state if $L = L_c = \pi/2\kappa$. In general, from Equation (11.13), the switch is at the CROSS state if

$$\frac{(L/L_c)^2}{(L/L_c)^2 + (2\delta L/\pi)^2} \sin^2\left[\frac{\pi}{4}\sqrt{(L/L_c)^2 + (2\delta L/\pi)^2}\right] = \tfrac{1}{2} \qquad \textbf{[11.15]}$$

where $\kappa = \pi/2L_c$ is substituted. The dependence of L/L_c on $2\delta L/\pi$ according to Equation (11.15) is shown in Figure 11.18. When $L = L_c$, the switch can be at the BAR state by increasing $2\delta L_c/\pi$ to $\sqrt{15} = 3.87$. From Equation (11.9), the required voltage is

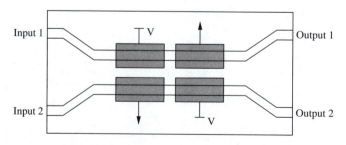

Figure 11.17   A reversal-β waveguide switch.

$$V = \frac{\lambda}{\pi\gamma}\delta = \frac{\lambda}{\pi\gamma}\frac{1.94\pi}{L_c} = \frac{1.94\lambda}{\gamma L_c}.$$ **[11.16]**

LiNbO₃ REVERSAL-$\Delta\beta$ COUPLER   Consider the same LiNbO₃ directional waveguides as in Example 11.5 with the reversal-β electrode structure. From Equation (11.16), the required voltage to go to the BAR state is   **Example 11.6**

$$V_{TE} = \frac{1.94 \times 0.633}{2.3 \times 10^{-15} \times 1570} = 34 \text{ V}$$

for the TE polarization and

$$V_{TM} = \frac{1.94 \times 0.633}{6.6 \times 10^{-15} \times 1570} = 12 \text{ V}$$

for the TM polarization. The required voltages are higher than those given in Example 11.5. ■

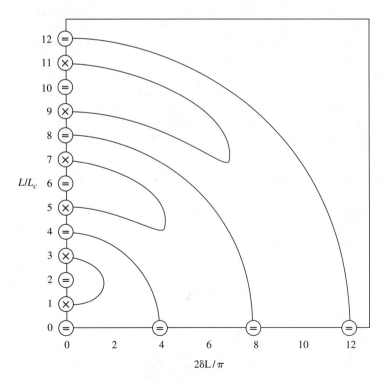

Figure 11.18   Relationship between L/L_c and δL for a complete switchover of the reversal-β directional couplers.

SOURCE: Reprinted, by permission, from Kogelnik and Schmidt, "Switched Directional Couplers with Alternating $\Delta\beta$," *IEEE Journal of Quantum Electronics*, vol. 12, no. 7 [18]. ©1976 by IEEE.

Polarization-Independent Couplers   Because of the electro-optic effect illustrated in Examples 11.5 and 11.6, the required voltage to change the switching state is polarization dependent. As a result, there can be an incomplete switching and large crosstalk when the designed voltage is used for a different polarized wave. To solve this problem, various techniques for polarization-independent couplers have been proposed [24]–[29].

One proposal is for a reversal-β design with a *weighted* coupling, shown in Figure 11.19 [24]. A weighted coupling allows the switch to have slightly different κ or L_C values for the TE and TM modes. As shown in Figure 11.20, the two L/L_C values can be adjusted so that

$$\frac{\delta_{TM}}{\delta_{TE}} = \frac{\gamma_{33}}{\gamma_{13}}. \qquad \textbf{[11.17]}$$

Under this condition and from Equation (11.9), the same voltage can be used to change the switch to the BAR state. A crosstalk of –23 dB was achieved from this design [24].

Other designs can achieve different $L/L_C - \delta L$ dependencies for the two polarization modes [25][26]. As shown in Figure 11.21, four electrodes can be used for better $\Delta \delta L$ control [26]. A low crosstalk around –30 dB was reported for this design [29].

In addition to the above approaches that modify the switchover characteristic $L/L_C - \delta L$, there are other polarization-independent couplers based on different principles. The refractive index change, Δn, for both the TE and TM modes can be made the same at the same bias voltage by properly selecting the Ti concentration [27]. As shown in Figure 11.22, the waveguides can be made of asymmetric dimensions so that switching is done through **propagation mode conversions** [28][29]. The required refractive index change of this switch exhibits a step-function characteristic as shown in Figure 11.23 . Because of this step-function characteristic, the switch is called a **digital optic switch** (DOS). When the bias voltage is large enough, both polarizations can be switched equally.

11.2.4   BISTABLE DEVICES

Waveguide switches are planar or two-dimensional (2D) switches in which all switching elements are interconnected in the same plane. For a larger switch size, a three-dimensional (3D) switch can be formed by first placing switching elements in 2D planes and then

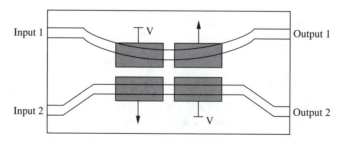

Figure 11.19   A polarization independent waveguide switch using β-reversal and weighted coupling.

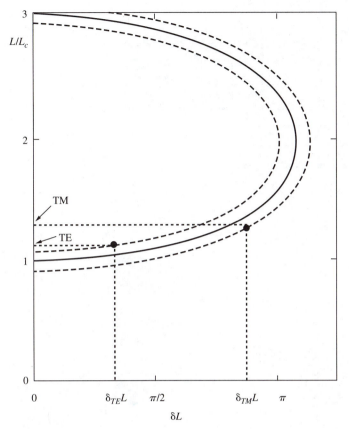

Figure 11.20   By having two slightly different L_c values for the TE and TM polarizations, $\delta_{TM}\delta_{TE} = \gamma_{TM}/\gamma_{TE}$ can be achieved at −20 dB crosstalk. The two dotted lines represent a crosstalk of −20 dB.

SOURCE: Reprinted, by permission, from Alferness, "Polarization-Independent Optical Directional Coupler Switch Using Weighted Coupling," *Applied Physics Letters*, vol. 35, no. 10 [24]. ©1979 by American Institute of Physics.

interconnecting them over free space [30]. This arrangement avoids many crossovers that are needed in a planar switch. To direct light propagation over free space, however, various reflecting and/or grating optics are needed instead.

To build 2D switching elements, bistable semiconductor devices have been studied. A typical bistable device has an input–output characteristic shown in Figure 11.24. There is an input range within which an input can map to three different output values. In general, the middle value is unstable, and the output can stay at either of the other two according to the operating history. As illustrated in Figure 11.24a, it will be in the low state if the input

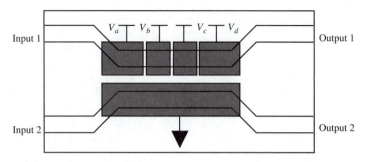

Figure 11.21   Use of multiple electronics for polarization-independent switching.

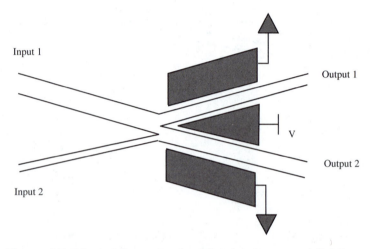

Figure 11.22   Polarization-independent digital optic switch (DOS).

comes from a high value and will be in the high state if the input comes from a low value.
The loop shown is frequently referred to as the **hysteresis loop** from magnetism.

In general, bistable devices are based on the principle of **nonlinear feedback.** This
can be intuitively understood as follows. If T is the transfer factor between the input x and
output y of a bistable device,

$$y = T x.$$

When the device has a nonlinear feedback, T is a nonlinear function of y. That is,
$T = T(y)$. At a given input x, a device can have multiple output values y if

$$x = \frac{T(y)}{y} \qquad\qquad \textbf{[11.18]}$$

has multiple solutions.

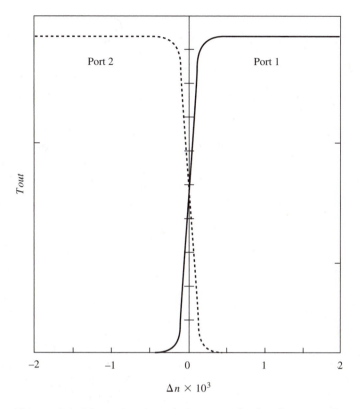

Figure 11.23 Switching characteristic of a digital optic switch.

SOURCE: Reprinted, by permission, from Silberberg and Perlmutter, "A Digital Electrooptic Switch," *Photonic Switching*, edited by Gustafson and Smith, Springer-Verlag [28]. ©1988 by Springer-Verlag.

BISTABLE FP DEVICES As shown in Figure 11.25, a Fabry-Perot resonator made of an EO crystal can be configured as a bistable device. From Equation (3.28), the transmissivity of an FP resonator is given by

$$T = \frac{T_0}{1 + (2\mathcal{F}/\pi)^2 \sin^2(2\pi n L/\lambda)}$$

where $\mathcal{F}$ is the finesse of the FP resonator, n is the refractive index of the crystal, and L is the longitudinal length of the FP resonator. If the output is photodetected and used to modulate the refractive index of the EO crystal, the refractive index according to the Pockel EO effect, discussed in Chapter 14, is given by

$$n = n_0 + n_1 I_{out}$$

Example 11.7

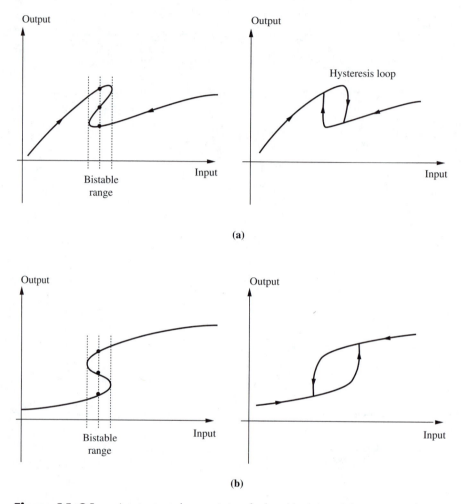

Figure 11.24   Input-output characteristics of a bistable device: (a) inverting and (b) noninverting.

where n_2 is a constant proportional to the EO coefficient of the crystal. From the above results, the transmissivity is a function of the output power given by

$$T(I_{out}) = \frac{T_0}{1 + (2\mathcal{F}/\pi)^2 \sin^2(2\pi n_1 I_{out} L/\lambda + \phi_0)}$$

where $\phi_0 = 2\pi n_0 d/\lambda$. Given this, the FP resonator has a bistable input–output characteristic illustrated in Figure 11.26. Large arrays of FP bistable devices have been used as logic gates for photonic computing and switching [44]. ■

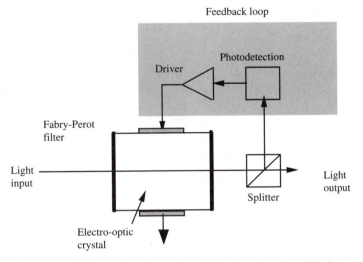

Feedback loop

Figure 11.25   Use of a nonlinear Fabry-Perot as a bistable device.

BISTABLE LASERS   A bistable laser, shown in Figure 11.27, has been proposed for fast switching [45]. As shown, the device has two active sections separated by a gap. To turn on the first section as a laser, a threshold current, I_1, is required. Once the laser is turned on, the output light will pass through the gap and into the second active section. By providing a proper injection current to the second section so that its gain is higher than the loss from the middle gap, the light feedback to the first section can provide a positive gain to the first section. As a result, the laser can still be on though the injection current is reduced below I_1. As shown in Figure 11.27, the laser has a "turn-off" current, I_2, smaller than the "turn-on" current, I_1. When the first section is biased at a current between I_1 and I_2, the device is bistable. To change the state from one to another, as shown, either a reset current pulse or a set light pulse can be used. ∎

Example 11.8

The importance of bistable devices is that they can be used as logic gates or flip-flops. For example, as shown in Figure 11.28a, the output can go from high to low if both inputs are high. Therefore, logically it is a NAND gate. Alternatively, the device can be biased as shown in Figure 11.28b. By providing either a "set" or "reset" signal, the state of the device can be switched to either high or low.

When bistable devices are configured as logic gates, they can be used for photonic switching and computing. Groups of bistable devices for certain logic functions are called **smart pixels** [31]. As illustrated in Figure 11.29, a 2×2 switch can be formed by using four AND gates and two OR gates.

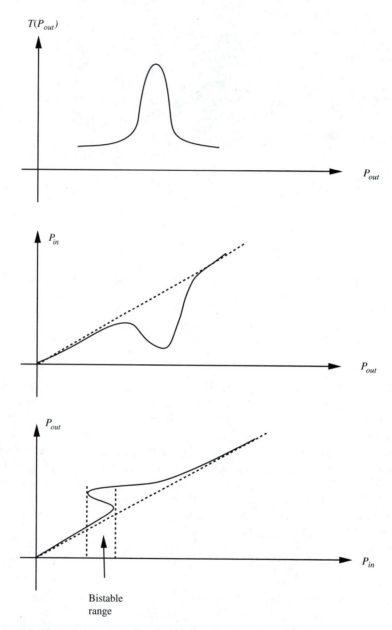

Figure 11.26 Bistable characteristic of a Fabry-Perot device.

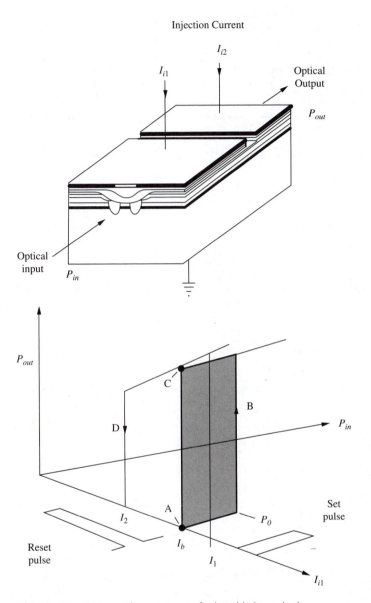

Figure 11.27 Characteristics of a bistable laser diode.

SOURCE: Reprinted, by permission, from Suzuki et al., "An Experiment on High-Speed Optical Time-Division Switching," *Journal of Lightwave Technology*, vol. 4 [45]. ©1986 by IEEE.

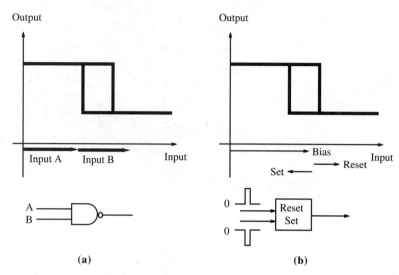

Figure 11.28   The use of bistable devices as logic gates: (*a*) NOR gate and (*b*) flip-flop.

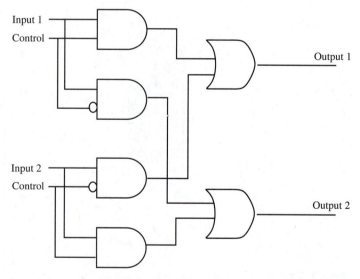

Figure 11.29   A 2-to-2 switch using a combination of AND or OR gates.

11.2.5 SELF–ELECTRO-OPTIC EFFECT DEVICES

One important bistable device used in photonic switching is called the **self–electro-optic effect device** (SEED). As shown in Figure 11.30, a SEED is a PIN photodiode with a multiple quantum-well (MQW) structure in its intrinsic region. When the SEED is at a reverse bias, there is a large electric field in its intrinsic MQW region (see Chapter 5). Because of the Stark effect [32], the large electric field can shift the energy bandgap and affect the photon absorption. This effect of the energy shift in the MQW structure is called the **quantum confined Stark effect** (QCSE) [33] and is the principle behind the SEED's bistability.

The bistability of SEEDs can be understood as follows. In Figure 11.31 first note that the responsivity of photodetection is a function of the incident photon energy or wavelength. Because of the QCSE, there are also different responsivity curves at different bias voltages. If the incident wavelength is at point B in Figure 11.31, an increase of the reverse bias can result in a smaller responsivity. At this wavelength, the responsivity of the same SEED as a function of the bias voltage is shown in Figure 11.32. As shown, the responsivity decreases as the bias voltage increases. When the incident light is the input and the bias voltage is the output, the responsivity versus the bias voltage shown in Figure 11.32 provides the nonlinear feedback for SEEDs to be used as bistable devices.

In practice, a SEED is used in series with an electronic or electro-optic device to form a feedback loop [40]. For example, a SEED can be used in series with a resistor (called R-SEED) [34], with a field effect transistor (FET) (called F-SEED) [35], with a heterostructure photo transistor (HPT) (called H-SEED) [36], and with another SEED (called symmetric SEED or S-SEED) [37][38]. For more logical operations, multiple SEEDs can be integrated and called logic-SEED (L-SEED) [39]. These different combinations are illustrated in Figure 11.33.

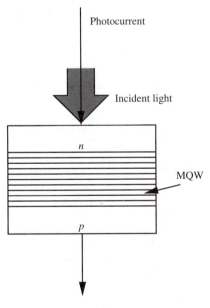

Figure 11.30   A self–electro-optic effect device.

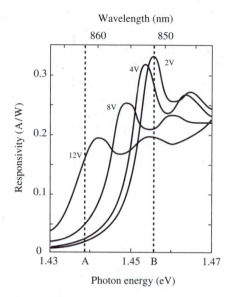

Figure 11.31   Responsivity of a SEED device as a function of its incident photon energy or wavelength.

SOURCE: Reprinted, by permission, from Miller et al., "The Quantum Well Self-Electrooptic Effect Device," *IEEE Journal of Quantum Electronics*, vol. 21, no. 9 [33]. ©1985 by IEEE.

R-SEED   For an R-SEED, as shown in Figure 11.33a, the output voltage is determined by the load equation

$$V = V_0 - R_L I_{ph} = V_0 - R_L \mathcal{R} P_{in} \qquad \text{[11.19]}$$

where R_L is the load resistance, I_{ph} is the photocurrent, and $\mathcal{R}$ is the photodetection responsivity of the SEED. Because $\mathcal{R}$ is a function of the output voltage, V,

$$\mathcal{R}(V) = \frac{V_0 - V}{R_L P_{in}}. \qquad \text{[11.20]}$$

Different load curves at different $\mathcal{R}P_{in}$ values are shown in Figure 11.32. As shown, when the slope $\mathcal{R}P_{in}$ is within a certain range, there are multiple intersections or solutions. Equation (11.20) can be rearranged to give

$$P_{in} = \frac{V_0 - V}{R_L \mathcal{R}(V)}. \qquad \text{[11.21]}$$

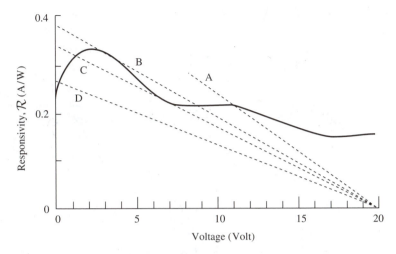

Figure 11.32   Responsivity of a SEED device as a function of the reverse bias voltage.

SOURCE: Reprinted, by permission, from Miller et al.,"The Quantum Well Self-Electrooptic Effect Device," *IEEE Journal of Quantum Electronics*, vol. 21, no. 9 [33]. ©1985 by IEEE.

This $P_{in}-V$ characteristic is illustrated in Figures 11.34*b* and 11.34*c*. It has a similar bistable characteristic to that shown in Figure 11.24*a*. From the light transmission coefficient, T, shown in Figure 11.35, there can be similar bistable characteristics of T versus P_{in} shown in Figure 11.34*d*, and P_{out} versus P_{in} shown in Figure 11.34*e* and Figure 11.36.

F-SEED   The FET used in an F-SEED functions as a switch. When the gate voltage is high, the FET is on and the bias voltage of the SEED is high. Depending on the wavelength of the incident light to the SEED (points A and B in Figure 11.31), the F-SEED can function as an inverting gate or noninverting gate. When the SEED is operated at point A of Figure 11.31, the responsivity increases as the bias voltage increases. As a result, when the FET is on, the reverse bias is high, the responsivity is high, and most of the incident light will be absorbed. On the other hand, if the FET is off, the bias voltage of the SEED is low, the responsivity is small, and most of the incident light can pass through. In this case, the F-SEED functions as an inverting gate.

When the SEED is operated at point B of Figure 11.31, the responsivity decreases as the bias voltage increases. As a result, when the FET is on, the responsivity is low and most of the incident light can pass through the SEED. When the FET is off, the bias voltage is low and most of the incident light will be absorbed because of a high responsivity.

Because the FET functions as a switch, the current from the bias can quickly flow to the SEED and change the state when it is turned on. This results in a shorter turn-on delay. Compared to R-SEEDs, F-SEEDs thus have a higher switching speed.

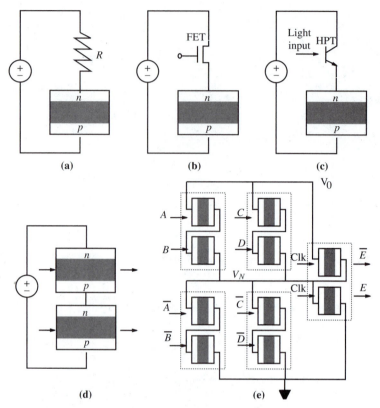

Figure 11.33   Use of SEEDs in different circuit configurations: (*a*) R-SEED, (*b*) F-SEED, (*c*) H-SEED, (*d*) S-SEED, and (*e*) L-SEED of logic function $E = AB + CD$.

H-SEED and Exciton Absorption Reflection Switch   The FET in the F-SEED design can be replaced by a phototransistor [36][42]. In this arrangement, the signal that controls the state is an optical input. Because of this optical-input and optical-output characteristic, an H-SEED can be used not only as a gate but also as an amplifier. As shown in Figure 11.38, when the HPT is properly biased, a small change at the input can result in a large change at the output. This power amplification can provide the critical power gain in photonic switching.

For device integration, a variation of H-SEEDs has been proposed to integrate a vertical-cavity surface emission laser diode (VCSEL) with an HPT [42]. To achieve a higher switching speed, another variation called an **exciton absorption reflection switch** (EARS) was also proposed [41]. As shown in Figure 11.39, the latter adds an additional

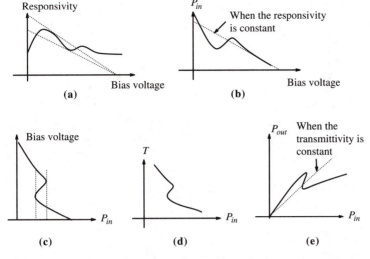

Figure 11.34 Output voltage versus input power of a reverse biased R-SEED.

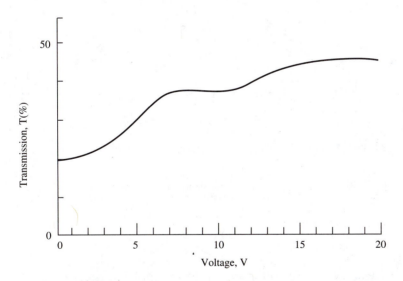

Figure 11.35 Transmission coefficient as a function of the reverse bias voltage.

SOURCE: Reprinted, by permission, from Miller et al., "The Quantum Well Self-Electrooptic Effect Device," *IEEE Journal of Quantum Electronics*, vol. 21, no.9 [33]. ©1985 by IEEE.

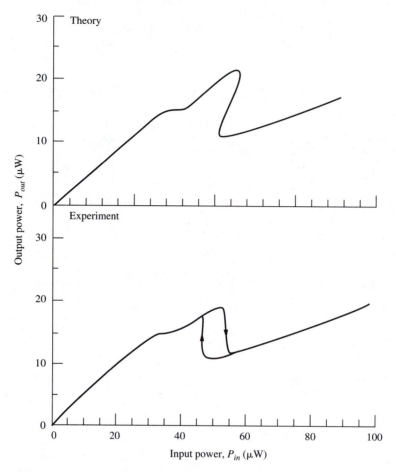

Figure 11.36   Output power versus input power of a reverse biased R-
SEED.

SOURCE: Reprinted, by permission, from Miller et al., "The Quantum Well Self-Electrooptic Effect Device," *IEEE Journal of Quantum Electronics*, vol. 21, no.9 [33]. ©1985 by
IEEE.

Bragg reflection layer to the SEED so that the control light will be reflected instead of
passing through. This design can reduce the power loss of the incident light and can increase the switching speed.

S-SEED   The use of two SEEDs in an S-SEED is similar to the CMOS (complementary
MOS) design in electronics. Because the same photocurrent, I_{ph}, passes through the two
SEEDs in series, their I_{ph}–V_{out} characteristics can be superimposed, as shown in Figure

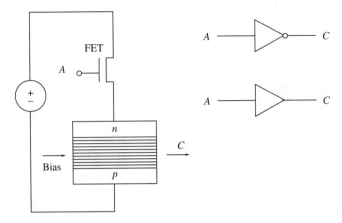

Figure 11.37   The use of an F-SEED as an AND gate.

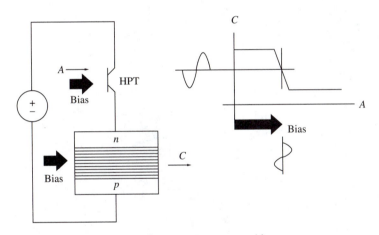

Figure 11.38   Use of an H-SEED as an amplifier.

11.40. From the similar I–V characteristic of a photodiode shown in Figure 5.7, note that each curve corresponds to an incident light power. As Figure 11.40 shows, there are three intersections when the two inputs to the two SEEDs are of the same power. Because the middle one is unstable, the output can be at either of the two points. This bistability results in the bistable characteristic as a function of $P_{in,1}$ as shown in Figure 11.41.

Because of the bistable characteristic, an S-SEED can be used as a flip-flop. As shown in Figure 11.42, a pair of light beams with a sufficiently large power ratio can be

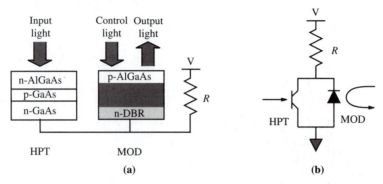

Figure 11.39   An exciton absorption reflection switch (EARS): (a) device structure and (b) equivalent circuit.

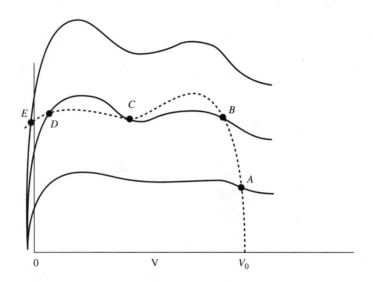

Figure 11.40   Load characteristics of S-SEED devices.

SOURCE: Reprinted, by permission, from Lentine et al., "Symmetric Self-Electrooptic Effect Device," *IEEE Journal of Quantum Electronics*, vol. 25, no.8 [38]. ©1989 by IEEE.

used to either set or reset the S-SEED. When the "set" signal is high in power and the "reset" signal is low in power, the output voltage is close to the bias voltage, V_0. As a result, the bias voltage of the upper SEED is small and that of the lower one is large. Consequently, the upper SEED has a large responsivity and the lower SEED has a small responsivity. When two "clocks" of equal power are used to probe the state of the S-SEED, the lower clock can pass through the lower SEED and the upper clock is ab-

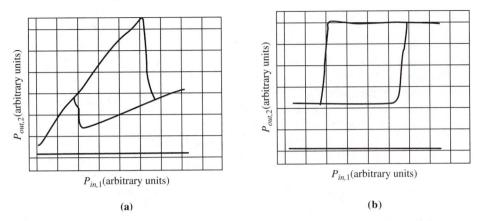

(a)   **(b)**

Figure 11.41   Bistable characteristics of S-SEED devices: (a) $P_{out,1}$ versus $P_{in,1}$ and (b) $P_{out,2}$ versus $P_{in,1}$.

SOURCE: Reprinted, by permission, from Lentine et al., "Symmetric Self-Electrooptic Device," *IEEE Journal of Quantum Electronics*, vol. 25, no. 8 [38]. ©1989 by IEEE.

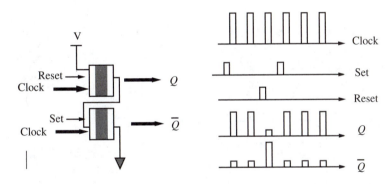

Figure 11.42   Use of S-SEEDs as a flip-flop.

sorbed. As a result, output Q is high and $\overline{Q}$ is low. To change the state of Q and $\overline{Q}$, as illustrated in Figure 11.42, a high power "reset" signal can be applied.

L-SEED   To perform various logic functions, multiple S-SEEDs can be integrated. This integration of S-SEEDs is called L-SEED. As an example, Figure 11.33*e* shows an integration of 10 S-SEEDs for a logic function $E = AB + CD$. The voltage V_N is high when either AB or CD is high. Therefore, it is a logic OR for AB and CD.

11.2.6 FREE-SPACE INTERCONNECTIONS

To form a 3D switch in terms of 2D switching elements such as SEED arrays, light propagation must be directed over free space according to a given interconnection architecture. As depicted in Figure 11.43, a 2 × 2 switch can be formed through a shuffle interconnection and the use of fan-ins, fan-outs, and AND gates. Depending on the switching devices and the interconnection architecture used, actual implementation of free-space interconnection can vary significantly (e.g., see the crossover network interconnection shown in Figure 11.11).

For large and flexible interconnections, holography is a practically attractive technique. As illustrated in Figure 11.44, a hologram is a 2D film whose transmission coefficient, t, is a complex function of the coordinate (x, y). By properly encoding $t(x, y)$, a hologram functions as a phase grating element that can direct incident light to the desirable direction.

According to the Fraunhofer diffraction [43], if the incident wave is a constant amplitude plane wave, the output field in the x–y plane and at a distance d from a hologram is given by

$$g(x, y) = E_0 \frac{j}{\lambda d} e^{-jkd} T\left(\frac{x}{\lambda d}, \frac{y}{\lambda d}\right) \qquad \textbf{[11.22]}$$

where the complex transmission coefficient $T(u, v)$ is the Fourier transform of $t(x, y)$ given by

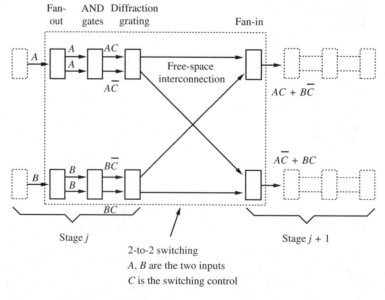

Figure 11.43   Free-space interconnection between two 2D arrays. The logic function shown is a 2-to-2 switch.

$$T(u, v) = \int\int_{-\infty}^{\infty} t(x, y)e^{-j2\pi(ux+vy)}dxdy. \qquad \textbf{[11.23]}$$

For a given incident light intensity I_{in}, the output light intensity I_{out} is thus

$$I_{out}(x, y) = I_{in}\left|T\left(\frac{x}{\lambda d}, \frac{y}{\lambda d}\right)\right|^2 \left(\frac{1}{\lambda d}\right)^2. \qquad \textbf{[11.24]}$$

LINEAR PHASE HOLOGRAM   Consider a rectangle hologram of a finite size $a \times a$. Its complex transmission coefficient is given by

$$t(x, y) = \begin{cases} e^{j2\pi(v_xx+v_yy)} & \text{if } |x| \le a/2 \text{ and } |y| \le a/2 \\ 0 & \text{otherwise.} \end{cases}$$

Example 11.9

Taking the Fourier transform gives

$$T(u, v) = a^2\text{sinc}\left[a\left(\frac{u}{\lambda d} - v_x\right)\right]\text{sinc}\left[a\left(\frac{v}{\lambda d} - v_y\right)\right].$$

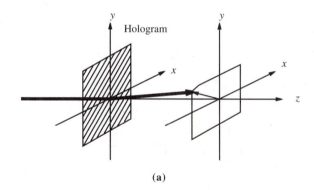

(a)

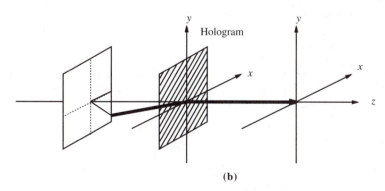

(b)

Figure 11.44   Use of holograms as light interconnection: (a) normal incidence and (b) oblique incidence.

The output pattern is thus

$$g(x, y) = j\frac{E_0}{\lambda d}e^{-jkd}a^2\text{sinc}\left[a\left(\frac{x}{\lambda d} - v_x\right)\right]\text{sinc}\left[a\left(\frac{y}{\lambda d} - v_y\right)\right]$$

and the output light intensity is

$$I_{out}(x, y) = I_{in}\left(\frac{a^2}{\lambda d}\right)^2\text{sinc}^2\left[a\left(\frac{x}{\lambda d} - v_x\right)\right]\text{sinc}^2\left[a\left(\frac{y}{\lambda d} - v_y\right)\right].$$

This result shows that the center of the output intensity is shifted to $\lambda d(v_x, v_y)$. Thus a linear phase hologram results in a linear spatial domain shift. ∎

Consider a laser beam that has a normal incidence to a hologram at position (x, y). If the beam has a small spot size compared to the hologram, from Example 11.9, it will be diffracted to position (x', y') with deviation from (x, y) given by

$$\Delta x = x' - x = \lambda dv_x(x, y) = \frac{\lambda d}{2\pi}\frac{\partial\psi(x, y)}{\partial\psi} \qquad \textbf{[11.25]}$$

and

$$\Delta y = y' - y = \lambda dv_y(x, y) = \frac{\lambda d}{2\pi}\frac{\partial\psi(x, y)}{\partial y}. \qquad \textbf{[11.26]}$$

In the above equation, $\psi(x, y)$ is the phase of $t(x, y) = e^{j\psi(x,y)}$ and

$$v_x = \frac{1}{2\pi}\frac{\partial\psi(x, y)}{\partial x}$$

$$v_y = \frac{1}{2\pi}\frac{\partial\psi(x, y)}{\partial y}$$

are the spatial frequencies. When the mapping from (x, y) to (x', y') is known, $\psi(x, y)$ can be solved from Equations (11.25) and (11.26).

Example 11.10   **FAN-IN** A fan-in interconnection, as shown in Figure 11.45a, requires that $(x', y') = (0, 0)$ for normal incident light at any position (x, y). In this case, $\Delta x = -x$ and $\Delta y = -y$. Therefore, solving Equations (11.25) and (11.26) gives

$$\psi(x, y) = -\frac{\pi(x^2 + y^2)}{\lambda d}. \quad ∎$$

When the laser beam has an oblique incidence as shown in Figure 11.44b, the effective transmission coefficient of the hologram needs to include an additional phase factor given by

$$\phi(x, y) = k[x \sin(\theta_x) + y \sin(\theta_y)] = (k_x x + k_y y).$$

Therefore, from Equations (11.25) and (11.26), the new beam deflection under oblique incidence is given by

$$\Delta x = x' - x = \frac{\lambda d}{2\pi} \left(\frac{\partial \psi(x, y)}{\partial x} + k_x \right) \qquad [11.27]$$

and

$$\Delta y = y' - y = \frac{\lambda d}{2\pi} \left(\frac{\partial \psi(x, y)}{\partial y} + k_y \right). \qquad [11.28]$$

FAN-OUT For the fan-out interconnection, shown in Figure 11.45b, $\Delta x = \Delta y = 0$. Because all oblique incident laser beams come from a point with distance d from the hologram, for a beam incident at (x, y),

$$k_x = \frac{2\pi x}{\lambda d}$$

and

$$k_y = \frac{2\pi y}{\lambda d}.$$

Using Equations (11.27) and (11.28), $\psi_x(x, y) = -k_x = -(2\pi x)/(\lambda d)$ and $\psi_y(x, y) = -k_y = -(2\pi y)/(\lambda d)$. The phase function (x, y) from these results is thus

$$\psi(x, y) = -\frac{\pi(x^2 + y^2)}{\lambda d}.$$

This is the same phase function as fan-in. From basic optics, this is not a surprise, because both cases can be implemented by the same convex lens. ∎

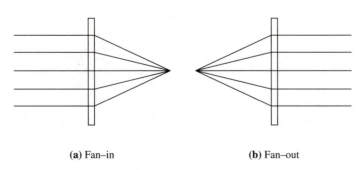

(a) Fan–in (b) Fan–out

Figure 11.45 Fan-in and fan-out using holograms.

11.3 **MULTIDIMENSIONAL PHOTONIC SWITCHING**

In addition to spatial-domain switching, traffic can be switched in the wavelength domain and time domain. To switch light signals from different physical lines, these different domain switchings are commonly integrated with spatial-domain switching. For lower spatial switching complexity and better match with TDoMA or WDoMA traffic, this integration into multidimensional switching is attractive.

Although switchings in different domains have different physical realizations, as pointed out in Chapter 2, they can be logically equivalent. Thus wavelength- and time-domain switches can be analyzed and constructed using various switching architectures discussed earlier. This equivalence will be made clearer as various wavelength- and time-domain switches are discussed below.

11.3.1 **WAVELENGTH-DOMAIN SWITCHING**

Wavelength-domain switching is commonly used in WDoMA. According to how wavelength channels are switched, there are two primary types: **broadcast and select** and **wavelength routing** [46]. As shown in Figure 11.46, the first type uses a star coupler to mix all wavelength inputs and broadcast them to all output ports (see Chapter 9). Using optical filters at the star coupler outputs allows nonblocking wavelength switching. To allow several wavelength switches to be used in series, **wavelength converters** (WCs) are added to perform necessary wavelength permutations.

For wavelength routing, as shown in Figure 11.47, a photonic switch consists of two arrays of WCs on the two sides and a waveguide grating router (WGR) [47] in between. According to the destination and the routing rule of the WGR, the WCs in the first stage are used to tune the wavelengths of input channels. From Chapter 9, if a wavelength channel at input port i needs to be routed to output port j, its wavelength needs to be first tuned to

$$\lambda_{i+j} = \lambda_0 - (i + j)\Delta\lambda \qquad \qquad \textbf{[11.29]}$$

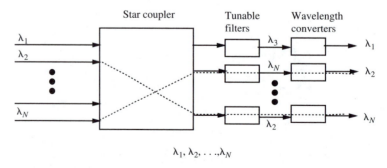

Figure 11.46   A broadcast-and-select wavelength switch.

where λ_0 is a reference wavelength determined by the WGR and $\Delta\lambda$ is the wavelength channel separation. At the output of the WGR, wavelengths may need to be converted again for subsequent switching and processing.

Comparing the above two wavelength switching methods, note that the broadcast-and-select method has simpler implementation but suffers a larger distribution loss. The wavelength routing method on the other hand has low power loss but requires precise wavelength control and conversion.

In the above switching methods, input wavelength channels are routed in the spatial domain. Alternatively, wavelength switching can be performed in the same wavelength domain. This is called **wavelength-channel interchange** (WCI) and is logically equivalent to the time-slot interchange (TSI) discussed in Chapter 2. As shown in Figure 11.48, a WCI consists of a wavelength demultiplexer, an array of WCs, and a coupler. This WCI performs wavelength switching within the same set of wavelength channels. Note that the WCI uses a coupler instead of a wavelength-dependent multiplexer because WCs can be set for different wavelength conversions. When the WCI is used together with WGRs, it can form a λ-S-λ or S-λ-S switch, as shown in Figures 11.48b and 11.48c. These two-dimensional switches are logically equivalent to the three-stage Clos switch shown in Figure 2.8.

11.3.2 TIME-DOMAIN SWITCHING

Time-domain switching is attractive to TDoMA where traffic is multiplexed in the time domain. Because photons cannot be easily stored and retrieved after a programmable delay, implementation of time-domain switching or time-slot interchange is not an easy task. A programmable time delay line that uses a fiber loop and a 2×2 photonic switch is shown in Figure 11.49a [48]–[51]. By designing a unit delay T (e.g., a packet duration) in the fiber loop, a programmable delay of multiple T's can be achieved by changing the state of the 2×2 switch. To do this, the switch is first set in the CROSS state for a duration of T to switch the input packet to the delay loop. After that, the switch is set in the BAR state for a duration of $(k - 1)T$, which then keeps the packet for another $(k - 1)T$ delay. At the end, the switch is reset to the CROSS state, and a total delay of kT is introduced.

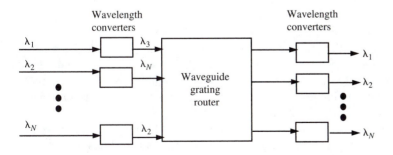

Figure 11.47   Wavelength switching from wavelength routing.

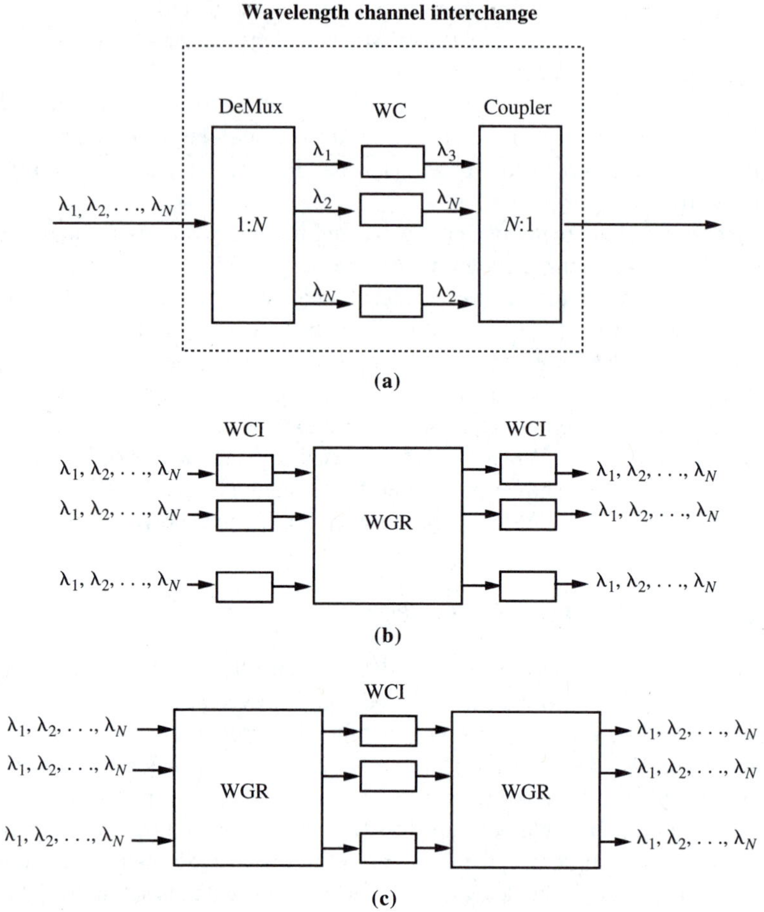

Wavelength channel interchange

(a)

(b)

(c)

Figure 11.48   (a) A wavelength channel interchange or λ switch, (b) a λ-S-λ switch, and (c) an S-λ-S switch.

Based on the programmable delay lines, a TSI can be implemented as shown in Figure 11.49b. In the first stage, a time-slot demultiplexer, as shown in Figure 11.49c, must be used to align all time slots in the time domain. After this, different delays can be introduced according to the TSI needed. At the end, the delayed slots are multiplexed by using a time-slot multiplexer, as shown in Figure 11.49d. In practice, TSIs are used with spatial- and/or wavelength-domain switching for multidimensional switching.

Because the programmable delay line discussed above can introduce a large power loss and timing errors after a long delay, a careful design is critical. When multidimensional switching is available, delay lines can be avoided and time-domain switching can be implemented in a different way. For example, a T-S-T switch can be achieved by using the

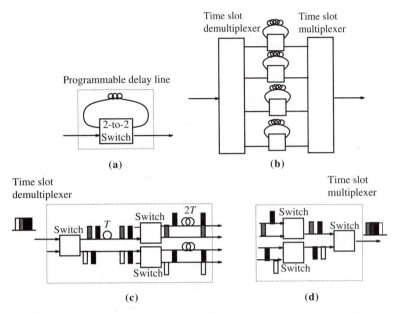

Figure 11.49 An implementation of a photonic time-slot change: (*a*) a basic programmable delay line, (*b*) the TSI, (*c*) implementation of a time-slot demultiplexer, and (*d*) implementation of a time-slot multiplexer.

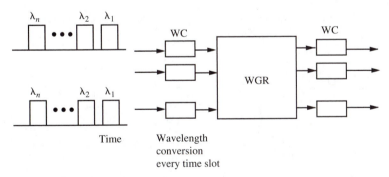

Figure 11.50 A T-S-T photonic switch using WC-WGR-WC.

same WC-WGR-WC combination discussed earlier. By converting the wavelengths of input channels every time slot, as shown in Figure 11.50, the spatial configuration can be rearranged every time slot, thus achieving T-S-T switching.

11.3.3   SELF-ROUTING AND ATM SWITCHING

To support ATM/B-ISDN networking, high-speed packet switching in an all-optical network has been an active research area. In this case, self-routing networks such as Batcher-Banyan, discussed earlier, can be used, and an optical implementation of address decoding is needed. As shown in Figure 11.51, the basic component in a self-routing optical network is a 2-to-2 switch whose switching state is determined by an optical address decoder. In practice, the address decoder can be implemented by an optical correlator consisting of fiber delay lines or by optical gates (smart pixels). Because there can be a switching conflict when both input packets need to be routed to the same output port, optical delay loops, shown in Figure 11.51*b*, can be used to reduce the blocking probability [50]–[51].

11.4   SUMMARY

1. Photonic switching can avoid the electronics speed bottleneck by providing optical-domain switching. To route optical signals, a photonic switch needs to be able to configure optical paths according to the traffic patterns. In practice, photonic switching can be done over the spatial, wavelength, and time domains.

2. Interconnection among switching elements in a photonic switch can be done by fibers, waveguides, and free space. In general, fibers and waveguides provide an easy solution when the switch size is small. However, when there are many crossovers among connections and when the switch size is large, three-dimensional free-space interconnection using prisms, mirrors, and grating devices becomes attractive.

3. A large photonic switch needs a good switching architecture to interconnect basic switching elements. To minimize cost and provide good switching performance, the architecture needs to minimize the number of crosspoints, the number of crossovers, the power loss, the crosstalk, and the internal blocking probability.

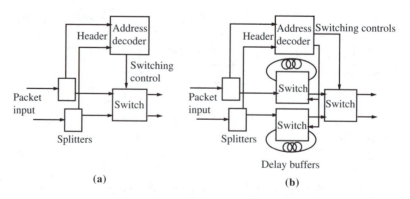

Figure 11.51   A (a) 2 × 2 self-routing photonic switch, and (b) the same switch with optical buffer.

4. For a given switching architecture, there might be no route for a given connection even when the output port is idle. This is called internal blocking. A switch is called strictly nonblocking when a route always exists and wide-sense nonblocking or re-arrangeably nonblocking when a route can be found if a proper switching control (i.e., an algorithm to set up routes) or a rearrangement of the existing switching configuration is used, respectively.

5. Crossbar is a wide-sense nonblocking switch that has no crossovers. For a switch of size N, its primary disadvantages include a large number of crosspoints (N^2) and a large power loss through many crosspoints (up to $2N - 1$). To reduce the power loss, double crossbar that has a constant number of crosspoints ($N + 1$) in every route can be used. However, its disadvantages are more crosspoints ($2N^2$) and crossovers. To reduce the number of crosspoints and avoid crossovers, an N-stage planar switch with only $N(N - 1)/2$ crosspoints can be used. One primary disadvantage of this switch is it is only rearrangeably nonblocking.

6. To reduce the number of crosspoints and power loss, the three-stage Clos switch can be used. By having a sufficiently large number of switches in the middle stage, the Clos switch is strictly nonblocking. Compared to the crossbar, it requires much fewer crosspoints but requires more crossovers. These crossovers can be avoided, however, by using a three-dimensional interconnection.

7. The Benes switch is a special case of the Clos switch with its middle stage consisting of two half-size Benes switches. In other words, the Benes switch is a recursive three-stage Clos switch. The Benes switch is important because it requires a very small number of crosspoints, close to the lower bound, $\log_2(N!)$. Because the Benes switch does not meet the Clos strictly nonblocking condition, it is only rearrangeably nonblocking. To avoid crosstalk, a variation of the Benes switch called the dilated Benes has been proposed.

8. In packet switching, self-routing of optical packets can avoid the speed bottleneck in switching control. There are several self-routing networks, including Banyan, baseline (half of the Benes), omega or shuffle exchange, and flip (inverse shuffle). They are all logically equivalent and can have internal blocking.

9. To avoid internal blocking, a Batcher sorting network can be used in front of a Banyan routing network. This Batcher-Banyan switch is nonblocking and requires a small number of crosspoints. With a three-dimensional free-space interconnection, its many crossovers can also be avoided.

10. To provide simple free-space interconnection, a crossover network that uses only prisms and mirrors is attractive. Because it is logically equivalent to self-routing networks, it can have internal blocking. A variation called extended generalized shuffle (EGS) that uses fan-in and fan-out to reduce the internal blocking probability is a good alternative.

11. A mechanical photonic switch is a spatial switch that uses a mechanical mechanism to configure optical paths between input fibers and output fibers. Because of the various physical limitations, mechanical switches are primarily used in applications such as automatic protection switching (APS) and self-healing rings that do not require high-speed re-configurations.

12. For high-speed switching, directional couplers that route optical signals based on the electro-optic (EO) effect can be used. For low propagation loss and a large EO effect, Ti-LiNbO$_3$ waveguides have been favorably considered, where the refractive index of waveguides made of Ti-LiNbO$_3$ can be modulated by an external voltage. As a result, the incident light can be switched to one of the output ports according to the applied voltage.

13. Based on a certain nonlinear feedback, bistable optical devices that have two stable outputs can be used as logic gates in optical computing and photonic switching. Important bistable optical devices include Fabry-Perot resonators and self–electro-optic effect devices (SEEDs).

14. SEEDs are PIN photodiodes whose intrinsic region has a multiple-quantum-well (MQW) structure. Because of an effect called the quantum confined stark effect (QCSE), the photodetection responsivity and transmissivity of a SEED is a function of its reverse biased voltage. When it is used with a resistor (R-SEED), an FET (F-SEED), a heterostructure photo transistor (H-SEED), or another SEED (S-SEED), it functions as a bistable device from the voltage feedback due to the QCSE.

15. In addition to spatial domain switching, input channels can be switched in the wavelength and time domains, where the wavelengths or time slots of input channels are switched. Therefore, they are called wavelength channel interchange (WCI) and time slot interchange (TSI), respectively. In general, WCI's and TSI's can be used in combination with spatial domain switches for multidimensional switching.

16. For future all-optical ATM switching, we need self-routing photonic switches that can buffer photons and decode the addresses. In this case, we need optical delay lines as buffers and optical logic gates to decode ATM packet addresses.

APPENDIX 11-A *N*-STAGE PLANAR WAVEGUIDE SWITCH

This appendix shows that the *N*-stage planar waveguide switch is rearrangeably nonblocking [8]. Without loss of generality, consider an 8–stage planar switch, as shown in Figure 11.4, and assume input ports 1, 2,..., 8 are connected to output ports $\pi_1, \pi_2, \ldots, \pi_8$. If some of the input ports are not active, they are arbitrarily assigned to unused output ports. Therefore, the output connections $i \to \pi_i$'s for $i = 1, \ldots, 8$ are simply a permutation of the sequence $1, 2, \ldots, 8$.

The state of each 2×2 switch is set up beginning with connection 1 to π_1. As illustrated in Figure 11.52*a*, the connection path from the input port will be a horizontal line until it reaches a point that all subsequent switches it goes through are in the CROSS state.

After the first connection is done, all the switches along the connection can be replaced by the corresponding lines shown in Figure 11.52*b*. By dropping the connection, the *N*-stage planar switch reduces to an $N - 1$ or 7-stage planar switch shown in Figure 11.52*c*. Now the same algorithm can be used to connect 2 to π_2. By repeating the same algorithm, all the connections can be completed, and the switch is thus rearrangeably nonblocking.

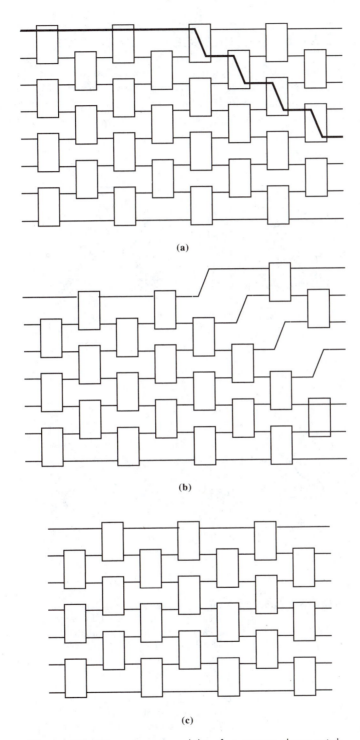

(a)

(b)

(c)

Figure 11.52   Rearrangeability of an *N*-stage planar switch.

APPENDIX 11-B   REARRANGEABLE NETWORK

This appendix verifies the rearrangeability condition, Equation (11.1), of the three-stage Clos network. For explanation, an address labeling scheme shown in Figure 11.53 is used, where the first-stage switches are indexed by i, i_1, etc., the middle-stage switches are indexed by j, j_1, etc., and the third-stage switches are indexed by k, k_1, etc. To build a con-

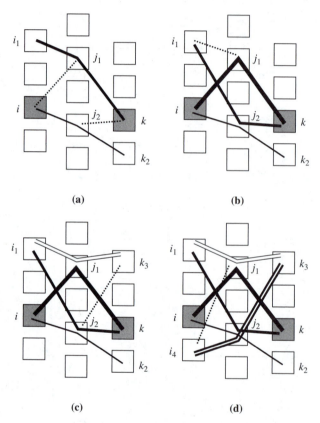

(a)   (b)

(c)   (d)

Figure 11.53   Rearrangeability of a three-stage Clos switch: (a) switch j_1 is available to i and switch j_2 is available to k (indicated by dotted lines); (b) j_1 is rearranged for connection between i and k (dark solid line) and j_2 (if available) is used for connection between i_1 and k; (c) another rearrangement if i_1–j_2 connection in the previous arrangement is unavailable; and (d) another rearrangement if j_1–k_3 connection in the previous arrangement is unavailable.

nection between switch i in the first stage and switch k in the third stage, there must be an available switch j in the middle stage.

If there is a switch j that is not used by the other $n - 1$ inputs of switch i and the other $n - 1$ outputs of switch k, it can be used to set up the connection without any rearrangement. If such a switch cannot be found, a middle switch j_l that is not used by other $n - 1$ inputs of switch i can be found. This is possible because $m > n - 1$ according to Equation (11.1). According to the assumption, switch j_1 is used by one of the existing outputs of switch k. Similarly, there is a switch j_2 in the middle stage that is not used by the outputs of switch k but is used by one of the existing inputs of switch i. As illustrated in Figure 11.53a, assume switch j_1 is used in the connection between switches i_1 and k, and switch j_2 is used for connections between switches i and k_2.

Once the middle switches j_1 and j_2 are found, the connection can be rearranged as follows. First, as shown Figure 11.53b, the middle switch j_1 is used for the new connection between i and k, and the middle switch j_2 is used for the existing connection between i_1 and k. From this rearrangement, the original connection between switch i_1 and j_1, shown as the dotted line in Figure 11.53b, is now made available.

The above rearrangement is complete if the line between i_1 and j_2 is available. If not, say it is used for connection from i_1 through j_2 to k_3, another rearrangement must be performed by replacing the connection between i_1 and j_2 with the connection between i_1 and j_1 (made available from the previous rearrangement) and replacing the connection between j_2 and k_3 with j_1 and k_3. As shown in Figure 11.53c, the connection between j_2 and k_3 is available after this rearrangement (dotted line). The above rearrangement is complete if the connection between j_1 and k_3 is available. Otherwise, the above rearrangement process can be repeated recursively.

In the rearrangement process described above, a *new* switch on either the first stage or third stage is introduced at each rearrangement step. For example, as illustrated in Figure 11.53, a new switch k_2 is introduced in step 2, k_3 is introduced in step 3, i_4 is introduced in step 4, etc. To see that k_3 is a new switch instead of one of the previous switches such as k or k_2, note that k_3 is originally connected to j_2. Because j_2 is connected to k and k_2, k_3 must be a different switch. Similarly, i_4 is different from i_1 and i because it is originally connected to j_1, which has connections with i_1 and i. Therefore, a new switch is added alternately from the first and third stages as the rearrangement process continues. This observation implies a finite number of rearrangements. Eventually, there is a successful rearrangement.

APPENDIX 11-C   SWITCHING CONTROL FOR A DILATED BENES NETWORK

This appendix describes the switching control for a dilated Benes network and verifies that it can ensure one active input per 2×2 switch [11]. For convenience, let π_i be the output port of input i, and let $\hat{i}$ be the **dual port** of i given by

$$\hat{i} \stackrel{\text{def}}{=} \begin{cases} i + 1 & \text{if } i \text{ is odd} \\ i - 1 & \text{if } i \text{ is even.} \end{cases} \qquad \textbf{[11.30]}$$

For example, ports 1 and 2 are dual ports of one another, and so are ports 3 and 4.

Control Algorithm   The switch setup algorithm is given below. Use Figure 11.54 for illustration.

1. For input $i = 1$ to N, choose the first one whose connection has not been set up.

2. Set $j = i$.

3. Connect input switch j in the first stage to the upper switch in the second stage, and connect input switch $\hat{j}$ to the lower switch.

4. Connect the output switch $\pi_{\hat{j}}$ in the third stage to the lower switch of the second stage. At this point, the connection between $\hat{j}$ and $\pi_{\hat{j}}$ is complete.

5. Connect the output switch $\hat{\pi_i}$ to the upper switch.

6. If π_j is the dual port of $\pi_{\hat{j}}$, connect the output switch π_j to the upper switch and go to step 1. If not, as shown in Figure 11.54, let k be the input for which π_k is the dual port of $\pi_{\hat{j}}$. Set $j = k$ and go to Step 3.

As illustrated in Figure 11.54, when $k \neq i$, the first round of Steps 3–6 of the algorithm forms an incomplete loop $i - \hat{i} - \pi_{\hat{i}} - \hat{\pi_i} - k$. If Steps 3–6 of the alogirhtm are repeated for another round, another loop is formed starting from k. This can be repeated until the final loop meets the original port i. From this looping characteristic in setting up connections, the control algorithm is referred to as the **looping algorithm** [11].

In Step 3 of the control algorithm, two dual inputs are connected to the two different middle switches. Therefore, all 2×2 switches at the first stage of the middle switches have

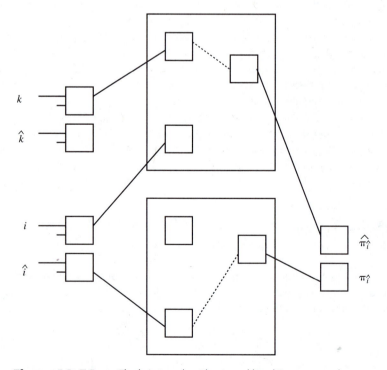

Figure 11.54   The looping algorithm in a dilated-Benes network.

only one active input. In Steps 4 and 5, the dual outputs are also connected to the two different middle switches. Therefore, the two middle switches are another two $N/2$ dilated Benes networks. From the recursive definition, then, all 2×2 switches have only one active input.

OUTER LOOP SETUP OF AN 8 X 8 DILATED BENES   Consider the 8×8 dilated Benes network shown in Figure 11.7c with inputs $1, 2, \ldots, 8$ switched to outputs $3, 7, 2, 5, 1, 8, 4, 6$, respectively. As a notation, let i_j be switch i at stage j. The looping algorithm gives the following steps:

> **Example 11.12**

1. In loop 1: 1_1 is connected to 1_2, 2_1 (2 is dual of 1) is connected to 5_2, 8_5 is connected to 7_6, 8_6 (8 is dual of 7) is connected to 4_5, and 3_2 is connected to 6_1.

2. In loop 2: 5_1 (5 is dual of 6) is connected to 7_2, 5_5 is connected to 1_6, 2_6 is connected to 1_5, and 2_2 is connected to 3_1.

3. In loop 3: 4_1 (4 is dual of 3) is connected to 6_2, 7_5 is connected to 5_6, 6_6 (6 is dual of 5) is connected to 3_5, and 4_2 is connected to 8_1.

4. In loop 4: 7_1 (7 is dual of 8) is connected to 8_2, 6_5 is connected to 4_6, 3_6 (3 is dual of 4) is connected to 2_5, and 1_2 is connected to 1_1. At this end, the four loops meet their ends, and all outer loop connections are done.

From the above setup, the two inner dilated Benes networks have mappings of $1, 2, 3, 4$ to $2, 1, 4, 3$ and $4, 3, 1, 2$, respectively. Interested readers can apply the same looping algorithm for the rest of the connections. ∎

APPENDIX 11–D   BATCHER SORTING NETWORK

This appendix explains the Batcher sorting algorithm that is the foundation for the Batcher sorting network shown in Figure 11.9. To apply the algorithm, the input sequence needs to be **bitonic.** A finite sequence is called bitonic if

1. It consists of two subsequences, one ascending and one descending, as shown in Figure 11.55a, or

2. It can be transformed to the above sequence by a certain number of cyclic shifts, as shown in Figure 11.55b.

Sorting Algorithm   To sort a bitonic sequence of length $2m$, first divide it into two equal halves and label them as $\{a_1, a_2, \ldots, a_m\}$ and $\{d_1, d_2, \ldots, d_m\}$. After this, compare each pair (a_i, d_i) and collect all the smaller ones in one subsequence and the larger ones in another. As shown in Figure 11.56, $\{u_1, u_2, \ldots, u_m\}$ is the subsequence of the smaller ones, and $\{l_1, l_2, \ldots, l_m\}$ is the subsequence of the larger ones. The two subsequences $\{u_i\}$ and $\{l_i\}$ can be proved to have the following two properties:

1. Both are bitonic.

2. The largest element in $\{u_i\}$ is not greater than the smallest element in $\{l_i\}$.

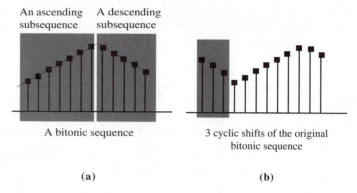

An ascending   A descending
subsequence   subsequence

A bitonic sequence   3 cyclic shifts of the original
                                      bitonic sequence

(a)   **(b)**

Figure 11.55   Bitonic sequences.

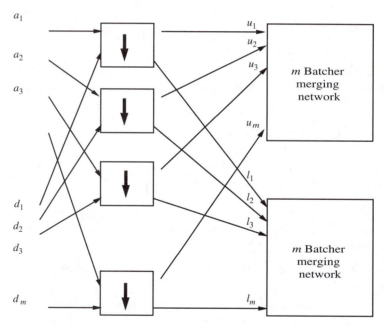

Figure 11.56   A $2m$ Batcher merging network in terms of two m Batcher merging networks.

According to the first property, the sequences can continue to be split and the same Batcher sorting algorithm applied for them. The second property allows the recursive Batcher sorting and merging shown in Figure 11.56.

Proof   For a bitonic sequence $\{b_1, b_2, \ldots, b_m\}$ consisting of two subsequences $\{a_i\}$ and $\{d_i\}$, the same set of m pairs (a_i, d_i) exits when shifts are performed on $\{b_i\}$. This is simply because of a constant separation (cyclically) between a_i and d_i. For a given number of cyclic shifts on $\{b_i\}$, the two subsequences $\{u_i\}$ and $\{l_i\}$ go through the same number of cyclic shifts. As a result, from the bitonic sequence definition, if $\{u_i\}$ and $\{l_i\}$ are bitonic, they are still bitonic if cyclic shifts are performed on $\{b_i\}$.

The above observations allow the following assumption without loss of generality:

$$b_1 \le b_2 \le \ldots \le b_j \ge b_{j+1} \ge b_{j+2} \ge \ldots \ge b_{2m}.$$

For convenience, assume $j > m$. In this case, $a_i = b_i \le b_{m+i} = d_i$, for $i = 1, \ldots, j - m$. Therefore, $u_i = a_i$ and $l_i = d_i$, for $i = 1, \ldots, j - m$. For the remaining comparisons, there are the following two scenarios.

First, if $b_m \le b_{2m}$, for $j - m < i \le m$,

$$b_i \le b_m \le b_{2m} \le b_{i+m} \le b_j.$$

Therefore, $u_i = a_i$ and $l_i = d_i$ for all $1 \le i \le m$. In this case, as illustrated in Figure 11.57a, $\max_i a_i = b_m \le \min(b_{m+1}, b_{2m}) \le \min_i d_i$, and the two properties are clearly true.

On the other hand, if $b_m > b_{2m}$, there is a value k in the range $j < k < 2m$ such that $b_i \ge b_{i+m}$ if $i \ge k - m$. This yields

$$\begin{cases} u_i = a_i \; l_i = d_i & \text{for } 1 \le i < k - m \\ u_i = d_i \; l_i = a_i & \text{for } k - m \le i \le m. \end{cases}$$

As a result,

$$\begin{cases} u_i \le u_{i+1} & \text{for } 1 \le i < k - m \\ u_i \ge u_{i+1} & \text{for } k - m \le i \le m \end{cases}$$

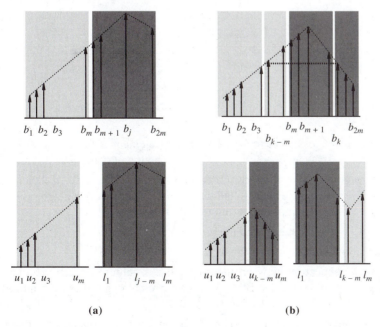

(a)   (b)

Figure 11.57   Two scenarios in merging two subsequences of a bitonic input: (a) $b_m \le b_{2m}$ and (b) $b_m > b_{2m}$.

and

$$\begin{cases} l_i \leq l_{i+1} & \text{for } 1 \leq i \leq j - m \\ l_i \geq l_{i+1} & \text{for } j - m < i < k - m \\ l_i \leq l_{i+1} & \text{for } k - m \leq i \leq m. \end{cases}$$

By definition, $\{u_i\}$ is a bitonic sequence. Because $l_m = b_{2m} \leq b_k \leq b_{k-m} \leq b_{m+1} = l_1$, $\{l_i\}$ is also bitonic. This proves the first property. Furthermore, $u_{k-m-1} = b_{k-m-1}$ or $u_{k-m} = b_k$ is the largest among the u_i's, and $l_{k-m-1} = b_{k-1}$ or $l_{k-m} = b_{k-m}$ is the smallest among the l_i's. Because $b_{k-1} \geq b_k$, $b_{k-m} \geq b_{k-m-1}$, $b_{k-m} \geq b_k$, and $b_{k-m-1} < b_{k-1}$ (the last two come from the definition of k), this proves the second property.

Recursive Construction of a Batcher Sorting Network   A Batcher network of size $N = 2^p$ consists of two stages. In the first stage, two $N/2$ Batcher networks are used to generate one ascending and one descending sequence. These two output subsequences from the first stage form one bitonic sequence, which can be merged according to the recursive Batcher algorithm described.

From the recursive construction, the total number of stages of a Batcher network can be determined below. Let the number of stages of a Batcher network of size $N = 2^p$ be M_p. From the recursive construction shown in Figure 11.9a, this gives

$$M_p = M_{p-1} + p.$$

Therefore,

$$M_p = \tfrac{1}{2}p(p+1) = \tfrac{1}{2}\log_2 N(\log_2 N + 1). \qquad \textbf{[11.31]}$$

PROBLEMS

Problem 11–1 Power Loss and Crosstalk of Crossbar: Consider a crossbar switch of size N.

    a. If the power loss of each 2×2 switching element is 0.5 dB and the worst case power loss that can be tolerated is 10 dB, find the maximum switch size N.

    b. Let the control algorithm illustrated in Figure 11.1b be used. If the crosstalk from each 2×2 switch is –40 dB and the tolerable crosstalk from input port 1 to output port 1 is –20 dB, find the maximum switch size N.

Problem 11–2 N-Stage Planar:

    a. Draw a four-stage planar switch.

    b. Draw a connection between input port 1 and output port 2 by having a CROSS state in the first stage and BAR states at the remaining stages (port numbering goes from 1 to 4).

    c. Show that there is blocking when input port 2 is to be connected to output port 3.

Problem 11–3 N-Stage Planar: From the switching algorithm discussed in Appendix 11–A, describe the connection setup of a planar switch of size 6 from 1 to 5, 2 to 4, 3 to 1, 4 to 6, 5 to 2, and 6 to 3.

Problem 11–4 Rearrangeably Nonblocking Clos: If all the switching modules in a rearrangeably nonblocking Clos switch are nonblocking crossbar switches, find the optimum n value that gives the minimum number of crosspoints. Also give the total number of crosspoints at the optimum n. For simplicity, ignore the conditions that n is an integer and a factor of N.

Problem 11–5 Switching Rearrangement of Clos: Consider a Clos switch that has $N = 6, n = 2, r = 3$, and $m = 2$.

a. Draw the interconnection architecture.

b. Use the rearrangement algorithm if necessary for the following connections: 1 to 1, 2 to 3, 3 to 6, 4 to 4, 5 to 2, and 6 to 5. Connect them in a *sequential* order.

Problem 11–6 Benes: Consider a Benes switch of size 8. Use the same rearrangement algorithm as for Clos to set up the following connections in a *sequential* order: 1 to 8, 2 to 6, 3 to 4, 4 to 2, 5 to 1, 6 to 3, 7 to 5, and 8 to 7.

Problem 11–7 Dilated Benes: Let M_p be the number of stages of a dilated Benes network of size $N = 2^p$. From the facts that $M_p = 2 + M_{p-1}$ and $M_1 = 2$, show that $M_p = 2p$.

Problem 11–8 Looping Algorithm: Continue Example 11.12 to set up connections in the two 4×4 dilated Benes subnetworks according to the looping algorithm.

Problem 11–9 Self-Routing: Consider the omega self-routing network shown in Figure 11.8. Give an algorithm to route input packets according to the interconnection architecture. Hint: For the three-stage omega network of size 8, if $[a_0, a_1, a_2]$ is the three-tuple input address at a certain 2×2 switch, it can be connected to either $[a_1, a_2, 0]$ or $[a_1, a_2, 1]$.

Problem 11–10 Batcher: Show that the number of stages of a Batcher network of size $N = 2^p$ is

$$M_p = \tfrac{1}{2} p(p + 1) = \tfrac{1}{2} \log_2 N (\log_2 N + 1).$$
[11.32]

Problem 11–11 Bitonic Sequence Sorting:

a. Consider a bitonic sequence {4, 7, 16, 30, 22, 17, 8, 5}. Explain how it can be sorted into an ascending sequence according to the Batcher algorithm.

b. Consider an arbitrary input {4, 20, 12, 52, 22, 42, 83, 17}. Explain how to sort it using the Batcher sorting network.

Problem 11–12 Waveguide Switches: Consider a LiNbO$_3$ waveguide switch that has a crossover length $L_c = 2$ mm.

a. Find the coupling constant, κ.

b. Find the required voltage to set the switch at the BAR state. Assume $\gamma = 3 \times 10^{-5}$ V^{-1} at $\lambda = 633$ nm.

Problem 11–13 Crosstalk in Reverse-β Directional Couplers: If a reversable-β waveguide switch with $L = L_c$ is set at the BAR state by applying a voltage given by Equation (11.16), find the crosstalk if the actual κ is 90 percent of the assumed value.

Problem 11–14 R-SEED: From Figure 11.32:

a. Find the range $R_L P_{in}$ that can have bistable output.

b. Using the middle value from the above range and setting $P_{in} = 50\ \mu$W, find the required load resistance.

c. From (b), find the P_{in} range for which V_{out} can have bistable output.

Problem 11–15 S-SEED: Consider the use of S-SEED devices as the basic 2-to-1 switching elements.

a. From the physical arrangement shown in Figure 11.58a, show that it has a logical representation shown in Figure 11.58b. Note that when the control signal is equal to the bias voltage, clock signals will be absorbed by the SEEDs.

b. From the logical representation given, explain how it can be used as the basic 2-to-1 switching element.

Problem 11–16 Hologram: To provide a one-dimensional crossover interconnection using a hologram with $x' = -x$ and $y' = y$, find the required phase function of the hologram.

Problem 11–17 Wavelength Router: Consider a wavelength router, as shown in Figure 11.47, of size four. If wavelength routing of the WGR used follows Equation (11.29), describe the wavelength conversions required so that wavelength channel inputs from ports 1–4 are switched to output ports 4, 2, 3, and 1, respectively.

Problem 11–18 Time-Slot Interchange: Consider the TSI shown in Figure 11.49, and assume the fiber delay loop has an attenuation of 0.5 dB/km.

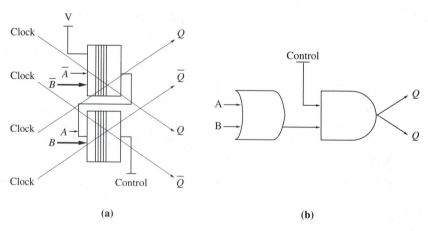

(a)   (b)

Figure 11.58   Use of S-SEEDs as 2-to-1 switches. (a) physical arrangement and (b) logical representation.

a. Find the fiber loss in each delay loop if the delay introduced is 500 nsec. Assume the light propagation velocity in the fiber is 2×10^8 m/sec.

b. If the total coupling loss at the two fiber ends of the delay loop is 0.1 dB, find the total loss including the fiber loss.

c. If the TSI is designed for a slot size of $N = 32$, find the worst case power loss.

REFERENCES

1. S. D. Personick, "Photonic Switching: Technology and Applications," *IEEE Communications Magazine,* vol. 25, no. 5 (May 1987), pp. 5–8.

2. H. S. Hinton and J. E. Midwinter, editors, *Photonic Switching,* IEEE Press, 1990.

3. P. R. Prucnal et al., "Photonic Switch with Optically Self-Routing Bit Switching," *IEEE Communications Magazine,* vol. 25, no. 5 (May 1987), pp. 50–55.

4. D. Blumenthal et al., "Photonic Packet Switches: Architectures and Experimental Implementations," *Proceedings of the IEEE,* vol. 82, no. 11 (November 1994), pp. 1650–67.

5. R. A. Spanke, "Architectures for Guided-Wave Optical Space Switching Systems," *IEEE Communications Magazine,* vol. 25, no. 5 (May 1987), pp. 42–48.

6. V. E. Benes, *Mathematical Theory of Connecting Networks and Telephone Traffic,* Academic Press, 1965.

7. M. Kondo et al., "32 Switch Elements Integrated Low-Crosstalk $LiNbO_3$ 4×4 Optical Matrix Switch," Integrated Conference on Integrated Optics and Optical Fiber Communication European Conference on Optical Communication 1985, pp. 361–64.

8. R. A. Spanke and V. E. Benes, "An N-Stage Planar Optical Permutation Network," *Applied Optics,* vol. 26, no. 7 (April 1987), pp. 1226–29.

9. A. M. Deguid, "Structural Properties of Switching Networks," Progress Report BTL–7, Brown University, 1959.

10. J. Hui, *Switching and Traffic Theory for Integrated Broadband Networks,* Kluwer Academic Publishers, 1990.

11. K. Padmanabhan and A. Netravali, "Dilated Networks for Photonic Switching," *IEEE Transactions on Communications,* vol. 35, no. 12 (December 1987), pp. 1357–65.

12. J. Jahns and M. J. Murdocca, "Crossover Networks and Their Optical Implementation," *Applied Optics,* vol. 27, no. 15 (August 1988), pp. 3155–60.

13. T. J. Cloonan, "Topological Equivalence of Optical Crossover Networks and Modified Data Manipulator Networks," *Applied Optics,* vol. 28, no. 13 (July 1989), pp. 2494–98.

14. T. Cloonan et al., "Free-Space Photonic Switching Architectures Based on Extended Generalized Shuffle Networks," *Applied Optics,* vol. 31, no. 35 (December 1992), pp. 7471–92.

15. K. E. Batcher, "Sorting Networks and Their Applications," American Federation of Information Processing Societies, Proceedings of Spring Joint Computer Conference, vol. 32 (1968) pp. 307–14.

16. W. C. Young and L. Curtis, "Single-Mode Fiber Switch with Simultaneous Loop-Back Feature," *Photonic Switching,* edited by T. K. Gustafson and P. W. Smith, Springer-Verlag, 1988, pp. 50–53.

17. R. C. Alferness, R. V. Schmidt, and E. H. Turner, "Characteristics of Ti-Diffused Lithium Niobate Optical Directional Couplers," *Applied Optics,* vol. 18, no. 23 (December 1979), pp. 4012–16.

18. H. Kogelnik and R. V. Schmidt, "Switched Directional Couplers with Alternating $\Delta\beta$," *IEEE Journal of Quantum Electronics,* vol. 12, no. 7 (July 1976), pp. 396–401.

19. L. Thylen, "LiNbO$_3$ and Semiconductor Guided Wave Optics in Switching and Interconnects," Chapter 1 of *Photonics Switching and Interconnects,* edited by A. Marrakchi, Dekker, 1994.

20. T. O. Murphy, C. T. Kemmerer, and D. T. Moser, "A 16×16 Ti:LiNbO$_3$ Dilated Benes Photonic Switch Module," Proceedings of OSA Topical Meeting on Photonic Switching, Salt Lake City, (1991), pp. 7–9.

21. J. A. Cavailles et al., "Integration of Detectors with InP/GaInAsP Carrier Depletion Optical Switches," *Electronics Letters,* vol. 26, no. 21 (1990), pp. 1783–84.

22. J. A. Cavailles et al., "First Digital Optical Switch Based on InP/GaInAsP Double Heterostructure Waveguides," *Electronics Letters,* vol. 27, no. 9 (1991), pp. 699–700.

23. J. F. Vinchant et al., "InP Digital Optical Switch: Key Element for Guided-Wave Photonic Switching," *IEE Proceedings J,* vol. 140, no. 5 (October 1993), pp. 301–07.

24. R. C. Alferness, "Polarization-Independent Optical Directional Coupler Switch Using Weighted Coupling," *Applied Physics Letters,* vol. 35, no. 10 (November 1979), pp. 748–50.

25. P. Granestrand et al., "Polarization Independent Switch and Polarization Splitter Employing $\Delta\beta$ and $\Delta\kappa$ Modulation," *Electronics Letters,* vol. 24, no. 18 (September 1988), pp. 1142–43.

26. P. Granestrand, "Four-Sectioned Polarization-Independent Directional Coupler with Extremely Relaxed Fabrication Tolerances," *IEEE Photonics Technology Letters,* vol. 4, no. 6 (June 1992), pp. 594–96.

27. M. Kondo et al., "Low-Drive-Voltage and Low-Loss Polarization-Independent LiNbO$_3$ Optical Waveguide Switches," *Electronics Letters,* vol.23, no. 21 (October 1987), pp. 1167–69.

28. Y. Silberberg and P. Perlmutter, "A Digital Electrooptic Switch," *Photonic Switching,* edited by T. K. Gustafson and P. W. Smith, Springer-Verlag, 1988, pp. 95–99.

29. P. Granestrand, "Novel Approaches to Polarization-Independent Switches," *IEE Proceedings J,* vol. 140 (October 1993), pp. 291–95.

30. F. B. McCormick, Jr., et al., "Design and Tolerancing Comparisons for S-SEED Based Free Space Switching Fabrics," *Optical Engineering,* vol. 31, no. 12 (December 1992), pp. 2697–2709.

31. T. J. Cloonan et al., "A Complexity Analysis of Smart Pixel Switching Nodes for Photonic Extended Generalized Shuffle Switching Networks," *IEEE Journal of Quantum Electronics,* vol. 29, no. 2 (February 1993), pp. 619–33.

32. C. Cohen-Tannoudji, B. Diu, and F. Laloe, *Quantum Mechanics*, vol. 2, Wiley Interscience, 1977.

33. D. A. B. Miller et al., "The Quantum Well Self-Electrooptic Effect Device: Optoelectronic Bistability and Oscillation, and Self-Linearized Modulation," *IEEE Journal of Quantum Electronics,* vol. 21, no. 9 (September 1985), pp. 1462–75.

34. D. A. B. Miller et al., "Novel Hybrid Optically Bistable Switch: The Quantum Well Self-Electro-Optic Effect Device," *Applied Physics Letters,* vol. 45 (1984), pp. 13–15.

35. F. B. McCormick et al., "Five-Stage Free-Space Optical Switching Network with Field-Effect Transistor Self-Electro-Optic-Effect-Device Smart-Pixel Arrays," *Applied Optics,* vol. 33, no. 8 (March 1994), pp. 1601–18.

36. P. Wheatley et al., "Hard Limiting Opto-Electronic Logic Devices," *Photonic Switching*, edited by T. K. Gustafson and P. W. Smith, Springer-Verlag, 1988, pp. 69–72.

37. A. L. Lentine et al., "Symmetric Self-Electro-Optic Effect Device: Optical Set-Reset Latch," *Applied Physics Letters,* vol. 52, no. 17 (April 1988), pp. 1419–21.

38. A. L. Lentine et al., "Symmetric Self-Electrooptic Effect Device: Optical Set-Reset Latch, Differential Logic Gate, and Differential Modulator/Detector," *IEEE Journal of Quantum Electronics,* vol. 25, no. 8 (August 1989), pp. 1928–36.

39. A. L. Lentine et al., "Photonic Switching Nodes Based on Self Electro-Optic Effect Devices," *Optical and Quantum Electronics,* vol. 24 (1992), pp. 443–64.

40. K. Kasahara, "Two Dimensional Optoelectronic Devices for Future Optical Switching and Information Processing," *Optical and Quantum Electronics,* vol. 24 (1992), pp. 783–800.

41. M. Yamaguchi et al., "Experimental Investigation of a Digital Free-Space Photonic Switch that Uses Exciton Absorption Reflection Switch Arrays," *Applied Optics,* vol. 33, no. 8 (March 1994), pp. 1337–44.

42. R. P. Bryan et al., "Hybrid Integration of Bipolar Transistors and Microlasers: Current-Controlled Microlaser Smart Pixels," *Applied Physics Letters,* vol. 62, no. 11 (March 1993), pp. 1230–32.

43. B. E. A. Saleh and M. C. Teich, *Fundamentals of Photonics,* Wiley Interscience,1991.

44. J. L. Jewell et al., "GaAs-AlAs Monolithic Microresonator Arrays," *Applied Physics Letters*, vol. 51, no. 2 (July 1987), pp. 94–96.

45. S. Suzuki et al., "An Experiment on High-Speed Optical Time-Division Switching," *Journal of Lightwave Technology,* vol. 4 (1986), pp. 894–99.

46. H. Obara et al., "Multiwavelength Routing Using Tunable Lasers and Arrayed-Wave-guide Grating Multiplexers for Wavelength-Division and Space-Division Multiplexed Crossconnects," *Electronics Letters,* vol. 28, no. 23 (November 1992), pp. 2172–74.

47. C. Dragone et al., "Integrated Optics $N \times N$ Multiplexer on Silicon," *IEEE Photonics Technology Letters,* vol. 3, no. 10 (October 1991), pp. 896–99.

48. R. A. Thompson, "Optimizing Photonic Variable-Integer-Delay Circuits," *Photonic Switching*, edited by T. K. Gustafson and P. W. Smith, Springer-Verlag, 1988, pp. 158–66.

49. J. G. Zhang, "New Architecture for Self-Routing Photonic ATM Switching with Self-Synchronization and Optically Processed Control," *Microwave and Optical Technology Letters,* vol. 7, no. 2 (February 1994), pp. 81–83.

50. Y. Shimazu and M. Tsukada, "Ultrafast Photonic ATM Switch with Optical Output Buffers," *Journal of Lightwave Technology,* vol. 10 (1992), pp. 265–72.

51. J. Spring and R. S. Tucker, "Photonic 2×2 Packet Switch with Input Buffers," *Electronics Letters,* vol. 29, no. 3 (February 1993), pp. 284–85.

In Part 2, we have discussed basic optical communication components. To provide higher bit-rate and longer distance transmission, there have been many significant breakthroughs. for example, to overcome power loss due to fiber attenuation, optical amplifiers have been developed and installed in practical systems; to increase receiver sensitivity, coherent communication and external modulation have been used; and to over-come fiber dispersion, single frequency light sources and soliton transmission have been developed.

In this fourth part, we address some advanced topics in detail. In particular, Chapters 12–14 cover some important modulation topics, including direct modulation, DFB laser diode modulation, and external modulation. From these chapters, we learn how to determine the modulation bandwidth of a light source, what are the relaxation oscillation and frequency chirping, and when we need external modulation.

Chapter 15 describes various coherent communication schemes and their detection methods. In contrast to direct detection discussed in Chapter 7, coherent detection mixes the received signal with a local optical signal before photodetection. This mixing can increase the receiver sensitivity and enables phase detection of the received signal. To compare various coherent signaling and detection schemes, we will derive their shot-noise limited performance.

In either direct or coherent detection, one fundamental block in a digital receiver that has not yet been discussed is bit timing recovery. As mentioned in Chapter 7, a bit clock extracted from the received signal is necessary in digital communication to sample the threshold detector output and regenerate original bits. In Chapter 16, we describe various binary line codes and scrambling techniques for high speed timing recovery in optical communications.

In the final two chapters, we discuss two recent advancements that bring us to the current generation of lightwave technology. In Chapter 17, we describe semiconductor and erbium-doped fiber amplifiers. They are being widely used for their high pumping efficiency, high amplification gain, and simple implementation. Chapter 18 explains how nonlinear optics can be used to overcome fiber dispersion in optical fiber communication. With a proper balance between fiber dispersion and optical nonlinearity, an optical pulse called optical soliton can propagate over thousands of kilometers with negligible pulse broadening.

12

DIRECT MODULATION

Important light sources for optical communications have been discussed in Chapter 3. To transmit information, the light output must be modulated in either amplitude, frequency, or phase. As illustrated in Figure 12.1, according to the position where modulation is performed, light modulation can be classified as either **direct** or **external** modulation. With direct modulation, light is directly modulated inside a light source. External modulation, on the other hand, uses a separate, external modulator.

Direct modulation is used in most optical communication systems for its simpler implementation than external modulation. Because of physical limitations, the light output under direct modulation cannot respond to the input signal instantaneously. Instead, there can be delays and oscillations when the input has large and rapid variations. Finding the light output under direct modulation requires using rate equations, which describe the dynamics of photons and carriers inside the active layer of the light source. Rate equations for both LEDs and Fabry-Perot LDs are discussed in this chapter. More advanced rate equations of DFB lasers will be discussed in Chapter 13. The light output and the modulation bandwidth under a certain bias condition can be determined from the rate equations.

Direct modulation has several undesirable effects such as **frequency chirping** and **linewidth broadening.** In frequency chirping, the spectrum of the light output is time varying because of refractive index modulation of the light source, and in linewidth broadening, the spectrum width is broader than that in the steady state. These effects can be the limiting factors in long-distance and high-speed communications. To reduce these effects, external modulation can be used. In this case, the bias current to the light source is constant, and a separate modulator is used to modulate the continuous wave (CW) output of the light source. A detailed discussion on external modulation is given in Chapter 14.

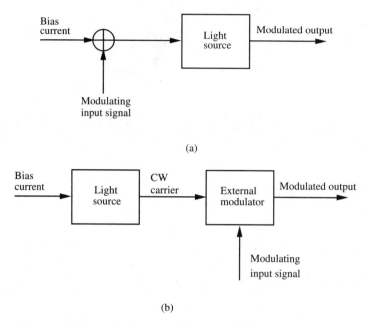

(a)

(b)

Figure 12.1   (a) Direct modulation and (b) external modulation.

12.1   DIRECT MODULATION FOR LIGHT EMITTING DIODES

As mentioned earlier, direct modulation uses the input current to modulate the output light intensity. Because the light output of an LED is incoherent, as discussed in Chapter 3, the phase or frequency content of the output is not of interest. Therefore, the following analysis considers only the intensity or power of the modulated light.

12.1.1   RATE EQUATION AND STEADY STATE SOLUTION

Whether in the steady state or under modulation, the light intensity output of an LED can be derived from a single rate equation that describes the dynamic relationship between the carrier density and the input current. If the active layer of an LED is N-type of donor concentration N_D, the rate equation is[1]

$$\frac{dN}{dt} = \frac{J}{qd} - B(NP - n_i^2) - \frac{N - N_D}{\tau_{nr}}$$ **[12.1]**

where N is the electron density (number of electrons per cubic meter), P is the hole density,[2] J is the current density, d is the thickness of the active layer, τ_{nr} is the nonradiative time decay constant for the electrons, and B is the electron–hole recombination coefficient.

---

[1] This equation neglects the lateral diffusion current that flows in the transverse direction of the p-n junction.

[2] To avoid the same notation for the electron density and refractive index, capitalized N and P here represent electron and hole carrier densities.

The above rate equation (12.1) can be understood from charge conservation. On the left hand, dN/dt is the net change rate of the electron density at the p-n junction. On the right-hand side are various sources for the rate change. The first term, J/qd, is the carrier pumping rate due to external current density J. The second term, $B(NP - n_i^2)$, is the net radiative electron–hole recombination (EHR) rate, where BNP is the EHR rate and Bn_i^2 is the electron–hole generation rate (n_i here is the intrinsic electron density). Finally, the third term is the net nonradiative carrier recombination rate inside the active layer.

Because it is the EHR of the second term on the right-hand side of Equation (12.1) that contributes to the spontaneous emission, the optical power output is

$$P(t) = \eta_{ext} hf V B(NP - n_i^2) \qquad \textbf{[12.2]}$$

where η_{ext} is the external quantum efficiency that represents the fraction of photons coupled to the output, hf is the photon energy, and V is the active layer volume.

In the steady state, $dN/dt = 0$. Therefore,

$$\frac{J}{qd} = B(NP - n_i^2) + \frac{(N - N_D)}{\tau_{nr}}.$$

According to charge neutrality,[3]

$$NP - n_i^2 = N(N - N_D + \frac{n_i^2}{N_D}) - n_i^2 \approx N^2 - N_D N. \qquad \textbf{[12.3]}$$

It is convenient to define

$$\tau_{rr} \overset{\text{def}}{=} \frac{1}{BN} \qquad \textbf{[12.4]}$$

where τ_{rr} is called the radiative recombination time constant. Note that it depends on the carrier density. With the further definition

$$\frac{1}{\tau_r} \overset{\text{def}}{=} \frac{1}{\tau_{rr}} + \frac{1}{\tau_{nr}} = BN + \frac{1}{\tau_{nr}} \qquad \textbf{[12.5]}$$

the rate equation in the steady state reduces to

$$\frac{J}{qd} = \frac{N - N_D}{\tau_r}. \qquad \textbf{[12.6]}$$

From Equation (12.3),

$$B(NP - n_i^2) = \frac{N - N_D}{\tau_{rr}} = \frac{\tau_r}{\tau_{rr}} \frac{J}{qd}. \qquad \textbf{[12.7]}$$

The ratio

$$\frac{\tau_r}{\tau_{rr}} = \frac{1/\tau_{rr}}{1/\tau_{rr} + 1/\tau_{nr}} \overset{\text{def}}{=} \eta_{int} \qquad \textbf{[12.8]}$$

---

[3] In thermal equilibrium, $NP = n_i^2$ when the bias current is zero. When the current is increased, because of charge neutrality, the numbers of electrons and holes increased must be the same and equal to $N - N_D$.

is called the internal quantum efficiency, meaning the ratio of the radiative recombination rate to the total recombination rate. From Equations (12.2), (12.7), and (12.8), the optical power output can be related to the input current by

$$P = \eta_{ext} hfVB(NP - n_i^2) = \eta_{ext}\eta_{int} hfV\frac{J}{qd} = \eta\frac{hf}{q}I = \eta\frac{1.24}{\lambda[\mu m]}I \qquad \textbf{[12.9]}$$

where

$$\eta = \eta_{ext}\eta_{int}$$

is the total quantum efficiency.

Example 12.1

STEADY STATE OUTPUT POWER   Consider an LED with the following parameters: input current $I = 50$ mA, wavelength $\lambda = 1.35$ μm, nonradiative time constant $\tau_{nr} = 2$ nsec, radiative recombination coefficient $B = 8 \times 10^{-11}$ cm^{3}sec^{-1}, N-type doping $N_D = 5 \times 10^{17}$ cm^{-3}, cavity width $w = 1$ μm, thickness $d = 0.1$ μm, length $L = 100$ μm, and external quantum efficiency $\eta_{ext} = 0.1$. Its output power in the steady state can be computed as follows.

We first find the carrier density increase $\Delta N = N - N_D$ in the steady state. Substituting τ_r^{-1} given by Equation (12.5) into the steady state condition Equation (12.6) gives

$$B(\Delta N + N_D)\Delta N + \frac{\Delta N}{\tau_{nr}} = \frac{J}{qd}.$$

This is a second-order equation in ΔN. The solution is

$$\Delta N = \frac{-(BN_D + 1/\tau_{nr}) + [(BN_D + 1/\tau_{nr})^2 + 4BJ/qd]^{1/2}}{2B}. \qquad [12.10]$$

Substituting the numerical values gives

$$\Delta N = 1.67 \times 10^{19} \text{ cm}^{-3}.$$

Thus, $N = 1.7 \times 10^{19}$ cm^{-3} and

$$\frac{1}{\tau_{rr}} = BN = 1.41 \times 10^9 \text{ sec}^{-1}.$$

The internal quantum efficiency is then

$$\eta_{int} = \frac{1.41}{1.41 + 0.5} = 0.74.$$

Using Equation (12.9),

$$P = 0.1 \times 0.74 \times \frac{1.24}{1.35} \times 50 = 3.39 \text{ mW}.$$

This result is consistent with the steady state output shown in Figure 12.2 when the LED is turned on by a pulse input. ∎

12.1.2 PULSE INPUT RESPONSE: DIGITAL SIGNAL MODULATION

As discussed in Chapters 1 and 7, on-off keying (OOK) is a common signaling scheme in digital communications. In this scheme, a pulse is sent to convey a bit "1," and nothing is sent to transmit a bit "0" for one bit interval. To know how fast an LED can be modulated for OOK, its pulse input response is studied below.

To generate a pulse, the bias current is first increased from a low value I_1 to a high value I_2 and then reduced back to I_1 after a certain duration (e.g., the bit interval when NRZ signaling is used). In general, when the input current to an LED goes up and down, there is a delay before the output light intensity follows. This is illustrated in Figure 12.2. From Equation (12.2), the basic reason for this delay is it takes time to build up the carrier density product NP from external current injection. Because these turn-on and turn-off delays can limit the final achievable transmission bit rate, this section quantifies them and examines how to reduce them.

To derive the turn-on and turn-off delays, one needs to solve the rate equation (12.1) for a two-step input: one goes from low to high, and one goes from high to low. Consider the first case, in which a step input goes from low (J_1) to high (J_2). The initial condition at time zero for J is

$$J(0) = J_1 = qd \left[B(N_1 P_1 - n_i^2) + \frac{N_1 - N_D}{\tau_{nr}} \right]$$

where

$$NP \mid_{t=0} \overset{\text{def}}{=} N_1 P_1.$$

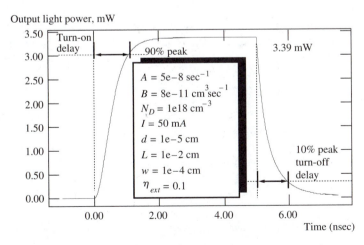

Figure 12.2   A typical pulse output of an LED. Data is generated from numerically solving the rate equation.

Similarly, the steady state condition for $J = J_2$ at $t = \infty$ is

$$J(\infty) = J_2 = qd \left[B(N_2 P_2 - n_i^2) + \frac{N_2 - N_D}{\tau_{nr}} \right]$$

where

$$NP \mid_{t=\infty} \overset{\text{def}}{=} N_2 P_2.$$

From charge neutrality, the numbers of electrons and holes generated are always the same. It is thus possible to define

$$\Delta N(t) \overset{\text{def}}{=} N(t) - N_1 = P(t) - P_1 \qquad \textbf{[12.11]}$$

as the carrier density increases from the initial value at $t = 0$. From Equations (12.1) and (12.11), for $t > 0$,

$$\frac{d[\Delta N(t)]}{dt} = \frac{J_2}{qd} - B(N_1 + \Delta N)(P_1 + \Delta N) + Bn_i^2 - \frac{1}{\tau_{nr}}(\Delta N + N_1 - N_D)$$

$$= \frac{J_2 - J_1}{qd} - B(N_1 + P_1 + \Delta N)\Delta N - \frac{\Delta N}{\tau_{nr}} = \frac{J_2 - J_1}{qd} - \frac{\Delta N}{\tau_{step}} \qquad \textbf{[12.12]}$$

where

$$\frac{1}{\tau_{step}} \overset{\text{def}}{=} B(N_1 + P_1 + \Delta N) + \frac{1}{\tau_{nr}}. \qquad \textbf{[12.13]}$$

Note that τ_{step} is a function of time and depends on $\Delta N(t)$. Therefore, Equation (12.12) in general cannot be solved analytically. When τ_{step} is constant, however, there is a simple solution. Consider this simple case first.

Constant τ_{step} If the doping level N_D of the active layer is much higher than ΔN, τ_{step} can be approximated as a constant. In this case, Equation (12.12) reduces to

$$\frac{1}{\tau_{step}} = BN_D + \frac{1}{\tau_{nr}} = \frac{1}{\tau_r} \qquad \textbf{[12.14]}$$

where the last equality comes from Equation (12.5) with $N \approx N_D$. The solution to Equation (12.12) can be readily written as

$$\Delta N(t) = \frac{J_2 - J_1}{qd} \tau_r (1 - e^{-t/\tau_r}) \qquad \textbf{[12.15]}$$

and the light output is

$$P(t) = \eta_{ext} hf V B(NP - n_i^2) \approx \eta_{ext} hf V B[N_D \Delta N(t) + (N_1 P_1 - n_i^2)]$$

$$= \eta_{ext} \frac{\tau_r}{\tau_{rr}} hf V \left[\frac{J_2 - J_1}{qd}(1 - e^{-t/\tau_r}) + \frac{J_1}{qd} \right]$$

or

$$P(t) = \eta \frac{1.24}{\lambda[\mu m]} [(I_2 - I_1)(1 - e^{-t/\tau_r}) + I_1] \qquad \textbf{[12.16]}$$

where η_{int} is defined by Equation (12.8).

In computation, the turn-on and turn-off delays are defined as the delay to reach 90 percent and 10 percent of the peak value, respectively. From Equation (12.15), the delay to reach 90 percent of the steady state level is when $1 - e^{-t_{on}/\tau_r} = 0.9$ or

$$t_{on} = \ln(10)\tau_r = 2.3\tau_r. \qquad \textbf{[12.17]}$$

Variable τ_{step} When τ_{step} strongly depends on $\Delta N(t)$, Equation (12.12) has no analytical solution. Using numerical computation, however, the turn-on and turn-off delays can be obtained according to the doping and current levels. For simplicity, let the low current density level $J_1 = 0$. By multiplying B on both sides of Equation (12.12), the equation can be normalized to

$$\frac{d\hat{N}(t)}{dt} = \hat{J} - \hat{N}(t)\left[\frac{1}{\tau_{r0}} + \frac{1}{\tau_{nr}} + \hat{N}(t)\right] \qquad \textbf{[12.18]}$$

where

$$\hat{N}(t) \stackrel{\text{def}}{=} B\Delta N(t)$$

$$\frac{1}{\tau_{r0}} \stackrel{\text{def}}{=} B(N_1 + P_1)$$

and

$$\hat{J} = \pm B\frac{J_2}{qd}.$$

$\hat{J}$ is positive in the turn-on delay calculation and negative in the turn-off delay calculation.

From Equation (12.18), note that the step response is only a function of $\tau_{r0}^{-1} + \tau_{nr}^{-1}$ and $\hat{J}$. Results of turn-on and turn-off delays as a function of $\hat{J}$ for various τ_{r0} and τ_{nr} are shown in Figures 12.3 and 12.4.

TURN-ON DELAY AT LARGE ΔN(t)   Using the same parameters as in Example 12.1, $\tau_{nr} = 2$ | **Example 12.2**
nsec,

$$\tau_{r0} = \frac{1}{BN_D} = \frac{1}{8 \times 10^{-11} \times 5 \times 10^{17}} = 25 \text{ nsec}$$

and

$$B\frac{J_2}{qd} = 8 \times 10^{-11} \times \frac{50 \times 10^{-3}}{1.6 \times 10^{-19} \times 10 \times 10^{-11}} = 2.5 \text{ nsec}^{-2}.$$

Turn-on delay
(nsec)

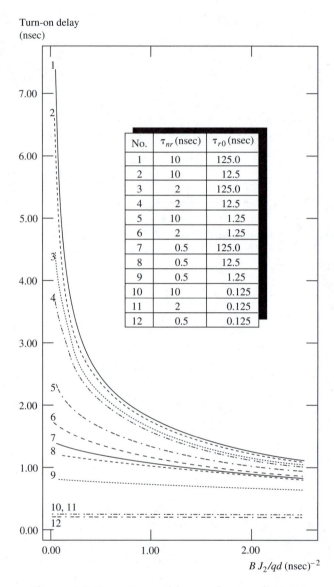

No.	τ_{nr} (nsec)	τ_{r0} (nsec)
1	10	125.0
2	10	12.5
3	2	125.0
4	2	12.5
5	10	1.25
6	2	1.25
7	0.5	125.0
8	0.5	12.5
9	0.5	1.25
10	10	0.125
11	2	0.125
12	0.5	0.125

$B J_2/qd$ (nsec)$^{-2}$

Figure 12.3   Turn-on delay as a function of $B J_2/qd$.

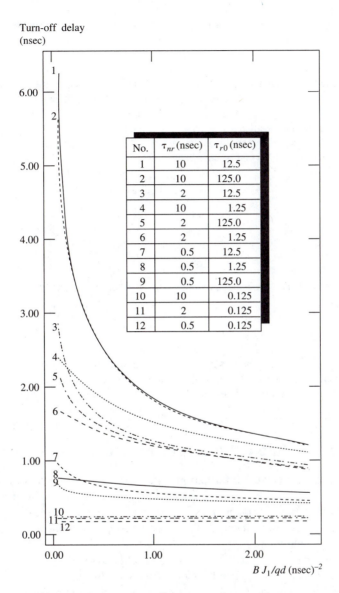

Figure 12.4   Turn-off delay as a function of BJ_1/qd.

Given these τ_{nr} and τ_{r0} values, from Figure 12.3, $t_{on} = 1.1$ nsec, and from Figure 12.4, $t_{off} = 0.9$ nsec. These delays are consistent with Figure 12.2. ∎

Example 12.3

TURN-ON DELAY REDUCTION   Continue from the previous example. To reduce both the turn-on and turn-off delays below 0.5 nsec, to what level should the doping level N_D and current density J_2 be increased?

Figure 12.3 shows that a small τ_{r0} is critical to a small turn-on delay. The definition of t_{r0} says a high doping level is needed. When this is the case and J_2 is not too large, $N_D \gg \Delta N$ and t_{step} is a constant. Thus Equation (12.17) can be used. This gives

$$\tau_r = \frac{t_{on}}{2.3} = 0.22 \text{ nsec}$$

and

$$N_D = \frac{1}{B\tau_r} = 5.75 \times 10^{19} \text{ cm}^{-3}$$

where τ_{nr} is neglected because it is large compared to τ_r. To ensure $N_D \gg \Delta N = J_2\tau_r/qd$,

$$I_2 \ll \frac{1}{\tau_r}qVN_D = (0.22 \times 10^{-9})^{-1} \times 1.6 \times 10^{-19} \times 1 \times 10^{-11} \times 5.75 \times 10^{19} = 0.42 \text{ A}$$

which can be met in practice.

From the above discussion, note that the turn-on and turn-off delays depend on only $\tau_{nr}^{-1} + \tau_{r0}^{-1}$ and $J_2 B$. In general, the delay decreases as these these two values decrease. When the doping level is high enough, delay is essentially determined by Equation (12.17) or BN_D. ∎

12.1.3   SMALL SIGNAL RESPONSE: ANALOG SIGNAL MODULATION

In analog communications, the information signal is added to a dc bias to form the total current input to a light source. From the nonlinear rate equation at a large current input discussed earlier, the signal component needs to be small compared to the dc bias to maintain a high end-to-end waveform linearity. Therefore, analog communications can be considered as small signal modulation.

The previous section analyzed turn-on and turn-off delays with pulse modulation. In analog communications, on the other hand, the modulation bandwidth for the small signal input is of interest. The time–frequency duality suggests that the delay and bandwidth analyses yield similar results. In fact, the subsequent discussion demonstrates that the smaller the delay of an LED in pulse modulation, the larger the 3 dB bandwidth in small signal modulation.

To proceed, consider a single tone input at frequency ω:

$$J(t) = J_0[1 + k_m \cos(\omega t)] \qquad \textbf{[12.19]}$$

where J_0 is the bias current density and k_m is the amplitude modulation index. Let N_1 be the carrier density at J_0, and let

$$N(t) \overset{\text{def}}{=} N_1 + \Delta N \cos(\omega t - \phi) \qquad \textbf{[12.20]}$$

where the second term is a small signal term due to the single tone input. From the above two equations, the rate equation (12.1) reduces to

$$-\Delta N \omega \sin(\omega t - \phi) = \frac{J_0}{qd} k_m \cos(\omega t) - \frac{1}{\tau_{ac}} \Delta N \cos(\omega t - \phi) \qquad \textbf{[12.21]}$$

where

$$\frac{1}{\tau_{ac}} \overset{\text{def}}{=} B(N_1 + P_1) + \frac{1}{\tau_{nr}}. \qquad \textbf{[12.22]}$$

Note that τ_{ac} defined here is different from what was defined previously in the dc and pulse analyses. This is because of the nonlinear characteristic of the rate equation. The solution to Equation (12.21) is

$$\Delta N = \frac{J_0}{qd} k_m \tau_{ac} \frac{1}{(1 + \omega^2 \tau_{ac}^2)^{1/2}} \qquad \textbf{[12.23]}$$

and

$$\phi = \cos^{-1} \left(\frac{1}{[1 + \omega^2 \tau_{ac}^2]^{1/2}} \right). \qquad \textbf{[12.24]}$$

From Equation (12.23), the output power is

$$
\begin{aligned}
P(t) = P_0 + \Delta P(t) &= \eta_{ext} hf V B[N(t)P(t) - n_i^2] \\
&\approx \eta_{ext} hf V B(N_1 P_1 - n_i^2) + \eta_{ext} hf V B(N_1 + P_1)\Delta N \cos(\omega t - \phi) \\
&= \eta hf \frac{I_0}{q} \left[1 + \frac{k_m}{(1 + \omega^2 \tau_{ac}^2)^{1/2}} \cos(\omega t - \phi) \right].
\end{aligned}
\qquad \textbf{[12.25]}
$$

Therefore, the signal part is

$$\Delta P(t) = \eta hf \frac{I_0}{q} k_m \frac{1}{(1 + \omega^2 \tau_{ac}^2)^{1/2}} \cos(\omega t - \phi). \qquad \textbf{[12.26]}$$

From Equation (12.26), the 3 dB optical signal bandwidth is

$$B_{opt, 3dB} = \frac{\sqrt{3}}{2\pi \tau_{ac}} = \frac{0.28}{\tau_{ac}}. \qquad \textbf{[12.27]}$$

Based on the final photocurrent signal on the receiver side, the 3 dB electrical signal bandwidth is[4]

$$B_{elec, 3dB} = \frac{1}{2\pi \tau_{ac}} = \frac{0.16}{\tau_{ac}}. \qquad \textbf{[12.28]}$$

---

[4] The 3 dB optical bandwidth is the value of ω that reduces the magnitude of $\Delta P(t)$ by a factor of 2. However, the 3 dB electrical bandwidth is the value of ω that reduces the magnitude of $\Delta P(t)$ by a factor of $\sqrt{2}$. Because the photocurrent is proportional to the received optical power, the factor $\sqrt{2}$ is used in determining the electrical 3 dB bandwidth.

The results show that the 3 dB frequency response is determined solely by the time constant τ_{ac}. Now consider two different cases to understand how to improve the modulation bandwidth.

Lightly Doped LEDs   First, consider the case where a light doping level is assumed. That is, $N - N_D \approx N$. This creates the following quiescent condition

$$\frac{J_1}{qd} \approx BN^2 + \frac{N}{\tau_{nr}}.$$

This approximation shows that N is a strong function of the bias current. Thus, according to Equation (12.22), the 3 dB bandwidth can be increased by increasing the bias current. Specifically, if the nonradiative term N/τ_{nr} is negligible,

$$\frac{J}{qd} \approx BN^2 = \frac{1}{4B}(2BN)^2 \approx \frac{1}{4B}\frac{1}{\tau_{ac}^2}$$

or

$$\frac{1}{\tau_{ac}} = 2\left(\frac{B}{qd}J\right)^{1/2}. \qquad\qquad \textbf{[12.29]}$$

This shows that the small signal modulation bandwidth of lightly doped LEDs is proportional to the square root of the bias current.

Heavily Doped LEDs   On the other hand, for heavily doped devices, τ_{ac} is independent of the bias current level. That is, from Equation (12.22),

$$\frac{1}{\tau_{ac}} \approx BN_D + \frac{1}{\tau_{nr}}.$$

Therefore, changing the bias current has no effect on the bandwidth, but increasing the doping level N_D can increase the bandwidth. When N_D increases, however, the thickness d of the p-n junction decreases, which increases the nonradiative recombination rate $1/\tau_{nr}$. From Equations (12.22) and (12.8), if $1/\tau_{nr}$ increases at a higher rate than the EHR rate, the internal quantum efficiency will decrease.

Example 12.4   **BANDWIDTH DEPENDENCY ON DOPING LEVEL AND BIAS CURRENT**   For illustration, use the same parameters of Example 12.1 to calculate the 3 dB electrical bandwidth of the LED biased at two different bias current levels: 10 and 40 mA.

From Equation (12.10), at $I_0 = 10$ mA,

$$\Delta N = 6.1 \times 10^{18} \text{ cm}^{-3}.$$

Thus

$$\frac{1}{\tau_{ac}} = B(2\Delta N + N_D) + \frac{1}{\tau_{nr}} = 1.6 \times 10^9 \text{ sec}^{-1}.$$

The 3 dB bandwidth is then 247 MHz. Similarly, at $I_0 = 40$ mA,

$$\Delta N = 1.46 \times 10^{19} \text{ cm}^{-3}$$

and

$$\frac{1}{\tau_{ac}} = 2.9 \times 10^9 \text{ sec}^{-1}.$$

The 3 dB bandwidth is increased to 465 MHz. Therefore, the increase of the bandwidth from 10 mA to 40 mA is 465/247 = 1.9 times, close to the square root of 4.

On the other hand, if N_D is increased to $1 \times 10^{20} \text{cm}^{-3}$,

$$\Delta N = 7.3 \times 10^{17} \ll N_D$$

at $I_0 = 10$ mA, and

$$\Delta N = 2.9 \times 10^{18} \ll N_D$$

at $I_0 = 40$ mA. Therefore,

$$\frac{1}{\tau_{ac}} \approx BN_D + \frac{1}{\tau_{nr}} = 8.5 \times 10^9 \text{sec}^{-1}$$

and the 3 dB bandwidth of the LED is 1.35 GHz for both cases. ■

12.2 RATE EQUATIONS OF LASER DIODES

Similar to LEDs, laser diodes can be directly modulated by varying the bias current. Because carriers interact with photons in the laser generation process, there are separate rate equations to describe the dynamics of carriers and photons. In this section, the rate equations of carrier and photon densities are given for FP laser diodes. These equations can quantify and explain various important phenomena such as turn-on delay, relaxation oscillation, chirping, and linewidth broadening. Advanced rate equations for DFB lasers are derived and discussed in Chapter 13.

12.2.1 DYNAMICS IN A LASER DIODE

Building on the laser principle discussed in Chapter 3, this section presents a deeper look at the dynamics of a laser diode, from which rate equations can be written to describe the time dependence among carriers, photons, and external current injection.

The carrier density and photon density in the laser cavity are two key parameters that determine the stimulated emission rate and, consequently, the output light power. These two densities are determined by various processes and interact through the stimulated emission process, by which the photon density is increased and the carrier density is decreased. Figure 12.5 illustrates many of these processes discussed in this section. In the

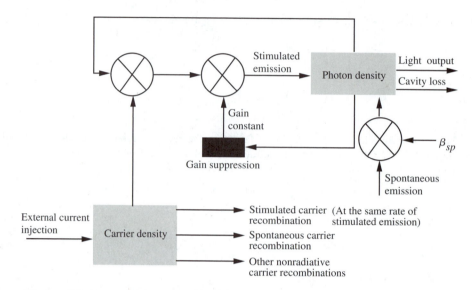

Figure 12.5   The dynamics of laser generation, where each ⊗ means multiplication.

steady state, the rate increase of the photon density due to stimulated emission is equal to the total rate decrease due to cavity loss and output light coupling.

For the carrier density, on the other hand, external current injection is the main source that contributes to its increase, and several carrier recombination processes contribute to its decrease. In addition to stimulated carrier recombination, which is the same process of stimulated photon emission, there are spontaneous carrier recombination and other nonradiative recombination processes.

To build up the photon density or generate laser, the stimulated emission rate initially needs to be higher than the total photon loss rate. That is, the laser medium should provide a positive gain to amplify the light intensity.[5] To achieve this, a high carrier density is necessary, which in turn requires a high level of external current injection. As a result, there is a **threshold current,** above which the carrier density can be built up and the net optical gain is positive. If the injection current is lower than the threshold current, the net optical gain is negative and the coherent light cannot be built up. In this case, the laser diode functions as an LED.

Although the optical gain is positive initially, the light amplification process cannot continue indefinitely. As the photon density increases, the stimulated carrier recombination rate also increases. This brings down the carrier density. Consequently, the stimulated emission rate is reduced, and eventually the net optical gain reduces to 0 dB in the steady state.

In the light amplification process described above, the initial photon density is assumed to be nonzero. Otherwise, no matter how large the carrier density is, the stimulated

---

| [5] Here, positive and negative gains are referred to in terms of dB.

emission rate is zero, and there is no possibility to generate laser. Fortunately, there is spontaneous emission due to radiative spontaneous carrier recombination. As a result, some of the photons generated serve as the *initial seeds* for stimulated emission.

The stimulated emission rate is also proportional to a gain constant determined by the medium. In practice, the gain constant can decrease as the photon density increases. This is called **gain suppression.** As a result, the laser generation process becomes less efficient as the laser operates at a higher current or output level.

12.2.2 LASER RATE EQUATION FOR CARRIER DENSITY

Based on the laser generation dynamics described, the rate equation for the carrier density can be written. Similar to the rate equation of LEDs, it can be expressed as

$$\frac{\partial N}{\partial t} = \frac{J(t)}{qd} - R(N, N_{ph}) = \frac{J(t)}{qd} - \frac{N}{\tau_e(N)} - \Gamma v_g g(N) N_{ph} \qquad \textbf{[12.30]}$$

where $R(N, N_{ph})$ is the total carrier recombination rate and is a function of the carrier density N and photon density N_{ph}. Specifically, for a lightly doped active layer, $R(N, N_{ph})$ can be expressed as [1]:

$$R(N, N_{ph}) = AN + BN^2 + CN^3 + \Gamma v_g g(N) N_{ph} = \frac{N}{\tau_e(N)} + \Gamma v_g g(N) N_{ph} \quad \textbf{[12.31]}$$

where

- $AN = N/\tau_{nr}$ is the nonradiative recombination rate.
- BN^2 is the radiative spontaneous emission rate.
- CN^3 is called the Auger (pronounced as [oh-zhay]) recombination rate [2].
- $1/\tau_e(N) \stackrel{\text{def}}{=} A + BN + CN^2$ is the effective recombination rate.
- $\Gamma v_g g(N) N_{ph}$ is the stimulated emission rate.

In the stimulated emission term given above, v_g is the group velocity, Γ is the **cavity confinement factor,**[6] and

$$g(N) = a(N - N_0) \qquad \textbf{[12.32]}$$

is the optical gain, with a being the gain constant.

To include the gain suppression effect, the gain constant can be expressed as [2]:

$$a = \frac{a_0}{1 + \eta_g N_{ph}} \approx a_0(1 - \eta_g N_{ph}) \qquad \textbf{[12.33]}$$

---

[6] The cavity confinement factor describes the fraction of photons generated by stimulated emission that contribute back to stimulated emission.

where the parameter η_g is called the **gain suppression coefficient.** The gain constant a decreases as the optical intensity increases. In Equation (12.33) η_g is in the unit of cm^3, which can also be expressed in units of 1/W if N_{ph} is replaced by the power inside the cavity. The conversion relationship is

$$\eta_g \ [1/W] = (v_g hf wd)^{-1}\eta_g \ [cm^3] \qquad \textbf{[12.34]}$$

where w and d are the width and thickness of the laser cavity, respectively, and $P = (v_g hf wd)N_{th}$ is the light power inside the cavity.

Example 12.5

GAIN SUPPRESSION   For an InGaAsP laser diode operated at $\lambda = 1.5$ μm, let η_g be 6×10^{-17} cm^3 (see Table 12.1 for typical parameter values) and $v_g = 7.5 \times 10^9$ cm/sec. If it has dimensions of $d = 0.1$ μm and $w = 10$ μm, the gain suppression coefficient in 1/W is

$$\eta_g = (7.5 \times 10^9 \times 10^{-8} \times 6.63 \times 10^{-34} \times 2 \times 10^{14})^{-1} \times 6 \times 10^{-17} = 6.0 \ W^{-1}.$$

This says that the gain suppression effect is important when the optical power inside is comparable to 0.16 W. ∎

Table 12.1 Typical values for the parameters used in the FP rate equations [2][3].

Parameters	Typical Value	Units
A	1×10^9	1/sec
B	1×10^{-10}	cm^3/sec
C	1×10^{-29}	cm^6/sec
a	1×10^{-16}	cm^2
N_o	1×10^{18}	$1/cm^3$
n_g	4.0	
α_{lw}	5	
β_{sp}	1×10^{-5}	
Γ	0.3	
η_g	6×10^{-17}	cm^3
τ_{sp}	1.1	psec

12.2.3 RATE EQUATION FOR PHOTON DENSITY

Similar to the carrier density rate equation, the photon density rate equation can be formulated according to the sources of its rate change. Because the photon density in a cavity is determined by the stimulated emission rate, spontaneous emission rate, and cavity loss, the following rate equation holds:

$$\frac{dN_{ph}}{dt} = \Gamma v_g g(N) N_{ph} - \frac{N_{ph}}{\tau_{ph}} + \beta_{sp} B N^2 \qquad \textbf{[12.35]}$$

where the parameter β_{sp} represents the percentage of the spontaneous emission that happens to be coherent with and in phase to that of the stimulated emission, and τ_{ph} is the photon decay constant related to the total cavity loss α_{tot} discussed in Chapter 3. Derivation of Equation (12.35) is given in Appendix 12–A. Typically, Γ is between 0.1 and 0.5 and β_{sp} is around 10^{-5}. Although the contribution of spontaneous emission is small, it is critical to the initial stimulated emission when $N_{ph} = 0$ in Equation (12.35).

The photon decay constant τ_{ph} can be expressed in terms of the total cavity loss α_{tot}. Because the photon decay over one trip in the cavity has a factor of $e^{-\alpha_{tot}L}$ and takes a time of L/v_g,

$$e^{-L/v_g\tau_{ph}} = e^{-\alpha_{tot}L}.$$

Therefore,

$$\boxed{\frac{1}{\tau_{ph}} = v_g\alpha_{tot}.} \qquad \textbf{[12.36]}$$

The rate equation (12.35) gives only the photon density or light intensity in the cavity. It does not describe the instantaneous phase or frequency of the light carrier. From Appendix 12–A, the instantaneous frequency can be expressed as

$$f(t) = \frac{n_0}{n_0 + \Gamma b N(t)} f_0 \qquad \textbf{[12.37]}$$

where n_0 is the refractive index of the laser active layer at $N(t) = 0$, b is a negative constant, and f_0 is the light output frequency of a longitudinal mode when $N(t) = 0$. By definition, b is a parameter such that the refractive index at the carrier density of $N(t)$ is $n_0 + \Gamma b N(t)$. From this, Equation (12.37) can be understood from the longitudinal mode condition (3.14), which says that the frequency–refractive index product is constant for a given longitudinal mode.

From Equation (12.37), the instantaneous frequency is a function of $N(t)$. When $N(t)$ is time varying under modulation, $f(t)$ is time varying. This phenomenon is called **frequency chirping.** Equation (12.37) shows that the larger the absolute value of b, the larger the chirping effect at a given $N(t)$. Therefore, it is desirable to minimize b. From Equation (12.113) derived in Appendix 12–A, the constant b is shown to be related to the gain constant a by

$$b = -\alpha_{lw}\frac{a}{2k} = -\alpha_{lw}a\frac{\lambda}{4\pi} \qquad \textbf{[12.38]}$$

where $k = 2\pi/\lambda$ and α_{lw} is the linewidth broadening factor defined by Equation (6.120) in Chapter 6. Therefore, α_{lw} must be reduced to reduce $|b|$. Multiple quantum-well lasers, discussed in Chapter 3, for example, can thus be used.

Parameter values defined above for a typical InGaAsP semiconductor laser diode are given in Table 12.1.

Example 12.6

FREQUENCY CHIRPING UNDER DIRECT MODULATION   From Equation (12.37), the frequency change ratio is approximately given by

$$\frac{f(t) - f_0}{f_0} = -\frac{\Gamma b N(t)}{n_0}.$$

For a 1.55 μm InGaAsP laser diode with a linewidth broadening factor $\alpha_{lw} = 5$ and a gain constant $a = 10^{-16}$ cm^2,

$$b = -5.0 \times 10^{-16} \times \frac{1.55 \times 10^{-4}}{4\pi} = -6.17 \times 10^{-21} \text{ cm}^3.$$

If $\Gamma = 0.5$, $n_0 = 3.5$, and $N(t) = 2 \times 10^{18}$ 1/cm^3, the frequency change ratio is 1.77×10^{-3}. Although this looks small, at $f_0 = c/\lambda = 1.94 \times 10^{14}$, the amount of frequency change is 342 GHz, which is large compared to the signal's bandwidth. This shows the importance of the chirping effect. ■

12.3 STEADY STATE SOLUTION OF LASER DIODES

The steady state solutions can easily be obtained from the rate equations by setting

$$\frac{dN}{dt} = \frac{dN_{ph}}{dt} = 0.$$

Under these conditions and using Equations (12.30) and (12.35),

$$N_{ph} = \frac{\beta_{sp} B N^2}{1/\tau_{ph} - \Gamma v_g g(N)} \qquad \textbf{[12.39]}$$

and

$$J = q d R(N, N_{ph}). \qquad \textbf{[12.40]}$$

These two equations make it possible to calculate the steady state values N_{ph} and J at a given N. The result is illustrated in Figure 12.6, where the steady state photon density and carrier density are normalized by factors $J_{th}\tau_{ph}/qd$ (see Equation [12.44]) and N_{th}, respectively. Note that when J is greater than the threshold current density J_{th}, N is essentially a constant and N_{ph} is a linear function of $J - J_{th}$. These properties are discussed in detail below.

From Equation (12.39), first note that there is a condition for N:

$$\Gamma v_g g(N) < \frac{1}{\tau_{ph}}.$$

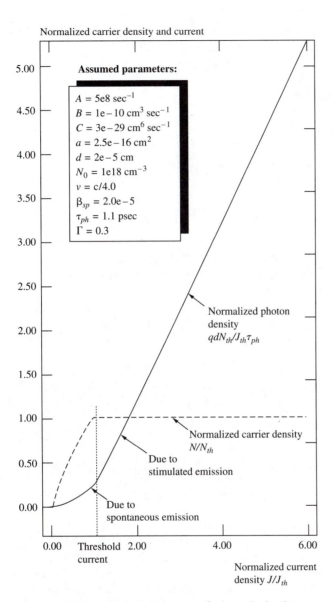

Normalized carrier density and current

Assumed parameters:

$A = 5e8 \ sec^{-1}$
$B = 1e-10 \ cm^3 \ sec^{-1}$
$C = 3e-29 \ cm^6 \ sec^{-1}$
$a = 2.5e-16 \ cm^2$
$d = 2e-5 \ cm$
$N_0 = 1e18 \ cm^{-3}$
$v = c/4.0$
$\beta_{sp} = 2.0e-5$
$\tau_{ph} = 1.1 \ psec$
$\Gamma = 0.3$

Normalized photon
density
$qdN_{th}/J_{th}\tau_{ph}$

Normalized carrier density
N/N_{th}

Due to
stimulated emission

Due to
spontaneous emission

0.00   Threshold 2.00   4.00   6.00
              current

Normalized current
density J/J_{th}

Figure 12.6   DC characteristics of a laser diode. The
photon and carrier densities are normalized.

This condition is necessary to ensure a positive N_{ph}. From this observation, there is an upper limit for the carrier density. Denoting this limit by N_{th},

$$\Gamma v_g g(N_{th}) = 1/\tau_{ph}. \qquad \textbf{[12.41]}$$

Combining Equations (12.32) and (12.41) gives

$$\boxed{N_{th} = N_0 + \frac{1}{\Gamma v_g a \tau_{ph}}.} \qquad \textbf{[12.42]}$$

From Equations (12.32), (12.39), and (12.41),

$$N_{ph} = \frac{\beta_{sp} B N^2}{\Gamma v_g a (N_{th} - N)}. \qquad \textbf{[12.43]}$$

This equation tells two important things. First, the steady value of N is always smaller than N_{th}. Second, at large N_{ph}, N is very close to the constant N_{th}. When $N \approx N_{th}$ is true, Equation (12.40) reduces to

$$J \approx qd \left[\frac{N_{th}}{\tau_e(N_{th})} + \Gamma v_g g(N_{th}) N_{ph} \right] \approx qd \left[\frac{N_{th}}{\tau_e(N_{th})} + \frac{1}{\tau_{ph}} N_{ph} \right].$$

With simple manipulation, this leads to

$$N_{ph} = \frac{\tau_{ph}}{qd}(J - J_{th}) = \frac{\tau_{ph} J_{th}}{qd}(\frac{J}{J_{th}} - 1) = \frac{\tau_{ph}}{\tau_e(N_{th})} N_{th}(\frac{J}{J_{th}} - 1) \qquad \textbf{[12.44]}$$

where

$$\boxed{J_{th} \overset{\text{def}}{=} \frac{qd}{\tau_e(N_{th})} N_{th} = qd N_{th}(A + B N_{th} + C N_{th}^2)} \qquad \textbf{[12.45]}$$

is called the **threshold current density.**

When $N \ll N_{th}$, from Equation (12.43), N_{ph} is negligible because β_{sp} is very small. In this case, most photons in the cavity are generated from spontaneous emission. Therefore, when $N \ll N_{th}$ or $J < J_{th}$, photons are incoherent and the laser diode is essentially an LED.

Equation (12.45) indicates that the threshold current J_{th} depends on the carrier recombination constant τ_e and threshold carrier density N_{th}, which depends on the confinement factor Γ and photon decay time constant τ_{ph}. Equation (12.42) shows that a smaller threshold carrier density N_{th} can be achieved by having a larger confinement factor or a larger decay constant τ_{ph} (or smaller cavity loss). Thus, according to Equation (12.45), there is a smaller threshold current. This observation is the motivation for the various cavity confinement structures discussed in Chapter 3.

The total power at the output of the laser diode can be expressed as:

$$P = \Gamma N_{ph} \times hf \times wd \times \frac{v_g}{2}(1 - r^2)$$

which is the rate of the photon energy flow that comes out of the laser diode. Note that a factor $\frac{1}{2}$ is used to account for half of the photons that propagate in one direction and another half in the opposite direction. Also the factor $1 - r^2 = 1 - R = T$ is the transmissivity of the light at the laser cavity end. From Equation (12.44),

$$P = \Gamma \frac{\tau_{ph} v_g}{2Lq} hf(1 - R)(I - I_{th})$$

$$= \frac{\Gamma}{2\alpha_{tot}L} \frac{hf}{q}(1 - R)(I - I_{th}) = \frac{\Gamma}{2\alpha_{tot}L}(1 - R)\frac{1.24}{\lambda[\mu m]}(I - I_{th}).$$

[12.46]

A STEADY STATE SOLUTION   Consider an InGaAsP laser diode of $d = 0.2$ μm, $w = 5$ μm, $L = 150$ μm, $\lambda = 1.55$ μm, distributed cavity loss 4000 m^{-1}, the refractive index $n = 3.4$, and the group refractive index $n_g = 4.0$. Other parameters of the diode are given in Figure 12.6. From these parameters, the threshold current and the output power at $I = 4I_{th}$ can be calculated as follows.

Example 12.7

First, calculate the photon decay constant τ_{ph}. From $n = 3.4$, the reflection coefficient is $r_1 = r_2 = 0.55$. Thus,

$$\alpha_{tot} = 4000 - \frac{1}{150 \times 10^{-6}} \times \ln(r_1 r_2) = 1.21 \times 10^4 \text{ m}^{-1}$$

and

$$\tau_{ph} = \frac{1}{v_g \alpha_{tot}} = 4.0/(3 \times 10^8 \times 12{,}100) = 1.1 \text{ psec}.$$

Therefore,

$$N_{th} = N_0 + \frac{1}{\Gamma v_g a \tau_{ph}}$$

$$= 1 \times 10^{18} + 4.0/(0.3 \times 3 \times 10^{10} \times 2.5 \times 10^{-16} \times 1.1 \times 10^{-12})$$

$$= 2.61 \times 10^{18} \text{ cm}^{-3}$$

and

$$J_{th} = qd(AN_{th} + BN_{th}^2 + CN_{th}^3) = 8070 \text{ A/cm}^2.$$

The corresponding threshold current is

$$I_{th} = wLJ_{th} = 61 \text{ mA}.$$

From Equation (12.44),

$$N_{ph,steady} = \frac{1.1 \times 10^{-12}}{1.6 \times 10^{-19} \times 2 \times 10^{-5}}(4J_{th} - J_{th}) = 8.1 \times 10^{15} \text{ cm}^{-3}$$

and the output power from Equation (12.46) is

$$P = \frac{1}{2} \times \frac{0.3(1 - 0.55^2)}{12{,}100 \times 150 \times 10^{-6}} \frac{1.24}{\lambda}(I - I_{th}) = 0.06 \times \frac{1.24}{\lambda}(I - I_{th}) = 8.6 \text{ mW.} \blacksquare$$

12.4 PULSE INPUT RESPONSE OF LASER DIODES: DIGITAL SIGNAL MODULATION

The rate equations given earlier can be used to study the pulse input response of laser diodes for digital transmission. A typical pulse input response from numerically solving Equations (12.30) and (12.35) is shown in Figure 12.7. Clearly, laser diodes respond quite differently from LEDs. On the rising edge, a turn-on delay is followed by an oscillation. On the falling edge, there is a sharp drop or negligible turn-off delay.

Before a detailed analysis is given, the behavior shown in Figure 12.7 can be qualitatively understood as follows. First, careful examination of Equation (12.35) shows that the rate of increase dN_{ph}/dt is essentially zero when N_{ph} is small. It will not become significantly positive until the net gain is positive:

$$\Gamma v_g g(N) - \frac{1}{\tau_{ph}} > 0$$

or

$$\Gamma g(N) > \alpha + \alpha_m.$$

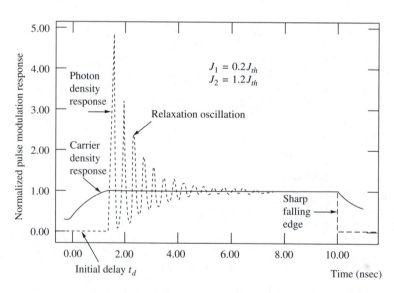

Figure 12.7   Pulse modulation response. The normalized carrier density shown is N/N_{th}, and the normalized photon density is $N_{ph}/N_{ph,steady}$.

From Equations (12.32) and (12.42), this condition is equivalent to

$$N > N_{th}.$$

Therefore, when the laser diode is turned on, the photon density due to stimulated emission will stay essentially zero until N reaches its threshold N_{th}. This can be clearly seen from Figure 12.7, where the normalized carrier density N/N_{th} is shown. The delay for the carrier density to reach N_{th} is called the turn-on delay. In this initial turn-on period, N continues to increase and passes the threshold point N_{th}.

Once $N > N_{th}$, the optical gain becomes positive. Consequently the photon density increases rapidly and quickly exceeds its steady state value. This rapid increase is caused by the nonlinear stimulated emission term $\Gamma v_g g(N) N_{ph}$ in Equation (12.35). According to Equation (12.30), once N_{ph} exceeds a certain value, dN/dt becomes negative. This brings the carrier density down and even below the steady state value. This interaction between N and N_{ph} forms an oscillation called the **relaxation oscillation.**

Finally, when the laser diode is turned off, the drop in current brings down the carrier density. As a result, the laser medium has a negative gain, and the output drops to zero rapidly.

The above qualitative explanation suggests analyzing the pulse input response by dividing the pulse modulation into three stages:

1. $0 < t < t_d$. In this period, $N_{ph} \approx 0$, and t_d is the turn-on delay until N first reaches the threshold value N_{th}.

2. $t_d < t < T_0$. During this interval, N_{ph} and N experience a relaxation oscillation.

3. $t > T_0$. In this case, the bias current drops back to the low value.

12.4.1   STAGE 1: $t < t_d$ AND $N_{ph} \approx 0$

In this first stage, $N_{ph} \approx 0$; therefore, the stimulated emission can be neglected and only the carrier density rate equation (12.30) is needed for output analysis. Thus

$$\frac{dN}{dt} \approx \frac{J_2}{qd} - \frac{N}{\tau_e(N)} \quad \text{for } 0 < t < t_d. \qquad \textbf{[12.47]}$$

Similar to the earlier analysis of LEDs, because of the carrier dependence term $\tau_e(N)$, Equation (12.47) is nonlinear and can only be solved numerically or approximately. To proceed, assume $\tau_e(N)$ is a constant between $\tau(N_1)$ and $\tau(N_{th})$, where $N_1 = N(0)$ is the initial carrier density. With this approximation, Equation (12.47) has the following solution:

$$N(t) \approx \frac{J_2}{qd} \tau_e (1 - e^{-t/\tau_e}) + N_1 e^{-t/\tau_e} \quad \text{for } 0 < t < t_d. \qquad \textbf{[12.48]}$$

Because $N(t_d) = N_{th}$ by definition, t_d satisfies the equation

$$\left(\frac{J_2}{qd} \tau_e - N_1 \right) e^{-t_d/\tau_e} = \frac{J_2}{qd} \tau_e - N_{th}.$$

Thus,

$$t_d = \tau_e \ln\left(\frac{J_2/qd - N_1/\tau_e}{J_2/qd - N_{th}/\tau_e}\right).$$

[12.49]

This result shows that if J_1 is biased close to J_{th}, N is close to N_{th}, and t_d is negligible. On the other hand, if $N_1 \ll N_{th}$, there will be a significant turn-on delay.

Example 12.8

TURN ON DELAY AT CONSTANT τ_e   If $B = C = 0$ in Equation (12.31), $\tau_e = 1/A$, a constant. Also, from the steady state conditions,

$$N_1/\tau_e = J_1/qd$$

and

$$N_{th}/\tau_e = J_{th}/qd.$$

Therefore,

$$t_d = \tau_e \ln\left(\frac{J_2 - J_1}{J_2 - J_{th}}\right).$$

If the initial bias current density $J_1 = J_{th}$, t_d is zero. ∎

Example 12.9

TIME-VARYING τ_e   The pulse response in Figure 12.7 is obtained with the same parameter values given in Figure 12.6. The low current value is 20 percent of the the threshold value, and the high value is 120 percent of the threshold value. The pulse response indicates a clear initial delay of $t_d \approx 1.3$ nsec. From Equations (12.45) and (12.49),

$$t_d = \tau_e \ln\left[\frac{1 - (J_{th}/J_2)[\tau_e(N_{th})/\tau_e](N_1/N_{th})}{1 - (J_{th}/J_2)[\tau_e(N_{th})/\tau_e]}\right].$$

[12.51]

From Figure 12.6, $N_1 \approx 0.33N_{th}$ at $J_1 = 0.2J_{th}$; therefore, $1 - N_1/N_{th} = .67$. From Example 12.7, $N_{th} = 2.61 \times 10^{18}$ cm^{-3}. Therefore,

$$\tau_e(N_{th}) = (A + BN_{th} + CN_{th}^2)^{-1} = 1.0 \text{ nsec}$$

and

$$\tau_e(N_1) = (A + BN_1 + CN_1^2)^{-1} = 1.6 \text{ nsec}.$$

τ_e is between 1.0 and 1.6 nsec. Using $\tau_e = 1.1$ nsec gives $t_d \approx 1.4$ nsec, which is consistent with Figure 12.7.

When $J_2 \gg J_{th}$, the expression of t_d given by Equation (12.51) can be approximated as

$$t_d \approx \tau_e(J_{th}/J_2)[\tau_e(N_{th})/\tau_e](1 - N_1/N_{th}) = (J_{th}/J_2)(1 - N_1/N_{th})\tau_e(N_{th}).$$

[12.52]

For example, if $J_1 = 0.8J_{th}$ and $J_2 = 2.0J_{th}$, $N_1 \approx 0.8N_{th}$ and $J_{th}/J_2 = 0.5$. The time delay is approximately

$$t_d = 0.5 \times 0.2 \times 1.0 = 0.1 \text{ nsec.}$$

This is close to what Figure 12.8 shows. ∎

12.4.2   STAGE 2: $t_d < t < T_0$, WHERE T_0 IS THE BIT PERIOD

Once the carrier density reaches the threshold value, the optical gain becomes positive and the photon density increases rapidly. As a result, the photon density can reach its steady state in a very short interval. After that, both the carrier density and photon density are high, and they start to interact through the common stimulated emission term in Equations (12.30) and (12.35). Because the stimulated emission term has opposite signs in the two equations, it causes one to increase and the other to decrease. As mentioned earlier, this interaction results in a relaxation oscillation, where the two densities oscillate around their steady state values.

To quantify the relaxation oscillation of the two densities, one can first linearize the two rate equations (12.30) and (12.35). To do this, define

$$\Delta N(t) \overset{\text{def}}{=} N(t) - N_{th} \qquad \qquad \textbf{[12.53]}$$

and

$$\Delta N_{ph}(t) \overset{\text{def}}{=} N_{ph}(t) - N_{ph,steady} \qquad \qquad \textbf{[12.54]}$$

where N_{th} is defined by Equation (12.42) and is close to the steady state value of $N(t)$, and $N_{ph,steady}$ is defined as the steady state value of $N_{ph}(t)$. From these definitions, $\Delta N(t)$ and $\Delta N_{ph}(t)$ are the small deviations of $N(t)$ and $N_{ph}(t)$ from their corresponding steady state values.

Substituting $N(t)$ and $N_{ph}(t)$ given by Equations (12.53) and (12.54), the rate equation (12.39) reduces to

$$\frac{d\Delta N(t)}{dt} = \frac{J_2}{qd} - \left[A(N_{th} + \Delta N) + B(N_{th} + \Delta N)^2 + C(N_{th} + \Delta N)^3\right]$$
$$- \Gamma v_g a(N_{th} + \Delta N - N_0)(N_{ph,steady} + \Delta N_{ph})$$
$$\approx \left[\frac{J_2}{qd} - (AN_{th} + BN_{th}^2 + CN_{th}^3) - \Gamma v_g g(N_{th})N_{ph,steady}\right]$$
$$- [A + 2B + 3C + v_g aN_{ph,steady}]\Delta N - \Gamma v_g g(N_{th})\Delta N_{ph}$$

where higher-order terms of ΔN and $\Delta N \Delta N_{ph}$ are dropped. Because N_{th} is close to the steady value of $N(t)$, the steady state condition (12.40) says that the first bracket term on the right-hand side is approximately zero. By defining

$$\frac{1}{\tau_{ac}} \overset{\text{def}}{=} A + 2BN_{th} + 3CN_{th}^2 + \Gamma v_g aN_{ph,steady} \qquad \qquad \textbf{[12.55]}$$

the rate equation reduces to

$$\frac{d}{dt}\Delta N(t) = -\frac{\Delta N}{\tau_{ac}} - \Gamma v_g g(N_{th})\Delta N_{ph}. \qquad \qquad \textbf{[12.56]}$$

Note that this is a linear equation of $\Delta N(t)$ and $\Delta N_{ph}(t)$.

Similarly, substituting $N(t)$ and $N_{ph}(t)$ given by Equations (12.53) and (12.54) into the photon density rate equation (12.35) gives

$$\frac{d}{dt}\Delta N_{ph} \approx -\frac{N_{ph,steady} + \Delta N_{ph}}{\tau_{ph}} + \Gamma v_g a (N_{th} + \Delta N - N_0)(N_{ph,steady} + \Delta N_{ph})$$

$$+ \beta_{sp} B N_{th}^2$$

$$= \left[-\frac{N_{ph,steady}}{\tau_{ph}} + \Gamma v_g g(N_{th}) N_{ph,steady} + \beta_{sp} B N^2 \right]$$

$$+ \left[-\frac{1}{\tau_{ph}} + \Gamma v_g g(N_{th}) \right] \Delta N_{ph} + \Gamma v_g a N_{ph,steady} \Delta N.$$

The first term in the bracket on the right is approximately zero because of the steady state condition (12.39), and the second term is also zero because of the definition of N_{th} given by Equation (12.42). Therefore, the rate equation of the photon density reduces to

$$\frac{d}{dt}\Delta N_{ph}(t) = \Gamma v_g a N_{ph,steady} \Delta N(t). \qquad \textbf{[12.57]}$$

Equations (12.56) and (12.57) are the two linear rate equations of $\Delta N(t)$ and ΔN_{ph} that can be used to study the relaxation oscillation. Eliminating ΔN leaves

$$\frac{d^2}{dt^2}\Delta N_{ph}(t) + 2\alpha \frac{d\Delta N_{ph}}{dt} + \omega_n^2 \Delta N_{ph} = 0 \qquad \textbf{[12.58]}$$

where

$$2\alpha \overset{\text{def}}{=} \frac{1}{\tau_{ac}} = A + 2B N_{th} + 3C N_{th}^2 + \Gamma v_g a N_{ph,steady} \qquad \textbf{[12.59]}$$

and

$$\omega_n^2 \overset{\text{def}}{=} \Gamma^2 v_g^2 a g(N_{th}) N_{ph,steady} = \frac{\Gamma}{\tau_{ph}} a v_g N_{ph,steady}. \qquad \textbf{[12.60]}$$

The second equality of Equation (12.60) comes from Equation (12.41). From Equations (12.44) and (12.45),

$$\omega_n^2 = \frac{1}{\tau_{ph}\tau_e(N_{th})}(J_2/J_{th} - 1)(a\Gamma v_g \tau_{ph} N_{th}).$$

Equation (12.42) then gives

$$\omega_n^2 = \frac{1}{\tau_{ph}\tau_e(N_{th})}\frac{J_2/J_{th} - 1}{1 - N_0/N_{th}}. \qquad \textbf{[12.61]}$$

Also, α given by Equation (12.59) can be expressed as

$$\alpha = \tfrac{1}{2}(A + 2B N_{th} + 3C N_{th}^2) + \tfrac{1}{2}\tau_{ph}\omega_n^2. \qquad \textbf{[12.62]}$$

It can be shown that the carrier density ΔN has the same form as the second-order differential equation (12.58). Because $\Delta N_{ph}(t_d) = N_{ph}(t_d) - N_{ph,steady} \approx -N_{ph,steady}$, the solution to Equation (12.58) can be expressed by

$$\Delta N_{ph}(t) = -N_{ph,steady} e^{-\alpha(t-t_d)} \cos(\omega_r[t - t_d]), \quad t > t_d \qquad \textbf{[12.63]}$$

where

$$\omega_r^2 = \omega_n^2 - \alpha^2. \qquad \textbf{[12.64]}$$

The circular frequency ω_r is called the **relaxation frequency**. Figure 12.7 shows that the relaxation oscillation has asymmetrical peak values with respect to the steady state value $N_{ph,steady}$. This is mainly because of the nonlinear effect, which the preceding analysis has neglected. As the oscillation amplitude decreases, the nonlinear effect decreases, and the oscillation looks more sinusoidal.

From Equation (12.63), the damping constant α is an important parameter that determines how fast ΔN and ΔN_{ph} settle to zero. Equation (12.59) shows that the larger the photon density in the steady state, the larger the damping constant α, and the faster the system reaches the steady state.

RELAXATION OSCILLATION   Using the same parameters as the previous example ($J_1 = 0.2J_{th}$ and $J_2 = 1.2J_{th}$), Equations (12.59) and (12.61) give

Example 12.10

$$\omega_n^2 = \frac{1}{1.1 \times 10^{-12} \times 1.0 \times 10^{-9}} \times \frac{1.2 - 1}{1 - 1.0 \times 10^{18}/2.61 \times 10^{18}} = 2.8 \times 10^{20} \text{ sec}^{-2}$$

and

$$2\alpha = A + 2BN_{th} + 3CN_{th}^2 + \Gamma v_g a N_{ph,steady} = A + 2BN_{th} + 3CN_{th}^2 + \omega_n^2 \tau_{ph}$$
$$= 5 \times 10^8 + 2 \times 1.0 \times 10^{-10} \times 2.61 \times 10^{18} + 3.0 \times 3 \times 10^{-29}$$
$$\times (2.61 \times 10^{18})^2 + 3.1 \times 10^8 = 1.94 \times 10^9 \text{ sec}^{-1}.$$

Therefore,

$$\omega_n = 1.67 \times 10^{10} \text{ sec}^{-1}$$

and

$$\omega_r = (\omega_n^2 - \alpha^2)^{1/2} \approx \omega_n = 1.67 \times 10^{10} \text{ sec}^{-1}.$$

Therefore, the relaxation frequency is $\omega_r/2\pi = 2.7$ GHz and the decay time constant is $1/\alpha = 1.0$ nsec. These results are consistent with what a careful examination of Figure 12.7 shows.

If $J_1 = 0.8J_{th}$ and $J_2 = 2.0J_{th}$,

$$\omega_n^2 = 1.4 \times 10^{21} \text{ sec}^{-2}$$

and

$$2\alpha = 3.17 \times 10^9 \text{ sec}^{-1}.$$

Therefore, the relaxation frequency increases to 6.0 GHz and the time decay constant reduces to 0.63 nsec. These can also be observed from Figure 12.8. ■

Equations (12.61) and (12.62) and Example 12.10 show that a higher J_2/J_{th} value can result in a higher ω_n or α value. This means a faster decay in oscillation. In digital pulse modulation, this means a higher achievable transmission rate. Specifically, for an oscillation $\Delta N_{ph}(t)$ within 10 percent of its steady value, the delay required because of relaxation oscillation is

$$t_{d,osc} = \frac{1}{\alpha}\ln(10) = \frac{2.3}{\alpha}.$$ **[12.65]**

Example 12.11

OOK TRANSMISSION   In OOK digital communications, if a given laser driver circuit has an initial turn-on delay t_d of 0.2 nsec and $\alpha = 1 \times 10^9$ 1/sec, find the achievable bit rate if the bit interval needs to be at least twice $t_d + t_{d,osc}$.

From Equation (12.65),

$$t_{d,osc} = 2.3 \text{ nsec.}$$

Therefore, the minimum bit interval is $2 \times (2.3 + 0.1) = 4.8$ nsec, and the achievable bit rate is 208 Mb/s. ∎

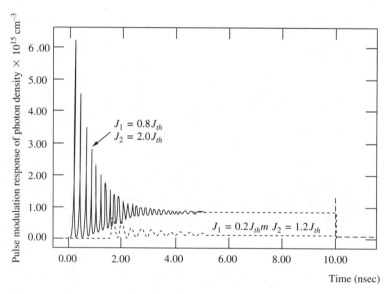

Figure 12.8   Two pulse modulation responses at different J_1 and J_2 values.

There can be a simple relationship between the damping constant α and the current density J_2 when $B = C = 0$. These are good assumptions when radiative and Auger recombinations are small compared to the nonradiative combination and N_0 is small compared to the threshold density N_{th}. Under these approximations and from Equations (12.61) and (12.62),

$$\alpha = \tfrac{1}{2}A + \tfrac{1}{2}A(J_2/J_{th} - 1) = AJ_2/J_{th}. \qquad \textbf{[12.66]}$$

This result shows a linear relationship between α and J_2/J_{th}. Thus, increasing J_2 reduces $t_{d,osc}$.

12.4.3 STAGE 3: $t > T_0$

When the diode is turned off, the carrier density drops below the threshold density N_{th} and the net optical gain becomes negative. As a result, the photon density drops rapidly. As shown in Figure 12.7, the turn-off delay is very small and can be neglected.

From the above analysis, to increase transmission bit rates for digital communications, one can (1) bias the current density J_1 just above J_{th} to reduce t_d, and (2) increase the output to increase the damping constant α. These points have been made earlier and can be seen by comparing two pulse modulation responses as shown in Figure 12.8.

12.4.4 PULSE RESPONSE MODELING

From Equation (12.63), the pulse output in pulse amplitude modulation (PAM) can be modeled by

$$p_s(t) = \begin{cases} 0 & \text{if } t < t_d \\ 1 - \cos(\omega_r[t - t_d])e^{-\alpha(t-t_d)} & \text{if } t_d < t < T_0 \quad \textbf{[12.67]} \\ \left[1 - \cos(\omega_r[T_0 - t_d])e^{-\alpha(T_0-t_d)}\right]e^{-\alpha_{off}(t-T_0)} & \text{if } t > T_0 \end{cases}$$

where T_0 is the pulse duration and α_{off} is the time decay constant when the laser is turned off. This model neglects the second-order nonlinear term from stimulated emission. Because the stimulated emission term $\Gamma a(N - N_0)N_{ph}$ is proportional to the gain constant a, the model is less accurate when the gain constant a is large. This dependence can be observed from Figure 12.9. There is a higher peak when a is large; when a is small, the oscillation is closer to a sinusoidal function.

Figure 12.9 also shows that the relaxation frequency and damping constants increase as the gain constant decreases. This is because the steady state carrier density N_{th} increases as the gain constant decreases (see Equation [12.42]). As a result, $1/\tau_e(N_{th}) = AN_{th} + BN_{th}^2 + CN_{th}^3$ increases. Equations (12.59)–(12.61) thus give a higher relaxation frequency and damping constant.

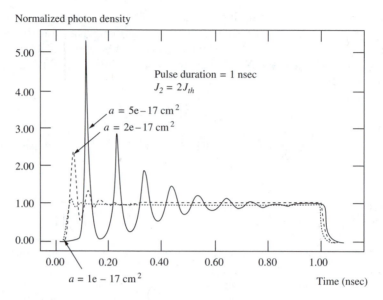

Figure 12.9   Pulse responses at different gain constants.

12.5 SMALL SIGNAL RESPONSE OF LASER DIODES: ANALOG SIGNAL MODULATION

Similar to LEDs, small signal analysis of laser diodes is useful for analog communications. A similar analysis can help explain the modulation bandwidth of a single tone current input.

For convenience, a single tone current input at the circular frequency ω_m is expressed by

$$J(t) = J_0[1 + k_{m,j} \exp(j\omega_m t)] \qquad \textbf{[12.68]}$$

where $k_{m,j}$ is the modulation index for the input current and J_0 is the bias current density. Note that instead of using a cosine function, as in the LED case, Equation (12.68) uses an exponential function for $J(t)$. The two are equivalent if only the real part of Equation (12.68) is considered.[7]

Similarly, the following forms can be assumed for the carrier and photon densities:

$$N(t) = N_{n,0}[1 + k_{m,n} \exp(j\omega_m t)] \qquad \textbf{[12.69]}$$

---

[7] The small signal analysis in Section 12.4.2 gives two first-order linear differential equations of $\Delta N(t)$ and $\Delta N_{ph}(t)$. If they are sinusoidal functions, it is a common practice to assume both have the exponential dependence $e^{j\omega_m t}$. In this case, their time derivatives are replaced by multiplications of $j\omega_m$. As a result, the differential equations reduce to algebraic equations, and $\Delta N(t)$ and $\Delta N_{ph}(t)$ can be solved easily. Because the equations are linear, the final results can be obtained from the real part of the solutions.

and

$$N_{ph}(t) = N_{ph,0}[1 + k_{m,ph}\exp(j\omega_m t)] \qquad \textbf{[12.70]}$$

where $k_{m,n}$ and $k_{m,ph}$ are the modulation indices of the modulated carrier and photon densities, respectively. In general, they can be complex to represent possible phase shifts with respect to $J(t)$.

When the current modulation index $k_{m,j}$ is small, the same perturbation equations (12.56) and (12.57) derived previously can be used to find $k_{m,n}$ and $k_{m,ph}$. In this case, the small term $\Delta N(t)$ in Equation (12.56) should be replaced by $k_{m,n}N_{n,0}e^{j\omega_m t}$, and the small term $\Delta N_{ph}(t)$ in Equation (12.57) should be replaced by $k_{m,ph}N_{ph,0}e^{j\omega_m t}$. Because the input current also has a small time varying term, $k_{m,j}J_0 e^{j\omega_m t}/qd$ must be added to Equation (12.56). Since each small signal term has a time dependent factor $e^{j\omega_m t}$, the time derivative can be substituted by $j\omega_m t$. As a result, the final rate equations can be written as

$$N_{n,0}k_{m,n}(j\omega_m) = \frac{J_0}{qd}k_{m,j} - \frac{1}{\tau_{ac}}N_{n,0}k_{m,n} - \Gamma v_g g(N_{th})N_{ph,0}k_{m,ph} \qquad \textbf{[12.71]}$$

and

$$N_{ph,0}k_{m,ph}(j\omega_m) = \Gamma a v_g N_{ph,0}N_{n,0}k_{m,n} \qquad \textbf{[12.72]}$$

where τ_{ac} is already defined by Equation (12.55). Solving the two equations for $k_{m,ph}$ gives

$$k_{m,n} = \frac{j\omega_m}{\Gamma a v_g N_{n,0}}k_{m,ph}$$

and

$$k_{m,ph} = \frac{J_0}{qd}\frac{k_{m,j}}{\Gamma v_g g(N_{th})N_{ph,0} + \frac{j\omega_m}{\tau_{ac}\Gamma a v_g} - \frac{\omega_m^2}{\Gamma a v_g}}.$$

Using the definitions given by Equations (12.59) and (12.60),

$$k_{m,ph} = \frac{J_0}{qd}\Gamma a v_g \frac{k_{m,j}}{\omega_n^2 - \omega_m^2 + j2\alpha\omega_m}. \qquad \textbf{[12.73]}$$

Clearly $k_{m,ph}$ is a complex number. Its magnitude is

$$|k_{m,ph}| = \frac{J_0}{qd\omega_n^2}\Gamma a v_g \frac{k_{m,j}}{\left[\left(1 - \frac{\omega_m^2}{\omega_n^2}\right)^2 + \left(\frac{2\alpha\omega_m}{\omega_n^2}\right)^2\right]^{1/2}}. \qquad \textbf{[12.74]}$$

From Equations (12.60) and (12.44), the response at dc ($\omega_m = 0$) is

$$|k_{m,ph}|_{dc} = \frac{J_0}{qd\omega_n^2}\Gamma a v_g k_{m,j} = \frac{J_0/qd}{N_{ph,0}/\tau_{ph}}k_{m,j} = \frac{J_0}{J_0 - J_{th}}k_{m,j}. \qquad \textbf{[12.75]}$$

Therefore, it is desirable to bias J_0 close to J_{th} for large response. However, if J_0 is too close, the small current signal will bring the total current below the threshold. This results in undesirable distortion, and the above small signal analysis will not hold.

When ω_m is at ω_n, the frequency response has a peak value equal to

$$| k_{m,ph} |_{peak} = \frac{J_0}{J_0 - J_{th}} \frac{\omega_n}{2\alpha} k_{m,j}. \qquad \textbf{[12.76]}$$

From Equations (12.59) and (12.60), Equation (12.76) can also be expressed as

$$| k_{m,ph} |_{peak} = \frac{J_0}{J_0 - J_{th}} \frac{\omega_n}{1/\hat{\tau}_e(N_{th}) + \omega_n^2 \tau_{ph}} k_{m,j} \qquad \textbf{[12.77]}$$

where

$$\hat{\tau}_e(N_{th}) = (A + 2BN_{th} + 3CN_{th}^2)^{-1}.$$

Equations (12.74)–(12.77) lead to the following observations:

1. The modulation bandwidth is determined by ω_n. According to Equation (12.61), it can be increased by increasing the bias current J_0. When $J_0 \gg J_{th}$, the bandwidth is approximately proportional to the square root of J_0 and consequently, to the square root of P_0. In other words, more dc power enables a higher ac bandwidth.

2. When J_0/J_{th} is large, the dc response is close to a constant $k_{m,j}$ independent of J_0. At the same time, from Equation (12.77), the peak to dc ratio is approximately proportional to $1/\omega_n$ or the square root of J_{th}/J. Therefore, a flatter response can be achieved at a larger dc power. This is illustrated in Figure 12.10.

Example 12.12

SMALL SIGNAL FREQUENCY RESPONSE   With the same conditions as in Examples 12.9–12.11, calculate the ratio $\omega_n/2\alpha$ with $J_0 = 2.0J_{th}$. If the current density J_0 is increased from $2.0 J_{th}$ to $20J_{th}$, calculate the new α, ω_n, and $\omega_n/2\alpha$.

From Example 12.11, the peak to dc response ratio at $J_0 = 2J_{th}$ is

$$\frac{\omega_n}{2\alpha} = 11.8.$$

If J is increased to $20J_{th}$,

$$\omega_n^2 = \frac{1}{1.1 \times 10^{-12} \times 1.0 \times 10^{-9}} \times \frac{20-1}{1 - 1.0 \times 10^{18}/2.61 \times 10^{18}} = 2.8 \times 10^{22} \text{ sec}^{-2}$$

and

$$2\alpha = A + 2BN_{th} + 3CN_{th}^2 + \Gamma v_g a N_{ph,steady} = A + 2BN_{th} + 3CN_{th}^2 + \omega_n^2 \tau_{ph}$$
$$= 5 \times 10^8 + 2 \times 1.0 \times 10^{-10} \times 2.61 \times 10^{18} + 3.0 \times 3 \times 10^{-29}$$
$$\times (2.61 \times 10^{18})^2 + 3.1 \times 10^{10} = 3.2 \times 10^{10} \text{ sec}^{-1}.$$

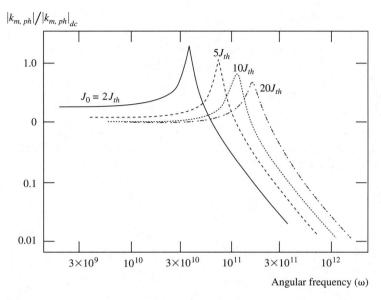

Figure 12.10 Small signal frequency responses at different bias current values. Other parameters have the same values as the previous figures.

Therefore,

$$\omega_n = 1.67 \times 10^{11} \text{ sec}^{-1}$$

and the peak to dc response ratio is

$$\frac{\omega_n}{2\alpha} = 5.2.$$

Compared to Example 12.11, the ratio is decreased by a factor of $11.8/5.2 = 2.3$ when the bias current is increased 10 times. ■

Equation (12.74) makes it possible to calculate the 3 dB optical bandwidth when the modulation index falls to 50 percent. Specifically,

$$\left(1 - \frac{\omega_{opt,3dB}^2}{\omega_n^2}\right)^2 + \left(\frac{2\alpha\omega_{opt,3dB}}{\omega_n^2}\right)^2 = 4. \qquad \textbf{[12.78]}$$

This can be simplified to

$$\left(\frac{\omega_{opt,3dB}}{\omega_n}\right)^4 - \left[2-4\left(\frac{\alpha}{\omega_n}\right)^2\right]\left(\frac{\omega_{opt,3dB}}{\omega_n}\right)^2 - 3 = 0.$$

In general, $\alpha \ll \omega_n$. Therefore,

$$B_{opt,3dB} \approx \sqrt{3}f_n = 1.73 f_n \qquad\qquad \textbf{[12.79]}$$

where $B_{opt,3dB} = \omega_{opt,3dB}/2\pi$ and $f_n = \omega_n/2\pi$. To derive the electrical 3 dB bandwidth, Equation (12.78) is modified to

$$\left(1 - \frac{\omega_{elec,3dB}^2}{\omega_n^2}\right)^2 + \left(\frac{2\alpha\omega_{elec,3dB}}{\omega_n^2}\right)^2 = 2. \qquad\qquad \textbf{[12.80]}$$

Under the same approximation, $\alpha \ll \omega_n$,

$$B_{elec,3dB} \approx (1 + \sqrt{5}/2)^{1/2} f_n = 1.46 f_n. \qquad\qquad \textbf{[12.81]}$$

The turn-on and turn-off delays and transmission bandwidths for LEDs and LDs are summarized in Table 12.2.

Table 12.2 Summary of direct modulation characteristics of LEDs and LDs.

Characteristics	LED	LD
Turn-on delay	$2.3\,\tau_r$	$t_d \approx \ln[(J_2 - J_1)/(J_2 - J_{th})]$
Turn-off delay	$2.3\,\tau_r$	Negligible
Relaxation damping within 10% of the steady state value	—	$2.3/\alpha$
3 dB optical bandwidth ($B_{opt,3dB}$)	$0.28/\tau_{ac}$	$1.73 f_n$
3dB electrical bandwidth ($B_{elec,3dB}$)	$0.16/\tau_{ac}$	$1.46 f_n$

12.6 LIMITATIONS OF DIRECT MODULATION

Although direct modulation is simple in implementation, the above analysis shows that it has several critical disadvantages. Equation (12.37), for example, shows that the instantaneous frequency of the output light is modulated by the carrier density $N(t)$. As mentioned earlier, this is called **frequency chirping**. In pulse modulation, frequency chirping results in a large frequency shift at the leading and trailing edges of each pulse. In addition to chirping, for FP lasers, a large signal modulation in digital communications or a high index modulation in analog communications can cause significant power fluctuation of side modes. This fluctuation results in mode partition noise as discussed in Chapter 6. These undesirable properties of direct modulation are discussed in detail below.

12.6.1 Frequency Chirping

Frequency chirping is the sweeping from one frequency to another of a carrier's instantaneous frequency. As mentioned earlier, it is caused by refractive index modulation by the carrier density. An example of frequency chirping is illustrated in Figure 12.11, where both the intensity (dotted line) and instantaneous frequency (solid line) of a modulated optical pulse are shown. In this illustration, the bias current is turned on and off between a low value of $0.5 J_{th}$ and a high value of $2 J_{th}$, and the parameters of the laser diode used have the same values as in the previous figures, except for the gain constant a.

The intensity curve shown in Figure 12.11 is normalized to its steady state so that it can be shown together with the frequency curve, which is multiplied by $2\pi \times 10^{-12}$ to reduce its scale. From the illustration, a chirping from a high frequency to a low frequency can be seen clearly at the initial turn-on. When the laser is turned off, there is a similar shift in frequency from its steady state value to a low frequency. This frequency curve is plotted between two points whose intensity values are 10 percent of the steady state. In addition to these frequency shifts, there is a small oscillation in frequency. This is due to the relaxation oscillation discussed earlier.

The change of output frequency from the steady state value can be quantified by using Equation (12.37):

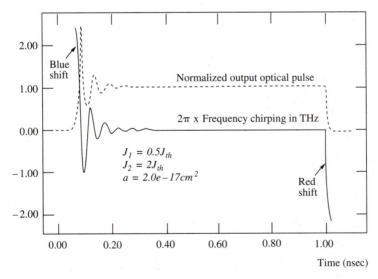

Figure 12.11 The chirping effect. The frequency shift shown goes from the 10 percent point of the steady state optical output at the rising edge to the 10 percent point at the falling edge.

$$f(t) - f_s = \frac{n_0}{n_0 + \Gamma b N(t)} f_0 - \frac{n_0}{n_0 + \Gamma b N_{th}} f_0 \approx \frac{\Gamma b}{n_0}[N_{th} - N(t)]f_0 \qquad \textbf{[12.82]}$$

where f_s is the steady state carrier frequency of the light output. This expression shows that the peak frequency deviation is proportional to the peak deviation of $N(t)$ from N_{th}. When $N(t) > N_{th}$ in the initial turn-on, $f(t)$ is greater than f_s because $b < 0$. This frequency increase is called the **blue shift** from radar terminology. When $N(t) < N_{th}$ in the final turn-off, $f(t)$ is lower than f_s, and it is called the **red shift**.

According to Equation (12.82), reducing either the constant b or the peak deviation of the carrier density will reduce the chirping effect. To reduce b, quantum-well laser diodes discussed in Chapter 3 can be used because of their more confined energy states [4]. Figure 3.26 shows that frequency chirping can be reduced approximately 50 percent by using quantum-well lasers compared to standard FP lasers.

Reducing the peak deviation of the carrier density requires reducing the initial turn-on rate, when the nonlinear stimulated emission is strong. Reducing the turn-on rate requires reducing the relaxation oscillation frequency ω_r. The earlier discussion on pulse modulation explains how to achieve this by decreasing J_2/J_{th}. This is illustrated in Figure 12.12, which shows that, when J_2/J_{th} gets larger, the chirping effect becomes more significant.

Because the nonlinear stimulated emission plays an important role in the initial density deviation, reducing the gain constant a will also reduce the chirping effect. This can be seen from Figure 12.12. When either J_2/J_{th} or the gain constant a is reduced to reduce the

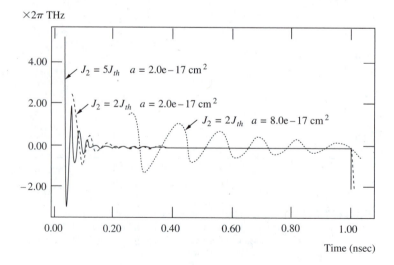

Figure 12.12   Chirping at different J_2 and gain constant (a) values.

chirping, there is a smaller damping constant α or a smaller relaxation frequency ω_r. This implies either a smaller output power (when J_2/J_{th} is reduced) or a smaller bandwidth (a smaller α and ω_r).

Although frequency chirping caused by refractive index modulation is undesirable in most cases, it is a useful property for frequency modulation. By switching the bias current between two levels (both higher than the threshold), the frequency output of the optical signal can be switched between two values. To increase the frequency separation, devices with larger b in Equation (12.37) become desirable. This direct frequency modulation makes frequency-shift keying (FSK) an attractive scheme in coherent communication. See Chapter 15 for further discussion.

12.6.2 MODE PARTITION

The pulse modulation analysis given earlier based on the rate equations (12.30) and (12.35) has assumed a single longitudinal mode output. Because FP laser diodes can generate multimodes, side modes should also be considered for higher accuracy.

When multimodes are considered, the rate equations can be extended to [1]:

$$\frac{\partial N}{\partial t} = \frac{J(t)}{qd} - \frac{N}{\tau_e(N)} - \Gamma v_g \sum_{i=-M}^{M} g_i(N) N_{ph,i} \qquad \textbf{[12.83]}$$

and

$$\frac{dN_{ph,i}}{dt} = \Gamma v_g g_i(N) N_{ph,i} - \frac{N_{ph,i}}{\tau_{ph}} + \beta_{sp} B N^2 \qquad \textbf{[12.84]}$$

where $i = -M, (M-1), \dots, M$. The above expressions are based on $2M+1$ modes (M modes on each side of the main mode). For simplicity, assume a parabolic gain profile:

$$g_i(N) = a(N - N_0)[1 - (i/M)^2]. \qquad \textbf{[12.85]}$$

From Equation (12.84), the photon density of mode i in the steady state is

$$N_{ph,i} = \frac{\beta_{sp} B N^2}{1/\tau_{ph} - \Gamma v_g g_i(N)}. \qquad \textbf{[12.86]}$$

If δ is defined as

$$\delta \overset{\text{def}}{=} \frac{1}{\tau_{ph}} - \Gamma v_g g_0(N)$$

then Equations (12.85) and (12.86) give

$$N_{ph,0} = \frac{\beta_{sp} B N^2}{\delta} \quad \text{or} \quad \delta = \frac{\beta_{sp} B N^2}{N_{ph,0}} \qquad \textbf{[12.87]}$$

and

$$N_{ph,i} = \frac{\beta_{sp}BN^2}{\delta + \Gamma v_g g_0(N)i^2/M^2}.$$

[12.88]

The **mode suppression ratio** of the ith mode is thus

$$\frac{N_{ph,0}}{N_{ph,i}} = \frac{\delta + \Gamma v_g g_0(N)i^2/M^2}{\delta}.$$

Using Equations (12.87) and (12.41) then gives

$$\frac{N_{ph,0}}{N_{ph,i}} = 1 + [\Gamma v_g g_0(N)/\beta_{sp}BN^2](i^2/M^2)N_{ph,0} = 1 + \frac{N_{ph,0}}{\tau_{ph}\beta_{sp}BN^2}\frac{i^2}{M^2}.$$

[12.89]

This result shows that the larger the density of the main mode, the stronger the mode suppression of side modes. One important observation from this fact is that when an FP diode is pulse modulated, side modes are stronger at the initial turn-on. This can be seen from Figure 12.13.

Equation (12.89) also shows that the stronger the spontaneous emission effect ($\beta_{sp}BN^2$), the smaller the side-mode suppression ratio and the stronger the side modes. In other words, random spontaneous emission is one important cause in side mode generation. A similar phenomenon is also observed in the discussion of DFB laser diodes in Chapter 13.

Example 12.13

STEADY STATE SIDE MODES   To demonstrate the side mode effect, consider a laser diode that has the same parameters given in Example 12.7 except that $\beta_{sp} = 2 \times 10^{-4}$ and $J_2 = J_{th}$. Let $N_{th} = 2.61 \times 10^{18}$ cm^{-3} and $\tau_{ph} = 1.1$ psec, as given in Example 12.7. From Figure 12.13, $N_{ph,0} = 3.0 \times 10^{15}$ cm^{-3} in the steady state. Assuming $M = 4$ and using Equation (12.89),

$$\frac{N_{ph,0}}{N_{ph,1}} = 1 + \frac{3.0 \times 10^{15}}{(1.1 \times 10^{-12}) \times (2 \times 10^{-4}) \times (1 \times 10^{-10}) \times (2.61 \times 10^{18})^2} \times \frac{1}{4^2}$$

$$= 1250.$$

Therefore,

$$N_{ph,1} = \frac{3.0 \times 10^{15}}{1250} = 2.4 \times 10^{12} \text{ cm}^{-3}$$

and $N_{ph,2} = N_{ph,1}/2^2 = 6.0 \times 10^{11}$ cm^{-3}, $N_{ph,3} = N_{ph,1}/3^2 = 2.7 \times 10^{11}$ cm^{-3}, and so forth. These results are consistent with what is shown in Figure 12.13. ■

Stronger side modes can occur not only in direct pulse modulation but also in direct analog modulation. As illustrated in Figure 12.14, a single-mode DFB laser is amplitude modulated at different modulation indices [5]. When the modulation index is greater than 80 percent, the spectrum of the modulated output changes from a single mode to multimodes.

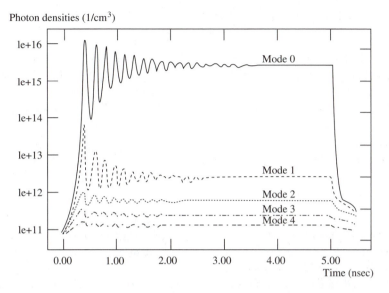

Figure 12.13   Photon densities of different longitudinal modes during pulse modulation. Data are obtained from numerically solving the multimode rate equations. $\beta_{sp} = 2.0 \times 10^{-4}$ cm^{-3}.

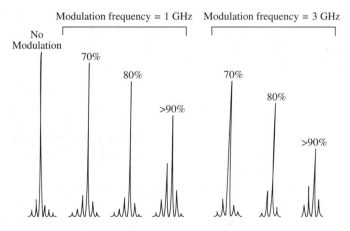

Figure 12.14   Mode partition in analog AM modulation.

SOURCE: Reprinted, by permission, from Lau et al., "Longitudinal Mode Spectrum," Figure 3*b* [5]. © 1984 by IEEE.

12.6.3 Linewidth Broadening

Because of phase noise, discussed in Chapter 6, the linewidth of a single-mode laser diode is nonzero. Even worse, when a laser diode is directly modulated, its bandwidth is broader than when it is at a constant bias. For example, a single-mode DFB laser biased at a constant current level may have a bandwidth of only 20 MHz. But if it is directly modulated, its bandwidth can increase to several GHz. The reason is similar to the cause of chirping, where the refractive index of the medium is modulated by the carrier density.

12.7 Summary

1. Light carrier modulation can be done by directly modulating the bias current or by using an external modulator. Direct modulation is more popular but has limitations, such as relaxation oscillation, chirping, mode partition, and linewidth broadening. As Chapter 14 will explain, external modulation avoids these disadvantages but is bulky and more expensive.

2. LEDs have a large linewidth because of spontaneous emission. Therefore, they are used only for intensity modulation. In the steady state, the output light intensity is linearly proportional to the bias current.

3. For pulse modulation, the speed of modulating an LED is limited by its turn-on and turn-off delays, which are primarily determined by the radiative time constant τ_r and non-radiative time constant τ_{nr}. By operating the diode at a high bias current or having a high-level doping, τ_r can be reduced to achieve a higher modulation bandwidth.

4. For small signal modulation of LEDs, the modulation bandwidth is inversely proportional to $\tau_{nr}^{-1} + BNP$. Therefore, similar to pulse modulation, the bandwidth can be increased by operating the diode at a high bias current or having a high-level doping.

5. LDs have a small linewidth compared to that of LEDs because of stimulated emission. In the steady state, the output light intensity is linearly proportional to the bias current minus the threshold current.

6. The threshold current of a laser diode is the bias current that makes the net optical gain in the cavity equal to 0 dB. In general, the threshold is large when either the cavity confinement is small or the cavity loss is large.

7. For pulse modulation of LDs, there is an initial turn-on delay to bring the optical gain to positive. Before the gain becomes positive, the photon density due to stimulate emission in the active layer is negligible.

8. For pulse modulation of LDs, because of the interaction between photons and carriers, there is a relaxation oscillation after the initial turn-on delay. In general, the larger the ratio of the final current to the threshold current, the higher the amplitude and the faster the oscillation.

9. Different from LEDs, when an LD is turned off, the falling edge has a sharp drop because of the nonlinear interaction between photons and carriers.

10. For small signal modulation of LDs, the modulation bandwidth is determined by the relaxation oscillation frequency. In general, the larger the bias current, the larger the bandwidth.

11. Chirping is a carrier frequency drift of the output light when an LD is turned on and off. It is caused by the modulation of the refractive index during direct modulation. Chirping is an undesirable phenomenon because it limits the transmission speed and distance.

12. The multiple longitudinal modes of FP LDs can have different power distributions during modulation. For digital communications, side modes are stronger during the initial pulse turn-on. This causes pulse broadening in fiber transmission. For analog communications, it causes signal distortion and limits the allowable modulation depth.

APPENDIX 12–A: FABRY-PEROT LASER DIODE RATE EQUATIONS

This appendix derives the FP rate equation given by Equation (12.35). The essence of the following derivation is to relate the carrier density and photon density by the electric field and the laser medium's susceptibility.

To start, the wave equation (4.71) given in Appendix 4–A is repeated here:

$$\nabla^2 \mathcal{E} - \frac{1}{c^2}\frac{\partial^2}{\partial t^2}\mathcal{E} = \mu \frac{\partial^2}{\partial t^2}\mathcal{P}. \qquad \textbf{[12.90]}$$

For simplicity, assume the electric field $\mathcal{E}$ in the laser cavity is a transverse magnetic (*TM*) mode with the following E_z field:

$$E_z(x, y, z, t) = E_T(x, y)\sin(\beta_z z)\Re\{E(t)e^{j\omega t}\} \qquad \textbf{[12.91]}$$

where $E_T(x, y)$ is the transverse factor of the field, $E(t)$ is a slow time-varying factor (compared to $e^{j\omega t}$), $\Re\{\cdot\}$ denotes the real part, and β_z is the propagation constant in the z direction and should satisfy the longitudinal boundary condition given by Equation (3.14).

For a given longitudinal mode or β_z, Maxwell's equations and propagation modes discussed in Appendix 4–A, lead to the definition:

$$\left(\frac{n_0\omega_0}{c}\right)^2 \overset{\text{def}}{=} \beta_0^2 = (\beta_z)^2 + \kappa_{TM}^2 \qquad \textbf{[12.92]}$$

where n_0 is the refractive index of the laser medium and κ_{TM} is the eigenvalue of the transverse mode E_T, both at zero external current pumping. From the definition, ω_0 is the angular frequency of the lightwave at zero pumping, and the transverse field E_T satisfies

$$\frac{\partial^2 E_T}{\partial x^2} + \frac{\partial^2 E_T}{\partial y^2} + \kappa_{TM}^2 E_T = 0. \qquad \textbf{[12.93]}$$

When there is external current injection, ω given by Equation (12.91) is different from but close to ω_0 given by Equation (12.92).

Wave Equation in terms of $E(t)$ The first step to derive the rate equation given by Equation (12.35) is to express Equation (12.90) in terms of $E(t)$. To do this requires substituting E_z, given by Equation (12.91), into each term of Equation (12.90). Substituting E_z into the first term of Equation (12.90) gives

$$\nabla^2 E_z = \left(\frac{\partial^2}{\partial x^2} + \frac{\partial^2}{\partial y^2} + \frac{\partial^2}{\partial z^2}\right) E_z = \left(\frac{\partial^2 E_T}{\partial x^2} + \frac{\partial^2 E_T}{\partial y^2} - \beta_z^2 E_T\right) \sin(\beta_z z) \Re\{E(t)e^{j\omega t}\}.$$

Similarly, for the second term of Equation (12.90),

$$\frac{1}{c^2}\frac{\partial^2}{\partial t^2} E_z = E_T(x, y)\sin(\beta_z z)\frac{1}{c^2}\Re\left\{\frac{\partial^2}{\partial t^2}[E(t)e^{j\omega t}]\right\}$$

$$\approx \frac{1}{c^2}E_T(x, y)\sin(\beta_z z)\Re\left\{\left[-\omega^2 E(t) + 2j\omega\frac{\partial E(t)}{\partial t}\right]e^{j\omega t}\right\} \qquad \textbf{[12.94]}$$

where the second-order term $\partial^2 E(t)/\partial t^2$ is dropped because $E(t)$ is slowly varying compared to $e^{j\omega t}$.

The last term of Equation (12.90) is a little tricky to obtain. First, note that the relationship $P(x, y, z, t) = \epsilon_0 \chi \mathcal{E}(x, y, z, t)$ given by Equation (4.69) is only an approximation. Taking into consideration the time delay between the electric field and the induced polarization, a more accurate form is given by [6]

$$\mathcal{P}(x, y, z, t) = \epsilon_0 \int \hat{\chi}(x, y, z, t')E_z(x, y, z, t - t')dt'.$$

If $E(t)$ is slowly time varying, $E_z(x, y, z, t - t')$ will expand into the following Taylor series with respect to t:

$$E_z(x, y, z, t - t') \approx E_T(x, y)\sin(\beta_z z)\Re\left\{\left[E(t) + (-t')\frac{\partial E(t)}{\partial t}\right]e^{j\omega t}e^{-j\omega t'}\right\}.$$

Therefore,

$$\mathcal{P}(x, y, z, t) \approx \epsilon_0 E_T(x, y)\sin(\beta_z z)\Re\left\{\left[\int \hat{\chi}(t')e^{-j\omega t'}dt'\right]E(t)e^{j\omega t}\right.$$

$$+ \left[\int (-t')\hat{\chi}(t')e^{-j\omega t'}dt'\right]\frac{\partial E(t)}{\partial t}e^{j\omega t}\right\}$$

$$= \epsilon_0 E_T(x, y)\sin(\beta_z z)\Re\left\{\left[\chi(\omega)E(t) - j\frac{\partial \chi(\omega)}{\partial \omega}\frac{\partial E(t)}{\partial t}\right]e^{j\omega t}\right\}.$$

From this result, the last term of Equation (12.90) reduces to

$$\mu_0\frac{\partial^2}{\partial t^2}\mathcal{P} \approx \frac{1}{c^2}E_T(x, y)\sin(\beta_z z)\Re\left\{-\chi(\omega)\omega^2 E(t)e^{j\omega t}\right.$$

$$+ j2\omega\left[\chi(\omega) + \frac{\omega}{2}\frac{\partial \chi(\omega)}{\partial \omega}\right]\frac{\partial E(t)}{\partial t}e^{j\omega t}\right\} \qquad \textbf{[12.95]}$$

where only the zero and first-order terms have been retained. From Equations (12.93)–(12.95), Equation (12.90) reduces to

$$
\left\{ \frac{\partial^2 E_T}{\partial x^2} + \frac{\partial^2 E_T}{\partial y^2} - \beta_z^2 E_T \right\} \sin(\beta_z z) E(t)
$$
$$
- \frac{1}{c^2} E_T(x, y) \sin(\beta_z z) \left\{ -\omega^2 E(t) + 2j\omega \frac{\partial E(t)}{\partial t} \right\}
$$
$$
= \frac{1}{c^2} E_T(x, y) \sin(\beta_z z) \left\{ -\chi(\omega)\omega^2 E(t) + j2\omega \left[\chi(\omega) + \frac{\omega}{2} \frac{\partial \chi(\omega)}{\partial \omega} \right] \frac{\partial E(t)}{\partial t} \right\}.
$$

Using Equation (12.93) for E_T gives

$$
\left(-\beta_0^2 + \frac{\omega^2}{c^2} \right) E(t) - \frac{1}{c^2}(2j\omega) \frac{\partial E(t)}{\partial t}
$$
$$
= \frac{1}{c^2} \left\{ -\chi(\omega)\omega^2 E(t) + 2j\omega \left[\chi(\omega) \frac{\omega}{2} \frac{\partial \chi(\omega)}{\partial \omega} \right] \frac{\partial E(t)}{\partial t} \right\}.
$$

This can be further simplified to

$$
\left[-\beta_0^2 + \frac{\omega^2}{c^2} \epsilon_r(\omega) \right] E(t) - \frac{2j\omega}{c^2} \left[\epsilon_r(\omega) + \frac{\omega}{2} \frac{\partial \epsilon_r}{\partial \omega} \right] \frac{\partial E}{\partial t} = 0 \qquad \textbf{[12.96]}
$$

where $\epsilon_r(\omega) = 1 + \chi(\omega)$.

Decomposition of ϵ_r Equation (12.96) is the wave equation for $E(t)$. To see how it is modulated by external pumping or current injection, the dielectric constant ϵ_r must be expressed in terms of various physical quantities in the laser cavity. Specifically, ϵ_r can be expressed as

$$
\epsilon_r = 1 + \chi = 1 + \chi_0 + \chi_p - j \frac{\sigma}{\epsilon_0 \omega} \qquad \textbf{[12.97]}
$$

where the susceptibility χ is decomposed into three components: (1) χ_0 is the susceptibility of the medium in the absence of external current pumping, (2) χ_p is the susceptibility of the medium due to external pumping, and (3) the imaginary term $-j(\sigma/\epsilon_0\omega)$ is used to account for the cavity loss. Therefore, χ_p is the only term depending on the injected carrier density.

Let $\epsilon_r \overset{\text{def}}{=} \epsilon_r' + j\epsilon_r''$, where

$$
\epsilon_r' = 1 + \Re\chi_0 + \Re\chi_p = \epsilon_b + \Re\chi_p = n_0^2 + \Re\chi_p \qquad \textbf{[12.98]}
$$

and

$$
\epsilon_r'' = \Im\chi_0 + \Im\chi_p - \frac{\sigma}{\epsilon_0 \omega} \qquad \textbf{[12.99]}
$$

denote the real and imaginary part of ϵ_r, respectively. From these definitions,

$$\frac{\omega^2}{c^2}\epsilon_r - \beta_0^2 = \frac{\omega^2}{c^2}\left(n_0^2 + \chi_0 + \chi_p - j\frac{\sigma}{\epsilon_0\omega}\right) - \beta_0^2$$

$$\approx \frac{(\omega^2 - \omega_0^2)}{c^2}n_0^2 + \frac{\omega^2}{c^2}\chi_p' + j\frac{\omega^2}{c^2}\left(\chi_0'' + \chi_p'' - \frac{\sigma}{\epsilon_0\omega}\right). \qquad \textbf{[12.100]}$$

For simplification, define

$$\alpha_{int} \overset{\text{def}}{=} \frac{\omega}{n_0 c}\frac{\sigma}{\epsilon_0\omega}. \qquad \textbf{[12.101]}$$

Also, for laser diodes, one can relate $\chi_0'' + \chi_p''$ by the following empirical equation [1]:

$$\Gamma a(N - N_0) = \frac{\omega}{n_0 c}(\chi_0'' + \chi_p''). \qquad \textbf{[12.102]}$$

Furthermore, if Δn_p is defined as the refractive index change caused by pumping, one has

$$\mathfrak{Re}_r = n_0^2 + \chi_p \overset{\text{def}}{=} (n_0 + \Delta n_p)^2. \qquad \textbf{[12.103]}$$

Therefore,

$$\chi_p' \approx 2n_0\Delta n_p. \qquad \textbf{[12.104]}$$

From Equations (12.100) − (12.104),

$$\frac{\omega^2}{c^2}\epsilon_r - \beta_0^2 = \frac{(\omega^2 - \omega_0^2)}{c^2}n_0^2 + 2\frac{\omega^2}{c^2}n_0\Delta n_p + j\frac{\omega n_0}{c}\left[\Gamma a(N - N_0) - \alpha_{int}\right]. \qquad \textbf{[12.105]}$$

Because $n^2(\omega) = \epsilon_r(\omega)$,

$$\epsilon_r(\omega) + \frac{\omega}{2}\frac{\partial\epsilon_r}{\partial\omega} = n^2(\omega) + \omega n(\omega)\frac{\partial n}{\partial\omega} = nn_g. \qquad \textbf{[12.106]}$$

Using Equations (12.105) and (12.106), Equation (12.96) reduces to

$$\frac{dE(t)}{dt} = \frac{c^2}{2j\omega n_0 n_g}\left\{2\omega(\omega - \omega_0)\frac{n_0^2}{c^2} + \frac{\omega^2}{c^2}\chi_p' + \frac{j\omega n_0}{c}\left[\Gamma a(N - N_0) - \alpha_{int}\right]\right\} E$$

or

$$\frac{dE(t)}{dt} = -j(\omega - \omega_0)\frac{n_0}{n_g}E - j\frac{\omega}{n_g}\Delta n_p E + \frac{1}{2}v_g\left[\Gamma a(N - N_0) - \alpha_{int}\right]E. \qquad \textbf{[12.107]}$$

Rate Equation of Photon Density   If the electric field $E(t)$ is expressed in terms of its amplitude and phase by

$$E \overset{\text{def}}{=} Ae^{j\phi} \qquad \textbf{[12.108]}$$

the real and imaginary parts of Equation (12.107) can be expressed by

$$\frac{dA}{dt} = \frac{1}{2}v_g[\Gamma g(N) - \alpha_{int}]A \qquad \textbf{[12.109]}$$

and

$$\frac{d\phi}{dt} = -\frac{n_b}{n_g}(\omega - \omega_0) - \frac{\omega}{n_g}\Delta n_p. \qquad \textbf{[12.110]}$$

Because the photon density N_{ph} is proportional to $|A|^2$, Equation (12.109) reduces to

$$\frac{dN_{ph}}{dt} = v_g[\Gamma g(N) - \alpha_{int}]N_{ph} + \beta_{sp}BN^2 \qquad \textbf{[12.111]}$$

where the $\beta_{sp}BN^2$ term is added to include the spontaneous emission contribution.

Assuming that the propagation delay within the cavity is short compared to the modulation speed, all the phase change caused by modulation can be quickly absorbed by the output frequency ω. In other words, $d\phi/dt \approx 0$ in Equation (12.110). This gives

$$\omega = \frac{n_0}{n_0 + \Delta n_p}\omega_0 = \frac{n_0}{n_0 + \Gamma bN}\omega_0. \qquad \textbf{[12.112]}$$

Relationship between Chirping Constant b and Linewidth Broadening Factor α_{lw} As shown below, the chirping constant b can be expressed in terms of the gain constant a and the linewidth broadening factor α_{lw} defined in Equation (6.120). When the imaginary part of the refractive index $\Im n = n''$ has a change due to a certain change of the carrier density,

$$(n + j\Delta n'')^2 \approx n^2 + 2nj\Delta n'' = \epsilon_r + j\Delta\chi_p''.$$

Therefore,

$$\Delta n'' = \frac{1}{2n}\Delta\chi_p'' = \frac{c}{2\omega}\Gamma a\Delta N$$

where the last equality comes from Equation (12.102). Therefore, from the definition of α_{lw} given by Equation (6.120),

$$\alpha_{lw} \stackrel{\text{def}}{=} -\frac{\Delta n''}{\Delta n'} = -\frac{c}{2\omega}\frac{\Gamma b\Delta N}{\Gamma a\Delta N}$$

or

$$b = -\frac{1}{2k}\alpha_{lw}a. \qquad \textbf{[12.113]}$$

where $k = \omega/c = 2\pi/\lambda \approx \omega_0/c$.

PROBLEMS

Problem 12–1 Propagation Delay in Cavity: A semiconductor light source has a cavity length of $L = 300$ μm. If the index of refraction of the active layer is 3.7, find the one-way propagation delay along the cavity. At a given bias, assume photons are uniformly distributed in the cavity and travel in either direction with equal possibility. If the LED is turned off instantaneously and all photon generation processes are cut off after the turn-off, how long does it take for the total photons in the cavity to reduce to the 10 percent level after the turn-off? This problem illustrates one fundamental speed limit in modulation. In solving the problem, neglect the cavity loss and assume only r^2 of the total photons remain after each one-way trip, where r is the reflection coefficient at the cavity end.

Problem 12–2 LED Internal Quantum Efficiency: An N-type LED biased at a constant current has a carrier density of $N = 2.0 \times 10^{19}$ cm^3. If the carrier recombination coefficient B is 1×10^{-10} cm^3/sec, calculate the radiative time constant and the total time constant. If the nonradiative time constant is 0.4 nsec, find the internal quantum efficiency.

Problem 12–3 LED Power Output: An LED is used to transmit a digital signal over 100 km. The wavelength is 1.5 μm. Assume the minimum power required for "1" at the receiver is -30 dBm and the fiber has an attenuation of 0.4 dB/km. If the quantum efficiency of the LED is 0.2, find the minimum current to drive the LED when a bit "1" is transmitted.

Problem 12–4 Carrier Density of LED: An N-type InGaAsP heterostructure LED has a doping level of $N_D = 2 \times 10^{18}$ cm^3 in the active layer. If the diode has $w = 10$ μm, $d = 0.2$ μm, and $L = 500$ μm, find the carrier density at a bias current of 100 mA. What is the corresponding net radiative recombination rate? Assume recombination coefficient B is 5×10^{-10} cm^3/sec and the nonradiative time constant is $\tau_{nr} = 0.2$ nsec.

Problem 12–5 Large Signal LED Modulation: A heterostructure LED is used to transmit a digital signal over 100 km. The wavelength is 1.5 μm. The diode has a dimension $w = 5$ μm, $d = 0.1$ μm, and $L = 1000$ μm.

a. Assume the minimum power required for "1" at the receiver is -35 dBm and the fiber has an attenuation of 0.3 dB/km. If the quantum efficiency of the LED is 0.1, find the minimum current to drive the LED when the input is "1." What is the corresponding output power?

b. If the LED has a P-type active layer with $N_A = 10^{18}$ cm^{-3} and $B = 10^{-10}$ cm^3/sec, find the delay of the carrier density reaching 90 percent of its steady state value when the diode is turned from off to on. Assume the nonradiative time constant is $\tau_{nr} = 1$ nsec.

c. With the same assumptions as in *b* and if the minimum bit interval required is 4 times the above delay, can the diode be used for a 50 Mb/s system? If not, how can the problem be solved?

Problem 12–6 Small Signal Modulation for LED: The same LED in Problem 12–5 is modulated by a current of the form $I = I_0 + I_1 \cos(\omega_1 t)$, where $I_0 = 10$ mA and $I_1 = 2$ mA. Find the output light intensity as a function of time in terms of ω_1. What is the 3 dB modulation bandwidth?

Problem 12–7 LED Modulation Bandwidth Improvement: For the same LED of Problem 12–6, to double the modulation bandwidth, what current level I_0 is needed?

Problem 12–8 LD Power Output: A laser diode has the following parameters: refractive index $n = 3$, group refractive index $n_g = 4.0$, cavity length $L = 500$ μm, operating wavelength $\lambda = 1.3$ μm, cavity distributive loss $\alpha = 1000$ dB/m, $N_0 = 2.0 \times 10^{18}$ cm^{-3}, gain constant $a = 5 \times 10^{-16}$ cm^2, active layer thickness $d = 0.1$ μm, cavity width $w = 10$ μm, confinement factor $\Gamma = 0.1$, and carrier recombination constants $A = 10^9$ sec^{-1}, $B = 10^{-10}$ cm^{-3}sec^{-1}, and $C = 0$. Find

    a. The total attenuation (dB/m) in the cavity.

    b. The threshold current.

    c. The output power if the input current is $10\,I_{th}$.

Problem 12–9 Laser Diode Steady State: An InGaAsP laser diode has dimensions $d = 0.1$ μm, $w = 5\,\mu$m, and $L = 500\,\mu$m. The operating wavelength and other laser diode parameters except the gain constant a are assumed to be the same as in Problem 12–8. Find the gain constant so that an output of 2.5 mW can be achieved at $J/J_{th} = 1.5$.

Problem 12–10 Large Signal LD Modulation: In a digital optical fiber communication link, a laser diode is used. If its output power must be greater than 2.5 mW to meet the power budget, perform the following computations. Use the same parameters as in Problem 12–8.

    a. At the 2.5 mW output, calculate the damping constant and the relaxation oscillation frequency.

    b. If it is required to have $e^{-\alpha T_0} < 0.1$ where T_0 is the bit interval, what is the speed limit in digital signal modulation?

This problem shows that when the bit rate is higher than the value computed in *b*, the speed of the system is not limited by the power budget but rather by the laser diode's modulation bandwidth.

Problem 12–11 Initial Turn-On Delay: A laser diode is turned on from zero bias to $5\,J_{th}$. Given the same parameter values as in Problem 12–9,

    a. Calculate $\tau_e(N_{th})$.

    b. Calculate the turn-on delay using Equations (12.51) and (12.52). Assume $N_1 = 0$ and $\tau_e(N_{th})/\tau_e = 0.9$. Is there any significant difference in the results?

    c. If $B = 0$, calculate the turn-on delay. From this, you will see that using $t_d = \tau_e \ln([J_2 - J_1]/[J_2 - J_{th}])$ gives a conservative estimate of the turn-on delay.

Problem 12–12 Small Signal LD Modulation: Assume a given laser diode is biased at $I_B = 5I_{th}$ and has the same parameter values as in Problem 12–8.

    a. Find the damping constant α and $\omega_n/2\pi$.

    b. Find the ratio of the peak value to dc of the frequency response.

Problem 12–13 LD Modulation Bandwidth: Using the same parameter values and bias current as in Problem 12–12, calculate the 3 dB modulation bandwidth.

Problem 12–14 Chirping:

    a. Given Equation (12.67), derive the expression for the carrier density using Equation (12.57).

b. Find the time point at which $\Delta N(t)$ has its peak value. Perform the numerical calculation with the same parameter values given in Problem 12–8.

c. Derive the peak frequency deviation in terms of the laser diode parameters and ΔN_{peak}. Use Equation (12.113) to find the constant b. Let $\alpha_{lw} = 5.5$. Also assume the same parameter values given in Problem 12–8.

Problem 12–15 Multimode LD:

a. At the steady state, assume $N_{th} = 3.0 \times 10^{18}\,cm^{-3}$ and $N_{ph,steady} = 3.0 \times 10^{15}\,cm^{-3}$. Also, assume $\tau_{ph} = 1.0\,psec$, $B = 1.0 \times 10^{-10}$, $\beta_{sp} = 1 \times 10^{-4}$, and there are 21 longitudinal modes ($M = 10$). Use Equation (12.89) to calculate the mode suppression ratio of the main mode to the first side mode.

b. If the bias condition of a is $I_B = 2I_{th}$, what should the bias current level be to double the suppression ratio? How much does the steady state power increase at the new bias level?

REFERENCES

1. G. P. Agrawal and N. K. Dutta, *Long-Wavelength Semiconductor Lasers*, Van Nostrand Reinhold, 1986.

2. P. Vankwikelberge et al., "CLADISS: A Longitudinal Multimode Model for the Analysis of the Static, Dynamic, and Stochastic Behavior of Diode Lasers with Distributed Feedback," *IEEE Journal of Quantum Electronics*, vol. 26, no. 10 (1990), pp. 1728–41.

3. R. S. Tucker, "High Speed Modulation of Semiconductor Lasers," *Journal of Lightwave Technology*, December 1985, pp. 1180–92.

4. K. Uomi et al, "Ultralow Chirp and High-Speed 1.55 μm Multiquantum Well $\lambda/4$-Shifted DFB Lasers," *IEEE Photonics Technology Letters*, vol. 2, no. 4 (April 1990), pp. 229–30.

5. K. Lau et. al, "Longitudinal Mode Spectrum of Semiconductor Lasers under High Speed Modulation," *IEEE Journal of Quantum Electronics*, vol. 20, no. 1 (January 1984), pp. 71–79.

6. M. Schubert and B. Wilhelmi, Chapter 1, "Electromagnetic Fields: Classical Description," *Nonlinear Optics and Quantum Electronics*, John Wiley and Sons, 1986.

DISTRIBUTED FEEDBACK LASER DIODES AND MODULATION

Chapter 12 discussed direct modulation of Fabry-Perot (FP) laser diodes. Because of their multimode properties, FP lasers are limited in systems that require single-mode transmissions. As mentioned in Chapter 3, distributed feedback (DFB) lasers have an internal feedback structure that can suppress side modes by Bragg reflection. Therefore, they are attractive for use in high-speed Gb/s systems that require low fiber dispersion. To understand the characteristics of DFB laser diodes, this chapter presents in more detail its various important properties at dc and under modulation.

Analyzing DFB laser diodes requires using the rate equations as in the case of FP lasers. Because of the distributed feedback structure, the rate equations in this case become more complicated. As will be explained shortly, the electric field in the cavity is represented by a pair of forward and backward traveling waves. These two waves are coupled to one another through the periodic structure in the cavity. The structure results in reflection of the forward traveling wave and adds it to the backward wave. Similarly, part of the backward traveling wave is reflected by the structure and added to the forward traveling wave. As a result, instead of one rate equation for the photon density, as in the case of FP lasers, there are two wave equations called the **coupled-mode wave equations** to describe interaction of the two opposite-traveling waves.

This chapter derives and explains the coupled mode wave equations. These equations and the carrier density rate equation allow the properties of DFB diodes at the steady state and under modulation to be studied. The analysis covers such important properties as threshold gain, emission wavelengths, single-mode condition, gain suppression, spatial hole burning, and chirping.

13.1 COUPLED-MODE RATE EQUATIONS

Appendix 12–A derived the rate equations for Fabry-Perot lasers. As mentioned earlier, the difference in deriving the rate equations for DFB laser diodes is the different representation of the electric field $\mathcal{E}(x, y, z, t)$. Instead of a standing wave given by Equation (12.91), the electric field in a DFB laser diode consists of a pair of forward- and backward-traveling waves:

$$\mathcal{E}(x, y, z, t) = E_T(x, y)\Re\left\{\sum_q E_q^+(z, t)e^{j(\omega_q t - \beta_B z)} + \sum_q E_q^-(z, t)e^{j(\omega_q t + \beta_B z)}\right\} \quad \textbf{[13.1]}$$

where q is the index for longitudinal mode q,[1] ω_q is the corresponding angular frequency,

$$\beta_B = \frac{2\pi n_b}{\lambda_B} \overset{\text{def}}{=} \frac{\pi}{\Lambda} \quad \textbf{[13.2]}$$

is the wave number at the Bragg wavelength given by Equation (3.16) with n_b being the refractive index of the laser medium, $E_q^+(z, t)e^{j(\omega_q t - \beta_B z)}$ is the forward-traveling wave in the $+z$ direction, and $E_q^-(z, t)e^{j(\omega_q t + \beta_B z)}$ is the backward-traveling wave in the $-z$ direction. The factors $E_q^+(z, t)$ and $E_q^-(z, t)$ are slowly varying in both the spatial domain (z) and the time domain (t). According to Equation (13.1), all waves are assumed to have the same transverse mode $E_T(x, y)$.

This use of two opposite-traveling waves allows the wave interactions in the periodic structure to be described. From Appendix 13–A, substituting $\mathcal{E}(x, y, z, t)$ of Equation (13.1) in the wave equation (4.71), produces the following rate equations for $E_q^+(z, t)$ and $E_q^-(z, t)$:

$$\frac{\partial E_q^+(z, t)}{\partial z} + \frac{1}{v_g}\frac{\partial E_q^+(z, t)}{\partial t} + \left\{j\Delta\beta_q - J_{sp,q}^+\right\}E_q^+(z, t) = -j\kappa^+ E_q^-(z, t) \quad \textbf{[13.3]}$$

and

$$-\frac{\partial E_q^-(z, t)}{\partial z} + \frac{1}{v_g}\frac{\partial E_q^-(z, t)}{\partial t} + \left\{j\Delta\beta_q - J_{sp,q}^-\right\}E_q^-(z, t) = -j\kappa^- E_q^+(z, t) \quad \textbf{[13.4]}$$

where v_g is the group velocity of the wave in the cavity; other variables will be defined shortly. Equations (13.3) and (13.4) describe the interdependence of the two traveling waves $E_q^+(z, t)$ and $E_q^-(z, t)$. Therefore, they are called the coupled-mode wave equations. For convenience, the units of the magnitude squared of the electric fields $E_q^+(z, t)$ and $E_q^-(z, t)$ are set to watts.[2]

Frequency Shift and Cavity Gain   In Equations (13.3) and (13.4), $\Delta\beta_q$ is a complex variable with the real part representing the frequency shift from the Bragg frequency

---

[1] Although DFB lasers have been known for their single-mode output, multimode rate equations are considered here for generality. Later in the chapter, conditions to have single-mode emission and techniques to suppress side modes will be discussed.

[2] This avoids additional factors to relate $|E_q^+(z, t)|^2$ or $|E_q^-(z, t)|^2$ to optical power.

and the imaginary part representing the net cavity gain. Specifically, from Appendix 13–A, $\Delta\beta_q$ is defined as

$$\Delta\beta_q \overset{\text{def}}{=} \frac{1}{v_g}(\omega_q - \omega_B) - \frac{1}{2}\Gamma a\alpha_{lw}N + \frac{j}{2}\left[-\alpha_{int} + \Gamma a(N - N_0)\right] \qquad \textbf{[13.5]}$$

where $\omega_B = \beta_B c/n_b$ is the Bragg frequency, and other parameters such as the carrier density N are defined the same as in Chapter 12.

Equation (13.5) shows that the first term of the real part comes from the difference between the emission frequency and the Bragg frequency, and the second term, $\Gamma a\alpha_{lw}N/2$, in Equation (13.5) represents the chirping effect discussed in Chapter 12. If the contribution from $\Gamma a\alpha_{lw}N/2$ is ignored, the real part of $\Delta\beta_q$ tells the frequency shift of propagation mode q from the Bragg frequency.

The imaginary part of $\Delta\beta_q$ is one-half of the net cavity gain due to stimulated emission ($\Gamma a[N - N_0]$) and distributed cavity loss (α_{int}). To sustain emission, the net cavity gain is greater than zero to compensate for additional loss such as facet reflection loss.

Spontaneous Emission   In Equations (13.3) and (13.4), $J_{sp}^{\pm}$ is the term representing spontaneous emission. It represents a certain fraction of spontaneous emissions that contribute to the emission of the qth mode. Because spontaneous emission is incoherent, its phase and frequency have a broad distribution. As a result, there is a small fraction (e.g., 0.01 percent) that has the same phase and frequency as the qth mode. As pointed out in Chapter 12, although the significance of spontaneous emission is small, its inclusion is critical to the initial stimulated emission when the laser is just turned on.

As derived in Appendix 13–A, $J_{sp,q}^{\pm}$ is given by

$$J_{sp,q}^{\pm} = \frac{I_{sp}}{2|E_q^{\pm}|^2} \qquad \textbf{[13.6]}$$

where

$$I_{sp} = \tfrac{1}{2}\beta_{sp}wd(h\omega_q/2\pi)BN^2 \qquad \textbf{[13.7]}$$

is the fraction of the spontaneous emission in W/m. Therefore, $J_{sp,q}^{\pm}$ has the unit of 1/m. Because this spontaneous emission term is added to the imaginary part of $\Delta\beta_q$, the terms $J_{sp,q}^{\pm}$ contribute equivalently to the total cavity gain.

Coupling Constants   In Equations (13.3) and (13.4), $\kappa^{\pm}$ are coupling constants of the two opposite-traveling waves. They are the new terms that do not exist in the FP rate equations. To see how they are related to the periodic structure, let the laser cavity have a length L from $z = -z_0$ to $z = L - z_0$, and assume the periodic part of the dielectric constant is of the form:

$$\Delta\epsilon_b(z) \approx 2\Delta\epsilon\cos(\theta_k + 2\pi[z - (L/2 - z_0)]/\Lambda) \qquad \textbf{[13.8]}$$

where $\Delta\epsilon$ is the magnitude of the periodic dielectric constant change, and θ_k is the phase of $\Delta\epsilon_b(z)$ at the center point of the cavity. Equation (13.8) can be expressed as

$$\Delta\epsilon_b(z) = \Delta\epsilon_+ e^{j2\pi z/\Lambda} + \Delta\epsilon_- e^{-j2\pi z/\Lambda}$$

with

$$\Delta\epsilon_{\pm} \overset{\text{def}}{=} \Delta\epsilon e^{\pm j[\theta_k - 2\pi(L/2 - z_0)/\Lambda]}. \qquad \textbf{[13.9]}$$

From above and the coupled mode theory discussed in Appendix 13–A, forward and backward coupling constants $\kappa^{\pm}$ are defined as

$$\kappa^{\pm} \overset{\text{def}}{=} \frac{\omega_B^2}{2c^2\beta_B} \frac{\int\int \Delta\epsilon_{\mp} E_T^2(x, y)dxdy}{\int\int E_T^2(x, y)dxdy} \overset{\text{def}}{=} \kappa_0 e^{\mp j\theta_k} e^{\pm j2\beta_B(L/2 - z_0)} \qquad \textbf{[13.10]}$$

where

$$\kappa_0 \overset{\text{def}}{=} \frac{\omega_B^2}{2c^2\beta_B} \frac{\int\int \Delta\epsilon E_T^2(x, y)dxdy}{\int\int E_T^2(x, y)dxdy} \qquad \textbf{[13.11]}$$

is the coupling constant. In general, $\Delta\epsilon$ in Equation (13.8) can be complex. If it is purely real, the DFB laser is called **index coupled**. On the other hand, if it is purely imaginary, it is called **gain coupled**. In the latter case, a periodic gain is introduced in the longitudinal direction of the cavity, which can be seen from the right-hand side of the coupled-mode equations (13.3) and (13.4). From Equation (13.10),

$$\kappa^- = \begin{cases} \kappa^{+*} & \text{for purely index-guided DFB lasers} \\ -\kappa^{+*} & \text{for purely gain-guided DFB lasers} \end{cases} \qquad \textbf{[13.12]}$$

where the superscript * denotes the complex conjugate.

Example 13.1

SIGNIFICANCE OF SPONTANEOUS EMISSION   Consider an InGaAsP DFB diode with $n_b = 3.5$. To have an emission wavelength of $\lambda_B = 1.55 \ \mu m$, from Equation (13.2),

$$\beta_B = \frac{\pi}{\Lambda} = \frac{2\pi n_b}{\lambda_B} = 1.42 \times 10^7 \ 1/m.$$

Therefore, the Bragg period should be $\Lambda = 221$ nm.

Assume the device has a cross-sectional area of $1 \ \mu m^2$, its spontaneous emission constant is $\beta_{sp} = 2 \times 10^{-5}$, and the spontaneous recombination constant is $B = 1 \times 10^{-16} \ m^3/sec$. From Equation (13.7), the spontaneous emission intensity at the carrier density $N = 1.2 \times 10^{24} \ 1/m^3$ is

$$I_{sp} = (1.0 \times 10^{-5}) \times (1.0 \times 10^{-12}) \times (6.62 \times 10^{-34}) \times (3 \times 10^8) \times (1.55 \times 10^{-6})^{-1}$$
$$\times (1 \times 10^{-16}) \times (1.21 \times 10^{24})^2 = 1.87 \times 10^{-4} \ W/m.$$

If the light power is $|E_q^+|^2 = 1$ mW, from Equation (13.6) there is an additional contribution to the total gain:

$$J_{sp,q}^+ = 9.5 \times 10^{-4} \ cm^{-1}.$$

On the other hand, the gain due to external pumping is

$$\tfrac{1}{2}\Gamma a(N - N_0) = 0.15 \times 2.5 \times 10^{-16} \times 0.2 \times 10^{18} = 7.5 \ cm^{-1}$$

where values for Γ, a, and N_0 are from Table 13.1. Therefore, the spontaneous emission contribution to the total gain is negligible compared to external pumping. When the light intensity is small, such as when the laser is just turned on, $|E_q|^2$ is small and the the contribution due to the spontaneous emission can be significant. ∎

Table 13.1 Typical parameters of a DFB laser diode, which are also used in the computations. [1]–[3]

Parameters	Values	Units	Description
Γ	0.3		Cavity confinement
n_g	4.0		Group refractive index
n_b	3.5		Bulk refractive index
α_{int}	4.0	1/cm	Distributive cavity loss
L	500	μm	Longitudinal length of the cavity
w	5	μm	Transverse width of the cavity
d	0.2	μm	Active layer thickness
Λ	650	nm	Bragg period
a	2.5×10^{-16}	cm^2	Medium gain constant
N_0	1×10^{18}	1/cm^3	Carrier density at zero gain
α_{lw}	5.0		Linewidth enhancement factor
η_g	1.6×10^{-17}	cm^3	Gain suppression constant
β_{sp}	2.0×10^{-4}		Spontaneous emission contribution
θ_k	0		Phase of the coupling coefficient
A	5×10^8	1/sec	Nonradiative recombination constant
B	1×10^{-10}	cm^3/sec	Spontaneous recombination constant
C	3×10^{-29}	cm^6/sec	Auger recombination constant

REQUIRED DIELECTRIC CONSTANT VARIATION From Equation (13.11),

Example 13.2

$$\kappa_0 \approx \frac{\omega_B^2}{2c^2 \beta_B} \Delta\epsilon = \frac{1}{2} \beta_B \frac{\Delta\epsilon}{\epsilon_b}.$$

For a typical value of $\kappa_0 L = 1.0$,

$$\beta_B L = \pi \frac{L}{\Lambda} = 2 \frac{\epsilon_b}{\Delta\epsilon}.$$

Thus the number of periods needed for a given normalized coupling constant is inversely proportional to the ratio of the dielectric constant change. If $L = 500\ \mu$m and $\Lambda = 0.2\ \mu$m, a dielectric constant change ratio of

$$\frac{\Delta\epsilon}{\epsilon_b} = \frac{2}{\pi}\frac{0.2}{500} = 0.25\%$$

is needed. This represents a small change ratio. ■

13.1.1   BOUNDARY CONDITIONS

Let r_L^0 and r_R^0 be the true physical reflection coefficients at the left- and right-hand facets of the cavity, respectively. According to Equation (13.1), the total z-dependent factor of the electric field is

$$E_{q,tot}^+(z) = E_q^+(z)e^{-j\beta_B z}$$

and

$$E_{q,tot}^-(z) = E_q^-(z)e^{j\beta_B z}.$$

Therefore, the boundary condition at the left-hand side is

$$E_q^+(-z_0)e^{j\beta_B z_0} = r_L^0 E_q^-(-z_0)e^{-j\beta_B z_0}.$$

The following definitions are useful:

$$\frac{E_q^+(-z_0)}{E_q^-(-z_0)} \overset{\text{def}}{=} r_L = r_L^0 e^{-j2\beta_B z_0} \qquad\qquad \textbf{[13.13]}$$

and

$$\frac{E_q^-(L-z_0)}{E_q^+(L-z_0)} \overset{\text{def}}{=} r_R = r_R^0 e^{-j2\beta_B(L-z_0)} \qquad\qquad \textbf{[13.14]}$$

From the defintions, r_L and r_R are the effective reflection coefficients for the electric fields E_q^+ and E_q^-.

From Equations (13.10), (13.13), and (13.14), note that $\kappa^{\pm}$, r_L, and r_R are z_0 dependent. Because physics is invariant of z_0 or the absolute coordinate of the z-axis, they individually do not determine the coupled-mode fields. Instead, as will be seen shortly in the next section, the following z_0-independent products determine the emission modes:

$$\kappa^+ r_R = (e^{-j\theta_k}\kappa_0) \times (e^{-j\beta_B L}r_R^0) \qquad\qquad \textbf{[13.15]}$$

$$\kappa^- r_L = (e^{j\theta_k}\kappa_0) \times (e^{-j\beta_B L}r_L^0) \qquad\qquad \textbf{[13.16]}$$

and

$$\kappa^+\kappa^- = \kappa_0^2. \qquad\qquad \textbf{[13.17]}$$

These products show that there are two important phase factors: θ_k and $\beta_B L$. They are associated with the coupling constants and reflection coefficients, respectively. As will be shown shortly, these phases can strongly affect the output wavelengths and the threshold current of DFB diodes. Therefore, extreme care needs to be taken in DFB fabrication to control these phases.

TOLERABLE DESIGN INACCURACY In practical DFB diode fabrication, assume there is an inaccuracy up to ± 0.1 μm in cleaving the two facets of the diode. Therefore, the actual diode length L can vary up to ± 0.2 μm. The phase variation range of the reflection coefficient is thus

$$\Delta(\beta_B L) = \pm 2 \times 10^{-7} \times \frac{2\pi n_b}{\lambda_B} = \pm 2.9 = \pm 46\% \text{ of } 2\pi$$

where the wavelength is assumed to be $\lambda_B = 1.5$ μm, and the refractive index is $n_b = 3.5$. This represents a significant variation. Therefore, it is critical to accurately cut the diode to control the phase $\beta_B L$.

When each facet of the cavity has an independent cutting error of ± 0.1 μm, the center position of the diode also has a ± 0.1 μm variation. Therefore, the phase of the coupling constants has a peak variation of

$$\Delta\theta_k = \pm 2\pi \times \frac{10^{-7}}{\Lambda} = \Delta(\beta_B L) = \pm 2.9$$

where $\Lambda = \lambda_B / 2n_b = 0.214$ μm. ∎

13.1.2 STEADY STATE EQUATIONS

From the rate equations, the steady state longitudinal modes can be found by applying proper boundary conditions at the cavity ends. Equations (13.3) and (13.4), dropping the time-derivative terms give

$$\frac{\partial E_q^+(z, t)}{\partial z} + \left\{ j\Delta\beta_q - J_{sp,q}^+ \right\} E_q^+(z, t) = -j\kappa^+ E_q^-(z, t) \qquad \textbf{[13.18]}$$

and

$$-\frac{\partial E_q^-(z, t)}{\partial z} + \left\{ j\Delta\beta_q - J_{sp,q}^- \right\} E_q^-(z, t) = -j\kappa^- E_q^+(z, t). \qquad \textbf{[13.19]}$$

These steady state coupled-mode equations are still difficult to solve because the spontaneous emission term $J_{sp,q}^{\pm}$ is a function of $E_q^{\pm}$ and the term $\Delta\beta_q$ is a function of the carrier density. As a result, the coupled-mode equations are nonlinear, and the $\Delta\beta_q$ term causes interdependence on the carrier density and field intensity in the cavity. Because the light intensity is spatially dependent, the carrier density is also spatially dependent. This spatial dependence of the carrier density on the photon intensity is called **spatial hole burning** [4].

13.2 THRESHOLD SOLUTIONS

The steady state computations can be simplified by first computing the threshold gain required for each mode. The required threshold gain is the necessary medium gain from stimulated emission to sustain a given mode against cavity loss. At the threshold, the field intensity is negligible. Therefore, the carrier density is a constant. As a result, from Equation

(13.5), $\Delta\beta$ is a constant. To further simplify the equations, neglect the small spontaneous emission term $J_{sp,q}$. This makes the equations linear, so they can be solved analytically.

With the above assumptions, Equations (13.18) and (13.19) reduce to first-order linear differential equations. From the basic linear differential equation theory, $E_q^{\pm}(z)$ can be expressed as linear combinations of $e^{\pm\gamma z}$, where γ is a certain spatial constant in the z direction to be determined. Taking boundary conditions into consideration, $E_q^{\pm}$ can be expressed as

$$E_q^+(z) = A\sinh[\gamma(z+z_0)] + r_L D\sinh[\gamma(z-L+z_0)] \qquad \textbf{[13.20]}$$

and

$$E_q^-(z) = Ar_R\sinh[\gamma(z+z_0)] + D\sinh[\gamma(z-L+z_0)] \qquad \textbf{[13.21]}$$

where A and D are unknown coefficients to be solved, and r_L and r_R are the reflection coefficients defined earlier.

As shown in Appendix 13–B, γ can be solved by substituting $E_q^{\pm}(z)$ given by Equations (13.20) and (13.21) into the coupled-mode equations (13.18) and (13.19). The result is

$$-\frac{\gamma^2}{\sinh^2(\gamma L)} + \gamma^2\frac{4r_L r_R}{(1+r_L r_R)^2}\frac{\cosh^2(\gamma L)}{\sinh^2(\gamma L)} - \frac{2\gamma(1-r_L r_R)}{(1+r_L r_R)^2}(j\kappa^+ r_R + j\kappa^- r_L)\frac{\cosh(\gamma L)}{\sinh(\gamma L)}$$

$$-\frac{1}{(1+r_L r_R)^2}(j\kappa^+ r_R + j\kappa^- r_L)^2 = \kappa^+\kappa^-. \qquad \textbf{[13.22]}$$

Equation (13.22) shows γ is a function of $\kappa^- r_L$, $\kappa^+ r_R$, $\kappa^+\kappa^-$, and $r_L r_R$, which are all z_0 independent. With γ solved, from Appendix 13–B, $\Delta\beta_q$ can be obtained from the following **dispersion equation:**

$$(\Delta\beta_q)^2 + \gamma^2 = \kappa^+\kappa^-. \qquad \textbf{[13.23]}$$

According to Equation (13.5), the real part of $\Delta\beta_q$ represents the emission frequency shift from the Bragg frequency, and the imaginary part represents the required medium gain.

According to Equations (13.15)–(13.17), γ depends on the magnitudes of the reflection coefficients, the coupling phase θ_k, and reflection coefficient phase $\beta_B L$. To explain the characteristics of DFB lasers from Equation (13.22), three important types are discussed below.

The first type has simple cleaving at both of its cavity ends. The magnitude of their reflection coefficients is

$$|r_L| = |r_R| = \frac{n_b - 1}{n_b + 1} \qquad \textbf{[13.24]}$$

where n_b is the dielectric constant of the cavity.

The second type has one cleaved cavity end and one zero-reflection end. The zero-reflection end can be made by either antireflection (AR) coating or a window structure, as shown in Figure 13.1 [5]. As shown, InP is used as an intermediate layer between the InGaAsP laser cavity and the air. Because the interface between InP and InGaAsP forms a heterostructure (see Chapter 3), carriers in the cavity can be confined. To further limit the current flow through the active layer, an additional n-InP structure is used. At the same time, because InP and InGaAsP have very close refractive indices, there is negligible reflection at the interface. Although there is reflection at the air-InP interface, the round-trip path from the InP–InGaAsP interface, through the InP intermediate layer, reflected at the air–InP interface, and back to InGaAsP has a large attenuation because of diffraction [5]. As a result, by having a large width of the InP intermediate layer, effective reflectivity can be greatly reduced.

The third type has zero reflection at both of its facets. Similar to the second type, this can be done by having either AR coating or a double window structure. Next, the threshold characteristics of these three types are discussed in detail.

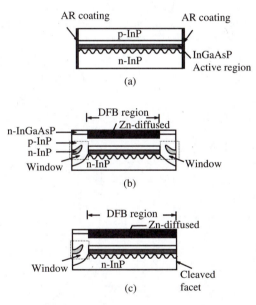

Figure 13.1　DFB lasers: (*a*) zero reflection at two ends attained with antireflection coating; (*b*) zero reflection at both ends attained with a double-window structure, where InP is used as the transparent material for its larger bandgap (the additional structures, such as Zn-diffusion on the top and n-InP at the two sides, are used for carrier confinement); (*c*) single-window structure, where one of the facets has a window structure and the other is done by simple cleaving.

13.2.1 ZERO-REFLECTION DFB LASERS

The first type of DFB laser considered has zero reflection at both its ends (i.e., $r_L = r_R = 0$). This is the case considered in the pioneering work by Kogelnik and Shank [6]. Equation (13.22) in this case reduces to

$$-\frac{\gamma^2}{\sinh^2(\gamma L)} = \kappa^+\kappa^-. \qquad\qquad \textbf{[13.25]}$$

By solving for γ in terms of the coupling constants and then using the dispersion equation (13.23), one can find $\Delta\beta_q$. The results are shown in Figure 13.2. Each curve in the figure corresponds to one longitudinal mode. Figure 13.2 suggests the following observations.

1. All longitudinal modes are symmetric about the Bragg frequency.[3] That is, for a longitudinal mode on the right of the Bragg frequency, there is a corresponding mode on the left with the same threshold gain and the same amount of frequency shift. This symmetry can also be observed from Equation (13.25).

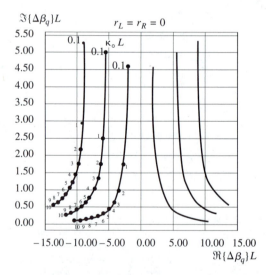

Figure 13.2   Threshold gains versus normalized frequency shift from the Bragg frequency of longitudinal modes of zero-reflection DFB lasers. $r_L = r_R = 0$.

---

[3] For convenience, the output is said to be "at" the Bragg frequency if $\Re\{\Delta\beta_q\} = 0$. This same terminology is used in the subsequent discussion, although there is a shift because α_{lw} is nonzero, as Equation (13.5) shows.

2. Equation (13.25) shows that γ cannot be either purely real or purely imaginary, because $\kappa^+\kappa^-$ is real and positive. Thus according to the dispersion equation, $\Delta\beta_q$ cannot be purely imaginary. This implies there is a nonzero frequency offset from the Bragg frequency for each longitudinal mode.

3. The required threshold gain decreases as the magnitude of the coupling constant increases. Because the main modes are those that have the lowest threshold gain, there are two main modes at the center and symmetric with respect to the Bragg frequency.

4. The separation of longitudinal modes on each side of the Bragg frequency is $|\beta_{q+1} - \beta_q|L \approx \pi$. This is consistent with the longitudinal mode condition discussed in Chapter 3. This mode separation is closer to π as the coupling constant decreases, which approaches the limit of Fabry-Perot lasers.

DIFFERENTIAL THRESHOLD GAIN From Figure 13.2, at $\kappa_0 L = 2.0$, the normalized threshold gain $\Im(\Delta\beta_q)L$ of the two main modes is 1.0, and the next two sides have a normalized threshold gain of 1.75. This represents a difference of 0.75 of the normalized threshold gain. The power gain difference over one trip of the cavity is

Example 13.4

$$e^{2\Im(\Delta\beta_q)L} = 10^{\Delta g_{dB}L/10}$$

where $\Delta g_{dB}L$ is the differential power gain in dB. By simple manipulation,

$$\Delta g_{dB}L = 2 \times 10\log_{10}(e) \times \Im(\Delta\beta_q)L = 8.68 \times \Im(\Delta\beta_q)L = 6.51 \text{ dB.}$$

This difference is large enough to suppress all side modes. As the normalized coupling constant increases, the differential gain decreases. This means there can be an optimal coupling constant for the maximum differential gain. ∎

13.2.2 SINGLE-WINDOW DFB LASERS

Because one important objective of using DFB lasers is to have only one longitudinal mode, the fact that zero-reflection DFB lasers have two main modes is undesirable. This can be solved by introducing some asymmetry in the cavity. The $\lambda/4$-shift DFB is one example [7]–[9]; its theory is explained in the next subsection.

The second type of DFB laser considered has only one facet of zero reflection, say $r_R = 0$. In this case, the longitudinal modes are no longer symmetric with respect to the Bragg frequency. Figure 13.1c illustrates its practical implementation. Equation (13.22) in this case reduces to

$$-\frac{\gamma^2}{\sinh^2(\gamma L)} - 2j\kappa^- r_L\gamma \frac{\cosh(\gamma L)}{\sinh(\gamma L)} + (\kappa^- r_L)^2 = \kappa^+\kappa^-. \qquad \textbf{[13.26]}$$

Some solutions to Equation (13.26) are shown in Figures 13.3 through 13.6. Figure 13.3 shows the dependence of $\Delta\beta_q$ on the phase $\Delta\beta_B L$ of the reflection coefficient r_L.

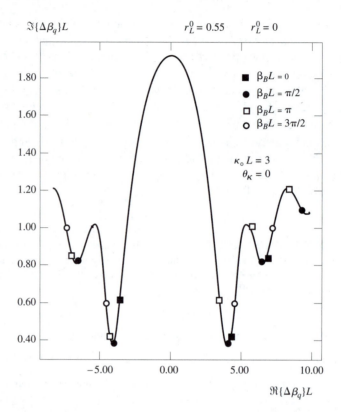

Figure 13.3   Dependence of the threshold gain and normalized frequency shift on the phase shift $\beta_B L$; $r_L^0 = 0.55$ and $r_R^0 = 0$.

Note that there are multiple solutions at the same phase $\Delta \beta_B L$, each of which corresponds to one longitudinal mode.

Figures 13.4 through 13.6 show how $\Delta \beta_q$ depends on the magnitude of the coupling constants $|\kappa^{\pm}|$, where the $\beta_B L$ values used are π, $5\pi/4$, and $3\pi/2$, respectively. In these figures, each curve corresponds to a longitudinal mode and the $\kappa_O L$ value is in the range from 0.1 to 10. Some important observations from these curves are summarized below.

1. As Figure 13.3 shows, the longitudinal modes depend strongly on the phase term of $\kappa^{-} r_L$. In this single-window type of DFB laser, all modes can be obtained by scanning the $\beta_B L$ value.

2. In general, depending on the phase of $\beta_B L$, the longitudinal modes are not necessarily symmetric about the Bragg frequency. Figures 13.4 and 13.5 show that only one main mode with the minimum threshold gain is possible.

3. In Figure 13.3, there is a solution that has zero frequency shift at $\beta_B L = 3\pi/2$ when $\theta_k = 0$. As Figure 13.6 shows, all the modes are symmetric with the center one at the exact

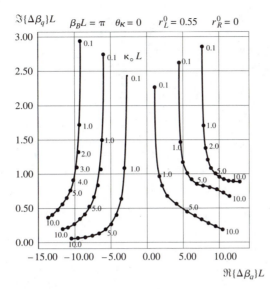

Figure 13.4   Dependence of the threshold gain and normalized frequency shift on the coupling constant κ_0, where $\theta_k = 0$ and $\beta_B L = \pi$; $r_L^0 = 0.55$ and $r_R^0 = 0$.

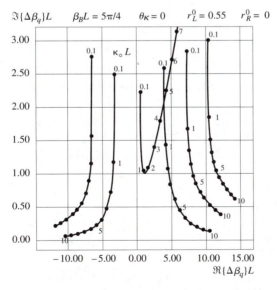

Figure 13.5   Dependence of the threshold gain and normalized frequency shift on the coupling constant κ_0, where $\theta_k = 0$ and $\beta_B L = 5\pi/4$; $r_L^0 = 0.55$ and $r_R^0 = 0$.

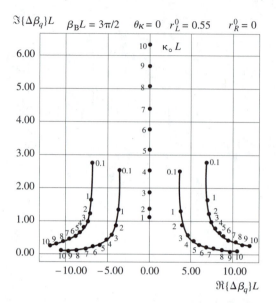

Figure 13.6   Dependence of the threshold gain and normalized frequency shift on the coupling constant κ_0, where $\theta_k = 0$ and $\beta_B L = 3\pi/2$; $r_L^0 = 0.55$ and $r_R^0 = 0$.

Bragg frequency. In general, depending on κ_0, the center mode is not necessarily the main mode. When $\kappa_0 L \leq 1$, it is the main mode of the minimum required gain. Once $\kappa_0 L \geq 2$, however, it has a higher required gain and is no longer the main mode. As a result, there are two main modes.

4. In Figures 13.4, 13.5, and 13.6, the solutions depend strongly on the magnitude of the coupling constant. For most modes, the required threshold gain increases as the magnitude of the coupling constants decreases. For some cases, such as in Figures 13.5 and 13.6, however, the required threshold gain of the center mode increases as coupling increases. Thus the main mode changes as coupling increases.

5. Equation (13.26) indicates that the dependence of the longitudinal modes on the phase of the coupling constant κ^- is similar to the dependence on the phase of the reflectivity r_L. More specifically, the solution is the same at the same $\theta_k + \beta_B L$ value.

13.2.3 $\lambda/4$-SHIFT DFB LASERS

For the single-window DFB lasers, consider a special case where $\theta_k = \pi/2$, $r_L^0 > 0$, and $\beta_B L$ is a multiple of 2π. According to Equation (13.16), this is equivalent to the case

$\theta_k = 0$, $\beta_B L = 3\pi/2$, and $r_L^0 > 0$. As shown in Figure 13.6, where $r_L^0 = 0.55$, there is a longitudinal mode at the Bragg frequency; however, it is a main mode only when κ_0 is small.

This special case is interesting because it reveals the possibility of single main mode output at the Bragg frequency. Therefore, it deserves more attention. First, assuming $\theta_k = \pi/2$, $r_L^0 > 0$, and $\beta_B L = 2m\pi$ (m is an integer), Equation (13.26) reduces to

$$-\frac{\gamma^2}{\sinh^2(\gamma L)} + 2\kappa_0 r_L^0 \gamma \frac{\cosh(\gamma L)}{\sinh(\gamma L)} - (\kappa_0 r_L^0)^2 = \kappa_0^2$$

or

$$\frac{\gamma^2}{\sinh^2(\gamma L)} - 2\kappa_0 r_L^0 \gamma \frac{\cosh(\gamma L)}{\sinh(\gamma L)} + [1 + (r_L^0)^2]\kappa_0^2 = 0. \qquad \textbf{[13.27]}$$

From this equation, a real solution γ can exist, which means there can be an output mode at the Bragg frequency.

Careful examination also reveals the dependence of $\Delta\beta$ on κ_0. First note from Equation (13.27) that $\gamma \to \infty$ as $\kappa_0 \to \infty$. When $\gamma \to \infty$, $\gamma/\sinh(\gamma) \to 0$ and $\cosh(\gamma L)/\sinh(\gamma L) \to 1$. Therefore, Equation (13.27) reduces to

$$\gamma = \frac{1 + (r_L^0)^2}{2r_L^0}\kappa_0 \qquad \text{when } \kappa_0 \gg 1.$$

Thus, from Equation (13.23),

$$\Delta\beta_q^2 = \kappa_0^2 - \gamma^2 = -\left[\frac{1 - (r_L^0)^2}{r_L^0}\right]^2 \kappa_0^2 \qquad \text{when } \kappa_0 \gg 1. \qquad \textbf{[13.28]}$$

Equation (13.27) says that (1) $\Delta\beta_q$ is purely imaginary and (2) the threshold gain increases when κ_0 increases except when $r_0 = 1$. This is what Figure 13.6 shows, where $r_L^0 < 1$.

To have the threshold gain increase as the coupling increases, r_L^0 must equal 1. In this case, $\Delta\beta_q^2$ can approach zero as $(\kappa_0 L)^2 \gg 1$. This is the case, as Figure 13.7 shows. Thus the special case $r_L^0 = 1$ is important because it can always result in a main mode at the Bragg frequency.

A DFB laser diode that has $\beta_B L = 0$, $\theta_k = -\pi/2$, and $r_L^0 = 1$ is shown in Figure 13.8a. Because the left-hand end of the cavity is simply a mirror when $r_L^0 = 1$, it is an equivalent zero-reflection DFB laser with a phase shift of $\pi/2$ from the center on both sides. As illustrated in Figure 13.8b, this phase-shift DFB laser is called a $\lambda/4$-shift DFB because of its $\pi/2$ phase shift with respect to a zero-phase DFB laser shown in Figure 13.8c.

DIFFERENTIAL THRESHOLD GAINS OF $\lambda/4$-DFB   From Figure 13.7, the normalized threshold gain difference between the main mode and the first side mode at $\kappa_0 L = 0.1$ is

$$(\alpha_1 - \alpha_0)L = 2.2 - 1.8 = 0.4.$$

The difference at $\kappa_0 L = 1$ is

$$(\alpha_1 - \alpha_0)L = 1.02 - 0.35 = 0.67$$

Example 13.5

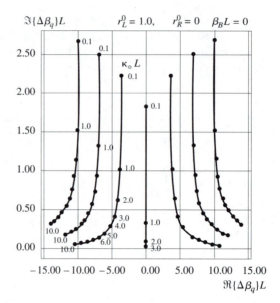

Figure 13.7 Dependence of the threshold gain and normalized frequency shift on the coupling constant κ_0, where $\theta_k = \pi/2$ and $\beta_B L = 0$; $r_L^0 = 1.0$ and $r_R^0 = 0$.

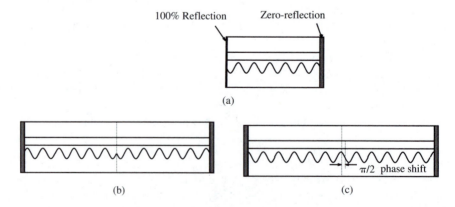

Figure 13.8 $\lambda/4$-phase-shift DFB lasers: (a) DFB laser with $\theta_k = \pi/2$, zero reflection at its right end, and 100 percent reflection at its left end; (b) $\lambda/4$-phase-shift DFB laser, which is equivalent to (a) because of mirror symmetry; (c) regular DFB laser with $\theta_k = 0$.

and the difference at $\kappa_0 L = 2$ is

$$(\alpha_1 - \alpha_0)L = 0.63 - 0.07 = 0.56.$$

As $\kappa_0 L$ continues to increase, the threshold difference decreases. From this, note that (1) the main mode is always at the Bragg frequency and (2) the maximum gain difference is around $\kappa_0 L = 1$. ∎

13.2.4 DOUBLE-CLEAVED DFB LASERS

Another common type of DFB laser has nonzero reflection coefficients at its two facets or $|r_L| = |r_R| \neq 0$. As mentioned earlier, this type of DFB laser can be fabricated by simply cleaving the two cavity ends.

Figure 13.9 shows the dependence of the longitudinal modes on the phase of the reflection coefficients (see Equation 13.22). Figures 13.10–13.12 show the dependence of $\Delta\beta_q$ on the magnitude of the coupling constant at different phases of the reflectivity. Figure 13.13 shows the dependence of $\Delta\beta_q$ on the phase of the coupling constant. These figures suggest the following observations.

1. Similar to the previous two cases, the longitudinal modes are strongly dependent on the magnitude of the coupling constants.

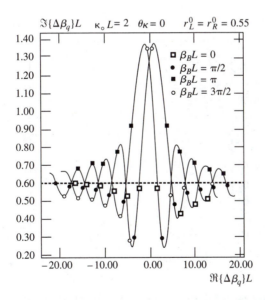

Figure 13.9 Dependence of the threshold gain and normalized frequency shift on the phase shift of $\beta_B L$, where $\kappa_0 L = 2$ and $\theta_K = 0; r_L^0 = r_R^0 = 0.55$.

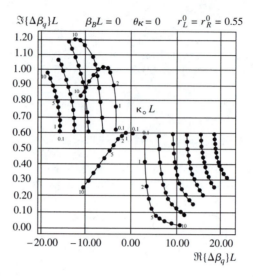

Figure 13.10 Dependence of the threshold gain and normalized frequency shift on the coupling constant κ_0, where $\theta_k = 0$ and $\beta_B L = 0$; $r_L^0 = r_R^0 = 0.55$.

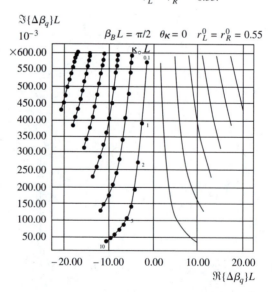

Figure 13.11 Dependence of the threshold gain and normalized frequency shift on the coupling constant κ_0, where $\theta_k = 0$ and $\beta_B L = \pi/2$; $r_L^0 = r_R^0 = 0.55$.

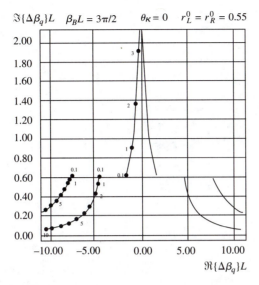

$\Im\{\Delta\beta_q\}L$ $\beta_B L = 3\pi/2$ $\theta_\kappa = 0$ $r_L^0 = r_R^0 = 0.55$

$\Re\{\Delta\beta_q\}L$

Figure 13.12   Dependence of the threshold gain and normalized frequency shift on the coupling constant κ_0, where $\theta_k = 0$ and $\beta_B L = 3\pi/2$; $r_L^0 = r_R^0 = 0.55$.

2. Similar to the single-window type DFB lasers, the required threshold gain for some modes can increase as the magnitude of the coupling constant increases.

3. The modes are in general asymmetric with respect to the Bragg frequency. As shown in Figures 13.11 and 13.12, however, they are symmetric at $\beta_B L = \pi/4$ and $3\pi/4$, respectively. At these phases all the coefficients of γ in Equation (13.22) are real.

4. When $\beta_B L$ is a multiple of 2π, as shown in Figure 13.10, side modes on the right hand of the Bragg frequency have smaller threshold gains than those on the left. In this case, therefore, the most important modes are above the Bragg frequency.

5. Figures 13.10–13.12 show that the required threshold gains of all modes approach 0.598 as the magnitude of the coupling constants approaches zero. This limiting value is equal to $-\ln(|r_L||r_R|)/2.0$. Equation (3.11) indicates that this is half of the required gain to overcome the mirror loss in FP laser diodes. This is consistent with the definition of the threshold gain given by the imaginary part of Equation (13.5).

6. Figure 13.13 shows that the phase of the coupling constant has negligible effect on the phase shifts of longitudinal modes; however, it can significantly affect the required threshold gain.

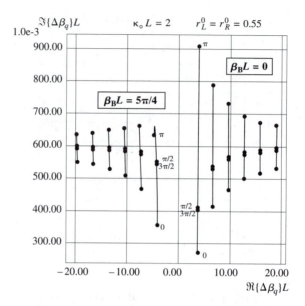

Figure 13.13   Dependence of the threshold gain and normalized frequency shift on the phase of the coupling constant κ_0, where $\kappa_0 L = 2$ and $\beta_B L$ is 0 on the right and $5\pi/4$ on the left of the Bragg frequency; $r_L^0 = r_R^0 = 0.55$.

13.3   DIRECT CURRENT CHARACTERISTICS

The threshold solutions obtained from Equations (13.23) and (13.22) give the emission frequency and the required threshold gain of each mode at $J = J_{th}$. This section explains how the carrier density and longitudinal modes interact with one another at different bias current levels.

To proceed, first note that the rate equations (13.18) and (13.19) plus the carrier density rate equation (12.30) are nonlinear once the field intensity becomes nonzero. Therefore, there is no simple expression for each longitudinal mode as a function of the bias current density. To discuss various important concepts thus requires using numerical computation to find the solutions. In the following, some important dc characteristics of DFB lasers are discussed. For illustration, the parameter values of a typical DFB laser given in Table 13.1 are used.

Threshold Current   The imaginary part of $\Delta\beta_q$ given by Equation (13.5) shows that the required carrier density can be determined from the required threshold gain. Specifically, if $\Im\{\Delta\beta_q\} \overset{\text{def}}{=} \alpha_q$ of the main mode at the threshold is known, the corresponding carrier density N can be calculated. Let α_0 be the threshold gain of the main mode. The carrier density at the threshold is

$$N_{th} \overset{\text{def}}{=} \frac{2\alpha_0 + \alpha_{int}}{\Gamma a} + N_0 \qquad \text{[13.29]}$$

and the corresponding current density from Equation (12.30) is

$$J_{th} \overset{\text{def}}{=} qd(AN_{th} + BN_{th}^2 + CN_{th}^3). \qquad \text{[13.30]}$$

From the above equations, note that N_{th} and J_{th} depend only on the main mode that has the smallest threshold gain obtained from the threshold analysis. Also note from the earlier discussion that the main mode strongly depends on the phase term $\beta_B L$ and the magnitude and phase of the coupling constants $\kappa^{\pm}$. Therefore, in practical DFB diode fabrication, the threshold current and the main mode may vary greatly. This results in a low yield of low threshold DFB laser diodes. Table 13.2 gives some numerical computation results for the threshold carrier density and current density.

Table 13.2 Some computation results of the threshold carrier density and current density.

$\kappa_0 L$	$|r_L|$	$|r_R|$	N_{th} $(1/\text{cm}^3)$	$J_{th}(\text{A/cm}^2)$
2.0	0.556	0.556	1.235×10^{18}	2.644×10^3
1.0	0.556	0.556	1.306×10^{18}	2.848×10^3
2.0	0.0	0.556	1.437×10^{18}	3.244×10^3
1.0	0.0	0.556	1.598×10^{18}	3.764×10^3
2.0	0.0	0.0	1.578×10^{18}	3.700×10^3

Find the threshold current of a DFB diode with parameters given in Table 13.1 and the fifth row of Table 13.2. Because $\alpha_0 L = 1.0$ at $\kappa_0 L = 2.0$ from Figure 13.2, the threshold gain of the main mode is

Example 13.6

$$\alpha_0 = \frac{1.0}{500 \times 10^{-4}} = 20 \text{ cm}^{-1}.$$

From Equation (13.29),

$$N_{th} = \frac{2\alpha_0 + \alpha_{int}}{\Gamma a} + N_0 = \frac{40 + 4}{0.3 \times 2.5 \times 10^{-16}} + 1 \times 10^{18} = 1.59 \times 10^{18} \text{ cm}^{-3}.$$

Therefore, from Equation (13.30),

$$J_{th} = qd(A + BN_{th} + CN_{th}^2)N_{th} = 3738 \text{ mA/cm}^2$$

and

$$I_{th} = wLJ_{th} = 93 \text{ mA}.$$

These results are consistent with those given in Table 13.2. ∎

Side Modes   The previous discussion considered only one mode. All other modes cannot exist because they require a higher threshold gain. From Equations (13.29) and (13.30), only the main mode that has the minimum threshold can start to emit at N_{th} and J_{th}. When J continues to increase, N is still around N_{th} because any additional N will be suppressed by stimulated emission (see Equation [12.30]). Consequently, all other modes still cannot be excited.

In reality, however, there are side modes. This is because there is additional gain contribution from spontaneous emission (i.e., $\beta_{sp} > 0$). As Equations (13.3) and (13.4) show, the spontaneous emission contribution is included through the terms $J_{sp,q}^{\pm}$. The definition given in Equation (13.7) indicates that $J_{sp,q}^{\pm}$ contribute to the total gain of the fields $E_q^{\pm}$ in their corresponding propagation directions. Therefore, they make up additional gain for side modes at the threshold. Because $J_{sp,q}^{\pm}$ is inversely proportional to $|E_q^{\pm}|^2$, the larger the $J_{sp,q}^{\pm}$ value required for the additional gain, the smaller the power $|E_q^{\pm}|^2$.

From the above observation, the side mode power can be estimated if it is assumed that the spatial dependence of the field intensity is small. That is, the field intensity is constant or

$$|E_q|^2 = |E_q^+(z)|^2 = |E_q^-(z)|^2.$$

At a high power level, the spatial hole burning effect is strong, and this spatial independence assumption may not be accurate. Under this assumption, Equations (13.3)–(13.5) lead to the following equality for each mode:

$$\frac{1}{2}[-\alpha_{int} + \Gamma a(N - N_0)] + J_{sp,q} = \frac{1}{2}[-\alpha_{int} + \Gamma a(N - N_0)] + \frac{I_{sp}}{|E_q|^2} = \alpha_q. \quad \textbf{[13.31]}$$

From the definition of N_{th}, the main mode has the following field density at a given $\Delta N \overset{\text{def}}{=} N_{th} - N$:

$$|E_0|^2 = \frac{2I_{sp}}{\Gamma a \Delta N}. \quad \textbf{[13.32]}$$

This equation says that (1) $\Delta N = N_{th} - N$ is always positive for finite output power, and (2) the output intensity is inversely proportional to ΔN. Therefore, the carrier density is always smaller than N_{th}; and the larger the output power, the closer N is to N_{th}. For side modes,

$$|E_q|^2 = \frac{I_{sp}}{\alpha_q - \alpha_0 + \Gamma a \Delta N/2}. \quad \textbf{[13.33]}$$

From Equations (13.32) and (13.33), the side-mode suppression ratio is given by

$$\frac{|E_0|^2}{|E_q|^2} = 1 + (\alpha_q - \alpha_0)\frac{|E_0|^2}{I_{sp}}. \quad \textbf{[13.34]}$$

Thus the larger the field intensity of the main mode, the larger the mode suppression. This is similar to what was discussed in the case of FP lasers. The difference is that side modes in DFB lasers are suppressed by the differential threshold gains $\alpha_q - \alpha_0$, and in FP lasers they are suppressed by the nonconstant gain profile.

REQUIRED MAIN MODE POWER FOR SIDE MODE SUPPRESSION Consider a zero-reflection DFB of $\kappa_0 L = 2.0$. Figure 13.2 shows that $\alpha_1 - \alpha_0 = 0.75/L$ between the main mode and the first side mode. A 20 dB side-mode suppression, according to Equation (13.34), thus requires approximately

Example 13.7

$$\frac{|E_0|^2}{I_{sp}} = \frac{99}{0.75}L = 130L.$$

If $I_{sp} = 0.1$ W/m and $L = 500\ \mu$m,

$$|E_0|^2 = 6.5 \text{ mW.} \ \blacksquare$$

Power–Current Characteristics In Figures 13.14–13.18, the output power of different longitudinal modes versus the bias current is shown for different coupling and reflection coefficients. Because the output power is defined to be either $|E_q^-(0)|^2$ or $|E_q^+(L)|^2$, an additional factor $1 - |r_L|^2$ or $1 - |r_R|^2$ must be multiplied to get the "true" output power.

In Figures 13.14, 13.16 and 13.18, multimode outputs are shown. One single mode dominates once the current is above the threshold current. Note that in Figure 13.18 there are two main modes at and below the threshold.

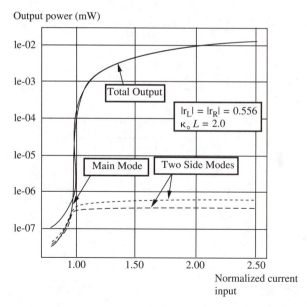

Figure 13.14 Multimode output $|E_q^-(0)|^2$ versus dc bias current.

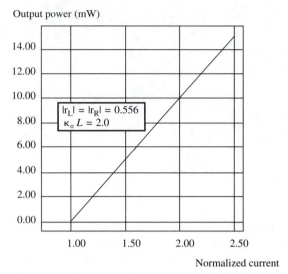

Figure 13.15   Total $|E_q^-(0)|^2$ power versus dc bias current.

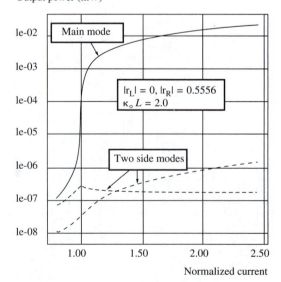

Figure 13.16   Multimode output $|E_q^-(0)|^2$ versus dc bias current.

Output power (mW)

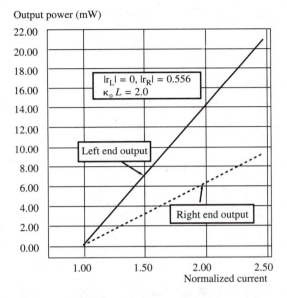

Figure 13.17 Total $|E_q^-(0)|^2$ power versus dc bias current.

Output power (mW)

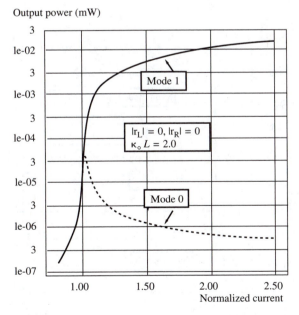

Figure 13.18 Two main-mode output power versus dc bias current.

In Figures 13.15 and 13.17, the total output power is linearly proportional to the bias current beyond the threshold current. The power–current slopes for different parameter values from computation are given in Table 13.3.

Table 13.3 Computation results of the power–current slope.

$\kappa_0 L$	$|r_L|$	$|r_R|$	$(1 - |r_L|^2) \times |E_q^-(0)|^2/(J - J_{th})$ $[\text{W} \cdot \text{cm}^2/\text{A}]$	$(1 - |r_R|^2) \times |E_q^+(L)|^2/(J - J_{th})$ $[\text{W} \cdot \text{cm}^2/\text{A}]$
2.0	0.556	0.556	2.61×10^{-6}	2.61×10^{-6}
1.0	0.556	0.556	2.81×10^{-6}	2.81×10^{-6}
2.0	0.0	0.556	4.50×10^{-6}	1.41×10^{-6}
1.0	0.0	0.556	2.66×10^{-6}	2.94×10^{-6}
2.0	0.0	0.0	3.18×10^{-6}	3.18×10^{-6}

Output Frequency versus Bias Current   A typical dependence of the propagation constant β_q of each mode on the bias current is shown in Figure 13.19. Note that the output frequency (linearly proportional to β_q) decreases in both directions from the threshold current, although the slope is smaller above the threshold. This property is different from Fabry-Perot lasers, where the frequency is essentially a constant above the threshold

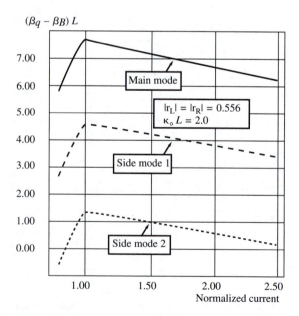

Figure 13.19   Normalized propagation constant.

current. This new frequency dependence comes from the spatial hole burning effect, where the carrier density is a function of the longitudinal field intensity distribution.

Field Distribution   Some typical power distributions of the main mode(s) are shown in Figures 13.20–13.22 for different coupling and reflection coefficients. From these figures, note that the power distributions over the laser cavity are quite different at different parameter values and at different bias currents. In general, the power distribution depends on the corresponding eigenvalue γ of the mode, which in turn strongly depends on the reflection and coupling constants.

Carrier Density Distribution   The carrier density distributions over the laser diode cavity for various coupling and reflection coefficients are shown in Figures 13.23–13.25. These figures show that the carrier density is modulated by the field intensity over the cavity. This demonstrates the spatial hole burning effect.

Note that when the cavity is symmetric, or $|r_L| = |r_R|$, total power is higher in the center of the cavity. Therefore, the carrier density is minimum in the center because of Equation (12.30). This can be clearly seen from Figures 13.23 and 13.25. When the laser cavity is asymmetric, carrier distribution is assymetric. This can be seen in Figure 13.24.

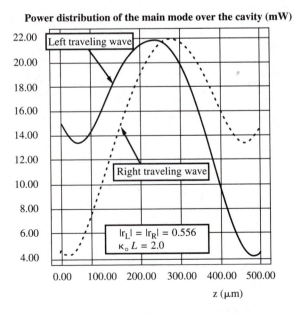

Power distribution of the main mode over the cavity (mW)

Left traveling wave

Right traveling wave

$|r_L| = |r_R| = 0.556$
$\kappa_o L = 2.0$

z (μm)

Figure 13.20   Power distribution of the main mode over the cavity. $I = 2.5 I_{th}$.

Power distribution of the main mode over the cavity (mW)

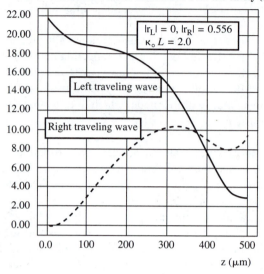

Figure 13.21 Power distribution of the main mode over the cavity. $I = 2.5I_{th}$.

Power distribution over the cavity of mode 1 (mW)

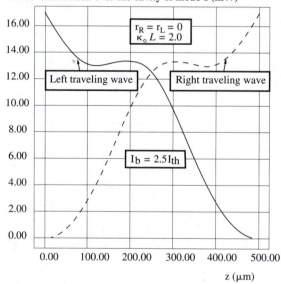

Figure 13.22 Power distribution of the main mode over the cavity. $I = 2.5I_{th}$.

Carrier density distribution over the cavity
in 1e18 1/cm^3

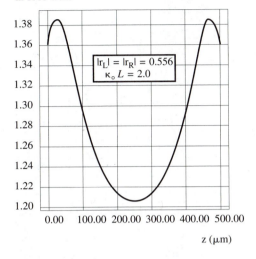

$|r_L| = |r_R| = 0.556$
$\kappa_o L = 2.0$

z (μm)

Figure 13.23 Carrier density distribution over the cavity.

Carrier density distribution over the cavity
in 1.0e18 1/cm^3

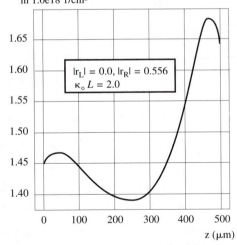

$|r_L| = 0.0, |r_R| = 0.556$
$\kappa_o L = 2.0$

z (μm)

Figure 13.24 Carrier density distribution over the cavity.

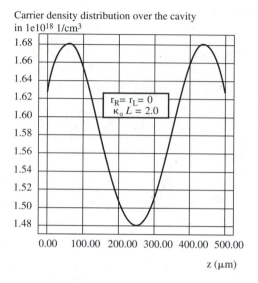

Carrier density distribution over the cavity
in 1e10^18 1/cm^3

$r_R = r_L = 0$
$\kappa_o L = 2.0$

z (μm)

Figure 13.25   Carrier density distribution over the cavity.

Trade-offs of Different DFB Designs

From the above discussion on the emission frequencies and threshold gains of different DFB designs, a trade-off summary is given in Table 13.4.

Table 13.4   Trade-offs summary of different DFB laser diode designs.

Types	Advantages	Disadvantages
Zero-reflection	1. Emission wavelengths and threshold gains independent of the phases $\beta_B L$ and θ_k.	1. Two main modes. 2. AR coating or window structure required. 3. High threshold gains.
Single-window	1. Possible single-mode emission. 2. Possible emission at the Bragg frequency.	1. AR coating or window structure required. 2. Emission wavelengths and threshold gains sensitive. to the phase $\theta_k + \beta_B L$.
Double-cleaved	1. Low threshold gains. 2. Simple cleaving implementation. 3. Possible single mode emission.	1. Emission wavelengths and threshold gains very sensitive to the phases θ_k and $\beta_B L$. 3. Possible mode switching as $\kappa_0 L$ varies slightly.
λ/4-shifted	1. Single-mode emission at the Bragg frequency. 2. Moderate threshold gains.	1. AR coating or window structure required. 2. Precision lithography and cleaving required.

13.4 MODULATION CHARACTERISTICS

In addition to the dc characteristics discussed, it is also important to know the characteristics of DFB laser diodes under direct modulation. Based on the coupled-mode equations and the carrier density rate equation, the power output and emission wavelength can be solved numerically as a function of time. For digital and analog communications, two types of modulation are considered below: pulse input and single-tone input.

13.4.1 PULSE MODULATION

In digital communications, the diode is turned on and off according to the input data. The modulation output of an individual pulse input is thus important to know. Below the modulation output of different types of DFB diodes where the bias current is turned on from $0.8I_{th}$ to $1.5I_{th}$ for 3 nsec is discussed.

Output Power   Typical power output from the pulse input is shown in Figures 13.26 and 13.27. These figures show a relaxation oscillation at a frequency around 4 GHz. There is also a large damping constant that quickly brings the oscillation to its steady state. The steady state output power is found to be consistent with the dc analysis results.

When there are two main modes in the case of zero-reflection DFB lasers, note from Figure 13.27 that the two modes can both be strong during the initial turn-on. However, once the steady state is reached, one of the main modes is suppressed by the other.

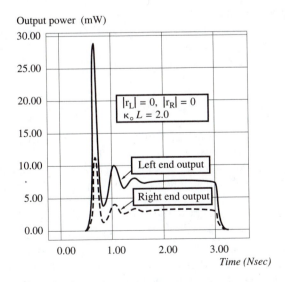

Figure 13.26   Output power due to a pulse input.

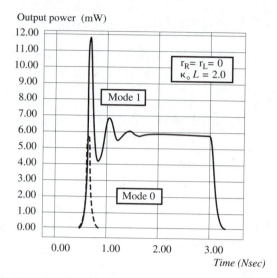

Figure 13.27   Output power due to a pulse input.

Output Frequency   A typical output frequency from the pulse input is shown in Figure 13.28. There is a large damping constant in the frequency oscillation. Interestingly, there is also a small oscillation when the laser is turned off. This is uncommon in normal Fabry-Perot lasers.

Carrier Density Response   A typical carrier density over the cavity due to the pulse input is shown in Figure 13.29. Because of the effect of spatial hole burning, the carrier density shown is an average over the cavity. Comparing these carefully with the output power reveals the push-pull interaction that causes the relaxation oscillation.

13.4.2   SINGLE TONE MODULATION

In addition to pulse modulation in digital communications, DFB diodes can be used for analog communications such as subcarrier multiplexing transmission (SCM). In this case, the output response due to a single-tone input at different modulation index values is important.

The output power from the single-tone input is shown in Figure 13.30. (Figures 13.30 and 13.31 illustrate a single-tone input of 1 GHz with amplitude modulation indices at 0.8, 1.0, and 1.2.) Clearly there is a reasonable sinusoidal output at a modulation index of 0.8. However, when the modulation indices are at 1.0 and 1.2, the input becomes a large signal. Thus there is strong distortion caused by the relaxation oscillation, as in the case of pulse modulation.

Figure 13.31 shows the normalized average carrier density as a function of time. The normalized carrier density is the actual average carrier density divided by N_{th}. Figure 13.31 shows that they are similar in waveform to the output power.

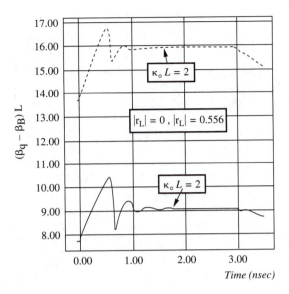

Figure 13.28   Normalized frequency output to a pulse input.

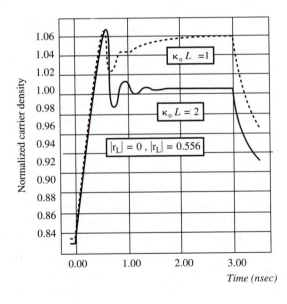

Figure 13.29   Carrier density response to a pulse input.

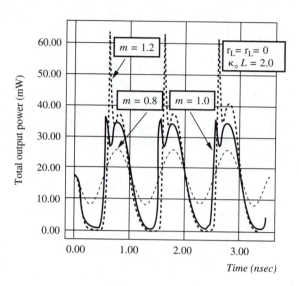

Figure 13.30   Total output power at various modulation indexes.

13.5   SUMMARY

1. Analyzing DFB laser diodes requires using the coupled-mode equations, which describe the interaction of opposite-traveling waves through a periodic structure inside the laser cavity.

2. In general, the coupled-mode equations are nonlinear. They can be made linear, however, if the spontaneous emission contribution is neglected and the diode is operated at its threshold, where the light intensity is zero. The solutions obtained under these conditions give the threshold gain required for each mode and the frequency shift from the Bragg frequency. The mode that has the lowest threshold gain is the main mode.

3. The solution of each longitudinal mode also strongly depends on the reflection coefficient at the two cavity ends and the phase shift of the corrugation structure of the DFB diode. In general, they should be carefully controlled to give low-threshold-current DFB lasers. Practical fabrication limitations to control the phase shift of the corrugation structure and the length of the cavity can cause a low yield rate of low-threshold DFB lasers.

4. Depending on the reflection coefficients at the two cavity ends, there are three important types of DFB lasers: zero-reflection, single-window, and double-cleaved. Zero-reflection DFB lasers have zero reflection at both their ends. This can be done by using either AR coating or a double-window structure. Because of symmetry, zero-reflection DFB lasers have two main modes at threshold.

5. Single-window DFB lasers have only one zero-reflection facet, and double-cleaved DFB lasers have both facets of nonzero reflection. Depending on their reflection coeffi-

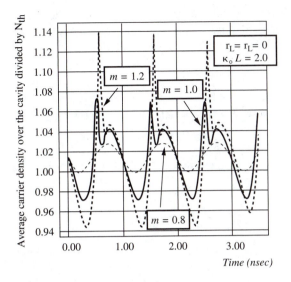

Figure 13.31   Carrier density response to a single-tone input at various modulation indexes.

cients and the phase shift of the corrugation structure, they can have only one main longitudinal mode and have their output at Bragg frequency.

6. The $\lambda/4$-phase-shift DFB laser is a special type of DFB laser that is equivalent to the single-window DFB laser with $\pi/2$ phase shift of its corrugation structure. The primary importance of the $\lambda/4$-phase-shift DFB laser is its single-mode output at the Bragg frequency.

7. When there is no spontaneous emission, side modes that have higher threshold gains cannot exist. Because there is spontaneous emission in reality, however, there are also side modes in the output. The side-mode suppression ratio depends on the difference of the threshold gains between the side modes and the main mode. In general, the larger the difference, the smaller the side modes. Therefore, a good DFB laser should have a large differential threshold gain.

8. When a DFB laser is operated above its threshold current, the field intensity can modulate the carrier density. Because the field intensity is not a constant but a function of z, the carrier density is not uniform along the cavity. This is called the spatial hole burning effect.

9. Similar to FP lasers, the emission frequency of a longitudinal mode is a function of the bias current, and it decreases as the bias current decreases below the threshold. However, different from FP lasers, the emission frequency also slightly decreases as the bias current increases above the threshold. This is in part due to the effect of spatial hole burning.

10. When a DFB laser is modulated by a pulse input, there are relaxation oscillations and chirping similar to the case for FP laser diodes.

11. When a DFB laser is modulated by a single-tone input, the output can have strong distortion when the modulation index is above 0.8. In this case, there is a large signal modulation, and the distortion is due to relaxation oscillation.

APPENDIX 13–A   DISTRIBUTED-FEEDBACK COUPLED-MODE EQUATIONS

This appendix derives the coupled-mode wave equations for DFB laser diodes. To start, here is the wave equation (4.71):

$$\nabla^2 \mathcal{E} - \frac{1}{c^2}\frac{\partial^2}{\partial t^2}\mathcal{E} = \mu \frac{\partial^2}{\partial t^2}\mathcal{P} \qquad \textbf{[13.35]}$$

where μ is the magnetic permeability, $\mathcal{P}$ is the induced polarization given by

$$\mathcal{P}(x, y, z, t) = \epsilon_0 \int \hat{\chi}(x, y, z, t - t')\mathcal{E}(x, y, z, t')dt'$$

and $\hat{\chi}$ is the time-dependent susceptibility (see Appendix 12–A).

Similar to the perturbation method used in Appendix 12–A, let

$$\mathcal{E} = E_T(x, y)\tilde{\mathcal{E}}(z, t)$$

where $E_T(x, y)$ is the transverse mode satisfying

$$\frac{\partial^2 E_T}{\partial x^2} + \frac{\partial^2 E_T}{\partial y^2} + \kappa_{TM}^2 E_T = \frac{\partial^2 E_T}{\partial x^2} + \frac{\partial^2 E_T}{\partial y^2} + \left(\frac{\omega_B^2 \bar{\epsilon}_b}{c^2} - \beta_B^2\right)E_T = 0 \qquad \textbf{[13.36]}$$

with κ_{TM} being the eigenvalue of the transverse mode. Also,

$$\omega_B \overset{\text{def}}{=} \frac{c}{\sqrt{\bar{\epsilon}_b}}\sqrt{\beta_B^2 + \kappa_{TM}^2} \approx \frac{c\beta_B}{n_b} = ck_0$$

is the center carrier frequency close to the Bragg frequency, and $\bar{\epsilon}_b$ is the dielectric constant at ω_B and zero external pumping.

To take forward- and backward-traveling waves into consideration, let

$$\tilde{\mathcal{E}}(z, t) \overset{\text{def}}{=} \Re\left\{\sum_q E_q^+(z, t)e^{j(\omega_q t - \beta_B z)} + \sum_q E_q^-(z, t)e^{j(\omega_q t + \beta_B z)}\right\} \qquad \textbf{[13.37]}$$

where $E_q^+(z, t)$ and $E_q^-(z, t)$ are slowly varying factors in z and t compared to $e^{j(\omega_q t - \beta_B z)}$ or $e^{j(\omega_q t + \beta_B z)}$.

With the above assumptions, the first term of Equation (13.35) becomes

$$\nabla^2 \mathcal{E} = \left(\frac{\partial^2}{\partial x^2} + \frac{\partial^2}{\partial y^2} + \frac{\partial^2}{\partial z^2}\right)\mathcal{E} \approx \left(\frac{\partial^2 E_T}{\partial x^2} + \frac{\partial^2 E_T}{\partial y^2} - \beta_B^2 E_T\right)\tilde{\mathcal{E}}(z, t)$$

$$+ 2E_T(x, y)\Re\left\{-j\sum_q \beta_B \frac{\partial E_q^+}{\partial z} e^{j(\omega_q t - \beta_B z)} + j\sum_q \beta_B \frac{\partial E_q^-}{\partial z} e^{j(\omega_z t + \beta_B z)}\right\}$$

[13.38]

where the second-order terms $\partial^2 E_q^\pm / \partial z^2$ have been dropped. From Equation (13.36),

$$\nabla^2 \mathcal{E} = -\frac{\omega_B^2 \bar{\epsilon}_b}{c^2}\tilde{\mathcal{E}}(z, t)$$

$$+ 2E_T(x, y)\Re\left\{-j\sum_q \beta_B \frac{\partial E_q^+}{\partial z} e^{j(\omega_q t - \beta_B z)} + j\sum_q \beta_B \frac{\partial E_q^-}{\partial z} e^{j(\omega_q t + \beta_B z)}\right\}.$$

[13.39]

The second term of Equation (13.35) on the left is

$$\frac{1}{c^2}\frac{\partial^2 \mathcal{E}}{\partial t^2} = \frac{1}{c^2}E_T(x, y)\frac{\partial^2}{\partial t^2}\tilde{\mathcal{E}}(z, t)$$

$$\approx \frac{E_T(x, y)}{c^2}\mathcal{R}\left\{-\sum_q \omega_q^2 E_q^+(z, t)e^{j(\omega_q t - \beta_B z)} - \sum_q \omega_q^2 E_q^-(z, t)e^{j(\omega_q t + \beta_B z)}\right.$$

$$\left. + 2j\sum_q \frac{\partial E_q^+}{\partial t}\omega_q e^{j(\omega_q t - \beta_B z)} + 2j\sum_q \frac{\partial E_q^-}{\partial t}\omega_q e^{j(\omega_q t + \beta_B z)}\right\}.$$

[13.40]

Here, the second-order terms $\partial^2 E_q^\pm / \partial t^2$ have similarly been dropped.

The term of Equation (13.35) on the right can similarly be treated as in Appendix 12 [10]. That is, from the Taylor series expansion of $\mathcal{E}(x, y, z, t - t')$ with respect to t,

$$\mathcal{P}(x, y, z, t) \approx \epsilon_0 E_T(x, y)\mathcal{R}\left\{\sum_q \left[\int \hat{\chi}(t')e^{-j\omega_q t'}dt'\right]\right.$$

$$\times \left[E_q^+(z, t)e^{j(\omega_q t - \beta_B z)} + E_q^-(z, t)e^{j(\omega_q t + \beta_B z)}\right]$$

$$+ \sum_q \left[\int (-t')\hat{\chi}(t')e^{-j\omega_q t'}dt'\right]$$

$$\left. \times \left[\frac{\partial E_q^+}{\partial t}e^{j(\omega_q t - \beta_B z)} + \frac{\partial E_q^-}{\partial t}e^{j(\omega_q t + \beta_B z)}\right]\right\}$$

$$\approx \epsilon_0 E_T(x, y)\Re\left\{\chi(\omega_q)\tilde{\mathcal{E}} - j\frac{\partial \chi(\omega_q)}{\partial \omega_q}\right.$$

$$\left. \times \sum_q \left[\frac{\partial E_q^+}{\partial t}e^{j(\omega_q t - \beta_B z)} + \frac{\partial E_q^-}{\partial t}e^{j(\omega_q t + \beta_B z)}\right]\right\}.$$

Therefore,

$$\mu \frac{\partial^2}{\partial t^2} \mathcal{P} \approx -\frac{E_T(x, y)}{c^2} \mathcal{R} \left\{ \sum_q \chi(\omega_q) \omega_q^2 \left[E_q^+(z, t) e^{j(\omega_q t - \beta_B z)} + E_q^-(z, t) e^{j(w_q t + \beta_B z)} \right] \right.$$

$$\left. -j \sum_q \left[2\chi(\omega_q) + \omega_q \frac{\partial \chi(\omega_q)}{\partial \omega_q} \right] \omega_q \left[\frac{\partial E_q^+}{\partial t} e^{j(\omega_q t - \beta_B z)} + \frac{\partial E_q^-}{\partial t} e^{j(\omega_q t + \beta_B z)} \right] \right\}$$

$$[\mathbf{13.41}]$$

where higher order terms have all been dropped.

Combining Equations (13.35)–(13.41) gives

$$2 E_T(x, y) \mathfrak{R} \left\{ -j \sum_q \beta_B \frac{\partial E_q^+}{\partial z} e^{j(\omega_q t - \beta_B z)} + j \sum_q \beta_B \frac{\partial E_q^-}{\partial z} e^{j(\omega_q t + \beta_B z)} \right\}$$

$$\approx \frac{E_T(x, y)}{c^2} \mathfrak{R} \left\{ -\sum_q \left[\epsilon_r \omega_q^2 - \bar{\epsilon}_b \omega_B^2 \right] \left[E_q^+(z, t) e^{j(\omega_q t - \beta_B z)} + E_q^-(z, t) e^{j(\omega_q t + \beta_B z)} \right] \right.$$

$$\left. + 2j \sum_q \left[\epsilon_r(\omega) + \frac{\omega_B}{2} \frac{\partial \epsilon_r}{\partial \omega_B} \right] \omega_q \left[\frac{\partial}{\partial t} E_q^+ e^{j(\omega_q t - \beta_B z)} + \frac{\partial}{\partial t} E_q^- e^{j(\omega_q t + \beta_B z)} \right] \right\}$$

$$[\mathbf{13.42}]$$

which uses the fact:

$$2j[1 + \chi(\omega)] + j\omega \frac{\partial \chi(\omega)}{\partial \omega} = 2j \left[\epsilon_r + \frac{\omega}{2} \frac{\partial \epsilon_r(\omega)}{\partial \omega} \right].$$

Because $\epsilon_r \approx \bar{\epsilon}_b = n_b^2$,

$$\epsilon_r + \frac{\omega}{2} \frac{\partial \epsilon_r(\omega)}{\partial \omega} \approx n_b^2 + n_b \omega \frac{\partial n_b}{\partial \omega} = n_b n_g \qquad [\mathbf{13.43}]$$

where $n_g = n_b + \omega \frac{\partial n_b}{\partial \omega}$ is the group velocity refractive index. Because ω_B is close to ω_q,

$$\epsilon_r \omega_q^2 - \bar{\epsilon}_b \omega_B^2 = \left[\bar{\epsilon}_b(\omega_q) + \Delta \epsilon_b + \chi_p' - j\alpha_{int} \frac{n_b}{k_0} + j(\chi_b'' + \chi_p'') \right] \omega_q^2 - \bar{\epsilon}_b(\omega_B) \omega_B^2$$

$$\approx [\Delta \epsilon_b + \chi_p' - j\alpha_{int} \frac{n_b}{k_0} + j(\chi_b'' + \chi_p'')] \omega_B^2 + 2\bar{\epsilon}_b(\omega_q - \omega_B)\omega_B + \frac{\partial \bar{\epsilon}_b}{\partial \omega}(\omega_q - \omega_B)\omega_B^2$$

$$[\mathbf{13.44}]$$

where $\Delta \epsilon_b$ is the periodic change of the refractive index of the DFB laser, and $\epsilon_b(\omega_q) \approx \epsilon_b(\omega_B) + (\omega_q - \omega_B)(\partial \epsilon_b / \partial \omega)$ is used.

For convenience, let

$$\Delta \beta_q \stackrel{\text{def}}{=} \frac{k_0}{n_b} \left(\frac{1}{2} \left[\chi_p' - j\alpha_{int} \frac{n_b}{k_0} + j(\chi_b'' + \chi_p'') \right] + n_b n_g \frac{\omega_q - \omega_B}{\omega_B} \right).$$

Thus, from Equations (13.43) and (13.44),

$$\epsilon_r \omega_q^2 - \bar{\epsilon}_b \omega_B^2 = \Delta \epsilon_b \omega_B^2 + \frac{2\omega_B^2 n_b}{k_0} \Delta \beta_q \qquad [\mathbf{13.45}]$$

where $k_0 \stackrel{\text{def}}{=} \beta_B/n_b$. Using $\omega_B = c\beta_B/n_b$, Equation (12.101), and the relationship between $\Delta\chi_p'$ and $\Delta\chi_p''$ defined by Equation (6.120),[4]

$$\Delta\beta_q = \frac{n_g}{n_b}(\beta_q - \beta_B) - \frac{1}{2}\Gamma a\alpha_{lw}N + \frac{j}{2}[-\alpha_{int} + \Gamma a(N - N_0)] \qquad \textbf{[13.46]}$$

$$= \frac{1}{v_g}(\omega_q - \omega_B) - \frac{1}{2}\Gamma a\alpha_{lw}N + \frac{j}{2}[-\alpha_{int} + \Gamma a(N - N_0)] \qquad \textbf{[13.47]}$$

where $v_g = c/n_g$. Note that in Equation (13.46) the real part of $\Delta\beta_q$ represents the frequency change and the imaginary part represents the net cavity gain.

From the definition of $\Delta\beta_q$ and Equations (13.43) and (13.45), Equation (13.42) reduces to

$$2E_T(x, y)\Re\left\{-j\sum_q \beta_B\frac{\partial E_q^+}{\partial z}e^{j(\omega_q t - \beta_B z)} + j\sum_q \beta_B\frac{\partial E_q^-}{\partial z}e^{j(\omega_q t + \beta_B z)}\right\}$$

$$\approx \frac{E_T(x, y)}{c^2}\sum_q \Re\left\{-\frac{n_b}{k_0}2\omega_B^2\Delta\beta_q\left[E_q^+(z, t)e^{j(\omega_q t - \beta_B z)} + E_q^-(z, t)e^{j(\omega_q t + \beta_B z)}\right]\right.$$

$$- \Delta\epsilon_b\omega_B^2\left[E_q^+(z, t)e^{j(\omega_q t - \beta_B z)} + E_q^-(z, t)e^{j(\omega_q t + \beta_B z)}\right] \qquad \textbf{[13.48]}$$

$$\left.+ 2j\omega_B(n_b n_g)\left[\frac{\partial}{\partial t}E_q^+(z, t)e^{j(\omega_q t - \beta_B z)} + \frac{\partial}{\partial t}E_q^-(z, t)e^{j(\omega_q t + \beta_B z)}\right]\right\}.$$

In Equation (13.48), $\Delta\epsilon_b(x, y, z)$ due to the periodic structure of the DFB laser is a periodic function of z. Therefore,

$$\Delta\epsilon_b(x, y, z) = \sum_i \Delta\epsilon_i e^{j2\pi i(z/\Lambda)} \approx 2\Delta\epsilon\cos\big(\theta_k + 2\pi[z - (L/2 - z_0)]/\Lambda\big)$$

$$= \Delta\epsilon_+ e^{j2\pi(z/\Lambda)} + \Delta\epsilon_- e^{-j2\pi(z/\Lambda)} = \Delta\epsilon_+ e^{j2\beta_B z} + \Delta\epsilon_- e^{-j2\beta_B z}$$

where $\Delta\epsilon_\pm$ are defined by Equation (13.9) and θ_k is the phase of $\Delta\epsilon_b$ at the center of the cavity $L/2 - z_0$. Given this, the forward and backward coupling coefficients can be defined by

$$\kappa^+ = \frac{\omega_B^2}{2c^2\beta_B}\frac{\int\int \Delta\epsilon_- E_T^2(x, y)dxdy}{\int\int E_T^2(x, y)dxdy} \qquad \textbf{[13.49]}$$

and

$$\kappa^- = \frac{\omega_B^2}{2c^2\beta_B}\frac{\int\int \Delta\epsilon_+ E_T^2(x, y)dxdy}{\int\int E_T^2(x, y)dxdy}. \qquad \textbf{[13.50]}$$

Comparing each $e^{j(\omega_q t - \beta_B z)}$ or $e^{j(\omega_q t + \beta_B z)}$ term gives

---

| [4] Note that $\Delta n_p''/\Delta n_p' = \Delta\chi_p''/\Delta\chi_p'$.

$$-j\frac{\partial E_q^+}{\partial z} + \frac{\omega_B^2}{c^2\beta_B}\left\{\frac{n_b}{k_0}\Delta\beta_q E_q^+ + \frac{n_b n_g}{\omega_B}\left[-j\frac{\partial}{\partial t}E_q^+(z,t)\right]\right\} = -\kappa^+ E_q^-$$

and

$$j\frac{\partial E_q^-}{\partial z} + \frac{\omega_B^2}{c^2\beta_B}\left\{\frac{n_b}{k_0}\Delta\beta_q E_q^- + \frac{n_b n_g}{\omega_B}\left[-j\frac{\partial}{\partial t}E_q^-(z,t)\right]\right\} = -\kappa^- E_q^+.$$

Because

$$\frac{\omega_B n_b n_g}{c^2\beta_B} = \frac{n_g}{c} = \frac{1}{v_g}$$

and

$$\frac{\omega_B^2}{c^2\beta_B} = \frac{\beta_B}{n_b^2} = \frac{k_0}{n_b}$$

the above equations reduce to

$$\frac{\partial E_q^+}{\partial z} + \frac{1}{v_g}\frac{\partial E_q^+}{\partial t} + j\Delta\beta_q E_q^+ = -j\kappa^+ E_q^- \qquad \textbf{[13.51]}$$

and

$$-\frac{\partial E_q^-}{\partial z} + \frac{1}{v_g}\frac{\partial E_q^-}{\partial t} + j\Delta\beta_q E_q^- = -j\kappa^- E_q^+. \qquad \textbf{[13.52]}$$

Equations (13.51) and (13.52) are the coupled-mode equations without considering the spontaneous emission, which can be added by defining

$$I_{sp} \overset{\text{def}}{=} \tfrac{1}{2}\beta_{sp}wd(h\omega_q/2\pi)BN^2. \qquad \textbf{[13.53]}$$

I_{sp} represents the spontaneous emission strength in W/m that contributes to the change of the field intensity [1], where β_{sp} is the spontaneous emission factor or the percentage of spontaneous emission that turns to the qth mode. The factor $\tfrac{1}{2}$ indicates that spontaneous emission is equally distributed between the forward and backward waves. As a result, when there is no cavity gain caused by external pumping, the spontaneous emission strength I_{sp} causes increases of $|E_q^\pm|^2$ in the waves' corresponding propagation direction given by

$$\frac{\partial |E_q^\pm|^2}{\partial z} = \mp I_{sp}$$

or

$$\frac{\partial E_q^\pm}{\partial z} = \mp\frac{I_{sp}}{2E_q^{\pm*}} \overset{\text{def}}{=} \mp J_{sp,q}^\pm E_q^\pm$$

where

$$J_{sp,q}^{\pm} \overset{\text{def}}{=} \frac{I_{sp}}{2|E_q^{\pm}|^2}.$$ **[13.54]**

Adding $J_{sp,q}^{\pm} E_q^{\pm}$ to Equations (13.51) and (13.52), respectively, gives the following coupled-mode equations:

$$\frac{\partial E_q^+}{\partial z} + \frac{1}{v_g}\frac{\partial E_q^+}{\partial t} + \left\{ j\Delta\beta_q - J_{sp,q}^+ \right\} E_q^+ = -j\kappa^+ E_q^-$$ **[13.55]**

and

$$-\frac{\partial E_q^-}{\partial z} + \frac{1}{v_g}\frac{\partial E_q^-}{\partial t} + \left\{ j\Delta\beta_q - J_{sp,q}^- \right\} E_q^- = -j\kappa^- E_q^+.$$ **[13.56]**

APPENDIX 13–B   THRESHOLD EQUATIONS OF DFB LASERS

This appendix derives the threshold equation from the coupled-mode wave equations [11]. By definition, the field intensity is essentially zero at the threshold $J = J_{th}$. Therefore, there is no spatial hole burning effect and the carrier density is a constant. As a result, from Equation (13.46), $\Delta\beta_q$ is a constant.

If the spontaneous emission contribution (i.e., $\beta_{sp} = 0$) is neglected, the rate equations (13.55) and (13.56) in the steady state reduce to

$$\frac{\partial E_q^+}{\partial z} + j\Delta\beta_q E_q^+ = -j\kappa^+ E_q^-$$ **[13.57]**

and

$$-\frac{\partial E_q^-}{\partial z} + j\Delta\beta_q E_q^- = -j\kappa^- E_q^+.$$ **[13.58]**

Note that the time derivative terms have been dropped at the steady state.

Without loss of generality, the longitudinal direction of the cavity can be assumed to go from $-z_0$ to $L - z_0$. The two boundary conditions thus are

$$E_q^+(-z_0) = r_L E_q^-(-z_0)$$ **[13.59]**

and

$$E_q^-(L - z_0) = r_R E_q^+(L - z_0)$$ **[13.60]**

where r_L and r_R are the reflection coefficients at the boundaries given by Equations (13.13) and (13.14).

From the boundary conditions given above, $E_q^+(z)$ and $E_q^-(z)$ can in general be expressed as

$$E_q^+(z) = A \sinh[\gamma(z + z_0)] + r_L D \sinh[\gamma(z - L_z)]$$ **[13.61]**

and

$$E_q^-(z) = Ar_R \sinh[\gamma(z + z_0)] + D \sinh[\gamma(z - L_x)] \qquad \textbf{[13.62]}$$

where $L_z \overset{\text{def}}{=} L - z_0$, and γ, A, and D are unknown coefficients to be solved. It can be easily verified that $E_q^{\pm}$ given above satisfy the boundary condition Equations (13.59) and (13.60).

From the definition of the hyperbolic sine function,

$$\begin{aligned}
E_q^+(z) &= \tfrac{1}{2}(Ae^{\gamma z_0} + r_L De^{-\gamma L_z})e^{\gamma z} - \tfrac{1}{2}(Ae^{-\gamma z_0} + r_L De^{\gamma L_z})e^{-\gamma z} \\
&= \tfrac{1}{2}(Ae^{\gamma L/2} + r_L De^{-\gamma L/2})e^{\gamma z}S^{-1} - \tfrac{1}{2}(Ae^{-\gamma L/2} + r_L De^{\gamma L/2})e^{-\gamma z}S
\end{aligned}$$

where

$$S \overset{\text{def}}{=} e^{\gamma(L/2 - z_0)}.$$

The similar expression for E_q^- is

$$E_q^-(z) = \tfrac{1}{2}(Ar_R e^{\gamma L/2} + De^{-\gamma L/2})e^{\gamma z}S^{-1} - \tfrac{1}{2}(Ar_R e^{-\gamma L/2} + De^{\gamma L/2})e^{-\gamma z}S.$$

Therefore,

$$\frac{\partial E_q^+}{\partial z} = \frac{\gamma}{2}(Ae^{\gamma L/2} + r_L De^{-\gamma L/2})e^{\gamma z}S^{-1} + \frac{\gamma}{2}(Ae^{-\gamma L/2} + r_L De^{\gamma L/2})e^{-\gamma z}S$$

and

$$\frac{\partial E_q^-}{\partial z} = \frac{\gamma}{2}(Ar_R e^{\gamma L/2} + De^{-\gamma L/2})e^{\gamma z}S^{-1} + \frac{\gamma}{2}(Ar_R e^{-\gamma L/2} + De^{\gamma L/2})e^{-\gamma z}S.$$

Substituting these expressions into the coupled-mode equations (13.57) and (13.58) gives

$$\begin{aligned}
&(\gamma + j\Delta\beta_q)(Ae^{\gamma L/2} + r_L De^{-\gamma L/2})e^{\gamma z}S^{-1} + (\gamma - j\Delta\beta_q)(Ae^{-\gamma L/2} + r_L De^{\gamma L/2})e^{-\gamma z}S \\
&= -j\kappa^+\left[(Ar_R e^{\gamma L/2} + De^{-\gamma L/2})e^{\gamma z}S^{-1} - (Ar_R e^{-\gamma L/2} + De^{\gamma L/2})e^{-\gamma z}S\right]
\end{aligned}$$

and

$$\begin{aligned}
&(-\gamma + j\Delta\beta_q)(Ar_R e^{\gamma L/2} + De^{-\gamma L/2})e^{\gamma z}S^{-1} + (-\gamma - j\Delta\beta_q)(Ar_R e^{-\gamma L/2} + De^{\gamma L/2})e^{-\gamma z}S \\
&= -j\kappa^-\left[(Ae^{\gamma L/2} + r_L De^{-\gamma L/2})e^{\gamma z}S^{-1} - (Ae^{-\gamma L/2} + r_L De^{\gamma L/2})e^{-\gamma z}S\right].
\end{aligned}$$

Equating the above components according to $e^{\gamma z}$ and $e^{-\gamma z}$ produces the following four equations:

$$(\gamma + j\Delta\beta_q)(Ae^{\gamma L/2} + r_L De^{-\gamma L/2}) = -j\kappa^+(Ar_R e^{\gamma L/2} + De^{-\gamma L/2}). \qquad \textbf{[13.63]}$$

$$(-\gamma + j\Delta\beta_q)(Ae^{-\gamma L/2} + r_L De^{\gamma L/2}) = -j\kappa^+(Ar_R e^{-\gamma L/2} + De^{\gamma L/2}). \qquad \textbf{[13.64]}$$

$$(-\gamma + j\Delta\beta_q)(Ar_R e^{\gamma L/2} + De^{-\gamma L/2}) = -j\kappa^-(Ae^{\gamma L/2} + r_L De^{-\gamma L/2}). \qquad \textbf{[13.65]}$$

$$(\gamma + j\Delta\beta_q)(Ar_R e^{-\gamma L/2} + De^{\gamma L/2}) = -j\kappa^-(Ae^{-\gamma L/2} + r_L De^{\gamma L/2}). \qquad \textbf{[13.66]}$$

Combining Equations (13.63) and (13.65) or Equations (13.64) and (13.66) gives the following dispersion equation:

$$(\gamma + j\Delta\beta_q)(-\gamma + j\Delta\beta_q) = (j\kappa^+)(j\kappa^-)$$

or

$$(\Delta\beta_q)^2 = \kappa^+\kappa^- - \gamma^2. \qquad \textbf{[13.67]}$$

This equation can be used to find the value of $\Delta\beta_q$ if γ is known. From Equation (13.63),

$$D = \frac{(\gamma + j\Delta\beta_q) + j\kappa^+r_R}{-j\kappa^+ - r_L(\gamma + j\Delta\beta_q)}e^{\gamma L}A. \qquad \textbf{[13.68]}$$

Substituting this into Equation (13.64) gives

$$\left\{-r_L(\gamma + j\Delta\beta_q)(-\gamma + j\Delta\beta_q) - j\kappa^+ \times [(\gamma + j\Delta\beta_q) + r_Rr_L(-\gamma + j\Delta\beta_q)] + \kappa^+\kappa^+r_R\right\}e^{\gamma L}$$

$$= \left\{-j\kappa^+[(-\gamma + j\Delta\beta_q) + r_Rr_L(\gamma + j\Delta\beta_q)] + \kappa^+\kappa^+r_R - r_L(\gamma + j\Delta\beta_q)(-\gamma + j\Delta\beta_q)\right\}e^{-\gamma L}$$

From the dispersion equation (13.67),

$$\left\{-r_L(j\kappa^+)(j\kappa^-) - j\kappa^+[\gamma(1 - r_Lr_R) + j\Delta\beta_q(1 + r_Rr_L)] - (j\kappa^+)(j\kappa^-)r_R\right\}e^{\gamma L}$$

$$= \left\{-j\kappa^+[-\gamma(1 - r_Lr_R) + j\Delta\beta_q(1 + r_Rr_L)] - (j\kappa^+)(j\kappa^+)r_R - (j\kappa^+)(j\kappa^-)r_L\right\}e^{-\gamma L}.$$

This gives

$$(1 + r_Lr_R)\sinh(\gamma L)(j\Delta\beta_q) + (j\kappa^+)r_R\sinh(\gamma L)$$
$$+ r_L(j\kappa^-)\sinh(\gamma L) + \gamma(1 - r_Lr_R)\cosh(\gamma L) = 0$$

or

$$j\Delta\beta_q = \frac{-1}{1 + r_Lr_R}\left[j\kappa^+r_R + j\kappa^-r_L + \gamma(1 - r_Lr_R)\cosh(\gamma L)/\sinh(\gamma L)\right].$$

$$\textbf{[13.69]}$$

Substituting this into the dispersion equation gives the following equation for γ.

$$(j\Delta\beta_q)^2 = \gamma^2 - \kappa^+\kappa^- = \frac{1}{(1 + r_Lr_R)^2}(j\kappa^+r_R + j\kappa^-r_L)^2$$

$$\times \frac{2\gamma(1 - r_Lr_R)}{(1 + r_Lr_R)^2}(j\kappa^+r_R + j\kappa^-r_L)\frac{\cosh(\gamma L)}{\sinh(\gamma L)} + \gamma^2\frac{(1 - r_Lr_R)^2}{(1 + r_Lr_R)^2}\frac{\cosh^2(\gamma L)}{\sinh^2(\gamma L)}$$

or

$$-\frac{\gamma^2}{\sinh^2(\gamma L)} + \gamma^2\frac{4r_Lr_R}{(1 + r_Lr_R)^2}\frac{\cosh^2(\gamma L)}{\sinh^2(\gamma L)} - \frac{2\gamma(1 - r_Lr_R)}{(1 + r_Lr_R)^2}(j\kappa^+r_R + j\kappa^-r_L)\frac{\cosh(\gamma L)}{\sinh(\gamma L)}$$

$$-\frac{1}{(1 + r_Lr_R)^2}(j\kappa^+r_R + j\kappa^-r_L)^2 = \kappa^+\kappa^-. \qquad \textbf{[13.70]}$$

PROBLEMS

Problem 13–1 DFB Diode Design:

a. If a given DFB diode is designed to have a Bragg wavelength $\lambda_B = 1.55$ μm, find its Bragg period at $n_b = 3.5$.

b. If L is approximately 500 μm and at the same time $\beta_B L$ is a multiple of 2π, find the exact L from a. What is the corresponding number of periods?

c. If the normalized coupling $\kappa_0 L$ is required to be 2.0, find the required ratio $\Delta\epsilon/\epsilon_b$ using L from b.

Problem 13–2 Spontaneous Emission Contribution: If the active layer of a given DFB diode has a width of 10 μm and width of 0.5 μm, find the spontaneous emission intensity I_{sp} at $N = 1.5N_0$. Use Table 13.1 for all unspecified parameter values.

Problem 13–3 Sensitivity of θ_k and $\beta_B L$:

a. Consider a DFB diode design where the accuracy of the phase $\beta_B L$ is required to be within $10°$. Find the accuracy requirement on the length L in terms of Λ.

b. If each DFB facet cut has an inaccuracy range of ± 10 percent of Λ, find the worst case error of θ_k.

Problem 13–4 Zero Reflection DFB Lasers: Use Figure 13.2:

a. At $|\kappa_0 L| = 0.1$, 1, and 2, find (approximately) the corresponding normalized frequency shifts $\Re(\Delta\beta_q L)$ of the three modes on the left of the Bragg frequency. Compare the differences of the frequency shifts with π. What can you tell from the comparisons?

b. Find the threshold gain difference between the main mode and the first side mode at $|\kappa_0 L| = 1$, 2, 3, and 4. From these results, how would you design the coupling constant for minimal side modes? Also, what is the total differential gain times the cavity length in dB?

Problem 13–5 Single Window DFB Lasers: Consider the DFB diode with parameters and modes shown in Figure 13.5.

a. What is the normalized frequency shift $\Re(\Delta\beta_q L)$ of the main mode at $|\kappa_0 L| = 1$?

b. What is the normalized frequency shift $\Re(\Delta\beta_q L)$ of the main mode at $|\kappa_0 L| = 2$?

c. From a and b, explain why the DFB laser considered is not a good design.

Problem 13–6 $\lambda/4$ Phase-Shift DFB Lasers: Consider a $\lambda/4$-phase-shift DFB diode shown in Figure 13.8b. If the normalized coupling constant is required to operate at the point of $|\kappa_0 L| = 2.0$ in Figure 13.7 and the cavity length L is set to be around 500 μm, give the design of the diode including the ratio $\Delta\epsilon/\epsilon_b$ and cavity length L. Assume $n_b = 3.5$ and the emission wavelength is 1.3 μm.

Problem 13–7 Double Cleaved DFB Lasers:

a. From Figures 13.10–13.12, note that as the coupling constant approaches zero, the normalized threshold gains all approach 0.60 and the mode separations in normalized frequency approach π. Explain the reason for this common limit.

b. From the same figures, explain which one you would choose in designing a single-mode output. From the choice, give a $\kappa_0 L$ value that would result in a large gain difference.

Problem 13–8 Threshold Current: From the parameter values given in Table 13.1, find the threshold current if the DFB diode is a $\lambda/4$-phase-shift diode as given in Figure 13.8*b*. To meet the conditions of $\lambda/4$-phase-shift diodes, note that the L value given in Table 13.1 is only an approximation. Also let $|\kappa_0 L| = 2.0$.

Problem 13–9 Side-Mode Suppression: If the normalized threshold gain difference between the main mode and the first side mode is 0.5, use Equation (13.34) to find the required ratio $|E_0|^2/(I_{sp}L)$ so that there is a 30 dB side-mode suppression.

REFERENCES

1. P. Vankwikelberge et al., "CLADISS: A Longitudinal Multimode Model for the Analysis of the Static, Dynamic, and Stochastic Behavior of Diode Lasers with Distributed Feedback," *IEEE Journal of Quantum Electronics*, October 1990, pp. 1728–41.

2. R. S. Tucker, "High Speed Modulation of Semiconductor Lasers," *Journal of Lightwave Technology*, December 1985, pp. 1180–92.

3. P. Vankwikelberge et al., "Analysis of the Carrier-Induced FM Response of DFB Lasers: Theoretical and Experimental Case Studies," *IEEE Journal of Quantum Electronics,* vol. 25, no. 11 (November 1989), pp. 2239–54.

4. A. E. Siegman, *Lasers*, University Science Books, 1986.

5. K. Utaka et al., "Effect of Mirror Facets on Lasing Characteristics of Distributed Feedback InGaAsP/InP Laser Diodes at 1.5 μm Range," *IEEE Journal of Quantum Electronics*, vol. 20, no. 3 (March 1984), pp. 236–45.

6. H. Kogelnik and C. V. Shank, "Coupled-Wave Theory of Distributed Feedback Lasers," *Journal of Applied Physics*, vol. 43, no. 5 (May 1972), pp. 2327–35.

7. H. A. Haus and C. V. Shank, "Asymmetric Tapers of Distributed Feedback Lasers," *IEEE Journal of Quantum Electronics*, vol. 12 (1976), pp. 532–39.

8. M. Murakami, "Analysis of Quarter-Wave-Shifted DFB Laser," *Electronics Letters,* vol. 20 (1984), p. 326.

9. S. L. McCall and P. M. Platzman, "An Optimized $\pi/2$ Distributed Feedback Laser," *IEEE Journal of Quantum Electronics*, vol. 21, no. 12 (December 1985), pp. 1899–1904.

10. M. Schubert and B. Wilhelmi, Chapter 1, "Electromagnetic Fields: Classical Description," *Nonlinear Optics and Quantum Electronics*, John Wiley and Sons, 1986.

11. W. Streifer, R. D. Burnham, and D. R. Scifres, "Effect of External Reflectors on Longitudinal Modes of Distributed Feedback Lasers," *IEEE Journal of Quantum Electronics*, vol. 11, no. 4 (April 1975), pp. 154–61.

14

EXTERNAL MODULATION

To avoid undesirable chirping and mode partitioning in direct modulation, external modulation is a good alternative. A basic external modulator in general consists of an optical waveguide in which the incident light passes through and the refractive index of the medium is modulated by the information bearing signal (not the incident light). According to the way the refractive index is modulated, there are two primary types of modulation: **electro-optic** (EO) and **acousto-optic** (AO), where the refractive index is modulated by either a voltage input or an acoustic wave, respectively. With proper arrangement, both EO and AO modulators can modulate the amplitude of incident light, while EO can also be used for phase modulation.

This chapter explains the basic principles and properties of light modulation based on the EO and AO effects. It also describes various modulator designs for amplitude and phase modulations. Their performance and operating characteristics, such as modulation bandwidths and switching power for high-speed optical communications, are discussed in detail.

14.1 DESIRABLE PROPERTIES FROM AN EXTERNAL MODULATOR

From the communication system point of view, a good modulator should have a large modulation bandwidth, large modulation depth, and minimal signal power loss. From the operation point of view, a modulator should also operate at a low voltage and consume small switching power. Some desirable properties of an external modulator are described below.

1. Large modulation bandwidth. A good external modulator should have a fast response to the the modulating input (not the incident light). The response speed is characterized by the modulation bandwidth, which can be limited by various physical properties. In EO modulators, for example, the modulation bandwidth is limited by the finite propagation delay through the modulator and finite electron charge or discharge time.

2. Large modulation depth. To provide a large transmission capacity and/or good detection performance, it is desirable to have a large dynamic range of the modulated quantity such as amplitude or phase. In amplitude modulation, a large amplitude variation with respect to the carrier magnitude is desirable. In phase modulation, on the other hand, a large phase change on the order of π is necessary.

3. High linearity. In analog communications, it is important to maintain a high linearity to achieve a low distortion level. In practical external modulators, phase modulation can be linear if the signal bandwidth is well within the modulation bandwidth. For amplitude modulation, on the other hand, the response is in general nonlinear unless the modulation index is small.

4. Small size. A small modulator size is desirable for practical system operation. The size of an external modulator in general depends on the material of the external modulator and is proportional to the required modulation depth. In general, materials with large electro-optic or elasto-optic coefficients are needed for an EO or AO modulator to achieve the same refractive index change in a smaller size.

5. Polarization independence. In general, electro-optic coefficients of electro-optic modulators and elasto-optic coefficients of acousto-optic modulators depend on the polarization of the incident light. To simplify polarization alignment, it is thus desirable to achieve polarization-independent operation. This can be done by choosing a medium with the necessary crystal symmetry.

6. Low insertion loss. Insertion loss consists of coupling loss at the modulator interface and medium loss of the modulator. Because it adds additional power penalty to the system power budget, it is important to keep the insertion loss as low as possible.

7. Low power consumption and low voltage operation. In general, external power consumption is proportional to the modulation speed, and the operating voltage is proportional to the required modulation depth. For practical system operation, it is desirable to keep both power consumption and operating voltage as low as possible.

Tables 14.1 and 14.2 give performance specifications of some commercially available external modulators. The tables show that EO modulators generally require a high voltage and

Table 14.1 Summary of characteristics of commercially available EO external modulators [1].

Manufacturer	Model No.	Material	Wavelength (μ m)	Bandwidth (MHz)	Modulation	Modulation Depth	Half-Wave Voltage (kV)
INRAD	101-020	KD*P	0.20–1.2	350	AM	1000	4.0
	641-010	LITaO$_3$	0.45–0.75	1000	Traveling wave	–	–
Conoptis	380	ADP	0.3–0.8	50	AM	500	0.117
	355	KD*P	0.3–1.1	75	AM	500	0.125
FastPulse	1039A/B	ADP	0.35–1.0	500	PM	–	–
	1039C/D	AD*P	0.32–1.2	500	PM	–	–
	3032	AD*P	0.34–1.2	100	AM	250	0.09
Quantum Technology	3200	ADP	0.40–0.80	200	AM	500	0.110
	11	LiTaO$_3$	0.6–1.8	1000	AM	50	0.13
GEC	Y–35–5395	LiNbO$_3$	1.3–1.53	8000	PM		0.25
Advanced Optical	Y–35–8391	LiNbO$_3$	1.3–1.55	8000	AM	500	6.0
	Y–35–8392	LiNbO$_3$	1.3–1.55	18,000	AM	500	14.0
Pilkington	PM3	LiNbO$_3$	0.85–2.3	8000	AM	10,000	0.005
Lasermetrics	1039A/B	ADP	0.35–1.0	500	PM	–	–
	3035	ADP	0.34–0.95	100	AM	250	0.12
Leysop	EM 10KD	KD*P	0.3–1.2	1000	AM	500	3.6
II-VI Inc.	EOS5	CdTe	2.0–16.0	1000	AM	500	> 1.5

Table 14.2 Summary of characteristics of commercially available AO external modulators[1].

Manufacturer	Model No.	Material	Wavelength (μ m)	Bandwidth (MHz)	Deflection Efficiency (%)	Driving Power (Watts)
Crystal Tech.	3500	TeO$_2$	0.4–1.5	125	65	1.5
Brimrose	TEM–100–30	TeO$_2$	0.44–0.83	300	35	1.0
	IPM–60–20	InP	1.0–1.6	200	30	1.0
	IPM–150–100	GaP	0.59–1.0	1000	10	1.0
	GPM–100–35	GaAs	1.0–1.6	350	20	1.0
Isomet	1250C	PbMoO$_4$	0.44–0.633	50	> 55	1.2
A.A SA	AA MB P9	PbMoO$_4$	0.476–0.850	100	30 or 75	3.0
	AA IR 20	PbMoO$_4$	1.06–1.35	20	85	6.0
GEC	Y–36–2761–01	LiNbO$_3$	0.780	1000	1	0.5

can be used for both amplitude and phase modulation. AO modulators, on the other hand, can be used only for amplitude modulation, and their deflection efficiency depends on the input acoustic power instead of the voltage. Definitions of the modulation bandwidth, depth, half-wave voltage, deflection efficiency, and driving power will be given in subsequent discussion.

14.2   PRINCIPLES OF EXTERNAL MODULATION

Before the physics and designs of various external modulators are described in detail, it is instructive to first know the basic principles of external modulation. As mentioned earlier, there are two primary types of external modulators: EO and AO modulators. In EO modulators, a *constant* refractive index change is introduced by an external voltage signal. In AO modulators, a *periodic* change of the refractive index is introduced by an acoustic wave. With proper arrangements, these different refractive index modulations can both be used to modulate the incident light.

Electro-Optic Modulators   An EO modulator can be as simple as an optical channel or waveguide through which incident light passes. For many media used in EO modulators, the incident light "sees" different refractive indices at different polarizations. As mentioned in the section of Chapter 4 on polarization-maintaining fibers, the polarization of a lightwave is the direction of its transverse electric field, which can stay in the same direction (linearly polarized) or rotate (circularly polarized) as the lightwave propagates.

As will be explained in detail shortly, a medium whose refractive index is input-polarization dependent is called **anisotropic.** In this case, light inside can have only two polarizations, each of which has its own propagation constant. As mentioned in Chapter 4, this phenomenon is called **birefringence.**

Let β_a and β_b be the two propagation constants, both of which can be modulated by an external voltage signal. The electric field at the waveguide output can thus be written as

$$\overline{E}_{out} = A_a e^{-j\beta_a L}\hat{s}_a + A_b e^{-j\beta_b L}\hat{s}_b \qquad \textbf{[14.1]}$$

where $\hat{s}_a$ and $\hat{s}_b$ are the unit vectors corresponding to the permissible polarizations, A_a and A_b are the corresponding complex amplitudes at the input of the modulator, and L is the longitudinal length of the modulator.

According to Equation (14.1), the phase or magnitude of the incident light can be modulated as follows. For phase modulation, simply set $A_b = 0$ and change the phase of $\overline{E}_{out}$ by modulating β_a. For amplitude modulation, set $A_a = A_b$ and modulate the difference $\beta_a - \beta_b$. If $\hat{s}_a$ and $\hat{s}_b$ are perpendicular to each other, there can be two orthogonal polarizations $\hat{s}_a \pm \hat{s}_b$ by setting $(\beta_a - \beta_b)L$ at either 0 or π. Therefore, by adding a polarizer at the external modulator output, one polarization is allowed to pass and the other is rejected. This achieves on-off-keying (OOK) modulation.

Section 14.3 will discuss the basic physics of wave propagation inside an anisotropic medium, explain why there are only two permissible polarizations, and derive the corresponding propagation constants. Section 14.4 will describe different types of EO crystals and modulators, from which the dependence of the propagation constants (i.e., β_a and β_b given in Equation [14.1]) on the external voltage can be obtained. From the basic physics and EO effects understood, Sections 14.5 and 14.6 will explain various arrangements to achieve phase and amplitude modulation.

Acousto-Optic Modulators   In AO modulators, the periodic modulation of the refractive index forms a grating. As a result, the incident light is diffracted. Thus the grating can be controlled to modulate either the through light or the diffracted light.

In general, the grating structure created in AO modulation is similar to the periodic Bragg reflector structure of DFB lasers discussed in Chapter 13. As a result, there are two waves inside the modulator,[1] one in the same direction as the incident wave and the other diffracted by the grating. These two waves interact as they propagate along the modulator and are similarly governed by the coupled mode equations described in Chapter 13. As a result, by modulating the coupling constant through the input acoustic wave, the light output can be modulated. Section 14.8 will describe various types of AO crystals and quantify their refractive index changes from an acoustic wave input. Section 14.9 will discuss wave interaction due to Bragg diffraction and analyze the modulated light output.

14.3   WAVE PROPAGATION IN ANISOTROPIC MEDIA

As mentioned earlier, a medium that responds differently to the different polarizations of incident light is called **anisotropic.** A medium that has the same response to different polarizations is called **isotropic.** When the medium of an external modulator is modulated, it can turn from isotropic to anisotropic. In fact, to achieve a large modulation depth and power efficiency, an external modulator should have a large anisotropic response to either the EO or AO effect. This point will become clear from the discussion in the next few sections.

14.3.1   ANISOTROPIC MATERIALS

As mentioned in Appendix 4–A, the response of a medium to incident light is characterized by its permittivity. For an anisotropic medium, its response depends on the polarization of the light. As a result, its permittivity is no longer a constant. Instead, it is a **tensor** or a three by three matrix through which the electric flux density $\overline{D}$ is related to the electric field $\overline{E}$ by

$$\overline{D} = \begin{bmatrix} D_x \\ D_y \\ D_z \end{bmatrix} = \begin{bmatrix} \epsilon_{xx} & \epsilon_{xy} & \epsilon_{xz} \\ \epsilon_{yx} & \epsilon_{yy} & \epsilon_{yz} \\ \epsilon_{zx} & \epsilon_{zy} & \epsilon_{zz} \end{bmatrix} = \overline{\overline{\epsilon}}\,\overline{E}. \qquad \textbf{[14.2]}$$

From basic physics, it can be verified that $\epsilon_{ij} = \epsilon_{ji}^*$ [2]. Therefore, it can be transformed to a diagonal matrix [3]. By choosing a good coordinate, $\overline{D}$ can become

$$\overline{D} = \begin{bmatrix} \epsilon_1 & 0 & 0 \\ 0 & \epsilon_2 & 0 \\ 0 & 0 & \epsilon_3 \end{bmatrix} \overline{E} \qquad \textbf{[14.3]}$$

The axes that result in the above equation are called the **principle axes.** In general, the three nonzero ϵ_i values ($i = 1, 2, 3$) can be identical or not. According to their relative values, there are three categories:

1. **Isotropic:** $\epsilon_1 = \epsilon_2 = \epsilon_3$.
2. **Uniaxial:** $\epsilon_1 = \epsilon_2 = \epsilon_0$ and $\epsilon_3 = \epsilon_e$, where $\epsilon_o \neq \epsilon_e$. When $\epsilon_o < \epsilon_e$, it is called *positive* uniaxial, when $\epsilon_o > \epsilon_e$, it is called *negative* uniaxial.
3. **Biaxial:** $\epsilon_1 \neq \epsilon_2 \neq \epsilon_3$.

| [1] There can be more diffracted waves when higher order diffractions are considered.

Most practical electro-optic external modulators such as ADP (ammonium dihydrogen phosphate or $[NH_4]H_2PO_4$) and KDP (potassium dihydrogen phosphate or KH_2PO_4) are uniaxial. In this case, the z-axis is generally called the **extraordinary axis,** and the two axes perpendicular to the z-axis are called the **ordinary axes.** Some important anisotropic materials are given in Table 14.3 according to the above classification.

14.3.2 PLANE WAVE PROPAGATION

As pointed out earlier, a plane wave inside an anisotropic medium can have two polarizations with different propagation constants. From the permittivity tensor defined above, the wave equations inside an anisotropic medium can be derived.

For a plane wave propagating in direction $\overline{\beta} = \beta\hat{s}$, the electric field $\mathcal{E}$ and magnetic field $\mathcal{H}$ can be written as

Table 14.3 Refractive indices of some important crystals [2].

Type	Materials	n_1	n_2	n_3
Istropic	CdTe		2.690	
$n_1 = n_2 = n_3$	NaCl		1.544	
	Diamond		2.417	
	Fluorite		1.392	
	GaAs		3.400	
Positive uniaxial:	Ice	1.309		1.310
$n_1 = n_2 = n_o$	Quartz	1.544		1.553
$n_3 = n_e$	BeO	1.717		1.732
$n_o < n_e$	Zicron	1.923		1.968
	Rutile	2.616		2.903
	ZnS	2.354		2.358
Negative uniaxial:	$(NH_4)H_2PO_4$ (ADP)	1.522		1.478
$n_1 = n_2 = n_o$	Beryl	1.598		1.590
$n_3 = n_e$	KH_2PO_4 (KDP)	1.507		1.467
$n_o > n_e$	$NaNO_3$	1.587		1.336
	Calcite	1.658		1.486
	Tourmaline	1.638		1.486
	$LiNbO_3$	2.300		2.208
	$BaTiO_3$	2.416		2.364
	Proustite	3.019		2.739
Biaxial:	Gypsum	1.520	1.523	1.530
$n_1 \neq n_2 \neq n_3$	Feldspar	1.522	1.526	1.530
	Mica	1.552	1.582	1.588
	Topaz	1.619	1.620	1.627
	$NaNO_2$	1.344	1.411	1.651
	SbSI	2.7	3.2	3.8
	$YAlO_3$	1.923	1.938	1.947

$$\mathcal{E}(t,\overline{r}) = \overline{E}e^{j(\omega t - \overline{\beta} \times \overline{r})}$$

and

$$\mathcal{H}(t,\overline{r}) = \overline{H}e^{j(\omega t - \overline{\beta} \times \overline{r})}$$

where $\overline{E}$ and $\overline{H}$ are constant vectors and $\overline{r}$ is the position vector. With the above expressions, the Maxwell equations given by Equations (4.60) and (4.61) in Appendix 4–A reduce to

$$\overline{\beta} \times \overline{E} = \omega\mu\overline{H} \qquad\qquad \textbf{[14.4]}$$

and

$$\overline{\beta} \times \overline{H} = -\omega\overline{D} = \omega\overline{\epsilon}\overline{E} \qquad\qquad \textbf{[14.5]}$$

where the current density is assumed to be zero ($J = 0$) in the anisotropic medium. From Equation (14.5), note that

$$\overline{\beta} \cdot \overline{D} = \frac{-1}{\omega}\overline{\beta} \cdot (\overline{\beta} \times \overline{H}) = 0 \qquad\qquad \textbf{[14.6]}$$

This shows $\overline{D}$ is perpendicular to $\overline{\beta}$. Similarly, $\overline{D}$ can be shown to be perpendicular to $\overline{H}$. Using the same argument with Equation (14.4) shows that $\overline{H}$ is perpendicular to $\overline{\beta}$ and $\overline{E}$. These orthogonal relationships are shown in Figure 14.1. Note that $\overline{\beta}$, $\overline{D}$, and $\overline{H}$ are orthogonal to each other.

If $\overline{H}$ given by Equation (14.4) is substituted into Equation (14.5),

$$\overline{\beta} \times (\overline{\beta} \times \overline{E}) + \omega^2\mu\overline{\epsilon}\overline{E} = 0. \qquad\qquad \textbf{[14.7]}$$

From the vector identity:

$$\overline{X} \times (\overline{Y} \times \overline{Z}) = \overline{Y}(\overline{X} \cdot \overline{Z}) - \overline{Z}(\overline{X} \cdot \overline{Y}) \qquad\qquad \textbf{[14.8]}$$

Equation (14.7) reduces to

$$\beta^2\overline{E} - \overline{\beta}(\overline{\beta} \cdot \overline{E}) = \beta^2\overline{E}_{\perp} = \beta^2 Proj_{\overline{\beta}}\{\overline{E}\} = \omega^2\mu\overline{\epsilon}\overline{E} \qquad\qquad \textbf{[14.9]}$$

where $\overline{E}_{\perp}$ denotes the transverse electric field perpendicular to $\overline{\beta}$, and $Proj_{\overline{\beta}}\{\cdot\}$ is the projection operator onto the plane perpendicular to $\overline{\beta}$. This is illustrated in Figure 14.1.

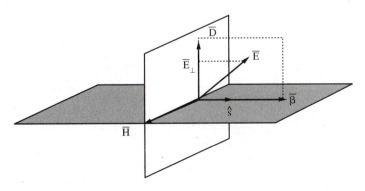

Figure 14.1   Relative directions of the wave vectors of a plane wave.

In matrix form, Equations (14.7) or (14.9) can be written as

$$
\begin{bmatrix}
\omega^2\mu\epsilon_1 - \beta_y^2 - \beta_z^2 & \beta_x\beta_y & \beta_x\beta_z \\
\beta_y\beta_x & \omega^2\mu\epsilon_2 - \beta_x^2 - \beta_z^2 & \beta_y\beta_z \\
\beta_z\beta_x & \beta_z\beta_y & \omega^2\mu\epsilon_3 - \beta_x^2 - \beta_y^2
\end{bmatrix}
\begin{bmatrix}
E_x \\ E_y \\ E_z
\end{bmatrix}
\overset{\text{def}}{=} \overline{A}\,\overline{E} = 0
$$

[14.10]

where

$$
\overline{A} \overset{\text{def}}{=}
\begin{bmatrix}
\omega^2\mu\epsilon_1 - \beta_y^2 - \beta_z^2 & \beta_x\beta_y & \beta_x\beta_z \\
\beta_y\beta_x & \omega^2\mu\epsilon_2 - \beta_x^2 - \beta_z^2 & \beta_y\beta_z \\
\beta_z\beta_x & \beta_z\beta_y & \omega^2\mu\epsilon_3 - \beta_x^2 - \beta_y^2
\end{bmatrix}
$$

[14.11]

and

$$
\Delta_i^2 \overset{\text{def}}{=} \omega^2\mu\epsilon_i - \beta^2 = \omega^2\frac{n_i^2}{c^2} - \omega^2\frac{n^2}{c^2} = \frac{\omega^2}{c^2}(n_i^2 - n^2)
$$

[14.12]

for $i = 1, 2,$ and 3. In Equation (14.12) β is defined as

$$
\beta = |\bar{\beta}| \overset{\text{def}}{=} \omega\frac{n}{c}
$$

[14.13]

and

$$
n_i^2 \overset{\text{def}}{=} \frac{\epsilon_i}{\epsilon_0}
$$

[14.14]

From Equation (14.10), there is a nontrivial solution $\overline{E} \neq 0$ only if the determinant of the matrix $\overline{A}$ is zero. This observation leads to the following condition:

$$
\Delta_1^2\Delta_2^2\Delta_3^2 + \Delta_2^2\Delta_3^2\beta_x^2 + \Delta_3^2\Delta_1^2\beta_y^2 + \Delta_1^2\Delta_2^2\beta_z^2 = 0
$$

[14.15]

which can be simplified and expressed in terms of n as

$$
(n^2 - n_2^2)(n^2 - n_3^2)n^2 s_x^2 + (n^2 - n_3^2)(n^2 - n_1^2)n^2 s_y^2
$$
$$
+ (n^2 - n_1^2)(n^2 - n_3^2)n^2 s_z^2 = (n^2 - n_1^2)(n^2 - n_2^2)(n^2 - n_3^2)
$$

[14.16]

with

$$
s_i \overset{\text{def}}{=} \frac{\beta_i}{\beta}
$$

[14.17]

for $i = x, y, z$. Because $s_x^2 + s_y^2 + s_z^2 = 1$, Equation (14.16) is a quadratic equation of n and thus has two solutions.

By dividing both sides by $n^2(n^2 - n_1^2)(n^2 - n_2^2)(n^2 - n_3^2)$, Equation (14.16) can be rewritten in a more popular form called **Fresnel's equation of wave normals:**

$$
\boxed{\frac{s_x^2}{n^2 - n_1^2} + \frac{s_y^2}{n^2 - n_2^2} + \frac{s_z^2}{n^2 - n_3^2} = \frac{1}{n^2}.}
$$

[14.18]

When none of the s_i's is zero, Equation (14.18) can be used to find the two solutions of n. However, when one of the s_i's is zero, it yields only one n value; and when two of the s_i's are zero, there is no solution. In these cases, other solutions can be easily found from Equation (14.16). This is illustrated below.

LIMITATIONS OF THE FRESNEL EQUATION   If $s_x = 0$, Equation (14.18) reduces to

Example 14.1

$$n^2(n_3^2 s_z^2 + n_2^2 s_y^2) = n_2^2 n_3^2.$$

In other words, there is only one solution to Equation (14.18). In this case Equation (14.16) needs to be used to give another solution: $n = n_1$.

Similarly, if $s_x = s_y = 0$, there is no solution to Equation (14.18). On the other hand, there are two solutions, $n = n_1$ and $n = n_2$, from Equation (14.16). ∎

14.3.3 BIREFRINGENCE

From the above discussion, it is clear that there are only two possible n or β values for a plane wave propagating in an anisotropic medium and in a given direction of $\hat{s} = (s_x, s_y, s_z)$. From Equation (14.12), there are two different sets of Δ_i^2's for the two possible n values. As a result, there are two $\bar{A}$ matrixes from Equation (14.11). Because Equation (14.10) can be interpreted as the condition that the electric field vector $\bar{E}$ is perpendicular to the two-dimensional plane spanned by the row vectors of $\bar{A}$ (not three-dimensional space because $\det \bar{A} = 0$), there are also only two $\bar{E}$ vectors or polarizations corresponding to the two n or β values. This phenomenon is called **birefringence.** From Problem 14–3, when n is known, the corresponding polarization can be shown to be in the direction of

$$\bar{E} \propto \begin{bmatrix} \frac{s_x}{n^2 - n_1^2} \\ \frac{s_y}{n^2 - n_2^2} \\ \frac{s_z}{n^2 - n_3^2} \end{bmatrix}.$$ **[14.19]**

When n is equal to one of the n_i's, $\bar{E}$ will be in the corresponding direction.

From the above observation, let β_a and β_b be the two propagation constants and n_a and n_b be the corresponding refractive indices. The birefringence $\mathcal{B}$ between the two polarizations is defined by

$$\boxed{\mathcal{B} \overset{\text{def}}{=} n_a - n_b = (\beta_a - \beta_b)\frac{\lambda}{2\pi}}$$ **[14.20]**

where λ is the free space wavelength. For a given birefringence $\mathcal{B}$, the two polarizations over a propagation distance L will have a phase difference $\Delta\phi$ given by

$$\Delta\phi = (\beta_a - \beta_b)L = (n_a - n_b)\frac{\omega}{c}L = \frac{\omega}{c}\mathcal{B}L.$$ **[14.21]**

As Example 14.2 illustrates, this phase difference or a nonzero birefringence can be used for external modulation.

Example 14.2

AMPLITUDE MODULATION Consider a plane wave propagating inside an anisotropic medium and over a distance L. From the concept of birefringence discussed, the output electric field can be written as

$$\mathcal{E} = E_a \cos(\omega_c t - \beta_a L)\hat{s}_a + E_b \cos(\omega_c t - \beta_b L)\hat{s}_b.$$

If $E_a = E_b = E_0$,

$$\mathcal{E} = E_0 \Re\left\{e^{j\omega_c t - \beta_b L}[e^{j\Delta\phi}\hat{s}_a + \hat{s}_b]\right\}$$

$$= E_0 \cos(\omega_c t - \beta_b L)[\cos(\Delta\phi)\hat{s}_a + \hat{s}_b] - E_0 \sin(\omega_c t - \beta_b L)\sin(\Delta\phi)\hat{s}_a$$

where $\Delta\phi$ is defined by Equation (14.21). To get a better picture of this electric field, define two new orthogonal vectors:

$$\hat{x} \overset{\text{def}}{=} \frac{1}{\sqrt{2}}(\hat{s}_a + \hat{s}_b).$$

$$\hat{y} \overset{\text{def}}{=} \frac{1}{\sqrt{2}}(-\hat{s}_a + \hat{s}_b).$$

Thus,

$$\mathcal{E} = \frac{E_0}{\sqrt{2}}[\cos(\omega_c t - \beta_b L + \Delta\phi) + \cos(\omega_c t - \beta_b L)]\hat{x}$$

$$- \frac{E_0}{\sqrt{2}}[\cos(\omega_c t - \beta_b L + \Delta\phi) - \cos(\omega_c t - \beta_b L)]\hat{y} \qquad \textbf{[14.22]}$$

$$= \sqrt{2}E_0 \cos(\Delta\phi/2)\cos(\omega_c t - \beta_b L + \Delta\phi/2)\hat{x}$$

$$-\sqrt{2}E_0 \sin(\Delta\phi/2)\sin(\omega_c t - \beta_b L + \Delta\phi/2)\hat{y}$$

Therefore, when $\cos(\Delta\phi/2)$ is ± 1, the output electric field is linearly polarized in $\pm\hat{x}$. In this case, $\Delta\phi = 2m\pi$, where m is an integer. On the other hand, when $\sin(\Delta\phi/2) = \pm 1$ or when $\Delta\phi = (2m + 1)\pi$, the output field is linearly polarized in $\pm\hat{y}$. When $|\cos(\Delta\phi/2)| = |\sin(\Delta\phi/2)| = 1/\sqrt{2}$, there is circular polarization. In other cases, the output is elliptically polarized. These different polarizations are illustrated in Figure 14.2.

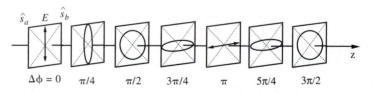

Figure 14.2   Polarization inside an anisotropic medium.

To perform external modulation, one can place a linear polarizer at the end of the anisotropic medium. Assume the polarizer is in the direction $\hat{x}$. If the anisotropic medium is modulated so that $\Delta\phi = \pi$, the wave will be rejected and the output is zero. On the other hand, if the medium is modulated so that $\Delta\phi = 2\pi$, the wave will pass through. This thus achieves on-off keying (OOK). ∎

14.3.4   NORMAL SURFACES

According to the above discussion, to find the two permissible plane waves propagating in a given direction requires using the Fresnel equation (14.18) to solve for the propagation constants and using Equation (14.19) to find the polarizations. These results, allow one to find the birefringence and design the external modulator.

Instead of using Equations (14.18) and (14.19) directly, this and next subsections discuss two instructive methods to "see" and solve wave propagation. In many cases, these methods can immediately provide the solutions without going through tedious mathematics.

The first method is the use of the so-called **normal surface,** which is defined as the set of all points (ns_x, ns_y, ns_z) with n satisfying Equation (14.18). Therefore, for a given propagation direction $\hat{s}$, n_a and n_b can be found from generating a ray in the same direction $\hat{s}$ from the origin. The distance of the intersection of the ray with the normal surface gives the corresponding n value.

The normal surface can be constructed as follows. For the special case that $s_z = 0$ or $\bar{\beta}$ is in the x–y plane, Equation (14.16) reduces to two equations

$$n^2 = n_3^2 \qquad\qquad \textbf{[14.23]}$$

and

$$\frac{1}{n^2} = \frac{s_x^2}{n_2^2} + \frac{s_y^2}{n_1^2}. \qquad\qquad \textbf{[14.24]}$$

Equations (14.23) and (14.24) allow the two curves to be drawn on the x–y plane as shown in Figure 14.3. There can be similar curves when $\bar{\beta}$ is in the y–z and z–x planes. In Figures 14.3b and 14.3c, note that there is a special axis called the **optic axis,** which is defined to be the propagation direction in which the two n values are the same. For uniaxial crystals, the optic axis is the same as the extraordinary axis. For biaxial crystals, the optic axis is in the plane perpendicular to one of the principal axes whose refractive index is between the other two refractive indices.

14.3.5   INDEX ELLIPSOID

Another useful method that can solve Equations (14.10) and (14.18) is the use of the so-called **index ellipsoid,** which is defined as the set of all electric flux density $\bar{D}$ vectors that have the same energy density. From [4], the energy density of an electromagnetic wave is given by

$$\frac{|\bar{D}|^2}{\epsilon_0 n^2} = \bar{E}^T \bar{D} = \epsilon_0^{-1} (\bar{\eta}\bar{D})^T \bar{D} = \bar{D}^T \bar{\eta}^T \bar{D} \qquad\qquad \textbf{[14.25]}$$

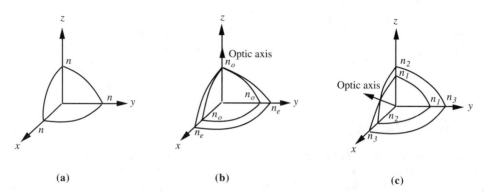

Figure 14.3   Normal surfaces of (a) isotropic, (b) uniaxial, and (c) biaxial crystals.

where $\bar{\eta}$ is the **impermeability matrix** or inverse matrix of the dielectric tensor $\bar{\epsilon}/\epsilon_0$ given by Equation (14.2), and $\bar{D}^T$ denotes the transpose of $\bar{D}$. When $\bar{D}$ is in the principal axis, Equation (14.25) reduces to

$$\frac{|\bar{D}|^2}{\epsilon_0 n^2} = \frac{D_x^2}{\epsilon_1} + \frac{D_y^2}{\epsilon_2} + \frac{D_z^2}{\epsilon_3} = \frac{1}{\epsilon_0}\left(\frac{D_x^2}{n_1^2} + \frac{D_y^2}{n_2^2} + \frac{D_z^2}{n_3^2}\right).$$ **[14.26]**

Normalizing Equation (14.26) gives the following ellipsoid equation:

$$\frac{x^2}{n_1^2} + \frac{y^2}{n_2^2} + \frac{z^2}{n_3^2} = \frac{1}{n^2}$$ **[14.27]**

where $\hat{d} = (x, y, z) = \bar{D}/|\bar{D}|$ is the unit vector of $\bar{D}$. The ellipsoid described by Equation (14.27) is called an index ellipsoid and is depicted in Figure 14.4a.

From Equation (14.27), n can be calculated if the direction of $\hat{d}$ is known. The following discussion describes two properties that make it possible to determine $\hat{d}$ at a given propagation direction $\hat{s}$.

From Equation (14.6), the first property is that $\bar{D}$ is perpendicular to the propagation direction $\hat{s}$. Therefore, as shown in Figure 14.4a, $\hat{d}$ is on the ellipse created by the intersection of the plane perpendicular to $\hat{s}$ and the index ellipsoid defined by Equation (14.27).

From the ellipse obtained by the first property, the second property says that the unit vector $\hat{d}$ is in fact in the direction of one of the two principal axes of the ellipse. This property will be verified shortly. As a result, the corresponding refractive index n can be solved geometrically. Specifically, if the two principal axes of the ellipse shown in Figure 14.4a have lengths n_a and n_b, n is equal to either n_a or n_b.

Example 14.3   **z-AXIS PROPAGATION**   If the propagation direction $\hat{s}$ is in the direction of the $\hat{z}$-axis, the two possible polarizations of $\bar{D}$ are in the direction of the other two principal axes, $\bar{x}$ and $\bar{y}$, with refractive index n equal to n_1 and n_2, respectively. In this special case, from Equation (14.3), $\bar{E}$ is in the same direction as $\bar{D}$ and is thus perpendicular to $\bar{\beta}$.

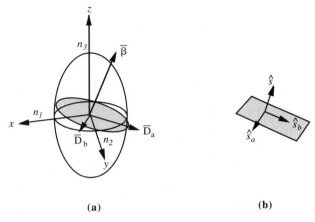

Figure 14.4   (a) The index ellipsoid and (b) the new orthogonal coordinate $[\hat{s}_a, \hat{s}_b, \hat{s}]$, where $\hat{s}_a$ and $\hat{s}$ are the two unit vectors of the principal axes of the ellipse from the intersection of the index ellipsoid and the plane perpendicular to $\hat{s}$.

For the special case in which the crystal is uniaxial, or $n_1 = n_2$, the polarization of $\bar{E}$ or $\bar{D}$ can be arbitrary in the plane of the ellipse. ∎

PROPAGATION IN THE $\hat{\mathbf{y}}$-$\hat{\mathbf{z}}$ PLANE   If the propagation direction $\hat{s}$ is perpendicular to the principal axis $\hat{x}$ of the crystal but not parallel to either of the other two principal axes, as shown in Figure 14.5, one solution has $\hat{D}$ in parallel with the principal axis $\hat{x}$:

$$\bar{D}_a^T = [D, 0, 0].$$ **[14.28]**

Example 14.4

The corresponding refractive index is $n_a = n_1$. The other solution has a refractive index given by

$$n_b = \sqrt{n_2^2 \cos^2\theta + n_3^2 \sin^2\theta}$$ **[14.29]**

where θ is the angle between $\bar{\beta}$ and the principal axis $\hat{y}$. For the second solution, $\bar{D}$ can be written as

$$\bar{D}_b^T = [0, -D\sin\theta, D\cos\theta]$$ **[14.30]**

and the corresponding electric field vector is

$$\bar{E}_b^T = \frac{1}{\epsilon_0}\left[0, -\frac{D}{n_2^2}\sin\theta, \frac{D}{n_3^2}\cos\theta\right].$$ **[14.31]**

Note that $\bar{E}_b$ is not perpendicular to the unit propagation vector $\hat{s} = [0, \cos\theta, \sin\theta]$. ∎

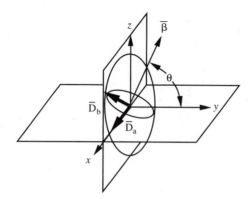

Figure 14.5   The propagation direction of a plane wave is perpendicular to only one of the principal axes.

From Example 14.4, when the propagation direction of the plane wave is perpendicular to one of the principal axes, the two possible polarizations can readily be solved using Equations (14.28)–(14.31).

Verification of the Second Property   To verify the second property that $\bar{D}$ is in the direction of the two principle axes of the ellipse, Equation (14.9) can be rewritten as an equation for $\bar{D}$:

$$Proj_{\hat{s}}\{\bar{\eta}\bar{D}\} = \frac{1}{n^2}\bar{D} \qquad \textbf{[14.32]}$$

where $\bar{\eta} = \epsilon_0 \bar{\epsilon}^{-1}$ is the impermeability tensor and $Proj_{\hat{s}}\{\cdot\}$ is the projection operator defined earlier. Equation (14.32) can be considered as an eigenvalue equation for $\bar{D}$ with operator $Proj_{\hat{s}}\{\bar{\eta}\cdot\}$ and an eigenvalue equal to $1/n^2$.

Equation (14.32) can be further simplified by using a new coordinate for the ellipsoid. The new coordinate is shown in Figure 14.4b, whose three orthogonal axes are $\hat{s}_a$, $\hat{s}_b$, and $\hat{s}$, where $\hat{s}_a$ and $\hat{s}_b$ are the two principle axes of the ellipse. Given this new coordinate, the ellipse orthogonal to $\bar{\beta}$ shown in Figure 14.4b satisfies the equation:

$$\frac{x'^2}{n_a^2} + \frac{y'^2}{n_b^2} = \frac{1}{n^2} \qquad \textbf{[14.33]}$$

where $(x', y', 0)$ is the new coordinate of a point on the ellipse. As a result, when the impermeability tensor $\bar{\eta}$ is represented in the same new coordinate, it should have the following general form:

$$\bar{\eta} = \begin{bmatrix} \frac{1}{n_a^2} & 0 & \eta_{13} \\ 0 & \frac{1}{n_b^2} & \eta_{23} \\ \eta_{31} & \eta_{32} & \eta_{33} \end{bmatrix} \qquad \textbf{[14.34]}$$

which is necessary so that Equation (14.25) reduces to Equation (14.33) when $z' = 0$.

From Equation (14.34), for a flux density $\bar{D}^T = [D_a, D_b, 0]$ perpendicular to $\hat{s}$, the eigenvalue equation, Equation (14.32), reduces to

$$Proj_{\hat{s}} \begin{bmatrix} \frac{D_a}{n_a^2} \\ \frac{D_b}{n_b^2} \\ \eta_{31} D_a + \eta_{32} D_b \end{bmatrix} = \begin{bmatrix} \frac{D_a}{n_a^2} \\ \frac{D_b}{n_b^2} \\ 0 \end{bmatrix} = \frac{1}{n^2} \begin{bmatrix} D_a \\ D_b \\ 0 \end{bmatrix}. \qquad \text{[14.35]}$$

Thus the two possible polarizations of $\bar{D}$ are in the directions of $\hat{s}_a$ and $\hat{s}_b$, with corresponding refractive indices equal to n_a and n_b, respectively.

14.4 ELECTRO-OPTIC MODULATION

The previous section describes the EO effect and explains how it can be used for external modulation. This section describes the basic principles of EO modulation. Design of phase and amplitude modulators based on the EO effect will be discussed in the next section.

14.4.1 MODULATION OF REFRACTIVE INDICES

When an external voltage is applied to an EO crystal, the electric field present in the crystal can modulate its refractive index tensor. The electro-optic effect can be characterized by the change of the impermeability tensor:

$$\Delta \eta_{ij}(\bar{E}) = \sum_k r_{(ij)k} E_k + \sum_{kl} s_{(ij)(kl)} E_k E_l \qquad \text{[14.36]}$$

where i, j, k, and l can be 1, 2, 3. Note that the first summation term on the right is linearly proportional to the electric field, and the second summation is a quadratic function of the electric field. The linear coefficients $r_{(ij)k}$ are called the **Pockels** coefficients, and the quadratic coefficients $s_{(ij)(kl)}$ are called the **Kerr** coefficients, in honor of their discoverers. In general, the Kerr effect is insignificant unless the Pockels coefficients are all zero. Crystals that have zero Pockels effect have a centrosymmetric crystal structure. For most practical EO modulators that are not centrosymmetric, only the linear Pockels effect must be considered.

Given the change of the impermeability from the external electric field, the index ellipsoid equation from Equation (14.25) can be expressed as

$$\left(\frac{1}{n_1^2} + \Delta \eta_{11} \right) x^2 + \left(\frac{1}{n_2^2} + \Delta \eta_{22} \right) y^2 + \left(\frac{1}{n_3^2} + \Delta \eta_{33} \right) z^2$$

$$+ 2\Delta \eta_{23} yz + 2\Delta \eta_{31} zx + 2\Delta \eta_{12} xy = \frac{1}{n^2}. \qquad \text{[14.37]}$$

In general, from the symmetry of $\Delta \eta_{ij} = \Delta \eta_{ji}$, the new index ellipsoid equation can be transformed into the canonical form given by Equation (14.27). This means the principal axis of the crystal can rotate in the presence of an external field.

Symmetry and Notation Convention   Because of the symmetry $\eta_{ij} = \eta_{ji}$, the following symmetries for the electro-optic coefficients exist:

$$r_{(ij)k} = r_{(ji)k}. \qquad\qquad \textbf{[14.38]}$$

$$s_{(ij)(kl)} = s_{(ji)(kl)}. \qquad\qquad \textbf{[14.39]}$$

$$s_{(ij)(kl)} = s_{(ij)(lk)}. \qquad\qquad \textbf{[14.40]}$$

From Equation (14.38), only six $r_{(ij)k}$ values must be specified for each k. A combined index $m = 1, \ldots, 6$ is thus commonly used in the literature. That is, for $r_{mk} = r_{(ij)k}$, m to (ij) mapping is given by

m	(ij)	Coefficient of
1	(11)	x^2
2	(22)	y^2
3	(33)	z^2
4	(23),(32)	yz
5	(13),(31)	zx
6	(12),(21)	xy

$$\textbf{[14.41]}$$

The quadratic coefficients can be similarly expressed by

$$s_{mn} = s_{(ij)(kl)} \qquad\qquad \textbf{[14.42]}$$

with m and n determined by Equation (14.41). By using the combined index, only 36 s_{mn} Kerr effect coefficients must be specified.

Important Types of Pockels Coefficients   In practice, many r_{mk}'s or s_{mn}'s of common electro-optic crystals are zero. For a given crystal, the electro-optic coefficients strongly depend on the point group of the crystal. When the crystal has additional rotational symmetry, inversion symmetry, or mirror symmetry, the electro-optic coefficients will also have the corresponding symmetry. Thus electro-optic crystals can be classified according to their crystal groups. Pockel coefficients of important EO crystals are given in Table 14.4.

Table 14.4 Important electro-optic crystals. In the table, $r_c = r_{33} - r_{13}(n_o^3/n_e^3)$, superscript T stands for response below audio frequency, and superscript S stands for high-frequency response [2].

Crystal System	International Symbols	Representative Crystals	Refractive Index	Electro-Optic Coefficients (10^{-12} m/V)		Wavelength (μm)
Triclinic	1	KIO_3	$n_1 = 1.700$ $n_2 = 1.828$ $n_3 = 1.832$	$r_{62} = 90$		0.5
	$\bar{1}$	Mica, Al_2SiO_5		All zero		
Monoclinic	m	$PbHPO_4$				
	2	KOH				
	2/m	$AgAuTe_4$, $PbSiO_3$		All zero		
Tetragonal	$\bar{4}2m$	ADP	$n_o = 1.5266$ $n_e = 1.4808$	$r_{41}^T = 23.76$ $r_{63}^T = 8.56$		0.546
			$n_o = 1.5222$ $n_e = 1.4773$	$r_{41}^T = 23.41$ $n_o^3 r_{63}^T = 27.6$		0.633
		AD*P	$n_o = 1.516$ $n_e = 1.475$	$r_{41}^T = 40$ $r_{63}^T = 10$		0.633
		KDP	$n_o = 1.5115$ $n_e = 1.4698$	$r_{41}^T = 8.77$ $r_{63}^T = 10.3$		0.546
			$n_o = 1.5074$ $n_e = 1.4669$	$r_{41}^T = 8$ $r_{63}^T = 11$		0.633
				$r_{41}^T = 9.7$	$n_o^3 r_{63}^T = 33$	3.39
		KD*P	$n_o = 1.5079$ $n_e = 1.4683$	$r_{41}^T = 8.8$	$r_{63}^T = 26.8$	0.546
			$n_o = 1.502$ $n_e = 1.462$	$r_{63}^T = 24.1$		0.633
	4mm	$BaTiO_3$ ($T < T_c$)	$n_o = 2.437$ $n_e = 2.365$	$r_{51}^T = 1640$ $r_c^T = 108$	$r_{51}^S = 820$ $r_c^S = 23$	0.546
	4/m	$AgIO_4$, NaIO, $KCuF_4$		All zero		
	4/mmm	TiO_2, GeO_2		All zero		
Trigonal	3m	$LiNbO_3$	$n_o = 2.286$ $n_e = 2.200$	$r_{13}^T = 9.6$ $r_{22}^T = 6.8$ $r_{33}^T = 30.9$ $r_{51}^T = 32.6$ $r_c^T = 20.1$	$r_{13}^S = 8.6$ $r_{22}^S = 3.4$ $r_{33}^S = 30.8$ $r_{51}^S = 28$	0.633
			$n_o = 2.229$ $n_e = 2.150$	$r_{22}^T = 5.4$ $r_c^T = 19$		1.15
			$n_o = 2.136$ $n_e = 2.073$	$r_{22}^T = 3.1$ $r_c^T = 18$ $r_{33}^S = 28$ $r_{51}^S = 23$	$r_{13}^S = 6.5$ $r_{22}^S = 3.1$	3.39

Table 14.4 Cont.

Crystal System	International Symbols	Representative Crystals	Refractive Index	Electro-Optic Coefficients (10^{-12} m/V)		Wavelength (μm)
		LiTaO$_3$	$n_o = 2.176$ $n_e = 2.180$	$r_{13}^T = 8.4$ $r_{22}^T = -0.2$ $r_{33}^T = 30.5$ $r_c^T = 22$	$r_{13}^S = 7.5$ $r_{22}^S = 1$ $r_{33}^S = 33$ $r_{51}^S = 20$	0.633
			$n_o = 2.060$ $n_e = 2.065$		$r_{13}^S = 4.5$ $r_{22}^S = 0.3$ $r_{33}^S = 27$ $r_{51}^S = 15$	3.39
	$\bar{3}$	S, Ge$_3$N$_4$, B$_2$O$_3$		All zero		
	$\bar{3}$m	Al$_2$O$_3$, CaCO$_3$, NaNO$_3$		All zero		
Orthorhombic	222	α-HIO$_3$	$n_1 = 1.837$ $n_2 = 1.984$ $n_3 = 1.960$	$r_{41}^T = 6.6$ $r_{52}^T = 7.0$ $r_{63}^T = 6.0$	$r_{41}^S = 2.3$ $r_{52}^S = 2.6$ $r_{63}^S = 4.3$	0.633
	2mm	KNbO$_3$	$n_1 = 2.280$ $n_2 = 2.329$ $n_3 = 2.169$	$r_{13}^T = 28$ $r_{42}^T = 380$ $r_{51}^T = 105$	$r_{23}^T = 1.3$ $r_{33}^T = 64$ $r_{42}^S = 270$	0.633
	mmm	CaCl$_2$, Al$_2$BeO$_3$		All zero		
Cubic	$\bar{4}$3m	CdTe	$n = 2.84$	$r_{41}^T = 4.5$		1.0
				$r_{41}^T = 6.8$		3.39
			$n = 2.60$	$r_{41}^T = 6.8$		10.6
			$n = 2.58$	$r_{41}^T = 5.47$		23.35
			$n = 2.53$	$r_{41}^T = 5.04$		27.95
		GaAs	$n = 3.60$	$r_{41} = 1.1$		0.9
			$n = 3.43$	$r_{41}^T = 1.43$		1.15
			$n = 3.3$	$r_{41}^T = 1.24$		3.39
			$n = 3.3$	$r_{41}^T = 1.51$		10.6
		GaP	$n = 3.66–3.08$	$r_{41}^T = -1.0$		0.55–1.3
			$n = 3.32$	$r_{41}^S = -0.97$		1.15
			$n = 3.10$	$r_{41}^S = -1.10$		3.39
			$n = 3.02$	$r_{41}^S = -0.97$		10.6
		β-ZnS	$n = 2.52$	$r_{41}^T = 1.1$		0.4
			$n = 2.42$	$r_{41}^T = 1.81$		0.5
			$n = 2.36$	$r_{41}^T = 2.1$		0.6
			$n = 2.35$		$r_{41}^S = -1.6$	0.633
					$r_{41}^S = -1.4$	3.39
		ZnSe	$n = 2.66$	$r_{41}^T = 2.0$		0.548
			$n = 2.60$	$r_{41}^S = 2.0$		0.633
			$n = 2.39$	$r_{41}^T = 2.2$		10.6

Table 14.4 Cont.

Crystal System	International Symbols	Representative Crystals	Refractive Index	Electro-Optic Coefficients (10^{-12} m/V)		Wavelength (μm)
		ZnTe	$n = 3.06$	$r_{41}^T = 4.51$		0.589
			$n = 3.01$	$r_{41}^T = 4.27$		0.616
			$n = 2.99$	$r_{41}^T = 4.04$	$r_{41}^S = 4.3$	0.633
			$n = 2.93$	$r_{41}^T = 3.97$		0.690
			$n = 2.70$	$r_{41}^T = 4.2$		3.41
			$n = 2.70$	$r_{41}^T = 3.9$		10.6
	23	$Bi_{12}GeO_{20}$	$n = 2.54$	$r_{41}^T = 3.22$		0.666
		$Bi_{12}SiO_{20}$	$n = 2.54$	$r_{41}^T = 5.0$		0.633
	432	$LiFe_5O_8$		All zero		
	m3	H_2S, $MnSe_2$, MgO_2		All zero		
	m3m	$BaTiO_3$ $(T > T_c)$		All zero		
Hexagonal	6	$LiIO_3$	$n_o = 1.8330$ $n_e = 1.7367$		$r_{13}^S = 4.1$ $r_{33}^S = 6.4$ $r_{41}^S = 1.4$ $r_{51}^S = 3.3$	0.633
	6mm	CdS	$n_o = 2.320$ $n_e = 2.336$	$r_{13}^T = 3.1$ $r_{33}^T = 3.2$ $r_c^T = 6.2$ $r_{51}^T = 2.0$		1.15
			$n_o = 2.276$ $n_e = 2.292$	$r_{13}^T = 3.5$ $r_{33}^T = 2.9$ $r_c^T = 6.4$ $r_{51}^T = 2.0$		3.39
		CdSe	$n_o = 2.452$ $n_e = 2.471$	$r_{13}^T = 1.8$	$r_{33}^S = 4.3$	3.39
		ZnO	$n_o = 1.990$ $n_e = 2.006$		$r_{13}^S = 1.4$ $r_{33}^S = 2.6$	0.633
			$n_o = 1.902$ $n_e = 1.916$		$r_{13}^S = 0.96$ $r_{33}^S = 1.9$	3.39
		α-ZnS (wurtzite)	$n_o = 2.347$ $n_e = 2.360$		$r_{13}^S = 0.9$ $r_{33}^S = 1.8$	0.633
	∞m	PbLa-(TiZr)O (PLZT)	$n_o = 2.55$	$n_e^3 r_{33} - n_o^3 r_{13} = 2320$		0.546
	6/m	$PbSb_2S_4$		All zero		
	6/mmm	BN, β-Al_2O_3, NiAs		All zero		

Tensor matrix for the electro-optic coefficients are given in Table 14.5 according to the crystal groups.

Table 14.5 Pockels electro-optic tensors of important crystal groups [2].

Crystal Group	Electro-Optic Tensor
Centrosymmetric	$\bar{1},2/m,mmm,4/m,4/mmm,\bar{3},\bar{3}m,6/m,6/mmm,m3,m3m,432$ $$\begin{bmatrix} 0 & 0 & 0 \\ 0 & 0 & 0 \\ 0 & 0 & 0 \\ 0 & 0 & 0 \\ 0 & 0 & 0 \\ 0 & 0 & 0 \end{bmatrix}$$
Triclinic	1 $$\begin{bmatrix} r_{11} & r_{11} & r_{11} \\ r_{21} & r_{21} & r_{21} \\ r_{31} & r_{31} & r_{31} \\ r_{41} & r_{41} & r_{41} \\ r_{51} & r_{51} & r_{51} \\ r_{61} & r_{61} & r_{61} \end{bmatrix}$$
Orthorhombic	222 $$\begin{bmatrix} 0 & 0 & 0 \\ 0 & 0 & 0 \\ 0 & 0 & 0 \\ r_{41} & 0 & 0 \\ 0 & r_{52} & 0 \\ 0 & 0 & r_{63} \end{bmatrix}$$ $\qquad$ $2mm$ $$\begin{bmatrix} 0 & 0 & r_{13} \\ 0 & 0 & r_{23} \\ 0 & 0 & r_{23} \\ 0 & r_{42} & 0 \\ r_{51} & 0 & 0 \\ 0 & 0 & 0 \end{bmatrix}$$
Tetragonal	$4mm$ $$\begin{bmatrix} 0 & 0 & r_{13} \\ 0 & 0 & r_{13} \\ 0 & 0 & r_{33} \\ 0 & r_{51} & 0 \\ r_{51} & 0 & 0 \\ 0 & 0 & 0 \end{bmatrix}$$ $\qquad$ $42m$ $$\begin{bmatrix} 0 & 0 & 0 \\ 0 & 0 & 0 \\ 0 & 0 & 0 \\ r_{41} & 0 & 0 \\ 0 & r_{41} & 0 \\ 0 & 0 & r_{63} \end{bmatrix}$$
Trigonal	$3m$ $$\begin{bmatrix} 0 & -r_{22} & r_{13} \\ 0 & r_{22} & r_{13} \\ 0 & 0 & r_{33} \\ 0 & r_{51} & 0 \\ r_{51} & 0 & 0 \\ -r_{22} & 0 & 0 \end{bmatrix}$$

Table 14.5 Cont.

Crystal Group	Electro-Optic Tensor
Cubic	$\bar{4}3m, 23$ $$\begin{bmatrix} 0 & 0 & 0 \\ 0 & 0 & 0 \\ 0 & 0 & 0 \\ r_{41} & 0 & 0 \\ 0 & r_{41} & 0 \\ 0 & 0 & r_{41} \end{bmatrix}$$
Hexagonal	6 $\qquad\qquad\qquad$ 6mm $$\begin{bmatrix} 0 & 0 & r_{13} \\ 0 & 0 & r_{13} \\ 0 & 0 & r_{33} \\ r_{41} & r_{51} & 0 \\ r_{51} & -r_{41} & 0 \\ 0 & 0 & 0 \end{bmatrix} \qquad \begin{bmatrix} 0 & 0 & r_{13} \\ 0 & 0 & r_{13} \\ 0 & 0 & r_{33} \\ 0 & r_{51} & 0 \\ r_{51} & 0 & 0 \\ 0 & 0 & 0 \end{bmatrix}$$

Important Types of Kerr Coefficients Tensor coefficients due to the Kerr electro-optic effect for important crystals are given in Tables 14.6 and 14.7.

Table 14.6 Important Kerr effect electro-optic crystals [2].

International Symbols	Representative Crystals	Refractive Index	Electro-Optic Coefficients, 10^{-18} $(m/V)^2$	Wavelength (μm)	Temperature $°C$
m3m	$BaTiO_3$	$n = 2.42$	$s_{11} - s_{22} = 2290$	0.633	$T > T_c = 120°C$
	$BaTiO_3$	$n = 2.42$	$n_o^3(s_{11} - s_{22}) = 72{,}000$ $n_o^3 s_{44} = 44{,}000$	0.500	$T \approx T_c$
	$K(Nb_{0.37}Ta_{0.63})O_3$	$n = 2.29$	$s_{11} - s_{22} = 2890$	0.633	20
	$KTaO_3$	$n = 2.24$	$s_{11} - s_{22} = 10$	0.633	-226
$\bar{4}2m$	KDP	$n_o = 1.5115$ $n_e = 1.4698$	$n_e^3(s_{33} - s_{11}) = 31$ $n_o^3(s_{31} - s_{11}) = 13.5$ $n_o^3(s_{12} - s_{11}) = 8.9$ $n_o^3 s_{66} = 3.0$	0.546	25
	ADP	$n_o = 1.5266$ $n_e = 1.4808$	$n_e^3(s_{33} - s_{11}) = 24$ $n_o^3(s_{31} - s_{11}) = 13.6$ $n_o^3(s_{12} - s_{11}) = 5.8$ $n_o^3 s_{66} = 2.0$	0.546	25

Table 14.7 Kerr electro-optic tensors of important crystal groups [2].

Crystal Group	Symbol	Kerr Tensor
Tetragonal	422, 4mm, $\bar{4}$2m, 4/mm	$$\begin{bmatrix} s_{11} & s_{12} & s_{13} & 0 & 0 & 0 \\ s_{12} & s_{11} & s_{13} & 0 & 0 & 0 \\ s_{31} & s_{31} & s_{33} & 0 & 0 & 0 \\ 0 & 0 & 0 & s_{44} & 0 & 0 \\ 0 & 0 & 0 & 0 & s_{44} & 0 \\ 0 & 0 & 0 & 0 & 0 & s_{66} \end{bmatrix}$$
Cubic	23,m3	$$\begin{bmatrix} s_{11} & s_{12} & s_{13} & 0 & 0 & 0 \\ s_{13} & s_{11} & s_{12} & 0 & 0 & 0 \\ s_{12} & s_{13} & s_{11} & 0 & 0 & 0 \\ 0 & 0 & 0 & s_{44} & 0 & 0 \\ 0 & 0 & 0 & 0 & s_{44} & 0 \\ 0 & 0 & 0 & 0 & 0 & s_{44} \end{bmatrix}$$
	432,m3m,$\bar{4}$3m	$$\begin{bmatrix} s_{11} & s_{12} & s_{12} & 0 & 0 & 0 \\ s_{12} & s_{11} & s_{12} & 0 & 0 & 0 \\ s_{12} & s_{11} & s_{11} & 0 & 0 & 0 \\ 0 & 0 & 0 & s_{44} & 0 & 0 \\ 0 & 0 & 0 & 0 & s_{44} & 0 \\ 0 & 0 & 0 & 0 & 0 & s_{44} \end{bmatrix}$$
Isotropic		$$\begin{bmatrix} s_{11} & s_{12} & s_{12} & 0 & 0 & 0 \\ s_{12} & s_{11} & s_{12} & 0 & 0 & 0 \\ s_{12} & s_{11} & s_{11} & 0 & 0 & 0 \\ 0 & 0 & 0 & (s_{11}-s_{12})/2 & 0 & 0 \\ 0 & 0 & 0 & 0 & (s_{11}-s_{12})/2 & 0 \\ 0 & 0 & 0 & 0 & 0 & (s_{11}-s_{12})/2 \end{bmatrix}$$

Example 14.5

CRYSTAL GROUP $\bar{4}$2M   From Table 14.4, note that crystals in the group $\bar{4}$2m, such as KDP and ADP, are uniaxial. Their z-axis is their optic axis. If an electric field is applied also in the z direction, the index ellipsoid equation is

$$\frac{x^2 + y^2}{n_o^2} + \frac{z^2}{n_e^2} + 2r_{63}E_z xy = \frac{1}{n^2}.$$ **[14.43]**

If the x–y plane is rotated by 45 degrees and two new coordinates:

$$x' = \frac{1}{\sqrt{2}}(x - y)$$ **[14.44]**

$$y' = \frac{1}{\sqrt{2}}(x + y)$$ **[14.45]**

are defined, then Equation (14.43) reduces to

$$\frac{x'^2}{n_1^2} + \frac{y'^2}{n_2^2} + \frac{z^2}{n_e^2} = \frac{1}{n^2} \qquad \textbf{[14.46]}$$

where

$$\frac{1}{n_1^2} \stackrel{\text{def}}{=} \frac{1}{n_o^2} - r_{63} E_z \qquad \textbf{[14.47]}$$

and

$$\frac{1}{n_2^2} \stackrel{\text{def}}{=} \frac{1}{n_o^2} + r_{63} E_z \qquad \textbf{[14.48]}$$

Therefore, the uniaxial property becomes biaxial under an electric field E_z. When $n_o^2 r_{63} E_z \ll 1$,

$$n_1 \approx n_o(1 + \tfrac{1}{2} n_o^2 r_{63} E_z) \qquad \textbf{[14.49]}$$

and

$$n_2 \approx n_o(1 - \tfrac{1}{2} n_o^2 r_{63} E_z). \qquad \textbf{[14.50]}$$

Therefore, the uniaxial crystal not only has a rotation of 45 degrees of its principal axis but also becomes biaxial. The birefringence between the two new indices n_1 and n_2 is

$$\mathcal{B} = n_1 - n_2 = n_o^3 r_{63} E_z. \ \blacksquare \qquad \textbf{[14.51]}$$

CRYSTAL GROUP 3M From Table 14.4, note that crystals in point group 3m such as LiNbO$_3$ are also uniaxial. Their z-axes are their optic axes. If an electric field is applied parallel to the z-axis, from Table 14.5, the index ellipsoid equation of these crystals is

Example 14.6

$$\frac{x^2 + y^2}{n_o^2} + \frac{z^2}{n_e^2} + r_{13} E_z x^2 + r_{13} E_z y^2 + r_{33} E_z z^2 = \frac{1}{n^2}.$$

This can be modified as

$$\frac{x^2}{n_o'^2} + \frac{y^2}{n_o'^2} + \frac{z^2}{n_e'^2} = \frac{1}{n^2} \qquad \textbf{[14.52]}$$

where

$$\frac{1}{n_o'^2} \stackrel{\text{def}}{=} \frac{1}{n_o^2} + r_{13} E_z \qquad \textbf{[14.53]}$$

and

$$\frac{1}{n_e'^2} \stackrel{\text{def}}{=} \frac{1}{n_e^2} + r_{33} E_z. \qquad \textbf{[14.54]}$$

Therefore, the uniaxial property is maintained under an electric field in the z direction, and there is no change of the principal axis.

From Equations (14.53) and (14.54), when the change of refractive index $r_{33} E_z$ is small compared to $1/n_o^2$ or $1/n_e^2$,

$$n_o' \approx n_o (1 - \tfrac{1}{2} n_o^2 r_{13} E_z) \qquad\qquad \textbf{[14.55]}$$

and

$$n_e' \approx n_e (1 - \tfrac{1}{2} n_e^2 r_{33} E_z). \qquad\qquad \textbf{[14.56]}$$

The birefringence between n_e' and n_o' is

$$\mathcal{B} = n_e' - n_o' = (n_e - n_o) - \tfrac{1}{2}(n_e^3 r_{33} - n_o^3 r_{13}) E_z. \ \blacksquare \qquad\qquad \textbf{[14.57]}$$

Example 14.7	**CRYSTAL GROUP $\bar{4}$3M** From Table 14.4, note that cubic crystals in the group $\bar{4}$3m such as GaAs, are isotropic. According to their EO coefficient tensors, they can become biaxial if an external electric field is applied. From Table 14.5, the new index ellipsoid equation under an electric field in the $\hat{z}$ direction is

$$\frac{1}{n^2}(x^2 + y^2 + z^2) + 2r_{41} E_z xy = \frac{1}{n^2}$$

or

$$\frac{x'^2}{n_1^2} + \frac{y'^2}{n_2^2} + \frac{z^2}{n^2} = \frac{1}{n^2} \qquad\qquad \textbf{[14.58]}$$

where the new coordinates x' and y' have the same definitions given by Equation (14.46), with

$$\frac{1}{n_1^2} \stackrel{\text{def}}{=} \frac{1}{n^2} + r_{41} E_z \qquad\qquad \textbf{[14.59]}$$

and

$$\frac{1}{n_2^2} \stackrel{\text{def}}{=} \frac{1}{n^2} - r_{41} E_z. \qquad\qquad \textbf{[14.60]}$$

Therefore,

$$n_{1,2} \approx n(1 \mp \tfrac{1}{2} n^2 r_{41} E_z) \qquad\qquad \textbf{[14.61]}$$

and the birefringence between n_1 and n_2 is

$$\mathcal{B} = n_1 - n_2 = -n^3 r_{41} E_z. \ \blacksquare \qquad\qquad \textbf{[14.62]}$$

Example 14.8	**KERR EFFECT IN ISOTROPIC CRYSTALS** Consider the Kerr effect in an isotropic crystal such as $BaTiO_3$. If the applied electric field is in the $\hat{z}$ direction, from Table 14.7, the index ellipsoid equation is

$$\left(\frac{1}{n^2} + s_{12}E_z^2\right)x^2 + \left(\frac{1}{n^2} + s_{12}E_z^2\right)y^2 + \left(\frac{1}{n^2} + s_{11}E_z^2\right)z^2 = \frac{1}{n^2}.$$

Therefore, the crystal is changed from isotropic to uniaxial with

$$n_o \approx n - \frac{1}{2}n^3 s_{12}E_z^2$$

and

$$n_e \approx n - \frac{1}{2}n^3 s_{11}E_z^2.$$

The birefringence is

$$\mathcal{B} = n_e - n_o = \frac{1}{2}n^3(s_{12}-s_{11})E_z^2.$$

For BaTiO$_3$ above its Curie temperature, $n = 2.42$ and $s_{11} - s_{12} = 2.290 \times 10^{-15}$ (m/V)^2. Therefore, the birefringence is

$$\mathcal{B} = n_e - n_o = 1.62 \times 10^{-14} \times E_z^2.$$

It is common to express the birefringence in terms of the so-called **Kerr constant**, K:

$$\mathcal{B} = n_e - n_0 = K\lambda E^2. \tag{14.63}$$

Therefore,

$$K = \frac{n^3}{2\lambda}(s_{12} - s_{11}).$$

For BaTiO$_3$ at $\lambda = 0.633$ μm,

$$K = \frac{1.62 \times 10^{-14}}{6.33 \times 10^{-7}} = 2.56 \times 10^{-8} \text{ m/V}^2. \blacksquare$$

14.4.2 LONGITUDINAL AND TRANSVERSE MODULATORS

According to the relative direction of the bias electric field and the lightwave propagation, an EO modulator can be classified into two categories: *transversal* and *longitudinal*. As illustrated in Figure 14.6, the bias electric field is perpendicular to the wave propagation direction in transverse modulation; and in longitudinal modulation, the bias electric field is in the same direction as the wave propagation.

For longitudinal modulators, from Equation (14.21) and the EO effect specified by equations such as (14.51), the phase change of a given permissible polarization is linearly proportional to the applied electric field E_z. Therefore, if the lightwave propagates in the z direction,

$$\Delta\phi = \frac{2\pi L}{\lambda}\Delta n = \frac{2\pi r}{\lambda}LE_z = \frac{2\pi r}{\lambda}V_B \tag{14.64}$$

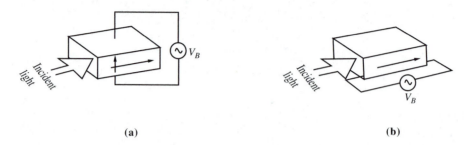

Figure 14.6 (a) Transverse and (b) longitudinal modulators.

where V_B is the external bias voltage and r is the electro-optic coefficient according to the wave polarization as given in Table 14.8.

Table 14.8 EO coefficients and birefringence $\mathcal{B}$ for different combinations of important crystal groups and modulation types. The applied electric field is in the $\hat{z}$ direction.

Crystal Group	Longitudinal	Transverse
$\overline{4}2m$	$r_{a,b} = \pm\frac{1}{2}n_o^3 r_{63}$	$r_a = \pm\frac{1}{2}n_o^3 r_{63}, \ r_b = 0$
	$\mathcal{B} = n_o^3 r_{63} E_z$	$\mathcal{B} = (n_e - n_o) \mp \frac{1}{2}n_o^3 r_{63} E_z$
$3m$	$r_a = r_b = -\frac{1}{2}n_o^3 r_{13}$	$r_a = -\frac{1}{2}n_o^3 r_{13}, \ r_b = -\frac{1}{2}n_e^3 r_{33}$
	$\mathcal{B} = 0$	$\mathcal{B} = (n_e - n_o) + \frac{1}{2}(n_o^3 r_{13} - n_e^3 r_{33})E_z$
$\overline{4}3m$	$r_{a,b} = \pm\frac{1}{2}n^3 r_{41}$	$r_a = \pm\frac{1}{2}n^3 r_{41}, \ r_b = 0$
	$\mathcal{B} = n^3 r_{41} E_z$	$\mathcal{B} = \mp\frac{1}{2}n^3 r_{41} E_z$
$m3m*$	$s_a = s_b = -\frac{1}{2}n^3 s_{12}$	$s_a = -\frac{1}{2}n^3 s_{12}, \ s_b = -\frac{1}{2}n^3 s_{11}$
	$\mathcal{B} = 0$	$\mathcal{B} = \frac{1}{2}n^3(s_{12} - s_{11})E_z^2$

| * Kerr Effect

On the other hand, if $\hat{z}$ is in the transverse plane of the wave propagation,

$$\Delta\phi = \frac{2\pi r}{\lambda}LE_z = \frac{2\pi r}{\lambda}\frac{V_B}{d}L \qquad \textbf{[14.65]}$$

where d is thickness of the EO crystal in the transverse direction.

From Equations (14.64) and (14.65), the classification of longitudinal and transverse modulations has two important performance implications: modulation depth and modulation bandwidth. These are discussed below.

Modulation Depth For longitudinal modulation, from Equation (14.64), the phase change is not a function of L. Therefore, the phase change or modulation depth can be increased only by increasing the bias voltage. Because the electro-optic coefficient r is small in general, this means a large voltage is required.

For transverse modulation, the phase change can be large at a small and fixed bias voltage if the ratio L/d is large. Therefore, the longitudinal length of the modulator can be linearly increased to achieve the required phase change.

LONGITUDINAL KDP MODULATOR   From Example 14.5 and Equation (14.51), if the incident lightwave propagates along the optic axis (z-axis), there are two polarizations: $\hat{x}'$ and $\hat{y}'$, with phase propagation constants $(\omega/c)n_1$ and $(\omega/c)n_2$, respectively. In other words, there can be a phase difference between the two permissible polarizations over distance L:

Example 14.9

$$\Delta\phi = \frac{\omega}{c}(n_1 - n_2)L \approx \frac{2\pi}{\lambda}n_o^3 r_{63} E_z L = \frac{2\pi}{\lambda}n_o^3 r_{63} V_B \qquad \textbf{[14.66]}$$

where V_B is the bias voltage.

For KDP, $n_o = 1.5$ and $r_{63} = 11 \times 10^{-12}$ m/V. Thus

$$\Delta\phi = \frac{2\pi}{\lambda} 3.7 \times 10^{-11} V_B.$$

A π phase change for λ at 1.5 μm requires a bias voltage

$$V_B = V_\pi = \frac{1.5}{2 \times 3.7 \times 10^{-5}} = 20 \text{ kV}$$

which is very high. ∎

TRANSVERSE LiNbO₃ MODULATOR   From Equation (14.57), if the incident lightwave propagates along the y-axis of the crystal, there can be two polarizations in the x and z directions, with the refractive index equal to n_o' and n_e', respectively. The phase difference of the two polarizations over distance L due to the refractive index change is

Example 14.10

$$\Delta\phi = \frac{\omega}{c}(n_o' - n_e')L \approx \frac{\pi}{\lambda}(n_e^3 r_{33} - n_o^3 r_{13})E_z L = \frac{\pi}{\lambda}n_e^3 r_c \frac{V_B}{d} L \qquad \textbf{[14.67]}$$

where V_B is the bias voltage applied in the transverse direction, d is the transverse thickness of the crystal, and

$$r_c \overset{\text{def}}{=} r_{33} - r_{13}\frac{n_o^3}{n_e^3}. \qquad \textbf{[14.68]}$$

For LiNbO₃, from Table 14.4, $n_o = 2.229$ and $n_e = 2.150$ at $\lambda = 1.15$ μm. Furthermore, $r_c = 19 \times 10^{-12}$ m/V. Thus

$$\Delta\phi = \frac{\pi}{\lambda} 1.89 \times 10^{-10} \times \frac{V_B}{d} L.$$

A π phase change requires a voltage

$$V_\pi = \frac{1.15}{1.89 \times 10^{-4}} \frac{d}{L} = 6084 \times \frac{d}{L}.$$

If $d/L = 0.01$, the required voltage for a phase change of π is only 60.8 V. Therefore, a transverse modulator needs a much smaller voltage than that in Example 14.9 when $L/d \gg 1$. ∎

Example 14.11

TRANSVERSE GaAs MODULATOR   From Example 14.7, when the propagation direction of the incident light is in the y' axis, there are two polarizations in the x' and z directions, with the refractive index equal to n_1 and n, respectively. The phase change over a propagation distance L is

$$\Delta\phi = \frac{\pi}{\lambda} n^3 r_{41} E_z L = \frac{\pi}{\lambda} n^3 r_{41} \frac{V_B}{d} L. \qquad \text{[14.69]}$$

Thus

$$V_B = V_\pi = \lambda \frac{d}{L} \frac{1}{n^3 r_{41}}. \qquad \text{[14.70]}$$

For GaAs, from Table 14.4, $n = 3.43$ and $r_{41} = 1.43 \times 10^{-12}$ m/V at $\lambda = 1.15\ \mu$m. Therefore,

$$\Delta\phi = 1.58 \times 10^{-4} \times \frac{L}{d} V_B$$

and

$$V_\pi = 2.0 \times 10^4 \times \frac{d}{L}.$$

If $d/L = 0.01$, $V_\pi = 20$ V. ∎

Modulation Bandwidth   The modulation bandwidth of an EO modulator is limited by two factors: transit delay throughout the modulator and the RC time constant to charge and discharge the modulator. The dependence of the bandwidth on the modulator length L is briefly pointed out here. Detailed discussion on the modulation bandwidth will be given in Section 14.7.

The phase transit delay is defined by

$$\tau_t = \frac{L}{v_p} \qquad \text{[14.71]}$$

where v_p is the phase velocity. Therefore, the transit delay is linearly proportional to the length of the modulator. Equations (14.64) and (14.65) show that a small transit delay can be achieved for longitudinal modulation because the phase change does not depend on L. For transverse modulation, a large phase change requires a large L, which results in a large transit delay and thus a smaller modulation bandwidth.

Because an EO modulator can also be considered as a dielectric capacitor, it takes time to charge and discharge during modulation. In general, the charge time is proportional to the capacitance C, which is proportional to L/d for transverse modulators and d/L for longitudinal modulators. Equation (14.65) shows that transverse modulators have a charge time inversely proportional to the phase change needed. This means a trade-off between modulation depth and bandwidth at a given bias voltage. For longitudinal modulators, because d/L is small, there is a very small capacitance and the charge time can be neglected.

14.5 ELECTRO-OPTIC PHASE MODULATORS

In the previous discussion on the electro-optic effect, a phase modulator was implemented by simply modulating the refractive index of the waveguide. This is illustrated in Figure 14.7, where the polarization of the incident light is aligned to one of the principle axes in the transverse plane, say $\hat{a}$. A polarizer filter may be added to reject any coupling to the other transverse propagation mode.

When only the linear Pockels effect is considered,

$$n_a = n_{a0} + \Delta n_a(t) = n_{a0} + r_a E_z \stackrel{\text{def}}{=} n_{a0} + K_a V_B \qquad \text{[14.72]}$$

where r_a is the EO coefficient that can be found from Table 14.8 for some important types of EO crystals. For longitudinal modulators,

$$K_a = r_a \frac{1}{L} \qquad \text{[14.73]}$$

and for transverse modulators,

$$K_a = r_a \frac{1}{d} \qquad \text{[14.74]}$$

where d is the transverse width of the modulator.

Over a propagation distance L, the phase change with respect to the phase at zero bias is

$$\Delta\phi_a = \frac{2\pi}{\lambda} \Delta n_a L = \frac{2\pi}{\lambda} K_a L V_B. \qquad \text{[14.75]}$$

Therefore, achieving a large phase change requires a large factor $K_a L V_B$.

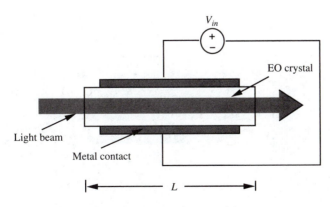

Figure 14.7   Electro-optic phase modulator.

Example 14.12

MATERIAL SELECTION FOR PHASE MODULATION   A large K_a factor at a given L and V_B requires a large r_a value. Thus a large refractive index and EO coefficients r_{ij} must be found in Table 14.8.

For example, for longitudinal modulators of the crystal group $\bar{4}$2m, a large $n_o^3 r_{63}$ value is needed. At wavelength $\lambda = 0.633$ μm, from Table 14.4, $n_o^3 r_{63}$ equals 27.6, 34.8, 37.7, and 81.7 for ADP, AD*P, KDP, and KD*P, respectively. Therefore, KD*P has the largest K_a coefficient. ∎

14.6 ELECTRO-OPTIC AMPLITUDE MODULATORS

There are three ways to implement amplitude modulation from the electro-optic effect: (1) polarization filtering, (2) wave interference, and (3) waveguide coupling. These methods are explained below.

14.6.1 POLARIZATION FILTERING

From Example 14.2, note that the output of an anisotropic crystal is in general elliptically polarized. By properly controlling the relative phase change between the two permissible polarizations, the output can be linearly polarized. Therefore, amplitude modulation can be performed by adding a polarizer at the modulator output, as illustrated in Figure 14.8.

In general, if the two permissible polarizations of the electric field in the EO modulator are $\hat{s}_a$ and $\hat{s}_b$, the output electric field is

$$\bar{E} = E_a \cos(\omega_c t - k_a L)\hat{s}_a + E_b \cos(\omega_c t - k_b L)\hat{s}_b \qquad \textbf{[14.76]}$$

where $k_{a,b} = n_{a,b}\omega/c$ are the propagation constants of the two polarizations.

From Equation (14.76), when $(k_a - k_b)L = 2m\pi$, where m is an integer, the output electric field is linearly polarized in the direction of $E_a\hat{s}_a + E_b\hat{s}_b$. When $(k_a - k_b)L$

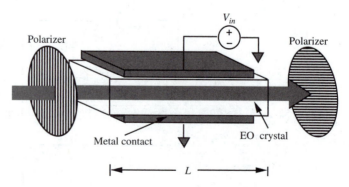

Figure 14.8   EO amplitude modulator using polarization filtering.

$= (2m + 1)\pi$, there is another linearly polarized output in the direction of $E_a\hat{s}_a - E_b\hat{s}_b$. Therefore, the two linearly polarized outputs can be expressed as

$$\hat{p}_1 = \cos\phi\hat{s}_a + \sin\phi\hat{s}_b \qquad \textbf{[14.77]}$$

and

$$\hat{p}_2 = \cos\phi\hat{s}_a - \sin\phi\hat{s}_b \qquad \textbf{[14.78]}$$

where

$$\cos\phi = \frac{E_a}{\sqrt{E_a^2 + E_b^2}}$$

and

$$\sin\phi = \frac{E_b}{\sqrt{E_a^2 + E_b^2}}.$$

In general, these two linearly polarized waves may not be orthogonal to each other. Because

$$\hat{p}_1 \cdot \hat{p}_2 = \cos^2\phi - \sin^2\phi \qquad \textbf{[14.79]}$$

they are orthogonal if $|E_a| = |E_b|$ at the input of the modulator.

OOK KDP MODULATOR   Consider a longitudinal KDP modulator. From Example 14.5, $\hat{s}_a$ and $\hat{s}_b$ are in the directions of $\hat{x} \pm \hat{y}$. If there is a linearly polarized wave in the direction of $\hat{x}$ at the modulator input, $E_a = E_b = E_x/\sqrt{2}$. Therefore, the two linearly polarized waves are orthogonal to each other. From Equations (14.77) and (14.78), the two linear polarizations are in the direction of $\hat{x}$ and $\hat{y}$. By having a relative phase change $(k_a - k_b)L$ equal to π, there can be a linearly polarized output in the $\hat{y}$ direction. Thus, if a polarizer filter is placed at the modulator output in parallel to $\hat{x}$, OOK modulation can be achieved by applying a bias voltage at either 0 or V_π. ∎

Example 14.13

14.6.2 FIELD INTERFERENCE

The basic idea of amplitude modulation using wave interference is to modulate the phase of one wave and add it to other waves. Modulating the phase can cause either constructive or destructive interference, which results in amplitude modulation.

For example, the Fabry-Perot interferometer discussed in Appendix 3–A can be used for amplitude modulation by modulating the refractive index of the resonant cavity. According to Equation (3.26) and Figure 3.33, the refractive index can be changed to modulate the output intensity.

A more important alternative called the Mach-Zehnder interferometer (MZI) [4] discussed in Chapter 9 and illustrated in Figure 14.9 is also commonly used for amplitude modulation. Assume the two beam splitters in Figure 14.9 are made such that the two split beams have a phase difference $\pi/2$:

$$r = \frac{1}{\sqrt{2}} e^{j\pi/4}$$

$$t = \frac{1}{\sqrt{2}} e^{-j\pi/4}$$

where r and t are the reflection and transmission coefficients. If there is a phase shift ϕ_1 in the path through mirror 1 and ϕ_2 through mirror 2,

$$E_1 = t E_i e^{-j\phi_1}$$

and

$$E_2 = r E_i e^{-j\phi_2}.$$

Therefore,

$$E_{o1} = r E_1 + t E_2 = rt E_i (e^{-j\phi_1} + e^{-j\phi_2}) \qquad \textbf{[14.80]}$$

and

$$E_{o2} = t E_1 + r E_2 = E_i (t^2 e^{-j\phi_1} + r^2 e^{-j\phi_2}). \qquad \textbf{[14.81]}$$

If $\Delta\phi \overset{\text{def}}{=} \phi_1 - \phi_2$ and

$$\phi_0 = {}^1\!/_2(\phi_1 + \phi_2)$$

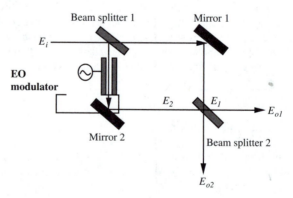

Figure 14.9   EO amplitude modulator based on the structure of the Mach-Zehnder interferometer.

Equations (14.80) and (14.81) reduce to

$$E_{o1} = E_i \cos(\Delta\phi/2)e^{-j\phi_0} \qquad \textbf{[14.82]}$$

and

$$E_{o2} = -E_i \sin(\Delta\phi/2)e^{-j\phi_0}. \qquad \textbf{[14.83]}$$

Therefore,

$$P_{o1} = P_{in} \cos^2(\Delta\phi/2) \qquad \textbf{[14.84]}$$

and

$$P_{o2} = P_{in} \sin^2(\Delta\phi/2). \qquad \textbf{[14.85]}$$

MZI MODULATION   The phase change is $\Delta\phi = (2\pi L/\lambda)K_a V_B$ if L is the modulator waveguide length in Figure 14.7 and V_B is the applied voltage. If the phase change $\Delta\phi$ is small, the output power P_{o1} is

Example 14.14

$$P_{o1} \approx P_{in}\left[1 - \left(\frac{\Delta\phi}{2}\right)^2\right] = P_{in}\left[1 - (\pi L K_a/\lambda)^2 V_B^2\right]. \qquad \textbf{[14.86]}$$

If $L = 150\,\mu$m, $\lambda = 1.5\,\mu$m, and $K_a = 1 \times 10^{-4}$ 1/V, $\pi L K_a/\lambda = 0.03$ 1/V. If

$$V_B(t) = k_m m(t)^{1/2}$$

where k_m is in units of volts and $m(t)$ has a peak value equal to unity,

$$P_{o1} = P_{in}\left[1 - (0.03k_m)^2 m(t)\right].$$

Therefore, the amplitude modulation index is $(0.03k_m)^2$. To have 50 percent modulation, k_m must equal 24 V. ∎

14.6.3   WAVEGUIDE COUPLING

Another amplitude modulation method uses two coupled waveguides, as shown in Figure 14.10, where an incident wave at one of the waveguide inputs can be coupled to the other waveguide [5]. To see this, express the total electric field as

$$\mathcal{E}(x, y, z, t) = E_1(z)E_{T,1}(x, y)e^{j(\omega t - \beta_1 z)} + E_2(z)E_{T,2}(x, y)e^{j(\omega t - \beta_2 z)} \qquad \textbf{[14.87]}$$

where $E_i(z)$ is the slowly varying factor of the electric field propagating in waveguide i, $E_{T,i}(x, y)$ is the transverse mode of waveguide i, and β_i is the corresponding propagation constant along the z-axis.

Appendix 14–A and [2] give the following coupled-mode equations for $E_1(z)$ and $E_2(z)$:

$$\frac{\partial E_1}{\partial z} = -j\kappa E_2 e^{j2\delta z} \qquad \textbf{[14.88]}$$

and

$$\frac{\partial E_2}{\partial z} = -j\kappa E_1 e^{-j2\delta z} \qquad \textbf{[14.89]}$$

where κ is the coupling constant and δ is the mismatch factor between the two waveguides. Equations (14.88) and (14.89) can be solved to yield the following solutions:

$$P_{o1} = P_{in} - P_{o2} \qquad \textbf{[14.90]}$$

and

$$P_{o2} = P_{in}\frac{\kappa^2}{\kappa^2 + \delta^2} \sin^2[(\kappa^2 + \delta^2)^{1/2}z] \qquad \textbf{[14.91]}$$

where P_{in} is the input power at waveguide 1 and $P_{oi} \overset{\text{def}}{=} |E_i|^2$ is the power at the output of waveguide i.

When no external bias voltage is applied, the two waveguides can be assumed to be the same. In this case, the mismatch factor δ is zero. It is then possible to design the waveguide length L to have zero output power at one of the waveguide outputs. To minimize the waveguide length, it is usually set at

$$L = L_{\pi/2} = \frac{\pi}{2\kappa}. \qquad \textbf{[14.92]}$$

In this case, there can be a complete power switchover at the zero bias.

When the bias voltage of the coupled waveguides is increased, the refractive indices of the two waveguides are changed. Because of the asymmetry, $\delta \neq 0$. If

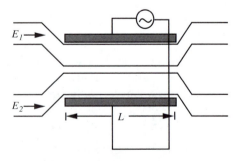

Figure 14.10   EO amplitude modulator using waveguide
coupling.

$$(\kappa^2 + \delta^2)^{1/2} L_{\pi/2} = \pi$$

or

$$\delta = \sqrt{3}\kappa \qquad \qquad \textbf{[14.93]}$$

there can be zero power output at the crossover arm. From Appendix 14–A, δ can be estimated by

$$\delta \approx \frac{1}{2}(\beta_1 - \beta_2) = \frac{2\pi}{\lambda}\Delta n = \frac{2\pi}{\lambda} r \frac{V_B}{d}.$$

Therefore, the required switchover voltage is

$$V_B = \sqrt{3}\frac{\kappa \lambda}{2\pi}\frac{d}{r}. \qquad \qquad \textbf{[14.94]}$$

LiNbO$_3$ WAVEGUIDE COUPLER   For a waveguide made of LiNbO$_3$ at $\lambda = 0.633$ μm, $r = 1.89 \times 10^{-10}$ m/V. Therefore, assuming $d = 10$ μm and $\kappa = 1.0 \times 10^3$ 1/m,

$$V_B = 9.2V. \blacksquare$$

Example 14.15

Alternating-$\Delta\beta$ Couplers   In the above discussion, the extinction ratio can be zero if $L = L_{\pi/2}$. In practice, the L value cannot be set precisely to $L_{\pi/2}$ because of various fabrication errors. Thus, from Equation (14.91), a δ value cannot be found such that $P_{o2} = P_{in}$. For example, to maximize the factor $\sin([\kappa^2 + \delta^2]^{1/2}L)$ requires a nonzero δ. However, when $\delta \neq 0$, $\kappa^2/(\kappa^2 + \delta^2) < 1$. Therefore, when $L \neq L_{\pi/2}$, the design error cannot be electrically compensated to have a 100 percent switchover. This thus reduces the achievable modulation depth.

To overcome this problem, alternating- $\Delta\beta$ or -δ couplers have been proposed [6]. This is illustrated in Figure 14.11. As derived in Appendix 14–A, the output power of the two waveguides can be expressed as

$$P_{o1}(L) = P_{in}\left(1 - \frac{2\kappa^2}{\kappa^2 + \delta^2}\sin^2[(\kappa^2 + \delta^2)^{1/2}L/2]\right)^2 \qquad \qquad \textbf{[14.95]}$$

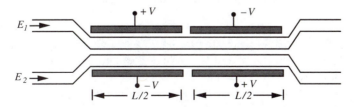

Figure 14.11   Alternating $\Delta\beta$ waveguides.

and

$$P_{o2}(L) = P_{in} - P_{o1}(L). \qquad \textbf{[14.96]}$$

Therefore, power can be completely transferred to the other waveguide if

$$\frac{2\kappa^2}{\kappa^2 + \delta^2} \sin^2[(\kappa^2 + \delta^2)^{1/2} L/2] = 1. \qquad \textbf{[14.97]}$$

This equation can be used to find the required δ for a given L.

Example 14.16

From Equation (14.97), if $\delta = 0$, there is a complete crossover if $L = \pi/2\kappa = L_{\pi/2}$. On the other hand, if $L = L_{\pi/2}(1 + \epsilon)$, a nonzero δ is needed to satisfy Equation (14.97). In other words,

$$\frac{1}{1 + (\delta/\kappa)^2} \sin^2 \left(\frac{\pi}{4} + \frac{\pi \delta^2}{8\kappa^2} + \frac{\pi}{4} \epsilon \right) = \frac{1}{2}.$$

This reduces to

$$\sin \left(\frac{\pi \delta^2}{4\kappa^2} + \frac{\pi}{2} \epsilon \right) = \frac{\delta^2}{\kappa^2}. \qquad \textbf{[14.98]}$$

When $\delta^2 \ll \kappa^2$ or $\epsilon \ll 1$,

$$\delta^2 \approx \frac{\pi/2}{1 - (\pi/4)} \kappa^2 \epsilon.$$

In other words, electrical compensation is possible if the error ϵ is positive. ∎

14.7 MODULATION BANDWIDTH AND SWITCHING POWER OF ELECTRO-OPTIC MODULATORS

In the previous discussion, the external bias voltage that modulates the permittivity tensor is assumed to be dc. When the modulating signal is rapidly changing or has a large bandwidth, the modulator may not respond fast enough, which results in a smaller modulation depth. Furthermore, because the modulator can be considered as a capacitor to the external voltage source, a high speed modulation also requires a high ac power. Because high-speed modulation is required in optical communications, this section discusses some important high-speed modulation effects.

Modulation Bandwidth and Depth of EO Modulators   As mentioned earlier, the modulation bandwidth of an EO external modulator is limited by two factors: (1) propagation delay through the modulator and (2) charge and discharge time (or simply the RC time constant) to change the bias electric field of the modulator.

To quantify the effect of finite propagation delay, consider a modulator of length L. The total phase change of an incident lightwave due to refractive index modulation can be expressed as

$$\phi(t) = \int_0^L \Delta\beta_z \left[t - (L - z)/v_p \right] dz = \int_0^L \frac{2\pi \Delta n(t - \tau_t + z/v_p)}{\lambda} dz \qquad \textbf{[14.99]}$$

where τ_t is the transit delay from Equation (14.71). If the modulator is used for binary phase-shift keying (PSK) and $\Delta n(t)$ is switched between

$$\pm\Delta n_p \stackrel{\text{def}}{=} \pm K_a V_B \qquad \textbf{[14.100]}$$

there can be a pulse train for $\Delta n(t)$, with the duration of each pulse equal to the bit period. This is illustrated in Figure 14.12. From Equations (14.99) and (14.100), the peak-to-peak phase difference can equal π if $\Delta n_p = \lambda/(2L)$ and $\tau_t < T_0$, where T_0 is the bit period. When the propagation delay is longer than the bit period, however, the peak-to-peak phase deviation is reduced to

$$\Delta\phi_p = \frac{2\pi}{\lambda} \Delta n_p (2T_0 - \tau_t) v_p = \pi \left(\frac{2T_0 - \tau_t}{\tau_t} \right) \qquad \textbf{[14.101]}$$

for $T_0 < \tau_t < 2T_0$. Equation (14.101) tells that a long propagation delay τ_t compared to T_0 will reduce the achievable phase change. For the pulse train of the phase change given in Figure 14.12a, the achievable peak phase $\Delta\phi_p$ is shown in Figure 14.13. In practice, in addition to the requirement $\tau_t < T_0$, the phase change must be stabilized over most of the bit period. For τ_t to be within 20 percent of the bit period,[2] the following speed limit applies:

$$R_b \leq \frac{1}{5\tau_t}. \qquad \textbf{[14.102]}$$

Consider a transverse GaAs waveguide phase modulator. Modulating the device for 1 Gb/s binary PSK transmission requires, from Equation (14.102),

Example 14.17

$$\tau_t < \frac{1}{5R_b} = 0.2 \text{ nsec.}$$

If the refractive index is $n = 3.43$, the pulse velocity is

$$v_p = \frac{c}{n} = 8.75 \times 10^7 \text{ m/sec.}$$

Therefore, the cavity length L should be within

$$L \leq v_p \tau_t = 175 \text{ mm.}$$

To achieve a phase change of π:

$$\Delta\phi = \pi = \frac{2\pi}{\lambda} r_a \frac{L}{d} V_B$$

it requires

---

[2] From Chapter 7, the total pulse rise time should be within 25 percent of the bit interval without significant power penalty. Considering other rise times in the system, a rise time of 20 percent of the bit interval is optimistically allowed here.

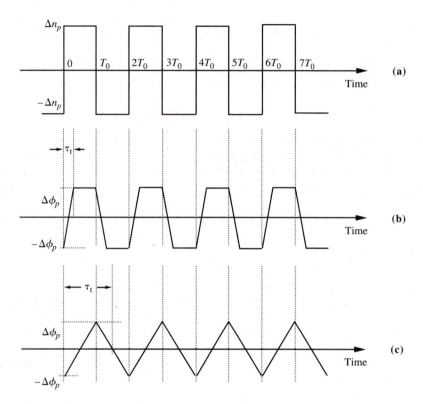

Figure 14.12   Effect of finite propagation delay on phase modulation:
(a) change of refractive index as a function of time,
(b) change of phase as a function of time when the transit
delay τ_t is smaller than the bit interval, and (c) change of
phase when $2T > \tau_t > T$.

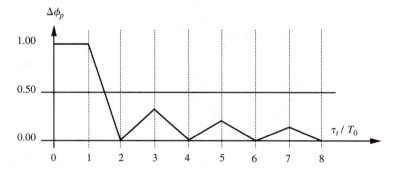

Figure 14.13   Peak phase as a function of τ_t / T_0.

$$V_B > \frac{d}{2r_a}\frac{\lambda}{L}.$$

For GaAs, $r_a = n^3 r_{41} = 5.77 \times 10^{-11}$ m/V at $\lambda = 0.633$ μm. Therefore, the required voltage is

$$V_B > 6.27 \times 10^4 d = 0.63 \text{ V}$$

at $d = 10$ μm. If L is set to 1 mm instead, the required voltage will be 110 V. ∎

The speed limit given by Equation (14.102) is derived from digital modulation where $\Delta n(t)$ is a pulse train. Similar conclusions can be drawn for analog modulation by considering a single-tone sinusoidal waveform for $\Delta n(t)$ instead. In this case,

$$\Delta n(t) = \Delta n_p \cos(\omega_m t) \qquad \textbf{[14.103]}$$

and

$$\Delta\phi(t) = \frac{2\pi v_p}{\lambda}\int_0^{\tau_t} \Delta n(t - t')dt' = (2\pi \Delta n_p)\frac{L}{\lambda}\text{sinc}(f_m \tau_t)\cos(\omega_m t). \qquad \textbf{[14.104]}$$

Therefore, there is a frequency dependent factor $\text{sinc}(f_m \tau_t)$ that causes the reduction of the peak-to-peak value of the phase function $\phi(t)$ as f_m increases. If the transmission bandwidth $f_m = B$ of the modulator is defined to be the 50 percent point, or $\text{sinc}(B\tau_t) = 0.5$,

$$B = \frac{0.6}{\tau_t}. \qquad \textbf{[14.105]}$$

Comparing this result with that given by Equation (14.102) for digital modulation shows that the bandwidth in both cases is inversely proportional to the transit delay.

From Equation (14.104), also note that the peak value of the phase function is proportional to

$$\Delta\phi_p \propto L\text{sinc}(f_m \tau_t) = L\text{sinc}(f_m L/v_p) \propto \sin(\pi f_m L/v_p). \qquad \textbf{[14.106]}$$

This result is similar to the case of pulse modulation shown in Figure 14.13. Therefore, unless $f_m = 0$ or is at dc, the peak phase change cannot be linearly increased by increasing L. The peak phase change is at

$$L_p = \frac{v_p}{2f_m} = \frac{c}{2nf_m} \qquad \textbf{[14.107]}$$

As a numerical example, at $f_m = 1$ GHz and $n = 3.0$, $L_p = 50$ mm.

Capacitor Charge Time   As mentioned earlier, another speed limiting factor is the time required to charge or discharge the dielectric capacitor made of the electro-optic modulator. For a transverse modulator, the capacitance is

$$C = n^2 \epsilon_0 \frac{wL}{d}.$$ [14.108]

If w and d are on the same order, C is primarily determined by L.

If a voltage source is used to switch the modulator, the charge time to 90 percent is $2.3RC$, where R is the output resistance of the voltage source. If the bit interval required should be at least five times the turn-on delay, this requires

$$R_b \le \frac{1}{5\tau_{on}} = \frac{1}{11.5RC} = \frac{1}{11.5R} \frac{d}{n^2 \epsilon_0 wL}.$$ [14.109]

This shows that the switching speed is inversely proportional to L for transverse modulators.

Example 14.18

Assume $w = 4d$, $L = 500$ μm, and $n = 3.5$. From Equation (14.108), $C = 0.22$ pF. If the output resistance of the voltage source is 100 Ω, the turn-on delay is

$$t_{on} = 2.3RC = 0.05 \text{ nsec.}$$

If the bit period must be at least five times the turn-on delay, the speed limit is

$$R_b < \frac{1}{5 \times 0.05} = 4 \text{ Gb/s.} \blacksquare$$

Total Delay   From Appendix 7–D, the propagation delay and turn-on delay can be combined by using the sum of squares. That is,

$$\tau_d^2 = \tau_t^2 + t_{on}^2$$ [14.110]

and the speed limit is given by

$$R_b \le \frac{1}{5\tau_d}.$$ [14.111]

Switching Power   Although the EO modulator does not consume dc power when the crystal is lossless, it does consume ac power to switch the voltage between two points V_1 and V_2. If the capacitance of the modulator is C, the change of the charge to switch the voltage level is

$$\Delta Q = C(V_2 - V_1).$$

Therefore, the required energy to charge or discharge the capacitor is

$$\Delta E = \Delta Q(V_2 - V_1) = C(V_2 - V_1)^2.$$

In digital communications, if the switching rate is R_b and the probability of a switch occurring every bit interval is 0.5, the average switching power required is

$$P_{ac} = \frac{1}{2} R_b C (V_2 - V_1)^2. \qquad \textbf{[14.112]}$$

Equation (14.112) shows that the switching power is proportional to the bit rate, waveguide length, and square of the change in voltage. Therefore, a high transmission bit rate or large modulation depth requires a high switching power.

AC POWER FOR MODULATION   As a numerical illustration, assume $V_2 - V_1 = 10$ V, and use $C = 0.23$ pF. At $R_b = 1$ Gb/s,

$$P_{ac} = 0.5 \times 10^9 \times 2.3 \times 10^{-13} \times 10^2 = 11.5 \text{ mW}.$$

Example 14.19

Because power consumption higher than 1 W is difficult to operate in practice, it can be a problem for external modulation at either larger modulation depths or higher speeds. ∎

14.8   ACOUSTO-OPTIC MODULATION

The interaction of sound and light was first predicted by Brillouin in 1922 [7]. Similar to electro-optic modulation, acousto-optic modulation uses sound waves to modulate the refractive index of the medium. The difference is that sound waves have periodic compression and rarefaction patterns that result in periodic variations of the medium's refractive index. This periodic variation of the refractive index acts as a phase grating that diffracts part or all of the incident light.

14.8.1   ELASTO-OPTIC COEFFICIENTS

Similar to the electro-optic coefficients, there are so-called **elasto-optic coefficients** that quantify the change of the permeability tensor under an acoustic wave.

For an acoustic wave $\bar{U}(\Omega t - \bar{K} \cdot \bar{r})$ in a medium with propagation constant $\bar{K}$, the **strain tensor** is defined as

$$S_{(ij)} = \frac{\partial U_i}{\partial r_j}. \qquad \textbf{[14.113]}$$

Because the acoustic wave $\overline{U}$ is in units of meters, the strain tensor $S_{(ij)}$ is dimensionless. Following the same notation given by Equation (14.41), a single index can be used for the strain tensor.

When the strain tensor due to an acoustic wave is known, the change of the permeability is described by

$$\Delta \eta_i = \sum_{j=1}^{6} p_{ij} S_j \qquad \textbf{[14.114]}$$

where p_{ij}'s are the AO coefficients and $i, j = 1, \ldots, 6$. Similar to the electro-optic coefficients, the p_{ij}'s strongly depend on the point group of the crystal used. The symmetry of elasto-optic tensors for different crystal groups [2] is given in Table 14.9. Values of p_{ij} and other important parameters of common acousto-optic crystals are given in Table 14.10. As shown, the interaction of the incident light and acoustic wave depends on their polarizations because the AO medium can become anisotropic.

Table 14.9 Symmetry of elasto-optic tensors of different crystal groups [2].

Crystal Group	Elasto-Optic Tensor
Triclinic	$$\begin{bmatrix} p_{11} & p_{12} & p_{13} & p_{14} & p_{15} & p_{16} \\ p_{21} & p_{22} & p_{23} & p_{24} & p_{25} & p_{26} \\ p_{31} & p_{32} & p_{33} & p_{34} & p_{35} & p_{36} \\ p_{41} & p_{42} & p_{43} & p_{44} & p_{45} & p_{46} \\ p_{51} & p_{52} & p_{53} & p_{54} & p_{55} & p_{56} \\ p_{61} & p_{62} & p_{63} & p_{64} & p_{65} & p_{66} \end{bmatrix}$$
Monoclinic	$$\begin{bmatrix} p_{11} & p_{12} & p_{13} & 0 & p_{15} & 0 \\ p_{21} & p_{22} & p_{23} & 0 & p_{25} & 0 \\ p_{31} & p_{32} & p_{33} & 0 & p_{35} & 0 \\ 0 & 0 & 0 & p_{44} & 0 & p_{46} \\ p_{51} & p_{52} & p_{53} & 0 & p_{55} & 0 \\ 0 & 0 & 0 & p_{64} & 0 & p_{66} \end{bmatrix}$$
Orthorhombic	$$\begin{bmatrix} p_{11} & p_{12} & p_{13} & 0 & 0 & 0 \\ p_{21} & p_{22} & p_{23} & 0 & 0 & 0 \\ p_{31} & p_{32} & p_{33} & 0 & 0 & 0 \\ 0 & 0 & 0 & p_{44} & 0 & 0 \\ 0 & 0 & 0 & 0 & p_{55} & 0 \\ 0 & 0 & 0 & 0 & 0 & p_{66} \end{bmatrix}$$
Tetragonal	$4,\bar{4},4/m$ $$\begin{bmatrix} p_{11} & p_{12} & p_{13} & 0 & 0 & p_{16} \\ p_{12} & p_{11} & p_{13} & 0 & 0 & -p_{16} \\ p_{31} & p_{31} & p_{33} & 0 & 0 & 0 \\ 0 & 0 & 0 & p_{44} & p_{45} & 0 \\ 0 & 0 & 0 & -p_{45} & p_{44} & 0 \\ p_{61} & -p_{61} & 0 & 0 & 0 & p_{66} \end{bmatrix}$$ $4mm,422,4/mmm$ $$\begin{bmatrix} p_{11} & p_{12} & p_{13} & 0 & 0 & 0 \\ p_{12} & p_{11} & p_{13} & 0 & 0 & 0 \\ p_{31} & p_{31} & p_{33} & 0 & 0 & 0 \\ 0 & 0 & 0 & p_{44} & 0 & 0 \\ 0 & 0 & 0 & 0 & p_{44} & 0 \\ 0 & 0 & 0 & 0 & 0 & p_{66} \end{bmatrix}$$

Table 14.9 Cont.

Crystal Group	Elasto-Optic Tensor	

Trigonal

$3,\bar{3}$

$$\begin{bmatrix} p_{11} & p_{12} & p_{13} & p_{14} & p_{15} & p_{16} \\ p_{12} & p_{11} & p_{13} & -p_{14} & -p_{15} & -p_{16} \\ p_{13} & p_{13} & p_{33} & 0 & 0 & 0 \\ p_{41} & -p_{41} & 0 & p_{44} & p_{45} & -p_{51} \\ p_{51} & -p_{51} & 0 & -p_{45} & p_{44} & p_{41} \\ -p_{51} & p_{51} & 0 & -p_{15} & p_{14} & (p_{11}-p_{12})/2 \end{bmatrix}$$

$3m,32,\bar{3}m$

$$\begin{bmatrix} p_{11} & p_{12} & p_{13} & p_{14} & 0 & 0 \\ p_{12} & p_{11} & p_{13} & -p_{14} & 0 & 0 \\ p_{13} & p_{13} & p_{33} & 0 & 0 & 0 \\ p_{41} & -p_{41} & 0 & p_{44} & 0 & 0 \\ 0 & 0 & 0 & 0 & p_{44} & p_{41} \\ 0 & 0 & 0 & 0 & p_{14} & (p_{11}-p_{12})/2 \end{bmatrix}$$

Hexagonal

$6,\bar{6},6/m$

$$\begin{bmatrix} p_{11} & p_{12} & p_{13} & 0 & 0 & p_{16} \\ p_{12} & p_{11} & p_{13} & 0 & 0 & -p_{16} \\ p_{31} & p_{31} & p_{33} & 0 & 0 & 0 \\ 0 & 0 & 0 & p_{44} & p_{45} & 0 \\ 0 & 0 & 0 & -p_{45} & p_{44} & 0 \\ -p_{61} & p_{61} & 0 & 0 & 0 & (p_{11}-p_{12})/2 \end{bmatrix}$$

$\bar{6}m2,6mm,622,6/mmm$

$$\begin{bmatrix} p_{11} & p_{12} & p_{13} & 0 & 0 & 0 \\ p_{12} & p_{11} & p_{13} & 0 & 0 & 0 \\ p_{31} & p_{31} & p_{33} & 0 & 0 & 0 \\ 0 & 0 & 0 & p_{44} & 0 & 0 \\ 0 & 0 & 0 & 0 & p_{44} & 0 \\ 0 & 0 & 0 & 0 & 0 & (p_{11}-p_{12})/2 \end{bmatrix}$$

Cubic

$23,m3$

$$\begin{bmatrix} p_{11} & p_{12} & p_{21} & 0 & 0 & 0 \\ p_{21} & p_{11} & p_{12} & 0 & 0 & 0 \\ p_{12} & p_{21} & p_{11} & 0 & 0 & 0 \\ 0 & 0 & 0 & p_{44} & 0 & 0 \\ 0 & 0 & 0 & 0 & p_{44} & 0 \\ 0 & 0 & 0 & 0 & 0 & p_{44} \end{bmatrix}$$

$\bar{4}3m,432,m3m$

$$\begin{bmatrix} p_{11} & p_{12} & p_{12} & 0 & 0 & 0 \\ p_{12} & p_{11} & p_{12} & 0 & 0 & 0 \\ p_{12} & p_{12} & p_{11} & 0 & 0 & 0 \\ 0 & 0 & 0 & p_{44} & 0 & 0 \\ 0 & 0 & 0 & 0 & p_{44} & 0 \\ 0 & 0 & 0 & 0 & 0 & p_{44} \end{bmatrix}$$

Isotropic

$$\begin{bmatrix} p_{11} & p_{12} & p_{12} & 0 & 0 & 0 \\ p_{12} & p_{11} & p_{12} & 0 & 0 & 0 \\ p_{12} & p_{11} & p_{11} & 0 & 0 & 0 \\ 0 & 0 & 0 & (p_{11}-p_{12})/2 & 0 & 0 \\ 0 & 0 & 0 & 0 & (p_{11}-p_{12})/2 & 0 \\ 0 & 0 & 0 & 0 & p_{14} & (p_{11}-p_{12})/2 \end{bmatrix}$$

Table 14.10 Values of important parameters of common acousto-optic crystals[2]. Note: Light polarization ⊥ or ∥ means perpendicular or parallel to the plane of the sound and light propagation vectors.

Crystal Group	Medium	λ (μm)	Elasto-Optic Coefficients	Refractive Index n	ρ (g/cm³)	Sound Polarization in Direction	Sound Velocity (km/sec)	Light Polarization in Direction	M 1.0e−15 (m²/W)
Isotropic	Fused SiO₂	0.63	$p_{11} = 0.121$ $p_{12} = 0.27$	1.46	2.2	Longitudinal Transverse	5.95 3.76	⊥ ⊥ or ∥	1.51 0.467
	H₂O	0.63	$p_{11} = 0.31$ $p_{12} = 0.31$	1.33	1.0	Longitudinal	1.5		160
	Ge₃₃Se₅₅As₁₂ (glass)	1.06	$p_{11} = 0.21$ $p_{12} = 0.21$	2.55	4.0	Longitudinal	2.5		246
Cubic: 4̄32 432, m3m	GaAs	1.15	$p_{11} = -0.152$ $p_{12} = -0.140$ $p_{44} = -0.072$	3.37	5.34	Longitudinal in [110] Transverse in [100]	5.15 3.32	= ∥ or ⊥ in [010]	104 46.3
	KRS5	0.63	$p_{11} = 0.18$ $p_{12} = 0.27$ $p_{44} = 0.15$	2.6	7.37	Longitudinal Longitudinal	2.11 2.11	⊥ =	180 254
Hexagonal 6mm	CdS	0.63	$p_{11} = -0.142$ $p_{12} = -0.066$ $p_{13} = -0.057$ $p_{31} = -0.041$ $p_{33} = -0.20$ $p_{44} = \pm0.054$	2.44	4.82	Longitudinal in [112̄0]	4.17	∥	12.1
Trigonal: 3m,32,3̄m	Al₂O₃	0.63	$p_{11} = -0.23$ $p_{12} = -0.03$ $p_{13} = -0.02$ $p_{14} = 0.00$ $p_{31} = -0.04$ $p_{33} = 0.20$ $p_{41} = -0.01$ $p_{44} = 0.10$	1.76	4.0	Longitudinal in [001]	11.15	∥ in [112̄0]	0.34

Table 14.10 Cont.

Crystal Group	Medium	λ (μm)	Elasto-Optic Coefficients	Refractive Index n	ρ (g/cm³)	Sound Polarization in Direction	Sound Velocity (km/sec)	Light Polarization in Direction	M 1.0e–15 (m²/W)
	LiNbO₃	0.63	$p_{11} = -0.026$ $p_{12} = -0.09$ $p_{13} = 0.133$ $p_{14} = -0.075$ $p_{31} = 0.179$ $p_{33} = 0.071$ $p_{41} = -0.151$ $p_{44} = 0.146$	2.20	4.7	Longitudinal in [11$\bar{2}$0]	6.57		6.99
	LiTaO₃	0.63	$p_{11} = -0.081$ $p_{12} = 0.081$ $p_{13} = 0.093$ $p_{14} = -0.026$ $p_{31} = 0.089$ $p_{33} = -0.044$ $p_{41} = -0.085$ $p_{44} = 0.028$	2.18	7.45	Longitudinal in [001]	6.19	∥ in [11$\bar{2}$0]	1.37
Tetragonal 4mm, $\bar{4}$2m, 422,4/mmm	ADP	0.63	$p_{11} = 0.296$ $p_{12} = 0.243$ $p_{13} = 0.208$ $p_{31} = 0.188$ $p_{33} = 0.228$	1.58	1.80	Longitudinal in [100] Transverse in [100]	6.15 1.83	∥ in [010] ∥or ⊥ in [001]	2.78 6.43
	KDP	0.63	$p_{11} = 0.254$ $p_{12} = 0.230$ $p_{13} = 0.233$ $p_{31} = 0.221$ $p_{33} = 0.212$ $p_{66} = -0.055$	1.51	2.34	Longitudinal in [100] Transverse in [100]	5.5	∥ in [010] ∥or ⊥ in [001]	1.91 3.83

Table 14.10 Cont.

Crystal Group	Medium	λ (μm)	Elasto-Optic Coefficients	Refractive Index n	ρ (g/cm³)	Sound Polarization in Direction	Sound Velocity (km/sec)	Light Polarization in Direction	M 1.0e-15 (m²/W)
	TeO₂	0.63	$p_{11} = 0.0074$	2.30	5.99	Longitudinal in [100]	2.98	[100] in [001]	0.48
			$p_{12} = 0.187$					[001] in [010]	10.6
			$p_{13} = 0.340$			Longitudinal in [001]	4.26	[100] in [010]	34.5
			$p_{31} = 0.0905$					[001] in [010]	25.6
			$p_{33} = 0.240$			Longitudinal in [110]	4.21	[110] in [$\bar{1}$10]	0.802
								[001] in [$\bar{1}$10]	3.77
			$p_{44} = -0.17$			Longitudinal in [101]	3.64	[010] in [$\bar{1}$01]	33.4
			$p_{66} = -0.0463$			Longitudinal in [010]	2.98	[101] in [$\bar{1}$01]	20.4
						Longitudinal in [$\bar{1}$10]	0.617	Arb. [001]	793
						Longitudinal in [$\bar{1}$01]	2.08	[001] in [010]	77
	TiO₂	0.63	$p_{11} = -0.011$	2.58	4.6	Longitudinal in [11$\bar{2}$]	7.86	$\perp$ in [001]	3.93
			$p_{12} = 0.172$						
			$p_{13} = -0.168$						
			$p_{31} = -0.0965$						
			$p_{33} = -0.058$						
			$p_{66} = \pm 0.072$						
Tetragonal $4,\bar{4},4/m$	PbMoO₂	0.63	$p_{11} = 0.24$	2.35	6.95	Longitudinal in [001]	3.98	[001] in [010]	7.5
			$p_{12} = 0.24$					[100] in [010]	24
			$p_{13} = 0.30$			[100] in [010]		[010] in [001]	24
			$p_{16} = 0.017$				2.2	[100] in [001]	12.8
			$p_{31} = 0.175$			Longitudinal in [001]	3.75	[100] in [010]	41
			$p_{33} = 0.300$					[001] in [010]	41
			$p_{44} = 0.675$						
			$p_{45} = -0.01$						
			$p_{61} = 0.013$						
			$p_{66} = 0.05$						

LONGITUDINAL WAVE IN WATER   Consider a longitudinal sound wave propagating inside water in the $\hat{z}$ direction. The sound wave can be described by

Example 14.20

$$\bar{U}(z,t) = A\cos(\Omega t - Kz)\hat{z}$$

where A is the amplitude (in meters) of the wave, Ω is the circular frequency, $K = 2\pi/\Lambda$ is the propagation constant, and Λ is the wavelength. Given the longitudinal wave above, the strain tensor S_i's are zero except S_3 or $S_{(33)}$:

$$S_3 = \frac{\partial U_z}{\partial z} = AK\sin(\Omega t - Kz) = S\sin(\Omega t - Kz)$$

where $S \overset{\text{def}}{=} AK$. From Table 14.10, note that water is isotropic. Therefore,

$$\Delta\eta_{11} = \Delta\eta_{22} = p_{12}S_3 = p_{12}S\sin(\Omega t - Kz)$$

and

$$\Delta\eta_{33} = p_{33}S_3 = p_{11}S\sin(\Omega t - Kz).$$

All other $\Delta\eta_{ij}$'s are zero. Hence the index ellipsoid equation can be written as

$$\left[\frac{1}{n_0^2} + p_{12}S\sin(\Omega t - Kz)\right]x^2 + \left[\frac{1}{n_0^2} + p_{12}S\sin(\Omega t - Kz)\right]y^2$$

$$+ \left[\frac{1}{n_0^2} + p_{11}S\sin(\Omega t - Kz)\right]z^2 = \frac{1}{n^2}.$$

From this equation, note that the principle axis remains the same and the refractive indices are modulated by a traveling wave:

$$n_1 = n_2 \approx n_0 - \tfrac{1}{2}n^3 p_{12}S\sin(\Omega t - Kz)$$

and

$$n_3 \approx n_0 - \tfrac{1}{2}n^3 p_{11}S\sin(\Omega t - Kz).$$

For water, $p_{11} = p_{12} = 0.31$ and $n = 1.33$. The velocity in water is $v = 1500$ m/sec. Therefore, if the sound wave is at 100 MHz,

$$\Lambda = \frac{v}{f} = 15 \ \mu\text{m}$$

and

$$K = \frac{2\pi}{\Lambda} = 4.2 \times 10^5 \ 1/\text{m}.$$

If the amplitude A is 1.0×10^{-10} m, $S = 4.2 \times 10^{-5}$ and

$$\Delta n = 1.53 \times 10^{-5}\sin(\Omega t - Kz). \ \blacksquare$$

TRANSVERSE WAVE IN WATER   Continue from Example 14.20 but now consider a *transverse* wave propagating in the $\hat{z}$ direction:

Example 14.21

$$\bar{U}(z,t) = A\cos(\Omega t - Kz)\hat{y}.$$

Here it is assumed the wave is polarized in the $\hat{y}$-axis direction. Therefore, the only nonzero strain tensor term is S_4:

$$S_4 = S_{(23)} = \frac{\partial U_2}{\partial z} = AK \sin(\Omega t - Kz) = S \sin(\Omega t - Kz).$$

Because $p_{11} = p_{12}$ in water, according to Table 14.9, there is no modulation of the refractive index. This example shows that only longitudinal sound waves can modulate the refractive index of water. ∎

For different polarizations of the acoustic wave and different elasto-optic tensors of the medium, tensor multiplication $[p_{ij}][S_j]$ can result in various different impermeability changes. In general, after coordination rotation to the new principal axis, one can obtain

$$\frac{1}{n^2} = \frac{1}{n_0^2} + p_{ao}S(t, \bar{r})$$

where n_0 is the refractive index in the absence of the acoustic wave and p_{ao} is the effective elasto-optic coefficient. When the term $p_{ao}S$ is small,

$$\Delta n \approx -\frac{1}{2} n_0^3 p_{ao} S(t, \bar{r}).$$

Therefore, the peak change of the refractive index is

$$\Delta n_p = \frac{1}{2} n_0^3 p_{ao} S_p \qquad\qquad \textbf{[14.115]}$$

where S_p is the peak value of the strain wave.

Example 14.22	**EFFECTIVE ELASTO-OPTIC COEFFICIENT** From Example 14.20 of the longitudinal wave in water, $p_{ao} = p_{11} = p_{12}$, and $S_p = AK$. ∎

14.8.2   BRAGG DIFFRACTION

A basic acousto-optic modulator, where an incident light beam can be diffracted into different directions, is shown in Figure 14.14. The condition between the incident angle and the output angle comes from the conservation of momentum as shown in Figure 14.15:

$$\bar{\beta}_{out} = \bar{\beta}_{in} \pm \bar{K}. \qquad\qquad \textbf{[14.116]}$$

For the positive sign, diffraction is *up-shifted* where the acoustic momentum is picked up by the incident optical momentum. For the negative sign, diffraction is *down-shifted* where

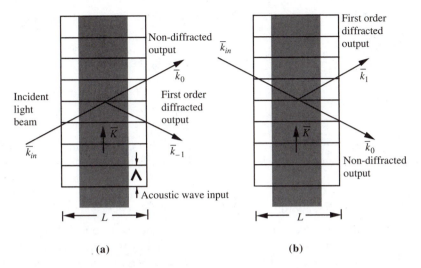

Figure 14.14 Acousto-optic modulator: (*a*) down-shifted Bragg diffraction and (*b*) up-shifted Bragg diffraction.

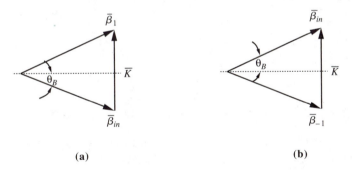

Figure 14.15 Conservation of momentum: (a) up-shifted and (b) down-shifted diffraction.

the acoustic momentum is canceled by the incident optical momentum. In either case, from the conservation of energy,

$$\omega_{out} = \omega_{in} \pm \Omega.$$ **[14.117]**

In other words, the output light signal also has a slight frequency shift by the amount of the acoustic frequency. This diffraction is well known as the **Bragg diffraction.**

Because the light frequency is much higher than the sound frequency, $\omega_{out} \approx \omega_{in}$. In addition, because

$$\frac{\omega_{in}}{|\bar{\beta}_{in}|} = \frac{\omega_{out}}{|\bar{\beta}_{out}|} = \text{light velocity in the medium}$$

it follows that

$$|\bar{\beta}_{in}| = |\bar{\beta}_{out}|. \qquad \textbf{[14.118]}$$

Combining Equations (14.117) and (14.118), one can obtain the condition θ_B for light and the acoustic wave to interact. Specifically, from the illustration of Figure 14.15, diffraction occurs when

$$\theta_B = \sin^{-1}(\lambda/2n\Lambda) \qquad \textbf{[14.119]}$$

where λ is the light wavelength in free space and Λ is the acoustic wavelength.

From the above discussion, when the incident light has an incident angle equal to θ_B, both energy and momentum conservations are met, and there is an interaction between the incident lightwave and the acoustic wave. As a result, the incident light is diffracted. If the incident angle is not equal to θ_B, the incident light passes through and is not diffracted. Consequently, the acoustic wavelength Λ can be used to modulate the output light.

Example 14.23	**BRAGG INCIDENT ANGLE** If the incident light has a wavelength $\lambda = 1.5\ \mu$m in an acousto-optic medium of refractive index $n = 1.5$ and the sound has a wavelength 10 μm, $$\theta_B = 0.05 = 2.8°.$$ In general, the Bragg angle is small because $\lambda \ll \Lambda$. ∎

14.8.3 RAMAN-NATH OR DEBYE-SEARS DIFFRACTION

If the ratio L/Λ of the modulator is not large enough, the acoustic wave will not be a plane wave of a single propagation vector $\bar{K}$. Specifically, when

$$\frac{\lambda}{\Lambda} \gg \frac{\Lambda}{L} \qquad \textbf{[14.120]}$$

is invalid, the Bragg diffraction is generalized to the so-called **Raman-Nath** or **Debye-Sears** diffraction [8]. In this case, there are multiple diffracted beams. The basic idea is shown in Figure 14.16. Because of the two acoustic waves $\bar{K}_1$ and $\bar{K}_{-1}$, a horizontal incident lightwave has two diffracted waves $\bar{\beta}_1$ and $\bar{\beta}_{-1}$, which will be diffracted by sound waves, $\bar{K}_2$ and $\bar{K}_{-2}$, to generate $\bar{\beta}_2$ and $\bar{\beta}_{-2}$. From Figure 14.16, the number of diffracted waves will depend on the ratio Λ/L to λ/Λ.

Example 14.24	**CONDITION FOR BRAGG DIFFRACTION** If the incident light has a wavelength of 1.5 μm in a medium of refractive index 1.5 and the acoustic sound has a wavelength of 50 μm, the Bragg angle is

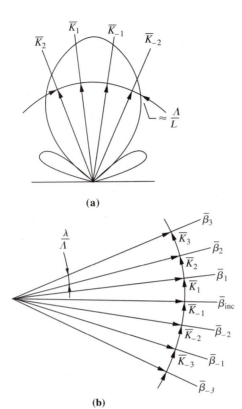

(a)

(b)

Figure 14.16 Raman-Nath diffraction. (a) Possible acoustic wave vectors that can result in diffraction (b) Diffracted light of different orders.

SOURCE: Reprinted, by permission, from Korpel, "Acousto-Optics: A Review of Fundamentals," *Proceedings of the IEEE*, January 1981, p. 49, Figure 4 [9]. ©1981 by IEEE.

$$\theta_B = \sin^{-1}(1.0/100) = 1.0 \times 10^{-2} = 0.57°.$$

The condition for the acousto-optic modulator to operate at the Bragg regime is

$$L \gg \Lambda^2/\lambda = 1.7 \text{ mm}.$$

This can be easily implemented in practice. ∎

14.9 Acousto-Optic Bragg Amplitude Modulators

When the Bragg diffraction condition is met (i.e., the incident angle is equal to the Bragg angle), as derived in Appendix 14–B, the incident and diffracted waves are described by the following coupled-mode equations:

$$\frac{\partial E_1(z)}{\partial z} = -j\kappa E_2(z) \qquad \textbf{[14.121]}$$

and

$$\frac{\partial E_2(z)}{\partial z} = -j\kappa E_1(z) \qquad \textbf{[14.122]}$$

where

$$\kappa = \frac{1}{2\cos(\theta_B)}\frac{2\pi}{\lambda}\Delta n_p \qquad \textbf{[14.123]}$$

and Δn_p is the peak deviation of the refractive index. Using Equation (14.115),

$$\kappa = \frac{1}{4\cos(\theta_B)}\frac{2\pi n_0^3}{\lambda}p_{ao}S_p. \qquad \textbf{[14.124]}$$

With the boundary conditions:

$$E_1(0) = E_0$$

$$E_2(0) = 0$$

the solutions are:

$$E_1(z) = E_0\cos(\kappa z) \qquad \textbf{[14.125]}$$

and

$$E_2(z) = -jE_0\sin(\kappa z). \qquad \textbf{[14.126]}$$

Therefore, the output powers of the straight-through and diffracted beams have forms similar to the case of electro-optic modulation:

$$P_{o1} = P_{in}\cos^2(\kappa L) \qquad \textbf{[14.127]}$$

$$P_{o2} = P_{in}\sin^2(\kappa L). \qquad \textbf{[14.128]}$$

Therefore, if the refractive index is modulated such that

$$\Delta n_p = 2\cos(\theta_B)\frac{\lambda}{4L} \qquad \textbf{[14.129]}$$

the incident power can be completely switched to the diffracted beam.

Example 14.25

ACOUSTIC AMPLITUDE MODULATION   If Δn_p is 1.0×10^{-4} in a given medium under modulation at the sound wavelength $\Lambda = 15\ \mu\text{m}$, the Bragg angle is $\theta_B = 0.05$ rad at light wavelength $1.5\ \mu\text{m}$. Therefore,

$$\kappa = \frac{1}{2\cos(\theta_B)} \frac{2\pi}{1.5 \times 10^{-6}} \times 1.0 \times 10^{-4} = 2.10 \times 10^2 \text{ 1/m}.$$

To have a complete switchover, the length L required is

$$L = \frac{\pi/2}{\kappa} = 7.5 \text{ mm} \quad \blacksquare$$

14.10 DEFLECTION EFFICIENCY, DRIVING POWER, AND BANDWIDTH OF ACOUSTO-OPTIC MODULATORS

In AO modulators, as shown in Table 14.3, important performance parameters include deflection efficiency, required driving power, and modulation bandwidth. These design parameters are explained below.

Deflection Efficiency   The deflection efficiency is defined as the ratio of the diffracted output power P_{o2} to the incident power P_{in}. From Equation (14.128),

$$\eta_{df} = \sin^2(\kappa L).$$

In practice, κ is commonly expressed in terms of the **acoustic wave intensity** $I_{acoustic}$ [W/m^2] and a material dependent factor called the figure of merit M. These two parameters are defined by

$$\boxed{I_{acoustic} \stackrel{\text{def}}{=} {}^{1}\!/_{2}\rho v^3 S^2} \qquad \textbf{[14.130]}$$

and

$$\boxed{M \stackrel{\text{def}}{=} \frac{n^6 p_{ao}^2}{\rho v^3},} \qquad \textbf{[14.131]}$$

where S is the acoustic strain amplitude, v is the acoustic wave velocity equal to Ω/K, and ρ is the mass density of the AO medium. From the above definitions and Equation (14.124),

$$\kappa = \frac{1}{\sqrt{2}\cos\theta_B} \frac{\pi}{\lambda} (M I_{acoustic})^{1/2} \qquad \textbf{[14.132]}$$

and

$$\boxed{\eta_{df} = \sin^2\left[\frac{\pi L}{\sqrt{2}\cos(\theta_B)\lambda} (M I_{acoustic})^{1/2}\right].} \qquad \textbf{[14.133]}$$

Consider a longitudinal acoustic wave propagating in [001] and at velocity 3.75 km/sec in lead molybdate (PbMO$_4$). From Tables 14.10 and 14.9, if the incident light wave propagates in [010], its effective elasto-optic coefficient is $p_{ao} = p_{13} = 0.30$, and its figure of merit is

Example 14.26

$$M = \frac{n^6 p_{ao}^2}{\rho v^3} = \frac{2.35^6 \times 0.30^2}{6.95 \times 10^3 \times (3.75 \times 10^3)^3} = 4.1 \times 10^{-14} \text{ m}^2/\text{W}.$$

For water, because it is isotropic, $p_{ao} = 0.31$, and the figure of merit is

$$M = \frac{n^6 p_{ao}^2}{\rho v^3} = \frac{1.33^6 \times 0.31^2}{1.0 \times 10^3 \times (1.5 \times 10^3)^3} = 1.58 \times 10^{-13} \text{ m}^2/\text{W}.$$

At an acoustic intensity of $I_{acoustic} = 10^6$ W/m^2 and $L = 1$ mm, the deflection efficiency for PbMO$_4$ is

$$\eta_{df} = \sin^2 \left(\frac{\pi}{\sqrt{2}} \frac{1000}{0.63} \sqrt{4.1 \times 10^{-8}} \right) = \sin^2(0.76) = 47.5\%$$

where the light wavelength is 0.63 μm. For water at the same acoustic intensity,

$$\eta_{df} = \sin^2(1.40) = 97\%. \quad \blacksquare$$

Driving Power   From Equation (14.133), we note that we need a large acoustic intensity to achieve a large deflection efficiency. This implies a large driving power, which is defined to be

$$P_a = (hL)I_{acoustic} \tag{14.134}$$

where h is the height of the modulator and hL represents the cross-sectional area of the acoustic wave. At a given acoustic power, the deflection efficiency is

$$\eta_{df} = \sin^2 \left(\frac{\pi}{\sqrt{2}\lambda} \sqrt{M P_a L / h} \right). \tag{14.135}$$

Equation (14.135) shows that the required power for a given acoustic power is not a function of the switching speed, a situation different from that in electro-optic modulation.

Modulation Bandwidth   From the Bragg condition given by Equation (14.119), note that if the acoustic wave changes to a different wavelength, a different Bragg incident angle is required for the incident light. In other words, if the Bragg condition is not met because the acoustic wavelength changes, there will be no diffraction and the incident light will completely pass through.

In practice, the incident light is not a plane wave but has a finite width, as shown in Figure 14.17. As a result, its incident angle has a nonzero range. If the incident laser beam has a spot size D at its waist, it has a finite angle range from the center of the beam [10]:

$$\Delta\theta = \frac{2\lambda}{\pi n D}. \tag{14.136}$$

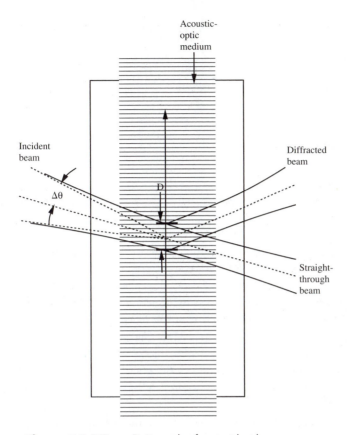

Figure 14.17   Finite angle of an incident beam.

This nonzero angle range allows a nonzero modulation bandwidth of the acoustic wave. From the Bragg condition (14.119), when θ_B is small,

$$\theta_B \approx \frac{\lambda}{2n\Lambda} = \frac{\lambda}{2nv} f_{sound}$$

where v and f_{sound} are the velocity and frequency of the acoustic wave, respectively. The achievable bandwidth B of the acoustic wave is defined in such a way that the acoustic frequency $f_{sound} \pm B$ meets the Bragg condition at $\theta_B \pm \Delta\theta/2$. Therefore,

$$B = \frac{2nv}{\lambda}\left(\frac{1}{2}\Delta\theta\right) = \frac{2v}{\pi D}. \qquad \textbf{[14.137]}$$

This is on the order of v/D, which is the inverse of the transit delay of the acoustic wave through the laser beam. From Equation (14.137), note that the bandwidth can be improved by having a larger acoustic velocity for a given beam spot size D.

Example 14.27 **AO MODULATION BANDWIDTH** In $LiNbO_3$, the velocity of sound is 7.4×10^3 m/sec. For a spot size of $D = 10$ μm,

$$B = \frac{2 \times 7.4 \times 10^3}{\pi \times 1 \times 10^{-5}} = 470 \text{ MHz}.$$

14.11 SUMMARY

1. The basic principle of external modulation is to modulate the refractive index of a waveguide through which a constant frequency lightwave passes. The refractive index can be modulated using an electrical or acoustic input signal, and the modulators are called electro-optic and acousto-optic modulators, respectively.

2. A good modulator should have a large modulation bandwidth and depth. A large modulation bandwidth is necessary for high bit rate transmission, and a large modulation depth gives a higher signal-to-noise ratio at detection. For analog communications, a high linearity is also important. Other desirable properties include small size, polarization independence, low insertion loss, and low operating power or voltage.

3. Modulating the refractive index using either the EO or AO effect requires crystals whose refractive index can be changed by a bias electric field or a sound wave. In general, the change of the refractive index depends on the polarization of the bias field. Materials that respond differently to different polarizations are called anisotropic materials. Otherwise, they are called isotropic.

4. For electro-optic materials, the change of the refractive index can be either a linear or quadratic function of the applied field. These are called Pockels and Kerr effects, respectively. In general, the Kerr effect can be ignored except when the crystal has zero Pockels effect because of its particular crystal symmetry.

5. Most electro-optic materials are anisotropic. In this case, an incident ray can have only two permissible polarizations, which may have different phase velocities. This difference is caused by two different refractive indices "seen" by the two different polarized waves. This phenomenon is called birefringence, which is also defined as the refractive index difference. The two permissible polarizations and the corresponding refractive indices can be found using the Fresnel's equation of wave normals and the index ellipsoid.

6. There are two primary types of electro-optic modulators: longitudinal and transverse. A longitudinal modulator has its bias electric field in the same propagation direction as the incident wave, and a transverse modulator has its bias field orthogonal to the propagation direction of the incident wave. In general, a longitudinal modulator requires a large bias voltage to achieve a high modulation index, but it can have a higher modulation bandwidth. A transverse modulator, on the other hand, can achieve a large modulation depth at a low voltage, but it has a lower modulation bandwidth because of the long propagation delay through the waveguide and a long charge/discharge time to change the bias field of the modulator.

7. Both phase and amplitude modulations can be achieved using electro-optic modulators. For phase modulation, one can simply modulate the refractive index, which will in turn modulate the propagation delay and phase change of the incident light. For amplitude modulation, (1) polarization filtering, (2) field interference, and (3) waveguide coupling techniques can be used to change the amplitude of the incident light. In general, the first two methods modulate the polarization or relative phase difference of the incident light by modulating the refractive index of the electro-optic waveguide, and the third method modulates the coupling property of the two waveguides. By providing proper polarization filtering, field interference, or change of coupling, amplitude modulation can be achieved.

8. Because the change rate of the bias electric field is proportional to the bit rate of the message signal, the ac power consumption of electro-optic modulators increases as the bit rate increases. In general, there is also a trade-off between the power consumption and modulation depth.

9. In acousto-optic modulators, the refractive index of the medium is modulated by a sound wave. The change of the refractive index is linearly proportional to the strain tensor of the sound wave. Because the sound wave is periodic in either time or space, there is a periodic change of the refractive index of the acousto-optic medium. This effectively introduces a grating for the incident light.

10. From the periodic change of the refractive index, the incident light can be diffracted if its incident angle satisfies the Bragg angle condition. When the sound wave is a plane wave, there is only one possible diffraction, called Bragg diffraction. When the sound wave is not strictly planar, there are multiple diffractions, called Raman-Nath or Debye-Sears diffraction.

11. An acousto-optic modulator is primarily used for amplitude modulation. In this case, the output of the modulator is the diffracted light. When the Bragg condition is not met, there will be no diffraction and the output is zero. When the Bragg condition is met, there will be a certain diffraction power. The ratio of the diffraction power to the incident light power is called the diffraction or deflection efficiency. Therefore, the diffraction efficiency is directly proportional to the modulation depth or signal-to-noise ratio at detection.

12. The diffraction efficiency is determined by the product of the acoustic wave intensity and a material dependent factor called the diffraction figure of merit. In general, the larger the product, the better the diffraction efficiency. Therefore, a large efficiency requires a higher acoustic wave driving power.

13. The modulation bandwidth of an acousto-optic modulator is determined by the frequency band of the acoustic wave within which the Bragg condition can be met. This is in turn determined by the incident angle range of the incident light. In general, the larger the angle or the smaller the spot size of the incident light beam at its waist, the larger the modulation bandwidth. Specifically, the bandwidth is on the order of the inverse of the transit delay of the sound wave traveling through the spot size of the incident beam.

APPENDIX 14-A: WAVEGUIDE COUPLING

This appendix derives the coupled-mode equations for coupling waveguides. From the equations, we show how the alternating-β waveguides can compensate for inaccurate waveguide design electrically. The refractive index profile of the coupling waveguides is shown in Figure 14.18. As in optical fibers, the refractive indices of the two waveguides have a higher value than that of the substrate. Thus the refractive index profile can be expressed as

$$n^2(x, y) = n_0^2 + \Delta n_1^2(x, y) + \Delta n_2^2(x, y) \qquad \textbf{[14.138]}$$

where $\Delta n_i^2 = \Delta \epsilon_i$ represents the increase of the dielectric constant due to waveguide i.

In general, the total electric field can be expressed as

$$\mathcal{E}(x, y, z, t) = E_1(z)E_{T,1}(x, y)e^{j(\omega t - \beta_1 z)} + E_2(z)E_{T,2}(x, y)e^{j(\omega t - \beta_2 z)} \qquad \textbf{[14.139]}$$

where $E_i(z)$ is the slowly varying factor of the electric field propagating in waveguide i, $E_{T,i}(x, y)$ is the transverse mode field distribution of waveguide i, and β_i is the corresponding propagation constant along the z-axis. By definition, $E_{T,i}(x, y)$ satisfies the following wave equations:

$$\left[\frac{\partial^2}{\partial x^2} + \frac{\partial^2}{\partial y^2} + \frac{\omega^2}{c^2}(n_0^2 + \Delta n_i^2) \right] E_{T,i}(x, y) = \beta_i^2 E_{T,i}(x, y) \qquad \textbf{[14.140]}$$

where $i = 1, 2$. Therefore, $\mathcal{E}_i = E_{T,i}(x, y)e^{j(\omega t - \beta_i z)}$ is a solution to the wave equation

$$\left[\nabla^2 - \frac{n_0^2 + \Delta n_i^2}{c^2} \frac{\partial^2}{\partial t^2} \right] \mathcal{E}_i = 0$$

when there is only waveguide i.

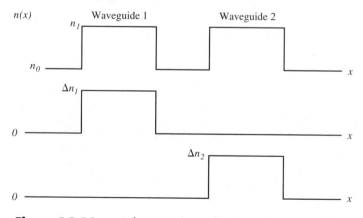

Figure 14.18   Refractive index profile of coupling waveguides.

When both waveguides are considered, the total field $\mathcal{E}$ given by Equation (14.139) should satisfy

$$\left[\nabla^2 + (n_0^2 + \Delta n_1^2 + \Delta n_2^2)\frac{\omega^2}{c^2}\right]\mathcal{E} = 0. \qquad \textbf{[14.141]}$$

Substituting $\mathcal{E}$ given by Equation (14.139) into Equation (14.141) and using Equation (14.140) gives

$$-2j\beta_1\frac{\partial E_1}{\partial z}E_{T,1}e^{-j\beta_1 z} - 2j\beta_2\frac{\partial E_2}{\partial z}E_{T,2}e^{-j\beta_2 z}$$
$$+ \frac{\omega^2}{c^2}\Delta n_2^2 E_1 E_{T,1}e^{-j\beta_1 z} + \frac{\omega^2}{c^2}\Delta n_1^2 E_2 E_{T,2}e^{-j\beta_2 z} = 0 \qquad \textbf{[14.142]}$$

where the second-order terms have been dropped. Multiplying each term in Equation (14.142) by $E_{T,1}^*(x, y)$ and integrating over the x–y plane, gives

$$\frac{\partial E_1}{\partial z} = -j\kappa_{12}E_2 e^{j\Delta\beta z} - j\kappa_{11}E_1 \qquad \textbf{[14.143]}$$

where $\Delta\beta \overset{\text{def}}{=} \beta_1 - \beta_2$ and

$$\kappa_{ij} \overset{\text{def}}{=} \frac{1}{2\beta_i}\frac{\omega^2}{c^2}\frac{\int E_{T,i}^* \Delta n_{3-j}^2 E_{T,j}dxdy}{\int |E_{T,i}|^2 dxdy}. \qquad \textbf{[14.144]}$$

From the definitions, note that

$$\kappa_{12} = \kappa_{21}^*. \qquad \textbf{[14.145]}$$

In getting Equation (14.143), it was assumed that:

$$\int E_{T,1}^* E_{T,2}dxdy \ll \int |E_{T,i}|^2 dxdy. \qquad \textbf{[14.146]}$$

Similar to Equation (14.143), one has

$$\frac{\partial E_2}{\partial z} = -j\kappa_{21}E_1 e^{-j\Delta\beta z} - j\kappa_{22}E_2. \qquad \textbf{[14.147]}$$

Equations (14.143) and (14.147) are the coupled-mode equations.
    For convenience, let

$$E_1(z) = \hat{E}_1(z)e^{-jz[\kappa_{11}-(\Delta\beta+\Delta\kappa)/2]} = \hat{E}_1(z)e^{-j\kappa_{11}z+j\delta z} \qquad \textbf{[14.148]}$$

and

$$E_2(z) = \hat{E}_2(z)e^{-jz[\kappa_{22}+(\Delta\beta+\Delta\kappa)/2]} = \hat{E}_2(z)e^{-j\kappa_{22}z-j\delta z} \qquad \textbf{[14.149]}$$

where

$$\Delta \kappa \overset{\text{def}}{=} \kappa_{11} - \kappa_{22}$$

and

$$\delta \overset{\text{def}}{=} \tfrac{1}{2}(\Delta\beta + \Delta\kappa) = \tfrac{1}{2}(\beta_1 + \kappa_{11} - \beta_2 - \kappa_{22}) \qquad \textbf{[14.150]}$$

is called the mismatch factor between the two factors. From the above definitions, the total electric field given in Equation (14.140) can be written as

$$\mathcal{E} = [\hat{E}_1(z)E_{T,1}(x, y) + \hat{E}_2(z)E_{T,2}(x, y)]e^{j(\omega t - \bar{\beta}z)}$$

where

$$\bar{\beta} = \tfrac{1}{2}(\beta_1 + \beta_2 + \kappa_{11} + \kappa_{22}).$$

Also, Equations (14.143) and (14.147) reduce to

$$\frac{\partial \hat{E}_1}{\partial z} = -j\kappa_{12}\hat{E}_2 - j\delta\hat{E}_1 \qquad \textbf{[14.151]}$$

and

$$\frac{\partial \hat{E}_2}{\partial z} = -j\kappa_{21}\hat{E}_1 + j\delta\hat{E}_2. \qquad \textbf{[14.152]}$$

Because these two equations are first-order linear differential equations, $\hat{E}_1(z)$ and $\hat{E}_2(z)$ are linear combinations of $e^{j\gamma z}$ and $e^{-j\gamma z}$, with γ satisfying the following dispersion equation:

$$\gamma^2 = \delta^2 + \kappa_{12}\kappa_{21}. \qquad \textbf{[14.153]}$$

If boundary conditions are imposed such that

$$\hat{E}_1(0) = E_{10} \qquad \textbf{[14.154]}$$

and

$$\hat{E}_2(0) = E_{20} \qquad \textbf{[14.155]}$$

the following solutions exist in matrix form:

$$\begin{bmatrix} \hat{E}_1(z) \\ \hat{E}_2(z) \end{bmatrix} = \begin{bmatrix} \cos(\gamma z) - j\frac{\delta}{\gamma}\sin(\gamma z) & -j\frac{\kappa_{12}}{\gamma}\sin(\gamma z) \\ -j\frac{\kappa_{21}}{\gamma}\sin(\gamma z) & \cos(\gamma z) + j\frac{\delta}{\gamma}\sin(\gamma z) \end{bmatrix} \begin{bmatrix} E_{10} \\ E_{20} \end{bmatrix}$$
$$\overset{\text{def}}{=} \begin{bmatrix} T(z) & -jR(z) \\ -jR^*(z) & T^*(z) \end{bmatrix} \begin{bmatrix} E_{10} \\ E_{20} \end{bmatrix} \qquad \textbf{[14.156]}$$

where

$$T(z) = \cos(\gamma z) - j\frac{\delta}{\gamma}\sin(\gamma z) \qquad \textbf{[14.157]}$$

and

$$R(z) = \frac{\kappa_{12}}{\gamma}\sin(\gamma z) = \frac{\kappa_{21}^{*}}{\gamma}\sin(\gamma z). \qquad \textbf{[14.158]}$$

For the special case that $E_{20} = 0$ and the incident power at the waveguide 1 input is P_{in}, the output powers are

$$P_{o2}(z) = P_{in}\frac{\kappa^2}{\kappa^2 + \delta^2}\sin^2(\gamma z) \qquad \textbf{[14.159]}$$

and

$$P_{o1}(z) = P_{in} - P_{o2}(z). \qquad \textbf{[14.160]}$$

From Equation (14.159), note that the complete switchover condition is

$$\frac{\kappa^2}{\kappa^2 + \delta^2}\sin^2(\gamma z) = 1. \qquad \textbf{[14.161]}$$

If the mismatch factor is nonzero or $\sin(\gamma z) \neq 1$, a complete switchover will be impossible.

Solutions given by Equation (14.156) can be easily extended to the case of alternating $\Delta\beta$ couplers. Because of the alternating polarity, the mismatch factor δ changes in sign for adjacent sections. Thus for a two-section alternating $\Delta\beta$ coupler of length $L/2$ each, as shown in Figure 14.11,

$$\begin{bmatrix} \hat{E}_1(L) \\ \hat{E}_2(L) \end{bmatrix} = \begin{bmatrix} T(L/2) & -jR(L/2) \\ -jR(L/2)^* & T(L/2)^* \end{bmatrix}\begin{bmatrix} T(L/2)^* & -jR(L/2) \\ -jR(L/2)^* & T(L/2) \end{bmatrix}\begin{bmatrix} E_{in} \\ 0 \end{bmatrix}.$$
$$\textbf{[14.162]}$$

Therefore,

$$P_{o1}(L) = P_{in}\left[|T(L/2)|^2 - |R(L/2)|^2\right]^2 = P_{in}\left[1 - \frac{2\kappa^2}{\kappa^2 + \delta^2}\sin^2(\gamma L/2)\right]^2 \quad \textbf{[14.163]}$$

and

$$P_{o2}(L) = P_{in} - P_{o1}. \qquad \textbf{[14.164]}$$

From Equation (14.162), note that a complete power switchover is

$$\frac{\kappa^2}{\kappa^2 + \delta^2}\sin^2(\gamma L/2) = \frac{1}{2}. \qquad \textbf{[14.165]}$$

Comparing this with Equation (14.161), shows that δ can be adjusted to achieve a complete switchover.

APPENDIX 14-B: ACOUSTO-OPTIC COUPLING

This Appendix analyzes the acousto-optic effect and derives the coupled-mode equations between the incident light and diffracted light. Because the interaction between the light wave and the acoustic wave is through refractive index modulation, it is necessary to first formulate the wave equation in terms of the change of the refractive modulation.

As illustrated in Figure 14.19, for simplicity it is assumed that the sound wave propagates in the $\hat{x}$ direction and the incident plane wave has its polarization in the $\hat{y}$ direction. The Maxwell equations (4.60) and (4.61) with zero conducting current give the wave equation for the electric field:

$$\nabla \times \nabla \mathcal{E} = \nabla \left(\nabla \times \mathcal{E} \right) - \nabla d^2 \mathcal{E} = -\frac{1}{c^2} \frac{\partial^2}{\partial t^2} \left(\frac{1}{\epsilon_0} \mathcal{D} \right). \tag{14.166}$$

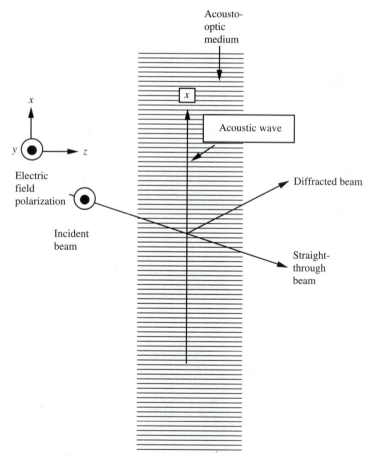

Figure 14.19 Interaction of the acoustic wave and the incident lightwave.

Also, from Equation (4.64),

$$\nabla \times \mathcal{D} = 0 = \epsilon(x,t)\nabla \times \mathcal{E} + \mathcal{E} \times \nabla\epsilon(x,t).$$

Therefore $\nabla \times \mathcal{E} = 0$ because $\mathcal{E} \times \nabla\epsilon = 0$ from the polarization assumption. This reduces Equation (14.166) to

$$\nabla^2 \mathcal{E} - \frac{1}{c^2}\frac{\partial^2}{\partial t^2}[n^2(x,t)\mathcal{E}] = 0. \qquad \textbf{[14.167]}$$

The electric field $\mathcal{E}$ can be assumed in the following form:

$$\mathcal{E}(x,z,t) = \sum_i E_i(z)e^{j(\omega_i t - \beta_{z,i}z - \beta_{x,i}x)}\hat{y} \qquad \textbf{[14.168]}$$

where $E_i(z)$'s are the slowly varying factor of the electric fields with their propagation constants satisfying

$$\beta_{z,i}^2 + \beta_{x,i}^2 = n_0^2\frac{\omega_i^2}{c^2}. \qquad \textbf{[14.169]}$$

In Equation (14.169), n_0 is the refractive index when there is no acoustic wave. Therefore, $e^{\omega_i t - \beta_{z,i}z - \beta_{x,i}x}\hat{y}$ is the plane wave satisfying the Maxwell equation (14.167) when there is no acoustic wave.

Substituting $\mathcal{E}$ given by Equation (14.168) into Equation (14.167) gives

$$\sum_i 2\beta_{z,i}\frac{\partial E_i(z)}{\partial z}e^{j(\omega_i - \beta_{z,i}z - \beta_{x,i}x)} = -j\Delta n(x,t)^2 \sum_i \frac{\omega_i^2}{c^2}E_i e^{j(\omega_i - \beta_{z,i}z - \beta_{x,i}x)} \quad \textbf{[14.170]}$$

where the second-order terms have been neglected. The refactive index $n(x,t)$ can be expressed as

$$n(x,t) = n_0 + \Delta n_p \cos(\Omega t - Kx) = n_0 + \tfrac{1}{2}\Delta n_p[e^{j(\Omega t - Kx)} + e^{-j(\Omega t - Kx)}] \quad \textbf{[14.171]}$$

where Ω is the acoustic wave frequency and $K = 2\pi/\Lambda$ is the corresponding propagation constant. Therefore, by neglecting the Δn_p^2 term,

$$\Delta n(x,t)^2 = n_0\Delta n_p[e^{j(\Omega t - Kx)} + e^{-j(\Omega t - Kx)}]. \qquad \textbf{[14.172]}$$

Substituting $\Delta n(x,t)^2$ given by Equation (14.172) into Equation (14.170) creates the following coupled-mode equation:

$$2\sum_i \beta_{z,i}\frac{\partial E_i}{\partial z}e^{j(\omega_i - \beta_{z,i}z - \beta_{x,i}x)} = -jn_0\Delta n_p\left[e^{j(\Omega t - Kx)} + e^{-j(\Omega t - Kx)}\right]$$

$$\textbf{[14.173]}$$

$$\times \sum_i \frac{\omega_i^2}{c^2}E_i e^{j(\omega_i - \beta_{z,i}z - \beta_{x,i}x)}$$

Among the many possible terms of the electric field components in the summation, we can consider two main terms: the incident wave and the diffracted wave. Imposing the Bragg diffraction conditions of Equations (14.116) and (14.117) gives

$$\beta_{z,1} = \beta_{z,2} \stackrel{\text{def}}{=} \beta_z$$

$$\beta_{x,1} \pm K = \beta_{z,2}$$

and

$$\omega_2 \pm \Omega = \omega_1.$$

Thus by considering $E_1(z)$ as the incident wave and $E_2(z)$ as the diffracted wave, Equation (14.173) reduces to

$$E_1(z) = -j\kappa E_2(z) \qquad \textbf{[14.174]}$$

and

$$E_2(z) = -j\kappa E_1(z) \qquad \textbf{[14.175]}$$

where κ is the coupling constant defined by

$$\kappa \stackrel{\text{def}}{=} \frac{\omega^2}{2c^2\beta_z} n_0 \Delta n_p. \qquad \textbf{[14.176]}$$

Note that because $\Omega \ll \omega_i$, $\omega_1 \approx \omega_2 \approx \omega$. Because

$$\beta_z = \frac{2\pi}{\lambda} n_0 \cos(\theta_B)$$

Equation (14.176) becomes

$$\kappa = \frac{1}{2\cos(\theta_B)} \frac{2\pi}{\lambda} \Delta n_p. \qquad \textbf{[14.177]}$$

PROBLEMS

Problem 14–1 Projection: Verify that $Proj_{\hat{s}}(\bar{E}) = \bar{E} - \hat{s}(\hat{s} \times \bar{E})$, where $Proj_{\hat{s}}(\bar{E})$ is the projection of $\bar{E}$ onto the plane perpendicular to $\hat{s}$. Hint: To do this, you need to verify $Proj_{\hat{s}}(\bar{E})$ is perpendicular to both (1) $\hat{s} = 0$ and (2) $\bar{E} - Proj_{\hat{s}}(\bar{E})$.

Problem 14–2 Fresnel's Equation Derivation: Derive Equation (14.15) from the condition $\det \bar{A} = 0$ and with $\bar{A}$ given by Equation (14.11).

Problem 14–3 Polarization Determination: When n is solved from the Fresnel equation, show that the polarization of the corresponding electric field is given by Equation (14.19).

Problem 14–4 Plane Wave in an Anisotropic Medium: Consider a plane wave propagating in KDP in the direction $[0, 1, 1]$.

  a. Find the phase velocity β/ω if the electric field of the plane wave is $[E_0, 0, 0]$.

  b. What is the other possible polarization and the corresponding refractive index?

Problem 14–5 Fresnel's Equation of Wave Normals: If a plane wave in topaz listed in Table 14.3 propagates in the direction [1,1,1], find the two possible refractive indices and the corresponding birefringence.

Problem 14–6 Optic Axis: For mica given in Table 14.3, find the direction of the optic axis and the corresponding refractive index.

Problem 14–7 Electro-Optic Modulation of Crystal Group $\bar{4}$2m: If an electric field E_0 is applied in the [0,1,0] direction inside ADP, find the new principal axis. Is it dependent on the magnitude of the electric field E_0? If yes, find the principle axis at $E_0 = 10^4$ V/m. Use values given in Table 14.4 at $\lambda = 633$ nm.

Problem 14–8 Electro-Optic Modulation of Crystal Group 3m: If an electric field E_0 is applied in direction [0,0,1] in LiNaO$_3$, find the birefringence in terms of E_0 for a plane wave propagating in [0,1,1]. Use $n_o = 2.286$, $n_e = 2.200$, $r_{13} = 9.6 \times 10^{-12}$ m/V, and $r_{33} = 30.9 \times 10^{-12}$ m/V at $\lambda = 633$ nm. Comment on how important E_0 is to the birefringence in this case.

Problem 14–9 Electro-Optic Modulation of Crystal Group $\bar{4}$3m: If we apply an electric field E_0 to GaAs in the direction [0,0,1], find the new optic axis.

Problem 14–10 Electro-Optic Modulation from Kerr Effect: If an electric field E_0 is applied in the direction [0,0,1] in KDP,

    a. Give the index ellipsoid equation that includes both the Pockels effect and the nonlinear Kerr effect. What are the new principal refractive indices in the new principal axis?

    b. How large should E_0 be so that the nonlinear Kerr effect causes a larger refractive index than the linear Pockels effect in either the new x' or y'-axis? Let $r_{63} = 1.0 \times 10^{-11}$ m/V and $s_{31} = 3 \times 10^{-18}$ (m/V)^2.

Problem 14–11 Longitudinal LiNbO$_3$ EO Modulator: Consider a longitudinal modulator made of LiNbO$_3$, where both the propagation direction and the electric field are in the [0,0,1] direction. Find the required voltage change for a phase modulation of $\pi/2$. Use $r_{13} = 7.0 \times 10^{-12}$ m/V and $n_o = 2.229$ at $\lambda = 1.15$ μm.

Problem 14–12 Transverse KDP EO Modulator: Consider a transverse modulator made of KDP. If the electric field is in the direction [0,0,1] and the incident wave propagates in [1,1,0] and has a polarization [–1,1,0], find the required voltage for a phase modulation of π. Assume the ratio of the longitudinal to transverse dimension is 1000 and use parameter values given in Example 14.9.

Problem 14–13 Transverse Kerr Modulator: Consider the Kerr effect illustrated in Example 14.8. If the applied electric field is in [0,0,1] and the incident wave propagates in [1,0,0], find the required voltage change for a phase change of π between the two eigen polarizations. Assume the longitudinal and transverse dimensions of the modulator are 10 mm and 0.1 mm, respectively.

Problem 14–14 EO Amplitude Modulator Using Polarization Filtering: Consider the use of polarization filtering shown in Figure 14.8 for amplitude modulation, where the input polarizer is aligned in [1,0,0], the output polarizer is aligned in [0,1,0], and the EO modulator in the middle is made of GaAs with its longitudinal direction aligned in [0,0,1]. Assume $n = 3.43$ and $r_{41} = 1.43 \times 10^{-12}$ m/V at $\lambda = 1.15$ μm.

   a. Consider a longitudinal modulator design where both the modulating electric field E_0 and the propagation direction of the incident wave are in [0,0,1]. Find the required voltage change for maximum peak-to-peak OOK modulation.

   b. From *a*, what is the corresponding phase change due to the applied voltage?

Problem 14–15 Mach-Zehnder Interferometer: Consider an MZI whose EO modulator section is made of KD*P. If the modulator is longitudinal (*z*-axis) and operated at $\lambda = 633$ nm, find

   (*a*) the $K_a L$ value and

   (*b*) the required voltage to switch the state of the interferometer.

Problem 14–16 Waveguide Couplers: If the mismatch factor is $\delta = 0.01\kappa$ at zero bias, find the minimum extinction ratio of P_{o1} from Equations (14.90) and (14.91). Assume the waveguide length is set at $L = \pi/2\kappa$ given by Equation (14.92).

Problem 14–17 Alternating-β Waveguide Couplers: For an alternating-β waveguide coupler with $L = 1.1 \times L_{\pi/2} = 1.1 \times \pi/2\kappa$, find the two δ values that give a complete crossover or zero crossover, respectively. Hint: Use Equation (14.98) to compute δ for a complete crossover.

Problem 14–18 Modulation Bandwidth and Depth of EO Modulators: Using as the modulation depth with Δn given by Equation (14.72), derive the expression for the bit-rate and modulation-depth product when the speed is limited by (*a*) capacitance charge time and (*b*) transit delay, respectively. For each case, consider both transverse and longitudinal EO modulators. Comment on which type of modulator is better from this bit-rate and modulation-depth product consideration.

Problem 14–19 AC Power Consumption of EO Modulators: Express the ac power for modulation at a given bit rate R_b, a total modulation depth $\Delta n L = \lambda$, and a voltage change $\Delta V = V_2 - V_1$. Consider both transverse and longitudinal modulators when the speed is limited by (*a*) capacitance charge time and (*b*) transit delay, respectively.

Problem 14–20 Acousto-Optic Effect: Consider a longitudinal acoustic wave in GaAs in the direction of [1,1,0] of the principal axis. Also assume the incident light is in the direction of [1, –1, 0] and polarized in [1, 1, 0].

   a. Find the effective elasto-optic coefficient p_{ao}.

   b. Find the deflection figure of merit.

Problem 14–21 Bragg Diffraction: For a longitudinal acoustic wave in water, the refractive index is 1.33 and the sound velocity is 1.5 km/sec. Find the Bragg angle θ_B if the incident lightwave is at $\lambda = 1.5$ μm and the acoustic wave is operated at 1 MHz.

Problem 14–22 Raman-Nath Diffraction: Consider an acousto-optic modulator made of LiTaO$_3$. If the input light wavelength is 0.63 μm, what is the condition for the width of the modulator so that Raman-Nath diffraction can be significant?

Problem 14–23 Deflection Efficiency and Modulation Bandwidth: For PbMoO$_2$ shown in Table 14.10, find the best arrangement that has the largest deflection efficiency and modulation bandwidth product at $I_{acoustic} = 10^5$ W/m^2. Assume $L/\lambda = 500$ and $\cos \theta_B \approx 1$.

Problem 14–24 Driving Power: For a longitudinal acoustic wave propagating in [1,1,0] in GaAs, find the modulating power to have a deflection efficiency of 20 percent. Assume the light wavelength is $\lambda = 1.5$ μm and the ratio $L/h = 20$.

REFERENCES

1. *Lasers and Optronics: Buying Guide, Industry and Product Directory,* 1991.

2. A. Yariv and P. Yeh, *Optical Waves in Crystals,* John Wiley and Sons, 1984.

3. K. Hoffman and R. Kunze, *Linear Algebra,* 2nd ed., Prentice-Hall, 1971.

4. M. Born and E. Wolf, *Principles of Optics,* 6th ed., Pergamon Press, 1980.

5. A. B. Buckman, *Guided-Wave Photonics,* Saunders College Publishing, 1992.

6. H. Kogelnik and R. V. Schmidt, "Switched Directional Couplers with Alternating $\Delta\beta$," *IEEE Journal of Quantum Electronics,* vol. 12 (1976), p. 396.

7. I. Brillouin, "Diffusion de la Lumiére et des rayons X par un corps transparent homogéne," Ann Phys (France), (1922) pp. 88–122.

8. P. P. Banerjee and T.-C. Poon, *Principles of Applied Optics,* Aksen Associates, 1991.

9. A. Korpel, "Acousto-Optics: A Review of Fundamentals," *Proceedings of the IEEE,* vol. 69, no. 1 (January 1981), pp. 48–53.

10. B. E. A. Saleh and M. C. Teich, *Fundamentals of Photonics,* John Wiley and Sons, 1991.

15

COHERENT DETECTION

Chapter 12 discussed incoherent detection, where only the intensity of the incident light is detected. Although incoherent detection is simple in implementation, it cannot detect the phase and frequency of the received signal. In other words, it can detect only amplitude modulated (AM) signals. When phase modulation (PM) or frequency modulation (FM) is desirable, such as when intensity noise is strong, coherent detection becomes a better choice. This is familiar from radio communications, where FM is much better than AM in transmission quality.

Coherent detection is also important in applications such as wavelength division multiplexing (WDM), where multiple channels are transmitted at the same time. As discussed in Chapter 9, coherent detection is one important technique used to tune in or select one particular frequency channel. Although passive tunable filters can be used to avoid coherent detection, a larger channel separation is necessary because of limited filter resolution.

In the history of lightwave technology development, a more important reason behind the active coherent detection research work is its ability to amplify the received signal optically for a better signal-to-noise ratio (SNR). As discussed in Chapters 6 and 12, photocurrent amplification using an avalanche photodiode (APD) can help to overcome thermal and receiver noise. Practical incoherent detection receivers, however, still have a performance far worse than the quantum limit because of the excess noise. Coherent detection can avoid this problem and at the same time provide signal amplification. As a result, coherent detection can have a performance close to the quantum limit.

Optical amplifiers developed over the last few years provide another attractive alternative. For example, Erbium-doped fiber amplifiers (EDFAs) can be easily inserted into regular optical fibers for a power gain of 20–30 dB and at a pumping efficiency of 5–10 dB/mW. One disadvantage is that the amplifier also introduces noise because of amplified spontaneous emission (ASE). Detailed discussion on optical amplifiers will be given in Chapter 17.

15.1   BASIC PRINCIPLES OF COHERENT DETECTION

Although coherent detection is relatively new in optical communications, it has been around in radio communications for a long time. In both radio and optical communications, the essence of coherent detection is to generate a product term of the received signal and a local carrier. As a result, the received passband signal can be demodulated or shifted back to baseband.

As an example, consider a passband signal $m(t)\cos(\omega_{inc}t)$ shown in Figure 15.1a. To recover the original baseband signal $m(t)$, the received signal is multiplied by a local oscillator $\cos(\omega_{loc}t)$. If the local carrier is synchronized to the received signal $m(t)\cos(\omega_{inc})$ in frequency, i.e.($\omega_{loc} = \omega_{inc}$,), the product term is

$$m(t)\cos(\omega_{inc}t) \times \cos(\omega_{loc}t) = \tfrac{1}{2}m(t) + \tfrac{1}{2}m(t)\cos(2\omega_{inc}t).$$

Therefore, the baseband signal can be recovered using a low-pass filter.

The above scheme is called **homodyning** because $\omega_{inc} = \omega_{loc}$. In practice, the local carrier frequency ω_{loc} does not have to be equal to ω_{inc}. In this case, the coherent detection scheme is called **heterodyning** and demodulation is performed in two stages. As will be explained in detail in this chapter, there are various techniques that can be used for the second-stage demodulation.

15.1.1   OPTICAL MIXING

Although the use of the multiplier to generate the product term is common in radio communications, it is not practical in optical communications. An alternative way is to mix the incident signal with a local optical carrier. As illustrated in Figure 15.1b, if the two signals have the same polarizations, the magnitudes of their fields can be scalarly added. In this case, because the photocurrent output is proportional to the combined intensity,

$$I_{ph} = \mathcal{R}[P_{inc} + P_{loc} + 2\sqrt{P_{inc}P_{loc}}\cos(\omega_{inc}t - \omega_{loc}t)] \qquad \textbf{[15.1]}$$

where $\mathcal{R}$ is the responsivity of the photodiode and P_{loc} is the local oscillator power. Among the three terms, P_{loc} is a constant term that can be simply filtered out by ac-coupling. The third term is the product term of interest. Because $P_{loc} \gg P_{inc}$, $\sqrt{P_{inc}P_{loc}}$ is much larger than P_{inc}. Therefore, the latter term can be dropped.

Example 15.1

SENSITIVITY INCREASE FROM COHERENT DETECTION   If a direct detection receiver has a receiver sensitivity of -20 dBm, a minimum received signal power of 10 μW is needed. If the receiver is dominated by the receiver noise instead of shot noise, the receiver sensitivity can be improved by using coherent detection and a high-power local oscillator. For example, a local optical carrier of power 1 mW can be generated, and the power of the incident light can be reduced to

$$P_{inc} = \frac{P_{rx,min}^2}{P_{loc}} = \frac{(10^{-5})^2}{10^{-3}} = 0.1 \ \mu\text{W}.$$

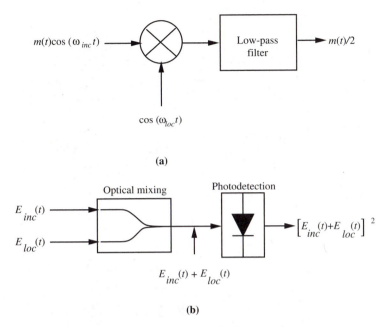

$m(t)\cos(\omega_{inc}t)$

Low-pass filter

$m(t)/2$

$\cos(\omega_{loc}t)$

(a)

Optical mixing

Photodetection

$E_{inc}(t)$

$E_{loc}(t)$

$E_{inc}(t) + E_{loc}(t)$

$\left[E_{inc}(t)+E_{loc}(t)\right]^2$

(b)

Figure 15.1   Coherent detection in (a) radio and (b) optical communications.

This means a receiver sensitivity of -40 dBm, or equivalently a 20 dB optical gain is achieved from coherent detection.

In practice, shot noise power is also increased because of a large P_{loc} term in Equation (15.1). Therefore, the actual optical gain is a little worse. ■

15.1.2 HOMODYNE AND HETERODYNE DETECTIONS

A more detailed block diagram of coherent detection is shown in Figure 15.2. As mentioned earlier, there are two different types: homodyne and heterodyne detection. In the latter case, the two frequencies differ by a radio frequency called **intermediate frequency** (IF) and denoted by $\omega_{IF} = \omega_{inc} - \omega_{loc}$. Also, the photocurrent output is filtered by an IF or bandpass filter. In general, it is easier to implement heterodyne detection because of simpler carrier synchronization (see Section 15.9). However, the trade-off is a lower receiver sensitivity by a few dBs.

As shown in Figure 15.2, there are some common blocks in both homodyne and heterodyne detection. In addition to photodetection and a local oscillator, they both use a carrier recovery loop for local carrier synchronization, a device for polarization control, and a hybrid for optical mixing. The functions of these common blocks are described below.

Carrier Recovery   In homodyne detection, the carrier recovery loop uses a photodetector output to drive the carrier loop. The photodetector output carries the phase difference information of the signal and the local oscillator. In heterodyne detection, on the other

Incident Light Signal

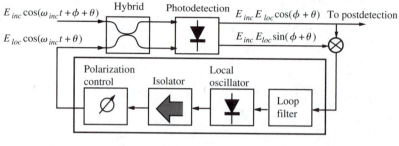

(a) Homodyne detection

Incident light signal

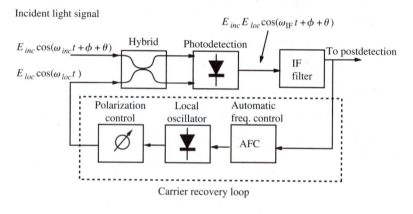

(b) Heterodyne detection

Figure 15.2   Block diagrams of coherent detection: (a) homodyne detection and (b) heterodyne detection.

hand, the output of the IF filter is used to drive an **automatic frequency control** (AFC) device in the carrier loop. The AFC generates an output that is proportional to the difference of the frequency of the IF filter output and the specified ω_{IF} value. This thus maintains the frequency difference between the local oscillator output and the received signal. Detailed discussion on carrier recovery is given in Section 15.9.

Polarization Control in Coherent Detection   As mentioned earlier, the photocurrent given in Equation (15.1) assumes the two light signals have the same polarization. In general, this may not be the case. Let $\bar{E}_{inc}(t) = S(t)\hat{x}$ be the electric field of the incident light, where $\hat{x}$ is the unit vector in the direction of the polarization, and let $\bar{E}_{loc} = L(t)\hat{x}'$ be the electric field of the local oscillator. When the two signals are mixed, the output photocurrent is proportional to

$$| \bar{E}_{inc} + \bar{E}_{loc} |^2 = | S(t)|^2 + | L(t)|^2 + 2\Re\{S(t)L(t)^*\}\hat{x} \cdot \hat{x}'$$

where $\hat{x} \cdot \hat{x}'$ is the inner product of the two unit vectors. As mentioned earlier, the cross term $2\Re\{S(t)L(t)^*\}\hat{x} \cdot \hat{x}'$ carries the signal information for detection. To maximize this term, it is desirable to maximize the inner product or align the two polarizations. Therefore, it is important to use polarization control to ensure a large product term.

EFFECT OF POLARIZATION ALIGNMENT If the polarizations of the two light signals are perpendicular to each other, there is no cross term, and the output power of the hybrid is simply the sum of the two input powers. Therefore, information carried by PM or FM signals will not be detectable.

    If polarization control is required to have the cross term within 90 percent of the peak value, the angle between the two polarizations should be within

$$\theta = \cos^{-1}(0.9) = 25.8°. \quad \blacksquare$$

| **Example 15.2** |

    To implement polarization control, polarization or Faraday rotators can be used. As described in Appendix 15–A, they are made of anisotropic media and have the similar birefringence property discussed in Chapter 14. Different from electro-optic modulators, whose birefringence is between two *linearly* polarized waves, polarization rotators have a birefringence between two opposite, *circularly* polarized waves.

    An alternative approach to polarization control is the use of a polarization diversity receiver, as shown in Figure 15.3. In this design, two **polarizing beam splitters** (PBSs) are used to separate the two orthogonally polarized beams of the local laser output and the incident light. From the separations, the same polarized beams from the incident light and local laser output are mixed and detected. The two photocurrent signals from the two orthogonal polarizations are then added. From this design, no matter what the polarization of the incident light, there is always mixing with the local carrier. Depending on the power partition among the two orthogonal polarizations, it can be shown that the diversity design can maintain 70 percent of the peak photocurrent (see Problem 15–1).

Hybrids The device that mixes two light signals is called a hybrid, which in general is a four-port device, whose two inputs and two outputs can be related by a 2×2 matrix:

$$\begin{bmatrix} E_{o1} \\ E_{o2} \end{bmatrix} = \begin{bmatrix} T_1 & X_1 \\ X_2 & T_2 \end{bmatrix} \begin{bmatrix} E_{inc} \\ E_{loc} \end{bmatrix} = \bar{H} \begin{bmatrix} E_{inc} \\ E_{loc} \end{bmatrix}. \qquad \textbf{[15.2]}$$

    Various practical hybrid designs are discussed in Appendix 15–B. In coherent detection, there are two important types of hybrids that deserve further consideration. The first type is called the 180° hybrid, with the transfer matrix given by

$$\bar{H}_{180} = \frac{1}{\sqrt{2}} e^{j\theta} \begin{bmatrix} 1 & 1 \\ 1 & -1 \end{bmatrix}. \qquad \textbf{[15.3]}$$

Note that there is a 180° phase shift between T_1 and T_2, and the hybrid is lossless because $|T_1|^2 + |X_2|^2 = |T_2|^2 + |X_1|^2 = 1$.

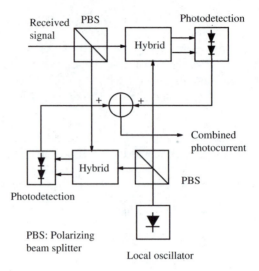

Figure 15.3 A polarization diversity receiver. A polarizing beam splitter separates two orthogonally polarized beams.

Another important kind of hybrid has a transfer matrix given by

$$\bar{H}_{90} = \frac{a}{\sqrt{2}} e^{j\theta} \begin{bmatrix} 1 & 1 \\ 1 & j \end{bmatrix}$$ [15.4]

where $0 < a < 1$ is a certain loss factor from practical implementation. This hybrid is called the $90°$ hybrid because there is a $90°$ phase shift between T_1 and T_2. As Section 15.9 explains, $90°$ hybrids are needed for carrier recovery based on the Costas loop.

In practical $90°$ four-port hybrid design, the loss factor a cannot be greater than $1/\sqrt{2}$ because of the limitation of physics (see Appendix 15–B). This implies at least a 3 dB power loss and is undesirable.

Fortunately, when hybrids are used for both signal detection and carrier recovery, a $90°$ six-port hybrid, illustrated in Figure 15.4, can be used [1]. In this design, 50 percent of the signal power is used for signal detection, and the remaining 50 percent is used for carrier recovery. In other words, the 3 dB power loss is transferred for the use of carrier recovery (Problem 15–13). See Section 15.9 and Appendix 15–C for detailed discussion on this six-port hybrid.

15.2 SIGNAL AND NOISE FORMULATIONS IN COHERENT DETECTION

After the two light signals are mixed by the hybrid, there are two main configurations used in photodetection: **single detection** and **balanced detection**. As illustrated in Figure 15.5, single detection uses only one photodiode. This is the same as in incoherent detection. In

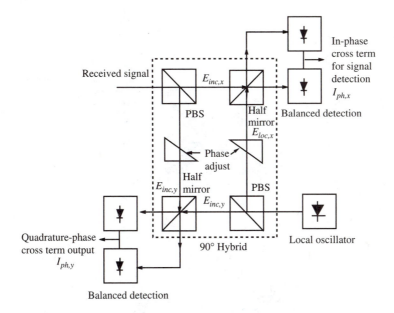

Figure 15.4   A six-port 90° hybrid with two input ports and four output ports. Each PBS splits the input according to its polarization. Each half-mirror functions as a four-port hybrid. The phase adjusters add necessary phase shifts so that the in-phase and quadrature-phase products can be obtained after balanced detection.

this case, one of the hybrid's outputs is not used and can be used for carrier recovery as discussed later. Balanced detection feeds the two outputs to two photodiodes whose current outputs are subtracted. As will be explained shortly, one major advantage of balanced detection is that it cancels the relative intensity noise (RIN) from the local oscillator.

Signal Formulations Using Balanced Detection Without loss of generality, consider the use of a 180° hybrid. The two outputs from the hybrid can thus be expressed as

$$E_{o1} = \frac{1}{\sqrt{2}}(E_{inc} + E_{loc})$$

and

$$E_{o2} = \frac{1}{\sqrt{2}}(E_{inc} - E_{loc}).$$

After photodetection,

$$I_{ph,1} = \frac{1}{2}\mathcal{R}\left\{P_{inc} + P_{loc} + 2\sqrt{P_{inc}P_{loc}}\cos[(\omega_{inc} - \omega_{loc})t + \phi(t)]\right\} \qquad \textbf{[15.5]}$$

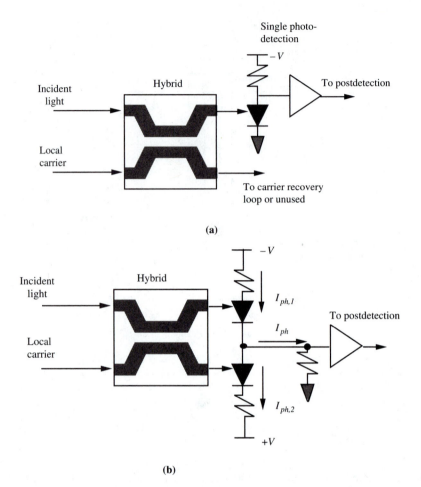

Figure 15.5   (a) Single detection versus (b) balanced detection.

$$I_{ph,2} = \frac{1}{2}\mathcal{R}\left\{P_{inc} + P_{loc} - 2\sqrt{P_{inc}P_{loc}}\cos[(\omega_{inc} - \omega_{loc})t + \phi(t)]\right\} \qquad \textbf{[15.6]}$$

where P_{inc} is the incident light power and P_{loc} is the local carrier power. In amplitude modulation, P_{inc} is modulated according to the transmitted data. Also, $\phi(t)$ is the phase of the carrier and can be used for phase modulation.

With balanced detection, the difference between the photocurrents is

$$I_{ph} = I_{ph,1} - I_{ph,2} = 2\mathcal{R}\sqrt{P_{inc}P_{loc}}\cos[(\omega_{inc} - \omega_{loc})t + \phi(t)]. \qquad \textbf{[15.7]}$$

This subtracted current has no dc terms and is twice that of the individual photodiode output. Therefore, use of single detection has a 3 dB (factor 1/2) power loss compared to balanced detection.

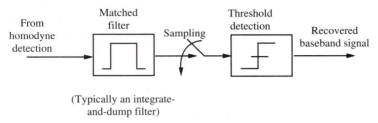

From homodyne detection → Matched filter (Typically an integrate-and-dump filter) → Sampling → Threshold detection → Recovered baseband signal

Figure 15.6 Postdetection for homodyne detection.

Based on the balanced detection, when homodyne detection is used or $\omega_s = \omega_{loc}$,

$$I_{ph,homo}(t) = 2\mathcal{R}\sqrt{P_{inc}P_{loc}}\cos[\phi(t)]. \qquad \textbf{[15.8]}$$

Similarly, when heterodyne detection is used, or $\omega_{inc} - \omega_{loc} = \omega_{IF}$,

$$I_{ph,hetero}(t) = 2\mathcal{R}\sqrt{P_{inc}P_{loc}}\cos[\omega_{IF}t + \phi(t)]. \qquad \textbf{[15.9]}$$

Signal Detection in Homodyne Detection In the case of homodyne detection, the photocurrent signal given by Equation (15.8) is a baseband signal and immediately ready for detection. Specifically, as discussed in Chapter 6 and shown in Figure 15.6, the photocurrent output from homodyne detection is first equalized by a matched filter and then followed by threshold detection. When the shot noise is approximated as Gaussian and there is no ISI, this matched filtering structure gives the optimum detection performance. When the input pulse is rectangular or a NRZ pulse, the matched filtering is equivalent to integrate-and-dump.

To convert the incident light signal directly to baseband, the carrier frequency of the local optical carrier needs to be synchronized by a carrier loop. As Section 15.9 explains, the loop has a feedback circuit that drives the local laser diode according to the photocurrent until the two carriers have the same optical frequency and a small but fixed phase difference.

Signal Detection in Heterodyne Detection In the case of heterodyne detection, the photocurrent signal given by Equation (15.9) is still a passband signal and consequently needs to be demodulated again. Because $\omega_{inc} \neq \omega_{loc}$, the carrier loop for frequency synchronization can be relaxed and only needs to ensure that the frequency difference is within the IF band (a fixed phase relationship is unnecessary). To perform postdemodulation, there are two methods: coherent and incoherent postdetections. As shown in Figure 15.7, an IF carrier loop is needed in coherent postdetection to generate a carrier that is in phase with the IF signal. On the other hand, in incoherent postdetection, envelope detection, which consists of a squarer and low-pass filter, is used. Incoherent postdetection can be used to detect amplitude and frequency modulated signals. These different techniques will be discussed in detail in the next few sections.

Noise Formulation in Balanced Detection The current outputs given in Equations (15.5) and (15.6) contain only signal terms. In practice, there are additional noise

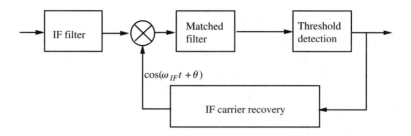

(a) Coherent post detection

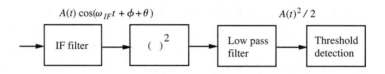

(b) Envelope detection

Figure 15.7   Use of (a) coherent detection and (b) envelope detection in postdetection for heterodyne detection.

terms that need to be added. In addition to receiver noise, two important noise terms are the shot noise from photodetection and the RIN from the local oscillator. Because the RIN power is proportional to the local optical power, which is much larger than the received signal power, the RIN can greatly affect detection performance. When balanced detection is used, the same RIN occurs at the two photodiode outputs. Therefore, by subtracting the two current outputs from balanced detection, the RIN can be cancelled [2].

Example 15.3

IMPORTANCE OF BALANCED DETECTION Using a $180°$ hybrid, the RIN power at each hybrid output is

$$\sigma_{RIN}^2 = \tfrac{1}{2} \times \text{RIN}(\mathcal{R}P_{loc})^2 B.$$

On the other hand, the shot noise power due to the local oscillator is

$$\sigma_{shot}^2 = q B \mathcal{R} P_{loc} B.$$

Therefore, the noise power ratio is

$$\frac{\sigma_{RIN}^2}{\sigma_{shot}^2} = \frac{\text{RIN}\mathcal{R}P_{loc}}{2q}.$$

When the ratio is comparable to 1 or larger, it is important to use balanced detection to cancel the RIN. As a numerical example, assume a local oscillator has a power output of 1 mW, the relative intensity noise is -130 dB/Hz, and photodiodes have a responsivity of 0.8. The ratio is

$$\frac{\sigma^2_{RIN}}{\sigma^2_{shot}} = \frac{10^{-13} \times 0.8 \times 10^{-3}}{2 \times 1.6 \times 10^{-19}} = 250 = 24 \text{ dB}.$$

Therefore, if the RIN is not cancelled, there can be a SNR drop of 24 dB. ∎

After the RIN is cancelled, the only noise term to consider is the shot noise because of the high local optical power. From Chapter 6, the two-sided power spectral density (PSD) of noise at each photodiode output is

$$S_{n,i}(\omega) = \tfrac{1}{2}q\mathcal{R}P_{loc}$$

where i is either 1 or 2. When the two current outputs are subtracted in balanced detection, the total noise power is

$$S_n(\omega) = S_{n,1}(\omega) + S_{n,2}(\omega) = q\mathcal{R}P_{loc}B. \qquad \textbf{[15.10]}$$

As discussed in Chapter 6, shot noise can be assumed to be Gaussian when the noise power is large. If an integrate-and-dump filter is used in Figure 15.6 as the matched filter for homodyne detection, the noise power at the threshold detector input is

$$\sigma^2_{n,homo} = q\mathcal{R}P_{loc}T. \qquad \textbf{[15.11]}$$

When heterodyning is used, an additional IF demodulation is needed. In the case of coherent IF demodulation, as in Figure 15.7a, an IF carrier $\cos(\omega_{IF}t)$ is used to multiply the combined photocurrent. The corresponding noise power after integrate-and-dump is scaled down by a factor of 2. That is,

$$\sigma^2_{n,hetero} = \tfrac{1}{2}q\mathcal{R}P_{loc}T. \qquad \textbf{[15.12]}$$

SNR IN HOMODYNE DETECTION   In homodyne detection, from Equations (15.8) and (15.11), | **Example 15.4**

$$\text{SNR} = \frac{(2\mathcal{R}\sqrt{P_{inc}P_{loc}}T)^2}{q\mathcal{R}P_{loc}T} = 4\eta\frac{P_{inc}T}{hf} = 4\eta N$$

where N is the average number of incident photons over T, η is the quantum efficiency, and $\mathcal{R} = q\eta/hf$. As will be shown, a SNR of 36 is needed to achieve a BER of 10^{-9} for phase-shift keying (PSK) ($\phi = 0$ or π in Equation [15.8]). If $\eta = 1$, N must equal $(P_{inc}T/hf) = 9$ photons per bit, which is the quantum limit using PSK homodyne detection. ∎

Digital Signaling Schemes   The photocurrent given by Equations (15.8) and (15.9) can have different forms to carry binary data. If its amplitude is modulated according to the information signal, the signaling scheme is called amplitude-shift keying (ASK). One special case of ASK is OOK, where the amplitude is either a high value or zero. In addition to ASK, the phase or frequency content of the photocurrent can also be modulated according to the information signal. The modulation scheme is then called phase-shift keying (PSK) or frequency-shift keying (FSK), respectively. When the phase change between two bit intervals is modulated, the signaling scheme is called differential PSK (DPSK). These signaling formats are illustrated in Figure 15.8, where the carrier frequencies shown are much lower than they would be in reality.

Recently, there have been active research studies on polarization modulation techniques called **polarization shift keying** (PolSK). In PolSK, the polarization is modulated according to the transmitted information. PolSK in general requires a completely different detection scheme called **Stokes detection**, where the Stokes parameters [3] of the polarized light are detected. Because the Stokes parameters are three dimensional, they provide more compact signaling at the same signaling distance. As a result, PolSK is attractive in multilevel signaling (i.e., more than two levels; OOK is a two-level scheme).

The next few sections discuss in detail the detection methods and performance of each signaling scheme.

15.3   ON-OFF KEYING

As Figure 15.8 shows, OOK transmits a pulse when the input bit is one, and transmits no pulse when the input bit is zero. This is the simplest signaling method because it can be implemented by direct modulation, as discussed in Chapter 12.

15.3.1 SIGNAL REPRESENTATION AND DEMODULATION

When OOK signaling is used, the signal power, $P_{inc}(t)$, in Equations (15.8) and (15.9) can be expressed as

$$P_{inc}(t) = \sum_k A_k p(t - kT)$$ **[15.13]**

where A_k can assume either a high or a zero value and $p(t)$ is an NRZ pulse. The phase term, $\phi(t)$, in Equation (15.9) is a constant. OOK can be extended to M-ary ASK, where A_k can be $-(M-1)A/2, -(M-3)A/2, \ldots, -A/2, A/2 \ldots, (M-1)A/2$, and M is a power of 2 integer.

If homodyne detection is used, as illustrated in Figure 15.6, the photocurrent is a baseband NRZ pulse train, and the transmitted data can be recovered by matched filtering and simple threshold detection. On the other hand, if heterodyne detection is used, as illustrated in Figure 15.7, the incoherent post-detection method or envelope detection can be used, or the coherent method can be used to demodulate the signal to baseband by an IF carrier.

In the case of envelope detection, as illustrated in Figure 15.7*b*, a squarer followed by a low-pass filter is commonly used. In this case,

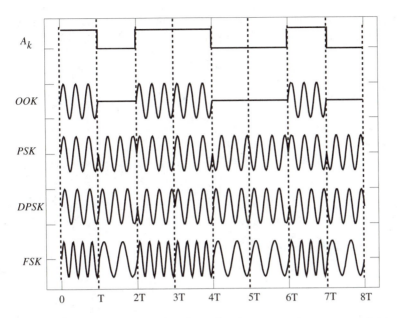

Figure 15.8 Various digital signaling formats in coherent communications.

$$[A cos(\omega_{IF} t)]^2 = \tfrac{1}{2} A^2 + \tfrac{1}{2} A^2 \cos(2\omega_{IF} t)$$

where $A = 2\mathcal{R}\sqrt{P_{inc} P_{loc}}$.

The first term is the baseband signal to be used for detection, and the second term is a high-pass signal that can be rejected by low-pass filtering.

In the case of coherent postdetection, an IF recovery loop is needed to generate the same carrier $\cos(\omega_{IF} t)$ of the IF filter output. By multiplying the IF filter output with the IF carrier, one has

$$A[\cos(\omega_{IF} t)]^2 = \tfrac{1}{2} A + \tfrac{1}{2} A \cos(2\omega_{IF} t)$$

where the first term is the term of interest, and the second term will be rejected by low-pass filtering.

15.3.2 OOK FUNDAMENTAL DETECTION PERFORMANCE

From the above discussion, the "fundamental" OOK detection performance based only on shot noise can be evaluated. When other degradation sources, such as phase noise and intersymbol interference are considered, the performance will be worse. The actual drop in performance depends on the relative importance of the shot noise and the other degradation sources.

Homodyne Detection When the photocurrent given by Equation (15.8) is integrated over one bit interval T, the output due to the transmission of bit "1" is:

$$N_1 = 2\mathcal{R}\sqrt{P_{inc}P_{loc}}T.$$

If bit "0" is transmitted,

$$N_0 = 0.$$

If the threshold detection discussed in Chapter 7 is used and the threshold is set at the middle between N_0 and N_1, from $\sigma_{n,homo}^2$ given in Equation (15.11), the error detection probability is

$$P_{E,OOK,homo} = Q\left(\frac{N_1/2}{\sigma_{n,homo}}\right) = Q\left(\sqrt{\frac{\mathcal{R}P_{inc}T}{q}}\right) = Q(\sqrt{N_s}) = Q(\sqrt{2N_b}) \quad \textbf{[15.14]}$$

where the Q-function is defined in Chapter 6,

$$\boxed{N_s \stackrel{\text{def}}{=} \frac{\mathcal{R}}{q}P_{inc}T = \frac{\eta}{hf}P_{inc}T} \quad \textbf{[15.15]}$$

represents the average number of "effective" photons over one bit interval when "1" is transmitted, and

$$N_b = \frac{N_s}{2} \quad \textbf{[15.16]}$$

is the average number of "effective" photons per bit. The adjective "effective" is used to account for the quantum efficiency η.

Example 15.5	**HOMODYNE OOK SENSITIVITY** To achieve $P_E = 10^{-9}$, from Equation (15.14), $\sqrt{2N_b}$ must equal 6. Therefore, $N_b = 18$, which is the quantum limit of homodyne OOK transmission. If the receiver noise power is nine times the shot noise power due to the local oscillator, the total noise power is actually 10 times higher. Therefore, the received signal power must be 10 times higher, or $N_b = 180$ photons/bit. ∎

Heterodyne Detection with Coherent Postdetection In heterodyne detection, as mentioned earlier, an additional IF demodulation is needed before integrate-and-dump detection. The final signal output when bit "1" is transmitted is

$$N_1 = \mathcal{R}\sqrt{P_{inc}P_{loc}}T.$$

When bit "0" is transmitted, $N_0 = 0$. Therefore, from $\sigma_{n,hetero}^2$ given in Equation (15.12), the error detection probability is

$$P_{E,OOK,hetero} = Q\left(\frac{N_1/2}{\sigma_{n,hetero}}\right) = Q\left(\sqrt{\frac{N_s}{2}}\right) = Q(\sqrt{N_b}) \qquad \textbf{[15.17]}$$

where N_s and N_b are defined by Equations (15.15) and (15.16), respectively. Comparing Equations (15.14) and (15.17) shows that heterodyning has a 3 dB penalty in fundamental performance compared to its homodyne counterpart. The trade-off of this worse performance is a simpler optical carrier recovery implementation.

HETERODYNE OOK SENSITIVITY   At a BER of 10^{-9}, N_b must equal 36. If the bit rate is 1 GHz and the quantum efficiency is 0.8, the fundamental receiver sensitivity at $\lambda = 1.55$ μm is   **Example 15.6**

$$P_{inc} = \frac{36}{0.8} \times hf \times 10^9 = 5.77 \text{ nW} = -52.4 \text{ dBm}.$$

This power input in the case of direct detection will generate a photocurrent of only 5.76 nA. Compared to practical current noise power at the receiver front-end, this signal current is quite small. Therefore, coherent detection becomes attractive by making the receiver noise relatively unimportant. ∎

Envelope Detection   Evaluating the performance of envelope detection requires knowing the probability distribution of the envelope signal when noise is included. Adding the shot noise to the photocurrent given by Equation (15.9) gives

$$I_{ph}(t) + n(t) = 2\mathcal{R}\sqrt{P_{inc}P_{loc}}\cos(\omega_{IF}t) + n(t) \qquad \textbf{[15.18]}$$

where $n(t)$ here is a filtered noise from ideal bandpass filtering of bandwidth $2/T$ centered at ω_{IF}. Therefore, the noise power is

$$\sigma_n^2 = S_{n,hetero} \times \frac{4}{T} = \frac{2}{T}q\mathcal{R}P_{loc} \overset{\text{def}}{=} \sigma_{n,envelope}^2. \qquad \textbf{[15.19]}$$

Because $n(t)$ is a bandpass noise, according to [4] and also Problem 15–6, $n(t)$ can be expressed as

$$n(t) = n_c(t)\cos(\omega_{IF}t) + n_s(t)\sin(\omega_{IF}t) \qquad \textbf{[15.20]}$$

where $n_c(t)$ and $n_s(t)$ are independent low-pass processes with variance

$$\sigma_{n_c}^2 = \sigma_{n_s}^2 = \sigma_{n,envelope}^2. \qquad \textbf{[15.21]}$$

From Equation (15.18),

$$I_{ph}(t) + n(t) = [2\mathcal{R}\sqrt{P_{inc}P_{loc}} + n_c(t)]\cos(\omega_{IF}t) + n_s(t)\sin(\omega_{IF}t)$$
$$= E(t)\cos[\omega_{IF}t + \psi(t)]$$

where

$$E(t) = \left[(2\mathcal{R}\sqrt{P_{inc}P_{loc}} + n_c)^2 + n_s^2\right]^{1/2} \qquad \textbf{[15.22]}$$

is the envelope of the total current and

$$\psi(t) = -\tan^{-1}\left(\frac{n_s}{2\mathcal{R}\sqrt{P_{inc}P_{loc}} + n_c}\right) \qquad \textbf{[15.23]}$$

is the phase component. From Appendix 15–D, the PDF of $E(t)$ is a Rician distribution with the following PDF:

$$f_{E,1}(E) = \frac{E}{\sigma^2}e^{-(E^2+A^2)/2\sigma^2}I_0\left(\frac{AE}{\sigma^2}\right) \qquad \textbf{[15.24]}$$

where $\sigma^2 = \sigma_{n,envelope}^2$, $A = 2\mathcal{R}\sqrt{P_{inc}P_{loc}}$ and $I_0(x)$ is the zero-order modified Bessel function of the first kind. Several curves of Rician distribution density functions are shown in Figure 15.9

As shown in Figure 15.9, when $A \gg \sigma$, $f_E(E)$ can be approximated as Gaussian:

$$f_E(E) \approx \frac{1}{\sqrt{2\pi}\sigma}e^{-(E-A)^2/2\sigma^2}.$$

When $A = 0$, $I_0(0) = 1$ and the Rician distribution reduces to the Rayleigh distribution:

$$f_{E,0}(E) = \frac{E}{\sigma^2}e^{-E^2/2\sigma^2}. \qquad \textbf{[15.25]}$$

In envelope detection, when the threshold is set at $A/2$, the error detection probability is

$$P_E = \frac{1}{2}P(E > A/2|0) + \frac{1}{2}P(E < A/2|1) = \frac{1}{2}\left[e^{-A^2/8\sigma^2} + Q\left(\frac{A/2}{\sigma}\right)\right]$$

where E is the envelope signal sampled at a certain time. Using the approximation

$$Q(x) \approx \frac{1}{\sqrt{2\pi}x}e^{-x^2/2} \qquad \textbf{[15.26]}$$

when $x \gg 1$,

$$P_{E,OOK,envelope} = \tfrac{1}{2}e^{-A^2/8\sigma^2} = \tfrac{1}{2}e^{-N_s/4} = \tfrac{1}{2}e^{-N_b/2}. \qquad \textbf{[15.27]}$$

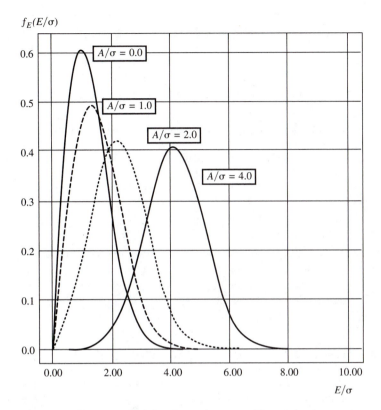

$f_E(E/\sigma)$

Figure 15.9   Probability density functions of Rician distribution.

OOK ENVELOPE DETECTION   According to Equation (15.27), N_b must equal 40 photons per bit at a BER of 10^{-9}. This represents a $40/36 = 1.11 = 0.46$ dB power penalty compared to the coherent postdetection case.

Example 15.7

In general, from the approximation given by Equation (15.26), note that the coherent postdetection performance of heterodyne detection given by Equation (15.17) can be approximated as

$$P_{E,OOK,hetero} \approx \frac{1}{\sqrt{2\pi N_b}} e^{-N_b/2}.$$

Comparing this with Equation (15.27) for envelope detection shows that

$$\frac{N_b'}{N_b} = \frac{1}{N_b} \ln\left(\frac{\pi N_b}{2}\right) + 1 \qquad \textbf{[15.28]}$$

to have the same BER, where N_b' is the required number of photons per bit using envelope detection. Note that the performance ratio N_b'/N_b approaches one when N_b is large. ■

15.4   **PHASE-SHIFT KEYING**

PSK transmits information by modulating the phase term in Equation (15.8) or (15.9), which can be achieved through external modulation, as discussed in Chapter 14. This section describes the demodulation process and analyzes the detection performance.

15.4.1   **SIGNAL REPRESENTATION AND DEMODULATION**

The phase term $\phi(t)$ given in Equations (15.8) and (15.9) in PSK can be generally expressed as

$$\phi(t) = \sum_k A_k p(t - kT) + \theta \qquad \textbf{[15.29]}$$

where θ is a constant term and A_k can be either 0 or π for binary PSK. In general, for M-ary PSK, $A_k = (2\pi j)/M$, where j can be 0, 1, ..., $M-1$.

In homodyne detection, similar to OOK, the photocurrent output can be matched filtered and detected with a local carrier, $\cos(\omega_{loc}t + \theta)$. Similarly, in heterodyne detection, the IF filter output can be demodulated by an IF carrier, $\cos(\omega_{IF}t + \theta)$. Because both the envelope and frequency of a PSK signal are constant, incoherent postdetection such as envelope detection cannot be used.

15.4.2   **BINARY PSK FUNDAMENTAL PERFORMANCE**

Binary PSK detection performance can be evaluated similarly to OOK. The only difference is that the amplitudes of 1's and 0's have opposite signs. As a result, at the same BER, or same peak-to-peak signal distance, the amplitude in PSK can be reduced by a factor of 2. This gives a 3 dB power advantage. Detailed analysis is given below.

Homodyne Detection   Following analysis similar to that for OOK signaling,

$$N_1 = -N_0 = 2\mathcal{R}\sqrt{P_{inc}P_{loc}}T.$$

Therefore, from $\sigma^2_{n,homo}$ given in Equation (15.11),

$$P_{E,PSK,homo} = Q\left(\frac{N_1}{\sigma_{n,homo}}\right) = Q\left(\sqrt{\frac{4\mathcal{R}P_{inc}T}{q}}\right) = Q(\sqrt{4N_s}) = Q(\sqrt{4N_b}).$$

$$\textbf{[15.30]}$$

Note that $N_b = N_s$ in PSK because bit 1's and 0's have the same transmission power. Comparing Equation (15.30) with Equation (15.14), one confirms that homodyne PSK has a 3 dB advantage over homodyne OOK in average power and also a 6 dB advantage in peak power. To achieve this, external modulation, discussed in Chapter 14 must be used.

Heterodyne Detection   Similar to the OOK heterodyning,

$$N_1 = -N_0 = \mathcal{R}\sqrt{P_{inc}P_{loc}}T.$$

Therefore, from $\sigma_{n,hetero}^2$ given in Equation (15.12),

$$P_{E,PSK,hetero} = Q\left(\frac{N_1}{\sigma_{n,hetero}}\right) = Q\left(\sqrt{\frac{2\mathcal{R}P_{inc}T}{q}}\right) = Q(\sqrt{2N_s}) = Q(\sqrt{2N_b}).$$

[15.31]

Again, comparing with Equation (15.17) shows that this is 3 dB better than the OOK counterpart. However, comparison with Equation (15.30) shows that it is 3 dB worse than PSK homodyne detection. The advantage of heterodyne PSK over homodyne PSK is its simplicity in carrier recovery.

15.5   DIFFERENTIAL PHASE-SHIFT KEYING

In PSK heterodyne detection, although there is no need to recover the original phase and frequency of the transmitter carrier in the optical loop, it must still be done in the IF loop. In order to simplify carrier recovery, *differential* PSK (DPSK) discussed below can be used.

Different from PSK, information in DPSK is transmitted through the *phase difference* of adjacent symbols. Specifically, if the transmitted bit is "0," A_k in Equation (15.29) is the same as the previous value A_{k-1}. If the transmitted bit is "1," there is a phase change of π between A_k and A_{k-1}. This is illustrated in Figure 15.8.

15.5.1   DPSK DEMODULATION

With differential phase modulation, the absolute phase θ is not of concern. Instead, only the phase change over two adjacent symbols must be detected.

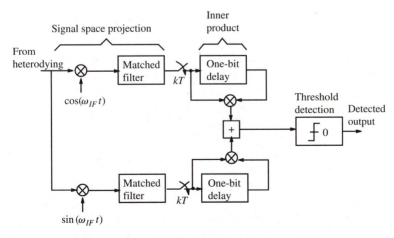

Figure 15.10   Block diagram of DPSK detection.

A block diagram of DPSK demodulation is illustrated in Figure 15.10. As shown, it consists of three stages: (1) signal space projection, (2) inner product calculation, and (3) threshold detection. These three steps are explained below.

Signal Space Projection   Because the phase term $\phi(t)$ carries the information, the first step of detection is to extract it from the received signal. For the purpose of subsequent detection, a one-to-one mapping is used between the phase $\phi(t)$ and the unit vector $\bar{u}(t) = [\cos\phi(t), -\sin\phi(t)]$. Since the signal after balanced detection is

$$y(t) = 2\mathcal{R}\sqrt{P_{inc}P_{loc}}\cos[\omega_{IF}t + \phi(t)]$$

the local carrier $\cos(\omega_{IF}t)$ and matched filter can be used to obtain $\cos[\phi(t)]$. Specifically, when $\phi(t)$ is an NRZ train, the matched filter is an integrate-and-dump filter over time duration T. Therefore, the matched filter output at the upper branch of Figure 15.10 at time $(k+1)T$ is

$$U_c[(k+1)T] = \int_{kT}^{(k+1)T} y(t)\cos(\omega_{IF}t)dt = I\cos[\phi(kT)]$$

where

$$I = \mathcal{R}\sqrt{P_{inc}P_{loc}}T \qquad\qquad \textbf{[15.32]}$$

and the high-frequency component is neglected because of its small dc average. Similarly, the sampled output at $(k+1)T$ and at the lower branch of Figure 15.10 is

$$U_s[(k+1)T] = \int_{kT}^{(k+1)T} y(t)\sin(\omega_{IF}t)dt = -I\sin[\phi(kT)].$$

The vector $\bar{U}_k = [U_c, U_s]$ sampled at time $(k+1)T$ thus represents the phase vector at time kT. That is,

$$\bar{U}_k = I[\cos\phi(kT), -\sin\phi(kT)]. \qquad\qquad \textbf{[15.33]}$$

Inner Product   With two adjacent phase vectors $\bar{U}_k$ and $\bar{U}_{k+1}$ obtained, one can detect the phase change of the two by calculating their inner product. Specifically, let

$$\phi(kT) \overset{\text{def}}{=} \phi_k + \theta.$$

Then

$$\bar{U}_k \cdot \bar{U}_{k-1} = I^2\cos[\phi(kT) - \phi(kT - T)] = I^2\cos(\phi_k - \phi_{k-1}) = I^2\cos(A_k). \quad \textbf{[15.34]}$$

Therefore, for binary A_k's of $\pm A$, the inner product is either $+1$ or -1.

Threshold Detection   The above discussion assumes no noise. Two noiseless phase vectors, $\bar{U}_k$ and $\bar{U}_{k+1}$, are illustrated in Figure 15.11. However, when there is noise, the ac-

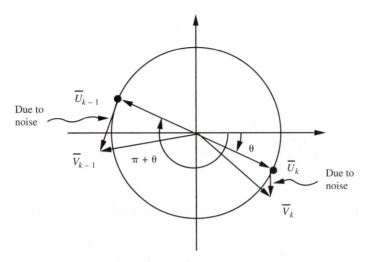

Figure 15.11.   Mapping of the phase information to a unit vector.

tual projected phase vectors can vary in both magnitude and phase, as illustrated in Figure 15.11. As a result, the inner product output can deviate from the actual value by ± 1. However, when the noise is not too strong or the phase deviation is within $\pm \pi/2$, the inner product has the same sign as when there is no noise. Therefore, a threshold detector of zero threshold can be used to detect A_k. When the inner product is positive, A_k is detected as zero; otherwise, it is detected as one. According to this threshold detection, one can have an error detection only when the phase noise is so large that it changes the sign of the inner product.

15.5.2 DPSK FUNDAMENTAL PERFORMANCE

If the noise term due to shot noise is added, the phase vector can be expressed as

$$\bar{V}_k = \bar{U}_k + \bar{n}_k$$

where $\bar{n}_k = [n_{c,k}, n_{s,k}]$ has the noise power

$$E[n_{c,k}^2] = E[n_{s,k}^2] = \sigma_c^2 = \sigma_s^2 = \sigma_{n,hetero}^2 \qquad \text{[15.35]}$$

from Equations (15.12) and (15.19). To evaluate the detection performance, without loss of generality, one can assume $A_k = A_{k-1}$. Therefore,

$$\bar{U}_k = \bar{U}_{k-1} = I[\cos\theta, -\sin\theta]$$

where I is given by Equation (15.32). The error detection probability is

$$P_E = P(\bar{V}_k \cdot \bar{V}_{k-1} < 0).$$

Because

$$4\bar{V}_k \cdot \bar{V}_{k-1} = |\bar{V}_k + \bar{V}_{k-1}|^2 - |\bar{V}_k - \bar{V}_{k-1}|^2$$

this can be written as

$$P_E = P(|\bar{V}_k + \bar{V}_{k-1}| < |\bar{V}_k - \bar{V}_{k-1}|).$$

Let

$$X_- = |\bar{V}_k - \bar{V}_{k-1}| = |\bar{n}_k - \bar{n}_{k-1}| = (n_{c,-}^2 + n_{s,-}^2)^{1/2}$$

and

$$X_+ = |\bar{V}_k + \bar{V}_{k-1}| = |2\bar{U} + \bar{n}_k + \bar{n}_{k-1}| = [(2I + n_{c,+})^2 + n_{s,+}^2]^{1/2}$$

where $n_{c,\pm} = n_{c,k} \pm n_{c,k-1}$ and $n_{s,\pm} = n_{s,k} \pm n_{s,k-1}$. Each of these newly defined noises has variance

$$\sigma^2 = E[(n_{c,k} - n_{c,k-1})^2] = 2\sigma_{n,hetero}^2.$$

Similar to what was discussed in OOK envelope detection, X_- is a Rayleigh random variable with the probability density function (PDF) given by Equation (15.25), and X_+ is a Rician distribution with the PDF given by Equation (15.24) and $A = 2I$. The error detection probability can thus be evaluated by

$$P_E = \int_0^\infty \int_{x_+}^\infty P_{E,0}(x_-) P_{E,1}(x_+) dx_- dx_+ = \int_0^\infty \int_{x_+}^\infty \frac{x_-}{\sigma^2} e^{-x_-^2/2\sigma^2} dx_- P_{E,1}(x_+) dx_+$$

$$= \int_0^\infty e^{-x_+^2/2\sigma^2} \frac{x_+}{\sigma^2} e^{-(x_+^2 + A^2)/2\sigma^2} I_0\left(\frac{Ax_+}{\sigma^2}\right) dx_+$$

$$= \frac{1}{2} e^{-I^2/2\hat{\sigma}^2} \int_0^\infty \frac{x_+}{\hat{\sigma}^2} e^{-(x_+^2 + I^2)/2\hat{\sigma}^2} I_0\left(\frac{Ix_+}{\hat{\sigma}^2}\right) dx_+ \qquad \textbf{[15.36]}$$

where $A = 2I$ and $\sigma^2 = 2\hat{\sigma}^2$. Because the integrand in the last integral is in the form of the Rician distribution, its integral is one. Therefore,

$$P_{E,DPSK} = {}^1\!/_2 e^{-A^2/4\sigma^2} = {}^1\!/_2 e^{-I^2/\sigma^2} = {}^1\!/_2 e^{-N_s} = {}^1\!/_2 e^{-\bar{N}_b} \qquad \textbf{[15.37]}$$

where the following fact is used:

$$\frac{I^2}{\sigma^2} = \frac{\mathcal{R}^2 P_{inc} P_{loc} T^2}{q \mathcal{R} P_{loc} T} = N_s.$$

Example
15.8

From the performance of DPSK given by Equation (15.37), 20 photons per bit are needed to achieve a BER of 10^{-9}. Compared to heterodyne PSK (see Figure 15.14), this is only 1 dB lower in performance. Because the IF carrier in DPSK does not need to be phase locked to the demodulated IF signal, there is a great advantage in using DPSK. ■

15.6 **FREQUENCY-SHIFT KEYING**

In FSK, the frequency of the transmitted optical carrier is not a constant but is modulated according to the transmitted data. It is a common modulation technique in coherent communication because of its incoherent postdetection ability. Specifically, instead of generating an IF carrier, two passband filters followed by envelope detection can be used in postdetection. When phase noise is important, this incoherent postdetection becomes even more critical to maintaining good detection performance.

15.6.1 **SIGNAL REPRESENTATION AND DEMODULATION**

For binary FSK, the angular frequency of the incident light can be expressed as

$$\omega_{inc} = \omega_0 \pm \frac{\Delta\omega_d}{2} = \omega_0 + \frac{\Delta\omega_d}{2}\sum_k A_k p(t - kT) \qquad \textbf{[15.38]}$$

where $\Delta\omega_d$ is the frequency separation of the two frequencies and A_k is either 1 or –1, according to the transmitted data. Because the frequency is not constant, only heterodyne detection is used in coherent detection, and the photocurrent in Equation (15.9) can be expressed as

$$I_{ph}(t) = 2\mathcal{R}\sqrt{P_{inc}P_{loc}}\cos[\omega_{IF}t + (\Delta\omega_d/2)t \times \sum_k A_k p(t - kT)]. \qquad \textbf{[15.39]}$$

To detect the above FSK current signal, one simple way is to use two bandpass filters centered at $\omega_{IF} \pm \Delta\omega_d/2$. If the frequency band of the two bandpass filters is smaller than the frequency separation, one of the filters has a high output and the other has a low output. Thus the transmitted data A_k can be detected by comparing the two outputs. In this approach, one only needs to ensure that the IF frequency ω_{IF} is in the middle of the two center frequencies of the filters. Otherwise, the filters cannot properly respond to the FSK current signal and generate wrong outputs.

Another easy way to demodulate the FSK signal is to use a frequency discriminator, which consists of a differentiator and an envelope detector. The discriminator obtains the time derivative of the IF signal. Thus its output has an amplitude proportional to the frequency of the carrier. After envelope detection, the transmitted frequency is converted to an amplitude signal and can be recovered by threshold detection.

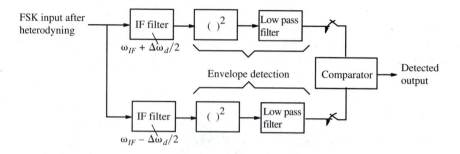

Figure 15.12   Envelope postdetection in FSK heterodyne detection.

Because both of the above two schemes use envelope detection, they belong to the category of incoherent postdetection. Alternatively, one can use two carrier recovery loops to generate the two frequencies $\omega_0 \pm \Delta\omega_d/2$ for coherent postdetection. This arrangement has a much more complex implementation and consequently is rarely used in practical systems.

15.6.2   FSK FUNDAMENTAL PERFORMANCE

The following sections discuss the detection performance of both coherent and incoherent postdetection.

Coherent Detection   In this case, the noise power at each IF demodulator output is the same, given by Equation (15.12). After subtraction, the noise power is doubled. Because

$$N_1 = -N_0 = \mathcal{R}\sqrt{P_{inc}P_{loc}}$$

the error detection probability is

$$P_{E,FSK} = Q\left(\sqrt{\frac{\mathcal{R}P_{inc}T}{q}}\right) = Q(\sqrt{N_s}) = Q(\sqrt{N_b}). \qquad \textbf{[15.40]}$$

Envelope Detection   Similar to envelope detection of OOK signaling, one of the envelope detector outputs in FSK follows the Rician distribution with variance equal to

$$\sigma^2 = \sigma^2_{n,envelope} = \frac{2}{T}q\mathcal{R}P_{loc}$$

and mean equal to

$$A = 2\mathcal{R}\sqrt{P_{loc}P_{inc}} \quad .$$

The other output follows the Rayleigh distribution with zero mean and the same variance. Therefore, the error probability can be evaluated in a similar way using Equation (15.36). With proper substitutions, one obtains

$$P_{E,FSK,envelope} = 1/2 e^{-A^2/4\sigma^2} = 1/2 e^{-N_s/2} = 1/2 e^{-N_b/2}. \qquad \textbf{[15.41]}$$

FSK SENSITIVITY USING BANDPASS FILTERING   At a BER of 10^{-9}, the required number of photons per bit is 36 and 40 for FSK coherent and envelope postdetection, respectively. From the best performance obtained by homodyne PSK, envelope detection is only 7 dB worse. Taking the significant simplicity in implementation into consideration, FSK envelope detection is an attractive modulation scheme in coherent communications. ■

Example 15.9

15.7 PERFORMANCE SUMMARY

Bit error probabilities of the various schemes discussed in the previous sections are summarized in Table 15.1. The corresponding BERs as a function of N_b are shown in Figure 15.13. Clearly PSK homodyne has the best fundamental performance, even 1 dB better than the quantum limit from direct detection. Because of implementation difficulty and phase noise in practice, however, PSK homodyne is seldom used.

Table 15.1 Performance summary for coherent optical communications.

Detection Scheme	P_E	N_S at $P_E = 10^{-9}$	$\bar{N}_b$ at $P_E = 10^{-9}$	Equation No.
Direct detection, quantum limit	$e^{-N_s}/2$	20	10	(6.27)
Homodyne OOK	$Q(\sqrt{N_s})$	36	18	(15.14)
Heterodyne OOK, coherent post-detection	$Q(\sqrt{N_s/2})$	72	36	(15.17)
Heterodyne OOK, envelope post-detection	$e^{-N_s/4}/2$	80	40	(15.27)
Homodyne PSK	$Q(\sqrt{4N_s})$	9	9	(15.30)
Heterodyne PSK	$Q(\sqrt{2N_s})$	18	18	(15.31)
Heterodyne DPSK	$e^{-N_s}/2$	20	20	(15.37)
Heterodyne FSK	$Q(\sqrt{N_s})$	36	36	(15.40)
Heterodyne FSK, envelope post-detection	$e^{-N_s/2}/2$	40	40	(15.41)

On the other hand, OOK and FSK envelope postdetections have the worst performance. As shown in Figure 15.14, they are approximately 7 dB worse than PSK homodyne at a BER of 10^{-9}. However, because they are simple to implement and insensitive to phase noise (see Section 15.10), they are more practically used.

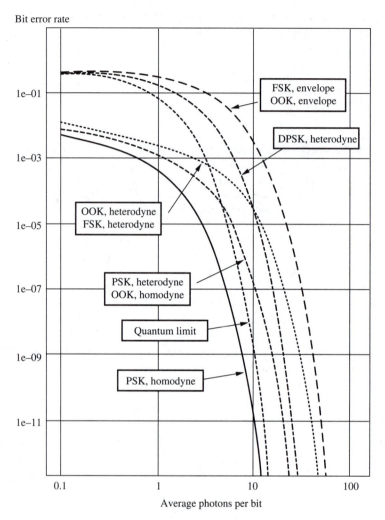

Figure 15.13   Summary of bit error rates of various detection schemes versus average number of photons per bit.

Other schemes have performance between the PSK homodyne and OOK/FSK envelope detection. They provide a compromise between performance and implementation difficulty. However, because of their coherent postdetection nature, they have an error floor due to phase noise. That is, the BER cannot be further reduced beyond a certain level even by continuing to increase the incident power. This error floor phenomenon will be explained in section 15.10.

Over the past decade, many experiments on both homodyne and heterodyne detections have been conducted. Table 15.2 summarizes some of the recently published results compared with their theoretical limits. The most popular scheme used is FSK. In practical

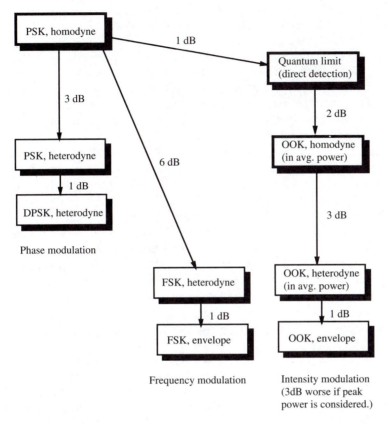

Figure 15.14 Relative performance in dB at bit error rate 10^{-9}.

implementation, PSK is not attractive because of its difficulty in carrier recovery, and OOK is not a preferred choice because of the chirping effect from direct modulation. In most FSK experiments, continuous phase FSK (CPFSK) is used for the nice continuous phase property using simple direct modulation.

Table 15.2 Some field experimental results using coherent detection.

Modulation	Detection	$\lambda\ (\mu m)$ (dBm)	Bit Rate (Gb/s)	Sensitivity Limit	Photons/Bit	Shot Noise	Reference
FSK	Envelope	1.545	2.5	-46.2	74	40	[5]
			4	-42.6	107	40	
FSK		1.548	1.187	-41.8 to -42.8	430–550	40	[6]
PSK	Homodyne	1.32	2.5	-47.5	47	9	[7]
DPSK	Differential	1.55	0.565	-50.2	86	20	[8]

15.8   POLARIZATION-SHIFT KEYING

The concept of polarization-shift keying (PolSK) was first proposed and demonstrated by [9] and [10]. Since then, much experimental and theoretical work has been conducted [11]–[20]. In contrast to the waveform modulation schemes discussed earlier (i.e., phase, frequency, and amplitude modulation), PolSK transmits information by modulating the **state of polarization** (SOP) of the light carrier. Thus, for accurate detection, it is important to maintain the SOP in transmission.

In general, various causes can distort the SOP during transmission. For example, a light signal can change its polarization when the fiber is bent. Furthermore, when signals of different polarizations suffer from different attenuations, a circularly polarized signal can become elliptically polarized, and the SOP is distorted [12]. For the above reasons, it is necessary to either use polarization maintaining fibers (PMFs) in Polsk transmission or lock the received polarization with a polarization controller at the received end.

On the other hand, PolSK can be attractive when multilevel signaling is used [13]. PolSK has a three-dimensional signal space, which allows a more compact constellation design at a given number of signal points and a given signal separation. To achieve an even higher multilevel signaling, amplitude modulation plus PolSK has also been suggested [14].

15.8.1   STATE OF POLARIZATION AND STOKES PARAMETERS

To understand polarization modulation and detection, one must first know how to express the polarization of a light carrier. In general, the transverse component of the electric field can be expressed as a linear combination of two mutually orthogonal components with a certain phase difference between them. Without loss of generality, the two components can be expressed as

$$E_x = \Re\{a_x(t)e^{j[\omega_{inc}t+\phi_x(t)]}\} \qquad \textbf{[15.42]}$$

$$E_y = \Re\{a_y(t)e^{j[\omega_{inc}t+\phi_y(t)]}\} \qquad \textbf{[15.43]}$$

where a_x and a_y are the amplitudes of the electric field components in the $\hat{x}$ and $\hat{y}$ directions, respectively, and ϕ_x and ϕ_y are the corresponding phase components. From Equations (15.42) and (15.43), the total transverse electric field is

$$\bar{E}_T = E_x\hat{x} + E_y\hat{y} = \Re\left\{[a_x\hat{x} + a_ye^{j\delta}\hat{y}]e^{j[\omega_{inc}t+\phi_x(t)]}\right\} \qquad \textbf{[15.44]}$$

where

$$\delta \overset{\text{def}}{=} \phi_y - \phi_x \qquad \textbf{[15.45]}$$

is the phase difference of the two orthogonal components.

Equation (15.44) shows that the SOP of the field is a function of the three variables a_x, a_y, and δ. A more common way to express the SOP is thus to use the following Stokes parameters S_i, $i = 0, 1, 2, 3$, which are defined by

$$S_0 \overset{\text{def}}{=} a_x^2 + a_y^2 \qquad \textbf{[15.46]}$$

$$S_1 \stackrel{\text{def}}{=} a_x^2 - a_y^2 \qquad\qquad \textbf{[15.47]}$$

$$S_2 \stackrel{\text{def}}{=} 2a_x a_y \cos \delta \qquad\qquad \textbf{[15.48]}$$

$$S_3 \stackrel{\text{def}}{=} 2a_x a_y \sin \delta. \qquad\qquad \textbf{[15.49]}$$

Because there are only three independent variables (i.e. a_x, a_y, and δ), the four Stokes parameters are not independent. Specifically, it is easy to verify that

$$S_0^2 = S_1^2 + S_2^2 + S_3^2. \qquad\qquad \textbf{[15.50]}$$

Some important SOPs and their Stokes parameters are given in Table 15.3.

Table 15.3 Some important SOPs and their Stokes parameters.

SOP	(S_1, S_2, S_3)
Horizontal ($E_y = 0$)	(1, 0, 0)
Vertical ($E_x = 0$)	(−1, 0, 0)
Right circular (RCP)	(0, 0, 1)
Left circular (LCP)	(0, 0, −1)

From the definitions of the Stokes parameters, it can be readily shown that

$$a_x = \sqrt{\frac{S_0 + S_1}{2}} \qquad\qquad \textbf{[15.51]}$$

$$a_y = \sqrt{\frac{S_0 - S_1}{2}}] \qquad\qquad \textbf{[15.52]}$$

$$\delta = \arctan\left(\frac{S_3}{S_2}\right) \qquad\qquad \textbf{[15.53]}$$

with range $-\pi < \delta < \pi$. For a given set of the Stokes parameters used for transmission, Equations (15.51)–(15.53) can be used to determine the amplitudes and relative phase difference of the two polarizations.

HORIZONTAL POLARIZATION For a SOP of $(S_1, S_2, S_3) = (1, 0, 0)$, Equation (15.50) says that $S_0 = 1$. According to Equations (15.51)–(15.53), $a_x = 1$, $a_y = 0$, and δ can be arbitrary. This corresponds to a linearly polarized light in the $\hat{x}$ or horizontal direction. ∎ | **Example 15.10**

Poincaré Sphere   At a given S_0 value, the three Stokes parameters S_1, S_2, and S_3 can be mapped to a point in a three-dimensional sphere of radius S_0. This sphere is the well-known Poincaré sphere. As shown in Figure 15.15, each point on the Poincaré sphere represents a SOP. From Table 15.3, note that all linear polarizations are on the equator, where $S_3 = 0$. Also, the north and south poles of the sphere represent the right and left circular polarization, respectively. The SOPs of other points have elliptic polarizations.

15.8.2 STOKES RECEIVER

Because the Stokes parameters are used to represent a SOP, a PolSK receiver needs to first extract the Stokes parameters from the received signal. Such a receiver is called a **Stokes receiver**, and its block diagram is shown in Figure 15.16.

At the receiver front, the PBS for the incident light is aligned so that it sends the $\hat{x}$ and $\hat{y}$ components of the incident optical signal to two coherent detectors. The local oscillator

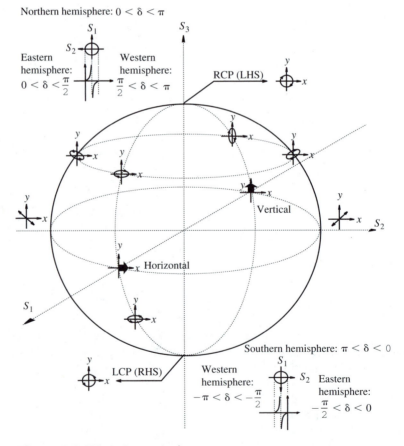

Figure 15.15   Poincaré sphere

is assumed to be linearly polarized with equal power in the $\hat{x}$ and $\hat{y}$ components. That is, it is assumed that

$$E_{loc,x} = E_{loc,y} = a_{loc} \cos (\omega_{loc} t + \phi_{loc}).$$ **[15.54]**

Assuming $180°$ hybrids are used, from Equation (15.9), the photocurrent at the two IF filter outputs can be expressed as

$$I_x = \mathcal{R} a_x a_{loc} \cos(\omega_{IF} t + \phi_{xd})$$

and

$$I_y = \mathcal{R} a_y a_{loc} \cos(\omega_{IF} t + \phi_{yd})$$

where $\phi_{xd} = \phi_x - \phi_{loc}$ and $\phi_{yd} = \phi_y - \phi_{loc}$. The Stokes parameters can thus be obtained by performing the following computations. For S_1, take the squares of I_x and I_y, then subtract. That is,

$$S_1 = I_x^2 - I_y^2 = \tfrac{1}{2}\mathcal{R}^2 a_{loc}^2 (a_x^2 - a_y^2)$$

where high-frequency components have been dropped using low-pass filtering. To get S_2, simply multiply the outputs of the two IF filters:

$$S_2' = \mathcal{R} a_x a_{loc} \cos (\omega_{IF} t + \phi_{xd}) \times \mathcal{R} a_y a_{loc} \cos (\omega_{IF} t + \phi_{yd}).$$

After low-pass filtering,

$$S_2 = \tfrac{1}{2}\mathcal{R}^2 a_{loc}^2 a_x a_y \cos \delta.$$

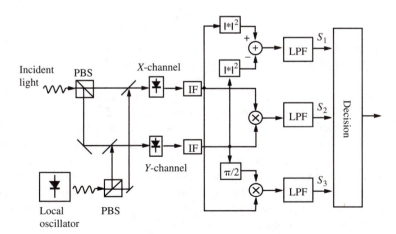

Figure 15.16   Block diagram of the Stokes receiver.

Similarly, S_3 can be obtained by multiplying I_y with a 90° phase shift and I_x. After low-pass filtering,

$$S_3 = \frac{1}{2}\mathcal{R}^2 a_{loc}^2 a_x a_y \sin\delta.$$

Once the three Stokes parameters are obtained, the SOP can be compared with a finite set of possible SOPs defined by the constellation design. In general, the detected output is one of the signal vectors that has the minimum distance to or angle of separation from the received signal.

Multilevel Signaling　As mentioned earlier, one primary motivation of using PolSK is because of its three-dimensional signal space. In M-ary PolSK, M points are allocated in the Poincaré sphere. To minimize the probability of error detection, the M points are allocated with maximum separation. Examples of quaternary and octonary constellation designs are illustrated in Figure 15.17.

Detection Performance　In general, detection performance of PolSK is difficult to analyze because the Stokes receiver introduces nonlinearity. The nonlinearity comes from the need of multiplications to extract the Stokes parameters (see Figure 15.16). Because each IF filter output contains both the signal and shot noise, each Stokes parameter extracted has a noise term due to the product terms from the signal and noise terms. Since the two IF filter outputs are used to generate the three Stokes parameters, the noise terms in the three Stokes parameters are also statistically dependent.

In the past, there have been extensive studies analyzing and optimizing the detection performance of PolSK [17]–[20]. In particular, [20] developed a noise distribution map on the Poincaré sphere. This map can help to optimize detection performance by properly allocating the signaling points on the Poincaré sphere.

15.9　CARRIER RECOVERY IN COHERENT DETECTION

As mentioned earlier, one critical component in coherent detection is the carrier recovery loop that generates a local carrier synchronized with the incident light signal. Specifically, in homodyne detection, the local carrier should be synchronized in both phase and frequency with respect to the incident light. In heterodyne detection, the local carrier should be synchronized in frequency (separated by a fixed ω_{IF} amount).

Compared to RF carrier recovery, the primary difficulty of optical carrier recovery comes from the need for a similar implementation in the optical domain. For example, optical sources in general have much larger phase noise than their RF counterparts. Therefore, a He-Ne laser instead of a semiconductor diode laser is needed in homodyne detection [21]. The difficulty can be further illustrated by the following example.

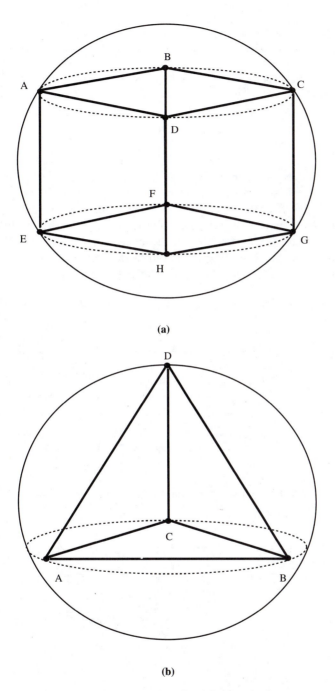

(a)

(b)

Figure 15.17   Examples of multilevel constellations:
(a) octonary cube, and (b) quaternary
tetrahedron.

Example 15.11   **FREQUENCY DOUBLER AND DIVIDER**   In RF binary PSK, one simple way to recover the incoming carrier is to use a frequency doubler and divider combination as shown in Figure 15.18. In the case of optical recovery, there are no simple counterparts for the frequency doubler and divider. It is true that a frequency doubler can be built using nonlinear optics. However, the nonlinear effects take place only when the carrier power is high, which is not practical in optical communications. ∎

Although there can be many different implementations in RF and optical communications, a carrier recovery loop in general has three components. As illustrated in Figure 15.19, they are (1) phase detector, (2) loop filter, and (3) voltage controlled oscillator (VCO). The VCO generates the local carrier, whose frequency and phase are determined by the voltage (or current) input to the oscillator. The loop filter is generally a low-pass filter. It is used to determine the time response for frequency locking and tracking. The phase detector is used to compare the phases of the received carrier and local carrier. In practice, most carrier recovery loops differ only in the phase detection implementation.

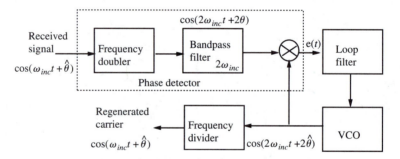

Figure 15.18   Use of frequency doubler and divider for binary PSK carrier recovery.

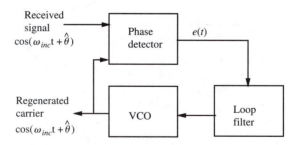

Figure 15.19   A block diagram of a carrier recovery phase-locked loop.

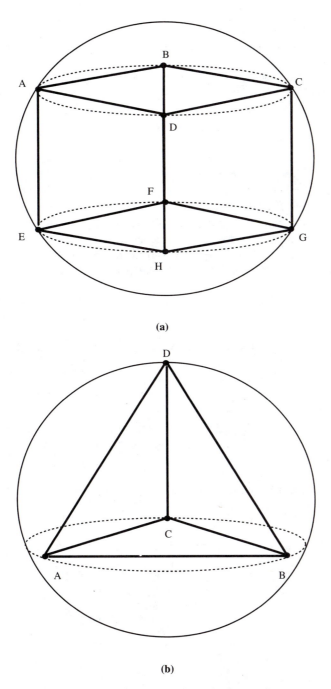

(a)

(b)

Figure 15.17   Examples of multilevel constellations: (a) octonary cube, and (b) quaternary tetrahedron.

Example 15.11

FREQUENCY DOUBLER AND DIVIDER   In RF binary PSK, one simple way to recover the incoming carrier is to use a frequency doubler and divider combination as shown in Figure 15.18. In the case of optical recovery, there are no simple counterparts for the frequency doubler and divider. It is true that a frequency doubler can be built using nonlinear optics. However, the nonlinear effects take place only when the carrier power is high, which is not practical in optical communications. ■

Although there can be many different implementations in RF and optical communications, a carrier recovery loop in general has three components. As illustrated in Figure 15.19, they are (1) phase detector, (2) loop filter, and (3) voltage controlled oscillator (VCO). The VCO generates the local carrier, whose frequency and phase are determined by the voltage (or current) input to the oscillator. The loop filter is generally a low-pass filter. It is used to determine the time response for frequency locking and tracking. The phase detector is used to compare the phases of the received carrier and local carrier. In practice, most carrier recovery loops differ only in the phase detection implementation.

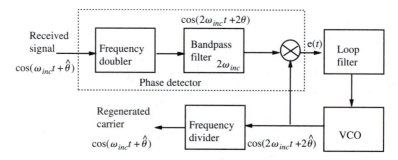

Figure 15.18   Use of frequency doubler and divider for binary PSK carrier recovery.

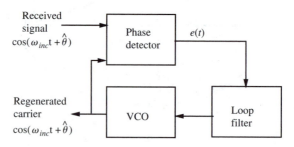

Figure 15.19   A block diagram of a carrier recovery phase-locked loop.

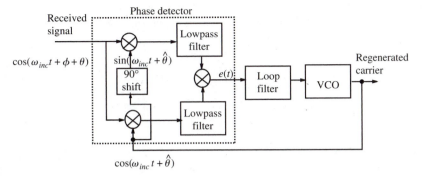

Figure 15.20   The Costas loop for carrier recovery.

COSTAS LOOP   The Costas loop is commonly used in RF communications and is illustrated in Figure 15.20. The phase detector consists of one 90° phase shifter, two low-pass filters, and three multipliers. Let the received carrier be

$$s(t) = A\cos(\omega_{inc}t + \phi + \theta).$$

Example 15.12

In the steady state, it can be assumed that the VCO output has the same frequency as the received signal:

$$c(t) = \cos(\omega_{inc}t + \hat{\theta})$$

where $\hat{\theta}$ is a certain phase. Because

$$s(t)c(t) = \frac{A}{2}\cos(\phi + \theta - \hat{\theta}) + \frac{A}{2}\cos(2\omega_{inc}t + \phi + \theta + \hat{\theta})$$

the low-pass filter output of the upper branch is $(A/2)\cos(\phi + \theta - \hat{\theta})$. Similarly, the lower low-pass filter output is $(A/2)\sin(\phi + \theta - \hat{\theta})$. Their product, $e(t)$, is thus

$$e(t) = \frac{A^2}{8}\sin(2\Delta\theta)$$

where the phase 2ϕ is dropped because it is either 0 or 2π, and

$$\Delta\theta = \theta - \hat{\theta}.$$

When the phase difference, $\Delta\theta$, is small, the phase detector output $e(t)$ is linearly proportional to the phase difference. In the steady state, if the VCO resonant frequency (at zero voltage input) is ω_0 and the dc gain of the loop filter is K, the steady phase difference is determined by

$$\frac{A^2}{8}\sin(2\Delta\theta)K = \omega_{inc} - \omega_0.$$

Thus the larger the phase loop gain, the smaller the steady phase difference. Note that it is nonzero unless the resonant frequency of the VCO is exactly the same as the received carrier frequency. ∎

The following sections explain phase detection techniques in optical carrier recovery and describe their operation in the steady state. Analysis of a carrier recovery loop for carrier acquisition is beyond the scope of this book.

Homodyne PSK Carrier Recovery   An implementation of the Costas loop for optical PSK homodyne detection is shown in Figure 15.21. To get the 90° phase shift from the regenerated carrier, a six-port 90° hybrid (shown in Figure 15.4) is used, where the two PBSs split each of the two inputs into two beams with orthogonal polarizations. In general, the input is assumed or made to be linearly polarized, and the beam splitter is set at 45° with respect to the input polarization. As a result, the two split outputs have equal power. Two half mirrors are then used to mix the output from the PBSs of the same polarization. With proper phase adjustment, a 45° phase shift can be introduced from each phase adjuster. After photodetection and balanced detection, the two outputs are proportional to $\cos(\phi + \Delta\theta)$ and $\sin(\phi + \Delta\theta)$, respectively, where $\Delta\theta$ is given by Equation (15.93). Detailed analysis is given in Appendix 15–C.

The cosine term, $\cos(\phi + \Delta\theta)$, can be used for subsequent detection. At the same time, the two terms $\cos(\phi + \Delta\theta)$ and $\sin(\phi + \Delta\theta)$ can be multiplied to give $2\sin(2\phi + 2\Delta\theta)$. This product term is information independent because ϕ is either 0 or π. Similar to the operation of the Costas loop discussed in Example 15.12, there is a small phase difference $\Delta\theta$, or small nonzero voltage to the VCO in the steady state. This small phase difference will result in a slight and insignificant signal level drop.

Because in practice there is additional noise such as shot noise, the recovered carrier does not have a constant phase $\hat{\theta}$. The random fluctuation away from $\hat{\theta}$ is called **phase jit-**

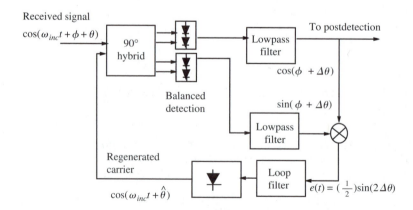

Figure 15.21   Costas loop implementation for homodyne PSK carrier recovery using a 90° hybrid.

ter or simply jitter. To reduce it, one modification of the Costas loop is shown in Figure 15.22 and is called a **decision feedback recovery loop** [22]. In this modification, the cosine term, $\cos(\phi + \Delta\theta)$, is replaced by its decision output. Because the detected output under correct detection is $A_k = \cos(\phi)$ and $\sin(\phi + \Delta\theta) = \pm\sin(\Delta\theta)$ (the sign is positive if $\phi = 0$ and negative if $\phi = \pi$), the product term $e(t)$ is $\sin(\Delta\theta)$, which can be used as the phase error term input to the VCO in the Costas loop.

In this decision feedback implementation, error-free detection is assumed. Because the probability of error detection is small in normal operation, this assumption is reasonable. If there is an occasional detection error, the resultant sudden phase change is rejected by the low-pass loop filter and has little effect on the output of the local carrier.

Heterodyne Carrier Recovery In heterodyne detection, the requirement in carrier recovery is much relaxed. For example, it is unnecessary to lock the receiver carrier in phase. Instead, it is necessary only to ensure that the frequency difference of the two carriers be close to the IF frequency. The phase difference is either unimportant in envelope detection or can be taken care of by coherent postdetection.

To lock onto the frequency difference, as shown in Figure 15.23, an **automatic frequency controller** (AFC) can be used to drive the local oscillator. The AFC consists of a frequency discriminator and a voltage comparator. The frequency discriminator generates an output voltage proportional to the frequency of the input signal [23]. Comparing the output with a reference voltage enables one to drive the local oscillator output to the correct frequency.

15.10 EFFECTS OF PHASE NOISE

The previous sections discussed the fundamental detection performance due to shot noise. In practice, however, phase noise also plays an important role in limiting performance. As

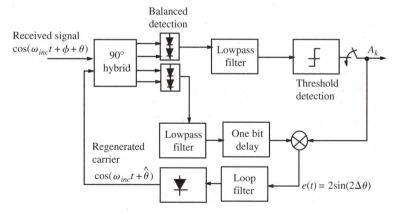

Figure 15.22 Decision feedback implementation for homodyne PSK carrier recovery.

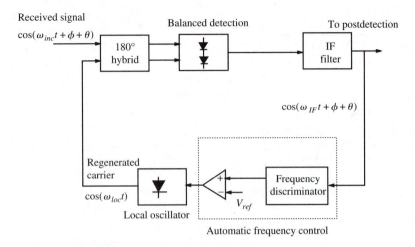

Figure 15.23   Heterodyne PSK carrier recovery.

explained in Chapter 6, phase noise comes from random spontaneous emissions in laser diodes. In contrast to phase noise in radio communications, where it is insignificant, phase noise in laser diodes can cause linewidth broadening of tens of MHz.

One immediate consequence of phase noise in coherent communications is the additional random phase in the output phase of the detected photocurrent. That is, Equations (15.8) and (15.9) should be modified as

$$I_{ph,homo}(t) = 2\mathcal{R}\sqrt{P_{inc}P_{loc}}\cos[\phi(t) + \phi_n(t)] \qquad \textbf{[15.55]}$$

and

$$I_{ph,hetero}(t) = 2\mathcal{R}\sqrt{P_{inc}P_{loc}}\cos[\omega_{IF}t + \phi(t) + \phi_n(t)] \qquad \textbf{[15.56]}$$

where $\phi_n(t)$ is the phase noise. Clearly, if the signal is phase modulated, the random phase will corrupt the phase information term $\phi(t)$ and affect the subsequent detection performance. Signals that are amplitude or frequency modulated can also be affected. For example, in heterodyne FSK, the random phase results in a random frequency called frequency noise, which results in errors in detecting the transmitted frequency.

The effects of phase noise in coherent communications can be understood from the signal corruption in three different aspects: amplitude, frequency, and phase. In amplitude, the effect can be a certain power penalty [24] or an error floor [25] when envelope detection is used. In frequency and phase, the result is an error floor. These different effects are explained in detail below.

15.10.1 EFFECT OF PHASE NOISE IN DPSK

In DPSK, as mentioned earlier, detection is based on the phase change of two adjacent projected vectors. When there is no noise, the phase change is either zero or π. Neglecting shot noise and considering only phase noise allows one to assume an arbitrary phase for the vector $\bar{V}_{k-1}$ with constant magnitude. If the following vector $\bar{V}_k$ has no phase change caused by the transmitted data (i.e., bit "0" is transmitted), the error detection probability is the probability that the amount of average phase change over T due to phase noise is greater than $\pi/2$ Because the phase change is caused by only phase noise under the above assumption,

$$P_E = P \left\{ \left| \frac{1}{T} \int_0^T \phi_n(t' + T) - \phi_n(t') dt' \right| > \frac{\pi}{2} \right\}.$$

Let

$$\overline{\Delta\phi_n} \overset{\text{def}}{=} \frac{1}{T} \int_0^T [\phi_n(t + T) - \phi_n(t)] dt = \frac{1}{T} \int_0^T \int_t^{t+T} \dot{\phi}_n(t') dt' dt. \qquad \textbf{[15.57]}$$

The error detection probability can be expressed as

$$P_E = P\{|\overline{\Delta\phi}_n(T)| > \frac{\pi}{2}\}.$$

Chapter 6 shows that the time derivative of phase noise, $\dot{\phi}(t)$, is a Gaussian random variable at any time t. Therefore, $\overline{\Delta\phi}_n$ is a zero mean Gaussian random variable, and

$$P_E = 2Q \left(\frac{\pi/2}{\sigma} \right) \qquad \textbf{[15.58]}$$

with σ^2 being the variance of $x = \overline{\Delta\phi}_n(T)$. From Equation (15.57),

$$\sigma^2 = E[x^2] = E \left[\frac{1}{T^2} \int_0^T \int_t^{t+T} \dot{\phi}_n(t') dt' dt \int_0^T \int_\tau^{\tau+T} \dot{\phi}_n(\tau') d\tau' d\tau \right].$$

Using Equation (6.126),

$$R_{\dot{\phi}}(\tau) = E[\dot{\phi}(t + \tau)\dot{\phi}(t)] = 2\pi \Delta f_{3dB} \delta(\tau).$$

This gives

$$\sigma^2 = 2\pi \Delta f_{3dB} \frac{1}{T^2} \int_0^T \int_t^{t+T} \int_0^T \int_\tau^{\tau+T} \delta(t' - \tau') d\tau' d\tau dt' dt.$$

For a given pair of t and τ, there are two cases: $\tau < t$ and $t < \tau$. For the first case, because the integrand is zero except $t' = \tau'$,

$$\int_t^{t+T} \int_\tau^{\tau+T} \delta(t' - \tau') d\tau' dt' = \int_t^{\tau+T} \int_t^{\tau+T} \delta(t' - \tau') d\tau' dt' = \tau + T - t.$$

Similarly, for the second case,

$$\int_t^{t+T} \int_\tau^{\tau+T} \delta(t' - \tau') d\tau' dt' = T + t - \tau.$$

Therefore

$$\sigma^2 = \frac{2\pi \Delta f}{T^2} \left\{ \int_0^T \int_0^t (T + \tau - t) d\tau dt + \int_0^T \int_0^\tau (T - t + \tau) dt d\tau \right\} = \frac{4\pi \Delta f_{3dB} T}{3}.$$

[15.59]

From Equation (15.58),

$$P_{E,DPSK,floor} = Q\left(\sqrt{\frac{3\pi}{16\Delta f_{3dB} T}} \right).$$

[15.60]

Note that the phase noise width Δf_{3dB} is contributed from both the transmitter and the local oscillator. If the contributions are equal, the required Δf_{3dB} for each laser should be half. If the BER floor is set at one-tenth of the required BER, a BER of 10^{-9} requires

$$\sqrt{\frac{3\pi}{16\Delta f_{3dB} T}} > 6.36$$

or

$$\Delta \nu_{tx}, \Delta \nu_{loc} \leq 0.0073 R_b$$

[15.61]

where $\Delta \nu_{tx} = \Delta \nu_{loc} = \Delta f_{3dB}/2$ is assumed.

Example 15.13

LINEWIDTH REQUIREMENT IN DPSK   If the bit rate R_b is 1 Gb/s, the combined FWHM linewidth should be within 14.5 MHz. For each laser, the linewidth should be less than 7.3 MHz. This can be achieved by state-of-the-art single-frequency laser diodes. ∎

15.10.2 EFFECT OF PHASE NOISE IN ENVELOPE DETECTION

The effect of phase noise in envelope detection can manifest itself in two ways. First, because of the phase noise, the IF signal has a broader spectral density. To accommodate this, the IF filter bandwidth can be increased, which then passes more noise power through. This thus translates into a power penalty [24].

Alternatively, the same IF filter bandwidth could be used. Over a certain bit interval, because the phase noise can cause a random frequency shift, the signal's power spectrum can thus have a random frequency shift away from its central IF frequency. This results in a random peak value at the IF filter output [25]. When the peak value is lower than the threshold, an error is possible. Because the variation of the random peak is proportional to the signal level, this results in an error floor in detection.

As pointed out by [24], these two approaches yield approximately the same condition on the laser linewidth. In fact, the first approach of increasing the IF filter bandwidth allows a little more relaxed condition on the linewidth. For this reason, the linewidth condition is derived below from the power penalty consideration.

To find the power penalty, it is necessary first to quantify the effect of spectrum broadening. Using the complex envelope of the photocurrent in Equation (15.56):

$$\hat{I}_{ph}(t) = 2\mathcal{R}\sqrt{P_{inc}(t)P_{loc}}\, e^{j[\phi(t)+\phi_n(t)]}$$

the autocorrelation of the complex envelope photocurrent is

$$R_{\hat{i}}(\tau) = E[\hat{I}_{ph}^*(t)\hat{I}_{ph}(t+\tau)]$$

$$= E\left[4P_{loc}\sqrt{P_{inc}(t)P_{inc}(t+\tau)}\, e^{[\phi(t+\tau)-\phi(t)]}e^{j[\phi_n(t+\tau)-\phi_n(t)]}\right].$$

Therefore,

$$R_{\hat{i}}(\tau) = R_{\hat{i}}(\tau)|_{\text{ no phase noise}} \times R_{\phi_n}(\tau).$$

That is, the autocorrelation of the total current is the product of the autocorrelation of the current when there is no phase noise and the autocorrelation of the phase noise.

Because the power spectrum density is the Fourier transform of the autocorrelation function, the spectrum of the photocurrent is the convolution of the photocurrent spectrum when there is no phase noise and the spectrum of the phase noise. According to the basic concept of Fourier transforms, the convolution of two pulse functions will result in a broader pulse. Therefore, the current spectrum is broader than when there is no phase noise.

The resultant current spectrum can be approximately expressed as the sum of squares of the spectral widths of the phase noise and original signal bandwidth. That is,

$$B_{tot}^2 = B_{sig}^2 + B_{ph}^2 \qquad \textbf{[15.62]}$$

where B_{sig} and B_{ph} are the spectral widths of the signal and phase noise, respectively. When the IF filter has a bandwidth of B_{tot} instead of B_{sig}, the noise power is increased by the following factor:

$$10\log_{10}\frac{B_{tot}}{B_{sig}} = 10\log_{10}\sqrt{1+\left(\frac{B_{ph}}{B_{sig}}\right)^2}. \qquad \textbf{[15.63]}$$

For a given signal bandwidth B_{sig} and a certain tolerable power penalty, the condition on the phase noise bandwidth B_{ph} is

$$B_{ph} < B_{sig}[10^{PP/5}-1]^{1/2} \qquad \textbf{[15.64]}$$

where PP is the optical power penalty in dB. When NRZ is used for the pulse waveform, $B_{sig} \approx 3R_b$ is needed to cover 95 percent of the signal power [24][1]. Similarly, to cover 95 percent of the phase noise power, using the Lorentzian spectrum,

---

[1] In this case, B_{sig} is the IF filter bandwidth used to pass the signal. If the signal is NRZ modulated at the IF frequency, f_{IF}, the signal's power spectral density is proportional to $\text{sinc}^2([f-f_{IF}]/R_b)$. Therefore, to pass 95 percent of the signal power using ASK and NRZ, the actual bandwidth required is $4.16R_b$. A bandwidth of $3R_b$ can pass only 93 percent of the total power.

$$\frac{1}{\pi f_{3dB}} \int_{-B_{ph}/2}^{B_{ph}/2} \frac{1}{1 + (2f/\Delta f_{3dB})^2} df = 0.95 = \frac{2}{\pi} \arctan(B_{ph}/\Delta f_{3dB}).$$

This gives

$$B_{ph} = \tan(0.95\pi/2)\Delta f_{3dB} = 12.7\Delta f_{3dB}. \qquad \textbf{[15.65]}$$

From Equations (15.64) and (15.65),

$$\Delta \nu_{tx}, \Delta \nu_{loc} = \frac{\Delta f_{3dB}}{2} = \frac{B_{ph}}{25.4} < \frac{3}{25.4}[10^{PP/5}-1]^{1/2} R_b. \qquad \textbf{[15.66]}$$

At a power penalty of 1 dB,

$$\Delta \nu_{tx}, \Delta \nu_{loc} < 0.09 R_b. \qquad \textbf{[15.67]}$$

15.10.3 EFFECT OF PHASE NOISE IN FSK

For heterodyne FSK demodulation, envelope detection can be used in the postdetection, as discussed earlier. In this case, the phase noise effect results in a power penalty as discussed in the previous subsection. Alternatively, a frequency discriminator can be used to detect the transmitted frequency. That is, the discriminator will generate an output proportional to $\omega_{IF} \pm \Delta\omega_d/2$ when there is no phase noise.

When there is phase noise, the frequency discriminator has an output proportional to

$$x(t) = \omega_{IF} \pm \Delta\omega_d/2 + \dot{\phi}_n(t).$$

To maximize the detection performance, matched filtering or integrate-and-dump is used. The output is

$$y = \int_0^T x(t)dt = (\omega_{IF} \pm \Delta\omega_d/2)T + \int_0^T \dot{\phi}_n(t)dt.$$

Because the phase noise $\dot{\phi}$ term is Gaussian, from Equation (6.126), its variance is

$$E\left[\left(\int_0^T \dot{\phi}_n(t)dt\right)^2\right] = 2\pi\Delta f_{3dB}T.$$

The detection performance is thus

$$P_E = Q\left(\sqrt{\frac{\Delta\omega_d^2 T}{8\pi\Delta f_{3dB}}}\right) = Q\left(\sqrt{\frac{\pi\Delta f_d^2 T}{2\Delta f_{3dB}}}\right) \qquad \textbf{[15.68]}$$

where Δf_d is the frequency separation of the two possible frequencies. If the bit error floor is set at 10^{-10},

$$\frac{\pi}{2} \frac{(\Delta f_d T)^2}{\Delta f_{3dB} T} \geq 40$$

is needed. This implies

$$\Delta v_{tx}, \Delta v_{loc} < \frac{\pi}{160} (\Delta f_d T)^2 R_b = 0.019 (\Delta f_d T)^2 R_b. \qquad \textbf{[15.69]}$$

Comparing this result to the condition using envelope detection given by Equation (15.67) shows that when $\Delta f_d T > 2.2$, using frequency discrimination in postdetection affords a larger linewidth Δv. On the other hand, if $\Delta f_d T < 2.2$, envelope detection can allow for a larger linewidth.

15.10.4 EFFECTS OF PHASE NOISE IN OTHER COHERENT DETECTION TECHNIQUES

In other homodyne or heterodyne detection schemes, phase noise has a similar error floor phenomenon due to random phase error. For example, in homodyne PSK the detected current output after matched filtering is proportional to

$$x = \pm \int_0^T \cos[\phi_n(t)] dt.$$

If the phase noise, $\phi_n(t)$, causes a negative integration value, there is an error in detection. In general, the error detection probability depends on the statistics of $\phi_n(t)$, which in turn depend on the carrier loop implementation. The analysis is complicated and is beyond the scope of this book. According to [22], the linewidth requirement for homodyne PSK is

$$\Delta v_{tx}, \Delta v_{loc} < 3.1 \times 10^{-4} R_b. \qquad \textbf{[15.70]}$$

In other reports [26][27], the requirement is similar and in the range between $2 \times 10^{-4} R_b$ and $5 \times 10^{-4} R_b$.

15.11 SUMMARY

 1. In contrast to direct or intensity detection, coherent detection has the capability to detect the phase, frequency, amplitude, and even polarization of the incident light signal. Therefore, information can be transmitted via phase, frequency, amplitude, or polarization modulation. When the intensity noise in the transmission is strong, coherent communication using PSK or FSK becomes attractive.

 2. Also in contrast to direct detection, one unique characteristic of coherent detection is the use of a local optical carrier, which is locked to the incident light signal in phase and/or frequency. The incident light signal is mixed with the local carrier by a device called hybrid. This mixing down shifts the light carrier frequency either directly to baseband (homodyne) or to an intermediate frequency (heterodyne) in the radio frequency range.

3. More important, using a local carrier can help to bring the detection performance close to its quantum limit. Because the local carrier is strong in power, the noise at the photodetector output is dominated by the shot noise of the local oscillator. This effectively suppresses other noise sources such as thermal noise and receiver noise. This ability to reach the quantum limit by using coherent detection was a primary motivation behind the rapid development of the coherent communication technology.

4. According to the frequency difference between the incident light and the local carrier, there are two coherent detection techniques: homodyne and heterodyne. In homodyne detection, the local carrier has the same frequency as the incident signal; in heterodyne detection, the local carrier has a finite nonzero frequency difference from the incident light. The frequency difference is called the intermediate frequency (IF).

5. To ensure proper mixing of the incident signal and the local carrier, their polarizations must be aligned. If their polarizations are orthogonal to each other, there will be no product term. Other than polarization control, polarization diversity can be used to ensure a nonzero product output.

6. A hybrid generally is a four-port device with two input ports and two output ports. There are two important types of hybrids in optical communications: 180° and 90° hybrids. In the first type, the two output ports generate $E_{inc} \pm E_{loc}$. In the second type, the two mixed outputs have a relative phase difference of 90°. In general, 180° hybrids are commonly used in heterodyne detection, and 90° hybrids are commonly used in homodyne detection for carrier recovery.

7. Because the local carrier has a large power, its intensity noise is large. To reduce this noise, balanced detection is used, where the two hybrid outputs are detected and subtracted by two photodetectors. The intensity noise is cancelled by the subtraction.

8. In general, homodyne detection performs better than heterodyne detection by at least 3 dB. This is because heterodyne uses an IF filter, whose bandwidth is twice that of the low-pass filter used in homodyne detection. As a result, the noise power is also twice that of heterodyne detection.

9. Homodyne detection, on the other hand, requires a more complicated implementation because both the frequency and phase must be synchronized between the incident signal and the local carrier. Furthermore, the performance is more sensitive to phase noise. Thus both laser sources and local oscillators are required to have a small spectral width compared to the bit rate.

10. When homodyne detection is used, the photodetector output is a baseband signal. Thus it is ready for detection. In heterodyne detection, another demodulation stage is needed to convert the IF photocurrent to baseband. In general, this can be done either by another step of coherent detection at the IF frequency, by incoherent postdetection such as envelope detection, or by weakly synchronous postdetection, where a local IF carrier is recovered and locked only in frequency. The trade-off of these methods is performance versus implementation complexity.

11. In general, a PSK signal has to be synchronously detected, and DPSK can be detected by weakly synchronous postdetection. FSK and OOK signals can be detected first by heterodyne and then by envelope detection. The combination of heterodyne and envelope detection is the simplest implementation scheme in coherent detection.

12. Homodyne PSK has the lowest quantum limit (9 photons/bit at a BER of 10^{-9}), and heterodyne/envelope FSK and OOK have the highest quantum limit (40 photons/bit). In practice, heterodyne/envelope FSK is the most commonly used scheme because it is simple to implement in both modulation (direct modulation is possible) and detection (no IF carrier recovery is needed).

13. PolSK transmits information by modulating the polarization of the incident light signal. Because the state of polarization (SOP) can be described by the three Stokes parameters, a received signal can be represented by a three-dimensional vector according to its Stokes parameters. A PolSK receiver that derives the Stokes parameters of the received signal is called a Stokes receiver.

14. The three Stokes parameters of a given SOP can be mapped to a three-dimensional sphere called the Poincaré sphere. A transmitted symbol in PolSK can thus be mapped to a point in a Poincaré sphere. Because of the three-dimensional representation, PolSK plus amplitude modulation can have more freedom or larger minimum distance in M-ary signaling.

15. Carrier recovery in homodyne detection requires both phase and frequency synchronization. Implementation is in general based on the Costas loop, which has a phase detector generating a phase error signal with an amplitude proportional to the phase difference of the incident light signal and the local carrier.

16. To generate the phase error signal in the Costas loop, a six-port 90° hybrid with balanced detection is commonly used, where four ports are used as output, two each for one balanced detection.

17. In heterodyne detection, the local carrier only needs to be synchronized with the incident signal in frequency. Therefore, instead of using the Costas loop, an automatic frequency control (AFC) with input from the IF signal is used. An AFC consists of a frequency discriminator, whose output is proportional to the frequency of the input. The AFC output is thus used as a feedback to drive the local oscillator.

18. Coherent detection performance can also be strongly subject to phase noise from both the source laser and local carrier. Except for heterodyne detection using envelope detection, there is an error floor in detection performance because of phase noise. This is because the phase noise directly corrupts the phase and/or frequency content of the carrier.

19. In homodyne detection, phase noise corrupts not only the phase of the demodulated output but also the performance of the carrier recovery loop. Therefore, the linewidths of the source laser and local oscillator are critical to detection performance. Depending on the carrier loop implementation, the 3 dB spectral widths of the source laser and local carrier at an error floor of 10^{-10} need to be within 0.02–0.05 percent of the bit rate.

20. In DPSK and FSK using heterodyne detection, depending on the postdetection implementation (except envelope detection), the 3 dB spectral width of the source laser and local carrier at an error floor of 10^{-10} is required to be on the order of 1 percent of the bit rate.

21. In OOK and FSK using envelope detection, phase noise results in a larger spectral width of the IF signal. Thus the IF filter bandwidth can be increased to maintain the same envelope output. Because this increase of the bandwidth passes more noise power through, there is a power penalty due to phase noise. At a power penalty of 1 dB, the 3 dB spectral width of the source laser and local carrier at an error floor of 10^{-10} is required to be within 9 percent of the bit rate.

APPENDIX 15-A: POLARIZATION CONTROLLERS AND ISOLATORS

Some anisotropic media such as quartz cause a linearly polarized wave to rotate. This phenomenon is called **optical activity**, and the ability to rotate the linearly polarized wave is characterized by ρ, the **rotary power** in deg/cm. In other words, for a medium that has a rotary power of ρ, the linearly polarized wave inside will rotate ρL over a distance L. This appendix explains the theory and use of such anisotropic media for polarization control and reflected light isolation.

From Equation (14.9) derived in Chapter 14, a plane wave inside an anisotropic medium is governed by the following wave equation:

$$\frac{n^2}{c^2} Proj_{\bar{\beta}}\{\bar{E}\} = \bar{\mu}\bar{\epsilon}\bar{E} \qquad \text{[15.71]}$$

where n is the polarization-dependent refractive index, $\bar{\beta}$ is the propagation vector, $\bar{\epsilon}$ is the permittivity tensor, and the magnetic permeability is now replaced by a permeability tensor $\bar{\mu}$ for generality.

For a medium that exhibits optical activity, its $\bar{\mu}\bar{\epsilon}$ tensor can be written as

$$\bar{\mu}\bar{\epsilon} = \frac{n_0^2}{c^2}\begin{bmatrix} 1 & j\mu_1 & 0 \\ -j\mu_1 & 1 & 0 \\ 0 & 0 & 1 \end{bmatrix}. \qquad \text{[15.72]}$$

In this case, if $\bar{E}^T = [E_1, E_2, E_3]$, wave equation (15.71) reduces to

$$n^2\begin{bmatrix} E_1 \\ E_2 \\ 0 \end{bmatrix} = n_0^2\begin{bmatrix} 1 & j\mu_1 & 0 \\ -j\mu_1 & 1 & 0 \\ 0 & 0 & 1 \end{bmatrix}\begin{bmatrix} E_1 \\ E_2 \\ E_3 \end{bmatrix} = n_0^2\begin{bmatrix} E_1 + j\mu_1 E_2 \\ -j\mu_1 E_1 + E_2 \\ E_3 \end{bmatrix}.$$

Therefore, the two possible refractive indices n are

$$n_\pm^2 = n_0^2(1 \pm \mu_1) \qquad \text{[15.73]}$$

with the corresponding electric field vectors given by

$$\bar{E}_\pm = E_0\begin{bmatrix} 1 \\ \mp j \\ 0 \end{bmatrix}. \qquad \text{[15.74]}$$

Equation (15.74) says that the two eigen polarizations in a medium with a joint tensor given by Equation (15.72) are opposite, circularly polarized.

Rotary Power   When the two circularly polarized waves given by Equation (15.74) propagate in the direction $\hat{z}$ and over a certain distance L, they experience a phase difference

$$\Delta\phi = \frac{2\pi L}{\lambda}(n_- - n_+) \stackrel{\text{def}}{=} 2\rho L \approx \frac{2\pi n_0 \mu_1}{\lambda} L \qquad \textbf{[15.75]}$$

where

$$\rho \stackrel{\text{def}}{=} \frac{\pi(n_- - n_+)}{\lambda} \qquad \textbf{[15.76]}$$

is the rotary power. Therefore, if the incident field is a linearly polarized wave given by

$$\bar{E}_{in} = E_0 \begin{bmatrix} \cos(\phi_0) \\ \sin(\phi_0) \\ 0 \end{bmatrix} = \frac{1}{2} E_0 e^{j\phi_0} \begin{bmatrix} 1 \\ j \\ 0 \end{bmatrix} + \frac{1}{2} E_0 e^{-j\phi_0} \begin{bmatrix} 1 \\ -j \\ 0 \end{bmatrix}$$

the output wave over distance L from the decomposition is given by

$$\bar{E}_{out} = \frac{e^{-j\phi_1}}{2} E_0 e^{j(\phi_0 + \Delta\phi/2)} \begin{bmatrix} 1 \\ j \\ 0 \end{bmatrix} + \frac{e^{-j\phi_1}}{2} E_0 e^{-j(\phi_0 + \Delta\phi/2)} \begin{bmatrix} 1 \\ -j \\ 0 \end{bmatrix}$$

$$= e^{-j\phi_1} E_0 \begin{bmatrix} \cos(\phi_0 + \Delta\phi/2) \\ \sin(\phi_0 + \Delta\phi/2) \\ 0 \end{bmatrix}$$

where $\phi_1 = (\pi L/\lambda)(n_+ + n_-)$ is the average phase shift. The above result shows that the linearly polarized wave is rotated by an angle $\Delta\phi/2 = \rho L$. Equation (15.75) says that this rotation is due to the difference between n_- and n_+, which is called **circular birefringence.**

Faraday Effect   Many crystals exhibit optical activity when a magnetic flux density, B, is applied in the direction of the wave propagation. This phenomenon is called the **Faraday effect**. In this case, the rotary power is characterized by

$$\rho = VB \qquad \textbf{[15.77]}$$

where V is called the **Verdet constant**. Verdet constants of some materials are shown in Table 15.4.

The Verdet constant in general has units of deg/G·mm or mim/Oe·cm, where G or Gauss is the Gaussian unit for the magnetic induction (B), and Oe or oersted is the Gaussian unit for the magnetic field (H). For conversions between Gaussian units and SI units, note that 1 tesla (T) = 1 Wb/m^2 = 10^4 Gauss (G), 1 A/m = $4\pi \times 10^{-3}$ oersted (Oe), and $\mu_0 = 4\pi \times 10^{-7}$ H/m for the vacuum permeability. Therefore, for a medium that has a Verdet constant V in deg/G·mm,

Table 15.4   Values of the Verdet constants of some important materials.

Substance	Temperature	V in deg/Gauss$\cdot$mm
Water	20°C	2.18×10^{-5}
Glass (crown)	18°C	2.68×10^{-5}
Glass (flint)	18°C	5.28×10^{-5}
Carbon disulfide (CS$_2$)	20°C	7.05×10^{-5}
Phosphorus	33°C	2.21×10^{-4}
Sodium chloride (NaCl)	16°C	6.0×10^{-5}
Quartz	20°C	2.77×10^{-5}
TbAlG		-1.93×10^{-3}

Most values given are at $\lambda = 589.2$ nm except TbAlG, which is at 500 nm [28]–[30].

$$V[\text{deg/G}\cdot\text{mm}] \times 10^4[\text{G}\cdot\text{m}^2/\text{Wb}] \times \mu_0[\text{Wb/m}\cdot\text{A}] \times (4\pi \times 10^{-3})^{-1}[\text{A/m}\cdot\text{Oe}]$$
$$= V[\text{deg/Oe}\cdot\text{mm}].$$

This is not a coincidence, because $\mu_0 = 1$ or $B = H$ in the Gaussian units. On the other hand,

$$V[\text{deg/G}\cdot\text{mm}] \times 10^4[\text{G/T}] = 10^4 V[\text{deg/T}\cdot\text{mm}].$$

Example 15.14

FARADAY ROTATION   From Table 15.4, water at 20°C has a Verdet constant of 2.18×10^{-5} deg/G$\cdot$mm or deg/Oe$\cdot$mm. If the applied magnetic field is 10^4 Oe, or 1 tesla, the angle of rotation over a length of 1 mm is 0.218 or $0.218 \times 180°/\pi = 12.5°$.

For TbAlG, the angle of rotation in the same magnetic field and over the same length is −19.3 or more than 3 turns. According to the convention, a negative V means a left-hand rotation pointing to the magnetic field direction, and a positive V means a right-hand rotation pointing to the magnetic field direction, both independent of the propagation direction (i.e., same as or opposite to the magnetic field) of the linearly polarized wave. ∎

Polarization Controller   From Equation (15.77), B can be used to control the rotary power, which in turn can determine the rotation of the polarization. Therefore, a Faraday rotator can be used as a polarization controller, which is an important component in coherent detection.

Isolator   When a linearly polarized wave passes through a Faraday rotator, it experiences a certain rotation, say θ. If it is reflected back, it will *not* rotate back to its original polarization. Instead, it will experience another θ rotation. This is because of the reversed magnetic field with respect to the new propagation direction. Therefore, the total rotation over the round trip is 2θ.

This observation leads to the isolator design shown in Figure 15.24. As shown, the rotation over the Faraday rotator is set to 45°. Therefore, the round-trip rotation is 90°. If a polarizer is added at the input of the Faraday rotator, the reflected wave will be rejected because of its orthogonality to the input polarizer.

APPENDIX 15-B: **FOUR-PORT HYBRIDS**

A four-port hybrid can be made of either a simple beam splitter or combinations of beam splitters and couplers, as illustrated in Figure 15.25. When a single beam splitter is used, as shown in Figure 15.25a, it is at 45° to the two incident beams. Each incident beam is split into two output beams, one transmitted and one reflected. Proper design can produce the desired mixing of the two input signals.

SINGLE BEAM-SPLITTER HYBRID   The transmitted and reflected beams of an incident beam onto a beam splitter can be characterized by the transmission and reflection coefficients r and t, respectively. According to [3], they can be written as

$$r = \frac{r_0(1 - e^{j2\beta})}{1 - r_0^2 e^{j2\beta}} \qquad [15.78]$$

and

$$t = \frac{(1 - r_0^2)e^{j\beta}}{1 - r_0^2 e^{j2\beta}} \qquad [15.79]$$

Example 15.15

where $0 < r_0 < 1$ is the reflection coefficient at the splitter interface, and β is the phase shift through the beam splitter. It can be easily verified that $|r|^2 + |t|^2 = 1$, which is consistent with conservation of energy. Furthermore, the ratio r to t is given by

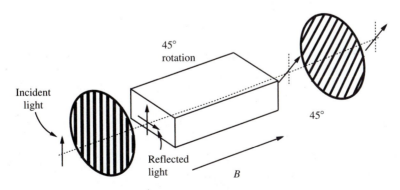

Figure 15.24   Use of a Faraday rotator for reflected light isolation.

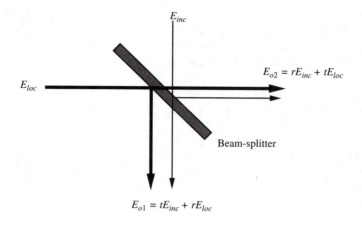

$$E_{o2} = rE_{inc} + tE_{loc}$$

Beam-splitter

$$E_{o1} = tE_{inc} + rE_{loc}$$

(a)

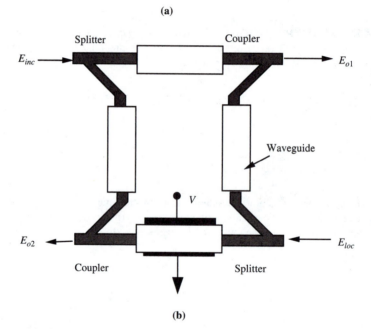

(b)

Figure 15.25   Hybrid implementation. (a) single beam splitter and (b) combination of waveguides, splitters, and couplers.

$$\frac{r}{t} = \frac{-2j\sin(\beta)r_0}{1 - r_0^2}.$$ **[15.80]**

To have an equal power partition, or $|r/t| = 1$, requires

$$|2r_0\sin(\beta)| = 1 - r_0^2.$$

This implies the condition $r_0 > \sqrt{2} - 1$.

Because r_0 depends on the the dielectric constant of the beam splitter and β depends on the thickness of the splitter, the mixing can be controlled by adjusting these two parameters. From Equation (15.80), note that there is always a 90° phase shift between the transmitted and reflected beams. ■

As shown in Figure 15.25b, the second type of implementation consists of two splitters and two couplers, where their interconnections can be done by either waveguides, free space, or optical fibers. In the configuration shown, the phase shift of each branch can be individually controlled by using electro-optic materials such as $LiNbO_3$, discussed in Chapter 14.

HYBRID OF COUPLERS AND SPLITTERS   For symmetric splitters and couplers with equal phase shift on each waveguide branch except the lower input branch of E_{loc}, as shown in Figure 15.25b, the hybrid output can be expressed as

Example 15.16

$$E_{o1} = 1/2 (E_{inc} + E_{loc}) e^{j\theta}$$

and

$$E_{o2} = 1/2 (E_{inc} + e^{j\phi} E_{loc}) e^{j\theta}$$

where θ is the total phase shift over the hybrid and ϕ is the additional shift of the input branch of E_{loc} with respect to other waveguide branches. By adjusting the additional phase shift ϕ, the desired mixing for subsequent signal detection can be attained.

In this implementation, note that the total output power due to E_{inc} is half of the incident power of E_{inc}. Therefore, the price of having the ability to adjust the phase shift ϕ is a 3 dB power loss. ■

Lossless Hybrids   As shown in Equation (15.2), a four-port hybrid is characterized by its transfer matrix. For a lossless hybrid, the coefficients of the matrix cannot be arbitrary. In fact, the matrix must be unitary [31]. That is, its inverse is the same as its complex transpose or

$$\begin{bmatrix} T_1^* & X_2^* \\ X_1^* & T_2^* \end{bmatrix} \begin{bmatrix} T_1 & X_1 \\ X_2 & T_2 \end{bmatrix} = \begin{bmatrix} 1 & 0 \\ 0 & 1 \end{bmatrix}. \tag{15.81}$$

This condition can be verified from conservation of energy. First, for the special case $E_{in,2} = 0$ or the second input is zero, to have the incident power equal to the total output power requires that

$$|T_1|^2 + |X_2|^2 = 1. \tag{15.82}$$

Similarly, if $E_{in,1} = 0$ or the first input is zero,

$$|X_1|^2 + |T_2|^2 = 1. \qquad \textbf{[15.83]}$$

Finally, if $E_{in,1} = e^{j\theta} E_{in,2}$, where θ is arbitrary, energy conservation and Equations (15.82) and (15.83) give

$$0 = \Re\{X_1^*(e^{j\theta}T_1)\} + \Re\{T_2^*(e^{j\theta}X_2)\}. \qquad \textbf{[15.84]}$$

The special cases $\theta = 0$ and $\pi/2$ give

$$T_1 X_1^* + T_2^* X_2 = T_1^* X_1 + T_2 X_2^* = 0. \qquad \textbf{[15.85]}$$

It can be easily verified that Equations (15.82), (15.83), and (15.85) are equivalent to the unitary condition given by Equation (15.81).

Example 15.17

The transfer matrices $\bar{H}$ of Examples 15.15 and 15.16 can be respectively expressed as

$$\bar{H}_1 = \begin{bmatrix} t & r \\ r & t \end{bmatrix}$$

and

$$\bar{H}_2 = \frac{1}{2} \begin{bmatrix} 1 & 1 \\ 1 & 1 \end{bmatrix}.$$

Because $|t|^2 + |r|^2 = 1$, the transfer matrix $\bar{H}_1$ is unitary. Because of the 3 dB power loss mentioned earlier, however, the second-type hybrid, $\hat{H}_2$, is not unitary. ∎

Important Types of Hybrids   In practical system design, there are several important types of hybrids that deserve further consideration. The first kind is called **symmetric hybrids**. In this case, $T_1 = T_2$ and $X_1 = X_2$.

Example 15.18

From Equations (15.81) and (15.82), a lossless symmetric hybrid can be expressed as

$$\begin{bmatrix} T_1 & X_1 \\ X_2 & T_2 \end{bmatrix} = \begin{bmatrix} T & X \\ X & T \end{bmatrix} = e^{j\theta} \begin{bmatrix} x & \sqrt{1-x^2}e^{j\alpha} \\ \sqrt{1-x^2}e^{j\alpha} & x \end{bmatrix} \qquad \textbf{[15.86]}$$

where $0 < x < 1$ is used to characterize the power partition and θ is the phase shift, which can be arbitrary. From Equation (15.84), it can be verified that α can be only $\pm\pi/2$ and $0 < x < 1$.

A lossless symmetric hybrid can be made of the single beam splitter discussed in Example 15.15. As noted in that example, there is a relative 90° shift between the transmission and reflection beams. This is consistent with the condition of $\alpha = \pm\pi/2$. ∎

There are also important types of hybrids that are not symmetric. One special type has the properties $T_1 = e^{j\beta} T_2$ and $X_1 = X_2$. The transfer matrix can be generally written as

$$\bar{H} = \begin{bmatrix} T_1 & X_1 \\ X_2 & T_2 \end{bmatrix} = ae^{j\theta} \begin{bmatrix} x & \sqrt{1-x^2}e^{j\alpha} \\ \sqrt{1-x^2}e^{j\alpha} & e^{j\beta}x \end{bmatrix} \qquad \textbf{[15.87]}$$

where $0 < a < 1$ is included to account for any possible power loss. If the hybrid is lossless, $a = 1$, and from the unitary condition

$$e^{-j\alpha} + e^{j(\alpha-\beta)} = 0$$

or

$$2\alpha - \beta = (2n+1)\pi$$

where n is an integer. Therefore, for a given β,

$$\alpha = \frac{\beta}{2} + \frac{2n+1}{2}\pi. \qquad \textbf{[15.88]}$$

180° HYBRID   As a special case, if $\beta = \pi$, $\alpha = 0$. For equal power partition, or $x = 1/\sqrt{2}$,

$$\bar{H}_{180} = \frac{1}{\sqrt{2}}e^{j\theta} \begin{bmatrix} 1 & 1 \\ 1 & -1 \end{bmatrix}. \qquad \textbf{[15.89]}$$

Example 15.19

This is called a 180° hybrid. One way to implement this lossless 180° hybrid is to use a single beam splitter symmetric hybrid and two additional phase shift waveguides at the lower input and output of the hybrid. Each waveguide has a 270° phase shift. Therefore, the combined hybrid has the following transfer matrix

$$\bar{H}_{180} = \frac{1}{\sqrt{2}}e^{j\theta} \begin{bmatrix} 1 & 0 \\ 0 & -j \end{bmatrix} \begin{bmatrix} 1 & j \\ j & 1 \end{bmatrix} \begin{bmatrix} 1 & 0 \\ 0 & -j \end{bmatrix} = \frac{1}{\sqrt{2}}e^{j\theta} \begin{bmatrix} 1 & 1 \\ 1 & -1 \end{bmatrix}. \; \blacksquare$$

90° HYBRID   Another special case of the hybrid given by Equation (15.89) has $\beta = \pi/2$ and $\alpha = 0$. Equation (15.88) says that this type of hybrid cannot be lossless. For equal power partition or $x = 1/\sqrt{2}$, it is called a 90° hybrid and can be expressed as

Example 15.19

$$\bar{H}_{90} = \frac{a}{\sqrt{2}}e^{j\theta} \begin{bmatrix} 1 & 1 \\ 1 & j \end{bmatrix}.$$

From Example 15.16, this hybrid can be implemented with $a = 1/\sqrt{2}$. In other words, this type of hybrids suffers a 3 dB power loss. ∎

APPENDIX 15-C: SIX-PORT 90° HYBRID ANALYSIS FOR CARRIER RECOVERY

This appendix analyzes the operation of the six-port hybrid shown in Figure 15.4. To start, let the received signal be

$$E_{inc} = \sqrt{2P_{inc}} \cos[\omega_{inc}t + \phi(t) + \theta],$$

and let the local oscillator output be

$$E_{loc}(t) = \sqrt{2P_{loc}} \cos(\omega_{loc}t + \hat{\theta}).$$

The two inputs to one of the half mirrors can thus be expressed as

$$E_{inc,x}(t) = \frac{1}{\sqrt{2}} \sqrt{2P_{inc}} \cos[\omega_{inc}t + \phi(t) + \theta]$$

and

$$E_{loc,x}(t) = \frac{1}{\sqrt{2}} \sqrt{2P_{loc}} \cos(\omega_{loc}t + \hat{\theta} + \pi/4).$$

From the property of hybrids made of a single half mirror discussed in Appendix 15–B, there is a 90° phase shift in one of the mixed outputs. Specifically, the half mirror yields the following two outputs:

$$E_{x1} = \frac{1}{2}\sqrt{2P_{inc}} \cos[\omega_{inc}t + \phi(t) + \theta + \pi/2] + \frac{1}{2}\sqrt{2P_{loc}} \cos(\omega_{loc}t + \hat{\theta} + \pi/4). \quad \textbf{[15.90]}$$

$$E_{x2} = \frac{1}{2}\sqrt{2P_{inc}} \cos[\omega_{inc}t + \phi(t) + \theta] + \frac{1}{2}\sqrt{2P_{loc}} \cos(\omega_{loc}t + \hat{\theta} + 3\pi/4). \quad \textbf{[15.91]}$$

Therefore, the balanced detection output is

$$I_{ph,x} = \mathcal{R}[|E_{x1}|^2 - |E_{x2}|^2] = \mathcal{R}\sqrt{P_{inc}P_{loc}} \cos[\phi(t) + \Delta\theta] \quad \textbf{[15.92]}$$

where $\omega_{loc} = \omega_{inc}$ for homodyne detection and

$$\Delta\theta \stackrel{\text{def}}{=} \theta - \hat{\theta} + \pi/4. \quad \textbf{[15.93]}$$

The photocurrent at the other balanced detector output can be obtained similarly. Because the two inputs to the other half mirror are

$$E_{inc,y}(t) = \frac{1}{\sqrt{2}} \sqrt{2P_{inc}} \cos[\omega_{inc}t + \phi(t) + \theta + \pi/4]$$

and

$$E_{loc,y}(t) = \frac{1}{\sqrt{2}} \sqrt{2P_{loc}} \cos(\omega_{loc}t + \hat{\theta})$$

the half mirror yields the following two outputs:

$$E_{y1} = \frac{1}{2}\sqrt{2P_{inc}} \cos[\omega_{inc}t + \phi(t) + \theta + \pi/4] + \frac{1}{2}\sqrt{2P_{loc}} \cos(\omega_{loc}t + \hat{\theta} + \pi/2).$$

$$E_{y2} = \frac{1}{2}\sqrt{2P_{inc}} \cos[\omega_{inc}t + \phi(t) + \theta + 3\pi/4] + \frac{1}{2}\sqrt{2P_{loc}} \cos(\omega_{loc}t + \hat{\theta}).$$

Therefore, the balanced detection output is

$$I_{ph,y} = \mathcal{R}[|E_{y1}|^2 - |E_{y2}|^2] = \mathcal{R}\sqrt{P_{inc}P_{loc}} \sin[\phi(t) + \Delta\theta]. \qquad \text{[15.94]}$$

The output photocurrent $I_{ph,x}$ given by Equation (15.92) can be used for subsequent signal detection. At the same time, it can be multiplied with $I_{ph,y}$ given by Equation (15.94) for carrier recovery. Because

$$I_{ph,x}I_{ph,y} = \mathcal{R}^2 P_{inc}P_{loc} \sin[2\phi(t) + 2\Delta\theta] = \frac{1}{2}\mathcal{R}^2 P_{inc}P_{loc} \sin(2\Delta\theta)$$

the product can be used as a feedback signal to drive the local laser diode in the Costas loop.

From Equations (15.90)–(15.92), also note that the ratio of the signal power to the shot noise power is 3 dB less than that obtained before using a lossless 180° hybrid (see Problem 15–13). This is because 50 percent of the incident power is used for carrier recovery.

APPENDIX 15-D: RICIAN AND RAYLEIGH DISTRIBUTIONS

In envelope detection, Rician and Rayleigh are two important probability distributions in evaluating the bit error probability. This appendix shows that the envelope function $E(t)$ given by Equation (15.22) follows the Rician distribution given by Equation (15.24).

The definitions of $E(t)$ and $\psi(t)$ given by Equations (15.22) and (15.23) give

$$n_c^2 + n_s^2 = E^2 - A^2 - 2An_c = E^2 - 2A(A + n_c) + A^2 = E^2 - 2AE \cos \psi(t) + A^2 \quad \text{[15.95]}$$

where

$$A = 2\mathcal{R}\sqrt{P_{inc}P_{loc}}.$$

Also, because the Jacobian $\partial(n_c, n_s)/\partial(E, \psi)$ is

$$\frac{\partial n_c}{\partial E}\frac{\partial n_s}{\partial \psi} - \frac{\partial n_c}{\partial \psi}\frac{\partial n_s}{\partial E} = E \cos^2(\psi) + E \sin^2(\psi) = E$$

the joint PDF of E and ψ can be written as

$$f_{E,\psi}(E, \psi) = f_{n_c,n_s}(n_c, n_s) \frac{\partial(n_c, n_s)}{\partial(E, \psi)} = \frac{E}{2\pi \sigma_n^2} e^{-[E^2 + 2AE\cos(\psi) + A^2]/2\sigma_n^2}$$

where $\sigma_n^2 = E[n_c^2] = E[n_s^2]$. If the joint PDF is integrated from 0 to 2π with respect to ψ, the marginal PDF of E is

$$f_E(E) = \frac{E}{\sigma^2} e^{-(E^2 + A^2)/2\sigma^2} I_0\left(\frac{AE}{\sigma^2}\right) \qquad \textbf{[15.96]}$$

where $I_0(x)$ is the zero order modified Bessel function of the first kind given by

$$I_0(x) = \frac{1}{2\pi} \int_0^{2\pi} e^{x\psi} d\psi. \qquad \textbf{[15.97]}$$

For the special case that $A = $ zero,

$$I_0(0) = \frac{1}{2\pi} \int_0^{2\pi} d\psi = 1. \qquad \textbf{[15.98]}$$

Therefore, the density function $f_E(E)$ in Equation (15.96) reduces to

$$f_E(E) = \frac{E}{\sigma^2} e^{-E^2/2\sigma^2}. \qquad \textbf{[15.99]}$$

This is called the Rayleigh distribution with mean $\sqrt{2\pi\sigma^2}$.

PROBLEMS

Problem 15–1 Polarization Diversity Receiver: Consider the polarization diversity receiver shown in Figure 15.3. Assume the local oscillator power is equally divided by its PBS.

    a. What is the largest possible photocurrent after balanced detection? What is the corresponding condition for the polarization of the incident light signal?

    b. What is the smallest possible photocurrent after balanced detection? What is the corresponding condition for the polarization of the incident light signal?

    c. What can you conclude from *(a)* and *(b)* in terms of the photocurrent deviation due to misalignment of polarization?

Problem 15–2 Hybrid: Consider a half mirror used as the hybrid. Its transfer function can be expressed as

$$\bar{H} = \frac{1}{\sqrt{2}} \begin{bmatrix} j & 1 \\ 1 & j \end{bmatrix}. \qquad \textbf{[15.100]}$$

This is the type of hybrid used in the six-port 90° as shown in Figure 15.4.

    a. Show that the hybrid is unitary.

    b. If balanced detection is used, derive the photocurrent output.

Problem 15–3 Local Oscillator Power:

    a. At a given NEP W/Hz$^{1/2}$ of a photodetector, find the required local oscillator power so that the shot noise power due to the local oscillator is 10 times the NEP of the photodetector.

    b. For a typical NEP value of 10^{-11} W/Hz$^{1/2}$, calculate the required local oscillator power from (*a*). Assume the responsivity of the photodetector is $\mathcal{R} = 0.8$ A/W.

Problem 15–4 RIN Noise and Balanced Detection:

    a. If single detection is used, calculate the intensity noise power per Hz at the photodiode output. Assume that the local oscillator output is 0.5 mW and has a RIN of −130 dB/Hz, and that the photodiode has a responsivity of 0.8.

    b. From (*a*), calculate the improvement of the signal-to-noise ratio when balanced detection is used.

Problem 15–5 Super Quantum Limit: In homodyne PSK using balanced detection,

    a. Calculate the quantum limit when the local oscillator has the same power as the incident light signal. Assume bits "1" and "0" are equally likely.

    b. Under what practical conditions can the above limit be achieved?

Problem 15–6 Bandpass Noise: Consider a bandpass noise $n_b(t)$ that is the filtered output of an ideal low-pass filter from a white noise source input. Assume the white noise input, $n(t)$, has a spectral density of N_0 and the ideal bandpass filter has the form

$$h_b(t) = h(t)\cos(\omega_0 t)$$

where $h(t)$ is the impulse response of an ideal LPF of bandwidth B. Let

$$n_c(t) = [n(t)\cos(\omega_0 t)] \otimes h(t).$$

$$n_s(t) = [n(t)\sin(\omega_0 t)] \otimes h(t).$$

    a. Show that both the power spectral densities of $n_c(t)$ and $n_s(t)$ are given by

$$S_{n,c}(\omega) = S_{n,s}(\omega) = \frac{N_0}{2}|H(\omega)|^2.$$

    b. Show that $n_c(t)$ and $n_s(t)$ are uncorrelated. Because they are Gaussian, they are also independent.

    c. Show that $n_b(t)$ can be expressed as

$$n_b(t) = n_c(t)\cos(\omega_0 t) + n_s(t)\sin(\omega_0 t).$$

    d. From the above results, show that

$$\sigma_{n,b}^2 = \sigma_{n,c}^2 = \sigma_{n,s}^2 = N_0 B.$$

Problem 15–7 Envelope Detection of OOK: From the equation before Equation (15.26), calculate the error detection probabilities $P(e \mid 0)$ and $P(e \mid 1)$. What is the ratio

of the two probabilities? Use the ratio A/σ at which the average error detection probability is 10^{-9}.

Problem 15–8 Homodyne PSK: Consider a homodyne PSK system where the balanced detection has a NEP of 10^{-11} W/Hz$^{1/2}$ and the local oscillator output power is -10 dBm.

   a. Find the SNR at the integrate-and-dump output in terms of P_{inc}. Let the bit rate be 2.5 Gb/s, Assume the responsivity of the photodiode is 1.0.

   b. Find the BER if P_{inc} is -50 dBm.

Problem 15–9 Differential PSK: In DPSK detection, if the local IF carrier is $\cos(\omega_{IF}t + \phi_e)$ instead of $\cos(\omega_{IF}t)$, show that the inner product is the same as that given by Equation (15.34).

Problem 15–10 Heterodyne FSK: Consider a heterodyne FSK system that uses envelope detection. If the balanced photodetection has a NEP of $10^{-11}W/\text{Hz}^{1/2}$ and the local oscillator output power is -5 dBm, find the receiver sensitivity at 1 Gb/s. Assume the photodiode has a quantum efficiency of 0.8 and the light is at wavelength 1.55 μm. How many dB is it higher than the quantum limit of heterodyne FSK?

Problem 15–11 Poincaré Sphere:

   a. Show that all points on the equator of the Poincaré correspond to linearly polarized input.

   b. Show that the two points on the north and south pole correspond to circularly polarized input.

Problem 15–12 Polarization-Shift Keying: For the quaternary constellation shown in Figure 15.17*b*, assume the four points have the coordinates:

$\bar{A} = (\frac{\sqrt{3}}{2}, 0, -\frac{1}{2})$, $\bar{B} = (-\frac{3}{4}, \frac{\sqrt{3}}{4}, -\frac{1}{2})$, $\bar{C} = (-\frac{3}{4}, -\frac{\sqrt{3}}{4}, -\frac{1}{2})$, and $\bar{D} = (0, 0, 1)$.

   a. Express the corresponding electric fields.

   b. From (*a*), how can you design the modulator at the source side?

Problem 15–13 Carrier Recovery: Assume the six-port hybrid shown in Figure 15.4 is used in the Costas loop for carrier recovery, where each four-port hybrid has the transfer matrix given in Problem 15–2.

   a. Derive the shot noise power of the in-phase photocurrent.

   b. Express the error detection probability in terms of N_b.

Problem 15–14 Decision Feedback Costas Loop: Draw the block diagram of the Costas loop using decision feedback when QPSK (four phase PSK) is used. Give necessary analysis to verify the block diagram.

Problem 15–15 IF Frequency Consideration: Because an IF filter is a bandpass filter, it can be characterized by a parameter called the Q-factor (see Chapter 16 for details), which is defined to be the ratio of the central frequency to its bandwidth.

   a. If a large Q-factor is desirable in implementing the IF filter, how would you choose the IF frequency?

   b. In dense wavelength division multiplexing (WDM) applications where channel separation should be as small as possible, how would you choose the IF frequency?

Problem 15–16 Automatic Frequency Control: For the AFC implementation using a frequency discriminator shown in Figure 15.23, let the discriminator output be $v_f = G_f(\omega_{inc} - \omega_{loc})$. Therefore, the input to the loop filter that drives the local laser diode is $v_d = v_f - v_{ref}$, where v_{ref} is set at ω_{IF}/G_f. If the emission frequency of the laser diode is $G_d v_d + \omega_0$, find the required loop gain $G_d G_f$ so that the frequency difference between the local carrier frequency and the incident signal is maintained within 10 percent of the desired IF frequency. For numerical calculation, assume the incident light wavelength is 1510 nm, local carrier wavelength at zero v_d is 1540 nm, and $\omega_{IF} = 2\pi \times 2 \times 10^9$ rad/sec.

Problem 15–17 Error Floor Due to Phase Noise: If the spectral widths of the source laser and local oscillator are both equal to 2 MHz, what should be the minimum bit rate of DPSK so that the BER floor is at 10^{-10}?

Problem 15–18 Power Penalty due to Phase Noise: If the tolerable power penalty is 3 dB in heterodyne/envelope FSK, find the minimum bit rate if both the source laser and local oscillator have the same spectral width of 2 MHz.

Problem 15–19: For a heterodyne FSK transmission system, the frequency separation, Δf_d, is set at 5 times the bit rate. Find the upper bound of the total 3dB spectral width for an error floor of 10^{-10} at $R_b = 2$ Gb/s. Assume frequency discrimination is used in post FSK detection.

REFERENCES

1. T. Miyazaki, S. Ryu, Y. Namihira, and H. Wakabayashi, "Optical Costas Loop Experiment Using a Novel Optical 90° Hybrid Module and a Semiconductor-Laser-Amplifier External Phase Adjustor," Digest of International Conference on Optical Fiber Communication, 1991. Optical Society of America 1991, p. 99.

2. G. L. Abbas, V. W. S. Chan, and T. K. Yee, "A dual-Dector Optical Heterodyne Receiver for Local Oscillator Noise Suppression," Journal of Lightwave Technology, vol. 3, no. 5 (October 1985), pp. 1110-22.

3. Max Born and Emil Wolf, Section 1.6.4 of *Principles of Optics*, 6th ed., Pergamon Press, 1980.

4. B. P. Lathi, *Modern Digital And Analog Communication Systems*, 2nd ed., Holt, Rinehart and Winston, 1989.

5. T. Chikama et al., "Optical Heterodyne Continuous Phase FSK Transmission Experiment Up to 4 Gb/s," *Proceedings of European Conference on Optical Communications (ECOC)*, 1990, pp. 65–68.

6. S. Ryu, "Field Demonstration of 195km-Long Coherent Unrepeatered Submarine Cable System Using Optical Booster Amplifier," *Electronics Letters,* vol. 28, no. 21 (1992), pp. 1965–67.

7. E. Gottwald et al., "2.5 Gb/s PSK Homodyne System with Nonlinear Phase-Locked Loop," *European Conference on Optical Communications,* 1990, pp. 331–34.

8. B. Biotteau et al., "Highly Sensitive 565 Mb/s DPSK Heterodyne Transmission Experiment Using DC Modulation of a DFB Laser Transmitter," Digest of International Conference on Optical Fiber Communication, 1991. Optical Society of America 1991, pp. 94.

9. R. Calvani et al., "Polarization Phase-Shift Keying: A Coherent Transmission Technique with Differential Heterodyne Detection," *Electronics Letters.*, vol. 23, no. 10 (April 9, 1987), pp. 421–22.

10. E. Dietrich et al., "Heterodyne Transmission of a 560 Mbit/s Optical Signal by Means of Polarization Shift Keying," *Electronics Letters*, vol. 24 (May 1988), pp. 642–43.

11. S. Betti et al., "State of Polarization and Phase Noise Independent Coherent Optical Transmission System Based on Stokes Parameter Detection," *Electronics Letters*, vol. 24, no. 23 (November 10, 1988), pp. 1461–62.

12. S. Betti et al., "Dichroism Effect on Polarization-Modulated Optical Systems Using Stokes Parameters Coherent Detection," *Journal of Lightwave Technology*, vol. 8, no. 11 (November 1990), pp. 1762–68.

13. S. Betti et al., "Multilevel Coherent Optical System Based on Stokes Parameters Modulation," *Journal of Lightwave Technology*, vol. 8, no. 7 (July 1990), pp. 1127–36.

14. S. Benedetto and P. Poggiolini, "Combined Amplitude and Polarization Shift Keying Optical Coherent Modulation," *Electronics Letters*, vol. 26, no. 13 (June 1990), pp. 918–19.

15. S. Betti et al., "Phase Noise and Polarization State Insensitive Optical Coherent Systems," *Journal of Lightwave Technology*, vol. 8, no. 5 (March 1990), pp. 756–67.

16. Y. Imai et al., "Phase-Noise-Free Coherent Optical Communication System Utilizing Differential Polarization Shift Keying (DPolSK)," *Journal of Lightwave Technology*, vol. 8, no. 5 (May 1990), pp. 691–97.

17. S. Benedetto and P. Poggiolini, "Theory of Polarization Shift Keying Modulation," *IEEE Transactions on Communications*, vol. 40 (April 1992), pp. 708–21.

18. S. Benedetto and P. Poggiolini, "Performance Evaluation of Polarization Shift Keying Modulation Schemes," *Electronics Letters*, vol. 26, no. 4 (March 1990), pp. 256–58.

19. S. Benedetto and P. Poggiolini, "Performance Evaluation of Multilevel Polarization Shift Keying Modulation Schemes," *Electronics Letters*, vol. 26, no. 4 (February 1990), pp. 244–46.

20. Jaeyon Kim, "Analysis of a Polarization Shift Keying System by Monte Carlo Simulation and Optimum Constellation Design," master's thesis, Department of Electrical and Computer Engineering, University of Arizona, August 1994.

21. D. J. Malyon et al., "PSK Homodyne Receiver Sensitivity Measurements at 1500 nm," *Electronics Letters,* vol. 19 (1983), 144–46.

22. L. G. Kazovsky, "Decision-Driven Phase-Locked Loop for Optical Homodyne Receivers," *Journal of Lightwave Technology,* vol. 3, no. 6 (December 1985), pp. 1238–47.

23. S. Haykin, *Communication Systems*, 2nd ed., John Wiley and Sons, 1983.

24. L. G. Kazovsky, "Impact of Laser Phase Noise on Optical Heterodyne Communication System," *Journal of Optical Communications,* vol. 7, no. 2 (1986), pp. 66–78.

25. G. Jacobson and I. Garrett, "Error-Rate Floor in Optical ASK Heterodyne Systems Caused by Nonzero (Semiconductor) Laser Linewidth," *Electronics Letters,* vol. 21, no. 7 (1985), pp. 268–70.

26. I. Garret and G. Jacobson, "The Effect of Laser Linewidth on Coherent Optical Receivers with Nonsynchronous Demodulation," *Journal of Lightwave Technology,* vol. 5, no. 4 (April 1987), pp. 551–60.

27. K. Iwashita, "Multi-Gbit/s Coherent Optical Fiber Transmission Technologies," Digest of International Conference on Optical Fiber Communication, 1991. Optical Society of America 1990, p. 207.

28. A. Yariv and P. Yeh, *Optical Waves in Crystals*, John Wiley and Sons, 1984.

29. B. E. A. Saleh and M. C. Teich, *Fundamentals of Photonics*, John Wiley and Sons, 1991.

30. E. Hecht, *Optics*, 2nd ed., Addison-Wesley, 1987.

31. I. Bar-David and J. Salz, "On Dual Optical Detection: Homodyne and Transmitted-Reference Heterodyne Reception," *IEEE Transactions on Communications*, vol. 36, no. 12 (December 1985), pp. 1309–15.

chapter
16

TIMING RECOVERY AND LINE CODING

In digital transmissions, a bit clock must be used to sample the received signal. Because the clock should be locked in both phase and frequency, the clock must be derived from the received signal. This clock derivation is called bit timing recovery, and is unique to digital communications (in contrast to analog communications).

Instead of deriving the clock from the received signal, one may ask, why not use a local clock of the same frequency at the receiver end to sample the received signal? In practice, because of the finite accuracy of crystal fabrication and oscillator circuit design, it is not possible to have a local clock of exactly the same frequency. When there is a slight difference in frequency, no matter how small, after a certain time of transmission, the frequency offset can cause errors and loss of synchronization. Example 16.1 illustrates this problem.

WHY NOT USE A LOCAL CLOCK?   Assume the transmitter clock is 10 MHz and the receiver clock is $10\text{MHz} + 1\text{ppm}$ or $10\text{MHz} + 10\text{Hz}$. For a transmission of 1 second, the number of input bits is 10 Mbits, but the receiver will "receive" 10 Mbits plus 10 extra bits due to the higher local clock. Clearly, there are errors in detection. More importantly, when the transmitted bits are in a time-division multiplexing (TDM) frame structure, such as T-carrier or SONET frames, additional bits detected will cause wrong framing or loss of synchronization (see chapter 8). As a result, bits received will be incorrectly interpreted. ∎

Example 16.1

Example 16.1 shows that it is impractical to use a separate local clock to sample the received signal. Since it is also impractical to send the transmitter clock over a long distance because of both high cost and relative phase wander, the clock must be derived from the received signal. To facilitate this, bit timing must be encoded into the transmitted bits. This means a frequent signal level transition, at least every few bits, is needed. If the signal level were constant over a long sequence of 1's or 0's, it would be difficult for the receiver to recognize the clock.

There are several ways to ensure a frequent level transition. One important technique is to use **line codes.** Generally speaking, a line code is a rule that maps a sequence of *binary* bits into a sequence of *waveform* symbols. The NRZ (Non-Return to Zero) code discussed in Chapter 1 is one simple example, where bit "1" is transmitted as a high-level signal and "0" is transmitted as a low-level signal. It is clear that the NRZ code is not adequate for timing recovery, because it cannot prevent a long sequence of 1's or 0's. Various line codes good for timing recovery in optical communications will be described later in the chapter.

Use of line coding can also maintain **dc balance.** As pointed out in Chapter 7, when the receiver is ac coupled, the received signal needs to be dc balanced to minimize inter-symbol interference (ISI). A good example is the biphase code discussed in Chapter 7. In general, when the overall transmission channel cannot pass the dc component of the signal, a dc-balanced line code is necessary.

In addition to the need for timing recovery and dc balance, a good line code in high-speed optical communications must meet other conditions. For example, its implementation must be *very* simple. As mentioned in Chapter 2, the transmission speed in optical communications is in general already at the speed limit of electronics (Gb/s). A difficult line code implementation would be impractical in optical communications. For the same reason of speed limitation, a line code should not introduce excessive redundancy. High redundancy means a large increase in transmission bandwidth, which can be expensive in high-speed communications. For example, although the biphase code is excellent in dc balance, it has 100 percent redundancy. Therefore, it is not a good choice in Gb/s optical communications. Another condition for line codes in optical communications is they have to be two-level. This is different from cable and radio transmissions, where multiple levels can be used. The primary reason for this constraint is that most optical transmission systems are binary. As a result, some good ternary (three level) codes cannot be used directly, such as the **alternative mark inversion** (AMI) code that has been used in T-carrier systems [1]. Some two-level variations of the AMI code will be discussed later.

Other than the use of line codes, another technique for timing recovery and dc balance is **scrambling,** which maps a long sequence of 1's or 0's into a sequence of random 1's and 0's. This technique is used in the SONET fiber optics transmission system [1]. One primary advantage of scrambling over line coding is there is no transmission redundancy added as in the case of line codes. Its main disadvantage, however, is the possibility for a certain input bit sequence to be mapped into a long sequence of 1's or 0's. Use of line coding, on the other hand, can guarantee a frequent signal level transition for any input data pattern.

When the transmitted signal is either line coded or scrambled, bit timing can be recovered by simple bandpass filtering. In high-speed optical communications, this bandpass timing recovery is commonly implemented by a **surface acoustic wave** (SAW) filter. A SAW filter is a very narrow bandpass filter that can have its resonant frequency above GHz. Therefore, they are good for timing recovery above Gb/s. **Phase-locked loops** (PLLs) are another alternative for bandpass filtering implementation. Because of their more complex structure, however, PLLs are rarely used when the bit rate is above 50 or 100 Mb/s.

This chapter explains the basic principle and important properties of bandpass filtering for timing recovery. It also discusses important two-level line codes and scrambling techniques for bit timing recovery and dc balance. Their trade-offs between transmission efficiency and implementation simplicity will be addressed. For illustration, some examples used in practical transmissions, such as SONET and fiber distributed data interface (FDDI), will be considered.

16.1   BANDPASS FILTERING FOR TIMING RECOVERY

As mentioned earlier, bandpass filtering is a basic technique for timing recovery. As illustrated in Figure 16.1, the basic component used in this method is a narrow bandpass filter. As a result, as long as the Fourier transform (not the power spectral density) of the received signal has a nonzero frequency content at the clock frequency and within the frequency band of the filter, the bandpass filter can reject other frequency components and regenerate a single frequency output at the bit clock. This use of a very narrow bandpass filter for timing recovery is called the **spectrum-line method** [2] and is the basic principle behind many timing recovery implementations.

PRINCIPLE OF SPECTRUM-LINE TIMING RECOVERY   Consider the return-to-zero (RZ) code discussed in Example 1.13. If the transmitted bits are random independent 1's and 0's with equal probability, the transmitted waveform can be considered to be the sum of a periodic clock sequence with half of the amplitude and a random sequence with zero mean as shown in Figure 16.2. The Fourier transform of the clock component has a peak at the bit frequency, and the Fourier transform of the random component is zero at the bit frequency. Therefore, if there is a narrow bandpass filter at the receiver with the received signal as the input, the clock component will pass through and the random part will be rejected. The output is thus a pure sinusoidal output at the clock frequency. ■

Example 16.2

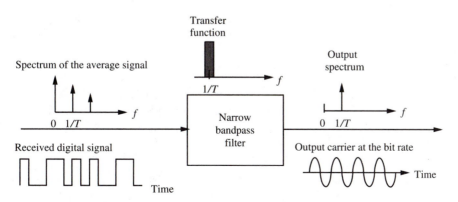

Figure 16.1   The bandpass filtering principle for bit timing recovery.

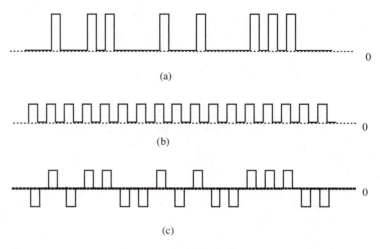

Figure 16.2　　(a) An RZ signal, (b) the clock component, and (c) the random zero-mean component.

<table>
<tr><td>**Example 16.3**</td><td>**FOURIER SERIES EXPANSION**　　The periodic component of the RZ signal illustrated in Example 16.2 can be expressed as a Fourier series:</td></tr>
</table>

$$\frac{1}{2}\sum_{k=1}^{\infty} p(t - kT_0) = \frac{1}{4} + \sum_{k=1}^{\infty} a_k \sin(2\pi kt/T_0)$$

where $p(t)$ is the unit amplitude RZ pulse (i.e., equal to 1 if $0 < t < T_0/2$ and zero otherwise), and a_k is the amplitude at frequency $2\pi k/T_0$. After the total signal is sent to the narrow bandpass filter centered at frequency $1/T_0$, the dc term and all components with $k > 1$ are rejected. Therefore, the filter output is

$$v_{out}(t) = a_1 \sin(2\pi t/T_0)$$

where

$$a_1 = \frac{1}{T_0} \int_0^{T_0/2} \sin(2\pi t/T_0)dt = \frac{1}{\pi}. \quad \blacksquare$$

Example 16.3 suggests the following generalization. Consider a PAM signal given by $r(t) = \sum_k A_k p(t - kT_0)$. If $r(t)$ is the received signal and $E[r(t)]$ is its average component, $E[r(t)] = E[A_k] \sum_k p(t - kT_0)$. Therefore, the average component is a periodic signal with period T_0. If $E[A_k] \neq 0$ and

$$z_1 = \frac{1}{T_0} \int_0^{T_0} p(t)e^{-j2\pi t/T_0}dt \neq 0 \qquad \textbf{[16.1]}$$

the signal at the bandpass filter output is a sinusoidal signal given by

$$v_{out}(t) = E[A_k]\{z_1 e^{j2\pi t/T_0} + z_{-1} e^{j2\pi t/T_0}\} = 2E[A_k] \mid z_1 \mid \cos(2\pi t/T_0 + \theta_z) \quad \textbf{[16.2]}$$

where $z_1 \overset{\text{def}}{=} \mid z_1 \mid e^{j\theta_z}$. To obtain a square pulse train from the sinusoidal signal for bit clock, a simple comparator circuit can be used.

16.2   THE *Q*-FACTOR IN BANDPASS FILTERING

One important parameter in bandpass filtering design is called the quality factor or simply **Q-factor**. To understand its definition and physical meaning, consider an LC bandpass circuit illustrated in Figure 16.3. This circuit is sometimes referred to as a **tank circuit** or **resonant circuit** because energy is stored either in the form of an electric field in the capacitor or in the form of a magnetic field in the inductor. To account for energy loss in the tank circuit, a resistor R is also included.

If a step-input current $I_0 u(t)$ drives the circuit, simple circuit analysis [3] says that the output voltage is

$$v_{out}(t) = u(t)\sqrt{\frac{L}{C}} I_0 \frac{\omega_0}{\omega_d} e^{-\alpha t} \sin(\omega_d t) \quad \textbf{[16.3]}$$

where $u(t)$ is the unit step function, $\alpha = 1/(2RC)$ is the damping constant, $\omega_0 = 1/\sqrt{LC}$ is the resonant frequency, and

$$\omega_d = \sqrt{\omega_0^2 - \alpha^2} \quad \textbf{[16.4]}$$

is the damped oscillation frequency of the tank circuit. When $R \to \infty$, α is zero and $\omega_d = \omega_0$. This means the circuit can oscillate forever at the resonant frequency.

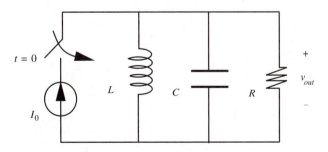

Figure 16.3   A bandpass filter based on an RLC tank circuit.

For a given tank circuit, the quality factor is defined as

$$Q \stackrel{\text{def}}{=} \frac{\omega_0}{2\alpha}. \qquad \textbf{[16.5]}$$

From this definition, when Q is large, Equation (16.3) can be approximated as

$$v_{out}(t) \approx u(t)\sqrt{\frac{L}{C}} I_0 e^{-\omega_d t/(2Q)} \sin(\omega_d t). \qquad \textbf{[16.6]}$$

Therefore, the larger the Q-value, the more cycles it takes for the oscillation to decay. In fact, it can be shown that $Q/(2\pi)$ is the ratio of the energy stored to the energy loss over one oscillation cycle due to damping (see Problem 16–1 and [3]). Therefore, the quality factor divided by 2π can be considered as the number of cycles for the tank circuit to dissipate all the energy from one unit step input.

Example 16.4

PULSE INPUT TO A TANK CIRCUIT   Consider a tank circuit of $Q = 10$. From Equation (16.3), the step response is shown in Figure 16.4. By linear superposition, if the input pulse $p(t) = u(t) - u(t - T_0/2)$, where $T_0 = 2\pi/\omega_d$, the output can be constructive. In other words, the oscillation output can essentially be doubled at frequency $1/T_0$. If the input pulse $p(t) = u(t) - u(t - T_0)$, the oscillation will be canceled at the end of the pulse. This shows why RZ is more important than NRZ for timing recovery.

If the pulse train is given by $x(t) = \sum_k p(t - kT_0)$, where $p(t)$ is an RZ pulse, the output will be a superposition of all step-input responses:

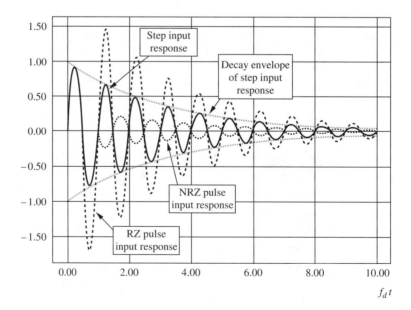

Figure 16.4   Responses of the tank circuit at $Q = 10$.

$$v_{out}(t) = \sum_{k=-\infty}^{\infty} e^{-\alpha(t-kT_0)} u(t - kT_0) \sqrt{\frac{L}{C}} I_0 \frac{\omega_0}{\omega_d} \sin(\omega_d t).$$

Without loss of generality, consider $0 < t < T_0$. Therefore,

$$v_{out}(t) = e^{-\alpha T_0/4} \sum_{k=-\infty}^{0} e^{k\alpha T_0} \sqrt{\frac{L}{C}} I_0 \frac{\omega_0}{\omega_d} \sin(\omega_d t).$$

Because $\alpha T_0 = 2\pi\alpha/\omega_d \approx 2\pi/Q$,

$$e^{-\alpha T_0/4} \sum_{k=-\infty}^{0} e^{k\alpha T_0} = \frac{e^{-\alpha T_0/4}}{1 - e^{-\alpha T_0}} = \frac{e^{-\pi/2Q}}{1 - e^{-2\pi/Q}} \approx \frac{Q}{2\pi}$$

when $Q/2\pi \gg 1$. Therefore,

$$v_{out}(t) = \frac{Q}{2\pi} \sqrt{\frac{L}{C}} I_0 \frac{\omega_0}{\omega_d} \sin(\omega_d t). \qquad \textbf{[16.7]}$$

The result shows that we see the steady state output from a periodic RZ pulse train has an amplitude proportional to Q, the quality factor. ∎

Example 16.4 shows that the quality factor Q represents the ability to store the clock information. In other words, the larger the Q, the larger the clock output that can be built up. Therefore, regenerating a strong and stable clock requires a large Q. Because it takes $Q/(2\pi)$ cycles for the oscillation to decay, a reasonable clock output can also be maintained as long as the next signal level transition comes within an interval small compared to $Q/(2\pi)$ clock cycles. As a result, when Q is large, the clock can also be sustained over a long interval in which there is no level transition. For further qualitative illustration, see Problem 16–1.

A large Q-factor is also important because it can tolerate level transitions that are not exactly at the bit interval. As pointed out in Chapter 7, timing variation (i.e., jitter) of level transitions can come from fiber dispersion and intersymbol interference. In the worst case, there can be a half-cycle timing jitter, which results in an out-of-phase contribution to the clock output. At a large Q, one such negative contribution is unimportant.

The discussion shows the importance of a large Q in timing recovery. However, there is a trade-off. It can be shown from circuit analysis that the tank circuit considered earlier has a 3 dB bandwidth equal to

$$\Delta f_{3dB} = \frac{1}{2\pi} \frac{\omega_0}{Q}. \qquad \textbf{[16.8]}$$

Therefore, the larger the Q, the smaller the frequency band of the narrow bandpass filter. When the transmitter bit clock is not exactly at the center frequency of the band, clock output can be zero. In other words, the larger the Q, the more sensitive the output clock is to the frequency deviation. Therefore, although a large Q can provide a large and stable clock output, it is not good when the bit rate of the received signal has a large variation. In bit timing recovery, the ability to recover the clock of an input signal over a wide frequency range is called **frequency acquisition,** and the ability to tolerate timing jitter and a long interval of zero transition is called **frequency tracking.** Therefore, there is a trade-off between frequency acquisition (needing a small Q) and frequency tracking (needing a large Q). This trade-off is illustrated in Figure 16.5.

Example 16.5	**LORENTZIAN BANDPASS FILTER** Assume a bandpass filter has the following spectrum for amplitude squared:

$$|H(\omega)|^2 = \frac{1}{1 + (\omega - \omega_0)^2/\Delta\omega_{3dB}^2}.$$

If the input signal is at a frequency of $2\Delta\omega_{3dB}$ away from the center frequency ω_0, the output clock amplitude is attenuated by a factor of $1/\sqrt{5}$ or 0.45. ∎

16.3   SURFACE ACOUSTIC WAVE FILTERS

As mentioned earlier, SAW filters are narrow bandpass filters. Because of their ability for high-speed timing recovery, they are commonly used in optical communications. A typical structure of a SAW filter is illustrated in Figure 16.6. As shown, it has several toothlike periodic structures interleaved with each other called **interdigital transducers** (IDTs). In operation, one of the IDTs is connected to the input, and the other is connected to the output. The input IDT converts the input voltage signal to an acoustic wave. Because the acoustic wave is in response to the input voltage, it can be a wideband signal. When it travels to the second IDT, however, the second IDT responds only to the frequency components within the narrow band of its resonant frequency. As a result, bandpass filtering is performed in the acoustic domain, and a sinusoidal voltage signal is generated at the second IDT.

Various SAW filter structures have been designed for better responsivity and lower insertion loss [4]-[6]. Some important characteristics of SAW filters are given in Tables 16.1 and 16.2. Basically, they are easy to build and are reliable against aging and temperature. On the other hand, they require special design for a given frequency and have insertion loss because of acoustic wave conversions. For comparison, Tables 16.1 and 16.2 also give characteristics of phase-locked loops, which are another implementation of timing recovery discussed next.

Table 16.1 Advantages of SAW filters over PLLs.

SAW Filters	Phase-Locked Loops
Simple to implement	IC design difficult above 50–100 MHz
Reliable performance possible	Performance somewhat unpredictable
Aging and temperature changes manageable	False lock, jitter peaking because of design errors

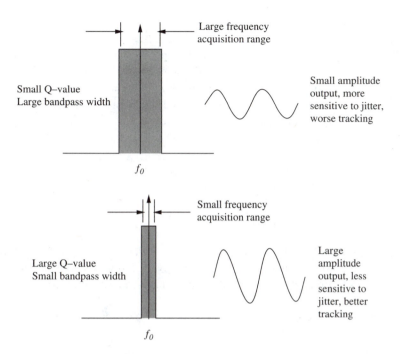

Figure 16.5   The trade-off between frequency acquisition and frequency tracking.

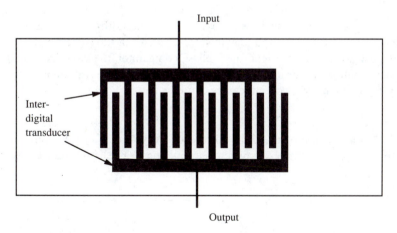

Figure 16.6   A surface acoustic wave (SAW) filter.

Table 16.2   Advantages of PLLs over SAW filters.

SAW Filters	Phase-Locked Loops
Center frequency set by pattern	Center frequency broadly adjustable
Center frequency may shift over time	Track clock automatically
Bandwidth controlled by pattern	Bandwidth independently controllable
High loss, additional amplification required	Low loss
Special SAW substrate required	Monolithic IC possible

16.4   PHASE-LOCKED LOOPS

As shown in Figure 16.7, a PLL consists of a (1) **phase detector** (PD), (2) **loop filter** (LF), and (3) **voltage-controlled oscillator** (VCO). When the PLL is locked to the frequency of the input signal, its VCO output $v(t)$ generates a continuous sinusoidal clock at the same frequency.

The operation of the PLL for timing recovery can be understood as follows. Let the input signal $y(t)$ be expressed as

$$y(t) = A_y \cos[\omega_0 t + \theta(t)] \qquad \text{[16.9]}$$

and the VCO output be

$$v(t) = A_v \cos[\omega_0 t + \phi(t)] \qquad \text{[16.10]}$$

where ω_0 is the natural or free-running frequency of the VCO and $\theta(t)$ and $\phi(t)$ are the phases of the two signals, respectively. When $y(t)$ is at a different frequency, the phase term $\theta(t)$ is a linear function of time with slope equal to 2π times the frequency offset.

When the two signals are sent to the phase comparator, the phase comparator generates a voltage output proportional to the phase difference of the two input signals. Mathematically, the phase detector output can be expressed as

$$e(t) = d(\theta - \phi) \qquad \text{[16.11]}$$

where $d(x)$ is a function of the phase difference. A typical $d(x)$ function is depicted in Figure 16.8. In general, the phase difference function $d(x)$ should have a positive slope

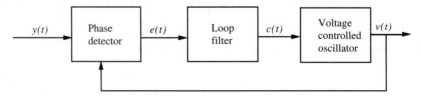

Figure 16.7   Block diagram of a PLL.

$d_\theta > 0$ and zero value at $x = 0$. This condition is needed to form a feedback loop for the VCO to regenerate the clock. Therefore, when $|\theta(t) - \phi(t)|$ is small,

$$e(t) \approx d_\theta[\theta(t) - \phi(t)].$$ **[16.12]**

The phase detector output is sent to a loop filter, which can be of different forms. The loop filter controls the frequency tracking and acquisition in phase locking the input signal. In general, the choice of the loop filter in a PLL determines the order of the PLL. For example, a first-order PLL has a constant gain for its loop filter:

$$L(s) = K_L$$ **[16.13]**

and the second-order PLL has its loop filter in the form

$$L(s) = K_L \frac{s + K_1}{s + K_2}$$ **[16.14]**

where $L(s)$ is the Laplace transform of the filter. The relationship between the loop filter and the PLL frequency response will be shown shortly.

The loop filter output is then used to drive the VCO, whose instantaneous frequency output is proportional to the input voltage. That is,

$$\frac{d}{dt}[\omega_0 t + \phi(t)] = \omega_0 + c(t)$$

or

$$\frac{d\phi(t)}{dt} = c(t)$$ **[16.15]**

where $c(t)$ is the loop filter output.

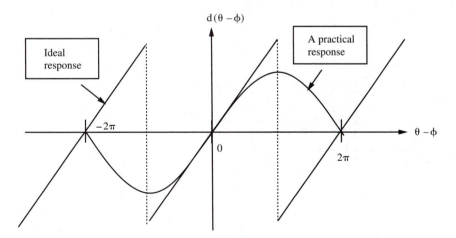

Figure 16.8   Characteristic function of a typical phase detector.

From Equation (16.15), taking the Laplace transform on the both sides gives

$$s\Phi(s) = C(s) = L(s)E(s)$$

if

$$|\theta(t) - \phi(t)| < \pi. \qquad \textbf{[16.16]}$$

When the approximation given by Equation 16.12 is valid,

$$s\Phi(s) = d_\theta L(S)[\Theta(s) - \Phi(s)]$$

which results in

$$\Phi(s) = \frac{d_\theta L(s)}{s + d_\theta L(s)}\Theta(s). \qquad \textbf{[16.17]}$$

Therefore, the frequency response of the input phase $\Theta(s)$ is

$$H(s) = \frac{\Phi(s)}{\Theta(s)} = \frac{s\Phi(s)}{s\Theta(s)} = \frac{d_\theta L(s)}{s + d_\theta L(s)}. \qquad \textbf{[16.18]}$$

This is a low-pass response. Because this is the frequency response with respect to ω_0, we see the frequency response of a PLL is equivalent to a bandpass filter. This equivalence is illustrated in Figure 16.9, where the phase detector first performs a downward frequency shift before phase detection.

Example 16.6

FREQUENCY ACQUISITION RANGE OF A PLL　　Assume that a PLL is locked to the phase of an input signal $\cos(\omega_{in}t + \theta)$. The phase difference between the input signal and the VCO output is thus a constant. If the difference is δ, the total phase of the VCO output is

$$\omega_0 t + \phi(t) = \omega_0 t + \omega_v t + \theta + \delta$$

where $\omega_v = \omega_{in} - \omega_0$ is the frequency offset between the input signal and the natural frequency of the VCO. Because the phase difference is δ, the VCO input is $c = L(0)d(\delta)$, with $L(0)$ being the dc gain of the loop filter. Because

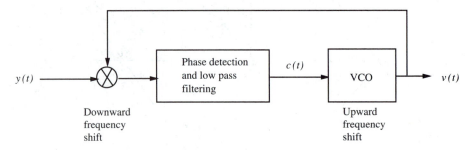

Figure 16.9　　Equivalence of a PLL to a bandpass filter. The carrier is first shifted down in frequency, low-pass filtered, and then shifted up again.

$$c = \frac{d\phi(t)}{dt} = \omega_v$$

the frequency offset is

$$\omega_v = L(0)d(\phi) = K_L d(\delta).$$

Thus the frequency offset, $|\omega_v|$, should be within $d_p L(0)$, where d_p is the peak value of the phase detector output. This suggests two observations. First, the frequency acquisition range is proportional to the dc gain of the loop filter. Therefore, the larger the dc gain, the larger the input frequency range that the PLL can acquire. Second, when the phase function $d(\delta)$ has a positive slope, the phase offset δ is inversely proportional to K_L at a frequency offset. In other words, the phase offset is less sensitive to input frequency variation when K_L is large. These two observations illustrate the tradeoff between frequency acquisition and tracking. ∎

BANDWIDTH OF THE PLL   Assume a first-order PLL is used. That is, $L(s) = K_L$. In this case, the transfer function of the PLL is   **Example 16.7**

$$H(s) = \frac{1}{1 + s/(d_\theta K_L)}.$$

This shows the PLL has a 3 dB bandwidth of $d_\theta K_L$ in rad/sec within which the clock can be recovered. This is consistent with the observation made in Example 16.6. ∎

16.5   PREPROCESSING FOR BANDPASS FILTERING

In general, most digital signals cannot be directly input to a narrow bandpass filter or PLL for bit timing recovery. If the signal has zero component at the bit rate, direct use of bandpass filtering results in zero output. To solve this problem, some nonlinear preprocessing can be used. Depending on the specific type of digital signal, there are various ways of preprocessing.

Decision Feedback   One method of preprocessing uses the detected output to demodulate the received signal. The demodulated output is then sent to a bandpass filter or PLL for timing recovery. This is illustrated in Example 16.8.

BIPHASE CODE   For biphase coded data, 1's and 0's have opposite transitions. Earlier discussion explained that the bandpass outputs caused by opposite transitions cancel each other. One way to solve this problem based on decision feedback is shown in Figure 16.10, where the detected output is used to change the transition direction of 1's. To compensate for the delay due to detection, the received signal sent to the XOR gate is delayed by one bit interval. Because the low-to-high transitions at the nonlinear preprocessing output are determined by the received signal or original clock in the implementation, a precise delay of one bit interval is not critical. ∎   **Example 16.8**

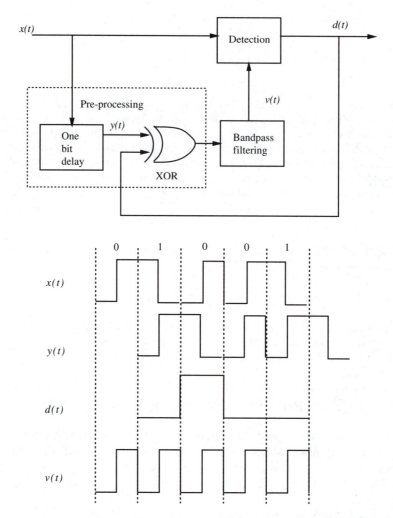

Figure 16.10   Decision feedback preprocessing for timing recovery.

Exclusive-Or   For some line codes, the received signal can be used directly to exclusive-or a time-delayed version of itself. This provides necessary level transitions for timing recovery.

<table>
<tr><td>**Example 16.9**</td><td>**NRZ CODE**   Because the average of NRZ is a constant, it has zero frequency content at the bit rate. An exclusive-or (XOR) circuit can solve this as shown in Figure 16.11. The function of the cir-</td></tr>
</table>

cuit is essentially to convert the NRZ signal to RZ, which can then be used for timing recovery from bandpass filtering. ∎

Squaring   For signals such as AMI codes that have opposite polarities, one common preprocessing technique is to square the received signal as shown in Figure 16.12. This can remove mutually destructive level transitions for timing recovery.

AMI CODE   Consider the AMI code, where 1's have alternate signs of RZ pulses, and 0's are simply zero. Without preprocessing, pulses that alternate in sign result in zero output at the bandpass filtering output. In this case, simply taking the square will remove the sign. ∎ | **Example 16.10**

The recovered clock from squaring can be quantified as follows. For a PAM signal $r(t) = \sum_k A_k p(t - kT_0)$ with data values A_m and A_n that are statistically independent and of zero mean, one has

$$E[A_m A_n^*] = \begin{cases} A^2 & \text{if } n = m \\ 0 & \text{otherwise.} \end{cases}$$

Therefore,

$$E[|r(t)|^2] = A^2 \sum_{m=-\infty}^{\infty} |p(t - mT_0)|^2.$$

Because this is a periodic signal, it has the following Fourier series expansion:

$$x(t) = \sum_{m=-\infty}^{\infty} |p(t - mT_0)|^2 = \frac{1}{T_0} \sum_n z_n e^{j2\pi nt/T_0}$$

where

$$z_n = \int_0^{T_0} |p(t)|^2 e^{-j2\pi nt/T_0} dt = \int_0^{T_0} p(t)p^*(t)e^{-j2\pi nt/T_0} dt$$

$$= \frac{1}{2\pi} \int_{-\infty}^{\infty} P(\omega)P^*(\omega - 2\pi n/T_0)d\omega.$$

[16.19]

If $z_1 \neq 0$ the clock output is nonzero and equal to $2\Re\{z_1 e^{j2\pi t/T_0}\}A^2/T_0$.

16.6   LINE CODES FOR TIMING RECOVERY

The above discussion shows that the key to timing recovery is to ensure a frequent level transition in the transmitted signal. By introducing a certain redundancy, a line code can map an input bit sequence to an output sequence with sufficient level transitions.

As mentioned earlier, because the data rate is already high in optical communications, minimum increase in transmission bandwidth and simple timing recovery are important

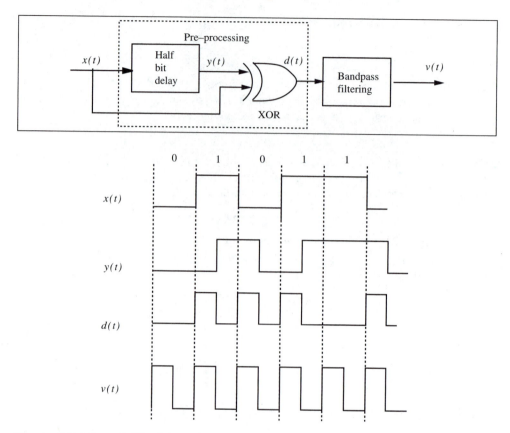

Figure 16.11   Half-bit delay and XOR preprocessing for timing recovery.

criteria to a good line code. To reduce the bandwidth increase with simple encoding and decoding, various mBnB codes [7], mB1C codes [8], and DmB1M codes [9] have been introduced for optical communications. All these codes are block codes. The parameter m in the above notations denotes the number of input bits per block, n denotes the output block size, C or M denotes either the **complementary bit** or **mark bit** added, and D denotes **differential encoding.** The coding efficiency of these block codes is m/n or $m/(m+1)$. With a large m or a large m/n ratio, the bandwidth inefficiency can be made small. These codes are explained in detail below.

mB1M Codes   An mB1M code is a block code. For every input block of m bits, one mark bit (i.e., 1) is added to the end of the block. For example, a 4B1M block code adds a "1" bit at the end of every four input bits. If the input sequence were 0010 1000, the output

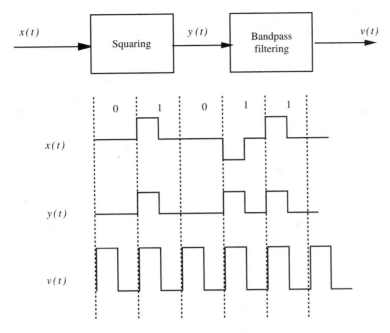

Figure 16.12   Squaring preprocessing for timing recovery.

would be 00101 10001, where the mark bits are in bold. It is easy to calculate that this code has a transmission efficiency of 80 percent.

In general, the mB1M code is used with RZ pulse transmission. The mark bit thus ensures a level transition at least every $m + 1$ bits.

If the RZ pulse is used, the worst case mB1M coded sequence for timing recovery is 0000100001 . . . , where $m = 4$ is assumed. If a narrow bandpass filter of a quality factor Q is used for timing recovery, the sinusoidal signal at the filter output has a magnitude proportional to $Q/(m + 1)$. Therefore, at a given received signal power, the Q to m ratio must be large for a strong and stable clock recovery. At a given Q-value, there is thus a tradeoff between clock recovery and transmission efficiency. ∎

**Example
16.11**

---

mB1C Codes   The complementary bit used in mB1C codes [8] is opposite to the last bit of the m information bits. For example, for a 5B1C code and an input block of 01001, the encoded block is 01001**0**. If the input block is 01000, the encoded block is 01000**1**. This code ensures there is one transition every $m + 1$ bits. By using proper preprocessing before bandpass filtering, a bit clock can be reliably recovered.

mBnB Codes   In the previous mB1M or mB1C codes, a redundant bit is added at the end of each block. In general, the redundancy can be added through mapping of an m-bit input block to an n-bit output block with $n > m$. This class of codes is called mBnB codes. Some important examples of mBnB codes are illustrated below in Examples 16.12–16.14.

Example 16.12	**4B5B IN FDDI** A fiber distributed data interface (FDDI) network uses a 4B5B code for transmission. The mapping is given in Table 16.3. In this table, each 5-bit codeword has 2 to 4 1's. In other words, there are no all-zero or all-one blocks. This ensures level transitions within each block. ∎

Table 16.3   4B5B code in FDDI.

4B Input	5B Output
0000	11110
0001	01001
0010	10100
0011	10101
0100	01010
0101	01011
0110	01110
0111	01111
1000	10010
1001	10011
1010	10110
1011	10111
1100	11010
1101	11011
1110	11100
1111	11101

One important observation from the above example is that the dc average of each output block is between 40 percent and 80 percent. This is in contrast to the dc average ranging from 0 to 100 percent without coding. In other words, in addition to ensuring transitions, the use of the code reduces the dc variation by 40 percent.

Compared to mB1C or mB1M codes, there is a tradeoff between implementation complexity and dc balance. First we note that mBnB codes require memory access to get the translation between m-bit input and n-bit output. Since memory access time (e.g., 10 nsec) can be slow compared to the transmission bit rate, there is a potential speed limit for mBnB codes. On the other hand, mB1M and mB1C codes have a dc value from $1/(1 + m)$ to 100 percent. Therefore, when m is large, they have a poor dc balance.

ZERO PARITY mBnB CODE   A special class of mBnB codes has an even number of bits in every *n*-bit block and there are $n/2$ 0's and 1's each per block [10]. For example, for $n = 8$, there are

$$N = \frac{8!}{4!4!} = 70 > 2^6 = 2^m$$

different code words with equal 1's and 0's. Therefore, there can be $m = 6$ information bits per block, and the coding efficiency is 75 percent. ∎

Example 16.13	

5B6B CODE   Some undersea optical fiber transmission systems in Europe use a 5B6B code with the code table given in Table 16.4. The encoding table shows that the code can have two possible codewords for a given input block. The choice of the two possible codes depends on the most recent codeword block whose number of 1's is not equal to three. If the most recent block has four 1's, the choice will be the codeword of two 1's. If the most recent block has two 1's, the choice will be the codeword of four 1's. This encoding method ensures dc balance around $1/2$, and is called **bimode mapping**. ∎

Example 16.14	

Table 16.4   Bimode mapping of dc balance in the 5B6B code.

5B Input	6B Output	5B Input	6B Output
00000	011101/100010	10000	111010/000101
00001	101110/010001	10001	100011
00010	010111/101000	10010	100101
00011	000111	10011	100110
00100	101011/010100	10100	101001
00101	001011	10101	101010
00110	001101	10110	101100
00111	001110	10111	011011/100100
01000	110101/001010	11000	110001
01001	010011	11001	110010
01010	010101	11010	110100
01011	010110	11011	101101/010010
01100	011001	11100	111000
01101	011010	11101	110011/001100
01110	011100	11110	101101/010010
01111	110110/001001	11111	100111/011000

Code Mark Inversion Codes   To avoid bit redundancy in mBnB codes, another important family of line codes for both timing recovery and dc balance in optical communications is called the **code mark inversion** (CMI) code. This code is the counterpart of the AMI code in cable and radio transmissions. As illustrated in Figure 16.13, for the AMI code, +1 and −1 alternate for bit 1's. Therefore, the dc average is zero. However, because the AMI code has three levels: +1, 0, and −1, it cannot be applied directly to optical communications. Some variations from the three-level AMI code for dc balance are illustrated in Figure 16.13.

To avoid transition in every bit interval, as in the case of biphase code, the CMI code has no transition for 1's. Instead, it alternates between a high and low level. For 0's, on the other hand, there is always a transition from low to high at the middle of the bit interval. This transition every bit 0 ensures proper timing recovery. Figures 16.13*d* and 16.13*e* give other variations. In both cases, 1's alternate between 1 and 0 as in the CMI code, and the direction of transition for "0" is not fixed. In Figure 16.13*d*, the direction of transition ensures a transition at every bit boundary. In Figure 16.13*e*, the direction of transition minimizes the frequency of transitions at the bit boundary. In other words, the direction of transition maintains a continuity from the previous bit. In general, the higher the transition frequency, the larger the high-frequency content of the signal's power spectrum. Therefore, Figures 16.13*d* and 16.13*e* present a trade-off between transmission bandwidths and timing contents. The CMI code is a compromise choice. (For more detailed discussion of line coding, readers may find [11]–[13] useful.)

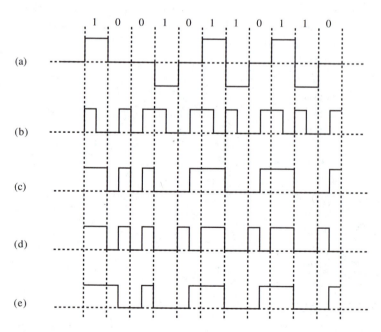

Figure 16.13   DC balance codes: (*a*) AMI code, (*b*) biphase or Manchester code, (*c*) code mark inversion code (CMI), and (*d*) and (*e*) other two-level AMI codes.

16.7 FIXED TRANSITION CODES

Line codes are all designed to ensure frequent transitions. With sufficient transitions, the signal can be sent to a bandpass filter for timing recovery. As mentioned earlier, when the transmission speed is high, SAW filters are used. However, one limitation of SAW filters is their inability to lock signals of different frequencies. In the case of multiple access, where transmitter clocks have different frequencies, this becomes a problem for the receiver in timing recovery.

To solve this problem, a special kind of line code called **fixed transition** (FT) codes can be used [14]. An (n,k) FT code has n-bit codewords with the following two properties:

1. The number of transitions from 0 to 1 in every n-bit block is always k.
2. The first bit of each block is always 1, and the last bit is always 0. This ensures a 0 to 1 transition at the block boundary.

As an example, permissible codewords of the (12,4) FT code are illustrated in Figure 16.14. Because the number of transitions is fixed regardless of the transmitted data, the block timing can be recovered by simply using a divide-by-k counter that divides the number of transitions by k. As illustrated in Figure 16.15, if the phase of the countdown is correct, the output waveform will be a square wave synchronized with the signal. The period of the recovered clock is slower than the bit clock by a factor $2n$. By using exclusive-or processing on the output of the counter and a delayed version, a square wave clock that is a factor of n lower in frequency can be generated. This recovered clock is the block clock because each block has n bits.

In this implementation, the block timing can be recovered by using simple counters and logic gates. Because the counter only counts the number of transitions, a FT code can recover timing without respect to the input signal frequency. Therefore, FT codes are attractive in high-speed optical local area networks, where transmitter frequencies are different.

Parallel Data Latching   Because the clock recovered is the block clock, we need to generate its delayed versions to latch all bits within the same block. An implementation is

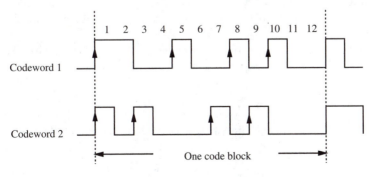

Figure 16.14   A (12,4) fixed transition code.

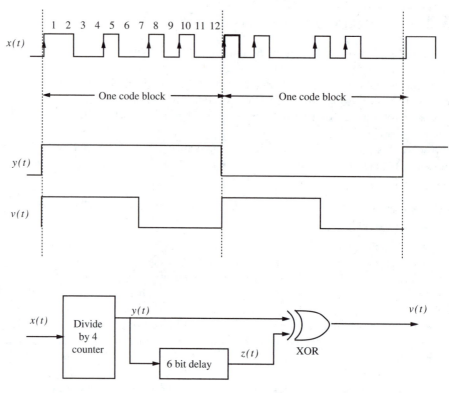

Figure 16.15   Block timing for the fixed transition code.

shown in Figure 16.16, where bits are successively latched by the delayed clocks. From this, we note the serial bit stream is also automatically transformed into a parallel stream, which is desirable since we can reduce the high speed requirement in subsequent processing.

Coding Efficiency and Complexity   One important question in using FT codes is their transmission efficiency. To calculate it, the number of possible codewords for a given (n, k) pair must be found.

To do so, note from Figure 16.16 that there are $2k - 1$ possible transitions (both 0 to 1 and 1 to 0) among $n - 1$ positions, where the first transition at the beginning of the block is fixed. Consequently, the number of possible codewords is

$$S = C(n - 1, 2k - 1)$$ **[16.20]**

where $C(n, m) = \frac{m!(n-m)!}{n!}$ is the combinatorial function. Therefore, the coding efficiency is

$$\eta(n, k) = \frac{\lfloor \log_2 S \rfloor}{n} = \frac{\lfloor \log_2 C(n - 1, 2k - 1) \rfloor}{n}.$$ **[16.21]**

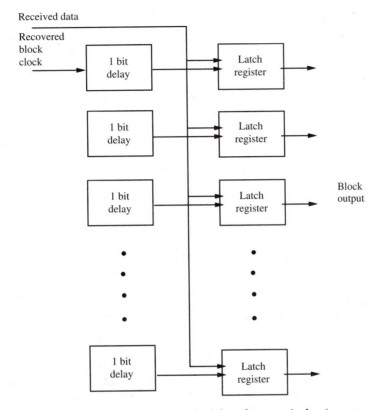

Figure 16.16   Parallel delay latch lines for using the fixed transition code.

The efficiency is shown in Figure 16.17 for different values of n. For reasonable block sizes (say $n = 8$ to 20), the efficiency ranges from 60 percent to 80 percent.

Implementing these codes raises other interesting design aspects such as how to identify the first transition of each code block. Detailed discussion can be found in [14][15]. Some experimental results are shown in Figure 16.18.

16.8   SCRAMBLING

All the binary line codes discussed earlier use redundancy to ensure frequent transitions. Another important technique, which does not add redundancy but can help timing recovery, is called **scrambling.** In principle, scrambling maps data one-to-one to a scrambled sequence. If the input data has a long output sequence of 0's or 1's, the output will look like a random 1's and 0's sequence. Because scrambling does not introduce any redundancy,

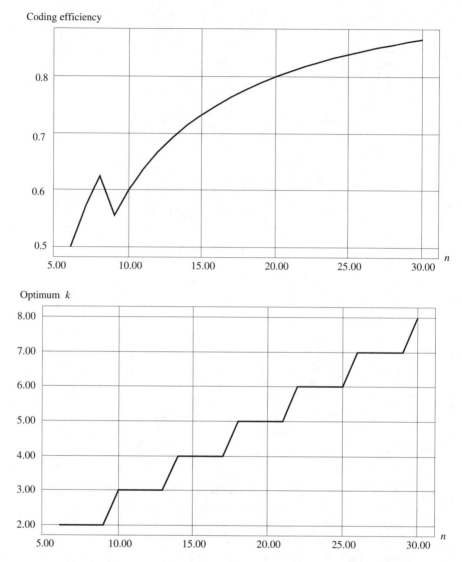

Figure 16.17   Optimum efficiency for different (n, k) fixed transition codes.

there can be an input sequence that generates a long sequence of 0's or 1's; however, in practice this is unlikely unless the input sequence matches the random sequence exactly.

In implementation, there are two different scrambling techniques: **self-synchronized** and **frame-synchronized** scramblers. Both types of scramblers use a **maximum-length shift register** (MLSR) to generate a periodic but seemingly random sequence. As a result, the output sequence from a MLSR is called a **pseudo random sequence.** As discussed in

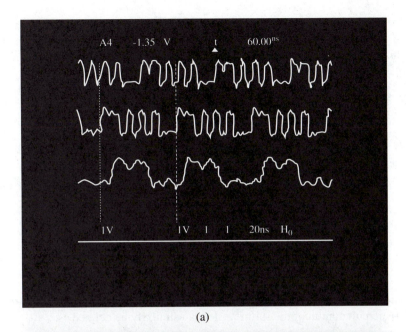

(a)

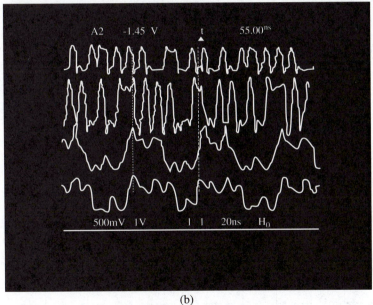

(b)

Figure 16.18   Experimental results of recovered block timing from (*a*) a fixed transition pattern and (*b*) different patterns at 200 Mb/s, where the top row is the transmitted data, the second row is the received data, the third row is the recovered block, and the fourth row is the clock delayed by 11 bits (only shown in [*b*]). A (12,4) code is used, with each bit equal to 5 nsec.

Appendix 16–A, a pseudo-random sequence generated by an n-bit MLSR has a period of $r = 2^n - 1$. The remainder of this section explains the structure of a MLSR and the self-synchronized and frame-synchronized scramblers.

16.8.1 MAXIMUM-LENGTH PSEUDO-RANDOM SEQUENCE GENERATION

A MLSR is a shift register with a feedback structure shown in Figure 16.9, where h_i can be either 1 or 0. From the structure, the sequence follows the recursive relationship:

$$x_k = h_1 x_{k-1} \oplus h_2 x_{k-2} \oplus \ldots \oplus h_n x_{k-n} \qquad \textbf{[16.22]}$$

where $\oplus$ is the modulo-2 summation.

For the random sequence $\{x_k\}$, $(k \geq 0)$, its binary D-transform is defined as

$$X(D) = \sum_{k=0}^{\infty} x_k D^k. \qquad \textbf{[16.23]}$$

This is similar to the Z-transform. The operator D is used to indicate a one-bit delay. The characteristic polynomial of the shift register can similarly be defined as:

$$H(D) = 1 + h_1 D + \ldots + h_n D^n. \qquad \textbf{[16.24]}$$

From Equations (16.22)–(16.24), $X(D)$ can be expressed in terms of the initial values in the shift register and $H(D)$. That is,

$$\begin{aligned}
X(D) &= \sum_{k=0}^{\infty} \sum_{i=1}^{n} h_i x_{k-i} D^k = \sum_{i=1}^{n} h_i D^i \sum_{k=0}^{\infty} x_{k-i} D^{k-i} \\
&= \sum_{i=1}^{n} h_i D^i \left[x_{-i} D^{-i} + \ldots + x_{-1} D^{-1} + X(D) \right].
\end{aligned}$$

Combining $X(D)$ and using modulo–2 addition,

$$X(D) = \frac{\sum_{i=1}^{n} h_i D^i \left(x_{-i} D^{-i} + \ldots + x_{-1} D^{-1} \right)}{H(D)} \overset{\text{def}}{=} \frac{I(D)}{H(D)} \qquad \textbf{[16.25]}$$

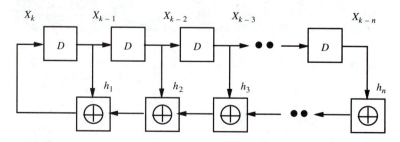

Figure 16.19   A maximum length shift register structure.

where

$$I(D) = \sum_{i=1}^{n} h_i D^i (x_{-i} D^{-i} + \ldots + x_{-1} D^{-1}) \qquad \textbf{[16.26]}$$

is called the initial polynomial of the shift register. Equation (16.25) shows that long division can be used to compute $\{x_k\}$ if the initial polynomial $I(D)$ and the characteristic polynomial $H(D)$ are known.

A 3-BIT MLSR   Consider a MLSR with $H(D) = 1 + D + D^3$. In other words, the MLSR is a three-bit shift register. If $I(D) = 0$, or $x_{-1} = x_{-2} = x_{-3} = 0$, from Equation (16.25), the output sequence is all zero. On the other hand, if $x_{-1} = x_{-2} = 0$ and $x_{-3} = 1$, $I(D) = 1$ and $X(D) = 1/H(D)$. Taking long division gives   **Example 16.15**

$$X(D) = (1 + D + D^2 + D^4) + D^7(1 + D + D^2 + D^4) + \ldots.$$

It can be noted that the output sequence has a period of 7 with the periodic pattern $(1,1,1,0,1,0,0)$. ∎

In general, for an n-bit shift register and a given feedback, there can be at most 2^n different possible values or states in its shift registers. At each clock shift, the shift register can go from one state to another. Because the number of states is finite, however, it will repeat the same transitions once it goes back to the same state. According to the feedback structure of the MLSR shown in Figure 16.19 or Equation (16.25), if the system is in the all-zero state (i.e., the shift registers have all 0's), it will remain in the same state forever. Therefore, the largest cycle of an n-bit shift register is $2^n - 1$. A feedback shift register that can have the largest cycle is called a MLSR. Various important properties of a MLSR are given in Appendix 16–A.

16.8.2 FRAME-SYNCHRONIZED SCRAMBLER

A frame-synchronized scrambler is shown in Fig. 16.20. This scrambler scrambles the input sequence $\{b_k\}$ by

$$c_k = b_k \oplus x_k \qquad \textbf{[16.27]}$$

where x_k is the MLSR output and c_k is the scrambled output sent to the channel. At the receiver, if the same MLSR is used and at the same phase of the transmitter MLSR,

$$c_k \oplus x_k = b_k \oplus x_k \oplus x_k = b_k. \qquad \textbf{[16.28]}$$

Therefore, this is called a frame-synchronized scrambler because the two MLSR's must be synchronized.

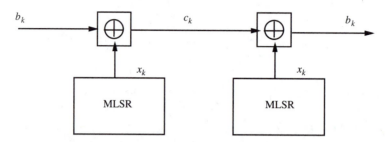

Figure 16.20   Frame-synchronized scrambler and descrambler.

Example 16.16   **SONET**   In SONET, a 7-bit frame-synchronized scrambler is used with $H(D) = 1 + D^6 + D^7$. The shift registers are reset with all 1's at the beginning. To help synchronize the state of the scramblers, scrambling is not performed over the framing bytes (A1 and A2) and the STS–1 ID byte (C1) of the SONET frame (see Chapter 8 for details). The framing bytes have a fixed framing pattern for the scrambler to recognize the start of the scrambling point. ∎

16.8.3   SELF-SYNCHRONIZED SCRAMBLER

A self-synchronized scrambler is shown in Figure 16.21. Mathematically,

$$c_k = b_k \oplus h_1 c_{k-1} \oplus \ldots \oplus h_n c_{k-n}.$$

A derivation similar to that discussed for the maximum sequence generation shows that

$$C(D)H(D) = B(D) + I(D)$$

or

$$C(D) = \frac{B(D)}{H(D)} + \frac{I(D)}{H(D)}. \qquad \textbf{[16.29]}$$

Therefore, $C(D)$ consists of two parts: one is called the **zero-state** response (the first term), and the other is called the **zero-input** response.

To descramble the scrambled sequence at the receiver, as shown in Figure 16.21, the output sequence $\hat{B}(D)$ is related to $C(D)$ by

$$\hat{B}(D) = C(D)H(D) + I'(D) = B(D) + I(D) + I'(D). \qquad \textbf{[16.30]}$$

Therefore, if the initial seed, or the state, is the same (i.e., $I[D] = I'[D]$), the original data can be recovered. If $I(D) \neq I'(D)$, there will be some initial bit errors, which are usually not important.

Propagation Errors   The advantage of the self-synchronized scrambler over the frame synchronized scrambler is that there is no need to synchronize the scrambler with re-

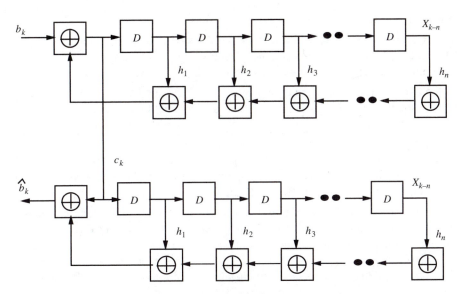

Figure 16.21   Self-synchronized scrambler and descrambler.

spect to the input data. However, the self-synchronized scrambler has an error propagation problem. If one bit error is received in sequence $\{c_k\}$, say the mth bit, then

$$\hat{B}(D) = [C(D) + D^m]H(D) + I'(D) = B(D) + I(D) + I'(D) + D^m H(D). \quad \textbf{[16.31]}$$

Therefore, even in the case of $I(D) = I'(D)$, there are a total of t errors generated because of the single error, where t is the number of nonzero coefficients in $H(D)$ and is always odd for a MLSR polynomial. (Why?) Therefore, the number of additional errors is always even.

ERROR PROPAGATION   If $H(D) = 1 + D + D^3$, one error at the mth bit will result in three errors at the mth, $(m + 1)$–th, and $(m + 3)$–th bits. ∎

Example 16.17

16.9 SUMMARY

1. To recover bit timing, two fundamental steps are: (1) use a narrow bandpass filter with its center frequency close to the bit rate, and (2) ensure the input signal to the filter has a nonzero frequency content at the bit rate. Specifically, one needs

$$z_1 = \frac{1}{T_0} \int_0^{T_0} E[r(t)]e^{j2\pi t/T_0} dt \neq 0$$

where $E[r(t)]$ is the average signal input to the filter.

2. If z_1 defined above is zero, preprocessing is needed to generate a signal with nonzero z_1. Depending on the specific signaling format of the input signal, preprocessing techniques include: decision feedback modulation, exclusive-or, and squaring.

3. The Q-factor is an important parameter in characterizing the performance of a narrow bandpass filter or tank circuit. The Q-value divided by 2π is the ratio of the energy stored in the circuit to the energy loss over one oscillation cycle. Therefore, the larger the Q value, the longer the tank circuit can sustain oscillation.

4. The Q-factor is also related to the 3 dB bandwidth of the narrow bandpass filter. Specifically, it is the ratio of the center resonant frequency to the 3 dB bandwidth. Therefore, the larger the Q, the smaller the 3 dB bandwidth.

5. The choice of the Q value represents a trade-off between frequency acquisition and frequency tracking in bit timing recovery. In general, the larger the Q value, the better the output clock holds up against timing jitter and long intervals without transitions. This provides a better frequency tracking. On the other hand, the smaller the Q value, the larger the 3 dB bandwidth. This provides better frequency acquisition. This trade-off is also true for PLLs because they are equivalent to narrow bandpass filtering.

6. In optical communications, SAW filters are commonly used for bit timing recovery. They are narrow bandpass filters consisting of two interdigital transducers (IDTs) of the same resonant frequency. Because the resonant frequency is high, SAW filters can provide timing recovery for speeds higher than Gb/s.

7. PLLs are another implementation of narrow bandpass filters for timing recovery. In general, they can lock onto the phase of the input signal over a wider frequency range than SAW filters. Because of their feedback structure, however, it is difficult to operate PLLs higher than 100 Mb/s.

8. To ensure a frequent transition of the transmitted signal for timing recovery, there are two primary techniques: line coding and scrambling. Line coding can guarantee a frequent transition for any transmitted data. The price paid is a certain transmission inefficiency. On the other hand, scrambling one-to-one maps an input sequence to a scrambled sequence. Therefore, it adds no redundance but can generate a long sequence of 0's or 1's for certain input patterns.

9. There are two types of binary codes for timing recovery. The first type ensures a minimum frequency of transitions. Examples of this type are mB1M, mB1C, and mBnB codes. The second type has a fixed number of transitions in every fixed size block. This type of code is called a fixed transition code. The first type of code needs a narrow bandpass filter for timing recovery. For the fixed transition codes, on the other hand, a simple divide-by-k counter can generate the block timing of the received signal, where k is the number of transitions per block.

10. Fixed transition codes can be used in multiple access optical local area networks where the bit rate is high and the transmitter clocks are different. In contrast to narrow bandpass filtering, the same timing recovery circuit can be used for different clock input. The limitation of this approach, on the other hand, is its sensitivity to timing jitter.

11. There are two types of scramblers: frame-synchronized scramblers and self-synchronized scramblers. Frame-synchronized scramblers require synchronization between the scrambler and descrambler. Self-synchronized scramblers require no synchronization, but they are subject to error propagation.

12. Both types of scramblers require the use of a maximum-length shift register (MLSR). A MLSR has an n-bit shift register and a feedback structure. According to the feedback structure, a MLSR can be characterized by a characteristic polynomial $H(D)$. An n-bit MLSR generates a periodic sequence of period $2^n - 1$ and its characteristic polynomial is a primitive polynomial.

APPENDIX 16–A: PROPERTIES OF MAXIMUM-LENGTH SEQUENCES

This appendix presents some important properties of a MLSR.

1: Irreducibility of H(D). From Equation (16.25), if $H(D)$ is not an irreducible polynomial or $H(D) = H_1(D)H_2(D)$, then $X(D) = 1/H_2(D)$ if $I(D) = H_1(D)$. This implies a smaller period sequence. Therefore, irreducibility of $H(D)$ is one necessary condition to have a maximum-length sequence.

2: Expression of Periodic Sequences. If, and only if, $X(D)$ has a period of p, $X(D) = X_0(D)/(1 + D^p)$, where $X_0(D)$ is a polynomial of degree less than p.

This property can be seen as follows. First, if, and only if, $X(D)$ has a period of p, then

$$X(D) = X_0(D) + D^p X_0(D) + D^{2p} X_0(D) + \dots$$

for some polynomial $X_0(D)$ of degree less than p. Because the right-hand side of the above equation is a geometric series with ratio D^p, its sum is equal to

$$X(D) = \frac{X_0(D)}{1 + D^p}.$$

3: Period of an Irreducible Polynomial. An irreducible binary polynomial $H(D)$ of degree n divides the polynomial $1 + D^{2^n-1}$. Proof of this property is quite involved and is not given.

IRREDUCIBLE POLYNOMIALS OF DEGREE 3 Consider $H(D) = 1 + D + D^3$. It is an irreducible polynomial. Because $1 + D^7 = H(D)(1 + D + D^2 + D^4)$, $H(D)$ is a factor of $1 + D^7$, where $7 = 2^3 - 1$.   **Example 16.18**

On the other hand, another polynomial $H(D) = 1 + D + D^2 + D^3$ is not an irreducible polynomial because $H(D) = (1 + D)(1 + D + D^2)$. Therefore, it cannot be expected to be a factor of $1 + D^7$. In fact, it is a factor of $1 + D^4$, which is not a factor of $1 + D^7$. ■

From Property 1, note that the characteristic polynomial $H(D)$ of degree n of a MLSR must be irreducible. Property 3 says that $H(D)Q(D) = 1 + D^{2^n-1}$ for some $Q(D)$. From Equation (16.25),

$$X(D) = \frac{I(D)}{H(D)} = \frac{I(D)Q(D)}{1 + D^{2^n-1}}.$$

From Property 2, therefore, the sequence generated from an irreducible polynomial must have a period of $2^n - 1$. However, this may not be the minimum period. It can have a smaller period p with p being a factor of $2^n - 1$.

Example 16.19

IRREDUCIBLE POLYNOMIAL NOT GOOD FOR MLSR   Consider $H(D) = 1 + D + D^2 + D^3 + D^4$. It is an irreducible polynomial. Therefore, it is a factor of $1 + D^{15}$. However, it is also a factor of $1 + D^5$. Therefore, this $H(D)$ cannot generate a maximum length of 15. ■

The above discussion suggests the following definition:

Definition: Primitive Polynomial. A polynomial is called a primitive polynomial if it is an irreducible polynomial and is not a factor of $1 + D^p$ with $p < 2^n - 1$.

According to the definition, a primitive polynomial is the necessary and sufficient condition to generate a maximum-length sequence. If an irreducible polynomial is not a primitive polynomial, from the discussion, its period must be a factor of $2^n - 1$. Therefore, we can have the following property.

4: Sufficient Condition for an Irreducible Polynomial to be also a Primitive Polynomial.   For an irreducible polynomial of degree n, it is also a primitive polynomial if $2^n - 1$ is irreducible.

The above properties describe the conditions for a feedback shift register to generate a maximum-length sequence. There are two other important properties that describe the dc balance and spectrum properties of the maximum-length sequence itself.

5: Balance.   For a maximum-length sequence of period $2^n - 1$, there are $(2^{n-1} - 1)$ 0's and 2^{n-1} 1's. This follows from the basic fact that all states of the shift register are reached during the length of $2^n - 1$ except the all zero state. If $r = 2^n - 1$, the number of 1's is $(r + 1)/2$, and the number of 0's is $(r - 1)/2$. Therefore, when r is large, the numbers of 1's and 0's are about the same.

6: Shift-and-Add.   If a maximum-length sequence from $-\infty$ to ∞ is added to a phase-delayed version of itself, the new sequence is another phase delay of the original sequence.

This property can be verified as follows. From the feedback structure of the shift register, note that $x_k = \sum_{i=1}^{n} h_i x_{k-i}$. From the modular-2 summation, this is equivalent to $\sum_{i=0}^{n} h_i x_{k-i} = 0$, where $h_0 = 1$. Taking the D-transform gives $H(D)X(D) = 0$.

When $X(D)$ is binary and added by its shift version $D^l X(D)$, the combined sequence is $X'(D) = (1 + D^l)X(D)$. Because $H(D)X(D) = 0$, $H(D)X'(D) = (1 + D^l)H(D) \times X(D) = 0$. Therefore, the combined sequence also follows the feedback property of the shift register. Therefore, there should exist an m such that $D^m X(D) = X'(D) = (1 + D^l)X(D)$.

The balance property and the shift-and-add property can help to explain the spectral property of the maximum-length sequence discussed below. First, map the binary sequence $\{x_k\}$ into an antipodal sequence $\{s_k\}$, where $s_k = -1$ if $x_k = 0$, and $s_k = 1$ if $x_k = 1$. Time average autocorrelation of the binary antipodal maximum sequence is

$$R_s(l) = \frac{1}{r} \sum_{k=0}^{r-1} s_k s_{k+l}.$$

Because $s_k s_{k+l}$ is 1 if s_k and s_{k+l} are of the same sign, and $s_k s_{k+l}$ is -1 if s_k and s_{k+l} are of different signs,

$$s_k s_{k+l} = 1 - 2x_k \oplus x_{k+l}.$$

From the shift-and-add property,

$$R_s(l) = 1 - \frac{2}{r} \sum_{k=0}^{r-1} x_k \oplus x_{k+1} = \begin{cases} 1 - \frac{2}{r} \sum_{k=0}^{r-1} x_{k+m} & \text{for some } m \text{ if } l \neq 0 \\ 1 & \text{if } l = 0. \end{cases}$$

From the balance property,

$$R_s(l) = \begin{cases} 1 & \text{if } l = 0 \\ -\frac{1}{r} & \text{if } l \neq 0. \end{cases} \qquad \textbf{[16.32]}$$

Because the autocorrelation function is discrete and has a period r, the power spectrum of the maximum-length sequence is also periodic and discrete. By performing the discrete Fourier transform (DFT), one has

$$\Phi(m) = \sum_{0}^{r-1} R_s(l) e^{-j2\pi ml/r} \quad 0 \leq m \leq r - 1$$

$$= 1 + \frac{1}{r} - \frac{1}{r} \sum_{0}^{r-1} e^{-j2\pi ml/r} = \begin{cases} \frac{1}{r} & \text{if } m = kr, k \text{ is an integer} \\ 1 + \frac{1}{r} & \text{if } m \neq kr. \end{cases}$$

Note that the distance between two adjacent spectral points is $1/rT_0$. Therefore, in the limit r goes to infinity, the spectrum approaches white (i.e., constant). The autocorrelation function and the spectrum of a maximum-length sequence are shown in Figure 16.22.

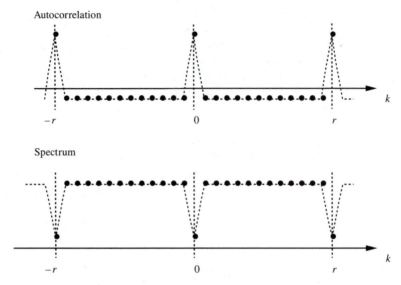

Figure 16.22 Autocorrelation function and spectrum of a maximum-length sequence output.

PROBLEMS

Problem 16–1 Physical Meaning of Quality Factor: Consider the tank circuit shown in Figure 16.3. Turning on and off the current produces an initial current that will oscillate for some time.

a. If $R \to \infty$, the oscillation will last forever and $\omega_d = \omega_0$. Thus you can assume the voltage signal output has the form $V = V_0 \cos(\omega_0 t)$. Show that the instantaneous power that flows into the capacitor is the same as the power that flows out of the inductor and given by $P_C = -\frac{1}{2} C V_0^2 \omega_0 \sin(2\omega_0 t)$.

b. From (a), show that the total energy stored in either the capacitor or inductor is $\frac{1}{2} C V_0^2$.

c. Over one clock cycle, $2\pi/\omega_0$, what is the total energy dissipation over the resistor R? Assume the energy dissipation is small compared to the energy stored in L or C so that the same voltage expression $V = V_0 \cos(\omega_0 t)$ given in (a) can be used.

d. From (b) and (c) and the definition of the quality factor given by Equation 16.5, show that

$$Q = 2\pi \frac{E_s}{E_d}$$

where E_s is the total energy stored in the inductor and capacitor and E_d is the energy dissipated by R over one cycle.

Problem 16–2 Zero Transition Tolerance: Consider a received signal $x(t) = \sum_k A_k p(t - kT_0)$ input to a tank circuit of $Q = 100$, where $p(t)$ is an RZ pulse and A_k can be either 1 or 0. During the initial transmission, assume all 1's are transmitted so that the tank circuit output reaches its steady state given by Equation (16.7). Once the steady state is reached, consecutive 0's are transmitted.

    a. What is the largest number of consecutive 0's that can be transmitted before the peak value of the tank circuit output goes down to 50 percent of the peak value at its original steady state?

    b. Do the same computation as in (*a*) for 10 percent of the original peak value.

Problem 16–3 Trade-off Between Frequency Acquisition and Tracking: Consider a binary transmission system where RZ is used for signaling and a narrow bandpass filter like that shown in Figure 16.3 is used for bit timing recovery.

    a. If 0's and 1's are equally likely in transmission, what is the average peak value of the filter output with respect to that given by Equation (16.7)?

    b. Assume at a certain time point the oscillation output of the bandpass filter is at its average level from (*a*). How many zero bits can be tolerated before the peak value of the oscillation decreases to $x \times 100$ percent of its peak average? Give the answer in terms of x and Q.

    c. Under the scenario given by (*b*), to tolerate up to 30 bits of consecutive 0's, what is the lower limit of the Q-value if the peak oscillation will not decrease below the average peak value given by Equation (16.7) when $Q = 20$?

    d. If the input bit clock can fluctuate $\pm 10^{-4}$ of its nominal bit clock from the central frequency of the bandpass filter, find the upper limit of the Q value so that the corresponding peak value variation is within 3 dB.

    e. From (*c*) and (*d*), what can you say about the trade-off between the clock acquisition and tracking?

Problem 16–4 First Order PLL: Consider a PLL with a loop filter of a constant transfer function. That is, $L(s) = K_L$. Also assume the phase detector has a slope of d_θ. The phase error is defined as $\phi_e(t) = \theta(t) - \phi(t)$. If the PLL is turned on at $t = 0$, the input phase $\theta(t)$ of a constant frequency input can be generally described as

$$\theta(t) = \omega_v t + \theta_0$$

where ω_v is the difference between the input signal's frequency and the PLL's resonant frequency. From the assumptions, find the steady state phase error $\phi_e(\infty)$ using the final value property of the Laplace transform:

$$x(\infty) = \lim_{s \to 0} s X(s). \qquad\qquad \textbf{[16.33]}$$

Problem 16–5 Second-Order PLL: Consider a second-order PLL with $L(s) = (K_1 + s)/(K_2 + s)$.

    a. Derive the transfer function $\Phi(s)/\Theta(s)$. Show that there is a zero at $-K_1$ and two poles of product $d_\theta K_L K_1$.

    b. From different relative locations of the zero to the two poles, plot corresponding qualitative transfer functions of $\Phi(s)/\Theta(s)$. What condition results in a peak in one of the cases?

  c. What is the frequency acquisition range?

  d. Use Equation (16.33) to find the steady state phase error $\theta - \phi$. Assume $\theta(t) = \omega_v t + \theta_0$ for the phase of the received signal. From the result and (*c*), comment on the trade-off between frequency tracking and frequency acquisition.

  e. How does the trade-off in (*d*) affect the peak of the transfer function in (*b*)? What are possible undesirable effects?

Problem 16–6 Decision Feedback: If the XOR gate used in Figure 16.10 is replaced by an OR gate for biphase codes, will the bit timing recovery still work? If yes, what will be the difference?

Problem 16–7 Exclusive-Or: If the time delay used in Figure 16.11 for NRZ codes is not exactly half of the bit period, will the bit timing recovery still work? If yes, what will be the difference? Use Equation (16.19) for a quantitative analysis.

Problem 16–8 Squaring Preprocessing: If squaring is used for preprocessing an AMI signal for timing recovery, find the coefficient z_1 from Equation (16.19).

Problem 16–9 Line Code for Sufficient Transitions: For the 5B1C code discussed, what is the minimum frequency of transition from 0 to 1 or 1 to 0? What is the maximum frequency of transition? Give scenarios for all these cases.

Problem 16–10 Line Codes for DC Balance: The dc average over a certain time interval T of signal $x(t)$ is defined as

$$x_{dc}(t) \stackrel{\text{def}}{=} \frac{1}{T} \int_{T-t}^{t} x(t')dt'.$$

Find the peak dc variation for the NRZ code, AMI code, biphase code, and CMI code at (*a*) $T = 2T_0$ and (*b*) $T = 10T_0$.

Problem 16–11 FDDI: For the FDDI code table given in Table 16.3:

  a. Find the largest possible dc value over a long interval. Give an example input sequence.

  b. Find the smallest possible dc value over a long interval. Give an example input sequence.

  c. If the dc value is calculated as the average of the last 10 encoded bits, find the largest possible dc variation.

Problem 16–12 Bimode Mapping: For the 5B6B code given by Table 16.4, if the dc value is calculated as the average of the last 12 encoded bits, find the largest possible dc variation.

Problem 16–13 Fixed Transition Code:

  a. From Figure 16.17, find the minimum codeword size that has a coding efficiency of at least 80 percent.

  b. From (*a*), if the coding is performed by using a codeword table, how large must the memory size be?

  c. If the highest available speed of PLLs is 100 Mb/s and bipolar electronics for memory and logic gates can operate at 500 Mb/s, find the maximum achievable bit rate using the FT code from (*a*).

  d. From (*a*)-(*c*), comment on the net transmission bit rate with or without using the FT code.

Problem 16–14 Initial Polynomial: If the primitive polynomial of a MLSR is $H(D) = 1 + D + D^3$, calculate the initial polynomial for $x_{-1} = 1$, $x_{-2} = 1$, and $x_{-3} = 0$. Also compute x_i for $i = 0$–7.

Problem 16–15 Frame Synchronized Scrambler:

a. Let the MLSR given in Problem 16–14 be used as a frame-synchronized scrambler. If it has the same initial polynomial, find the output sequence for an input sequence of all 1's. If the MLSR used in the descrambler has an initial polynomial of $I(D) = 1$, find the descrambled output.

b. As mentioned in the text, "scrambled output" is not always random for some input sequences. Find input sequence examples that result in the scrambled output being (i) a period of 2 sequence and (ii) an all 1's sequence.

Problem 16–16 Shift-and-Add Property and Code Division Multiple Access:

a. From the shift-and-add property, show that the descrambled output of a frame synchronized scrambler is another scrambled output of the same type MLSR if the scrambler and descrambler have two different initial polynomials.

b. Assume the frame-synchronized scrambler of Problem 16–15 is used and consider an input sequence of "blocks" of bits. Each block is 7 identical bits (i.e., $2^n - 1$). Therefore, each block can be considered as a bit of "1" or "0" of the bit period equal to the period of the MLSR. If the scrambler and descrambler have two different initial polynomials, from (a), what will the scrambled output look like if the scrambler and descrambler have two different initial polynomials? You may show an example. The importance of having the same initial polynomial in frame-synchronized scrambling allows an initial polynomial to be used as a key in scrambling. Unless the descrambler has the same key, the original input cannot be easily recovered. This concept of using scrambling and encoding data by keys is called **direct sequence** code-division multiple access.

Problem 16–17 Self-Synchronized Scrambler: Consider a MLSR of the characteristic polynomial $H(D) = 1 + D^3 + D^4$.

a. If the polynomial is $I(D) = 1$, calculate the zero-input output of the self synchronized scrambler.

b. If the input polynomial is $B(D) = D/(1 + D^5)$, find the zero-state output of the scrambler for the first 10 bits.

c. Find the total scrambled output from (a) and (b). Also find the initial polynomial of the descrambler that results in the most initial errors.

Problem 16–18 Error Propagation of Self-Synchronized Scrambler: For the same output computed in Problem 16–17b, if the sixth bit has a transmission error, find the descrambled output. How many errors will result?

REFERENCES

1. John Bellamy, *Digital Telephony*, 2nd ed. John Wiley and Sons, 1991.

2. E. A. Lee and D. G. Messerschmitt, *Digital Communication*, 2nd ed. KAP, 1994.

3. Charles A. Desor and Ernest S. Kuh, *Basic Circuit Theory,* McGraw-Hill, 1969.

4. A. J. Budreau and P. H. Carr, "Narrow Band Surface Wave Filters at 1 GHz," *Proceedings of Ultrasonics Symposium*, 1972, pp. 218–19.

5. R. L. Rosenberg et al., "Optical Fiber Repeated Transmission Systems Utilizing SAW Filters," *IEEE Transactions on Sonics and Ultrasonics*, vol. 30, no. 3 (May 1983), pp. 119–26.

6. J. De Klerk and B. R. McAvoy, eds., *Collected Papers on Surface Acoustic Waves and Signal Processing*, Piscataway, NJ: IEEE Press, 1979.

7. Y. Takasaki et al. "Optical Pulse Formats for Fiber Optical Digital Communications," *IEEE Transactions on Communications*, vol. 24 (April 1976), pp. 404–13.

8. N. Yoshikai et al., "mB1C Code and Its Performance in an Optical Communication System," *IEEE Transactions on Communications*, vol. 32 (February 1984), pp. 163–68.

9. S. Kawanishi et al., "DmB1M Code and Its Performance in a Very High Speed Optical Transmission System," *IEEE Transactions on Communications*, vol. 36 (August 1988), pp. 951–56.

10. J. N. Franklin and J. R. Pierce, "Spectra and Efficiency of Binary Codes without DC," *IEEE Transactions on Communications*, vol. 20, no. 6 (December 1972), p. 1182.

11. B. P. Lathi, *Modern Digital and Analog Communication Systems*, 2nd ed., Holt, Rinehart and Winston, 1989.

12. E. A. Lee and D. G. Messerschmitt, *Digital Communication*, KAP, 1988.

13. J. G. Proakis, *Digital Communications*, 2nd ed., McGraw-Hill, 1989.

14. M. K. Liu and D. G. Messerschmitt, "A Fixed Transition Coding for High Speed Timing Recovery at 200 Mb/s in Fiber Optics Networks," *Proceedings of International Conference on Communication*, by IEEE, 1987, pp. 188–92.

15. M. K. Liu, "Low-Cost High-Speed General Service Fiber Optic Network," Ph.D. dissertation, Department of Electrical Engineering and Computer Science, University of California, Berkeley, 1987.

chapter

17

OPTICAL AMPLIFICATION

As discussed in Chapter 4, power loss in fiber transmission places a fundamental limit on the speed and distance product. When various couplings and splittings are used in an optical network or a photonic switch, as discussed in Chapters 2 and 11, power loss can also limit the network size and switch throughput.

To overcome the power loss problem, optical amplifiers can be used. Compared to electronic amplifiers that amplify electrical signals, optical amplifiers have several important advantages. First, they have a much larger amplification bandwidth. An optical fiber amplifier, for example, can have a bandwidth of several thousand GHz. Therefore, they are attractive to all-optical networking, where speed bottlenecks from electronics are removed by optics implementation. Second, optical amplifiers can amplify multiple optical inputs at different wavelengths simultaneously. Therefore, they are attractive to applications such as wavelength-division multiplexing (WDM).

There are two primary types of optical amplifiers: **semiconductor amplifiers** and **fiber amplifiers** [1]. A semiconductor amplifier is a laser diode operated below threshold. Therefore, it can amplify input signals but cannot generate a coherent light by itself. A fiber amplifier is a fiber section that has a positive medium gain. To achieve this, the fiber is doped with ions such as Er^{+3}. When carriers of the doped ions are excited by external optical pumping, they can be stimulated back to the ground state by the incident light. This results in stimulated emission and provides the positive optical gain. Among all optical fiber amplifiers, erbium-doped fiber amplifiers (EDFA) that amplify light at around 1.55 μm are the most mature [1]. For amplification at around 1.3 μm, neodymium- and praseodymium-doped fiber amplifiers have also been recently developed [2]–[4]. Compared to EDFA's, they are relatively immature but are promising.

17.1   SYSTEM APPLICATIONS

An optical amplifier can be placed in different parts of a communication system. Depending on their locations in a transmission link, optical amplifiers can be used as (1) power amplifiers, (2) in-line amplifiers, and (3) receiver amplifiers. These three uses are illustrated in Figure 17.1.

Power Amplifiers   A power amplifier is placed right after a light source to boost the transmitted signal power. It is used when the light source has limited output power. If the power from the light source is already high, the amplifier can saturate and introduce distortion.

Receiver Amplifiers   In contrast to power amplifiers, receiver amplifiers amplify weak signals received before photodetection. In this application, power saturation is insignificant because of the weak power. Because of amplified spontaneous emission (ASE) noise of optical amplifiers, however, a minimum incident power is still required for a satisfactory SNR.

In-line Amplifiers   When the transmission distance is long, a number of in-line amplifiers need to be used. In this case, optical amplifiers are inserted periodically in the

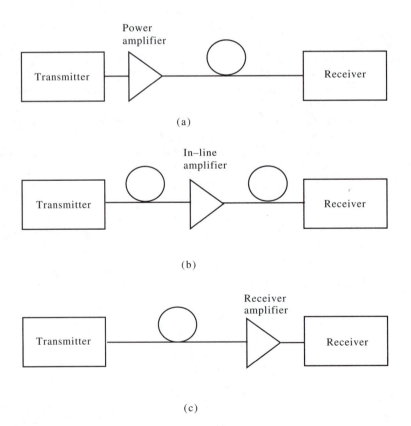

Figure 17.1   Different uses of optical amplifiers.

transmission line. In fiber **soliton** transmission, where optical pulses can propagate without broadening, in-line amplifiers are used to maintain a minimal power level for optical non-linearity (see Chapter 18).

USE OF RECEIVER AMPLIFIERS   Consider a transmission link where the total transmission loss is 50 dB. If the receiver sensitivity for the given transmission link is –20 dBm and the available light source power is 10 dBm, determine the use of the following two optical amplifiers: (1) an ideal optical amplifier of 20 dB gain, and (2) an optical amplifier of 20 dB gain but which saturates at 15 dBm output.

> **Example 17.1**

From the given condition, a total $50 - [10 - (-20)] = 20$ dB power gain is required. For the first case, the amplifier can be put anywhere in the system because the ideal amplifier provides the necessary 20 dB gain.

The second amplifier cannot be used as the power amplifier, because it saturates at 15 dBm. At the receiver side, however, the incident power is only –40 dBm, so it can be used to boost the signal to –20 dBm without saturation. ∎

USE OF IN-LINE AMPLIFIERS   In Example 17.1, if a total gain of 100 dB is required, at least five 20 dB amplifiers are needed. Because ASE noise is generated in each amplifier and is proportional to the amplifier gain (see Section 17.5), a high signal power input to each amplifier needs to be maintained. As a result, the amplifiers should be used as in-line amplifiers. If the transmission system is used for optical soliton transmission, their use as in-line amplifiers is also necessary to keep a high optical nonlinearity. ∎

> **Example 17.2**

17.2   SYSTEM CRITERIA

Example 17.1 shows that power saturation is a problem in optical amplification. Noise and crosstalk are other degradation factors. Below, important criteria in optical amplifier design are discussed.

1. High Power Gain. A large power gain is the main purpose of using optical amplifiers. Depending on the input power, a power gain of 10–30 dB can be achieved [5]. As noted earlier, gain saturation reduces the gain as the input power increases.

2. High External Pumping Efficiency. The required external power is proportional to the required amplification gain. To achieve a large gain at a small external power, a high external pumping efficiency is needed. This requirement leads to the development of EDFAs that surpass their predecessors based on the stimulated Raman scattering effect. A typical EDFA has a pumping efficiency of 6–10 dB/mW.

3. Small Saturation Effect. As mentioned earlier, the amplifier gain decreases as the incident power increases because of the gain saturation effect. It is thus desirable to have a small effect or gain drop. As will be shown later, gain saturation is not critical in semiconductor amplifiers but is significant in fiber amplifiers.

4. Large Bandwidth. An optical amplifier of a large amplification bandwidth is desirable for two important reasons. First, it can be used to amplify multiple signals of different wavelengths simultaneously. This is important to wavelength-division multiplexing

(WDM) applications. Second, at a large bandwidth, the amplifier gain will be insensitive to the wavelength of the incident signal. This allows the transmission system to be robust against a wide range of wavelength drift.

5. Polarization Independence. In general, the power gain also depends on the polarization of the incident light. This is caused by different cavity confinement factors of the different polarizations. To overcome this problem, two amplifiers can be combined together as shown in Figure 17.2.

6. Low Added Noise. Because of spontaneous emission inside the amplifier channel, fiber amplifiers also add noise to the incident signal. Moreover, because of the amplifier gain, the spontaneous emission noise is also amplified. As mentioned earlier, this noise is called amplified spontaneous emission (ASE) noise. As will be shown later, it adds a minimum power penalty of 3 dB in detection. For amplifiers not properly designed, the power penalty due to ASE noise can be even worse.

7. Small Crosstalk. When an optical amplifier is used to amplify multiple incident light signals at different wavelengths, it is important to make sure there is no interference from one signal to another. If the amplifier gain is independent of the total input signal power, there will be no interchannel interference (ICI) or crosstalk. Because of gain saturation, however, the amplification gain is input signal power dependent. As a result, when the power of one channel goes down, other channels can experience a larger power gain. This results in ICI or crosstalk.

In practice, the average power of input signals is constant, and only their simultaneous power can change because of intensity modulation. Therefore, as long as the gain of the amplifier does not follow immediately with the simultaneous power of input signals, the amplifier power gain should remain a constant. As will be shown, EDFAs meet the above condition because the carriers have a long lifetime at the excited metastable state.

8. Proper Operating Wavelength. As mentioned in Chapter 4, two important wavelengths used in optical transmissions are 1.3 μm and 1.55 μm. At 1.3 μm, fiber dispersion is minimal, and at 1.55 μm, fiber attenuation is minimal. Because optical amplifiers can only overcome attenuation, it is desirable to operate amplifiers at 1.3 μm. In general,

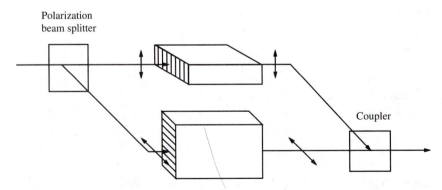

Figure 17.2   Polarization-independent amplification using two separate amplifiers for two orthogonally polarized waves.

this is not a problem if semiconductor amplifiers made of III–V compounds are used. When EDFAs are used, however, they can only amplify light at around 1.55 μm because of the energy bands of erbium. This motivates the search for other types of fiber amplifiers at 1.3 μm [2]–[4].

9. Low Coupling Loss. When an optical amplifier is used in an optical link, it adds additional coupling loss. A low coupling loss can be achieved when the amplifier and optical fibers have a good optical match. Because they have the same fiber structure, fiber amplifiers are attractive from this consideration.

According to the above criteria, Table 17.1 shows the characteristics of semiconductor amplifiers and EDFAs. These two types of optical amplifiers will be discussed in detail in the next two sections.

Table 17.1 Comparison between semiconductor and erbium-doped fiber amplifiers.

Properties	Semiconductor Amplifiers	EDFAs
Power gain	Good	Good
Effect of gain saturation	Small	Large
Pumping efficiency	High	High
Bandwidth	Small for FP's	Large
Polarization dependence	Yes	Yes
ASE	Small	Large
Crosstalk	Large	Negligible
Operating wavelength	1.3–1.55 μm	1.55 μm
Coupling loss	A few dB	Negligible

17.3   SEMICONDUCTOR AMPLIFIERS

As mentioned earlier, semiconductor amplifiers are laser diodes that are biased below the threshold current. To provide amplification, the active layer of a semiconductor amplifier has a positive medium gain but not large enough for laser emission. This section describes and analyzes various semiconductor amplifier characteristics. In particular, the section quantifies the medium gain at a given current pumping, explains the gain saturation effect, characterizes the interchannel interference in multichannel amplification, derives the amplifier gain and bandwidth, and discusses two types of semiconductor amplifiers: Fabry-Perot (FP) and traveling wave (TW).

17.3.1   EXTERNAL PUMPING AND RATE EQUATION

Similar to laser diodes, a positive optical gain in semiconductor amplifiers comes from external current injection. From the rate equation of the carrier density given by Equation (12.30),

$$\frac{\partial N(t)}{\partial t} = R_p(t) - R_s(t) - \frac{N(t)}{\tau_r} = \frac{J(t)}{qd} - \Gamma v_g a[N(t) - N_{th}]N_{ph}(t) - \frac{N(t)}{\tau_r} \quad \text{[17.1]}$$

where

$$R_p(t) = \frac{J(t)}{qd} \quad \text{[17.2]}$$

is the external pumping rate from current injection,

$$R_s(t) = \Gamma a v_g [N - N_{th}]N_{ph} \quad \text{[17.3]}$$

is the net stimulated emission rate, and τ_r is the combined time constant due to spontaneous emission and various carrier recombination mechanisms. From Equations (3.11) and (12.32), $R_s = v_g g(N)N_{ph}$ with $g(N)$ given by

$$g(N) = \Gamma a(N - N_0) - \alpha_m \stackrel{\text{def}}{=} \Gamma a(N - N_{th}) \quad \text{[17.4]}$$

where α_m is the distributed medium loss, Γ is the confinement factor, v_g is the group velocity of the incident light, and N_{th} is the threshold carrier density to have a positive gain.

In the steady state, $\partial N/\partial t = 0$, and

$$R_p = R_s + \frac{N}{\tau_r} = v_g N_{ph}g(N) + \frac{N - N_{th}}{\tau_r} + \frac{N_{th}}{\tau_r} = \left[v_g N_{ph} + \frac{1}{\Gamma a \tau_r}\right]g(N) + \frac{N_{th}}{\tau_r}.$$

Therefore,

$$g(N) = \frac{J/qd - N_{th}/\tau_r}{v_g N_{ph} + 1/(\Gamma a \tau_r)} = \frac{g_0}{1 + N_{ph}/N_{ph,sat}} \quad \text{[17.5]}$$

where

$$N_{ph,sat} \stackrel{\text{def}}{=} \frac{1}{\Gamma a v_g \tau_r} \quad \text{[17.6]}$$

is called the **saturation photon density** and

$$g_0 = \Gamma a \tau_r \left\{\frac{J}{qd} - \frac{N_{th}}{\tau_r}\right\} \quad \text{[17.7]}$$

is the medium gain at zero photon density.

From the definition given by Equation (17.6), it is desirable to have a small $\Gamma a \tau_r$ product to have a large $N_{ph,sat}$. Example 17.3 shows that $N_{ph,sat}$ is large in semiconductor amplifiers. Therefore, gain saturation is in general not a problem.

Example 17.3

EFFECT OF GAIN SATURATION   Consider an InGaAsP semiconductor amplifier of dimension $L = 200$ μm, $w = 5$ μm, and $d = 0.5$ μm. Assume it has a gain constant $a = 1.0 \times 10^{-20}$ m^2, confinement factor $\Gamma = 0.3$, group velocity $v_g = 2.0 \times 10^8$ m/sec, recombination constant

$\tau_r = 1$ nsec, and threshold carrier density $N_{th} = 1.0 \times 10^{24}$ m^{-3}. If 100 mA dc current is supplied to the amplifier, the pumping rate is

$$R_p = \frac{I}{qwdL} = 1.25 \times 10^{33} \ (\text{m}^3\text{sec})^{-1}.$$

The zero-power medium gain is thus

$$g_0 = \Gamma a(R_p\tau_r - N_{th}) = 750 \ \text{m}^{-1}$$

and the saturating photon density is

$$N_{ph,sat} = \frac{1}{\Gamma a v_g \tau_r} = 1.25 \times 10^{21} \ \text{m}^{-3}.$$

If the incident light power P_{in} is 1 μW at wavelength 1.5 μm, the photon density is

$$N_{ph} = \frac{P_{in}}{v_g h f(wd)} = \frac{1.0 \times 10^{-8} \times 1.5 \times 10^{-6}}{2 \times 10^8 \times 6.626 \times 10^{-34} \times 3 \times 10^8 \times 2.5 \times 10^{-12}}$$

$$= 1.5 \times 10^{16} \ \text{m}^{-3}.$$

Because this is much smaller than $N_{ph,sat}$, gain saturation is insignificant here. ∎

17.3.2 AMPLIFIER GAIN, PUMPING EFFICIENCY, AND BANDWIDTH

When the medium gain $g(N)$ is known, the light power $P(z)$ as a function of z is determined by the following differential equation:

$$\frac{dP(z)}{dz} = g(N)P(z). \qquad \textbf{[17.8]}$$

From Equation (17.5), N in turn is a function of N_{ph} or $P(z)$. Therefore, $g(N)$ is an implicit function of z. The one-trip amplifier gain within the amplifier is defined as

$$G_0 \overset{\text{def}}{=} \frac{P(L)}{P(0)} = e^{\int_0^L g(N)dz}. \qquad \textbf{[17.9]}$$

If gain saturation is negligible, $g(N) = g_0$ is a constant and $G_0 = e^{g_0 L} \overset{\text{def}}{=} G_{0,no\ sat}$.

Amplifier Gain Considering Gain Saturation   When gain saturation is considered, from Equations (17.5) and (17.8),

$$dP = g(z)P(z)dz = g_0 dz \frac{P(z)}{1 + P(z)/P_{sat}}$$

where $P_{sat} = N_{ph,sat}(hf)(wd)v_g$ is the saturation optical power. With simple rearrangement,

$$g_0 dz = \left[\frac{1}{P(z)} + \frac{1}{P_{sat}}\right]dP.$$

Integrating the above equation from $z = 0$ to $z = L$ gives

$$G_0 = 1 + \frac{P_{sat}}{P_{in}} \ln\left(\frac{G_{0,no\ sat}}{G_0}\right). \qquad \textbf{[17.10]}$$

When $G_0 \gg 1$, Equation (17.10) can be rearranged as

$$10\log_{10}\left(\frac{G_{0,no\ sat}}{G_0}\right) \approx 4.34\frac{P_{in}}{P_{sat}}G_0. \qquad \textbf{[17.11]}$$

This gain expression shows that the gain penalty $G_{0,no\ sat}/G_0$ in dB is linearly proportional to the actual amplifier gain G_0 and the power ratio P_{in}/P_{sat}. This gain penalty dependence is shown in Figure 17.3.

Example 17.4

GAIN PENALTY   Figure 17.3 shows that at $G_{0,no\ sat} = 30$ dB, the actual gain is $G_0 = 30 - 7.5 = 22.5$ dB at $P_{in}/P_{sat} = 0.01$. According to Equation (17.11), the power penalty at $G_0 = 22.5$ dB or 178 is $4.34 \times 178 \times 0.01 = 7.7$ dB, which is close to the 7.5 dB observed from Figure 17.3.

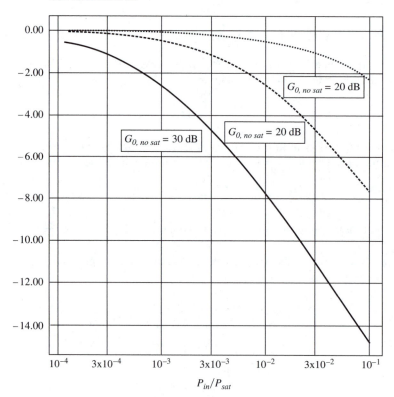

Figure 17.3   Gain reduction due to gain saturation of traveling wave semiconductor amplifiers.

From the above calculation, if an optical amplifier of $G_{0,no\ sat} = 30$ dB and $P_{sat} = 1$ W is used as a power amplifier at a transmitter output of power 10 mW, there will be only 22.5 dB gain. If the receiver sensitivity is -30 dBm, a total transmission power loss

$$\text{Total loss} = 10 + 22.5 - (-30) = 62.5 \text{ dB}$$

can be tolerated. On the other hand, if the amplifier is used as a receiver amplifier, a total transmission power loss close to

$$\text{Total loss} = 10 - (-30) + 30 = 70 \text{ dB}$$

can be tolerated where $G_0 \approx G_{0,no\ sat} = 30$ dB. If the fiber attenuation is 0.2 dB/km, this means an increase of 37.5 km in transmission distance. ∎

Upper Bound of Amplifier Gain   In general, to avoid laser emission, the amplifier gain G_0 cannot be arbitrarily large. Specifically, G_0 is bounded by

$$G_{rd} \stackrel{\text{def}}{=} G_0^2 R_L R_R < 1 \qquad \textbf{[17.12]}$$

where G_{rd} is the round-trip gain and $r_L^2 = R_L$ and $r_R^2 = R_R$ are the reflectivities at the two cavity facets.

PRACTICAL GAIN LIMIT   Consider a low reflectivity semiconductor amplifier with $R_L = R_R = 0.001$. From Equation (17.12), the gain G_0 of the amplifier is limited to 1000 or 30 dB. In practice, from Equation (17.18 discussed later), G_0 should be even lower to avoid a large peak-to-peak variation in the gain spectrum. ∎

Example 17.5

Pumping Efficiency   From Equation (17.9), it appears that the amplifier gain can be increased by increasing the cavity length L. From Equation (17.7), however,

$$g_0 L = \Gamma a \tau_r \left\{ \frac{J}{qd} - \frac{N_{th}}{\tau_r} \right\} L = \Gamma a \tau_r \left\{ \frac{I}{qwd} - \frac{N_{th}}{\tau_r} L \right\}.$$

Therefore, the gain in fact will decrease as L increases at a given injection current.[1] When gain saturation is negligible, $G_0 = G_{0,no\ sat}$ in dB is

$$G_{0,no\ sat}\ [\text{dB}] = 10 \log_{10} G_0 = 10 \log_{10} e^{g_0 L}$$

$$= 4.34 g_0 L \approx 4.34 \Gamma a \left[\frac{\tau_r}{qwd} I - N_{th} L \right] \qquad \textbf{[17.13]}$$

---

[1] In reality, L cannot be too small for various reasons. For example, a high current density due to a small L at a given injection current I can reduce the lifetime of the amplifier.

and the pumping efficiency η_i in dB/A is

$$\eta_i = 4.34\frac{\Gamma a \tau_r}{qwd} \text{ dB/A.}$$ **[17.14]**

**Example
17.6**

TYPICAL EFFICIENCY   Consider the same semiconductor amplifier given in Example 17.3. The pumping efficiency given by Equation (17.14) is

$$\eta_i = 4.34 \times \frac{0.3 \times 10^{-20} \times 10^{-9}}{1.6 \times 10^{-19} \times 2.5 \times 10^{-12}} = 32.55 \text{ dB/A.}$$

At 100 mA, the amplifier gain from the computed pumping efficiency is 3.26 dB. In reality, when the loss term N_{th} is considered, from Example 17.3, the amplifier gain is only $4.34g_0L = 0.65$ dB. ∎

Gain Bandwidth   As mentioned in Chapter 12, the gain constant a is frequency dependent. Therefore, the amplifier gain is also frequency dependent. From the exponential relationship between g and G_0 given by Equation (17.9), the full-width half-magnitude (FWHM) gain bandwidth of G_0 can be determined from the gain profile $g(f)$. Consider Example 17.7 for illustration.

**Example
17.7**

GAIN DEPENDENT BANDWIDTH   Assume a Lorentzian gain profile given by

$$g(f) = \frac{g_0}{1 + 4(f - f_0)^2/(\Delta f)^2}$$

where Δf is the FWHM of the gain profile $g(f)$. At half of the peak amplifier gain G_0 and ignoring the effect of gain saturation,

$$e^{gL} = \tfrac{1}{2}e^{g_0L}.$$

Taking the logarithm,

$$g = g_0 - \frac{1}{L}\ln 2 = \frac{g_0}{1 + 4(f - f_0)^2/(\Delta f)^2}.$$

After some manipulation,

$$\frac{2 \mid f - f_0 \mid}{\Delta f} = \left(\frac{1}{g_0L/\ln 2 - 1}\right)^{1/2} = [\log_2(G_0/2)]^{-1/2}.$$

This result shows that the FWHM gain of the optical amplifier is reduced by a factor $[\log_2(G_0/2)]^{1/2}$ with respect to the spectrum width of the gain profile. Therefore, the larger the peak amplifier gain G_0, the larger the reduction of the FWHM bandwidth. Thus there is a trade-off between the amplifier gain and bandwidth. ∎

17.3.3 FABRY-PEROT AMPLIFIERS

Because the two cavity facets of an amplifier can cause reflections, incident light can be bounced back and forth within the amplifier. Amplifiers that have strong internal reflections are called Fabry-Perot (FP) amplifiers. In this case, the one-trip amplifier gain G_0 is not the actual amplifier gain. Amplifiers that have negligible internal reflection or $R_L R_R \approx 0$ are called traveling-wave (TW) amplifiers. In general, FP amplifiers have poor time and frequency response. As a result, they are not attractive as compared to TW amplifiers.

To find the amplifier gain of FP amplifiers, assume a certain optical power distribution $P(z)$ in the cavity. If $P(z)$ is known, the medium gain $g(z)$ can be obtained from Equation (17.8). If $g(z)$ is known, $P(z)$ can be expressed as

$$P(z) = (1 - r_L^2)|E^+(z) + E^-(z)|^2 \qquad \textbf{[17.15]}$$

where

$$E^+(z) = \sqrt{P_{in}}e^{\int_0^z g(z')dz'/2} \sum_{m=0}^{\infty} (G_0 r_L r_R)^m e^{j(\beta z + m\theta_0)}$$

and

$$E^-(z) = \sqrt{P_{in}}\sqrt{G_0} r_R e^{\int_z^L g(z')dz'/2} e^{j\theta_0/2} \sum_{m=0}^{\infty} (G_0 r_L r_R)^m e^{j[\beta(L-z) + m\theta_0]}$$

represent the positive and negative traveling waves, respectively. Also in the above equations, θ_0 is the round-trip phase shift defined by

$$\theta_0 \overset{\text{def}}{=} 2\beta L = \frac{2\pi n}{\lambda} L$$

and G_0 is the one-trip gain given by Equation (17.9). With some manipulation, Equation (17.15) can be simplified as

$$P(z) = P_{in}(1 - r_L^2)\left|\frac{1}{1 - G_0 r_L r_R e^{j\theta_0}}\right|^2 \left\{G(z) + \frac{G_0^2 r_R^2}{G(z)} + 2r_R G_0 \cos(2\beta z - \theta_0)\right\} \qquad \textbf{[17.16]}$$

with

$$G(z) \overset{\text{def}}{=} e^{\int_0^z g(z')dz'}. \qquad \textbf{[17.17]}$$

From Equation (17.6), note that $G(z)$ is a function of $P(z)$. Therefore, Equations (17.16) and (17.17) form a pair of integral equations for $P(z)$ and can be solved numerically.

Once $P(z)$ and $G(z)$ are solved, from Equation (17.16), the net amplification gain of the FP amplifier is

$$G_{FP} = (1 - r_L^2)(1 - r_R^2)\frac{|E^+(L)|^2}{P_{in}} = (1 - r_L^2)(1 - r_R^2)\frac{G_0}{|1 - G_0 r_R r_L e^{j2\beta L}|^2}. \qquad \textbf{[17.18]}$$

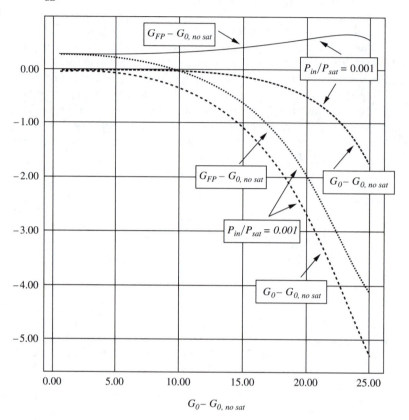

Figure 17.4   Changes of G_{FP} and G_0 in dB with respect to $G_{0, no\ sat}$ as a function of $G_{0,\ no\ sat}$ at $r_L^2 = r_R^2 = 0.001$ and $\beta L = m\pi$, where $G_{0,no\ sat}$ is the gain when $r_R = r_L = 0$ and there is no saturation effect or $P_{sat} \to \infty$.

This equation shows a strong frequency dependence when $G_0 r_R r_L$ is large. Some computation results are shown in Figures 17.4–17.6. In Figures 17.4 and 17.5, the gain drops of G_{FP} and G_0 in dB with respect to $G_{0,no\ sat}$ at zero reflection and saturation are shown. The larger the gain $G_{0,no\ sat}$ and input power P_{in}, the larger the gain drop. In Figure 17.6, the gain is also strongly dependent on the round-trip phase when $G_{0,no\ sat}$ is large. Because the round-trip phase $2\beta L$ is frequency dependent, this means the gain is strongly carrier frequency dependent.

To characterize the gain variation due to the round-trip phase dependence, the following maximum to minimum gain ratio is defined:

$$C = \left(\frac{1 + G_0 r_L r_R}{1 - G_0 r_L r_R} \right)^2 \qquad\qquad \textbf{[17.19]}$$

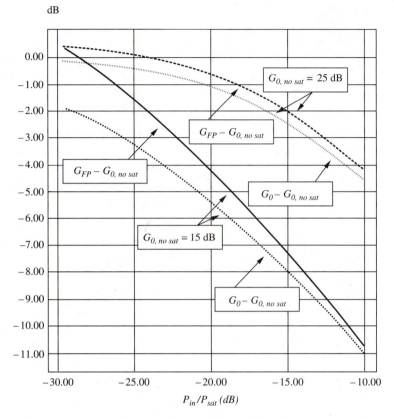

Figure 17.5   Changes of G_{FP} and G_0 in dB with respect to $G_{0,no\ sat}$ as a function of P_{in}/P_{sat} at $r_L^2 = r_R^2 = 0.001$ and $\beta L = m\pi$.

where the maximum gain is reached when $2\beta L = 2m\pi$ and the minimum gain is reached when $2\beta L = (2m + 1)\pi$. Equation (17.19) shows that when $1 - G_0 r_L r_R$ is small, there is a large gain deviation.

IMPORTANCE OF LOW FACET REFLECTIVITY   Consider a FP amplifier of one-trip gain $G_0 = 100 = 20$ dB. If the peak-to-peak deviation C is required to be within 1 dB,

Example 17.8

$$10^{0.1} = 1.26 = \left(\frac{1 + G_0 r_L r_R}{1 - G_0 r_L r_R}\right)^2.$$

This requires $r_L r_R = 5.67 \times 10^{-4}$ at $G_0 = 100$. When r_L and r_R are the same, this requires $r_L^2 = r_R^2 = 5.67 \times 10^{-4}$, a very small value.

If $r_L r_R = 0.005$, on the other hand, the peak-to-peak variation at $G_0 = 100$ is 9 or 9.5 dB. This is a large gain variation. ∎

$G_{FP} - G_{0, \, no \, sat}$ in dB

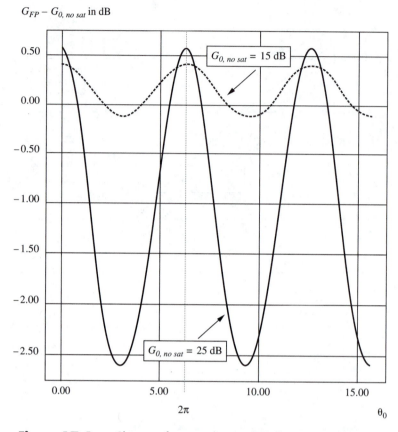

Figure 17.6   Changes of G_{FP} and G_0 in dB with respect to $G_{0,no \, sat}$
as a function of $\theta_0 = 2\beta L$ at $r_L^2 = r_R^2 = 0.001$ and
$\beta L = m\pi$.

Reduction of Reflectivity   To reduce the phase or frequency dependence of the amplifier gain requires a very small $r_R r_L$ value ($\ll 0.001$). Several techniques that can achieve a low reflectivity are depicted in Figure 17.7. As shown, the first technique uses antireflection coating to reduce reflection, and the second technique introduces a tilt of the cavity with respect to the cavity facets.

To see how zero reflection is achieved in the second technique, consider a transverse magnetic (TM) wave at an incident angle θ_1 and refracted angle θ_2. In this case, the reflection coefficient is

$$r = \frac{n_2 \cos(\theta_1) - n_1 \cos(\theta_2)}{n_2 \cos(\theta_1) + n_1 \cos(\theta_2)}.$$

From Snell's law,

$$n_1 \sin(\theta_1) = n_2 \sin(\theta_2).$$

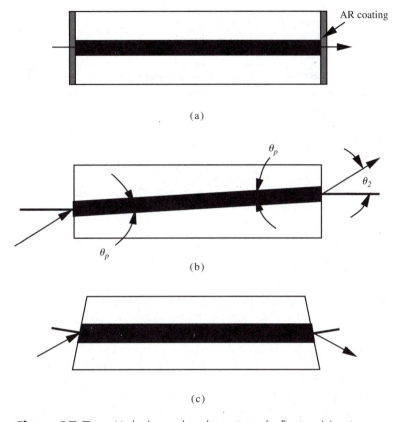

(a)

(b)

(c)

Figure 17.7 Methods to reduce the cavity end reflection: (a) antire-flection coating, (b) cavity tilted at the Brewster angle, and (c) cavity facet tilted at the Brewster angle. In (b) and (c), note that the incident and output light is not par-allel to the longitudinal direction of the cavity.

Combining the above two equations,

$$r = \frac{n_2 \cos \theta_1 - n_1 \sqrt{1 - (n_1/n_2)^2 \sin^2 \theta_1}}{n_2 \cos \theta_1 + n_1 \sqrt{1 - (n_1/n_2)^2 \sin^2 \theta_1}}.$$ **[17.20]**

A zero-reflection condition can thus be achieved at $\theta_1 = \theta_p$ if

$$1 = \left(\frac{n_2}{n_1}\right)^2 \cos^2 \theta_p + \left(\frac{n_1}{n_2}\right)^2 \sin^2 \theta_p$$

or

$$\tan \theta_p = \frac{n_2}{n_1}.$$ **[17.21]**

The angle θ_p is called the **Brewster angle.**

**Example
17.9** | **BREWSTER ANGLE OF SEMICONDUCTOR AMPLIFIERS**   For semiconductor ampli-
fiers at $n_1 = 3.5$ and $n_2 = 1.0$, $\theta_p = 15.9°$. This gives a refracted angle $\theta_2 = 73.5°$, which is
large. ∎

17.3.4 INTERCHANNEL INTERFERENCE

When either R_s or R_p in Equation (17.1) is time varying, the time constant τ_r in the rate
equation also plays an important role in interchannel interference (ICI) in multichannel
amplification. Intuitively, the time constant determines how fast the carrier density $N(t)$
follows the change of R_s or R_p. As discussed in Chapter 12, it is desirable to have a small
τ_r to reduce the rise time and fall time in direct modulation. In optical amplification, however, a large τ_r is needed to reduce ICI.

To see the effect of τ_r on ICI, consider an amplitude change of one wavelength channel and see how it affects the change of the medium gain. Let ΔN_{ph} be the step change of
one channel and let $N_{ph,0}$ be the average photon density of all channels. If the total number of wavelength channels is large, ΔN_{ph} is small compared to $N_{ph,0}$. As a result, the corresponding change of the carrier density $\Delta N(t)$ is also small compared to its steady state
value N. In this case, Equation (17.1) can be made linear, producing the following small
signal equation:

$$\frac{\partial}{\partial t} \Delta N = -\Gamma v_g a (N - N_{th}) \Delta N_{ph} - \left[\Gamma v_g a N_{ph,0} + \frac{1}{\tau_r} \right] \Delta N.$$

With the initial condition $\Delta N(t) = 0$, it is easy to solve for $\Delta N(t)$:

$$\Delta N(t) = -\Gamma a v_g \tau' (N - N_{th}) \Delta N_{ph} (1 - e^{-t/\tau'})$$ **[17.22]**

where

$$\frac{1}{\tau'} \stackrel{\text{def}}{=} \frac{1}{\tau_r} + \Gamma v_g a N_{ph,0} = \frac{1}{\tau_r} \left(1 + \frac{N_{ph,0}}{N_{ph,sat}} \right).$$ **[17.23]**

From Equation (17.4), the medium gain $g(N)$ has a change given by

$$\Delta g = \Gamma a \Delta N = (\Gamma a)^2 v_g \tau' (N - N_{th}) \Delta N_{ph} (1 - e^{-t/\tau'})$$
$$= g(N) [\Gamma a v_g \tau' \Delta N_{ph}] (1 - e^{-t/\tau'}).$$ **[17.24]**

Using $N_{ph,sat}$ defined by Equation (17.6), one obtains

$$\Delta g = g(N) \frac{\tau'}{\tau_r} \frac{\Delta N_{ph}}{N_{ph,sat}} (1 - e^{-t/\tau'}) \stackrel{\text{def}}{=} \Delta g_0 (1 - e^{-t/\tau'})$$ **[17.25]**

where

$$\Delta g_0 = g(N)\frac{\tau'}{\tau_r}\frac{\Delta N_{ph}}{N_{ph,sat}} = g(N)\frac{\Delta N_{ph}}{N_{ph,sat} + N_{ph,0}}. \qquad \textbf{[17.26]}$$

Because the change ΔN_{ph} is random, Δg_0 is random. When the wavelength channels are asynchronous, the time t between the change and observation is also random. If the number of channels is large, a uniform distribution of t between 0 and T (the bit interval) can be assumed. As a result, the variance of Δg is given by

$$E[\Delta g^2] = E[\Delta g_0^2]\frac{1}{T}\int_0^T (1 - e^{-t/\tau'})^2 dt \approx \begin{cases} E[\Delta g_0^2] & \text{when } T \gg \tau' \\ E[\Delta g_0^2]\frac{(T/\tau')^2}{3} & \text{when } T \ll \tau'. \end{cases} \qquad \textbf{[17.27]}$$

Thus it is desirable to have a large τ' compared to T to reduce the gain fluctuation.

Consider an amplification of L 1 Gb/s OOK wavelength channels. In this case, $\Delta N_{ph} = \pm\frac{2}{L}N_{ph,0}$. If the average photon intensity is one-half of the saturating density or $N_{ph,0} = 0.5 N_{ph,sat}$, $\tau' = 2\tau/3$ from Equation (17.23). Using Equation (17.25), one obtains

Example 17.10

$$\Delta g_0 = \pm\frac{2}{3} \times \frac{2}{L} \times \frac{g(N)}{2} = \pm\frac{2}{3L}g(N)$$

and

$$E[\Delta g_0^2] = \frac{1}{2} \times \frac{4}{9L^2}g(N)^2$$

where the factor $1/2$ is used to account for the 50 percent probability of transition.

For semiconductor amplifiers, τ_r is typically around 0.1 nsec. Therefore, at 1 Gb/s, T is much larger than τ or τ'. From Equation (17.27), the variance of Δg is $(2/9L^2)g(N)^2$. Adding gain variation from all channels, the total variance is $(2/9L)g(N)^2$. For 100 channels, the total variance is $2.2 \times 10^{-3}g(N)^2$. Reducing the gain variation requires that $T \ll \tau$, which thus requires a high bit-rate transmission. ∎

17.4   ERBIUM-DOPED FIBER AMPLIFIERS

Although the use of rare-earth ions as a gain medium for optical fiber amplification was noted as early as 1964 [6], erbium-doped fiber amplifiers (EDFAs) were not practical until low-loss doped fibers were made possible [7][8]. Use of EDFAs in optical fiber communications is illustrated in Figure 17.8, where one small fiber section is doped with erbium ions, Er^{+3}, as the agency for stimulated emission. To excite the electrons of Er^{+3} to higher energy states, external optical pumping through a directional coupler is used.

17.4.1   OPTICAL PUMPING

To excite carriers to a higher energy level for stimulated emission, external pumping needs to be operated at a higher frequency than that of the amplified signal. The energy diagram

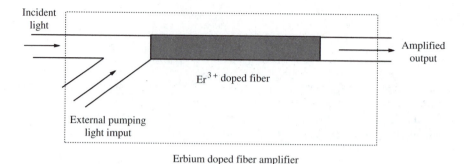

Figure 17.8   Erbium-doped fiber amplifier (EDFA).

of Er^{+3} is shown in Figure 17.9, where the ground level is labeled as $^4I_{15/2}$, and the metastable level (stimulated emission level) is $^4I_{13/2}$. The energy difference between these two levels gives an emission wavelength of 1530 nm.

In order to pump carriers from the ground level to the metastable level, a pumping source at wavelength 1450 nm, 980 nm, or 800 nm can be used. These will excite the carriers to $^4I_{13/2}$, $^4I_{11/2}$ or $^4I_{9/2}$, respectively. Excited carriers at $^4I_{11/2}$ or $^4I_{9/2}$ will quickly move down to the metastable level $^4I_{13/2}$ because of their short lifetime. At 1450 nm pumping, because of the Stark splitting effect that causes both the metastable level $^4I_{13/2}$ and the ground level $^4I_{15/2}$ to consist of several finer separated levels as shown in Figure 17.10 [9], carriers are excited from the lower band of the ground level to the higher band of the metastable level. From thermal equilibrium or Boltzman distribution, excited carriers will quickly move down to the lower band of $^4I_{13/2}$.

The efficiency of external pumping is determined by the absorption spectrum of Er^{+3} ions. The absorption spectrum of a silicate glass is illustrated in Figure 17.11, where the absorption wavelengths correspond exactly to the energy level differences from the ground level shown in Figure 17.9.

Although external pumping at a wavelength lower than 700 nm has a higher absorption efficiency, the difficulty of finding good semiconductor sources limits pumping to only 800, 980, and 1470 nm. Because of the excited-state absorption (ESA) from $^4I_{13/2}$ to $^2H_{11/2}$ shown in Figure 17.9, pumping at 800 nm is not good. Therefore, only 980 and 1470 nm pumpings are used practically. In general, semiconductor sources at 1470 nm are relatively more available and are used in early EDFA systems. Pumping at 980 nm, on the other hand, has a higher pumping efficiency (around 10 dB/mW) compared to 1470 nm pumping (around 6 dB/mW). In addition, 980 nm pumping has a lower pumping noise. As a result, as advanced lasers at 980 nm become more available, more systems are using 980 nm pumping.

Longitudinal Optical Pumping   Different from current injection in semiconductor amplifiers, optical pumping in EDFAs is in the same direction as the incident light. As illustrated in Figure 17.12, when the pumping direction is perpendicular to the propagation

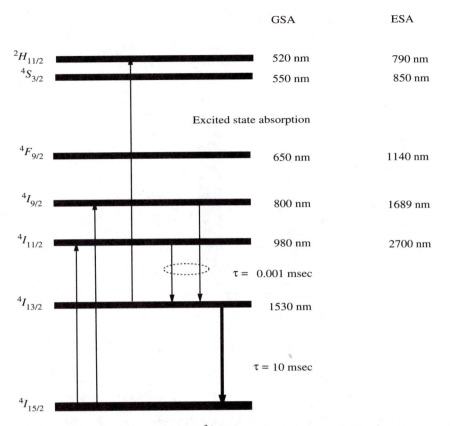

	GSA	ESA
$^2H_{11/2}$	520 nm	790 nm
$^4S_{3/2}$	550 nm	850 nm

Excited state absorption

$^4F_{9/2}$	650 nm	1140 nm
$^4I_{9/2}$	800 nm	1689 nm
$^4I_{11/2}$	980 nm	2700 nm

$\tau = 0.001$ msec

$^4I_{13/2}$ 1530 nm

$\tau = 10$ msec

$^4I_{15/2}$

Figure 17.9 Energy levels of Er^{3+}. For each level, the ground state absorption (GSA) wavelength is the light wavelength needed to excite carriers from the ground state to the given level, and the excited state absorption (ESA) wavelength is the light wavelength needed to excite carriers from the given level to the metastable state $^4I_{13/2}$.

direction, as in semiconductor amplifiers, it is called **transverse** pumping. When the pumping direction is parallel to the incident light, it is called **longitudinal** pumping. In the latter case, the pumping rate is stronger at the input side of the amplifier. As power is transferred from the pumping light to the signal light, the pumping rate decreases along the light propagation direction.

Absorption and Emission Cross Sections To quantify the absorption efficiency in external pumping, a parameter called the **absorption cross section** σ_a is used. By definition, if the pumping power is P_p and the ground state population is N_1, the pumping rate is $W_p N_1$, where

$$W_p \stackrel{\text{def}}{=} \frac{\sigma_a P_p}{h f_p A} \text{ sec}^{-1} \qquad \textbf{[17.28]}$$

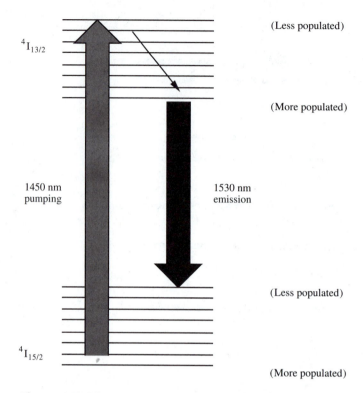

$^4I_{13/2}$

1450 nm
pumping

1530 nm
emission

$^4I_{15/2}$

(Less populated)

(More populated)

(Less populated)

(More populated)

Figure 17.10   1450 nm pumping. Because of the Stark effect, there are splittings at the ground state and the metastable state. At thermal equilibrium, both states have a higher population at their lower bands. Because both the pumping rate and the stimulated emission rate are proportional to the population difference of the two levels, pumping takes place between the lower band of the ground state and the upper band of the metastable state (1450 nm), and stimulated emission takes place between the lower band of the metastable state and the upper band of the ground state (1530 nm).

hf_p is the photon energy of external pumping at frequency f_p, and A is the core area of the EDFA fiber. From Equation (17.28), a large absorption cross section produces a high pumping efficiency. Absorption cross sections at 800 nm, 980 nm, and 1450 nm are shown in Figures 17.13–17.15, respectively.

Because of longitudinal pumping, P_p given in Equation (17.28) is also spatially dependent. At a given absorption cross section, the amount of power decrease over a short distance dz is

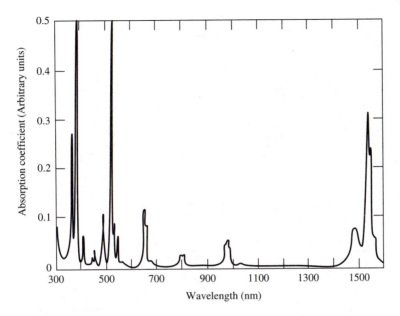

Figure 17.11   Absorption spectrum of Er^{3+}.

Source: Reprinted by permission, from Miniscalco, "Erbium-Doped Glasses for Fiber Amplifiers at 1500 nm," Figure 2 [10]. © 1991 by IEEE.

$$dP_p(z) = -\sigma_a P_p(z) N_1 dz.$$

When $\sigma_a N_1$ is constant along the fiber, $P_p(z)$ has an exponential decay. In practice, N_1 increases with z because of a lower pumping power. As a result, $P_p(z)$ drops even faster.

In addition to the absorption cross section that determines the pumping rate, there is an **emission cross section** that determines the medium gain. Specifically, if σ_e is the emission cross section, the medium gain is given by

$$g = \sigma_e(N_2 - N_1) \qquad\qquad \textbf{[17.29]}$$

where N_2 and N_1 are the carrier densities at the metastable and ground states, respectively. From Equation (17.29), the stimulated emission rate is

$$R_s = v_g g N_{ph} = \frac{\sigma_e P_{in}}{h f_s A}(N_2 - N_1) \stackrel{\text{def}}{=} W_s(N_2 - N_1) \qquad\qquad \textbf{[17.30]}$$

where $P_{in} = v_g N_{ph} A$ is the incident light power, $h f_s$ is the photon energy of the input signal, and

$$W_s \stackrel{\text{def}}{=} \frac{\sigma_e P_{in}}{h f_s A} \text{ sec}^{-1}. \qquad\qquad \textbf{[17.31]}$$

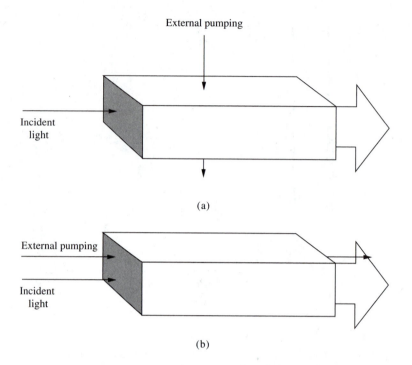

Figure 17.12 Two types of pumping: (a) transverse and (b) longitudinal.

The emission cross section at 1540 nm is given in Figure 17.16.

17.4.2 RATE EQUATIONS AND AMPLIFIER GAIN

Because the metastable energy level $^4I_{13/2}$ has a much longer lifetime than its upper levels,[2] the energy diagram of Er^{+3} can be approximated as a two-level system, where $^4I_{15/2}$ is the ground level and $^4I_{13/2}$ is the upper level. The carrier rate equation of an EDFA can thus be written as [11]:

$$\frac{\partial N_2}{\partial t} = W_p N_1 - W_s(N_2 - N_1) - \frac{N_2}{\tau_{sp}} = -\frac{\partial N_1}{\partial t}. \qquad \textbf{[17.32]}$$

The first term, $W_p N_1$, on the right-hand side is the pumping rate from the lower state to the upper state; the second term, $W_s(N_2 - N_1)$, is the net stimulated emission rate; and the third term, N_2/τ_{sp}, is the spontaneous recombination rate from the upper state to the lower state. The time constant τ_{sp} of EDFA is typically 10 msec [10]. Typical values of the above parameters are given in Table 17.2.

| [2] This is still the case even at 1450 nm pumping because of Stark splitting, discussed earlier.

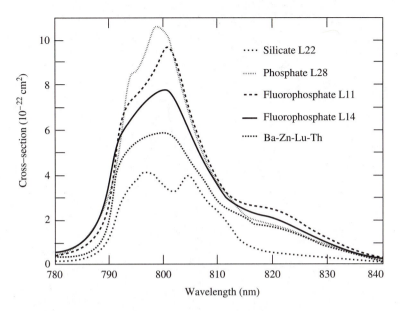

Figure 17.13   Absorption cross section of Er^{3+} at 800 nm.

Source: Reprinted, by permission, from Miniscalco, "Erbium-Doped Glasses for Fiber Amplifiers at 1500 nm," Figure 11 [10]. © 1991 by IEEE.

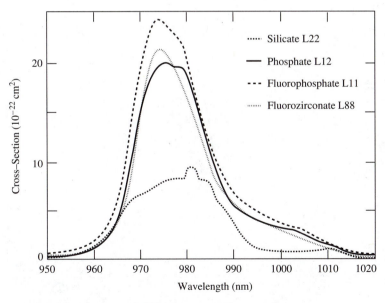

Figure 17.14   Absorption cross section of Er^{3+} at 980 nm.

Source: Reprinted, by permission, from Miniscalco, "Erbium-Doped Glasses for Fiber Amplifiers at 1500 nm," Figure 12 [10]. © 1991 by IEEE.

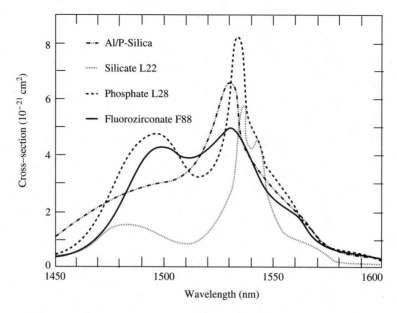

Figure 17.15   Absorption cross section of Er^{3+} at 1450 nm.

Source: Reprinted, by permission, from Miniscalco, "Erbium-Doped Glasses for Fiber Amplifiers at 1500 nm," Figure 7 [10]. © 1991 by IEEE.

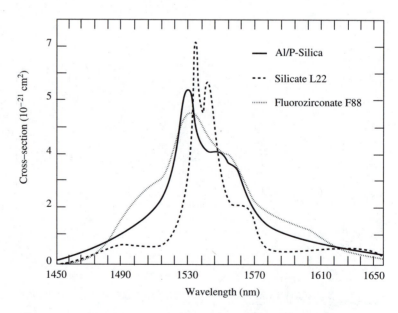

Figure 17.16   Emission cross section of Er^{3+} at 1540 nm.

Source: Reprinted, by permission, from Miniscalco, "Erbium-Doped Glasses for Fiber Amplifiers at 1500 nm," Figure 8 [10]. © 1991 by IEEE.

Table 17.2   Typical EDFA parameters, which can strongly depend on the materials doped.

Parameter	Typical Value
τ_{sp}	10 msec
σ_a	2.5×10^{-21} cm^2 @ 980 nm
	1.8×10^{-21} cm^2 @ 1480 nm
σ_e	5×10^{-21} cm^2 @ 1540 nm
$N_t = N_1 + N_2$	8×10^{18} cm^{-3}
Emission bandwidth	30 nm (FWHM)

In the steady state, the rate equation (17.32) gives

$$N_2 - N_1 = \frac{W_p - 1/\tau_{sp}}{W_p + 2W_s + 1/\tau_{sp}} N_t \qquad \textbf{[17.33]}$$

where $N_t \stackrel{\text{def}}{=} N_1 + N_2$ is the total carrier density. When the pumping rate is high enough, or $W_p \gg W_s$ and $W_p \gg 1/\tau_{sp}$, $N_2 - N_1 \approx N_t$. In this case, the medium gain is approximately

$$g = \sigma_e(N_2 - N_1) \approx \sigma_e N_t \stackrel{\text{def}}{=} g^* \qquad \textbf{[17.34]}$$

where g^* is the upper limit of the medium gain constant. From Equation (17.53) and the definition of g^* given by Equation (17.34),

$$g = g^* \frac{W_p - 1/\tau_{sp}}{W_p + 2W_s + 1/\tau_{sp}}. \qquad \textbf{[17.35]}$$

PUMPING AT 980 NM   Assume an EDFA of length 5 m has $N_t = 8 \times 10^{18}$ cm^{-3}, the emission cross section is $\sigma_e = 5 \times 10^{-21}$ cm^2, the absorption cross section at 980 nm pumping is 2.0×10^{-21} cm^2, and the spontaneous emission time constant is $\tau_{sp} = 10$ msec. The upper limit of the medium gain at large pumping is thus

Example 17.11

$$g^* = 5 \times 10^{-21} \times 8 \times 10^{18} = 40 \times 10^{-3}\text{cm}^{-1} = 4 \text{ m}^{-1} = 17 \text{ dB/m}.$$

where a factor of 4.34 is included for conversion to dB/m. If the EDFA has a core area $A = 50$ μm^2, to ensure $W_p \gg 1/\tau_{sp}$,

$$P_p \gg \frac{hf_p A}{\sigma_a \tau_{sp}} = 5 \text{ mW}.$$

Assuming there is an external pumping of 10 mW, the actual medium gain at zero W_s is

$$g = g^* \frac{W_p - 1/\tau_{sp}}{W_p + 1/\tau_{sp}} = 1.3 \text{ m}^{-1} = 5.6 \text{ dB/m}.$$

Over a total length of 5 m, a gain of 28 dB can be achieved. The pumping efficiency is thus $28/10 = 2.8$ dB/mW. ∎

Example 17.11 assumes the pumping power is constant over the fiber amplifier channel. As mentioned earlier, because of its longitudinal pumping, the pumping rate W_p is spatially dependent. Because

$$\frac{dP_p}{dz} = -\sigma_a N_1 P_p \qquad\qquad [17.36]$$

and

$$\frac{dP_{in}}{dz} = g P_{in} \approx \sigma_e (N_2 - N_1) P_{in} \qquad\qquad [17.37]$$

from Equations (17.33) and (17.34),

$$\frac{dP_p}{dz} = -(\sigma_a N_t) P_p \frac{W_s + 1/\tau_{sp}}{W_p + 2W_s + 1/\tau_{sp}} \qquad\qquad [17.38]$$

and

$$\frac{dP_{in}}{dz} = g^* \frac{(W_p - 1/\tau_{sp})}{W_p + 2W_s + 1/\tau_{sp}} P_{in} = \frac{g_0}{1 + W_s/W_{sat}} P_{in} \qquad\qquad [17.39]$$

where

$$g_0 = g^* \frac{W_p - 1/\tau_{sp}}{W_p + 1/\tau_{sp}} \qquad\qquad [17.40]$$

is the medium gain at zero incident signal and

$$W_{sat} = \frac{1}{2}(W_p + 1/\tau_{sp}) \qquad\qquad [17.41]$$

is the saturation rate. Because W_{sat} becomes smaller as W_p gets smaller along the light propagation direction, gain saturation effect is stronger at the output end of the amplifier. When $W_p < 1/\tau_{sp}$ or $N_2 < N_1$, the gain can even be negative.

Example 17.12

GAIN SATURATION IN EDFA   Consider an EDFA with the numerical values given in Table 17.2. From Equation (17.41), if $W_p = 3 \times 10^2$ sec^{-1},

$$W_{sat} = \frac{1}{2}(3 \times 10^2 + 1 \times 10^2) = 2 \times 10^2 \text{ sec}^{-1}.$$

If P_{in} is 1 mW at the amplifier output, from Equation (17.31),

$$W_s = \frac{5 \times 10^{-21} \times 10^{-3}}{6.63 \times 10^{-34} \times (3 \times 10^8 / 1.54 \times 10^{-6}) \times 50 \times 10^{-8}} = 77.1 \text{ sec}^{-1}.$$

Comparing this with W_{sat} illustrates that gain saturation is critical in EDFAs. ∎

The gain saturation effect in fiber amplification can also be seen from Figure 17.17, where the amplifier gain increases as the pumping power increases. However, increasing the length of the fiber amplifier does not necessarily increase the gain. When the length is beyond a certain limit at a given pumping power, the gain starts to decrease. This occurs when $N_2 < N_1$ or when the pumping rate becomes so small that it can no longer invert the population. Figure 17.17 indicates that the optimum length is approximately linearly proportional to the pumping power.

OPTIMAL EDFA LENGTH   Finding the optimum length requires solving Equations (17.38) and (17.39). In general, they do not yield simple analytical expressions. However, they can easily be solved for the special case that W_s is large. That is, assume $W_s \gg W_p$ and $W_s \gg 1/\tau_{sp}$. As a result, from Equation (17.38),

Example 17.13

$$\frac{dP_p}{dz} \approx -\frac{\sigma_a N_t}{2} P_p.$$

Therefore,

$$P_p(z) = P_p(0)e^{-\sigma_a N_t z/2}.$$

Because the optimum length L is at the point $W_p(L) = 1/\tau_{sp}$ or $N_2 = N_1$,

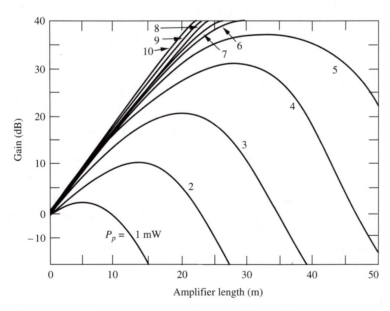

Figure 17.17   EDFA gain as a function of the amplifier length.

Source: Reprinted, by permission, from Giles and Desurvire, "Modeling Erbium-Doped Fiber Amplifiers," Figure 8b [12]. © 1991 by IEEE.

$$L = \frac{2}{\sigma_a N_t} \ln[P_p(0)\sigma_a \tau_{sp}/hf_p A].$$

As a numerical example, using the parameter values given in Table 17.2 at 980 nm pumping, L at $P_p(0) = 10$ mA and $A = 50$ μm^2 is

$$L = \frac{2}{1.8 \times 10^{-21} \times 8 \times 10^{18}} \ln 2 = 96 \text{ cm}.$$

This is a small length. To increase it, a higher pumping power is needed. ∎

17.5   NOISE FROM OPTICAL AMPLIFICATION

Because spontaneous emission comes together with optical amplification, noise is added when a light signal passes through an amplifier. As mentioned earlier, this noise is called the amplified spontaneous emission (ASE) noise because it is also amplified. This section shows the power spectral density of the ASE noise and quantifies its effect on SNR degradation using the noise figure.

17.5.1   AMPLIFIED SPONTANEOUS EMISSION NOISE

Photons that contribute to the ASE noise can have different transverse modes in the amplifier and different polarizations. The one-sided[3] power spectral density of the ASE noise that is of the same mode and polarization as the incident light signal was first derived by Kogelnik and Yariv [14] and can be expressed as

$$\boxed{S_{ASE}(f) = (G - 1)n_{sp}\chi hf.}$$ **[17.42]**

In the expression, G is the amplifier gain, hf is the photon energy, and

$$n_{sp} = \frac{N_2}{N_2 - N_1}$$ **[17.43]**

is a parameter describing how complete the external pumping that depletes the ground state population is. When a large population inversion is achieved, such as in semiconductor amplifiers, n_{sp} is close to 1. Otherwise, it is a parameter higher than 1. The parameter χ is also greater than 1 and is used to account for the nonuniform carrier density distribution due to gain saturation. For derivation and detailed discussion, see Appendix 17–A.

---

[3] Chapters 6 and 12 use two-sided spectral density functions according to the convention in the telecommunications literature. Here the one-sided spectral density is used because it is used in the optical amplifier literature.

17.5.2 Noise Figures

When the light signal is converted to photocurrent from photodetection, there are noise terms due to ASE noise and its interaction with the signal. This section explains the various noise terms and uses the **noise figure** (NF) to quantify their total effect.

Noise Figure in Direct Detection For simplicity, first consider the case that the light signal is directly detected by a photodiode. If the incident power to the amplifier is P_{in} and the amplifier has a gain G, the output power is

$$P_{out} = P_{in}G.$$

Therefore, the photocurrent is

$$I_{ph} = \mathcal{R}P_{out} = \mathcal{R}P_{in}G.$$

In addition to shot noise from photodetection, it was first shown by Olsson [15] that there are noise terms due to ASE noise. Specifically, the total noise power at the photodiode output is

$$\sigma_n^2 = \sigma_{th}^2 + \sigma_{shot}^2 + \sigma_{sig=ASE}^2 + \sigma_{ASE=ASE}^2 \qquad \text{[17.44]}$$

where σ_{th}^2 is the thermal noise power, σ_{shot}^2 is the shot noise power, $\sigma_{sig=ASE}^2$ is the signal-ASE beat noise power due to signal and ASE noise interaction, and $\sigma_{ASE=ASE}^2$ is the noise power due to ASE alone. From Appendix 17–B, they can be expressed by

$$\sigma_{shot}^2 = 2q\mathcal{R}(P_{in}G + S_{ASE}B_{opt})B \qquad \text{[17.45]}$$

$$\sigma_{sig=ASE}^2 = 4(\mathcal{R}GP_{in})(\mathcal{R}S_{ASE}B) \qquad \text{[17.46]}$$

$$\sigma_{ASE=ASE}^2 = \mathcal{R}^2 S_{ASE}^2 (2B_{opt} - B)B. \qquad \text{[17.47]}$$

In the above equations, $\mathcal{R}$ is the photodiode responsivity, B is the front-end amplifier bandwidth, and B_{opt} is the optical bandwidth of the optical amplifier.

Among the noise sources given above, the beat noise $\sigma_{sig=ASE}^2$ in general is the most important term. This can be understood as follows. First, the thermal noise can be generally neglected when the amplifier gain is large enough. Also, because GP_{in} is in general much larger than the ASE noise power, $S_{ASE}B_{opt}$, $\sigma_{ASE=ASE}^2$ can be dropped when it is compared to the beat noise, $\sigma_{sig=ASE}^2$. Finally, because $\mathcal{R} = (\eta q)/(hf)$, where η is the quantum efficiency of the photodiode,

$$\mathcal{R}S_{ASE} = \eta q n_{sp} \chi (G - 1) \gg q \quad \text{when } G \text{ is large.}$$

Therefore, the first term of shot noise given by Equation (17.45) is much smaller than the beat noise given by Equation (17.46). From the above discussion, the signal-to-noise ratio at the photodetector output is approximately

$$\text{SNR} \approx \frac{I_{ph}^2}{\sigma_{sig=ASE}^2} = \frac{P_{in}}{4hf n_{sp} \chi B} = \frac{N_b}{4n_{sp}\chi} \qquad \textbf{[17.48]}$$

where

$$N_b \overset{\text{def}}{=} \frac{P_{in}}{hfB}$$

is the number of photons per bit. Equation (17.48) gives the achievable upper limit of the SNR. Therefore, in order to have a good SNR at the photodetection output, the light signal must be amplified before P_{in} becomes too weak. For a given SNR required, from Equation (17.48), the incident light power is required to be

$$P_{in} > 4hf B n_{sp}\chi\,\text{SBR} \quad \text{or} \quad N_b > 4n_{sp}\chi\,\text{SNR}. \qquad \textbf{[17.49]}$$

Example 17.14	**SENSITIVITY DEGRADATION DUE TO ASE NOISE** If $n_{sp}\chi = 5$, in order to have an SNR of 16, the number of incident photons per bit should be at least $N_b = 320$. This is 20 times higher than the quantum limit. ∎

From Equation (17.48), the noise figure as the ratio of the SNR_{ref} to SNR can be computed, where SNR_{ref} is the SNR when only shot noise is considered. That is,

$$\text{SNR}_{ref} = \frac{\mathcal{R}P_{in}}{2qB}. \qquad \textbf{[17.50]}$$

Therefore, the noise figure (NF) is

$$\boxed{NF \overset{\text{def}}{=} \frac{\text{SNR}_{ref}}{\text{SNR}} = 2\eta n_{sp}\chi.} \qquad \textbf{[17.51]}$$

The NF given above is a true value only when $G \gg 1$ or when other noise components such as σ_{th}^2 can be ignored. If this is not the case, the NF will be much higher.

Equation (17.51) shows that the NF of an optical amplifier is 3 dB when $\eta n_{sp}\chi = 1$. When $\eta n_{sp}\chi > 1$ because of incomplete pumping and/or nonuniform carrier density distribution, the NF is worse. To reduce the NF, a higher pumping power can be used to reduce the product $n_{sp}\chi$. This is shown in Figure 17.18.

Noise Figure in Coherent Detection   In the case of coherent detection, the signal component of the output photocurrent is

$$I_{ph} = 2\mathcal{R}\sqrt{G P_{in} P_{loc}}$$

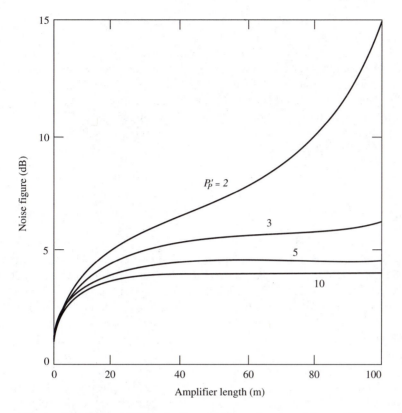

Figure 17.18   EDFA noise figure (NF) as a function of the amplifier length.

and the beat noise power is

$$\sigma^2_{sig=ASE} = 4(\mathcal{R}P_{loc})(\mathcal{R}S_{ASE}B)$$

where P_{loc} is the local oscillator power. Therefore, the signal-to-noise ratio is

$$\text{SNR} = \frac{I^2_{ph}}{\sigma^2_{sig=ASE}} = \frac{P_{in}}{hf n_{sp}\chi B} = \frac{N_b}{n_{sp}\chi} \qquad \textbf{[17.52]}$$

when $G \gg 1$. If no optical amplifier is used, the reference SNR is

$$\text{SNR}_{ref} = \frac{2\mathcal{R}P_{in}}{qB} = \frac{2\eta P_{in}}{hf B}. \qquad \textbf{[17.53]}$$

Therefore, the NF of coherent detection is the same as that of direct detection given by Equation (17.51).

From Chapter 15, note that coherent detection and optical amplification both can amplify incident light signals to overcome the thermal noise and receiver noise. From the 3 dB noise figure, it is thus pointless to use both optical amplification and coherent detection at the same time. Instead, there is a trade-off between performance and implementation complexity. That is, a system can either use optical amplification to avoid the implementation complexity of coherent detection or use coherent detection to avoid the 3 dB noise figure penalty.

17.6 SYSTEM DESIGN

This chapter has presented several important concepts of optical amplification, including amplifier gain and ASE noise. This section discusses when and where optical amplifiers should be used. Before the discussion, note that optical amplifiers can only help to overcome the attenuation problem. When a transmission system has a large fiber dispersion, transmission performance can be limited by intersymbol interference (see Chapter 7), and use of optical amplifiers alone is insufficient. In this case, one must either resort to the conventional approach using repeaters or use the recent optical fiber soliton technology (see Chapter 18).

Designing a transmission system using optical amplifiers requires answering three questions. First, is optical amplification needed? Second, if optical amplification is needed, where should the amplifier be placed: as a power amplifier, an in-line amplifier, or a receiver amplifier? When the system requires a large power budget and use of one optical amplifier is still insufficient, the third question is, How many amplifiers are needed and where should they be placed? These three questions are discussed below.

When Is Optical Amplification Needed?   For a given transmission system where the transmitter power and required BER or SNR are given and the total transmission power loss and noise power are known, one can determine whether optical amplification is needed. Specifically, from Chapter 7, the received SNR without amplification can be expressed by

$$\text{SNR} = \frac{(\alpha \mathcal{R} M P_{tx})^2}{(\text{NEP}^2 + 2q\alpha \mathcal{R} P_{tx} M^2 F) B} \qquad \textbf{[17.54]}$$

where P_{tx} is the transmitter power, α is the total transmission power loss, NEP is the noise equivalent power (see Chapter 6), M is the APD gain ($M = 1$ if a PIN diode is used), F is the excess noise factor of the APD, and B is the receiver bandwidth. When the received SNR cannot meet the specified value even when a large gain APD is used, optical amplification is needed.

RECEIVED POWER TOO WEAK   Assume the transmission power is 10 mW, the total trans- **Example 17.15** mission loss is 100 dB, and the required received SNR is 20 dB. If the receiver responsivity is $\mathcal{R} = 0.5$, $NEP = 0$, and the signal bandwidth is $B = 100$ MHz, one has

$$\text{SNR} = \frac{(0.5 \times 10^{-10} \times 0.01)^2}{2 \times 1.6 \times 10^{-19} \times 0.5 \times F \times 10^{-10} \times 0.01 \times 10^8} = 1.56 \times 10^{-2} F^{-1}.$$

Thus the SNR cannot be greater than 100 even when $F = 1$. Therefore, optical amplification is needed in this case. ∎

Where Should the Amplifier Be Placed?   If optical amplification is needed, the next question is, Where should the amplifier be placed? From the gain saturation and ASE noise discussed, the decision is based on the required amplifier gain and the final SNR.

Because of the effect of gain saturation, it is best to place the amplifier at the receiver end. In this case, the effect of gain saturation is minimized. On the other hand, because of ASE noise, placing the amplifier at the receiver end has the smallest SNR. From Equation (17.48), use of the amplifier as the receiver amplifier may not even be possible when P_{in} becomes too weak.

Therefore, to decide where to place the amplifier, one must first check whether the SNR given by Equation (17.48) meets the required SNR using $P_{in} = \alpha P_{tx}$. If it does, the amplifier can be used as the receiver amplifier. Otherwise, the amplifier must be moved closer to the transmitter side.

USE AS IN-LINE AMPLIFIER   Continue from Example 17.15. If the light wavelength is 1.55 **Example 17.16** μm and the amplifier has $n_{sp}\chi = 10$, the received SNR from Equation (17.48) is

$$\text{SNR} = \frac{10^{-10} \times 10^{-2} \times 1.55 \times 10^{-6}}{40 \times 6.63 \times 10^{-34} \times 3 \times 10^8 \times 10^8} = 1.9 \times 10^{-3}.$$

Therefore, the amplifier cannot be used as a receiver amplifier. On the other hand, the amplifier can be used at the middle point of the transmission link as an in-line amplifier. In this case, the ASE noise is attenuated by 50 dB from the second half of transmission, and the SNR can be boosted by 50 dB if other noise can be still neglected. Therefore, the final received SNR is 190 or 23 dB. This meets the required 20 dB. ∎

How Many Amplifiers Are Needed?   When the system has an extremely large power loss, use of a single optical amplifier may still be insufficient. In this case, multiple amplifiers are needed.

Example 17.17

STRONG THERMAL NOISE   Continue from Example 17.16. If the amplifier is at the middle of the transmission link with a gain of 30 dB, the beat noise power at the receiver is

$$\sigma^2_{sig=ASE} = 4(\mathcal{R} P_{tx} \times 10^{-7})(\mathcal{R} n_{sp} \chi h f B \times 10^3 \times 10^{-5}) = 1.28 \times 10^{-21} A^2.$$

On the other hand, if a high-impedance receiver with load resistance of 100 kΩ is used, the thermal noise power is

$$\sigma^2_{th} = \frac{4kTB}{R} = 1.7 \times 10^{-17} A^2.$$

Therefore, the beat noise is much smaller than the thermal noise and consequently the NEP, and the use of a single in-line amplifier is still insufficient. ∎

To have a system design when multiple amplifiers are needed, consider the use of amplifiers as shown in Figure 17.19. Assuming that N amplifiers are used, there are $N + 1$ sections in the transmission link, with attenuations of $\alpha_1, \ldots, \alpha_{N+1}$. Therefore, the total power loss is

$$\alpha = \prod_{i=1}^{N+1} \alpha_i.$$

If the amplifier gain of the ith amplifier is $G^{(i)}$, the total amplifier gain is

$$G_{tot} = \prod_{i=1}^{N} G^{(i)}.$$

From the above assumptions, the received signal power is

$$P_{in} = P_{tx} \alpha G_{tot}$$

and the total ASE power spectral density at the receiver input is

$$S_{ASE,tot} = (hf) n_{sp} \chi \left[\sum_{i=1}^{N-1} (G^{(i)}-1) \prod_{j=i+1}^{N} (G^{(j)} \alpha_j) + (G^{(N)}-1) \right] \alpha_{N+1} \qquad \textbf{[17.55]}$$

where it is assumed that each amplifier has the same $n_{sp} \chi$ value.

Equation (17.55) gives a general expression for calculating the total ASE power spectral density. To minimize $S_{ASE,tot}$, one can lump all attenuation to the last section, or set $\alpha_N = \alpha$. This means lumping all amplifiers at the transmitter side however, which is not practically possible because of gain saturation.

Therefore, a practical design is to distribute amplifiers over the entire transmission line. That is, the N amplifiers can be uniformly distributed between the transmitter and receiver, thus resulting in identical power loss between adjacent amplifiers. If each amplifier is also assumed to have the same gain, G, one can have the following definitions:

$$r = G\alpha^{1/(N+1)}$$

and

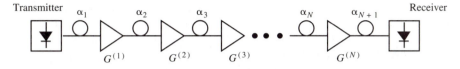

Figure 17.19   Use of a series of optical amplifiers.

$$S_{ASE,tot}^{(N)} = E_a(G-1)\alpha^{1/(N+1)}\frac{1-r^N}{1-r} \approx E_a r \frac{1-r^N}{1-r} \qquad \textbf{[17.56]}$$

where

$$E_a \overset{\text{def}}{=} (hf)n_{sp}\chi. \qquad \textbf{[17.57]}$$

The received SNR is then

$$\text{SNR}^{(N)} = \frac{(\mathcal{R}\alpha G^N P_{tx})^2}{\sigma_{th}^2 + 4\mathcal{R}^2 \alpha G^N P_{tx} S_{ASE,tot}^{(N)} B}. \qquad \textbf{[17.58]}$$

According to the above equation, at the given α, P_{tx}, σ_{th}^2, E_a, and amplifier gain G, increasing N will increase r, which can make $S_{ASE,tot}$ large enough compared to σ_{th}^2 and at the same time small enough compared to the signal power.

USE OF TWO AMPLIFIERS   In Exampie 17.17, $N = 1$ and the received SNR does not meet the 20 dB requirement. Now consider $N = 2$. In this case,

$$r = 10^{-10/3}10^3 = 0.46$$

and

$$S_{ASE,tot}^{(2)} = r(1+r)E_a = 8.7 \times 10^{-19}.$$

Therefore,

$$\text{SNR}^{(2)} = \frac{(0.5 \times 10^{-12} \times 10^6)^2}{1.7 \times 10^{-17} + 10^{-10+6-2+8} \times 8.7 \times 10^{-19}} = 2400 = 34 \text{ dB}.$$

This is greater than the 20 dB requirement. ∎

Example 17.18

17.7 SUMMARY

1. When a transmission system is power limited, using optical amplifiers can improve the received SNR and increase the repeater distance. This use of optical amplification can avoid the excess noise of APDs and can have a simpler implementation than coherent detection.

2. Depending on its position in a transmission line, an optical amplifier can be used as a power amplifier (at the transmitter side), an in-line amplifier (middle in the transmission line), or receiver amplifier (at the receiver side). Care must be taken in placing the amplifier to trade off between the gain saturation and ASE noise.

3. In addition to high power gain and pumping efficiency, a good optical amplifier should have low noise, small crosstalk, minimal coupling loss, wide bandwidths, and a flexible input wavelength range that can be amplified.

4. There are two important types of optical amplifiers: semiconductor amplifiers and erbium-doped fiber amplifiers (EDFAs). They are important for their large gain (around 30 dB) and a high pumping efficiency.

5. Both semiconductor and erbium-doped fiber amplifiers are based on the principle of stimulated emission. Different from lasers, they are operated below the threshold so that there is no internal oscillation or lasing. For example, a semiconductor amplifier is a laser diode biased below its threshold current. Semiconductor amplifliers have lower noise power than EDFAs and a flexible operating wavelength.

6. Based on the principle of stimulated emission, the gain of an optical amplifier depends on the carrier density at the higher energy level. Because of stimulated recombination from the incident light, the carrier density at the higher energy level decreases when the incident light power increases. This reduces the gain, and the effect is called gain saturation.

7. The incident light signal can be reflected back and forth between the two ends of a semiconductor amplifier. If the round-trip gain including the reflection is strong, the amplifier is called a Fabry-Perot amplifier. Otherwise, it is a traveling-wave amplifier. Because reflected waves interfere in the amplifier, the FWHM bandwidth of a Fabry-Perot amplifier is too small to be practically useful. To have a traveling-wave amplifier, however, care must be taken to ensure a small reflectivity (around 10^{-4}) at a large amplifier gain (around 30 dB).

8. An EDFA inverts the population of the energy levels of Er^{+3} for stimulated emissions. Because the energy levels of Er^{+3} cannot be changed, EDFAs are limited to amplifying optical signals of wavelengths around 1.53 μm. Nevertheless, EDFAs are attractive for their large gain, high pumping efficiency, low crosstalk, and low coupling loss. Other fiber amplifiers such as neodymium- and praseodymium-doped amplifiers are being studied for emission at 1.3 μm.

9. An EDFA can be pumped at several wavelengths, including 800 nm, 980 nm, and 1470 nm. Because of excited-state absorption (ESA) in the Er^{+3} energy levels, 800 nm has a low pumping efficiency. The trade-off between 980 nm and 1470 nm pumping is a high pumping efficiency at 980 nm (10 dB/mW versus 6 dB/mW) versus easier availability of light sources at 1470 nm.

10. Because of spontaneous emissions from the higher energy level, an optical amplifier also adds noise to the incident signal. Because the spontaneous emission is amplified by the amplifier too, it is called amplified spontaneous emission (ASE) noise. In general, the ASE noise power is proportional to the amplifier gain.

11. When the combined amplified optical signal and noise are detected by a photodiode, the current noise includes not only shot noise but also signal and ASE beat noise. As a result, the beat noise power is proportional to the square of the amplifier gain and can become the dominating term at large gains.

12. The noise characteristics of an optical amplifier can be quantified by its noise figure, which is defined as the reduction of the SNR in dB at the photodetection output when only shot noise is considered. If the quantum efficiency of the photodiode is 1, the minimum noise figure is 3 dB. The noise figure of a typical EDFA is around 10 dB and can be reduced by a higher external pumping power.

13. When a lightwave transmission system has a large power loss and needs power amplification, it is necessary to decide where to place the amplifiers and how many amplifiers are needed. In general, when gain saturation is a concern, the amplifier must be placed toward the receiver side. When the beat noise is a concern, the amplifier must be moved toward the transmitter side. When more than one amplifier is needed, they should be placed uniformly along the transmission line to achieve the best combination of the overall power gain and final SNR.

APPENDIX 17-A: AMPLIFIED SPONTANEOUS EMISSION NOISE DERIVATION

This appendix derives the ASE noise in an optical amplifier. First, based on the two-level model, if the carrier density at the higher energy level is N_2, the spontaneous emission contribution from position z and in the propagation direction is

$$dP_{ASE}(z) = hfA\frac{N_2(z)}{\tau_{sp}}\Omega dz \qquad\qquad \textbf{[17.59]}$$

where A is the cross-sectional area of the amplifier and Ω is a certain solid angle within which the spontaneous emission falls. Specifically, for propagation along the amplifier [14],

$$\Omega = \frac{\lambda_a^2}{4\pi^2 A} \qquad\qquad \textbf{[17.60]}$$

where λ_a is the emission wavelength of the amplifier.

   If the medium gain is $g(z)$, the total gain for the spontaneous emission contribution at z is

$$G(z) = e^{\int_z^L g(z')dz'}$$

and the total spontaneous emission power as a result is

$$P_{ASE} = \int_0^L dP_{ASE}(z)G(z) = hfA\Omega\int_0^L \frac{N_2(z)}{\tau_{sp}}G(z)dz. \qquad\qquad \textbf{[17.61]}$$

For the simple case that N_2 is independent of z, the gain g is constant and

$$G(z) = e^{g(L-z)}.$$

Therefore,

$$P_{ASE} = hfA\Omega\int_0^L \frac{N_2}{\tau_{sp}}e^{g(L-z)}dz = hfA\Omega\frac{N_2}{g\tau_{sp}}(G-1).$$

From the Einstein equation, the net stimulated emission rate is

$$R_s = B_{21} \frac{hf N_{ph}}{B_{opt}}(N_2 - N_1) = g v_g N_{ph}$$

where B_{opt} is the optical bandwidth and $hf N_{ph}/B_{opt}$ is the photon energy density per volume per Hz. Therefore,

$$g v_g = \frac{B_{21} hf}{B_{opt}}(N_2 - N_1).$$

From $\tau_{sp} = 1/A_{21}$,

$$\frac{1}{g \tau_{sp}} = \frac{A_{21} v_g}{hf B_{21}} B_{opt} \frac{1}{N_2 - N_1} = \frac{8\pi f^2 n^2}{c^2} B_{opt} \frac{1}{N_2 - N_1} = \frac{8\pi}{\lambda_a^2} B_{opt} \frac{1}{N_2 - N_1}$$

where $A_{21}/B_{21} = 8\pi hf^3 n^3/c^3$ is substituted. Therefore,

$$P_{ASE} = hf A\Omega \frac{N_2}{N_2 - N_1} \frac{8\pi}{\lambda_a^2}(G - 1)\Delta f. \qquad \textbf{[17.62]}$$

From the solid angle given by Equation (17.60), the one-sided ASE noise power spectral density per mode and per polarization is

$$S_{ASE}(f) = \frac{P_{ASE}}{2B_{opt}} = hf n_{sp}(G - 1) \qquad \textbf{[17.63]}$$

where

$$n_{sp} \stackrel{\text{def}}{=} \frac{N_2}{N_2 - N_1}.$$

When the gain is not uniform due to saturation, the medium gain, g, is higher at $z = 0$ than at $z = L$. Because spontaneous emission on the $z = 0$ side contributes the most to the noise power, the nonuniform gain results in a larger ASE noise power. Therefore, an additional factor $\chi > 1$ is included to account for the nonuniform gain effect. The final ASE power spectral density is

$$S_{ASE}(f) = hf \frac{N_2}{N_2 - N_1} \chi(G - 1). \qquad \textbf{[17.64]}$$

APPENDIX 17-B:　NOISE POWER AFTER PHOTODETECTION

This appendix considers various noise components after photodetection caused by shot noise and ASE noise.

When the ASE noise is added to the light signal, the total output light field is

$$E_{tot}(t) = \sqrt{2G\,P_{in}}\,\cos(\omega_o t) + E_{ASE}(t)$$

where E_{ASE} is the field due to ASE and can be expressed as

$$E_{ASE}(t) = \lim_{\delta f \to 0} \sum_{i=-M}^{M} \sqrt{2S_{ASE}\delta f}\,\cos[(\omega_o + 2\pi i\delta f)t + \phi_i].$$

In the above expression, E_{ASE} is assumed to have an optical bandwidth

$$B_{opt} = (2M+1)\delta f$$

around the center frequence ω_o. If direct detection is performed, the total photocurrent output is

$$i_{tot}(t) = \mathcal{R}\,|\,E_{tot}(t)\,|^2 + i_{shot}$$

$$= \mathcal{R}G\,P_{in} + 2\mathcal{R}\sum_{i,\,|\,i\delta f\,|\,\le B}\sqrt{G\,P_{in}}\sqrt{S_{ASE}\delta f}\,\cos[(2\pi i\delta f)t + \phi_i]$$

$$+ \mathcal{R}\sum_{i,k,\,|\,i-k\,|\,\delta f \le B} S_{ASE}\cos[2\pi(i-k)\delta f t + \phi_i - \phi_k]\delta f + i_{shot}$$

$$\overset{\text{def}}{=} \mathcal{R}G\,P_{in} + i_{ASE=sig} + i_{ASE=ASE} + i_{shot}$$

where

$$i_{ASE=sig}(t) \overset{\text{def}}{=} 2\mathcal{R}\sum_{i,\,|\,i\delta f\,|\,\le B}\sqrt{G\,P_{in}}\sqrt{S_{ASE}\delta f}\,\cos[(2\pi i\delta f)t + \phi_i] \qquad \textbf{[17.65]}$$

$$i_{ASE=ASE}(t) \overset{\text{def}}{=} \mathcal{R}\sum_{i,k,\,|\,i-k\,|\,\delta f \le B} S_{ASE}\cos[2\pi(i-k)\delta f t + \phi_i - \phi_k]\delta f$$

$$= 2\mathcal{R}S_{ASE}\delta f \sum_{i,k,0<(i-k)\delta f=j\delta f<B}\cos[(2\pi j\delta f)t + \phi_i - \phi_k] \qquad \textbf{[17.66]}$$

and i_{shot} is the shot noise current with variance

$$\sigma_{shot}^2 = 2qR(G\,P_{in} + S_{ASE}B_{opt})B. \qquad \textbf{[17.67]}$$

Finding the noise power of $i_{ASE=sig}$ and i_{ASE} requires examining their power spectral densities. From the definition of $i_{ASE=sig}$ given by Equation (17.66), its autocorrelation function is

$$R_{ASE=sig}(\tau) = E[i_{ASE-sig}(t)i_{ASE-sig}(t+\tau)]$$

$$= 2\mathcal{R}^2 G\,P_{in}S_{ASE}\delta f \sum_{i,\,|\,i\delta f\,|\,\le B}\cos[(2\pi i\delta f)\tau].$$

Thus, the power spectral density $S_{ASE=sig}(f)$ or the Fourier transform of $R_{ASE=sig}(\tau)$ is

$$S_{ASE=sig}(f) = \mathcal{R}^2 G P_{in} S_{ASE} \delta f \sum_{i,\,|i\delta f|\,\leq B} [\delta(f - i\delta f) + \delta(f + i\delta f)].$$

Taking the limit $\delta f \to 0$ gives

$$S_{ASE=sig}(f) = \begin{cases} 2\mathcal{R}^2 G P_{in} S_{ASE} & \text{if } |f| < B \\ 0 & \text{if } |f| > B \end{cases}. \qquad \textbf{[17.68]}$$

This gives the noise power

$$\sigma^2_{ASE=sig} = 4\mathcal{R}^2 G P_{in} S_{ASE} B. \qquad \textbf{[17.69]}$$

Similarly, from the definition of $i_{ASE=ASE}(t)$ given by Equation (17.66),

$$R_{ASE=ASE} = 2(\mathcal{R} S_{ASE} \delta f)^2 \sum_{i,k,0<(i-k)\delta f=j\delta f<B} \cos[(2\pi j\delta f)\tau].$$

Taking the Fourier transform gives

$$S_{ASE=ASE}(f) = (\mathcal{R} S_{ASE} \delta f)^2 \sum_{i,k,0<(i-k)\delta f=j\delta f<B} [\delta(f - j\delta f) + \delta(f + j\delta f)].$$

Considering all possible combinations of (i, j) to give a certain j, there are $2M$ terms for $j = 1$, $2M - 2$ terms for $j = 2, \ldots$, and 1 term for $j = 2M$. Therefore, when $\delta f \to 0$,

$$S_{ASE=ASE}(f) = \mathcal{R}^2 S^2_{ASE}(B_{opt} - f) \qquad \textbf{[17.70]}$$

where $|f| < B_{opt}$. This is illustrated in Figure 17.20. Taking the integration of the spectrum from dc to B gives the following noise power:

$$\sigma^2_{ASE=ASE} = \mathcal{R}^2 S^2_{ASE}(2B_{opt} - B)B. \qquad \textbf{[17.71]}$$

PROBLEMS

Problem 17–1 Amplifier Bandwidth: Consider an optical amplifier used for a WDM system where 100 wavelength channels are simultaneously amplified. If the channel separation is 20 GHz and the central wavelength is 1550 nm, find the minimum required amplifier linewidth in nm.

Problem 17–2 Amplifier Gain: To have a repeaterless transmission across the Pacific Ocean, find the required gain to compensate for the transmission loss. Assume the distance is 5000 km, fiber attenuation plus other loss is 0.3 dB/km, the transmitter output power is 10 dBm, and the receiver sensitivity is –20 dBm. If the maximum achievable gain per amplifier is 30 dB, how many are needed?

Problem 17–3 Gain and Loss of Semiconductor Amplifiers: Consider a semiconductor amplifier with a confinement factor $\Gamma = 0.5$, gain constant $a = 5 \times 10^{-20}$ m^2, recombination time constant $\tau_r = 0.2$ nsec, and $N_0 = 8 \times 10^{23}$ m^{-3}.

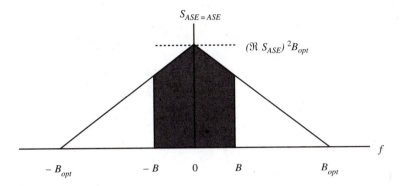

Figure 17.20   Power spectral density function of the ASE noise.

a. Find the threshold carrier density, N_{th}, if the amplifier medium has a distributed loss of $\alpha_m = 2000$ 1/m.

b. If the medium gain at zero saturation, g_0, is required to be 1000 1/m, find the required current density. Assume the thickness of the active layer of the amplifier is $d = 0.1\ \mu$m.

Problem 17–4 Gain Saturation: From Equation (17.6), note that it is desirable to have a smaller gain constant, a, to increase the saturation power. However, this will result in a smaller gain.

a. Use Equation (17.5) to find the medium gain, $g(N)$ as $a \to 0$. From this, will it be good to increase the saturation power P_{sat} by reducing a?

b. The same Equation (17.5) shows that the gain coefficient $g(N)$ is inversely proportional to P as $a \to \infty$. In this case, what can you say about the amplifier gain, G, as a function of its length and input power at a given current density, J?

Problem 17–5 Gain Saturation: Consider a semiconductor amplifier with a confinement factor of $\Gamma = 0.3$, threshold carrier density $N_{th} = 10^{24}$ 1/m³, gain constant $a = 5 \times 10^{-20}$ m², and time constant $\tau_r = 0.1$ nsec.

a. To have a net gain of $G_0 = 25$ dB, calculate the needed nonsaturated gain $G_{0,no\ sat}$ when $P_{in}/P_{sat} = 0.001$.

b. Use Equations (17.11) and (17.13) to find the injection current, I, for a gain of $G_0 = 30$ dB at $P_{in}/P_{sat} = 0, 10^{-3}$, and 10^{-2}. Assume the semiconductor has dimensions $d = 0.1\ \mu$m, $w = 2\ \mu$m, and $L = 250\ \mu$m.

Problem 17–6 FWHM Linewidth of Gain: If the gain profile of an optical amplifier is

$$g(\lambda) = g_0 e^{-(\lambda-\lambda_0)^2/2\Delta\lambda^2}$$

where $\Delta\lambda = 25$ nm, find the FWHM of the amplifier gain, G, if the peak gain at λ_0 is 30 dB.

Problem 17–7 Finite Facet Reflection:

a. If the gain variation due to finite facet reflectivity must be limited to 3 dB, find the required reflectivity with $G_0 = 30$ dB. Hint: use Equation (17.19).

b. If N such amplifiers are in series in a transmission line, what is the required reflectivity product, $r_L r_R$, as a function of N when the worst case peak-to-peak variation is still required to be 3 dB?

Problem 17–8 Fabry-Perot Amplifiers: Use Equation (17.18) to find the required product $r_L r_R$ so that the maximum G_{FP} gain is the same as $G_{0,no\ sat}$, the gain at no saturation and zero reflection. Assume $G_0 = 20$ dB, 5 dB below $G_{0,no\ sat}$. At this value, what is the peak-to-peak variation, C?

Problem 17–9 Brewster Angle:

a. Find the derivative of the expression given by Equation (17.20) with respect to θ_1 and evaluated at θ_p.

b. If the Brewster angle is used to achieve zero reflection, from Equations (17.20) and (17.21), what will be the reflection $R = r^2$ if there is an alignment error such that θ_1 is $\pm 1°$ from the Brewster angle, θ_p? Assume $n_1 = 3.5$ and $n_2 = 1.0$.

Problem 17–10 Pumping Efficiency of an EDFA:

a. From Equation (17.35), find $(\tau_{sp} g^*)^{-1} dg/dW_p$ in terms of $\tau_{sp} W_p$ at $W_s = 0$.

b. Evaluate the derived expression in (a) for $g = 0.1g^*$, $0.2g^*$, and $0.5g^*$, respectively, at $W_s = 0$. What is the trade-off to have a large g, according to these results?

Problem 17–11 Gain Saturation of EDFA: Repeat Problem 17–10 with $W_s \neq 0$. For part (b), assume $W_s \tau_{sp} = 2$.

Problem 17–12 Interchannel Interference in EDFAs: Similar to semiconductor amplifiers, there is also interchannel interference (ICI) in EDFAs when they are used for multichannel amplification. Because of a much larger time constant, τ_{sp}, however, ICI is negligible in EDFAs.

a. From the rate equation given by Equation (17.32), show that the carrier density change, ΔN_2, due to a small stimulated emission rate change, ΔW_s, follows the following small signal equation:

$$-\frac{\partial}{\partial t}\Delta N_2 = -\frac{\Delta N_2}{\tau'} - (N_2 - N_1)\Delta W_s$$

where

$$\frac{1}{\tau'} = W_p + 2W_s + \frac{1}{\tau_{sp}}.$$

b. Show that the solution of the above equation is

$$\Delta N_2 = -\Delta W_s (N_2 - N_1)\tau'(1 - e^{-t/\tau'}).$$

c. From Equation (17.34), show the corresponding medium gain change is

$$\Delta g(t) = -2g\frac{\Delta W_s}{W_p + 2W_s + 1/\tau_{sp}}(1 - e^{-t/\tau'}).$$

d. Use a discussion similar to that in Section 17.3.4 to argue that ICI in EDFAs is negligible.

Problem 17–13 Beat Noise: Consider the use of a receiver amplifier of gain 20 dB before a PIN photodetector that has a responsivity of 0.7 A/W and noise equivalent power (NEP) of 10^{-11} W/Hz$^{1/2}$. Find the input power P_{in} below which the beat noise is smaller than the signal independent noise power. Assume $\chi n_{sp} = 10$ and wavelength $\lambda = 1540$ nm.

Problem 17–14 Noise Figure: The noise figure given by Equation (17.51) shows that the use of optical amplifiers is at least 3 dB worse in SNR in either direct detection or coherent detection. If this is the case, why use optical amplifiers? For the photodetector considered in Problem 17–13, find the range of the incident power P_{in} within which the SNR at photodetection output is greater than 20 dB and it is worth to use optical amplification. Assume $B = 1$ GHz in calculation.

Problem 17–15 System Design: Consider a transmission system that has a total transmission loss of 50 dB, the transmitter has an output power of 1 mW, and the receiver is the same as that in Problem 17–13.

a. Check whether an optical amplifier is needed at the receiver input if the required SNR is 30 dB at $B = 1$ GHz and the responsivity is $\mathcal{R} = 0.9$ A/W. Assume a PIN diode is used in the receiver.

b. If an optical amplifier of gain 20 dB at the receiver input is used, find the SNR at the photodetector output at $B = 1$ GHz. Assume the amplifier has a noise figure of 7 dB.

Problem 17–16 System Design: Consider a transmission system that has a total transmission loss of 200 dB.

a. Ignoring the gain saturation effect, design the use of optical amplifiers according to Figure 17.19 to achieve a final SNR of at least 30 dB at the output of the photodetection. Assume the transmitter output is 10 mW, $B = 1$ GHz, the same photodetection circuit as in Problem 17–13 is used, and each optical amplifier has a gain of 20 dB and a noise figure of 5 dB.

b. Using optical amplifiers of 30 dB gain and noise figure of 7 dB, do the design again for the same conditions given in (*a*).

REFERENCES

1. Special Issue on Optical Amplifiers, *Journal of Lightwave Technology,* vol. 9, no. 2 (February 1991).

2. P. H. Howerton, "Diode-Pumped Amplifier/Laser Using Leaky Wavefiber Coupling: An Evaluation," *IEEE Journal of Quantum Electronics,* vol. 28, no. 4 (1992), pp. 1081–87.

3. K. Kikushima, "Distortion and Noise Properties of a Praseodymium-Doped Fluoride Fiber Amplifier in 1.3 μm AM-SCM Video Transmission Systems," *IEEE Photonics Technology Letters,* vol. 6, no. 3 (1994), pp. 440–42.

4. T. Whitley, "High Output Power from an Efficient Praseodymium-Doped Fluoride Fiber Amplifier," *IEEE Photonics Technology Letters,* vol. 5, no. 4 (1993), pp. 401–3.

5. Graham R. Walker et al., "Erbium-Doped Fiber Amplifier Cascade for Multichannel Coherent Optical Transmission," *Journal of Lightwave Technology,* vol. 9, no. 2 (February 1991), pp. 182–93.

6. C. J. Koester and E. Snitzer, "Amplification in a Fiber Laser," *Applied Optics*, vol. 3 (1964), p. 1182.

7. R. J. Mears et al., "Low Noise Erbium-Doped Fiber Amplifier Operating at 1.54 μm," *Electronics Letters*, vol. 23 (1987), p. 1026.

8. E. Desurvire et al., "High-Gain Erbium-Doped Traveling-Wave Fiber Amplifier," *Optics Letters,* vol. 12 (1987), p. 888–90.

9. C. R. Pollock, *Fundamentals of Optoelectronics*, Burr Ridge, IL: Richard D. Irwin, 1995.

10. W. J. Miniscalco, "Erbium-Doped Glasses for Fiber Amplifiers at 1500 nm," *Journal of Lightwave Technology,* vol. 9, no. 2 (February 1991), pp. 234–50.

11. G. P. Agrawal, *Fiber-Optic Communication Systems,* John Wiley and Sons, 1992.

12. C. R. Giles and E. Desurvire, "Modeling Erbium-Doped Fiber Amplifiers," *Journal of Lightwave Technology,* vol. 9, no. 2 (February 1991), pp. 271–83.

13. K. Kikuchi, "Generalized Formula for Optical-Amplifier Noise and Its Application to Erbium Doped Fiber Amplifier," *Electronics Letters*, vol. 26 (1990), p. 1851.

14. H. Kogelnik and A. Yariv, "Considerations of Noise and Schemes for Its Reduction in Laser Amplifiers," *Proceedings of the IEEE,* February 1964, pp. 165–73.

15. N. A. Olsson, "Lightwave Systems with Optical Amplifiers," *Journal of Lightwave Technology,* vol. 7, no. 7 (July 1989), pp. 1071–82.

18

OPTICAL FIBER SOLITON TRANSMISSION

Previous discussion pointed out two fundamental limits in optical fiber transmission: attenuation and dispersion. Optical amplification can overcome the attenuation limit, as discussed in Chapter 17. This chapter discusses the recent development of fiber soliton technology, which turns fiber dispersion liability into a positive asset.

The word **soliton** [1] was derived from the name **solitary wave**, which was first observed and discussed by Scottish scientist J. Scott Russel [2]. In his studies on the Edinburgh–Glasgow canal in 1834, Russel first observed that a large solitary wave was generated when a canal boat suddenly stopped. The wave is a rounded, smooth, and well-defined heap of water that can travel over many miles without changing its form or speed.

Russel's initial observation attracted many scientists' interests. One important milestone was the discovery of the KdV equation by Korteweg and de Vries [3], which describes the solitary wave discovered by Russel. Because the KdV equation can be applied not only to water waves but also to other fields such as plasma where the nonlinearity is strong, active research work was done to understand why its solution can maintain the same form as it propagates.

In 1965, Zabusky and Kruskal [1] discovered an **inverse scattering** technique that transforms the nonlinear KdV equation into a set of *linear* equations, which can then be solved using standard techniques. In this technique, the nonlinear equation is transformed to a wave equation, and the pulse function, or the soliton in the KdV equation, is given a different physical meaning: a time-varying "energy potential." According to the wave function, the "potential" determines how an incident wave is "scattered." From the scattered data of the incident wave, the inverse scattering technique then finds the potential, or the soliton. This transformation technique of using the scattered data to find the potential is similar to the Fourier transform that describes a time-domain pulse in terms of its spectral content. Because the wave equation is linear after transformation, the solution to the KdV equation can be expressed as a sum of eigenfunctions, each of which is a soliton with its unique eigenvalue. Because of the linear nature, when two solitons are traveling toward each other, they can pass through each other with only a possible phase change.

In 1972, Zakharov and Shabat [4] used the same inverse scattering technique to solve the nonlinear Schrödinger equation (NLSE), which can be used to describe wave propagation inside an optical fiber when nonlinearity is strong. From this discovery, Hasegawa and Tappert [5] first suggested in 1973 that optical solitons could exist in optical fiber transmission by taking advantage of both fiber dispersion and nonlinearity. Since then, active research has been conducted around the world to make fiber soliton transmission a reality.

This chapter derives the NLSE that describes wave propagation in an optical fiber. To help readers understand the meaning of the equation, the chapter explains the physical effect of each term. This will help us to explain the existence of solitons and their important properties. Based on the NLSE, some important solutions, including the fundamental soliton and higher order modes, are discussed. At the end, recent soliton transmission experiments and important technical issues in practical implementation are described.

18.1 FIBER NONLINEARITY AND WAVE EQUATIONS

As mentioned earlier, wave propagation in an optical fiber with nonlinearity can be described by the NLSE. This can be derived from the wave equations given in Appendix 4–A. To see this, a nonlinear induced polarization term is added to wave equation (4.71). The new equation is

$$\nabla^2 \mathcal{E} - \frac{1}{c^2}\frac{\partial^2}{\partial t^2}\mathcal{E} = \mu_0 \frac{\partial^2}{\partial t^2}(\mathcal{P}_L + \mathcal{P}_{NL}) \qquad \textbf{[18.1]}$$

where $\mathcal{P}_{NL}$ denotes the nonlinear polarization due to the nonlinear Kerr effect (see Chapter 14). When $\mathcal{E}$ is a wave packet, it can be expressed as

$$\mathcal{E}(z,t) = A(z,t)e^{j(\omega_0 t - \beta_0 z)} \qquad \textbf{[18.2]}$$

where $A(z,t)$ is the envelope of the wave packet that is slowly varying in both time and space compared to the phase factor $e^{j(\omega_0 t - \beta_0 z)}$.

From Equation (18.2), the first term in Equation (18.1) can be approximated as

$$\nabla^2 \mathcal{E}(z,t) = \left(-\beta_0^2 A - 2j\beta_0 \frac{\partial A}{\partial z}\right)e^{j(\omega_0 t - \beta_0 z)} \qquad \textbf{[18.3]}$$

where higher order terms have been ignored.

To further simplify Equation (18.1), let

$$\mathcal{X}(z,t) = -\frac{1}{c^2}\frac{\partial^2}{\partial t^2}(\mathcal{E} + \frac{1}{\epsilon_0}\mathcal{P}_L) = -\frac{1}{\epsilon_0 c^2}\frac{\partial^2}{\partial t^2}\left[\mathcal{E} + \int \hat{\chi}(t-t')\mathcal{E}(z,t')dt'\right]$$

where $\hat{\chi}$ is the time dependent susceptibility (see Appendix 12-A). Taking Fourier transform on both sides gives

$$\tilde{\mathcal{X}}(z,\omega) = \frac{\omega^2}{c^2}\left[\tilde{\mathcal{E}}(z,\omega) + \int \hat{\chi}(t-t')\mathcal{E}(z,t')dt' \, e^{-j\omega t}dt\right] \qquad \textbf{[18.4]}$$

$$= \frac{\omega^2}{c^2}\left[\tilde{\mathcal{E}}(z,\omega) + \int \hat{\chi}(t-t')\mathcal{E}(z,t')e^{-j\omega t'}e^{-j\omega(t-t')}dtdt'\right]$$

$$= \frac{\omega^2}{c^2}n^2(\omega)\tilde{\mathcal{E}}(z,\omega) = \beta(\omega)^2\tilde{\mathcal{E}}(z,\omega)$$

where $n^2(\omega) = 1 + \chi(\omega)$, $\beta(\omega) = \omega n(\omega)/c$, and $\tilde{\mathcal{E}}(z, \omega)$ is the Fourier transform of $\mathcal{E}(z, t)$:

$$\tilde{\mathcal{E}}(z, \omega) = \int A(z, t) e^{-j(\omega - \omega_0)t} dt \, e^{-j\beta_0 z} = \tilde{A}(z, \omega - \omega_0) e^{-j\beta_0 z}. \qquad \textbf{[18.5]}$$

Expanding $\beta(\omega)$ into a Talyor series gives

$$\beta(\omega) = \beta_0 + \beta_1(\omega - \omega_0) + \frac{\beta_2}{2}(\omega - \omega_0)^2 + \dots \qquad \textbf{[18.6]}$$

where $\beta_0 \stackrel{\text{def}}{=} \beta(\omega_0)$,

$$\beta_1 \stackrel{\text{def}}{=} \left. \frac{\partial \beta}{\partial \omega} \right|_{\omega_0} = \frac{1}{v_g} \qquad \textbf{[18.7]}$$

is the inverse of group velocity and

$$\beta_2 \stackrel{\text{def}}{=} \left. \frac{\partial^2 \beta}{\partial \omega^2} \right|_{\omega_0} \qquad \textbf{[18.8]}$$

is the group velocity dispersion. From the expansion,

$$\beta(\omega)^2 \approx \beta_0^2 + 2\beta_0\beta_1(\omega - \omega_0) + \beta_0\beta_2(\omega - \omega_0)^2.$$

Equation (18.4) thus reduces to

$$\tilde{\mathcal{X}}(z, \omega) \approx \beta_0 \left[\beta_0 + 2\beta_1(\omega - \omega_0) + \beta_2(\omega - \omega_0)^2 \right] \tilde{\mathcal{E}}(z, \omega).$$

Transforming this back to the time domain,

$$\mathcal{X}(z, t) = \beta_0 \left[\beta_0 A(z, t) - 2j\beta_1 \frac{\partial A}{\partial t} - \beta_2 \frac{\partial^2 A}{\partial t^2} \right] e^{j(\omega_0 t - \beta_0 z)}. \qquad \textbf{[18.9]}$$

From the nonlinear Kerr effect described by Equation (14.36), the nonlinear term $\mathcal{P}_{NL}$ can be expressed as

$$\mathcal{P}_{NL} = \epsilon_0 n^2 \times (-n^2 s |\mathcal{E}|^2) \times \mathcal{E} = -\epsilon_0 n^4 s |A|^2 A e^{j(\omega_0 - \beta_0 z)} \qquad \textbf{[18.10]}$$

where s is the Kerr coefficient. Therefore,

$$\mu \frac{\partial^2}{\partial t^2} \mathcal{P}_{NL} \approx \frac{\omega_0^2}{c^2} n^4 s |A|^2 A e^{j(\omega_0 - \beta_0 z)}. \qquad \textbf{[18.11]}$$

Substituting the above results from Equations (18.3), (18.9), and (18.11) into Equation (18.1) gives

$$-2j \frac{\partial A}{\partial z} - 2j\beta_1 \frac{\partial A}{\partial t} - \beta_2 \frac{\partial^2 A}{\partial t^2} = -2\gamma |A|^2 A \qquad \textbf{[18.12]}$$

where

$$\gamma \overset{\text{def}}{=} -\frac{\beta_0}{2} n^2 s. \qquad \textbf{[18.13]}$$

Because

$$\beta_2 = \frac{\partial}{\partial \omega} \frac{1}{v_g} = \frac{\partial \lambda}{\partial \omega} \frac{\partial}{\partial \lambda} \frac{1}{v_g} = -\frac{\lambda}{\omega_0} D_{intra} \qquad \textbf{[18.14]}$$

Equation (18.12) reduces to

$$\frac{\partial A}{\partial z} + \frac{1}{v_g} \frac{\partial A}{\partial t} - \frac{j\beta_2}{2} \frac{\partial^2 A}{\partial t^2} = \frac{\partial A}{\partial z} + \frac{1}{v_g} \frac{\partial A}{\partial t} + \frac{j\lambda D_{intra}}{2\omega_0} \frac{\partial^2 A}{\partial t^2} = -j\gamma |A|^2 A. \qquad \textbf{[18.15]}$$

This is the NLSE that describes pulse propagation in a nonlinear fiber.

18.2   PHYSICAL MEANING OF THE NONLINEAR SCHRÖDINGER EQUATION

In Equation (18.15), it is clear that the first two terms on the left-hand side describe pulse propagation at a group velocity v_g in the $+\hat{z}$ direction. The third term on the left and the nonlinear term on the right describe pulse and spectrum broadening, respectively. This section elaborates these points and shows that a pulse can propagate with the same shape when pulse dispersion and spectrum broadening are in balance.

18.2.1 v_g^{-1}: PULSE PROPAGATION

If there is no dispersion or fiber nonlinearity, Equation (18.15) reduces to

$$\frac{\partial A}{\partial z} + \frac{1}{v_g} \frac{\partial A}{\partial t} = 0. \qquad \textbf{[18.16]}$$

Clearly, it has the following general solution

$$A(z, t) = A(z - v_g t). \qquad \textbf{[18.17]}$$

This means that the envelope of the wave packet propagates at a speed of v_g. From this observation, it is possible to define

$$t_1 \overset{\text{def}}{=} t - \frac{z}{v_g} \qquad \textbf{[18.18]}$$

and

$$A(z, t) = A[z, t_1 + (z/v_g)] \overset{\text{def}}{=} A_1(z, t_1).$$

As a result,

$$\frac{\partial A_1(z, t_1)}{\partial z} = \frac{\partial A}{\partial z} + \frac{1}{v_g} \frac{\partial A}{\partial t} \bigg|_{t=t_1+z/v_g}$$

and Equation (18.15) reduces to

$$\frac{\partial A_1}{\partial z} - \frac{j\beta_2}{2}\frac{\partial^2 A_1}{\partial t_1^2} = \frac{\partial A_1}{\partial z} + \frac{j\lambda D_{intra}}{2\omega_0}\frac{\partial^2 A_1}{\partial t_1^2} = -j\gamma|A_1|^2 A_1. \qquad \textbf{[18.19]}$$

This equation describes wave propagation in a new time coordinate $t_1 = t - z/v_g$. When there is no dispersion or nonlinearity, the solution to Equation (18.19) is spatially invariant or $A_1(z, t_1) = A_1(0, t_1)$.

18.2.2 β_2 OR $-(\lambda/\omega)D_{intra}$: PULSE BROADENING

When there is only fiber dispersion, Equation (18.19) reduces to

$$\frac{\partial A_1}{\partial z} + \frac{j\lambda D_{intra}}{2\omega_0}\frac{\partial^2 A_1}{\partial t_1^2} = 0. \qquad \textbf{[18.20]}$$

To see the effect of pulse broadening, first note that $A_1(z, t_1)$ given by Equation (18.20) can be expressed as

$$A_1(z, t_1) = \frac{1}{2\pi}\int \tilde{A}_1(0, \omega)e^{j[\omega t_1 + (\lambda D_{intra}/2\omega_0)\omega^2 z]}d\omega \qquad \textbf{[18.21]}$$

where $\tilde{A}_1(0, \omega)$ is the Fourier transform or spectrum of $A_1(0, t_1)$ at $z = 0$. By taking the Fourier transform on both sides,

$$\tilde{A}_1(z, \omega) = \tilde{A}_1(0, \omega)e^{j(\lambda D_{intra}/2\omega_0)\omega^2 z}. \qquad \textbf{[18.22]}$$

This gives the spatial evolution of the pulse in the frequency domain and shows that the dispersive fiber channel has a transfer function for $A_1(z, t_1)$:[1]

$$H_{fiber}(\omega) = e^{j(\lambda D_{intra}/2\omega_0)\omega^2 z}. \qquad \textbf{[18.23]}$$

The phase of $H_{fiber}(\omega)$ varies faster as the frequency increases.

From the above observation, the cause of pulse broadening can be intuitively understood as follows. Equation (18.21) indicates that the phase of the integrand is around zero at a certain time t_1 when the frequency ω is around

$$\omega_c \overset{\text{def}}{=} -\frac{2\omega_0}{\lambda D_{intra} z}t_1.$$

Thus, outside a certain small frequency band $\Delta\omega$ around ω_c as illustrated in Figure 18.1, the phase variation is large and the contribution to the integration is negligible. From this, $A_1(z, t_1)$ can be approximated as

$$A_1(z, t_1) \approx \Delta\omega\tilde{A}(\omega_c) = \Delta\omega\tilde{A}\left(-\frac{2\omega_0 t_1}{\lambda D_{intra} z}\right).$$

This result shows that the pulse becomes broader as z increases.

---

[1] Because $A_1(z, t_1)$ is complex, note that the corresponding impulse response is complex. This transfer function is different from that discussed in Chapter 4 for the *power* or $|A_1|^2$ of the pulse.

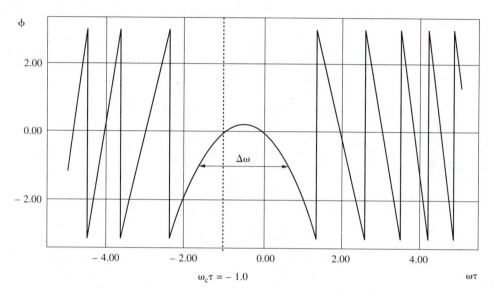

Figure 18.1   Illustration of phase $\phi(\omega) = \omega t_1 + (\lambda D_{intra}/2\omega_0)\omega^2 z \overset{\text{def}}{=} \omega(\omega_c - \omega)\tau^2$ as a function of $\omega\tau$, where $\omega_c \overset{\text{def}}{=} -\frac{2\omega_0}{\lambda D_{intra}z}t_1$ and $\tau^2 = -t_1/\omega_c$. In the illustration, $\omega_c\tau = -1$ is assumed.

Example 18.1

GAUSSIAN PULSE   To see more quantitatively the pulse broadening effect, consider a Gaussian pulse input. In this case,

$$A_1(0, t_1) = e^{-t_1^2/2\sigma_0^2}$$

where σ is the root mean square (RMS) width of the pulse. From this input, its Fourier transform is

$$\tilde{A}_1(0, \omega) = \sqrt{2\pi\sigma_0^2}\,e^{-\omega^2\sigma_0^2/2}.$$

Substituting this into Equation (18.21),

$$A_1(z, t_1) = \frac{\sigma_0}{\sqrt{2\pi}} \int e^{-\omega^2\sigma_0^2/2 + j\omega t_1 + j(\lambda D_{intra}/2\omega_0)\omega^2 z}\,d\omega$$

$$= \frac{\sigma_0}{\sigma(z)} e^{-t^2/2\sigma^2(z)}$$

where

$$\sigma^2(z) = \sigma_0^2 - j(\lambda D_{intra}/\omega_0)z \overset{\text{def}}{=} \sigma_0^2(1 - jz/z_D)$$

and

$$z_D = \frac{\omega_0}{\lambda D_{intra}}\sigma_0^2.$$

Therefore, the magnitude square of $A_1(z, t_1)$ is

$$|A_1(z, t_1)|^2 = \frac{1}{[1 + (z/z_D)^2]^{1/2}} e^{-t_1^2/\sigma_0^2[1+(z/z_D)^2]}.$$

As illustrated in Figures 18.2 and 18.3, this expression shows that the pulse in the time domain (but not in the frequency domain) broadens as z increases. ∎

18.2.3 $j\gamma|A_1|^2$: SELF–PHASE MODULATION AND SPECTRUM BROADENING

When only fiber nonlinearity is considered, Equation (18.19) reduces to

$$\frac{\partial A_1}{\partial z} = -j\gamma|A_1|^2 A_1. \qquad\qquad \textbf{[18.24]}$$

Therefore, $A_1(z, t_1)$ can be approximated as

$$A_1(z, t_1) \approx e^{-j\gamma|A_1(z,t_1)|^2 z} A_1(0, t_1). \qquad\qquad \textbf{[18.25]}$$

From the expression, note that the phase shift depends on the light intensity $|A_1|^2$. This is called **self–phase modulation** (SPM). Because the time derivative of the phase change results in a frequency change, SPM can result in a change of the spectrum. Some interesting phenomena due to SPM include: **self-focusing** [6], **pulse narrowing** [7], and **spectrum broadening** [8].

If Equation (18.25) is compared with Equation (18.22) and the nonlinear term $-\gamma|A_1|^2$ is substituted with the dispersive term $(\lambda D_{intra}/2\omega_0)\omega^2$, it can be seen that they are very similar in form. The difference is Equation (18.25) gives the spatial evolution of the pulse in the time domain and Equation (18.22) gives the spatial evolution of the pulse in the frequency domain. From the frequency–time duality, the pulse will experience spectrum broadening because of fiber nonlinearity. As illustrated in Figures 18.4–18.6, a Gaussian pulse input has the same shape in the time domain but broadens in the frequency domain as it propagates.

18.2.4 BALANCE BETWEEN FIBER DISPERSION AND NONLINEARITY

When both fiber dispersion and nonlinearity exist, the spatial evolution of the pulse magnitude can stay unchanged if there is a balance between the phase changes due to dispersion and nonlinearity. This can be understood as follows. From Equations (18.21) and (18.25), $A_1(z, t_1)$ can be expressed as

$$A_1(z, t_1) = \frac{1}{2\pi} e^{-j\gamma|A_1|^2 z} \int \tilde{A}_1(0, \omega) e^{-j\omega(t_1 + \beta_2\omega z/2)} d\omega \stackrel{\text{def}}{=} |A_1| e^{j\phi(z,t_1)}. \quad \textbf{[18.26]}$$

If $|A_1|$ is unchanged as z increases,

$$\frac{\partial A_1}{\partial z} = j\frac{\partial\phi}{\partial z} A_1 = -j\gamma|A_1|^2 A_1 - j\frac{\beta_2}{2}\frac{1}{2\pi}\int \omega^2 \tilde{A}_1(0, \omega) e^{-j\omega(t_1 + \beta_2\omega z/2)} d\omega$$

$$= -j\gamma|A_1|^2 A_1 + j\frac{\beta_2}{2}\frac{\partial^2 A_1}{\partial t_1^2}.$$

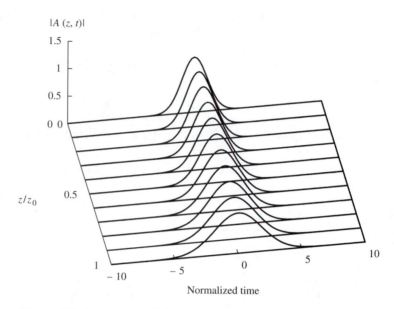

Figure 18.2   Spatial evolution of the magnitude of a Gaussian pulse when only fiber dispersion is considered. The pulse width becomes broader as z increases.

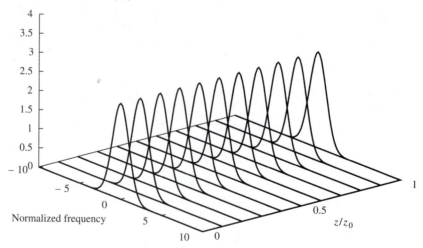

Figure 18.3   Spatial evolution of the magnitude of the spectrum of the Gaussian pulse when only fiber dispersion is considered. It is spatially invariant. Note, however, that the phase of the spectrum increases along the propagation and is faster at large ω (not shown).

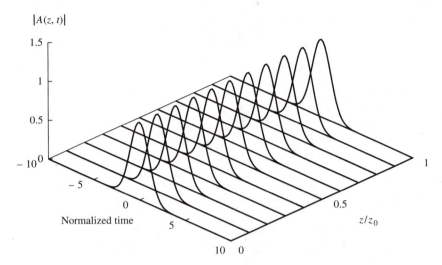

Figure 18.4 Spatial evolution of the magnitude of a Gaussian pulse under fiber nonlinearity. Fiber dispersion is ignored here.

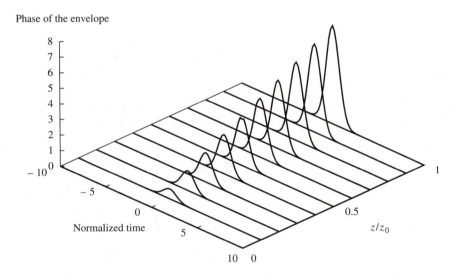

Figure 18.5 Spatial evolution of the phase of the Gaussian pulse under fiber nonlinearity. Fiber dispersion is ignored here.

Magnitude of Fourier transform of $A(z, t)$

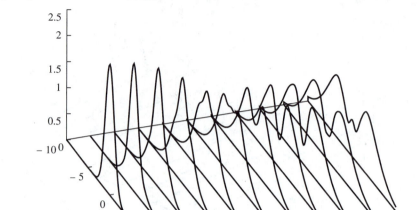

Figure 18.6   Spatial evolution of the magnitude of the spectrum of the Gaussian pulse under fiber nonlinearity. Fiber dispersion is ignored here.

Thus,

$$\frac{\partial \phi}{\partial z} = -\gamma |A_1|^2 + \frac{\beta_2}{2A_1} \frac{\partial^2 A_1}{\partial t_1^2}.$$

This expression makes it clear that the phase change with respect to z is a result of both fiber nonlinearity and dispersion. If the two have a good balance so that

$$-\gamma |A_1|^2 + \frac{\beta_2}{2A_1} \frac{\partial^2 A_1}{\partial t_1^2} = \text{constant} \qquad \text{[18.27]}$$

the spatial evolution of $A_1(z, t_1)$ is invariant other than a linear phase shift. Thus the physical meaning of the NLSE given by Equation (18.19) is to ensure the phase balance given by Equation (18.27).

18.3 ONE-DIMENSIONAL SOLITON SOLUTIONS

Based on the physical meaning of the NLSE, this section describes the soliton solution. To simplify the explanation, only several special cases are considered here. Detailed discussion on solving Equation (18.15) using the inverse scattering method is given in Appendix 18–A.

Normalization   It is convenient to first transform Equation (18.15) to a dimensionless expression. To do so requires first defining the following normalized time and space variables:

$$T \overset{\text{def}}{=} \frac{t - z/v_g}{T_0} \qquad \textbf{[18.28]}$$

$$Z \overset{\text{def}}{=} \frac{z}{L_D} \qquad \textbf{[18.29]}$$

where T_0 is a certain time value called the soliton time constant, and

$$L_D \overset{\text{def}}{=} \frac{T_0^2}{|\beta_2|} \qquad \textbf{[18.30]}$$

is called the **soliton distance**. To normalize the nonlinearity, another important parameter is defined:

$$N^2 \overset{\text{def}}{=} \gamma A_p^2 L_D = \frac{1}{|\beta_2|} \gamma A_p^2 T_0^2. \qquad \textbf{[18.31]}$$

Because it is proportional to γ, we see N^2 represents the strength of the nonlinearity.

From the above definitions, the normalized envelope U can be defined as

$$U(Z, T) \overset{\text{def}}{=} N \frac{A(z, t)}{A_p} \qquad \textbf{[18.32]}$$

where A_p is the peak value of $|A(z, t)|$. Therefore, $U(Z, T)$ has a peak power of N and

$$A(z, t) = \frac{A_p}{N} U(Z, T) = \frac{A_p}{N} U\left(\frac{z}{L_D}, \frac{t - z/v_g}{T_0}\right). \qquad \textbf{[18.33]}$$

Substituting Equation (18.33) into Equation (18.15), gives:[2]

$$\frac{\partial U}{\partial Z} = j\left[\frac{1}{2}\frac{\partial^2 U}{\partial T^2} + |U|^2 U\right]. \qquad \textbf{[18.34]}$$

This is the canonical form of the NLSE. Comparing Equations (18.15) and (18.34), note that $\beta_2 < 0$ has been assumed. This is an important condition for ensuring the existence of solitons. The condition of negative β_2 is equivalent to positive D_{intra}, which is true in ordinary glass optical fibers when $\lambda > 1.30\ \mu$m (see Chapter 4).

TYPICAL SOLITON DISTANCE   From Equation (18.31), the soliton distance L_D is

$$L_D = \frac{N^2}{\gamma P}$$

Example 18.2

---

[2] The sign for j is changed here because of different phaser representations in the literature. In electrical engineering, the phaser of an EM wave is given by $e^{j(\omega_0 t - \beta_0 z)}$. This is the convention used in the previous sections and the rest of the book. In physics and soliton literature, unfortunately, the phaser is given by $e^{i(\beta_0 z - \omega_0 t)}$, where $j = i = \sqrt{-1}$. To follow the convention used in the soliton literature, the sign for j must be changed here. Readers can identify which convention is used from the context.

where $P = A_p^2$ is the peak power of the soliton. For a typical silica fiber, $\gamma = 2 \times 10^{-3}$ $(\text{m·W})^{-1}$. At $N = 1$ and $P = 50$ mW, $L_D = 10$ km. Because L_D is linearly proportional to $1/P$, L_D can be increased at a smaller peak power. ■

Fundamental Soliton   A special and important solution to Equation (18.34) is

$$U(Z, T) = \frac{2}{e^T + e^{-T}} e^{jZ/2} = \text{sech}(T)e^{jZ/2}. \qquad \textbf{[18.35]}$$

This is called the fundamental soliton because $N = 1$. From Equation (18.33), the corresponding denormalized envelope is

$$A(z, t) = A_p \text{sech}\left(\frac{t - z/v_g}{T_0}\right) e^{jz/(2L_D)}. \qquad \textbf{[18.36]}$$

Figures 18.7 and 18.8 illustrate the propagation of the soliton. This solution says that the soliton maintains the same waveform and spectrum as it propagates. The only change is its phase, which is a linear function of Z. Verification of the solution (18.35) is given by Problem 18–4.

Example 18.3

SOLITON PULSE WIDTH   When $N = 1$,

$$T_0 = \left(\frac{|\beta_2|}{\gamma}\right)^{1/2} \frac{1}{A_p} = \left(\frac{|\beta_2|}{\gamma P}\right)^{1/2} \qquad \textbf{[18.37]}$$

where P is the peak power of the light pulse. Therefore, given the nonlinearity coefficient γ, dispersion coefficient β_2, and the peak envelope A_p, T_0 can be determined for the fundamental soliton. Because T_0 is inversely proportional to the peak amplitude A_p, the larger the pulse power, the smaller the pulse width. This is consistent with the pulse compression concept pointed out earlier.

As a numerical example, assume $\lambda = 1.55$ μm and $D_{intra} = 15$ ps/nm·km.

$$\beta_2 = -\frac{\lambda}{\omega} D_{intra} = -\frac{\lambda^2}{2\pi c} D_{intra} = -1.9 \times 10^{-26} \text{ sec}^2/\text{m}.$$

For a typical silica fiber at $\lambda = 1.55$ μm, γ is around 2 $(\text{km·W})^{-1}$. Therefore, from Equation (18.37) and assuming $P = 10$ mW,

$$T_0 = \left(\frac{1.9 \times 10^{-26}}{2 \times 10^{-3} \times 10^{-2}}\right)^{1/2} = 30 \text{ psec}.$$

To increase the transmission bit rate, it is desirable to have as small a T_0 as possible. At a given transmission power, from Equation (18.37), reducing $|\beta_2|$ will reduce T_0. For example, reducing β_2 by a factor of 100 reduces T_0 to 3 psec. This explains why dispersion-shifted fibers are used in most soliton transmission experiments (see Table 18.1). ■

Soliton Propagation, N = 1

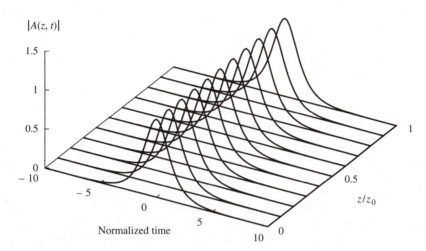

Figure 18.7   The magnitude of soliton propagation at $N = 1$.

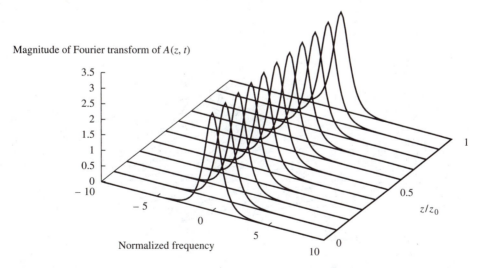

Figure 18.8   Spatial evolution of the magnitude of the Fourier transform of the soliton pulse at $N = 1$.

Higher Order Solitons When N is an integer larger than 1, the solution to Equation (18.34) is a higher order soliton. A soliton solution for $N = 2$ is illustrated in Figures 18.9 and 18.10. The illustrations show that both the envelope and spectrum evolve as the pulse propagates. Interestingly, the pulse recovers its original shape after a period z_0, which is given by

$$z_0 = \frac{\pi}{2} L_D. \qquad \textbf{[18.38]}$$

For $N = 2$, this can be verified from Equation (18.108) derived in Appendix 18–A. In general, for any N, the soliton has the same period z_0 given above [4]. Therefore, z_0 is called the **soliton period**.

18.4 FIELD EXPERIMENTS

The first fiber soliton transmission experiment was conducted in 1988 by Mollenauer and Smith over a distance of 4,000 km [10]. To compensate for fiber transmission loss, Raman amplification was used. Afterward, as shown in Table 18.1, various experiments using EDFAs and dispersion-shifted fibers have been conducted for longer distance and higher bit rates [11]–[22]. As explained in Chapter 17, EDFAs can compensate for fiber transmission loss. This is necessary to maintain the sufficient nonlinearity in soliton transmission. It is shown that if the repeater separation is well within the soliton period z_0 [14], soliton transmission can be maintained. As pointed out in earlier examples, dispersion-shifted fibers can reduce the pulse width (T_0) for a higher transmission bit rate. Equations (18.30) and (18.31), show that the only way to reduce T_0 at the same pulse power and soliton distance L_D is to reduce $|\beta_2|$.

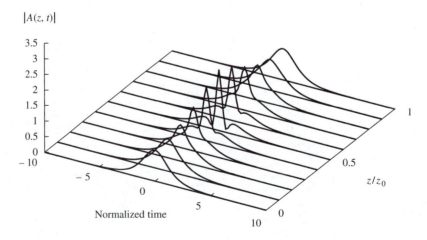

Figure 18.9   The magnitude of soliton propagation at $N = 2$.

Table 18.1 Some fiber soliton transmission experiments.

Distance (km)	Bit Rate (Gb/s)	Remarks	Reference
15,000/11,000	5/10	EDFAs used, WDM of two 5 Gb/s channels for the second case	[14]
1200	10	24 EDFAs used, dispersion-shifted fibers	[15]
1020	20	24 EDFAs used every 50 km, dispersion-shifted fibers	[16]
90	32	24 EDFAs used every 30 km, dispersion-shifted fibers, 8 multiplexed channels of 4 Gb/s each	[17]
65	40	4 multiplexed channels of 10 Gb/s each, dispersion-shifted fibers	[18]
3000	5	91 EDFAs used, dispersion-shifted fibers	[19]
80	80	Time/polarization multiplexed channels of 10 Gb/s, dispersion-shifted fibers	[20]
10^6	10	Soliton control in frequency and time, dispersion-shifted fibers	[21]

Magnitude of Fourier transform of $A(z, t)$

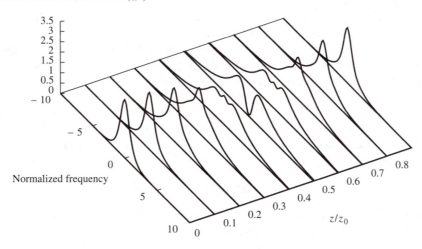

Figure 18.10 Spatial evolution of the magnitude of the Fourier transform of the soliton pulse at $N = 2$.

18.5 APPLYING SOLITONS FOR DIGITAL TRANSMISSION

From the NLSE given by Equation (18.34), only the single soliton case is considered in the earlier discussion. In practical digital communications, multiple soliton pulses must be generated and transmitted for multiple bit transmission. This section explains (1) how to generate soliton pulses and how the chirping effect from direct modulation can affect soliton transmission, (2) how to place optical amplifiers to maintain soliton transmission against fiber attenuation, (3) how large the achievable bit-rate and distance product due to the spontaneous emission noise from optical amplifiers is, and (4) how closely consecutive pulses can be placed because of the nonlinear Kerr effect.

18.5.1 SOLITON GENERATION

To provide soliton transmission, one immediate and practical question is how to generate fundamental soliton pulses given by Equation (18.35). This involves two questions. First, if the initial pulse waveform is not a hyperbolic secant function, can it eventually evolve into a fundamental soliton? Second, if the spectral content of the pulse is not chirp-free, how will the pulse propagation be affected?

When the initial waveform deviates either in power or shape, the resulting pulse can eventually evolve into a fundamental soliton if N in Equation (18.34) is within (0.5,1.5) [23]. For example, an incident Gaussian pulse $U(0, T) = e^{-T^2/2}$ with $N = 1$ can evolve into a fundamental soliton after several L_D. This is shown in Figure 18.11. Also, as shown in Figure 18.12, numerical simulation indicates that, after some oscillation in peak power and pulse width, a hyperbolic secant function with $N = 1.4$ can eventually evolve into a fundamental soliton with $N = 1$ after $10L_D$.

The above observation can be understood from the inverse scattering theory. For a given initial pulse $U(0, T)$, a set of eigenfunctions given by Equations (18.91) and (18.92) can be deremined. If the eigenvalue η of an eigenfunction has an imaginary part, the function will decrease to zero at large Z, and it is called a **dispersive** mode. As a result, if the initial pulse $U(0, Z)$ contains only one nondispersive eigenfunction, the pulse will eventually evolve into a fundamental soliton.

Another question of pulse generation is how the chirping effect discussed in Chapter 12 can affect pulse propagation. When the pulse width is on the order of psec, frequency chirping is a common phenomenon. To investigate the effect, consider an initial pulse of a linear frequency chirp [24]:

$$U(0, T) = N \text{sech}(T) e^{j\phi T^2} \qquad \textbf{[18.39]}$$

where ϕ is called the chirping intensity. Taking the time derivative of the phase term and dividing it by 2π leaves a linear frequency change as a function of time:

$$f(T) = \phi \frac{T}{\pi T_0}.$$

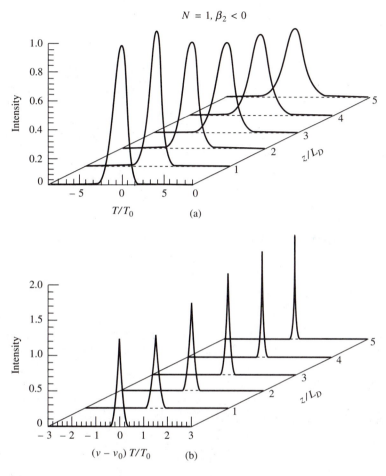

Figure 18.11   Pulse evolution from a Gaussian pulse to a fundamental soliton: (a) time domain pulse and (b) power spectral density.

SOURCE: Reprinted, by permission, from Agrawal, *Fiber-Optic Communication Systems*, Figure 9.2 [9]. ©1992 by John Wiley and Sons.

To investigate pulse propagation from the initial pulse given by Equation (18.39), the inverse scattering technique has been used. The objective is to find the condition of ϕ for soliton transmission. It is found in [24] that there is an upper limit of ϕ above which the initial pulse cannot evolve into a fundamental soliton. For $N = 1$, for example, the upper limit of ϕ is 0.82. When ϕ is within its limit, the pulse will eventually evolve into

$$U(Z, T) = \eta \text{sech}(\eta T)e^{-\eta^2 Z/2} \qquad \textbf{[18.40]}$$

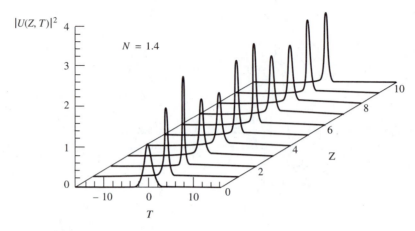

Figure 18.12   Pulse evolution from a hyperbolic secant pulse with $N = 1.4$ to a fundamental soliton with $N = 1.0$.

SOURCE: Reprinted, by permission, from Agrawal, *Fiber-Optic Communication Systems*, Figure 9.3 [9]. ©1992 by John Wiley and Sons.

where η is a function of N and ϕ and can be determined from Figure 18.13. When ϕ approaches its limit, η reduces to zero. This means the initial pulse cannot evolve into a soliton pulse.

Although the pulse with ϕ within the limit can evolve into a soliton, the price of the chirping effect is a smaller pulse energy. Specifically, when $\eta > 0$, the ratio of the final pulse energy to the initial pulse energy can be easily calculated by

$$\frac{\int [\eta \operatorname{sech}(\eta T)]^2 dT}{\int |U(0, T)|^2 dT} = \frac{\eta}{N^2}. \qquad [18.41]$$

Figure 18.13 shows that the larger the ϕ, the smaller the η. Therefore, the initial pulse is more dispersive when ϕ increases. Figure 18.13 also shows that a larger N can allow for a larger ϕ. This is because a larger N results in a larger nonlinearity, which means a higher pulse compression ability to overcome the frequency chirp.

Example 18.4   **PULSE BROADENING DUE TO CHIRPING**   If $N = 1.0$, from Figure 18.13, $\eta = 0.6$ at $\phi = 0.5$. Therefore, the final pulse energy is only 60 percent of the original. Furthermore, the pulse width is broadened by $(1/\eta) - 1$ or 67 percent. ∎

18.5.2   FIBER ATTENUATION AND OPTICAL AMPLIFICATION

To compensate for fiber loss, optical amplifiers must be used to maintain the power level. Otherwise, the nonlinear effect becomes weaker along the propagation, and fiber disper-

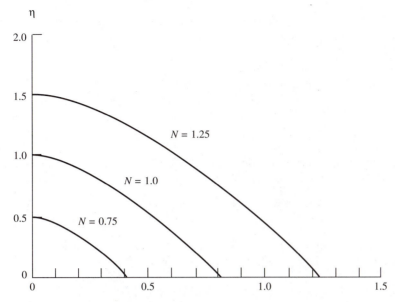

Figure 18.13 η versus ϕ for a given N.

SOURCE: Reprinted, by permission, from Desem and Chu, "Effect of Chirping on Soliton Propagation in Single-Mode Optical Fibers," Figure 1 [24]. ©1986 by Optical Society of America.

sion will eventually take over. As mentioned earlier, Raman amplification was used in the initial soliton transmission experiments [10]. With the introduction of EDFAs, such an amplifier can be placed at certain intervals. This use of lumped amplification poses one immediate question: How close should the amplifier spacing be to maintain soliton transmission?

Similar to the chirping effect in pulse propagation discussed earlier, the amplifier spacing is determined by the evolution of the eigenvalue η of the nondispersive mode given in Equation (18.41). If it reaches zero, the soliton will disappear and cannot be regenerated. It is found that if the amplifier spacing, L_a, is well within the soliton period z_0, lumped amplification can be used to provide essentially indefinite transmission [14]. In other words, transmission requires

$$L_a \ll z_0 = \frac{\pi}{2} \frac{T_0^2}{|\beta_2|}.$$

Assuming the transmission bit rate is $B = 1/q_0 T_0$, where $q_0 > 1$ is the minimum soliton pulse separation with respect to T_0, and adopting the condition $L_a < z_0/\pi$ gives the following bound:

$$\boxed{B^2 L_a < (2q_0^2 |\beta_2|)^{-1}.}$$ **[18.42]**

Example 18.5	**REQUIRED AMPLIFIER SPACING** Consider an ordinary silica fiber of $\beta_2 = -20$ psec^2/Km at 1.55 μm. If $q_0 = 10$ and $B = 2$ Gb/s, then

$$L_a < 62.5 \text{ km.}$$

To increase the amplifier spacing, dispersion-shifted fibers can be used. For example, if $|\beta_2|$ is reduced by a factor of 10, L_a increases to 625 km. ∎

To see how lumped amplification can sustain soliton transmission, consider the following modified NLSE that includes fiber attenuation:

$$\frac{\partial U}{\partial Z} = j\frac{1}{2}\frac{\partial^2 U}{\partial T^2} + j|U|^2 U - \frac{\alpha_f L_D}{2}U \qquad \textbf{[18.43]}$$

where α_f is the fiber attenuation in 1/m (not dB/km as used in Chapter 4). To take fiber attenuation into consideration, $U(Z, T)$ can be decomposed as

$$U(Z, T) = U_0(Z, T)e^{-\alpha_f L_D Z/2}e^{jZ/2}.$$

Therefore, if there is no fiber attenuation, $U_0(Z, T)$ should be a hyperbolic secant function. Substituting $U(Z, T)$ given above into Equation (18.43),

$$\frac{\partial U_0}{\partial Z} = j\left(\frac{1}{2}\frac{\partial^2 U_0}{\partial T^2} + e^{-\alpha_f L_D Z}|U_0|^2 U_0 - \frac{1}{2}U_0\right). \qquad \textbf{[18.44]}$$

Over a certain distance L_a that U_0 is essentially unchanged, the total pulse $U = U_0 e^{-\alpha L_D Z/2 + jZ/2}$ experiences only attenuation and phase change. Therefore, taking the average of each term in Equation (18.44) over the distance L_a gives

$$\frac{\partial U_0}{\partial Z} \approx j\left(\frac{1}{2}\frac{\partial^2 U_0}{\partial T^2} + \rho|U_0|^2 U_0 - \frac{1}{2}U_0\right) \qquad \textbf{[18.45]}$$

where

$$\rho = \frac{1}{L_a}\int_0^{L_a/L_D} e^{-\alpha_f L_D Z} dZ = \frac{1 - e^{-\alpha_f L_a}}{\alpha_f L_a}. \qquad \textbf{[18.46]}$$

Equation (18.45) shows that soliton transmission can be maintained using lumped amplification if

$$U_0(Z, T) = \frac{1}{\sqrt{\rho}}\text{sech}(T). \qquad \textbf{[18.47]}$$

This means the initial pulse should be boosted by a power factor $1/\rho$ with respect to the fundamental soliton.

With the above analysis lumped amplification can be designed as follows. First, solitons given by Equation (18.47) are launched. Specifically, for a given soliton pulse of width T_0, from Equations (18.37) and (18.47), the initial peak power should be

$$P_{tx} = \frac{1}{\rho} P = \frac{1}{\rho} \frac{|\beta_2|}{\gamma T_0^2}.$$ [18.48]

Over a distance L_a, the peak soliton power decreases from $1/\rho$ to

$$\frac{e^{-\alpha_f L_a}}{\rho} = \frac{\alpha_f L_a}{1 - e^{-\alpha_f L_a}} e^{-\alpha_f L_a} = \frac{\alpha_f L_a}{e^{\alpha_f L_a} - 1} < 1.$$

Therefore, the power drops below the normal level. To compensate for the power loss caused by fiber attenuation over distance L_a, an amplifier of gain

$$G = e^{\alpha_f L_a}$$ [18.49]

is placed every L_a km, where $L_a \ll z_0$ is used to ensure little change of U_0. This amplification design is depicted in Figure 18.14.

POWER PLANNING Consider a fiber of attenuation 0.2 dB/km at 1550 nm. If the soliton pulse is designed to have $T_0 = 50$ psec, and assuming $\gamma = 2$ (km·W)$^{-1}$ and $|\beta_2| = 20$ psec^2/km, the soliton peak power is

Example 18.6

$$P = \frac{|\beta_2|}{\gamma T_0^2} = 4 \text{ mW}.$$

Because the soliton period is

$$z_0 = \frac{\pi}{2} \frac{T_0^2}{|\beta_2|} = 196 \text{ km}$$

the amplifier spacing can be set at $L_a = 100$ km. Therefore, the amplifier gain should be $0.2 \times 100 = 20$ dB. From Equation (18.49), we have $\alpha_f L_a = \ln(100) = 4.6$. Using Equation (18.46),

$$\rho = \frac{1 - 0.01}{4.6} = 0.21.$$

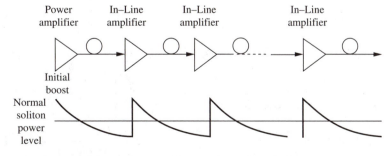

Figure 18.14   Lump amplification design for soliton transmission.

Therefore, the initial peak power at the transmitter output should be

$$P_{tx} = \frac{1}{\rho}P = 18.6 \text{ mW}.$$

Taking into consideration the dispersive power loss effect due to chirping, as given by Equation (18.42), a larger initial power boost is needed. ∎

18.5.3   AMPLIFIER NOISE AND TIMING JITTER

When optical amplifiers are used to compensate for power loss in soliton transmission, they also introduce ASE noise, as discussed in Chapter 17. The random ASE noise can cause a random change of the waveform and frequency content of the soliton pulse. As a result, it causes a random shift of the propagation velocity. Over a long distance, this random shift or jitter can become significant compared to the bit interval. As a result, the end-to-end transmission distance will be limited by the ASE noise. This limit is called the **Gordon-Haus limit** after its discoverers and derivers [25].

The Gordon-Haus limit can be seen from the following discussion. First, from Appendix 18–B, the RMS variation of v_g^{-1} due to ASE can be shown to be

$$E[\delta(v_g^{-1})^2] = \frac{hfT_0}{3A_p^2L_D^2}(G-1) = \frac{hf\gamma|\beta_2|}{3T_0}(G-1) \qquad \textbf{[18.50]}$$

where G is the amplifier gain. If the transmission distance is L and there are m in-line amplifiers with uniform separation, the total mean square timing jitter is

$$\sum_{i=1}^{m}\left(i\frac{L}{m+1}\right)^2 E[\delta(v_g^{-1})^2] = \frac{m(m+1)(2m+1)}{6(m+1)^2}L^2 \times \frac{hf\gamma|\beta_2|}{3T_0}(G-1)$$
$$\approx \frac{m}{9T_0}L^2(G-1)hf\gamma|\beta_2|. \qquad \textbf{[18.51]}$$

As a fundamental upper limit (see Problem 18–7), $(G-1)$ can be approximated as

$$G - 1 = e^{\alpha_f L/(m+1)} - 1 \approx \frac{1}{m+1}\alpha_f L. \qquad \textbf{[18.52]}$$

At the bit rate B, Equation (18.51) thus reduces to

$$\frac{1}{9T_0}\alpha_f L^3 hf\gamma|\beta_2|B^2 < \epsilon^2$$

where ϵ is the fraction of the bit interval that the total RMS jitter should be within. Therefore, the final Gordon-Haus limit can be expressed as

$$\boxed{(LB)^3 < \frac{9\epsilon^2 T_0 B}{\alpha_f hf\gamma|\beta_2|} = \frac{9\epsilon^2}{q_0\alpha_f hf\gamma|\beta_2|} = \frac{18\pi\epsilon^2}{q_0\alpha_f h\lambda\gamma D_{intra}}} \qquad \textbf{[18.53]}$$

where $q_0 T_0$ is the inverse of the bit rate. From the result, note that the Gordon-Haus limit due to ASE can be improved by using a fiber with small $|\beta_2|$ (i.e., a dispersion-shifted fiber) and small attenuation (α_f). A smaller $|\beta_2|$ reduces the dependence of the group velocity on frequency shift, and a smaller α_f allows a smaller required amplifier gain at a given amplifier spacing. Also note that a smaller nonlinearity γ can increase the limit. This is because a larger power is then needed to have the same $N = 1$, which means ASE is relatively unimportant to the soliton pulse.

TYPICAL DISTANCE BIT RATE PRODUCT   Assume $\epsilon = 0.2$, $q_0 = 10$, $\alpha_f = 0.2$ dB/km or 0.046 1/km, $D_{intra} = 2$ psec/km·nm, and $\gamma = 10$ (W·km)$^{-1}$. At $\lambda = 1550$ nm, | **Example 18.7**

$$(LB) < \left(\frac{18 \times \pi \times 0.04}{10 \times 4.6 \times 10^{-5} \times 6.63 \times 10^{-34} \times 1.55 \times 10^{-6} \times 10^{-2} \times 2.0 \times 10^{-6}} \right)^{1/3}$$

$$r = (2.4 \times 10^{50})^{1/3} = 6.2 \times 10^{16} \text{ m} \cdot \text{b/s}.$$

For a 10 Gb/s, this means $L < 6200$ km. ∎

Noise Control   To overcome the Gordon-Haus limit for longer transmission, several different approaches have been proposed. One basic approach is to insert filters to limit the noise and resynchronize pulses periodically by using a built-in modulator [26][27]. Filtering can effectively restore the spectrum of the soliton distorted by ASE.

Another approach uses a closer soliton separation to reduce the effect of ASE [28]. This comes from the observation that the effect of ASE can be made relatively unimportant when the soliton interaction force is strong. In other words, reducing the soliton separation reduces the effect of ASE. When solitons get closer together, however, their relative separations can vary periodically (see discussion in the next subsection). Because this variation is deterministic, the position variation can be later restored by spatial equalization.

18.5.4   TRANSMISSION BIT RATE

The bit rate of soliton transmission is limited by how closely consecutive solitons can be transmitted. Because the nonlinear Kerr effect is involved, a close separation of two solitons can affect their subsequent transmission. For a given initial separation and with relative phases and amplitudes, multiple soliton pulses can "push-pull" along their propagation. With two initial solitons given by

$$U(0, T) = \text{sech}(T - q_0) + a\,\text{sech}(a[T + q_0])e^{j\theta} \qquad \textbf{[18.54]}$$

Figures 18.15 and 18.16 show that soliton interaction can be strongly dependent on their relative phase difference [29]. In particular, when $a = 1$ and $\theta = 0$, the soliton separation oscillates over a certain period. Figure 18.15 shows that the separation becomes zero after a certain distance and the two solitons reduce to a single one.

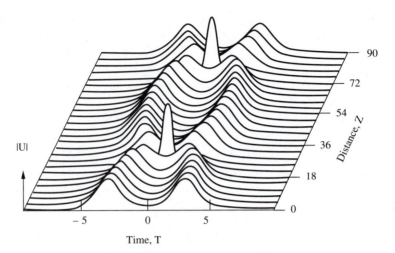

Figure 18.15   Propagation of two solitons with $q_0 = 3.5, \theta = 0$, and $a = 1$.

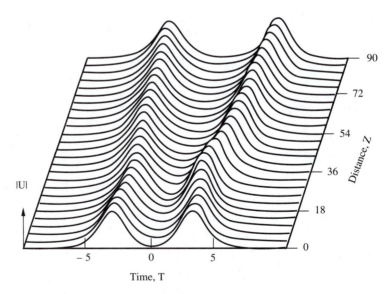

Figure 18.16   Propagation of two solitons with $q_0 = 3.5, \quad \theta = \pi/4$, and $a = 1$.

Because the transmission bit rate is $B = 1/(2q_0 T_0)$, it is desirable to have as small a value of q_0 as possible. To achieve this, one must know the dependence of the required q_0 on θ and a. For the special case that the two initial solitons are identical (i.e., $\theta = 0$ and $a = 1$), the separation is periodic, as shown by Figure 18.15. The oscillation period is found to be [9][29]:

$$L_p = e^{q_0} z_0 = \frac{\pi}{2} e^{q_0} L_D.$$ **[18.55]**

Therefore, the initial q_0 can be increased to ensure $L \ll L_p$ or

$$L \ll \frac{\pi}{2} e^{q_0} L_D = \frac{\pi}{2} e^{q_0} \frac{T_0^2}{|\beta_2|}.$$

Because the bit rate in this case is $B = 1/(2q_0 T_0)$, the necessary distance would then be

$$L \ll \frac{\pi e^{q_0}}{8 q_0^2 |\beta_2|} B^{-2}.$$ **[18.56]**

REQUIRED DISTANCE FOR INSIGNIFICANT SOLITON INTERACTION For $q_0 = 5$ and $|\beta_2| = 2$ psec^2/km, | **Example 18.8**

$$LB^2 \ll 1.16 \times 10^6 \ (\text{Gb/s})^2 \cdot \text{km}.$$

$B = 10$ Gb/s requires that

$$L \ll 11,600 \text{ km}.$$

This is a large distance in practice. ∎

To further reduce the soliton separation, alternating amplitudes, or $a \neq 1$, can be used. From [31], it is known that a slight increase in a, or $a > 1$, can maintain good soliton separation over a long distance at a smaller q_0. For example, with $a = 1.175$ and $2q_0 = 3.5$, the minimum separation is around 3.0. As illustrated in Figure 18.17, there is essentially no limit to transmission distance in this case. This unequal amplitude approach, however, requires careful power control in practice.

18.6 Summary

1. Soliton transmission has been actively studied and experiments performed for its ability to overcome fiber dispersion over thousands of kilometers and to achieve bit rates greater than 10 Gb/s. Its principle is based on the balance of negative group velocity dispersion (GVD) ($\beta_2 < 0$ or $D_{intra} > 0$) and the nonlinear Kerr effect.

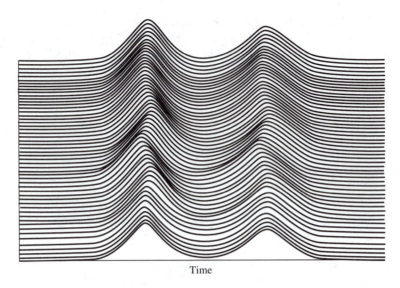

Time

Figure 18.17   Propagation of two solitons with $2q_0 = 3.5, \theta = 0$, and $a = 1.175$.

SOURCE: Reprinted, by permission, from Chu and Desem, "Mutual Interaction between Solitons of Unequal Amplitudes in Optical Fiber," [31]. ©1985 by IEE.

2. In general, the negative GVD tends to broaden the pulse, and the nonlinear Kerr effect tends to compress the pulse. When these two forces are balanced, the pulse waveform remains unchanged as it propagates.

3. A fundamental soliton in an optical fiber is an optical pulse with a hyperbolic secant waveform that has a perfect balance between the negative GVD and the nonlinear Kerr effect.

4. The equation that governs the pulse propagation in an optical fiber is the nonlinear Schrödinger equation (NLSE). In addition to the fundamental soliton solution, there can be higher order solutions, which consist of N soliton pulses and represent an integer number of eigenfunctions.

5. An important technique to solve the NLSE is called the inverse scattering method. It is the same method used to solve the KdV equation that describes the first solitary wave observed. The importance of the inverse scattering method is that it considers the original pulse function as a potential and transforms the nonlinear equation into a set of linear wave equations. The wave equations can then be used to solve for the scattered wave with a given potential. The inverse of this problem is to solve for the potential when the scattered field is known. Because the potential represents the desired light pulse, the inverse scattering method allows the nonlinear problem to be solved using linear wave equations.

6. For higher order solitons, the total pulse waveform evolves periodically as it propagates along the fiber. Furthermore, they all have the same period, given by $\pi L_D/2$, where $L_D = T_0^2/|\beta_2|$ is the soliton distance and $1.76T_0$ is the FWHM of the fundamental soliton in the time domain.

7. In soliton transmission, it is important to have a large L_D to maintain soliton transmission over a large distance. Therefore, for a given T_0, it is desirable to reduce $|\beta_2|$. This can be achieved by using dispersion-shifted fibers at 1550 nm.

8. The required peak power in soliton transmission is inversely proportional to T_0^2. Therefore, to reduce T_0 or to increase the bit rate, a larger transmission power is needed. However, the required power can be reduced with a larger nonlinearity or a smaller negative GVD.

9. Many successful soliton transmission experiments have been reported. In all of these experiments, dispersion-shifted fibers are used to reduce $|\beta_2|$, and a 1550 nm wavelength is used to match the EDFAs' operating regime.

10. Important technical issues to apply soliton transmission to practical digital communications include: (1) low chirp pulse generation, (2) periodic power amplification, (3) ASE noise control, and (4) close soliton separation.

11. A pulse with a hyperbolic secant waveform may not propagate as a soliton if its spectral content has a frequency chirp, which is common in short pulse modulation. It is found that soliton transmission can persist if the chirp is within a certain limit.

12. Power amplification is necessary in soliton transmission to overcome fiber attenuation. There are two types of amplification: distributed and lumped. Before the wide use of EDFAs, distributed Raman amplification was used in early experiments. Now, for its convenience, lumped EDFA amplification is the primary choice. When the amplifier spacing is well within the soliton period z_0, lumped amplification is sufficient for transmission over thousands of kilometers.

13. When power amplification is used, ASE from optical amplifiers also adds to the signal. The ASE noise distorts the original frequency content and results in a random variation of the propagation velocity. Over a long distance, this random speed variation can result in a significant timing variation of the received bits. For a given tolerable timing variation and transmission bit rate, there is thus an upper limit for the transmission distance. This limit due to the ASE noise is called the Gordon-Haus limit. In general, the limit can be improved by using a fiber with a smaller fiber attenuation (α_f), nonlinearity (γ), and dispersion $|\beta_2|$.

14. Because the nonlinear Kerr effect plays a critical role in soliton transmission, pulses of too close a separation can push-pull as they propagate. Ways to reduce the interaction between adjacent pulses include (1) increasing the minimum pulse separation, (2) using different amplitudes between adjacent pulses, and (3) introducing nonzero relative phases between adjacent pulses.

APPENDIX 18-A: INVERSE SCATTERING TECHNIQUE

This appendix explains the inverse scattering technique used by Zakharov and Shabat [4] to solve the nonlinear Schrödinger equation (NLSE). As mentioned earlier in the chapter, the inverse scattering technique was first discovered by Zabusky and Kruskal [1] to solve the nonlinear KdV equation. Although the equations are different, the concept of the inverse scattering technique is the same. As a result, for nonlinear equations that can be formulated by the inverse scattering technique, their solutions all have the similar soliton properties. In addition to the KdV and NLSE equations, modified KdV and sine-Gordon equations can be solved similarly [32].

Concept of the Inverse Scattering Technique   To understand the basic concept of the inverse scattering technique, the envelope function $U(Z, T)$ given by Equation (18.34) must now be associated with a different physical meaning: a *potential*. According to wave physics, an incident wave can be scattered by a potential. The scattered wave is determined by the potential and a *linear* wave equation (not the same equation for $U[Z, T]$ but related) that governs the wave. Therefore, the concept of the inverse scattering technique is to find $U(Z, T)$ from the scattered wave.

The concept of the inverse scattering technique is its transformation of a nonlinear problem to a linear one. This is illustrated in Figure 18.18. As we can see, it consists of three steps described below.

1. First, find the initial scattered wave at $Z = 0$ for the potential $U(0, T)$ at $Z = 0$. This is sometimes called the **forward scattering problem.** In general, the initial scattered wave can be expressed as a linear combination of N eigenfunctions, which are fundamental solutions to the governing equation. Therefore, the forward scattering problem is to find the corresponding N linear coefficients and the N eigenvalues of the eigenfunctions. When there are N eigenfunctions in the linear combination, the soliton solution is called an N-soliton solution.

2. From the N initial eigenfunctions at $Z = 0$, their values can easily be found at any other Z. Their linear superposition gives the total scattered wave at any $Z > 0$.

3. From the scattered wave, the Marchenko equation can be used to find the potential $U(Z, T)$. This is called the **inverse scattering problem.** As will be shown shortly, the Marchenko equation [33] is also a linear equation. Therefore, it can be solved straightforwardly.

The following discussion describes the wave operators used by Zakharov and Shabat (ZS) that involve the potential $U(Z, T)$ and explains in detail how to execute the inverse scattering technique outlined above.

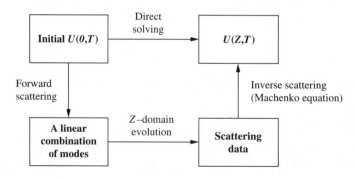

Figure 18.18   The inverse scattering technique.

Wave Operators for the NLSE   According to ZS, the following two wave operators that describe the wave motion can be constructed from the normalized NLSE given by Equation (18.34),

$$\bar{\Delta}^{(1)} \stackrel{\text{def}}{=} \left(\frac{j}{3} \frac{\partial}{\partial Z} - \frac{1}{2} \frac{\partial^2}{\partial T^2} \right) \bar{I} - \begin{bmatrix} \frac{1}{3}|U|^2 & \frac{\sqrt{2}}{3} U_T \\ -\frac{\sqrt{2}}{3} U_T^* & \frac{2}{3}|U|^2 \end{bmatrix} \stackrel{\text{def}}{=} \frac{j}{3} \frac{\partial}{\partial Z} \bar{I} - \bar{M} \qquad \textbf{[18.57]}$$

$$\bar{\Delta}^{(2)} \stackrel{\text{def}}{=} \begin{bmatrix} \sqrt{2} & 0 \\ 0 & -\frac{1}{\sqrt{2}} \end{bmatrix} \frac{\partial}{\partial T} + \begin{bmatrix} 0 & U \\ U^* & 0 \end{bmatrix} \stackrel{\text{def}}{=} \bar{L}. \qquad \textbf{[18.58]}$$

Note that both wave operators are functions of the potential $U(Z, T)$. When $|T|$ is very large, it is assumed that U is negligible or $|U| \to 0$. This limiting case produces two definitions:

$$\bar{\Delta}_0^{(1)} = \lim_{|T| \to \infty} \bar{\Delta}^{(1)} = \left(\frac{j}{3} \frac{\partial}{\partial Z} - \frac{1}{2} \frac{\partial^2}{\partial T^2} \right) \bar{I} \qquad \textbf{[18.59]}$$

$$\bar{\Delta}_0^{(2)} = \lim_{|T| \to \infty} \bar{\Delta}^{(2)} = \begin{bmatrix} \sqrt{2} & 0 \\ 0 & -\frac{1}{\sqrt{2}} \end{bmatrix} \frac{\partial}{\partial T}. \qquad \textbf{[18.60]}$$

These $U(Z, T)$ independent wave operators are called **undressed** wave operators as compared to their dressed counterparts $\bar{\Delta}^{(1)}$ and $\bar{\Delta}^{(2)}$. By definition, these undressed wave operators describe wave motion when the potential is zero.

The reason for defining the above operators will be explained shortly. In the ZS approach, two more operators $\bar{J}$ and $\bar{J}_F$ are defined. These operators all have physical meanings in the inverse scattering process, which are discussed next.

From the two dressed operators $\bar{\Delta}^{(i)}, i = 1, 2$, the scattered wave $\bar{\psi}_{out}$ for a given incident wave $\bar{\psi}_{in}$ can be found by

$$\bar{\psi}_{out} = \bar{\Delta} \bar{\psi}_{in}.$$

Here the superscript of $\bar{\Delta}$ is dropped to show only the physical meaning. If $U(Z, T)$ is known, $\bar{\Delta}$ can be used to find the scattered wave directly. Alternatively, the following indirect method can be used.

First, let $(\bar{I} + \bar{J}_F)$ be an operator that describes the scattered wave at a time point when $|U|$ is negligible.[3] This happens when $|T| \to \infty$ and $|U| \to 0$. As a result, when $|T|$ is large enough, the wave motion can be described by the undressed operators. Once the asymptotic behavior of the wave at large $|T|$ is known, it can be moved back again to smaller $|T|$ values by another operator $(\bar{I} + \bar{J})$. This gives the final scattered wave. Therefore, $\bar{J}_F$ is called the far-field operator, and $\bar{J}$ is the near-field operator. Thus

$$\bar{\psi}_{out} = \bar{\Delta} \bar{\psi}_{in} = (\bar{I} + \bar{J}) \bar{\Delta}_0 (\bar{I} + \bar{J}_F) \bar{\psi}_{in}.$$

---

[3] In the original NLSE considered by [4], the role of Z and T are switched. Therefore, the asymptotic wave at $|Z| \to \infty$ is considered. This is why it is called the *scattered* wave.

From the above formulation, note that $(\bar{I} + \bar{J}_F)\tilde{\psi}_{in}$ is the incident wave at infinite time and $\bar{\Delta}_0(\bar{I} + \bar{J}_F)\tilde{\psi}_{in}$ is the scattered wave at infinite time. This is illustrated in Figure 18.19. This observation leads to the following identity:

$$(\bar{I} + \bar{J})\bar{\Delta}_0^{(i)}(\bar{I} + \bar{J}_F) = \bar{\Delta}^{(i)}. \qquad \textbf{[18.61]}$$

The physical meaning of $\bar{J}$ and wave operators $\bar{\Delta}^{(i)}$ also produces the identity:

$$\bar{\Delta}^{(i)}(\bar{I} + \bar{J}) = (\bar{I} + \bar{J})\bar{\Delta}_0^{(i)}. \qquad \textbf{[18.62]}$$

This can be understood when the above operators are used on a far incident field. From the physical meanings of $\bar{I} + \bar{J}$, $\bar{\Delta}^{(i)}$, and $\bar{\Delta}_0^{(i)}$ given earlier, note that the combined operator on the left first moves the far incident field to the near incident field and then finds the scattered wave. On the other hand, the combined operator on the right first finds the scattered field at the far end and then moves it to the near end. Therefore, both give the scattered wave at the near field. Later, it will be shown that Equation (18.62) leads to the Marchenko equation. Comparing Equation (18.61) and (18.62) gives another identity:

$$(\bar{I} + \bar{J})(\bar{I} + \bar{J}_F) = (\bar{I} + \bar{J}_F)(\bar{I} + \bar{J}) = \bar{I}. \qquad \textbf{[18.63]}$$

Relationship between the NLSE and Wave Operators   Because both operators $\bar{J}$ and $\bar{J}_F$ depend on the potential function $U(Z, T)$, Equation (18.63) is an implicit equation of $U(Z, T)$. Therefore, Equations (18.34) and (18.63) should be equivalent. This can be verified briefly. First, from the undressed operators $\bar{\Delta}_0^{(i)}$ given by Equations (18.59) and (18.60), note that they commute with each other. That is,

$$\bar{\Delta}_0^{(1)}\bar{\Delta}_0^{(2)} - \bar{\Delta}_0^{(2)}\bar{\Delta}_0^{(1)} \stackrel{\text{def}}{=} [\bar{\Delta}_0^{(1)}, \bar{\Delta}_0^{(2)}] = 0.$$

From Equations (18.61) and (18.63), it can be verified that

$$[\bar{\Delta}^{(1)}, \bar{\Delta}^{(2)}] = (\bar{I} + \bar{J})[\bar{\Delta}_0^{(1)}, \bar{\Delta}_0^{(2)}](\bar{I} + \bar{J}_F) = 0. \qquad \textbf{[18.64]}$$

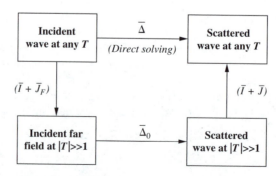

Figure 18.19   Physical meaning of the ZS operators.

If the operators $\bar{L}$ and $\bar{M}$ defined in Equations (18.57) and (18.58) are used,

$$[\bar{\Delta}^{(1)}, \bar{\Delta}^{(2)}] = \frac{j}{3}\frac{\partial \bar{L}}{\partial Z} + [\bar{L}, \bar{M}] = 0. \qquad \textbf{[18.65]}$$

This is called the **Lax equation**, and $\bar{L}$ and $\bar{M}$ are called the **Lax pair**. Substituting for $\bar{L}$ and $\bar{M}$ defined in terms of U, it can be shown that Equation (18.65) is simply the NLSE (18.34) (see Problem 18–8). This equivalence explains why Zakharov and Shabat defined the operators given by Equations (18.57) and (18.58).

Marchenko Equation　So far the physical meanings and properties of the wave operators J and J_F have only been described. They now can be defined specifically by how they operate on a wave function ϕ:

$$\bar{J}\bar{\psi} \stackrel{\text{def}}{=} \left[\int d\tau \bar{K}(Z, T, \tau)\right]\bar{\psi} = \int \bar{K}(Z, T, \tau)\bar{\psi}(Z, \tau)d\tau. \qquad \textbf{[18.66]}$$

$$\bar{J}_F\bar{\psi} \stackrel{\text{def}}{=} \left[\int d\tau \bar{F}(Z, T, \tau)\right]\bar{\psi} = \int \bar{F}(Z, T, \tau)\bar{\psi}(Z, \tau)d\tau. \qquad \textbf{[18.67]}$$

Because the wave function $\bar{\psi}$ is a 2×1 column vector, $\bar{K}$ and $\bar{F}$ are 2×2 matrixes. Furthermore, because the near-field operator $\bar{J}$ uses the far field at τ to find the near field at T, $\bar{K}$ has the following causality condition:

$$\bar{K}(Z, T, \tau) = 0 \text{ if } \tau < T. \qquad \textbf{[18.68]}$$

This condition means the far field at τ must be generated from the near field that occurs sometime earlier because of the finite speed of propagation. Thus from the definitions of $\bar{J}$ and $\bar{J}_F$ and the condition (18.63),

$$\int \bar{K}(Z, T, \tau)\bar{\psi}(Z, \tau)d\tau + \int \bar{F}(Z, T, \tau)\bar{\psi}(Z, \tau)d\tau$$

$$+ \int \left[\int_t^\infty \bar{K}(Z, t, t')\bar{F}(Z, t', \tau)dt'\right]\bar{\psi}(Z, \tau)d\tau = 0.$$

For any arbitrary $\bar{\psi}$, this leads to the following Marchenko equation:

$$\boxed{\bar{K}(Z, T, \tau) + \bar{F}(Z, T, \tau) + \int_t^\infty \bar{K}(Z, T, t')\bar{F}(Z, t', \tau)dt' = 0.} \qquad \textbf{[18.69]}$$

See Problem 18–9 for verification. With the Marchenko equation (18.69), one can solve for $\bar{K}$ (the near-field operator) from a known F (the far field operator). Physically, this means the near-field scattered wave can be found from the far-field scattered wave.

Properties of $\bar{F}$ and $\bar{K}$ and Inverse Scattering　The final step in the inverse scattering process is to find the potential from the scattered field. Specifically, the potential $U(Z, T)$ must be found from the kernel function $\bar{K}(Z, T, \tau)$.

Consider some other properties of F and K. First, note that the dependence of the scattered wave on the potential U should decrease as $|T|$ increases. In other words, the scattered wave at the far field is independent of U. The physical meaning of $\bar{J}_F$ thus suggests the following identity:

$$(\bar{I} + \bar{J}_F)\bar{\Delta}_0^{(i)} = \bar{\Delta}_0^{(i)}(\bar{I} + \bar{J}_F).$$

For an incident near field, the right-hand side first computes the far field and then computes its scattered wave. Assuming $U = 0$, the left-hand side first computes the scattered field and then computes the far field. Because the scattered far field is not a function of the potential U as $|T| \to \infty$, the above identity holds true. This identity can also be expressed for convenience in terms of commutation:

$$[\bar{J}_F, \bar{\Delta}_0^{(i)}] = \bar{J}_F \bar{\Delta}_0^{(i)} - \bar{\Delta}_0^{(i)} \bar{J}_F = 0. \qquad \textbf{[18.70]}$$

From Problem 18–9, Equation (18.70) can be explicitly expressed as

$$\frac{j}{3}\bar{F}_Z(Z, T, \tau) - \frac{1}{2}\bar{F}_{TT}(Z, T, \tau) + \frac{1}{2}\bar{F}_{\tau\tau}(Z, T, \tau) = 0 \qquad \textbf{[18.71]}$$

and

$$\begin{bmatrix} \sqrt{2} & 0 \\ 0 & -\frac{1}{\sqrt{2}} \end{bmatrix} \bar{F}_T(Z, T, \tau) + \bar{F}_\tau(Z, T, \tau) \begin{bmatrix} \sqrt{2} & 0 \\ 0 & -\frac{1}{\sqrt{2}} \end{bmatrix} = 0. \qquad \textbf{[18.72]}$$

The above two equations are linear equations in $\bar{F}$. Therefore, a linear combination of solutions is another solution. A family of fundamental solutions called eigenfunctions will be derived shortly, while solving the N-soliton case.

Another important property involves $\bar{K}$. Using Equation (18.62), it can be shown that

$$\bar{U}(Z, T) = \frac{3}{\sqrt{2}}\bar{K}_{12}(Z, T, T) \overset{\text{def}}{=} \frac{3}{\sqrt{2}}\hat{K}_{12}(Z, T). \qquad \textbf{[18.73]}$$

The proof is given in Problem 18–11. Equation (18.73) says that $U(Z, T)$ can be found once $\bar{K}$ or $\hat{K}$ is solved from the Marchenko equation (18.69).

Summary of the Inverse Scattering Method   From the above discussion, the procedure of solving the NLSE based on the inverse scattering method can be summarized as follows.

1. Find the wave scattering operators $\bar{\Delta}^{(1)}$ and $\bar{\Delta}^{(2)}$. For the NLSE, they are given by Equations (18.57) and (18.58).

2. Find the far-field operator $\bar{I} + \bar{J}_F$, which gives the far field at $T \gg 1$ when it operates on the incident wave. In the case of the NLSE, the function $\bar{F}(Z, T, \tau)$ of $\bar{J}_F$ can be obtained by solving Equations (18.71) and (18.72).

3. Find the near-field scattering operator $\bar{I} + \bar{J}$, which gives the scattered field for any T. Specifically, solve the Marchenko equation (18.69).

4. Find the potential $U(Z, T)$ that causes the scattered field. Specifically, we can simply use Equation (18.73) once $\bar{K}$ associated with the operator $\bar{J}$ is obtained.

Several special cases below illustrate the use of the inverse scattering technique.

One-Soliton Solution   First, consider the single-soliton case. Assume

$$\bar{F}(Z, T, \tau) = \begin{bmatrix} 0 & r(Z, T, \tau) \\ s(Z, T, \tau) & 0 \end{bmatrix}.$$ [18.74]

From Equation (18.72),

$$\begin{bmatrix} 0 & \sqrt{2}r_T \\ -\frac{1}{\sqrt{2}}s_T & 0 \end{bmatrix} + \begin{bmatrix} 0 & -\frac{1}{\sqrt{2}}r_\tau \\ \sqrt{2}s_\tau & 0 \end{bmatrix} = 0.$$

Combining Equation (18.71) gives the general solutions for $r(Z, T, \tau)$ and $s(Z, T, \tau)$:

$$r(Z, T, \tau) = Re^{\rho(T+2\tau)/3 + j\rho^2 Z/2}.$$ [18.75]

$$s(Z, T, \tau) = Se^{\sigma(2T+\tau)/3 - j\sigma^2 Z/2}.$$ [18.76]

The solution given by Equation (18.74) with r and s given by Equations (18.75) and (18.76) is an eigenfunction of Equation (18.70). The parameter values R, S, ρ, and σ can in general be determined by the initial potential $U(Z, T)$ at $Z = 0$.

With $\bar{F}(Z, T, \tau)$ obtained, the Marchenko equation (18.69) can be used to solve for $\bar{K}$. Define

$$\bar{K}(Z, T, \tau) \overset{\text{def}}{=} \begin{bmatrix} A(Z, T, \tau) & B(Z, T, \tau) \\ C(Z, T, \tau) & D(Z, T, \tau) \end{bmatrix}.$$

By examining Equation (18.69) and the dependence of $r(Z, T, \tau)$ and $s(Z, T, \tau)$ on τ from Equations (18.75) and (18.76), the following expressions can be introduced.

$$A(Z, T, \tau) = a(Z, T)e^{\sigma\tau/3}.$$ [18.77]

$$B(Z, T, \tau) = b(Z, T)e^{2\rho\tau/3}.$$ [18.78]

$$C(Z, T, \tau) = c(Z, T)e^{\sigma\tau/3}.$$ [18.79]

$$D(Z, T, \tau) = d(Z, T)e^{2\rho\tau/3}.$$ [18.80]

Substituting Equations (18.75)–(18.80) into the Marchenko equation (18.69), one obtains

$$a(Z, T) + S\int_T^\infty b(Z, T)e^{2\rho t'/3}e^{2\sigma t'/3}e^{-j\sigma^2 Z/2}dt' = 0$$ [18.81]

$$b(Z, T) + Re^{\rho T/3 + j\rho^2 Z/3} + R\int_T^\infty a(Z, T)e^{(\sigma+\rho)t'/3 + j\rho^2 Z/2}dt' = 0.$$ [18.82]

Solving the above two equations,

$$b(Z, T) = \frac{-Re^{\rho T/3}e^{j\rho^2 Z/2}}{1 - \frac{9RS}{2(\rho+\sigma)^2}e^{(\rho+\sigma)T}e^{j(\rho^2-\sigma^2)Z/2}}. \qquad \textbf{[18.83]}$$

Following the same procedure,

$$c(Z, T) = \frac{-Se^{2\sigma T/3}e^{-j\sigma^2 Z/2}}{1 - \frac{9RS}{2(\rho+\sigma)^2}e^{(\rho+\sigma)T}e^{j(\rho^2-\sigma^2)Z/2}}. \qquad \textbf{[18.84]}$$

As a result,

$$B(Z, T, \tau) = \frac{-Re^{\rho(T+2\tau)/3}e^{j\rho^2 Z/2}}{1 - \frac{9RS}{2(\rho+\sigma)^2}e^{(\rho+\sigma)T}e^{j(\rho^2-\sigma^2)Z/2}} \qquad \textbf{[18.85]}$$

$$C(Z, T, \tau) = \frac{-Se^{\sigma(T+2\tau)/3}e^{-j\sigma^2 Z/2}}{1 - \frac{9RS}{2(\rho+\sigma)^2}e^{(\rho+\sigma)T}e^{j(\rho^2-\sigma^2)Z/2}}. \qquad \textbf{[18.86]}$$

From Equation (18.73), $B(Z, T, T) = -C(Z, T, T)^* = (\sqrt{2}/3)U(Z, T)$. Comparing Equations (18.83) and (18.84) thus gives

$$-R^* = S = m$$

and

$$\rho = \sigma^* = -p + jq. \qquad \textbf{[18.87]}$$

Therefore,

$$U(Z, T) = \frac{3}{\sqrt{2}}B(Z, T, T) = \frac{3}{\sqrt{2}}\frac{me^{(-p+jq)T}e^{j(p^2-q^2-2jpq)Z/2}}{1 + \frac{9m^2}{8p^2}e^{-2pT}e^{2pqZ}}.$$

A pulse that is symmetric with respect to $T = 0$ requires that

$$9m^2 = 8p^2.$$

Thus,

$$U(Z, T) = p \times \text{sech}[p(T - qZ)]e^{jqT}e^{j(p^2-q^2)Z/2}. \qquad \textbf{[18.88]}$$

Equation (18.88) shows that the magnitude of $U(Z, T)$ is a hyperbolic secant function. Without loss of generality, it can be assumed that $q = 0$. Hence,

$$U(Z, T) = p \times \text{sech}(pT)e^{jp^2 Z/2}. \qquad \textbf{[18.89]}$$

This is the general form of the fundamental soliton. Note that a large peak power or p results in a smaller pulse width. For the special case that $p = 1$,

$$U(Z, T) = \text{sech}(T)e^{jZ/2}. \qquad \text{[18.90]}$$

This is the well-known single-soliton solution to Equation (18.34).

N-Soliton Solution   The process of finding the single-soliton solution can be easily generalized to the N-soliton case because Equations (18.71) and (18.72) and the Marchenko equation (18.69) are linear. In particular, for N solitons, $F(Z, T, \tau)$ can be expressed in terms of a linear combination of N eigenfunctions:

$$r(Z, T, \tau) = \sum_{n=1}^{N} r_n e^{\rho_n(T+2\tau)/3 + j\rho_n^2 Z/2}. \qquad \text{[18.91]}$$

$$s(Z, T, \tau) = \sum_{n=1}^{N} s_n e^{\sigma_n(T+2\tau)/3 - j\sigma_n^2 Z/2}. \qquad \text{[18.92]}$$

Because $B(Z, T, T) = -C(Z, T, T)^*$, there are the following equalities analogous to the single-soliton case:

$$r_n^* = -s_n$$

$$\sigma_n = \rho_n^*$$

for $n = 1, \ldots, N$.

Therefore, similar to Equations (18.77)–(18.80) that define the kernel $K(Z, T, \tau)$, one can have

$$A(Z, T, \tau) = \sum_{n=1}^{N} a_n(Z, T)e^{\sigma_n \tau/3} \qquad \text{[18.93]}$$

and

$$B(Z, T, \tau) = \sum_{n=1}^{N} b_n(Z, T)e^{2\rho_n \tau/3}. \qquad \text{[18.94]}$$

Substituting the above definitions into Equations (18.81) and (18.82),

$$a_n + \sum_{l}^{N} \epsilon_{nl} b_l = 0 \qquad \text{[18.95]}$$

and

$$b_n + r_n e^{\rho_n T/3 + j\rho_n^2 Z/2} + \sum_{l=1}^{N} \delta_{nl} a_l = 0 \qquad \text{[18.96]}$$

where

$$\epsilon_{nl} = -\frac{3}{2} \frac{e^{2\rho_l T/3}}{(\rho_n^* + \rho_l)} e^{2\rho_n^* T/3 - j(\rho_n^*)^2 Z/2} r_n^* \qquad \text{[18.97]}$$

and

$$\delta_{nl} = 3\frac{e^{\rho_l^* T}}{(\rho_l^* + \rho_n)}e^{\rho_n T/3 + j\rho_n^2 Z/2}r_n. \qquad \textbf{[18.98]}$$

From the above two linear equations, solving for each b_n allows one to obtain $U(Z, T)$. In matrix form, Equations (18.95) and (18.96) become

$$[a_n] + [\epsilon_{nl}][b_l] = 0 \qquad \textbf{[18.99]}$$

and

$$[b_n] + [r_n e^{\rho_n T/3 + j\rho_n^2 Z/2}] + [\delta_{nl}][a_l] = 0. \qquad \textbf{[18.100]}$$

These two equations can be further simplified as follows. By defining

$$\lambda_n \overset{\text{def}}{=} (3r_n/2\sqrt{2})^{1/2}e^{\rho_n T/2 + j\rho_n^2 Z/4} \qquad \textbf{[18.101]}$$

$$a_n \overset{\text{def}}{=} (2\sqrt{2}r_n^*/9)^{1/2}e^{\rho_n^* T/6 - j\rho_n^{*2}Z/4}\Psi_{1n} \qquad \textbf{[18.102]}$$

$$b_n \overset{\text{def}}{=} -(\sqrt{2}r_n/3)^{1/2}e^{-\rho_n T/6 + j\rho_n^2 Z/4}\Psi_{2n} \qquad \textbf{[18.103]}$$

it can be verified that (see Problem 18–12)

$$\boxed{\Psi_{1n} + \sum_l \frac{\lambda_l \lambda_n^*}{\eta_l + \eta_l^*}\Psi_{2l} = 0} \qquad \textbf{[18.104]}$$

$$\boxed{\Psi_{2n} - \sum_l \frac{\lambda_l^* \lambda_n}{\eta_l^* + \eta_n}\Psi_{1l} = \lambda_n} \qquad \textbf{[18.105]}$$

where $\eta_n = \rho_n/2$.

From $U(Z, T) = (3/\sqrt{2})B(Z, T, T)$ and using Equation (18.94), it can be shown that (see Problem 18–13)

$$U(Z, T) = -2\sum_n \lambda_n \Psi_{2n}. \qquad \textbf{[18.106]}$$

From Equation (18.101), there are two undetermined variables, r_n and ρ_n, for each λ_n. Without loss of generality, η_n can be assumed to be purely real [4][34]. Furthermore, to have a symmetric pulse with respect to $T = 0$, it can be shown that r_n needs to satisfy the following condition [35]:

$$\frac{3r_n}{2\sqrt{2}} = -\frac{\prod_{l=1}^N |\eta_n + \eta_l|}{\prod_{l\neq n}^n |\eta_n - \eta_l|}. \qquad \textbf{[18.107]}$$

For N solitons, $\eta_1 = -1/2, \eta_2 = -3/2, \cdots$ are used to give the standard soliton expressions. See the following example for $N = 2$.

TWO SOLITONS For $N = 2$,

Example 18.9

$$\eta_1 = -1/2 \quad \text{and} \quad \eta_2 = -3/2.$$

From Equation (18.107),

$$\frac{3r_1}{2\sqrt{2}} = -\frac{1 \times 2}{1} = -2$$

and

$$\frac{3r_2}{2\sqrt{2}} = -\frac{2 \times 3}{1} = -6.$$

Therefore, $r_1 = -4\sqrt{2/3}, r_2 = -4\sqrt{2}$,

$$\lambda_1 = \sqrt{-2}e^{-T/2+jZ/4}$$

and

$$\lambda_2 = \sqrt{-6}e^{-3T/2+j9Z/4}.$$

From Equation (18.104),

$$\begin{bmatrix} \Psi_{11} \\ \Psi_{12} \end{bmatrix} + \begin{bmatrix} 2e^{-T} & \sqrt{3}e^{-2T}e^{j2Z} \\ \sqrt{3}e^{-2T}e^{-j2Z} & 2e^{-3T} \end{bmatrix} \begin{bmatrix} \Psi_{21} \\ \Psi_{22} \end{bmatrix} = 0.$$

From Equation (18.105),

$$\begin{bmatrix} \Psi_{21} \\ \Psi_{22} \end{bmatrix} - \begin{bmatrix} 2e^{-T} & \sqrt{3}e^{-2T}e^{-j2Z} \\ \sqrt{3}e^{-2T}e^{j2Z} & 2e^{-3T} \end{bmatrix} \begin{bmatrix} \Psi_{11} \\ \Psi_{12} \end{bmatrix} = \begin{bmatrix} \lambda_1 \\ \lambda_2 \end{bmatrix}.$$

The above two matrix equations can be solved to obtain Ψ_{21} and Ψ_{22}. Using Equation (18.106),

$$U(Z, T) = 4\frac{\cosh(3T) + 3e^{4jZ}\cosh(T)}{\cosh(4T) + 4\cosh(2T) + 3\cos(4Z)}e^{jZ/2}. \qquad \textbf{[18.108]}$$

This is verified in Problem 18–14. At $Z = 0$,

$$U(0, T) = 4\frac{(e^T + e^{-T})^3}{(e^T + e^{-T})^4} = 2\text{sech}(T).$$

In other words, the initial pulse at $Z = 0$ has the same waveform as the fundamental soliton, but the magnitude is doubled ($N = 2$). ■

APPENDIX 18–B: DERIVATION OF THE GORDON-HAUS LIMIT

This appendix derives the RMS of the v_g^{-1} variation due to ASE. To start, it is neccessary to first derive the dependence of the soliton pulse on its carrier frequency. For a given reference frequency ω_0, the carrier frequency ω can be related to it by

$$\omega = \omega_0 + \Delta\omega$$

where $\Delta\omega$ is the frequency deviation from the reference frequency. From Equation (18.36) and because

$$\frac{1}{v_g} = \frac{1}{v_{g0}} + \beta_2 \Delta\omega$$

the envelope of the soliton pulse can be expressed as

$$A(z, t) = A_p \operatorname{sech} \left(\frac{t - z/v_{g0}}{T_0} - \frac{\beta_2 \Delta\omega z}{T_0} \right) e^{jz/(2L_D)}. \qquad \textbf{[18.109]}$$

Because the total wave is

$$E(z, t) = A(z, t)e^{j(\beta z - \omega t)}$$

Equation (18.6) can be used to give

$$E(z, t) = A(z, t)e^{-j\Delta\omega(t - z/v_g) + j\beta_2 \Delta\omega^2 z/2} e^{j(\beta_0 z - \omega_0 t)}.$$

Next, define a new envelope function that includes all the frequency dependent factors:

$$\hat{A}(z, t) = A(z, t)e^{-j\Delta\omega(t - z/v_{g0}) + j\beta_2 \Delta\omega^2 z/2}. \qquad \textbf{[18.110]}$$

Combining Equations (18.109) and (18.110) and using a new time variable t_1 to substitute for $t - z/v_{g0}$,

$$\hat{A}(z, t) = A_p \operatorname{sech} \left(\frac{t_1}{T_0} - \frac{\beta_2 \Delta\omega z}{T_0} \right) e^{-j\Delta\omega t_1 + jz\beta_2(\Delta\omega^2 - 1/T_0^2)/2} \qquad \textbf{[18.111]}$$

where Equation (18.30) is used for L_D.

For a given envelope function $\hat{A}$, the pulse energy is

$$E = \int |\hat{A}(z, t)|^2 dt = 2A_p^2 T_0$$

where the fact that $\int \operatorname{sech}(x)^2 dx = 2$ is used (see Problem 18–15). Also, the mean frequency (with respect to ω_0) of the pulse can be calculated by

$$E[\Delta\omega] = \frac{1}{E} \Im \int \hat{A} \frac{\partial}{\partial t} \hat{A}^* dt = \Delta\omega \qquad \textbf{[18.112]}$$

where $\Im$ means to take the imaginary part.

Therefore, when an ASE noise, δA, is added to $\hat{A}$, the new pulse energy becomes

$$E' = \int |\hat{A} + \delta A|^2 dt \approx E + 2\Re \int \hat{A} \delta A^* dt$$

where $\Re$ means to take the real part, and the shift of the mean frequency is now

$$\delta(\Delta\omega) = \frac{1}{E'}\Im \int (\hat{A} + \delta A)\frac{\partial}{\partial t}(\hat{A} + \delta A)^* dt - \Delta\omega$$

$$\approx \frac{2}{E}\left\{\Im \int \delta A\frac{\partial}{\partial t}\hat{A}^* dt - \Delta\omega\Re \int \hat{A}^*\delta A dt\right\}.$$

Substituting $\hat{A}$ from Equation (18.111) and because $\Im(jX) = \Re X$ for any complex X,

$$\delta(\Delta\omega) = \frac{2}{ET_0}\Im \int \tanh(t/T_0 - \beta_2\Delta\omega z/T_0)\hat{A}^*\delta A dt. \qquad \textbf{[18.113]}$$

This frequency shift results in a variation of $1/v_g$ given by the expression

$$\delta(v_g^{-1}) = \beta_2\delta(\Delta\omega) = \frac{2\beta_2}{ET_0}\Im \int \tanh(t/T_0 - \beta_2\Delta\omega z/T_0)\hat{A}^*\delta A dt \qquad \textbf{[18.114]}$$

$$= -\frac{1}{A_p^2 L_D}\Im \int \tanh(t/T_0 - \beta_2\Delta\omega z/T_0)\hat{A}^*\delta A dt.$$

Chapter 17 explained that the noise power of each mode is $(G-1)hf$ (excess factor is ignored here), where G is the amplifier gain. Considering Equation (18.114), there can be one noise mode given by

$$\delta A(z, t) = j\epsilon[\tanh(t/T_0 - \beta_2\Delta\omega z/T_0)]\hat{A} \stackrel{\text{def}}{=} j\epsilon n_A(z, t) \qquad \textbf{[18.115]}$$

where ϵ is a zero-mean, real, random variable whose variance is to be determined, and

$$n_A(z, t) = \tanh(t/T_0 - \beta_2\Delta\omega z/T_0)]\hat{A}.$$

Because all of the other modes are orthogonal to the given mode, Equation (18.114) reduces to

$$\delta(v_g^{-1}) = -\frac{1}{A_p^2 L_D}\epsilon \int |n_A|^2 dt.$$

Because ϵ is real (ϵ should be complex in general), the noise mode, $n_A(z, t)$, given by Equation (18.115) has only half of the ASE energy, $(G-1)hf/2$. In other words,

$$E[\epsilon^2] \int |n_A|^2 dt = \frac{1}{2}(G-1)hf.$$

Thus

$$E[\delta(v_g^{-1})^2] = \left(\frac{1}{A_p^2 L_D}\right)^2 E[\epsilon^2]\left(\int |n_A|^2 dt\right)^2$$

$$= \left(\frac{hf}{2A_p^4 L_D^2}\right)(G-1)\left(\int |n_A|^2 dt\right).$$

From Problem 18–15,

$$\int |\tanh(x)\text{sech}(x)|^2 dx = \frac{2}{3}.$$

Therefore,

$$\int |n_A|^2 dt = A_p^2 T_0 \int |\tanh(x)\text{sech}(x)|^2 dx = \frac{2}{3} A_p^2 T_0$$

and

$$E[\delta(v_g^{-1})^2] = \frac{hf T_0}{3 A_p^2 L_D^2}(G-1) = \frac{hf\gamma|\beta_2|}{3 T_0}(G-1) \qquad \textbf{[18.116]}$$

where the last equality makes use of substitutions from Equations (18.30) and (18.31) with $N = 1$.

PROBLEMS

Problem 18–1 Pulse Width of Fundamental Soliton: For the fundamental soliton given by Equation (18.35), show that the FWHM of the pulse is $1.76 T_0$.

Problem 18–2 Reduction of T_0: From Equation (18.37), find the required $|\beta_2|$ so that T_0 is only 10 fsec at the peak power of 100 mW and $\lambda = 1.55\mu$m. What is the corresponding D_{intra} value? Assume $\gamma = 2 \times 10^{-3}$ (m·W)$^{-1}$.

Problem 18–3 Soliton Distance: Find the peak power of the fundamental soliton ($N = 1$) so that its L_D is 30 km. Assume $\gamma = 2 \times 10^{-3}$ (m·W)$^{-1}$.

Problem 18–4 Fundamental Soliton: From the fundamental soliton solution given by Equation (18.35), show:

a. $\frac{\partial U}{\partial T} = -U \tanh(T)$.

b. $\frac{\partial^2 U}{\partial T^2} = -2|U|^2 U + U$.

c. Verify that U given by Equation (18.35) satisfies Equation (18.34).

Problem 18–5 Frequency Chirping Effect:

a. For an initial soliton pulse with a chirping intensity $\phi = 0.6$, use Figure 18.13 to find the power loss percentage if the initial soliton has a normalized peak value $N = 1.25$. With respect to the case $\phi = 0.0$, also calculate the percentage of pulse broadening.

b. If the initial normalized peak value of a soliton is 1.0, find the maximum chirping intensity ϕ if the power loss should be within 10 percent. What is the final soliton pulse?

Problem 18–6 Amplifier Spacing:

a. Design the spacing of EDFAs for a soliton transmission of 15,000 km at $T_0 = 100$ psec, $D_{intra} = 2$ psec/km·nm, $\gamma = 2$ (W·km)$^{-1}$, $\alpha_f = 0.2$ dB/km, and operating wavelength = 1550 nm. In the design, assume the achievable amplifier gain is not greater than 30 dB and the amplifier spacing should be less than $z_0/10$.

b. Find the peak power at the initial transmitter output.

Problem 18–7 Gordon-Haus Limit: The Gordon-Haus limit given by Equation (18.53) is based on the approximation in Equation (18.52). Instead, if the amplifier spacing is L_a and $m = L/L_a$, show that a general expression for the limit is

$$(LB)^3 < \frac{18\pi\epsilon^2}{q_0 h \lambda \gamma D_{intra}} \frac{L_a}{e^{\alpha_f L_a} - 1}. \qquad \textbf{[18.117]}$$

From this expression, show that this new limit is lower than the limit given by Equation (18.53).

Problem 18–8 Equivalence of Equation (18.63) to the NLSE:

a. By substituting the definitions of $\bar{\Delta}^{(1)}$ and $\bar{\Delta}^{(2)}$ from Equations (18.57) and (18.58) in terms of $\bar{L}$ and $\bar{M}$, show that the condition Equation (18.64) implies Equation (18.65). Note that

$$\frac{\partial}{\partial Z}(\bar{L}\bar{\psi}) = \frac{\partial \bar{L}}{\partial Z}\bar{\psi} + \bar{L}\frac{\partial \bar{\psi}}{\partial Z}.$$

b. Show that

$$\bar{L}\bar{M} = \frac{1}{2}\begin{bmatrix} \sqrt{2} & 0 \\ 0 & -\frac{1}{\sqrt{2}} \end{bmatrix}\frac{\partial^3}{\partial T^3} + \frac{1}{2}\begin{bmatrix} 0 & U \\ U^* & 0 \end{bmatrix}\frac{\partial^2}{\partial T^2} + \begin{bmatrix} -\frac{\sqrt{2}}{3}UU_T^* & \frac{2}{3}|U|^2U \\ \frac{1}{3}|U|^2U^* & \frac{\sqrt{2}}{3}U_TU^* \end{bmatrix}$$

$$+ \begin{bmatrix} \frac{\sqrt{2}}{3}[UU_T^* + U_TU^* + |U|^2\frac{\partial}{\partial T}] & \frac{2}{3}[U_{TT} + U_T\frac{\partial}{\partial T}] \\ \frac{1}{3}[U_{TT}^* + U_T^*\frac{\partial}{\partial T}] & -\frac{\sqrt{2}}{3}[UU_T^* + U_TU^* + 6|U|^2\frac{\partial}{\partial T}] \end{bmatrix}.$$

c. Show that

$$\bar{M}\bar{L} = \frac{1}{2}\begin{bmatrix} \sqrt{2} & 0 \\ 0 & -\frac{1}{\sqrt{2}} \end{bmatrix}\frac{\partial^3}{\partial T^3}$$

$$+ \frac{1}{2}\begin{pmatrix} 0 & U_{TT} + 2U_T\frac{\partial}{\partial T} + U\frac{\partial^2}{\partial T^2} \\ U_{TT}^* + 2U_T^*\frac{\partial}{\partial T} + U^*\frac{\partial^2}{\partial T^2} & 0 \end{pmatrix}$$

$$+ \begin{pmatrix} \frac{\sqrt{2}}{3}U_TU^* & \frac{1}{3}|U|^2U \\ \frac{2}{3}|U|^2U^* & -\frac{\sqrt{2}}{3}UU_T^* \end{pmatrix} + \begin{pmatrix} \frac{\sqrt{2}}{3}|U|^2\frac{\partial}{\partial T} & -\frac{1}{3}U_T\frac{\partial}{\partial T} \\ -\frac{2}{3}U_T^*\frac{\partial}{\partial T} & -\frac{2}{3}|U|^2\frac{\partial}{\partial T} \end{pmatrix}.$$

d. From (b) and (c), show that

$$j\frac{1}{3}\frac{\partial \bar{L}}{\partial Z} + (\bar{L}\bar{M} - \bar{M}\bar{L}) = \begin{bmatrix} 0 & NLSE/3 \\ -NLSE^*/3 & 0 \end{bmatrix}$$

where NLSE is the left-hand side of the NLSE equation given by Equation (18.34).

Problem 18–9 Equations for the Far-Field Operator:

a. From Equation (18.70) for $i = 1$, show that

$$\frac{j}{3}\bar{F}_Z(Z, T, \tau) - \frac{1}{2}\bar{F}_{TT}(Z, T, \tau) + \frac{1}{2}\bar{F}_{\tau\tau}(Z, T, \tau) = 0.$$

b. From Equation (18.70) for $i = 2$, show that

$$\begin{pmatrix} \sqrt{2} & 0 \\ 0 & -\frac{1}{\sqrt{2}} \end{pmatrix} \bar{F}_T(Z, T, \tau) + \bar{F}_\tau(Z, T, \tau) \begin{pmatrix} \sqrt{2} & 0 \\ 0 & -1/\sqrt{2} \end{pmatrix} = 0.$$

Problem 18–10 Marchenko Equation:

Let

$$\bar{V} \overset{\text{def}}{=} \bar{\Delta}^{(2)} - \bar{\Delta}_0^{(2)} = \begin{pmatrix} 0 & U \\ U^* & 0 \end{pmatrix}$$

From Equation (18.62) for $i = 2$, verify the following.

a.

$$\bar{V} = \begin{pmatrix} \sqrt{2} & 0 \\ 0 & -\frac{1}{\sqrt{2}} \end{pmatrix} \hat{K} - \hat{K} \begin{pmatrix} \sqrt{2} & 0 \\ 0 & -\frac{1}{\sqrt{2}} \end{pmatrix}.$$

where

$$\hat{K}(Z, T) = \bar{K}(Z, T, T).$$

b.

$$V K + K_\tau \begin{pmatrix} \sqrt{2} & 0 \\ 0 & -1/\sqrt{2} \end{pmatrix} + \begin{pmatrix} \sqrt{2} & 0 \\ 0 & -1/\sqrt{2} \end{pmatrix} K_T = 0.$$

c.

$$\bar{V} = \frac{3}{\sqrt{2}} \begin{pmatrix} 0 & K_{12}(Z, T, T) \\ -K_{21}(Z, T, T) & 0 \end{pmatrix}.$$

Problem 18–11 Marchenko Equation: Show that Equation (18.62) for $i = 1$ can result from Equations (18.61), (18.63), and (18.62) for $i = 2$. In other words, the equation for $\bar{K}$ and U derived in Problem 18–10 is consistent with Equation (18.62) when $i = 1$.

Problem 18–12 N Solitons:

a. From the definitions given by Equations (18.101)–(18.103), verify Equation (18.104) for $n = 1, \ldots, N$.

b. Similarly, verify Equation (18.105) for $n = 1, \ldots, N$.

c. Show that the final solution $U(Z, T)$ to Equation (18.34) of $N = 1$ can be expressed as

$$U(Z, T) = \frac{3}{\sqrt{2}} \sum_n b_n e^{2\rho_n T/3} = -2 \sum_n \lambda_n^* \Psi_{2n}.$$

Problem 18–13 Expression of $U(Z, T)$ **for N Solitons:** Verify Equation (18.106) using Equations (18.94), (18.101), and (18.103).

Problem 18–14 Two-Soliton Solution: Verify the soliton solution for $N = 2$ given by Equation (18.108).

Problem 18–15 Energy of a Soliton Pulse: Use the dummy variable substitution $y = e^x$ and partial integration to show that

a. $\int_{-\infty}^{\infty} \text{sech}(x)^2 dx = 2$

b. $\int_{-\infty}^{\infty} \tanh(x)^2 \text{sech}(x)^2 dx = \frac{2}{3}$. Hint: Use $\tanh(x)^2 = 1 - \text{sech}(x)^2$.

REFERENCES

1. N. J. Zabusky and M. D. Kruskal, "Interactions of Solitons in a Collisionless Plasma and the Recurrence of Initial States," *Physical Review Letters,* vol. 15, (1965), pp. 240–43.

2. J. S. Russel, "Reports on Waves," *Reports of the 14th Meetings of the British Association for the Advancement of Science,* London: John Murray, 1844, pp. 311–90.

3. D. J. Korteweg and G. de Vries, "On the Change of Form of Long Waves Advancing in a Rectangular Canal, and On a New Type of Long Stationary Waves," *Phil. Mag.,* vol. 5, (1895), pp. 422–43.

4. V. E. Zakharov and A. B. Shabat, "Exact Theory of Two-Dimensional Self-Focusing and One-Dimensional Modulation of Waves in Nonlinear Media," *Soviet Physics, Journal of Experimental and Theoretical Physics,* vol. 34, (1972), pp. 62–69.

5. A. Hasegawa and F. Tappert, "Transmission of Stationary Nonlinear Optical Pulses in Dispersive Dielectric Fibers," *Applied Physics Letters,* vol. 23, (August 1973), pp. 142–44.

6. J. H. Marburger, "Self-Focusing Theory," *Progress in Quantum Electronics,* vol. 4, (1975), pp. 35–110.

7. L. F. Mollenauer, R. H. Stolen, and J. P. Gordon, "Experimental Observation of Picosecond Pulse Narrowing and Solitons in Optical Fibers," *Physical Review Letters,* vol. 45, no. 13, (September 1980), pp. 1095–98.

8. R. H. Stolen and C. Lin, "Self-Phase Modulation in Silica Optical Fibers," *Physical Reviews A,* vol. 17, (1978) p. 1448.

9. G. P. Agrawal, *Fiber-Optic Communication Systems,* John Wiley and Sons, 1992.

10. L. F. Mollenauer and K. Smith, "Demonstration of Soliton Transmission over More than 4,000 km in Fiber with Loss Periodically Compensated by Raman Gain," *Optics Letters,* vol. 13, (August 1988), pp. 675–77.

11. K. Smith and L. F. Mollenauer, "Experimental Observation of Soliton Interaction over Long Fiber Paths: Discovery of a Long Range Interaction," *Optics Letters,* vol. 14, (November 1989) pp. 1284–86.

12. L. F. Mollenauer et al., "Experimental Study of Soliton Transmission over More than 10,000 km in Dispersion Shifted Fiber," *Optics Letters,* vol. 15, (November 1990), pp. 1203–05.

13. L. F. Mollenauer et al., "Demonstration of Soliton Transmission at 2.4 Gbit/s over 12,000 km," *Electronics Letters,* vol. 27, (January 1991), pp. 178–79.

14. L. F. Mollenauer et al., "Demonstration of Error-Free Soliton Transmission over More than 15,000km at 5 Gb/s Single-Channel, and over More than 11,000 km at 10 Gb/s in Two-Channel WDM," *Electronics Letters,* vol. 28, no. 8 (April 1992), pp. 792–4.

15. M. Nakazawa, "10 Gb/s, 1200 km Error-Free Soliton Data-Transmission Using Erbium-Doped Fiber Amplifiers," *Electronics Letters,* vol. 28, no. 9, (1992), pp. 817–18.

16. M. Nakazawa, "20 Gb/s, 1020 km Penalty-Free Soliton Data-Transmission Using Erbium-Doped Fiber Amplifiers," *Electronics Letters,* vol. 28, no. 9, (1992), pp. 1046–47.

17. P. Andrekson, "32 Gb/s Optical Soliton Data-Transmission over 90 km," *IEEE Photonics Technology Letters,* vol. 4, no. 1, (1992), pp. 76–79.

18. K. Iwatsuki, "40 Gb/s Optical Transmission over 65 km," *Electronics Letters,* vol. 28, no. 19, (1992), pp. 1821–22.

19. H. Taga, "5 Gb/s Optical Soliton Transmission Experiment over 3000 km Employing 91 Cascaded Er-Doped Fiber Amplifier Repeaters," *Electronics Letters,* vol. 28, no. 24, (1992), pp. 2247–48.

20. K. Iwatsuki, "80 Gb/s Optical Transmission over 85 km with Time Polarization Division Multiplexing," *IEEE Photonics Technology Letters,* vol. 5, no. 2, (1993), pp. 245–48.

21. M. Nakazawa, "Experimental Demonstration of Soliton Data-Transmission over Unlimited Distances with Soliton Control in Time and Frequency Domains," *Electronics Letters,* vol. 29, no. 9, (1993), pp. 729–30.

22. L. F. Mollenauer et al., "Long-Distance Soliton Propagation Using Lumped Amplifiers and Dispersion Shifted Fibers," *Journal of Lightwave Technology,* vol. 9, no. 2, (1991), pp. 184-306.

23. J. Satsuma and N. Yajima, "Initial Value Problems of One-Dimensional Self-Modulation of Nonlinear Waves in Dispersive Media," *Progress in Theoretical Physics Supplement,* vol. 55, (1974), pp. 184–306.

24. C. Desem and P. L. Chu, "Effect of Chirping on Soliton Propagation in Single-Mode Optical Fibers," *Optics Letters,* vol. 11, no. 4, (April 1986), pp. 248–50.

25. J. P. Gordon and H. A. Haus, "Random Walk of Coherently Amplified Solitons in Optical Fiber Transmission," *Optics Letters,* vol. 11, no. 10, (October 1986), pp. 665–67.

26. M. Nakazawa et al., "10 Gb/s Soliton Transmission over One Million Kilometers," *Electronics Letters,* vol. 27, (July 1991), pp. 1270–72.

27. H. A. Haus, "Optical Fiber Solitons, Their Properties and Uses," *Proceedings of the IEEE,* vol. 81, no. 7, (July 1993), pp. 970–83.

28. J. Arnold, "Soliton Pulse-Position Modulation," *IEE Proceedings, J,* vol. 140, no. 6, (1993), pp. 359–69.

29. J. P. Gordon, "Interaction Forces among Solitons in Optical Fibers," *Optics Letters,* vol. 8, (1987), pp. 596–98.

30. C. Desem and P. L. Chu, "Reducing Soliton Interaction in Single-Mode Optical Fibers," *IEE Proceedings, J,* vol. 134, (1987), p. 145.

31. P. L. Chu and C. Desem, "Mutual Interaction between Solitons of Unequal Amplitudes in Optical Fiber," *Electronics Letters,* vol. 21, no. 24, (October 1985), pp. 1133–34.

32. P. G. Drazin and R. S. Johnson, *Solitons: An Introduction,* Cambridge University Press, 1989.

33. V. A. Marchenko, "On the Reconstruction of the Potential Energy from Phases of the Scattered Waves," *Dokl. Akad. Nauk SSSR,* vol. 14, (1955), pp. 695–98.

34. G. P. Agrawal, *Nonlinear Fiber Optics,* Academic Press, 1989.

35. H. A. Haus and M. N. Islam, "Theory of the Soliton Laser," *IEEE Journal of Quantum Electronics,* vol. 21, (1985), p. 1172.

IMPORTANT PHYSICAL
AND MATHEMATICAL CONSTANTS

Constants	Descriptions	Values
c	Speed of light	2.99792×10^8 m/s
e	Base of natural logarithm	2.71828
h	Planck constant	6.62617×10^{-34} J·s
k	Boltzmann constant	1.38066×10^{-23} J/K
m_0	Stationary electron mass	9.11×10^{-31} kg
q	Unit electron charge	1.602×10^{-19} C
$\epsilon_0 = 1/\mu_0 c^2$	Vacuum permittivity	8.85418×10^{-12} F/m
μ_0	Vacuum permeability	$4\pi \times 10^{-7} = 1.25663 \times 10^{-6}$ H/m
π	Area of unit circle	3.1415926
eV	Unit electron volt	$1.602 \times 10^{-19}\,(q)$ J
kT/q	Thermal voltage	0.0259 Volt at 300 K
kT	Thermal energy	4.14198×10^{-21} at 300 K
hc/q	Wavelength of photons of energy 1 eV	1.23977 μm

Important Conversion Factors

1 mil	0.001 inch = 25.4 μm
1 Å	10^{-10} m
1 eV	1.602×10^{-19} J
$\log_{10} e$	0.43429
$\log_e 10 = \ln 10$	2.30259

B

INTERNATIONAL SYSTEM OF UNITS (SI)

Base Units

Quantity	Unit	Symbol
Length	meter	m
Mass	kilogram	kg
Time	second	s
Current	ampere	A
Temperature	kelvin	K

Secondary Units

Quantity	Unit	Symbol	Dimension
Force	newton	N	$kg \cdot m/s^2$
Frequency	hertz	Hz	$1/s$
Energy	joule	J	$N \cdot m = kg \cdot (m/s)^2$
Power	watt	W	J/s
Electric Charge	coulomb	C	$A \cdot s$
Potential	volt	V	$J/C = W/A$
Resistance	ohm	Ω	V/A
Conductance	siemens	S	A/V
Capacitance	farad	F	C/V
Magnetic Flux	weber	Wb	$V \cdot s$
Magnetic Induction ($\mathcal{B}$)	tesla	T	Wb/m^2
Inductance	henry	H	Wb/A

appendix

C

IMPORTANT PHYSICAL CONSTANTS OF III–V COMPOUNDS

III, IV, and V Atoms

Group III Atoms			Group IV Atoms			Group V Atoms		
Symbol	**Name**	**Atom No.**	**Symbol**	**Name**	**Atom No.**	**Symbol**	**Name**	**Atom No.**
B	Boron	5	C	Carbon	6	N	Nitrogen	7
Al	Aluminum	13	Si	Silicon	14	P	Phosphorus	15
Ga	Gallium	31	Ge	Germanium	32	As	Arsenic	33
In	Indium	49	Sn	Tin	50	Sb	Antimony	51

Recombination Coefficient[4]

Compound	B_r **cm**^{3}**/s**
GaAs	7.21×10^{-10}
GaSb	2.39×10^{-10}
InAs	8.5×10^{-11}
InSb	4.58×10^{-11}
Si	1.79×10^{-15}
Ge	5.25×10^{-14}
GaP	5.37×10^{-14}

Intrinsic Carrier Density n_i^2 $(1/\text{cm}^{-3})$

GaAs	3.2×10^{-12}

[4] From John Senior, *Optical Fiber Communications, Principles and Practice,* (Prentice-Hall, 1985).

Important III-V Compound Constants[5]

III-V Compound Name		E_g (eV)		Band	Mobility $300°K$, cm^2/V·s		Eff. Mass m*/m$_0$		$n^2 = \epsilon_r$
	•	**300°K**	**0°K**		**Electron**	**Hole**	**Electron**	**Hole**	
Binary Compounds									
AlSb	Aluminum antimonide	1.58	1.68	I	200	420	0.12	0.98	14.4
BN	Boron nitride	≈7.5		I					7.1
BP	Boron phosphide	2.0							
GaN	Gallium nitride	3.36	3.50		380		0.19	0.60	12.2
GaSb	Gallium antimonide	0.72	0.81	D	5000	850	0.042	0.4	15.7
GaAs	Gallium arsenide	1.42	1.52	D	8500	400	0.067	0.082	13.1
GaP	Gallium phosphide	2.26	2.34	I	110	75	0.82	0.60	11.1
InSb	Indium antimonide	0.17	0.23	D	80000	1250	0.0145	0.4	17.7
InAs	Indium arsenside	0.36	0.42	D	33000	460	0.023	0.40	14.6
InP	Indium phosphide	1.35	1.42	D	4600	150	0.077	0.64	12.4

Ternary Compounds			
$Ga_xIn_{1-x}P$	$1.351 + 0.643x + 0.786x^2$	D	Note 1
$Ga_xIn_{1-x}As$	$0.36 + 1.064x$	D	
$Ga_xIn_{1-x}Sb$	$0.172 + 0.139x + 0.415x^2$	D	
$Al_xIn_{1-x}P$	$1.351 + 2.23x$	D	
$Al_xIn_{1-x}As$	$0.36 + 2.012x + 0.698x^2$	D	
$Al_xIn_{1-x}Sb$	$0.172 + 1.621x + 0.43x^2$	D	
$Al_xGa_{1-x}As$	$1.424 + 1.247x + f(x)$	D	Note 2
$Al_xGa_{1-x}Sb$	$0.726 + 1.129x + 0.368x^2$	D	
InP_yAs_{1-y}	$0.36 + 0.891y + 0.101y^2$	D	
GaP_yAs_{1-y}	$1.424 + 1.15y + 0.176y^2$	D	
$InAs_ySb_{1-y}$	$0.18 - 0.41y + 0.58y^2$	D	
$GaAs_ySb_{1-y}$	$0.726 - 0.502y + 1.2y^2$	D	

Quaternary Compounds		
$Al_xGa_{1-x}As_ySb_{1-y}$	0.7–2.2	D
$In_xGa_{1-x}As_yP_{1-y}$	0.4–1.4	D

Note 1: D for direct energy bandgap and I for indirect energy bandgap.
Note 2: $f(x) = 1.147(x - 0.45)^2$ is added when $x > 0.45$.

[5] Adapted from (1) S. M. Sze, *Physics of Semiconductor Devices,* 2nd Edition (Wiley, 1981) and (2) H. C. Casey and M. B. Panish, *Heterostructure Lasers* (Academic Press, 1978).

IMPORTANT VARIABLE DEFINITIONS

Chapter 1: Introduction

Parameter	Unit	Description
$c(t)$		carrier signal
f_c	Hz	carrier frequency
$f(t)$	Hz	total instantaneous frequency of a modulated sinusolidal signal
k_{AM}		modulation index of AM
k_{FM}		modulation index of FM
k_{PM}		modulation index of PM
L	km	fiber length
$m(t)$		baseband source signal
P_E		error probability in digital transmission
P_{in}	W	incident power
P_{out}	W	output power
P_{ref}	W	reference power
r_k		sampled received signal at the kth bit interval
$S_{AM}(\omega)$		Fourier transform of $s_{AM}(t)$
$s_{AM}(t)$		amplitude modulated signal
$s_{FM}(t)$		frequency modulated signal
$s_{PM}(t)$		phase modulated signal
T_0	sec	bit interval in digital transmission
x_k		impulse response of a communication channel at the kth bit interval
α	dB/km	fiber attenuation
γ		signal to noise ratio
$\phi(t)$	rad	phase component of a sinusoidal signal
ω_c	rad/sec	circular frequency of the carrier
$\Delta\omega$	rad/sec	circular frequency shift
$\theta(t)$	rad	total phase function of a modulated sinusoidal signal

Chapter 2: From Point-To-Point to Networking

Parameter	Unit	Description
c	m/sec	speed of light
DR		dynamic range
$e_i(t)$		encoded output by the ith key in CDMA
N		an integer number
N_c		number of crosspoints
m		the number of middle switches in a three-stage circuit switch
n		the switch size of the first stage in a three-stage circuit switch
P_0	W	transmission power
P_{min}	W	minimum possible received power
P_{max}	W	maximum possible received power
r		the number of first stage swtiches in a three-stage circuit switch
T_f	sec	frame size
T_g	sec	guard time
T_s	sec	time slot size
x		coupling coefficient from the bus to a user node or vice versa
x_{opt}		optimum coupling coefficient from the bus to a user node or vice versa
α		coupling power loss
η		network access utilization
η_{bus}		total power loss in a bus topology
$\eta_{r.bus}$		total power loss in a re-entrant bus topology
η_{star}		total power loss in a star topology
λ	m	wavelength
λ_i	m	wavelength of channel i
$\phi_i(t)$'s		a set of orthonormal functions in time

Chapter 3: Light Sources

Parameter	Unit	Description
A_{21}	1/sec	spontaneous emission rate from energy level 2 to 1
B_{12}	m^3(joule $\cdot$ sec^2)	stimulated absorption coefficient
B_{21}	m^3(joule $\cdot$ sec^2)	stimulated emission coefficient
c	m/sec	speed of light in vacuum
$c(t)$		carrier signal
$c_{loc}(t)$		local carrier of the receiver
D		one way phase shift factor
d	m	thickness of the active layer of a semiconductor light source
E_c	eV	energy level of the conduction band

Chapter 3: Light Sources (continued)

Parameter	Unit	Description
E_f	eV	Fermi level
E_v	eV	energy level of the valence band
E_g	eV	energy bandgap between the conduction band and valence band
f	Hz	frequency
Δf	Hz	spectrum width of a light source
Δf_{long}	Hz	spectrum separation of longitudinal modes
$\mathcal{F}$		finesse
g	1/m	gain constant in a laser cavity
h	joule · sec	Planck constant
I	Amp	bias current of a light source
I_{th}	Amp	threshold current of a light source
k	joule · sec	Planck constant
L	m	cavity length in the longitudinal direction
N_1, N_2	1/m³	carrier densities at energy levels 1 and 2
m_e	gram	effective mass of electrons in a given semiconductor
m_h	gram	effective mass of holes in a given semiconductor
m_0	gram	stationary mass of electrons
n, n_1, n_2		refractive index
P_{in}	watt	input power to an FP resonator
P_{out}	watt	output power of an FP resonator
$p(t)$		transmitted pulse
q	Columb	electron charge
R_1, R_2		reflectivity and equal to $\mid r_1 \mid^2$ and $\mid r_2 \mid^2$
R, R'		reflectivities equal to $\mid r \mid^2$ and $\mid r' \mid^2$
$\bar{R}$		$(RR')^{1/2}$
r_1, r_2		reflection coefficient at the two sides of a laser cavity
r, r'		reflection coefficients at the left and right ends of a FP cavity
rect(t,T₀)		unit rectangle pulse from t = 0 to T₀
S	joule/m³ · Hz	photon energy density in a cavity
T	K	temperature
T		transmissivity
T_0	sec	bit interval
T_c	K	characteristic temperature of a laser diode
t, t'		transmission coefficients at the left and right ends of a FP cavity
Δv_g	m/sec	change in group velocity
w	m	cavity width in the transversal direction
α	1/m	absorption constant in a laser cavity
α_{dB}	dB/m	cavity loss in dB/m
α_m	1/m	eqivalent absorption due to reflection loss at the cavity ends

Chapter 3: Light Sources (continued)

Parameter	Unit	Description
α_{tot}	1/m	total distributed cavity loss
β_z	1/m	propagation constant in the longitudinal direction of a laser cavity
δ		round trip phase shift in an FP cavity
$\Delta\delta$		FWHM of a fringe of an FP resonator
ϵ		residual round trip phase shift of δ in an FP cavity
Λ	m	grating period in a DFB laser diode
λ	m	wavelength
λ_B	m	Bragg wavelength
λ_m	m	wavelength of the mth longitudinal mode
$\Delta\lambda$	m	linewidth of a light source
$\Delta\lambda_{long}$	m	longitudinal mode separation in wavelength
ω_c	rad/sec	circular frequency of a carrier
$\omega_{c,i}$	rad/sec	circular frequency of longitudinal mode i
$\Delta\omega$	rad/sec	circular frequency shift
$\phi_i(t)$	rad	phase noise of longitudinal mode i
$\phi_n(t)$	rad	phase noise of a light source
τ_i	sec	propagation delay of longitudinal mode i

Chapter 4: Optical Fibers

Parameter	Unit	Description
$A(z,t)$		envelop of a wave packet
$A_i(r,\theta)$		field distribution of transverse mode i
a	m	core diameter
$\mathcal{B}$		birefringence
B	b/sec	bit rate
B_0	b/sec	reference bit rate
B_{max}	b/sec	maximum achievable bit rate
B_{fiber}	Hz	fiber bandwidth
b		a parameter in weakly guided fibers
c	m/sec	speed of light in vacuum
c_R	dB/km $\cdot (\mu m)^4$	Rayleigh scattering coefficient
$\mathcal{D}$	C/m^2	displacement or electric flux density
D_{intra}	sec/km $\cdot$ nm	intramodal dispersion
D_{modal}	sec/km	intermodal or modal dispersion
D_{total}	sec/km	total fiber dispersion
$D_{waveguide}$	sec/km $\cdot$ nm	waveguide dispersion

Chapter 4: Optical Fibers (continued)

Parameter	Unit	Description
$D_{material}$	sec/km·nm	material dispersion
$\mathcal{E}$	V/m	electric field
E_x, E_y, E_z	V/m	x, y, z components of an electric field
Δf	Hz	spectrum width
$\mathcal{H}$	A/m	magnetic field
H_x, H_y, H_z	A/m	x, y, z components of a magnetic field
h	1/m	coupling constant of a polarization maintaining fiber
J	A/m^2	current density
k	1/m	propagation constant in free space
k_b		bandwidth expansion factor in light modulation
L	km	fiber length
L_c	km	critical fiber length of mode coupling
L_{max}	km	maximum transmission distance due to attenuation or dispersion
M		number of modes in a multimode fiber
NA		numerical aperature
n_1		core refractive index
n_2		cladding refractive index
n_{1g}		group refractive index of the core
n_{2g}		group refractive index of the cladding
n_x, n_y		refractive indices of a birefrigent fiber
$\mathcal{P}$	V/F	induced polarization
P_0	W	reference receiver sensitivity
P_{min}	W	minimum required received power or receiver sensitivity
P_{tx}	W	transmitter output power
$p(t), p(t, \lambda_i, m)$		optical pulse function of time, wavelength, and mode
$Q(x)$		the Q function
V		normalized frequency
v_g	m/sec	group velocity in a dielectric medium
v_{gi}	m/sec	group velocity of transverse mode i
$v_{g,max}$	m/sec	maximum group velocity
$v_{g,min}$	m/sec	minimum group velocity
v_{gz}	m/sec	group velocity along the longitudinal direction of a waveguide
v_p	m/sec	phase velocity
v_z	m/sec	z-component velocity of propagation rays in a fiber
Δw	sec	RMS width of a pulse
α		refractive index profile parameter of a multimode fiber
$\alpha_{coupling}$	dB	coupling loss
α_{fiber}	dB/km	fiber attenuation
α_R	dB/km	Rayleigh scattering loss
β	1/m	propagation constant in a dielectric medium

Chapter 4: Optical Fibers (continued)

Parameter	Unit	Description
$\bar{\beta}$	1/m	average propagation constant of a wave packet
β_z	1/m	propagation constant in the longitudinal direction
β_{zi}	1/m	longitudinal propagation constant of transverse mode i
β_x, β_y	1/m	propagation constants in the transverse directions
β_1	1/m	propagation constant in the core
β_2	1/m	propagation constant in the cladding
ϵ	F/m	permittivity
γ		signal to noise ratio
Δ		refractive index change ratio in a fiber
ϵ_r		dielectric constant
$\kappa_i, \kappa_{m,n}$		eigenvalue of transverse mode i or (m, n) in a waveguide
λ	m	wavelength
λ_c	m	waveguide cutoff wavelength
λ_0	m	reference wavelength
$\Delta\lambda$	m	linewidth of a light source
μ	H/m	magnetic permeability
$\Psi_i(r, \theta, z)$		field function of transverse mode i
θ_{crit}		critical angle
θ_{in}		incident angle to the fiber
θ_1, θ_2		angles at the core-cladding boundary
σ		conductivity
τ_g	sec/km	proprogation delay per km
τ_t	sec	rise time of the optical transmitter
τ_r	sec	rise time of the optical receiver
Ω		solid angle
ω	rad/sec	circular frequency
$\bar{\omega}$	rad/sec	average circular frequency of a wave packet
χ		susceptibility

Chapter 5: Light Detection

Parameter	Unit	Description
A	m^2	light reception area of a photodetection device
B_{3dB}	Hz	3 dB bandwidth
c	m/sec	speed of light
d	m	thickness of the absoprtion layer of a photodetection device
E	V/m	electric field
E_{max}	V/m	peak electric field in a photodiode
E_{IP}	V/m	electric field at the interface of the intrinsic and p-type layers

Chapter 5: Light Detection (continued)

Parameter	Unit	Description
E_c	eV	energy level of the conduction band
E_g	eV	engergy bandgap
E_v	eV	energy level of the valence band
f	Hz	frequency
G		current gain
G_c	S	conductance of a photoconductor
ΔG_c	S	change of conductance of a photoconductor
h	joule $\cdot$ sec	Planck constant
I_d	Amp	dark current
I_{ph}	Amp	photocurrent due to incident light signal
I_{tot}	Amp	total photocurrent
Δi	Amp	current change
J	A/m^2	output photocurrent density
J_{ac}	A/m^2	average ac current density
J_{PIN}	A/m^2	photocurrent density from the intrinsic layer
J_n	A/m^2	electron current density
J_p	A/m^2	hole current density
J_{out}	A/m^2	average output photocurrent density
k		ratio of hole ionization coefficient to that of electrons in an APD
k_m		amplitude modulation index
L_d	m	total depletion width of a PIN diode
L_m	m	gain multiplication width of an APD
M_{apd}		APD multiplication gain
$M_{apd,n}$		n-type APD multiplication gain
$M_{apd,0}$		n-type APD multiplication gain at dc
N		a parameter in APD emperical frequency response modeling
N_A	1/m^3	doping level of the p-type layer
N_D	1/m^3	doping level of the n-type layer
N_I	1/m^3	doping level of the intrinsic layer
n	1/m^3	electron density in a semiconductor
n_B		empirical parameter used to relate the gain to the bias voltage of an APD
n_i	1/m^3	intrinsic carrier density in a semiconductor
Δn	1/m^3	change of electron density in a semiconductor
p	1/m^3	hole density in a semiconductor
Δp	1/m^3	change of hole density in a semiconductor
P_{in}	watt	incident light power
q	C	electron charge
R		reflectivity
$\mathcal{R}$		responsivity
r		reflection coefficient

Chapter 5: Light Detection (continued)

Parameter	Unit	Description
R_c	Ω	resistance of a photoconductor
R_F	Ω	load resistance in photodetection
ΔR_c	Ω	change of resistance of a photoconductor
T		transmissivity
V	m^3	volumn of the absorption layer of a photodetection device
$V(x)$	V	voltage as a function of position x
V_B	V	breakdown voltage of an APD
V_{DD}	V	bias voltage of a photoconductor
V_{PIN}	V	bias voltage of a PIN diode
V_{bi}	V	built-in junction voltage at a p-n junction
V_T	V	thermal voltage equal to kT/q
V_{min}	V	minimum voltage to deplete the multiplication region of an APD
v_n	v/m	electron drift velocity
v_p	v/m	hole drift velocity
W_N	m	width of the n-doped layer
W_I	m	width of the intrinsic layer
W_{dN}	m	depletion width in the n-doped layer
W_{dP}	m	depletion width in the p-doped layer
α	1/m	absorption coefficient
α_N	1/m	absorption coefficient in the n-doped layer
α_I	1/m	absorption coefficient in the intrinsic layer
$\alpha(x)$	1/m	electron ionization coefficient of an APD
$\beta(x)$	1/m	hole ionization coefficient of an APD
Δ		voltage drop ratio over the intrinsic layer with respect to the peak electric field
ϵ_r		dielectric constant
η		photodetection quantum efficiency
η_{msm}		quantum efficiency of a MSM device
η_{pin}		quantum efficiency of a PIN diode
λ	m	wavelength
μ_n		mobility of electrons in a semiconductor
μ_p		mobility of holes in a semiconductor
$\rho(x)$	C/m^3	charge density
σ_c	S/m	conductivity of a semiconductor
$\Delta\sigma_c$	S/m	change of conductivity of a semiconductor
τ_t	sec	transit delay
τ_e	sec	relaxation time constant of a photoconductor
ω_{3dB}	rad/sec	3 dB bandwidth times 2π of a photodiode
ω_m	rad/sec	circular frequency of a modulating carrier

Chapter 6: Noise in Optical Communications

Parameter	Unit	Description
a		transmission loss factor
a_i		relative power of mode i of a multimode laser
a, b		parameters of an APD
B	Hz	bandwidth
$E[X]$		expectation of random variable X
$\mathcal{F}$		collection of subsets of the sample space Ω
F_{apd}		excess noise factor
$F_X(s)$		probability accumulation function of random variable X
$f_X(n)$		PDF of random variable X
f_b	Hz	peaking frequency of RIN
$G = 1/R$	S	conductance
$H(\omega)$		transfer function of a channel
$H_{eq}(\omega)$		transfer function of the receiver equalizer
$H_{opt}(\omega)$		optimum transfer function of the equalizer
$H_{pre}(\omega)$		transfer function of the pre-equalizer
$H_{post}(\omega)$		transfer function of the post-equalizer
h	joule · sec	Planck constant
$h(t)$		impulse response of the channel
$h_{eq}(t)$		impulse response of the equalizer
$h_{opt}(t)$		impulse response of the optimum equalizer
$h_{pin}(t)$		normalized impulse response of a PIN diode
I		normalized number of total photons in a laser cavity
I_B	Amp	bias current
I_{th}	Amp	threshold current
$I_{ph}(t)$	Amp	average photocurrent
$i_\delta(t)$	Amp	photocurrent when $h_{PIN} = \delta(t)$
I_d	Amp	dark current
$\mathcal{K}_{mpn}$	dB/Hz	MPN coefficient of $S_{MPN}(\omega)$
K_{mpn}	dB	MPN coefficient of MPN noise power
k	joule/K	Botlzman constant
k		hole to electron ionization ratio
k_{mpn}		parameter in characterizing MPN
k_m		amplitude modulation index
L	km	fiber length
$M_1(s)$		moment generating function of $P(1, r)$
M_{apd}		APD gain
$M_{apd,n}$		N-type APD gain
$M_{apd,0}$		dc gain of an APD
$M_v(s)$		moment generating function of receiver equalizer output
$M_X(s)$		moment generating function of random variable X

Chapter 6: Noise in Optical Communications (continued)

Parameter	Unit	Description
MSE		mean square error
N_q		quantum limit
n_{apd}		APD noise
n_δ		shot noise current when $h_{PIN} = \delta(t)$
n_f		refractive index of the fiber
n_{mpn}		MPN noise
n_{out}		noise at the equalizer output
n_{rin}		relative intensity noise
n_{th}		thermal noise
n_{shot}		shot noise
P_E		bit error probability
P_n		noise power
$P(\mathcal{A})$		probability function
$P(n, r)$		probability of a total r EHPs generated from n primary EHPs
$P(\omega)$		Fourier transform of $p(t)$
P_{in}		power of the incident light signal
$P[N]$		probability of having N EHPs generated over T_0
$p(t)$		input pulse to the receiver equalizer
p_1, p_0		prior probabilities of sending bit "1" and "0", respectively
$p_{out}(t)$		$p(t) \otimes h(t)$
$Q(x)$		the Q-function
$\hat{q}$	Amp	$q \times (1\text{Hz})$
R	Ω	resistance
$R_n(\tau)$		autocorrelation function of $n(t)$
R_{sp}	1/sec	spontaneous emission rate
$\mathcal{R}$	A/W	responsivity
RIN	dB/Hz	relative intensity noise coefficient
$r(t)$		received signal
r_k		kth samples value of $s(t)$
S_{rin}		two sided PSD of laser relative intensity noise
S_{apd}		two sided PSD of APD noise
S_{shot}		two sided PSD of PIN diode shot noise
S_T		two sided PSD of thermal noise
$S_{\dot{\phi}_r}$		two sided PSD of $\dot{\phi}_r$ or frequency noise
$S_n(\omega)$		two sided PSD of noise $n(t)$
$S_s(\omega)$		two sided PSD of signal $s(t)$
$S(t)$		transmitted signal
T	K	temperature
T_0	sec	bit interval

Chapter 6: Noise in Optical Communications (continued)

Parameter	Unit	Description
t_{coh}	sec	coherence time of a laser output
V_T	V	thermal voltage
v		APD output
x		parameter for excess noise of an APD
α_{lw}		linewidth broadening factor
$\Gamma(x)$		the gamma function
$\delta(t)$		the δ function
η		quantum efficiency of the photodiode
η_X		mean of random variable X
Λ		average number of incident photons over a certain interval
$\phi(t)$	rad	random phase due to a spontaneous emission
$\phi_r(t)$	rad	the zero mean random phase term of each spontaneous emission
$\Delta\phi_i$	rad	random phase change due to the ith spontaneous emission
σ^2		noise power
σ_X^2		variance of random variable X
Ω		sample space of all possible events
$\Delta\omega_{3dB}$	rad/sec	3 db spectrum width due to phase noise

Chapter 7: Incoherent Detection

Parameter	Unit	Description
A		open loop transistor gain
A_H	Amp	high photocurrent value for bit 1
A_L	Amp	low photocurrent value for bit 0
A_{pp}		peak to peak difference at the equalizer output due to "1" and "0"
B	Hz	receiver bandwidth
B_{fiber}	Hz	fiber bandwidth
CNR		carrier to noise ratio
C_{in}	F	total input capacitance
C_d	F	diode junction capacitance
C_s	F	stray capacitance
C_a	F	front-end amplifier input capacitance
C_{gs}	F	gate-source capacitance
D_{total}	nsec/km	total fiber dispersion
D_{intra}	nsec/(km·nm)	intramodal fiber dispersion
DR	dB	dynamic range

Chapter 7: Incoherent Detection (continued)

Parameter	Unit	Description
F_{apd}		excess noise factor of an APD
f_T	Hz	cut-off frequence of a transistor
G	S	transimpedance amplifier gain
G_{in}	S	input conductance
g_m	S	equivalent transconductance of the transistor
$g_s(\lambda - \lambda_0)$		output spectrum of a light source
$H(\omega)$		transfer function of the receiver equalizer
h		ratio of the high signal dependent noise power to thermal noise power
$h(t)$		impulse response of the equalizer
$h_{fiber}(t)$		effective impulse response of an optical fiber
$h_{LD}(t), h_{LED}(t)$		impulse response of a laser diode or a LED
$h_{ph}(t)$		impulse response of a photodiode
I_0	Amp	dc current component in analog communications
I_B	Amp	base current
I_d	Amp	dark current of a photodiode
I_G	Amp	gate current
i_F	Amp	thermal noise due to the feedback resistor
ISI_k		ISI at the k-th sampling
i_a	Amp	input current noise source of the amplifier
i_n	Amp	total noise input at the front-end amplifier
$i_{ph}(t)$	Amp	photocurrent due to the incident light signal
J_i		ith moment of the normalized transfer function of the equalizer
k	Joule/K	Boltzman constant
k		APD ionization ratio
k_m		amplitude modulation index
L	km	fiber length
M_{apd}		current gain of an APD
$m(t)$		message signal
$\bar{N}$		receiver sensitivity in terms of the average number of photons per bit
NEP	W/Hz$^{1/2}$	noise equivalent power
$\bar{P}_{in}$	W	receiver sensitivity in terms of average received power
P_E		end-to-end bit error probability
$P_{E,r}$		BER at each repeater stage
$P_{out}(\omega)$		Fourier transform of the equalized pulse
p_T	sec	integration of $p(t)$ over a bit interval
$p(t)$		the received pulse
p_0, p_1		prior probabilities for bits 0 and 1
$p_m(t)$		modulating pulse input to a light source
$p_s(t)$		pulse at a light source output
$\hat{p}_s$		equalized output

Chapter 7: Incoherent Detection (continued)

Parameter	Unit	Description
$p_{out}(t)$		output pulse of the receiver equalizer
PP_{ISI}		power penalty due to *ISI*
$Q(x)$		the *Q*-function
$\mathcal{R}$	W/A	responsivity
R_F	Ω	feedback resistance
R_{in}	Ω	total input resistance
$R_b = 1/T_0$	b/sec	bit rate
R_d	Ω	output resistance of the photodiode
R_L	Ω	load resistance
R_a	Ω	front-end amplifier input resistance
RIN	dB/Hz	relative intensity noise factor
$rect(t, T_0)$		unit rectangle function of duration from 0 to T_0
S_a		total PSD of the equivalent front-end amplifier
S_v		PSD of the equivalent voltage noise source input of the amplifier
S_i		PSD of the equivalent current noise source input of the amplifier
$S_{n,ph}$		PSD of the noise output from the photodiode
$S_{n,in}(\omega, t)$		total noise PSD at the equalizer input and time t
$S_{n,out}$		noise PSD at the equalizer output
$S_x(\tau)$		either $S_H(\tau)$ or $S_L(\tau)$ at sampling time τ
SNR		signal to noise ratio
T	K	temperature
T_0	sec	bit interval
t_d	sec	initial turn-on delay of a laser diode
V_D	V	dc bias
v_a	V	input voltage noise source of an amplifier
x_{min}		minimum argument value for the Q-function for a given BER
$y_s(t)$		signal component of the equalizer output
$y_{out}(t)$		equalizer output
$y_{out,k}$		k-th sampled value at the equalizer output
$y_{n,out}(t)$		noise component of the equalizer output
$y_{n,k}$		k-th sampled noise value at the equalizer output
y_{th}		threshold for detection at the equalizer output
y_H		equalizer output when A_H is sent
y_L		equalizer output when A_L is sent
Z_{in}	Ω	input impedance of the front-end amplifier
α	1/sec	damping constant of the relaxation oscillation
α_{lw}		linewidth broadening factor
α_{off}	1/sec	time decay constant when the laser is turned off
β		current gain of a BJT
β_{chirp}		ratio of the peak wavelength shift due to chirping

Chapter 7: Incoherent Detection (continued)

Parameter	Unit	Description
Γ		material dependent parameter of an FET
γ		reference SNR
δ	sec	pulse broadening parameter
δ_H^2, δ_L^2		normalized noise power
ϵ		extinction ratio
η		quantum efficiency of a photodetector
η_{eq}		performance comparison parameter between integration-and-dump and raised cosine
λ	nm	wavelength
λ_0	nm	reference wavelength
$\Delta\lambda$	nm	linewidth of the light source
$\Delta\lambda_c(t)$	nm	wavelength shift due to chirping
$\zeta = \delta/T_0$		normalized pulse broadening parameter
σ_H^2, σ_L^2		noise power of y_n when $A_k = A_H, A_L$, respectively
σ_a^2		noise power due to the front-end amplifier
σ_{si}^2		signal independent noise power term at the receiver output
σ_{sd}^2		signal dependent noise power term at the receiver output
$\sigma_{n,out}^2$		total noise power at the equalizer output
τ	sec	relative sampling time
$\tau_g(\lambda)$	sec	propagation delay at λ
τ_{g0}	sec	reference propagation delay at the reference wavelength λ_0
τ_{LD}	sec	rise time of a laser diode
τ_{LED}	sec	rise time of an LED
τ_{tx}, τ_{rx}	sec	turn-on or off delays of the transmitter and receiver
τ_{RC}	sec	RC time constant
ω_m	rad/sec	circular frequency of the modulating carrier
ω_r	rad/sec	relaxation oscillation circular frequency
ξ		parameter that determines the relative importance between σ_{si}^2 and σ_{sd}^2

Chapter 8: Time Domain Medium Access

Parameter	Unit	Description
B_s	b/sec	bit rate of a constant bit rate input
D	sec	token rotation time in FDDI in the absence of traffic
f_o	Hz	relaxation oscillation frequency when a laser is turned on
Δf	Hz	frequency difference in TDM multiplexing
f_w	Hz	write frequency of an elastic store

Chapter 8: Time Domain Medium Access

Parameter	Unit	Description
L_{tx-i}	km	distance between the transmitter and the interface point in SONET
L_{rx-i}	km	distance between the receiver and the interface point in SONET
N		number of channels, nodes or time slots
PB	dB	power budget
P_I	W	optical power at the interface point in SONET
R	b/sec	instantaneous bit in TDMA
r		negative stuffing ration in TDM
T_f	sec	frame time in TDMA or TDM
T_g	sec	guard time in TDMA
T_{pg}	sec	propagation delay
$T_{pg,max}$	sec	maximum propagation delay over a given network
T_{ref}	sec	reference burst time in TDMA
T_s	sec	slot time in TDMA
$T_{s,oh}$	sec	overhead in each slot in TDMA
$T_{s,pload}$	sec	payload in each slot in TDMA
THT	sec	token holding time in FDDI
TRT	sec	token rotation time in FDDI
TTRT	sec	target token rotation time in FDDI
α_{c1}, α_{c2}	dB	coupling loss
η_{TDMA}		access efficiency in TDMA
η_{FDDI}		access efficiency in FDDI
$\eta_{FDDI,s}$		synchronous traffic only access efficiency in FDDI
$\eta_{FDDI,a}$		asynchronous traffic only access efficiency in FDDI

Chapter 9: Wavelength Domain Medium Access

Parameter	Unit	Description
$a_i(t)$		amplitude function that modulates the optical carrier of channel i
b	m	fiber spacing
$\mathcal{F}$		finesse of a Fabry-Perot filter
Δf	Hz	wavelength channel separation in frequency
FSR	nm or Hz	free spectral range
H		maximum number of hops in a deBruijn configuration
$\bar{H}$		average number of hops in a logical WDMA configuration
$H(\omega)$		transfer function of the filter following photodetection
$h_j[i]$		frequency response of channel i when the optical filter is tuned to channel j
$i_{ph}(t)$	A	photocurrent

Chapter 9: Wavelength Domain Medium Access (continued)

Parameter	Unit	Description
K_λ	rad/nm	angular dispersion factor at λ
k		number of stages in a perfect shuffle network
k	1/m	free space propagation constant or $2\pi/\lambda$
$L_{\pi/2}$	m	coupling length for a switchover
ΔL_{eff}	nm	effective length difference in a MZI
N		number of nodes or channels in a WDoMA system
N_{ch}		total available channel number in a WDM system
N_λ		total number of wavelength channels in a WDMA network
n, n_1, n_2		refractive indices
n_B		refractive index in a DBR system
Δn_B		step difference of refractive indices in a DBR array
$n_{coupler}$		refractive index in a star coupler
n_{wgr}		refractive index of a waveguide in a WGR
P_{bk}		blocking probability of a circuit switching WDMA network
P_E		bit error probability
P_{ICI}	A^2	total ICI power
P_{inc}	W	incident optical power at a receiver
P_{loc}	W	local optical power at a coherent detection receiver
P_p		power penalty due to interchannel interference
p		number of transceivers per WDMA node
p		active probability of each WDMA node
R	m	radius of a WGR
$\mathcal{R}$	A/W	responsivity of a photodiode
S		ratio of the total number of nodes to the total number of wavelength channels
$S_a(\omega)$	sec	power spectral density of $a_i(t)$
$S_a^{(2)}(\omega)$	sec	self-convolution of $S_a(\omega)$
T		transmissivity
SIR		signal to interference power ratio
SNR		signal to noise power ratio
SNR_0		signal to noise power ratio in the absense of ICI
α	rad	incident angle to a grating
α_{tot}	dB	total power loss of a star coupler
α_{excess}	dB	excess power loss of a star coupler
β	rad	reflected angle from a grating
$\Delta\beta$	rad	reflected angle separation
γ		a BER performance parameter for different coherent modulations
κ	1/m	coupling constant in a directional coupler
σ_n^2	A^2	photocurrent noise power in the absense of ICI
σ_{n0}^2	A^2	photocurrent noise power in the absense of ICI and optical filtering

Chapter 9: Wavelength Domain Medium Access (continued)

Parameter	Unit	Description
σ_{tot}^2	A^2	total photocurrent noise power including ICI
Λ	m	period of a grating structure
λ_i	m	wavelength of channel i
$\Delta\lambda$	nm	wavelength channel separation
ϕ_i	rad	phase of the carrier of channel i
$\Delta\phi$	rad	phase difference between two propagation paths
θ_B	rad	Blazed angle or Bragg angle
ω_{IF}	rad/sec	IF circular frequency in coherent detection
ω_i	rad/sec	circular frequency of channel i
$\Delta\omega$	rad/sec	wavelength channel separation in circular frequency

Chapter 10: Subcarrier Multiplexing

Parameter	Unit	Description
a_n		coefficient of order n in the series expansion of a laser I-P characteristic function
B	Hz	baseband bandwidth
B_{AM}	Hz	passband AM transmission bandwidth
B_{FM}	Hz	passband FM transmission bandwidth
$\text{CIMP}_\nu^{(n)}$		carrier power to the intermodulation product power of order n and at frequency ν
CNR		received carrier to noise ratio
CNR$_{FM}$		received carrier to noise ratio in FM transmission
CSO		ratio of the carrier power to all nonlinear distortion power at the CSO frequency
CTB		ratio of the carrier power to all nonlinear distortion power at the carrier frequency
F		excess noise factor of an APD diode
f_c	Hz	carrier frequency
f_i's	MHz	carrier frequencies of CATV channels
Δf	Hz	peak frequency deviation in FM
G_{FM}		detected CNR gain factor of FM transmission with respect to CNR$_{FM}$
G_{FM-AM}		detected CNR gain factor of FM transmission with respect to AM
$H_h(f)$		Hilbert transfer function
$H_n(x)$		Hermite function of order n
I	A	dc component of the photocurrent detected in SCM transmission
I_b	A	bias current of a laser diode in SCM transmission
I_{th}	A	threshold current of a laser diode

Chapter 10: Subcarrier Multiplexing (continued)

Parameter	Unit	Description
$K_v^{(n)}$		total number of product terms of order n at frequency v
k_f	Hz	frequency modulation parameter
k_m		amplitude modulation index of individual SCM channels
k_w		gain factor in FM transmission using pre-emphasis and filtering
$m(t)$		baseband message signal
$m_c(t)$		in-phase baseband message signal
m_p		peak value of the message signal
$m_s(t)$		quadrature-phase baseband message signal
N		total number of channels
NEP	W/Hz$^{1/2}$	noise equivalent power
P_{NLD}	W	total nonlinear distortion power
P_b	W	dc component of the output light power in SCM transmission
P_c	A^2	received carrier power
P_{out}	W	total output optical power in SCM transmission
$P_v^{(n)}$	A^2	n-th order distortion power at frequency v
$Q(x)$		the Q-function
RIN	dB/Hz	relative intensity noise of a laser diode
$\mathcal{R}_{ld}$	W/A	responsivity of a laser diode
$\mathcal{R}_{pd}$	A/W	responsivity of a photodiode
$X_{AM}(\omega)$		Fourier transform of $x_{AM}(t)$
$X_{FM}(\omega)$		Fourier transform of $x_{FM}(t)$
$X_{SSB}(\omega)$		Fourier transform of $x_{SSB}(t)$
$x_{AM}(t)$		an AM modulated signal
$x_{FM}(t)$		an FM modulated signal
$x_{SSB}(t)$		a SSB-AM modulated signal
$x_{tot}(t)$		total SCM signal
x_p		peak value of the VSB-AM video signal
α_f	dB/km	fiber attenuation
β_{FM}		frequency modulation index or ratio of Δf to B
Δ		step size in QAM transmission
μ		total modulation depth
σ_n^2	A^2	total receiver noise power
ω_c	rad/sec	carrier cyclic frequency

Chapter 11: Photonic Switching

Parameter	Unit	Description
d	m	distance between the image plane and the hologram
E_0	V/m	electric field

Chapter 11: Photonic Switching (continued)

$\mathcal{F}$		finesse of a FP resonator
$g(x,y)$	V/m	output electric field from a hologram
I_{in}, I_{out}		input and output light intensities of a hologram dual port of port i
L	m	waveguide length
L_c	m	crossover length of coupling waveguides ($\pi/2\kappa$)
M		number of stages in a multistage switch
m		number of switches in the middle stage of a Clos witch
N		switch wize
n		refractive index
n		number of input ports of switches in the first stage of a Clos switch
Δn		refractive index difference of coupling waveguides
P_{in}	W	input optical power
P_{out}	W	output optical power
p		$\log_2 N$
$\mathcal{R}$	A/W	photodiode responsivity
R_L	Ω	load resistance
r	m/V	Pockel EO coefficient
S	W	signal power
T		transmissivity
T_0		peak transmissity of a FP resondtor
$t(x,y)$		complex transmission coefficient of a hologram
X	W	crosstalk power
Y	W	total power due to both crosstalk and the signal
α		crosstalk
$\Delta\beta$	1/m	difference of propagation constants
δ	1/m	mismatch factor in coupling waveguides
γ	1/V	EO constant
κ	1/m	coupling constant
π_i		output port address of input i
$\phi(x, y)$		phase function of the transmission coefficient of $t(x, y)$
ν_x, ν_y	1/m	spatial frequencies of a hologram

Chapter 12: Direct Modulation

Parameter	Unit	Description
A	1/sec	nonradiative carrier recombination rate
A	V/m	amplitude of an electric field E
a	m^2	gain constant
a_0	m^2	gain constant at zero light power
b	m^3	refractive index modulation coefficient
B	m^3/sec	radiative spontaneous recombination coefficient

Chapter 12: Direct Modulation (continued)

Parameter	Unit	Description
$B_{elec,3dB}$	Hz	electrical circular 3dB bandwidth of small signal modulation
$B_{opt,3dB}$	Hz	optical circular 3dB bandwidth of small signal modulation
C	m^6/sec	Auger recombination coefficient
d	m	thickness of the active layer of a light source
E_1, E_2	joule	energy levels
E_z	V/m	z component electric field
E_T	V/m	transverse factor of an electric field
$\mathcal{E}$		electric field
f_0	Hz	light carrier frequency at zero light power
f_s	Hz	light carrier frequency at a certain steady state
f_n	Hz	natural frequency in relaxation oscillation
$g(N)$	m^{-1}	optical gain as a function of the carrier density
h	joule • sec	Planck constant
I	A	current
J	A/m^2	current density
$\hat{J}$	sec^{-2}	a normalized current density defined by BJ/qd
J_{th}	A/m^2	threshold current density
k	1/m	propagation constant in free space equal to $2\pi/\lambda$
k_m		amplitude modulation index
$k_{m,j}$		modulation index for the current density
$k_{m,n}$		modulation index for the carrier density
$k_{m,ph}$		modulation index for the photon density
L	m	longitudinal length of a light source
N	1/m^3	n-type carrier density
N_0	1/m^3	carrier density above which $g(N)$ is positive
N_D	1/m^3	n-type doping level
N_{ph}	1/m^3	photon density
$N_{ph,steady}$	1/m^3	steady state photon density
N_{th}	1/m^3	upper limit carrier density
n		refractive index
n_b		bulk refractive index of a medium, excluding external pumping
n_0		refractive index at zero light power
n_g		group refractive index
n_i	1/m^3	intrinsic carrier density
Δn_p		refractive index change due to external pumping
$\Delta n''$		imaginary part of the change of refractive index
P	1/m^3	p-type carrier density

Chapter 12: Direct Modulation (continued)

Parameter	Unit	Description
$P(t)$	W	output power of a light source
$p_s(t)$		laser pulse output for PAM transmission
$\mathcal{P}$	V/F	induced polarization by an external electric field
q	C	charge constant
r, r_1, r_2		reflection coefficients at the laser cavity ends
R		reflectivity at the laser cavity ends
S	joule/m^3·Hz	photon energy density
T		transmissivity of the laser cavity ends
T_0	sec	bit interval
t_d	sec	initial turn-on delay of a laser diode
$t_{d,osc}$	sec	time delay in relaxation oscillation
t_{off}	sec	turn-off delay
t_{on}	sec	turn-on delay
V	m^3	volume of the active layer
w	m	transverse width of a light source
α	1/sec	damping constant in relaxation oscillation
α_{lw}		linewidth broadening factor
α_{int}	1/m	internal cavity loss
α_{tot}	1/m	total distributed cavity loss
β_{sp}		fraction of spontaneous emission contributing to stimulated emission
β_z		z-direction propagation constant
β_0		propagation constant at zero power
Γ		confinement factor
δ	1/sec	a parameter defined by $\tau_{ph}^{-1} - \gamma v_g g_0(N)$
ϵ_0	F/m	vacuum permittivity
ϵ_r		dielectric constant
$\epsilon_r', \epsilon_r''$		real and imaginary parts of ϵ_r
η		total quantum efficiency
η_g	m^3	gain suppression coefficient
η_{int}		internal quantum efficiency
η_{ext}		external quantum efficiency
κ_{TM}	1/m	eigenvalue of a given transverse mode
σ	1/(Ω·m)	conductivity
τ_{ac}	sec	recombination time constant in ac analysis
τ_e	sec	effective recombination time constant in a laser diode
τ_{nr}	sec	nonradiative recombination time constant
τ_{ph}	sec	photon decay constant in a laser cavity
τ_{rr}	sec	radiative recombination time constant

Chapter 12: Direct Modulation (continued)

Parameter	Unit	Description
τ_r	sec	total radiative recombination time constant
τ_{r0}	sec	a time constant defined by $B(N + P)$
τ_{step}	sec	time constant of step input
ω_0	rad/sec	circular frequency of laser output at zero power
ω_m	rad/sec	circular frequency of a single tone input to a light source
ω_n	rad/sec	natural circular frequency of relaxation oscillation
ω_r	rad/sec	circular frequency of relaxation oscillation
$\omega_{elec,3dB}$	rad/sec	electrical circular 3dB bandwidth of small signal modulation
$\omega_{opt,3dB}$	rad/sec	optical circular 3dB bandwidth of small signal modulation
χ		susceptibility
χ_0		susceptibility of a medium at zero external pumping
χ_0', χ_0''		real and imaginary parts of χ_0
χ_p		susceptibility due to external pumping
χ_p', χ_p''		real and imaginary parts of χ_p

Chapter 13: DFB Laser Diodes and Modulation

Parameter	Unit	Description
a	m^2	gain constant
B	m^3/sec	radiative spontaneous recombination coefficient
c	m/sec	speed of light in free space
d	m	thickness of the active layer of the diode
$\mathcal{E}(x, y, z, t)$	$W^{1/2}$	total electric field
$\tilde{E}(z, t)$	$W^{1/2}$	z and t dependent electric field factor
$E_T(x, y)$		transversal electric field factor
$E_q^\pm(z, t)$	$W^{1/2}$	slowly varying electric field factor propagating of mode q in the $\pm z$ direction
Δg_{dB}	dB/m	differential threshold gain
I_{sp}	W/m	spontaneous emission strength
$J_{sp,q}^\pm$	1/m	term in the coupled mode equations due to spontaneous emission
J_{th}	A/m^2	threshold current density
L	m	longitudinal length of the laser cavity
N	$1/m^3$	carrier density
N_0	$1/m^3$	carrier density at which the optical gain $g(N)$ is zero
N_{th}	$1/m^3$	carrier density at which the total gain in zero in dB
n_b		bulk refractive index
n_g		bulk group refractive index
$\mathcal{P}$	$F \cdot W^{1/2}/m$	polarization
r_L^O, r_R^O		actual reflection coefficients at the two ends of the cavity

Chapter 13: DFB Laser Diodes and Modulation (continued)

Parameter	Unit	Description
r_L, r_R		equivalent complex reflection coefficients at the two cavity ends
v_g	m/sec	group velocity
w	m	transverse width of the laser cavity
$-z_0$	m	z coordinate of the left-end of the laser cavity
α_{lw}		linewidth broadening factor
α_{int}	1/m	internal cavity loss
α_q	1/m	threshold gain of mode q
β_B	1/m	wave number at the Bragg frequency
β_{sp}		fraction of spontaneous emission contributing to stimulated emission
$\Delta\beta_q$	1/m	a complex parameter in the coupled mode equations
Γ		confinement factor
γ	1/m	spatial constant of $E_q^\pm(z, t)$
$\bar{\epsilon}_b(z)$		bulk dielectric constant at zero external pumping
ϵ_0	F/m	vacuum permittivity
ϵ_r		dielectric constant at nonzero pumping
$\Delta\epsilon$		peak change of $\Delta\epsilon_b(z)$
$\Delta\epsilon_b(z)$		change of dielectric constant due to the periodic structure
$\Delta\epsilon_\pm$		first harmonic of $\Delta\epsilon_b(z)$
κ_0	1/m	$\mid \kappa^\pm \mid$
κ^+	1/m	coupling constant from E_q^- to E_q^+
κ^-	1/m	coupling constant from E_q^+ to E_q^-
Λ	m	period of the periodic Bragg structure
λ_B	m	free space Bragg wavelength
μ	H/m	magnetic permeability
θ_k		phase of $\Delta\epsilon_b$ at the center of the cavity
ω_B	rad/sec	Bragg circular frequency
ω_q	rad/sec	circular frequency of longitudinal mode q
$\hat{\chi}$	1/sec	time dependent susceptibility
$\chi(\omega)$		susceptibility at frequency ω
χ_p'		real part of susceptibility due to external pumping
χ_p''		imaginary part of susceptibility due to external pumping
χ_b''		imaginary part of the susceptibility of the medium due to loss

Chapter 14: External Modulation

Parameter	Unit	Description
A	m	amplitude of an acoustic wave
A_a, A_b	V/m	electric fields of two possible polarizations
$\mathcal{B}$		birefringence equal to $n_a - n_b$

Chapter 14: External Modulation (continued)

Parameter	Unit	Description
B	Hz	modulation bandwidth
C	F	capacitance
c	m/sec	speed of light in free space
$\bar{D}$	VF/m^2	constant displacement vector of a plane wave
D	VF/m^2	magnitude of the displacement vector
D	m	spot size of a laser beam
d	m	thickness of the external modulator waveguide
$\bar{E}$	V/m	constant electric field vector of a plane wave
$\mathcal{E}$	V/m	time and space dependent electric field of a plane wave
ΔE	joule	change of energy to have a charge change ΔQ
f	Hz	modulation frequency
$\bar{H}$	A/m	constant magnetic field vector of a plane wave
$\mathcal{H}$	A/m	time and space dependent magnetic field of a plane wave
h	m	height of an AO modulator
$I_{acoustic}$	W/m^2	acoustic wave intensity
K	m/V^2	Kerr constant
K	1/m	propagation constant of an acoustic wave
K_a	m/V	EO modulation cosntant
k_m		amplitude modulation index
L	m	longitudinal length of an external modulator
L_p	m	longitudinal length that results in peak phase change
M	m^2/W	figure of merit in AO external modulation
n		refractive index seen by a plane wave propagating in direction $\hat{s}$
n_1, n_2, n_3		refractive indices of the three principal axes
n_a, n_b		two possible refractive indices of a plane wave in an anisotropic medium
n_e, n_o		refractive indices of the extraordinary and ordinary axes
Δn_p		peak deviation of the refactive index
P_a	W	driving power for an AO modulator
P_{ac}	W	ac power to modulate an external modulator
P_{in}	W	input power to an external modulator
P_{o1}, P_{o2}	W	output power of an external modulator
P_{ao}		effective elasto-optic coefficient
p_{ij}		elasto-optic coefficients
ΔQ	C	change of charge of a capacitor
R	Ω	resistance
R_b	b/sec	modulation bit rate
r	m/V	effective Pockel coefficient for a given polarization and modulation
r		reflection coefficient
r_c	m/V	a parameter defined for the 3m group by $r_c = r_{33} - r_{13}n_0^3/n_e^3$
r_{ij}'s	m/V	Pockel EO coefficients

Chapter 14: External Modulation (continued)

Parameter	Unit	Description
$S_{(ij)}$ or S_i		strain tensor in AO modulation
$\hat{s}$		unit vector of $\bar{\beta}$
$\hat{s}_a, \hat{s}_b$		unit vectors of two possible polarizations
(s_x, s_y, s_z)		coordinates of unit vector $\hat{s}$
s_{ij}'s	$(m/V)^2$	Kerr EO coefficients
T_0	sec	bit interval
t		transmission coefficient
$\bar{U}$	m	acoustic wave vector
u	joule/m^3	energy density
V_B	V	bias voltage in EO external modulation
V_π	V	bias voltage that results in a phase change of π
v	m/sec	acoustic wave velocity
v_p		velocity of a light pulse
w	m	width of the external modulator waveguide
β	1/m	propagation constant equal to $\bar{\beta}$
$\bar{\beta}$	1/m	propagation vector
β_a, β_b	1/m	propagation constants of two possible polarizations
$\bar{\beta}_{in}$	1/m	propagation vector of incident lightwave in AO modulation
$\bar{\beta}_{out}$	1/m	propagation vector of output lightwave in AO modulation
Δ_i^2	1/m^2	a parameter defined by $\omega^2 \mu \epsilon_i - \beta^2$
δ	1/m	mismatch factor in waveguide coupling
$\bar{\epsilon}$	F/m	dielectric tensor
ϵ_0	F/m	vacuum electric permittivity
$\epsilon_1, \epsilon_2, \epsilon_3$	F/m	permittivities of the three principal axes
η_{df}		deflection efficiency in AO modulation
$\bar{\eta}$		impermeability tension equal to $\epsilon_0 \bar{\epsilon}^{-1}$
$\Delta \eta_{ij}$'s		change of $\bar{\eta}$
$\Delta \phi$		phase change due to birefirgence or path difference
$\Delta \phi_p$		peak phase change
μ	H/m	magnetic permeability
κ, κ_{ij}	1/m	coupling constants
Λ	m	wavelength of an acoustic wave
λ	m	wavelength of a lightwave
θ_B		Bragg diffraction angle
ρ	kg/m^3	acoustic medium mass density
τ_t	sec	transit delay through an external modulator
τ_{on}	sec	turn-on time
τ_d	sec	total delay in external modulation
Ω	rad/sec	circular frequency of an acoustic wave
ω_{in}	rad/sec	circular frequency of incident lightwave in AO modulation

ω_{out}	rad/sec	circular frequency of output lightwave in AO modulation
ω_m	rad/sec	modulation circular frequency

Chapter 15: Coherent Detection

Parameter	Unit	Description
A_k		signal value for bit k
$a_{loc}(t)$		electric field amplitude of the local oscillator
$a_x(t)$		electric field amplitude of $\hat{x}$ component
$a_y(t)$		electric field amplitude of $\hat{y}$ component
B_{ph}	Hz	95% energy phase noise bandwidth
B_{sig}	Hz	95% energy signal bandwidth
B_{tot}	Hz	95% energy total modulated carrier bandwidth
$\bar{E}_{inc}$	$W^{1/2}$	electric field of the incident light signal
$\bar{E}_{loc}$	$W^{1/2}$	electric field of the local oscillator
$\bar{E}_{o1}, \bar{E}_{o2}$	$W^{1/2}$	two electric fields at the output of a hybrid
Δf_d	Hz	frequency separation in FSK
Δf_{3dB}	Hz	3 dB bandwidth of the photocurrent due to phase noise
$I_0(x)$		zero order modified Bessel function
I_{ph}	A	photocurrent output
$I_{ph,homo}$	A	photocurrent output from homodyne detection
$I_{ph,hetero}$	A	photocurrent output from heterodyne detection
$I_{ph,1}, I_{ph,2}$	A	two photocurrent outputs in balance detection
$\hat{I}_{ph}$	A	complex envelope of the photocurrent I_{ph}
$\bar{H}$		2×2 matrix of a hybrid
$\bar{H}_{90}$		2×2 matrix of a $90°$ hybrid
$\bar{H}_{180}$		2×2 matrix of a $180°$ hybrid
M		number of signaling levels in digital transmission
$m(t)$		modulating baseband signal
N		number of photons
N_b		number of photons per bit to meet a specified BER performance
N_s		number of photons for bit one to meet a specified BER performance
N_o	joule	power spectral density of white noise
N_o	C	integrated output of photocurrent due to bit "0"
N_1	C	integrated output of photocurrent due to bit "1"
n^+, n^-		refractive indices of positive and negative circularly polarized waves
$n_c(t)$		in-phase noise
$n_s(t)$		quadrature-phase noise
P_E		error detection probability

Chapter 15: Coherent Detection (continued)

Parameter	Unit	Description
P_{inc}	W	power of the incident light signal
P_{loc}	W	power of the local oscillator
PP	dB	optical power penalty
$Q(x)$		the Q function
q	C	electron charge
$\mathcal{R}$	A/W	responsivity of a photodiode
R_b	b/sec	transmission bit rate
RIN	dB/Hz	relative intensity noise
S_0, S_1, S_2, S_3		Stokes parameters
S_n	joule	two-side noise power spectral density
T	sec	bit interval
T_1, T_2		in-line coupling coefficients of a hybrid
$\bar{U}_k$		noiseless phase vector from signal space projection
V	deg/G • mm	Verdet constant
$\bar{V}_k$		phase vector from signal space projection
X_1, X_2	F/m	cross coupling coefficients of a hybrid
δ		phase difference of the $\hat{x}$ and $\hat{y}$ components of the received light signal
$\bar{\epsilon}$	F/m	permittivity tensor
η		quantum efficiency of a photodiode
$\bar{\mu}$	H/m	magnetic permeability tensor
$\phi(t)$	rad	phase component of the incident light signal
$\phi_n(t)$	rad	phase noise
ρ	rad/m	rotary power
σ_c^2		in-phase noise power in heterodyne detection
σ_s^2		quadrature-phase noise power in heterodyne detection
$\sigma_{n,homo}^2$		shot noise power from homodyne detection
$\sigma_{n,hetero}^2$		shot noise power from heterodyne detection
$\sigma_{n,envelop}^2$		shot noise power from envelope detection
σ_{RIN}^2		RIN noise power
σ_{shot}^2		shot noise power
ω_{IF}	rad/sec	intermediate circular frequency
ω_{inc}	rad/sec	circular frequency of the incident light signal
ω_{loc}	rad/sec	circular frequency of the local oscillator
$\Delta\omega_d$	rad/sec	circular frequency separation in FSK
$\Delta\nu_{loc}$	Hz	3 dB bandwidth of the local oscillator due to phase noise
$\Delta\nu_{tx}$	Hz	3 dB bandwidth of the transmitter laser due to phase noise

Chapter 16: Timing Recovery and Line Coding

Parameter	Unit	Description
A_k		modulated amplitude for bit k in PAM transmission
a_k		Fourier series coefficients of $\sin(2\pi k/T_0)$
b_k		binary input sequence to an encoder
C	F	capacitance
c_k		binary output sequence of a scrambler
$c(t)$		VCO control input
d_θ		slope of the phase detector of a PLL
$e(t)$		error signal at the phase detector output
Δf_{3dB}	Hz	3 dB bandwidth of a bandpass filter
$H(s)$		Laplace transfer function of a PLL
$H(D)$		characteristic polynomial of a MLSR
h_i's		feedback coefficients of a MLSR
$I(D)$		initial polynomial of a MLSR
L	H	inductance
$L(0)$		dc gain of the loop filter of a PLL
$L(s)$		Laplace transfer function of the loop filter
$p(t)$		pulse function in PAM
Q		quality factor
$R_s(l)$		autocorrelation funtion of a sequence S_k
r		period of a MLSR
T_0	sec	bit interval
$u(t)$		unit step function
v_{out}		bandpass filter voltage output
x_k		binary output sequence of a MLSR
z_k		complex Fourier series coefficients of $e^{j2\pi k/T_0}$
α	1/sec	damping constant of a tank circuit
$\eta(n, k)$		coding efficiency of an (n, k) block code
ω_0	rad/sec	resonant circular frequency of a tank circuit or a PLL
ω_d	rad/sec	damped oscillation frequency of a tank circuit
ω_{in}	rad/sec	circular frequency of the input signal
ω_v	rad/sec	$\omega_{in} - \omega_0$

Chapter 17: Optical Amplification

Parameter	Unit	Description
A	m^2	cross section area of an EDFA
a	m^2	gain constant
B	Hz	signal bandwidth
B_{21}	$(m/_{sec})^3 w^{-1}$	Einstein stimulated emission constant

Chapter 17: Optical Amplification (continued)

Parameter	Unit	Description
B_{opt}	Hz	optical bandwidth of an optical amplifier
C		ratio of the maximum to minimum optical gain
d	m	thickness of the amplifier channel
$E^{+}(z)$	joule$^{1/2}$	$+z$ traveling electric field in the amplifier
$E^{-}(z)$	joule$^{1/2}$	$-z$ traveling electric field in the amplifier
ΔE	joule	energy difference between the ground state and excited state
F		APD excess noise factor
f_0	Hz	center frequency of the gain profile
f_p	Hz	pumping frequency in an EDFA
f_s	Hz	signal frequency input to an amplifier
G_0		one-trip amplifier gain
$G_{0,no\ sat}$		amplifier gain G_0 at zero saturation
G_{FP}		Fabry-Perot amplifier gain
G_{tot}		total power gain of all amplifiers in a chain
$G^{(i)}$		amplifier gain of the ith amplifier in a chain
G_i		amplifier gain when there are i input signals
g	1/m	medium gain
g_0	1/m	medium gain at zero photondensity
g^{*}	1/m	upper limit of the medium gain in an EDFA
h	joule/Hz	Planck constant
I_{ph}	A	signal photocurrent
$i_{ASE-ASE}$	A	ASE noise current
$i_{ASE-sig}$	A	beat noise current due to the ASE noise and the signal
i_{shot}	A	shot noise current
J	A/m^2	current density
L	m	amplifier longitudinal length
M		APD current gain
N	1/m^3	carrier density
N_1, N_2	1/m^3	carrier densities at energy levels 1 and 2
N_b		number of photons per bit
$N_p(z)$	1/m^3	external pumping photon density in an EDFA
N_{ph}	1/m^3	photon density in an amplifier
$N_{ph,sat}$	1/m^3	saturation photon density
N_t	1/m^3	total carrier density $N_1 + N_2$
N_{th}	1/m^3	threshold carrier density at which G is zero
NF		noise figure
n, n_1, n_2		refractive indices
n_{sp}		parameter in ASE noise power due to incomplete population inversion
$P(z)$	W	light power in the amplifier cavity

Chapter 17: Optical Amplification (continued)

Parameter	Unit	Description
P_{ASE}	W	spontaneous emission power
P_{in}	W	incident light power
P_{loc}	W	local oscillator power in coherent detection
P_p	W	external pumping power in an EDFA
P_{sat}	W	saturation power of an optical amplifier
P_{tx}	W	transmission power
$\mathcal{R}$	A/W	responsivity of a photodiode
q	C	electron charge
$R_{ASE-sig}(\tau)$	A^2	correlation function of the beat noise $i_{ASE-sig}$
$R_{ASE-ASE}(\tau)$	A^2	correlation function of $i_{ASE-ASE}$
R_L		reflectivity at the left end cavity
R_R		reflectivity at the right end cavity
R_p	$1/(m^3sec)$	external pumping rate
R_s	$1/(m^3sec)$	stimulated recombination rate
r_L		reflection coefficient at the left end cavity
r_R		reflection coefficient at the right end cavity
$S_{ASE}(f)$	joule	one-sided ASE noise PSD
$S_{ASE,tot}(f)$	joule	accumulated ASE noise PSD from amplifiers in a chain
SNR		signal to noise ratio at the photodetector output
$SNR^{(N)}$		SNR at the end of an N-amplifier chain
SNR_{ref}		SNR due to only shot noise
T_0	sec	bit rate
W_p	1/sec	external pumping constant
W_s	1/sec	stimulated recombination constant
W_{sat}	1/sec	saturation constant
w	m	width of the amplifier channel
v_g	m/sec	propagation velocity
α		total transmission power loss
α_i		power loss of section i of the transmission line
α_m	1/m	distributed cavity loss
β	1/m	propagation constant in the amplifier
Γ		cavity confinement factor
η		quantum efficiency of a photodiode
η_i	dB/A	pumping efficiency of semiconductor amplifiers
σ_a	m^2	absorption cross section
σ_e	m^2	emission cross section
σ_n^2	A^2	total current noise power at photodetection output
σ_{shot}^2	A^2	shot noise power at photodetection output
$\sigma_{sig-ASE}^2$	A^2	signal-ASE beat noise power at photodetection output

Chapter 17: Optical Amplification (continued)

Parameter	Unit	Description
$\sigma^2_{ASE-ASE}$	A^2	ASE noise power at photodetection output
σ^2_{th}	A^2	thermal noise power
λ_a	m	emission wavelength of an optical amplifier
θ_0	rad	round trip phase change in an amplifier
θ_p	rad	Brewster angle
Ω		solid angle that the spontaneous emission of a mode falls within
τ_0	sec	round trip propagation delay within the amplifier cavity
τ_r	sec	recombination time constant
τ_{sp}	sec	spontaneous emission time constant
χ		parameter in ASE noise power due to non-uniform pumping

Chapter 18: Optical Fiber Soliton Transmission

Parameter	Unit	Description
$A(z,t)$	W$^{1/2}$	envelope function of a pulse
$A_1(z,t_1)$	W$^{1/2}$	equal to $A(z,t)$ envelope function with $t_1 = t - z/v_g$
$\tilde{A}, (z,w)$	W$^{1/2} \cdot$ sec	Fourier transform of $A_1(z,t_1)$
$\hat{A}(z,t)$	W$^{1/2}$	frequency dependent envelope function
A_p	W$^{1/2}$	peak amplitude of the soliton envelope
B	Gb/s	transmission bit rate
D_{intra}	psec/km·nm	fiber intramodal dispersion
$E(z,t)$	W$^{1/2}$	electric field
$\tilde{E}(z,w)$	W$^{1/2}$	Fourier transform of $E(z,t)$
$F(Z,T,\tau)$		kernel function of the far field operator $\bar{J}_F$
$\bar{G}$		optical amplifier gain
$\bar{I}$		identity operator
$\bar{J}, \bar{J}_F$		near and far field operators
$K(Z,T,\tau)$		kernel function of the near operator $\bar{J}$
L	km	fiber length or transmission distance
$\bar{L}, \bar{M}$		Lax pair of wave operators $\bar{\Delta}^{(1)}, \bar{\Delta}^{(2)}$
L_a	km	amplifier spacing
L_D	km	soliton distance
N		order of the soliton
n		refractive index
n_0		refractive index when there is no field intensity
P	W	peak soliton pulse power
$P(\omega)$	W$^{1/2}$	Fourier transform of $p(z,t)$ at $z = 0$

Chapter 18: Optical Fiber Soliton Transmission (continued)

Parameter	Unit	Description
P_{tx}	W	initial transmission power
P_L	$W^{1/2}\,{}^m/_F$	linear induced polarization
P_{NL}	$W^{1/2}\,{}^m/_F$	nonlinear polarization
$p(z, t)$	$W^{1/2}$	a lightwave pulse
s	1/W	nonlinear Kerr coefficient
T		normalized time
T_B	sec	bit interval
T_0	sec	normalization constant for the fundamental soliton width
T_{FWHM}	sec	FWHM of the soliton width
t_i	sec	$t_1 = t - {}^z/_{V_g}$
$U(Z, T)$		normalized envelope of $A(z, t)$
$U_0(Z, T)$		normalized envelope excluding the phase shift factor and fiber attenuation
v_g	m/sec	group velocity
Z		normalized distance
z_0	km	soliton period
α_f	1/m	fiber attenuation in 1/m, equal to $0.23\,\alpha_{fiber}$ in dB/km
$\beta(\omega)$	1/m	propagation constant as a function of frequency ω
β_0	1/m	reference propagation constant at frequency ω_0
β_1	sec/m	$\partial\beta/\partial\omega$ or inverse of the group velocity
β_2	sec²/m	$\partial^2\beta/\partial\omega^2$ or group velocity dispersion
γ	$1/(W\cdot km)^{-1}$	nonlinearity constant or $\pi n_2/\lambda$
$\bar{\Delta}^{(1)}, \bar{\Delta}^{(2)}$		scattering wave operators
$\bar{\Delta}_0^{(1)}, \bar{\Delta}_0^{(2)}$		undressed wave operators of $\bar{\Delta}^{(1)}, \bar{\Delta}^{(2)}$
ϵ		fraction of a bit interval within which timing jitter can be tolerated
$\delta(v_g^{-1})$	sec/km	variation of unit distance propagation delay due to ASE
$\Delta\phi$	rad	phase change
ϕ		chirping strength
$\phi(z, t)$	rad	phase of $A(z, t)$
η		eigenvalue of a soliton mode
λ	m	wavelength
ρ		average fiber attenuation factor
$\bar{\psi}$		wave function
$\sigma^2(z)$	m²	RMS pulse width of a Gaussian pulse
ω_0	rad/sec	reference circular frequency
ω_c	rad/sec	circular frequency at which $\tilde{A}(0, \omega)$ has zero phase

E

USEFUL MATHEMATICAL FORMULAS

A. TRIGNOMETRIC EQUALITIES

$\sin^2 x + \cos^2 x = 1$

$\cos^2 x - \sin^2 x = \cos 2x$

$\cos 2x = 2\cos^2 x - 1 = 1 - 2\sin^2 x$

$\sin x \sin y = \frac{1}{2}[\cos(x - y) - \cos(x + y)]$

$\cos x \cos y = \frac{1}{2}[\cos(x - y) - \cos(x + y)]$

$\sin(x \pm y) = \sin x \cos y \pm \cos x \sin y$

$\cos(x \pm y) = \cos x \cos y \pm \sin x \sin y$

$\cosh^2 x - \sinh^2 x = 1$

$1 - \tanh^2 x = \text{sech}^2 x$

B.   TAYLOR SERIES EXPANSIONS

$$e^x = 1 + x + \frac{x^2}{2} + \frac{x^3}{6} + \ldots = \sum_{n=0}^{\infty} \frac{x^n}{n!}$$

$$\ln(1 + x) = x - \frac{x^2}{2} + \frac{x^3}{3} + \ldots = 1 + \sum_{k=1}^{\infty} (-1)^{k-1} \frac{x^k}{k} \quad \text{if } |x| \ll 1$$

$$(1 + x)^a = 1 + ax + \frac{a(a - 1)}{2} x^2 + \cdots \quad \text{if } |ax| < 1$$

$$\sin x = x - \frac{x^3}{3!} + \frac{x^5}{5!} + \ldots = \sum_{n=0}^{\infty} (-1)^n \frac{x^{(2n+1)}}{(2n + 1)!}$$

$$\cos x = 1 - \frac{x^2}{2!} + \frac{x^4}{4!} + \ldots = \sum_{n=0}^{\infty} (-1)^n \frac{x^{(2n)}}{(2n)!}$$

$$\sinh x = x + \frac{x^3}{3!} + \frac{x^5}{5!} + \ldots = \sum_{n=0}^{\infty} (-1)^n \frac{x^{(2n+1)}}{(2n + 1)!}$$

$$\cosh x = 1 + \frac{x^2}{2!} + \frac{x^4}{4!} + \ldots = \sum_{n=0}^{\infty} \frac{x^{(2n)}}{(2n)!}$$

$$Q(x) = \frac{e^{-x^2/2}}{\sqrt{2\pi x^2}} \left[1 - \frac{1}{x^2} + \frac{1 \times 3}{x^4} - \frac{1 \times 3 \times 5}{x^6} + \cdots \right]$$

C.   SERIES SUMMATIONS

$$\sum_{k=1}^{N} a^k = a \frac{a^N - 1}{a - 1}$$

$$S_1 \stackrel{\text{def}}{=} \sum_{k=1}^{N} k = \tfrac{1}{2} N(N + 1)$$

$$S_2 \stackrel{\text{def}}{=} \sum_{k=1}^{N} k^2 = \tfrac{1}{6} N(N + 1)(2N + 1)$$

$$S_3 \stackrel{\text{def}}{=} \sum_{k=1}^{N} k^3 = \tfrac{1}{4} N^2 (N + 1)^2$$

$$S_m \stackrel{\text{def}}{=} \sum_{k=1}^{N} k^m = \frac{1}{m + 1} \left[(N + 1)^{m+1} - 1 - \sum_{i=0}^{m-1} \frac{(m + 1)!}{i!(m + 1 - i)!} S_i \right]$$

D. INTEGRALS

$$\int \sin x dx = -\cos x$$

$$\int \cos x dx = \sin x$$

$$\int x \sin x dx = \sin x - x \cos x$$

$$\int x \cos x dx = \cos x + x \sin x$$

$$\int e^x dx = e^x$$

$$\int x e^x dx = e^x (x - 1)$$

$$\int e^{ax} \sin(bx) dx = \frac{e^{ax}}{a^2 + b^2} [a \sin(bx) - b \cos(bx)]$$

$$\int e^{ax} \cos(bx) dx = \frac{e^{ax}}{a^2 + b^2} [a \cos(bx) - b \sin(bx)]$$

E. FOURIER TRANSFORM PAIRS

$g(t)$	$G(\omega) = \int_{-\infty}^{\infty} g(t) e^{-j\omega t}$
$\delta(t)$	1
1	$2\pi \delta(\omega)$
$\cos(\omega_0 t)$	$\pi[\delta(\omega - \omega_0) + \delta(\omega + \omega_0)]$
$\sin(\omega_0 t)$	$-j\pi[\delta(\omega - \omega_0) - \delta(\omega + \omega_0)]$
$2B\,\text{sinc}(2Bt)$	$rect(\omega/4\pi B, -2\pi B)$
$rect(t/\tau, -\tau/2)$	$\tau\,\text{sinc}(\omega\tau/2\tau)$
$e^{-a\,\|t\|}$	$\frac{2a}{a^2 + \omega^2}$
$\sum_{k=-\infty}^{\infty} \delta(t - kT)$	$\frac{2\pi}{T} \sum_{k=-\infty}^{\infty} \delta(\omega - 2\pi k/T)$

ACRONYMS

ACI	Adjacent Channel Interference
ADM	Add Drop Multiplexer
ADP	Ammonium Dihydrogen Phosphate
AF	Audio Frequency
AFC	Automatic Frequency Control
AGC	Automatic Gain Control
AM	Amplitude Modulation
AMI	Alternative Mark Inversion
APD	Avalanche Photodiode
AR	Antireflection
ASE	Amplified Spontaneous Emission
ASK	Amplitude Shift Keying
ATM	Asynchronous Transfer Mode
B-B	Batcher-Banyan
BER	Bit Error Rate
BH	Buried Heterostructure
B-ISDN	Broadband Integrated Services Digital Network
BJT	Bipolar Junction Transistor
BSC	Binary Symmetric Channel
C^3	Cleaved Coupled Cavity
CATV	Community Antenna Television
CBR	Constant Bit Rate
CDMA	Code Division Multiple Access
CIMP	Carrier to Intermodulation Product
CMI	Code Mark Inversion
CMOS	Complementary Metal Oxide Semiconductor
CNLD	Carrier to Nonlinear Distortion
CNR	Carrier to Noise Ratio
CPFSK	Continuous Phase Frequency Shift Keying
CSMA/CD	Carrier Sense Multiple Access with Collision Detection
CSO	Composite Second Order
CTB	Composite Triple Bit
CW	Continuous Wave
DBR	Distributed Bragg Reflector

DC	Depressed Cladding
DCP-BH	Double Channel Planar Buried Heterostructure
DFB	Distributed Feedback
DFT	Discrete Fourier Transform
DH	Double Heterostructure
DPSK	Differential Phase Shift Keying
DS*n*	Digital Signal Level *n*
DSB	Double Side Band
DTE	Data Terminal Equipment
ECL	Emitter Coupled Logic
EDFA	Erbium Doped Fiber Amplifier
EHP	Electron Hole Pair
EHR	Electron Hole Recombination
ELF	Extreme Low Frequency
EM	Electromagnetic
EM-BH	Etched-Mesa Buried Heterostructure
EMI	Electromagnetic Interference
EO	Electro-Optic
ESA	Excited State Absorption
ETR	External Timing Reference
FCC	Federal Communications Commission
FDDI	Fiber Distributed Data Interface
FDM	Frequency Division Multiplexing
FDMA	Frequency Division Multiple Access
FET	Field Effect Transistor
FFOL	FDDI Follow On LAN
FITL	Fiber in the Loop
FM	Frequency Modulation
FP	Fabry-Perot
FPI	Fabry-Perot Interferometer/Interferometry
FSK	Frequency Shift Keying
FSR	Free Spectral Range
FSS	Frame-Synchronized Scrambler
FTC	Fixed Transition Code
FTTH	Fiber to the Home
FTP	File Transfer Protocol
FWHM	Full Width Half Magnitude
GVD	Group Delay Dispersion
HDTV	High Definition Television
HF	High Frequency
HPT	Hetero Phototransistor
HRC	Hybrid Ring Control
ICI	Interchannel Inteference
IDT	Interdigital Transducer
IMP	Intermodulation Product

IS	Inverse Scattering
ISDN	Integrated Services Digital Network
ISI	Intersymbol Interference
JFET	Junction Field Effect Transistor
KDP	Potassium Dihydrogen Phosphate
KdV	Korteweg de Vries
LAN	Local Area Network
LD	Laser Diode
LED	Light Emitting Diode
LF	Low Frequency
LTE	Line Terminating Equipment
MAC	Medium Access Control
MAP	Maximum a Posteriori
MC	Matched Cladding
MF	Medium Frequency
MFD	Mode Field Diameter
MOS	Metal Oxide Semiconductor
ML	Maximum Likelihood
MLSR	Maximum Length Shift Register
MMF	Multimode Fiber
MPN	Mode Partition Noise
MQW	Multiple Quantum Well
MUX	Multiplexer
MVC	Maintenance Voice Channel
MZI	Mach-Zehnder Interferometer/Interferometry
NEP	Noise Equivalent Power
NF	Noise Figure
NLSE	Nonlinear Schrodinger Equation
NNI	Network Network Interface
NRZ	Nonreturn to Zero
NTSC	National Television System Committee
OEIC	Opto-Electronic Integrated Circuit
OOK	On-Off Keying
ONI	Optical Network Interface
OSI	Open System Interconnect
PAM	Pulse Amplitude Modulation
PC	Personal Computers
PC	Photoconductive
PCM	Pulse Code Modulation
PD	Photodiode
PDF	Probability Density Function
PDG	Packet Data Group
PIN	P-type Intrinsic N-type
PLL	Phase Lock Loop
PM	Phase Modulation

PMF	Polarization Maintaining Fiber
PolSK	Polarization Shift Keying
POTS	Plain Old Telephone Services
PP	Power Penalty
PSD	Power Spectral Density
PSK	Phase Shift Keying
PSN	Perfect Shuffle Network
PTE	Path Terminating Equipment
PV	Photovoltaic
QCSE	Quantum Confined Stark Effect
QPSK	Quadrature Phase Shift Keying
RF	Radio Frequency
RIN	Relative Intensity Noise
RMS	Root Mean Square
RV	Random Variable
RZ	Return to Zero
SAM	Separate Absorption and Multiplication
SAW	Surface Acoustic Wave
SCM	Subcarrier Multiplexing
SDH	Synchronous Digital Hierachy
SEED	Self Electro-optic Effect Device
SMF	Single Mode Fiber
SNR	Signal to Noise Ratio
SONET	Synchronous Optic Network
SOP	State of Polarization
SPE	Synchronous Payload Envelope
SPM	Self-Phase Modulation
SRS	Stimulated Raman Scattering
SSB	Single Sideband
STS	Synchronous Transmission Signal
TDM	Time Division Multiplexing
TDMA	Time Division Multiple Access
TDoMA	Time Domain Medium Access
THT	Token Holding Time
TRT	Token Rotation Time
TSI	Time Slot Interchange
TSS	Time Slot Switching
TTL	Transistor Transistor Logic
TTRT	Target Token Rotation Time
TW	Traveling Wave
UHF	Ultra High Frequency
UNI	User Network Interface
VBR	Variable Bit Rate
VCI	Virtual Circuit Identifier
VCO	Voltage Control Oscillator

VCSEL	Vertical Cavity Surface Emission Laser
VHF	Very High Frequency
VLF	Very Low Frequency
VPI	Virtual Path Identifier
VSB	Vestigial Side Band
WBC	Wide Band Channel
WC	Wavelength Converter
WCI	Wavelength Channel Interchange
WDM	Wavelength Division Multiplexing
WDMA	Wavelength Division Multiple Access
WDoMA	Wavelength Domain Medium Access
WGR	Waveguide Grating Router
XOR	Exclusive OR
ZS	Zakharov and Shabat

INDEX

A

Absolute frequency stabilization, 448–449
Absorption coefficient, 183–184
Absorption cross section, 871–873
Access efficiency, 366–368
Accumulation function, 262
Acoustic Bragg reflection, 470
Acoustic wave intensity, 737
Acoustic wave (SAW) structure, 477
Acousto-optic Bragg amplitude modulators, 736–737
Acousto-optic Bragg diffraction, 464
Acousto-optic coupling, 746–748
Acousto-optic modulation, 476, 685, 688–689
  bandwidth, 738–740
  Bragg diffraction, 733–734
  Debye-Sears diffraction, 734–735
  deflection efficiency, 737–738
  driving power, 738
  elasto-optic coefficients, 725–732
  figure of merit, 737
  Raman-Nath diffraction, 734–735
Acousto-optic modulators, 735–740
Acronyms, 985–989
Active layer, 80
Adaptive routing, 431–432
Add-drop multiplexers (ADM), 436–437, 468
Adjacent channel interference (ACI), 225
ADP, 690, 701–706
Advanced light-detection devices
  dual wavelength photodetectors, 216–217
  integrated PIN/FET receivers, 214
  metal-semiconductor-metal photodetectors, 211–214
  phototransistors, 215
  separate absorption and multiplication photodetectors, 214
Advanced optical fibers, 151–157
Allowable dynamic range, 339–341
ALOHA, 42
  slotted versus time-division multiple access (TDMA), 44
Alternating current (ac) coupling, 292
  and direct current (dc) wander, 318–322
  by raised cosine (rc) filtering, 318–322

Alternative mark inversion (AMI) code, 829
Ammonium dihydrogen phosphate (ADP), 690, 701, 706
Amplified spontaneous emission (ASE) noise, 225, 880
  derivation, 889–890
Amplifiers
  bipolar junction transistor, 334–335
  Fabry-Perot, 863–868
  fiber, 853
  field effect transistor, 335–336
  front-end, 333–341
  gain considering saturation, 859–861
  high-impedance, 333–336
  in-line, 854
  noise and timing jitter, 918–919
  power, 854
  receiver, 854
  semiconductor, 853
  transimpedance, 336–339
  traveling-wave, 863
Amplitude modulated passband signal, 7
Amplitude modulation, 9, 490–494
  signal-to-noise ratio and carrier-to-noise ratio in, 497–498
Amplitude-shift keying (ASK), 10, 761–762
Analog communications, 10–11
  effects of noise and distortion in, 227–228
    Wiener filtering in, 234–236
Analog signal detection, 288–290
Analog signal modulation and small signal responses,
  of LDs, 620–624
  of LEDs, 600–603
Analog TV transmission, 499
Angular dispersion factor, 455
Anisotropy, 157, 688
  materials, 689
Application data processing, 35, 36
Application layer, 36
Architectures, switch, 47–49
ARPANET, 32
Asynchronous time division multiplexing (TDM), 376
Asynchronous traffic, 398–399
Asynchronous transfer mode (ATM), 362, 403–406

Attenuation
  limits of, 121, 133–135
  mode partition noise caused by, 253
  sources of, 126–131
  system limited by, 332
Aurora, 65
Autocorrelation, 267
Automatic frequency control (AFC), 753–787
Automatic protection switching (APS), 386, 539
Avalanche breakdown, 200
Avalanche photodiode (APD)
  current multiplication, 200–205
  electric field distribution, 198–200
  excess noise factor derivation, 272–274
  frequency response, 205–211
    derivation, 218–219
  gain optimization, 322–325
  multiplication gain optimization, 322–325
  noise in, 243–246
    power and spectral density, 245

B

Balanced detection, 756
  noise formulation in, 759–761
  signal formulations in, 757–759
Bandpass filtering
  preprocessing, 827–829
  Q-factor in, 819–822
  for timing recovery, 817–819
Banyan routing network, 532
Baseband transmission, 6–7
Baseline routing network, 532
Basic mode, 400
Basic optical fiber communication system, 4
Batcher-Banyan network, 534
Batcher-Banyan switch, 50
Batcher sorting network, 533–534, 579–582
Bayesian detection, 261
Bayes' theorem, 261
Bending loss, 130
Benes network, 524, 528–529
  dilated, 529–531
  switching control for dilated, 577–579
Bias current versus output frequency, 664–665

Biaxial materials, 689
Bimode mapping, 833
Binary digital signal detection, 290–292
Binary phase shift keying (PSK),
 fundamental performance of,
 768–769
Binary pulse amplitude modulated (PAM)
 signals, 267
Binary symmetric channel (BSC) model,
 259
Biphase code, 320–321, 827, 834
Bipolar junction transistor (BJT)
 amplifier, 334–335
Birefringence, 154, 688, 693–695
 circular, 797
Bistable devices, 546–554
Bistable Fabry-Perot devices, 549–551
Bistable lasers, 551
Bit clock, 815
Bit error rate (BER), 76, 131, 225, 229
Bit error rate (BER)
 including intersymbol interface,
  297–302
 neglecting intersymbol interference,
  295–297
 worst case, 297
Bit rate
 dependence of receiver sensitivity on,
  133–134
 fiber dispersion
  independent of, 148
  proportional to, 149
Bit rate dependence, 305
Bit rate squared, fiber dispersion
 proportional to, 150
Bit stuffing, 376, 377–380
 gapped clock, 380
 stuffing ratio, 379
 waiting time jitter, 381-382
Bit timing recovery, 815
Blanca, 65
Blazed grating, 454–455
Blocking
 internal, 46
 probability, 46
Blue shift, 346, 626
Boltzmann constant, 228
Boundary conditions, 644
Bragg diffraction, 732–734
Bragg filter, 109
Bragg-reflection add-drop multiplexers,
 468–470
Bragg-reflection grating, 464, 467–468

Bragg reflector, 109
Breakdown voltage, 200
Brewster angle, 868
Brillouin scattering, 129
 loss, 127
Broadband integrated services digital
 network (B-ISDN), 362, 402–407
Broadband network, 403–405
Broadcasting, 47
Built-in junction voltage, 194–195
Buried-heterostructure, 95
Bus topology, 52–53

C

Call, 34
Canent injection for positive gain, 91
Capacitance-distance product, 18
Capacitor charge time, 724
Carrier density
 distribution, 665
 laser rate equation for, 605–606
Carrier power to the nth-order
 intermodulation product power
 (CIMP), 505–506
Carrier recovery
 in coherent detection, 782–787
 six-port 90° hybrid analysis for,
  804–805
Carrier-sense multiple access (CSMA), 33
 with collision detection, 42, 362
Carrier-to-nonlinear-distortion ratio
 (CNLD), 504–505
Carrier-to-intermodulation-product power
 (CIMP), 505–506
Carrier-to-noise ratio (CNR), 287, 289
 in AM transmission, 497–498
 analysis for FM transmission, 514–515
 in FM transmission, 498
 in analog TV transmission, 289
Carson's rule, 494–495
Casa, 65
CATV, see Community Antenna TV
Cavity confinement, 92–95, 605
 gain guided, 92–94
 index guided, 94–95
CCITT recommendation G.652, 126
CCITT recommendation G.733, 373
Cell format of ATM, 404–405
Cell loss propity (CLP), 404
Centralized star, 364
Central limit theorem, 266
Centrosymmetric crystal structure, 699
Channel, 4

Channel coding, 5
Characteristic function, 264
Characteristic temperature, 106
Chirping effect
 frequency, 607, 624, 625–627
 received pulse determination
  considering, 346–351
Chromatic dispersion, see Material
 dispersion
Circuit switching, 35
 versus packet switching, 50–51, 422
Circular birefringence, 797
Circular fibers, 155
Circularly polarized, 153
Cleaved-coupled-cavity (C³) lasers, 100
Clipping, 496–497
 nonlinear power below, 504
Clos switch, 524, 528
Code division multiple access (CDMA),
 43
Code-domain multiple access, 43
Code mark inversion codes, 833–834
Coding, 4
 channel coding, 5, 25
 line coding, 812
 source coding, 5
Coding efficiency and complexity,
 836–837
Coding gain, 279
Coherence time, 250, 277
Coherent communications, phase noise
 in, 250
Coherent detection, 12, 13, 287, 751,
 974–975
 basic principles of, 752–756
 optical mixing, 752–753
 carrier recovery in, 782–787
 differential phase-shift keying
  demodulation, 769–771
  fundamental performance, 771–773
 effects of phase noise, 787–793
 four-port hybrids, 800–804
 frequency-shift keying in
  fundamental performance,
  774–775
  signal representation and
  demodulation, 773–774
 homodyne and heterodyne detections,
  753–756
 noise figure in, 881–884
 on-off keying in
  fundamental detection performance,
  763–767

Coherent detection—(*con't*)
  signal representation and
      demodulation, 762–763
  optical mixing in, 752–753
  performance summary, 775–777
  phase-shift keying in
    binary fundamental performance,
        768–769
    signal representation and
        demodulation, 768
  polarization control in, 754–755
  polarization controllers and isolators
      in, 796–799
  polarization-shift keying in
    state of polarization and Stokes
        parameters, 778–780
    Stokes receiver, 780–782
  Rician and Rayleigh distributions in,
      805–806
  signal and noise formulations in,
      756–762
  six-port 90° hybrid analysis for carrier
      recovery in, 804–805
  and transmission performance in
      wavelength-division
      multiplexing, 441–443
Coherent postdetection, heterodyne
    detection with, 764–765
Communication
  importance of, in daily lives, 3
  process of, 3
Communication engineers, primary task
    of, 3
Communication network, 4
  basic needs from, 32–33
  basic process, 34
  high-speed applications, 64–65
  information exchange in, 34–37
  medium access control, 38–43
  signaling in, 34
  speed bottlenecks in, 58–60
    design solutions to, 60–64
  switching, 45–52
  topology, 52–58
Communication systems, 4–6
  analog versus digital, 9–12
  baseband versus passband, 6–9
    basic optical fiber, 4
  coherent versus incoherent, 12–14
  modulation and line coding, 14–15
Community antenna TV (CATV)
  channel allocation, 500
  nonlinear distortion in, 290, 499–503
  systems, 64–65, 489

Complementary bit, 830
Complementary error function, 231
Component selection guidelines, 150-151
Composite second order (CSO) distortion,
    290, 501–503
Composite triple beat (CTB) distortion,
    290, 501–503
Compression delay, 366–368
Concentrator, 33
Conditional probability, 259
Conductivity, 162
Connectivity, 32
Constant cross-correlation, 252
Continuous bit rate (CBR) traffic, 406
Continuous phase FSK (CPFSK), 777
Continuous wave (CW), 166
Conversion factors, 943
Costas loop, 785–787
Cost sharing, 32
Coupled-cavity lasers, 100–101
Coupled-mode rate equations, 639–643
  boundary conditions, 644–645
  steady state, 645
Coupler, 423
Coupling
  constants, 641–642, 677, 718
  frequency-independent, 449–453
  waveguide, 738–745
Coupling loss, 130–131, 450-453
  and optical amplification, 370–371
Coupling theory, 541–544
Crossbar switch, 45, 525–527
Crossover and extended perfect shuffle,
    534
Crosstalk, 225, 530-531
Current gain and power penalty in
    multiple access, 325–329
Cutoff wavelengths, 122
Cycles,
  in FDDI II, 399
  formats of, 402

D

Dark current, 191
Data communications, OSI protocol
    layers in, 35–38
Datagram, 34
Data-link layer, 37
Data processing
  applications in, 35, 36
  transmitted, 35, 36
DeBruijn network, 426–428
Debye-Sears diffraction, 734–735

Decibel (dB), 22–24
Decision feedback recovery loop, 787
Demultiplexers, 424–425
  destuffing at, 380–381
Dense WDoMA, 417
Density functions
  normal or Gaussian distribution, 264
  Poisson distribution, 265
  uniform distribution, 264–265
Depressed-cladding (DC) fibers, 124
Design issues in digital transmissions,
    322–332
Design solutions to speed bottlenecks,
    60–64
Destuffing at demultiplexer, 380–381
Detection, 229, 287
  analog signal, 288–290
  binary digital signal, 290–292
Deterministic, 44
  access, 361
Dielectric constant, 161
Dielectric medium, waves in, 161–162
Differential encoding, 830
Differential phase-shift keying (DPSK),
    762, 769
  demodulation, 769–771
  effect of phase noise in, 788–790
  fundamental performance, 771–773
Differential polarization fibers, 155
Diffraction grating, 464–467
Digital communications, 9–12
  advantage of, 11–12
  effects of noise and distortion in, 228–229
  matched filtering in, 235–237
Digital image transmission, 5
Digital modulation, 495, 761-782
Digital optic switch (DOS), 546
Digital signaling schemes, 761–762
Digital signal modulation, 612–620
  and pulse input response, 595–600
Digital subcarrier multiplex transmission,
    508–510
Digital telephony for plain old telephone
    service (POTS), 35
Digital transmission
  applying solitons for, 912–921
  bit error rate in, 131
  design issues in, 322–332
Digitized image transmission, 5
Dilated Benes, 529–531
Diodes
  Fabry-Perot laser, 96–99
  light-emitting, 85–88
  single mode laser, 99–103

Direct bandgap, 81
  materials, 84, 947–948
Direct current (dc)
  balance, 292, 816
  characteristics of, 658–668
  coupling, 292
  wander, 292
Direct detection, 287
Direct direction, noise figure in,
  881–882
Direct modulation, 77, 591, 967–970
  Fabry-Perot laser diode rate equations,
    631–635
  for light-emitting diodes, 592
    pulse input response to digital
      signal modulation, 595–600
    rate equation and steady state
      solution, 592–594
    rate equations of laser diodes,
      603–607
    small signal response to analog
      signal modulation, 600–603
  limitations
    frequency chirping, 624, 625–627
    linewidth broadening, 630
    mode partition, 627–629
  pulse input response of laser diodes,
    612–620
  small signal response of laser diodes,
    620–624
  steady state solution of laser diodes,
    608–611
Direct recombination, 81
Direct sequence spread spectrum, 43
Discreteness of message, 9
Dispersion
  of graded-index fibers, 171–173
  group velocity (GVD), 140–141, 899,
    901
  intermodal, 143–144
  intramodal, 141–142
  modal, at longer distance, 145–146
  system limited by, 330
  total fiber, 145
Dispersion
  equation for, 138, 646
  limits in, 121, 146–150
Dispersion flattened fibers, 124–125
Dispersion relationship, 164
Dispersion-shifted fibers, 124, 151–153
Dispersive mode, 912
Displacement, 159
Distributed Bragg reflector (DBR) lasers,
  76, 100

Distributed-feedback (DFB) coupled-
    mode equations, 674–679
Distributed-feedback (DFB) laser diodes
    and modulation, 639, 970–971
  coupled-mode rate equations,
    639–643, 674–679
    boundary conditions, 644–645
    steady state, 644
  direct current characteristics, 658–668
  modulation characteristics
    pulse, 669–670
    single-tone, 670–672
  threshold equations of DFB lasers,
    679–682
  threshold solutions, 644–647
    double-cleaved DFB lasers,
      655–660
    $\lambda/4$-shift DFB lasers, 652–655
    single-window DFB lasers, 649–651
    zero-reflection DFB lasers, 648–649
Distributed-feedback (DFB) lasers, 76,
    99–100
  double-cleaved, 655–658
  $\lambda/4$-shift, 652–655
  single-window, 649–651
  threshold equations of, 679–682
  zero-reflection, 648–649
Distribution loss, 450
Double-cleaved distributed feedback
    (DFB) lasers, 654–659
Double crossbar switch,
    525–527
Double heterostructure (DH), 82
Dual port, 577
Dual-ring topology and clock distribution,
    393–395
Dual wavelength photodetectors, 216–217
Dynamic interface power requirement,
    393
Dynamic range, 57–58
  allowable, 339–341
Dynamic range bus topology, 58
Dynamic tuning, 421
  and wavelength division multiple
    access, 432–433
  equivalent spatial switching networks,
    434
  probability flow, 435

E

Edge emitting, 87
Effective waveguide length, 458
Eigenvalue, 138, 165
Elasto-optic coefficients, 725–732

Electric flux density, 159
Electric susceptibility, 160
Electromagnetic spectrum, 11
Electron-hole recombination (EHR) rate,
    81, 593
Electro-optic amplitude modulators
  field interference, 716–717
  polarization filtering, 714–715
  waveguide coupling, 718–720
Electro-optic filters, 477
Electro-optic modulation, 685,
    687–688
  longitudinal and transverse modulators,
    709–713
  of refractive indices, 699–709
Electro-optic phase modulators,
    713–714
E-mail, 32–33
Emission cross section, 873
Emission spectrum
  of LEDs, 86
  of LDs, 94, 104, 106
Emission wavelengths
  of GaAs, 82
  of quantum-well lasers, 105
Emitting
  edge, 87
  surface, 87
Energy bandgap, 81–84
  III-IV compounds, 948
  quantum wells, 105
Envelope detection, 767–769
  effect of phase noise in, 792–794
Equalizer, 234
Equivalent thermal voltage and current
    noise sources, 241
Erbium-doped fiber amplifiers (EDFA),
    22, 372
  optical pumping, 869–874
  rate equations and gain, 874–880
Error function, 231
Error multiplication, 25
Error propagation, 842–843
Error probability, 262
Ethernet, 33, 39, 42, 64
Event, 257
Excess bandwidth ratio, 346
Excess (avalanche gain) noise, 225, 243-
    246, 272–274
Excess loss, 450
Exciton absorption reflection switch
    (EARS), 558
Exclusive-or, 828
Expectation, 264

Exponential distribution, 263
Exponential pulse, 352
Extended generalized shuffle (EGS) network, 534
External blocking, 46
External modulation, 77, 971–974
  acousto-optic, 725
    Bragg diffraction, 733–734
    elasto-optic coefficients, 725–732
    Raman-Nath or Debye-Sears diffraction, 734–735
  acousto-optic Bragg amplitude modulators, 736–737
  acousto-optic coupling, 746–750
  acousto-optic modulators
    deflection efficiency, 737–738
    driving power, 738
    modulation bandwidth, 738–740
  amplitude modulation, 694–695
  bandwidth and switching power of electro-optic modulators, 720–724
  commercially available modulators, 687
  desirable properties in, 685–687
  electro-optic amplitude modulators
    field interference, 716–717
    polarization filtering, 714–715
    waveguide coupling, 718–720
  electro-optic modulation
    longitudinal and transverse modulators, 709–713
    of refractive indices, 699–709
    electro-optic phase modulators, 713–714
  principles of, 687–689
  waveguide coupling, 738–745
  wave propagation in anisotropic media
    birefringence, 673–695
    index ellipsoid, 695–699
    materials, 689
    normal surfaces, 695
    plane wave, 690–693
External pumping, 88–89
External quantum efficiency, 593–594
External timing reference (ETR), 399
Extinction ratio, 292, 329–330
Extraordinary axis, 690
Extremely low frequency (ELF), 8
Extrinsic absorption, 127
Extrinsic photoconductors, 186
Eye diagram, 319

F

Fabry-Perot (FP) amplifiers, 863–868
Fabry-Perot (FP) interferometry, 471–473, 716

Fabry-Perot (FP) laser diode rate equations, 631–635
Fabry-Perot (FP) laser diodes, 96–99, 639
Fabry-Perot (FP) resonators, 16–17, 112–115
Faraday effect, 799–800
Feedback resistor, PSD of, 338
Fiber amplifiers, 853
Fiber attenuation and optical amplification, 914–918
Fiber bandwidth, 147, 415–416
Fiber dispersion, 75, 140–151
  balance between nonlinearity and, 903–906
  independent of bit rate, 148
  proportional to bit rate, 149
  proportional to bit rate squared, 150
Fiber distributed data interface (FDDI), 22, 362, 393–402
  4B5B in, 832
  dual-ring topology, 394
  frame and token formats, 397–398
  medium access and efficiency, 398
  optical component specifications, 394–397
  target token rotation time (TTRT), 398
Fiber distributed data interface (FDDI)-II and fiber distributed data inferface (FDDI) follow-on LAN, 399–402
Fiber-in-the-loop (FITL), 22, 362, 406
Fiber nonlinearity and wave equation, 898–900
Fiber-to-the-home (FTTH), 22, 362, 406, 489
Field distribution, 665
Field effect transistor (FET) amplifier, 335–336
Field interference, 716–717
Figure of merit, 737
File transfer protocol (FTP), 36
Filtering
  matched, in digital communications, 236–237
  raised-cosine, 314–316
  Wiener, in analog communications, 234–236
Filters
  electro-optic, 477
  surface acoustic, 477
  Finesse of FP resonators, 114
5B6B code, 833
Fixed transition codes, 835–837
Fixed tuning, 420–421

Fixed tuning wavelength division multiple access (WDMA), logical configurations and routing in, 425–432
Flip routing network, 533
Floating payload, 382
Forward scattering problem, 924
4B5B in fiber distributed data interface (FDDI) network, 832
FM threshold, 131
Fourier transform pairs, 983
Four-port hybrids, 801–806
Frames, 40
  structure of TDM, 372–376
  structure of TDMA, 362
Frame-synchronized scrambler, 838, 841–842
Free-space interconnections, 566–569
Free spectral range (FSR), 464
  FP, 472
  grating, 464
  MZI, 473
Frequency acquisition, 822
Frequency acquisition range of phase-locked loops, 826–827
Frequency chirping, 591, 607, 624, 625–627
Frequency division multiplexing (FDM), 8–9, 108, 415, 454
  grating, 454–457
  Mach-Zehnder interferometry, 457–461
  waveguide grating router, 461–463
Frequency domain, 42
  discrimination in, 470–475
  medium access, 42
Frequency-independent coupling, 449–453
Frequency justification, 40, 371, 376–382
  bit stuffing, 377–382
  demultiplexing, 380
  slip control, 376–378
Frequency modulation (FM), 8, 494–495, 627
  threshold, 131
  transmission
    carrier-to-noise ratio analysis for, 516–517
    SNR and CNR in, 498
Frequency modulation (FM) index, 494
Frequency response,
  APDs, 205–211
  LEDs 600–603
  LDs 620–624
  PIN diodes, 196–197
Frequency reuse, 433–438

Frequency-shift keying (FSK), 764, 775
  effect of phase noise in, 794–795
  fundamental performance, 776–777
  signal representation and
    demodulation, 775–776
Frequency tracking, 822
Frequency tuning and stabilization,
  446–449
Fresnel's equation of wave normals,
  692–693
Front-end amplifiers, 333–341
  BJT, 334–335
  FET, 335–336
  high-impedance, 333–336
  transimpedance, 336–339
F-SEED, 557–558
FTP, 36
Full-width half-maximum (FWHM), 85
  of laser linewidth due to phase noise,
    249
Fully connected, 421–422
Fundamental soliton, 908

G

GaAs, emission wavelength of, 82
Gain bandwidth, 862
Gain constant, 605
Gain coupled, 642
Gain-guided lasers, 92–93
Gain saturation, amplifier gain
  considering, 859–861
Gain suppression, 605
Gain suppression coefficient, 606
Gapped clock, 380
Gaussian distribution, 265
Gaussian gain profile, 98, 116
Gaussian noise, 230
Gaussian pulse, 902–903
Geometrical optics, signal propagation by,
  135–137
Gordon-Haus limit, 918
  derivation of, 933–936
Graded-index fibers, 124, 143–144
  dispersion of, 171–173
Graded-index (GRIN) lens, 456
Grating, 454–457
  angular dispersion factor, 455
  blazed, 454
  Littrow configuration, 455
  Bragg-reflection, 467–468
  definition of, 464
  diffraction, 464–467
Group refractive index, 140
Group velocity, 140, 165–167

Group velocity dispersion (GVD),
  140–141, 899, 901
Guard time, 40

H

Heavily doped light emitting diode
  (LED), 602
Hermite function, 506
Heterodyne carrier recovery, 789
Heterodyne detection, 755–758, 770–771
  with coherent postdetection, 766–767
  signal detection in, 761
Heterodyning, 754
Heterogenous communications, 37
Heterojunction, 82
Heterostructures, 82–85
  buried, 95
  InP, 85
High-definition TV (HDTV), 65
Higher order solitons, 910
High-impedance, 292
High-impedance amplifier, 333–336
High performance computing, 65
Hilbert transform or filter, 491
Hollow cathod lamp (HCL), 448
Hologram, 565
Homodyne detection, 755–758, 766, 770
  signal detection in, 761
Homodyne phase-shift keying (PSK)
  carrier recovery, 788–789
Homodyning, 754
H-SEED and exciton absorption reflection
  switch (EARS), 560
Hybrid, 52, 757–758
  of couplers and splitters, 803
  lossless, 803–804
  90°, 806
  90° six-port, 758
  180°, 805
  single beam-splitter, 801–803
  six-port 90° analysis, for carrier
    recovery, 806–807
Hybrid
  symmetric, 804–805
Hybrid mode, 400
Hybrid ring control (HRC), 400
Hypercube configuration, 425–426
Hysteresis-loop, 548

I

III-V compounds, physical constants of,
  947–948
Incoherent detection, 12, 13, 287,
  439–441, 959–962

Incoherent detection—(con't)
  alternating current (ac) coupling and
    direct current (dc) wander,
    318–322
  analog signal detection, 288–290
  binary digital signal detection,
    290–292
  bit error rate including intersymbol
    interface, 297–302
  bit error rate neglecting intersymbol
    interference, 295–297
  design issues in digital transmissions,
    322–332
  front-end amplifiers, 333–341
  pulse-broadening analysis, 351–353
  received pulse determination, 309–312
    and chirping effect, 346–351
  receiver sensitivity, 302–309
  receiver transfer function design,
    312–317
  signal, intersymbol, interference, and
    noise formulation, 292–295
  spectrum and power of signal
    dependent noise, 344
  and transmission performance in
    wavelength-division
    multiplexing, 439–441
  zero intersymbol interference, 344–345
Incoherent light, 85
Independent events, 260
Index coupled, 642
Index ellipsoid, 695–699
Indirect bandgap, 81
  silicon, 81–82
Induced polarization, 159
Information exchange, 34–37
InGaAsP laser, 85
  characteristics, 78–79
In-line amplifiers, 854
In-phase baseband signal, 490
InP heterostructure, 85
Integrals, 983
Integrated PIN/FET receivers, 214
Integrated services digital network (ISDN)
  broadband, 402–407
  U-interface of, 10
Integration-and-dump filtering, 239,
  313–314
INTELSAT, 41, 367
Interchannel interference, 868–869
Interdigital transducer (IDT), 477, 822
Interdigitated structure, 212
Interferometry
  Fabry-Perot, 471–473
  Mach-Zehnder, 457–461, 473–474

Intermediate frequency (IF), 755
Intermodal dispersion, 143–144
Intermodulation distortion, 496
Intermodulation products, 500–503
Internal blocking, 46
Internal quantum efficiency, 594
International system of units (SI), 945
Internet, 32–33
Intersymbol interference (ISI), 5
    bit error rate including, 297–302
    fiber dispersion as cause of, 287,
        293–295
    and jitter, 256
    and signal distortion, 225, 228
Intramodal dispersion, 141–142
Intrinsic loss, 127
Intrinsic photoconductor, 186
Intrinsic relative intensity noise (RIN),
    247–248
Inverse shuffle, 532
Inverse scattering, 897, 923–933
Isolator, 801
Isotropic crystals, Kerr effect in, 709
Isotropic materials, 689

J

Jitter, 225, 789
    random, 256
    systematic, 256
    waiting time, 383

K

KDP, 690, 701, 706
KdV equation, 897
Kerr coefficients, 699
    important types of, 705–709
Kerr effect
    in isotropic crystals, 709
    nonlinear, 899

L

LAMBDANET, 60, 422
Laser arrays, tunable, 444–445
Laser diode (LD), 4, 80
    Fabry-Perot laser rate equations for,
        631–635
    phase noise from, 248–250
    pulse input response of, 608–616
    rate equations of, 599–604
    relative intensity noise in, 246–248
    small signal response of, 616–620
    steady state solution of, 604–607
        for Synchronous Optic NETwork
            (SONET), 389

Laser noise, kinds of, 76
Laser rate equation for carrier density,
    601–602
Laser(s)
    coupled-cavity, 100–101
    distributed Bragg reflector (DBR), 100
    distributed feedback (DFB), 99–100
    Fabry-Perot, 96–99
    gain-guided, 92–93
    principles of, 88–92
    quantum-well, 104–107
    strongly index-guided, 95
    threshold gain for, 97
    tunable, 108–110
    weakly index-guided, 94
Lax equation, 927
Lax pair, 927
Lee's approximation for blocking
        probability, 433
Light amplification, 89–90
Light detection, 954–956
    advanced devices
        dual wavelength photodetectors,
            216–217
        integrated PIN/FET receivers, 214
        metal-semiconductor-metal
            photodetectors, 211–214
        phototransistors, 215–216
        separate absorption and
            multiplication (SAM)
            photodetectors, 214
    avalanche photodiodes
        current multiplication, 200–205
        electric field distribution, 198–200
        frequency response, 205–211
    photoconductors, 186–189
    photodiodes, 189–191
    PIN diodes, 191–197
        electric field distribution, 193–195
        frequency response, 196–197
        reverse bias, 193–195
    quantum efficiency and responsibility,
        183–186
Light-emitting diodes (LEDs), 4, 80,
    85–88
    direct modulation for, 587
    edge emission, 88
    emission spectrum, 86
Light-emitting diodes (LEDs)—(con't)
    heavily doped, 602
    lightly doped, 602
    surface emission, 87
Lightly doped light-emitting diode
    (LED), 598

Light propagation in optical fibers,
    135–140
Light pulse at transmitter output, 308–309
Light sources, 950–952
    cavity confinement, 92–95
    criteria for, in optical communications,
        74–79
    Fabry-Perot laser diodes, 96–99
    laser principles, 88–92
    light-emitting diodes, 85–88
    quantum-well lasers, 104–107
    semiconductor, 79–85
    single (longitudinal) mode laser diodes,
        99–103
    tunable lasers, 108–110
Lightwave technology development, 18–22
Line terminating equipment (LTE), 384
Linearly birefringence fibers, 156–157
Linearly polarized, 153
Line codes, 816
    and timing recovery, 829–834, 976
    CMI, 833–834
    5B6B, 833
    fixed transition, 835–837
    4B5B in FDDI, 832
    mB1C, 831
    mB1M, 830
    mBnB, 832
    modulation code, 14
    zero parity, 833
Linewidth, temperature dependence of, 87
Linewidth broadening
    definition of, 107
    and direct modulating, 591
    and phase noise, 249, 274–279
    factor, 276
LiNB0$_3$ switch, 543, 690, 701, 707–708
Littrow configuration, 455
Local area network (LAN), 33
Local carrier or oscillator, 12, 752
Local clock, reasons for not using, 815
Local loop, 405–407
    alternatives to, 406
Local oscillator, see local carrier
Logical topology, 54
Longitudinal and transverse modulators,
    709–713
Longitudinal modes, 74, 98
    separation, 98–99
Longitudinal modulators, 709
Longitudinal optical pumping, 871–872
Longitudinal potassium dihydrogen
    phosphate (KDP) modulator, 711
Longitudinal wave in water, 726

Loop filter (LF), 824
Looping algorithm, 578
Lorentzian spectrum, 249, 277, 793
Lossless hybrids, 803–804
Lossy dielectric medium, 161–162
L-SEED, 563

M

Mach-Zehnder interferometry (MZI),
    457–461, 473–475, 716
Mach-Zehnder modulation, 717
Main modes, 74
Maintenance voice channel (MVC), 400
Marchenko equation, 927
Mark bit, 830
Matched-cladding (MC) fibers, 124
Matched filtering in digital
    communications, 235–237
Material absorption loss, 127
Material dispersion, 140–142
Mathematical formulas, 981–983
Maximum a posteriori probability (MAP)
    detection, 261
Maximum-length pseudo-random
    sequence generation, 840–841
Maximum-length sequences, properties
    of, 845–848
Maximum-length shift register, 838
    properties, 845–848
Maximum likelihood (ML) detection, 261
Maximum switching speed, 46
Maximum throughput, 46
Maximum-to-minimum gain ratio, 862
Maxwell equations, 159
mB1C codes, 831
mB1M codes, 830–831
mBnB codes, 832
Mean, 263
Mean square error (MSE), 227, 234
Mechanical switches, 539–540
Medical imaging, 64
Medium access
    deterministic versus statistic, 44
    shared resources in, 39–42
    and time compression, 364–366
Medium access control (MAC), 37, 38–43
Metal-semiconductor-metal
    photodetectors, 211–214
Mie scattering, 129
Mie scattering loss, 127
Minimum blocking probability, 46
Minimum delay and loss probability,
    46–47
Minimum number of crosspoints, 46

Minimum Nyquist bandwidths, $12n$
Mismatch factor of waveguide couplers,
    744
Modal dispersion at longer distance,
    145–146
Mode field diameter (MFD), 124
Mode partition, 627–629
Mode partition noise (MPN), 76, 225,
    251–254
    caused by attenuation, 253
    caused by fiber dispersion at high
        speeds, 253
Mode suppression ratio, 628
Modulation bandwidth and switching
    power of electro-optic modulators,
    720–725
Modulation
    amplitude, 7, 490–494
    bandwidth and switching power of EO
        modulators, 720–725
    codes, 14
    depth, 710–712, 720
    digital, 495
    frequency, 8, 494–495, 627
    phase, 14
Moment generating function, 243–244, 264
    of APD noise, 243
Moments, 264
Monochromatic wave, 165
Multicasting, 47
Multicladding fibers, 124
Multidimensional photonic switching, 568
    time-domain, 569–571
    wavelength-domain, 568–569
Multihop, 422
Multimedia, 65
Multimode fibers (MMF), 122
Multimode sources,
    FP, 96–99
    problems of, 74–75
Multiple access, 38–39
    current gain and power penalty in,
        325–329
    in optical communications, 44
Multiple quantum, 107
Multiple-stage switches, 47–48
Multiplexer, 38, 423
Multiplexing, 38–39, 59, 406
Multiply clad fibers, 153

N

Narrow band FM, 495
Narrow-band optical amplification,
    474–475

Near-far problem, 43
Nectar, 65
Negative stuffing, 388
Negative stuffing ratio, 379
Network access, 35, 37
Network layer, 37
Network-network interface (NNI), 404
90° hybrid, 806
90° six-port hybrid, 758
Noise, 4, 957–959
    in coherent detection, 882–884
    in direct direction, 881–882
    formulation of, in balanced detection,
        761–763
    Gaussian, 230–231
    in optical amplication, 880–884
    in optical communications, 225–226
        avalanche, in APDs, 243–246
        avalanche photodiode excess noise
            factor derivation, 272–274
        characterization, 229–232
        and distortion reduction techniques,
            234–237
        effects of, and distortion, 227–229
        intersymbol interference and
            jitter, 256
        mode partition, 251–254
        phase, 274–279
        phase noise from laser diodes,
            248–250
        probability, 257–266
        random process and power spectral
            density, 267–270
        and random variables, 257–266
        relative intensity in laser diodes,
            246–248
        shot noise from PIN diodes,
            237–240
        shot noise power spectral density,
            270–272
        summary of, 226
        thermal, 240–243
        total, 254–256
    shot, 190
    time domain, 225
    white, 232
Noise equivalent power (NEP), 242–243
    using avalanche photo diode (APD),
        246
Noise Figures, 879–882
Noise power after photodetection,
    890–892
Non-blocking TST switch, 49
Noncausal Wiener filter, 235

Noncircular symmetric fibers, 126
Nonlinear distortion, 499–503
    analysis of, 503–508, 515–518
Nonlinear feedback, 548
Nonlinearity, balance between fiber
    dispersion and, 903–906
Nonlinear Kerr effect, 899
Nonlinear Schrödinger equation (NLSE),
    897–898
    normalization, 907
    physical meaning of, 900–906
    and relationship between wave
        operators, 926–927
    wave operators for, 925–926
Non-return-to-zero (NRZ) codes, 14, 816,
    828–829
Nonzero intersymbol interference (ISI),
    and extinction ratio, 307–309
Normal distribution, 265
Normalized frequency, 152
Normal surfaces, 695
n-P heterojunction, 82
N-soliton solution, 931–932
N-stage planar, 527
N-stage planar waveguide switch, 574–575
Numerical aperture (NA), 137
Nyquist bandwidth, 12n, 345
Nyquist rate, 345

O

Omega routing network, 532
One-dimensional soliton solutions,
    906–910
180° hybrid, 805
One-soliton solution, 929–931
On-off keying (OOK), 238–239, 292,
    439, 441n
    and direct modulation, 595
    and external modulation, 695
    fundamental detection performance,
        765–769
    optical communications, 13
    signal representation and
        demodulation, 764–765
Open system interconnect (OSI) protocol
    layers in data communication,
    35–38
Optic axis, 695
Optical activity, 798
Optical amplification, 976–979
    and coupling loss, 370–371
    erbium-doped fiber amplifiers
        optical pumping, 869–874
        rate equations and amplifier gain,
            874–880

Optical amplification—(*con't*)
    and fiber attenuation, 914–918
    narrow-band, 474–475
    noise from, 880–884
    noise power after photodetection,
        890–892
    semiconductor amplifiers
        amplifier gain, pumping efficiency,
            and bandwidth, 859–862
        external pumping and rate equation,
            857–859
        Fabry-Perot, 863–868
        interchannel interference, 868–869
        spontaneous emission noise derivation,
            889–890
    system applications, 854–855
    system criteria, 855–857
    system design, 884–887
Optical channel, 311–312
Optical communications
    advances in, 18–22
    advantages of, 16
    basic fiber system, 4
    components in, 16–17
    criteria for light sources in, 74–79
    multiple access in, 44
    noise in, 225–226
        avalanche, in APDs, 243–246
        avalanche photodiode excess noise
            factor derivation, 271–273
        characterization, 229–234
        and distortion reduction techniques,
            234–237
        effects of, and distortion, 227–229
        intersymbol interference and jitter,
            256
        mode partition, 251–254
        phase, 274–279
        phase noise from laser diodes,
            248–250
        probability, 258–266
        random process and power spectral
            density, 267–270
        and random variables, 258–266
        relative intensity in laser diodes,
            246–248
        shot noise from PIN diodes, 237–240
        shot noise power spectral density,
            270–272
        thermal, 240–243
        total, 254–256
    switching in, 51–52
    topology considerations in, 54–58
Optical domain demultiplexing, 371
Optical domain implementation, 60–61

Optical domain time division multiple
    access (TDMA), 368–371
Optical fibers, 122, 952–954
    advanced, 151–157
    CCITT recommendation G.652, 126
    dispersion, 140–151
    fiber attenuation and attenuation limits,
        126–135
    light propagation in, 135–140
    noncircular symmetric fibers, 126
    refractive index profiles, 124–125
    single-mode and multimode fibers,
        122–124
    for Synchronous Optic NETwork
        (SONET), 391–392
    video transmission over, 9
Optical fiber soliton transmission,
    893–894, 979–980
    applying solitons for digital
        transmission, 912
        amplifier noise and timing jitter,
            918–919
        fiber attenuation and optical
            amplification, 914–918
        soliton generation, 912–914
        transmission bit rate, 919–921
    derivation of Gordon-Haus limit,
        933–936
    fiber nonlinearity and wave equation,
        898–900
    field experiments, 910–911
    inverse scattering technique, 923–933
    one-dimensional soliton solution,
        906–910
    physical meaning of nonlinear
        Schrödinger equation, 900–906
Optical interface for Synchronous Optic
    NETwork (SONET), 390–393
Optical network communications, speed
    bottlenecks in, 58–60
Optical pumping, 869–874
Optical signal modulation, 59
Optimum threshold, 296–297
Optoelectronic integrated circuit (OEIC),
    181
    technology, 82
Orderwire byte, 385
Ordinary axis, 690
Output frequency, versus bias current,
    662–663

P

Packet data group (PDG), 399
Packets, 34

Packet switching, 35
  versus circuit switching, 50–51, 421
Parallel current noise sources, power
  spectral density of, 338
Parallel data latching, 835–836
Parallel implementation, 64
Parity check bits, 5
Partially connected, 422
Passband transmission, 6–9
Path terminating equipment, 384
Payload type (PT) of ATM, 404
Pedestal in FITL, 408
Permeability, 159
Permittivity, 159
Perfect shuffle network, 428–431
Phase detector (PD), 824
Phase-locked loop (PLL), 381, 824–827
  bandwidth of, 827
  frequency acquisition range of,
    826–827
Phase modulation (PM), 14
Phase noise, 76, 225, 274–279
  in coherent communications, 250
  effects of, 789–795
    in differential phase-shift keying
      (DPSK), 790–792
    in envelope detection, 792–794
    in frequency-shift keying (FSK),
      794–795
    in other coherent detection
      techniques, 795
  from laser diodes, 248–250
  linewidth broadening because of,
    249–250
Phase-shift keying (PSK), 764
  binary PSK fundamental performance,
    770–771
  signal representation and
    demodulation, 770
Phase velocity, 139, 165
Phone line concentration, 33
Photoconductive (PC) detection, 190
Photoconductors, 181, 186–189
  current gain, 188
  frequency response, 188–189
Photocurrent detection and carrier-to-
  noise ratio, 497–498
Photodetection, 287
  absorption coefficient, 183–184
  quantum efficiency, 191–193, 212
  noise power after, 890–892
Photodetector, 4
Photodiodes, 13, 181, 189–191
Photon counting, 13, 132
Photon decay constant, 607

Photon density, rate equation for,
  606–610
Photonic switching, 60, 61, 523–524,
  966–967
  architectures, 524
    Batcher-Banyan network, 534
    Batcher sorting network, 533–534,
      581–584
    Benes, 528–529
    Clos, 527
    crossbar and double crossbar,
      525–527
    crossover and extended perfect
      shuffle, 534
    dilated Benes, 529–531
    N-stage planar, 527
    self-routing, 531–533
    system considerations, 524–525
  multidimensional photonic
    switching, 568
    time-domain switching, 569–571
    wavelength-domain switching,
      568–569
  N-stage planar waveguide switch,
    574–575
  rearrangeable network, 576–577
  self-routing and asynchronous transfer
    mode switching, 572
  spatial-domain photonic switching, 538
    bistable devices, 546–554
    design criteria, 538–539
    free-space interconnections,
      564–567
    mechanical switches, 539–540
    self-electro-optic effect devices,
      554–563
    waveguide switches, 540–546
  switching control for dilated Benes
    network, 577–579
Photons, receiver sensitivity in, 305–306
Phototransistors, 215–216
Photovoltaic (PV) detection, 190
Physical and mathematical constants, 943
Physical constants of III-V compounds,
  947–948
Physical layer, 37
Physical topology, 52–53
PIN diodes, see P-type intrinsic N-type
  (PIN) diodes
Plain old telephone service (POTS),
  digital telephony for, 35
Planar waveguides, 452
Plane wave propagation, 690–693
Plesiochronous network, 388
P-N junction, 80–82

Pockels coefficients, 699
  importance types of, 700–705
Poincaré sphere, 782
Pointer processing, 62, 382
  encoding of H1, H2 bytes, 388
  for Synchronous Optic NETwork
    (SONET), 386–389
Point-to-point transmission link, 4
Poisson distribution, 265
Poisson process, 239
Polarization control in coherent detection,
  756–757
Polarization controller, 800
Polarization-domain demultiplexing,
  475–477
Polarization filtering, 714–715
Polarization-independent couplers, 546
Polarization-maintaining fibers, 126, 151,
  153–157
Polarization mode coupling mechanism,
  475
Polarization-shift keying (PolSK), 764
  state of polarization and Stokes
    parameters, 780–782
  Stokes receiver, 782–784
Polarization state, 153
Polynomial, primitive, 846
Population inversion, 90–92
Positive gain, canent injection for, 91
Positive optical gain, 90–92
Positive stuffing, 388
Positive stuffing ratio, 379
Potassium dihydrogen phosphate (KDP),
  690, 701, 706
Power amplifiers, 854
Power budget, 131
Power-current characteristics, 661–664
Power levels for Synchronous Optic
  NETwork (SONET), 392–393
Power loss, 55–57
  and gain, 96–98
  of star coupler, 57
Power penalty, 316
  due to ISI, 301, 309
  due to nonzero extinction ratio,
    308–309, 330
  in multiple access, 325–329
  in WDM, 440–441, 443
Power spectral density (PSD), 18, 76,
  230, 232–234, 267, 278
  of APD noise, 245
  of filter output, 269–270
  of phase noise, 249–250, 278–279
  of shot noise, 237–238
  of thermal noise, 240

Power spectral density (PSD)—*(con't)*
physical meaning, 269
total, 339
Preprocessing for bandpass filtering, 827–829
Presentation layer, 36
Primary EHPs, 198
Primitive polynomial, 846
Principle axes, 689
Probability
axiomatic approach to, 258
basic properties of, 259–262
conditional, 259
intuitive definition of, 258
and random variables, 258–266
independent events, 260
σ-field, 258
Probability accumulation function, 229
Probability density function, 230–232, 243–245
of APD noise, 243
Poisson, 265, 266
normal or Gaussian, 265
uniform, 265
Probability distribution, 263
Probability distribution function, 230
Probability function, 258
Probability space, 259
Propagatable, 164
Propagation delay and Taylor series expansion, 141
Propagation errors, 842–843
Propagation mode conversions, 546
Propagation modes, 138–140, 164
Pseudo random sequence, 838
P-type intrinsic *N*-type photodiode (PIN) diodes, 191–197
electric field distribution, 193–195
P-type intrinsic *N*-type photodiode (PIN) diodes
frequency response, 196–197
reverse bias, 193–195
shot noise from, 237–240
3dB bandwidth, 197
Pulse amplitude modulated (PAM) signal, 228
autocorrelation function of, 268
Pulse broadening, 147, 901
analysis, 351–353
Pulse input response
to digital signal modulation,
of LEDs, 595–600
of laser diodes, 612–620
Pulse modulation, 669–670

Pulse narrowing, 903
Pulse response modeling, 619–620
Pumping
efficiency, 861–862
longitudinal optical, 870–871
transverse, 871

Q

Q-factor in bandpass filtering, 819–822
physical meaning, 821
Q-function, 231
Quadrature amplitude modulated (QAM) signal, 490
Quadrature-phase baseband signal, 490
Quantum confined Stark effect (QCSE), 555
Quantum efficiency, 191–192
and responsivity, 183–186
Quantum limit, 14, 238–240
Quantum-well lasers, 104–107
emission wavelengths of, 105
multiple (MQW), 107

R

Radioactive recombination time constant, 593
Radio frequency (RF) mixing and laser modulation, 496–497
RAINBOW, 60
Raised-cosine filter, 314–316
Raised-cosine family, 345
Raman-Nath diffraction, 734–735
Raman scattering, 129
Raman scattering loss, 127
Random jitter, 256
Random process, 266
and power spectral density, 267–270
wide-sense stationary, 267
Random variables, 262–263
probability and, 257–266
Rate equation
of LEDs, 592
derivations of FP LDs, 631–635
derivations of DFB LDs, 674–679
and amplifier gain, 874–880
of laser diodes, 603–608
for photon density, 606–608
and steady state solution, 592–594
Rayleigh distribution, 807–808
Rayleigh scattering, 129
Rayleigh scattering loss, 127
Reach-through voltage, 195
Rearrangeable network, 576–578

Rearrangeably nonblocking, 525
Received pulse, 312
Received pulse determination, 309–312
considering chirping effect, 346–351
Receiver, 4
Receiver amplifiers, 854
Receiver sensitivity, 131–133, 302–309
dependence of, on bit rate, 133–134
gain from MSM PD, 213–214
degradation due to ASE noise, 880
improvement of, 306–307
in photons, 305–306
increase from coherent detection, 752
Receiver transfer function design, 312–317
Red shift, 346, 626
Re-entrant bus loss, 56
Reference burst, 362
Reflection, acoustic Bragg, 470
Refractive index, 129
modulation of, 699–709
profile, 124
Register, 33
Relative frequency, 258
stabilization, 449
Relative intensity noise (RIN), 76, 225
due to reflection, 248
intrinsic, 247
Relaxation frequency, 617
Relaxation oscillation, 613, 615
Relaxation phase shift, 277
Repeaters, use of, 330–332
Resonant circuit, 819
Resonator, Fabry-Perot, 112–115
Response speed, improving, 197
Responsivity
of photodiodes, 185
of laser diodes, 496
Return-to-zero (RZ) codes, 14, 817
Return-to-zero (RZ) signaling, 15
Reversal-β directional couplers, 544–545
Reverse-bias detection, 193
Rib waveguide, 94
Rician distribution, 807–808
Ridge waveguide, 94
Ring topology, 52–53
Robbered bits, 375
Rotary power, 798, 799
Routing networks, 531–533
R-SEED, 556–557

S

Saleh's fundamental limit, 506, 515
Sample space, 258

Satellite communications, time-division multiple access in, 41
Scalability, 47
Scalable switches, 49
Scattering
  Brillouin, 129
  inverse, 897
  loss, 127
    Mie, 129
  Raman, 129
  Rayleigh, 129
  stimulated Raman, 130
Schottky barrier, 213
Scrambling, 816, 837–840
  frame-synchronized, 841–842
  maximum-length pseudo-random sequence generation, 840–841
Section terminating equipment, 385
Self-electro-optic effect devices, 554–563
Self-focusing, 903
Self-healing ring, 52
Self-phase modulation (SPM), 903
Self-routing, 531–533
  and asynchronous transfer mode (ATM) switching, 572
Self-synchronized scramblers, 838
Semiconductor amplifiers, 853
  external pumping and rate equation, 857–862
  Fabry-Perot, 863–868
  gain, pumping efficiency, and bandwidth, 859–862
  interchannel interference, 868–869
Semiconductor light sources, 79–85
Sensitivity, see Receiver sensitivity
Separate absorption and multiplication (SAM) photodetectors, 214
Series summations, 982
Session, 34
Session layer, 36–37
Shared medium, 363–364
Shared resources, in medium access, 39–42
Shift-and-add property, 847
Shot noise, 190, 225
  from P-type intrinsic N-type photodiode (PIN), 237–240
  limit in coherent detection, 21, 775
Shot noise power spectral density, 270–272
Shuffle exchange network, 532–533
Side modes, 74
λ-shift DFB lasers, 652–655
σ-field, 258–259

Signal, intersymbol interference, and noise formulation, 292–295
Signal detection
  in heterodyne detection, 761
  in homodyne detection, 761
Signal formulations, balanced detection in, 759–761
Signaling, 34
Signal propagation by geometrical optics, 135–138
Signal representation and demodulation, 770
Signal space projection, 770
Signal-to-noise ratio (SNR), 225, 227, 289
  in AM transmission, 497–498
  in FM transmission, 498
  simultaneous peak frequency deviation, 494
Single beam-splitter hybrid, 801–803
Single-bus loss, 56
Single-bus topology, 52
Single detection, 758
Single hop, 421–422
Single (longitudinal) mode laser diodes, 99–103
Single-mode fibers (SMF), 122
Single-polarization, 155
Single sideband (SSB), 491
Single tone modulation, 670–672
Single-window distributed Braff reflector (DFB) lasers, 649–651
Six-port 90° hybrid analysis for carrier recovery, 806–807
Slip control, 376–377
Slot size, 366–368
Small signal response
  to analog signal modulation, 598–602
  of laser diodes, 620–624
Smart pixels, 554
Solid angle, 137
Solitary wave, 897
Soliton, 897
  distance, 907–908
  experiments, 21–22, 910–911
  fundamental, 908
  generation, 912–914
  higher order, 910
  period, 910
SONET. See Synchronous Optic NETwork (SONET)
Source coding, 5, 25
Sparse WDoMA, 417
Spatial-domain demultiplexing, 464–470

Spatial-domain photonic switching
  bistable devices, 546–554
  design criteria, 538–539
  free-space interconnections, 564–567
  mechanical switches, 539–540
  self-electro-optic effect devices, 554–563
  waveguide switches, 540–546
Spatial hole burning, 645
Special efficiency, 12n
Spectral width, and line width concession, 85
Spectrum and power of signal dependent noise, 344
Spectrum broadening, 903
Spectrum-line method, 817
Speed bottlenecks
  design solutions to, 60–64
  in optical network communications, 58–60
Splicing loss, 130–131
Splitters, 424–425
Spontaneous emission, 89
Squaring, 829
S-SEED, 561–562
Star coupler, power loss of, 57
Star topology, 53
State of polarization (SOP), 780
Statistical multiplexing, 361–362
Statistic multiple access, 44
Steady state solution,
  of DFB LDs, 645
  of FP LD, 608–611
  of LEDs, 593–594
Step-index fibers, 124, 143
Stimulated absorption, 89
Stimulated emission, 89
Stimulated Raman scattering (SRS), 130
Stokes receiver, 782–784
Strain tensor, 725–727
Stress-induced polarization-maintaining fibers, 157
Strictly non-blocking, 525
Strongly index-guided lasers, 95
Stuffing
  negative, 388
  positive, 388
Subcarrier multiplexing (SCM), 9, 965–966
  analog TV transmission, 499
  basic system in, 489–490
  carrier-to-noise ratio analysis for FM transmission, 514–515

Subcarrier multiplexing (SCM)—(con't)
  combination of subcarrier multiplexing and wavelength-domain medium access, 510–512
  combining with wavelength-domain medium access, 510–512
  digital subcarrier multiplex transmission, 508–510
  modulation schemes, 490–496
  nonlinear distortion, 499–503
  nonlinear distortion analysis, 503–508, 515–518
  photocurrent detection and carrier-to-noise ratio, 497–498
  RF mixing and laser modulation, 496–497
Superframes, 373
Surface acoustic wave (SAW) filter, 477, 816, 822–824
Surface emitting, 87
Switches
  architectures, 47–49
  Batcher-Banyan, 50
  Benes, 528–529
  Clos, 47–48
  self-routing, 531–533
  criteria of, 45–47
  crossbar, 45, 525–527
  double crossbar, 525–527
  multiple-stage, 47–48
  non-blocking TST, 49
  scalable, 49
  wavelength division multiplexing (WDM), 49
Switching, 45–52
  circuit, 35
  circuit versus packet, 50–51, 422
  fabric, 45, 47–49, 524–538, 568–572
  in optical communications, 51–52
  packet, 35
  photonic, 60, 61
  time-slot, 63–64
  traffic, 37, 59
Switching control for dilated Benes network, 577–579
Symbol error rate, 229
Symmetric hybrids, 804–805
Synchronous Optic NETwork (SONET), 62–63, 361, 382–393, 842
  frame and layered structure, 383–386
  optical interface, 389–393
  pointer processing, 386–389
Synchronous payload envelope (SPE), 384

Synchronous time division multiplexing (TDM), 376
Synchronous traffic, 398
Synchrotron orbital radiation, 445
Systematic jitter, 256
System limited
  by attenuation, 332
  by dispersion, 332

T

Tank circuit, 819
Target token rotation time (TTRT), 398
Taylor series expansion, 141, 982
T-carriers, 373–376
Telephone network, 32
Telnet (remote login to another computer), 36
Temperature dependence of linewidth, 87
Thermal equilibrium, emission at, 91
Thermal noise, 225, 240–243
  equivalent voltage and current sources, 241
3dB bandwidth, 280
  of APD, 209
  of LEDs, 601–603
  of LDs, 249, 623–624
  of PIN diodes, 197
Threshold,
  optimum, 296, 300–301
Threshold current, 77, 604, 658–661
  density, 610
Threshold detection, 229, 293
Threshold equations of DFB lasers, 677–680
Threshold gain for laser emission, 97
Time-division multiple access (TDMA), 39, 40–41, 361, 362–368
  efficiency, 41
  centralized start, 364
  compression delay, 366
  guard time, 40, 363–364
  medium access and time compression, 364–366
  optical domain, 368–371
  reference burst, 362–363
  shared medium, 363–364
  timing skew, 364
  in satellite communications, 41
  versus slotted ALOHA, 44
Time-division multiplexing (TDM), 39–40, 361, 371–382
  frame structure, 372–376
  CEPT- or E-carriers, 375–376

Time-division multiplexing (TDM)—(con't)
  frequency justification, 376–382
  hierarchy, 375
  SONET or SDH, 283–393
  T-carriers, 373–376
  tributary signals, 371
Time domain, 39
Time-domain medium access, 962–963
  broadband integrated services digital network (B-ISDN), 402–407
  fiber distributed data interface, 393–402
  optical domain TDMA, 368–371
  Synchronous Optic NETwork (SONET), 382–393
  frame and layered structure, 383–386
  optical interface, 389–393
  pointer processing, 386–389
  plesiochronous network, 388
  synchronous payload envelope, 384
  time-division multiple access, 362–368
  time-division multiplexing, 371–382
Time-domain medium access (TDoMA), 415
Time domain noise or jitter, 225
Time-domain switching, 569–571
Timed token passing, 398
Time-slot interchange (TSI), 48, 523
Time slots, 40, 362
Time-slot switching, 63–64
Time-space-time (TST) switch, 48, 523
Timing jitter, and amplifier noise, 918–919
Timing recovery, line codes for, 815–817, 829–834
  bandpass filtering for, 817–819
  fixed transition codes, 835–837
  frame-synchronized scrambler, 841–843
  lines codes for timing recovery, 829–834
  phase-locked loops, 824–826
  preprocessing for bandpass filtering, 827–829
  properties of maximum-length sequences, 845–848
  Q-factor in bandpass filtering, 819–822
  scrambling, 837–841
    maximum-length pseudo-random sequence generation, 840–841
  surface acoustic wave filters, 822–824
Timing skew, 364
Token holding time, 398

Token rotation time (TRT), 398
Topology, 52–58
    consideration in optical
        communications, 54–58
    dynamic range bus, 58
    logical, 54
    physical, 52–53
Total fiber dispersion, 145
    derivation, 173–174
Total noise, 254–256
Total power spectral density (PSD), 339
Traffic switching, 35, 37, 59
Transimpedance amplifier, 292,
    336–339
Transmission bit rate, 919–921
Transmission inefficiency, simple
    processing in exchange for, 62
Transmission performance in wavelength-
    division multiplexing, 438–443
Transmitted data processing, 35, 36
Transmitter, 4
Transmitter output, light pulse at,
    310–311
Transport equations,
    PIN diodes, 196
    APd, 200–202, 205
Transport layer, 37
Transverse electric (TE) waves, 164–165
Transverse GaAs modulator, 712
Transverse LiNbO$_3$, 711–712
Transverse magnetic (TM) waves, 164
Transverse mode, 122
Transverse modulators, 709–713
Transverse pumping, 871
Transverse wave in water, 727
Traveling-wave (TW) amplifiers, 863
Tributary signals, 371
Trigonometric equalities, 981
Tunable laser arrays, 444–445
Tunable lasers, 108–110
Tunable light sources, 422–423
Turn-on delay
    of LEDs, 597–600
    of LDs, 613–615
TV transmission
    analog, 499
    community antenna, 64–65, 290
Two-dimensional switches, 48
Two-polarization, 156–157

U

U-interface of integrated services digital
    networks (ISDN), 10
Uniaxial materials, 689

Uniform distribution, 265
Unit distance propogation delay, 141
User network interface (UNI), 404–405

V

Variable definitions, 949–980
Variable bit rate (VBR) traffic, 406
Variance, 264
Velocity, group, 165–167
Verdet constant, 799
Vertical cavity surface emission laser
    diode (VCSEL), 558
Vestigial sideband amplitude modulated
    (VSB-AM) signal, 492
Video conferencing, 65
Video transmission over optical fibers, 9
Virtual circuit, 34
Virtual circuit identifier (VCI), 34
Virtual path identifier (VPI), 404
Vistanet, 65
Voltage-control oscillator (VCO), 381,
    824
Voltage noise source, PSD of, 338

W

Waiting time jitter, 381
Water
    longitudinal wave in, 726
    transverse wave in, 727
Wave equation, 159–160
    and fiber nonlinearity, 898–900
Waveform domain, 225
Waveguide, waves in, 162–165
Waveguide coupling, 718–720, 736–745
Waveguide dispersion, 167–171
Waveguide grating router, 461–463
    and optical amplifiers, 446
Waveguide surface (Mie), 129
Waveguide switches, 540–546
    coupling theory, 541–543
    reversal-directional couplers, 544-545
    polarization independent, 546
Wavelength, 77
Wavelength-channel interchange (WCI),
    523
Wavelength converters (WC), 436, 438,
    568
Wavelength-division multiple access
    (WDMA) networks, 22, 42, 417
    deBruijn, 426–428
    dynamic tuning, 432–433
    frequency reuse, 433–438
    hypercube, 425–426
    perfect shuffle, 428–432

Wavelength-division multiplexing
    (WDM), 9, 16, 42, 64, 77, 108,
    216–217, 853
    switch, 49
    switching network, 17
    transmission performance in, 438–443
Wavelength-domain medium access
    (WDoMA), 415–416, 489, 963–965
    components
        demultiplexers and splitters,
            424–425
        multiplexers and couplers, 423–424
        tunable light sources, 422–423
    frequency-dependent multiplexing, 454
    grating, 454–457
        Mach-Zehnder interferometry,
            457–461
        frequency-independent coupling,
            449–453
        waveguide grating router, 461–463
    polarization-domain demultiplexing,
        475–477
    spatial domain demultiplexing,
        464–470
        frequency-domain discrimination,
            470–475
    subcarrier multiplexing combining
        with, 510–512
    system characteristics, 416
        coherent detection versus incoherent
            detection, 418–420
        dense versus sparse WDoMA,
            417–418
        fixed tuning versus dynamic tuning,
            420–421
        packet switching versus circuit
            switching, 422
        physical versus logical topology, 417
        single-hop versus multihop,
            421–422
        WDM versus WDMA, 417
    transmission performance in
        wavelength-division
        multiplexing, 438–443
        coherent detection, 441–443
        incoherent detection, 439–441
    tunable sources, 443–444
        frequency tuning and stabilization,
            446–449
        laser arrays, 444–445
        waveguide grating router and optical
            amplifiers, 446
    wavelength-division multiple access
        network access and routing

Wavelength-domain medium access (WDoMA)—(*con't*)
  dynamic tuning WDMA, 432–433
  frequency reuse, 433–438
  logical configurations and routing in fixed tuning WDMA, 425–432
Wavelength-domain switching, 568–569
Wave operators
  for nonlinear Schrödinger equation (NLSE), 925–926
  and relationship between nonlinear Schrödinger equation (NLSE), 926–927
Wave propagation, 159–165
  in anisotropic media, 689

Wave propagation—(*con't*)
  birefringence, 693–695
    index ellipsoid, 695–699
    materials, 689
    normal surfaces, 695
    plane wave, 690–693
Wave(s)
  in dielectric medium, 161–162
  in waveguides, 162–165
Weakly index-guided lasers, 94
Wideband channels (WBC), 400
White Gaussian noise, 240
White noise, 232
Wideband FM, 495
Wide-sense nonblocking, 525

Wide-sense stationary process, 267
Wiener filtering in analog communications, 234–236
  non-casual filter, 235

Z

z-direction propagation constant, 138–139
z-direction propagation velocity, 139
Zero-forcing equalizer, 314
Zero intersymbol interference (ISI), 344–345
  and extinction ratio, 303–307
Zero parity mBnB code, 833
Zero-reflection DFB lasers, 648–649
Zero substitution, 15